CROWELL'S HANDBOOK OF *Elizabethan & Stuart* LITERATURE

CROWELL'S HANDBOOK OF *Elizabethan & Stuart* LITERATURE

James E. Ruoff

THOMAS Y. CROWELL COMPANY
New York / Established 1834

 Published simultaneously in Canada by Fitzhenry & Whiteside Limited, Toronto.

Designed by Ingrid Beckman

Manufactured in the United States of America

1 2 3 4 5 6 7 8 9 10

Library of Congress Cataloging in Publication Data

Ruoff, James E

Crowell's handbook of Elizabethan and Stuart literature.

1. English literature—Early modern (to 1700)—Dictionaries. I. Title. II. Title: Handbook of Elizabethan and Stuart literature.

PR19.R8 820'.9'003 73-22097

ISBN 0-690-22661-6

For Deanie, Matt, and Amy

Preface

It is hoped that this book will serve the dual purpose of providing an informative introduction to the English Renaissance for general readers and a useful reference work for students and teachers of the period. The authors, works, and literary genres, movements, and terms described in these pages pertain to the Elizabethan, Jacobean, Stuart, and Commonwealth eras, the period 1558-1660, from the accession of Elizabeth I to the Restoration. These time limits are, of course, approximate rather than exact demarcations. Sir Thomas More is included although he occupies a place outside the periphery, and John Dryden is omitted in spite of the technicality that he composed in 1658 his "Heroic Stanzas" on the death of Oliver Cromwell. Milton's *Paradise Lost, Paradise Regained,* and *Sampson Agonistes* receive considerable attention even though they were published after 1660. No doubt such whimsical distinctions can be justified by recourse to some arcane literary logic, but they are in fact the results of my own arbitrary and intuitive judgments about which authors and works on the historical borders conspired to produce the complex and wondrous phenomenon described in these pages as the English Renaissance. Looking back over this work, I can see that in spite of its sheen of alphabetized objectivity, it might well be called "*one* man's view of the English Renaissance" in its essentially subjective emphases and selectivity. Confronted by this deplorable necessity, I can only hope that the view presented here is, in spite of its inevitable limitations, comprehensive, coherent, and lucid.

A principal aim of this book—and, hopefully, its unique value—is to give information about authors and works not to be found in one place elsewhere, and to accomplish this end within the confines of a single volume, I have dealt with titans such as Spenser, Shakespeare, and Milton more concisely and less expansively than their intrinsic greatness might otherwise deserve. The reader should not be surprised to discover that *The Spanish Tragedy* receives as much emphasis as *Hamlet,* or that Beaumont and Fletcher are treated as fully as Spenser. In this book I attempt to present other English Renaissance writers in a way comparable to the treatment of the major authors in H. S. V. Jones, *A Spenser Handbook* (1930); James Holly Hanford, *A Milton Handbook* (1926; rev. ed., 1933); and *The Reader's Encyclopedia of Shakespeare,* ed. by Oscar James Campbell and Edward G. Quinn (1966).

For the sake of accuracy and uniformity,

I have based publication dates on *The Cambridge Bibliography of English Literature,* ed. by F. W. Bateson, 4 vols. (1940), and its *Supplement,* ed. by G. Watson (1957), except in rare instances in which this bibliography errs. In presenting titles, I have tried to avoid the lengthy Elizabethan "puff titles" often cited in the *CBEL* and followed, instead, the most familiar forms for titles as they appear in a standard work such as *A Literary History of England,* ed. by Albert C. Baugh (1948).

In providing dates of composition for dramatic works, I have followed E. K. Chambers, *The Medieval Stage,* 2 vols. (1903) for plays written before 1558; E. K. Chambers, *The Elizabethan Stage,* 4 vols. (1923) for plays written 1558-1603; G. E. Bentley, *The Jacobean and Caroline Stage,* 7 vols. (1941-67) for plays written 1603-1660. In dating Shakespeare's plays I have relied upon E. K. Chambers, *William Shakespeare: A Study of Facts and Problems* (1930) as corrected by James G. McManaway in "Recent Studies in Shakespeare's Chronology," *Shakespeare Survey 3* (1950). All such dates of composition must therefore be assumed to be approximate and tentative—merely an arbitrary means of avoiding lengthy and tedious discussions of dating in the drama entries.

In each instance a date in parenthesis after a title indicates first publication unless otherwise noted. The following abbreviations are used with dates: c.—around, approximately; perf.—performed; rev.—revised; wr.—written. Question marks with dates denote great uncertainty regarding an author's birth, death, or dating of a work.

I wish to express my sincere gratitude to the indefatigable editors who helped make this book possible. Mr. Patrick Barrett did more than offer good advice; he drove the work forward from beginning to end with unflagging diligence and infallible judgment. Mrs. Dorothy Duffy caught a thousand contradictions and errors, suggested many new titles for the bibliographies, and made highly creative suggestions that improved the manuscript immeasurably.

I am much indebted, also, to Miss Wendy Hill for her help in preparing the manuscript. Several of my friends and colleagues at The City College of New York read various entries and offered comments and corrections—Professors Thomas King, Philip Miller, Samuel I. Mintz, and Edward G. Quinn. I am equally grateful for the generous assistance of Professor Allan Chester, University of Pennsylvania; Professor Tetsumaro Hayashi, Ball State University; and Professor James Mirollo, Columbia University.

James E. Ruoff
The City College of New York

Abbreviations of Periodicals

CL	Comparative Literature
CritQ	Critical Quarterly
DUJ	Durham University Journal
EA	Etudes Anglaises
E&S	Essays and Studies by Members of the English Association
EHR	English Historical Review
EIC	Essays in Criticism (Oxford)
ELH	Journal of English Literary History
ES	English Studies
ETJ	Educational Theatre Journal
HLQ	Huntington Library Quarterly
HudR	Hudson Review
JEGP	Journal of English and Germanic Philology
Library	The Library
MLN	Modern Language Notes
MLQ	Modern Language Quarterly
MLR	Modern Language Review
MP	Modern Philology
N&Q	Notes and Queries
PMLA	Publications of the Mod. Lang. Assn. of America
PQ	Philological Quarterly (Iowa City)
RenD	Renaissance Drama (Northwestern U.)
RenP	Renaissance Papers
RES	Review of English Studies
SB	Studies in Bibliography; Papers of the Bibliographical Society of the University of Virginia

SEL	Studies in English Literature, 1500-1900
ShakS	Shakespeare Studies (U. of Cincinnati)
ShS	Shakespeare Survey
SJW	Shakespeare-Jahrbuch (Weimar)
SoR	Southern Review (Louisiana State U.)
SP	Studies in Philology
SQ	Shakespeare Quarterly
SR	Sewanee Review
SRen	Studies in the Renaissance
SSF	Studies in Short Fiction (Newberry Coll., S.C.)
TDR	The Drama Review [formerly Tulane Drama Review]
TLS	[London] Times Literary Supplement
TSE	Tulane Studies in English
TSL	Tennessee Studies in Literature
UR	University Review (Kansas City, Mo.)
UTQ	University of Toronto Quarterly
VQR	Virginia Quarterly Review
YR	Yale Review
YSE	Yale Studies in English

CROWELL'S HANDBOOK OF *Elizabethan & Stuart* LITERATURE

A

Acts and Monuments of These Latter and Perilous Days, Touching Matters of the Church, etc. A history of Christian martyrs written by John Foxe. It was first published in Latin at Strasbourg in 1554 as *Commentarii rerum in ecclesia gestarum,* and again at Basel in a much-enlarged edition in 1559. The English version, *Acts and Monuments of the Christian Church,* was first printed in 1563. The edition of 1776 was the first to be entitled *The Book of Martyrs,* the title used in many subsequent editions. Foxe himself published in 1570 a revised English version, with many additions and omissions, entitled *The Ecclesiastical History*. Today his history is usually referred to as "Foxe's Book of Martyrs."

The *Commentarii* published in 1554 deals chiefly with the Lollards; this edition was enlarged in the Latin version of 1559 to include the famous account of the persecution of Protestants under Mary Tudor. The English edition entitled *Acts and Monuments* (1563), which was not translated by Foxe, contains much information about the Marian massacres that Foxe collected from witnesses during his exile on the Continent and after his return to England in the early years of Elizabeth's reign. His *Ecclesiastical History* is the only version that reaches as far back the apostolic martyrdoms.

As an English prose stylist, Foxe is of little significance, for he wrote most effectively in Latin; the English versions of his history are largely the work of several translators. As a historian, however, he produced in his *Book of Martyrs* a work of enormous religious and political influence. Queen Elizabeth ordered a copy to be placed in every cathedral church along with the Book of Common Prayer, and Foxe's work proved extremely effective in sustaining hatred and fear of Roman Catholicism throughout the Tudor period. The role of a divisive propagandist, however, was not one that the mild-tempered Foxe relished, for he strongly advocated mercy for both heretics and Catholics.

Foxe's work was vehemently refuted as a tissue of lies by Catholics during the sixteenth century and defended by Protestants as gospel truth. The Elizabethan Protestant view was argued in the Victorian period by Foxe's editor, G. Townsend, in his debate with S. R. Maitland, who attacked Foxe's book as a medley of hearsay, specious documentation, and outright anti-Catholic propaganda. More recently, however, J. F. Mozley and others have restored Foxe's reputation as an essentially honest though fallible historian who made a genuine attempt to sift facts from hysterical prejudice. Mozley has established that when an account stood against what Foxe knew to be the truth, Foxe invariably rejected it.

Foxe's history grew to massive proportions through additions and exfoliations by other writers in later editions, in spite of the fact that the 1563 edition was in its time one of the bulkiest and most discursive histories in any language. In the 1563 edition the narrative is arranged into six books corresponding to the six main periods of Catholic persecutions after the Middle Ages. Each book is stuffed with legal documents in both Latin and English, anti-at Catholic martyr "accused and condemned and grisly woodcuts depicting burnings and mutilations. Foxe's accounts of the martyrdoms of Sir John Oldcastle, John Wyclif, and Jan Hus are especially vivid, but as his history reaches his own times and the terrible fires of the Smithfield massacres under Mary Tudor, his writing grows exceptionally dramatic. Foxe's zealous Protestant bias is most evident when his peremptory account of Sir Thomas More, as Catholic martyr "accused and condemned of treason" by Henry VIII, is compared with his patiently detailed and beautifully emotive story of the reformed bishops Nicholas Ridley and Hugh Latimer, burned together at Cambridge during the Marian executions. Bishop Ridley is seen comforting his friends and relatives the night before the execution; the composure and dignity of the martyrs is conveyed in eloquent dialogue like Latimer's poignant "Be of good cheer, Master Ridley, for we shall light such a candle in England this day as I daresay shall never be put out." There are horrors, too, meticulously recounted with almost journalistic understatement:

> Then the smith took a chain of iron and brought the same about both Doctor Ridley and Master Latimer's middles. And as he was knocking in a staple, Doctor Ridley took the chain in his hand, and shaked the same, for it did gird in his belly, and looking aside to the smith, said, "Good follow, knock it in hard, for the flesh will have his course."

From one perspective, Foxe's *Book of Martyrs* is a conduct book; for if Castiglione's *Il Cortegiano* taught Elizabethans how to make love and Lyly's *Euphues* how to converse elegantly, Foxe's *Book of Martyrs* taught them how to die like Christians.

The standard edition is by S. R. Cattley and G. Townsend, 8 vols. (1837-41). The 1843-49 edition contains Townsend's vindications of Foxe as a reliable historian. For S. R. Maitland's position, see his *Notes on the Contributions of... G. Townsend* (1841-42) and *Remarks on... S. R. Cattley's Defence of His Edition* (1842). The best critical analysis of Foxe's work is by J. F. Mozley, *John Foxe and His Book* (1940).

Advancement of Learning. See BACON, FRANCIS; CRITICISM, LITERARY.

Adventures of Master F. J., The. A prose tale by George GASCOIGNE, first published anonymously in 1573 in Gascoigne's *A Hundred Sundry Flowers,* a collection of poems. In the second version of the story, which appeared in *The Posies* (1575), Gascoigne expurgated some of the more risqué passages and changed the setting from northern England to Italy, perhaps to avoid any identification of the characters with actual persons. *The Adventures of Master F. J.* is often described as the first, or among the earliest, novels in English; it portrays social customs of the time with considerable realism and takes deep interest in the complex motives of its characters. No source is known.

In the revised version of the tale, Ferdinando Jeronimi, a rich Venetian gentleman "delighting more in hawking, hunting, and such other pastimes than he did in study," accepts an invitation to spend several months at the Lord of Velasco's country house in Lombardy. The Lord of Velasco secretly hopes to match him with his eldest daughter Frances, an intelligent, beautiful, and modest girl; but Ferdinando falls passionately in love with his host's daughter-in-law Elinor, "and forgetting the courtesy that the Lord of Velasco had showed him in entertaining him and his servants, with their horses, by the space of four months (which is a rare courtesy nowadays, and especially in such a country), he sought by all means possible to make the heir of Velasco a *becco*" (i.e., a cuckold).

Unlike Frances, Elinor is a vain and wanton courtesan; she has already taken her secretary as a lover, but when he departs for Venice on business she responds eagerly to Ferdinando's passionate sonnets and *billets-doux*. When the secretary returns, she promptly jilts Ferdinando, who becomes jealous and depressed, and finally physically ill for several weeks. Elinor nurses him faithfully and tries to raise his spirits, but when he recovers he bitterly rejects her and all "courtesies" and returns to Venice, "spending the rest of his days in a dissolute kind of life." Elinor continues her fickle ways, and Frances, after languishing in grief over Ferdinando's ingratitude, dies of consumption. At the conclusion Gascoigne states his moral: ". . . thus we see that where wicked lust doth bear the name of love, it doth not only infect the light-minded, but it may also become confusion to others which are vowed to constancy."

The standard edition is in *The Works,* ed. J. W. Cunliffe, 2 vols. (1907-10), I, which contains the revised version; Cunliffe's text is reprinted in *Elizabethan Fiction,* ed. Robert Ashley and Edwin Moseley (1953). The original version is in C. T. Prouty's edition of *A Hundred Sundry Flowers* (1942). For critical analyses, see C. T. Prouty, *George Gascoigne: Elizabethan Courtier, Soldier, and Poet* (1942); R. P. Adams, "Gascoigne's *Master F. J.* as Original Fiction," *PMLA,* LXXIII (1958); Richard A. Landham, "Narrative Structure in Gascoigne's *F. J.,*" *SSF,* IV (1966); and Lynette F. McGrath, "George Gascoigne's Moral Satire: The Didactic Use of Convention in *The Adventures Passed by Master F. J.,*" *JEGP,* LXX (1971).

Aethiopica. A late Greek romance attributed to Heliodorus of Emesa in Syria (fourth century A.D.), reputed to have been a bishop. Heliodorus' prose romance was translated into English by Thomas Underdowne in 1569 from a Latin translation by Stanislavs Warschewiczki (1551). Underdowne's version served as a source for plays by John Fletcher, Shakespeare, and other dramatists. Sir Philip Sidney drew extensively on the *Aethiopica* in his *Arcadia.*

The plot of the *Aethiopica* is so episodic and tangled as to defy summary. Persine, wife of an Ethiopian king, bears a white daughter, Chariclea, whose skin had been made pale by an alabaster statue during the mother's pregnancy. To foil scandal, Persine gives Chariclea in trust to a Pythian priest, who establishes her as a priestess of Apollo at Delphi, where Theagenes falls in love with her and carries her away. They have many adventures involving pirates, invading armies, wild animals, and so forth, until at last Chariclea returns to Ethiopia. She is about to be sacrificed when her real identity is discovered at the last moment.

The best translation is still that by Thomas Underdowne, available in the Tudor Translations (1895) as *An Aethiopian History.* For the influence of the *Aethiopica,* see S. L. Wolff, *Greek Romances in Elizabethan Prose Fiction* (1912).

Alabaster, William (1567-1640). English divine and Latin poet. Alabaster was educated at Westminster School and Trinity College, Cambridge; he became chaplain to the earl of Essex in 1596 and accompanied him on the Cádiz expedition. During 1588-92 Alabaster wrote two long Latin poems, an unfinished epic on Queen Elizabeth (not published), and a Latin tragedy, *Roxana* (1632), a condensed version of the Italian play *La Dalida* (1567) by Luigi Groto. Alabaster's epic is praised by Spenser in *Colin Clout's Come Home Again.*

After his conversion to Roman Catholicism in 1597, Alabaster was defrocked and imprisoned, and during this period he composed his sonnets (not printed until 1959), which are considered by some scholars to be among the earliest religious lyrics in the metaphysical style. In 1613-14 he returned to the Anglican Church and became Doctor of Divinity and chaplain to James I. His last years were devoted to theological studies and to the compilation of a Hebrew dictionary.

Alabaster's sonnets were edited by G. M. Story and Helen Gardner in the Oxford English Monographs series, No. 7 (1959).

Alaham. A tragedy by Fulke GREVILLE, first printed in 1633 but written some years earlier.

The villainous Alaham deposes his father, the king of Ormus, and orders him and an older brother, Zophi, blinded. The old king's virtuous daughter Caelica rescues them, but later Alaham has all three burned at the stake. At the conclusion of the play the people rebel against Alaham's tyranny. A *nuntius* (messenger) relates these grisly events to the audience.

The standard edition is in *The Poems and Dramas,* ed. G. Bullough, 2 vols., II (1939). For criticism, see R. N. Cushman, "Concerning Fulke Greville's Tragedy," *MLN,* XXIV (1909).

Alarum Against Usurers, An. LODGE. Thomas. See SATIRE.

Alchemist, The. A comedy by Ben JONSON, written in 1610 and printed in 1612. For the plot Jonson consulted a variety of sources, including Plautus' *Mostellaria,* Erasmus' *De alcumista,* and Giordano Bruno's *Il candelaio.* The character of Subtle may have been suggested by the real-life Simon Forman, an astrologer and charlatan of the time. The scene is the Blackfriars district of London during the plague of the summer of 1610.

Doctor Subtle, a professional cheat, and his whore Doll Common persuade Lovewit's butler Jeremy to allow them to set up their alchemical laboratory in Lovewit's house while the master is away in the country. Subtle and Jeremy, the latter disguised as Face, gull a whole series of dupes and scoundrels, including Abel Drugger, who consults Face about the proper way of setting up a tobacco shop; Dapper, a gambler; two sanctimonious Puritans called Ananias and Tribulation Wholesome; Sir Epicure Mammon, a miserly lecher, and one Kastril, a country bumpkin who aspires to swagger and fight like a city gallant. Subtle's factory of intrigue and quackery ends with the return of Lovewit, himself something of a wily character, who disposes of the rogues and appropriates their winnings—all except those acquired by Face, who manages to provide Lovewit with a rich wife. More concentrated than either *Volpone* or *Epicoene, The Alchemist* is among Jonson's most brilliant satiric comedies. Consistent with the classical unities, all of the action occurs at Lovewit's house, the events do not exceed a single day, and every character and gesture combine to focus on the single motive also stressed in *Volpone*—the perversity of greed and the obsession of every character to get something for nothing. Unlike *Volpone,* however, *The Alchemist* treats this theme without moral indignation or harsh poetic justice.

The standard edition is in *Ben Jonson,* ed. C. H. Herford and Percy and Evelyn Simpson, 11 vols. (1925-53), V. Douglas Brown has edited *The Alchemist* in a New Mermaid edition (1966); F. H. Mares in the Revels Plays series (1967); and Sidney Musgrove for the Fountainwell Drama Series (1968). Important critical analyses are those by Edward B. Partridge, *The Broken Compass* (1958), and Robert E. Knoll, *Ben Jonson's Plays* (1964). Jonson's esoteric allusions and vocabulary are explained in articles by Johnstone Parr, *PQ,* XXIV (1945), and E. H. Duncan, *PMLA,* LXI (1946). See also Judd Arnold, "Lovewit's Triumph and Jonsonian Morality: A Reading of *The Alchemist,*" *Criticism,* XI (1969); Myrddin Jones, "Sir Epicure Mammon: A Study in 'Spiritual Fornication,'" *Ren Q,* XXII (1969); and Alan C. Dessen, *Jonson's Moral Comedy* (1971).

alchemy. The medieval pseudo-science that sought to change base metals into gold by use of a "philosopher's stone," and to cure the sick and prolong life by means of an "elixir," or chemical panacea. Alchemy was based on the theory that there were four elements, each with its dominant "properties": air (hot and moist), earth (cold and dry), fire (hot and dry), and water (cold and moist). Gold, the one "perfect" metal, was thought to be the product of a precise balance of these elements; similarly, by correspondence, health in humans was achieved by a perfect mixture of these elements as they were manifest in the four humours. Hence medicine and natural philosophy concurred in the alchemist's assumption that all reactions were derived from the dynamic effects of elemental "properties."

Although some sixteenth-century intellectuals scorned alchemists, as did Ben Jonson in his satiric comedy *The Alchemist,* their claims were widely accepted by many. One notable alchemist, John DEE, for a time enjoyed the patronage of Queen Elizabeth.

For a general discussion of the subject, see J. E. Mercer, *Alchemy, Its Science and Romance* (1921), and Paul H. Kocher, *Science and Religion in Elizabethan England* (1953); for the philosophical bases of alchemy, see Wayne Shumaker, *The Occult Sciences in the Renaissance: A Study of Intellectual Patterns* (1973) and Peter J. French, *John Dee: The World of an Elizabethan Magus* (1972).

Alexander, Sir William, earl of Stirling (1567-1640). Scottish statesman, poet, and dramatist. After attending the universities of Glascow and Leyden, he went on a lengthy tour of France, Spain, and Italy. In 1604 he published *Aurora,* a listless sonnet sequence in the Petrarchan mode, and in 1603 *The Tragedy of Darius,* the first of four Senecan tragedies on Darius, Alexander the Great, Croesus, and Caesar that he later published as *The Monarchic Tragedies* (1607). These were based on French neoclassic models introduced into England by the countess of Pembroke. He also wrote a poorly received translation of the Psalms.

He held a number of high offices, including that of viscount of Canada, a position which actually gave him all the territories of Canada as his own property. His enthusiasm for colonial investments and adventures is evident from his book *Encouragement to Colonies* (1624), later published with the title *The Map and Description of New England* (1630).

The standard edition of the verse is by L. E. Kastner and H. B. Charlton, 2 vols. (1921-29), which includes a full bibliography. There is a biographical and critical study by T. H. McGrail, *Sir William Alexander* (1940).

Allegro, L', and Il Penseroso. Companion poems by John MILTON, written about 1632. Both are in tetrameter couplets. *L'Allegro* ("the cheerful man" in Italian) celebrates the joys of spring, pastoral poetry, rural scenery, and urban excitement, and concludes with a tribute to Ben Jonson's "learned sock" (comedy). Shakespeare is described as "fancy's child" whom the poet longs to hear "warble his native wood-notes wild." *Il Penseroso* pays tribute to manners and moods totally opposite—melancholy, contemplation, tragedy, and "the hairy gown and mossy cell." By the title "Penseroso" Milton intended to mean "contemplative" (actually spelled "pensieroso" in Italian). What Milton contrasts by these two poems has long been debated by scholars. Certainly *L'Allegro* and *Il Penseroso* oppose contrasting moods of gaiety and melancholy; it has also been suggested, by E. M. W. Tillyard and others, that they represent adaptations into verse of Latin prolusions, or college rhetorical exercises, on opposing subjects such as the virtues of day versus night, comedy versus tragedy, rural versus urban. Both poems owe something to Robert Burton's *Anatomy of Melancholy,* which prescribes pleasure as an antidote for chronic depression. William Blake's illustrations of the two poems are reproduced in the Nonesuch edition, *Milton's English Poems* (1954), and in Adrian Van Sinderin's *Blake, the Mystic Genius* (1949).

The edition by Merritt Y. Hughes in *Complete Poems and Major Prose* (1957) is fully annotated. There is a survey of criticism by J. B. Leishman in *E & S,* New Series, IV (1951); and a casebook, *L'Allegro and Il Penseroso,* ed. Elaine B. Safer and Thomas L. Erskine (1970).

All Fools. A comedy by George CHAPMAN, written in 1599 and performed the same year by the Lord Admiral's Men at the Rose Theatre and the Blackfriars. It was first printed in 1605. Chapman's play was adapted from two comedies by Terence, *Heautontimoroumenos* ("The Self-Tormentor") and *Adelphi* ("The Brothers"). The story takes place in Florence at some unspecified time.

Marc Antonio and Gostanzo are two fathers of totally different temperaments and parental methods. Marc Antonio is easygoing, lenient, and honest; Gostanzo is dictatorial, tight-fisted, and Machiavellian. Marc Antonio's elder son Fortunio clandestinely courts Bellanora, Gostanzo's only daughter, and Gostanzo's son Valerio, although duping his father into believing he is dutiful and thrifty, is secretly married to a penniless beauty named Gratiana and spends all his spare time at "dice, cards, tennis, wenching, dancing, and what not."

The scene of Valerio's revels is sometimes at the house of the social-climbing merchant Cornelio, a husband so madly jealous of his wife Gazetta that he keeps her virtually a prisoner in his house and falsely accuses her of infidelity with the score of gallants he lavishly entertains. The subplot of Cornelio and Gazetta contrasts a couple who live in open matrimony without love with Fortunio and Bellanora, and Valerio and Gratiana, who experience genuine passion but must conceal their love.

Rinaldo, Marc Antonio's younger son and Valerio's best friend, is a wily prankster who begins his first intrigue in the play by tricking Gostanzo into believing that Fortunio is secretly married to Gratiana, a device to throw the old man off the scent of Gratiana's real husband. As Rinaldo anticipates, Gostanzo promptly takes this information to Marc Antonio, whom he roundly berates for his foolish leniency in raising Fortunio. To demonstrate the efficacy of his own harsh parental conduct, Gostanzo offers to take Fortunio home to live with him, where the supposedly errant son will profit from the example of the "dutiful and thrifty" Valerio. Gostanzo also invites Gratiana to perform as a "proper lady" with whom Valerio will illustrate for Fortunio's benefit the most elegant and chaste conduct. Thus Rinaldo dupes Gostanzo into bringing both sets of lovers to dwell under the same roof.

During one of his parties Cornelio humiliates Valerio by ridiculing the young man's lack of singing ability, and Valerio and Rinaldo conspire to prey upon Cornelio's jealousy until he divorces his wife. Maddened by Valerio's innuendoes, Cornelio challenges his prime suspect, the courtier Dariotto, to a duel, but the merchant is so ignorant of the art of swordsmanship that he is lucky to escape with some slight wounds.

Meanwhile Gostanzo is alarmed to discover his supposedly proper son in the arms of Gratiana, and unwisely chooses to consult Rinaldo, who suggests he send the girl to Marc Antonio's house posing as Valerio's (not Fortunio's) wife, presumably married without Gostanzo's knowledge. By this stratagem Gostanzo will remove Gratiana (unknown to Marc Antonio) from his house without losing face with Fortunio. Later Valerio appears at Marc Antonio's, where his father has gone, and confesses that he is in fact married to Gratiana. Mollified by his son's apparent humbleness and Marc Antonio's eloquent plea for compassion, Gostanzo forgives Valerio and accepts his new daughter-in-law.

Cornelio's stormy relations are not so easily calmed. He hires a notary to draw up articles of divorce, which he insists upon reading to an assembled company of gallants. A friend of Dariotto's proclaims Gazetta's innocence and reveals the plot against Cornelio by Valerio and Rinaldo. These revelations are sufficient to forestall the divorce but not enough to ease Cornelio's nagging jealousy. In revenge against Valerio, he falsely reports to Rinaldo that Valerio has been arrested for debt and detained by officers at the Half Moon Tavern, Valerio's favorite carousing ground. As Cornelio expects, Rinaldo brings Gostanzo to the tavern with money for Valerio's release, and there Gostanzo discovers his "dutiful and thrifty" son at the height of his revels. Marc Antonio soon appears to announce that Fortunio and Bellanora have married, and Gostanzo, considerably humbled by these multiple discoveries, realizes that he can no longer chide Marc Antonio for his parental leniency, nor continue to boast of his own harsh discipline as an effective control for youthful passions. Also to the tavern comes Cornelio, reconciled with Gazetta and determined to keep his chronic jealousy to himself. At the conclusion of the play a tipsy Valerio mounts a chair and delivers a witty speech in praise of family harmony.

Chapman's comedy is an artful adaptation of Terentian characters and situations. Rinaldo is an updated version of Terence's scheming slave; the contrast between the two fathers, one lenient and the other strict, is also taken from Terence. Except for Gostanzo, who is often genuinely comic as a domestic Machiavellian hoist by his own petard, Chapman's characters have little dramatic vitality, perhaps because they are so thoroughly manipulated by the superlatively intelligent Rinaldo. Another weakness of the play is its plot, which is often convoluted and difficult to follow. Nevertheless, *All Fools* remains, for the most part, a lively social comedy tinged with satire that is almost equal to Chapman's other efforts in the same mode, *The Gentleman Usher* and *Monsieur D'Olive.*

The standard edition is by T. M. Parrott, *The Comedies,* 2 vols. (1914). II: More recent editions are by Frank Manley for the Regents Renaissance Drama series (1970), and Allan Holaday (1970). For criticism, see Paul V. Kreider, *Elizabethan Comic Character Conventions as Revealed in the Comedies of George Chapman* (1935).

All's Well That Ends Well. A comedy by William SHAKESPEARE, written about 1602-04 and first printed in the 1623 Folio. The source is the ninth novel of the third day in Boccaccio's *Decameron,* which Shakespeare read in William Painter's *Palace of Pleasure* (1566-67). No source has been found for the subplot. Like *Measure for Measure* and *Troilus and Cressida, All's Well* is considered one of Shakespeare's "problem plays," a term used to describe the comedies of a more saturnine outlook and abrasive tone than the romantic comedies of the 1590s.

Helena, orphan of a renowned physician and ward of the countess of Rousillon, is in love with the countess's son Bertram, but has no hope of marrying so far above her own station. When Bertram is called to the king's court in Paris, Helena finds an excuse to follow him: the king is ailing and she will cure him with one of her father's prescriptions. She makes a bargain with the king: her life will be forfeit if the medicine fails, but she can have her pick of the bachelors in the court if it succeeds. The king is cured, and Helena claims Bertram. He objects to the marriage as unsuitable to his rank but consents rather than risk the anger of the king. Immediately after the wedding, with the encouragment of his braggart friend Parolles, Bertram hastens away to the wars in Tuscany.

Bertram sends Helena a cruel letter in which he states that he will never act as her husband unless she is able to take a ring from his finger and to conceive his child during his absence. While in Florence on a pilgrimage Helena meets Diana, whom Bertram has been trying to seduce, and Helena persuades her to help fulfill the seemingly impossible conditions of Bertram's letter. Diana gets the ring from Bertram on the promise of an assignation. Helena is substituted for Diana in bed, the plot succeeds, and when Bertram learns the truth he laments his former cruelty, repudiates Parolles, and is reunited with his wife.

In *All's Well* Shakespeare innovated on two traditional types of medieval tales: the so-called virtue narrative, in which a wife must prove her worth to a contemptuous husband before he will consummate the marriage; and the "bed trick," in which the heroine is substituted in bed for another woman—an episode Shakespeare employed again in *Measure for Measure.* To modern audiences, neither of these episodes is especially entertaining, and *All's Well* has not been one of Shakespeare's most popular plays on the stage. Moreover, the main characters of the play are unsavory and the satiric tone savage in the manner of Juvenal. Bertram is not sufficiently noble to warrant Helena's irrational devotion, his friend Parolles is degraded and coarse, and even the clown lacks wit and gaiety.

The standard edition is in the New Cambridge edition, ed. Arthur Quiller-Couch and J. Dover Wilson (1929). For critical discussions, see W. W. Laurence, *Shakespeare's Problem Comedies* (1931); E. M. W. Tillyard, *Shakespeare's Problem Plays* (1949); James L. Calderwood, "The Mingled Yarn of *All's Well,*" *JEGP,* LXII (1963); and Roger Warren, "Why Does It End Well? Helena, Bertram, and The Sonnets," *Sh S,* XXII (1969).

Amoretti. A sequence of eighty-eight sonnets by Edmund SPENSER, written in 1593 and first published with the wedding song *Epithalamion* in 1595. Spenser adopts a variety of rhyme schemes, the most prevalent being the linked quatrains, *abab bcbc cdcd ee.* Although the sequence reflects the influence of Petrarch, especially in the conventional portrayal of the dedicated, passionate lover and his cruel, ungrateful mistress, Spenser instilled the sonnets with a great deal of his own Platonic and Christian ideals regarding love; hence the sequence, in its dramatization of an ideal love culminating in the Christian sacrament of marriage, is sometimes thought to have been written in reaction to Sir Philip Sidney's more courtly and passionate *Astrophel and Stella.*

Tradition holds that the sequence describes Spenser's difficult courtship of his second wife, Elizabeth Boyle, although the lady in the sequence is not named. In one sonnet the poet explains that she repulsed his early impetuous ardor; in another he expresses concern over their differences of age, the poet being forty, the lady much younger. Two sonnets (33, 80) lament the poet's slow progress on *The Faerie Queen.* The concluding sonnets rejoice over the lady's acceptance of the poet's love, and the *Epithalamion,* appended to the edition of 1595, celebrates their marriage.

Thus *Amoretti* is somewhat more specific in autobiographical allusions than either Sidney's *Astrophel and Stella* or Shakespeare's Sonnets. Sonnet 5 comments on the poet's reactions to criticism of the lady's pride; 46 refers to her chastising him for staying too late during a visit, probably at her brother's house at Youghal, thirty miles from Spenser's Kilcolman; 64 refers to their first kiss; 75 to an episode in which he writes her name in the sand; and 87 to a brief separation before their marriage. Spenser notes, too, that she is somewhat proud and not a little vain (79) and and must be gently schooled in virtues (84). The relationship described in *Amoretti* is that of a sacramental union of soul with soul, occasionally threatened by carnal desires. Spenser's conflict between this ideal conception of love and his passionate temptation to settle for less parallels Petrarch's familiar struggle of reason and passion. (For further discussion of Petrarchan themes, see SONNET SEQUENCES.)

The standard edition is in *The Works,* ed. E. A. Greenlaw, F. M. Padelford, *et. al.,* 10 vols. (1932-49). II. A well-annotated edition with critical commentary is *Edmund Spenser's Poetry,* ed. Hugh Maclean (1968). For criticism, see L. C. John, *The Elizabethan Sonnet Se-*

quences: Studies in Conventional Conceits (1938); Louis L. Martz, "*The Amoretti:* 'Most Goodly Temperature,'" in *Form and Convention in the Poetry of Edmund Spenser: Selected Papers from the English Institute,* ed. William Nelson (1961); William Nelson, *The Poetry of Edmund Spenser* (1963); and R. Kellogg, "Thought's Astonishment and the Dark Conceits of Spenser's *Amoretti,*" *Ren P*(1965).

Anatomy of Melancholy, The. See BURTON, ROBERT.

Andrewes, Lancelot (1555-1626). Anglican preacher and theologian. Born in London, Andrewes attended the Merchant Taylors' School and Pembroke Hall, Cambridge. After taking orders in 1580, he became vicar of St. Giles', Cripplegate, and later prebendary of St. Paul's. For the last twenty years of his life he was vicar in Southwell. He rose to his highest office, bishop of Winchester, in 1618. He was frequently consulted about theology and church matters by Queen Elizabeth (for whom he served as chaplain), James I, and Charles I. Among the fifty-four divines chosen by James I to translate the Authorised Version of the Bible, Andrewes was the most formidable linguistic scholar, with a knowledge of Hebrew, Syriac, Chaldee, Greek, Latin, and at least ten additional languages (see BIBLE TRANSLATIONS). All his voluminous writings are homiletic and theological, many highly esoteric or technical in nature. His prose style has been praised by T. S. Eliot for its intellectual complexity, economy, and wit. With John Donne and Jeremy Taylor, Andrewes was among the foremost Anglican preachers of his age.

Ninety-Six sermons (1870-74; 5 vols.) is the only complete edition of Andrewes' sermons. The fullest collection of Andrewes' works is in *The Library of Anglo-Catholic Theology,* 11 vols. (1841-54). See also *The Sermons,* ed. G. M. Story (1967). Critical commentaries include K. N. Colville, *Fame's Twilight* (1923); T. S. Eliot's appreciation. "For Lancelot Andrewes" (1928; repr. in *Selected Essays,* 1950); W. F. Mitchell, *English Pulpit Oratory from Andrewes to Tillotson* (1932); and John Webber, "Celebration of Word and World in Lancelot Andrewes' Style." *JEGP,* LXIV (1965). For biography, see H. Ross Williamson, *Four Stuart Portraits* (1949); and P. A. Welsby, *Lancelot Andrewes, 1555-1626* (1958).

Angler, The Compleat. A contemplative discourse on fishing by Izaak Walton, first published in 1653. The fifth edition (1676) contains additions by Charles Cotton that have become an integral part of the text; also added to the 1676 edition are portions of Robert Venables' *Experienced Angler* (1662). Walton's tone is modest, serene, genial; his style is detailed, concise, often vivid, particularly in his descriptions of nature. His treatise has little practical value as a manual on fishing, but the three hundred or more editions that have appeared since 1653 suggest that the book represents more to readers than simply a guide to fishing. Walton's genial charm is manifest everywhere; appropriately, the subtitle is "The Contemplative Man's Recreation" and is addressed to the "honest angler."

The principal characters of the discourse include Auceps, a falconer; Piscator, a fisherman; and Venator, a hunter. At the beginning of the book Auceps, Piscator, and Venator meet one May morning and each extols the virtues of his particular sport, or sporting "element" (i.e., earth, water, and air). As Auceps leaves to look at his hawk, Piscator accompanies Venator in hunting the otter, after which Piscator instructs Venator in the art of angling. The first day is spent fishing for chub and preparing them for dinner, the second with trout fishing and the mysteries of bait, lines, flies, and some discussion of excellent fishing locations—all larded with erudite quotations from the Bible, classical literature, and Bacon's works.

Part II, added to the fifth edition by Cotton, features the discourses of Piscator Junior and Viator, both ardent anglers, and much discussion of fly tying and trout cooking. It is not as lively as the first part.

The Compleat Angler is in *The Compleat Walton,* ed. Geoffrey. L. Keynes (1929), and was edited separately by J. Buchan (1935). The work is treated at length by R. B. Marston, *Walton and Some Earlier Writers on Fish and Fishing* (1894); and Peter Oliver, *A New Chronicle of The Compleat Angler* (1936). See also H. J. Oliver, "The Composition and Revisions of *The Compleat Angler,*" *MLN,* XLII (1947); and M. S. Goldman, "Izaak

Walton and *The Arte of Angling,* (1577)," *Studies in Honor of T. W. Baldwin* (1958). Arnold Wood, *A Bibliography of The Complete Angler* (1900) is still helpful; for more recent scholarship, see Dennis G. Donovan, "Recent Studies in Burton and Walton," *EIR,* I (1971).

anti-Masque. See MASQUE.

Antony and Cleopatra. A tragedy by William SHAKESPEARE, written about 1606-07 and first printed in the 1623 Folio. The principal source is Thomas North's translation of Plutarch's *Lives of the Noble Grecians and Romans* (1579; see TRANSLATIONS).

In Alexandria Mark Antony idles away his time with the beautiful Egyptian queen Cleopatra. Recalled to Rome by the death of his wife, he attempts to mend his growing rift with Octavius Caesar by marrying Caesar's sister Octavia, whom he soon abandons to rejoin Cleopatra. At Actium Antony, backed by Egyptian forces, fights Octavius' forces at sea. When Cleopatra flees with her ships, Antony deserts his followers and ignominiously follows her. Octavius Caesar presses his victory by pursuing Antony to Alexandria, where Antony is decisively beaten. Deserted by his faithful general Enobarbus and most of his followers, and desolated by a false report of Cleopatra's death, Antony falls upon his sword. He is taken to the monument where Cleopatra is in hiding, and dies in her arms. Cleopatra, fearing that she will be transported to Rome as a spectacle to grace Octavius' victory, has asps smuggled to her in a bowl of fruit and applies the fatal vipers to her arm and breast. The play concludes with Octavius' tribute to the dead lovers. Of Shakespeare's tragedies *Antony and Cleopatra* is the most episodic, lyrically intense, and morally neutral. In the first scene Antony declares his irresponsible passion with the words "Let Rome in Tiber melt, and the wide arch / Of the rang'd empire fall! Here is my space." Thereafter he is chided by Octavius Caesar and Lepidus, and even by his closest friend Enobarbus, as a "fool," yet neither his transgression nor the many examples of disloyalty in the play are treated in terms of moral evil. Instead, Antony's all-consuming passion for Cleopatra symbolizes an exalted vision of life in opposition to the mundane workaday world of Rome, with its political intrigues, wars, and struggles for power. Yet some readers cannot accept Antony's sensuality as an obsession worthy of a true tragic hero. Hence G. B. Harrison refuses to view Antony seriously because he "throws an empire into the lap of a harlot," and Bernard Shaw dismisses the play as a comedy because it turns "hogs into heroes." Others, however, have viewed the play as representing the ancient theme of a hero's choice of love over empire, a lyrical celebration of a passion that transcends reason, morality, and time. After the Restoration, *Antony and Cleopatra* was temporarily eclipsed by Dryden's adaptation *All for Love,* first performed in 1678.

The standard edition is in the New Cambridge edition, ed. J. Dover Wilson (1950). Characterizations are treated in detail by Levin L. Schücking, *Character Problems in Shakespeare's Plays* (1922), and imagery by Caroline Spurgeon, *Shakespeare's Imagery and What It Tells Us* (1935). For other important commentary, see G. Wilson Knight, *The Imperial Theme* (1930); F. R. Leavis, *"Antony and Cleopatra* and *All for Love," Scrutiny,* V (1936); S. L. Bethell, *Shakespeare and the Popular Dramatic Tradition* (1944); J. F. Danby, *Poets on Fortune's Hill* (1952); Maurice Charney, *Shakespeare's Roman Plays: The Function of Imagery in the Drama* (1961); and Julian Markels, *The Pillar of the World: Antony and Cleopatra in Shakespeare's Development* (1968).

Apology for Actors (Thomas Heywood). See CRITICISM, LITERARY.

Apology for Poetry, An (Sidney). See CRITICISM, LITERARY.

Arbasto, the Anatomy of Fortune. See GREENE, ROBERT.

Arcades. A pastoral entertainment in verse by John MILTON, written about 1633. Milton's friend Henry Lawes, the musician, composed the music. The subtitle describes the conditions of the performance: "Part of an entertainment presented to the countess dowager of Derby at Harefield by some noble persons of her family." The countess, the former Lady Alice Spencer, was the widow of the fifth earl of Derby, and related to Edmund Spenser, who dedicated to her "The Tears of the Muses" and lamented the death of her husband in *Colin Clout's Come Home Again.* In 1600 she married Sir Thomas Egerton and became the stepmother of Sir John Egerton, Lord Bridgewater, whose investiture as Lord President of Wales is celebrated in Milton's *Comus.* The countess' estate at Harefield was eight miles from Horton, where Milton resided.

The Arcades of the title are the denizens of Arcadia, the Greek state in the Peloponnesus idealized by Giacomo Sannazaro, Sir Philip Sidney, and numerous other Renaissance pastoralists. They begin the entertainment by addressing the "shining throne" of the countess:

Look Nymphes, and Shepherds look,
What sudden blaze of majesty
Is that which we from hence descry,
Too divine to be mistook:
 This, this is she
To whom our vows and wishes bend,
Here our solemn search hath end.

The Genius of the Wood (probably played by Lawes, who performed in *Comus* as the Attendant Spirit) then steps forward to descant for fifty or more lines of decasyllabic couplets on the music of the spheres and harmonious natural laws—a lyrical tribute to the powers of music—and the entertainment concludes with two brief songs in praise of the countess.

Arcades is so brief (109 lines) and purely lyrical that most scholars hesitate to describe it as a masque, preferring the term of the subtitle, an "entertainment"—a short masque—like dramatization used as a greeting or tribute. In contrast to *Comus,* which is lengthy and philosophical, *Arcades* is a simple and ingenuous work in the carefree spirit of *L'Allegro* and *Il Penseroso.*

The standard edition is in *The Works,* ed. Frank A. Patterson, 18 vols. (1931-38), I. For other well-annotated editions, see *The Complete Poetry and Selected Prose,* ed. Merritt Y. Hughes (1957); *The Complete English Poetry,* ed. John T. Shawcross (1963); and *The Complete Poetical Works,* ed. Douglas Bush (1965). For comment on Milton's collaboration with Lawes, see Willa McClung Evans, *Henry Lawes, Musician and Friend of Poets* (1941).

Arcadia, The. A pastoral romance by Sir Philip SIDNEY. It exists in two different versions. The "Old" *Arcadia* Sidney composed around 1580 for the amusement of his sister Mary, countess of Pembroke, describing it in his dedication to her in the 1590 edition as "an idle work"... "a trifle, and that triflingly handled." The "Old" *Arcadia* is a complete work consisting of five books or "acts" separated by commentary and narration in verse and prose which Sidney called "eclogues." Sidney's principal sources in *The Arcadia* are the late Greek romances of Achilles Tatius and Heliodorus. Giacomo Sannazaro's *Arcadia* (1504), and Jorge de Montemayor's *Diana enamorada* (c. 1550). The "Old" *Arcadia* survives in six manuscripts first collated by Bertram Dobell in 1909 and published in 1926 by A. Feuillerat. Before Feuillerat's edition, the "Old" *Arcadia* had been published only in incomplete and corrupt texts.

Around 1584 Sidney began a thorough revision of *The Arcadia,* and by the time of his death in 1586 he had completed two books and part of a third. According to his friend and biographer Fulke Greville, Sidney requested on his deathbed that the work be destroyed. When Greville learned that printers eager to exploit Sidney's fame were planning unauthorized editions, he secured a license of publication for Jacob Ponsonby, who in 1590 printed the incomplete, revised "New" *Arcadia* from Greville's manuscript. In 1593 the countess of Pembroke, obviously convinced that her brother's romance was more than "a trifle," arranged for the publication of the revised version, to which she added a completed Book III and Books IV and V improvised from portions of the "Old" *Arcadia.* This 1593 version, carefully edited and in parts thoroughly altered by the countess of Pembroke, became *The Arcadia* most widely read and often reprinted before Feuillerat's edition in 1926.

The "Old" *Arcadia* is a suspenseful adventure story of intrigue, love, and mystery. An oracle has predicted that within the year Duke Basilius of Laconia will be replaced on his throne by a foreigner, his young wife Gynecia will commit adultery, and his two beautiful daughters Pamela and Philoclea will be stolen from him. To escape this dire prophecy, Basilius leaves his trusted minister Philanax in charge of the kingdom and retires to Arcadia to wait out the year in seclusion with his wife and daughters. To Arcadia come two young princes, Pyrocles and Musidorus, son and nephew of Evarchus, king of Macedon. During their adventures in Asia Minor, they heard of Basilius' predicted fate and of the celebrated beauty of his daughters; to learn more about the situation in Arcadia without being detected, they don disguises—Pyrocles as an Amazon called Zelmane, Musidorus as a simple shepherd named Doras. By the conclusion of Book I Basilius has become enamored of Zelmane, as have both Gynecia and Philoclea, who, unlike Basilius, have penetrated Pyrocles' disguise. Musidorus and Pamela fall in love at first sight, but Musidorus, in an effort to conceal his ardor from Basilius and the others, pretends to woo Mopsa, daughter of Basilius' rustic servant Dametas.

Courted passionately by both Basilius and Gynecia, Pyrocles tricks them into making love in the darkness of a cave, each thinking the other to be Zelmane, while he spends the night in the arms of Philoclea. Meanwhile Musidorus elopes with Pamela, and Dametas, searching for the missing Pamela, comes across Pyrocles and Philoclea asleep together. Pyrocles is arrested for rape and Philoclea for treason. In the cave Basilius and Gynecia realize the deception, repent of their folly, and pledge loyalty to each other in the future. To seal their oaths Gynecia gives her husband a love potion she had prepared for Pyrocles, and Basilius falls into a deathlike coma.

The lovers Musidorus and Pamela also experience difficulties. They are captured by brigands while eloping to Thessalia, rescued by Philanax's soldiers, and brought back to Arcadia as prisoners to stand trial for treason. At this point King Evarchus arrives in Arcadia looking for his son and is appointed judge in a tense trial involving Gynecia for the supposed murder of Basilius, Pyrocles for rape, Musidorus, Philoclea, and Pamela for treason (thus fulfilling the prophecy that a foreigner would rule in Basilius' place). After their long absence, Evarchus does not recognize the princes, and condemns both of them to death. Gynecia, Evarchus decrees, is to be buried alive, and the daughter of Basilius sent to a nunnery. When a stranger arrives and identifies Musidorus and Pyrocles, Evarchus reluctantly proclaims that his harsh sentences must still be carried out in the name of justice. Tragedy is averted, however, when Basilius awakens and exonerates all the defendants. Thus, as Basilius realizes, the mysterious predictions of the oracle have all come to pass.

While Sidney was revising this tale he was strongly influenced by the neoclassic precepts of the countess of Pembroke and the Aristotelian commentator and critic Julius Caesar Scaliger (1484-1558), whose *Poetice* Sidney followed very closely in writing his *An Apology for Poetry,* a literary treatise which, most scholars believe, Sidney composed about the same time he was at work on the "New" *Arcadia.* In that treatise Sidney described such prose works as Xenophon's *Cyropaedia* and Heliodorus' *Aethiopica* as "absolute heroical poems." "It is not rhyming and versing that maketh a poet," Sidney observed in *An Apology for Poetry,* "but it is that feigning notable images of virtues, vices, and what else, with that delightful teaching, which must be the right describing note to know a poet by." These maxims are in essential agreement with Fulke Greville's explanation in *The Life of Sidney* of his friend's purpose in writing *The Arcadia:* "In all the creatures of his making, his intent and scope was, to turn the barren philosophy precepts into pregnant images of life. . ."

Sidney's "New" *Arcadia,* therefore, reflects his effort to turn a romance into "an absolute heroical poem" instilled with "notable images" of vices and virtues that would convey "delightful teaching." To convert "barren philosophy precepts into pregnant images of life," he changed the abstract speeches in the "Old" *Arcadia* into symbolic actions and characters in the "New"; he added concrete actions that represent moral concepts and new characters whose natures express extremes of good and evil. Whereas the "Old" *Arcadia* is primarily a love story, the "New" portrays love as but one motif among an orchestration of themes—politics, war, filial obligation, courtesy, and friendship—ideas touched upon in the "Old" *Arcadia* but given dramatic emphasis by action and characterizations in the "New." Consistent with the epic tradition, the "New" *Arcadia* begins not at the beginning with Basilius learning of the oracle's prophecy but *in medias res,* with two shepherds in conversation about the miraculous goddess Urania and with the unexplained shipwreck of Musidorus and Pyrocles. The "Old" *Arcadia* takes place in a single province, and the action, whether erotic or combative, is entirely personal; in the "New" the adventures of Musidorus and Pyrocles in Asia Minor are fully depicted, insurrections and wars rage throughout Greece and the Near East, and a host of new rulers are introduced to dramatize contrasting values of statecraft. Moreover, the language of the "New" *Arcadia* is considerably elevated in syntax and diction over the "Old"—some sentences of the "New" *Arcadia* reaching to 150 words or more—to give the tale a tone fitting to "an absolute heroical" prose poem.

The Arcadia was variously interpreted throughout the seventeenth century. Some read it as "a trifle, and that triflingly handled," a romance designed, like John Lyly's *Euphues,* to be read by genteel ladies (those enthusiastic disciples of *The Arcadia* whom Samuel Richardson appealed to when he named his novel *Pamela* after Sidney's heroine); others, like Fulke Greville, viewed *The Arcadia* as a profound moral and political narrative, a work intended, like Spenser's *Faerie Queene,* "to fashion a gentleman or noble person in virtuous and gentle discipline." Milton's condemnation of *The Arcadia* as a "vain, amatorious poem" in EIKONOKLASTES (1649) was motivated by political considerations, for in that tract he was answering the Royalist pamphlet *Eikon Basilike* ("The King's Image"), purported to be the death-watch meditations of Charles I on the night before his execution. As Milton pointed out, the king's pious and magnanimous words to his cruel oppressors were really those of Pamela during her imprisonment by her aunt Cecropia in Book III of *The Arcadia:* "Let calamity be the exercise, but not the overthrow, of my virtue; let their power prevail, but prevail not to destruction; let my greatness be their prey; let my pain be the sweetness of their revenge; let them (if so it seem good unto Thee) vex me with more and more punishment. But, O Lord, let never their wickedness have such a hand but that I may carry a pure mind in a pure body." Wisely, Sidney's plagiarists omitted Pamela's concluding request that God "preserve the virtuous Musidorus."

The main literary significance of *The Arcadia* is that, as the first pastoral romance in English, it not only helped to continue the vogue of the pastoral begun by Spenser's *The Shepherd's Calendar* in 1579 (see PASTORAL), but gave that mode a new prose dimension and established once and for all an English narrative fiction free of both medieval allegory and Lyly's absurd EUPHUISM. Almost equally important, Sidney's stately, flowing, and often graceful prose style served as forerunner to the architectonic, periodic paragraphs of seventeenth-century writers like Sir Thomas Browne and Jeremy Taylor. And although *The Arcadia* cannot be said to have led directly to the English novel, its psychological concern, sensuous descriptions, emphasis on irony of character and situation, and (contrary to general opinion) occasional humour and wit represent a sharp departure from earlier narratives and helped open much wider vistas for other types of fiction (see FICTION).

The Arcadia was closely imitated by Robert Greene and many other followers of Sidney; Shakespeare borrowed from it for his tale of Gloucester and his sons in *King Lear;* Beaumont and Fletcher based the character of Euphrasia in *Philaster* on Sidney's story of the real Zelmane (not Pyrocles disguised), who fell in love with Pyrocles, disguised herself as his page, and died of illness. In the 1630s James Shirley capitalized on the lingering popularity of Sidney's romance by dramatizing episodes from it in a play called *The Arcadia.* In the eighteenth century William Cowper and Samuel Johnson, poles apart on other aesthetic matters, both praised *The Arcadia* for its splendid style and noble sentiments, and in later years Sir Walter Scott did not hesitate to copy an entire descriptive passage from *The Arcadia* in writing *Ivanhoe.* Twentieth-century readers, inured to the brisk and laconic, may find Sidney's romance episodic and languorous, a *chef d'oeuvre* to be savored by the most desultory of palates, although there remains widespread admiration for many of the eighty poems of various experimental meters interspersed throughout the work; especially popular are such sonnets (later set to music) as "O stealing time, the subject of delay" and "My true love hath my heart, and I have his."

The definitive edition of *The Arcadia,* in both its versions, is in *The Complete Works,* ed. A. Feuillerat, 4 vols. (1912-26), IV. Sidney's sources are discussed by William Vaughan Moody, *An Inquiry into the Sources of Sir Philip Sidney's "Arcadia"* (1894); S. L. Wolff, *The Greek Romances in Elizabethan Fiction* (1912); and T. P. Harrison, "A Source of Sidney's *Arcadia,*" *University of Texas Studies in English,* VI (1926). The "Old" and "New" *Arcadia* are compared in R. W. Zandvoort, *Sidney's Arcadia: A Comparison Between the Two Versions* (1929); K. T. Rowe, "The Countess of Pembroke's Editorship of *The Arcadia,*" *PMLA,* LIV (1939); and A. G. D. Wiles, "Parallel Analyses of the Two Versions of Sidney's *Arcadia,*" *SP,* XXXIX (1942).

For other important commentary, see Mona Wilson, *Sir Philip Sidney* (1931); W. D. Briggs, "Political Ideas in Sidney's *Arcadia,*" *SP,* XXVIII (1931); M. S. Goldman, *Sir Philip Sidney and the Arcadia* (1934); Kenneth O. Myrick, *Sir Philip Sidney as a Literary Craftsman* (1935), and Walter R. Davis and Richard A. Lanham, *Sidney's Arcadia* (1965).

Arden of Feversham, The Lamentable and True Tragedy of. An anonymous tragedy based on an actual murder in Feversham, Kent, in 1551. The story is recounted in five pages of Raphael Holinshed's *Chronicles* (1577) and in John Stowe's *Annals* (1580). At various times the play has been assigned to Shakespeare, Christopher Marlowe, Thomas Kyd, and Anthony Munday. None of these attributions has been supported by any real evidence. First printed in 1592, *Arden of Feversham* represents the earliest example of a fully developed domestic tragedy. The 1592 quarto is divided into nineteen scenes without any act delineations.

Thomas Arden, a prosperous and avaricious landowner of Feversham, is grieved to discover that his beloved wife Alice is having an affair with Mosbie, a good-for-nothing rogue employed as a steward at a nearby estate; but Arden's friend Franklin persuades him to remain silent and attempt to win back Alice with kindness. Alice and Mosbie, meanwhile, are already plotting to murder Arden and have enlisted as accomplices young Michael, Arden's servant, and Clarke, a painter, who are lured into the conspiracy with false promises that their cooperation will lead to one of them marrying Susan, Mosbie's sister and Alice's maid. Arden's suspicions are aroused when he detects a strange taste to his broth (poisoned by Clarke); he quickly recovers after taking an antidote and credulously accepts Alice's protestations of innocence.

Alice and Mosbie gain another ally in Dick Greene, a neighbor who swears revenge when Arden deprives him of lands by certain legal maneuvers. Greene hires two cutthroats, Black Will and Shakebag, to ambush Arden while he is in London on business. After they bungle several attempts on Arden's life, Mosbie begins to question whether his accomplices are capable of the murder, and if they are, whether they can be trusted not to blackmail him. He is further disquieted by Arden's uncanny luck, fears about Alice's loyalty, and constant bickering between Michael and Clarke over Susan. Alice, meanwhile, remains the driving force of the conspiracy, constantly attempting to reassure her wavering lover while quieting the suspicions of her incredibly uxorious husband.

It is Arden who finally provides the murderers with their best opportunity for success. After a bitter quarrel with Alice and Mosbie, Arden magnanimously arranges a large supper party to celebrate what he foolishly believes is a reconciliation. While Arden is preoccupied with a game of backgammon with Mosbie, Black Will attacks him from behind and Alice, Mosbie, and Shakebag join in stabbing him to death. Susan, Michael, and Clarke carry the body to the countinghouse. Later Susan and Alice take the body into the fields, where it is discovered by Franklin, who follows bloody traces left in the snow. The corpse bleeds anew in the presence of Alice and Mosbie (believed to be a sure sign of guilt) and they confess to the murder. Alice, Mosbie, Susan, and Michael are executed. The fates of the remaining culprits are narrated in an epilogue spoken by Franklin: Shakebag was murdered in Southwark; Black Will burned at the stake for another crime; and Greene finally caught and hanged in Osbridge. Only Clarke escaped punishment, for he was never seen again. As for Arden's body, the epilogue observes ironically, it was laid to rest in the very ground Arden managed to wrest from a business competitor just before the murder.

The epilogue describes the play as a "naked tragedy"

> Wherein no filed points are foisted in
> To make it gracious to the ear or eye.

This abstention from the Senecan rhetoric, titanic characterizations, and stately spectacles of most Elizabethan tragedies is not indicative of the playwright's lack of art but of his deliberate effort to relate a story with all the stark episodic simplicity of modern cinema verité. Commenting on this effect, Louis Gillet has observed: "The result is a very special kind of drama, with a minimum of construction, that gives the impression of happening right before our eyes . . ." Indeed, the playwright chose to render the details of Holinshed's account very much as he found them, and on the few occasions where he departs from his source he does so to heighten some vital aspect of characterization. In Holinshed, for example, Arden is consistently aware of Alice's infidelity and malice, but pretends to ignore her conduct in order to remain on good terms with her wealthy family. For this somewhat tawdry motive the playwright substitutes Arden's almost perverse credulity: he becomes not an opportunist but an uxorious husband totally blinded by his need to see his wife as innocent. Although this change from the source occasionally strains credibility, it conveys a much profounder relationship than the one between Holinshed's cynical husband and wife. Again modifying his source, the dramatist further complicates Arden's character—and enlarges the theme of his tragedy—by giving him an avaricious nature that links motives and reactions to social class. For Arden's fatal obsession is the bourgeois need to *possess*—to possess his own illusions about his wife's goodness, to possess the image of his own saintly capacity to forgive any offense, and to possess another man's lands by legal chicanery. Significantly, his death comes shortly after he has duped a man out of his lands, as if the stars themselves had wearied of his avarice. At the end of the play Arden's wife laments that she was "bewitched" into deception and murder by Mosbie; actually, she seduces herself by somehow equating the virile young Mosbie with "freedom" from Arden's narrow cash-and-carry world. With a sure sense of irony, the playwright makes her lover a mediocre, indolent upstart who languidly tolerates her jaded passion in the wavering hope that somehow the affair will liberate him from his lower-class confinement. Basically shabby and unimaginative, he has no more of Iago's satanic villainy than Arden has of Othello's soul-shaking ferocity. Unlike Shakespeare, the author of *Arden of Feversham* focuses exclusively on what Hannah Arendt, in describing our own times, calls "the banality of evil"—the sordid meanness and tedium in the real-life tragedies we read about in our daily newspapers.

Well-annotated editions are in *The Shakespeare Apocrypha,* ed. C. F. Tucker Brooke (1918) and *Elizabethan Plays,* ed. A. H. Nethercot, C. R. Baskervill, and V. B. Heltzel (1971). For commentary, see H. H. Adams, *English Domestic or Homiletic Tragedy, 1675-1642* (1943); Louis Gillet, *"Arden of Feversham"* in *Shakespeare's Contemporaries,* ed. Max Bluestone and Norman Rabkin (1961); and Sarah Youngblood, "Theme and Imagery in *Arden of Feversham,*" *SEL,* III (1963).

Areopagitica. A prose pamphlet in defense of unlicensed printing by John MILTON. It was first published in 1644 and addressed, in the form of a classical oration, to Parliament. The title derives from the ancient Greek court of the Areopagus, a prestigious body of three hundred judges that presided on the hill of Ares above Athens. The immediate occasion for Milton's pamphlet was Parliament's ordinance for the licensing of the press on June 14, 1643, and the decree of August 24 of that year that the Stationers' Company strictly enforce the new law. The previous censorship law under Charles I, passed on July 11, 1637, had required that all licensing authority reside with the archbishops of Canterbury and York, the bishop of London, and the chancellors of Oxford and Cambridge universities. As Milton pointed out in his pamphlet, this law, revived during the Civil War, had been especially odious to Puritans and parliamentarians. Milton was also motivated to write the pamphlet because, as the author of several unlicensed divorce tracts (see THE DOCTRINE AND DISCIPLINE OF DIVORCE) that had caused scandal, he had been cited by name in the 1643 ordinance and made the subject of a sermon before Parliament by a Presbyterian minister, Herbert Palmer, on August 14, 1644.

Milton does not argue for complete liberty *per se,* but against licensing or censorship prior to publication. In his most stately prose, Milton reviews the history of such censorship since the time of ancient Athens, pausing for special emphasis on the Inquisition. His primary assumption in the pamphlet is that the meaning of virtue depends on freedom of choice in a world where good and evil "grow up together almost inseparably; and the knowledge of good is so interwoven with the knowledge of evil . . ." Taking his text from St. Paul, Milton defines Christian virtue in terms of trial and ordeal, and in a famous passage proclaims: "I cannot praise a fugitive and cloistered virtue, unexercised and unbreathed, that never sallies out and sees her adversary, but slinks out of the race where that immortal garland is to be run for, not without dust and heat. Assuredly we bring not innocence into the world, we bring impurity much rather: that which purifies us is trial, and trial is by what is contrary."

Some scholars have found a foreshadowing of *Paradise Lost* in Milton's treatment of sin in Adam and Eve: "Many there be that complain of divine providence for suffering Adam to transgress. Foolish tongues! When God gave him reason, he gave him freedom to choose, for reason is but choosing; he had been else a mere artificial Adam, such an Adam as he is in the motions" (i.e., puppet shows).

Elsewhere Milton refers to his having visited Galileo, "a prisoner to the Inquisition for thinking in astronomy otherwise than the Franciscan and Dominican licensers thought." He expresses his own vision of a new reformation and milennium in England, "when not only our seventy elders, but all the Lord's people, are become prophets," and his supreme confidence in the ultimate power of Truth, "next to the Almighty" in puissance.

Scholarly and well-annotated editions of *Areopagitica* are in *The Works of John Milton,* ed. Frank A. Patterson, 18 vols. (1931-38), IV; *The Complete Prose Works,* ed. D. M. Wolfe, 5 vols. (1953-71) II: *Complete Poems and Major Prose,* ed. Merritt Y. Hughes (1957); and *The Prose of John Milton,* ed. J. Max Patrick (1967). For commentary, see Harold Laski, "*Areopagitica* after Three Hundred Years," in *Freedom of Speech,* ed. Herman Ould (1945); Herbert Read, *The Areopagitica: A Coat of Many Colors* (1945); and William Haller, *Liberty and Reformation in the Puritan Revolution* (1955).

Areopagus (lit., Ares' hill). A low hill in Athens and also the name of the highest ancient court for political and religious matters, which met there. Hence Milton entitled his address to Parliament *Areopagitica* (1644).

The name is also used by Edmund Spenser in a letter to Gabriel Harvey, dated October 5, 1580, in which Spenser describes what appears to have been a meeting of a literary coterie to discuss reforms in English prosody: "And now they have proclaimed in their [Areopagus] a general surceasing and silence of bald rhymers—and also of the very best too: instead whereof, they have, by authority of their whole senate, prescribed certain laws and rules of quantities of English syllables for English verse, having had thereof already great practice, and drawn me to their faction." In his response on October 23, Harvey wrote: "Your new-founded [Areopagus] I honor more than you will or can suppose, and make greater accompt of the two worthy gentlemen than of two hundredth *Dionisii Areopagitae* or the very notablest senators that ever Athens did afford of that number."

Harvey's "two worthy gentlemen" were probably two among the several writers known to have frequented the Sidney circle at Leicester House (from which Spenser's letter was written) in the 1570s—Sir Philip Sidney himself, Fulke Greville, Thomas Drant, Sir Edward Dyer, and Thomas Lodge. Some scholars maintain that the two references above are insufficient evidence to indicate the existence of anything more formal than an occasional gathering of friends to discuss poetry; others cite the letters to show that Harvey and Sidney were leaders in a conscious effort to reform English versification by the adaptation of classical quantitative scansion. It is generally agreed that both Sidney and Spenser eventually repudiated the idea of employing classical meters and came to favor the native English accent.

For discussion, see G. H. Maynadier, "The Areopagus of Sidney and Spenser," *MLR,* IV (1909) and Edward Fulton, "Spenser, Sidney, and the Areopagus," *MLN,* XXXI (1916).

Argenis. A prose romance in Latin by John Barclay (1582-1621), written around 1617 and published in Paris and London in 1621 and 1622, respectively. English versions were done by Kingsmill Long (1625) and Sir Robert Le Grys (1628). An English translation by Ben Jonson, written in 1623, is lost. *Argenis* was translated into ten languages and went through forty editions in the seventeenth century. The sensational adventures and tangled love affair of Barclay's heroic Argenis and Poliarchus take place at some indefinite time in an unhistorical and mythical Sicily; the plot employs most of the characters and events found in late Greek romances like Heliodorus' AETHIOPICA Barclay's romance has long been interpreted as a thinly veiled allegory in defense of monarchial absolutism, with Argenis symbolizing the throne of France; Poliarchus and Archombrotus as two different sides of Henry of Navarre (later Henry IV of France);

Meleander as Henry III; Mauritania as England; Hyanisbe as Queen Elizabeth; and Radirobanes as Philip II of Spain. *Argenis* is significant as a political satire and as an influence on the development of the heroic romance, especially in France and Spain, where it was far more popular than in England. Grotius, Cardinal Richelieu, Rosseau, and Leibnitz all read it with enthusiasm. The plot, although extremely episodic and complex, is skillfully woven, as Samuel Taylor Coleridge—one of Barclay's last admirers in England—observed in his praise of the work. For continental writers in the seventeenth century, *Argenis* became something of a model of the sophisticated heroic romance that blends exciting action and political allegory.

Argenis is not available in any modern English version, Edward Bensly discusses it at length in the *Cambridge History of English Literature,* IV, Chap. 13 (1909). Other accounts are in G. Waterhouse, *Literary Relations of England and Germany* (1914), and Ernest A. Baker, *A History of the English Novel,* 10 vols. (1924-39), III.

Arraignment of Paris, The. A mythological, pastoral drama by George PEELE performed before Queen Elizabeth by the Children of the Chapel in 1582 or 1583 and first published anonymously in 1584. The source is the familiar myth in the *Iliad* of Paris' awarding of the golden apple in the contest among the three goddesses Juno, Pallas Athene, and Venus.

In the Vale of Ida, where the shepherd Paris and his love Oenone swear fidelity in song, the three goddesses Juno, Pallas Athene, and Venus are thrown a golden apple by Ate, goddess of discord, which is inscribed "Let this unto the fairest given be." The goddesses engage Paris to award the apple. Juno offers him kingdoms and riches, Pallas wisdom, honor, and glory in war; but Venus promises Paris her own towering beauty, Cupid's aid in love, and, in a vision of Helen of Troy attended by four Cupids, "a face that hath no peer." To the outrage of the other goddesses, Paris awards the apple to Venus.

Before the gods assembled at Diana's Bower, Paris must defend his choice against complaints by Juno and Pallas Athene. He pleads that he is only a simple mortal whose eyes were dazzled by beauty, and that, besides, he had been charged with choosing "the fairest" and not the greatest or most wise. In a quandary, the gods turn the matter over to Apollo, who suggests that the problem be solved by Diana, in whose country the contest occurred. Instead of awarding the apple to one of the three goddesses, Diana steps out of role and presents the apple to Queen Elizabeth, "the noble phoenix of our age, / Our fair Eliza, our Zabeta fair."

Peele's play is loosely constructed, especially in its subplot involving Thestylis, Colin, and other shepherds, who are arbitrarily dropped from the story. Their presence in the play may reflect the influence on Peele of Spenser's recently popular *The Shepherd's Calendar* (1579). Nevertheless, the play employs masque-like effects skillfully and displays considerable lyric variety. Peele's songs, written for the queen's choirboys, are especially charming.

The standard edition is in *The Works,* ed. C. T. Prouty, 3 vols., III: *The Arraignment of Paris,* ed. R. Mark Benbow (1970). The play is in *Elizabethan Plays,* ed. A. H. Nethercot, C. R. Baskervill, and V. B. Hetzel (rev. ed., 1971). It is discussed by P. H. Cheffaud, *George Peele* (1913); V. M. Jeffery, *Italian and English Pastoral Drama* (1924); and David H. Horne, *The Life and Minor Works of George Peele* (1952).

Art of English Poesy (George Puttenham). See CRITICISM, LITERARY; INKHORN TERMS.

Art of Rhetoric (Thomas Wilson). See CRITICISM, LITERARY; INKHORN TERMS.

Ascham, Roger (1515-1568). Classical scholar and educator. Ascham entered St. John's College, Cambridge, at fifteen, where he began the Greek and Latin studies that became the passion of his life. In 1538 he was appointed Greek reader at St. John's, and in 1540 the first Regius Professor of Greek at Cambridge. In 1548 he was made tutor to Princess Elizabeth, then sixteen, and afterward secretary to Sir Richard Moryson, ambassador to the court of Charles V. In 1559 Queen Elizabeth appointed him prebend of Wetwang in York Cathedral, where he spent his last years.

His two principal works are *Toxophilus* (1545), a lively dialogue in praise of the sport of archery and *The Schoolmaster* (1570), a manual for private tutors on the subject of teaching Latin to upper-class boys (see COURTESY

LITERATURE). In *Toxophilus* he extols archery (with the English longbow) as the queen of sports in every way superior to others, and especially to all unmanly indoor forms of recreation. The relaxed, intimate style of the book reveals a personality that was imaginative, intensely nationalistic and perhaps a little xenophobic, highly romantic about Merry England and yet scholarly and classical to the bone. *The Schoolmaster* contains a great deal of parenthetical literary criticism in which Ascham praises Chaucer, attacks the Arthurian romances, derides rhyme as an invention of "Goths and Huns," and recommends poetry be written in imitation of classical examples. He also argues for a "plain" style of English devoid of "inkhorn terms," foreign importations, and excessive elaboration. Other interests of Ascham include his efforts at the regularization of English spelling and the improvement of handwriting.

The Whole Works, ed. J. A. Giles, 4 vols. (1864-65), is still standard. *The English Works* was edited by W. A. Wright for the Cambridge Classics (1904). There is an excellent biographical and critical study by L. V. Ryan, *Roger Ascham* (1963), and a Concise Bibliography by S. A. and D. A. Tannenbaum (1946), updated in "Roger Ascham (1946-66)," ed. R. C. Johnson, in *Elizabethan Bibliographies Supplements,* IX (1968).

Astrophel and Stella. A sonnet sequence of 108 sonnets and eleven songs by Sir Philip Sidney. Sidney's sequence was first published in 1591 in a pirated edition with a preface by Thomas Nashe beginning *"Tempus adest plausus aurea pompa venit* [The time for applause is here; the golden procession comes] : so ends the scene of idiots, and enter Astrophel in pomp." Nashe's ebullient words proved to be prophetic, for Sidney's sequence inspired a wave of imitations throughout the 1590s. Sidney is believed to have written most of *Astrophel and Stella* during the period 1581-83 before the "Stella" of the sequence, Penelope Devereux, the earl of Essex's eldest daughter, married Lord Rich (to whom Sidney refers contemptuously in Sonnets 24, 35, and 37), and Sidney's own marriage to Frances Walsingham in 1583.

In the first several sonnets Sidney denies any influence of "Petrarch's long-deceased woes," insisting that his sonnets are inspired by simple passion and a desire to entertain his beloved Stella. In Sonnet 1 Astrophel proclaims:

Loving in truth, and fain in verse my love to show,
That she, dear she, might take some pleasure of my pain,
Pleasure might cause her read, reading might make her know,
Knowledge might pity win, and pity grace obtain,
I sought fit words to paint the blackest face of woe,
Studying inventions fine, her wits to entertain,
Oft turning others' leaves, to see if thence would flow,
Some fresh and fruitful showers upon my sunburned brain.
But words came halting forth, wanting invention's stay;
Invention, nature's child, fled step-dame study's blows;
And others' feet still seemed but strangers in my way.
Thus great with child to speak, and helpless in my throes,
Biting my truant pen, beating myself for spite:
"Fool!" said my muse to me, "look in thy heart and write."

Sidney's protest that he is "no pick-purse of another's wit" in *Astrophel and Stella* is more theatrical than actual, for the sequence is heavily indebted to Petrarch and his Italian and French imitators. Moreover, the tortuous struggle within Astrophel of reason against passion, the central conflict of the sequence, may represent a literary borrowing from the Petrarchan tradition rather than an autobiographical account of Sidney's actual relations with Penelope Devereux. What is highly original in *Astrophel and Stella,* however, is its *energia,* that quality of "forcibleness" and verisimilitude which Sidney had found totally absent from English love lyrics when he wrote in his *An Apology for Poetry:*

> But, truly, many of such writings as come under the banner of unresistible love, if I were a mistress, would never persuade me they were in love; so coldly they apply fiery speeches, as men that had rather read lover's writings, and so caught up certain swelling phrases—which hang together like a man that once told me the wind was at northwest and by south, because he would be sure to name winds enough—than that in truth they feel those passions,

> which easily, as I think, may be bewrayed by the same forcibleness, or "energia" (as the Greeks call it), of the writer.

Sidney instills *energia* in his sonnet sequence by creating a rounded and interesting personality in Astrophel, an arrogant, volatile, and brilliant young courtier who is part Sidney and part Sidney's imaginative creation, and by intensifying dramatic situations and events involving the lover's deep-felt tension between reason and passion, virtue and desire. Moreover, in spite of Astrophel's insistence that he writes for Stella alone, he is always conscious of the larger world of court affairs, literary ideas, and political events, and this gregarious quality of the sequence is still another aspect of Sidney's *energia.* Unlike Petrarch or Surrey, whose love poems are nostalgic and retrospective "emotion recollected in tranquillity," Sidney resembles Wyatt and Donne in his dramatic immediacy:

Fly, fly, my friend! I have my death's wound, fly!
See there that boy, that murdering boy, I say...

Whereas Surrey had written lyrics recalling tournaments years before at Windsor, Sidney writes: "Having *this day* my horse, my hand, my lance, / Guided so well that I obtained the prize..." This sustained impression of an alert and energetic consciousness in response to an ever-changing present is an essential feature of Sidney's dramatic method, and another prop in the theatrical illusion that Astrophel's "truant" pen is guided by nature rather than art.

Sidney's colloquial informality, sense of drama, and sheer fullness of conception make *Astrophel and Stella* a landmark separating the drab and prosaic verse of the early Tudor poetry from the truly golden verse of the 1580s and 1590s. One virtue especially noted by his contemporaries was his virtuosity in the sonnet form—a form only partially mastered by Wyatt and Surrey in their translations and adaptations from Italian and French writers. (See SONNET SEQUENCES). *Astrophel and Stella* has 85 sonnets using the Italian octave (*ab ba ab ba*) followed by the so-called English, or Shakespearean, sestet introduced by Surrey (*cd cd ee*). Sidney often employs the closing couplet with greater variety and to better effect than Shakespeare. Occasionally he uses it to clinch a climactic paradox (Sonnets 5, 45, 46, 60, 61, 63); or to exclaim dramatically (1, 19, 71, 103, 107), interpret the psychology of a situation he has developed in the sonnet (57); give a mocking jibe (70, 104); reverse the progression of an idea by a perplexed question (72, 76, 78); or conclude with a witticism, such as "My lips are sweet, inspired with Stella's kiss" (74) and "Sweet lip, you teach my mouth with one sweet kiss" (80). His instinctive mode of expression is the Petrarchan *concetto,* the "conceit," and in some sonnets (9 and 29, for example) the poem develops into a single extended metaphor arising from the initial *concetto.* All of the amorous paraphernalia of Petrarch and his disciples appear again in *Astrophel and Stella*—the passion-sick, masochistic lover and his cold, imperious lady; the obsession with paradoxes and irrational "contrarieties" of "living deaths," "dear wounds," "fair storms," and "freezing fires"; the invocations to therapeutic sleep; the images of religion in the service of a sacramental love; and the lover's professed conviction of his peculiar isolation from others, his lament on the futility of language to convey his passion, and his helpless admission that reason cannot restrain his illicit obsession. Many of these elements are apparent in Sonnet 28:

You that with allegory's curious frame
Of others' children changelings use to make,
With me those pains, for God's sake, do not take;
I list not dig so deep for brazen fame.
When I say "Stella," I do mean the same
Princess of beauty for whose only sake
The reins of love I love, though never slake,
And joy therein, though nations count it shame.
I beg no subject to use eloquence,
Nor in hid ways to guide philosophy;
Look at my hands for no such quintessence;
But know that I in pure simplicity
Breathe out the flames which burn within my heart,
Love only reading unto me this art.

No poet before Sidney was able to transplant the Petrarchan conventions to native soil with such spontaneity, imagination, and graceful dexterity, and until well into the seventeenth century his *Astrophel and Stella* remained the paradigm of Petrarchan love poetry.

Like Shakespeare's Sonnets, Sidney's sequence has been interpreted in any number of different ways. To Charles Lamb it is Sidney's candid autobiography—"the story of Hamlet in love"—but to Sidney Lee, the Victorian scholar, it is merely an eclectic literary exercise in Petrarchan conventions without any basis in actual experience. To C. S. Lewis it is a symphony of variegated themes without narrative continuity—love and virtue, literary criticism, court affairs, Platonic love. Whether Astrophel's conflict of passion and reason is meant to be real or imaginary, it did not, however, conclude with the two sonnets of Christian resignation and repudiation of secular love, "Thou blind man's mark" and "Leave me, O love." These did not appear until the publication of *Certain Sonnets* in 1598 and are therefore not part of Astrophel's feverish love affair with Stella.

The standard edition of *Astrophel and Stella* is in *The Poems,* ed. William A. Ringler, Jr. (1962). Lamb's critical essay "Some Sonnets of Sir Philip Sidney" is in his *Last Essays of Elia,* ed. F. Page (1929). Two excellent modern studies are in David Kalstone, *Sidney's Poetry* (1965), and Neil Rudenstine, *Sidney's Poetic Development* (1967).

As You Like It. A romantic comedy by William SHAKESPEARE written about 1599-1600 and first printed in the 1623 Folio. It was based on Thomas Lodge's pastoral novel ROSALYNDE, *or Euphues' Golden Legacy* (1590). Although shakespeare followed Lodge's novel closely, he changed the names of most of the characters and added Jaques, Touchstone, Audrey, William, and Sir Oliver Martext.

At the court of Duke Frederick, who has usurped the throne from his brother Duke Senior, the new duke's daughter Celia and his niece Rosalind, daughter of the banished duke, attend a wrestling match in which Orlando, son of Sir Rowland de Boys, defeats a professional wrestler. Rosalind and Orlando at once fall in love. When Duke Frederick learns that Orlando is the son of his old enemy and friend of the usurped duke, he angrily exiles Rosalind from the court. Rosalind disguises herself as a young boy named Ganymede, and Celia disguises herself as Ganymede's sister Aliena; accompanied by Touchstone, the court clown, they flee to the Forest of Arden, where Rosalind's father, the former duke, and his loyal followers maintain a court in exile. There they are joined by Orlando, who has been driven from home by his cruel elder brother Oliver.

In the Forest of Arden, Ganymede (the disguised Rosalind) instructs the love-stricken Orlando on the best ways to woo his "absent" Rosalind, while less romantic types like Touchstone and the rural Audrey, and Silvius and Phebe also contribute to the satire on love. When Oliver comes to the forest to kill Orlando, the latter saves his life, and the reformed Oliver later becames betrothed to Aliena. The tangled love affairs are not straightened out until the final assembly scene, when Rosalind and Celia throw off their disguises. News arrives that Duke Frederick has experienced a religious conversion and returned the ill-gotten throne to his brother, the rightful heir; Orlando gets his Rosalind; Oliver chooses Celia; Phebe settles for Silvius (after learning Ganymede is Rosalind); and the clown Touchstone takes Audrey as wife. The cynical, melancholy Jaques, the banished duke's attendant, resolves henceforth to join Duke Frederick and his followers in religious life.

As You Like It is one of Shakespeare's truly "golden" comedies, a festive celebration of love and pastoral idealism that never succumbs to either cynicism or sentimentality, although both extremes are amply represented in the characters. The most cynical of these is Jaques, the waspish ex-traveler who could "suck melancholy from an egg." But the melancholy vision of Jaques's famous "Ages of Man" speech, with its disillusioned peroration in which man declines at the end of life into a hopeless wreck, "sans teeth, sans eyes, sans taste, sans everything," is not to be confused with Shakespeare's world view. At the other end of the philosophical spectrum is Orlando, the hopelessly idealistic Renaissance lover, both adored and scorned by his Rosalind, who rejoices in love and yet perceives its ludicrous excesses in herself as well as others. It is Rosalind, Shakespeare's most vivacious comic heroine, who, in her clear sanity, satiric wit, and joy in living, carries the essence of the play to the audience.

The standard edition is the New Cambridge edition, ed. Arthur Quiller-Couch and J. Dover Wilson (1926). Important critical interpretations include Zera Fink, "Jaques and the Malcontent Traveler," *PQ,* XIV (1935); J. O. Campbell, *Shakespeare's Satire* (1943); C. L. Barber, *Shakespeare's Festive Comedy* (1959);

Bertrand Evans, *Shakespeare's Comedies* (1960); J. Dover Wilson, *Shakespeare's Happy Comedies* (1962); Michael Jamieson, *Shakespeare: As You Like It* (1965); Peter G. Phialas, *Shakespeare's Romantic Comedies* (1966); Sylvan Barnet, "'Strange Events': Improbability in *As You Like It*," *ShakS*, IV (1969); and Helen Gardner, *"As You Like It,"* in *More Talk About Shakespeare*, ed. John Garnett (1969).

Atheist's Tragedy, The; or The Honest Man's Revenge. A tragedy attributed to Cyril TOURNEUR; it was probably written about 1607-10 and printed anonymously in 1611. No source is known.

The atheist and arch-villain is D'Amville, brother of the extremely virtuous Lord Montferrers. With the help of his treacherous servant Borachio, D'Amville plots to increase his power and wealth. First, he persuades his nephew, Montferrers' son and heir Charlemont, to leave for the wars, after which he forces Charlemont's betrothed, Castabella, daughter of Lord Belforest and Lady Levidulcia, into marriage with his own son Rousard, a sickly and unattractive wretch. Only Sebastian, D'Amville's younger son, opposes this stratagem for uniting the two houses of Belforest and D'Amville at poor Castabella's expense.

At the wedding banquet for Rousard and Castabella, Borachio appears among the guests disguised as a wounded soldier and gives a false report of Charlemont's death. The bereaved Montferrers, with the assistance of Lord Belforest's hypocritical Puritan chaplain Languebeau Snuffe, rewrites his will and names his brother D'Amville sole heir. Later that night D'Amville and Borachio murder Montferrers in such a way as to make it appear an accident. In another scene Castabella's stepmother Levidulcia begins an affair with young Sebastian, who narrowly escapes detection when her husband arrives home unannounced. Meanwhile Montferrers' ghost appears to Charlemont, exposes the murderers, and urges Charlemont to return to France; but he also cautions him to be patient and leave revenge to heaven: "Attend with patience to the success of things, / But leave revenge unto the King of Kings."

Charlemont returns home and receives confirmation from Castabella of the ghost's account of D'Amville's perfidy. Charlemont bursts in upon his uncle and Sebastian as they are quarreling over Sebastian's allowance, which D'Amville has withheld as punishment for his son's opposition to the marriage of Castabella and Rousard. As Charlemont attacks his uncle, the ghost intervenes, again cautioning Charlemont against revenge, but not before Sebastian is wounded defending his father. Charlemont is imprisoned by D'Amville, then released by Sebastian, who secretly gives his allowance to secure Charlemont's freedom. In a second confrontation with D'Amville, Charlemont regrets his earlier assault, believing D'Amville has forgiven him and paid for his release, and the two are reconciled. D'Amville deceitfully pledges to be Charlemont's guardian and benefactor. From Castabella and Rousard, D'Amville and Charlemont learn that the impotent Rousard has not consummated the marriage. Thus D'Amville's hopes for an heir now appear futile.

At the shop of Cataplasma, a flagrant bawd, Levidulcia meets with Sebastian while the hypocritical Puritan chaplain Snuffe enjoys himself with Soquette, Cataplasma's seamstress. Meanwhile D'Amville plots to murder Charlemont and seduce Castabella in order to produce an heir. Borachio ambushes Charlemont, who slays his assailant. Charlemont then hides in a tomb, to which D'Amville happens to bring Castabella with intentions of rape. As Charlemont rises from a grave, D'Amville takes him for a ghost and flees. When D'Amville returns with his men, they discover the exhausted lovers asleep together. Charlemont is arrested for Borachio's murder, and Castabella, to be with her lover in prison, falsely confesses to fornication.

When Belforest learns of Levidulcia's infidelity, he fights with Sebastian, and both men are slain. Levidulcia commits suicide. Meanwhile the sickly Rousard dies and D'Amville is left childless and distracted. D'Amville sends Charlemont to the block, but as D'Amville raises the executioner's ax, it slips from his grasp and gives him a fatal wound. The atheist confesses his crimes, pays tribute to divine justice, and dies. Charlemont and Castabella are again betrothed, and in his new-found happiness Charlemont acknowledges the truth of the ghost's moral— that "patience is the honest man's revenge."

The Atheist's Tragedy is one of the most abrasive, violent, and fast-moving of Senecan tragedies. Until the wholly contrived and melodramatic conclusion, the play is credibly motivated by D'Amville's Machiavellian intrigues. Obviously influenced by Kyd's *Spanish Tragedy*, and perhaps by Shakespeare's *Titus Andronicus* as well, Tourneur's play strangely modifies the Elizabethan Senecan revenge formula by its denunciation of the code, its pervasive satiric characterizations, and its liberal use of situations derived from Jacobean comedies of intrigue (see SENECAN TRAGEDY).

Irving Ribner's edition for the Revels Plays (1964) contains an important introduction and extensive bibliography. The standard edition is in *The Works*, ed. Allardyce Nicoll (1930; repr. 1963). Lawrence J. Ross has edited the play for the Regents Renaissance Drama series (1970). For commentary, see Harold Jenkins, "Cyril Tourneur," *RES,* XVII (1941); Fredson Bowers, *Elizabethan Revenge Tragedy 1587-1642* (rev. ed., 1959); and Peter B. Murray, *A Study of Cyril Tourneur* (1964).

Aubrey, John (1626-1697). Biographer and antiquary. Aubrey's antiquarian interests began with his early research of the people, folkways, and environs of his native Wiltshire. His one celebrated work, *Brief Lives,* was intended as a contribution to Anthony à Wood's biographical collection *Athenae Oxonienses,* but after quarreling with Wood, Aubrey withheld his notes, which were published in 1813 as a separate collection of biographies. Aubrey's *Brief Lives* is not distinguished for its thoroughness or its accuracy, but it reveals the author's incisive use of effective details and his intuitive grasp of significant clues to character. The only other works by Aubrey are his *Miscellanies* (1696), a collection of folk tales and ghost stories, and natural histories of Surrey and Wiltshire.

It is often observed that Aubrey worked through local records, birth and death registers, legal documents, and tombstones to learn the most personal aspects of his subjects. Hence his accounts of such notables as John Florio, George Herbert, Thomas Hobbes, John Milton, William Shakespeare, Ben Jonson, and Sir Walter Raleigh are both factual and imaginative, objective and penetratingly interpretative. He is full of tidbits revealing quirks of personality, some of these legendary, others based on personal observation. He repeats the apocryphal tale of Shakespeare as a butcher's apprentice making a speech "in high style" whenever he killed a calf—it is false, perhaps, but a tale most readers would not relinquish. Aubrey was not only a student of human personality, but a scholar with a wide range of knowledge in geography, politics, architecture, and literature. Many of his *Brief Lives* conclude with acute analyses of his subject's works.

Aubrey's *Brief Lives* was edited by Andrew Clark, 2 vols. (1898); *Brief Lives and Other Selected Writings* by Oliver Lawson Dick (1949) is an excellent one-volume edition. J. Britton wrote a memoir of Aubrey for the Wiltshire Topographical Society (1845). Aubrey's biography is by A. Powell, *John Aubrey and His Friends* (1948).

autobiography. Before the eighteenth century, the shortcomings of autobiographies and biographies were largely the same. They were excessively formal, unrevealing, or merely forensic. Although John Lydgate, Thomas Hoccleve, and other medieval writers wrote autobiographical verse, most of it is in the form of palinodes—lamentations for wasted youth or frivolous secular life—and none approaches the psychological intensity and range of St. Augustine's *Confessions*. Autobiography in the Renaissance reached unprecedented greatness in the egocentric personal accounts of Benvenuto Cellini, the soul-searching of Petrarch, and the imaginative introspection of Montaigne, but no English autobiographer of the sixteenth or seventeenth century came close to matching the achievements of these three.

Autobiography in England developed very gradually from its kindred forms in letters, travel accounts, religious meditations, and quasi- or pseudo-confessional tracts like Robert Greene's A GROATSWORTH OF WIT. Among the earliest separately printed prose autobiographies in English was John BALE'S *The Vocation of John Bale* (1553), which describes Bale's career in the church from the time he was appointed bishop in 1552 until his ouster and flight to Holland after Mary Tudor came to the throne. As is to be expected, Bale's work is bitterly anti-Catholic and argumentative—perhaps more of a religious polemic than an autobiography. Of a quite different nature is *The Autobiography of Thomas Whythorne*, written around 1576 but not published until 1961. Whythorne, born in 1528, served as secretary to the dramatist John Heywood from 1545 to 1548, and was acquainted with the literary circle of Sir Thomas More. A composer and musician, he wrote *Songs of Three, Four, and Five Voices* (1571), the earliest English book of madrigals, and his autobiography may well be, as his modern editor claims, "the earliest autobiography in the English language." It is certainly the first autobiography in English of any human interest, for unlike Bale's work, Whythorne's discusses personalities and public affairs, relates anecdotes, expounds the author's personal philosophy, and intersperses his narrative with poems. His paraphrase of John Heywood's lost interlude *Of the Parts of Man* is the only existing account of that play. Unfortunately, like Sir John Cheke, Whythorne believed in the reform of English spelling, and composed his autobiography in a kind of phonetic shorthand. His "sonnet" on the relationship of wit and wisdom illustrates his eccentric orthography—and his meager poetic talents:

> When witt doth seek vys to embras
> ƀen witt him self doth much defas
> for witt and wizdom diffreth so
> az witt from wizdom needs must go . . .

Less appealing than Whythorne's is the brief and sober autobiography of Sir Thomas Bodley, written around 1609 and published in 1647. Brisk, factual, and impersonal, Bodley's is of interest chiefly for its account of the founding of the BODLEIAN LIBRARY at Oxford.

A totally different tone characterizes the memoirs of Robert Carey, earl of Monmouth, written around 1623 and first printed by Horace Walpole in 1759. The author gives a brief description of his childhood, tells of his career as a soldier in Holland and as Warder of West Marches, and boasts ingenuously of his heroic battles against Spaniards and outlaws and of his several interviews with Queen Elizabeth and James I. Although Carey is admirably frank and informative, he lacks those characteristics essential to autobiography—sensitivity, introspection, and humor. Nevertheless, Walpole praised his work, and Sir Walter Scott used Carey's memoirs as a source for episodes in several of his novels.

Like Carey's memoirs, the *Autobiography* of Edward HERBERT. lord of Cherbury, was first published by Walpole (1764). Brother of the poet George, Lord Herbert was a serious philosopher, historian, and statesman. His Latin treatise *De veritate,* the first extensive study of metaphysics by an Englishman, reveals a crisp, rational mind, and his religious writings have earned him praise as a founder of deism and a humane disciple of latitudinarianism. None of these admirable qualities is apparent, however, in his *Autobiography,* a tissue of tedious anecdotes boasting of his own courage, *savoir faire*, and personal charm. The *Autobiography* was written in the 1640s, when Herbert was past sixty; it takes the reader from his birth to his return from a diplomatic mission in France in 1624. Most of the details in the *Autobiography* are devoted to laborious accounts of Herbert's social and political encounters at the French court, his several duels and rivalries and feuds, and, most of all, his courtly amours. He seems to have needed a topic outside himself to refine the impurities of his narcissism and adolescent bravado. Curiously, of all his writings his *Autobiography* is the least complimentary and worthy of his name.

Equally eccentric but totally fascinating is Sir Kenelm DIGBY'S Private Memoirs, written around 1632 but not published until 1827. Digby's work is a pseudo-autobiography of fanciful and elegant sentiments derived from the Greek romances and Sir Philip Sidney's *Arcadia,* an idealized account mingling facts and fancies in which the author refers to himself as Theagenes and his bride Venetia Stanley as Stelliana, Digby's own re-creation of the female cynosure of Sidney's sonnet sequence *Astrophel and Stella.* Like Montaigne, Digby purports to write "only for my own private content" and "to please myself in looking back upon my past and sweet errors." Digby's account of his courtship of his wife Venetia, herself a notorious eccentric and "fantastical," is the narrative framework for a book adorned with philosophical dialogues, Platonic treatises, elegant epistles, and vivid descriptions of the author's life and times.

In contrast to Digby's whimsical mixture of fact and fancy is *The Life of Edward Hyde, Earl of Clarendon,* a stringently objective political autobiography told in the third person (See HYDE, EDWARD). Written during the period 1668-72 and first published in 1759, it covers the same period as Clarendon's famous *History of the Rebellion,* from his birth in 1609 to his exile in France in 1667. Written to be read exclusively by his family, Clarendon's *Life* omits any details of his domestic life and relationships and focuses exclusively on his political career. Like his *History of the Rebellion,* the *Life* abounds with formal descriptions of people, places, and events, and is characterized by an aloof, aristocratic detachment. The *Life* contains interesting portraits of Ben Jonson, John Selden, Sir Kenelm Digby, and most of the important political figures of the early seventeenth century. From the heights of his aristocratic stoicism, Clarendon looks down upon a world in which, he concludes, "nothing is lasting but the folly and wickedness of the inhabitants . . ."

A book of totally different philosophical and social outlook from Clarendon's *Life* is one that represents the high point of autobiographical writing in the seventeenth century, John BUNYAN'S powerful and searching *Grace Abounding to the Chief of Sinners,* first printed in 1666 and so popular that it went through seven editions by 1692. Bunyan's spiritual autobiography is one of the most candid and introspective in the language, the first English autobiography to equal the forthright self-revelation of Augustine's *Confessions*, The first part of *Grace Abounding* treats of Bunyan's religious conversion, the second of his call to the ministry. And yet these landmarks in his life are arrived at by way of a piligrimage as tortuous and fascinating as that of Everyman in PLIGRIM'S PROGRESS—Bunyan's mean birth and anxious childhood, his earliest encounters with sin, his adventures as a soldier in Cromwell's army, and his painfully slow awakening to the religious life as a result of reading two evangelical tracts given to him by his wife. Written in a forceful, concrete, and colloquial style, *Grace Abounding* throbs with all the extremes of fear and elation. Bunyan's greatest agony is that the weight of his terrible sins has dropped him too deep for God to raise him:

> Now was the Word of the Gospel forced from my soul; so that no promise or encouragement was to be found in the Bible for me. And now would that saying work upon my spirit to afflict me, "Rejoice not, O Israel, for Joy as other people." [Hosea 9:1] For I saw indeed, there was cause of rejoicing for those that heed to Jesus; but as for me, I had cut myself off by my transgressions, and left myself neither foothold nor hand-hold amongst all the stages and props in the precious World of Life.

Grace Abounding is full of such candid passages. It also contains realistic, occasionally awesome vignettes, as when Bunyan fears that the village church steeple will tumble on his head, or when he tries to perform miracles, or when he encounters a passage in the New Testament that allays his terror and fills him with inexpressible joy and conviction of salvation.

The first woman to write an autobiography was that inestimable and ingenuous bluestocking Margaret CAVENDISH, duchess of Newcastle, in "A True Relation of My Birth, Breeding, and Life" in her *Nature's Pictures* (1656). Her work expresses all the euphoric garrulity of those mimeographed family news letters sent to friends during the Christmas season. As in her *Life of William Cavendish,* she portrays her husband as nothing less than a demigod, and her account of her own family is almost pedantic in egotistical niceties and pompous discriminations. Her lengthy self-analysis is conducted with scrupulous regard for her own intelligence, talents, and achievements, and, in a quixotic and revealing conclusion, she confesses that her one abiding vanity in life was an unquenchable thirst for fame.

This rather spotty and uneven record of Renaissance autobiographies concludes with perhaps the most "modern" and sophisticated work of the period—Abraham COWLEY'S "Of Myself," first published with his *Works* in 1668. Few authors before Wordsworth have written so perceptively of childhood. Here Cowley attempts to explain the origins of his love for poetry:

> But how this love came to be produced in me so early is a hard question. I believe I can tell the particular little chance that filled my head first with such chimes of verse as have never since left ringing there. For I remember when I began to read, and to take some pleasure in it, there was wont to lie in my mother's parlor (I know not by what accident, for she herself never in her life read any book but of devotion) Spenser's works; this I happened to fall upon, and was infinitely delighted with the stories of the knights, and giants, and monsters, and

brave houses, which I found everywhere there (though my understanding had little to do with all this) and by degrees with the tinkling of the rhyme and dance of the numbers, so that I think I had read him all over before I was twelve years old, and was thus made a poet as immediately as a child is made an eunuch.

A thoughtful, introspective, and yet fast-moving account of his youth and apprenticeship as a poet, Cowley's "Of Myself" is both intimate and informative, vivid and psychologically perceptive. For its informal directness and artistry, it looks forward to the flowering of autobiography in the eighteenth century.

Individual autobiographies are listed in *CBEL,* I, 840 ff. Tudor and Stuart autobiographies are discussed by Donald A. Stauffer, *English Biography before 1700* (1930), and James W. Thompson, *A History of Historical Writing,* 2 vols., I (1942). See also the chapters by C. Whibley and Sir A. W. Ward in *The Cambridge History of English Literature,* III (1908) and VII (1910); and Paul Delany, *British Autobiography in the Seventeenth Century* (1969), which contains an extensive bibliography.

B

Bacon, Francis (1561-1626). Statesman, philosopher, essayist. Born in London the youngest son of Sir Nicholas Bacon, Queen Elizabeth's lord keeper of the Great Seal, Bacon enrolled at Trinity College, Cambridge, when only twelve years old and remained two years, after which he entered Gray's Inn. After a tour of France he returned to face mounting debts left by his father's death. From 1584 he made his career in law and Parliament, but advancement proved slow: his kinsmen the Cecils, though powerful at court, did nothing to promote his career, and the queen bitterly resented his opposition to one of her tax requests and disliked him for his obvious ambition. Bacon's chief patron became Essex, the queen's favorite, who generously dispensed influence and money. When Essex fell in 1601, Bacon represented the prosecution during the trial of his former friend and patron, earning the opprobrious epithet bestowed on him by Alexander Pope as "the wisest, brightest, meanest of mankind."

Upon the accession of James I, Bacon's fortunes improved: knighthood in 1603, Solicitor General in 1607, Attorney General in 1613, Privy Councilor in 1616, and Lord Chancellor in 1621. He was created Lord Verulam in 1618, Viscount St. Albans in 1621. But his betrayal of Essex and great favor with the king earned him many enemies. In 1621 he was tried and convicted in the House of Lords for accepting bribes while a judge in Chancery suits. Accepting gifts from suitors was common practice for judges, but it was technically a felony, and Bacon's political career was ruined. He retired to his family estate at Gorhambury to study philosophy, conduct scientific experiments, and continue work on his philosophical treatise *Instauratio magna*.

During Bacon's lifetime three editions of his famous *Essays* appeared, each edition substantially enlarged (1597, 1612, with a complete edition in 1625). (See ESSAYS.) His *Advancement of Learning* (1605) is divided into two parts, the first a tribute to man's intellectual capabilities when free of the "peccant humours" of superstitions and false learning, the second a detailed proposal for educational reforms; his *Advancement* was much enlarged upon in the Latin version, *De augmentis scientiarum* (1623). *De sapientia veterum* (1609), translated in 1619 as *The Wisdom of the Ancients*, interprets classical myths as symbolic expressions of scientific truths and well illustrates Shelley's observation that "Lord Bacon was primarily a poet." The incomplete *Novum organum* (1620) proposes induction, observation, and experiment as methods of inquiry to replace Aristotelian philosophy. *The History of the Reign of King Henry VII* (1622) is a brilliant and admiring biography of a coldly efficient Tudor administrator very much like Bacon himself (see BIOGRAPHY). *Apophthegms New and Old* (1625) is a wise and whimsical collection of anecdotes showing Bacon's lighter side (see JESTBOOKS). His fanciful utopia of the new science was published posthumously as THE NEW ATLANTIS (1627). Bacon's canon is vast and varied: miscellaneous poems, selected versions of the Psalms, an encyclopedic natural history (*Sylva sylvarum,* 1627), legal briefs and maxims, prefaces to *Instauratio magna,* and voluminous personal and official correspondence (the last not published until 1734).

Bacon's achievements were immense. More than any one man, he was responsible for hastening the widespread application of inductive reasoning and scientific methods, and his condemnation of Aristotelian scholasticism, superstitions, and theological polemics accelerated the steady and inevitable secularization of his age. His writings and personal influence inspired the guidelines of the Royal Society and helped systemize scholarship throughout Europe. Neither an inventor nor scientist himself, he was an eloquent theorist whose vision inspired others; he used his political power and prestige to advance the cause of science, and he did so in a number of contrasting roles—as archly practical publicist, cool persuader, and zealot of unquenchable enthusiasm and imagination. He once wrote that he had taken all knowledge for his province, and his *Instauratio magna,* which was never completed, indicates the epic magnitude of his philosophical design. The work was to consist of six parts in Latin (presumably a more permanent and universal language than English). The first part was to divide scientific activities into branches of inquiry and eliminate intellectual areas of speculation (religious dispute, superstitions, alchemy, astrology, etc.); Bacon completed this part of his project in *De augmentis scientiarum.* The second part of *Instauratio* was to be the formulation of principles for the interpretation of nature, a work only partially represented in the incomplete *Novum organum.* The third was to be a compendium of natural phenomena suitable for observation and analysis (color, heat, motion, etc.), a plan begun in small part with *Sylva sylvarum.* The last three parts of *Instauratio* were, of course, never brought down to earth from the airy heights of philosophical speculation—a report on all of nature's multiform operations observable in the universe; Bacon's own illuminations as a result of his close observations of nature; and, finally, a work to be done by future disciples of the new science —by "posterity" itself—on natural discoveries achieved through systematic observation, induction, and experimentation. Thus Bacon's *Instauratio,* like Raleigh's *History of the World* and Spenser's *The Fairie Queene.* is a work of such colossal scale as to baffle the modern mind, with its reverence for specialization and humility in the face of complexities.

Nor was Bacon very well-equipped for his heroic task. He knew scarcely any mathematics and was therefore unable to comprehend some of the paramount theories and discoveries of his age. He rejected Copernicus and remained totally ignorant of the medical research of his personal physician, William Harvey. He repudiated alchemy and astrology, but retained a stock of other "peccant humours"—including belief in witchcraft. Moreover, he placed excessive confidence in his inductive method as a panacea for all intellectual disorders, and he grossly simplified scientific inquiry by stressing the "forms" of nature—color, heat, and motion—insisting that these were like letters in nature's alphabet that, once mastered, would enable man to decipher her language. He was acutely aware of the pitfalls of metaphors, or what our modern age calls "semantics," but was himself too thoroughly a product of his time to avoid succumbing to this "peccant humour."

These are minor faults when viewed against his great achievements. He systematically refuted the medieval obsession with "correspondences" based on vanity and wishful-thinking and effectively discredited pseudo-sciences and pretentious esoterica disguised as learning. Many of his predecessors had inveighed against the inane facade of scholarship erected in the name of Aristotle, but none argued his case with Bacon's clear perception of the issues and crisp phraseology. His pithy wit and dramatic flare are always evident, and nowhere more so than in Book I of *Novum organum* where he classifies the four "idols" of false learning as the Idols of the Tribe, those agreed-upon illusions which bind men to false security rather than truth; Idols of the Cave, the errors arising from conditioned responses and habitual associations rather than valid perceptions; Idols of the Marketplace, the inexact and mindless words that obscure rather than illuminate or describe; and Idols of the Theatre, the schools and systems of thought to which men pledge allegiance rather than seek out truth freely and objectively. As the above description suggests, Bacon was able to combine the myth-making sensibilities of a poet with the incisive cognition of a philosopher. Perhaps his crowning achievement in the name of the new learning was best described by Douglas Bush in *English Literature of the Seventeenth Century:* "He not only summoned men to research, he brought the Cinderella of science out of her partial obscurity and enthroned her as queen of the world."

The standard edition of *The Works* is by J. Spedding, R. L. Ellis, and D. D. Heath, 7 vols. (1857-59), supplemented by Spedding's *The Letters and the Life,* 7 vols. (1861-74). The best selection of Bacon's writings in English was edited by J. M. Robertson (1905). There are excellent biographies by Mary Sturt (1932); Bryan Bevan (1960), and J. Max Patrick (1961). Two well-written introductions to Bacon's ideas are C. D. Broad, *The Philosophy of Francis Bacon* (1926) and the work by Benjamin Farrington of the same title (1964). Alfred North Whitehead's discussion of Bacon in *Science and the Modern World* (1925) is of exceptional interest. Other commentary is cited in the *CBEL,* I: R. W. Gibson, *Francis Bacon: A Bibliography of His Works and of Baconiana to the Year 1750* (1950; supplement, 1959); and "Francis Bacon, 1926-66." ed. J. Kemp Houck in *Elizabethan Bibliographies Supplements,* XV (1968).

Baldwin, William (fl. 1547). Poet and miscellanist. Almost nothing is known of Baldwin's life, and his fame derives entirely from his supervision of the first editions of the verse chronicle A MIRROR FOR MAGISTRATES (1559, with many enlarged editions). He was born in the western part of England, spent some time at Oxford, and began his career in London as a corrector for the printer Edward Whitechurch. Baldwin's first known work, *A Treatise of Moral Philosophy, Containing the Sayings of the Wise* (1547), was dedicated to the earl of Hertford and later enlarged by Thomas Palfreyman in the 1556 edition. By the middle of the seventeenth century it had gone through about thirty editions. Baldwin's work is divided into four sections. The first section relates the lives of the ancient philosophers; the second explains and classifies their precepts; the third lists philosophers' maxims and proverbs, some in verse; and the fourth defines some effective metaphors and figures of rhetoric employed by great Roman philosophers. Hence Baldwin's book is a clever appeal to a large audience, for it popularizes an esoteric subject and also provides a handy manual for students of oratory and rhetoric.

Baldwin's other works include a metrical version of Scripture, *The Canticles or Ballads of Solomon* (1549), some court entertainments prepared for Edward VI and Mary Tudor, and an anti-Catholic satiric verse bestiary, offset with many merry tales and jests, *A Marvelous History Entitled Beware the Cat* (1561). If any conclusion can be drawn from these various publications, it is that Baldwin had highly developed commercial instincts.

For Baldwin's role in preparing *A Mirror for Magistrates* and information about later editions of that work, see the entry under that title. Baldwin's *A Treatise of Moral Philosophy* was edited in the Scholars' Facsimiles and Reprints series by R. H. Bowers (1967). William P. Holden has edited *Beware the Cat and The Funerals of King Edward the Sixth by William Baldwin* (1963). For biographical information, see W. F. Trench, "William Baldwin," *MLQ,* I (1899); Eveline I. Feasey, "William Baldwin," *MLR,* XX (1925); and Arthur Freeman, "William Baldwin: The Last Years," *N & Q,* VIII (1961).

Bale, John (1495-1563). Dramatist, historian, and religious reformer. Born of poor parents in Suffolk. Bale attended Jesus College, Cambridge, where he graduated in divinity in 1529. At first a Roman Catholic, he became a zealous Protestant reformer during the early reign of Henry VIII. In 1534 he was in trouble with authorities for his anti-Catholic sermons. In 1540, after his patron Thomas Cromwell fell from royal favor, Bale and his family fled to Germany. He returned in 1547 and was made rector of a small church and in 1552 elevated to a bishopric in Ireland, where several of his morality plays were first performed. With the accession of Mary Tudor, Bale again fled, this time to Holland, then later to Basel. When Queen Elizabeth restored the Anglican Church, he returned to England and was made prebendary of Canterbury, where he died in 1563.

Bale was writer of several morality plays which, although loosely constructed and often carelessly written, are considered important as links between the medieval morality play and the Tudor chronicle or history play (see MORALITY PLAY; CHRONICLE PLAY). The best known of his moralities is *King John* (cir. before 1540), a source Shakespeare consulted in writing his play by that title. His bibliographical work, *Illustrium majoris Britanniae scriptorum summarium* (1548) is of considerable merit. Bale was most prolific, however, as the author of acrimonious religious treatises (see AUTOBIOGRAPHY).

Selections from Bale's voluminous religious tracts are in the *Selected Works,* ed. H. Christmas for the Parker Society (1849). *The Dramatic Writings of John Bale* was edited by J.S. Farmer (1907). The definitive biography is by J.W. Harris, *John Bale: A Study in the Minor Literature of the Reformation* (1942). There is a bibliography by W.T. Davies in *Oxford Bibliographical Society Proceedings and Papers,* V, Pt. 4 (1940).

Bandello, Matteo (1480-1562). Italian author of the *Novelle* (1554), 214 prose romances translated into French by Francois de Belleforest and Pierre Boaistuau (or Boisteau) in 1559 as *Histoires tragiques* and later into English by Sir Geoffrey Fenton as *Certain Tragical Discourses* (1567), a work that became a primary source for the plots of Shakespeare and other Elizabethan dramatists. William Painter's *The Palace of Pleasure* (1566-67), another collection of tales used as a source by Elizabethan playwrights, takes several of its stories from Bandello. Arthur Brooke's poem *Romeus and Juliet* (1562), on which Shakespeare based his play, was derived from a tale in Boaistuau's translation. Barnabe Rich's "Apolonius and Silla" in his collection *Rich His Farewell to Military Profession* (1581), a chief source of Shakespeare's *Twelfth Night,* is based on a story in Belleforest's translation. The Hero-Claudio plot in *Much Ado About Nothing* is also from Bandello. Bandello's tales of love became an ultimate source (often via Fenton or Painter) for other dramatists besides Shakespeare —Thomas Heywood in *A Woman Killed with Kindness* and *The Royal King and the Loyal Subject*, John Marston in *The Dutch Courtesan* and John Webster in *The Duchess of Malfi.* In general, Bandello's stories are characterized by domestic conflicts, intrigue, and realism.

Bandello was born at Castelnuova Scrivia in Torona, Lombardy, and became a priest, a soldier, and a politician. After fleeing Italy for political reasons, he was made bishop of Agen, France, by Francis I.

Bandello's novellas were translated and edited by John Payne, 6 vols. (1890). See also Rene Pruvost, *Matteo Bandello and Elizabethan Fiction* (1937).

Barclay, Alexander (1475-1552). Scottish poet, scholar, and theologian. Little is known for certain of his life. He graduated from Oriel College, Oxford, and may also have attended Cambridge. While chaplain of the College of Ottery St. Mary, Devonshire, he translated—very freely and with additions of his own—Sebastian Brant's *Das Narrenschiff* (1494) as *The Ship of the Fools* (1509). While a Benedictine monk at Ely, he wrote the first book of pastoral poems in English, his *Eglogues* (pr. c. 1515), which are moral and satiric poems attacking the evils of court life and celebrating the carefree innocence of the English rural scene. They are modeled after Mantuan's eclogues and Aeneas Sylvius' *Miseriae curialium*.

Barclay translated Brant's *Das Narrenschiff* from Latin, French, and Dutch versions, and gave the whole an English setting. As in Brant's work, Barclay describes how fools are deported from their own land to live in a Land of Fools; each group of fools is identified by social class and mocked for follies. Barclay's English translation (1520) of Sallust's *Bellum Jugurthinum* is more literal. In 1521 he published a textbook, *The Introductory to Write and to Pronounce French.* Of another work, *The Castle of Labor,* first printed in Paris (1503?), only a fragment survives.

Barclay's *Eglogues* was edited by Beatrice White (1928). For biographical accounts, see J. M. Berdan, "Alexander Barclay, Poet and Preacher," *MLR*, VIII (1913); J. R. Schultz, "The Life of Alexander Barclay," *JEGP*, XVIII (1919); and William Nelson, "New Light on Alexander Barclay," *RES*, XIX (1943). For critical commentary, see C. H. Herford, *Studies in the Literary Relations of England and Germany in the Sixteenth Century*

(1886); J. M. Berdan, *Early Tudor Poetry, 1485–1647* (1920); and B. White, *The Eclogues of Alexander Barclay* (1928).

Barclay, John (1582-1621). See ARGENIS.

Barnavelt, Sir John Van Olden. A historical play by John FLETCHER and Philip MASSINGER, written around 1619. There is no record of publication in the seventeenth century, and the existence of the play was not known until A. H. Bullen first published it in 1883 from a manuscript in the British Museum. A letter from Thomas Locke to Sir Dudley Carelton at The Hague reveals that on August 14, 1619, the play was suppressed just before it was to be performed (probably by the King's Men). In another letter Locke informed Carelton that on August 27 the players "found the means to go through with the play of Barnavelt, and it had many spectators and received applause."

The downfall of the Dutch patriot Barnavelt was the subject of several pamphlets which Fletcher and Massinger may have consulted in writing the play. The scene of the play is Holland in 1618-19, the last year of Barnavelt's life.

Barnavelt, a great Dutch patriot who led his people in throwing out the Spanish invaders, burns with resentment and a sense of injured justice because the prince of Orange enjoys support of the army and is chief power in the state. Once a great hero, the aged Barnavelt now destroys himself with envy and ambition. He locks the prince out of a council meeting, gathers a force of rebels, and blatantly declares himself a disciple of Arminianism, a feared heresy. Barnavelt and another former hero of the Spanish wars, Leidenberch, are defeated by the prince and his followers. Leidenberch commits suicide and Barnavelt is beheaded. To the end the proud rebel protests his innocence and defies his enemies.

The standard edition, which contains an informative discussion of sources and historical background, is by Wilhelmina P. Frijlinck (1922). For additional criticism, see Samuel C. Chew, "*Lycidas* and the Play of Barnavelt," *MLN*, XXXVIII (1923); E. H. C. Oliphant, *The Plays of Beaumont and Fletcher* (1927); and Henri J. Makkink, *Philip Massinger and John Fletcher* (1966).

Barnes, Barnabe (1571-1609). Poet and dramatist. Born in York, the son of the bishop of Nottingham, Barnes attended Brasenose College, Oxford, but left without taking a degree. In 1591 he accompanied Essex on the campaign in Normandy. His first work, a volume of sonnets called *Parthenophil and Parthenophe*, appeared in 1593 with a dedicatory sonnet addressed to the earl of Southampton, Shakespeare's patron. In 1595 Barnes published a collection of religious poems, *A Divine Century of Spiritual Sonnets* (see SONNET SEQUENCES.) In 1598 he was charged by the Star Chamber with attempted murder, but escaped from Marshalsea prison before his trial. Perhaps because of influential friends no attempt was made to recapture him. In 1607 the King's Men performed at court Barnes's anti-Catholic tragedy. *The Devil's Charter,* which may have furnished a source for one scene (V, *iv*) of Shakespeare's *Cymbeline.* Nothing is known of Barnes between 1607 and his burial in 1609.

The Devil's Charter was edited by R. B. McKerrow in *Bang's Materialien*, VI (1904); *Parthenophil and Parthenophe* by Sir Sidney Lee in *Elizabethan Sonnets*, I (1904) and by Victor A. Doyno (1971); and *A Divine Century* by A.B. Grosart (1875). For biographical and critical accounts, see Mark Eccles, "Barnabe Barnes," in *Thomas Lodge and Other Elizabethans,* ed. C. J. Sisson (1933); and E. K. Chambers, *The Elizabethan Stage*, 4 Vols. (1923)

Barnfield, Richard (1574-1627). Poet. Born in Shropshire of landed gentry, Barnfield graduated B.A. at Oxford in 1592. He was a friend of Michael Drayton, Thomas Watson, and Shakespeare. About 1600 Barnfield gave up writing and became a prosperous landowner in Staffordshire. His chief poems include *The Affectionate Shepherd* (1594), a PASTORAL in imitation of the second eclogue of Vergil and dedicated to Lady Rich (the "Stella" of Sir Philip Sidney's *Astrophel and Stella*), and *Cynthia, with Certain Sonnets* (1595; see SONNET SEQUENCES). Two lyrics in Shakespeare's *The Passionate Pilgrim* (1599)—"As it fell upon a day" and "He that is thy friend indeed"—were long attributed to Shakespeare but are, in fact, Barnfield's. His *Encomion of Lady Pecunia* (1598) is a satiric poem on the worthlessness of money and profit motives.

Barnfield's poems were edited by A. B.

Grosart for the Fuller Worthies' Library (1876) and by A. H. Bullen in *Some Longer Elizabethan Poems* (1903). The definitive edition of the poems is by Montague Summers (1936). There is a biographical and critical study by Harry Morris, *Richard Barnfield, Colin's Child* (1963).

Bartholomew Fair. A comedy by Ben JONSON, written in 1614 and printed in 1631. No source is known.

The scene is Smithfield, London; the time August 24, St. Bartholomew's Day, and to Bartholomew Fair come a colorful array of characters: John Littlewit, a scatterbrained lawyer of the ecclesiastical courts who aspires to see a puppet show he has secretly written for the fair; Littlewit's puritanical wife, Win-the-Fight Littlewit, who, being pregnant, yearns for a taste of Bartholomew pig (barbecued pork); Littlewit's equally puritanical mother-in--law, Dame Purecraft; her suitor Winwife; and her minister, Zeal-of-the-Land Busy, who resolves to gorge himself on Bartholomew pig to demonstrate his repudiation of Judaism. Awaiting them at Smithfield are a flock of "Bartholomew birds"—balladmongers, bullies, cutpurses, prostitutes, stallkeepers, peddlers of wares—and Jonson's play depends less on plot than on the sheer exuberance of these vivid characters in their several confrontations. Master Bartholomew Cokes, an idiotic magistrate, finds himself carried off to the stocks; there are amorous mixups and confused couplings, and the play concludes at the puppet show contrived by Master Littlewit in imitation of Christopher Marlowe's poem *Hero and Leander,* which Littlewit explains, he has made "a little easy and modern for the times":

> As for the Hellespont, I imagine our Thames here; and then Leander I make a dyer's son about Puddle Wharf; and Hero a wench o' the Bankside, who, going over one morning to Old Fish Street, Leander spies her land at Trig Stairs, and falls in love with her. Now do I introduce Cupid, having metamorphos'd himself into a drawer [server in a tavern], and he strikes Hero in love with a pint of sherry. And other pretty passages there are o' the friendship that will delight you, sir, and please you of judgment.

Littlewit's hilarious dramatization also mixes in a bit of Damon and Pythias, equally "metamorphos'd" into banal characters and setting, and the production is enthusiastically received until the arrival of the Puritan Zeal-of-the-Land Busy, who refuses to endure such "profanations" as plays and puppet shows:

> I will remove Dagon there, I say, that idol, that heathenish idol, that remains, as I may say, a beam, a very beam—not a beam of the sun, nor a beam of the moon, nor a beam of a balance, neither a house-beam, nor a weaver's beam, but a beam in the eye, in the eye of the brethren, a very great beam, an exceeding great beam; such as are your stage-players, rhymers, and morris dancers, who have walked hand in hand, in contempt of the brethren and the cause, and been borne out by instruments of no mean countenance.

Brother Busy soon becomes involved in a ludicrous debate with Dionysius, one of the puppets, who not only refutes the Puritan but converts him into a "beholder" of plays: "Let it go," Busy concedes, "for I am chang'd, and will become a beholder with you!"

In the last scene of *Bartholomew Fair* Justice Adam Overdo, who has disguised himself as a madman in order to ferret out the vices of the fair, reveals his identity to the assembled company and points out the moral "enormities" of all the rascals at the fair. In keeping with the good-natured tolerance of Jonson's tone in this comedy, however, Overdo admits to his own frailties and invites everyone to his house for supper. Thus Jonson's *Bartholomew Fair* is among his most joyous and festive comedies, much less acerbic than *Volpone* and even more genial than *The Alchemist.* Tightly classical in structure, the comedy observes the unities of time, place, and action, but Jonson bases his characters on his own acute observation of contemporaries rather than on types found in Roman comedy. The characterizations are more individuated than in Jonson's other plays, and his ear for contemporary colloquialisms, cant, and rhythms of speech is astonishing.

The standard edition is in *Ben Jonson,* ed. C. H. Herford and Percy and Evelyn Simpson, 11 vols. (1925-53), VI. *Bartholomew Fair* has been edited by E. A. Horsman for the Revels Plays (1960); Eugene M. Waith in the Yale Ben Jonson series (1963); Edward B. Partridge in the Regents Renaissance Drama series (1964); and Maurice Hussey in a New Mermaid edition (1964). For commentary, see Freda L. Townsend, *Apologie for Bartholmew Fayre: The Art of Jonson's Comedies* (1947); Jonas A. Barish, *Ben Jonson and the Language of Prose Comedy* (1960); *James E. Robinson, "Bartholomew Fair:* Comedy of Vapors," *SEL,* I (1961); Robert E. Knoll, *Ben Jonson's Plays: An Introduction* (1964); Richard Levin, "The Structure of *Bartholomew Fair,*" *PMLA,* LXXX (1965); and Joel H. Kaplan, "Dramatic and Moral Energy in Ben Jonson's *Bartholomew Fair,*" *Ren D,* New Series, III (1970).

Basilikon Doron (James I). See COURTESY LITERATURE.

Baxter, Richard (1615-1691). English nonconformist theologian and religious writer. After years of studying independently without formal education, Baxter taught school and studied divinity at Worcestershire, where he was ordained in 1638. Although a chaplain in Cromwell's army, Baxter was an individualistic Presbyterian who objected as much to Puritans as to Anglicans, and his cardinal theme was always that of reconciliation, humility, and reason. In 1660 he served as chaplain to Charles II, under whom he not only refused a bishopric but also balked at signing the king's Uniformity Act, whereupon he was forbidden to teach and was jailed for several months. After the Toleration Act under William and Mary, Baxter's final years were free of persecution. He wrote over a hundred works, all on religious topics. His best-known books are *The Saints' Everlasting Rest* (1650) and *Call to the Unconverted* (1657), two long evangelical meditations. He wrote an equally long spiritual autobiography and meditative miscellany, *Reliquiae Baxterianae* (1696).

Over one hundred of Baxter's writings are listed in the bibliography by A.G. Matthews, *The Works of Richard Baxter* (1933). The definitive biography is by F. J. Powicke, *A Life of the Reverend Richard Baxter,* 2 vols. (1924, 1926). There is an abridged edition of *Reliquiae Baxterianae* by J. M. L. Thomas (1925).

Beaumont, Francis (c. 1584-1616). Poet and dramatist. Born of an ancient and distinguished Leicestershire family, Beaumont was the third son of Francis Beaumont, a justice of the Common Pleas; the dramatist's elder brother was the minor poet Sir John Beaumont (c. 1582-1627), author of *The Metamorphosis of Tobacco* (1602), a mock-heroic poem dedicated to Michael Drayton, and *Bosworth Field* (1629), a lengthy historical poem in couplets dedicated to Drayton and Ben Jonson.

Francis Beaumont entered Oxford at twelve and left without a degree when his father died in 1598. In 1600 he was at the Inner Temple, where he began writing poems and plays, possibly with the encouragement of Michael Drayton, a family friend. Beaumont's earliest work, published anonymously, was *Salmacis and Hermaphroditus* (1602), a mythological poem of the type made popular by Marlowe's *Hero and Leander* and Shakespeare's *Venus and Adonis.* One of the few other poems that can be attributed to Beaumont with any certainty is an encomiastic verse epistle, written around 1612, to Sir Philip Sidney's daughter Elizabeth, countess of Rutland. Collections of poems with Beaumont's name were published in 1618, 1640, and 1653, but these are actually miscellanies written by several authors other than Beaumont.

Beaumont's first play, THE WOMAN HATER, written for the Children of Paul's around 1606, is a comedy of humours strongly influenced by Ben Jonson. Although Jonson told William Drummond in 1619 that "Francis Beamount loved too much himself and his own verses," that judgment could not have represented Jonson's prevailing opinion. Never one to dispense praise casually, he expressed an uncharacteristic deference to Beaumont in *Epigrams.* "How I do fear myself," Jonson wrote in "To Francis Beaumont," "that am not worth / The least indulgent thought thy pen drops forth!" According to John Dryden in his *Essay of Dramatic Poesy,* Jonson "submitted all his writings to his [Beaumont's] censure, and 'tis thought, used his judgment in correcting, if not contriving, all his plots." Even allowing for Dryden's well-known penchant for exaggeration, Jonson seems to have held Beaumont in the highest regard. Both Beaumont and John Fletcher contributed commendatory verses to the first edition of Jonson's *Volpone* (1607). It is more difficult to date Beaumont's famous verse epistle of eighty lines to Jonson. Written when Beaumont was living in the country, perhaps at his family estate, Grace-Dieu, in Leicestershire, Beaumont's poem complains of weak rural wines and tedious companions, and recalls the festive times in London at the Mermaid Tavern with Jonson and other wits:

What things have we seen
Done at the Mermaid! heard words that have been
So nimble and so full of subtle flame,
As if that everyone from whom they came
Had meant to put his whole wit in a jest,
And had resolved to live a fool the rest
Of his dull life; then when there has been thrown
Wit able to justify the town
For three days past, wit that might warrant be
For the whole city to talk foolishly
Till that were cancelled, and when we were gone
We left an air behind, which was alone
Able to make the two next companies
Right witty, though they were downright cockneys . . .

Beaumont's earliest comedy imitates his master's comedy of humours to the point of farce; but Beaumont's prose is often vivid, his characterizations amusing, and his observations of contemporary society exceptionally keen for a dramatist of only twenty-three. (For comment on comedy of humours, see JONSON, BEN.) His next play, The KNIGHT OF THE BURNING PESTLE, was an uproarious satire performed about 1608 by the Children of the Queen's Revels at Blackfriars. The first full-length mock-heroic play on the English stage, it is a genial and sophisticated burlesque of the chivalric romances and bourgeois dramas currently beloved of the London citizenry. Not even Bottom and his "mechanicals" in Shakespeare's *A Midsummer Night's Dream* are more entertaining than Beaumont's obstreperous grocer and busybody wife, who interrupt the performance at Blackfriars to put on their own drama with their apprentice in the title role—a mock-heroic drama that burlesques the whole range of middle-class favorites from Thomas Kyd's *The Spanish Tragedy* to Thomas Heywood's rambling chronicle plays exalting London's apprentices and merchants. The preface to the first edition of Beaumont's masterpiece, published anonymously in 1613, notes that it was "begot and born in eight days" and "utterly rejected" by the public.

It is perhaps significant that Beaumont's friend John FLETCHER experienced a similar failure with *The Faithful Shepherdess* about the same time. In any event, it was in about 1608 that Beaumont and Fletcher decided to pool their talents; their collaboration lasted five years and produced a half dozen of the most popular plays on the Stuart stage. If the seventeenth-century antiquarian John Aubrey is to be believed, their collaboration was more than literary, for in his *Brief Lives* he repeats a story that Beaumont and Fletcher "lived together on the Bankside, not far from the playhouse, both bachelors; lay together; had one wench in the house between them, which they did so admire; the same clothes and cloak, etc., between them." The date of their earliest collaboration may be significant because in 1608 the Children of the Queen's Revels was dissolved by the authorities for satirizing the court in George Chapman's *Conspiracy and Tragedy of Charles, Duke of Byron,* and they surrendered their lease of Blackfriars to the King's Men. Thus the King's Men took over one of the private theaters, previously used exclusively by the children's companies, and required a repertory that would appeal to audiences more sophisticated than those attending their alternate playhouse, the Globe. In view of their social status, courtly taste, and previous experience at Blackfriars, Beaumont and Fletcher were eminently qualified to provide just such a repertory for the King's Men.

The earliest results of their collaboration, *Four Plays in One* (perf. c. 1608) and THE COXCOMB (perf. c. 1608-10), were in the proper vein but too disjointed and unfocused to be very successful. Their initial triumph was a tragicomedy, PHILASTER, OR LOVE LIES A-BLEEDING, written and performed around 1610. The play proved to be as seminal to the later Stuart drama as Kyd's *The Spanish Tragedy* was to the Elizabethan stage. Although *Philaster* resembles *Hamlet* in its portrayal of a restive and brooding prince deprived of the throne by a suave antagonist, Beaumont and Fletcher's hero is not haunted by ghosts, madness, or reflection, but by certain perverse notions of love and honor which other characters in the tragicomedy extol as symptomatic of his "godly nobility." More important to its success, *Philaster* provides a savor of tragedy without requiring any of the emotional or cerebral demands of that difficult and disturbing genre; instead of mystery, pity, and terror, Beaumont and Fletcher's blander surrogate offers complex courtly intrigues, pathos, and suspense.

Philaster contains many of the ingredients found in Beaumont and Fletcher's subsequent plays at Blackfriars—THE MAID'S TRAGEDY (perf. c. 1611); A KING AND NO KING (perf. 1611); and *Cupid's Revenge* (perf. c. 1612). Except for THE SCORNFUL LADY (perf. c. 1613-16), a comedy of manners in which E. K. Chambers and others have found only "traces" of Beaumont, the typical Beaumont and Fletcher drama after *Philaster* features in various degrees a morbid and indecisive, boastful yet "lily-livered" hero; a virtuous and long-suffering heroine; a single character or pair of lovers dedicated to Platonic love; and a scheming tyrant who strains the hero's adherence to the political principle of monarchial "divine right." Even in a tragedy such as *The Maid's Tragedy,* Beaumont and Fletcher employed the same devices used in their tragicomedies—false starts, sudden reversals of motivation, spectacular scenes, gratuitous accidents, sharp contrasts of good and evil characters, and climaxes achieved by emotive rhetoric rather than action.

It has proved extremely difficult to distinguish Beaumont's contributions from those of Fletcher. Because Fletcher, the more prolific of the two, continued to write plays until he died in 1625, whereas Beaumont retired from the stage around 1612-13, Fletcher's style is more easily recognized. He writes a facile, slack blank verse often bordering on rhythmic prose, with many end-stopped lines and feminine endings. He shows little talent for construction of plot, but is ingenious in contriving intrigues and individual scenes of pathos or suspense; his penchant for extravagance and artifice, cynicism and intrigue, causes him to favor comedies of manners such as THE WILD-GOOSE CHASE or totally escapist fantasies like THE ISLAND PRINCESS.

Since Beaumont wrote only two plays on his own (both in prose), and few poems that can be assigned to him with any certainty, his style is more difficult to characterize, especially if that style has to be distinguished from those of other dramatists who are known to have worked closely with Fletcher. Most scholars, however, agree that Beaumont's verse is more compressed and regulated than Fletcher's; that Beaumont employs much fewer end-stopped lines and fewer stressed syllables at the beginning of lines. Beaumont is accredited with more profundity in the creation of characters, and with more coherence and continuity in construction of plots. Thus in Beaumont and Fletcher's *The Coxcomb*, Fletcher is usually identified as the author of the farcical plot of Antonio's effort to exchange his wife's virtue for Mercury's friendship, and his wife's intrigue in bringing the coxcomb to his senses; Beaumont is given credit for the sentimental and rather well-made story of Ricardo and Viola. Most but certainly not all scholars agree that Beaumont contributed the greater share in the collaborations, including the planning of the plays. The fact remains, however, that in spite of the best efforts of scholars, beginning in 1874 with F.G. Fleay's attempt to make close distinctions between Beaumont and Fletcher by "metrical tests," problems of attribution remain bewildering and disagreements abound among very competent authorities.

The team was dissolved around 1612-13 when Beaumont married an heiress and retired from the theater to manage her estates in Kent. He died on March 6, 1616, and was buried in what is now Poet's Corner in Westminster Abbey, an honor not previously accorded any poet except Chaucer and Spenser.

Beaumont's place of burial attests as much to his social connections as to his literary achievement. By 1637 others of his circle with fame among the gentry had joined Beaumont in Westminster Abbey, including his brother Sir John, Michael Drayton, and Ben Jonson. Beaumont's easy relations with the aristocracy is well illustrated by his last dramatic work, *The Masque of the Inner Temple and Gray's Inn*, performed in February 1613 by over a hundred members of the two Inns in celebration of the marriage of Princess Elizabeth to the elector palatine. The masque was held in the king's new banqueting hall at Whitehall, with the assistance of Francis Bacon, his Majesty's solicitor general and a member of Gray's Inn, and with stage machinery and sets invented by Inigo JONES, Ben Jonson's collaborator on court masques. Beaumont's masque employs the appropriate theme of the marriage of the Thames and Rhine rivers, an idea similar to that expressed in Spenser's stately *Prothalamion*, and reflects the influence of Jonson in its staging of two elaborate anti-masques accompanied by a lengthy dumb show. (For anti-masque, see MASQUE.)

The first anti-masque is presented by Mercury, who shows four Naiads, four Hyades, four

Cupids, and four statues; in the second anti-masque, Iris presents a rustic assembly of types, including a pedant, a May lord and lady, a serving-man and chambermaid, a shepherd and country wench, a host and hostess, a he-baboon and she-baboon, and he-fool and she-fool. The contrasting dances of Mercury and Iris both pay tribute to the house of Stuart. Also featured in the masque are twelve white-robed priests, each with a lute, who sing before Jupiter's altar while above, as if in the temple of Jove, fifteen "Olympian" knights appear in robes of silk and gold. At the conclusion, the masquers step down from their settings and dance with their ladies in the audience.

In a letter of John Chamberlain, the leisurely scholar whose prodigious private correspondence describes many events of the period, Francis Bacon is named as the "chief contriver" of this lavish spectacle and the generous patron who donated hundreds of pounds to pay for the costumes. The records of the time show personal assessments made of each of the "gentlemen-masquers" who performed, but Bacon himself is said to have supplemented their donations out of his own purse, and Beaumont's dedication to Bacon in the printed version of the masque expresses gratitude for the solicitor-general's generosity. The Venetian ambassador, who witnessed Beaumont's masque, described in a letter something of its sumptuous elegance:

> The knights were in long robes of silk and gold, the priests in gold and silver. The knights danced, their robes being looped up with silver, and their dance represented the introduction of the Olympian games into this kingdom. After the ballet was over their Majesties and their Highnesses passed into a great hall especially built for the purpose, where were long tables laden with comfits and thousands of mottoes. After the King had made the round of the tables everything was in a moment rapaciously swept away.

In retrospect, it seems possible that Beaumont and Fletcher's plays provided the Stuart gentry at Blackfriars with at least something of the lively spectacle that enthralled James I and his court at Whitehall. Their tragedies and tragicomedies, like Beaumont's masque, are more lavish of emotions and more extravagant in actions, spectacles, and sensational characters and turns of story than any of their contemporaries were capable of or even willing to attempt. The music of the plays, the songs and dances interlarding the action, the frequency of such "noble and symbolical" events as the stately masque in *The Maid's Tragedy*—all these contributed toward making Beaumont and Fletcher the most popular fare both at court and at private theaters until the demise of such elegance and the closing of the playhouses in 1642. George Bernard Shaw, without dismissing their artistic competence, comments in *Plays and Players* that Beaumont and Fletcher express "no depth, no conviction, no religious or philosophical basis, no real power or seriousness." These absences were not from fatuity but by ingenious design, for Beaumont and Fletcher gave an increasingly sensate but myopic privileged class the fullest possible perception of what it was still capable of experiencing—a glittering surface without depth or interior form.

The largest collection of Beaumont and Fletcher's plays is in *The Works of Francis Beaumont and John Fletcher,* ed. Arnold Glover and A. R. Waller, 10 vols. (1905-12). The incomplete Variorum Edition of Beaumont and Fletcher's plays, under the general editorship of A. H. Bullen, 4 vols. (1904-13), contains only twenty plays. Seven plays—including Beaumont's *The Knight of the Burning Pestle,* ed. Cyrus Hoy; *The Masque of the Inner Temple and Gray's Inn.* ed. Fredson Bowers; and *The Woman Hater,* ed. G. W. Williams—are in *The Dramatic Works in the Beaumont and Fletcher Canon,* ed. Fredson Bowers, 2 vols. (1966, 1970). Fletcher's collaboration with Beaumont and other dramatists is analyzed closely by Cyrus Hoy in a series of articles in *SB,* VIII (1956); IX (1957); XI (1958); XII (1959); XIII (1960); XIV (1961); and XV (1962). The standard biography of Beaumont is still the one by C. M. Gayley, *Beaumont, the Dramatist* (1914). Important critical studies include A. H. Thorndike, *The Influence of Beaumont and Fletcher on Shakespeare* (1901); E. H. C. Oliphant, *The Plays of Beaumont and Fletcher: An Attempt to Determine Their Respective Shares and the Shares of Others* (1927); Lawrence B. Wallis, *Fletcher, Beaumont, and Company* (1947); Eugene M. Waith, *The Pattern of Tragicomedy in Beaumont and Fletcher* (1952); and W. W. Appleton, *Beaumont and Fletcher: A Critical Study* (1956). There is a Concise Bibliography of Beaumont and Fletcher by S. A. Tannenbaum

(1938), supplemented by D. R. Tannenbaum (1946) and updated in "Beaumont and Fletcher (1937-65)," ed. C. A. Pennel and W. P. Williams, in *Elizabethan Bibliographies Supplements,* VIII (1968).

Beggars' Bush. A tragicomedy by John FLETCHER and Philip MASSINGER. It was first published in 1647 but produced on the stage as early as 1622. No source is known.

Goswin, a wealthy merchant at Bruges, does not realize that he is really Florez, earl of Flanders, stolen away by his stepfather Gerrard in order to escape death at the hands of Wolfort, who usurped Florez's earldom. Gerrard remains nearby in Bruges, disguised as a beggar, to watch over Florez's interests. Florez is in love with Bertha, presumed to be the daughter of the burgomaster of Bruges but in reality Gertrude, daughter of the duke of Brabant and betrothed in childhood to Florez. Like Florez, Gertrude is ignorant of her true identity. As the play opens, an honest courtier of Flanders named Hubert is apprehended by Wolfort's men—always suspicious of treason—as he attempts to depart for Bruges, a city which still refuses to surrender to Wolfort, One reason for Hubert's flight is to find his sweetheart Jacqueline, Gerrard's daughter; Wolfort is so touched by Hubert's tale of lost love that he sends his captain, Hempskirke, to help Hubert find the girl.

At Beggars' Bush, meanwhile, the merchant Goswin helps his friend Clause (really Gerrard in disguise) to become elected king of beggars. Goswin, Clause, Hubert, Hempskirke, and Bertha all meet at the house of Van Dunck, burgomaster of Bruges and supposed father of Bertha. Hempskirke recognizes Bertha as being really Gertrude, kidnaped heiress of Brabant, but he keeps the knowledge to himself. Hempskirke and Goswin quarrel, and the next day, at the place appointed for the duel, Goswin is rescued from Hempskirke's band of ruffians by the merry beggars, who show Hempskirke to be a knavish spy and plotter against Hubert's life.

A new danger threatens Goswin. He faces bankruptcy and debtors' prison unless his ships arrive in port the next day. He is saved again by Clause and his crew of beggars when they arrive with thousands of gold crowns. Clause lends the beggars' fortune to Goswin on the condition the merchant give the beggar a ring he wears and, when Clause wishes it, to grant him one boon. Just as Goswin pays his debts, his delayed ships arrive safely in port and Goswin prepares to marry Bertha, whereupon Clause appears with Goswin's ring and takes him away.

Meanwhile Hubert, disguised as a huntsman, locates Jacqueline, then enters into a feigned plot with his prisoner Hempskirke to betray the nobles in Bruges. Bertha, Goswin, and Clause are all captured by Hubert (pretending villainy), Wolfort, and Hempskirke. The beggar Clause reveals his true identity and that of Goswin and of Bertha, Van Dunck arrives with merchants and beggars to liberate the party from Wolfort, and all ends happily. Hubert marries Jacqueline, Wolfort and Hempskirke are banished, and Florez and Gertrude join the two kingdoms of Flanders and Brabant with their marriage.

The play is in the anthology by C. F. T. Brooke and N. B. Paradise, *English Drama, 1580-1642* (1933) and edited, with notes and commentary, by J. H. Dorenkamp (1967). It is discussed by E. H. C. Oliphant in *The Plays of Beaumont and Fletcher* (1927). See also John P. Cutts, "A Newly Discovered Musical Setting from Fletcher's *Beggar's Bush,*" *Comp D,* V (1971).

Belleforest, Francois de (1530-1583). French translator of *Histoires tragiques* (Paris 1559), a continuation in seven volumes of Matteo Bandello's *Novelle,* a small part of which had previously been translated from the Italian by Pierre Boaistuau (or Boisteau; d. 1566). Belleforest's translation includes many stories other than Bandello's. It was translated into English by Geoffrey Fenton under the title *Certain Tragical Discourses* (1567; see TRANSLATIONS). Both Fenton and Belleforest were widely used as sources by Elizabethan dramatists. One of Belleforest's tales is a legend translated from Saxo Grammaticus that may have been a source of HAMLET. Belleforest's stories were also sources for Shakespeare's ALL'S WELL THAT ENDS WELL, MUCH ADO ABOUT NOTHING, and TWELFTH NIGHT.

Fenton's translation of Belleforest's tales was edited by R. L. Douglas and H. Harris (1924). Belleforest's Volume V, Third story, the analogue of *Hamlet,* is translated by Joseph Satin in *Shakespeare and His Sources* (1966).

Bellman of London, The. A rogue pamphlet

in prose by Thomas DEKKER, first published in 1608. As sources Dekker used an early "beggar book" by Thomas Harman, *A Caveat or Warning for Common Cursitors* (1566), a collection of anecdotes revealing the villainies of "cursitors" (vagabonds). Dekker also made liberal use of Robert GREENE'S "coney-catching" pamphlets, such as *A Notable Discovery of Cosenage* and *The Black Book's Messenger,* and many other sources (see ROGUE LITERATURE). Indeed, as Frank W. Chandler has stated, "Dekker's work is an unblushing plagiarism from several sources, prefaced by an original and interesting narrative" (*The Literature of Roguery,* I [1907], p. 107).

In the beginning narrative the author comes to a cottage in the English countryside where a band of beggars have gathered for a feast. Here he observes their initiation ceremonies and listens to their "canting" underworld speeches in praise of beggary. Afterward the author returns to London to discover a multitude of ruses and tricks practiced by beggars and coney-catchers (confidence men), and provides "a discourse of all the idle vagabonds of England, their conditions, their laws among themselves, their decrees and orders, their meetings, and their manners of living."

The "bellman" of the title refers to the nightwatchman appointed under Queen Elizabeth to patrol the London streets to guard against fire, theft, and violence. His official cry was "Remember the clocks, / Look well to your locks, / Fire and your light, / and God give you good night, / For now the bell ringeth."

Dekker's *Bellman of London* is in A. B. Grosart's edition of *The Non-Dramatic Works,* 5 vols. (1884-86) III, and O. Smeaton's edition for the Temple Classics (1905). Dekker's many sources are treated by F. Aydelotte, *Elizabethan Rogues and Vagabonds* (1913).

Berners, John Bourchier, second **Baron** (1467-1533). Statesman and translator. Lord Berners' most famous work is his translation of Jean Froissart's *Chronicles* (1523, 1525), which provided Shakespeare and other dramatists with a source for their history plays. Berners also translated the romance *Huon of Bordeaux* (1534) and *The Golden Book of Marcus Aurelius* (1534), the latter an important source of the prose style called EUPHUISM. Berners spent most of his life in diplomatic posts under Henry VII and Henry VIII.

Berners' translation of Froissart was edited by W. P. Ker for the Tudor Translation series, 6 vols. (1901-03), and reissued by the Shakespeare Head Press, 8 vols. (1927-28). For a biography, see W. P. Ker, *Essays in Medieval Literature* (1905), and J. H. McDill, "The Life of Lord Berners," *TLS* (April 17, 1930).

Bible translations. The great Authorized Version of 1611 was the culmination of almost a century of assiduous Biblical scholarship. The first translation of the Bible into English was by the Lollard John Wyclif, whose Early Version appeared about the time of his death in 1384, the much greater Latin Version in about 1395-97. Wyclif's was the last translation until the Protestant Reformation inspired scholars to depart from the hopelessly inaccurate Latin Vulgate texts on which all medieval translations had been based. After 1488 the Hebrew of the Old Testament became available in print, and in 1516 Erasmus made another advance by translating the Greek of the New Testament into Latin.

It was the spirit of Luther that prompted William TYNDALE to translate into English the New Testament (1525), as well as the Pentateuch (c. 1530) and the Book of Jonah (1531). Hounded out of Cologne by Catholic officials in 1525, he completed his translation of the New Testament at Worms, whence copies were smuggled into England past Cardinal Wolsey's agents. Tyndale published the Pentateuch and Jonah texts at Marburg and issued a definitive new edition of his entire translation at Antwerp in 1534, complete with polemical anti-Catholic prologues and glosses. His work was never completed, but his lucid, vigorous English became an important influence on the prose style of the 1611 translation. Tyndale's version of the Sermon on the Mount illustrates his direct, idiomatic style:

> Think not that I am come to destroy the law or the prophets: No, I am not come to destroy them but fulfill them. For truly I say unto you, till heaven and earth perish, one jot or one tittle of the law shall not scape till all be fulfilled.
>
> Whosoever breaketh one of these least commandments and teacheth men so,

he shall be called the least in the kingdom of heaven. But whosoever observeth and teacheth, the same shall be called great in the kingdom of heaven.

Even before Tyndale's martyrdom in 1536 at Vilvorde, near Brussels, Miles Coverdale (1488-1568) had compiled a complete version of the Bible (1535) based on the Latin Vulgate, Tyndale's Old Testament, and the German and Swiss versions of Luther and Zwingli. Two years later appeared the so-called Matthew's Bible under the pseudonym "Thomas Matthew" (probably John Rogers, a London rector martyred in Mary Tudor's reign), a translation derived from those of Tyndale and Coverdale. This translation and the second edition of Coverdale's (1537) were printed in England with the approval (however temporary) of Henry VIII. The so-called Taverner's Bible (1539) by Richard Taverner (c. 1505--1575) was merely plagiarized from Matthew's Bible.

At the beginning of the 1530s Henry VIII formed a committee to prepare an approved translation of the Bible, but the project came to nothing untill 1538, when Thomas Cromwell and Archbishop Cranmer urged Coverdale and Richard Grafton, a London printer, to collate Tyndale's work and Matthew's Bible. This new version, called the Great Bible (1539), was first published in a huge black-letter folio bearing a front piece showing Henry VIII presenting the "Word of God" to Cromwell and Cranmer for distribution to the English people. Seven editions came out in the next two years, the second with a lengthy preface by Cranmer (hence the version is often referred to as "Cranmer's Bible"). The Twenty-third Psalm from the Great Bible illustrates the somewhat taut, occasionally stilted English of this translation:

> The Lord is my shepherd; therefore can I lack nothing. He shall feed me in a green pasture and lead me forth beside the waters of comfort. He shall convert my soul and bring me forth in the paths of righteousness for his name's sake. Yea, though I walk through the valley of shadow of death I will fear no evil, for thou art with me; thy rod and thy staff comfort me.
>
> Thou shalt prepare a table before me against them that trouble me; thou hast anointed my head with oil, and my cup shall be full.

The next great translation was the Geneva Bible (1560), often called the "Breeches Bible" because of its rendition of Genesis 3:7, "They sewed fig leaves together and made themselves breeches." It was largely the product of English Protestants in exile during the reign of Mary Tudor and was derived from the New Testament of Erasmus and Tyndale and the Greek and Hebrew scholarship of Protestant reformers. It was the first English translation of Scripture to employ Roman type rather than black letter, to divide chapters into verses, and to give explanatory notes in italics. Because of its dogmatic and anti-Catholic marginalia, it became a favorite of Puritans and was officially prohibited by the Anglican Church. Despite its proscription, it went through 150 editions by 1644.

It was partly the popularity of the Geneva Bible that caused the Anglican bishops under the supervision of Archbishop Matthew Parker (1504-1575) to compile the Bishops' Bible (1568; rev. ed., 1572), which became the principal basis for the Authorized Version. The Bishops' Bible is scholarly and accurate but utterly lacking in the literary qualities of the Authorized Version:

> God is my shepherd; therefore I can lack nothing. He will cause me to repose myself in pasture full of grass, and he will lead me unto calm waters.
>
> He will convert my soul; he will bring me forth into the paths of righteousness for his name sake.
>
> Yea, though I walk through the valley of the shadow of death, I will fear no evil, for thou art with me; thy rod and thy staff be the things that do comfort me.
>
> Thou wilt prepare a table before me in the presence of mine adversaries; thou hast anointed my head with oil, and my cup shall be brimful.

In response to these Protestant translations a group of English Catholics under the direction of two priests, Gregory Martin and William Allen, began work at Rheims on their own versions, the Douai-Rheims edition. The New Testament was printed at Rheims in 1582, the Old Testament at Douai in 1609. The complete edition of both Old and New Testaments did not appear until 1635. Based on the Vulgate, it is Latinate and stilted, almost totally barren of grace and eloquence:

> Our Lord ruleth me, and nothing shall be wanting to me; in place of pasture there he hath placed me.
>
> Upon the water of reflection he hath brought me up; he hath converted my soul; he hath conducted me upon the paths of justice for his name.
>
> For although I shall walk in the middes of the shadow of death I will not fear evils, because thou art with me; thy rod and thy staff they have comforted me.
>
> Thou hast prepared in my sight a table against them that trouble me. Thou hast fatted my head with oil, and my chalice inebriating, how goodly is it!

The greatest of these Biblical translations was the Authorized Version, or King James Version. This monumental work arose from the Hampton Court conference of Anglicans and Puritans in 1604 who had convened to discuss "things pretended to be amiss in the church" and shortly adjourned with little accomplished except a proposal agreed upon by King James, his bishops, and the Puritans that a definitive translation of the Old and New Testaments, together with the Apocrypha, might profitably be executed "by the best learned in both the universities."

After five months of deliberations, fifty-four scholars were chosen for the project from Oxford, Cambridge, and Westminster. They represented both Anglicans and Puritans, and included such divines as Lancelot Andrewes, William Bedwell, John Overall, Thomas Sanderson, Sir Henry Saville, and John Spenser. (For a complete list of the translators, see the *Encyclopedia Britannica,* 11th ed.) They were divided into six committees, or "companies," each assigned a portion of the text and each reporting to the bishops, the Privy Council, and the king. As guidelines the translators followed the Bishops' Bible "as little altered as the truth of the original will permit," adhered to orthodox ecclesiastical diction (employing "church" rather than "congregation," for example), and avoided the kind of provocative glosses found in the Geneva Bible. (The aims and methods of the translators were set forth in the preface to the first edition by Miles Smith and are reprinted in the Clarendon Press edition [1833].) In addition to the Bishops' Bible, they consulted the Tyndale and Coverdale versions, the Geneva Bible, and the Douai-Rheims texts. After the completion of the translation, the whole work was brought together for three years of revision. The printer, Robert Barker, spent nine months preparing it for publication.

The result was a truly magnificent achievement of English prose, a stately and eloquent climax to over a century of stylistic development from Sir Thomas More to Richard Hooker. The style of the Authorized Version is not, as is often assumed, in "ordinary Elizabethan English" but in a consciously elevated, rhythmic, and incantatory prose written by gifted and devout translators who believed that every syllable formed the living Word of God. The miracle of their accomplishment is their amazing consistency of diction, tone, and rhythm, as if every translator had worked in harmony with a common orchestration, a common tempo and scale. The influence of the Authorized Version on the English language can scarcely be exaggerated; the work occupies such a unique place in literature that the whole stress and texture of the language might well have been different—and certainly less beautiful—without the inspired scholarship of the 1611 edition.

A standard work on 16th and 17th century Biblical translations is B. F. Wescott, *A General View of the History of the English Bible* (rev. ed. by W. A. Wright, 1905). Also valuable is A. W. Pollard, *Records of the English Bible . . . 1525-1611* (1911). The story of the Authorized Version is told in two important works: C. C. Butterworth, *The Literary Lineage of the King James Bible* (1941), and David Daiches, *The King James Version of the English Bible* (1941). See also *The Cambridge History of the Bible,* III: *The West from the Reformation to the Present Day,* ed. S. L. Greenslade (1963).

biography. Renaissance English biography evolved from medieval saints' lives and from translations of such classical biographers as Plutarch, Suetonius, and Tacitus. Both influences are clearly evident in the earliest English biography. Sir Thomas MORE'S version of Pico della Mirandola's *Life of John Picus, Earl of Mirandola,* printed in black letter by Wynkyn de Worde around 1510, follows the tradition of medieval saints' legends in being adulatory and didactic. More's greater work, RICHARD THE THIRD (wr. 1513-14), is probably based on a lost Latin original by More's friend John Morton, archbishop of Canterbury, which, in turn, seems to have been modeled upon works by Suetonius and Tacitus. Although More's *Richard the Third* represents an unfinished and hasty rough draft, it remains the most fascinating and compelling biography of the sixteenth century, and one that Shakespeare consulted in writing his history play *Richard III* (see CHRONICLE PLAY). More's instinct for drama and human interest is everywhere apparent, especially in such vivid scenes as Buckingham's farcical efforts to get Richard elected by affirmation and the famous episode of the bishop of Ely's strawberries just before Hastings' arrest and execution. More's was the first biography in English to convey any real psychological interest in its subject; repelled as he was by Richard's fiendish cruelty, More was nevertheless concerned with tabulating his quirks of character and tempestuous changes. After Richard has the young princes murdered in the Tower, More shows him experiencing a tormenting conscience:

> For I have heard by credible report of such as were secret with his chambers, that after this abominable deed done, he never had quiet in his mind; he never thought himself sure. Where he went abroad, his eyes whirled about, his body privily fenced, his hand ever on his dagger, his countenance and manner like one always ready to strike again. He took all rest a nights, lay long waking and musing, sore wearied with care and watch, rather slumbered than slept; troubled with fearful dreams, suddenly sometime start up, leap out of his bed and run about the chamber . . .

Almost as effective is the biography of More himself by his son-in-law William Roper (1496-1578), whose *Life of More,* written during the reign of Mary Tudor, was first published in Paris in 1626 with the title *The Mirror of Virtue in Worldly Greatness.* Roper is laudatory and almost solemnly respectful, yet sensitive to the nuances of his subject's character, and like More, he shows an admirable talent for dramatic anecdote. He relates numerous incidents illustrating More's humor and portrays his subject in little scenes fraught with significance. After walking in his garden at Chelsea with Henry VIII, for example, More encounters his son-in-law, who expresses pleasure over More's close friendship with the king. "Howbeit, son Roper," More replies, "I have no cause to be proud, for if my head would win him a castle in France . . . it should not fail to go." The scene of More's deathwatch with his family in the Tower just before his execution is especially vivid and poignant, not only for its compassionate portrait of the serene and self-possessed Catholic martyr, but also for its subtle delineation of More's family relationships—his awkward alienation from his unsympathetic wife, his devotion to his daughter, and his touching warmth for Roper, whom he once rejected as a prospective son-in-law because of Roper's Protestant beliefs. There were other biographies of More in the sixteenth century, including the very thorough and scholarly one in Latin by Thomas Stapleton, *Tres Thomae* (first printed in 1588), but none, even to this day, has proved as readable and revealing as Roper's classic.

Another great early biography is *The Life and Death of Thomas Wolsey* by George CAVENDISH. Although written during the reign of Mary Tudor, the first edition did not appear until 1641, and then in a badly altered text edited by a Puritan who wished to point up the parallel between the Catholic Cardinal Wolsey and the Anglican Archbishop William Laud. During the sixteenth and early seventeenth centuries, however, Cavendish's biography, circulating in several manuscript versions, continued to have a great influence. John Stowe incorporated several extracts from Cavendish's biography in his *Annals*, and Shakespeare and John Fletcher used it as an important source for HENRY VIII. Cavendish knew his subject personally, having served as Wolsey's gentleman-usher for the last five years of the cardinal's life, and although he describes briefly Wolsey's humble birth and early education, it is the cardinal's later period of magnificence and opulence that Cavendish emphasizes. In his prologue, Cavendish claims that his biography was prompted by a desire to explain away the "diverse sundry surmises and imagined tales" of Wolsey's last years, but Cavendish's work actually originated in the more literary inspiration of John Lydgate's *Fall of Princes* and in Cavendish's view of Wolsey as the proud, fated hero of a medieval tragedy. After describing Wolsey's "ascending by fortune's favor to high honors, dignities, promotions, and riches," and portraying in great detail his many progresses and lavish banquets, he lingers over Wolsey's abrupt and miserable fall, concluding his biography as an *exemplum* illustrative of the vanity of human wishes:

> Here is the end and fall of pride and arrogancy of such men, exalted by fortune to honors and high dignities; for I assure you, in his time of authority and glory he was the haughtiest man in all his proceedings that then lived, having more respect to the worldly honor of his person than he had to his spiritual profession; wherein should be all meekness, humility, and charity . . .

Another Tudor biography, *The Life of Fisher,* written in 1559 and usually attributed to Richard Hall, owes less to medieval tragedy than to the saint's legend. Its portrait of Bishop John Fisher, executed in the time of More and for the same reasons, shows a humble and pious man of God caught up in the brutal intrigues of the king's divorce. Vehemently anti-Protestant, the biography is notable for its use of letters and its protracted and grisly depiction of Fisher's execution. This same influence of the saints' legends is apparent in John Foxe's famous ACTS AND MONUMENTS ("Book of Martyrs"; Latin version published in 1554, English in 1563), which, although purporting to be a history, is essentially a Protestant calendar of saints designed to supersede the R man Catholic literature on the same subject.

Adding to these influences of medieval tragedy and saints' legends was the stream of translations of classical biographies, beginning with Arthur GOLDING'S translation of Caesar's *Civil Wars* in 1565 and continuing with Sir Thomas NORTH'S Plutarch in 1579, Sir Henry Savile's four books of Tacitus (including "The Life of Agricola") in 1591, and Philemon Holland's Suetonius (*History of Twelve Caesars*) in 1606. These and other translations gave English biographers much-needed examples of form and style. Hence Sir George Paule used Plutarch as the model for his biography of John Whitgift (1612), and Peter Smith did the same in his life of the Protestant reformer Andrew Willet (1634). Similarly Bacon modeled his HENRY VII (1622) after Tacitus' *Annals,* with the result that it is more a history than a biography, for his account of Henry's life from Bosworth Field to his accession concentrates on such matters as finances, laws, diplomacy, and political intrigues to the exclusion of personal or domestic details. To Tacitus' example in organizing minute data and careful observations, Bacon brings a wealth of insight and experience about English history, law, and political institutions. Bacon's brief sketch of Queen Elizabeth, first printed in English from Latin by William Rawley in 1657, is equally perceptive but less critical, for in this sketch he intended an encomium to a queen whose statesmanship he admired.

By the beginning of the seventeenth century English biography had proliferated into a variety of types—royal biographies, ecclesiastical biographies, prefatory collections, and even bourgeois biographies. An example of the last is the anonymous *London's Dove, or A Memorial of the Life and Death of Master Robert Dove, Citizen and Merchant-Taylor of London* (1612), which like a saint's legend, provides a worthy "mirror," an ideal example for businessmen to emulate. "God stir up the hearts of rich and able men to follow his steps," exhorts the author, "and give them grace to imitate his good example." The bourgeois pseudo-biographies, such as Thomas DELONEY'S romantic fictions about tradesmen in THOMAS OF READING, JACK OF NEWBURY, and THE GENTLE CRAFT, all written between 1596 and 1600, represent the increasing popularity of biography as a form of entertainment.

The old tradition of encomia or condemnation—of writing biography to illustrate an ideal life to be emulated or a wicked one to be avoided—continued unabated in spite of experimentation with different types. An especially distinguished biography of the traditional kind is Fulke GREVILLE'S tribute, *The Life of Sidney,* first printed in 1652 but written much earlier. Greville's work is neither systematic nor comprehensive, but its energy, eloquence, and unquestionable sincerity make it one of the great achievements of English Renaissance biography. Like Plutarch, Greville finds in his subject's life a powerful theme—the Stoic concept of virtue's sole importance—and he integrates this motive with vivid portraits not only of Sidney but of such notables as Queen Elizabeth, and with dramatic accounts of episodes in Sidney's life, such as his confrontation with the earl of Oxford on a tennis court and his heroic death at Zutphen.

It is not, however, the scholarly statesman and courtier Fulke Greville who emerges as the most distinguished biographer of the early seventeenth century, but a simple Fleet Street draper named Izaak WALTON, whose Boswellian hero worship settled entirely on Anglican divines. He published a biography of John DONNE in 1640, of Sir Henry Wotton in 1651, of Richard HOOKER (see LAWS OF ECCLESIASTICAL POLITY) in 1665, of George HERBERT in 1670, and of Robert Sanderson in 1678. Originally Walton commissioned Wotton to write the Donne book, but when Wotton died, Walton took over the project by writing a seventeen-page introduction to eighty of Donne's sermons, and then enlarged upon this beginning. The result is still the definitive biography of Donne. Hardly a scholar by training. Walton was nevertheless the most thorough and resourceful biographer of the period. He interviewed friends and acquaintances, ransacked public records, collected letters, perused his subject's poems, sermons, and treatises; and to this diversified data he brought his lively imagination, direct and concrete style, and passionate conviction of the towering greatness of these five ministers of the church. In his preface to the life of Herbert he calls each of these biographies "a free-will offering, and writ chiefly to please myself." Walton's greatest work is his biography of Donne, with its accounts of Donne's early life as a "frequenter of ladies," his arduous intellectual training, his marriage and consequent poverty, his inspiring sermons at St. Paul's (where, Walton recalls from experience, Donne "preached like an angel on a cloud"), and the macabre preparations for his death. The best of the "intimate" biographers, Walton provides anecdotes and commentary from his own point of view, often names his sources, and frequently interlards his narrative with personal letters and imaginary conversations. To a greater extent than any biographer of the seventeenth century, Walton combines the assiduous scholarship, literary imagination, and subjective passion that were to become the salient qualities of the genre in the Victorian period.

The Civil Wars in England led to several noteworthy biographies of military heroes. Perhaps the strangest of these came from the pen of inimitable Margaret CAVENDISH, Duchess of Newcastle, whose panegyric *Life of William Cavendish, Duke of Newcastle* (1667), written and published while her subject was still alive, celebrates her husband's role in the Royalist armies in the north and concludes with his exile in France and Holland. A whole volume is devoted to Cavendish's particular achievements, virtues, and talents ("the finest lyric and dramatic poet of his age"), another to a collection of "my noble Lord and Husband's" favorite slogans and wise sayings. Here, as elsewhere in the duchess's turgid writings, she exhibits an exuberant verbosity that feeds voraciously on thinnest air. A somewhat less ebulient performance is the Puritan Lucy Hutchinson's *Memoirs of the Life of Colonel Hutchinson,* written around 1670 but not published until 1806. Her work is an ardent defense of her husband, who died in 1664 as a result of political persecution by the Royalists, but it also contains accounts, in the third person, of her early life, her scholarly interests and aspirations, and her courtship by her future husband, who, like William Cavendish, is presented as a paragon of the age.

At the end of the English Renaissance biography took a new and more antiquarian turn with an outpouring of biographical collections such as Thomas FULLER'S *Worthies of England* (1662); Edward Phillips' *Theatrum poetarium* (1674), biographical sketches of ancient and contemporary poets; William Winstanley's *Lives of the Most Famous English Poets* (1687); and Gerard Langbaine's *Account of the English Dramatic Poets* (1691). The greatest of these was Anthony à Wood's comprehensive work whose title indicates the magnitude of his project, *Athenae Oxonienses, An Exact History of All the Writers and Bishops Who Had Their Education in . . . Oxford from . . . 1500 to the End of the Year 1690* (1691-92). Clearly, the new age of exact biographical scholarship had begun.

The best single-volume study, with extensive bibliography, is. Donald A. Stauffer, *English Biography Before 1700* (1930). See also J. C. Major, *The Role of Personal Memoirs in English Biography and Novel* (1935) and J. W. Thompson, *A History of Historical Writing,* 2 vols. (1942).

Black Book's Messenger, The. See GREENE, ROBERT.

Bodleian Library. The library at Oxford University founded by Sir Thomas Bodley

(1545-1613) and first opened in 1602, when it contained about two thousand volumes. In 1610 the Stationers' Company agreed to give the Bodleian a copy of every book printed in England. Subsequently the Bodleian received substantial donations from the libraries of Archbishop William Laud, Oliver Cromwell, Robert Burton, and, more recently, Edmund Malone (1741-1812), who contributed from his Shakespeare library forty-three early quartos, two First Folios, three Second Folios, one Third Folio, and two Fourth Folios. Today the Bodleian possesses an immense collection of over half a million early books and manuscripts, many of them from the Elizabethan period. Some notable accessions include the libraries of Bishop Jerome Osorius and John Selden, and the Rawlinson and Canonice manuscripts. Under a copyright law of 1911 the Bodleian is authorized to require a copy of every book printed in the United Kingdom.

Sir Thomas Bodley was educated at Geneva, the son of a prominent family exiled during the persecutions of Protestants under Mary Tudor. He received his college degree at Magdalen College, Oxford, and from 1588 to 1596 held a diplomatic post at The Hague. He spent most of his life developing the great library that bears his name.

Bodley's letters to Thomas James, the first keeper of the Bodleian, were edited by G. W. Wheeler (1926), who also edited *The Letters of Sir Thomas Bodley to the University of Oxford, 1598-1611* (1927). This correspondence contains much information about the founding and development of the library. See also *The Cambridge History of English Literature,* ed. A. W. Ward and A. R. Waller, 14 vols. (1907-16), IV.

Bodley, Sir Thomas (1545-1613). See AUTOBIOGRAPHY, BODLEIAN LIBRARY.

Bondman, The. A tragicomedy by Philip MASSINGER, written around 1623, first performed in 1623, and printed in 1624. For his plot Massinger read the "Life of Timoleon" in Plutarch's *Lives,* translated by Sir Thomas North (1579). Several other historians, including Herodotus, tell the same story.

When the great Corinthian general Timoleon arrives in Syracuse (fourth century, B.C.), he finds the city ill-prepared for its war against Carthage. The rich are indifferent to the public good, and the people weakened by riot and luxury. After much difficulty Timoleon raises an army and departs for Carthage, leaving behind in the city mostly women, children, old men, and slaves. In Timoleon's absence the Theban gentleman Pisander, disguised as a bondman, or slave, leads a successful revolt, chiefly to win the love of Cleora, whose father has contemptuously denied his suit, and partly from compassion for the slaves. Cleora, however, remains loyal to Leosthenes, who is away in the army with Timoleon. When Timoleon returns victorious from Carthage, he finds the slaves in control of Syracuse. Pisander and his followers fight valiantly at first, but are routed when Timoleon has his men exchange their swords for whips. Pisander is discovered hiding in Cleora's bedchamber, and the jealous Leosthenes insists upon believing the worst in spite of Cleora's pleas of innocence. In court Pisander and Leosthenes confront each other with their rival claims, and Leosthenes conducts himself basely in contrast to Pisander, who acts with great courage and dignity. Finally Pisander reveals himself to be a proper gentleman, Cleora joyfully accepts him as a husband, and her father concurs. Pisander and his slaves are pardoned by Timoleon.

Scholars have interpreted the play as a political allegory in which Syracuse represents England and Carthage, Spain. Timoleon has been identified with Prince Maurice of Orange, and the weakness of Syracuse with the laxity of James I's government. *The Bondman,* however, cannot be read too literally as an allegory.

One of the most popular of Massinger's plays, it continued to be performed well into the Restoration period with the famed Thomas Betterton in the title role. Samuel Pepys saw the play several times and recorded in his diary (July 28, 1664): "There is nothing more taking in the world with me than that play." Like Massinger's *The Roman Actor. The Bondman* contains swift action and fiery political speeches pertaining to liberty and justice. Its heroic characterizations and variegated action made it a forerunner to the heroic plays of the Restoration. William Cartwright made extensive use of Massinger's play in writing his popular heroic tragicomedy *The Royal Slave.*

There is an excellent modern edition of *The Bondman* by B. T. Spencer (1932). For critical analyses, see T. A. Dunn, *Philip Massinger: The Man and the Playwright* (1957), and Philip

Edwards, "The Sources of Massinger's *The Bondman,*" *RES,* XV (1964).

Book of Common Prayer, The. A manual of rituals, devotions, and ecclesiastical observances appointed by law for use in the Anglican Church. The Prayer Book, although largely the work of Thomas Cranmer, archbishop of Canterbury from 1533 to 1556, developed gradually, from several sources during the sixteenth century. Before the English Reformation, church rituals and practices were based on a variety of texts, including breviaries (books of canonical and public prayers), missals (books of ritual for the Mass), manuals (books of observances governing ceremonies of baptism, communion, marriage, etc.), and pontificals (books of ceremonies performed by bishops, such as ordination). One popular guide to prayers and rituals was the so-called Use (i.e., ritual), especially the Use of Sarum (Salisbury), though the Uses of Bangor, Exeter, Hereford, St. Paul's, Wells, and York might also be employed. All these Uses were in Latin and hence incomprehensible to laymen.

The English break with Rome and the rendering of the Anglican Mass into English necessitated a uniform system of worship that could be understood by everyone, but Henry VIII, arch conservative in matters of church doctrine and discipline, did not authorize a uniform service until 1542, and even then permitted merely a modification of the medieval Use of Sarum. The extent of Henry's reforms was the authorization in 1544 for one chapter of Scripture in English to be read each Sunday in church and the use of a brief litany written by Cranmer.

The first complete Book of Common Prayer was approved by Parliament and published in 1549, during the brief period of religious reforms under Edward VI. Its basis was the Use of Sarum, the principal source for its morning and evening prayers, collects, epistles, gospels, consecration service, and rites of the sacraments. In addition, it was modeled after the Catholic Mass, retaining traditional late-medieval vestments and wafer bread, as well as on the so-called Mozarabic missal and manuals of litany by Luther and other Protestant reformers. However eclectic its form, its prose is graced by Cranmer's lucid and sonorous style:

> In the midst of life we be in death. Of whom may we seek for succor but of thee, O Lord, which for our sins justly art moved? Yet O Lord God most holy, O Lord most mighty, O holy and most merciful savior, deliver us not into the bitter pains of eternal death! Thou knowest, Lord, the secrets of our hearts; shut not thy merciful eyes to our prayers, but spare us, Lord most holy, O God most mighty, O holy and merciful savior, thou most worthy judge eternal. Suffer us not at our last hour for any pains of death to fall from thee.[*Order for the Burial of the Dead,* 1549 edition.]

By the Act of Uniformity (1549) Cranmer's Book of Common Prayer was adopted as the "one convenient and meet order, rite, and fashion of common and open prayer and administration of the sacraments." All local Uses, Latin manuals, Apocrypha, and saints' lives were proscribed. In 1552 this first Prayer Book was revised to keep pace with the increasingly anti-Catholic sentiments of the Anglican prelates. Altars and vestments (except surplices) were eliminated, portions of the canon were excised, and the sacrament of communion became increasingly symbolic rather than literal.

After the suppression of the Prayer Book of 1552 by Catholic Mary Tudor, Elizabeth restored this version with minor alterations by her Act of Uniformity in 1559. Slight changes were again made in 1561, which merely added some rules regarding holy days; otherwise, the 1559 version was adhered to until 1645, when a Puritan-dominated Parliament officially abolished its use. Although the preface to the 1559 version had proclaimed its purpose as the achieving of "the mean between the extremes," it became in fact a hot-bed of controversy between Anglicans and Puritans because of its prescriptions regarding church ornaments, priestly vestments, and other observances attacked by Puritans as "Romish" (see PURITANISM).

Next to the Authorized Version of the Bible, no single religious work has exceeded the literary influence of the Book of Common Prayer. Its echoes are heard everywhere in the plays and poems of Elizabethan and Stuart writers—a fact not surprising when one considers that baptisms, church services, burials, and scores of other everyday religious and social rituals followed its words and cadences.

Various versions of the Prayer Book between 1549 and 1662 are published with commentary in E. C. Ratcliff, *The Book of Common Prayer:*

Its Making and Revisions (1945). There is an excellent study by Francis Proctor and W. H. Frere, *New History of the Book of Common Prayer* (rev. ed., 1914).

Book of Martyrs. See ACTS AND MONUMENTS.

Book of the Ocean to Cynthia, A. See RALEIGH, SIR WALTER.

Bourchier, John, Second Berners. See BERNERS, JOHN BOURCHIER.

Bowge of Court, The. A verse dream-allegory and SATIRE by John SKELTON. Using rhyme royal, personification, and a prologue in which the narrator dreams the events of the poem, Skelton attacks the hypocrisy and cruelty of court life by symbolizing the state as a ship called "The Bowge of Court" ("bowge" means court rations), which is owned by Sans Peer and mastered by Captain Fortune. In his dream of a voyage aboard the ship, the narrator (Dread) tells how he is accosted by Danger, the favorite of Sans Peer, and soothed by Desire, who persuades him to stay aboard the ship. After this prologue, the main body of the poem describes the dialogue between Dread and seven of the ship's passengers: Favel (flattery), Suspect, Harvey Hafter, Disdain, Riot, Dissimulation, and Deceit. The one individuated character is Harvey Hafter, a trite jokester who calms the other passengers. Assaulted by every kind of vice, the narrator jumps overboard and awakens. In his conclusion, Dread points out that although what he has described is no more than a dream, dreams can express some grain of truth.

A standard text is in the *The Poetical Works,* ed. Alexander Dyce (1843, and several times reprinted). There are modernized versions edited by Philip Henderson (1931; rev. ed., 1948), and Robert Kinsman (1969). For critical discussion, see William Nelson, *John Skelton, Laureate* (1939); I. A. Gordon, *John Skelton, Poet Laureate* (1943); Arthur R. Heiserman, *Skelton and Satire* (1961); and Judith Sweitzer, "What is *The Bowge of Court?*" *JEGP*, LXI (1962).

Braithwait, Richard (1588?-1673). See COURTESY LITERATURE

Breton, Nicholas (1545?-1626?). Poet, pamphlet writer, miscellanist. The stepson of the poet George Gascoigne, Breton may have attended Oxford and afterward traveled abroad, though little is known of his early years. The countess of Pembroke, Sir Philip Sidney's sister, was his patron until 1601. Breton was a voluminous writer of pastorals, satires, dialogues, religious meditations, characters, and anthologies. He even wrote a lengthy book on fishing, *Wit's Trenchmour* (1597). Much of his verse is doggerel, but he wrote some admirable lyrics for the collections *England's Helicon* (1600) and *The Passionate Shepherd* (1604). Under the pseudonym "Pasquill," he produced a number of satires and burlesques.

Breton began his career as early as 1577 with a collection of poems called *A Flourish upon Fancy*, won some acclaim as author of two long and worshipful allegories of over 2,500 lines in six-line stanzas called *The Pilgrimage to Paradise, Joined with the Countess of Pembroke's Love* (1592), and lived to "croak on," as Thomas Nashe contemptuously noted, through the entire reign of James I. During that lengthy period he worked in a variety of genres in prose and verse, occasionally achieving a few notable lyrics of sweetness but more often producing a kind of persistently mediocre verse. His writings connect with almost every fashion of his time except the drama—CHARACTERS, ESSAYS, LETTER-WRITERS, PASTORALS, MARTIN MARPRELATE tracts, and COURTESY LITERATURE. His most enduring contribution is probably his immensely popular *A Post with a Packet of Mad Letters,* (pr. 1602; enl. ed., 1603; second part, 1606) a lively letter-writer that went through at least a dozen editions after its first publication in 1602.

Breton's *Works* was edited by A. B. Grosart, 2 vols. (1879). *A Mad World My Masters* and fourteen other prose pamphlets were edited by Ursula Kentish-Wright, 2 vols. (1929). There is a critical study by N. E. Monroe (1929) and a Concise Bibliography by S. A. and D. R. Tannenbaum (1946).

broadside ballads, or **"broadsides."** Ballads printed on folio sheets, two pages to a sheet and two columns to a page. This method of publication was an appropriately rapid and inexpensive way of disseminating these ephemeral forerunners of modern "yellow journalism." The subjects of the broadside ballads were varied but usually appealed to whatever was of current popular interest—religious controversy, tales of New World discoveries, miraculous events, anti-popish harangues, attacks on or defenses of women, the last words of executed criminals, popular songs, and so forth. Printed in black letter and often decorated with woodcuts, broadsides were hawked on the streets for a penny during the sixteenth and seventeenth centuries.

For collections of broadsides, see those edited by Hyder E. Rollins: *Old English Ballads 1553-1625* (1920); *A Pepsyian Garland 1595-1639* (1922); and *Cavalier and Puritan 1640-1660* (1923). Other collections are listed in *CBEL,* I. For a discussion of broadsides, see Rollins, "The Black-Letter Broadside Ballad," *PMLA.* XXXIV (1919); and Louis B. Wright, *Middle-Class Culture in Elizabethan England* (1935).

Broken Heart, The. A tragedy by John FORD, probably written sometime between 1627 and 1631 and printed in 1633. No source is known. The scene is ancient Sparta at some indeterminate time.

Years before the play opens, the present king of Sparta, Amyclas, sought to end a feud between Crotolon and Thrasus by betrothing Thrasus' only daughter Penthea to Crotolon's son Orgilus. When Thrasus died, however, the motive for the match ended, and in spite of the fact that Penthea and Orgilus were deeply in love, Thrasus' son Ithocles set aside the engagement and forced his sister to marry Bassanes, a rich and insanely jealous old nobleman. As the play opens, Orgilus takes leave of his sister Euphranea, whom he causes to swear never to marry without his permission. Orgilus pretends to journey to Athens but in reality disguises himself as a poor scholar in the service of the great philosopher Tecnicus. In this disguise he can remain in Sparta to watch over Penthea and observe how well Euphranea keeps her vow.

Meanwhile Ithocles, Penthea's proud brother, returns in triumph from the wars and is hailed by the king's beautiful daughter Calantha. In Ithocles' company of warriors is his friend Prophilus, who falls in love with Euphranea. In his disguise as a scholar, Orgilus agrees to act as a go-between for the two lovers. In this same disguise Orgilus encounters Penthea, to whom he reveals his identity, reiterates his love, and asserts the validity of their original betrothal. The noble, ethereal Penthea affirms her love but rejects his advance, advises him to marry another, and states that even if she were widowed, she could not in conscience defame Orgilus with "a second bed." For Penthea the past is hopeless and the future a tragedy of martyrdom to her own ideals.

In another interview, Penthea's brother Ithocles expresses sincere repentance for having forced her into her miserable enslavement to Bassanes, and she promises to help him in his own secret love for Calantha. Penthea's agony is underscored further when Bassanes, suspicious of incest, bursts in with dagger in hand to end this discussion between Penthea and Ithocles.

Orgilus appears in his own identity at court, where he is cordially welcomed by his former foe Ithocles and gives apparent approval to Euphranea's marriage to Prophilus. At court, too, arrives Nearchus, prince of Argos, whom Amyclas has approved as suitor for the hand of Calantha. The ailing Penthea, meanwhile, tells Calantha that she is to be executrix of her will. Calantha must dispose of three legacies bequeathed by Penthea: her youth Penthea would leave to "virgin wives," her fame to "memory" and "truth," and her brother Ithocles to Calantha herself. Although in tears, Calantha makes no response to Penthea's request.

Foreboding of tragedy deepens when the philosopher Tecnicus arrives at court with a cryptic message from the Delphian oracle. To Ithocles the oracle states: "The lifeless trunk shall wed the broken heart." To Orgilus the oracle says: "Revenge proves its own executioner." To the king, who has fallen gravely ill, the oracle proclaims: "But from the neighboring elm a dew / Shall drop, and feed the plot anew." Nobody at court is able to understand these ominous prophecies.

For the lovers, events seem at first auspicious. The king sets Nearchus' suit aside and promises Calantha to Ithocles, and Euphranea and Prophilus are duly betrothed. Penthea's agony increases, however; she starves herself, goes mad, and dies. As Ithocles and Orgilus mourn beside her body. Orgilus traps Ithocles in a mechanical chair and stabs him to death.

As Calantha dances at the wedding of Euphranea and Prophilus, she learns in succession the news of her father's death, Penthea's, and Ithocles'; but she continues to dance, apparently unmoved. Then, with stoical calm, as ruler in her father's stead, she sentences Orgilus to be his own executioner. The youth chooses to bleed himself to death, thus fulfilling the oracle's prophecy about revenge. At last, dressed all in white and with her lover's body beside her, Calantha deliberately completes the last prophecy by naming Nearchus king of Sparta, Crotolon ruler of Messene, and Bassanes marshal of Sparta; then she places her mother's ring on Ithocles' finger—fulfilling the first of the prophecies, that "that lifeless trunk shall wed the broken heart"—and drops dead with grief.

In the *dramatis personae* of the first edition Ford's characters are assigned such exotic epithets as "Flower of Beauty" (Calantha), "Honor of Loveliness" (Ithocles), "Complaint" (Penthea), and "Vexation" (Bassanes), thus pointing up Ford's esoteric and aristocratic code of love and honor, his rather vague Platonism, and his debt to the love pathology described in Robert Burton's ANATOMY OF MELANCHOLY. As in Ford's 'TIS PITY SHE'S A WHORE, the tragedy vacillates between quiet, unobstrusive conversations and such unexpected explosions of violence as Ithocles' death in the mechanical chair. As in *'Tis Pity,* also, Ford's theme is the marriage of true minds in abrasive conflict with tawdry political considerations (Ithocles) or base jealousy and possessiveness (Bassanes). Against these obstacles sanctioned by society, the lovers pit their mysterious and exalted personal conceptions of love and honor.

There is a modern edition by Donald K. Anderson for the Regents Renaissance Drama series (1970). For a discussion of Ford's psychology, see S. Blaine Ewing, *Burtonian Melancholy in the Plays of John Ford* (1940). Concise analyses are provided by Glenn H. Blayney, "Convention, Plot, and Structure in *The Broken Heart,*" *MP,* LVI (1958). R. J. Kaufmann, "Ford's 'Waste Land'; *The Broken Heart,*" *Ren D,* III (1970); Michael J. Kelly, "The Values of Action and Chronicle in *The Broken Heart,*" *MP,* LVI (1958); and Thelma Greenfield, "The Language of Process in Ford's *The Broken Heart,*"*PMLA,* LXXXVII (1972).

Brome, Richard (c. 1590-1652?). Dramatist. Almost nothing is known of Brome's life, and even his times of birth and death must be conjectured. His name first appears in Ben Jonson's *Bartholomew Fair* (1614), where he is described as being a servant of Jonson. Jonson again refers to Brome as his servant in verses affixed to Brome's *The Northern Lass,* and it was as a loyal "son of Ben" that Brome became known throughout the seventeenth and eighteenth centuries.

Brome's earliest recorded play is the lost *A Fault in Friendship,* entered in 1623 in the office book of Sir Henry Herbert, Charles I's master of the revels, who names "Young Jonson" as collaborator (believed to be neither Ben Jonson nor his son, but some unknown playwright). Before 1635 Brome wrote at least some plays for the Red Bull theater. In 1635 he signed a contract with the Salisbury Court theater to write exclusively for that playhouse three plays a year for three years at a set fee plus proceeds from the first day's gate receipts. The contract was offered again in 1638, but Brome chose to sign a similar contract with the Cockpit theater. Since Brome refers in 1652 to his *A Jovial Crew* as "this issue of my old age" and his name appears in no theatrical records as being alive after this date, it is generally assumed that he died in 1652 or 1653.

There is almost as much guessing about the dates of composition for Brome's plays as about his life. The extant plays attributed to Brome include *The Antipodes* (wr. 1638); *The City Wit* (wr. 1637-39?); *The Court Beggar* (wr. 1639-40); *The Damoiselle, or The New Ordinary* (wr. 1637-38?); *The English Moor, or The Mock Marriage* (wr. 1637); A JOVIAL CREW, or *The Merry Beggars* (wr. 1641); *The Late Lancashire Witches* (wr. 1634), with Thomas Heywood; *The Lovesick Court, or The Ambitious Politique* (wr. c. 1632-40); *A Mad Couple Well Matched* (wr. 1637?-39); *The New Academy, or The New Exchange* (wr. after 1640); THE NORTHERN LASS, (wr. 1629); *The Novella* (wr. 1632); *The Queen and Concubine* (wr. 1635-39?); *The Queen's Exchange* (wr. 1631-32?), also called *The Royal Exchange; The Sparagus Garden* (wr. 1635); and *The Weeding of the Covent Garden, or The Middlesex Justice of Peace* (wr. 1632; rev. c. 1642). There are also several lost plays assigned to Brome, two of these in collaboration with Thomas Heywood and one with George Chapman.

With the exception of *The Lovesick Court,* in which Brome either imitated or satirized the heroic dramas popular at court in the 1630s, all his extant plays are festive romantic comedies somewhat in the manner of Thomas Dekker's or satiric comedies of manners very obviously in imitation of Ben Jonson's. His best comedies are *The Northern Lass. The Sparagus Garden,* and *A Jovial Crew*—all closely woven and skillful comedies of manners—and his share in *The Late Lancashire Witches,* a superb melodrama reflecting Brome's occasional touches of realism. Although he lacked his master Jonson's energy of characterization and language, Brome was a masterful designer of plots with a simple integrity totally lacking among most other playwrights during the last decade before the closing of the theaters in 1642.

The Dramatic Works was edited by R. H. Shepherd, 3 vols. (1873). There is a biography by Clarence E. Andrews, *Richard Brome: A Study of His Life and Works* (1913). For critical analyses, see Herbert F. Allen, *A Study of the Comedies of Richard Brome, Especially as Representative of Dramatic Decadence* (1912), and R. J. Kaufmann, *Richard Brome, Caroline Playwright* (1961). The dating of Brome's plays and his relations with other dramatists and with the Salisbury Court and Cockpit theaters are studied by G. E. Bentley, *The Jacobean and Caroline Stage*, 7 vols. (1941-67), III; and John Freehafer, "Brome, Suckling, and Davenant's Theatre Project of 1639," *TSLL,* X (1968).

Browne, Sir Thomas (1605-1682). Author and physician. Born in London and educated at Winchester School and Broadgates (later Pembroke College), Oxford, Browne studied medicine at Montpellier, Padua, and Leyden. In 1633 he began his medical practice in Yorkshire, then in 1637 moved to Norwich, where he remained the rest of his life. In 1641 he married Dorothy Mileham, who bore him ten or twelve children (the exact number being unknown). During the Civil War he sympathized with the Royalist cause but took no active part in the conflict. He was knighted in 1671 during a royal visit to Norwich.

A man of enormous learning and prodigious memory. Browne was also whimsical, eccentric, and superstitious—a paradoxical mixture of medieval lore, Baconian science, and great intellectual curiosity. It is perhaps a significant clue to his strange sensibilities that in 1644, the year he was elected to the College of Physicians, he offered testimony that condemned two women accused of witchcraft. His first work, *Religio medici,* is expressive of this blend of rationality and mysticism. Intending it as a spiritual autobiography for his own use, Browne did not plan to publish the work until a pirated edition appeared in 1642, whereupon he brought out his own authorized version the following year. Instantly popular, it was translated into Latin and widely read abroad, where it was received as both atheistical and devout, and placed on the papal Index. Actually, it is the work of a genial and tolerant (albeit speculative) Anglican entirely comfortable with his religion and with himself. If its avowed purpose is to reconcile "skepticism and belief," the religious doubts are seen as having been youthful errors long since corrected by steadily maturing faith. What distinguishes the book is the author's amazingly energetic imagination and eloquent prose style—a complex yet lyrical manner of writing that some modern critics have deemed "metaphysical."

Browne's next work, *Pseudodoxia epidemica* (or *Vulgar Errors*), published in 1646, employs his encyclopedic knowledge and sharp powers of observation to refute certain ideas entertained by credulous minds. Characteristically, his inquiry ranges freely over topics as disparate as an Aristotelian metaphysical precept to the question of whether or not elephants have bones, and although on some questions Browne is as systematically scientific as Bacon, on others he argues *ex cathedra,* chops logic, and invokes his intuition or mystical "reason," *Hydriotaphia, or Urn Burial* was first published with his *Garden of Cyrus* in 1658. The occasion for the first work was the discovery of ancient burial urns in Norwich. Speculation regarding the origin of the sepulchers inspires Browne's lyrical digressions on ancient burial customs, man's fear of death and longings for immortality. As in *Religio medici,* the tone is stoic, self-possessed, and philosophically serene, the style often soaring and majestic.

The Garden of Cyrus is a complex treatise on the merits of the five-pointed figure of the quincunx (⁚·⁚), the arrangement of trees in antiquity, and especially the design of the gardens of Cyrus as described by Xenophon. Characteristically, Browne takes Xenophon's description as a starting point from which to launch quaint speculations about the quincunx in the Garden of Eden (with the Tree of Knowledge planted in the center), in architecture, and in military formations and tactics. The dissertation concludes with a discussion of the mysterious symbolic implications of the number five. Browne's last work, *Christian Morals,* a philosophical meditation blending stoicism and Christian piety, was not published until 1716. It was edited by Samuel Johnson in 1756.

Browne's religious position in *Religio medici* and his other works is that of a cultivated, tolerant Roman stoic thoroughly knowledgeable of Bacon's foolish idols but emotionally aligned to the ceremonial and ritualistic Anglican religion of John Donne, George Herbert, and Lancelot Andrewes. His *Religio medici* covers much the same ground as Richard Hooker's OF THE LAWS OF ECCLESIASTICAL POLITY, but does so with the brilliant speculations of Montaigne coupled with his own characteristic tone of "love and wonder." For Browne there is no tension between faith and reason, and doubt is not agony but occasion for paradoxical joy. In *Religio medici,* Browne is a relaxed Pascal who delights in the fact that reason puts his faith to the test:

> As for those wingy mysteries in Divinity, and airy subtleties in religion, which have unhinged the brains of better heads, they never stretched the *Pia Mater* of mine; methinks there be not impossibilities enough in religion for an active faith; the deepest mysteries ours contains have not only been illustrated but maintained by syllogism and the rule of reason. I love to lose myself in a mystery, to pursue my reason to an *O altitudo*! 'Tis my solitary recreation to pose my apprehension with those involved enigmas and riddles of the Trinity, with Incarnation and Resurrection. I can answer all the objections of Satan, and my rebellious reason, with that odd resolution I learned of Tertullian: *Certum est quia impossible est.* ["It is certain because it is impossible."] I desire to exercise my faith in the difficultest point, for to credit ordinary and visible objects is not faith but persuasion.

In *Religio medici,* the sustained metaphor is that of the circle, for as the above quotation suggests, Browne remains serenely convinced that any speculation, whether it begins with reason or faith, will take him back to a point in Christian revelation and truth. Browne's prose, therefore, is in the "loose" or "Attic" style, a pliant syntax of unraveling clauses that open out on the page into speculations and probings from an initial point in independent clauses. This anti-Ciceronian, Senecan style of Browne and other seventeenth-century prose writers has been thoroughly analyzed by M. W. Croll.

The standard edition of Browne's works and correspondence was edited by Geoffrey Keynes, 6 vols. (1928-31). The best biography is by J. S. Finch, *Sir Thomas Browne* (1950). For Browne's thought, see R. Sencourt, *Outflying Philosophy* (1924); Egon Merton, *Science and Imagination in Sir Thomas Browne* (1949); W. P. Dunn, *Sir Thomas Browne, A Study in Religious Philosophy* (rev. ed., 1950); and F. L. Huntley, *Sir Thomas Browne* (1962). For M. W. Croll's analysis of Browne's style, see *SP,* XVI (1919) and XVIII (1921), and *PMLA,* XXXIX (1924). A bibliography by Keynes (1925) has been updated in "Sir Thomas Browne (1924-66)," ed. Dennis Donovan, in *Elizabethan Bibliographies Supplements,* X (1968).

Browne, William (1591?-1643?). Poet and courtier. Born in Devonshire, which he later celebrated in verse, Browne entered Exeter College, Oxford, in 1603, left without a degree, and studied law at the Inner Temple. An admirer of Spenser and a friend of Michael Drayton and George Wither, Browne wrote mostly pastoral verse in the style of Spenser, and is remembered chiefly for the seven eclogues he contributed to *The Shepherd's Pipe* (1614) (see PASTORAL), a work he collaborated on with Wither. Milton annotated a copy of Browne's poems, and Browne's pastorals may have influenced Milton's *Lycidas.* Other works by Browne include *Two Elegies* (1613), on the death of Henry, prince of Wales; *Britannia's Pastorals,* Part I (1613) and Part II (1616); Part III (1852 in a Percy Society edition); and *The Inner Temple Masque* (1614). His collected works were not published until 1772.

G. Goodwin edited Browne's *Works* for the Muses' Library, 2 vols. (1894). The fullest critical study is F. W. Moorman, *William Browne* (1897).

Bryskett, Lodowick (1571?-1611?). For comment on his *A Discourse of Civil Life,* see FAERIE QUEENE, THE.

Buchanan, George (1506-1582). Scottish poet, classical scholar, and educator. After graduating B.A. and M.A. at the University of Paris, Buchanan won the favor of James V of Scotland, who secretly assigned him the dangerous task of writing verses against the Franciscans. Abandoned by the king, Buchanan was imprisoned for these satires, escaped, and fled to Bordeaux, where he taught Latin for three years at the College de Guyenne. Montaigne was one of his pupils there. Afterward Buchanan was appointed head of a college in Coimbra, Portugal. Accused of heresy by the Inquisition, he hid in a monastery for nearly three years (1549-51), during which time he wrote a Latin version of the Psalms.

By the time he returned to Scotland in 1560 he was an ardent Calvinist, and although Mary Queen of Scots had been his pupil, as a member of the Scottish General Assembly he helped prosecute her for high treason. Later (1570-78) he became tutor to James VI (the future James I of England) and was subsequently made director of Chancery and lord of the Privy Seal. Almost all of Buchanan's works are in Latin, a language he employed with polish and brilliance. For many years he championed the cause of making Latin Scotland's literary and scholarly language. He wrote many Latin love poems and at least two tragedies, *Baptistes* (1544) and *Jephthes* (1544), the latter translated into French, Polish, Italian, German, and finally, in 1750, English. The principal works of his later years were *De jure regni apud Scotos* ("Concerning the King's Law in Scotland," 1579) and a highly regarded history, *Rerum Scoticarum historia* ("History of Scotland," 1582). His Latin poems were read by Sidney, Spenser, and others in their circle, and may have directly influenced some of Milton's Latin elegies.

Buchanan's vernacular writings were edited by P. H. Brown (1892). There is a biography by D. Macmillan (1906) and a collection of critical studies in *George Buchanan, A Memorial, 1506-1906,* ed. D. A. Miller (1907). See also James E. Phillips, "George Buchanan and the Sidney Circle," *HLQ,* XII (1948-49).

Bunyan, John (1628-1688). Puritan writer and preacher. Born near Bedford the son of a tinsmith, Bunyan was pressed into Cromwell's army at sixteen. In 1653 he joined the Baptist church in Bedford and began preaching and writing. His first two works, *Some Gospel Truths Opened* (1656) and *A Vindication of Gospel Truths* (1657), were written to refute the teachings of a group of Quaker mystics in Bedford. When nonconformist preachers were banned at the Restoration, Bunyan defied the edict against preaching and was imprisoned intermittently for twelve years (1660-72), during which time he wrote *The Holy City, or The New Jerusalem* (1665) and his spiritual autobiography, *Grace Abounding* (1666; see AUTOBIOGRAPHY). *Grace Abounding* is a moving, frank account of the author's "misspent youth"—much exaggerated by his hypersensitive conscience—and describes his experiences as a soldier, his constant temptations to evil, and his final salvation. Like all Bunyan's works, it reflects his assiduous study of the Authorized Version of the Bible and of nonconformist evangelical writings.

When Charles II proclaimed the Act of Indulgence tolerating Catholics and nonconformists, Bunyan was released from prison. He returned to preaching in Bedford. After the withdrawal of the act in 1675, he was again jailed, this time for six months, and it was during this period that he began his major work, PILGRIM'S PROGRESS (1678), a pious Christian allegory. This was followed by two distinctly inferior allegories, THE LIFE AND DEATH OF MR. BADMAN (1680) and *The Holy War* (1682).

Bunyan's lack of formal education, his humble vocation, and his narrow range of allusions (chiefly to the Bible and evangelical writings) in his allegorical and autobiographical works all combine to suggest that he was an unlettered and isolated rustic. Bunyan was, however, not only widely read in Spenser, Milton, medieval pulpit literature, Foxe's *Book of Martyrs*, and emblem books, but was part of a great religious, literary, and social movement in which the humble workingman and open-communion Baptist preacher symbolized to his thousands of Puritan supporters the ideals of authentic apostolic inspiration and the priesthood of all true believers. Hence Bunyan used the most humble language derived from ordinary working-class life and wedded it to the sacred eloquence of the Authorized Version to convey to his readers an apocalyptic vision of Christian aspirations. Devoid of formal education and class privileges, the "mechanic preacher" represented the natural graces of God's Elect in their purest form. To restive sectarians his energetic spirit revealed the living word, the inspired message of a radical "saint" promising a revolutionary millennium and a New Jerusalem.

There is no satisfactory modern edition of Bunyan's voluminous works, which range from verses written for children to pietistic meditations and esoteric theological disputations. These are listed in *A Bibliography of the Works of John Bunyan*, ed. F. M. Harrison (1938). There are two distinguished biographies: John Brown, *John Bunyan: His Life, Times, and Work* (1885; rev. 1928 by F. M. Harrison), and G. B. Harrison, *John Bunyan: A Study in Personality* (1928). Bunyan's philosophical and literary significance is explored by William York Tindall in *John Bunyan, Mechanick Preacher* (1934). The most comprehensive analyses are by H. Talon, *John Bunyan: The Man and His Work* (1951); and Roger Sharrock, *John Bunyan* (rev. ed., 1968), which contains an extensive bibliography.

Burton, Robert (1577-1640). Author of the medical treatise *The Anatomy of Melancholy* (1621). The facts of Burton's life can be dispensed with briefly. Born in Lindley, Leicestershire, he entered Brasenose College, Oxford, in 1593 and remained there for the rest of his life. He was vicar of St. Thomas', Oxford, and later rector of Segrave, Leicestershire, but these were merely sinecures; his sole residence was his room at Oxford, his one occupation keeper of the college library. Although he wrote an anti-Catholic Latin comedy, *Philosophaster* (acted at Oxford in 1618), and contributed Latin verses to college publications, the one major product of his eccentric life was his *Anatomy of Melancholy,* a long and serious study of the causes, symptoms, and cures of the "black distemper" from which, reportedly, the author himself suffered. There is a legend that he foretold the day of his own death, January 25, by casting his horoscope.

The erudite Oxford scholar who never married or even traveled "but in map or card" put all of his life in *The Anatomy of Melancholy,* a work so profusely documented with thousands of allusions to authors from Galen to Bacon as to suggest that for Burton the choicest part of living was reading. His treatise is systematically divided into three principal parts: causes, symptoms, and prognoses of melancholy; cures and alleviations of melancholy; and symptoms of love and religious melancholy, the two classic manifestations of the malady. Burton's tripartite arrangement, however, does not prevent him from engaging in long digressions on human anatomy and the nature of spirits, observations on manners and morals, or descriptions of his own ideal commonwealth. For most readers, Burton's didactic or satiric anecdotes and well-placed allusions, however digressive, constitute one of the chief allurements of his book. Few readers have regretted the fact that although Burton was thoroughly conversant with Bacon and the "new science," and sympathetic with its aims, he could not resist imposing on every problem his own eccentric and restless imagination. Nor could he, for all his scientific values, overcome his peculiar conceptions of logic and his penchant for proving a case by the medieval method of totaling masses of authorities on either side of a given question.

The result is a book that can be picked up or put down as one wishes, a discursive and continuously charming repository of speculations on everything under the sun. It was a book Samuel Johnson kept by his bedside, that was praised by Charles Lamb as being admirably "fantastic," and that the historian Sir William Osler called the finest medical treatise written by a layman. Like his master Bacon, Burton is a superb prose stylist. Under clouds of profuse quotations and allusions, his sentences are firm and direct, curt and pithy, his diction concrete and often colloquial, as in this passage where Burton digresses on melancholia induced by learning:

> How much time did Thebet Benchorat employ, to find out the motion of the eighth sphere! forty years and more, some write. How many poor scholars have lost their wits, or become dizards (fools), neglecting all worldly affairs and their own health, wealth, being and well-being, to gain knowledge? For which, after all their pains, in the world's esteem they are accounted ridiculous and silly fools, idiots, asses,

> and (as oft they are) rejected, condemned, derided, doting, and mad! Look for examples in Hildesheim, read Trincavellius, Montanus, Gareus, Mercurialis, Prosper Calenus in his Book On Black Bile. Go to Bedlam and ask. Or if they keep their wits, yet they are esteemed scrubs [base fellows] and fools by reason of their carriage because they cannot ride an horse, which every clown can do; salute and court a gentlewoman, carve at table, cringe, and make congies [departing bows] which every common swasher can do, &c. they are laughed to scorn, and accounted silly fools by our gallants. Yea, many times, such is their misery, they deserve it: a mere scholar, a mere ass.

His epigrammatic first clauses enable Burton to pile modifiers, quotations, and allusions on the end of the sentences—an appropriate syntactical device to accommodate his wide-ranging imagination and well-stored scholar's memory. His insatiable intellect devours whole libraries at a gulp, and many of his sources will never be traced through the wilderness of his esoteric reading. Miraculously, however, under his ingenious pedantry is a curious, compassionate, and observant sensibility delicately responsive to whatever is universal in human experience.

Burton continued to add to the five editions of *The Anatomy* published during his lifetime. The sixth edition (1651) contains the last of his revisions. The standard edition is by H. Jackson, 3 vols. (1932). The complete text is also edited by F. Dell and P. Jordan-Smith, 2 vols. (1927), which provides translations of the numerous Latin quotations. Sir William Osler's appreciation is in *Robert Burton and the Anatomy of Melancholy,* ed. F. Madan (1926). Burton's medical importance is also stressed by Bergen Evans, *The Psychiatry of Robert Burton* (1944). The influence of Burton on John Ford is described by S.B. Ewing, *Burtonian Melancholy in the Plays of John Ford* (1941). Burton's literary sources are traced by H. J. Gottleib, *Robert Burton's Knowledge of English Poetry* (1937). See also Lawrence Babb, *Sanity in Bedlam* (1959), and David Renaker, "Robert Burton's Tricks of Memory," *PMLA,* LXXXVII (1972). There is an extensive bibliography by P. Jordan-Smith, *Bibliographia Burtoniana* (1931), which has been updated in "Robert Burton (1924-66)," ed. Dennis Donovan, in *Elizabethan Bibliographies Supplements,* X (1968). See also Donovan, "Recent Studies in Burton and Walton," *ELR*, I (1971).

Bussy D'Ambois. A tragedy by George CHAPMAN, written in about 1604 and first printed in 1607. It is based on both historical events and contemporary gossip about the exploits of the titular hero at the court of Henry III of France, whose reign (1574-89) was marked by intense strife between Catholics and Huguenots. Chapman's chief source was probably his kinsman William Grimestone's *General Inventory of the History of France* (1607), which Chapman may have read before publication. Some scholars also note the influence of Marlowe's play *The Massacre of Paris*. In 1691 Thomas D'Urfey revised Chapman's play as *Bussy D'Ambois, or The Husband's Revenge,* and in 1846 Alexandre Dumas made Bussy the subject of a novel, *La Dame de Monsoreau.*

A proud but poor Bussy D'Ambois is brought from obscurity into the French court of Henry III by the politic Monsieur (the duke D'Alençon), who secretly aspires to the throne. At the court the haughty Bussy deliberately antagonizes the powerful duke of Guise. In a later altercation, Bussy engages in a duel with three other courtiers, and only Bussy survives. To the disgust of Guise, King Henry exonerates Bussy of murder and begins to praise him publicly as the cynosure of virtue and courage. Meanwhile, with the aid of an old friar as go-between, Bussy enters into a secret love affair with the count of Montsurry's wife Tamyra, who has been spurning the advances of Monsieur. As Bussy's star rises at court and the king continues to lavish honors on him, Monsieur bitterly regrets having sponsored his former protege and joins with Montsurry and Guise in a conspiracy to destroy this "proud mushroom shot up in a night."

The agent of Bussy's downfall is Tamyra. From Tamyra's maid, Monsieur learns of the love affair and informs Montsurry. Tortured by her jealous husband, Tamyra is forced to send for Bussy as if for a rendezvous; but she writes the message in blood as a warning to her lover. Montsurry's cruelty to Tamyra is witnessed by the old friar, Tamyra's confessor, who drops dead from shock and grief; his ghost hastens to warn Bussy of the trap set by Montsurry and Guise. The proud Bussy, however, chooses to disregard the ghost's warning, as well as that issued by a spirit called Behemoth; he interprets Tamyra's blood-written letter as a testimony of her love. When he hastens to Tamyra's room, he is ambushed by armed assailants. The friar's ghost at first frightens off Bussy's attackers, but they counterattack under the leadership of Montsurry. Although Bussy defeats Montsurry in personal combat, he magnanimously spares him at Tamyra's pleading. Finally Bussy is mortally wounded by a pistol shot in the back. He nobly forgives his assailants, urges the reconciliation of Tamyra and Montsurry, and dies. Tamyra asks Montsurry's forgiveness, but vows to live alone in loyalty to Bussy's memory. The sequel to these events Chapman kept for a later play, THE REVENGE OF BUSSY D'AMBOIS.

Chapman's tragedy portrays an idealist corrupted in his futile effort to compromise with worldly ambitions and temptations. From Chapman's Neo-Platonic view, the allurements of the flesh are represented by the beautiful Tamyra, whose relationship with the hero is joyless and guilt-ridden; like Bussy, she submits to "fate" rather than to any well-considered motives or even her own rational preferences. For Chapman, presumably, the only means of preserving integrity is in total withdrawal from the irresistible temptations of corrupt society. Hence Bussy's titanic passion only clouds his reason; his heroism only imbues him with a reckless pride that drives him to his fall.

Maurice Evans has edited the play for the New Mermaid series (1966), N. S. Brooke for the Revels plays (1964), and R. J. Lordi in the Regents Renaissance Drama series (1965). Two important critical studies are in T. M. Parrott's scholarly edition, *The Tragedies of Chapman* (1910), and Jean Jacquot's critical biography, *George Chapman* (1951). See also Peter Ure, "Chapman's Tragedies," *The Jacobean Drama, Stratford-Upon-Avon Studies* I (1960); Irving Ribner, *Jacobean Tragedy: The Quest for Moral Order* (1962); and Eugene M. Waith, *The Herculean Hero in Marlowe, Chapman, Shakespeare, and Dryden* (1962).

Byrd, William (1543-1623). English composer and musician. In 1563 Byrd was appointed organist at Lincoln Cathedral and in 1569 joint organist of the Chapel Royal. In 1588 he composed the first English madrigals (see SONGBOOKS). Byrd and his early teacher, Thomas Tallis, were awarded monopolies by Queen Elizabeth to print and sell music. Some of their chief song collections include *Psalms, Sonnets, and Songs of Sadness and Piety* (1588), *Songs of Sundry Natures* (1589), and *Psalms, Songs, and Sonnets* (1611).

Byrd's madrigals were edited by E. H. Fellowes, *Collected Madrigals,* vols. 14-16 (1920). There are two important critical studies: E. H. Fellowes, *William Byrd* (1923), and F. Howes, *William Byrd* (1928).

C

Cambises, King of Persia. A tragedy attributed to Thomas PRESTON. *Cambises* was entered in the Stationers' Register in 1569; the earliest extant edition is that of 1584. Hence the dates of composition and first publication remain uncertain. In contrast to such early Senecan plays as *Gorboduc,* this early tragedy is a medley of crude farce, allegory, and abstract characters from the MORALITY PLAYS. It became synonymous with rant and bombast among later Elizabethan dramatists (see Shakespeare's 1 *Henry IV,* II, *iv,* 425). In theme Preston's play was influenced by Boccaccio's *De casibus virorum illustrium* and John Lydgate's *Fall of Princes;* the story of Cambises, son of Cyrus the Great, was based on two passages in Herodotus, Books III and IV.

While the vainglorious Cambises campaigns in Egypt, Ambidexter the Vice corrupts Sisamnes, a judge whom Cambises leaves behind to rule Persia. Upon his return Cambises hears the character Commons' Cry condemn Sisamnes' venality, and Cambises sits in judgment of his minister with Commons' Cry, Proof, and Trial as accusers. Sisamnes' son Otian is ordered by Cambises to witness his father's execution.

The wars in Egypt have made Cambises cruel and vicious. He petulantly murders a courtier's son; he sets Cruelty and Murder upon his brother Smirdis, and at his own wedding he executes the prospective bride when she rebukes him for the murder of Smirdis. Divine Justice condignly punishes Cambises when his sword slips from its scabbard and mortally wounds him. The main cause behind Cambises' misdeeds, the play concludes, is treacherous Ambidexter.

Although *Cambises* is of trifling merit aesthetically, it is of great interest to scholars for exemplifying Elizabethan tragedy at an early stage of transition. Its allegorical abstractions—Ambidexter (meaning "plays with both hands"), Commons' Complaint, Murder, Preparation, Shame, and others—link it with the morality plays. The demise of the tyrant at the apex of his pride reflects its affinities to the medieval concept of tragedy expressed in Lydgate's *Fall of Princes,* Chaucer's "Monk's Tale," and *A Mirror for Magistrates,* and its theme of political treachery shows Elizabethan tragedy at a stage of development when it was still indistinguishable from the history play (see CHRONICLE PLAY). Although *Cambises* is not divided into acts and scenes, the Senecan influence may be apparent in the use of "fourteeners" in King Cambises' speeches, for that verse form was employed by Seneca's English translators in

1581 (see SENECAN TRAGEDY; POULTER'S MEASURE). These stately speeches are contrasted to the colloquial language of Ambidexter and slapstick scenes involving the ruffian soldiers Huf, Ruf, and Snuf. Although the later Elizabethans' reviled *Cambises* as crude dramaturgy and absurd bombast, its mingling of farce and solemnity characterised much of English tragedy down to the Restoration.

The best critical edition is by J. M. Manley, *Specimens of the Pre-Shakespearean Drama* (1897). A well-annotated edition with a critical introduction is in *Elizabethan Plays,* ed. A. H. Nethercot, C. R. Baskervill, and V. B. Heltzel (rev. ed., 1971). The influence of the morality plays and interludes on *Cambises* is treated by D. M. Bevington, *From Mankind to Marlowe* (1962); the Senecan elements by H. B. Charlton, *The Senecan Tradition in Renaissance Tragedy* (1946); and the history play in context with tragedy by Irving Ribner, *The English History Play in the Age of Shakespeare* (rev. ed., 1965).

Cambridge Platonists. See HOBBES, THOMAS.

Campaspe. A prose comedy by John LYLY, first published in 1584 as *A Most Excellent Comedie of Alexander, Campaspe, and Diogenes.* The source is probably Pliny's *Historia naturalis.*

Alexander the Great returns to Athens from his conquest of Thebes with a number of captives, among them the beautiful Campaspe. With the wars temporarily at an end, Alexander gathers together a brilliant court of philosophers—Aristotle, Chrysippus, Crates, Plato, and others. Only the malcontent Diogenes refuses to participate; he emerges from his tub only to seek food or to rail at the Athenian populace. Alexander confesses to his officer Hephestion that he has fallen in love with Campaspe. He commissions an artist, Apelles, to paint her portrait. Soon the Theban girl proclaims in a soliloquy that she prefers the poor young painter to the world's conquerer. When Alexander learns that Campaspe and Apelles are in love, he orders them to marry, they joyously accept, and Alexander departs for Persia. The play is noted for its lyric "Cupid and my Campaspe played, / At cards for kisses..."

The play is included in *The Complete Works,* ed. R. W. Bond, 3 vols. (1902). The best critical studies are A. Feuillerat, *John Lyly, Contribution à l'histoire de la Renaissance en Angleterre* (1910); G. Wilson Knight, "Lyly," *RES*, XV (1939); and Peter Saccio, *The Court Comedies of John Lyly: A Study in Allegorical Dramaturgy* (1969).

Campion, Thomas (1567-1620). Musician and poet. Campion was born in London of wealthy parents who died when he was still a boy. He attended Peterhouse College, Cambridge (1581-84), but left without taking a degree and attended Gray's Inn. According to contemporary accounts, at Cambridge he was an indifferent scholar and at Gray's Inn he was more interested in music and poetry than the law. In 1591-92 he accompanied Essex on a military expedition to France. He published several brief lyrics in the surreptitious edition of Sir Philip Sidney's *Astrophel and Stella* that appeared in 1591. Sometime after 1595 he converted to Roman Catholicism.

He seems to have been of a restless, indecisive temperament. Sometime between 1602 and 1606 he studied medicine abroad and returned to practice in London. He wrote a number of masques, which are weak in story but distinguished for their mellifluous, graceful songs. Unlike most Elizabethan composers, Campion wrote both music and lyrics to his airs, madrigals, and songs, combining an infallible ear for music with a classical, epigrammatic diction and syntax derived from Catullus, Martial, and Propertius. Because, by his own statement, his poems "couple words and notes lovingly together," they may appear spare and anemic without musical accompaniment. His lovely lyric "There is a garden in her face, / Where roses and white lilies grow" with its refrain "Till 'Cherry-ripe' themselves do cry" is justly famous, and illustrates Campion's remarkable ability to fuse classical verse and folk ballad. (See SONGBOOKS). "My sweetest Lesbia, let us live and love," like many of Jonson's songs, is derived from Catullus, and "The man of life upright" echoes Horace:

> The man of life upright,
>   Whose guiltless heart is free
> From all dishonest deeds
>   Or thought of vanity...

Campion's characteristic mood is more in the light-hearted vein of "When to her lute Corinna sings," "Rose-cheeked Laura," and "Maids are simple," ditties of lightest love and amorous frolic. His world is that of the Roman love lyrists, bright and cheerful, and like Robert HERRICK, he often tints his classical verses with native English touches:

> Jack and Joan, they think no ill,
> But loving live, and merry still;
> Do their week-days' work and pray
> Devoutly on the holy day;
> Skip and trip it on the green,
> And help to choose the summer queen;
> Lash out, at a country feast,
> Their silver penny with the best.

Campion's principal works include *Poemata* (1595), a collection of amorous Latin epigrams, and his several books of airs (lyrics written for a single voice accompanied by a lute or bass-viol): *A Book of Airs* (1601), the second half of which was composed by the musician Philip Rosseter; *Two Books of Airs* (1613); *The Third and Fourth Book of Airs* (c. 1617); and a treatise on musical composition, *A New Way of Making Four Parts in Counterpoint* (wr. c. 1618). Campion's literary essay, *Observations in the Art of English Poesy* (1602), an attack on rhyme and a proposal for adapting classical quantitative prosody to English, was answered effectively by Samuel DANIEL in his *Defense of Rhyme* (see CRITICISM, LITERARY).

The standard edition of Campion's complete works is by P. Vivian (1907) and includes the masques. The best biographical and critical studies are M. M. Kastendieck, *England's Musical Poet: Thomas Campion* (1938), and Edward Lowbury, Timothy Salter, and Alison Young, *Thomas Campion: Poet, Composer, Physician* (1970).

Cardinal, The. A tragedy by James SHIRLEY, written around 1641 and first printed in 1652. No source is known, but the play is patterned on the conventional Elizabethan formula of Senecan tragedy, with its revenge motive, Machiavellian villain, real or feigned madness, bombast, and lurid homicides (see SENECAN TRAGEDY). Hence Shirley's play is often described as the last Elizabethan tragedy.

The Machiavellian Cardinal, the real power behind the throne of Navarre, has arranged for his nephew Columbo, a violent and choleric soldier, to wed a beautiful widow, the Duchess Rosaura, who is already in love with the gallant and graceful Count d'Alvarez, whose engagement to Rosaura was broken off by the weakling king at the urgings of the Cardinal. When war breaks out with Aragon, Columbo, as general, must postpone his marriage, and while he is absent Rosaura writes to be released from her troth. In his reply the enraged Columbo pretends not to have received the letter and saves face by sending her a brief note canceling their engagement. At the same time Columbo quarrels violently with an aide, Colonel Hernando, whose injured honor provides motivation for a later revenge.

Armed with Columbo's letter, Rosaura wins permission from the king to marry Alvarez, and Columbo returns in triumph from the war just in time to join the wedding party. With his followers he performs a masque during which Alvarez is lured offstage and murdered. For this outrage the timid king merely imprisons Columbo for a few days, not for the murder, which is found to be "justifiable," but for committing violence in the presence of the king.

Soon afterward Hernando joins Rosaura in wreaking revenge upon Columbo, whom Hernando kills in a duel. Hernando, pursued by the Cardinal's henchmen, goes into hiding. Rosaura meanwhile feigns madness to deceive her oppressors. The Cardinal, however, suspecting Rosaura's part in his nephew's death, cannot be kept from his revenge. Granted her wardship during her "madness," he determines to rape her, poison her, and then announce that she committed suicide. Hernando arrives in time to conceal himself behind the arras in Rosaura's chamber, and during supper, as the Cardinal attacks Rosaura, Hernando fatally wounds him and then kills himself. The villainous Cardinal manages a final stratagem by tricking Rosaura into taking poison before he himself dies.

Written only a year before the closing of the theaters in 1642, *The Cardinal* conveys some few echoes of the old Elizabethan dramatic vitality. Shirley's verse, however, lacks the timbre and resonance of Webster or even Ford; his characters, and particularly the Cardinal, have the vitality engendered by total wickedness, but they are for the most part devoid of complexity or consciousness. Hence the tragedy conveys more a sense of sensationalism than of any authentic spirit or tragic vision.

The Cardinal is in *The Dramatic Works and Poems,* ed. William Gifford and Alexander Dyce, 6 vols. (1833), and in *English Drama*

1580-1642, ed. C. F. Tucker Brooke and N. B. Paradise (1933). It is studied in R. S. Forsythe, *The Relations of Shirley's Plays to the Elizabethan Drama* (1914); Arthur Nason, *James Shirley, Dramatist* (1915), and Fredson Bowers, *Elizabethan Revenge Tragedy 1587-1642* (rev. ed., 1959).

Carew, Thomas (1594?-1639?). Poet. Born in Cornwall of a distinguished family, his father being master in Chancery and a famous lawyer, Carew went to Merton College, Oxford (B.A., 1611), and later to the Middle Temple. He showed little scholarly aptitude or enthusiasm for the law, and judging from several extant letters, he was the despair of his father. According to Izaak Walton, Carew was "a great libertine in his life and talk," although the earl of Clarendon referred to him more kindly as "a person of a pleasant and facetious wit." Carew served as secretary to Sir Dudley Carelton in Italy (1613) and at The Hague (1616), but was accused of slandering Carelton in a satire and dismissed from service. In 1619 he accompanied Lord Edward Herbert to Paris, and in 1628 received the first of several minor offices at court, where he made friends with most of the literary lights he addresses in his verse epistles—Ben Jonson, George Sandys, Walter Montagu, Aurelian Townshend, and Sir William Davenant. He was especially intimate with James Howell and Sir John Suckling. At court Carew translated songs from Giovanni Battista Marino and studied Petrarch, Ronsard, Jonson, and Donne. In "Session of the Poets" Suckling good-naturedly satirized Carew:

. . . he had a fault
That would not well stand with a Laureate;
His Muse was hard bound, and th'issue of's
  brain
Was seldom brought forth but with trouble
  and pain.

Carew's graceful masque *Coelum Britannicum,* with elaborate stage designs by Inigo Jones, was performed at court to great applause in 1634. He fought for the king in the first Bishops' War in 1639 and died that year. His poems and *Coelum Britannicum* (1634) were published together in a posthumous edition in 1640, which was enlarged in subsequent editions of 1642 and 1651.

Although Pope referred to Carew as "a lesser Waller," Carew was actually more intelligent, poised, and complex than either Edmund Waller or most other CAVALIER POETS. From his master Jonson he learned a classical economy, compression, and precision, and from Marino, whom he may have known in Paris, the art of chiseling witty conceits, hyperboles, and metaphysical "strong lines" (See METAPHYSICAL POETS). Donne's influence, although always apparent, was not as essential as that of Jonson, Marino, Petrarch, Ronsard, and the classical poets Propertius and Catullus. In his famous "Song" Carew revives the purest cadences of Jonson:

Ask me no more where Jove bestows,
When June is past, the fading rose;
For in your beauty's orient deep,
These flowers as in their causes, sleep.

To the familiar theme of mutability and invitations to virgins to make the most of time, Carew brings a genuinely passionate sensibility and occasionally white-hot wit. His lines quiver with all the perfervid eroticism of Marvell's "To His Coy Mistress" or Donne's amorous elegies, but his themes, unlike theirs, pertain to sybaritic pleasures sacrificed to paltry motives of honor. His "A Rapture" is a bedroom pastoral, Celia's surrender to passion being equated with a liberation from social restraints and escape into "Love's Elisium":

No wedlock bonds unwreathe our twisted
  loves;
We seek no midnight arbor, no dark groves
To hide our kisses; there the hated name
Of husband, wife, lust, modest, chaste, or
  shame
Are vain and empty words, whose very sound
Was never heard in the Elisian ground.
All things are lawful there, that may delight
Nature, or unrestrained appetite.
Like, and enjoy, to will, and act, is one,
We only sin when Love's rites are not done.

Carew's poetry brings together Petrarch's diction, Marino's hyperboles and conceits, Donne's logic, Jonson's finely spun rhetoric and syntax, and Carew's own sensual temperament. In contrast to contemporaries like Cleveland and Lovelace, who were courtly amateurs, Carew obviously worked hard at verses and thought seriously about his craft. His elegy on Donne represents the most pithy criticism on metaphysical poetry before Samuel Johnson's essay on Cowley in 1779. In that elegy he acknowledged Donne's originality, "spirit and heat," and condemned his own dessicated age (Cowley and others, by implication) for substituting the "mimic fury" of Anacreonic verses and Pindaric odes for Donne's "rich and pregnant fancy." Carew's elegy on Donne suggests that if he had written literary essays, he would have proved to be a foremost apologist for metaphysical poetry.

Carew's poems are available in *Minor Poets of the Seventeenth Century,* ed. R. G. Haworth, Everyman Edition (1931), and in *The Poems of Thomas Carew,* ed. Rhodes Dunlap (1949). Carew's verse is analyzed by George Williamson, *The Donne Tradition* (1930); F. R. Leavis, *Revaluation* (1936); Louis L. Martz, *The Wit of Love: Donne, Carew, Crashaw, Marvell* (1969); and D. F. Rauber, "Carew Redivivus," *TSLL,* XIII (1971).

Carey, Robert, earl of Monmouth (1560?-1639). See AUTOBIOGRAPHY.

Caroline (or **Cavalier**) **drama.** The drama of the reign of Charles I (1625-42). Shortly after the accession of Charles and his marriage to the French princess Henrietta Maria, a new group of court dramatists appeared upon the scene whose egregious influence hastened the decline of the popular theaters on the Bankside and turned the stage into an almost exclusively aristocratic pastime. The courtiers rushed forth with plays to satisfy the taste of the queen, who had been raised in the care of Mme. de Monglat and her daughter Mme. St. George at the salon at the Hotel de Rambouillet, the residence near the house of Marquise Catherine de Vivonne Pisani (1588-1665), who founded in 1615 a refined coterie in imitation of the one at Urbino depicted in Castiglione's *Il Cortegiano* (see THE COURTIER). As for Charles I himself, his literary taste was as romantic as his queen's, for he was an avid reader of Beaumont and Fletcher's tragicomedies, pastoral romances, and French and Spanish heroic tales. As the office book of his master of the revels Sir Henry Herbert illustrates, Charles took a personal interest in the theater, often encouraging his courtiers to write plays and masques, and on at least one occasion, even collaborating with a dramatist in the preparation of a manuscript.

As John Massinger observed in his *Emperor of the East* (1630), Henrietta Maria and her dilettante husband soon turned the court into "a kind of academy" and "school of virtue" over which the queen and her ladies reigned as "sovereign abbesses." By 1634 James Howell was writing that at court there was "a love called Platonic love, which much sways there of late . . . This love sets the wits of town on work." By 1638 so many courtly wits had come forth to gorge the presses with pastoral dramas, masques, and heroic plays on the subject of Platonic love that William Cartwright had a character exclaim in *The Siege:*

> I will turn
> Poet myself. It is in fashion, lady.
> He's scarce a courtier now that hath not
> Writ his brace of plays.

The first courtier to offer his services to the queen was Walter Montagu with *The Shepherd's Paradise* (perf. 1632), a rambling pastoral in rhythmic prose that reads like a lame parody of Honoré d'Urfé's *L'Astrée,* the interminable pastoral romance that had served as a kind of Arcadian textbook of eloquent gallantries at the Hotel de Rambouillet. *The Shepherd's Paradise,* a seminal play of its kind, portrays a whole society of garrulous nymphs and "pretty boys" in a "paradise of chastity" ruled over by the Platonic votaress Queen Fidamira, who is, of course, Henrietta Maria herself. Montagu's *tour de théâtre,* rehearsed by the queen and her ladies for four months before its presentation at court, helped to establish the characteristics of the Caroline tragicomedy described as the "Cavalier romance"—witless preciosity, pseudo-Platonic philosophizing, niceties of "love and honor," and tortuously inept prose that printers often arranged on the page to make it appear to be blank verse. The Cavalier romance invariably takes place in "Euboea" or "Tasminia," or some other equally remote kingdom of the late Greek and continental heroic tales, and although the stage shakes with battles and the collapse of empires, all that really matters are the subtle vacillations of a *débat de coeur* between a pedantic, imperious mistress and her supine royal wooer. The issues in the Cavalier romance spring from an insulated aristocratic culture that viewed reality as synonymous with vulgarity: Will a farewell kiss jeopardize the spiritual integrity of love? Does a mistress have the authority to release her lover to serve a friend? As Alfred Harbage has pointed out, the Cavalier romance is not "decadent" because of its sexual license (these are, in fact, the "cleanest" plays of the Renaissance), but the genre is intrinsically decadent for its vacuous improbabilities, formless dramaturgy, total disregard for artistic integrity, contempt for reality and human values, and brutal ignorance of life.

In addition to Montagu, the chief practitioners of the Cavalier romance were Lodowick Carlell, Sir Aston Cokayne, William Cartwright, Henry Glapthorne, William Habington, Henry and Thomas Killigrew, Richard Lovelace, Jasper Mayne, and Sir John Suckling. On the periphery of this group of courtiers, and infinitely superior to any of them, were Sir William DAVENANT and James SHIRLEY. Davenant began his court plays with *The Temple of Love,* performed in 1635 at Whitehall by the queen, nine lords, and fifteen ladies, and "set out with the most stately scenery, machines, and dresses" by Ben Jonson's former collaborator in stage design, Inigo Jones. Davenant followed up this triumph with a series of tragicomedies in the manner of Beaumont and Fletcher's *Philaster—Love and Honor* (perf. 1634), *The Platonic Lovers* (perf. 1635), *The Fair Favorite* (perf. 1638), and *The Unfortunate Lovers* (perf. 1638). In addition to these, he wrote several comedies, one of which, *The Wits* (perf. 1634), is a masterpiece in the comedy of manners. Made poet laureate in 1638, later imprisoned and rendered bankrupt for his Royalist loyalties, Davenant survived the Civil War to write the heroic poem *Gondibert* (1651; see CRITICISM, LITERARY) and the influential heroic opera *The Siege of Rhodes* in 1656 (Part II, 1659), a drama that links the Cavalier romances with the heroic plays of Dryden and Orrery in the Restoration period.

Although James Shirley also dabbled in the pernicious Cavalier romance, he was a genuinely gifted playwright of considerable versatility, writing tragedy in *The Maid's Revenge* (perf. 1626), *The Traitor* (perf. 1631), *Love's Cruelty* (perf. 1631), and *The Cardinal* (perf. 1641); Jonsonian comedy of manners in *The Lady of Pleasure* (perf. 1635), and romantic comedy in the Shakespearean mode in *Hyde Park* (perf. 1632). In his tragedies Shirley revived most of the elements of the old popular Elizabethan tragedies—revenge, Machiavellian villainy, introspective soliloquies—and yet by the 1630s and 1640s the ancient recipe produced a rather tasteless concoction. Plays like Shirley's *The Cardinal* attest that tragedy is not a formula but a way of perceiving the world, and by 1641 tragedy was no longer possible on the London stage. English society, like the drama, was spiritually exhausted. Richard BROME, Nathan Field, and Shakerley Marmion wrote a few comedies that kept alive the tradition of Jonson. Brome's *The Antipodes* (perf. 1638) and *A Jovial Crew* (perf. 1641) are worthy of his master for wit and realism. Another disciple of Jonson, Thomas RANDOLPH, contributed *Aristippus, or The Jovial Philosopher* (perf. 1625-26), which disputes in loose dramatic form the relative merits of ale and sack, and *The Muses' Looking Glass* (perf. 1630), a rollicking anti-Puritan satire that compares favorably with Jonson's *Bartholomew Fair*. Randolph's most popular play at court was *Amyntas, or The Impossible Dowry* (perf. 1630), an elaborate pastoral in five acts.

The two greatest dramatists of the Caroline period were Philip MASSINGER and John FORD. Massinger's best comedies are *A New Way to Pay Old Debts* (perf. 1621-1622) and *The City Madam* (perf. c. 1632?). Unlike most of his contemporaries, Massinger was a master of intricate plots, ingenious scenes, and lively characterization, hence a worthy disciple of Beaumont and Fletcher in tragicomedy and of Jonson in comedy of manners. If Massinger looks back in his best work to the Elizabethan masters (*A New Way* is a redaction of Thomas Middleton's *A Trick to Catch the Old One*), John Ford, in some ways the most "modern" of the Caroline dramatists, looks forward to the psychological drama of the twentieth century. Although his recurring theme is the "love and honor" dichotomy worn threadbare by the Cavalier romances, he gives the conflict new meaning by linking it to the psychopathology of medical treatises like Robert Burton's *Anatomy of Melancholy*. Hence his main characters are neither heroes nor villains, but strangely disoriented victims of self-destruction, and his interest centers compassionately on love as sickness, and honor as some ineffable urge known only to his mysteriously obsessed characters. In *'Tis Pity She's a Whore*, Ford deals sympathetically with incest, in *Love's Sacrifice* with imagined or symbolic adultery, in *The Broken Heart* with erotic frustration and repressed hatred. In his incomprehensible and esoteric moral concerns, Ford is an experimental, totally unpredictable dramatist. His fourth tragedy, *Perkin Warbeck* (1634), acted by the Queen Henrietta company, is one of the finest examples of the English CHRONICLE PLAY, a genre thoroughly moribund since the early 1600s but one Ford endowed with fresh meaning by his subtle characterizations and haunting irony.

With Ford the great heritage of the Elizabethan stage comes to an end. By 1642 the popular theaters on the Bankside were crumbling, and Shakespeare's old company, the King's Men, performed exclusively for courtly audiences at Blackfriars or Whitehall. When, on September 2, 1642, Parliament decreed that "public plays shall cease and be foreborne," the proclamation meant little more than a *coup de grace* administered to what was already a corpse.

The main history of the period, including biographical data, stage and publication information, is by G. E. Bentley, *The Jacobean and Caroline Stage,* 7 vols. (1941-68). A good general introduction is by F. S. Boas, *An Introduction to Stuart Drama* (1946). The court dramatists are treated at length by Alfred Harbage, *The Cavalier Drama* (1936).

Cartwright, William (1611-1643). Poet and dramatist. Cartwright was born near Tewkesbury, the son of a gentleman landowner who later became an innkeeper at Cirencester, where Cartwright attended school. He thereafter attended Westminster School, and went in 1628 to Christ Church, Oxford, graduating B.A. in 1632 and M.A. in 1635. In 1638 he took holy orders and in 1642 became reader in metaphysics. The remainder of his life was spent at Oxford, where he became nationally famous as a philosopher, orator, and poet. At the beginning of the Civil War in 1642 he was imprisoned for his Royalist sympathies, and died at Oxford the following year.

Cartwright wrote four plays, all except *The Siege* originally produced at Oxford and later adapted to the London stage: *The Lady Errant* (wr. c. 1628-43); *The Ordinary, or The City Cozener* (wr. 1634); *The Royal Slave* (wr. 1636); and *The Siege, or Love's Convert* (wr. c. 1628-43). *The Lady Errant* combines the artful plotting of Fletcher's tragicomedies with some comic characters derived from Aristophanes; *The Ordinary* is a comedy of humours in imitation of Jonson's *The Alchemist* together with some speeches taken from Chaucer. Both plays were revived in the Restoration period. Cartwright's most popular play, *The Royal Slave,* is a tragicomedy resembling Massinger's *The Bondman* and derives its details from the late Greek romances and Persian history. Cartwright's ineffectual hero, his use of love and honor as a theme, and his fatuous rhetoric probably owe something to Beaumont and Fletcher's *Philaster*, although that play's rapid pace and cleverly contrived situations are totally absent from *The Royal Slave,* which is so static in action and full of mere spectacle as to resemble a masque or heroic opera. The action is slow, the long speeches stilted and ornate. It was first performed as one in a series of three plays produced at Oxford in honor of a visit by Charles I and Queen Henrietta Maria in August 1636. The king pronounced it "the best that ever was acted," and the queen ordered the Persian costumes to be sent to Hampton Court so that it could be performed by her own company. Contemporary accounts in the office books of the Master of the Revels and in the Calendar of State Papers indicate that the court was enamored of Cartwright's tragicomedy chiefly because of its dances, exotic Persian costumes, and elaborate stage designs.

There is no evidence that Cartwright's other heroic tragicomedy, *The Siege*, was ever performed. Cartwright's dedication in the posthumous edition of 1648 states that he was dissuaded from destroying the play by the personal intervention of Charles I.

For the author of but four mediocre plays, Cartwright's great reputation among his contemporaries as a poet and dramatist is difficult to explain. The 1651 edition of his *Works* appeared with no fewer than fifty commendatory poems, and there are more references to Cartwright between his death and the turn of the century than there are to Fletcher, Jonson, or Shakespeare. Anthony à Wood refers to Cartwright as "the most noted poet, orator, and philosopher of his time"; doubtless Cartwright's fame as a speaker on metaphysics and theology at Oxford helped to obscure his salient deficiencies as a dramatist and poet.

As a poet Cartwright is, at best, competent and restrained—a cut below Sir John Suckling and James Shirley in talent, and probably even less gifted than Sir William Davenant. The thin volume of his verses consists chiefly of songs from the plays, epistolary poems in the manner of Ben Jonson, and quiet philosophical verses in heroic couplets. His best poems are occasional, such as his fine tribute to Ben Jonson in the memorial volume *Jonsonus Virbius* (1638).

The definitive biography, critical study, and texts are in the splendid edition of Cartwright's complete works by G. Blakemore Evans (1952), which supersedes the *Life and Poems* (1918) by R. Cullis Goffin. Evans' edition contains an exhaustive bibliography. There is another bibliographical study by J. P. Danton, "William Cartwright and His Comedies, Tragi-Comedies, with Other Poems, 1651," *Library*, XII (1942).

Case Is Altered, The. A comedy by Ben JONSON, written sometime between 1597 and 1609, and first printed in 1609. It is modeled after Plautus and the COMMEDIA DELL'ARTE.

Count Ferenze's son Paulo and Ferenze's general Maximilian fight an indecisive battle against the French general Chamont. Maximilian captures Chamont and Chamont's friend Gasper, but Paulo is taken prisoner by the other side. It is agreed that Paulo will be exchanged for Gasper, but Chamont himself escapes disguised as Gasper. As Ferenze prepares to execute Gasper, Chamont returns with Paulo and reveals that Gasper is, in fact, Ferenze's long-lost son Camillo. A farcical subplot concerns an absurd beggar named Jaques de Prie and a clown called Antonio Balladino, a character obviously satiric of the playwright Anthony Munday. Another farcical character, Juniper, speaks in an affected, pedantic manner that Jonson may have intended as a spoof at the expense of Gabriel Harvey. Aside from these peripheral interests, the play is fast-moving on both narrative levels, but it lacks the tight plot of Jonson's best comedies.

The standard edition, with much scholarly information, is in *Ben Jonson,* ed. C. H. Herford and Percy and Evelyn Simpson, 11 vols., III. (1925-53). There is a critical edition by W. E. Selin (1917). For commentary, see John J. Enck, "*The Case Is Altered:* Initial Comedy of Humours," *SP,* L (1953); and C. G. Thayer, *Ben Jonson: Studies in the Plays* (1963).

Castiglione, Baldassare (1478-1529). Italian diplomat and courtier to Guidobaldo, duke of Urbino. His treatise *Il Cortegiano* (1528) became the foremost Renaissance manual of courtesy. See THE COURTIER: COURTESY LITERATURE; HOBY, SIR THOMAS; TRANSLATIONS.

Cavalier drama. See CAROLINE DRAMA.

Cavalier poets. Poets writing during the reign of Charles I whose verses are characterized by imitations of Anacreonic and Horatian odes, songs of Catullus, and poems of Ben JONSON. The chief Cavalier poets were Thomas CAREW, John CLEVELAND, Sidney Godolphin, William Habington, Robert HERRICK (the only poet of the group not a courtier), Richard LOVELACE, Sir John SUCKLING, and Edmund WALLER. Carew, Cleveland, and Lovelace are sometimes classified with the METAPHYSICAL POETS.

In reaction against the ethereal, humid language of the Petrarchans of the 1590s, most Cavalier poets attempted to write amorous lyrics that were lighthearted, direct and realistic, cool and graceful. The typical Cavalier lyric combines the simple Elizabethan songs popularized by Wyatt, Jonson's lean classical imitations of Catullus, and some of Donne's angular wit, conceits, and realism. In "Mediocrity in Love Rejected," Carew imposes a classical polish and a direct, unromantic tone, together with his own stanzaic improvisation, on the tradition sonnet form. The treatment owes much to Jonson and perhaps a little to Donne:

Give me more love, or more disdain;
  The torrid, or the frozen, zone.
Bring equal ease unto my pain;
  The temperate affords me none:
Either extreme, of love or hate,
Is sweeter than a calm estate.

Give me a storm; if it be love,
  Like Danae in that golden shower,
I swim in pleasure; if it prove
  Disdain, that torment will devour
My vulture hopes; and he's possessed
Of Heaven, that's but from Hell released;
  Then crown my joys, or cure my pain;
  Give me more love, or more disdain.

Like the Petrarchans before them, the Cavalier poets alternately woo and admonish their cherry-lipped Celia, sportive Castara, or chaste Corinna; but the influences of Donne and Jonson add renewed vitality to this traditional love motif. Carew captures some of this vitality—and much of Jonson's polished grace—in "To a lady that desired I would love her":

Now you have freely given me leave to love,
  What will you do?
Shall I your mirth, or passion move
  When I begin to woo?
Will you torment, or scorn, or love me too?

In contrast to Carew, Sir John Suckling abjures both polish and careful structure; his few fine lyrics are characterized by careless spontaneity as in his famous song from *Aglaura:*

> Why so pale and wan, fond lover,
> Prithee, why so pale?

Lacking Donne's verbal athleticism, Suckling rarely attempts very complex metaphysical conceits. Instead, he strives for the easier effects of "Go and catch a falling star" and other of Donne's libertine lyrics:

> Out upon it, I have loved
> Three whole days together,
> And am like to love three more,
> If it prove fair weather.

Most of Edmund Waller's lyrics celebrating his cool pursuit of Saccharissa employ a wit devoid of metaphysical tensions and hard paradoxes; Like most Cavalier poets, he is in the spirit of the "tribe of Ben" and strives for restrained, concise diction:

> Go, lovely rose,
> Tell her that wastes her time and me,
> That now she knows,
> When I resemble her to thee,
> How sweet and fair she seems to be.

The greatest of the Cavalier poets was Robert Herrick, who wrote most of his verses in the rural environs of "dull Devonshire" among country bumpkins, "hock-carts, wassails, wakes." The bulk of his poems were inspired by halycon memories of the "tribe of Ben" and his reading of Catullus, Martial, Horace, and the Renaissance Latin poet Joannes Secundus. To these ingredients he added a totally imaginary mythology of Devonshire damsels with names like Anthea, Corinna, and Perilla. This entirely literary world of lithesome lasses, bacchanalian feasts, and summer frolics he celebrates with joyous epicureanism in his *Hesperides* (1648):

> I sing of brooks, of blossoms, birds, and bowers;
> Of April, May, of June, and July flowers.
> I sing of Maypoles, hock-carts, wassails, wakes,
> Of bridegrooms, brides, and of their bridal cakes.
> I write of youth, of love, and have access
> By these, to sing of cleanly wantonness.

Like many Cavalier poets, Herrick is a master of the pure, unadorned song in the tradition of Catullus and Jonson:

> Cherry-ripe, ripe, ripe, I cry,
> Full and fair ones, come and buy.
> If so be, you ask me where
> They do grow, I answer, there,
> Where my Julia's lips do smile.
> There's the land, or cherry-isle
> Whose plantations fully show
> All the year, where cherries grow,

Herrick's poetry is the last flowering of the Elizabethan courtly lyric that combines the romantic native tradition with classical epigrams. In contrast to Carew and Cleveland, Herrick shows little inclination for wreathing Donne's "iron pokers into true-love-knots." In addition to imitating simple folk songs, he was influenced by Horatian odes, Catullian songs and epithalamia, Martial-like epigrams, Jonsonian verse epistles, epigrams, and epitaphs. Although sensuous, he has neither Spenser's descriptive talent nor Sidney's spontaneous passion; within a broad range of lyric types he expresses an animated restraint—a quality found in most of the Cavalier poets.

The major Cavalier poets are in the editions by George Saintsbury, *Minor Poets of the Caroline Period,* 3 vols. (1905-21), and Robin Skelton, *The Cavalier Poets* (1970). For the influence of the classics, especially on Herrick, see Pauline Aiken, *The Influence of the Latin Elegists on English Lyric Poetry 1600-50* (1932); and for social background, see C. H. Hartmann, *The Cavalier Spirit and Its Influence on the Life and Work of Richard Lovelace* (1925).

Cavendish, George (1500-1561?). Tudor courtier and author of *The Life and Death of Thomas Wolsey.* The elder son of Thomas Cavendish, a clerk in the Exchequer, George Cavendish married Margery Kemp, a niece of Sir Thomas More. Beginning as a gentleman usher at the court of Henry VIII, he grew to become a close personal friend of Cardinal Wolsey. When Wolsey was disgraced in 1530, Cavendish was interrogated by the Privy Council about the cardinal's dying words but was released with the favor of the king. He remained a Roman Catholic during the Reformation, spending most of his declining years at his estate at Glensford, Sussex, where he wrote his great biography, a work that contrasts Wolsey's glorious achievements and sumptuous living with his ignominious fall, much in the manner of John Lydgate's *Fall of Princes* and A MIRROR FOR MAGISTRATES. A biography so favorable to Wolsey could not be published during Elizabeth's reign, but the manuscript was widely circulated and perhaps read by Shakespeare and Fletcher before they wrote their history play HENRY VIII. Cavendish's *Life of Wolsey* was first published, in a careless text, as *The Negotiations of Thomas Wolsey* (1641); a genuine text did not appear until 1810 (see BIOGRAPHY).

The standard edition of Cavendish's life of Wolsey is in *Two Early Tudor Lives,* ed. Richard S. Sylvester (1962).

Cavendish, Margaret, duchess of Newcastle (1624?-1674). Biographer and author of poems, plays, and essays. Born at St. John's near Colchester, Essex, the daughter of a country gentleman and a mother who had been a popular beauty at the court of Elizabeth, Margaret became a maid of honor at the court of Charles I, and she was in attendance with Queen Henrietta Maria in Paris when she met and married a widower, William CAVENDISH, first duke of Newcastle, an amateur playwright and royalist general. After 1644 Margaret and her husband lived in France until the Restoration. With the accession of Charles II she resumed her activities at court, where she became notorious for her eccentric behavior and esoteric intellectual passions. Samuel Pepys described her as "a mad, conceited, ridiculous woman," but others thought her brilliant and erudite. Although she was a prolific author in various genres (see AUTOBIOGRAPHY; LETTER-WRITERS), her one masterpiece is a biography of her husband, *The Life of William Cavendish, Duke of Newcastle* (1667), a vivid account of Stuart life and times (see BIOGRAPHY).

The Life of William Cavendish was edited by Sir Charles H. Firth (1886). For biographical data, see H. T. E. Perry, *The First Duchess of Newcastle and her Husband as Figures in Literary History* (1921).

Cavendish, William, first **duke of Newcastle** (1592-1676). Royalist general, dramatist, and patron of the arts. He left St. John's College, Cambridge, without taking a degree and entered diplomatic service under Sir Henry Wotton. In 1638 Charles I appointed him to the Privy Council and placed him in charge of the Prince of Wales, later Charles II. During the Civil War his military ability and zeal in raising money for the Royalist cause made him objectionable to Parliament, and after the severe Royalist defeat at Marston Moor in 1644 he left England and remained in Paris until the Restoration. After his first wife Elizabeth died in 1643, he married Margaret CAVENDISH, the prolific authoress and eccentric personality. After the Restoration Cavendish received many honors for his loyalty, notably a dukedom and the Order of the Garter. Cavendish avoided court life, however, preferring farming, playwriting, and horsemanship (about which he wrote a treatise in France in 1658).

A patron of Ben Jonson in the 1620s, Cavendish gave money generously to other writers as well—to William Davenant, Thomas Shadwell and the philosophers Hobbes and Descartes. He collaborated with James Shirley on the play *The Country Captain* and with Dryden on *Sir Martin Mar-all.* Two of his best comedies are *The Humorous Lovers* (1667) and *The Triumphant Widow* (1674-75). As a poet and playwright, Cavendish can be described as a modestly talented but enthusiastic amateur.

The standard biographical and critical study is H. T. E. Perry, *The First Duchess of Newcastle and Her Husband as Figures in Literary History* (1921). Selections from Cavendish's work are in *The Cavalier and His Lady,* ed. E. Jenkins (1872).

Certain Notes of Instruction (George Gascoigne). See CRITICISM, LITERARY.

Chamberlain, John (1553-1627). Letter writer. Chamberlain was born in London, the son of Richard Chamberlain, an ironmonger and once sheriff of London. He matriculated at Trinity College, Cambridge, in 1570, but left without a degree because of delicate health and resided for a time at Gray's Inn. As he often observed in his letters, he spent his life as a bachelor gentleman of leisure, pursuing no occupation except the cultivation of friends and the observance of public events. He seldom left London except for visits to country houses; significantly, perhaps, in view of his unstable health, he resided most of his life with physicians or with his brother Richard. In 1596 he lodged with Sir William Gilbert, physician and author of the first treatise on magnetism, and when Gilbert was called to court, stayed for several years with another physician, Mark Ridley. The last twenty years or so of his life he lived at his brother Richard's house, a few minutes' walk from St. Paul's Cathedral, where he heard Dr. John Donne deliver his sermons. There were, in spite of Chamberlain's dislike of travel, several brief trips abroad: to France in 1579 and 1581, to Ireland in 1597, and to Venice in 1610 to visit his friend Sir Dudley Carelton, the English ambassador.

The bulk of Chamberlain's famous correspondence was addressed to Carelton, a diplomat twenty years Chamberlain's junior, while Carelton served in Venice, Paris, and The Hague during the period 1597-1626. Chamberlain took responsibility for keeping his friend informed of events in England during this time in letters he wrote on the average of twice monthly, and he gives informative accounts of the Gunpowder Plot, the troubles in Ireland, Francis Bacon's fall from power, the Overbury trials, the proposed match of Prince Charles with the Infanta of Spain, and many other momentous events. He also reports on the activities and personalities of people he observed firsthand at court or at the great houses of London (as well as at the Mermaid Tavern, where he often dined with literati): Lancelot Andrewes, Francis Bacon (whom he distrusted), Thomas Bodley, William Camden, Sir Robert Cecil, Edward Coke, John Donne, Inigo Jones, Ben Jonson, Sir Walter Raleigh, Sir Henry Savile, Sir Ralph Winwood, Sir Henry Wotton, and many others of equal note.

Although Chamberlain loved gossip, he was instinctively cautious, a very detached, often wry observer and meticulous recorder of facts. He was not, unfortunately for students of literature, a frequenter of playhouses, as was Samuel Pepys, nor especially fond of poetry. Sending Carelton a copy of one of Donne's poems, he conceded that it was witty enough, but added, "Yet I wish a man of his years and place would give over versifying." He was self-consciously reportorial—"I love not altogether idle and empty letters," he stated to Carelton—and his voluminous correspondence has become a rich source of information for historians of the Stuart period.

The standard and only complete edition of the letters is *The Letters of John Chamberlain*, ed. Norman E. McClure, 2 vols. (1939). There is a well-annotated edition by Elizabeth M. Thomson, *The Chamberlain Letters: A Selection of Letters of John Chamberlain Concerning Life in England from 1597 to 1626,* with preface by A. L. Rowse (1965). Chamberlain's life is described by Wallace Notestein in *Four Worthies* (1957).

Changeling, The. A tragedy by Thomas MIDDLETON and William ROWLEY, written in 1622 and published in 1653. The Beatrice-Joanna and De Flores plot is taken from a didactic tale in John Reynolds' *The Triumph of God's Revenge Against the Crying and Execrable Sin of...Murder* (1621). No source has been found for the subplot which is believed to have been written mainly by Rowley. The scene is Spain in the sixteenth century.

Although Beatrice-Joanna, beautiful daughter of Vermandero, governor of Alicante, is to be married to Alonzo de Piracquo within the week, she finds herself in love with a new suitor, Alsemero, a gentleman from Valencia. When Alsemero threatens to challenge Alonzo to a duel, Beatrice, fearing for her new lover's life, arranges for her father's gentleman-servant De Flores to murder Alonzo. Once the murder is accomplished, De Flores, a deformed and lecherous brute, refuses the money Beatrice offers as his reward and demands that she bed with him, threatening to reveal her complicity in Alonzo's murder unless she acquiesces. Although she has long scorned and detested the man, Beatrice submits to De Flores to gratify two powerful desires—concealment of her guilt and marriage to Alsemero.

In the subplot that farcically counterpoints these illicit passions, old Doctor Alibius and his assistant Lollio manage a lunatic asylum, to which come two gallants disguised as lunatics, Antonio and Franciscus, who solicit Lollio's aid in attempting to seduce the doctor's young and beautiful wife. Inspired by their daring, Lollio begins to woo Isabella on his own behalf, threatening to reveal the subterfuges of Antonio and Franciscus to her husband, who is so insanely jealous he keeps her guarded like a prisoner. The level-headed Isabella stoutly defies Lollio's attempt at blackmail just as she contemptuously spurns the inane overtures of Antonio and Franciscus.

In the main story, Beatrice, having forfeited her virginity to the loathsome De Flores in order to marry Alsemero, now fears that her husband will discover her loss of maidenhead and substitutes her servant Diaphanta, a virgin, in the bridal bed; Beatrice is able to accomplish this ruse by convincing her husband that she is too shy to consummate the marriage except in total darkness. The eager Diaphanta lingers too long in Alsemero's bedchamber, and the jealousy-stricken Beatrice conspires with De Flores to kill the girl when she returns to her own room. Beatrice's marriage rapidly deteriorates as she develops an almost affectionate attachment to the once detested man who has unhesitatingly attended to her every wish. Eventually she and De Flores are discovered by Alsemero in an act of intimacy, and both their adultery and the murders of Alonzo and Diaphanta are brought to light. Confronted by an outraged Alsemero and Beatrice's father, as well as Alonzo's vengeance-seeking brother, De Flores stabs Beatrice and then himself.

Meanwhile Antonio and Franciscus, whose absence from the governor's castle and disguises as madmen have been construed as indications of their guilt, have been arrested for the murder of Alonzo, and the two madcap gallants escape the hangman only through Isabella's embarrassing explanation of their real activities at the asylum. Thus, although the title of the play refers to Antonio, whose feigned madness resembles that of a changeling or idiot child substituted by fairies for a normal child stolen from the cradle, the changes wrought in the other characters are equally evident: Beatrice's change from disgust with De Flores to a kind of strange love; Alsemero's love and ignorance to abhorrence and total revelation; and Doctor Alibius' idiotic suspicions of Isabella's infidelity to an informed and sane trust in her integrity.

The antics of Isabella and her wooers in the madhouse are trifling episodes in contrast to the tragic story of Beatrice's ferocious struggle to gratify her desires and at the same time elude the relentless pursuit of De Flores. In this passionate clash between freedom and possession, Middleton achieves some shattering moments of irony as Beatrice steadily sinks to join De Flores in depravity. Middleton's tracing of this conflict shows his dramatic genius at its greatest.

The Changeling has been edited in the New Mermaid series by Patricia Thomson (1964) and in the Regents Renaissance Drama series by G. W. Williams (1970). There are important critical studies by Samuel Schoenbaum, *Middleton's Tragedies: A Critical Study* (1955); Christopher Ricks, "The Moral and Political Structure of *The Changeling,*" *ETC,* X (1960); Edward Engleberg, "Tragic Blindness in *The Changeling* and *Women Beware Women,*" *MLQ,* XXIII (1962); and Robert Jordan, "Myth and Psychology in *The Changeling,*" *Ren D,* III (1970).

chapbook. A small book or pamphlet sold by itinerant dealers, or "chapmen," throughout the sixteenth, seventeenth, and eighteenth centuries. Chapbooks aimed at satisfying popular taste for religious tracts, ballads, travel tales, sentimental stories, biographies, and such old romances as *Bevis of Hampton* and *Guy of Warwick.* They were usually illustrated with wood blocks, published in octavos of sixteen pages or duodecimos of twenty-four pages and sold at a penny to sixpence a copy. Chapbooks had their greatest vogue during the eighteenth century, especially in Scotland and the north of England.

See E. Pearson, *Banbury Chap Books and Nursery Toy Book Literature* (1890), and Charles Gerring, *Notes on Printers and Booksellers* (1900).

Chapman, George (c. 1559-1634). Poet, dramatist, classical scholar, and translator. Born in the small town of Hitchin, Hertfordshire, about thirty miles north of London, Chapman attended Oxford, left without a degree, and may have taught school briefly in Hitchin. Like Jonson, Chapman taught himself classical scholarship; like Jonson also, he served as a soldier in the Low Countries. By 1596 he was employed as a dramatist for the Lord Admiral's Men at Philip Henslowe's Rose Theatre. Since Francis Meres describes him in *Palladis Tamia* (1598) as among "our best for tragedy" and since no tragedies before this date survive, it is evident that many of Chapman's plays are lost. His first notable successes were in comedies like *The Blind Beggar of Alexandria* (1598), produced by the Admiral's Men in February 1596, and *An Humourous Day's Mirth* (1599), a play resembling Jonson's comedy of humours (see JONSON, BEN).

Chapman supplied three cantos to Marlowe's *Hero and Leander,* left unfinished at Marlowe's death in 1593. The first edition (1598) includes lines in which Chapman proclaims his admiration and affection for the dead poet. About this time Chapman began his translation of Homer's *Iliad* and *Odyssey,* a task which was to absorb him for the remainder of his life (see TRANSLATIONS).

About 1600 Chapman began writing plays

for the Children of the Chapel (after 1603, the Queen's Revels) at Blackfriars, where he found an aristocratic audience more suited to his often esoteric and intellectual style than that at the popular theaters on the Bankside. The plays written during this period include THE GENTLEMAN USHER; ALL FOOLS; MONSIEUR D'OLIVE; *May Day;* and *The Widow's Tears.* His collaboration with Jonson and Marston on EASTWARD HO! in 1605 resulted in a term in prison for both Chapman and Jonson when James I personally objected to a slur against the Scots in that play. Marston somehow avoided arrest, but the other two were left to seek the help of influential friends in order to escape punishment. Eventually the offending remark was excised and the play was performed with considerable success by the Queen's Revels.

Chapman's principal tragedies are philosophical commentaries on contemporary political figures and events. The greatest of these, BUSSY D'AMBOIS, shows the defeat of a heroic idealist by his own moral blindness and the corruption of his society. Its sequel, THE REVENGE OF BUSSY D'AMBOIS (wr. c. 1610), is a less successful effort in the same direction. Another tragedy, this one in two parts called *The Conspiracy and Tragedy of Charles, Duke of Biron* (wr. c. 1608), incited a formal protest from the French ambassador because of its harsh view of French politics and court life.

After 1608 Chapman's dramatic output decreased, probably because he devoted his time increasingly to his translation of Homer. With the personal patronage of Prince Henry, Chapman published Books I, II, VII-XI of the *Iliad* in 1598, twelve books in 1609, and the complete twenty-four books in 1611. Prince Henry's death in 1612 left Chapman without a patron, but he continued to work on the *Odyssey* until its completion and publication in 1615. After this date Chapman wrote little except occasional pieces or partial translations. He died in poverty and was buried in St. Giles-in-the-Field, May 1634. His old friend Inigo Jones paid for the monument in his honor.

Although Chapman has been identified as the "Rival Poet" of Shakespeare's Sonnets 80, 85, and 86, and as the real author of Shakespeare's *Timon of Athens,* there is little evidence to support either claim. Indeed, there is little to tie Chapman to Shakespeare at all except the frail link that some of the verses in Chapman's opaque and erudite poem THE SHADOW OF NIGHT (1594) are addressed to the earls of Southampton and Pembroke, who were Shakespeare's patrons. Chapman has been read into the character of Holofernes in Shakespeare's *Love's Labour's Lost,* but with little if any justification.

Chapman was an occasionally brilliant dramatist, especially in a few of his best tragedies, such as *Bussy D'Ambois;* for the most part, his plays and poems derive from stoic and neo-Platonic conceptions that require a background in classical philosophy to understand. A fiercely self-conscious intellectual, he makes few allowances in his plays for an audience, and in such poems as *The Shadow of Night* he makes none whatever for his reader. Consistently neglected after his own times, his plays have enjoyed renewed interest because modern scholars have been willing to devote painstaking care to Chapman's often difficult language and arcane philosophical ideas.

The standard edition of Chapman's works is by T. M. Parrott, *The Plays and Poems,* 2 vols.: *The Tragedies* (1910), *The Comedies* (1914). The *Poems* has been edited by Phyllis B. Bartlett (1941, repr. 1962), *The Comedies* by Allan Holaday (1970). The definitive critical study is by Jean Jacquot, *George Chapman . . . sa vie, sa poésie, son théâtre, sa pensée* (1951). There is a Concise Bibliography by S. A. Tannenbaum (1938), updated by "George Chapman (1937-65)," ed. C. A. Pennel, *Elizabethan Bibliographies Supplements,* IV (1968). See also George W. Ray, "George Chapman: A Checklist of Editors, Biography, and Criticism, 1946-65," *RORD,* XI (1968).

characters and character books. Brief sketches describing the "typical" qualities of a person, occupation, or thing. Most often the subject is a social type such as the courtier, the gull, the schoolteacher, or the lawyer, with emphasis on the representative rather than the unique. The first known book of characters was by Theophrastus (372-287 B.C.), whose *Ethical Characters* describes thirty unsavory Athenian types. Theophrastus may have written contrasting favorable types, but these have not survived. A disciple of Aristotle and his master's successor as head of the Peripatetic school in Athens, Theophrastus conceived of vice as a violation of moderation, the golden mean praised in Aristotle's *Ethics,* and all his characters represent the follies of excessive conduct and temperament.

Theophrastus' character book was translated into Latin by Isaac Casaubon (1592, 1599), and the first English character, Joseph Hall's *Characters of Virtues and Vices* (1608), was based on Theophrastus. Hall departed from his source by including good as well as bad characters; of the twenty-four original portraits in Hall's collection, nine are virtuous and fifteen wicked or unattractive. Hall's tone is more didactic and less psychological than that of Theophrastus. Hall also reflects the influences of late sixteenth-century satiric verse and epigrams, and possibly the broad contemporary characterizations set forth on the stage in Jonson's *Every Man Out of His Humour* and *Cynthia's Revels*.

Hall's character "The Malcontent" illustrates his curt, epigrammatic style:

> What he hath he seeth not, his eyes are so taken up with what he wants; and what he sees he cares not for because he cares so much for that which is not. When his friend carves him the best morsel, he murmurs that it is a happy feast wherein each one may cut for himself. When a present is sent him, he asks, "Is this all?" and "What, no better?"

The vogue for characters did not begin with Hall but with *A Wife: Now the Widow of Sir Thomas Overbury* (1614), which contained Overbury's poem "A Wife" and twenty-two characters composed by Overbury and "other learned gentlemen his friends." Actually the publication was a successful effort of several writers to exploit the scandal surrounding Overbury's mysterious death in the Tower in September, 1613. By 1622 the "Overbury" characters had increased from twenty-two to eighty-three, some of these by such well-known writers as Dekker, Donne, and Webster. Unlike Hall's collection, most of the Overbury characters are more social than moral, more witty and fanciful than didactic, the stress being on liveliness of style rather than on edification. "A Puritan" illustrates the Overbury penchant for conceits and hyperboles.

> Where the meat is best, there he confutes most, for his arguing is but the efficacy of his eating; good bits, he holds, breed good positions, and the pope he best concludes against in plum-broth. He is often drunk, but not as we are, temporally, nor can his sleep then cure him, for the fumes of his ambition make his very soul reel, and that small beer that should allay him (silence) keeps him more surfeited . . .

Many imitations followed from the popularity of the Overbury characters, including those by John Stephens, *Satirical Essays, Characters, and Others* (1615); Nicholas Breton, *Characters upon Essays, Moral and Divine* (1615); and Richard Braithwait, *Whimsies, or A New Cast of Characters* (1631). Inevitably, variations on the customary characters were written, such as the character book devoted exclusively to prison types, Geoffrey Minshull's *Essays and Characters of a Prison and Prisoners* (1618).

The art of character writing reached a zenith in John Earle's *Microcosmography* (1628), which grew to include seventy-eight portraits in the course of its continuous publication. A fellow at Oxford, Earle drew many of his types from college life but also included such variations as "A Tavern" and "A Child." Earle is polished, urbane, witty, and genially subjective; his informal, epigrammatic style links him to Bacon's *Essays* and anticipates the cool sophistication and grace of Addison and Steele's *Tatler* essays. Here is a passage from his character "A Pretender to Learning":

> His business and retirement and caller-away is his study, and he protests no delight to it comparable. He is a great *Nomenclator* of authors, which he has read in general in the catalogue, and in particular in the title, and goes seldom as far as the dedication. He never talks of anything but learning, and learns all from talking . . .

The affinities of the character to its several kindred genres are well illustrated in Thomas Fuller's *The Holy State and the Profane State* (1642), a miscellany containing forty-eight characters of such social types as the elder brother, the good schoolmaster, and the good yeoman, all interlarded with commentary on Biblical lives and historical personages. Fuller's collection also contains characters of inanimate things such as clothes ("Of Apparel"), architecture and landscaping ("Of Building"), and human faculties ("Of Fancy"), and some of these are virtually indistinguishable from the Baconian essay. The fifth and last of Fuller's books contrasts some "profane" characters with the "holy" in sketches like "The Atheist" and "The Witch," Still others contrast "holy" personages from history such as Queen Elizabeth with "profane" ones like Cesare Borgia and thus blend the character and the short historical biography. Fuller's collection also links with courtesy literature, for his sketches invariably teach proper conduct and morals, as in "The Good Yeoman":

> He wears russet clothes, but makes golden payment, having tin in his buttons and silver in his pocket. If he chance to appear in clothes above his rank it is to grace some great man with his service, and then he blusheth at his own bravery. Otherwise he is the surest landmark, whence foreigners may take aim of the ancient English customs; the gentry more floating after foreign fashions.

As Coleridge observed in *Miscellanies, Aesthetic and Literary,* "Wit was the stuff and substance of Fuller's intellect." To an extent far greater than any other writer of characters, that faculty enabled Fuller to write unified and coherent characters drawn from scores of peripheral genres—courtesy literature, philosophical and theological treatise, biography, historical chronicle, familiar essay, and many others. Fuller's ability to accumulate details is amazing—he writes with as much authority on planting trees as on analyzing historical developments in the reign of Henry VII—but his equally astonishing wit, combined with a powerful moral imagination, gives his characters a sense of purposive design and unity. He combines a major requirement of the familiar essayist—the ability to convey the complexities of human consciousness—with a major requirement of the character writer—the capacity for close and objective observation.

The character underwent several mutations. During the Civil Wars such satiric portraits as "A Puritan" in the Overburian collection were used in religious and political pamphlets. The character was also easily absorbed into historical writing; in *History of the Rebellion,* Edward Hyde, the earl of Clarendon, sketches brief, vivid portraits of such notables as Lord Falkland, Charles I, Pym, Hampden, and others. Certainly the character exerted an influence in the shaping of the ESSAY and to a lesser extent, in the development of FICTION. (See also BIOGRAPHY.)

See Gwendolen Murphy, *A Bibliography of English Character-Books, 1608-1700* (1925). Two of the best collections of characters are Murphy, *A Cabinet of Characters* (1925), and Richard Aldington, *A Book of Characters* (1924). The most detailed study of the genre is by Benjamin Boyce, *The Theophrastan Character in England to 1642* (1947). See also E. N. S. Thompson, "Character Books," in *Literary Bypaths of the Renaissance* (1924).

Characters of Virtues and Vices. See HALL, JOSEPH; CHARACTERS.

Chettle, Henry (1560?-1607?). Poet and playwright. Little is known of Chettle except that he was the son of a London dyer, Robert Chettle, and began his career as a printer's apprentice and rose to become a partner with the printers John Danter and William Hoskins. (In 1594 Danter printed the first quarto of Shakespeare's *Titus Andronicus;* he also printed the so-called bad quarto of *Romeo and Juliet* in 1597.) Chettle edited Robert Greene's GROATSWORTH OF WIT (1592), the pamphlet containing the famous attack on Shakespeare as "an upstart crow." In the following year he published a pamphlet of his own, *Kind Hart's Dream,* which contains in its dedicatory epistle an apology for Greene's abusive remarks and some words of praise for Shakespeare's character. Soon afterward Chettle turned to writing plays, chiefly in collaboration with John Day, Thomas Dekker, Michael Drayton, William Haughton, Ben Jonson, and Anthony Munday. Henslowe's diary attributes forty-eight plays to Chettle as collaborator for the Lord Admiral's Men during the period 1598-1603, of which only half a dozen are extant. Although Francis Meres in *Palladis Tamia* (1598) describes Chettle as being among "the best for comedy," the only surviving play that can be attributed exclusively to him is *The Tragedy of Hoffman; or, A Revenge for a Father.*

As one of "Henslowe's hacks" and a "play-doctor" of others' plays, Chettle seems to have struggled unsuccessfully against poverty and debtors' prison. One of Henslowe's entries lists an advance to free him from Marshalsea prison, another to get one of his plays out of pawn. To commemorate the death of Queen Elizabeth, Chettle wrote *England's Mourning Garment* (1603), a poem exhorting several contemporary writers under various pseudonyms to join him in writing elegies. Chettle's address to "Melicert" is often read as being intended for Shakespeare. Chettle's death is inferred from Thomas Dekker's pamphlet *Night's Conjuring* (1607), in which Chettle is humorously described as joining Chaucer, Spenser, and others in Elysium.

The anonymous plays *The Trial of Chivalry* and *The Weakest Goeth to the Wall,* as well as Robert Yarington's *Two Lamentable Tragedies,* have been assigned to Chettle. He has also been identified as having been the so-called "A Hand" in the manuscript fragment attributed in part to Shakespeare, *The Book of Sir Thomas More.* These attributions have not been supported by much evidence. Somewhat more convincing, but by no means certain, is the recent theory that the famous pamphlet *A Groatsworth of Wit,* hitherto assumed to have been by Robert Greene, was actually written by Chettle (see below). According to this theory Chettle's apology in *Kind Hart's Dream* for Greene's slurs against Shakespeare was an effort to conceal the true author of *A Groatsworth.* The hypothesis rests chiefly on computerized vocabulary tests comparing writings by Chettle and Greene.

The Tragedy of Hoffman was edited by R. A. Ackermann (1894), *Kind Hart's Dream* by G. B. Harrison (1923), and *England's Mourning Garment* by Thomas Park, in *Harleian Miscellany,* III (1809). There is a critical biography by Harold Jenkins, *The Life and Work of Henry Chettle* (1934), and some new biographical data added by Celeste T. Wright, "Munday and Chettle in Grub Street," *BUSE,* V (1961). For Chettle's supposed authorship of *A Groatsworth,* see Louis Marder, "Chettle's Forgery of the *Groatsworth of Wit* and the 'Shakes-scene' Passage," *Sh N,* XX (1970), and Austin Warren, "Technique of Chettle-Greene Forgery: Supplementary Material in the Authorship of the *Groatsworth of Wit," Sh N,* XX (1970).

Christianopolis (Johann Andreae Valentin). See UTOPIAN FICTION.

Christ's Tears Over Jerusalem. See NASHE, THOMAS.

Christ's Victory. See FLETCHER, GILES, THE YOUNGER.

chronicle play. A play based on the accounts of English history in the sixteenth-century chronicles. Entirely of native origin, the chronicle play became popular shortly before the Spanish Armada and continued in vogue until around 1606. During this period over 150 chronicle plays appeared, about half of which are extant.

The earliest origins of the chronicle play are to be found in the comic, realistic, and secular elements of the medieval miracle and mystery plays, and in early dialogues, pageants, and INTERLUDES. One of the earliest pageants on record is that of St. George and the dragon, acted in 1416 before Henry V at Windsor. A simple presentation, it dramatized the arming of St. George, his fight with the dragon, and his rescue of the English king's daughter.

Sackville and Norton's GORBODUC, a seminal play in so many of its aspects, also provided an impetus to the chronicle play, for it imposed English historical material on a Senecan dramatic form (see SENECAN TRAGEDY). Equally influential among intellectual circles was a Latin play derived from Sir Thomas More's great biography of Richard III, Thomas Legge's *Richardus Tertius Tragedia,* acted at St. John's College, Cambridge, in 1579. Legge's play enjoys the distinction of being the earliest recorded drama of actual English history. In 1588, Thomas Hughes and others at Gray's Inn presented before Queen Elizabeth at Greenwich *The Misfortunes of Arthur,* which, like *Gorboduc,* combined elements found in both Seneca and Geoffery of Monmouth's *Historia regum Britanniae.* A cruder play than *Gorboduc, The Misfortunes* tells of Mordred's incestuous love for his stepmother Queen Guenevera, his revolt against Arthur, and his usurpation of the throne and subsequent defeat.

The enthusiasm for chronicle plays evolved naturally out of several related political and literary developments—the centralization of monarchy by Henry VII after the Wars of the Roses; the proliferation of English chronicles by such writers as Robert Fabyan, Joseph Hall, Raphael Holinshed and Richard Grafton; and the increased popularity of narrative and dramatic poems such as A MIRROR FOR MAGISTRATES (1559), which combines the medieval conception of tragedy found in John Lydgate's *Fall of Princes* with the historical data of the chronicles, especially characters and events from the Wars of the Roses.

The internecine struggles of the houses of Lancaster and York constitute the subject of Shakespeare's first tetralogy of history plays, *Henry VI,* Parts I-III, and *Richard III,* although the first of these is chiefly concerned with a jingoistic celebration of Lord Talbot's incredible feats of heroism against the French army, led by Joan of Arc. *Henry VI,* Part I, which may have been written and performed as early as 1590, was preceded by a number of chronicle plays based on recent English history, the earliest being the nonextant anonymous drama *The Tragedy of the King of Scots,* performed at court in 1567, and *The Famous Victories of Henry the Fifth,* acted by the Queen's Men around 1585-86, a crude play in prose that served as a source for Shakespeare's later *Henry IV,* Parts I and II, and *Henry V.* There was also the anonymous play *The Troublesome Reign of John, King of England*—probably performed around the time of the initial staging of Marlowe's *Tamburlaine* in about 1588—which influenced the writing of Shakespeare's *King John.* Another early chronicle play of uncertain date is the anonymous *The Life and Death of Jack Straw,* a four-act drama on the Peasant's Revolt of 1381. More of an interlude than a fully developed play, its blank verse of four-stress lines suggests that the work was written before Marlowe and Shakespeare established iambic pentameter as the dominant metrical form.

Before Marlowe and Shakespeare, the chronicle plays conformed to a simple chronological rather than dramatic order. The playwrights, according to Felix E. Schelling, "accepted whatever they found [in the chronicles] and used it as they found it." Shakespeare's *Henry VI* plays, with their episodic structure, thematic diffuseness, and uncertainties of characterization, reflect the chief elements of the chronicle play at its inchoate stage.

A new phase of development begins with Marlowe's EDWARD II and Shakespear's RICHARD II, both written around 1592. Whether *Edward II* or *Richard II* came first is a matter of dispute, but it would appear that Marlowe's technique of concentrating on a single dramatic character in such early plays as *Tamburlaine* provided the essential means of unifying the chaotic details in the chronicles. Equally important for both dramatists was the maturing genre of Elizabethan tragedy, a development that encouraged authors of chronicle plays to view historical events in the chronicles with close attention to certain significant aspects of characterization—e.g., the conflicts of antithetical personalities—as well as economy of plot and concentration of themes. Out of the dramatically unpalatable facts of the chronicles, Marlowe conjures up in *Edward II* a Machiavellian Mortimer who steals Edward's queen and plots to usurp the throne, and from a bare hint in history he raises Edward's favorite, Gaveston, to the role of the paramour who becomes the agent of the king's destruction. Marlowe reduces the tangled events of the chronicles to a dramatic tension within Edward's character between his desire for personal gratification as a man and the requirements of public responsibilities as a king; with an irony not found in the annals, he portrays Mortimer rising at the expense of Edward, but Edward's stature increasing as his fortunes decline.

This instinct for effective drama at the expense of historical fact is equally apparent in Shakespeare's *Richard II,* which includes most of the dramatic contrasts found in Marlowe's play but intensifies the conflict of two irreconcilable conceptions of statecraft personified by the weak but legitimate monarch Richard and the competent but unsanctioned usurper Bolingbroke. Like Marlowe, Shakespeare gives additional impulse to the plot with the tragic element of "nemesis," the conflict between two "mighty opposites," one fortuitous, the other doomed, and—departing from the fatalistic obsession of medieval tragedy—locates the ingredients of disaster and triumph in the motives of his principal characters. Thus both plays carry a previously cumbersome and episodic genre to a point where distinction between chronicle play and tragedy is almost imperceptible. In Shakespeare's *Richard III.* on the other hand, the Marlovian concentration on a single character and his Machiavellian exploits is so pronounced that chronicle becomes fused with melodrama on the order of Marlowe's JEW OF MALTA.

In spite of the great vogue for chronicle plays during the 1590s, no dramatist advanced the genre beyond the artistic innovations of Marlowe's *Edward II* and Shakespeare's *Richard II.* A chief practitioner of the type in addition to Shakespeare was the prolific Thomas HEYWOOD, who combined chronicle play and domestic tragedy in *Edward IV,* Parts I and II (1600). Heywood also produced another chronicle play in two parts, *If You Know Not Me, You Know Nobody* (Part I, 1605; II, 1616). Part I opens during the reign of Mary Tudor shortly after the execution of Sir Thomas Wyatt and Lady Jane Grey, stresses Bishop Gardiner's persecution of Elizabeth and other Protestants, and concludes triumphantly with Elizabeth's coronation. Part II, with Sir Thomas Gresham as its hero, is actually a comedy of London merchant life with garnishes of historical scenes depicting the duke of Medina in council before the Armada, Elizabeth's review of her troops at Tilbury, the building of the Royal Exchange, the reactions of both Spanish and English to the defeat of the Armada, and the queen's reception of the victorious Drake and Frobisher.

Heywood's *If You Know Not Me* illustrates the diffuse nature of the dramatized chronicle biography. Another dramatized biography is the anonymous BOOK OF SIR THOMAS MORE, preserved in a fragmentary manuscript written by several hands, parts of which some handwriting experts have attributed to Shakespeare. What remains of the manuscript indicates that it focused on More's career as under-sheriff of London, his association with Erasmus, and his humor and benevolence ("the best friend the poor ever had"). Another laudatory biography is the anonymous *Life and Death of Lord Cromwell,* entered in the Stationers' Register in 1602 and reprinted in the Third Folio—with much less probability than the manuscript of *Sir Thomas More*—as being by Shakespeare. Like Heywood's *If You Know Not Me, Cromwell* is zealous Protestant propaganda based largely on the fabulous account of Thomas Cromwell, Henry VIII's scheming chancellor, in Foxe's *Book of Martyrs.* Cromwell is shown to be a pious, contemplative, and honorable minister whose deceit and ruthlessness are necessary to extirpate the evils of Roman Catholicism:

> Yes, the abolishing of Anti-Christ
> And of his Popish order from our realm!
> I am no enemy to religion,
> But what is done, it is for England's good!

Equally interesting is the anonymous *History of Captain Thomas Stukeley,* first referred to in 1596 by Philip Henslowe as "Stewtly." In this account of an Elizabethan soldier of fortune reputed to be the natural son of Henry VIII, chronicle biography joins with chivalric romance and ROGUE LITERATURE to describe Stukeley's varied and far-flung adventures in England, Ireland, Spain, and Morocco. To add to this episodic diffusion, the author introduces, with the exception of the hero, a whole new *dramatis personae* with each act.

The vogue of the chronicle play was well over by 1612, when Shakespeare collaborated with John Fletcher in writing *Henry VIII* for the King's Men at the Globe. The last significant production of its kind was the experimental masterpiece by John Ford, PERKIN WARBECK, acted at the Phoenix around 1633 and first printed a year later. The prologue to Ford's *Perkin Warbeck* acknowledged that the chronicle play had long been out of fashion:

> Studies have, of this nature, been of late
> So out of fashion, so unfollowed, that
> It is become more justice to revive
> The antic follies of the times, than strive
> To countenance wise industry . . . .

The definitive study is by Felix E. Schelling, *The English Chronicle Play* (1902), which contains a bibliography of extant and non-extant plays based on English history. See also Ernest Talbert, *The Problem of Order* (1962); Irving Ribner, *The English History Play in the Age of Shakespeare* (rev. ed., 1965); and Hardin Craig, "The Origin of the History Play," *Arl.Q,* III (1968).

Churchyard, Thomas (1520?-1604). Poet. Born the son of a farmer near Shrewsbury, Churchyard spent his boyhood as a page in the household of Henry Howard, earl of Surrey, whom he later celebrated in many poems. Around 1541 Churchyard began a career as a soldier (another favorite subject of later verses), serving in various engagements in Scotland, Ireland, the Low Countries, and France. He began writing poetry in the reign of Henry VIII; incredibly, he was still composing verses, without perceptible change of style, during the time of James I.

Most of what is known of Churchyard's life is based on autobiographical passages in his numerous books of verses, many of them with alliterative titles like *Churchyard's Chips* and *Churchyard's Charge*. According to *Churchyard's Challenge* (1593), he contributed "many things" to Tottel's *Miscellany* (1557), but these verses have not been identified. He is known to have arranged pageants for the queen's progresses in 1574 and 1578; one of his shorter pieces offended her, and he sat out the storm in Scotland for three years. Apparently forgiven, he received a small pension from the queen in 1593. Churchyard's most famous poem, and one of considerable merit, is the verse narrative in the 1563 edition of A MIRROR FOR MAGISTRATES, "Shore's Wife," the "complaint" of the ill-fated Jane Shore, mistress of Edward IV who was forced by Richard III to do public penance for adultery. Churchyard's lines lamenting the influence of Jane's venal friends became justly praised: "They brake the boughs and shak'd the tree by sleight, / And bent the wand that might have grown full straight." Churchyard's couplet might have been forgotten, however, if Christopher Marlowe had not appropriated it in his epilogue to *Doctor Faustus:* "Cut is the branch that might have grown full straight."

Churchyard's poetry, a voluminous imposition from the drab age of Tottel's *Miscellany* and gone to vinegar in the effervescent time of Spenser and Marlowe, has suffered condign neglect. His awkwardly inverted and faltering verses revolve with painful prolixity around subjects not calculated to inflame many human fancies—the glories of the earl of Surrey, Sir Humphrey Gilbert, or Queen Elizabeth; descriptions of Wales or of a paper mill in Dartford; lamentations over time wasted in the wars in Flanders. Churchyard wrote on any subject that happened to interest him, and his interests meandered everywhere, often in the same poem.

There is, mercifully, no edition of Churchyard's complete works. Individual poems were printed in nineteenth-century collectanea: in Thomas Park's *Heliconia*, III (1815); H. Huth and W. C. Hazlitt's *Fugitive Tracts*, Series 2 (1875); and *Satirical Poems of the Time of the Reformation*, ed. James Cranstoun, 2 vols. (1891-93), which contains a bibliography of Churchyard's political poems. The standard biography is by H. W. Adnit (1884).

City of the Sun, The (Tommaso Campanella). See UTOPIAN FICTION.

Cleveland, John (1613-1658). Poet. The son of a clergyman, Cleveland grew up in Leicestershire, where his father was a vicar, and attended Christ's College, Cambridge, where his classmates were John Milton and Henry More. He graduated B.A. in 1631, M.A. in 1635, and became a fellow of St. John's and Reader in Rhetoric. He opposed Cromwell's election as member of Parliament for Cambridge in 1640, and when the Civil War broke out in 1642, supported the king's cause with great courage and integrity. As judge advocate at Newark, he held the town against the Scots in 1646. Imprisoned in 1655 on trumped-up charges, he appealed to Cromwell for amnesty but refused to repudiate his Royalist convictions. He died at Gray's Inn shortly after his release from prison.

According to John Dryden, Cleveland was a "strong-lined man" and metaphysical fantastic, but this extravagance made Cleveland an excellent satirist, an exuberant versifier, and one of the most popular poets of the mid-seventeenth century (see CAVALIER POETS). His collected *Poems* (1651) went through over twenty editions before the Restoration. Cleveland's anti-Puritan satire *The Rebel Scot* represents only one of his many journalistic propaganda efforts on the king's behalf during the Civil Wars. His elegies on Jonson and Edward King and his amatory verses to "Phillis" are boisterously obscure, archly witty and conceited. What Dryden condemned as "Clevelandism" consists of clever word games in imitation of Donne's conceits but without much of Donne's combined passion and profundity. Hence with Cleveland's poetry the once robust metaphysical tradition weakens into verbal tricks and self-mockery. Cleveland is always a satirist, always mockingly cynical, and none of his verse, not even his epigrammatic elegies and epitaphs, is without some tinge of self-conscious cleverness and rakish posing. His elegy on the drowning of Edward King, published in the same volume with Milton's great pastoral elegy LYCIDAS, is "copied out in grief's hydrography" where the sea, Cleveland states, is "too rough for verse." In his love poems he deliberately courts the grotesque and incongruous, always striving for easy shock effects. Occasionally he reads like a travesty of Donne, as in his "To the State of Love," where he invokes the navigation imagery and astronomical conceits of Donne's *Elegy 19:*

> My sight took pay, but (thank my charms),
> I now empale her in mine arms,
> (Love's Compasses) confining you,
> Good angels, to a compass too.
> Is not the Universe strait-lac'd,
> When I clasp it in the waist?
> My amorous folds about thee hurl'd,
> With Drake, I compass in the world.
> I hoop the firmament, and make
> This my embrace the Zodiac.

Although Cleveland was a very literal follower of Donne's metaphors, his levity and superficial conceits do not so much recall the early METAPHYSICAL POETS as anticipate the irreverent and satiric wits of the Restoration. In "The Anti-Platonic" he stands somewhere between Jack Donne the rake and the earl of Rochester, but always a head shorter than either of them:

> Give me a lover bold and free,
> Not eunucht with formality;
> Like an ambassador that beds a queen
> With the nice caution of a sword between.

J. M. Berdan's edition of *The Poems* (1911) is superseded by that of Brian Morris and Eleanor Withington (1967). There is also a selection in *Minor Poets of the Caroline Period,* ed. George Saintsbury, 3 vols. (1905-21), III. For criticism, see George Williamson, *The Donne Tradition* (1930); S. V. Gapp, "Notes on John Cleveland," *PMLA,* XLVI (1931); and A. Alvarez, *The School of Donne* (1961). Cleveland's influence in the seventeenth century is discussed by Paul J. Korshin, "The Evolution of Neoclassic Poetics: Cleveland, Denham, and Waller as Poetic Theorists," *ECS,* II (1968), and James Sutherland, "Anne Greene and the Oxford Poets," in *The Augustan Milieu; Essays Presented to Louis A. Landa,* ed. H. K. Miller, et al. (1970). See also Brian Morris' bibliography.

Colin Clout's Come Home Again. A pastoral dialogue by Edmund SPENSER, published in 1595 and occasioned by the poet's journey to England with Sir Walter Raleigh in 1589 to publish the first three books of *The Faerie Queene.*
Elizabeth as the cynosure of virtue, wisdom, and beauty.

In one passage (376 ff.) Spenser pays tribute to twelve contemporary English poets, only two of whom are referred to by name (William

Colin Clout (Spenser), as a humble shepherd, describes his impressions at the court of Queen Elizabeth. Some characters from *The Shepherd's Calendar* (1579) reappear, such as Hobbinol (Gabriel Harvey). Raleigh is depicted as the Shepherd of the Ocean. Temporarily out of favor with the queen, Raleigh complains of his "usage hard" in the service of Cynthia, the Lady of the Sea. In conclusion Colin mildly berates the court for its materialism, sensuality, unseemly competition for favor, neglect of the arts, and general frivolity; but he praises Queen Alabaster and Samuel Daniel). Among the others scholars have found allusions to Michael Drayton, Sir Edward Dyer, Abraham Fraunce, Thomas Lodge, and Shakespeare. The list of poets is followed by a roll call of distinguished ladies at court, including, as Urania, Sir Philip Sidney's sister Mary, countess of Pembroke.

Spenser's reaction to court life is carefully balanced. He is attracted by its beauty and power, but realizes they are not of the types to rouse a poet's inspiration or sustain his genius. The brilliant lords and ladies serving the queen have, he observes without harshness, a greater moral potential than they demonstrate: "For God his gifts there plenteously bestowes, / But gracilesse men them greatley do abuse."

The standard edition is in *The Works,* ed. Edwin A. Greenlaw, F. M. Padelford, et al., 10 vols. (1932-49), I. For criticism, see B. E. C. Davis, *Edmund Spenser, A Critical Study* (1962); William Nelson, *The Poetry of Edmund Spenser* (1963); and Samuel Meyer, *An Interpretation of Edmund Spenser's Colin Clout's Come Home Again* (1969).

Comedy of Errors, The. A comedy by William SHAKESPEARE, written around 1592-93 and first printed in the 1623 Folio. As sources Shakespeare relied on two comedies of Plautus, *Menaechmi* and *Amphitruo,* with some characters and incidents taken from a late Greek romance, *Appollonius of Tyre,* a work Shakespeare also consulted in writing *Pericles.* As in Roman comedy, the "errors" of the title refers to mistaken identities.

In Ephesus it is decreed that any Syracusan found in the city must pay a heavy ransom or be put to death, and an old Syracusan merchant, Aegeon, is arrested and brought before Duke Solinus, to whom Aegeon relates a tragic story. Many years before, Aegeon had twin boys, both named Antipholus, and twin slaves to attend them, both called Dromio. During a shipwreck Aegeon was separated from his wife, an infant son, and one of the slave twins, all of whom he saw rescued and taken away in a Corinthian ship. With his other son and the other slave child, Aegeon was rescued by a second vessel and eventually settled at Syracuse. Eighteen years later Antipholus and his slave departed from Syracuse to search for their brothers. When they did not return after five years, Aegeon set out to find them in Ephesus. Upon hearing this story, the sympathetic duke allows the old man until evening to raise the required ransom.

Unknown to Aegeon, Antipholus of Syracuse and his slave have arrived in Ephesus, where the other Antipholus and Dromio have lived since the shipwreck. Since each pair of twins not only look alike but are identically named, confusion abounds whenever chance brings them together. When the Ephesian Dromio happens to encounter Antipholus of Syracuse at an inn, he takes him to be his master and is beaten for his strange behavior. When Dromio of Syracuse denies to his master that they met at the inn, the Syracusan Antipholus beats him for impertinent lying. Matters become even more confusing when the Ephesian Antipholus' wife Adriana and her sister Luciana take Antipholus of Syracuse and slave to dinner at the house of Antipholus of Ephesus, where the Syracusan Antipholus is soon making love to Luciana and his slave is accosted by a serving wench who claims to be his wife. When the rightful master of the house arrives in the company of the other Dromio and his friends Angelo and Balthazar, he is ordered away by voices from behind locked doors. Angry and baffled, he invites his guests to dine with him at the house of a courtesan, and to avenge his wife's conduct still further, sends Angelo after a gold chain he had intended to give Adriana but now declares he will bestow on the harlot. As Angelo is returning with the chain, he encounters the Syracusan Dromio, sent out on an errand, and forces the chain upon him with orders to give it to his master.

When Angelo later demands payment for the chain, Antipholus of Ephesus denies he ever received it, and the enraged Angelo has him arrested. When the Syracusan Dromio appears, Antipholus of Ephesus sends him to Adriana for money to secure his release from custody. When this Dromio meets his real master on the way to Adriana's, Antipholus of Syracuse can make no sense out of his slave's talk about money, nor can he understand the courtesan's angry demand of the gold chain that hangs about his neck. His strange behavior sends the courtesan to Adriana with news of her husband's madness, and Adriana employs Doctor Pinch, a schoolmaster learned in exorcism, to drive out the devils possessing her husband. The conjurer is beaten for his efforts by the enraged husband who, after his debt is paid by Adriana, is taken away by officers to be confined at home as a lunatic. Upon returning from his house, the officers happen to meet the Syracusans on their way to their ship, and, of course, they assume this Antipholus to be an escaped prisoner. The ensuing melee is further confused by the appearance of Angelo, who demands the chain around Antipholus' neck. To these afflictions is added the plague of a shrewish virago when Adriana attacks the Syracusan Antipholus for his loose behavior with the courtesan. Both Syracusans flee to the sanctuary of a priory, where the aged abbess refuses to surrender them to Adriana and her friends on grounds that the wife's jealousy caused her husband's madness. Adriana appeals her case to the duke, who is leading to execution the hapless Aegeon, and while these matters are in progress the Ephesian Antipholus and his slave, having escaped from their confinement, arrive to make their complaints to the duke. All these "errors" are not corrected until the abbess appears with Antipholus of Syracuse and his Dromio, and Aegeon recognizes her as his long-lost wife. The two pairs of brothers are reunited, Aegeon is pardoned by the duke, and Antipholus of Syracuse announces his intentions of marrying Luciana.

Shakespeare's comedy is his most thoroughly academic, representing the type of play students translated from Latin and performed on school holidays. It bears most of the characteristics of Shakespeare's earliest comedies. The plot is meticuously constructed; the verse is rhetorical rather than colloquial, and there is liberal use of end-stopped lines, rhyme, "fourteeners," and stichomythia. Exposition is bald and prolix, as in Aegeon's lengthy narration to the duke at the beginning of the play. Although there is little depth of characterization, Plautine types are modulated by some rather vivid English portrayals, especially that of Adriana, whose shrewish ways are contrasted to the softer domestic theories of Luciana. As in Plautus, the main comedy depends on mistaken identities and mistimings, but the action is given a decidedly native romantic hue by the domestic relations of Adriana and her husband, and the budding love affair of Luciana and the Syracusan Antipholus.

A standard text is the new Arden edition, ed. R. A. Foakes (1962). Sources are printed and analyzed by Geoffrey Bullough, *Narrative and Dramatic Sources of Shakespeare,* 7 vols. (1972), I. For criticism, see G. R. Elliott, "Weirdness in *The Comedy of Errors,*" *UTQ,* IX (1939); Nevill Coghill, "The Bases of Shakespearean Comedy," *E & S,* New Series,

III (1950); M. C. Bradbrook, *The Growth and Structure of Elizabethan Comedy* (1955); Derek Traversi, *Shakespeare's Early Comedy* (1960); T. W. Baldwin, *On the Compositional Genetics of The Comedy of Errors* (1965); A. C. Hamilton, *The Early Shakespeare* (1967); and Richard Henze, "*The Comedy of Errors:* A Freely Binding Chain," *SQ,* XX (1971).

commedia dell'arte. A form of improvised Italian popular comedy in which the actors performed from a scenario rather than written dialogue. Besides improvisation of lines, the distinguishing feature of the type was its stock characters: the buffoon (*zanni*); the braggart soldier (*miles gloriosus*); the passionate young lovers (*amorosos* and *amorosas*); the heroine's resourceful nurse (*balia*); the elderly father or guardian, usually a rich merchant (*pantalone,* or "pantaloon"); and the *pantalone's* gullible old crony (*dottore*). Several of these types, such as the MILES GLORIOSUS, were derived from the Roman comedy of Plautus. In *Love's Labour's Lost,* Berowne enumerates some of the stock characters of the *commedia dell'arte* when he refers to "The pedant, the braggart, the hedgepriest, the fool and the boy" (V, *ii*). Another familiar character was the harlequin, who interrupted the play with farcical monologues, dancing, singing, or acrobatics; a farce in which the harlequin was the main character was known as a *harlequinade.* The stock character of primary interest was the *zanni.* Although the *zanni* might be a shrewd, conniving servant or a thick-witted oaf, he was invariably a buffoon who amused plebeian audiences with obscene jokes and gestures, acrobatics, and pratfalls—his routine being known as a *lazzi.*

Except for the young lovers in the *commedia dell'arte,* all the actors wore masks and were distinguishable by their conventional garb, such as the broad cape and huge black hat of the *dottore.* The masks were no impediment to expression because the actors employed energetic body movements, strong vocal intonations, and liberal pantomime and mimicry—acting qualities that enabled them to be understood when performing in foreign countries. The scenarios usually described complications arising from disguises or mistaken identities; a standard plot might concern the confusions caused by two sets of twins or a lover who disguises himself as a servant in the household of the *pantalone* in order to save the *pantalone's* daughter from an enforced marriage to an old man. Variations on these plots can be seen in Shakespeare's *Comedy of Errors* and *Twelfth Night* and in Thomas Dekker's *The Shoemaker's Holiday.*

The *commedia dell'arte* is of obscure origins. It has been traced to the Roman comedies of Plautus and Terence; Asiatic mimes; farces and soties interpolated into medieval mystery plays; and the so-called Atellan fables (*Atellanae fabulae*), comedies named for the Italian village of Atella in Campania that became known in the Middle Ages for its amateur performances of farce and pantomime. The *commedia dell'arte* began to be presented by professional actors at the beginning of the sixteenth century, and by 1550 professional dramatic companies acting exclusively in this form had become established in Mantua, Modena, and Padua. Italian troupes are known to have visited England as early as 1546, and their appearances became quite regular in the seventeenth century. Their influence on such Elizabethan plays as George Chapman's *An Humorous Day's Mirth* and Ben Jonson's *The Case Is Altered* and *Volpone* would appear obvious, except that plot situations and characterizations of both Elizabethan and Italian popular comedy often stem from and closely resemble a common source in Plautus and Terence. In England the *commedia dell'arte* came into its greatest vogue in the eighteenth century with the introduction of pantomimes in which serious legends, accompanied by lavish scenery, songs, and dances, were burlesqued by the stock characters of Italian comedy.

Scenarios of the Commedia Dell'Arte, ed. Henry Salerno (1967) is a translation of Flaminio Scala's collection of plots in *Il teatro delle favole rappresentative* (1611). For an account of the development and influence of the *commedia dell'arte*, see Allardyce Nicoll, *Masks, Mimes, and Miracles* (1931) and *The World of Harlequin* (1963); Kathleen M. Lea, *Italian Popular Comedy* (1934); Marvin T. Herrick, *Italian Comedy in the Renaissance* (1960); and Charles S. Felver, "The *Commedia dell'Arte* and English Drama in the Sixteenth and Early Seventeenth Centuries," *Ren D,* VI (1963).

Commonwealth of Oceana (James Harrington). See UTOPIAN FICTION.

Complaints, The; Containing Sundry Small Poems of the World's Vanity. A collection of poems, chiefly narrative, by Edmund SPENSER published in 1591. These include *The Ruins of Time,* a tribute dedicated to Sir Philip Sidney's memory, in which time destroys all man's achievements except, perhaps, the "eternizing" powers of poetry; *The Tears of the Muses,* in which each of the nine muses laments the sad condition of English poetry, and where Spenser expresses aesthetic ideas derived from his reading of the French poets of the PLÉIADE; *Prosopopoia, or Mother Hubberd's Tale,* a bestiary which, like *Virgil's Gnat,* is a satire on political and social intrigues at court before 1580 (see MOTHER HUBBERD'S TALE); *Virgil's Gnat,* an imitation of the pseudo-Vergilian *Culex; The Ruins of Rome,* an early translation of Du Bellay's *Antiquités de Rome; Muiopotmos, or The Fate of the Butterfly,* another satire on court life similar in style to *Virgil's Gnat; Visions of the World's Vanity,* twelve sonnets, most on the irony of how the weak in nature and society often conquer the strong (in a rhyme pattern of *ab ab bc bc cd cd ee*); and *The Visions of Bellay* and *The Visions of Petrarch,* early translations by Spenser of sonnets by Du Bellay and of Marot's translation of Petrarch's sixth *canzone.*

Spenser's collection of poems was intended to appeal to the current taste for melancholy didacticism in the manner of Boccaccio's *De casibus virorum illustrium,* Lydgate's *Fall of Princes,* and Sackville's lugubrious Induction to *A Mirror for Magistrates,* all of which, like Spenser's poems, are "complaints and meditations of the world's vanity, very grave and profitable." Few of the selections have any genuine artistic merit; Spenser may have rushed them to the printer to capitalize on the favourable response to the first three books of *The Faerie Queene* the year before. Some of the *Complaints* date back in composition to Spenser's Cambridge period or shortly after (1570-76), others to his first residence in London (1576-80), and a few to the early years in Ireland (1580-83).

The standard edition is in *The Works,* ed. Edwin A. Greenlaw, F. M. Padelford, et al., 10 vols. (1932-49), VIII. There is another excellent edition by W. L. Renwick (1928). For commentary, see H. S. V. Jones, *A Spenser Handbook* (1930), and Harold Stein, *Studies in Spenser's Complaints* (1934).

Complete Gentleman, The. A courtesy book by Henry Peacham (1576?-1643?), first published in 1622. Peacham's book was a chief authority on polite conduct throughout the seventeenth century, and as recently as the nineteenth century. Washington Irving had his Squire Bracebridge in *The Sketch Book* state that from childhood he "took honest Peacham for his text-book instead of Chesterfield." Peacham's book is a compilation on morals and manners from such familiar authorities as Plutarch, Erasmus, Vives, ELYOT, ASCHAM, and Castiglione (see THE COURTIER). To these Peacham brings his experience in foreign travel and his considerable knowledge of classical literature, music, painting, and poetry.

Like Castiglione, Peacham defines a gentleman as one having "honour of blood," but also one who contributes to the welfare of the state. Hence true nobility is not established solely by birth, for in some cases it can be achieved entirely by honorable or heroic deeds. In a famous passage Peacham concludes: "Riches are the ornament, not the cause of nobility." In considering the various professions, he observes that some are more "honorable" than others. Lawyers and physicians are especially worthy of respect, but the status of businessmen and merchants is dubious; common mechanics and menials are excluded from any consideration as gentry.

After praising learning as a prime requisite of gentility, Peacham discusses at length his conception of an ideal education. He criticizes teachers for being too strict and for disregarding individual differences, and parents for sending their sons to the university at too early an age, failing to spend enough money on education, and neglecting to stress religious training. Unlike Sir Thomas ELYOT in *A Book Named the Governor,* Peacham stresses educational content rather than teaching methods. Assuming some preparation in classical languages, he dwells at length on the vital importance of classical literature in providing examples of oratory and rhetoric. Next to the study of elocution and rhetoric, he values history, which he divides into the four branches of geography, chronology, genealogy, and history proper. He also praises geometry, which he believes of practical use in constructing war machines and fortifications. Less practical but equally heuristic is poetry, "the noblest of the arts," and among the ancients he praises Vergil, Horace, Plautus, and Terence; among the English writers, Chaucer, More, Gower, Lydgate, Wyatt, Surrey, and Spenser.

Peacham discourses at length on his own favorite pastimes of music and painting. Singing and playing the viol or lute he considers a necessity for any gentleman, and he invokes Aristotle to justify the study of painting. In the third edition Peacham added instructions on how to mix colors and some allegorical interpretations of Biblical and historical figures in the paintings of the Italian masters. He is equally technical in his discussion of heraldry, giving detailed instructions on how to design a coat of arms.

Like Elyot, Ascham, Castiglione, and Milton (*Of Education*), Peacham insists that physical training is as necessary as intellectual discipline, and commends in particular horsemanship, archery, hunting, and running at tilt. Unlike Elyot, however, he highly recommends foreign travel and (an inveterate traveler himself) gives advice on dining, conversing, and making friends while in France and Spain.

In summary, Peacham's book is a practical, encyclopedic guide to all the various activities that befit gentility; he even includes chapters on fishing and military operations. Whatever subject he takes up, it invariably reveals an inquisitive, bustling, and pragmatic personality, an author of wit, charm, and immense vitality. These were the qualities that endeared *The Complete Gentleman* to generations of English readers (see COURTESY LITERATURE).

The Complete Gentleman, together with Peacham's *The Truth of Our Times* and *The Art of Living in London,* are edited with an informative introduction and extensive bibliography by Virgil B. Heltzel (1962). There is another modern edition of *The Complete Gentleman* by G. S. Gordon (1906). For a discussion of its sources and influence, see D. T. Starnes, "Elyot's *The Governour* and Peacham's *Compleat Gentleman,*" *MLR,* XXII (1927). See also Robert R. Cawley, *Henry Peacham: His Contribution to English Poetry* (1971).

Comus. A masque by John MILTON, first published anonymously in 1637 with the title "A Mask Presented at Ludlow Castle, 1634" and followed by a dedication to John, son of the earl of Bridgewater, by the musician and composer Henry Lawes, who had written the music for the songs and acted the part of the Attendant Spirit at the performance at Ludlow Castle, home of the earl of Bridgewater. (The title "Comus" was first given to the masque by John Dalton in his edition of 1738.) Some of the many suggested sources and influences on *Comus* include the Circe episode in Homer's *Odyssey,* X; George Peele's OLD WIVES' TALE; Torquato Tasso's pastoral drama *Aminta;* Ben Jonson's masque *Pleasure Reconciled to Virtue;* and John Fletcher's *The Faithful Shepherdess.* Most scholars consider *Comus* more of a "pastoral entertainment" than a masque in the strictest sense. (For other examples, see MASQUE.)

Milton's main character, the Lady, separated in a forest at night from her two brothers, encounters Comus and his revelers, who lure the Lady to a nearby cottage and attempt to seduce her with wine, gallant words, and gaiety. When her brothers arrive, the friendly Attendant Spirit, disguised as the shepherd Thyrsis, gives them a magic herb to protect them from Comus' spell. Meanwhile the Lady easily resists the blandishments of her enticers; she stoutly proclaims the virtues of chastity and denounces the revelers for their hypocrisy. After the brothers put Comus and his Bacchanalian crew to flight, the Lady remains frozen in Comus' enchanted chair, from which she is at last freed by Sabrina and her water nymphs, spirits inhabiting the region of the River Severn. At the conclusion of the play the brothers and the Lady proceed to Ludlow Castle to attend the celebration of the earl of Bridgewater's investiture as president of Wales.

Except for a sonnet on Shakespeare, *Comus* was Milton's first published work, and it well illustrates the growth of his lyric and philosophical powers during the period between the *Nativity Ode* in 1629 and *Lycidas* in 1637. The masque, introduced from Italy into the court of Henry VIII and perfected during the reign of James I by Ben Jonson, had fallen into artistic decline in Milton's time. In *Comus* Milton demonstrates a thorough knowledge of the salient features of the masque, with its allegory, mythology, dances, and songs, and injects into the conventional form several improvisations—expansion of the usually brief dialogue into moralizing debates and orations, emphasis on intellectual themes, and sustained and relatively dramatic interaction of characters representative of philosophical ideas—and Milton accomplishes all of this without totally sacrificing the lyric grace and congenial humor achieved by Jonson. The differences between Jonson's masques and *Comus* are of degree rather than kind: *Comus* is less scenic, less imaginative in presentation of action, much less gregarious and whimsical. And none of Jonson's masques places such singular concentration on a philosophical theme. In Jonson's *Pleasure Reconciled to Virtue* (1619), Comus is merely a farcical glutton; in Milton's masque he becomes a philosophical idea of hedonism in conflict with Platonic soul.

As in Spenser's *Faerie Queene,* Book III, Milton has a woman personify the ideal of chastity, and his theme is the complete inviolability of virtue when set upon by the emotional and physical violence represented by Comus. Thus, while in search of the Lady, the Elder Brother lectures the Second Brother, a neophyte in Platonic philosophy, on how their sister, "clad in complete steel" of divine chastity, must remain secure from any evil (lines 453-63):

> So dear to Heav'n is Saintly chastity,
> That when a soul is found sincerely so,
> A thousand liveried Angels lackey her,
> Driving far off each thing of sin and guilt,
> And in clear dream and solemn vision
> Tell her of things that no gross ear can hear,
> Till oft converse with heav'nly habitants
> Begin to cast a beam on th'outward shape,
> The unpolluted temple of the mind,
> And turns it by degrees to the soul's essence,
> Till all be made immortal . . .

Comus anticipates many of the same concerns as AREOPAGITICA, PARADISE LOST, and PARADISE REGAINED: the theme of temptation, the paradoxical relationship of the physical and the spiritual (in *Comus* the physical being, as in the above passage, the outward manifestation of the inner essence of soul—a Platonic concept), the self-destructive nature of evil, and the view of reason as enlightened moral choice. One shortcoming of *Comus* in contrast to these other works is that in Milton's masque there is, in fact, no temptation and little genuine conflict: the Lady perceives Comus' true nature at once and, unlike Eve when confronted with Satan in *Paradise Lost,* she is not only instinctively repelled by his blandishments but justifiably contemptuous of his inferior mentality. Although Comus courts her as woman, he soon learns that she is a rather pedantic and refractory philosopher with exceptional skills in logic and oratory—a confrontation that conveys sparse dramatic tension. Indeed, the thrust of Milton's *Comus,* especially in the first half of the work, is toward putting philosophical ideas to the task of conveying sensuous entertainment—a purpose that only partially succeeds, contrary to the euphoric words of the Second Brother (lines 476-80):

> How charming is divine Philosophy!
> Not harsh and crabbed as dull fools suppose,
> But musical as is Apollo's lute,
> And a perpetual feast of nectar'd sweets,
> Where no crude surfeit reigns.

The standard edition is in *The Works of John Milton,* ed. Frank A. Patterson, 18 vols. (1931-38), I. There are quite well-annotated editions in *John Milton: Complete Poems and Major Prose*, ed. Merritt Y. Hughes (1957), and *Comus and Other Poems,* ed. F. T. Prince (1968). *Comus* is studied from various perspectives by Enid Welsford, *The Court Masque* (1927); E. M. W. Tillyard, *Studies in Milton* (1951); John Arthos; *On a Masque Presented at Ludlow Castle by John Milton* (1954), which has an extensive bibliography; John G. Demaray, *Milton and the Masque Tradition* (1968); and Angus Fletcher, *The Transcendental Masque* (1971). There is a collection of critical essays, with bibliography, in *A Masque at Ludlow: Essays on Milton's Comus,* ed. John J. Diekhoff (1968).

conduct books. See COURTESY LITERATURE.

coney-catching pamphlets. See GREENE, ROBERT; ROGUE LITERATURE.

Constable, Henry (1562-1613). Poet, Born of a distinguished family in Warwickshire, he received his degree at St. John's College, Cambridge, in 1580, and resided for a time at Lincoln's Inn before securing employment with Sir Francis Walsingham, the secretary of state, through the combined influence of his kinsmen the earl of Rutland, Sir Edward Stafford, and Gilbert Talbot, seventh earl of Shrewsbury. In 1583 Constable accompanied Walsingham to the court of James VI of Scotland and went with the king to Denmark during the marriage negotiations with representatives of the future Queen Anne. In December of that year he was on a mission to Paris, and during 1584-88 traveled extensively as an emissary in Germany, Poland, and Italy. In 1589 he wrote in Paris a treatise published anonymously as *Examen pacifique de la doctrine de Huguenots,* a work purporting to be by a French Roman Catholic urging his Catholic countrymen to tolerate the Huguenots and support their Protestant monarch Henry IV. The tract was published posthumously in England as *The Catholic Moderator, or A Moderate Examination of the Doctrine of the Protestants* (1623), translated by "W.W."

Constable's conversion to Roman Catholicism in 1590 made his presence extremely awkward when he accompanied the earl of Essex on the English expedition to France in 1591 to assist Henry IV in the civil war, and after several *contretemps* with his countrymen, Constable went to Rome, returning to Paris in 1595 to establish residence at Mignon College, where he lived between trips to Scotland, Rome, Antwerp, and Brussels. It is evident from his letters to Essex during the period 1595-97 that Constable was assiduously weaving plots with various influential people to effect a reconciliation between Rome and England, and that he conceived the first step in his grandiose design to be the conversion of James VI to Catholicism. A Catholic James I on the English throne, he reasoned, would then unite with Henry IV, recently converted to Catholicism, in a formidable alliance against Spain. Among English recusant exiles, Constable joined with that faction which was strongly patriotic, anti-Spanish, and deeply theological (in ways inimical to the Jesuits, who were identified with Spanish intrigues). It was a combination of piety and pedantry certain to appeal to his friend James VI, and in July 1599 Constable landed in Scotland determined to convert the king to the Old Faith. Cordially received but totally failing in his mission, Constable returned to Paris in November and set to work on two pamphlets defending James VI's right to the English crown.

With the accession of the Scottish king to the English throne in 1603, Constable hastened to London where he enjoyed considerable royal favor until the Privy Council clapped him in the Tower in April 1604 for editing "seditious" letters of a religious nature. Released through the intercession of influential friends, he spent the next six years in London under trying circumstances. He returned to Paris in 1610 and died at Liège on October 9, 1613, while on a mission to convert an English Protestant to Catholicism.

All the poems that can be attributed to Constable with any certainty are in the form of sonnets. His first collection, *Diana* (1592), included twenty-three sonnets, enlarged to seventy-six in the next edition (1594), although only twenty-seven of these are assigned to Constable. Four additional sonnets were printed in the 1595 edition of Sir Philip Sidney's *Apology for Poetry.* The four pastoral poems signed "H.C." in *England's Helicon* (1600), often attributed to Constable, are now believed to have been written by Henry Chettle. All of Constable's secular poems were written before 1591, circulated for several years in manuscript, and printed piecemeal without his supervision. As a man of affairs rather than a poet, he took no interest in the publication of his verses.

His religious sonnets were relatively unknown among his contemporaries. Entitled "Spiritual Sonnets: to the honor of God and his saints" in manuscript, they were first published in 1815 by Thomas Park. Deriving from no particular literary source, the more cerebral religious poems express the Counter Reformation theme of the guilt-stricken, earth-bound soul in perfervid longing of heavenly joys, and the eclectic Petrarchan court mistresses of *Diana* are replaced by flaming visions of Mary Magdalen. "To God the Father" conveys an authentic voice and unique persona:

> Great God: within whose single essence, we
> Nothing but that, which is Thyself, can find;
> When on Thyself thou did'st reflect thy mind,
> Thy thought was God, which took the form of
> Thee.

Such wit can hardly be called "metaphysical," yet at least one of Constable's sonnets, "To Our Blessed Lady," is sinewy enough to have been mistakenly included in the 1635 edition of John Donne's poems.

Constable's *Diana* was the first SONNET SEQUENCE to follow Sidney's *Astrophel and Stella* (*Diana* antedating Samuel Daniel's *Delia* by several months), and several of Constable's poems are written to Penelope Rich, the "Stella" of Sidney's sequence. Constable's usual rhyme scheme is *ab ba ab ba* in the octave, and about half his sonnets end in couplets.

Besides Petrarch, his master was the French poet Philippe Desportes (1546-1606). Constable's sonnets are closely woven, superior in total design and general craftsmanship to Thomas Watson's but markedly inferior to Sidney's and Spenser's in energy and originality. Constable's lucid diction and syntactical smoothness compare with "well-languaged" Samuel Daniel's, and his best sonnets are characterized by a fairly competent and uninspired reiteration of Petrarchan images and conceits rather than any personal fire or ingenuity. Constable's sonnets were widely admired by his contemporaries for their sweetness. In later years, however, the followers of Jonson and Donne found little to praise in Constable's plain style and unsophisticated Petrarchanisms.

The best edition, with biography, notes, and commentary, is by Joan Grundy, *The Poems of Henry Constable* (1960). See also George Wickes, "Henry Constable: Courtier Poet," *RenP* (1956); and J. W. Lever, *The Elizabethan Love Sonnet* (1956).

Conversations of Ben Jonson with Drummond. See JONSON, BEN.

Cooper's Hill. See DENHAM, SIR JOHN.

Corbet (or Corbett), Richard (1582-1635). Poet and clergyman. Later bishop of Oxford and Norwich, Corbet was born in Ewell, Surrey, the only son of Vincent Corbet, a wealthy landowner who, for reasons unknown, took the surname Poynter. (Ben Jonson has an epitaph on the father in *Underwoods*). Richard Corbet was educated at Westminster School and at both Broadgates Hall (later Pembroke College) and Christ Church, Oxford. He graduated M.A. in 1605 and spent the next three decades at Oxford, where he became dean of Christ Church (1620), bishop of Oxford (1628), and bishop of Norwich (1632). The antiquary John Aubrey makes Corbet the subject of one of his most humorous portraits in his *Brief Lives* (1813), describing Corbet as a rollicking jokester, an extemporizer of verses, and frequenter of the Devil and Mermaid taverns. Thomas Fuller (*Worthies,* 1662) pictures Corbet as a "high wit and most excellent poet," more given to amusing companionship than solitary piety, and Corbet's fifty or so short poems, begun in 1609, tend to corroborate Aubrey's portrait of the "jolly Doctor."

Corbet published none of his verses during his lifetime, but circulated them in manuscript among his friends at Oxford and at court. He wrote on a variety of subjects—on an ugly woman who seduced him in his rooms at Oxford, on the virtues of Francis Beaumont, John Donne, and others—but his best-known poem is a frolicsome anti-Puritan satire lamenting the passing of Merry England, "The Fairies' Farewell; or, God-a-Mercy Will":

Lament, lament, old abbeys,
  The fairies lost command:
They did but change priests' babies,
  But some have chang'd your land;
And all your children sprung from thence
  Are now grown Puritans...

Corbet's poems were published posthumously in *Certain Elegant Poems* (1647) and *Poetica Stromata* (1648). The standard edition, which contains a biography, is *The Poems of Richard Corbett,* ed. J. A. W. Bennett and H. R. Trevor-Roper (1955). There is a biographical account by J. E. V. Crofts, " A Life of Bishop Corbett," *E&S,* X (1924).

Coriolanus. A tragedy by William SHAKESPEARE, written around 1607-1608 and first printed in the 1623 Folio. The principal source is the life of Caius Marcius Coriolanus in Sir Thomas North's translation of Plutarch's *Lives of the Noble Grecians and Romans* (1579).

Caius Marcius, a haughty Roman aristocrat, conquers the Volscians and almost single-handedly captures Corioli, for which he receives the title "Coriolanus." His suave and diplomatic friend Menenius and his fiercely ambitious mother Volumnia persuade him to appeal to the people to make him consul, but his arrogance and his violent contempt for the Roman rabble, together with the intrigues of the jealous tribunes, soon cause the fickle populace to demand his death. Banished, Coriolanus seeks out his arch-enemy among the Volscians, a wily general called Aufidius, who accepts Coriolanus' help against the Romans while awaiting the most propitious moment to destroy him. Arriving at the gates of Rome in command of a Volscial army, Coriolanus is persuaded by his mother to spare the city, but his double treason causes the Volscians, spurred on by Aufidius, to tear him to pieces. The play concludes with Volumnia's triumphant return to a grateful

Rome and Aufidius' eulogy over the body of the slain Coriolanus.

Coriolanus is the least conscious, flexible, and intellectual of Shakespeare's tragic heroes. He is essentially simple, a man of great physical courage who judges everything from the perspective of his own narrow and mindless principles. Hence he proves a dupe to his own pride and lack of self-knowledge, and to the fierce ambitions of his virago mother Volumnia; even down to the moment of his destruction he remains oblivious of his true situation. Basically, his flaw is immaturity; godlike in valor, he remains a child tied to his mother's apron strings.

Yet Coriolanus cannot be understood without reference to the society that produced him, and as in *Richard III* and *Julius Caesar,* that society is shown to be deathly sick. Menenius' seriocomic telling of the myth of the belly of the state (I, *i*) provides a central metaphor by which the grave illness of the commonwealth can be gauged. In *Coriolanus* Rome is shown to be a jungle in which each faction preys on the other; the aristocrats devour the people, who are in turn cynically manipulated by their demagogues, and Coriolanus, although always appealing to some vague ideal of "honor," really lives only to feed his own insatiable vanity engendered by his mother. With the exception of Coriolanus' simple wife Virgilia, no character in the play is sympathetically portrayed. Menenius is shallow and glibly cynical; Volumnia so swollen with false pride she would prefer her son dead rather than deaf to the hollow praise that drives him on in pursuit of glory. Coriolanus' enemy Aufidius resembles Achilles in *Troilus and Cressida* in that Aufidius would win by any foul means in order to preserve his shallow "honor," and the populace of Rome is shown to be, as in *Julius Caesar,* a pack of fickle dogs.

Coriolanus is a uniform and well-made play; there are no subplots, peripheral scenes, digressions, or comic interludes. In some respects it resembles Jonson's lackluster *Sejanus,* for it achieves a formal integrity of structure and language, but its unsavory characters and banal hero reduce its human interest to a minimum.

The standard text is the New Cambridge edition, ed. J. Dover Wilson (1960). Important criticism is by A. C. Bradley, "Coriolanus," *PBA,* (1911-12); O. J. Campbell, *Shakespeare's Satire* (1943); J. C. Maxwell, "Animal Imagery in *Coriolanus,*" *MLR,* XLII (1947); Leonard F. Dean, "Voice and Deed in *Coriolanus,*" *UR,* XXI (1955); D. A. Traversi, *Shakespeare: The Roman Plays* (1963); Kenneth Burke, "Language as Symbolic Action," *HudR,* XIX (1966); and James L. Calderwood, "*Coriolanus:* Wordless Meanings and Meaningless Words," *English Literature,* VI (1966). See also *Twentieth Century Interpretations of Coriolanus: A Collection of Critical Essays,* ed. James E. Phillips (1970).

Cornwallis, Sir William (d. 1631). See ESSAYS.

courtesy literature, or conduct books. Works setting forth standards of morality and social behavior considered appropriate or ideal to a certain class, usually the aristocracy and upper-middle class. Courtesy books have many kindred relationships in other literary types; from one perspective, for example, *The Faerie Queene,* the "general end" of which Spenser described as "to fashion a gentleman or noble person in virtuous and gentle discipline," can be read as a courtesy book comparable to a more apparent manual of polite conduct such as Castiglione's *Il Cortegiano*. According to John E. Mason, courtesy literature in general falls into four not entirely distinct categories: parental advice; polite conduct; civility (including education); and policy (statecraft and government). The following discussion concerns the first three of these types as representing the essence of courtesy literature—moral and social conduct rather than political practice or theory.

An example of the conduct book of parental advice is the influential *Basilikon Doron,* written in 1599 for Prince Henry by King James I. Limited to seven copies in the first printing, it appeared in a full edition in 1603. The author's sources include the medieval "king's mirror" (*exemplum* for monarchs) as well as John Gower's *Confessio Amantis,* Sir Thomas Elyot's *A Book Named the Governor,* and Aristotle's *Ethics* and *Politics.* A practical and personal manual of princely behavior, *Basilikon Doron* was intended solely for family reading, and includes not only philosophical discussions of what constitutes the ideal ruler and the evil tyrant but also advice regarding food, reading, sports, and church observances. The prince is advised to practice moderation in all things—to be strict in punishing witches, counterfeiters, and murderers but lenient in dealing with misdemeanants; to worship God with sincere humility but to avoid fanaticism (typified by the Puritans); to be learned in the Bible, history, law, and science, but to spurn pedantry or excessive bookishness; and to maintain a sensible balance of power among the three estates of clergy, nobility, and middle class.

There were many imitators of *Basilikon Doron,* a notable one being John Cleland's *Heropaideia, or The Institution of a Young Nobleman* (1607), which, although dedicated to James I's son, broadens the subject to include sons of the aristocracy in general, and provides an encyclopedic treatment of courtly conduct in six sections: (1) the duty of parents to their children; (2) the importance of tutors; (3) the importance of religious education; (4) the proper relationship of parents to tutors; (5) the conduct of civil conversation; and (6) the role of travel in education of the young. Although Cleland's work moves away from the category of parental advice *per se,* its affinities to the type are evident in its sustained emphasis on the responsibilities of parents and the vital importance of tutors.

Long before *Basilikon Doron,* the conduct book of parental advice was well established, and the enduring vogue is evident in the lengthy and didactic advice bestowed on the hero by his elders in John Lyly's *Euphues* (1578, 1580). It remained for the middle-class, however, to give parental advice the self-righteous and complacent tone of Polonius' speech to Laertes in *Hamlet.* A step in that direction was Nicholas Breton's A POST WITH A PACKET OF MAD LETTERS (1602; see LETTER-WRITERS), which contains several pontificating epistles of a father to his son, and, in the same year, Breton's *The Mother's Blessing,* "a little tract of moral discipline" in doggerel verse, supposedly by a mother to her courtier son, advising him on proper behavior at court, wise choice of friends, courtship of a wife, conduct at games, and worship of God. Breton's maternal philosopher is, like Polonius, more sententious than practical:

Take hold of Time, the glass is quickly run;
Trust not to Fortune, for she will deceive thee;
What ere thou art, let not the world perceive thee;
Know God, love Him, be governed by His will,
And have no doubt of good, nor fear of ill.

Breton's work was soon challenged by *The Mother's Blessing* (1616) by Dorothy Leigh, a mother of three fatherless children whose chiefly negative counsel warns her offspring against "papists," Catholic priests, "pagan customs," unchastity, and other temptations of the devil. At the other end of the moral scale is Francis Osborn's *Advice to a Son* (Part I, 1656; Part II, 1658), which is as cynical in its outlook as Machiavelli's *The Prince* or Lord Chesterfield's letters. Osborn's class consciousness, instincts for self-preservation, and total pragmatism prompt him to view morality largely in terms of strategy. "Conscience should be subordinate not only to a superlative authority," he advises, "but also our own honest, safe, and wholesome conveniences." Hence he endorses religion so long as it does not inhibit one's career, and cautions obedience to those in authority because submission is invariably profitable. Learning, he observes, can be valuable if it is related to some financially remunerative profession; in this way, modern history is more practical than ancient, and music and the other arts are simply a waste of time. Even more provocative is Part II, which is concerned chiefly with love and marriage. For the most part, Osborn concludes, love is an energy-consuming illusion and marriage, except under certain financial conditions, an unprofitable investment. (In fairness to the opposite sex, Osborn provides a postscript "To the Woman Reader" in which he gives reasons why women too ought to remain single.) In short, Osborn's urbane *Advice to a Son* is the *reductio ad absurdum* of Bacon's essays, particularly those on career and marriage, which were denounced by Blake as "good advice for Satan's worshippers." Blake's reaction would have been more appropriate with reference to Osborn's work, for of all the conduct books from Machiavelli's *Il Principe* to Dale Carnegie's *How to Win Friends and Influence People,* Osborn's is the manual *par excellence* on the slippery arts of Getting Ahead.

Another type of courtesy literature, the manual of polite conduct, became established in England by the middle of the sixteenth century. An early example is the anonymous *The Institution of a Gentleman* (1555), a treatise on the origins and nature of "true nobility" and a classification of the descending order of mankind: (1) "gentle gentle," those of both aristocratic birth and moral integrity; (2) "gentle ungentle," those of noble birth and vicious living; (3) "ungentle gentle," those of humble origin but exalted virtue; and (4) "ungentle ungentle," those cads and churls both basely born and morally destitute.

The courtesy literature on the subject of polite conduct often constitutes an extended definition of the ideal prince or courtier as a moral and social human being, and the classic among these is Baldassare Castiglione's *Il Cortegiano,* composed during the period 1508-16 and translated into English as THE COURTIER by Sir Thomas Hoby in 1561. Under the leadership of Elisabeth Gonzaga, the duke of Urbino's intellectually lively wife, Castiglione's brilliant coterie devotes four days—and four books—of eloquent conversation to the many-faceted question of what qualities are essential to the ideal courtier. By the conclusion of Book IV, which marks the dawn of the fifth day, the disputants have pursued this one question through a myriad of related topics, including education, ethics, literature, politics, psychology, and sociology. The climax of these discussions, led by the articulate and often rhapsodic Peter Bembo, is given over entirely to the subject of love. Bembo's Platonic discourse on true beauty and divine love had, in different ways, important influences on later Elizabethan poets like Sidney, Spenser, Shakespeare, and Donne.

An Italian work of lesser importance was by Stephen Guazzo, three books of which were translated as *Civil Conversation* by George Pettie in 1581, with the fourth book translated by Bartholomew Young in 1586. Guazzo's manual of polite conduct covers such practical matters as clothes, social deportment, and polite conversation as well as the usual definition of what constitutes the "ideal" aristocrat.

The only book in English to rival the popularity of Castiglione's masterpiece was Sir Thomas Elyot's *A Book Named the Governor* (1531: see GOVERNOR), a treatise devoted to the education of those who "hereafter may be deemed worthy to be governors of the public weal." That Elyot was steeped in educational and moral philosophy is probative from his translations of Plutarch's *The Education of Children* (trans. c. 1535) and Isocrates' *Ad Nicoclem,* rendered around 1534 as *The Doctrinal of Princes,* and by his evident familiarity with Aristotle's *Nichomachean Ethics,* Quintilian's *Institutio oratoria,* and several Renaissance works like Erasmus' *Institutio principis Christiani* (1516). In spite of its debts to classical and continental sources, Elyot's is a thoroughly English book in its chauvinism, xenophobia, enthusiasm for the vernacular, and delightfully idiomatic excursions into manners and morals. Although a rigorous scholar, Elyot is invariably humane, always tempering discipline with delights:

> The discretion of a tutor consisteth in temperance; that is to say, that he suffer not the child to be fatigate with continual study or learning, wherewith the delicate and tender wit may be dulled or oppressed; but that there may be therewith interlaced and mixed some pleasant learning and exercise, as playing on instruments of music, which, moderately used and without diminution of honor . . . is not to be condemned.

A book similar to Elyot's was by another humanist of the following generation, Roger ASCHAM, whose *The Schoolmaster,* originally planned as a guide for Latin tutors, was composed with many additions from 1563 to 1568 and published posthumously in 1570. Ascham had published in 1545 his *Toxophilus,* a dialogue in praise of the edifying effects of archery with the English longbow, a subject providing the occasion for numerous digressions on educational theory, English customs, and moral conduct. In *The Schoolmaster* Ascham deals not only with formal education but also with manners and morals of the young after the completion of school. In a simple, idiomatic, and forceful style that set a standard for generations of prose writers, Ascham argues for a humanistic education that will mold athletic, intellectual, and socially graceful men. His vision is formed by the ancient Greek academies, his values are thoroughly classical, and his eccentricities entirely English. In passages sparkling with wit and learning, he inveighs against travel to Italy, loafing at court in search of preferment, pedantry in all forms, and the use of legal jargon and INKHORN TERMS in writing. He praises Castiglione's *Il Cortegiano,* "which book, advisedly read and diligently followed but one year at home in England, would do a young gentleman more good, I wis, than three years' travel abroad spent in Italy."

A flood of pedagogical conduct books followed Ascham's classic, but none matches his brisk anecdotal style, learning, and intimacy. Characteristic of these limping imitations is Edmund Coote's *The English Schoolmaster* (1596), which discusses the raising of children from the teacher's perspective. Some of Coote's doggerel verse is aimed at how children should behave in school:

Your clothes unbuttoned do not use,
Let not your hose ungartered be,
Have handkerchief in readiness,
Wash hands and face, or see not me.

One of the most popular conduct books of civility was Henry Peacham's discursive but fascinating *The Complete Gentleman* (1622). As a jack-of-all-trades—having been teacher, traveler, angler, antiquary, and draftsman as well as dabbler in heraldry, science, and literary scholarship—Peacham combines ponderous esoterica with homely anecdotes, didacticism with instructions on tying trout flies or drawing heraldic designs. His readers were class-conscious country gentlemen, grown in power and number during the Tudor monarchy, who apparently liked their information on social deportment mixed with edifying, moralizing and practical instructions on everything from child psychology to foreign and domestic travel.

In the seventeenth century the most prolific writer for upper-middle-class readers was Richard Braithwait, author of *The English Gentleman* (1630), *The English Gentlewoman* (1631), and *The Turtle's Triumph* (1641), this last being on the subject of marriage and marital duties. In Braithwait's *English Gentleman* the chief interests are both professional and familial—on the public duties of the soldier, statesman, and justice of the peace, and on the private responsibilities of the husband, father, and householder. Like most advice-givers of the time, Braithwait counsels moderation—the "golden mean" in everything, including attendance at plays—and he shows a special interest in sports (the chief occupation of country gentlemen). He recommends hawking and small doses of history as appropriate pastimes for the gentleman. Modern women will grind their teeth reading his *English Gentlewoman,* which recommends for ladies very brief books of moral edification that will not stagger their minds, and stresses the virtues of humility, chastity, obedience, and industry. "Choose rather with Penelope to weave and unweave," he suggests "than to give idleness the least leave."

In these middle-class primers of civility the Justice Shallows and Squire Boobys learned the class privileges, obligations, and conduct that finally converted them into the restrained ladies and gentlemen in the novels of Jane Austen and Anthony Trollope. For matters of state policy and executive strategies there was Machiavelli's *Il Principe,* and for the abiding values of humanist education and moral philosophy the works of Castiglione, Elyot, and Ascham. Increasingly, however, the growing middle class found the profundities of the humanist scholars tedious, and consulted, instead, the encyclopedic manuals of Cleland, Peacham, and Braithwait to learn the practical niceties of dress, conversation, and deportment.

The two most distinguished studies of courtesy literature in the English Renaissance are by Ruth Kelso, *The Doctrine of the English Gentleman in the Sixteenth Century* (1929), and John E. Mason, *Gentlefolk in the Making: Studies in the History of English Courtesy Literature and Related Topics from 1531 to 1774* (1935).

Courtier, The. A translation into English of Baldassare Castiglione's *Il Cortegiano* (pr. Italy, 1528) by Sir Thomas HOBY (1561). The book grew out of Castiglione's experience at the elegant court of Urbino during the years 1505-08 and purports to be a literal account of conversations extending over four evenings in which a number of ladies and gentlemen discuss the qualities of the ideal courtier. Like Thomas Elyot's *The Governor,* it is a "courtesy book," a manual of proper aristocratic deportment. (see COURTESY LITERATURE). The leader of the coterie at Urbino, and a central figure in the dialogues, was Duchess Elisabeth Gonzaga (1471-1526), wife of Duke Guidobaldo. Other main characters who appear in the dialogues include the duchess's friend and confidante, Lady Emilia Pia, the only other woman in the group; Peter Bembo, a poet, scholar, and later cardinal; Bernardo Bibbiena, a courtier about whom little is known; Lodovico Canossa, later archbishop of Bayeaux, addressed in the book as "Count Lewis"; Federico Fregoso, later archbishop of Salerno, called "Sir Frederick"; Cesar Gonzaga, Castiglione's cousin, called "Lord Cesare"; Giuliano de Medici, son of Lorenzo the Magnificent, addressed as "Julian"; Morello da Ortona, a courtier and musician; Gasparo Pallavicino, called "Lord Gaspar"; and Francesco Maria della Rovere, Duke Guidobaldo's cousin and heir.

In the first book the circle at Urbino discuss specific activities required of the ideal courtier and decide he must be exceptionally skilled in dancing, hunting, riding, fencing, and gymnastics as well as accomplished in poetry and oratory. Moreover, in engaging in these activities he must at all times exhibit *sprezzatura,* i.e., an attitude of effortless, almost careless mastery of difficult things.

The second book emphasizes the courtier's uses of language—proper modes of address and conversation, appropriate diction in different social situations—and concludes with a long discussion of jokes by Bibbiena.

The third book centers on the courtier's lady, and what is expected of her socially, intellectually, and morally. Considerable attention is given to the subject of chastity.

The fourth and last book begins with the courtier's responsibilities in advising and guiding his prince, then turns to a lengthy discussion of Platonic love by Peter Bembo. This book became the chief inspiration for Edmund Spenser's *Four Hymns* and served as a major point of reference for many Renaissance Platonists.

The standard edition of *The Courtier* in Hoby's translation is by Walter Raleigh in the Tudor Translations (1900), which contains a lengthy and informative introduction. For valuable background, see T. F. Crane, *Italian Social Customs of the Sixteenth Century* (1920), and Ruth Kelso, *The Doctrine of the English Gentleman in the Sixteenth Century* (1929). For Castiglione's life and times, see Julia Cartwright, *Baldassare Castiglione*, 2 vols. (1902).

courtly makers. A group of poets during the reign of Henry VIII who brought the so-called new poetry to England from Italy and France. The courtly makers usually include William Cornish, Lord Vaux, George Boleyn, Sir Thomas Chaloner, Robert Cooper, Robert Fairfax, John Heywood, Sir Thomas WYATT, and Henry HOWARD, earl of Surrey. Even Henry VIII himself wrote some lively and elegant songs. Although few of these poets troubled to publish their works—since they considered themselves courtiers and statesmen rather than primarily poets—some of their pieces appeared in the first edition of Tottel's *Miscellany* in 1557.

Like Wyatt and Surrey, the most gifted of the group, the courtly makers helped to free poetry from its medieval shackles in allegory and narrative. They polished and refined native lyrics and songs, experimented with Italian and French verse forms, and opened England to the Renaissance with their paraphrases and translations of Italian and French literature.

Two important studies of the group are John Berdan, *Early Tudor Poetry, 1485-1547* (1920), and Raymond Southall. *The Courtly Makers: An Essay on the Poetry of Wyatt and His Contemporaries* (1964).

Cowley, Abraham (1618-1667). Poet. Born in London of a wealthy middle-class family, Cowley attended Westminster School and in 1636 matriculated at Trinity College, Cambridge, where he was a close friend of Richard Crashaw and William Harvey, the great medical genius and personal physician of Francis Bacon. The last of the METAPHYSICAL POETS, Cowley was also the most precocious. While still at Cambridge and only fifteen, he published *Poetical Blossoms,* a collection of competent verses reflecting his childhood enchantment with Spenser's *The Shepherd's Calendar* and *The Faerie Queene,* which he again recalled in his autobiography. At Cambridge he also wrote a pastoral drama, a Latin comedy, and a realistic comedy of manners called *The Guardian* (1642), later revised as *Cutter of Coleman Street.* Cowley's *The Mistress* (1647) is an imitation of Donne's *Songs and Sonnets.* Thus Cowley is the only metaphysical poet to imitate all three of the principal English Renaissance poets—Donne, Spenser, and Jonson.

Like Crashaw, Cowley resigned his fellowship at Cambridge in 1643. He joined the king's court at Oxford, then accompanied Queen Henrietta Maria into exile at Paris in 1644-46. He returned to England in 1654, possibly as a Royalist secret agent, was imprisoned in 1655, and released after making peace with Cromwell. Upon his release he studied medicine at Oxford, earning the M.D. in 1657. In 1656 he published his *Poems,* which contained the *Miscellanies* (Pindaric odes and long elegies on William

Harvey and Crashaw), Anacreonics, and the unfinished Biblical epic *Davideis.*

After the Restoration, Queen Henrietta Maria restored Cowley to his fellowship at Cambridge and granted him land in Barn Elms and Chertsey, to which he retired to study botany and to work on his familiar essays. With Bishop Thomas Sprat and Thomas Hobbes, he was among the founders of the Royal Society, although he never became a member. After his death Bishop Sprat wrote a laudatory biography and edited both the English and Latin poems (1668). Throughout the seventeenth century Cowley's harsh and irregular Pindaric odes, his metaphysical *The Mistress,* and his concrete, vivid essays established a lofty reputation, only to be systematically reduced by eighteenth-century neoclassic critics like Dryden, Pope, and Addison, and then totally leveled by the romantics—a critical process made inevitable by Samuel Johnson's brilliant and immensely influential attack in his essay on Cowley in *The Lives of the Poets* (1779).

Johnson chose Cowley as a target because he considered him the weakest, least defensible practitioner of *discordia concors,* false wit, and far-fetched obscurities. Johnson's acerbic comments are justified except when he confuses Donne the master with Donne's pupil, for as Douglas Bush has succinctly stated, "Donne's fever of the bone has become a case of measles" in Cowley's poetry. Nothing better illustrates this observation than a comparison of Donne's *Songs and Sonnets* with Cowley's *The Mistress,* in which the metaphysical conceit has ceased to be symptomatic of multiple perspectives and fusion of thought and feeling but, as Cowley himself defined the conceit, merely "an ornament." Characteristically, Cowley approaches Donne's poetry with scholarly thoroughness, learning each rhetorical device and trick of wit, but it all turns out like a master chef's recipe prepared in a laboratory. In Cowley's "Written in Juice of a Lemon" and "Platonic Love" Donne's ingredients are there but the savor is gone. In "The Change" Cowley achieves but a pale imitation of Donne's passionate logic:

Oh, take my heart, and by that means you'll prove
  Within, too stor'd enough of Love.
Give me but yours, I'll by that change so thrive
  That Love in all my parts shall live.
So powerful is this change, it render can
My outside Woman, and your inside Man.

Johnson accurately described the effect of Cowley's love poetry: "Cowley's mistress has no powers of seduction . . . His poetical account of the virtues of plants and colors of flowers is not perused with more sluggish frigidity. The compositions are such as might have been written for penance by a hermit, or for hire by a philosophical rhymer who had only heard of another sex."

Hence, in spite of the boldness of Cowley's metaphors, they are not informed by tension or passion, as are Donne's and Herbert's, but by a calculated effort to imitate Pindar's "harsh and uncouth" verse (according to Cowley's own statement in the preface to his 1656 edition), and his dissonance is "metaphysical" only in a rhetorical sense. Under the veneer of a mimic fury, his poems are devoid of passion, partly because the Cambridge don, botanist, and fraternal intellectual (as in his elegies to Crashaw and Harvey, and in his drinking songs) found solace in the conventional amenities of society. It is instructive in this regard to contrast Cowley's "The Extasie" with Donne's poem of the same title, or Cowley's "The Wish" with Marvell's "The Garden." Cowley's garden is not the *hortus conclus* of meditation and passionate metaphysical speculation but a cozy rural retreat. He would retire to pleasant fields, a well-cultivated garden, several excellent books, and "since Love ne'er will from me flee, / A mistress moderately fair." In "The Wish," as in Cowley's poetry as a whole, there is neither transcendence nor dynamic commitment, but merely a sensible man's careful adjustment to the existing values of his society.

Perhaps another reason for Cowley's tepid style is that he moved with his age away from the passionate visions of the Elizabethans toward the reason, restraint, and decorum of the Augustans. To quote Douglas Bush's unkind quip, he was "the enfeebled grandson of Donne and the enfeebled grandfather of Dryden." The extent to which he was a poet in transition is apparent from his unfinished *Davideis,* the first English Biblical epic before Milton's *Paradise Lost.* In dealing with a topic profoundly religious, Cowley manages to be almost totally secular. Indeed, there is nothing in the prosaic decasyllabic couplets of *Davideis* that Hobbes, with his aversion to the supernatural, or any other gentleman of the Age of Reason could not accept. (For further comment on *Davideis,* see CRITICISM, LITERARY.)

Cowley's prose works, in contrast to his poetry, are written in a simple, direct, and brisk style. His tract *The Advancement of Experimental Philosophy* (1661) shows him to be a Baconian in style as well as content, and his *Essays* is written with the familiar, easy grace that came to characterize the prose of Addison and Steele in another generation (see ESSAYS). His essay "Of Myself" is easily one of the finest of its kind, a landmark in the art of candid, graceful AUTOBIOGRAPHY. Thus the early disciple of Donne concluded his career as a forerunner of the Enlightenment in his Pindaric odes, not in his metaphysical verse, and as an imitator of Pindar he worked a great influence on Dryden and other writers in the Restoration.

The standard edition of Cowley's works is by A. R. Waller, 2 vols. (1905). The best collection of his selected poems is edited by John Sparrow, *The Mistress with Other Select Poems* (1926). There is a critical biography by A. H. Nethercot, *Cowley: The Muse's Hannibal* (1931). See also the critical analyses of the poems by George Williamson, *The Donne Tradition* (1930), and by T. S. Eliot, "A Note on Two Odes of Cowley," in *Seventeenth Century Studies Presented to Sir Herbert Grierson* (1938). For a full critical study, see R. B. Hinman, *Abraham Cowley's* World of Order (1960).

Coxcomb, The. A comedy by Francis BEAUMONT and John FLETCHER, written around 1608-10 and first printed in 1647. The plot may have been suggested by Jean Baudouin's French version (1608) of *El curioso impertinente,* a story in the first part of Cervantes' *Don Quixote.* The Maria-Antonio plot may have been influenced by the Candido subplot of Thomas Dekker's THE HONEST WHORE, Part I.

The comedy contrasts two pairs of lovers: the beautiful young Viola and her beloved Ricardo, good-hearted but headstrong; and the shrewd, vivacious Maria and her witless husband Antonio, the coxcomb of the story. Arriving home after a long journey together, Antonio and Mercury are about to go their separate ways when Antonio pesters his reluctant companion into accompanying him home. At Antonio's house Mercury meets Maria and immediately becomes infatuated with her. An honorable man, Mercury candidly informs Antonio of his passion and serves notice to the coxcomb that he must either depart the house at once or succumb to desire for Maria. The coxcomb magnanimously offers his wife to Mercury as a token of noble masculine friendship.

In the other story Viola steals from her father's house to elope with Ricardo, who has arranged to meet her at a certain street corner. An hour before the rendezvous, however, he goes to a tavern and becomes roaring drunk. When he encounters Viola on the street, he takes her for a prostitute and knocks her down. Viola wanders grief-stricken to the outskirts of town, where she is kidnaped and robbed by a brutal tinker and his trull. Viola is rescued by a country gentleman, Valerio, who proposes that she become his mistress, and when she refuses, Valerio angrily departs. Meanwhile Ricardo sobers up and shamefully recalls his mistreatment of Viola; he goes to her father's house, makes a full confession of his former plan to elope with Viola, and receives her father's promise to help him find the girl.

Antonio continues his absurd effort to exchange his wife's virtue for Mercury's friendship. The coxcomb even writes a letter, purporting to be by Mercury, in which he berates himself and extols Mercury. When Antonio delivers the letter to Maria, he appears disguised as an Irish footman, but the wily wife easily penetrates the disguise and, pretending to take him for an intruder, has him beaten and jailed. She then slyly informs Mercury that Antonio is missing and probably murdered, and asks Mercury to take her to some secluded place where she might grieve in private. The delighted Mercury takes her to his house in the country.

To Mercury's country manor comes Viola seeking employment as a milkmaid. Antonio also appears, this time disguised as a post rider bearing a letter from Antonio urging Maria to give her favors to Mercury. Only Maria knows that the post rider is really Antonio, a secret she keeps to herself. Finally, more out of determination to teach the coxcomb a lesson than amorous desire. Maria agrees to spend the night with Mercury.

In their pursuit of Viola, Ricardo and her father meet Valerio, who repents of his rude treatment of her and joins in the search. At Mercury's house Ricardo discovers Viola working as a milkmaid; he begs her forgiveness, and the lovers are united. Her father, grateful at finding her safe, bestows his blessings on the pair. Antonio's cousin arrives with a writ for the arrest of Maria and Mercury for the murder of the missing Antonio, who saves them from a hanging judge by throwing off his disguise. Feigning joyous surprise at this timely arrival of her "savior," Maria gratefully embraces her foolish husband, who now expresses a new appreciation of his spouse. As for Mercury, the night with Maria has cured him of his lust, and he is secretly relieved to see husband and wife reconciled. At the conclusion of the play the main characters happily depart to enjoy a banquet prepared by Mercury.

The Coxcomb is not one of Beaumont and Fletcher's best comedies. The two plots are only loosely related, and no meaningful idea emerges from a contrast of the two pairs of lovers. The comedy has several scenes of excellent farce, especially those in which Antonio tries to deceive his all-knowing wife, but Maria's artful stratagems are never very clear, and Antonio's strange monomania is never convincing and only rarely humorous. Mercury's mean contempt for the coxcomb and lust for Maria are morally abrasive rather than genuinely funny. The love story of Viola and Ricardo is ponderously sentimental in spite of the heroine's occasional flashes of vivacity.

The Coxcomb is edited by Irby B. Cauthen, Jr., in *The Dramatic Works in the Beaumont and Fletcher Canon,* ed. Fredson Bowers, 2 vols. (1966, 1970), I. For criticism, see C. M. Gayley, *Beaumont, the Dramatist* (1914); W. W. Appleton, *Beaumont and Fletcher: A Critical Study* (1956), and Ian Fletcher, *Beaumont and Fletcher* (1967).

Cranmer, Thomas (1489-1556). Archbishop of Canterbury and Marian Martyr; See BOOK OF COMMON PRAYER.

Crashaw, Richard (1612?-1649). Poet. Crashaw was born in London of devout Anglican parents who, although not Puritans, were exceptionally strict in their religious observances. Crashaw received his early education at Charterhouse (1629-31), where he began his apprenticeship in poetry by translating Greek and Latin verses, then proceeded to Pembroke College, Cambridge, graduating B. A. in 1634. The college was then dominated by the High Church views of Archbishop William Laud. In 1635 Crashaw was made a fellow of Peterhouse, a center for the most Laudian of Cambridge intellectuals, and here he devoted several years to a study of baroque art and music as well as to continental devotional literature. He became especially interested in the employment of ornate art and music to the liturgy, a practice then in general disrepute because of the Puritan influence. Crashaw also participated in devotions with the ascetic Anglican community at Little Gidding, established by George Herbert's friend Nicholas Ferrar. About this time appeared Crashaw's first collection of poems, *Epigrammatum sacrorum liber* (1634), some of which were revisions of Latin epigrams written as early as the Charterhouse period. In 1639 Crashaw was ordained in the Anglican Church.

By 1643 it was no longer possible for a clergyman of Crashaw's High Church beliefs to hold a fellowship at Cambridge. After his resignation he traveled to Holland, a country he loathed for its Protestant austerity; he also may have spent some part of the same year, 1644, at the king's camp at Oxford. During the period 1645-46 he was in Paris with his former classmate at Cambridge, Abraham Cowley, and Queen Henrietta Maria and the countess of Denbigh. His conversion to Roman Catholicism in 1645 gave occasion for one of his best poems, "To the Noblest and Best of Ladies, the Countess of Denbigh," in which he urged his patroness to follow his example:

> Yield then, O yield, that love may win
> The fort at last, and let life in.
> Yield quickly, lest perhaps you prove
> Death's prey, before the prize of love.
> This Fort of your fair self, if't be not won,
> He is repuls'd indeed, but you're undone.

With a letter of introduction from the Queen, Crashaw journeyed to Rome, where he met with frustrating delays in his petitioning for some ecclesiastical office. Finally Cardinal Pallotta assigned him to a post at Loretto, where he died of fever the same year. His *Steps to the Temple,* containing most of his mature work, was published in 1646 and again in an enlarged edition in 1648. His other major collection of poems, *Carmen Deo Nostro,* was printed in Paris in 1652.

George HERBERT was one of Crashaw's leading masters, with John Donne not far behind (see METAPHYSICAL POETS); but Crashaw's febrile and humid metaphors, florid superlatives, and ecstatic freedom from intellectual discipline owe far less to the English metaphysical poets than to the lavish sensuousness of the Italian poet Giovanni Battista Marino, to the continental EMBLEM BOOKS, and to the spiritual exercises prescribed by Ignatius Loyola for the Jesuits. Marino's influence is joyously indulged in *The Suspicion of Herod* (wr.c.1637), Crashaw's translation from Book I of Marino's *La strage degli innocenti* (1633), in which he faithfully reproduces the Italian's fulsome hailstorms of blood and gore. Marino's penchant for rich metaphors also has a share in Crashaw's "The Weeper" (c. 1634), a "rosary poem" with the notorious conceit that traces Mary Magdalene's tears "upwards" to heaven, where they fall into "milky rivers" and rise to the surface there like "cream." Such strange ethereal chemistry leads to Crashaw's still stranger vignette:

Every morn from hence
A brisk Cherub something sips
Whose sacred influence
Adds sweetness to his sweetest lips.
Then to his music. And his song
Tastes of this breakfast all day long.

To the ornate and hyperbolic diction of Marino, Crashaw brings a terse, epigrammatic syntax learned from the Latin poets, and combines with these a metaphysical stress on paradoxes. In Crashaw's poetry, unlike Donne's or Herbert's, paradoxes are hung on poems like tinsel on Christmas trees. Thus the chorus celebrates the Christ child in "The Holy Nativity":

Welcome, all WONDERS in one sight!
Eternity shut in a span.
Summer in Winter. Day in Night.
Heaven in earth and GOD in MAN.
Great little one! whose all-embracing birth
Lifts earth to heaven, stoops heav'n to earth.

A poem like "To the Name Above Every Name, the Name of Jesus" from *Carmen Deo Nostro,* reflects the combined influence of emblem books and Spanish and French mysticism. Nothing could be more alien to English sensibilities than Crashaw's turtledoves, seraphim, "gorgeous nests," "beds of spices," "balmy showers," "ruby windows," and "bosoms big with love." It is not such incongruities as Crashaw's equating Mary Magdalene's tears with "portable and compendious oceans" that account for this alienation—other English metaphysical poets use almost equally incongruous metaphors without becoming deracinated. It is his verbal intoxication and the single-minded ecstasy of his metaphors that cast him outside the English vernacular and make his lines read as if they were being strained through the foreign sensibilities of Marino, the continental emblemists, St. Ignatius Loyola, and the Spanish mystics. The result is, inevitably, an impression of cloying overripeness. His point of reference is in the Counter Reformation movement and its baroque style, wherein art contrives to beguile the five senses so to perceive the infinite by way of the finite—the spiritual through the erotic, the abstract by way of the concrete, the infinite via the temporal—but this self-consciously irrational synthesis is totally foreign to the English temperament. The spongy lines of Crashaw's "The Weeper" measures the passage of time by the evaporation of Mary Magdalene's tears:

So do perfumes expire.
So sigh-tormented sweets, oppressed
With proud, unpitying fire.
Such tears the suff'ring rose that's vexed
With ungentle flames does shed,
Sweating in a too warm bed.

The catachreses, eccentric typography, and violations of sense in Crashaw's poetry are motivated by an assumption that mystical experience is ineffable, that language itself must explode under the pressure of visions. Indeed, Crashaw's poetry serves as a reminder that although mysticism may be portrayed artistically, as in Bernini's sculpture *The Ecstasy of St. Teresa* or in the gaunt countenances of El Greco's figures (baroque works of art, which Crashaw's poetry is always striving to effect), the mystical experience itself, from the inside, baffles any effective efforts at verbal communication. Crashaw's failure to realize the limits of language separates him from other metaphysical poets such as Donne, Marvell, Herbert, and even the most mystically inclined of Donne's followers, Henry Vaughan.

The standard edition is *Poems, English, Latin, and Greek,* ed. L. C. Martin (1927; 2d ed. 1957). *The Complete Poetry* was edited by George W. Williams (1970). For criticism, see T. S. Eliot, *For Lancelot Andrewes* (1928); Ruth Wallerstein, *Richard Crashaw: A Study in Style and Poetic Development* (1935);

Austin Warren, *Richard Crashaw: A Study of Baroque Sensibility* (1957); Mario Praz, *The Flaming Heart* (1958); and Louis L. Martz, *The Wit of Love: Donne, Carew, Crashaw, Marvell* (1969). For other critical studies, see Theodore Spencer and Mark Van Doren, *Studies in Metaphysical Poetry* (1939), which has been added to by "Richard Crashaw and Thomas Traherne: A Bibliography, 1938-1966," ed. Edward E. Samaha, Jr., *SCN,* XXVII (1969).

criticism, literary. Elizabethan and Stuart criticism is, for the most part, sparse and fragmentary, with little awareness of the richness of English literature or concern for concrete analysis of particular works. The greatest critical achievement of the period, Sir Philip Sidney's *An Apology for Poetry* (1595, also called *The Defense of Poesy*) was not only the first literary essay in English but also the last of its kind until John Dryden's *Essay of Dramatic Poesy* in 1668. The interim of almost a century between Sidney's work and Dryden's was one of tentative formulations and uncertain theorizing in preparation for the greater age of criticism in the eighteenth century.

Joel E. Spingarn, the chief authority on English Renaissance criticism, views sixteenth- and seventeenth-century criticism as developing in five stages: (1) purely rhetorical study; (2) metrical studies and classifications; (3) philosophical and apologetic criticism, much of it reflecting tensions between literature and Puritanism; (4) formalist invocation of general principles and "rules"; and (5) philosophical reactions to the French influence, especially during the 1650s and 1660s. As Spingarn notes, only the last of these developments is characterized by genuine originality, yet such critics as Sidney and Jonson, however eclectic, express their views with great insight and vitality.

The earliest stage of English Renaissance criticism, the purely rhetorical, is represented by Leonard Cox's *The Art or Craft of Rhetoric,* written around 1524, and Richard Sherry's *A Treatise of Schemes and Tropes* (1550). The former is largely derived from a rhetoric by the German humanist Melanchthon (1497-1560), and both works deal mainly with classical tropes and locutions rather than critical theory or belles-lettres, and treat poetry in the Horatian context of oratory. The first popular work of this type was Thomas Wilson's *Art of Rhetoric* (1553), which went through no fewer than eight editions by 1585. Although he adhered closely to all the pedagogical commonplaces of Cicero and Quintilian (the commanders of Renaissance rhetoricians), Wilson aimed at something more broadly appealing than an academic textbook and interlarded his formal principles of eloquence with witty anecdotes, critical *obiter dicta,* sample speeches and letters, and unabashed Protestant propaganda. Like Roger Ascham, Wilson was a student of the humanist Sir John Cheke, and like them he advocated an apt, clear, and simple English style. Like them, too, he inveighed against INKHORN TERMS, words grotesquely combining English with other languages, To illustrate "inkhorn terms", Wilson cited a letter, supposedly written by a Lincolnshire man, that would have done credit to Holofernes in *Love's Labour's Lost:*

> Pondering, expanding, and revoluting with myself your ingent affability and ingenious capacity for mundane affairs, I cannot but celebrate and extol your magnifical dexterity above all other. For how could you have adopted such illustrate prerogative and dominical superiority if the fecundity of your ingeny had not been so fertile and wonderful pregnant?

Wilson's *Art of Rhetoric,* divided into three books, follows the methods and terminology of Quintilian. Book I is devoted to basic definitions in rhetoric and to the proper training of the orator; Book II analyzes the different parts of an oration, such as entrance, narration, digression, peroration, etc.; and Book III, much of which is derived from Cicero, emphasizes, with many examples, the oratorical elements of elocution, memory, and expression. More than any English writer of the sixteenth century, Wilson was responsible for the continuous Elizabethan enthusiasm for classical rhetoric, and his book was followed by almost equally popular treatises such as Henry Peacham's *The Garden of Eloquence* (1577); Abraham Fraunce's *Arcadian Rhetoric* (1584); and Charles Butler's *The English Grammar* (1634).

The earliest critical treatise on prosody in English begins the second stage, a concern for meter and verse classifications. George

Gascoigne's *Certain Notes of Instruction* (1575) a ten-page pamphlet taken from Ronsard's *Abrégé de l'art poëtique français* (1565), cites sixteen rather whimsical points "in making of a delectable poem," many of which are illustrated from Chaucer. Gascoigne discusses caesura, rhyme royal, Latin prosody, and such larger matters as inkhorn terms and poetic license. His argument on behalf of using monosyllables is characteristically idiosyncratic:

> First, the most ancient English words are of one syllable, so that the more monosyllables that you use the truer Englishman you shall seem and the less you shall smell of the inkhorn.

William Webbe's *Discourse of English Poetry* (1586) is as discursive as Gascoigne's treatise, but far more pointed and comprehensive. Webbe was among the first critics to give a brief survey or "roll call," of English poets, beginning with "the first of our English poets that I have heard of," John Gower, and proceeding to Chaucer, John Lydgate, the author of *Piers Plowman,* John Skelton ("a pleasant, conceited fellow"), Gascoigne, the earl of Surrey, Thomas Tusser, Thomas Churchyard, John Heywood, and many others. Webbe reserves special praise for "the rightest English poet that ever I read," Spenser, for his *Shepherd's Calendar.* Although little is known about Webbe's life, he seems to have been conversant with some of the literary issues of the Harvey-Sidney-Spenser circle, for he takes Harvey's side by recommending the use of classical meters in English poetry, and to illustrate his argument he converts some of Spenser's April eclogues in *The Shepherd's Calendar* into wretched sapphics and renders two Vergilian eclogues into hexameters.

This futile campaign to adopt Latin quantitative prosody, chiefly hexameters, to English poetry in order to "discipline" the restive native accent seems to have originated with a suggestion in Ascham's *The Schoolmaster.* Richard Stanyhurst had translated the first four books of the *Aeneid* in hexameters (see TRANSLATIONS), and the cause for quantitative meter was earnestly pressed on a skeptical Spenser by Gabriel Harvey in *Three Proper and Witty Familiar Letters* and *Two Other Very Commendable Letters* (both 1580). In these "long, large, lavish, luxurious, laxative letters" (Harvey's words)—two by Spenser and three by Harvey—the two writers are found at their worst, Spenser glib and obviously aglow after his triumph with *The Shepherd's Calendar* the year before, and Harvey, the Cambridge don, majestically pronouncing on "proper" trochees and "licentious" iambics, all punctuated by self-congratulatory digressions about "certain great and serious affairs." As letters, these are as stilted and pompous as Pope's carefully edited self-revelations; as criticism, they fully warrant the virulent contempt meted out by Thomas Nashe in *Strange News* (1592): "Immortal Spenser, no frailty hath thy fame but the deputation of this idiot's friendship!"

To be classified with this second stage of criticism only because it treats mainly of the technicalities of verse is the most comprehensive and, in some ways, the finest Elizabethan critical study after Sidney, George Puttenham's *Art of English Poesy* (1589). In three books of seventy-four brief chapters, Puttenham analyzes the various literary genres such as tragedy, epic, comedy, and pastoral (Book I), classifies the prosodic forms currently in use by English poets (Book II), and explores the rhetorical devices and ornaments of classical, continental, and English verse (Book III). Puttenham follows the Italian critic Julius Caesar Scaliger (1484-1558) and Sidney in his conception of the poet as the divine "maker" who creates an ideal world out of disorder and imperfection: the poet's themes should be toward the glorification of God and edification of men—to praise of virtue and condemnation of vice. In his "roll call" of the English poets, Puttenham passes rapid judgment on fifty or more writers after Chaucer. This method of reviewing quickly with well-placed adjectives served in the sixteenth century as a principal technique for evaluating contemporaries:

> For ditty and amorous ode I find Sir Walter Raleigh's vein most lofty, insolent and passionate. Master Edward Dyer for elegy most sweet, solemn, and of high conceit. Gascoigne for the good meter and for a plentiful vein. Phaer and Golding for a learned and well-corrected verse...

Philosophical and apologetic criticism begins with the greatest literary essay of the sixteenth century, Sidney's *An Apology for Po-*

etry, written in 1581-83. Sidney's essay may have been occasioned by Stephen Gosson's pamphlet *The School of Abuse* (1579), a Puritan diatribe against stage plays that Gosson had the temerity to dedicate to Sidney, "and was for his labor scorned," according to Spenser in a letter to Harvey. Gosson was answered in a pamphlet by Thomas Lodge, *Reply to Stephen Gosson Touching Plays,* and also in the preface to Lodge's *Alarum Against Usurers* (1584), both of which are restrained and temperate pleas, not for freedom of artistic expression, but for the proper employment of literature for man's moral instruction. "I like not of an angry Augustus which will banish Ovid for envy," Lodge states. "I love a wise senator which in wisdom will correct him and with advice burn his follies."

Neither Lodge's pamphlet nor Sidney's essay stemmed the moral objections to literature, and especially to stage plays, and Puritan attacks increased in ferocity in the seventeenth century. Of the hundreds of pamphlets concerned with this controversy, two represent the extremes of sublime and absurd. Perhaps the most learned, incisive, and comprehensive defense of the theater against the Puritans is Thomas Heywood's *Apology for Actors* (1622), which stresses the educational values of drama. Himself a scholar, playwright, and actor, Heywood was ideally qualified to discuss elocution, language, and audience response, and his *Apology,* significantly dedicated to both the patron and actors of his own company, fairly glows with sincere love of the theater. In contrast is one of the most absurd Puritan attacks on the stage, William Prynne's *Histrio-mastix* (1632), an enormous tome that traces all the evils of the theater from ancient Roman times to his own day. A pedantic, bitter and garrulous Puritan, Prynne despised all forms of drama because he instinctively associated plays and masques with the "papist" antics of Queen Henrietta Maria's coterie at court.

One slip of the pen out of the more than a thousand pages of *Histrio-mastix* almost cost Prynne his life. Unknown to Prynne, a week before the publication of his book the queen had performed in a masque at court, and Prynne's enemies were quick to seize on his unguarded statement that any woman who acted on the stage was a whore. For this indiscretion Prynne had his nose split, was deprived of his living, harshly fined, and thrown in the stocks. Prynne's Puritan sympathizers made a political event of his punishment, following him to the stocks with hymns and prayers, and a week later the queen appeared again in an even more lavish masque in defiance of her outraged critics.

By the 1630's the Puritan attack on literature had grown from moral revulsion to explosive rebellion. Nevertheless, it would be erroneous to assume that all Puritans objected to secular literature. The word "Puritan" (and "precision") was employed from the end of the sixteenth century to the middle of the seventeenth as a pejorative term describing any Protestant opposing Anglican episcopacy; hence "Puritans" represented a variety of people with very different social attitudes and temperaments (see PURITANISM), and no doubt Puritans such as Milton and Marvell would have considered William Prynne's diatribe as absurd as Sidney and Spenser (both of whom had some "Puritan" leanings) found Stephen Gosson's *School of Abuse*. Puritans of the morally austere, stiff-necked variety were lampooned by Nashe, Jonson, and Beaumont and Fletcher, but these Puritans made up a comparatively small minority. Still, they held important municipal offices, and dramatists had good cause to fear them. Puritans were among the most acrimonious of the London aldermen, magistrates, and leading merchants who wished to close the theaters because they considered them a public nuisance. The theaters were habituated by pickpockets, prostitutes, and "common rogues"—and the conservative authorities tended to include actors and playwrights in this last class. Moreover, the city fathers, even if they were not Puritans, objected to playhouses in general because they instinctively disliked the idea of large gatherings except at church services or traditional civic ceremonies. Then, too, the theaters held afternoon performances that lured apprentices from their workbenches. Although most of these city fathers happened to be anti-episcopal and reformist in their religious views, their hostility to the drama was mainly practical.

During the reign of Charles I, however, this situation altered significantly. The popular theaters declined steadily in the early 1630's as the Caroline courtiers took over the drama, and acting companies began to perform almost exclusively at Whitehall, Hampton Court, and the new and fashionable Blackfriars (see

CAROLINE DRAMA). As Queen Henrietta Maria and her aristocratic coterie, dominated by Roman Catholics, became increasingly conspicuous as indulgent patrons of the drama, plays began to assume political and religious connotations for the angry Puritan opponents of Archbishop William Laud and his Anglican bishops. As the research of William Haller and G. F. Sensabaugh has shown, Puritans like William Prynne came to identify plays and masques as the arrogant fripperies of an immoral "papist" clique. Hence Prynne's attack against plays in the 1630's has quite a different context from Stephen Gosson's during the reign of Queen Elizabeth. Gosson seems to have been writing while in the throes of the personal religious conversion that caused him to repudiate all his earlier vanities; Prynne's attack, however furtively addressed, was aimed at a Roman Catholic queen famous for her enthusiasm for plays and at her bevy of cavalier dramatists and lady masquers.

It is doubtful that Sidney wrote his *Apology for Poetry* in direct response to the Puritan objections to literature. Although Gosson's *School of Abuse* may have prompted its completion, Sidney's thoughtful and polished essay is concerned with universal aesthetic questions transcending any ephemeral issues, and the work was probably in preparation long before Gosson's pamphlet appeared. Spenser had written a literary essay, now lost, called *The English Poet,* and Sidney's may have originated from his discussions about literature with Spenser, Harvey, Lodge, and others in the so-called AREOPAGUS. Hardly an occasional work, Sidney's essay derives from most of the principal sources of Renaissance literary criticism: Plato's *Ion, Symposium, Phaedrus, Sophist, Phaedo,* and *Republic;* Aristotle's *Poetics, Ethics,* and *Rhetoric;* Cicero's epistles and orations; Horace's *Ars poetica;* the Italian critics Castelvetro and Minturno; and especially Julius Caesar Scaliger, from whose *Poetics* Sidney appropriates whole sections. In defending poetry against the familiar charge that Plato banished poets from his Republic, Sidney adopts the strategy of enlisting Plato's own metaphysics and Aristotle's aesthetics to show that poetry is an imitation, or *mimesis,* not of the world as it is but as it ought to be:

> Nature never set forth the earth in so rich tapestry as divers poets have done; neither with so pleasant rivers, fruitful trees, sweet-smelling flowers, nor whatsoever else may make the too-much-loved earth more lively; her world is brazen, the poets only deliver a golden.

Like Milton's *Areopagitica,* Sidney's essay is organized in the form of a classical oration divided into seven parts: (1) the *exordium,* or entrance—here in form of an anecdote praising the horsemanship of the Italian Pugliano; (2) the *narratio*— a description of how poetry served a constructive moral influence during ancient Greek and Roman times; (3) the *propositio*, or statement of thesis—here Sidney defines poetry as *mimesis,* an "imitation, a speaking picture" calculated to delight and instruct, to idealize reality in order to deliver forth an ideal truth and beauty; (4) the *partitio,* or division—Sidney describes the distinctions among the three types of poetry; (5) the *confirmatio,* or proof—he argues that poetry teaches virtue more effectively than either history or philosophy; (6) the *reprehensio,* or refutation—he presents the four principal objections to poetry (it lies, wastes time, corrupts morals, invites Plato's condemnation) with his answer to each of these; and (7) the *peroratio,* or conclusion—Sidney pays tribute to the powers of verse in bestowing immortality.

Since the *peroratio* was traditionally preceded by a digression, Sidney makes it the occasion for his "roll call" of English poets, sifting out for special praise Chaucer, the *Mirror for Magistrates,* the earl of Surrey, and Spenser's *Shepherd's Calendar.* Adopting Lodovico Castelvetro's emendation of Aristotle's *Poetics* as a valid criterion of dramatic order, he chastises Sackville and Norton for violating the unities of time, place, and action in *Gorboduc,* "notwithstanding as it is full of stately speeches and well-sounding phrases, climbing to the height of Seneca his style." Sidney looks to these "rules" and the example of classical dramatists for the means to reform the "excesses" of the English stage—the disregard for the three unities, the mingling of tragedy and comedy, the portrayal of actions better reported by a *nuntius.* Although thoroughly classical, he nevertheless expresses a wish that English love poetry were more convincing of its passion, and in a famous passage he confesses to having been touched deeply by the simplest romantic ballads:

> Certainly, I must confess mine own barbarousness; I never heard the old song of Percy and Douglas that I found not my heart moved more than with a trumpet; and yet it is sung by some blind crowder, with no rougher voice than rude style...

Sidney was the first English critic to invoke the three unities, falsely attributed to Aristotle by Castelvetro in Italy in 1570 and introduced into France by Jean de la Taille in 1572. Less doctrinaire but equally influential in establishing these "rules" as synonymous with classicism was Ben Jonson, whose prefaces, prologues, dedicatory poems, and commonplace book TIMBER (1640) make up a coherent body of neoclassic criticism. From the popular stage, where his ideas could have maximum ventilation, he expounded his conviction that classical order and restraint were needed to curb the romantic extravagances of his age. In the prologue to *Volpone,* for example, he held up his own play as exemplary of such order:

> As best critics have designed,
> The laws of time, place, persons he observeth,
> From no needful rule he swerveth.

In *Timber* Jonson's classicism is less dogmatic than in his public statements, and although scholars have traced about four-fifths of *Timber* to Horace, Cicero, Quintilian, Seneca, Petronius, Erasmus, Justus Lipsius, Scaliger, and other sources, it is nevertheless impressive for its consistency and wholeness. In Jonson's discussion of writing the recurring words are "diligence," "exercise," and "industry" ("he who casts to write a living line must sweat," he wrote elsewhere); and yet, he states repeatedly, energy, revision, and learning, however necessary, can never substitute for the *sine qua non* of imagination and wit. Though Aristotle and Horace serve as reliable guides, he observes, they must never become a writer's "commanders." Hence Jonson is less rigidly classical than Sidney, more open to alternatives, more flexible and independent of authority.

Following Jonson, English Renaissance criticism became increasingly philosophical, combining attention to formalist "rules" with stress on general aesthetic principles. The metrical, apologetic, and "roll call" criticism, however, continued to flourish. A notable example of apologetic criticism in the age of Jonson is Sir John Harington's preface to his translation of *Orlando Furioso* (1592). Assuming that Sidney and Puttenham have conclusively settled the problem of defining genres, Harington proceeds to discuss literature as "a veil of fables" in allegorical form, an arcane and edifying tonic in the medieval sense of being a sugared moral pill. Thus Harington's brief essay represents a minor landmark in being the first to assume an established English tradition of literary criticism.

The encyclopedic "roll call" is represented again by Francis Meres's *Palladis Tamia* (1598), a commonplace book making no contribution whatever to criticism but now highly valued for its two paragraphs on the plays and poems of "mellifluous and honey-tongued Shakespeare" in a section entitled "A Comparative Discourse of Our English Poets with the Greek, Latin, and Italian Poets." Although Meres's work purports to be a collection of original apothegms on religion, ethics, and the arts, Don Cameron Allen has shown it to be little more than a plagiarized compendium lifted from several standard reference books known to every Elizabethan undergraduate and from passages in works by Ascham, Sidney, Webbe, and Puttenham (*Francis Meres's Treatise "Poetrie": A Critical Edition* [1933]). A "roll call" more original but little more heuristic as criticism is Sir John Suckling's "Session of the Poets" in his *Fragmenta Aurea* (1646), a verse satire twitting Suckling's contemporaries in the manner of Byron's later *English Bards and Scotch Reviewers*.

The earlier argument on behalf of adopting classical meters to English, together with the denigration of rhyme as a "barbarous invention," carried on by Harvey and the Areopagus group, was revived in Thomas Campion's *Observations in the Art of English Poesy* (wr.1591, pr. 1602) and Samuel Daniel's rejoinder, *A Defense of Rhyme* (1603). Against the use of sonnets, ottava rima, and other rhyming verse forms from Italy, Campion argues in favor of classical elegiacs, hexameters, and sapphics. Although he wisely dismisses a consistent use of dactyls as "against the nature of our language," he nevertheless recommends eight classical meters as in "consent with the nature of our English syllables." As for rhyme, he rejects it as "superfluous" and "absurd." Perhaps the most arresting aspect of Campion's essay is the extent to which pedantry drives him to contradict his own poetry and fine musician's ear.

Samuel Daniel's refutation of Campion rests on "custom that is before all law, nature that is above all art," and in a single passage he lays to rest the whole anachronistic question of classical meters:

> For as Greek and Latin verse consists of the number and quantity of syllables, so doth the English verse of measure and accent. And though it doth not strictly observe long and short syllables, yet it most religiously respects the accent; and as the short and the long make number, so the acute and grave accent yield harmony.

Daniel systematically refutes Campion's proposed eight classical meters, insists on the independence of the native prosody ("all our understandings are not to be built by the square of Greece and Italy"), and defends rhyme used in moderation as "a most excellent instrument to serve us."

The sixteenth-century preoccupation with rules, classical precepts, grammar, and meter—ever threatening to become more narrow and academic in spite of the larger issues raised by Sidney and Jonson—ends with the philosophical criticism of Bacon's *Advancement of Learning* (1605), the first original effort in English to establish the relationship of literature to other forms of learning (notwithstanding Sidney's eclectic passages on the subject). Bacon finds that literature, history, and philosophy correspond, respectively, to the three mental faculties of imagination, memory, and reason. Whereas philosophy (by which Bacon intends a word similar to the modern term "science") "doth buckle and bow the mind unto the nature of things," literature is "feigned imagination," a kind of coherent, articulate fantasy motivated by the writer's dissatisfaction with the real world. Like Freud, therefore, Bacon saw art in terms of psychological compensation, and his classification of literature as an irrational activity—allying it to alchemy and astrology rather than to philosophy—must be understood in the context of Bacon's effort to dislodge science from its medieval fixation with metaphors, "vain words," and "correspondences." Nevertheless, his hard-headed separation of poetry and reason inevitably sapped the spiritual vigor of literature and the other arts and helped to strip them of the divine sanctions claimed by earlier Renaissance critics. A less modern expression of Bacon's complex sensibilities is apparent in his *De sapientia veterum* (1609), translated by Sir Arthur Gorges as *The Wisdom of the Ancients* (1619), in which Bacon employs the Augustinian and medieval method of allegorical interpretation to explain how many of his own political and scientific ideas are parabolically revealed in thirty myths, such as those of Prometheus, Oedipus. Cassandra, and Typhon.

During the reign of Charles I and the Interregnum the stringent neoclassicism of the French Boileau, Corneille, and Racine introduced an unprecedented regard for rationalism, restraint, and curtailment of free imagination. Dryden's *Essay of Dramatic Poesy* (1668) is the progeny of this new emphasis on discipline and authority, but a much earlier manifestation of the new rationalism appears in the lengthy prefatory essays in 1650 by Sir William Davenant and Thomas Hobbes to Davenant's heroic poem *Gondibert* (1651). Davenant's solemn analysis of meters, genres, and literary creativity bears the same relationship to Sidney's inspired criticism as does his *Gondibert* to *The Faerie Queene* or *Paradise Lost;* it is all like a once richly colorful tapestry hanging faded and bleakly gray on a museum wall. In spite of his occasional rhapsodies on poetic inspiration and imagination, Davenant treats poetry as a form of social expression, a product of class values, and a moral surrogate for the declining power of orthodox religion. The imagination, seen by Renaissance critics as a divine mystery, Davenant discusses as "wit," a discriminating adjunct of critical reason. Thus, for its emphasis on reason, its ambivalence about free imaginative expression, and its conception of art as manifold social behaviorism, Davenant's preface moves directly towards the aesthetics of the Augustan age.

Hobbes's reply to Davenant is equally rationalistic, discussing the creative process in terms of Hobbes's own mechanistic psychology. The faculty of wit discerns unity in apparent dissimilarity; judgment apprehends dissimilarity in apparent unity. Hobbes defines the function of creativity quantitatively and mechanistically: "Time and education beget experience; experience begets memory; memory begets judgment and fancy; judgment begets the strength and structure, and fancy begets the ornaments of a poem." As for the relative significance of various poetic genres—a hierarchy dear to Sidney and Puttenham—Hobbes explains them as coordinate manifestations of "manners of men," heroic poetry and epics reflecting the cultural values and experience of the court, comedy and satire of the city, and pastoral verse of the country. Characteristically, he makes no allowance for the lyric, which he defines as an amorphous fragment, and he dismisses any use of the supernatural as patently immature.

The rational, common sense values of Bacon, Davenant, and Hobbes are at once apparent in Abraham Cowley's preface to his heroic poem in couplets, *Davideis* (1656), and in the poem itself, praised by Cowley's contemporaries as being the first neoclassic epic in English. Cowley's stated preference for Biblical history over mythological "fables and fancies" may represent a timid concession to the Puritans; on the other hand, *Davideis* conforms in all particulars to the rational strictures of Hobbes in its studious imitation of Vergil, its scholarly notes, its confinement to a reality the senses can grasp, its scrupulous credibility and conformity to rational taste.

In retrospect, the achievements of Elizabethan and Stuart criticism are difficult to assess. Certainly the early humanist scholars and grammarians like Ascham succeeded in establishing the vernacular, and later critics such as Sidney and Puttenham liberated criticism from its preoccupation with oratory, rhetoric, and grammar. It is possible but by no means certain that classical concepts of form, converted into specific "rules" by French and Italian critics, had some beneficial effect on curtailing libertine romantic impulses in poetry and drama. Perhaps the cardinal achievement of Renaissance criticism, with its discursive treatment of everything from tropes to poetic inspiration and poetic license, was planting seeds that came to bloom in the neoclassic and romantic periods that followed.

Important sixteenth-century English criticism is in *Elizabethan Critical Essays,* ed. G. G. Smith, 2 vols. (1904); later works are in *Critical Essays of the Seventeenth Century,* ed. Joel E. Spingarn, 2 vols. (1908). There are three essential studies: Joel E. Spingarn, *A History of Literary Criticism in the Renaissance* (1899); C. S. Baldwin, *Renaissance Literary Theory and Practice* (1939); and Vernon Hall, *Renaissance Literary Criticism: A Study of Its Social Content* (1945).

Crowley, Robert (1518?-1588). Puritan printer, satirist. See SATIRE.

Cymbeline. A play by William SHAKESPEARE, written in 1609-10 and first printed in the 1623 Folio. As sources Shakespeare consulted Holinshed's *Chronicles* (1587 ed.), "The Complaint of Guiderius" in Thomas Blenerhasset's *The Second Part of the Mirror for Magistrates* (1578), and "The Tragedy of Guiderius" by John Higgins in a later edition (1587) of the same collection. For the wager plot Shakespeare read the ninth novel of the second day in Boccaccio's *Decameron.* The source often suggested for the Belarius story is a romantic play of unknown authorship called *The Rare Triumphs of Love and Fortune* (1589).

Imogen, daughter of the British king Cymbeline, has clandestinely married Posthumus Leonatus. Her stepmother, who had planned a union between Imogen and her unworthy son Cloten, treacherously misrepresents the marriage to the king, who banishes Posthumus. In Rome, Posthumus boasts of his wife's virtue to Iachimo, a cynic who wagers a fortune that he can seduce Imogen. The indignant Posthumus accepts the challenge, wagering a diamond ring given to him by Imogen. When he comes to Cymbeline's court, Imogen spurns Iachimo, but he returns to Rome with contrived evidence of her infidelity. Posthumus surrenders the ring and vows revenge. He writes to Imogen asking her to meet him in Wales, then orders his servant Pisanio to kill Imogen during the journey. Convinced of Imogen's innocence, Pisanio shows her Posthumus' letter and, as a means of getting her to Rome to confront Posthumus, persuades her to pose as a lad and seek a place in the service of the Roman general Caius Lucius. Lucius is returning angrily to Rome after failing to exact tribute from Cymbeline.

As the boy Fidele, Imogen sets out to find the general; lost in the mountains of Wales, she is befriended by old Morgan and two youths who live with him in a cave. Morgan is really Belarius, a lord unjustly exiled years ago by Cymbeline; the youths are actually Imogen's brothers Guiderius and Arviragus, abducted by Belarius as infants and reared as his own sons. Cloten forces information from Pisanio and sets out intending to ravish Imogen and kill Posthumus; at the cave, however, Guiderius kills Cloten.

Caius Lucius, leading an army of invasion, happens upon the disguised Imogen and makes her his page. The Romans are defeated in battle, and Morgan and the two youths are presented to Cymbeline as heroes of the fight. Roman prisoners are brought before the king; they include Iachimo, the entourage of Caius Lucius, and Posthumus. Posthumus had come to England with the Romans, adopted the disguise of a peasant to fight against them, and was mistakenly seized as a Roman. On the entreaties of Caius Lucius, Cymbeline spares the page Fidele and grants the lad a boon. Instead of pleading for Lucius, as the general expects, the page asks that Iachimo be made to reveal how he came by the ring he wears. Iachimo penitently confesses his treachery; Posthumus and Imogen are reconciled; and Cymbeline makes peace with the Romans, forgives Imogen, Posthumus, Belarius, and even Iachimo, and is reunited with his long-lost sons.

Cymbeline has all the familiar elements of a fairy tale—an innocent young girl heartlessly mistreated by a wicked stepmother, falsely suspected of adultery, pursued by a brute, and exiled by a misunderstanding father. In addition, there are multiple disguises and uncouth mountaineers who turn out to be, miraculously, the forlorn girl's long-lost brothers. To these and other equally improbable events Shakespeare adds a panoply of stock characters from the late Greek and Spanish heroic romances—the faithful servant, the repentant villain, ghosts, noble Romans, and heroic Britons. Finally, he brought to *Cymbeline* the same theme of reconciliation he employed in two other romances. *The Winter's Tale* and *The Tempest.* Like Hermione in *The Winter's Tale,* Imogen is a faithful and loving wife abused by her husband. A similar situation is exploited for its sentimental potential in a popular tragicomedy by Beaumont and Fletcher, *Philaster, or Love Lies A-Bleeding.*

In *Cymbeline* characterization is superficial and events patently contrived in the manner of Beaumont and Fletcher's heroic tragicomedies. The play is noted, however, for its lyrical speeches and songs. One memorable lyric is sung by Guiderius (IV, *ii*):

> Fear no more th' heat o' th' sun,
> Nor the furious winter's rages.
> Thou thy worldly task hast done,
> Home art gone and ta'en thy wages.
> Golden lads and girls all must,
> As chimney-sweepers, come to dust.

The standard text is in the New Arden edition, ed. J. M. Nosworthy (1955), and the New Cambridge edition, edited by J. C. Maxwell with notes and commentary (1960). Important criticism is by E. M. W. Tillyard, *Shakespeare's Last Plays* (1938); G. Wilson Knight, *The Crown of Life* (1947); E. C. Pettet, *Shakespeare and the Romance Tradition* (1949); Derick R. Marsh, *The Recurring Miracle: A Study of Cymbeline and the Last Plays* (1969); and William B. Thorne, "*Cymbeline:* 'Lopp'd Branches' and the Concept of Rejuvenation," *SQ,* XX (1969).

D

Daniel, Samuel (1562-1619). Dramatist and poet. Born in Somerset, the son of John Daniel, a musician, he left Oxford without taking a degree and traveled in France and Italy. Upon his return around 1586 he was employed as a tutor to the son of William Herbert, earl of Pembroke (Shakespeare's patron), whose wife was the sister of Sir Philip Sidney and a famous patroness of literature. His first printed efforts in poetry were twenty-eight sonnets included in the first, unauthorized edition of Sidney's *Astrophel and Stella* (1591), and the next year Daniel brought out his own complete collection entitled *Delia,* with a dedication to the countess of Pembroke (see SONNET SEQUENCES). The fifty sonnets in *Delia* are, for the most part, in the form of three quatrains and a couplet, the formula introduced by Surrey and later used by Shakespeare. Inspired by the sonnets of Philippe Desportes and Torquato Tasso rather than by any real-life "Delia," Daniel's poems are passionless but precise, rhetorically effective without emotional conviction; yet their graceful technical mastery and conscious craftsmanship inspired Edmund Spenser to refer to Daniel in *Colin Clout's Come Home Again* as the "new shepherd late upsprung, the which doth all before him far surpass." Included in the 1592 edition of *Delia* was the popular "The Complaint of Rosamond," which Shakespeare admired enough to echo in his own *Rape of Lucrece, Love's Labour's Lost,* and *Romeo and Juliet. Delia* was followed by a Senecan closet drama, *The Tragedy of Cleopatra* (1594), which tells of Cleopatra's life after Antony's death. Like Shakespeare but unlike Plutarch, Daniel views Cleopatra sympathetically, and treats her death as a magnificent display of tragic heroism. Shakespeare echoes some passages of Daniel's play in his own *Antony and Cleopatra.* Daniel's second tragedy based on Plutarch, *Philotas* (1605), concerns the trial for treason of an ambitious and vain favorite of Alexander the Great. Daniel's contemporaries saw analogies to the ill-fated Earl of Essex, and although the playwright protested in his "apology" to *Philotas* that he had composed at least three acts before the Essex rebellion of 1601, he was brought before the Privy Council to explain his intentions. Like *Cleopatra, Philotas* is closely woven on the Senecan pattern popularized by the French dramatist Robert Garnier (1534-90), a favorite playwright of Sir Philip Sidney's sister, the countess of Pembroke (to whom Daniel dedicated *Cleopatra*). Both of Daniel's tragedies employ a chorus, lengthy speeches, a *nuntius,* and abundance of rhyme.

In 1599 appeared *Musophilus, or Defense of Learning,* a long philosophical dialogue in six and eight-line stanzas between Musophilus, representing humanistic, theoretical knowledge and moral edification, and Philocosmus, arguing on behalf of practical arts and values. Meanwhile Daniel had turned his energies toward writing an epic on the Wars of the Roses. The first four books of his *Civil Wars* appeared in 1595, and by 1609 he had published eight books, bringing his account to the marriage of Edward IV. His original intention was to carry his story down through the reign of Henry VII; instead, he discontinued the epic and wrote his prose *History of England,* the first part of which appeared in 1612, the second part in 1617.

In 1604 Daniel was appointed licenser of the Children of the Queen's Revels by James I, a post that did not require residence in London, and about that time he moved to a farm at Beckington, a country town near Devizes. For the Children of the Queen's Revels he wrote several masques, the most notable being *The Vision of the Twelve Goddesses* (wr. 1604), *The Queen's Arcadia* (wr. 1605), *Tethys' Festival* (wr. 1610), and *Hymen's Triumph* (wr. 1615). Most of these were written for Queen Anne and her ladies in a characteristically didactic and solemn tone, in verse that is smooth, dignified, and cooly precise. They well express Coleridge's judgment that Daniel was a poet of sharp critical taste rather than spontaneous genius.

In addition to his *History of England,* Daniel's major prose work is *A Defense of Rhyme* (1603), written in answer to Thomas Campion's *Observations in the Art of English Poesy* (1602). To Campion's attack on "the vulgar and unartifical [inartistic] custom of riming," Daniel replied that anything, including rhyme, was as appropriate in English as in any of the classical languages (see CRITICISM, LITERARY).

By his own statement, Daniel was a minor poet. Affirming that view, Michael Drayton described him as "too much historian in verse. His manner better fitted prose." And it was William Browne, another contemporary, who fitted him with the epithet "well-languaged Daniel." Certainly Daniel lacked the flash and fire of Marlowe or Shakespeare, but he was, nevertheless, an easy, graceful writer with extraordinary control of diction and rhetoric. Where restraint is appropriate, as in the philosophic poem *Musophilus,* Daniel's occasional wit and invariable lucidity compensate for the absence of passion.

Daniel's poems and *Defense of Rhyme* have been edited by A. C. Sprague (1930). *Philotas* is edited by Laurence Michel (1970). There are two excellent critical biographies by Joan Rees (1964) and Cecil Seronsky (1967). A Concise Bibliography by S. A. Tannenbaum (1942) is continued by "Samuel Daniel (1942-65)," ed. G. R. Guffey in *Elizabethan Bibliographies Supplements,* VII (1967).

Davenant (or **D'Avenant), Sir William** (1606-1668). Poet and playwright. Born at Oxford, the son of an innkeeper there, Davenant attended Lincoln College briefly, then left Oxford to become a page in the household of the duchess of Richmond and, later, of Fulke Greville, Lord Brooke. By 1626 Davenant was at court writing plays, his first effort being the unacted *Albovine, King of the Lombards* (1629). After Ben Jonson's death Davenant succeeded to the quasi-official position of "poet laureate" at court, a title accompanied by a modest pension and the unenviable task of supplying plays and masques for the amusement of Queen Henrietta Maria and her coterie. *The Temple of Love,* a masque performed in 1635 by the queen and her ladies at court, established him as a royal favorite among the Cavalier dramatists, but *The Wits* (wr. c. 1633) a comedy of manners, proved to be his masterpiece. According to Sir Henry Herbert, master of the revels, Charles I himself helped "correct" Davenant's play before its first performance in 1634. A sophisticated, fast-moving comedy about the efforts of a young rake to dupe the older generation, and set in contemporary London, *The Wits* anticipated the type of comedy popular after the Restoration. Davenant's tragicomedy LOVE AND HONOR, performed in 1634, was equally popular in the Restoration period.

During the civil war, Davenant was knighted (1643) for valor at the siege of Gloucester and remained unwavering in his loyalty to the throne. In 1650 he was imprisoned in the Tower for over a year by Parliament, during which time he wrote his romantic epic *Gondibert* (1651). In 1650 his *Preface to Gondibert* was published in Paris with a critical rejoinder by Thomas Hobbes (see CRITICISM, LITERARY). An episodic poem of 1,700 quatrains, *Gondibert* describes the tangled love affairs of Duke Gondibert at the court of King Aribert in Lombardy. Before the plot even crystallizes, Davenant declares himself bored with the work, and left it unfinished. The poem is characteristic of the rambling heroic tales that supplied the Cavalier dramatists with sources for their speechifying plays during the 1630s (see CAROLINE DRAMA). After his release from prison Davenant produced several dramas in spite of the legal ban against plays. Among these are *The First Day's Entertainment at Rutland House* (wr. 1656) and *The Siege of Rhodes,* Part I (wr. 1656) and Part II (wr. 1659?). *The Siege of Rhodes* represents one of the first operas performed in England.

After the Restoration, Davenant and Thomas Killigrew were awarded royal patents to form the only two acting companies allowed by the government. Davenant's group, the Duke's Company, performed several heroic plays, operas, Shakespearean adaptations, and comedies of manners. Thus Davenant is generally recognized as a vital link between the courtly drama of Charles I and the new theater of the Restoration. His opera *Siege of Rhodes* was clearly a forerunner of the heroic plays of John Dryden in the 1660s; his *The Wits* anticipated the Restoration comedy of manners; and his own particular style of writing established during the 1630s—his exaggerated characterizations and penchant for spectacle —was carried over with great influence into the Restoration period.

In collaboration with John Dryden, Davenant adapted Shakespeare's *The Tempest* in 1667, a version that held the stage into the eighteenth century. Davenant's *Macbeth* (pr. 1674) was adapted for the stage in 1663 and revised by David Garrick in 1744. In rewriting Shakespeare's plays, Davenant retained the main features of the plot but extensively simplified the language. Davenant's admiration for Shakespeare was so great that he advertised himself as Shakespeare's natural son. Although Shakespeare may have visited the inn of Davenant's father at Oxford, the legend that Davenant was Shakespeare's illegitimate son, or even his godson (both claimed by Davenant), has no basis whatever in fact.

The standard biographies of Davenant are those by Alfred Harbage, *Sir William Davenant, Poet Venturer 1606-68* (1935), and Arthur H. Nethercot, *Sir William D'Avenant, Poet Laureate and Playwright-Manager* (1938). The definitive edition of the plays is *The Dramatic Works of William D'Avenant,* ed. James Maidment and W. H. Logan (1872, repr. 1964). There is a modern edition of *Gondibert* by David F. Gladish (1971). Geoffrey Bush has edited *The Selected Poems* (1943). Davenant's *Preface to Gondibert* and *Hobbes' Answer* are in *Critical Essays of the Seventeenth Century,* ed. Joel E. Spingarn, 3 vols. (1908-09), II; these are studied by Cornell M. Dowlin, *Sir William Davenant's Gondibert, Its Preface and Hobbes' Answer* (1934), and by Clarence D. Thorpe, *The Aesthetic Theory of Thomas Hobbes* (1940). Davenant's version of *Macbeth* was edited by Christopher Spencer (1961); Davenant and Dryden's *The Tempest, or The Enchanted Island* is in *After The Tempest,* ed. George R. Guffey (1969).

Davideis. See COWLEY, ABRAHAM; CRITICISM, LITERARY.

Davies, Sir John (1569-1626). Poet and lawyer, Davies was born in Tisbury, Wiltshire, the son of a lawyer who died when Davies was a child. He attended Winchester School and Queen's College, Oxford (B. A. 1590), and proceeded to the Middle Temple in 1587. Called to the bar in 1595, he was disbarred two years later for assaulting Richard Martin, a fellow member of the Middle Temple.

Most of Davies' major poetry was written at Oxford or at court from the time of his disbarment in 1597 until his reinstatement in 1601. Poetry for Davies was a pleasant avocation rather than a serious commitment, and although he was widely read and moderately gifted in literature, his principal interests were the law and public affairs. After his reinstatement, he represented Corfe Castle in Parliament. Francis Bacon became a personal friend, and the new monarch James I expressed admiration for Davies' philosophical poem *Nosce teipsum.* In 1603 he began a long career in Irish politics with his appointment as solicitor-general of Ireland. In a prose tract dedicated to James I, *A Discovery of the True Causes Why Ireland Was Never Entirely Subdued* (1612), Davies advocated harsh measures against Catholic priests and stricter repression of religious dissenters in Ireland. For several years he was speaker of the house in the Irish Parliament and the *bête noire* of pro-Catholic factions. He died of apoplexy shortly after Charles I named him chief justice. Curiously, in view of Davies' own rationalism and orthodoxy, his wife Mary seems to have been a religious mystic. She wrote two books of prophecy, *The Stay of the Wise* (1643) and *Tobit's Book* (1652), and was jailed briefly in 1633 for recusancy by Archbishop William Laud's commission.

Davies' earliest publication, *Epigrams and Elegies* (undated; pr. 1590? 1600?), appeared with Marlowe's translations of Ovid. Davies' caustic and salacious Martialian epigrams were confiscated and burned by the ecclesiastical authorities in 1599. The chief targets of Davies' satires were town gallants, tobacco, and Puritans. His satiric bent is also apparent in his "gulling sonnets" parodying the Petrarchan love poetry of the 1590s. These were not published until the nineteenth century. His *Hymns of Astraea* (1599) consists of twenty-two acrostical poems, each on the name "Elisabetha Regina," and if the obtrusive capitals can be ignored, some few have genuine lyric grace.

The two best-known poems by Davies are *Orchestra, or A Poem . . . of Dancing* (1596) and *Nosce teipsum: This Oracle Expounded in Two Elegies* (1599). In *Orchestra,* which Davies dedicated to Richard Martin, the barrister he had attacked at the Middle Temple, Davies asserts the all-encompassing significance of dancing by linking it to the measured order of family, society, statecraft, and cosmology. A long and leisurely poem of 130 seven-line stanzas (*ab ab bcc*), *Orchestra* begins remotely enough from its real subject with a playful episode in which Ulysses' faithful Penelope refuses to dance with her suitor Antinous, whereupon "that fresh and jolly knight" undertakes to explain to her that dancing is the oldest and most significant of all the arts:

Dancing, bright lady, then began to be
When the first seeds whereof the world did spring,
The fire, air, earth, and water, did agree,
By Love's persuasion, Nature's mighty king,
To leave their first disordered combating,
And in a dance such measure to observe
As all the world their motion should preserve.

From the origins of dancing in the Creation, Antinous traces all of its diverse manifestations of order on earth and in heaven down to "our golden age" in the reign of Elizabeth. He finds dancing in the music of the spheres, the motions of the planets, the undulations of the sea and seasons of the year, in ceremonies of state, natural law, and even death itself:

For when pale Death your vital twist shall sever,
Your better parts must dance with them forever.

Davies' *Nosce teipsum* ("Know thyself"), dedicated to Queen Elizabeth, is one of the longest and most ambitious philosophical poems of the English Renaissance. Written in epigrammatic, almost prosaic quatrains, it examines the purpose of life in two sections, "Of Human Knowledge" and "Of the Soul of Man and the Immortality Thereof." The first part discourses on man's frailty and error, his ironic ignorance and pride, and concludes with the famous stanza:

I know my life's a pain and but a span;
I know my sense is mock'd with everything;
And, to conclude, I know myself a man,
Which is a proud and yet a wretched thing.

In Part II, the longer of the two, Davies attempts to "justify the ways of God to man" by stressing man's unworthiness because of original sin; he discourses further on man's ignorance and pride, dissects the various faculties of the soul, argues repetitiously for its immortality, and concludes with a didactic exhortation:

Cast down thyself, and only strive to raise
The glory of thy maker's sacred name;
Use all thy powers that blessed power to praise;
Which give the power to be, and use the same.

Nosce teipsum comes to no original philosophical conclusions, but presents a compendium of philosophical truisms from neo-Platonism, stoicism, and orthodox Christian doctrine. Although so prosaic as to be at times almost sub-poetical, it is also flowing and lucid. *Nosce teipsum* remained popular for many years; subsequent editions were printed in 1602, 1608, 1619, and 1622.

The Works was edited by A. B. Grosart, 2 vols. (1876), *The Poems* by Clare Howard (1941). The best edition of *Orchestra* is by E. M. W. Tillyard (1945). Other poems by Davies are available in Gerald Bullett's *Silver Poets of the Sixteenth Century* (1947) and in *Poetry of the English Renaissance,* ed. J. William Hebel and H. H. Hudson (1929). Hershey E. Sneath closely studied *Nosce teipsum* and edited the work in *Philosophy in Poetry: A Study of Sir John Davies's Poem "Nosce Teipsum"* (1903). See also M. D. Holmes, *The Poet as Philosopher: A Study of Nosce Teipsum* (1921); E. M. W. Tillyard, *Five Poems, 1470-1870* (1948); and G. A. Wilkes, "The Poetry of Sir John Davies," *HLQ,* XXV (1962).

Day, Angel (fl. 1586). For comment on his *The English Secretary,* see LETTER-WRITERS.

Day, John (c. 1574-c. 1640). Dramatist. Born at Cawston, Norfolk, Day attended Caius College, Cambridge, for one year and was expelled for theft in 1593. From 1598 to 1603 he was employed by the Lord Admiral's Men as one of Philip Henslowe's regular playwrights, working in collaboration with Thomas Dekker. In 1599 he killed the playwright Henry Porter in a quarrel. From 1604 to 1608 Day left Henslowe to work alone, and during this period wrote *Law Tricks* (1604), *The Isle of Gulls* (1606), and *Humour Out of Breath* (1608). Day's best work is not a play but a series of delicate pastoral dialogues called *The Parliament of Bees* (pr. 1641, wr. much earlier), in which the bees represent various vices and virtues. Without justification, Day has been suggested as the author of the PARNASSUS PLAYS and as Shakespeare's collaborator in the first and third scenes of Act II of *Pericles.*

Little is known of Day after *Humour Out of Breath* in 1608, and even the date of his death is conjectural. In his *Conversations with Drummond,* Jonson mentions that Day, along with Dekker and others, "were all rogues." Day seems to have been an irregular and needy hack in the employ of inferior dramatic companies. According to G. E. Bentley, most of Day's plays were written in collaboration with Dekker.

Day's *Complete Works,* including sixteen plays, most of doubtful attribution, was edited by A. H. Bullen, 2 vols. (1881). For a concise summary of biographical facts, see G. E. Bentley, *The Jacobean and Caroline Stage,* 7 vols. (1941-67), III. *The Parliament of Bees* is studied by S. R. Golding, *"The Parliament of Bees," RES,* III (1927). See also M. E. Borish, "John Day's *Humour out of Breath,*" *Harvard Studies & Notes in Philology and Literature,* XVI (1934).

Day (or Daye, Daie), John (1522-1584). English printer. For his militant publishing of Protestant religious tracts under Edward VI. Mary Tudor's authorities imprisoned Day for several years. Under Queen Elizabeth he became the most successful printer of the times, holding royal monopolies on metrical psalms, catechisms, and hornbooks (ABC primers). He printed the first church-music book in English (1560) and the first English edition of Foxe's *Acts and Monuments* (1563). At the request of Archbishop Matthew Parker, Day designed special type to make the first printing ever done in Old English.

There is an account of Day by J. G. Nichols, "John Day, the Printer," *Gentleman's Magazine,* CII (1832); see also Ronald B. McKerrow, *A Dictionary of Printers and Booksellers, 1557-1640* (1910).

Death's Duel. A sermon by John DONNE, preached before Charles I at St. Paul's on February 25, 1631. The first edition of 1632 was prepared by Richard Redmer with the title *Death's Duel; or, A Consolation to the Soul, Against the Dying Life, and Living Death of the Body.* Written a month before Donne's death, it is described by Redmer as Donne's "own funeral sermon." The topic of the text is Psalm 68: 20: "And unto God the Lord belong the issues from death." Donne constructs his sermon on the ambiguity of the Scriptural "issues," which he explores for three possible meanings, each related to a different person of the Trinity. Hence "issues of death" can mean deliverance from death by the Father, manner of death and afterlife imposed by the Holy Ghost, or transcendence of the flesh, represented by Jesus in the Incarnation and Resurrection.

The first section of the sermon examines how man passes in life from one death to another (i.e., how he lives the "dying life" of the subtitle). All living is a relentless march toward the grave, and each step in life is accompanied by pains and evils equal to death itself.

The second section deals with the impossibility of man predicting the quality of the soul and its destiny after death. Many thought to be sinners will be saved; many thought to be saints will be damned. Only God in His infinite wisdom knows the true value of soul.

The third and climactic section proclaims that men are only delivered from death by the merciful suffering of Christ in the mystery of the Incarnation. Much of Donne's wonder focuses on the enigmatic paradox that "this Lord, the Lord of Life, could die," and that man could only have been exalted by the agonies of God himself. The sermon concludes with a contemplation of Christ upon the cross:

> There now hangs that sacred body upon the cross, rebaptized in his own tears and sweat, and embalmed in his own blood alive. There are those bowels of compassion which are so conspicuous, so manifested as that you may see them through his wounds. There those glorious eyes grew faint in their light, so as the sun, ashamed to survive them, departed with his light too . . . . There we leave you in that blessed dependency, to hang upon him that hangs upon the cross; there bathe in his tears, there suck at his wounds and lie down in peace in his grave, till he vouchsafe you a resurrection and an ascension into that kingdom which he hath purchased for you with the inestimable price of his incorruptible blood. Amen.

For standard text and essential commentary, see *The Sermons,* ed. G. R. Potter and Evelyn M. Simpson, 10 vols. (1953-62). See also John Sparrow, "John Donne and Contemporary Preachers," *E&S,* XVI (1931); W. F. Mitchell, *English Pulpit Oratory* (1932); and W. R. Mueller, *John Donne: Preacher* (1962).

Dee, John (1527-1608). Alchemist, astrologer, and mathematician. Although Dee drew up his own flattering genealogy, claiming descent from a ninth-century Welsh king, his parentage remains vague. He was probably the son of a gentleman server to Henry VIII, or perhaps of a London vintner. Little is known of his life until his matriculation in 1542 at St. John's College, Cambridge (B.A., 1544), where he studied Greek vigorously. He became known as something of a conjurer and magician at St. John's after producing an Aristophanic comedy in which a scarabaeus, or large beetle, was made to fly as if by magic to Jupiter's palace "with a man and his basket of victuals on his back." By Dee's own statement, "Many vain reports spread abroad of the means how that was effected." Although Dee devoted later years to a systematic study of mathematics and science, he was never able to shake free of this unwanted—and undeserved—reputation as a necromancer and wizard of the black arts.

After taking an M.A. at Trinity College, Dee went to the Low Countries in 1547 to study civil law, astronomy, and mathematics at Louvain, and returned with two great globes of the world done by Gerard Mercator and an astronomer's ring of brass made by Gemma Frisius. In subsequent years Dee became an ardent collector of esoteric treatises, glass perspectives, astronomers' staffs, and other scientific paraphernalia, some of which are now in the British Museum. His science library at Mortlake, one of the greatest in Europe, held over four thousand volumes.

In 1550 Dee went to the College of Rheims at Paris, where he lectured on Euclid before huge audiences. In 1551 he was offered a lecturership at the college, but instead he returned to England, where Sir John Clarke introduced him to William Cecil (later Lord Burghley) and John Cheke's pupil, Edward VI. At the beginning of Mary Tudor's reign Dee was arrested on trumped-up charges of plotting to poison the queen, but was soon discharged after examination by the Star Chamber. Dee came to the attention of Mary Tudor again when he made the imaginative but futile proposal of founding a national library by retrieving the books and manuscripts that had been scattered throughout England and the Continent after the dissolution of the monasteries and religious houses in Henry VIII's reign.

At the accession of Elizabeth, Dee was on familiar terms with William Herbert, earl of Pembroke, and Robert Dudley, earl of Leicester, for whom Dee cast a horoscope to determine the most auspicious day for the queen's coronation. During the early 1560s he traveled widely on the continent, collecting mathematical and hieroglyphic literature and visiting royal courts. He purchased a copy of the *Steganographia* by John Trithemius, one of the earliest works on writing in cipher, and presented a copy of his own *Monas hieroglyphica,* a compendium of hieroglyphics, to Emperor Maximilian II of Hungary. Returning to England in 1564, he disclosed some of the "secrets" of *Monas hieroglyphica* to Queen Elizabeth, who became an ardent admirer of Dee's esoteric and occult discoveries in alchemy, astrology, hieroglyphics, and mathematics. Dee tried to establish a reputation as a scientist and philosopher as well as a magician. In the preface to Henry Billingsley's English translation of Euclid, Dee wrote learnedly of Greek mathematics and protested his own notoriety as a magician.

During the 1570s Dee was consulted by the queen on a number of matters—the appearances of new stars and comets, geography, and Elizabeth's own health. In 1577 he was called to Windsor for consultations regarding a waxen image of the queen, stuck with pins, that was discovered in Lincoln's Inn Fields; Dee was able to reassure the jittery queen. On several occasions Elizabeth visited his home at Mortlake to see his library, view his famous magic glass, and receive lessons in occultism. Although the queen treated Dee with unusual kindness, her promises of academic positions and court sinecures did not materialize. In 1578 he journeyed to Germany to consult with experts there about Elizabeth's medical afflictions, especially her rheum and toothaches. Upon his return he drew up a hydrographical and geographical table of the queen's possessions abroad, which he presented to her in 1580. Two years later Dee proposed to Lord Burghley the adoption of his modification of the new Gregorian calendar based on his own calculations as to the position of the sun at the hour of Christ's birth, but the Anglican bishops rejected the new calendar because of its "Romish" associations.

After 1580 Dee became increasingly engrossed in experiments in conjuring and magic, claiming to hold conversations with angels and devils seen in a crystal globe. After several months of such experiments with his "magic glass," he was visited at Mortlake by one Edward Kelley, alias Talbot, a convicted forgerer, who persuaded Dee that the angel Uriel had appeared to him and proclaimed that Kelley and Dee should become collaborators. For the next twenty-five years Kelley and Dee worked as partners, Kelley manipulating the magic glass and Dee acting as "recorder" in conjuring up and transcribing "conversations" with such spirits as "Lundrumguffa," and especially one called "Il," whom Dee describes in his diary as "a merry creature, apparelled like Vice in a play."

At Mortlake in 1583 Dee was visited by Prince Albert Laski, the bankrupt palatine of Siradz in Bohemia, who sought Dee's aid in finding the fabulous "philosopher's stone" that would convert base metals into gold. Dee and Kelley accompanied Laski to his palace near Cracow to conduct experiments, but the nobleman soon wearied of the pair and sent them to the court of Prague, where they failed to impress Emperor Rudolph II with their magic glass. Later they visited King Stephen Bathory of Poland, who is said to have ignominiously dismissed them as frauds.

While in Poland in 1587 Kelley informed Dee that a female spirit, "Madimi," revealed to him that he and Dee must share all things in common, including their wives, and Dee reluctantly consented. The bizarre domestic arrangement terminated in the dissolution of the partnership several months later, although Dee continued to correspond with Kelley on friendly terms for several years. The worst that can be said of Dee in this affair was that he was an honest dupe; Kelley, however, was a self-serving charlatan.

Upon Dee's return to Mortlake in 1588 he was visited by Queen Elizabeth. After he had lodged several complaints of poverty with her ministers, she finally granted him the wardenship of Manchester College in 1596. The post proved to be an unhappy one, with Dee quarreling interminably with faculty and townspeople. He resigned his post in 1604 and died in retirement at Mortlake under conditions of extreme poverty.

Dee was a complex mixture of scientist, mathematician, and necromancer, and his almost eighty volumes (few of which were printed during his lifetime) reflect a brilliant and whimsical erudition. He wrote prodigiously on a variety of subjects, including astrology, astronomy, mathematics, medicine, spiritualism, mysticism, navigation, cartography, and hieroglyphics. His *Monas hieroglyphica* was published in Antwerp (1564) and Frankfort (1591). His recondite study of Roger Bacon's occult science, *Roger Baconis . . . Naturae* (Hamburg, 1618), was translated by "T.M." as *Friar Bacon and His Discovery of the Miracles of Art, Nature and Magic* (1659). One of Dee's few books in English was *General and Rare Memorials . . . of Navigation* (1577).

Few modern scholars share the nineteenth-century view of Dee as a charlatan. His vast library at Mortlake, stocked with books and manuscripts in a dozen languages on everything from heraldry and Arthurian legends to cartography and Hermetic philosophy, has been likened to the Platonic academies of Renaissance Florence and More's residence at Chelsea. To Mortlake came not only Queen Elizabeth, Walsingham, Sir Christopher Hatton, and Lord Burghley, but also Sir Philip Sidney, Edward Dyer, and other members of the Sidney circle to hear the master discourse on alchemical, mathematical, and cabalistic theories. Dee also influenced the Tudor historians William Camden and John Stowe with his antiquarian studies, especially in his efforts to revive credence in the Arthurian legends—an effort which may have indirectly encouraged Spenser's *Faerie Queene.* On matters pertaining to cartography, geography, mathematics, and navigation, Dee was often consulted by Sir Walter Raleigh and Sir Humphrey Gilbert, and Sir Humphrey's brother Sir John Gilbert is known to have studied with Dee in planning expeditions in search of the Northwest Passage. Dee's famous preface to Henry Billingsley's English version of Euclid has been compared to Bacon's *Advancement of Learning* as a manifesto for the promotion of science. Indeed, a recent Dee scholar, Peter J. French, testifies that after several years of studying Dee's life and works, he has only begun to perceive the extent of Dee's influence on Renaissance thought.

Dee's *Private Diary,* with a catalog of collected manuscripts, was edited by J. O. Halliwell-Phillips for the Camden Society (1842). Additional lists of manuscripts owned by Dee were compiled by M. R. James in *Transactions of the Bibliographical Society,* Supplement I (1921). There is a life and study of Dee's works by G. M. Horst, *Dr. John Dee: Elizabethan Mystic and Astrologer* (1922), and Denis Meadows has a lively and informative account of Dee's life and works in *Elizabethan Quintet* (1956). For Dee's intellectual sources and amazing range of knowledge, see Frances A. Yates, *Theatre of the World* (1969), and Peter J. French, *John Dee: The World of an Elizabethan Magus* (1972).

Defense of Poesy (Sir Philip Sidney). See CRITICISM, LITERARY.

Defense of Rhyme, A (Samuel Daniel). See CRITICISM, LITERARY.

Dekker, Thomas (1572?-?1632). Dramatist and pamphleteer. With the exception of John Webster's, less is known of Dekker's life than of any other prominent Elizabethan writer. He may have been born in 1570, or possibly in 1572; guesses as to the year of his death range from 1631 to 1641. His name first appears in Henslowe's Diary in 1597 as the author of a nonextant book called *Phaethon,* and thereafter Dekker appears frequently in the records as a dramatist for the Lord Admiral's Men and Worcester's Men, as one of Henslowe's debt-haunted hacks, and as an assiduous collaborator on over forty plays with Chettle, Day, Drayton, Ford, Massinger, Middleton, Munday, Rowley, Webster, Robert Wilson, and others. It is estimated that Dekker wrote sixteen plays with Michael Drayton, fifteen with Henry Chettle, and nine with Robert Wilson. In Jonson's *The Poetaster* Dekker is scorned as "Demetrius Fannius, the dresser of plays."

Dekker's most original and imaginative plays were written during the period 1596-1604, beginning with the old-fashioned but charming OLD FORTUNATUS, which was performed at court in December, 1599, after Dekker had thoroughly revised it. This episodic dramatization of folklore with its multiplicity of plots, far-fetched actions, and unabashed sentimentality harks back to such plays by

Robert Greene as *Friar Bacon and Friar Bungay.* The neat tribute to the queen at the conclusion recalls George Peele's *Arraignment of Paris:* Dekker's Virtue kneels before Elizabeth and humbly states, "I am a counterfeit, you are the true."

Having been in debtors' prison in 1598, Dekker worked furiously to avert poverty. In 1599, the same year as *Old Fortunatus,* he collaborated with Chettle on a play called *Troilus and Cressida,* and in 1600 with Ben Jonson on *The Page of Plymouth,* a domestic tragedy, and with Anthony Munday on a lost play called *Jepthah.*

It was in these hard-pressed times that Dekker wrote his masterpiece THE SHOEMAKER'S HOLIDAY, payment for which Henslowe records in his Diary on July 15, 1599. In this play Dekker made supreme artistic use of his thorough knowledge of London, his affection for the honest and hard-working trades, his genuine attachment to the ideal of Merry England, and his great talent for writing lovely songs, lively characterizations, and energetic scenes. A truly festive comedy that blends realism and romance, laughter and pathos, *The Shoemaker's Holiday* is the most thoroughly unified of Dekker's plays.

In 1601 appeared Dekker's (and to an unknown extent, Marston's) contribution to the so-called War of the Theaters, SATIROMASTIX, OR THE UNTRUSSING OF THE HUMOROUS POET, performed by the Paul's Boys at a private theater. Dekker's twitting of Jonson was devastating; Dekker satirizes him for his pock-marked face, his sensitivity about having been a bricklayer, his flattering of social superiors, and his notorious slowness in composing a play. Jonson was roused to retaliation, but Dekker chose to abandon satire and join Webster in composing two rather inferior and loosely woven tragicomedies, *Westward Ho!* (wr. 1604) and *Northward Ho!* (wr. 1605). (For comment on the War of the Theaters, see JONSON, BEN.)

The enormous popularity of *The Shoemaker's Holiday* was repeated in 1604 with THE HONEST WHORE, Part I, on which Dekker may have collaborated with Thomas Middleton, and in 1605, Part II. Like most sequels, Part II is not nearly equal to Part I, except in its portrayal of Bellafront, the reformed prostitute who reappears as a courageous and loyal wife in Part II. *The Honest Whore* is rich in characterization, with many compelling scenes; it fails, however, in plot (Dekker's chief area of weakness), for it attempts to dramatize no fewer than three fully developed, independent stories ranging from bittersweet tragicomedy to rollicking farce. The first of these is a romantic story of two lovers, Hippolito and Infelice, who, like Romeo and Juliet, are separated by feuding families but, unlike Shakespeare's star-crossed lovers, are reunited after Infelice recovers from a sleeping potion. In the second story the courtesan Bellafront falls in love with Hippolito after the supposed death of Infelice; in the third tale, a shopkeeper's wife farcically tests the patience of her sanguine husband.

Around 1610 Dekker collaborated with Middleton on THE ROARING GIRL, a play based on the career of Mary Frith, alias Moll Cutpurse, who dressed like a man, was adept with a sword, and consorted with the toughs of London's underworld. In Dekker's play she is a free-wheeling spirit with a generous heart who succors lovers in distress and punishes bullies and hypocrites. At about the same time Dekker wrote *If It Be Not Good, the Devil Is in It,* a rambling dramatization of a folk tale printed in 1567 as *The Pleasant History of Friar Rush,* and *Match Me in London,* a tragicomedy in the manner of Beaumont and Fletcher, but neither of these plays proved especially successful. It would appear that after *The Honest Whore* Dekker began to experiment with several styles ranging from almost grimly realistic tragicomedy to comedy of manners, genres not really suited to his talents.

During the period 1603-10 Dekker also produced a number of pamphlets based on various aspects of the London he knew so intimately. The first of these was THE WONDERFUL YEAR (1603), begun as a commemoration of Queen Elizabeth's death and James I's succession but extending to include the subject of the plague that raged in London that year. *The Wonderful Year* is a vivid, brutal account of the agony, stench, and horrors of pestilence. Like Daniel Defoe in *Journal of the Plague Year,* Dekker demonstrates a capacity for combining powerful, detailed descriptions and seriocomic anecdotes.

In his next pamphlet, *The Seven Deadly Sins of London* (1606), he imitates the satiric, self-righteous posture of Thomas Nashe in describing an imaginary pageant of sin's disciples through the streets of London. The sins Dekker attacks are not theological but sociological; abstractions such as Politic Bankruptcy (discharge of debts by legal maneuvering), Shaving (profiteering), and Cruelty (extortion) are lustily cheered by their equally unscrupulous followers. *News from Hell* (1606) is as vividly descriptive as *The Wonderful Year.* In *News* a messenger travels through Paris, Venice, and London, then into hell to report on a number of trials wherein dead souls are convicted by a grisly jury made up of personifications of the loathsome crimes of the defendants.

THE BELLMAN OF LONDON (1608), in spite of its title, has for its scene a rural setting outside London where the narrator comes across a band of vagabonds and rogues holding a feast to initiate new members into their various organizations of cardsharps, shoplifters, and pickpockets. The cunning practices of these felons are described in a way similar to that of Robert GREENE'S famous "coney-catching" pamphlets. A somewhat similar subject is taken up in a very different manner in Dekker's next pamphlet LANTERN AND CANDLELIGHT (1608), in which a devil makes a tour of his followers in London—usurers, extortionists, gamblers—and is delighted with their prosperity and loyal devotion to his cause. Dekker's underworld pamphlets are more satiric than informative, less in the way of exposés than of didactic sermons, and he often resorts to anecdotes trimmed with expressions of moral indignation. (For these and other pamphlets like them, see ROGUE LITERATURE.)

The latent reformer and manifest moralist is implicit in the motto of Dekker's *Work for Armorers* (1609): "God help the poor, the rich can shift!" In this allegory depicting a conflict between the two queens Money and Poverty, Dekker again reveals his persistent concern for the suffering of the poor and indifference of the rich, the cruelty of the powerful and misery of the weak—a compassion that extends to include the mistreatment of animals in London's cockpits and bear-baiting arenas.

Dekker's best-known pamphlet was THE GULL'S HORNBOOK (1609), which satirically describes a single day in the life of a typical "gull," or affected young fop who would pass himself off as a *bon vivant* and sophisticate in his choice of friends, entertainment, clothes, and manners. Of particular interest is the chapter "How a Gull Should Conduct Himself in the Popular Playhouse," a humorous invective that throws considerable light on the conditions of the Elizabethan stage. Hence Dekker's "hornbook" is both a mock primer for would-be gallants and a device for administering proper chastisement to those affected young men who fluttered about London's taverns, bookstalls, and theaters.

During the long period 1613-19, when Dekker may have been in prison for debt, he wrote little if anything, and his appeals to former patrons and actors went largely unheeded. His last pamphlet before this period was probably *A Strange Horse Race* (1613), which elaborates ingeniously on the single conceit of racing, presenting everything in terms of this one idea—astronomy as a race of planets, physiology as a race of humours, alchemy as a race of elements, and morality as a race of vices and virtues. Consistent with Dekker's penchant for social satire, occupations are also described as racing contests—the lawyer against his conscience, the vicar in pursuit of benefices, and the tailor hot after his own pride.

After nearly seven years away from the stage, Dekker returned to collaborating with Ford, Massinger, Rowley, and Webster. With Massinger he wrote *The Virgin Martyr* (wr. c. 1620) and with Ford and Rowley, THE WITCH OF EDMONTON (wr. c. 1621). The latter is based on the last years of Elizabeth Sawyer, an old woman burned as a witch in 1621. For this play Ford may have written the romantic scenes; to Dekker and Rowley can be attributed the grimly realistic story of how Dame Sawyer was tormented into hysteria and witchcraft by her merciless and superstitious neighbors.

With Rowley and Webster, Dekker collaborated on one of his last dramatic works, a masque-like pageant called *The Sun's Darling* (wr. c. 1623), which traces the maturity of Raybright, child of the sun god, through the four seasons of the year. It may represent merely a revision of Dekker's first recorded play, the nonextant *Phaethon,* which he wrote as early as 1597. In all probability the dramatist was the "Thomas Decker, householder" buried August 25, 1632, as St. James's, Clerkenwell.

Most of the adjectives employed to describe Dekker's work and temperament derive from his single festive comedy, *The Shoemaker's Holiday,* and certainly there is much in his other works to confirm the impression of a writer who was joyous, optimistic, and compliant. To these adjectives must be added courage, piety, and simple faith, those virtues clearly evident in Dekker's devotional tract *Four Birds of Noah's Ark* (1609), of which one scholar has observed that probably no prayer book in the language from a single hand can compare with it for simplicity and beauty. This view of Dekker as a simple idealist is not, however, the entire picture. Like Greene, Nashe, and Jonson, he knew the common life of England intimately, and he often recoiled in disgust at the cruelties and injustices of his time. Like Defoe, he inclined toward realistic journalism, and like Dickens, he was both fascinated and repelled by the ebb and flow of London life. In spite of his remarkable sense of life, he seems to have been a tough-minded realist with few illusions. "What's this whole world but a gilt, rotten pill?" asks one of his characters, "for at the heart lies the old core still."

The definitive edition of Dekker's plays is by Fredson Bowers, 4 vols. (1953-61). Four of Dekker's best pamphlets—*The Wonderful Year; The Gull's Hornbook; Penny-wise, Pound Foolish;* and *Lantern and Candlelight*—are available in a single, well-annotated volume edited by E. D. Pendry for the Stratford-upon-Avon Library (1967). There are two excellent critical studies: J. H. Conover, *Thomas Dekker: An Analysis of Dramatic Structure* (1969), and G. R. Price, *Thomas Dekker* (1969). S. A. Tannenbaum has a Concise Bibliography (1939), continued in "Thomas Dekker (1945-65)," ed. Dennis Donovan, in *Elizabethan Bibliographies Supplements,* II (1967).

Deloney, Thomas (c. 1543-c. 1600). Silk weaver, ballad writer, pamphleteer, and author of middle-class romances. Very little is known for certain of Deloney's life except that he was a member of the London clothiers' guild. His earliest known writings were three ballads (1588) celebrating the defeat of the Spanish Armada. He also published two poetical miscellanies, *The Garland of Good Will* (entered in the Stationers' Register, 1593; earliest extant edition, 1631), containing poems by Sir Walter Raleigh, Nicholas Breton, and others (including several falsely assigned to Shakespeare), and *The Strange Histories of Kings, Princess, Dukes, etc.* (1602), a collection of ballads and sonnets more appropriately entitled *The Royal Garland of Love and Delight* after the 1674 edition.

Deloney's fame rests on three extremely popular prose narratives which represent the earliest distinctively middle-class fiction in English. Deloney's heroes are not knights but common artisans who rub shoulders with royalty and who participate, often heroically, in the great national events described in the chronicles. These romances were so popular they were literally used up in early editions; hence the first extant edition of one of Deloney's works usually represents a relatively late issue. *The Pleasant History of John Winchcomb... called Jack of Newbury* (see JOHN WINCHCOMB) was entered in the Stationers' Register in 1597, but the first extant edition—described on the title page as the eighth—is dated 1619. Similarly, Deloney's THOMAS OF READING was entered in 1600, but the first known edition—described as the fourth—is 1612. On the other hand THE GENTLE CRAFT, Part I, was entered in 1597, and printed in 1598 although the first complete extant edition is dated 1635. Deloney wrote all three of these romances around 1596.

One reason for the phenomenal popularity of Deloney's fiction was that English middle-class readers had grown weary of courtly romances such as John Lyly's *Euphues* and Sir Philip Sidney's *Arcadia.* Popular taste was swinging toward anecdotal JESTBOOKS, Greene's "coney-catching" pamphlets, and the fast-paced journalism of Nashe and Dekker, and Deloney exploited this development by combining most of the features of these genres, including some from the courtly romances, into a form that appeared to be original, timely, and highly realistic. Deloney retained much of the polyphonic narration and vagarious events and characterizations still attractive about the courtly romances, but he made ingenious improvisations on the old values by glorifying the craft of shoemaker or weaver as thoroughly as Sidney and Spenser had apotheosized true courtesy. Deloney turned the knights and ladies of the courtly romances into fun-loving artisans and lively wenches, and placed them in the familiar environs of Berkshire, Norwich, or London rather than in Fairyland or Mauritania. Instead of casting his adventures in the mythical kingdoms of the late Greek romances, he described them against the background of English history gleaned from Holinshed's

Chronicles. Instead of the esoteric idealism of Sidney, Deloney provided all the rustic pieties dear and familiar to ordinary Elizabethans —chauvinism and xenophobia, Protestantism and anti-Catholicism, class pride and social complacency—and he couched these sentiments in homely, colloquial dialogue (though his aristocrats often speak in the style of Lyly's *Euphues*). From the jestbooks Deloney derived far-fetched, humorous episodes strung out like beads on a string; his *Jack of Newbury* has eleven chapters of separate tales that somewhat resemble elongated jokes rather than a coherent, unified story.

Deloney is sometimes praised for his "realism," but it is a very selective realism confined chiefly to dialogue. In any event, it was not so much Deloney's realism as the gratifying nature of his fantasies that endeared him to middle-class readers, for his three romances proclaim that honest hard work coupled with a little ingenuity and manipulation can overcome the obstacles of a rigidly stratified society. If Deloney was aware of class tensions, social injustice, and ordinary human misery, his ebullient optimism never permits these realities to spoil his picture of a Merry England in which the apprentice clever enough to marry his master's widow can rise to such giddy pinnacles as to hobnob with kings and queens. Although Deloney's fiction lacks the social complexity, psychological interest, and coherence of plot most readers require of fully developed novels, his work is nevertheless interesting as an example of Elizabethan fiction at a stage of evolution where it gathers together many heterogeneous elements before solidifying. From another perspective, Deloney's fiction attests to the durability of the same middle-class spirit that inspired Poor Richard's euphoric almanacs and the muscular optimism of Horatio Alger.

The standard edition of Deloney's complete works was edited by Francis O. Mann (1912). There is a more recent edition of the fiction by Merritt E. Lawlis, *The Novels of Thomas Deloney* (1961), which contains much biographical and critical commentary. See also Lawlis' *An Apology for the Middle Class: The Dramatic Novels of Thomas Deloney* (1961). Deloney's style is studied by T. Dahl, *An Inquiry into Aspects of the Language of Deloney* (1951). An excellent study of Deloney's cultural milieu is Louis B. Wright, *Middle-Class Culture in Elizabethan England* (1935).

Denham, Sir John (1615-1669). Poet. Born in Dublin, where his father was chief baron of the Exchequer, Denham attended Trinity College, Oxford (1631-34), where he gained notoriety as a gambler and daydreamer. He entered Lincoln's Inn in 1634 and was admitted to the bar in 1639. His first literary work was a much-acclaimed historical tragedy of Turkish court life, *The Sophy* (1642). He was at court during the outbreak of the Civil War, a somewhat rakish courtier of dissolute habits, a friend of Abraham Cowley, Edmund Waller, Thomas Killigrew, and William Cartwright, and a writer of occasional verses and neoclassic satires in the manner of the Cavalier poets and other disciples of Ben Jonson. An unswerving Royalist, he was imprisoned in London in 1642, held several important posts under Charles I during the wars, and lost most of his property with the failure of the Royalist cause. After another term in prison in 1645, he lived abroad during the period 1648-52. With the Restoration he became surveyor of works, succeeding Inigo Jones, and dispatched his duties with imagination and energy, renovating Burlington House and Greenwich Palace and improving the pavements in London. He was knighted and made a member of Parliament in 1661. In 1663 he became one of the first members of the Royal Society. Toward the end of his life he became insane, reputedly because his young second wife, whom he had married in 1665, became the mistress of the duke of York. Before his death, Denham recovered sufficiently to translate the fifth act of Mrs. Katherine Philips' version of Corneille's *Horace* (1669).

Denham's reputation and influence rest on one work, *Cooper's Hill* (1642), a topographical poem in heroic couplets combining descriptions of natural scenery with moral and philosophical reflections. The best-known lines from *Cooper's Hill* are those on the River Thames:

O could I flow like thee, and make thy stream
My great example, as it is my theme!
Though deep, yet clear; though gentle, yet not dull,
Strong without rage, without o'erflowing full!

Denham's quatrain is a concise summary of his own poetic style, one that "flows" energetically and at an acceptable level of competence, contains reflections and speculations on philosophy, religion, and politics, and yet avoids the obscure "strong lines" of the metaphysical poets. It was a style Samuel Johnson praised as having "strength," a stolid conciseness, rational clarity, and precise regularity that became the much-imitated model of Restoration and eighteenth-century neoclassicists. With Edmund Waller, to whom John Dryden, Alexander Pope, and Samuel Johnson also paid tribute, Denham was celebrated as the unrivaled master of the closed couplet and the dignified, restrained philosophical reflection. In praising Denham's apostrophe to the Thames, Johnson summarized the peculiar virtues of a style that commanded so much admiration in the Augustan Age:

> So much meaning is comprised in so few words, the particulars of resemblances are so perspicaciously collected, and every mode of excellence separated from its adjacent fault by so nice a line of limitation; the different parts of the sentence are so accurately adjusted; and the flow of the last couplet so smooth and sweet . . .

Unlike the metaphysical poets, Denham is "smooth" rather than "rough," his observations on life clear and not obscure, his sensibilities "gentle," not tortured, eccentric, or in any way fantastical. And yet, by comparison with seventeenth-century poets like Donne or even Cleveland and Cowley, Denham is at best only tolerably mediocre, and his *Cooper's Hill,*—with its review of English history inspired by Windsor Castle seen from Denham's home at Egham, Surrey, its description of a royal stag hunt and the battle of Runnymede, and its unobtrusive reflections on the majesty of kings and the honor of the English nation—all enclosed in jogging couplets—provided just the right entertainment for the disciples of Descartes and Hobbes, who preferred sober restraint and unequivocal order to the wild cries of troubled and isolated souls.

The best edition of Denham's poems is by T. Howard Banks, Jr., *The Poetical Works of Sir John Denham* (2d ed., 1969), which contains a biography, a survey of criticism, and *The Sophy.* The influence of *Cooper's Hill* is fully discussed by R. A. Aubin, *Topographical Poetry in Eighteenth-Century England* (1936). Brendan O Hehir has a biography, *Harmony from Discords* (1968) and a critical study with annotated edition of *Cooper's Hill, Expans'd Hieroglyphicks: A Study of Sir John Denham's Cooper's Hill* (1969).

De veritate. See HERBERT, EDWARD.

Dialogue of Proverbs, The. See HEYWOOD, JOHN.

Digby, Sir Kenelm (1603-65). Diplomat, miscellanist, philosopher. Born at the ancestral estate at Gayhurst, Buckinghamshire, Digby was the son of Sir Everard Digby, executed as a conspirator in the Gunpowder Plot. At fourteen Digby accompanied his uncle Sir John Digby (later first earl of Bristol) to Spain to negotiate a marriage between Prince Charles and the Infanta. Upon his return in 1618, he entered Worcester College, Oxford, and left in 1620 to travel for three years in France, Italy, and Spain (where he joined his uncle, Prince Charles, the marquis of Buckingham, and their numerous English retainers in a last abortive effort to secure a Spanish match). In 1623 the king knighted Digby for his services in Spain.

Before leaving on the grand tour Digby had fallen in love with Venetia Stanley, a neighbor at Gayhurst and daughter of Sir Edward Stanley of Shropshire. The vicissitudes of that anguished and ecstatic courtship of almost ten years is the main theme of Digby's *Private Memoirs* (not printed until 1827). The antiquary John Aubrey describes Venetia as "a celebrated beauty and courtesan," a perilous combination perhaps, but one in which Digby rejoiced because, he states in his memoirs, her promiscuity gave him an opportunity to defend her highly vulnerable reputation. Digby described his *Private Memoirs* as "loose fantasies," and those portions pertaining to his wooing of Venetia as "castrations." The element of fantasy is stressed by Digby's use of allegory and pseudonyms; throughout the autobiography he refers to himself as Theagenes (hero of the late Greek romance *Aethiopica*) and Venetia as Stelliana (from Sir Philip Sidney's *Astrophel and Stella*). Their courtship totally characterizes the temperament of the author, which is best described as "baroque"—a bizarre mixture of ethereality and raw sex wherein apostrophic grandiloquence redolent of Platonic love invariably follows hard upon the most lascivious couplings.Their marriage in 1625, Digby proclaims in his memoirs, provided him with the ideal woman—experienced but not bored, well-trained but not worn out. By the time of her death in 1633, she had borne him five children and much felicity.

His *Journal of a Voyage into the Mediterranean,* written in 1628, describes his privateering expedition against the French, an adventure secretly approved by the king and climaxed by Digby's destruction of a French fleet at Scanderoon (now Alexandretta, a bay between Cyprus and the southern coast of Asia Minor). Upon his return to England he was feted as a hero, made a commissioner of the navy, and granted several lucrative monopolies. He surrounded himself with such literary luminaries as Endymion Porter, Abraham Cowley, John Aubrey, Thomas Randolph, Edmund Waller, Sir William Davenant, and Richard Crashaw. He was widely known as an avid book collector and eloquent conversationalist on literature, occultism, and science. A close friend and admirer was Ben Jonson, who chose Digby to supervise the publication of his complete works in 1640 and commemorated the death of Digby's wife in ten lengthy elegies entitled "Eupheme." An eccentric but enthusiastic literary critic, Digby wrote the first detailed essay on Edmund Spenser, *Observations on the 22nd Stanza in the 9th Canto of the 2nd Book of Spenser's Faery Queen* (wr. 1628; pr. 1643), exploring Spenser's stanza comparing the Castle of Alma with the geometrical structure of man's body and soul, a metaphor Digby interprets as a Platonic allegory. Digby also wrote a criticism of Sir Thomas Browne, *Observations upon Religio medici* (1643), in which he rebukes the Norwich physician for his neglect of experimentation, unscientific beliefs, and facile religious ideas.

Born and raised a Roman Catholic, Digby converted to the Anglican faith in the early 1630s under the influence of his friend archbishop William Laud, then he returned to Catholicism after his wife's death. In his grief he sequestered himself for two years (1633-35) at Gresham College, London, where he dabbled in alchemy and occultism but also gave himself over diligently to more systematic studies such as chemistry (with Robert Boyle), magnetism (with William Gilbert), and medicine (with William Harvey). His experiments in chemistry led him to the discovery of the necessity of oxygen to plant life. After his studies at Gresham College he returned to Paris, where he resided until 1660. There he wrote a preface to Sir Tobie Matthews' English version of St. Augustine (1636), discussed philosophy with Thomas Hobbes and René Descartes, and frequented the intellectual salon at the Hôtel de Rambouillet. By 1640 he had begun his philosophical magnum opus, later published in Paris with the title *Two Treatises, in the One of which, the Nature of Bodies; in the Other, the Nature of Man's Soul, is looked into: in way of discovery of the Immortality of Reasonable Souls* (1644). The first treatise is a massive compilation derived mainly from Aristotle, Galen, Galileo, Descartes, Gilbert, and Harvey with a view toward demonstrating the Cartesian concept of nature as extension and motion. Digby's belief that all material phenomena can be explained, known, and measured by experimentation is as optimistic as Bacon's; his psychology is as mechanistic as his friend Hobbes', his metaphysics as atomistic as Descartes'. Unlike them, however, he is totally incapable of sustaining a coherent pattern of ideas, and the treatise frequently dissolves into fragmentary digressions on small points of embryology, magnetism, and physiology still left partially undigested from his years at Gresham College.

The second treatise, on the immortality of the soul, is more unified and fluent, though less original. He argues that the immortality of the soul is proved by its manifest irrelevance to those material workings of nature described in the first treatise: the soul apprehends without sense data or extension, functions independently of motion, and perceives infinity. In essence, he makes no real distinction between soul and mind. *Two Treatises* illustrates the peculiar bent of Digby's dualism. Unlike Hobbes and Descartes, he creates out of the tensions between body and soul a symbiosis rather than a synthesis, and the hallmark of his baroque sensibilities is his capacity for occupying antithetical worlds simultaneously. Digby's biographer Robert T. Petersson describes him accurately as a "bewildered dualist . . . half-medieval, half-modern, partly devoted to experimentation, partly to the traditional framework of thought."

A related aspect of that mentality was an incongruous mixture of credulity and skepticism, intellectual integrity and purest charlatanism. In 1657, for example, he delivered a lecture at Montpellier before an audience of physicians on the efficacy of "sympathetic powders" in the treatment of wounds. According to this theory, a cut could be healed by applying powders or salves to the knife blade causing the wound, or even to a bloodied garment, rather than to the wound itself. Published as *Discours fait en une Célèbre Assemblée* (Paris, 1658), Digby's theory of "sympathetic powders" created a sensation throughout Europe. Two English translations appeared the same year; the book was rendered into Dutch, German (ten versions), and Latin, and went through twenty-nine editions.

During Queen Henrietta Maria's exile in France, Digby acted as her chancellor, representing her in Rome on two fruitless missions (1645-47) aimed at raising money for the Royalist cause. Returning to England in 1654 to claim his estates, he developed a close personal friendship with his former enemy Oliver Cromwell. Two works during this period, *A Discourse Concerning Infallibility* (1652) and *Of Adhering to God* (1654), the latter an English version of Albertus Magnus, attest his Roman Catholic orthodoxy. With the Restoration he returned to live in England, where he published his findings on chemical processes in plants, *A Discourse Concerning the Vegetation of Plants* (1661), and became a charter member of the Royal Society. One of his most popular works, published posthumously, was an eccentric but characteristically fascinating cookbook, *The Closet of the Eminently Learned Sir Kenelm Digby Kt. Opened* (1677).

Separate editions of Digby's works are listed in the *CBEL,* I. E. W. Bligh reprints several items in *Sir Kenelm Digby and his Venetia* (1932), including the criticism of Spenser. Digby's Mediterranean account was edited by James Bruce for the Camden Society (1868), his unpublished poems by H. A. Bright (1877), and his cookbook by Anne Macdonell (1910). The standard biography is by Robert T. Petersson, *Sir Kenelm Digby, the Ornament of England: 1603-65* (1956). Criticism of Browne by Digby and Alexander Ross (1590-1654) is studied by James N. Wise, *Sir Thomas Browne's Religio Medici and Two Seventeenth Century Critics* (1973). See also Catherine A. Acherman, "Fashionable Platonism in Sir Kenelm Digby's *Private Memoirs,*" *CLAJ,* V (1961).

Discovery of a New World (Joseph Hall). See UTOPIAN FICTION.

Discovery of...Guiana, The. See RALEIGH, SIR WALTER.

Doctor Faustus. A tragedy by Christopher Marlowe, probably written around 1588. There was an edition prior to the first extant edition of 1592. Others followed in 1601, 1604, 1609, and 1610. Marlowe's play is the earliest dramatization of the ancient German Faust legend and was probably derived from the "English Faustbook," *The History of the Damnable Life and Deserved Death of Dr. J. Faustus,* which may have been printed earlier than the only surviving edition of 1592. This book is a translation from the German *Historia von D. Johann Fausten,* published in 1587. Many variations on the legend appeared in Germany after 1587. The historical figure behind these legends is perhaps the shadowy one of a magician named Georg Faust (1480?-1538), about whom little of certainty is known.

Marlowe's play survives in two quite different but almost equally corrupt editions, the so-called A and B texts. The A text, the earlier of the two, contains over two hundred lines not found in B, together with several farcical scenes which some scholars have attributed to Thomas Nashe, William Rowley, and others. In recent years confidence has grown in the B text, which many scholars accept as the more authentic—but still very erroneous and marred—version of Marlowe's original play. (The synopsis that follows refers, for the most part, to the B text.)

Doctor Faustus begins with a long soliloquy in Faustus' study as he broods over the "four faculties" of humanistic studies—philosophy, medicine, law, and divinity. He has gained easy mastery over them all, and concludes that all learning is banal and simplistic except magic. Faustus conjures up a devil, Mephistophilis, Satan's minion, and offers to sell his soul in exchange for twenty-four years of luxurious living and complete obedience from Mephistophilis. In spite of the admonitions of his good angel to "lay that damned book" of magic aside and console himself with Holy Scripture, Faustus heeds his evil angel and determines to command the elements like a god. In parody of these grim matters, Faustus' silly assistant Wagner tries to persuade a village oaf to bind himself for seven years and actually succeeds in conjuring up two minor devils. These comic scenes with Wagner are interspersed throughout the play, and some scenes of buffoonery involve Faustus as well as his assistant.

At midnight in his study Faustus signs in blood his forbidden contract, but as he writes the blood ominously congeals, and Mephistophilis is required to make it flow again with hot coals. Faustus debates about astronomy, philosophy, and divinity with Mephistophilis, and is disillusioned to hear "questions that even Wagner can decide." To amuse him, Lucifer presents, ironically, a grotesque pageant of the seven deadly sins. Much of the remainder of the play shows Faustus enjoying his magic powers abroad. In Rome he plays tricks on the pope, and at the court of Emperor Charles V he astonishes everyone with his feats.

Back at Wittenberg twenty-four years later, Faustus waits in agony for Lucifer to exact his payment. He feasts and carouses, turns a deaf ear of despair to the pleadings of his good angel, and in a memorable scene, raises a vision of Helen of Troy ("Was this the face that launched a thousand ships, / And burnt the topless towers of Illium?"). At the stroke of midnight the fiends carry Faustus to hell, and the play concludes:

Cut is the branch that might have grown full straight,
And burned is Apollo's laurel bough
That sometime grew within this learned man.

Doctor Faustus is a powerful reworking of the traditional morality-play conflict between good and evil in man's soul. In spite of the implorings of the good angel, who counsels Faustus to the very end, he cannot repent of sin because he cannot believe in God's forgiveness. Faustus falls into sin through vanity and pride, and he is ultimately damned by *accidia,* or despair.

There were many renditions of the Faust story after Marlowe's. Goethe's play *Faust,* in two parts, was mainly inspired by a puppet show Goethe saw as a boy, although he later read Marlowe's version and exclaimed, "How carefully it is all planned!" Thomas Mann's novel *Doktor Faustus* employs the story of Faust as a sustained myth paralleling the fall of his hero, Adrian Leverkühn. Several operas have been based on the Faust legend: Boito's *Mefistofele* (1866), Gounod's *Faust* (1859), Berlioz's *La Damnation de Faust* (1893), and Busoni's *Doktor Faust* (1925).

The A and B texts have been edited in the same volume by W. W. Greg for the Clarendon Press (1950). The more authoritative B version is the basis of the edition in the Revels Plays series by John D. Jump (1962) and in *The Complete Plays,* ed. Irving Ribner (1963). Important criticism is in *The Works and Life,* ed. R. H. Case, 6 vols. (1930-33). See also Harry Levin, *The Overreacher, A Study of Christopher Marlowe* (1952); J. B. Steane, *Marlowe, A Critical Study* (1964); and Michael Hattaway, "The Theology of Marlowe's *Doctor Faustus,*" *Ren D,* III (1970). See also *Twentieth-Century Interpretations of Doctor Faustus,* ed. Willard Farnham (1969).

De doctrina Christiana ("On Christian Doctrine"). A religious treatise in Latin by John MILTON. Of very uncertain date, but probably composed between 1656 and 1660, *De doctrina* was not published during Milton's lifetime. His secretary, Daniel Skinner, a young Oxford graduate, made tentative plans to print Milton's manuscript in Amsterdam in 1675, but Skinner finally desisted after being warned that publishing such a controversial religious work might impair his political career. The manuscript remained in the London Public Records Office until 1823, when it was discovered by a clerk; two years later, by command of King George IV, it was edited for publication, with notes and an English translation, by Bishop Charles R. Sumner for the Cambridge University Press.

It is evident why Milton chose not to publish *De doctrina* during his lifetime, and especially after the re-establishment of the Anglican episcopacy in 1660, and why Daniel Skinner feared the work would damage his reputation. Addressed to "all churches of Christ," *De doctrina* is not only anti-Anglican and anti-Calvinist, but boldly free-thinking by any orthodox standards in its wide-ranging discussion of the creation, the trinity, revelation, the sacraments, predestination, natural law and teleology, man before and after the Fall, and many other points of faith and theology.

Consistent with the views of the Dutch Protestant theologian Jacobus Arminius (1560-1609), and contrary to Calvinist doctrine, Milton strongly argues for freedom of will and denies predestination and even the irrevocability of God's decrees (a theological position known as "Arminianism"). Moreover, Milton also rejects the concept of the trinity, describing the Son as inferior to the Father, and the Holy Ghost as little more than a symbol or figure of speech (a unitarian view implicit in *Paradise Lost*). He also repudiates as unessential or superstitious all formalities and rituals of worship not expressly prescribed by Scripture, condones divorce on grounds other than adultery (as he had done in his divorce tracts), and insists that polygamy is not forbidden in either the Old or New Testament. The work is written in a plain, coldly rational Latin heavily larded with Scriptural references and quotations, and has little intrinsic literary merit; nevertheless, it provides a fascinating, essential source for a study of Milton's religious ideas in his major poems.

The standard edition is in the so-called "Columbie Milton," *The Works of John Milton,* ed. Frank A. Patterson, 18 vols. (1931-38), XIV-XVI. *John Milton: Complete Poems and Major Prose,* ed. Merritt Y. Hughes (1957), follows Patterson's English text (based on Bishop Sumner's translation) in reproducing Book I, Chapters 1-10 and 27, and Book II, Chapter 9, of Milton's treatise. The most authoritative analysis is by Maurice Kelley, *This Great Argument: A Study of De Doctrina Christiana as a Gloss upon Paradise Lost* (1941). See also Arthur Sewell, *A Study of Milton's Christian Doctrine* (1939; rev. ed., 1967), and G. N. Conklin, *Biblical Criticism and Heresy in Milton* (1949).

Doctrine and Discipline of Divorce, The. The first of several divorce tracts by John MILTON. *The Doctrine and Discipline* was first published anonymously in 1643; a second edition in 1644 added chapter divisions and considerably more material. Other of Milton's divorce tracts include *The Judgment of Martin Bucer Concerning Divorce* (1644), *Tetrachordon,* and *Colasterion* (both 1645). The immediate occasion for *The Doctrine and Discipline* was Milton's separation from his first wife, Mary Powell, in 1642, and the erosion of their marriage. Faced with church laws allowing divorce on no grounds except adultery, Milton attempts in these tracts to alter the laws.

In resting his case on Scripture, Milton's task was formidable, for in the New Testament he confronted two passages by Jesus opposing divorce, especially *Matthew* V:32: "Whosoever shall put away his wife, saving for the cause of fornication, causeth her to commit adultery." Milton contended that this restriction did not cancel the law of Moses in Deuteronomy XXIV:1-2: "When a man hath taken a wife and married her, and it come to pass that she shall find no favor in his eyes, because he hath found some uncleanness in her; then let him write her a bill of divorcement, and give it in her hand, and send her out of his house." In effect, Milton contended for divorce on grounds of incompatibility. Moreover, since true marriage is not a physical union that can be effected by the physical power of the state, it cannot be maintained except by the two people involved; thus "love in marriage cannot live or subsist unless it be mutual; and where love cannot be, there can be left of wedlock nothing but the empty husk of an outside matrimony, as undelightful and unpleasing to God as any other kind of hypocrisy." Like Christ's words describing the Sabbath in Mark II:27, marriage "was made for man, not man for marriage." For Milton, England's divorce laws represented violation of Christ's humane intentions, corruption of reason and "tyranny of custom."

Milton's *Doctrine and Discipline* created a furor; he was branded a domestic anarchist and a threat to public morals, and his name was cited in Parliament to justify the new censorship laws of 1643. Milton replied with AREOPAGITICA (1644), a pamphlet in defense of liberty of the press.

Milton's divorce tracts are in editions by F. A. Patterson, *The Student's Milton* (rev. ed., 1933), and *Complete Poems and Major Prose,* ed. Merritt Y. Hughes (1957); both are fully annotated. Their role in Milton's development is treated by Denis Saurat, *Milton: Man and Thinker* (rev. ed., 1944). See also John Halkett, *Milton and the Idea of Matrimony:*

A Study of the Divorce Tracts and Paradise Lost (1970); and Ann Keplinger, "Milton: Polemics, Epic, and the Woman Problem Again," *Cithara,* X (1971).

domestic tragedy. A tragedy dealing with ordinary people in a domestic conflict rather than with kings and princes. English domestic tragedy has its origins in the medieval MORALITY PLAYS, with their solemn moral struggles involving ordinary and representative types rather than aristocrats, as in the morality *Everyman* (c. 1500), and received later impetus from the CHRONICLE PLAYS, which dealt sympathetically with such middle-class characters as Jane Shore, the much-maligned mistress of Edward IV. At the peak of its vogue in the 1590s, English domestic tragedy featured middle-class characters in a contemporary English setting, a realistic atmosphere offset by occasional farce and scenes of low comedy, and a moralizing, pietistic tone.

Following the morality plays, several Tudor interludes such as John Phillips' *Patient Grissil* (wr. c. 1558-61) and Thomas Garter's *Virtuous and Godly Susanna* (wr. c. 1569), although ending happily, treat domestic problems with moral gravity. George Whetstone's PROMOS AND CASSANDRA (1578), a full-length early Elizabethan play, and the chief source of Shakespeare's MEASURE FOR MEASURE, deals compassionately with main characters of less than noble stature. Unlike the fully developed domestic tragedies of later years, however, Whetstone's play does not have a contemporary English setting.

The first great tragedy of ordinary life is the anonymous ARDEN OF FEVERSHAM (1592), a dramatization from an account of about six pages in Raphael Holinshed's *Chronicles* of an actual murder in Feversham, Kent, in 1551. *Arden* is grimly realistic and brutal, the characterization of Alice Arden and her lover Mosbie vividly portrayed. In the end all the culprits are punished, and Alice, like most transgressors in domestic tragedy, expresses her repentance in pietistic language:

Leave now to trouble me with worldly things,
And let me meditate upon my savior Christ,
Whose blood must save me for the blood I shed.

Another murder, this one in 1573 of a London merchant named George Saunders, provided the subject for an equally realistic domestic tragedy, *A Warning for Fair Women,* (perf. c. 1599), the story of which the anonymous playwright found in a pamphlet by Anthony Munday, *A View of Sundry Examples. A Warning for Fair Women* is described by its author as a "true and home-born tragedy," and like *Arden of Feversham,* the murder of a husband results from the wife's adultery. Like *Arden* also, the murder is discovered by a miraculous event, for "Divine Providence" enables the only witness, a small boy, to live long enough to name the culprits. Such abstract characters as Charity and Lust point up the affinities of *A Warning* to the morality plays.

In Robert Yarington's *Two Lamentable Tragedies* (perf. c. 1599), which deals with the murder of a London merchant, Thomas Beech, in 1594, avarice rather than lust motivates the crime. After Beech is murdered for his money by Thomas Merry and his sister Rachel, and they are hanged for the murder, Beech's young heir Pertillo is killed in Italy by his uncle Fallerio, who hopes to possess the estate. Appropriately in this crude and sordid tale of multiple murders, the prologue is given by the morality-type characters Avarice, Homicide, and Truth.

An equally crude but far more popular and enduring domestic tragedy is A YORKSHIRE TRAGEDY, first published in 1608 with Shakespeare's name on the title page. Subsequent editions bearing Shakespeare's name appeared in 1619 and in the 1664 and 1685 folios, but few scholars are willing to assign the play, with its doggerel verse and awkward prose, to a dramatist of Shakespeare's stature. Based on an actual murder in 1605 recounted in John Stowe's *Annals, A Yorkshire Tragedy* tells of a man who, in love with one woman but forced into marriage with another, sinks into a life of dissipation and finally breaks out in violence, stabbing his wife and murdering two of their children. The author views the husband's crime as the inevitable outcome of a series of vices that put him in the hands of the devil and enable Satan to force the murder. In another play based on this crime, THE MISERIES OF ENFORCED MARRIAGE by George Wilkins, only the first part of the tale in Stowe's *Annals* is presented. After the hero's marriage and subsequent prodigality, he receives a large inheritance and resolves to mend his life.

Tragedies of domestic crime waned in popularity toward the end of James I's reign. The last notable domestic tragedy was by Dekker, Ford, and Rowley, THE WITCH OF EDMONTON, performed in 1621 but not published until 1658. It tells a tale of "Forced marriage, murder; murder blood requires; / Reproach, revenge; revenge, hell's help desires." As in *A Yorkshire Tragedy*, demonic passion is evident in both the plot of Mother Sawyer, the witch, and the story of Frank Thorney, who murders his wife while under the magic spell of a black dog.

The most artistic domestic tragedy is Thomas Heywood's A WOMAN KILLED WITH KINDNESS (perf. c. 1603; pr. 1607), a drama which, according to H. H. Adams, represents "the earliest of the extant plays to deal with a situation of family life divorced from the extravagance and sensationalism of murder." As a Christian gentleman, the hero Frankford represses his impulses toward a violent revenge when he discovers his wife Anne is guilty of adultery; instead of killing her, he vows to torment her conscience with charity and magnanimity:

. . . I'll not martyr thee,
Nor mark thee for a strumpet, but with usage
Of more humility torment thy soul,
And kill thee, even with kindness.

Stricken with guilt, Anne goes into total seclusion and experiences her repentance so rigorously she virtually starves herself to death. As she dies, her husband, observing "the duty of a merciful Christian," finally bestows his forgiveness with a last kiss that weds them "once again." In the subplot another "kindness" is dramatized in terms of class values. After Sir Charles Mountford is financially ruined by Sir Francis Acton, Sir Charles desperately offers his sister's virtue in exchange for the retention of his family estate, but Sir Francis gallantly refuses to exact revenge and, instead, releases his enemy from debt and honorably marries his virtuous sister. The subplot concludes happily with Sir Francis and his friends, secure in their solvency and mutual gains, grouped around the deathbed of Sir Francis' sister Anne, who expires joyously upon her husband's benevolent kiss:

Pardoned on earth, soul, thou in heaven art free;
Once more thy wife, dies thus embracing thee.

T. S. Eliot (in *Elizabethan Essays*) dismisses Heywood's play as being "not, in the highest sense, tragedy at all" because of its mixture of pathos and tragicomedy and its focus on narrow class values and sectarian morality to the exclusion of any cosmic significance. Other critics see these weaknesses as inherent in the genre of domestic tragedy. Whatever the limitations of the type, however, its characteristic elements of realism, solemnity, and family conflict left indelible traces in such masterpieces of the theater as *Othello*, *King Lear*, and *Macbeth*.

The definitive study of domestic tragedy is H. H. Adams, *English Domestic or Homiletic Tragedy, 1575-1642* (1943).

Donne, John (1572?-1631). Poet and divine. Donne was born in London of a distinguished Roman Catholic family. His father, who died when Donne was four, was a prosperous ironmonger. His mother was the daughter of John Heywood, the courtier-poet of Henry VIII, and granddaughter of Sir Thomas More's sister, Elizabeth Rastell. Two brothers of Donne's mother were Jesuits, and she remained a devout Catholic to the end of her life. In the same year Donne's father died, she married Dr. John Symmings, president of the Royal College of Physicians; he died in 1588, and she married again three years later, to one Richard Rainsford. Hence Donne was descended from a proud Catholic family, with a strong-willed, energetic mother. The impression is one of a brilliant, close-knit family drawn even closer together by virulent anti-Catholicism and official obstruction of opportunities.

A precocious scholar, Donne was sent to Oxford at twelve, where he remained until 1587, when he either transferred to Cambridge, as his early biographer Isaak WALTON, states, or fought against the Spanish in the Low Countries. By 1591 he was studying law, first at Thavies Inn and later, for a longer period, at Lincoln's Inn. During these early years he was, according to his own testimony and that of Walton, an omnivorous scholar and perhaps something of a rake. In the words of Sir Richard Baker, the Elizabethan historian, he was "not dissolute, but very neat, a great visitor of ladies, a great frequenter of plays, a great writer of conceited verses." He was also something of a soldier-adventurer. In 1596-97 he accompanied Essex on military expeditions to Cádiz and the Azores. There is a portrait of him in soldier's garb, believed to have been painted around 1591; the large, intelligent eyes are pensive but alert, the lips under a pencil mustache sensual, the face lean and swarthy.

According to Ben Jonson, Donne wrote "all of his best pieces ere he was twenty-five years old," and in all probability it was sometime during the middle or late 1590s that he wrote most of what were later called his *Songs and Sonnets,* the satires (see SATIRE), and the elegies. Certainly the very popular companion poems, "The Storm" and "The Calm," and several verse letters to Sir Henry Wotton were written during the expedition to the Azores. One passage from "The Calm," a description of a ship becalmed, Jonson liked so much he committed it to memory:

And all the tackling is a frippery.
No use of lanterns; and in one place lay
Feathers and dust, today and yesterday.
Earth's hollowness, which the world's lungs are,
Have no more wind than the upper vault of air.

Judging from *Satire III* and from his own later testimony, Donne went through a period of profound religious questioning, especially regarding Catholicism—a painful experience, no doubt, in view of his family background and the fact that his brother Henry died in prison in 1593 a martyr to the Catholic cause.

Upon his return from the Azores, Donne gained an appointment as secretary to Sir Thomas Egerton, the lord keeper, and his career began to flourish. In 1601 he was a member of Parliament, on familiar terms with poets and statesmen, and, no doubt in secret, composing his *Metempsychosis*, an eccentric poetic project in which, by Jonson's testimony, Donne intended to trace the soul of Eve's apple through "all the bodies of the heretics from the soul of Cain" down to the body of Calvin. Actually, it was Queen Elizabeth who was to receive this satirical apple. But the poem progressed no further than 500 lines or so of ferociously erotic verse, with the soul of the fatal apple still enroute through *Genesis.* By this time Donne had probably broken with Catholicism, and may even have been—in view of the progress of his career—a nominal Anglican; inside, however, he was restlessly skeptical, hostile to authority, and perhaps even defiantly sensual and promiscuous. In *Satire III* he treats the various religious sects, including Catholicism, in sexual metaphors:

. . . Careless Phrygius doth abhor
All, because all cannot be good, as one
Knowing some women whores, dares marry none.

The love poems associated with this period express an astonishing contrast of tones. "The Flea" is a strenuously witty exercise in verbal and logical athletics, "Song" ("Go and catch a falling star") a fleering denial of female virtue, and "The Indifferent" conveys a kind of adolescent bravado:

I can love both fair and brown,
Her whom abundance melts, and her whom want betrays,
Her who loves loneness best, and her who masks and plays,
Her whom the country formed, and whom the town,
Her who believes, and her who tries,
Her who still weeps with spungy eyes,
And her who is dry cork and never cries.
I can love her, and her, and you and you,
I can love any, so she be not true.

Other moods, as in *Elegy 15* ("To His Mistress Going to Bed"), are wildly erotic:

License my roving hands, and let them go,
Behind, before, above, between, below.
O my America! my Newfound-land,
My kingdom, safeliest when with one man manned,
My mine of precious stones, my Emperie,
How blest am I in this discovering thee!

Some lyrical notes, however, are as softly modulated as those of any Petrarchan lover:

Sweetest love, I do not go,
For weariness of thee,
Nor in the hope the world can show
A fitter love for me . . .

It is always perilous to quote Donne's poems in part, for they are tightly integrated and extremely concentrated, each line driving toward the next in explosive transitions, and just as it is impossible to predict from its inception how a poem will conclude, the whole can only be very dimly seen through any of its parts. Donne has been called metaphysical, a term first employed in a derogatory way to describe the "academic," intellectual quality of a verse that abjures both Ovidian mythology and Petrarchan metaphors and, instead, strives for precision of thought and feeling, often at the expense of congruity or conventional notions of decorum (see METAPHYSICAL POETS). In the love poems Donne writes out of his wealth of learning in Italian and Spanish literature, the medieval church fathers, the old disciplines of alchemy and astrology as well as the new speculations in logic, philosophy, astronomy, geography, and mathematics. His relentless pursuit of exactness, coupled with a white-hot wit, breathtaking capacity for speculation, and contempt for conformity allow for few compromises with shallow-minded readers or with those sentimentalists who insist upon a conventional vocabulary for love poetry. "He affects the metaphysics, not only in his satires, but in his amorous verses," Dryden complained of Donne in 1693, "and perplexes the minds of the fair sex with nice speculations of philosophy when he should engage their hearts, and entertain them with the softnesses of love." The result was what the Elizabethans termed "strong lines," or what Samuel Johnson described as *discordia concors,* in which "heterogeneous ideas are yoked by violence together," as in the oft-quoted stanzas of "A Valediction: Forbidding Mourning," where Donne compares the souls of parting lovers to twin compasses:

If they be two, they are two so
  As stiff twin compasses are two,
Thy soul, the fixed foot, makes no show
  To move but doth, if the other do.

And though it in the center sit,
  Yet when the other far doth roam,
It leans and hearkens after it,
  And grows erect, as that comes home.

To most Elizabethan poets a technical metaphor of this kind in a love poem would have appeared to be a violation of decorum; yet the image is a precise conceit in the metaphysical manner—ingenious, incongruous, and scrupulously extended. In "A Valediction: Of Weeping," similarly, Donne compares his tears at parting from his mistress to coins bearing her reflection; they have exceptional value because they were "minted" in her face. Such an extravagant conceit would have been a stopping point for most poets, but for Donne it is only the occasion for extending the metaphor by equating his tear with a "round ball," and that ball with a globe of the world:

  On a round ball
A workman that hath copies by, can lay
An Europe, Afric, and an Asia,
And quickly make that, which was nothing, all;
  So doth each tear,
  Which thee doth wear,
A globe, yea world by that impression grow,
Till thy tears mixed with mine do overflow
This world, by waters sent from thee, my heaven dissolved so.

Thus in a few brief lines the round O of the workman's globe (a "nothing") becomes an "all" (everything), and each tear bearing the lady's image becomes a world because she means everything to the poet. As in all Donne's poems, the initial metaphor is the first in a chain of closely connected, meaningful comparisons; the development is invariably linear, never massive as in Marlowe or Spenser, and no single phrase can be omitted, no metaphor relinquished, without impairing the poem as a steadily unfolding process.

Another feature of Donne's poetry, and one noted by his first twentieth-century editor, Sir. H. J. C. Grierson, is a rhetorical directness that confronts the reader with a dramatic situation rather than lures him into a receptive frame of mind. The language is colloquial, the tone abrupt: "For God's sake hold your tongue and let me love," or "Stand still, and I will read thee / A lecture, love, in love's philosophy," or:

I wonder by my troth, what thou, and I
Did, till we loved? Were we not weaned till then?

This is not emotion recollected in tranquility but response to an immediate dramatic situation, and as Helen Gardner has observed, most of Donne's poems are not only dramatic but argumentative, poems occasioned by lovers parting, a friend's upbraiding, a dream, or even a flea discovered on a lady's arm. In the religious poems the dramatic occasion can be Good Friday, when the poet finds himself on a journey, or it may be a piercing thought: "What if this present were the world's last night?" The salient point is that for Donne poetry meant a passionate intellectual response to immediate experience, not invocation of myth or remembrance of things past, and, for better or worse, his hungry wit is forever tossing and twisting an idea like a hungry dog worrying a bone. For Spenser the marrow of truth was accessible to reason and singular (like his symbol of truth, Una in *The Faerie Queene*); for Donne, afflicted by the dichotomies of the medieval and the modern, by the old scholasticism and the new learning that "calls all in doubt," it was multiple, ambiguous, inaccessible except by indirect pursuit:

On a huge hill,
Cragged, and steep, Truth stands, and he that will
Reach her, about must, and about must go . . .

Those poems which can be identified as early show that Donne's long quest after truth was already begun in the 1590s, and it was a journey through towering obstacles—religious allegiances combined with deep spiritual fears and anxieties, intellectual confusion resulting from a collision of scholastic training and new philosophy, an essentially religious temperament both tormented and inspired by powerful erotic impulses. But Donne's professional and economic ordeal began with what Walton calls "the remarkable error of his life," his impetuous marriage in December 1601 to Egerton's niece Ann More, then only seventeen. He was promptly dismissed from Egerton's service and imprisoned by the girl's father. ("John Donne, Anne Donne, Undone," the bridegroom quipped to his new wife in a letter from the Fleet prison.)

"God knows," observed Walton, "it proved to be true." For over fourteen years Donne struggled in poverty, having to rely upon a slender inheritance and the occasional generosity of patrons while his wife bore him twelve children, five of whom died. For a time in 1607-08 he assisted an Anglican bishop, Thomas Morton, in composing anti-Catholic polemics, and although Morton assured him of a profitable benefice if he took orders, Donne refused. About the same time, in what must have been his bleakest despair, he began *Biathanatos* (pr. c. 1646), an erudite and sophisticated prose work examining the historical and Scriptural compatibility of Christianity and suicide.

Donne's situation gradually improved after 1608, when his wife's wealthy father began to grant some financial assistance. Then, too, Donne was often invited to Twickenham, residence of the countess of Bedford and scene of several poems. There was also the friendship of the countess of Salisbury, Magdalene Herbert (the poet George Herbert's mother), and Sir Robert Drury, a wealthy benefactor whose daughter's death Donne eulogized in two long philosophical poems, *The First Anniversary* (1611) and *The Second Anniversary* (1612), which employ as their principal conceit the gradual deterioration of the world since the child's death. When Jonson complained that such extravagant adulation of a twelve-year-old girl was "profane and full of blasphemies," Donne's answer was that Elizabeth Drury symbolized "the Idea of Woman and not as she was." *The First Anniversary* is noteworthy for its moving expression of Donne's reaction to the "new science":

And new philosophy calls all in doubt,
The element of fire is quite put out;
The sun is lost, and the earth, and no man's wit
Can well direct him where to look for it.
And freely men confess that this world's spent,
When in the planets and the firmament,
They seek so many new; they see that this
Is crumbled out again to his atomies;
'Tis all in pieces, all coherence gone;
All just supply, and all relation . . .

In 1610 and 1611 Donne published two prose attacks on the Jesuits, *Pseudo-Martyr* and IGNATIUS HIS CONCLAVE (the latter in both Latin and English), which earned the notice of James I, who let it be known he would reward Donne's efforts providing he became ordained an Anglican priest. Nevertheless, Donne held out for several more years. Walton suggests that Donne felt unworthy, perhaps because of his early years as "John Donne the rake"; but there were doubtless other reasons as well—his religious perplexities, his sense of family loyalty and abhorrence of defection. He did not take Anglican orders until January 23, 1615, and only then with great humility and reservations. Soon afterward new honors came to him from the king—an honorary degree from Cambridge, two vicarages in Kent, and a year later, in 1616, a readership in divinity at Lincoln's Inn, where Donne had been a student years before and where he now began, with his *Essays on Divinity,* a new career as one of England's greatest divines.

In 1617, however, Donne was thrown into utter despair by the death of his wife after the birth of their twelfth child. He pledged himself to a life of charity and meditation, "crucified to the world," as he wrote. After a convalescent journey with Lord Duncaster to Germany in 1619, he returned to become dean of St. Paul's, the largest and most influential parish in England, from whose high pulpit, hourglass by his side, he delivered 160 of the most stirring sermons in the language. Meanwhile *Songs and Sonnets,* the collection of 55 amorous poems from his youth (of which, if Jonson is to be believed, Donne "repented on highly"), continued to circulate in manuscript.

After a serious illness in 1623 that prompted his *Devotions on Emergent Occasions* (1624), Donne was appointed vicar of St. Dunstan's in the West, where one of his parishioners was Isaak Walton, his future biographer. The remaining years he preached, added to his written sermons (most published posthumously), and produced the twenty-six poems collected in *Holy Sonnets.* At St. Paul's a month before his death in March 1631, he preached before Charles I his own funeral sermon, DEATH'S DUEL, "not to preach mortification by a living voice," Walton records, "but mortality by a decayed body and a dying face." Walton describes how in his last days Donne commissioned a portrait of himself in a winding sheet, "and caused it to be set by his bedside, where it continued, and became his hourly object till his death." It is appropriate that the poet who made death his lyrical obsession in both his sermons and spiritual poems, who chastised death as a proud but impotent tyrant, and who wrote such eloquent sermons on worms, graves and the spirit's transcendence, should have chosen this incongruous but effective way of expressing his supremacy over his life's omnipresent companion.

Most readers know Donne's prose only from the famous passage in his *Devotions:* "... and therefore never send to know for whom the bell tolls; it tolls for thee." The tone of this passage is not Donne's usual one, for he more often invokes the Augustinian and Counter-Reformation anxieties attendant upon recalling man's physical decay, disease, death, and depravity; the same "metaphysical shudder" of the poems, with their images of "bright bracelets about the bone" in tombs and their apocalyptic visions of the Last Judgment, is also found in the sermons. His prose style, sometimes referred to as "loose" or "baroque," is characterized by open ended coordinating conjunctions that pile up phrases as if into limitless expanse:

> My thoughts reach all, comprehend all. Inexplicable mystery, I their creator am in a close prison, in a sick bed, anywhere, and any one of my creations, my thoughts, is with the sun, and beyond the sun, overtakes the sun, and overgoes the sun in one pace, one step, everywhere...

As a poet Donne's influence among his contemporaries was as great as that of Spenser, Shakespeare, or Jonson, and Jonson's prediction that Donne would perish "for not being understood" did not begin to materialize until after the Restoration, when Donne's obscure conceits, "strong lines," and apparent metrical irregularity or "roughness" ("for not keeping the accent," Jonson had remarked, Donne "deserved hanging") proved incompatible with neoclassic standards of clarity, proportion, and propriety. Dryden's strictures have already been noted, and to these Samuel Johnson added his authoritative censure in his essay on Donne's leading disciple Abraham COWLEY in *The Lives of the Poets* (1779). By the end of the eighteenth century Donne's once prestigious name was all but forgotten.

In the romantic period Donne's orthodox theism and indifference to nature alienated all but a few antiquarians like those devotees of esoterica, Coleridge and Lamb. It was Coleridge who first sensed the interior harmony of Donne's prosody, writing admiringly of him as "wit's forge and fire-blast, meaning's press and screw":

> With Donne, whose muse on dromedary trots,
> Wreathe iron pokers into true-love knots...

The Victorians, on the other hand, objected to Donne's sexual realism and "Gothic irregularities," and Matthew Arnold, perhaps because he thought Donne lacked a prerequisite "high seriousness," omitted him entirely from his honor roll of English poets. Nevertheless, Robert Browning dissented from the majority, and Donne's other disciples kept his name alive, notably in successive editions of

Donne's poems by A. B. Grosart, Charles Norton, and E. K. Chambers, and in 1899 Sir Edmund Gosse produced what was to be for many years the standard biography.

Donne's great stature in the twentieth century began with the publication of his poems in 1912 by Sir Herbert J. C. Grierson, and with T. S. Eliot's enthusiastic reception to that edition. Other members of the disillusioned "lost generation" after World War I thought they saw in Donne a hard-boiled, rebellious compatriot, a proper anodyne to the philosophical raptures of Shelley and Wordsworth and the facile optimism of Tennyson. For the New Critics of the 1930s and 1940s, Donne's complexity provided a justification for their own analytical methods, and they elevated Donne into the ranks of Milton and Shakespeare, and sometimes even above them. Against these extravagant claims the historical critics frequently found themselves playing the awkward game of denigrating Donne in order to praise Milton.

More recently this internecine struggle between the New Critics and the literary historians has fortunately subsided, and Donne is seen more realistically from the diverse perspectives of mythic criticism, the history of ideas, linguistic study, and psychological criticism. Out of this comprehensive and systematic analysis, Donne has emerged as a poet not entirely alien to Milton in many respects, nor even to Spenser, and one whose limitations can now be freely acknowledged. He is not a poet particularly responsive to myth or nature; his images and themes are repetitious and restricted, his genius most comfortable with the brief lyric of erotic or religious passion. And yet, as Ben Jonson observed, he is, in spite of these limitations, "the first poet in the world in some things." At this juncture in literary history, Jonson's verdict would appear to be incontestable.

Besides his two-volume edition of the *Complete Poems* (1912), H. J. C. Grierson has done a convenient one-volume edition (1929). See also *The Complete Poetry,* ed. John T. Shawcross (1967). For the religious verse, *The Divine Poems,* ed. Helen Gardner (1952), is now standard. The definitive edition of Donne's *The Sermons* is by G. R. Potter and Evelyn M. Simpson, 10 vols. (1953-62). R. C. Bald's biography of Donne (1970) is the most concise and accurate, but Edmund Gosse's *Life and Letters,* (1899), is still an excellent introduction. For the vast accumulation of critical studies on Donne, too numerous to cite here, see Theodore Spencer and Mark Van Doren, *Studies in Metaphysical Poetry* (1939), which lists items for 1912-38; William White, *John Donne Since 1900: A Bibliography of Periodical Articles* (1942); Geoffrey L. Keynes, *A Bibliography of Dr. John Donne* (3d ed. 1958); and J. R. Roberts, *John Donne: An Annotated Bibliography of Modern Criticism, 1912-67* (1973).

Drant, Thomas (d. 1578?). For comment on his *A Medicinable Moral,* see SATIRE.

Drayton, Michael (1563-1631). Poet and dramatist. Born in Hartshill, Warwickshire, of yeoman stock, Drayton was raised as a page in the household of Sir Henry Goodere. Little is known of Drayton's life except from his prodigious and variegated literary works—sacred poems, historical narratives, odes, sonnets, epistles, mythological poems, pastoral verse, and plays. Drayton's first work was probably *The Harmony of the Church* (1591), paraphrases of the songs and prayers of the Old Testament and Apocrypha in wooden heptameters ("fourteeners"). By this date he had left the service of Sir Henry Goodere and of Goodere's brother Thomas and settled in London to begin a literary career. During the period 1597-99 the theater manager Philip Henslowe recorded almost two dozen plays by Drayton, all of them in collaboration with other dramatists, and in 1598 Francis Meres in *Palladis Tamia* judged him to be among the "best for tragedy." One of Henslowe's entries includes the play *Sir John Oldcastle* (1599), apparently written to correct the misrepresentation of the Protestant martyr Oldcastle as Falstaff in Shakespeare's *Henry IV* plays. Drayton later became affiliated with the Children of the King's Revels and with the Whitefriars theater (after about 1607), but none of his plays from this period has survived.

Drayton's eclogues, *Idea, the Shepherd's Garland Fashioned in Nine Eclogues* (1593) and *Muse's Elysium* (1630) clearly indicate that he was a disciple of Edmund Spenser, although the Platonism of these pastorals may have been derived from Claude de Pontoux's *L'Idée* (1579), a work that also influenced Drayton's sonnet sequence *Idea's Mirror* (1594). Drayton's sequence consists of 51 sonnets on "amours" in the Petrarchan mode in which the Platonic "idea," or symbol of absolute beauty, seems to have been Sir Henry Goodere's daughter Anne, later Lady Rainsford. All are in the so-called English or Shakespearean sonnet form of three quatrains and a couplet. Characteristically, Drayton continued to revise and amplify the sequence until the complete edition of 1619, adding eighteen sonnets to the 1602 edition, seven to the 1605, and ten to the 1619. These augmentations indicate a consistent development from a relatively spiritless imitation of Petrarch in 1594 toward an energetic, ironic, and colloquial style in 1619 that compares favorably with the best lyrics of Wyatt and Donne. Drayton's famous Sonnet LXI ("Since there's no help, come let us kiss and part") has been praised by Dante Gabriel Rossetti and others as being among the finest in the language; almost equally memorable are Sonnets VI ("How many paltry, foolish, painted things") and VIII ("There's nothing grieves me but that age should haste"). All of these first appeared in the 1619 edition.

Another major poem is Drayton's ENDYMION AND PHOEBE (1595), an Ovidian mythological narrative describing the shepherd Endymion's love for Phoebe, Platonic symbol of ideal beauty. (Keats consulted Drayton's poem in writing his own *Endymion* in 1818.) Unlike Marlowe's *Hero and Leander* or Shakespeare's *Venus and Adonis,* Drayton's poem owes less to Ovid's *Heroides* than to the French poet Du Bartas and to Spenser; Drayton's prolix description of the pastoral beauties of Latmos reflects the influence of Spenser's Garden of Adonis in *The Farerie Queene,* and his mythology is consistently treated as symbolic of Platonic ideas. At the climax of the story Phoebe reveals herself to Endymion to have been the nymph he had previously rejected out of loyalty to the goddess, and for his faith in her as a totally ethereal being, Endymion is rewarded with transcendent knowledge. Thus Phoebe symbolizes divine inspiration. The poem concludes with a tribute to Spenser, Samuel Daniel, and Thomas Lodge.

Drayton's first historical poem, *Piers Gaveston* (1594), also bears affinities to the Ovidian mythological tradition, for in this monologue the narrator, Gaveston, pours out lavish descriptions of his revelries with Edward II. Hence Drayton's nearly 300 six-line stanzas about Gaveston's illicit relationship with Edward owe as much to such erotic Ovidian epyllia as Shakespeare's *Venus and Adonis,* Marlowe's *Hero and Leander,* and Samuel Daniel's *Rosamond* as to the historical monologues in *A Mirror for Magistrates.* Apparently Drayton thought *Piers Gaveston* somewhat too flagrantly Ovidian, for in the 1596 edition he inserted three didactic stanzas pointing out the evils of a love in conflict with reason.

Drayton's next legend in monologue after *Piers Gaveston* was *Matilda* (1594), about the fair and chaste daughter of Lord Robert Fitzwater, in which he uses the rhyme royal of Shakespeare's LUCRECE. (In the second edition of 1596 Matilda refers to herself as "a second Lucretia.") Drayton's story of a girl who resists seduction by King John even at the cost of her life belongs, with Daniel's *Rosamond,* Shakespeare's *Lucrece,* and Willobie's *Avisa,* to the large body of Elizabethan literature glorifying chastity and denouncing lust. Unlike Tarquin, the brutal ravisher of Lucrece, or the lustful ogres in *The Faerie Queene,* John is a sweet-tongued Petrarchan lover with "words steeped in syrup of Ambrosia." Matilda dies with a prayer for him, forgiving him for his sinful desires, and he sincerely repents "love's affliction." Another monologue, or "complaint," is Drayton's *Tragical Legend of Robert, Duke of Normandy* (1596), which tells the misfortunes of William the Conqueror's eldest son and concludes with an allegorical debate between Fame and Fortune. Drayton's *Legend of Great Cromwell,* in which the ghost of Henry VIII's ill-starred minister laments his lofty aspirations and tragic fall, appeared in the last edition of *A Mirror for Magistrates* (1610).

Piers Gaveston may have been the first draft of Drayton's more ambitious historical narrative, the epical *Mortimeriados* ("the Story of Mortimer") in 1596, which Drayton revised as *The Barons' Wars* in 1603. *Mortimeriados* is in rhyme royal, *The Barons' Wars* in ottava rima, but the two versions differ only slightly in their didactic, slow-moving account of the same events and characters dramatized in Marlowe's play EDWARD II.

Drayton's combined interest in Ovid's *Heroides* and *A Mirror for Magistrates* led to the writing of *England's Heroical Epistles,* fictitious letters between famous English lovers beginning with Henry II and Rosamond and concluding with Lady Jane Grey and Guildford Dudley. The first edition of 1597 included nine pairs of lovers; Drayton added three more pairs in the editions of 1598 and 1599. All of the epistles are in heroic couplets. One noteworthy exchange is between the earl of Surrey and his lady Geraldine, an account of Surrey's imagined itinerary in France, Germany, and Italy that draws extensively on details from Surrey's poems and from Nashe's fiction *The Unfortunate Traveller.* The most popular of Drayton's poems, *England's Heroical Epistles* went through thirteen editions during his lifetime.

Drayton's *Poems Lyric and Pastoral* (1606) include his two most famous short historical narratives in verse, "Ode to the Virginia Voyage," a metrical rendition of several prose passages in Richard Hakluyt's "First Voyage to Virginia" in his *Principal Navigations,* and "The Battle of Agincourt," in eight-line stanzas based on several early ballads and on Holinshed's *Chronicles.* The latter poem is famous for its opening lines "Fair stood the wind for France, / When we our sails advance."

Drayton's most ambitious project was POLY-OLBION (Part I, 1612; Part II, 1622) a long topographical description in verse of the counties of England. This itinerary of English villages and rivers is an encyclopedic survey of each region's customs, legends, saints, notable families, and historical events, and was intended as an epic celebration of England's glories past and present. A monumental undertaking that Drayton never really completed, it absorbed much of his creative energy after 1603.

Drayton also wrote verse satires, *The Owl* (1604) and *The Moon-Calf* (1627), both patterned after Spenser's *Mother Hubberd's Tale;* but his best poem of ironic hyperbole is the mock-heroic verse narrative NYMPHIDIA, THE COURT OF FAIRY (1627), which describes the marital conflicts of the fairies Queen Mab and Oberon in delicate, finely wrought eight-line stanzas rhyming *aa ab cc cb.* Its style is derived from Chaucer's "Sir Thopas" in the *Canterbury Tales,* its characters and setting from the fairy world of Shakespeare's *A Midsummer Night's Dream.* (The title *Nymphidia* is from a Greek adjective meaning "bridal.")

In a late poem, an elegy entitled "To My Most Dearly Beloved Henry Reynolds" (1627), Drayton describes in couplets how, "much like a pigmy, scarce ten years old," he had begged his tutor to make him a poet, and his tutor had set him to reading Mantuan, the early sixteenth-century author of Latin eclogues, Vergil's eclogues, and Chaucer. What follows is a survey of English poets from Chaucer to Drayton's contemporaries in which he praises "great moral" Spenser, "noble" Sidney, Daniel, Shakespeare, "neat Marlowe, bathed in the Thespian Springs," and many others (see CRITICISM, LITERARY). As concise literary criticism, the poem compares favorably with Pope's *Essay on Criticism.*

Drayton died in 1631 and was buried in Westminster Abbey. There is a legend that Shakespeare fell ill and died after a drinking bout in Stratford with Drayton and Jonson. An equally dubious legend names Drayton as the Rival Poet of Shakespeare's Sonnets.

The definitive edition of Drayton's works is by J. William Hebel, Kathleen Tillotson, and Bernard H. Newdigate, 5 vols. (1931-41). All of Drayton's important poems are available in the shorter edition edited by C. Brett, *Minor Poems* (1907), and in *The Poems of Michael Drayton,* ed. John Buxton, 2 vols. (1950). The best life is Bernard H. Newdigate, *Michael Drayton and His Circle* (1941). Two significant critical studies are Oliver Elton, *Michael Drayton: A Critical Study* (1905), and R. Noyes, *Drayton's Literary Vogue Since 1631* (1935). There is a Concise Bibliography by S. A. Tannenbaum (1941), added to by "Michael Drayton (1941-65)," ed. G. R. Guffey, in *Elizabethan Bibliographies Supplements,* VII (1967).

Drummond, William, of Hawthornden (1585-1649). Scottish poet. Born at his father's estate at Hawthornden seven miles from Edinburgh, Drummond attended grammar school in Edinburgh and the newly founded University of Edinburgh. After graduating M.A. in 1605, he was sent to study law at Bourges and Paris. When Drummond's father died in 1610, he succeeded to become second laird of Hawthornden, abandoned any ambitions of a career in law, and spent his life reading, writing, and tinkering with inventions, most of them of a military nature.

Drummond's first publication was *Tears on the Death of Meliades* (1613), a eulogy on the death of Prince Henry in one hundred rhyming couplets followed by a sonnet; in the same year he wrote three more eulogies on Prince Henry's death in the collection *Mausoleum, or The Choicest Flowers of the Epitaphs.* He seems to have prepared a collection of poems for publication in 1614, then withdrew them for the later enlarged and revised *Poems: Amorous, Funeral, Divine, Pastoral, in Sonnets, Songs, Sextains, Madrigals* (1616), which includes fifty-five sonnets, sixty-five madrigals, and several pastorals and epigrams. About half of Drummond's *Poems* are paraphrases or translations of continental writers, especially the French poets Pierre de Ronsard (1524-1585) and Philippe Desportes (1546-1606), and the Italian poets Giacomo Sannazaro (1458-1530), Giovanni Battista Guarini (1537-1612), Torquato Tasso (1544-1595), and Giovanni Battista Marino (1569-1625)—and the list is far from complete. The overriding and consistent influence on the *Poems* is Sir Philip Sidney.

In his sonnets—Drummond's most accomplished poems—he uses liberally the Petrarchan conventions and figures of speech grown very shopworn indeed by 1616. His sonnets underscore his disadvantages of nationality and remoteness from London; Drummond was the first Scot to employ the London literary dialect exclusively in his poems, but he imitates a style in vogue a generation or more before his time. Moreover, he occasionally slips into Scotticisms and awkward locutions. For the most part, however, his sonnets are distinguished for their pronounced rhythm and emotional conviction, and poignant touches of melancholy. Drummond preferred three quatrains and a couplet, the so-called English or Shakespearean sonnet, although he varies this pattern, as did his master Sidney in *Astrophel and Stella.*

Drummond's poetry was deeply affected by the death in 1615 of his fiancée Mary Cunningham of Barns, whose loss may account for his pervasive melancholy and withdrawal from the world into a Platonism stressing preexistence, human transience, and immortality: "No wonder now I feel so fair a flame," he writes, "Sith I her loved ere on this earth she came."

His madrigals fuse Petrarch's and Sidney's amorous conceits with the pastoralism of Guarini and Tasso; in them his omnipresent melancholy is occasionally alleviated:

> Come, let us live, and love,
> And kiss, Thaumantia mine,
> I shall the elm be, be to me the vine.

It is impossible to determine whether Drummond intended his madrigals to be set to music; many are indistinguishable from the epigrams which Drummond, a skillful prosodist in the other poems, described as his "Skeltonical" verses, so named for the broken trimeters of John Skelton.

Drummond's literary friends were Sir William Alexander, earl of Stirling (1577?-1640) and author of the Senecan *Monarchial Tragedies,* and Michael Drayton, with whom Drummond corresponded but never met. Another was Ben Jonson, who came to Scotland on a walking tour in 1618, was warmly feted by dignitaries in Edinburgh, and stayed for two weeks with Drummond at Hawthornden. Drummond took careful notes of the great man's expansive conversations, published in the 1711 edition of Drummond's *Works* as "Heads of a Conversation betwixt the Famous Poet Ben Jonson and William Drummond of Hawthornden, January, 1619." Known simply as *Conversations with Drummond* (see JONSON, BEN), it is a priceless literary document and a rare portrait of Jonson, who, Drummond recorded, thought his host's verses "smelled too much of the schools and were not after the fancy of the time."

After 1616 Drummond wrote religious poetry exclusively. His last major publication of verse was *Flowers of Sion* (1623), consisting of several short devotional poems and a prose meditation of fifty pages, *A Cypress Grove.* Some of the poems are redolent of Marino's mannerist eroticism and hyperboles, but Drummond, who deplored both John Donne's "strong lines" and Richard Crashaw's raptures, employs a "sweetness" (the recurring word of critics describing his poems) without verbal extremes, a passionate tone without radical speculations or loss of restraint.

During the struggles between Parliament and Charles I, Drummond remained steadfastly Royalist, turning out biting epigrams on political subjects. His *History of Scotland from the Year 1423 until the Year 1542* was published posthumously in 1655 and included *A Cypress Grove,* several political tracts, and his correspondence.

The standard edition of the poems is *The Poetical Works of William Drummond of Hawthornden, with "A Cypress Grove,"* ed. L. E. Kastner, 2 vols. (1913). The fullest biography is by David Masson, *Drummond of Hawthornden: The Story of His Life and Writings* (1873; repr. 1969), although A. Joly's

William Drummond de Hawthornden (1934), in French, is more concise and interesting. For critical analyses of the poems, see F. R. Fogle, *A Critical Study of William Drummond of Hawthornden* (1952). The standard edition of Drummond's *Conversations* is in *Ben Jonson,* ed. C. H. Herford, Percy and Eveleyn Simpson, 11 vols. (1925-53), I.

Duchess of Malfi, The. A tragedy by John WEBSTER, written in 1613-14 and printed in 1623. It was based on a true account reported by Matteo Bandello and read by Webster in William Painter's *Palace of Pleasure* (1566-67). The Spanish dramatist Lope de Vega wrote a play about the duchess of Malfi before Webster, but there is no evidence that Webster read Lope's version. *The Duchess of Malfi* covers events that took place in Italy during the period 1504-13.

Although the widowed duchess of Malfi longs to remarry and has already selected as her next husband her steward Antonio Bologna, the duchess's two brothers, Ferdinand, duke of Calabria, and the cardinal, strongly oppose any second marriage, arguing that widows who remarry are lustful. To make sure she obeys, they employ a villainous adventurer, Bosola, to join her household as their spy. Because her steward Antonio is far beneath her in rank, the duchess must herself propose marriage; Antonio gratefully accepts, and they are secretly wed.

Some time later Bosola begins to notice signs of pregnancy in the duchess, but cannot guess the identity of the father. Antonio orders the servants to their rooms as the duchess gives birth to their child, a boy; but Bosola discovers a paper on which the child's horoscope has been cast. Still unable to name the father, Bosola informs the duchess's brothers that she has borne a child. They resolve to discover the father and exact revenge.

The duchess bears two more children without exposing her steward as the father. One night, however, her brother Ferdinand steals into her room and leaves a poniard as warning of his sinister intentions. When he departs, the duchess attempts to throw her brothers off the scent by accusing Antonio of embezzlement, but secretly arranges for him to flee to Ancona with their eldest son and there await her arrival with the other two children. When Bosola slyly defends Antonio's integrity to win her confidence, the duchess foolishly confides to him that Antonio is her husband. The duchess thus inadvertently places herself and her husband at the mercy of her ruthless brothers.

At the shrine of Our Lady of Loretto in Ancona, the cardinal prepares to fight a military campaign, and he acts out a ceremony of twofold symbolic meaning—his installation as a soldier, and his banishment of the duchess, Antonio, and their children. Antonio and the duchess take separate routs to Milan. Antonio arrives there safely with his little boy; but en route to join him, the duchess is arrested by Bosola and returned as a prisoner to Malfi.

Here her brother Ferdinand subjects the duchess to fiendish torments. He frightens her with a dead hand he claims is Antonio's; he presents to her waxen figures in the likeness of Antonio and her children; he keeps her awake with singing and dancing lunatics brought from a mental asylum. Finally, he has Bosola strangle the duchess, her maid Cariola, and the duchess's two younger children. For his crimes Bosola does not receive from Ferdinand the rewards he anticipated, but only a grudging "pardon" and release from service. Distraught with guilt, Ferdinand succumbs to lycanthropia, a disease in which the sufferer becomes like a wolf, prowls in churchyards at night, and digs up corpses.

Thus far the cardinal has not been suspected as an accomplice. When he orders Bosola to kill Antonio, he reveals no knowledge of the duchess's murder. His secret, however, is coaxed from him by his mistress Julia, and he seals her lips by a devilishly clever trick: he poisons the book that she kisses as a pledge of her discretion.

Antonio, still ignorant of the duchess's murder, foolishly hopes to be reconciled with her two brothers and therefore goes to the cardinal's palace. Bosola, meanwhile, arrives at the same place in the hope that he can atone for his crimes by saving Antonio's life. Ironically, however, he fatally stabs Antonio in the dark when he mistakes him for the cardinal. Bosola then attacks the cardinal; Ferdinand joins in the struggle, and all three men are killed. At the conclusion Antonio's friend Delio arrives to proclaim the ancestral rights of the duchess's little son.

The Duchess of Malfi is Senecan in its melancholy atmosphere, gloomy philosophical speeches, revenge motives, and macabre horrors, but more directly it recalls a host of Elizabethan dramatic and nondramatic writers in its echoes from Sir Philip Sidney's *Arcadia,* Montaigne's essays, John Donne's *Anatomy of the World,* and Shakespeare's tragedies. The language is highly concentrated in patterns of symbolic imagery derived from sickness and disease, animals, vegetation, and astronomy, but the plot is occasionally slack, especially in the handling of time. As many critics have noted, an entire year elapses between Acts I and II, and enough time between Acts II and III for the duchess to bear several children.

Only the duchess is a tragic character in the Shakespearean sense. Antonio is weak and vacillating, both inept and cautious, and he expresses no capacity for gratification other than living in peace with his wife and children. The duchess is of such stature that she "stains the time past, lights the time to come," and she fully realizes that when she chooses a husband below her social station she is "going into a wilderness, / Where I shall find nor path nor friendly clue / To be my guide." Nevertheless, she seizes her forbidden love on her own terms and dies as proudly as she lived, proclaiming at the end, "I am the duchess of Malfi still." Her decision to marry is an affirmation of life in opposition to the death and sterility represented by her brother Ferdinand, consumed by secret passion and poisoned in his soul by "foul melancholy."

The standard edition, which contains copious notes and commentary, is in *The Works,* ed. F. L. Lucas, 4 vols. (1927; rev. ed., 1958). *The Duchess of Malfi* was edited by John Russell Brown for the Revels Plays (1960) and by Elizabeth M. Brennan in the New Mermaid series (1966). Important critical studies are by Travis Bogard, *The Tragic Satire of John Webster* (1955); Inga-Stina Ekeblad, "The 'Impure Art' of John Webster," *RES,* IX (1958); R. W. Dent, *John Webster's Borrowing* (1960); Gunnar Boklund, *The Duchess of Malfi: Sources, Themes, Characters* (1962); and Clifford Leech, *The Duchess of Malfi* (1963). A collection of essays is in *Twentieth-Century Interpretations of "The Duchess of Malfi,"* ed. Norman Rabkin (1968).

dumb show. A dramatization in pantomime within a play. The device came into English drama by way of SENECAN TRAGEDY. In a dumb show the actors perform silently, often as allegorical characters similar to those employed in morality plays and masques. As a dramatic spectacle the dumb show was used to foreshadow impending events, to underscore the decisive nature of an action, or to express ironic or didactic comment on the action in a manner similar to that of a Greek chorus. In Elizabethan drama dumb shows were performed as prologues to plays, between the acts, or at some critical point within the play. Hence the functions of dumb shows are difficult to define specifically.

One of the earliest dumb shows occurs in the Senecan tragedy *Gorboduc* (1562) by Thomas Sackville and Thomas Norton, and thereafter they appear in over fifty plays before 1660, including Thomas Kyd's *The Spanish Tragedy,* Robert Greene's *James the Fourth,* John Marston's *The Malcontent,* John Webster's *The Duchess of Malfi,* and Thomas Middleton's *The Changeling*. The most famous and ingenious example is in *Hamlet* (III, *ii*), where the actors perform a brief dumb show summarizing the action of the "play-within-a-play" that follows.

The origins of the dumb show are discussed in J. W. Cunliffe's introduction to *Early English Classical Tragedies* (1912). See also B. R. Pearn, "Dumb-show in Elizabethan Drama," *RES,* XI (1935), and Dieter Mehl, *The Elizabethan Dumb Show* (1965).

Dutch Courtesan, The. A melodrama by John Marston, written in 1603-04 and first printed in 1605. For both the main story and comic subplot Marston used as his source Matteo Bandello's *Novelle* (1554-73), as translated either by Sir Geoffrey Fenton or William Painter. The scene is Elizabethan London.

Young Freevill, engaged to marry Sir Hubert Subboys' respectable daughter Beatrice, decides to dissolve his light affair with a Dutch prostitute, Franceschina, and to this end he is encouraged by his morally strict friend Malheureux. In the comic subplot a knavish vintner named Mulligrub begins his sustained skirmish with the wily Cocledemoy, who steals some goblets from Mulligrub's tavern. Their highjinks involve farcical assaults, disguises, false accusations, and, finally, after Mulligrub is convicted of theft, Cocledemoy's last-minute rescue of his rival and their good-humored reconciliation.

The main story is more melodramatic.

Malheureux, the "man of snow," falls in love with the Dutch courtesan, who tries to persuade him to murder Freevill, the lover who has spurned her in favor of the virtuous Beatrice. Not until Malheureux takes Freevill's ring from his dead hand will Franceschina accept another lover. Although Malheureux burns with desire for Franceschina, he reveals her plot to Freevill, who suggests a scheme by which his friend can enjoy the courtesan. Secretly, however, Freevill's plot is designed to cure Malheureux of his lust. The two friends feign a duel in which Freevill is presumed killed. Actually, Freevill disguises himself as Franceschina's pander, and in his plot to undo the courtesan and cure Malheureux of his passion, he allows Malheureux to be sentenced to death for murder. At the very point of execution, Freevill throws off his disguise and exonerates Malheureux. Franceschina is sentenced to whipping and jail, Malheureux is cured of his infatuation, and Freevill marries the virtuous Beatrice.

Characteristically of Marston, the main plot of *The Dutch Courtesan* is cynical and raw, as if he were consciously writing an acrid repudiation of Dekker's sentimental *The Honest Whore.* Like Marston's *The Malcontent. The Dutch Courtesan* is a "humours" play, especially in its characterization of the melancholy Malheureux. The minor plot involving "foulest mouthed, profane" Cocledemoy and the "sharking vintner" of Cheapside, Master Mulligrub, provides a farcical counterpoint to the elaborate intrigues of Freevill and Malheureux. Both plots are full of quick turns of action and narrowly averted disasters.

The Dutch Courtesan has been edited by M. L. Wine in the Regents Renaissance Drama series (1966) and by Peter Davison in the Fountainwell Drama books (1968). Important criticism is by Theodore Spencer, "Reason and Passion in Marston's *The Dutch Courtesan,*" *Criterion,* XIII (1934); R. K. Presson, "Marston's *Dutch Courtesan:* The Study of an Attitude in Adaptation," *JEGP,* LV (1956); Anthony Caputi, *John Marston, Satirist* (1961); and Philip J. Finkelpearl, *John Marston of the Middle Temple* (1969).

Dyer, Sir Edward (c. 1543-1607). Courtier and poet. Little is known of Dyer's early years. He was born in Weston, Somersetshire, the son of Sir Thomas Dyer, and was at Oxford by 1558, where he had the reputation of being an accomplished musician and singer. He left Oxford without taking a degree and traveled abroad after 1561, returning to England in 1565 when his father died. By 1566 he was at court in the service of Robert Dudley, earl of Leicester, the queen's powerful favorite, and Sir Francis Walsingham, the secretary of state. The queen granted Dyer life stewardship of Woodstock, Oxford, and a profitable tanning monopoly, but in 1571 he fell out of favor for some unknown offense. After a grave illness in 1572, he returned to court but was not totally restored to the queen's favor until July 1575, when Dyer helped prepare a royal entertainment at Woodstock highlighted by his plaintive lyric "The Song in the Oak," in which Dyer laments Elizabeth's coolness toward him and begs for her good will.

During the years 1575-80 Dyer was a frequent guest at Leicester House in the company of Sir Philip Sidney, Fulke Greville, and Edmund Spenser. Writing from Leicester House to Gabriel Harvey in 1580, Spenser refers to their literary circle as the AREOPAGUS and Harvey replies with much praise for "Master Dyer." In the tradition of the early Tudor courtly makers like Wyatt and Surrey, Dyer circulated his poems in manuscript and read them aloud to friends; he was primarily a courtier and man of affairs rather than a poet, and his verses, published anonymously, found their way long after composition into such poetic miscellanies as *The Phoenix Nest* (1593), *England's Helicon* (1600), and *A Poetical Rhapsody* (1602). Eleven of the fourteen or so lyrics that can be attributed to Dyer are believed to have been written in the 1570s, probably when he was active in the Sidney circle.

Like many Elizabethan courtiers, Dyer struggled to maintain a prosperous appearance on an insufficient income, and he devoted a great deal of time and effort to profit-making schemes. In 1575-77 he helped promote Martin Frobisher's expeditions in search of a Northwest Passage to the fabulous riches of Cathay, a venture that took him to Mortlake for consulations on geography and navigation with the famed alchemist and mathematician John DEE, whose *Private Diary* for these years describes visits by "worshipful Master Dyer" in the company of court luminaries such as Sir Francis Walsingham, the earl of Leicester, Sir Philip Sidney, and Sidney's sister the countess of Pembroke.

After Frobisher's failure to discover the Northwest Passage, Dyer turned to alchemy in his search for instant wealth. In 1590 he convinced the queen and Lord Burghley that Dee's assistant Edward Kelley had discovered the "philosopher's stone" by which base elements could be converted to gold, and the queen sent Dyer to Prague to persuade Kelley, then in the employ of Rudolph II of Bohemia, to return to England with his secret. Dyer remained in Prague with Kelley for five months, until Rudolph, angered by the charlatan's procrastination and suspicious that Dyer was stealing the priceless formula, placed both Kelley and Dyer under house arrest. Only the queen's hasty intervention prevented Dyer's imprisonment or execution.

In spite of Dyer's abortive mission to Prague, he continued to enjoy the favor of the queen and court notables such as Burghley and, later in the 1590s, the earl of Essex, although Dyer remained steadfastly loyal to the queen during the Essex rebellion. Nevertheless, Dyer failed to secure any more than powerless and largely titular offices at court. He served two terms in Parliament, and in 1596 was knighted and made chancellor of the Order of the Garter, a ceremonial office carrying only a small annual stipend. Dyer's fortunes declined sharply with the accession of James I, possibly because Dyer had gone to Denmark on a mission of surveillance for Queen Elizabeth when the Scottish king was negotiating his marriage with Anne of Denmark in 1589. In 1603 Dyer lost his lease to Woodstock and his tanning monopoly. He died in obscurity in London in 1607.

Although Dyer was praised as a poet by Gabriel Harvey, Edmund Spenser, William Puttenham, and Thomas Nashe, his reputation was kept alive chiefly by his connections to the Sidney circle and by two poems, his elegy on the death of Sidney (published in *The Phoenix Nest*) and his lyric "My mind to me a kingdom is," which William Byrd set to music in *Psalms, Sonnets, and Songs* (1588) and which continued to be popular as a song and broadside ballad throughout the seventeenth century. Like Sir Walter Raleigh's, Dyer's poems are melancholy and introspective, but with little of Raleigh's bitter cynicism. All Dyer's verses are in awkward "poulter's measure," lines of alternating six and seven stresses, and hark back to the drab age of Tottel's Miscellany and *A Paradise of Dainty Devices* rather than forward to the golden era of Sidney and Spenser.

The best biographical and critical study is by Ralph M. Sargent, *At the Court of Queen Elizabeth: The Life and Lyrics of Sir Edward Dyer* (1935), which reprints all Dyer's poems except the few attributed to him by B. M. Wagner in "New Poems by Sir Edward Dyer," *RES,* XI (1935). A. B. Grosart edited *The Writings in Verse and Prose of Sir Edward Dyer* (1872), which includes Dyer's correspondence. Several poems of Dyer's are in *Poetry of the English Renaissance, 1509-1660,* ed. J. William Hebel and H. H. Hudson (1929). A unique study by Alden Brooks, *Will Shakespeare and the Dyer's Hand* (1943), purports to show that Shakespeare's plays were written by Dyer.

E

Earle, John (1601?-1665). For comment on his *Microcosmography, see* CHARACTERS.

Eastward Ho! A comedy by George CHAPMAN, Ben JONSON, and John MARSTON, written and printed in 1605. No source is known. An imprudent reference to James I's "carpet knights" (royal favorites given knighthoods for a fee) caused Chapman and Jonson to be sent to prison. In 1685 Nahum Tate revised the play as *Cuckolds' Haven,* and Charlotte Lennox did an adaptation in 1775 called *Old City Manners*.

William Touchstone, a virtuous London goldsmith, employs two apprentices, the honest and industrious Golding, and the prodigal and reckless Quicksilver. Touchstone's two daughters are similarly opposite; Mildred is sensible and modest, Gertrude foolish and vain. To Mildred's marriage with Golding old Touchstone gives his fullest blessings; but to that of Gertrude to the impoverished fop Sir Petronel Flash—"one of my thirty-pound knights"—the wise father bestows his justified contempt. As for Quicksilver, he disgraces himself with his master by drunkenness and takes up a living with an unscrupulous old usurer named Security. While Sir Petronel makes plans to sell his bride's property to Security and flee to Virginia with the spoils, Quicksilver and Security plot to fleece the destitute knight of the estate he hopes to bamboozle from the social-climbing Gertrude, who believes Sir Petronel has a "castle in the country." Sir Petronel soon tricks Gertrude into signing away her land and deserts her for the company of Security's young wife Winifred.

As Golding's fortunes rise through honest hard work, the luck of the knaves founders on snobbery, mutual deceit, and greed. Sir Petronel and Winifred are prevented from embarking to Virginia by a storm that lands their boat back on the beach, and Quicksilver is arrested for counterfeiting. The prodigals all end in the Counter prison, where the virtuous Golding persuades Touchstone to acknowledge their penitence. After many confessions and good resolutions, the chastened Gertrude forgives her errant husband and is humbly reconciled with her father, who, for his part, accepts Sir Petronel providing the fool reforms; Quicksilver makes amends; and Security takes back his wife and returns Gertrude's lands, sold to him by Sir Petronel.

Eastward Ho! dramatizes the familiar myth of the prodigal son. Written in fluent prose, it defies any attempt to assign specific portions to a particular collaborator, although Jonson's hand seems evident in the prologue, in the discussions of alchemy in Act IV, Scene 1, and in parts of Act V. As the prologue indicates, *Eastward Ho!* was written in friendly rivalry to Dekker and Webster's *Westward Ho!* produced the year before. *Eastward Ho!* is especially noteworthy for its praise of the London citizenry, and can be seen as a ploy to attract middle-class audiences to the Blackfriars theater. The play gets it title from the cry of watermen who carried passengers across the Thames.

The standard edition is in *Ben Jonson,* ed. C. H. Herford and Percy and Evelyn Simpson, 11 vols. (1925-53), IV. A well-annotated edition is in *English Drama 1580-1642,* ed. C. F. Tucker Brooke and N. B. Paradise (1933). There is another edition, with extensive critical analysis, by J. Harris in the Yale Studies series (1926). For commentary, see R. E. Brettle, "*Eastward Ho!* 1605, by Chapman, Jonson, and Marston. Bibliography and Circumstances of Production," *The Library,* New Series, IX (1928); J. Q. Adams, "*Eastward Ho!* and Its Satire Against the Scots," *SP,* XXVIII (1931); and Richard Horwich, "*Hamlet and Eastward Ho!*" *SEL,* XI (1971).

Education, Of. A tract by John MILTON, first published in 1644 in a pamphlet of eight pages without author's name, date of publication, or publisher. The second edition (1673) has a dedicatory epistle by Milton to Samuel Hartlib, a progenitor of many schemes in education, agriculture, and science. Hartlib's treatise *A Reformation of Schools* (1642) is a broad translation of the educational theories of the Czech bishop and scholar John Amos Comenius (1592-1670). Hartlib brought Comenius to London to persuade Parliament to restructure the English educational system on a foundation of practical vocational training, a scheme Parliament largely ignored. It was Comenius who suggested that Milton write *Of Education.*

In *Of Education* Milton views the subject from two perspectives, the physical and the spiritual. The former view prevails in his concept of education as the training of gentlemen for national leadership—a view no doubt influenced by England's political crises in 1644: "I call therefore a complete and generous education that which fits a man to perform justly, skillfully, and magnanimously all the offices, both private and public, of peace and war." Equally practical is his stress on training in agriculture and military science, and his ardent belief that textbook learning must be supplemented by actual experience. In opposition to the strictly practical training advocated by Comenius and Hartlib, however, Milton stresses the kind of rigorous study of languages recommended in *De tradendis disciplinis* by the Spanish humanist Juan Luis Vives (1492-1540) and practiced at St. Paul's School, where Milton received his earliest formal education.

Although *Of Education* prescribes a curriculum for young men twelve to twenty years of age, no mention is made of university education or of the necessity for the subjects Milton so despised at Cambridge—Aristotelian logic and oratory. Milton's proposed course of study is heavily literary, and includes several years of Greek, Latin, Hebrew, Italian, and even Syriac, although these languages, he insists, are to be studied as a means to an end, with a view to mastering their content rather than memorizing grammatical forms. *Of Education* gives particular emphasis to motivation, to instilling a love of learning rather than acquiring a storehouse of facts. The spiritual perspective becomes most apparent in Milton's delineation of the ultimate purpose of education: "The end of learning is to repair the ruins of our first parents by regaining to know God aright, and out of that knowledge to love him, to imitate him, to be like him."

The standard edition is in *The Works of John Milton,* ed. Frank A Patterson, 18 vols. (1931-38), IV. There are also excellent editions in *John Milton: Complete Poems and Major Prose,* ed. Merritt Y. Hughes (1957); *The Complete Prose Works,* ed. D. M. Wolfe, 5 vols. (1953-71), II; and *The Prose of John Milton,* ed. J. Max Patrick (1967). For commentary, see E. N. S. Thompson, "Milton's *Of Education,*" *SP,* XV (1918); and Murry W. Bundy, "Milton's View of Education in *Paradise Lost,*" *JEGP,* XXI (1922). A helpful background study is by D. L. Clark, *Milton at St. Paul's School* (1948).

Edward II. A tragedy by Christopher MARLOWE, written about 1592. The 1594 edition is the second; the first, nonextant edition may have been printed in 1593. The play is based on the chronicles of Raphael Holinshed, Robert Fabyan, and John Stowe, and covers twenty-three years of English history (1307-30). Unlike Marlowe's other plays, *Edward II* does not focus exclusively on a single titanic hero, and there is much more stage action, less declamation, and fewer lengthy speeches. Shakespeare's RICHARD II, to which Marlowe's play is often favorably compared, was written at nearly the same time.

At the beginning of the play the upstart Piers Gaveston, who had been banished by Edward's father, King Edward I, hastens back to England when he receives the new king's invitation to share the kingdom. The English nobles greet Gaveston with bitter hostility, but Edward II welcomes him lovingly with extravagant gifts of powerful and honorific offices, whereupon the arrogant Gaveston avenges himself upon the bishop of Coventry, whom he believes responsible for his banishment, by throwing him in the Tower and confiscating his estates. Gaveston's misuse of power and Edward's unseemly passion for his minion cause Edward's queen, Isabella, profound grief and so enrage his chief nobles Warwick, Lancaster, and the Mortimers that they gather their powers and force the king to renew the decree of banishment. The queen, however, persuades the barons to again recall Gaveston because she pities her husband's unhappiness and desires his gratitude.

Gaveston's return from exile only precipitates further dissension. Edward foolishly betroths him to his niece, the earl of Gloucester's sole heir, and, in an equally rash action, refuses to ransom the elder Mortimer, captured by the Scots in Edward's war. The indignant barons capture Gaveston and put him to death. Queen Isabella leaves with her son to complain to her brother, the king of France.

Far from humbled, Edward selects a new favorite in young Spencer, who is as detested by the barons as was Gaveston. In the rebellion of the barons Edward is victorious, but he foolishly turns his triumph into disaster by executing Lancaster and Warwick but sparing his most dangerous enemy, Mortimer, who escapes from the Tower and flees to France to join the queen and gather a force against the king. In France the once loyal Isabella gradually turns away from Edward and toward Mortimer. Together they raise an army, invade England, and capture the king.

In defeat the suffering Edward assumes a new dignity, while Mortimer becomes increasingly ruthless and Machiavellian. Imprisoned at Berkeley Castle, the king is starved and tortured by Mortimer's sadistic hirelings, Gurney and Matrevis, to whom Mortimer sends a riddling letter borne by the professional killer Lightborn. The deliberately ambiguous letter reads, *"Edwardum occidere nolite timere bonum est."* Devoid of punctuation, or with a comma preceding the last two words, it means "Fear not to kill the king, 'tis good to die." If the single comma is moved back one word, however, it reads "Kill not the king, 'tis good to fear the worst." Thus Mortimer cleverly places any responsibility for the king's murder on Gurney and Matrevis. Edward's death is one of the most painful scenes in Elizabethan drama. Exhausted by his torment, he is coaxed to bed by Lightborn, his cries stifled by a pillow while he is slowly pressed to death with a table.

Incensed by the treachery of Mortimer and his mother, the newly crowned Edward III executes Mortimer and sends his mother to the Tower. The tragedy ends with peace and justice restored to the troubled realm.

Marlowe's *Edward II* is the greatest historical tragedy before Shakespeare's mature work, and equals in power of characterization the latter's *Richard II.* Unlike Shakespeare, Marlowe does not make his two great antagonists personifications of antithetical political concepts; as Edward's public fortunes decline, Mortimer's personal character deteriorates. *Edward II* is especially noteworthy as being the first historical tragedy that does not employ Senecan dramatic conventions (see CHRONICLE PLAY).

Edward II has been edited by W. Moelwyn Merchant for the New Mermaid series (1967) and by Russell Fraser in the Regents Renaissance Drama series (1971). Valuable for their notes and criticism are the editions by C. F. Tucker Brooke in Marlowe's *Works* (1910); Irving Ribner in *The Complete Plays* (1963); and Roma Gill in *The Plays* (1971). Important studies of genre are by Irving Ribner, "Marlowe's *Edward II* and the Tudor History Play," *ELH,* XXII (1955); and J. B. Steane, *Marlowe: A Critical Study* (1964). See also *Edward II: Text and Major Criticism,* ed. Irving Ribner (1970).

Eikonoklastes ("Image Breaker"). A political tract by John MILTON written and published in 1649 in response to a brief pamphlet entitled *Eikon Basilike,* purporting to have been composed by Charles I "in his solitudes and suffering" on the eve of his execution in January 1649. The real author of *Eikon Basilike* is now known to have been John Gauden, later bishop of Exeter under Charles II. The Royalist pamphlet became so enormously popular that the alarmed Council of State commissioned Milton, as secretary of foreign tongues, to counteract its effect on public opinion.

In *Eikonoklastes* Milton reviews the crimes and follies of the king, portraying him as a vainglorious tyrant, and demonstrates that the poignant prayer in *Eikon Basilike,* attributed to Charles I, was actually lifted from Sir Philip Sidney's *The Arcadia,* "stolen word for word from the mouth of a heathen fiction praying to a heathen God; and that in no serious book, but the vain amatorious poem of Sir Philip Sidney's *Arcadia*—a book in that kind full of worth and wit, but among religious thoughts and duties not worthy to be named, nor to be read at any time without good cautions, much less in time of trouble and affliction to be a Christian's prayer-book." S. B. Liljegren (*Studies in Milton* [1919]) argues, on rather tenuous grounds, that Milton himself wrote the prayer into *Eikon Basilike* to embarrass the Royalists.

The standard edition is in *The Works of John Milton* ed. Frank A. Patterson, 18 vols. (1931-38), V. Other excellent editions are in *The Complete Prose Works,* ed. D. M. Wolfe, 5 vols. (1953-71), III; and *John Milton: Complete Poems and Major Prose,* ed. Merritt Y. Hughes (1957). For commentary, see W. L. Lowenhaupt, "The Writing of Milton's *Eikonoklastes,*" *SP,* XX (1923); John S. Smart, "Milton and the King's Prayer," *RES,* (1925); F. F. Madan, *A New Bibliography of the Eikon Basilike of Charles I* (1950); and Timothy J. O'Keefe, "The Imaginal Strategy of John Milton's *Eikonoklastes,*" *BSUF,* XI (1971).

Elyot, Sir Thomas (1490?-1546). Classical scholar and diplomat. The son of a distinguished judge. Elyot boasted that after his twelfth year he was entirely self-taught in classical languages, law, and medicine. After 1511 he was a clerk of assize in his father's circuit, later a deputy for the peace for Oxfordshire (1522) and sheriff of Oxfordshire and Berkshire (1527). His enthusiasm for literature and moral philosophy brought him into the circle of Sir Thomas More, where he made friends with such humanists as Erasmus, Thomas Linacre, John Colet, and William Grocyn.

Elyot's first publication was his most famous, *A Book Named the Governor* (1531; see GOVERNOR), which helped to secure him an ambassadorship at the court of Charles V. Here Elyot's chief task was to persuade the emperor to take Henry VIII's side in the divorce proceedings against Katharine of Aragon. Elyot's position during the events following the divorce was paradoxical. A favorite of Queen Katharine, he worked on behalf of Anne Boleyn; under suspicion for his former friendship with More, he protested his loyalty to the new chancellor, Thomas Cromwell; formerly anti-Protestant in his writings, he signed the Oath of Supremacy rejected by More and even appropriated a confiscated religious house as his family manor. His last years were spent as a member of Parliament for Cambridgeshire.

Elyot's prolific writings deal mainly with education, political and moral philosophy, medicine, and classical translation. His *A Book Named the Governor,* dedicated to Henry VIII, prescribes the ideal education of a prince's minister (the "governor" of the title) and thus belongs with other aristocratic conduct books such as Castiglione's *Il Cortegiano,* Machiavelli's *Il Principe,* and Erasmus' *Institutio regis Christiani* (see COURTESY LITERATURE). Elyot begins by refuting the medieval prejudice against learning among the aristocracy, and he argues on behalf of Greek and Latin studies as sources of moral edification and for training in drawing, music, and other arts (as opposed to practical fields like law) as intrinsically valuable. Elyot's conception of "degree," or order, in the state is similar to Ulysses' famous speech on that subject in Shakespeare's *Troilus and Cressida* (I, ii); i.e., social and political stratification is a natural law vital to stability and harmony, and the ideal government is one ruled over by a powerful, virtuous monarch. Elyot's book is a landmark in the evolution of English prose because of its well-formed, rhythmic syntax and liberal use of new words.

A Book Named the Governor was followed by *Pasquil the Plain* (1533), a Platonic dialogue between Pasquil, representing free speech, and Gnato, a court flatterer and religious hypocrite, a garrulous Protestant who carries with him both the New Testament and Chaucer's "giddy romance" *Troilus and Cressyde. Of the Knowledge Which Maketh a Wise Man* (1533) and

The Image of Governance (1541) are on Elyot's favorite subjects of moral and political philosophy, the latter being a translation of a manuscript in Greek by Eucolpius, secretary to the emperor Alexander Severus. Another political tract, *The Doctrinal of Princes* (wr. c. 1534), is a translation from Isocrates. Not the least of Elyot's contributions was his popularization of the classics.

In 1539 was published Elyot's *The Castle of Health,* a layman's medical guide and primer that occasioned severe criticism by doctors because it was written by an amateur and in English instead of proper Latin. In the second edition Elyot defended his use of the vernacular and his informal, anecdotal style.

A Book Named the Governor was edited with a valuable biography by H. H. S. Croft, 2 vols. (1880). Important critical studies are L. C. Warren, *Humanistic Doctrines of the Prince from Petrarch to Sir Thomas Elyot* (1939), and James Wortham, "Sir Thomas Elyot and the Translation of Prose," *HLQ,* XI (1948).

emblem books. An emblem is a combination of motto, illustration, and brief poem used to express a moral or religious idea. The illustration (usually an engraving) is invariably symbolic, expressing some aspect of an idea treated in the accompanying epigram, sonnet, or madrigal. The vogue of emblems and emblem books derived partly from the new art of engraving in the sixteenth century, partly from the Counter Reformation and Baroque tendency to combine different art forms.

The earliest known emblem book was by an Italian jurist, Andrea Alciati, whose *Alciati emblematum fontes quatur* was published in Augsburg in 1531. It consisted of ninety-seven emblems accompanied by didactic Latin verses. Like many subsequent emblem writers, Alciati derived his material from beast fables, classical and medieval history, legend, and mythology. The first English emblem book was Geoffrey Whitney's *A Choice of Emblems and Other Devices* (1586), containing 248 devices, twenty-three by Whitney and the remainder by Alciati and other Italian emblem writers. A typical emblem in Whitney's collection shows an elephant leaning against a tree partly sawed through, and in black letter the commentary reads: "No state so sure, no seat within this life / But that may fall, though long the same have stood." Many of Whitney's didactic epigrams and mottoes are taken from Aesop's *Fables.*

The most celebrated collection of English emblems was by Francis QUARLES, whose *Emblems* (1635) went through several editions in the seventeenth century. In his "Epistle to the Reader" Quarles defines an emblem as "a silent parable" and defends its symbolic profundity: "What are the heavens, the earth, nay, every creature, but hieroglyphics and emblems of His Glory?" Of the five sections in Quarles's *Emblems* two are original, the remainder taken from Hermann Hugo's popular Latin collection *Pia desideria* (1624). Typical of Quarles's emblems is one showing a youth clutching á globe of the world as an angel looks wistfully at the heavenly rays falling on the boy's head. The motto underscores the moral: "Let not thy nobler thoughts be always raking / The world's base dunghill." Strongly influenced by George Herbert, Quarles wrote crude and simple verses that, in the words of Anthony à Wood, show him to be "the darling of our plebeian judgements."

Some emblem books confined selections to a single theme. Robert Farley's *Lychnocausia, Lights Moral Emblems* (1638) consists of fifty or more emblems pertaining somehow to light (hence the title "lighting of lamps"); George Stengel's *Ova Paschalia* (1635) presents all its illustrations in the shape of eggs; and Christopher Harvey's *Schola cordis* (1647) pertains entirely to hearts. Another innovation is Henry Peacham's *Minerva Britanna, or A Garden of Heroical Devices* (1612), a book of emblems symbolically praising such English worthies as Francis Bacon and Sir Henry Wotton.

Very few emblem books, including the enormously popular ones by Quarles, have any intrinsic literary value, although some rise above mere doggerel. Edmund Spenser's *Theatre of Voluptuous Worldlings* (1569) was partly translated from an emblem book in Dutch and French by John Van der Noodt. The sonnets in Spenser's *Theatre* are illustrated by woodcuts depicting scenes of grandeur and ruin followed by moralizing commentary in prose. Several of Spenser's other poems, such as *The Shepherd's Calendar* and *Muiopotmos,* also reflect the influence of emblem books.

Although they had only a brief vogue in England during the seventeenth century, emblem books left their traces in the poems of George HERBERT, Richard CRASHAW, and Henry

VAUGHAN. Many of John Donne's poems employ titles symbolically in the manner of emblems (e.g., "The Canonization," "The Extasie").

There is an excellent introduction to emblem literature by E. N. S. Thompson, *Literary Bypaths of the Renaissance* (1924). More detailed studies are by Mario Praz, *Studies in Seventeenth Century Imagery* (1939), and Rosemary Freeman, *English Emblem Books* (1948).

Endymion and Phoebe. A narrative poem in couplets by Michael DRAYTON. Written and first published in 1595, it is based on Ovid's *Metamorphoses,* with some conceptions of Platonism derived from the French poet Du Bartas. Like Lodge's *Scylla's Metamorphosis,* Marlowe's *Hero and Leander,* and Shakespeare's *Venus and Adonis,* Drayton's poem is classified as an Ovidian epyllion, an erotic narrative of some length based on Ovid's mythology. Drayton, however, employs Ovid's tale of the moon goddess Phoebe's love for the shepherd-prince Endymion only as the occasion for his own allegorical and philosophical improvisations.

Not realizing that the "green-garbed nymph" who woos him is really Phoebe, Endymion spurns her love because he is "Phoebe's servant sworn." After the nymph tells him he will someday regret this rejection and departs for her throne on Mount Latmos, Endymion experiences a change of heart and begins to long for the nymph. Later Phoebe returns to find Endymion wasted away in melancholy; she softly caresses him and breathes "the fiery nature of a heavenly muse" into his soul as he sleeps. When he awakens he tries to make love to her, believing her to be the nymph, whereupon the "queen of chastity" reveals her true identity and promises that "Great Phoebe's glory thou alone shalt see." She takes Endymion to Mount Latmos, where she rewards his chaste love with thirty years of glorious visions.

For Drayton this love of the moon goddess for Endymion, a mortal, symbolizes divine inspiration, and for his love of Phoebe he is rewarded with a divine power over nature in the form of knowledge of astronomy, a subject Drayton equates with the most sacred of mysteries. Hence the lover is not rewarded with sexual gratification, as in the conventional Ovidian epyllion, but with a surpassing vision, the fulfillment of the Platonic "ideal." (The subtitle of the poem, significantly, is *Idea's Latmos.*)

In spite of its Platonic orientation, Drayton's poem is as sensuous and erotic as Marlowe's *Hero and Leander,* for the dualism of his vision enables him to regard simultaneously both flesh and spirit. Drayton describes Endymion's beauty with Marlovian luxury, and Phoebe's physical charms are equally sensual in the manner of Spenser. Indeed, Drayton's rich description of Endymion's arbor on Mount Latmos owes nothing to Ovid's spare style but much to Spenser's rich descriptions of the Garden of Adonis and the Bower of Bliss in *The Faerie Queene.* In Drayton's tribute to English poets at the end of the poem, he indicates that Spenser (as "Colin") provided an inimitable ideal:

Dear Colin, let my muse excused be
Which rudely thus presumes to sing by thee,
Although her strains be harsh, untun'd, and ill,
Nor can attain to thy divinest skill.

The standard edition of the poem is in Drayton's *Works,* ed. J. William Hebel, Kathleen Tillotson, and Bernard H. Newdigate, 5 vols. (1931-41), I. It is discussed with other Ovidian epyllia by Hallett Smith, *Elizabethan Poetry* (1952). See also Oliver Elton, *Michael Drayton: A Critical Study* (1905) and C. L. Finney, "Drayton's *Endimion and Phoebe* and Keat's *Endymion,*" *PMLA,* XXXIX (1924).

Endymion, the Man in the Moon. A mythological comedy in prose by John LYLY, written in 1588 and first printed in 1591. The story of Endymion and Cynthia is from Lucian's *Dialogues of the Gods* and Ovid's *Metamorphoses.* Endymion is in love with Cynthia, goddess of the moon, while his friend Eumenides is secretly enamored of Semele, a lady of Cynthia's court. Tellus, an earth goddess, is enraged because Endymion spurns her love, and she seeks out Dipsas, a wicked old sorceress, to change Endymion's heart by charms and magic. Unable to affect his love, Dipsas casts a spell on Endymion that causes him to sleep for forty years.

Cynthia sends for soothsayers from Egypt, enchanters from Thessaly, and philosophers from Greece to find a remedy for Endymion's spell. Meanwhile Eumenides meets Geron, an old hermit, who tells him that Endymion's affliction can be cured by a magic well. Looking into the well, Eumenides reads the words that tell him his friend can be awakened only by Cynthia's kiss. At the same time a ridiculous knight, Sir Tophas, provides comic interludes by his clownish courtship of the ugly enchantress Dipsas.

In the last act Cynthia kisses Endymion, who awakens with gray hair and aged body. She restores his youth, and he vows to serve her forever. Eumenides confesses his love to Semele, who rejects him; Cynthia gives Tellus to a courtier; Dipsas reforms and is joined with Geron, who, it is discovered, was her husband years before; and the clown Sir Tophas joins Bagoa, Dipsas' assistant. The play ends with a tribute to Queen Elizabeth and her court.

Lyly's *Endymion* has been variously interpreted as a play signifying the relations of Elizabeth with the earl of Leicester or, perhaps, the earl of Oxford; as being about Elizabeth (Cynthia) and Mary Queen of Scots (Tellus); about the aspirations of James VI of Scotland to the English throne; or about a Platonic love in which Endymion disdains earthly beauty (Tellus) in search of divine beauty (Cynthia).

Endymion typifies Lyly's free handling of classical myth and his clever fashioning of love intrigue, pastoral setting, delicate songs, and sophisticated wit. His euphuistic prose dialogue had a marked influence on his contemporaries, including Shakespeare in such early comedies as *Love's Labour's Lost* (see EUPHUISM).

The standard edition is in *The Complete Works,* ed. R. W. Bond, 3 vols. (1902). Lyly's play is interpreted as an allegory by Josephine W. Bennett, "Oxford and *Endymion,*" *PMLA,* LVII (1942). The music in the play is studied by G. K. Hunter, *John Lyly: The Humanist as Courtier* (1962), and the love themes by G. Wilson Knight, "Lyly," *RES,* XV (1939). See also Peter Saccio, *The Court Comedies of John Lyly: A Study in Allegorical Dramaturgy* (1969).

Enemy of Idleness (William Fulwood). See LETTER-WRITERS.

England's Helicon. See MISCELLANIES, POETICAL; PASTORAL.

England's Heroical Epistles. See DRAYTON, MICHAEL.

English Secretary, The (Angel Day). See LETTER-WRITERS.

Epicoene; or The Silent Woman. A comedy by Ben JONSON, written and performed in 1609, and first printed in 1616. Jonson's sources include Plautus' *Casina* and Libanius' *Sixth Declamation* (fourth century, A.D.), wherein the character Morosus is plagued by a garrulous wife.

Morose, an old curmudgeon with an obsessive aversion to noise, plots to disinherit his nephew, the worthy Sir Dauphine Eugenie, by taking a wife and begetting an heir. To this end Morose has employed his barber Cutbeard to find a woman suitably silent, but unknown to Morose, Cutbeard is in collusion with Sir Dauphine. When the lady is brought before him, Morose discovers that she speaks barely six words a day, and these not above a whisper. Once married, however, the lady instantly turns into a loud and garrulous virago, and Morose appeals desperately to Sir Dauphine and his companion Truewit to procure a divorce at any cost. At the divorce hearings, where the learned doctor of laws and the astute theologian are really the ignoramuses Cutbeard and Dauphine's friend Captain Otter in disguise, poor Morose futilely seeks to slip the marital noose on a host of pleas, including impotence, and is finally driven to offer a settlement of five hundred pounds per annum plus a reversion of his property to Dauphine after his own death. Sir Dauphine thereupon pulls off Epicoene's disguise and reveals her to be a boy Dauphine has trained for the role of "wife."

Jonson's comedy is a sportive medley of classical devices and characters—the wily old man hoist by his own petard, the scheming servant, the virile and resourceful younger generation in conflict with their obtuse and greedy elders—and Jonson skillfully combines these elements with his own peculiar genius in giving characters dramatic vitality. As in all of Jonson's best comedies—*Every Man in His Humour, The Alchemist,* and *Volpone*—*Epicoene* exploits a single comic situation of intrigue that evolves hilariously into a dramatically effective climax of wild surprises and sudden reversals. One of his finest, most concentrated works, *Epicoene* combines comedy of humours, comedy of manners, and sheer farce. It held the stage well into the eighteenth century and earned the unqualified praise of John Dryden in his *Essay of Dramatic Poesy* (1668).

The standard edition is in *Ben Jonson,* ed. C. H. Herford and Percy and Evelyn Simpson,

11 vols. (1925-53), V. There are editions of *Epicoene* by L. A. Beaupline for the Regents Renaissance Drama series (1966) and by Edward Partridge for the Yale Ben Jonson series (1972). The play is analyzed by Helena W. Baum, *The Satiric and the Didactic in Ben Jonson's Comedy* (1947); John J. Enck, *Jonson and the Comic Truth* (1957); and Edward B. Partridge, *The Broken Compass: A Study of the Major Comedies of Ben Jonson* (1958).

Epigrams, The. See HEYWOOD, JOHN.

Epistles (Joseph Hall). See LETTER-WRITERS.

Epistolae Ho-Elianae (James Howell). See ESSAYS; LETTER-WRITERS.

Epitaphium Damonis ("Damon's Epitaph"). A pastoral elegy in Latin by John MILTON, written in 1639 on the occasion of the death of Milton's friend Charles Diodati, who died in August 1638. In the person of the shepherd Thyrsis (the name of the mourner for Daphnis in Theocritus' *Idyll I*), Milton complains of his loneliness after learning of Damon's (Diodati's) death; he notes that although Diodati's father was from the Tuscan city of Lucca, Charles was an exemplary Englishman whose life promised erudition and glory. Milton sees Diodati, "a stainless youth" who "did not taste the delight of the marriage-bed," crowned victoriously in the ecstatic "marriage of the Lamb" in *Revelation* XIX: 7. Following the examples of Bion's *Epitaph for Adonis* and Moschus' *Epitaph for Bion,* Milton gives unity to the poem with a refrain ("Go home unfed, for your master has no time for you, my lambs"). Toward the conclusion of the poem Milton bids farewell to pastoral poetry and promises to write an epic on Arthurian themes, to "tell of Igraine pregnant with Arthur by fatal deception, the counterfeiting of Gorlois's features and arms by Merlin's treachery."

Two well-annotated editions are *Milton's Lament for Damon and His Other Latin Poems,* tr. by W. W. Skeat and ed. by E. H. Visiak (1935), and "Epitaphium Damonis" in *John Milton: The Complete Poems and Major Prose,* ed. Merritt Y. Hughes (1957). Milton's classical sources are traced by W. A. Montgomery, "The 'Epitaphium Damonis' in the Stream of Classical Lament," in *Studies for William A. Read,* ed. N. M. Cafee (1940); the Italian influences are discussed by T. P. Harrison, Jr., "The Latin Pastorals of Milton and Castiglione," *PMLA,* L (1935). See also D. Dorian, *The English Diodatis: A History of Charles Diodati's Family and His Friendship with Milton* (1950).

Epithalamion. A nuptial poem by Edmund SPENSER, written in 1594 and published in 1595 with his sonnet sequence AMORETTI. It celebrates Spenser's marriage at Cork on July 11, 1594 ("St. Barnaby's Day") to Elizabeth Boyle, daughter of Stephen Boyle of Bradden, near Towcester, Northampton. Prior to her marriage she had lived with her kinsman, Richard Boyle, near the bay of Youghal, not far from Spenser's residence at Kilcolman.

In twenty-three stanzas and an envoy Spenser traces the passing hours of his wedding day: the rousing of the lovely bride at dawn, the preparations for the ceremony, the journey to the church, the joyous celebration among friends and neighbors, and the wedding night—all embellished with praises of the bride's beauty and virtue, invocations to the muses, nymphs, Hours, Graces, and starry heavens as well as fervent prayers to Cynthia, Juno, Genius, and Hebe. The first sixteen stanzas have for their refrain "The woods shall to me answer," which is modified in subsequent stanzas to "That all the woods may answer" and "The woods shall to you answer."

As Thomas M. Greene has shown, Spenser's chief models were the sixty-first and sixty-fourth odes of the Latin elegiac poet Catullus. Though few epithalamia had been written in English before Spenser's, he demonstrates his familiarity with its conventions among French and Italian poets—its basis of imitation in the odes of Catullus, its stress on time and specific events of the wedding day, and its portrayal of the bride and groom's community. All of these conventions Spenser observes, though he departs from tradition in some aspects—most notably by speaking in his own voice rather than creating a poetic observer.

A. Kent Hieatt was the first to comment at length on the significance of the correspondence of the twenty-four stanzas to hours of the day and that of the lines to days of the year. His ingenious hypothesis is too complex to summarize briefly; suffice to say that he has shown the poem to be an amazingly detailed system of numerical hieroglyphics. For Spenser these arcane numerical correspondences of lines and stanzas to the movement of the stars in the Ptolemaic astronomy and to the sun's orbit at the summer solstice on July 11 enabled him to see the event of his marriage in the context of a benevolent and vitalistic universe. The reader remains as unconscious of his emblematical numerology as most music lovers to the mathematical aspects of the scale while listening to classical music. The reader senses the pulsating rhythms of the varying long and short lines, the flowing verse paragraphs of sensuous images and euphonious allusions, the monumental synthesis of physical passion and spiritual inspiration, classical mythology and Irish folklore, pagan revelry and Christian ritual, mortal man and timeless nature. From all this comes not solemnity but triumphant joy:

Crowne ye God Bacchus with a coronall,
And Hymen also crowne with wreathes of vine,
And let the Graces daunce unto the rest;
For they can doo it best:
The whiles the maydens doe theyr carroll sing,
To which the woods shal answer and theyr eccho ring.

The standard edition is in *The Works,* ed. Edwin A. Greenlaw, F. M. Padelford, et al., 10 vols. (1932-49), II. For criticism, see Thomas M. Greene, "Spenser and the Epithalamic Convention," *CL,* IX (1957); L. W. Hyman, "Structure and Meaning in Spenser's *Epithalamion,*" *TSL,* III (1958); A. Kent Hieatt, *Short Time's Endless Monument: The Symbolism of Numbers in Edmund Spenser's Epithalamion* (1960); Enid Welsford, *Spenser: Fowre Hymnes, Epithalamion. A Study of Edmund Spenser's Doctrine of Love* (1967).

Erasmus, Desiderius (1466?-1536). Dutch-born Augustinian monk, humanist, classicist, Biblicist, linguist, traveler, translator, educator, and satirist. For comment on his *De conscribendis epistolis,* see LETTER-WRITERS.

essays. The sixteenth and seventeenth-century English essay had many congeners: the commonplace book, the epistle, the homily, the formal discourse, the philosophical dialogue, and the academic prolusion. Montaigne's great and influential essays evolved from the *leçon morale,* an informal collection of aphorisms on some single topic. Montaigne's first edition in 1580 included reflections on the whimsical topics usually associated with the *leçon morale*—"Of Chairs," "Of Smells and Odors," "Of Sleeping"—and he called attention to their provisional, informal nature by entitling them *essais* ("attempts"). In Montaigne's second, enlarged edition of 1588 the essays were more extended, spacious, and polished than in the first collection, but they retained their original digressive intimacy and informality. To emphasize the personal quality of these reflective pieces, Montaigne informs his reader that they were written entirely for his own amusement and self-enlightenment, that they contain nothing which could conceivably interest anyone but himself. Indeed, in his essays Montaigne often plays Hamlet in the graveyard scene and his reader is a Horatio, delighted and amazed by his friend's incredible powers of imaginative speculation.

The distinguishing features of Montaigne's essays are wit, imagination, and self-revelation—qualities that defy imitation—and Montaigne's first follower in English, the anonymous author of *Remedies Against Discontentment* (1596), did nothing toward popularizing the essay. Like Montaigne, his English disciple construes the essay to be an informal, subjective mode of writing and announces that his discursive observations were "only framed for mine own use; and that is the reason I took no great pain to set them forth any better."

The greatest English essayist of the seventeenth century was Francis Bacon. His *Essays, Religious Meditations, Places of Persuasion and Dissuasion* (1597) consists of ten short essays, "certain brief notes, set down rather significantly than curiously." The meditations in this first edition, entitled "*Meditations sacrae,*" are in Latin, the essays, entitled "Places," etc., in English. Although Montaigne was one of Bacon's models, these first essays were equally influenced by classical maxims and precepts recorded in his commonplace book; they resemble the laconic *sententiae* of the Roman philosophers, and, in fact, Bacon identifies one of his important sources as Seneca's *Epistles to Lucilius,* which he described as "dispersed meditations, though conveyed in the form of epistles." Hence Bacon's essays are derived from a variety of sources—the commonplace book, the philosophical epistle, the didactic maxims and epigrams of Latin writers. From the bare and unadorned *sententiae* of the 1597 edition, Bacon developed an essay as smooth and full as Montaigne's. In the second edition (1612) he revised nine of the first essays and added twenty-nine new ones, and the last edition (1625) contained fifty-eight. These additions and revisions after 1597 show clearly that Bacon began with *sententiae* and aphorisms as a bare-boned pattern and fleshed out this structure with illustrative quotations, anecdotes, and transitions. The original essay "Of Regiment of Health" consists of little more than about 250 words of gnomic, isolated statements: "Discern of the coming on of years, and think not to do the same things still," and "Despise no new accident in the body, but ask opinion of it." In an essay from the 1625 edition, "Of Studies," the aphorisms are made topic sentences for fully developed paragraphs:

> Read not to contradict and confute, nor to believe and take for granted, nor to find talk and discourse, but to weigh and consider. Some books are to be tasted, others to be swallowed, and some few to be chewed and digested; that is, some books are to be read only in parts; others to be read, but not curiously; and some few to be read wholly, and with diligence and attention. Some books also may be read by deputy, and extracts made of them by others; but that would be only in the less important arguments, and the meaner sort of books; else distilled books are like common distilled waters, flashy things. Reading maketh a full man, conference a ready man, and writing an exact man...

The differences of form and content between Bacon's essays and those of Montaigne point to their totally dissimilar temperaments. Unlike Montaigne, Bacon disliked abstract ethics and whimsical speculation; for Bacon, life, like politics, was the "art of the possible," and his essays are practical counsels to young, educated men of the ruling class on how best to succeed in a competitive, uncompromising world. Montaigne's essays are intimate, gossipy, directed at whatever is most human; even mothers of small children and lovers of cats find a friend in Montaigne. Bacon, on the other hand, is invariably formal, detached, intellectually exclusive; there is nothing in his essays that is relevant to women or children, the aged, the poor, or the powerless, and Blake's famous observation that Bacon's essays are "good advice for Satan's worshippers" is really another way of saying that they are practical guides to effective conduct for young men who, like Bacon himself, were chiefly concerned with success. Hence the essay "Of Discourse" treats of what a gentleman may and may not discuss effectively—"But some things are privileged from jest, namely religion, matters of state, great persons, any case that deserveth pity." In "Of Friendship," Bacon declares with astonishing practicality that friends are indeed more efficacious in alleviating melancholy than are medicinal remedies such as "sarza to open the livers, steel to open the spleen, flower of sulphur for the lungs . . ."

Like many ambitious aspirants to public office, Bacon was a disciple of Machiavelli, whose utilitarian advice appeared to be so much more enlightened and hard-headed than the other-worldly idealism of classical and medieval moralists. Like Machiavelli's *Il Principe,* Bacon's *Essays* is not so much innocuous entertainment as pragmatic instruction, a conduct or courtesy book designed for educated young men who would live prudently and govern wisely. In this authoritative role, Bacon never deigns to argue or prove a statement or idea; his advice is dispensed *ex cathedra,* adorned with attractive illustrations and perceptive nuances rather than with forensic heat or calculated logic. Unlike Montaigne, he shows little interest in the psychological aspects of a topic or in quaint human deviations or curious eccentricities. He charts a rational course between the impulses of the human heart and the objective necessities of social deportment and policy. In "Of Atheism" he views man's doubts and anxieties not from inside himself, as Montaigne had done, but from the magisterial heights of one who sees religious skepticism in terms of its social and political effects:

> So man, when he resteth and assureth himself upon divine protection and favor, gathereth a force and faith, which human nature in itself could not obtain. Therefore, as atheism is in all respects hateful, so in this, that it depriveth human nature of the means to exalt itself above human frailty. As it is in particular persons, so it is in nations . . .

In content Bacon's Essays are august and serene, the expression of a Roman stoicism firmly grounded in the conventional values of obedience, loyalty, piety, courage, truth, and honor. In style they represent an iconoclastic repudiation of prevailing Ciceronian prose, with its swelling, rotund periods, symmetrical constructions, and oratorical flourishes. Bacon modeled his prose after the concise, semi-colloquial examples of Seneca and Tacitus, and his Essays represent a clear break from the verbose and decorative Ciceronian prose of the sixteenth century toward a style that is lucid, crisp, and direct. That new style, combining the modes of Seneca and Tacitus and of their chief disciple Justus Lipsius, was called "Attic," and included the widely divergent qualities of Montaigne and Robert Burton, both considered "Attic libertines" for their discursiveness. Bacon and Jonson represent the "curt," or more disciplined, method; and, at still another extreme, Joseph Hall and Owen Felltham, are even more clipped, direct, and sententious than either Bacon or Jonson. For sheer polish, economy, and clarity, however, no prose writer of the seventeenth century surpassed Bacon's 1625 edition of the *Essays.*

Bacon's first imitator was Sir William Cornwallis, whose voluminous *Essays* (1600-01, in two parts; enl. ed., 1606-10; enl. ed. 1632) combines the practical advice of the conduct book with the personal tone of Montaigne. To a greater extent than Bacon, Cornwallis is concerned with the liberal education of a gentleman, and many of his essays bear the same titles as Bacon's—"Of Discourse," "Of Adversity," "Of Learning." Unlike Bacon or Montaigne, however, Cornwallis writes in a disjointed, terse prose:

> Affection begets extremities. Man is allowed only the middle way. He strayeth when he affects; his error is punished with deformity; whatsoever he performeth thus becoming disgraceful and uncomely. There is not any in this kind to be pardoned.

As one scholar has noted, the course of the essay in the seventeenth century resembles that of a whale followed by small fish, for no writer after Bacon contributed notably to the development of the genre. Robert Johnson's *Essays, or Rather Imperfect Offers* (1601) continues the tentative aspects of the form with observations on such subjects as education, courtesy, travel, and popular wisdom, whereas David Tuvill's enormous collections, *Essays Politic and Moral* (1608) and *Essays Moral and Theological* (1609), although properly Baconian in intention, are a wilderness of pedantic digressions and massive anecdotes from Greek and Roman historians and philosophers.

The fusion of the essay with such related genres as the CHARACTER and the LETTER-WRITER is illustrated in the 1614 edition of Sir Thomas Overbury's *Characters,* to which were appended several humorous essays on customs, travel, and foreign manners under the heading "News," and in Nicholas Breton's popular *Characters upon Essays* (1615), a collection of epistolary characters that also contains essays on such Baconian topics as courage, death, truth, and wisdom. Breton's earlier manual on the art of writing letters, *A Post with a Packet of Mad Letters* (1602; enlarged in many subsequent editions), also impinges on the essay in its treatment of such topics as education, marriage, and travel. Another collection of letters, JAMES HOWELL'S, *Epistolae Ho-Eliane* (1645, 1647, 1650, 1655), combines the various forms of commonplace book, diary, and epistle with the essay, for many of Howell's digressions on subjects like wine, language, religion, and science are virtually informal essays in the modern sense. Infinitely curious and gossipy, Howell is a kind of Samuel Pepys on a grand tour, a truly great journalist whose letters provide one man's vivid, energetic picture of his times—the common sights of Venice, the Overbury trial, Prince Charles's courtship of the Spanish Infanta, the siege of Rochelle, Platonic love at court, and even Ben Jonson boastfully displaying his learning at a dinner party. These vignettes, popular in their own time, helped to dislodge the essay from its original preoccupation with homiletic reflections, pious aphorisms, and notes on reading rather than accounts of lived experience.

The essays of Grey Brydges, fifth baron Chandos, *Horae subsecivae, Observations and Discourses* (1620), are so closely imitative of Bacon's aphoristic, sententious style in the 1597 edition that they were falsely attributed to Bacon himself. More distinctive and original in style is Owen Felltham's *Resolves Divine, Moral, Political* (1623?). Felltham describes the essay as "running discourse," and his ruminative style anticipates some of the stoical reflections of Sir Thomas Browne's *Religio medici* (1642) and *Urn Burial* (1658). Like Browne, Felltham was a moderate Anglican educated by his reading to value the Roman stoic's aristocratic virtues of education, tolerance, restraint, and magnanimity, all of which he combined with occasional impulsive flights into neo-Platonic mysticism. Both Felltham's *Resolves* and Browne's *Religio medici* illustrate the affinities of the essay form with the previously infra-literary religious and philosophical meditations that educated gentlemen recorded in their commonplace books for purposes of their own self-examination and edification. Henry Peacham's *The Truth of Our Times* (1638) bears a close affinity to personal meditation—like many essayists of the time, he announces that he writes only for himself—yet Peacham's essays are more extroverted than either Felltham's or Browne's, and his fleeting imagination congenially embraces every topic from fashions in dress to religious doctrines.

The religious meditation, the character, and the sermon *per se* are all combined in Thomas Fuller's *The Holy State and the Profane State* (1642), a miscellany of forty-eight characters of social types—the good child, the virtuous parent, and so forth—followed by Baconian essays on fame, travel, and marriage, many of which may represent Fuller's outlines for his sermons. These indefinite associations of the essay proper with any number of literary and infra-literary types are well illustrated in the title of Francis Osborn's work, *A Miscellany of Sundry Essays, Paradoxes, and Problematical Discourses, Letters, and Characters* (1659).

The essay joins with the commonplace book in Ben Jonson's TIMBER (1640-41) four-fifths of which has been found to be paraphrases or condensations of such diverse authors as Euripides, Quintilian, Horace, and Seneca, as well as some aphoristic commentaries on the art of writing and the works of Jonson's contemporaries. The close connection of the essay to literary criticism and classical dialogue is illustrated by Dryden's *Essay of Dramatic Poesy* (1668), in which several fictitious characters discuss, in brief essays, such subjects as the classical unities, Shakespeare's art, and heroic drama. Another famous example of the essay with roots in a kindred genre is Milton's *Areopagitica* (1644), which is couched in the form of a dignified oration based on classical principles.

The essay did not emerge as a truly distinct type until after 1660, in essays of Abraham Cowley, Addison and Steele, and others. Before 1660 the essay remained a combination of many forms related to philosophic and religious meditations, aphorisms, homilies, and conduct books. Written by upper class writers inclined to expound a conventional body of wisdom derived from Christian stoicism, the English essay was addressed chiefly to readers concerned with sharing common ideals of civilized and rational behavior. Hence the essay in the seventeenth century relates, also, to a large body of COURTESY LITERATURE.

There is a good collection of essays in *Prose of the English Renaissance,* ed. J. William Hebel, H. H. Hudson, et al. (1952). The standard edition of Bacon's *Essays* is by J. Spedding, R. L. Ellis, and D. D. Heath, 7 vols. (1857-59), VII. Studies of the essay include Hugh Walker, *The English Essay and Essayists* (1915); M. W. Croll, "Attic Prose: Lipsius, Montaigne, Bacon," *Schelling Anniversary Papers* (1923); E. N. S. Thompson, *The Seventeenth-Century English Essay* (1926); George Williamson, *The Senecan Amble* (1951); and R. J. Jones, *Triumph of the English Language* (1953).

Euphues. A prose romance by John LYLY. The first part, *Euphues, the Anatomy of Wit,* was printed in 1578; the second part, *Euphues and His England,* in 1580. Both are based in part on Sir Thomas NORTH'S *Dial of Princes* (1557), a translation of the Spanish writer Antonio de Guevara's *El relox de principes.* Lyly's first volume also combines the legend of the Prodigal Son and a tale of two friends similar to a story in Boccaccio's *Decameron* (X, 8). Other influences include Roger Ascham's *The Schoolmaster,* the romances of George Gascoigne (see FICTION), and George Pettie's *A Petite Palace of Pettie His Pleasure.*

Although some scholars regard *Euphues* as the first English novel of manners, the plots in both parts are slender and static, consisting chiefly of long stylized debates and ornate, flowery letters among the characters. In the first part the arrogant young Euphues, prodigal son of a rich Athenian, travels to Naples, where he meets Philautus, an Italian, and the two youths become close friends until Euphues brashly courts Philautus' sweetheart Lucilla. In the end the fickle Lucilla rejects both Euphues and Philautus for another lover, and the two friends are reunited. As Euphues departs for Athens, he writes Philautus a long letter of advice on love and life called "A Cooling Card for Philautus."

The second part, *Euphues and His England,* takes the two friends to London and the English court, where, in spite of Euphues' prudent advice, Philautus falls in love with an English lady and is rejected in favor of a "true-blue Englishman." A lengthy letter from Athens, addressed by Euphues to the ladies of Italy, bestows praise on Queen Elizabeth, the English court, and English institutions in general. The plot of the second part is even thinner than the first; both parts use the barest story line on which to hang the real substance of the work—highly affected language devoted to the lofty themes of love and courtship, masculine friendship, education, religion, manners and morals (see EUPHUISM).

The best edition of the two romances is edited by M. W. Croll and H. Clemons (1916). An important reference companion is M. P. Tilley, *Elizabethan Proverb Lore in Lyly's "Euphues" and Pettie's "Petite Palace"* (1926). An important essay is P. W. Long, "From *Troilus* to *Euphues*," *Kittredge Anniversary Papers* (1913). See also Rose Macaulay, "Lyly and Sidney" in *The English Novelists*, ed. D. Veschoyle (1936); and Shimon Sandbank, "Euphuistic Symmetry and the Image," *SEL*, XI (1971).

Euphuism. A prose style popularized by John LYLY in his two prose romances *Euphues, the Anatomy of Wit* (1578) and *Euphues and His England* (1580). The rhetorical devices characteristic of the style include elaborate syntactical parallelisms; abundant antitheses of phrases and clauses; strings of proverbs; profuse alliteration; exaggerated euphony and rhythm; melanges of questions; and pedantic or fantastic similes and metaphors, many drawn from mythology or the "unnatural natural history" of bestiary and lapidary lore. A brief passage from *Euphues, the Anatomy of Wit* will suffice to illustrate the peculiarities of the style:

> One drop of poison infecteth the whole tun of wine, one leaf of coloquintida maneth and spoileth the whole pot of porridge, one iron mold defaceth the whole piece of lawn. Descend into thine own conscience, and consider with thyself the great difference between staring and stark blind, wit and wisdom, love and lust. Be merry but with modesty, be sober but not too sullen, be valiant but not too venturous...

Lyly's "euphuistic" syntax is derived from the classical principles of *isocolon* (phrases and clauses of equal length), *parison* (symmetrical grammatical elements), and *paromoion* (successive syllables of corresponding sound). His ornamental figures of speech are equally traditional in classical rhetoric, consisting of *exempla* (illustrations from history, myth, and poetry), *sententiae* (proverbs and maxims), and *similea* (comparisons from pseudo-science or the "unnatural natural history" of Pliny, the medieval bestiaries and nature encyclopedias, or from the author's own fancy).

Thus Lyly popularized a style but by no means invented it. Characteristics of euphuism are evident in many late medieval sermons, in some of Sir Thomas More's prose, and in John Grange's romance *The Golden Aphroditis* (1577). Closest to Lyly in inspiration were Lord Berners' translation of Froissart's *Chronicles* (c. 1523-25), the Latin lectures of John Rainolds at Oxford (1572-78), and George Pettie's *A Petite Palace of Pettie His Pleasure* (1576), which contains twelve tales in imitation of William Painter's *The Palace of Pleasure*. Nevertheless, it was the resourceful Lyly who gave this grotesque style a local habitation and a name, and brought together in one work the rhetorical elements scattered throughout these sources.

For the origins and characteristics of euphuism, see William Ringler, "The Immediate Source of Euphuism," *PMLA,* LIII (1938); G. B. Parks, "Before Euphuism," *J. Q. Adams Memorial Studies* (1948); Walter A. King, "John Lyly and Elizabethan Rhetoric," *SP,* LII (1955); and Jonas Barish, "The Prose Style of John Lyly," *ELH,* XXIII (1956).

Evelyn, John (1620-1706). Diarist. Born in Wotton, Sussex, the second son of a prosperous landowner and sheriff of Sussex and Surrey, Evelyn attended school in Southover, where he was raised by his maternal grandmother, and proceeded to Balliol College, Oxford, in 1637. The next year he entered the Middle Temple, but was not admitted to the bar. With the death of his mother in 1635 and his father in 1640, he inherited a large fortune and traveled for a year on the Continent. His famous diary begins with this year (1641).

During the Civil War Evelyn remained steadfastly loyal to the king and to the Church of England, but took no part in the fighting. He did, however, serve as messenger for the royal family in France in 1643 and 1647. In the latter year he married Mary Browne, daughter of Charles I's representative in Paris, Sir Richard Browne. (The marriage was not consummated until several years later.) In 1648 Evelyn returned to England and settled in seclusion at Sayes Court near Deptford, where he spent most of his time improving the house and gardens at Sayes Court, studying agriculture, architecture, coins and medals, history, and literature.

With the Restoration Evelyn returned to public life, serving Charles II in several minor offices. During the Dutch War he acted as commissioner in charge of the sick and wounded; he remained in London on duty for the government during the terrible plague of 1665 and the great fire of 1666. During the years 1695 to 1703 he was treasurer of the hospital for aged sailors at Greenwich. He died at eighty-six at Wotton, the father of six sons and three daughters.

Evelyn's diary, which was not printed until 1818, is a priceless historical document describing many of the major events and personalities in England during the years 1641 to 1706. Although Evelyn was a quiet, cautious, and scholarly man, he was also a sharp observer and, in a sense, an extraordinarily active person. He knew and described in his diary many of the most distinguished men and women of his age—Charles I, Henrietta Maria, Charles II, James II, Christopher Wren, Samuel Pepys, Oliver Cromwell, William and Mary, Queen Anne, Jeremy Taylor, Robert Boyle, and many others. Although he resided quietly for most of his life at Sayes Court, he engaged periodically in momentous events and significant movements. He witnessed the Great Plague, the London fire, the Dutch War; he was a founder and secretary of the Royal Society; he brought the Arundel marbles to Oxford University; he worked with Christopher Wren on the reconstruction of London after the fire. In 1661 he published *Fumifugium,* a work attacking smoke pollution in London and recommending solutions. In another important work, *Silva* (1664), he proposed remedies for the depletion of English forests. Other publications include works on education, urban planning, horticulture, and chalcography.

His masterpiece, however, is his famous diary, in which he brings to bear the perceptions of an erudite, intellectually curious, and compassionate nature. A firm Royalist, devout Christian, and patriotic Englishman, he was nevertheless a tolerant and widely sympathetic recorder of his times. He describes public executions and other inhumane acts with repugnance; he loathed the dissolute habits of the court of Charles II, and although he feared and detested the Jesuits, he opposed punitive laws against Catholics and nonconformists. Unlike that of Pepys, Evelyn's diary is neither confessional nor especially revelatory; Evelyn is a cool, objective commentator on people and events. He was not a warm man, at least not in print, but his diary is rarely dull. Restrained and dignified, it is also a lucid and informative record of the period.

The Diary of John Evelyn, ed. E. S. De Beer, 6 vols. (1955) is standard. Geoffrey Keynes' *John Evelyn* (1937) is an exhaustive bibliography of Evelyn's many works, updated in "John Evelyn, 1920-68," ed. Dennis G. Donovan, *Elizabethan Bibliographies Supplements,* XVIII (1970). See also Jeanne K. Welcher, "A Survey of the Scholarship on John Evelyn," *BNYPL,* LXXIII (1969).

Every Man in His Humour. A satiric comedy by Ben JONSON. It was written in 1598, and first performed the same year by the Lord Chamberlain's Men with Shakespeare acting a part. Originally printed in 1600 with an Italian setting, it was revised by Jonson for the 1616 folio, giving the characters English names, changing the setting to London, and adding many allusions to Elizabethan life and manners. This was Jonson's first popular play, and the first to employ the so-called comedy of humours, a comedy portraying some one dominant "humour" or obsession in the main characters (see JONSON, BEN). Thus Captain Bobadill's "humour" is intemperate boasting, Stephen's stupidity, Knowell Senior's suspicion, and Kitley's and his wife's jealousy. Most of these "humours" or dispositions are "purged" by the therapeutic trickery of Knowell's scheming servant Brainworm. No one source for the play is known; but it is evident that Jonson drew extensively for his situations and characters from Roman comedy.

Old Edward Knowell's son Edward is scholarly and industrious, albeit too much given to "idle poetry." Knowell's nephew Stephen is a hare-brained prodigal given to hunting, swaggering, and idleness. One day Knowell opens a letter to Edward from Master Wellbred and discovers therein not only disparaging references to himself but an invitation to join Wellbred at the Windmill Tavern, where, Knowell now fears, Edward will fall in with dissolute companions. Old Knowell's wily servant Brainworm notifies Edward that Wellbred's letter has been intercepted, and Edward, in the company of his cousin Stephen, sets off for the Windmill with the intention of playing gaily on the old man's suspicions.

Meanwhile a fishmonger's son named Matthew and his companion Cob visit the lodgings of one Captain Bobadill, a boastful enthusiast of bombastic plays, tobacco, fencing, and fashionable cursing. Matthew has come to Captain Bobadill for some professional advice regarding the fine art of dueling, for the young fool has been threatened with a cudgeling by Squire Downright, Wellbred's volatile half-brother. Squire Downright and Wellbred have a virtuous sister, Mistress Kitely, lately married to an older man who is eaten with jealousy. Indeed, Master Kitely erroneously suspects that he has been made a cuckold.

Disguised as a disabled soldier, Brainworm meets Edward and Stephen, and sells to the latter an old sword he misrepresents as being "pure Toledo." Afterward Brainworm encounters Knowell and, still disguised as a soldier, is engaged by the old man as a servant. At the Windmill Tavern, Brainworm's "pure Toledo" is shown by Bobadill to be a poor quality rapier. Brainworm reveals his identity to Edward and warns him that his father, en route to the Windmill, has stopped briefly at the house of Justice Clement.

Edward Knowell confesses to Wellbred his love for Bridget, Master Kitely's sister, and Wellbred promises to aid in the suit. Meanwhile Kitely grows convinced that Edward Knowell is his young wife's lover. These several entanglements, including Kitely's jealousy and his wife's suspicions that he too is unfaithful, Old Knowell's suspicions of Edward's living habits and companions, and the humiliation of Bobadill and his friends at the hands of Downright—all are finally resolved at Justice Clement's house, where Brainworm throws off his disguise and informs the assembled characters of young Knowell's marriage to Mistress Bridget. The young lovers are forgiven, all discord gracefully eliminated by the merry Justice Clement, and the assembled company departs to supper and an evening of laughter and good fellowship.

Every Man in His Humour, Jonson's first mature comedy, is based on situations and characters in Terence: the gay, amiable young men, the possessive father, the cunning servant, and the attractive young girl looking to the youths to rescue her from a dull older generation. Yet Jonson gives his modicum of a plot exceptional dramatic interest by enlivening Terentian types with his own concept of the "humours" or obsessions dominating the main characters. Moreover, Jonson's dialogue is natural and witty, his plot neatly woven and unified.

The standard edition is in *Ben Jonson,* ed. C. H. Herford and Percy and Evelyn Simpson, 11 vols. (1925-53), III. Jonson's play has been edited by Martin Seymour-Smith in the New Mermaid series (1966) and by J. W. Lever in the Regents Renaissance Drama series (1971). Jonson's revisions in the 1616 edition are analyzed by J. A. Bryant, "Jonson's Revision of *Every Man in His Humour,*" *SP,* LIX (1962). For other commentary, see C. R. Baskervill, *English Elements in Jonson's Early Comedies* (1911); John J. Enck, *Jonson and the Comic Truth* (1957); and Jonas A. Barish, *Jonson and the Language of Prose Comedy* (1960).

Every Man Out of His Humour. A comedy by Ben JONSON, written in 1599 and published in 1600. The play was intended to exploit the success of Jonson's EVERY MAN IN HIS HUMOUR, written and produced a year before. No source has been found for Jonson's plot. The characters have Italian names but the scene is the "Fortunate Island," which is meant to represent England.

The bitter malcontent Macilente flees from the city to the country, where he overhears the cynical Carlo Buffone advising a wealthy young farmer, Sogliardo, that if he would be an accomplished gentleman he must spend his money freely, frequent taverns and theaters, increase his creditors, and affect a melancholy pose. After a few words with Macilente, the pair hurry off to the house of Puntarvolo, a fantastic, quixotic knight. Later Macilente hears Sordido, a miserly farmer, cursing predictions of fair weather because rain would increase the value of his hoarded grain. Sordido determines to hide his grain in spite of official orders that he bring it to market.

At Puntarvolo's house appears Sir Fastidious

Brisk, a swaggering fop whose stylish clothes so fascinate Fungoso, Sordido's son, that he asks his uncle Sogliardo to wheedle money from the miserly Sordido on the pretext of buying law books so that Fungoso can copy Brisk's finery.

Meanwhile the ridiculous Puntarvolo wagers five thousand pounds that he, his wife, and dog can travel to Constantinople and back, and although even Buffone views the wager as a joke, Brisk expresses a desire to put down a hundred pounds against Puntarvolo. In another development Macilente advises his merchant friend Deliro to stop doting on his wife Fallace, Fungoso's sister; the wife's petulance is made evident when, after being smitten by Brisk's courtly manners, she expresses dissatisfaction with her plain and ordinary husband. Fungoso arrives splendidly attired in a new suit, and is annoyed to find himself outdone by Brisk, who wears a new, more stylish outfit. Fungoso hastens away to borrow more money to add to his wardrobe.

Macilente, Fungoso, and Sogliardo venture to court, led by the confident Brisk, while Deliro chafes at his wife's infatuation with Brisk. Old Puntarvolo loses his wager—and his "humour"—when Macilente secretly poisons his dog. At a fray at the Mitre Tavern Puntarvolo assaults Buffone for mocking the dog's death, Brisk is seized by the bailiff for his debts, and Fungoso is required to pay the total tavern reckoning. Macilente sends Deliro to pay the bill and Fallace to debtors' prison to confront Brisk. At the assembling of the characters at the prison, Deliro realizes Fallace's infatuation for the ridiculous Brisk and is shaken out of his uxoriousness. Fungoso vows to renounce courtly ways, and Brisk resigns himself to a term in jail. Thus all the main characters are purged of their obsessional "humours."

The synopsis given above describes a plot much more coherent than the tangled episodes and confusing variety of characters actually portrayed in Jonson's comedy. Jonson seems less concerned with unraveling a plot than amassing absurd characters to enforce the more successful satiric methods of *Every Man in His Humour.* In this later play exaggerated social types are shown to be "out of humour" —that is, obsessed with some absurdity of the times: Fastidious Brisk and Fungoso with courtly dress and fashions; Sordido with almanacs and prognostications; Sogliardo with social status; Deliro with his wife; and Puntarvolo with his dog. In the fifth act—which is much faster in pace than the others—these "humorous" characters are scourged to the accompaniment of biting choral comments by Asper (representing Jonson) and several other characters stating various aspects of the author's moral views. Hence *Every Man Out of His Humour* is less unified and more didactic than *Every Man in His Humour;* the later comedy is more on the order of an episodic harangue. In the 1600 quarto Jonson provides a list of the "characters of the persons" in which each character's foibles are systematically described. For Jonson's comedy of humours, see JONSON, BEN.

The standard edition of Jonson's play is in *Ben Jonson,* ed. C. H. Herford and percy and Evelyn Simpson, 11 vols. (1925-53), III. For critical studies, see Helena W. Baum, *The Satiric and the Didactic in Ben Jonson's Comedy* (1947); John J. Enck, *Jonson and the Comic Truth* (1957); and Jonas A. Barish, *Ben Jonson and the Language of Prose Comedy* (1960).

F

Faerie Queene, The. An epic in six books by Edmund SPENSER. The first three books, dedicated to Queen Elizabeth with an epistle to Sir Walter RALEIGH, were published in 1590; the last three appeared in 1596. The first mention of *The Faerie Queene* occurs in a letter of Spenser to his friend Gabriel Harvey, dated April 1580, in which Spenser refers to having sent Harvey portions of the manuscript. In his reply the same month, Harvey writes disapprovingly of Spenser's "Hobgoblin" romantic epic as being a futile imitation of Ariosto's *Orlando Furioso.* Like many Renaissance critics, Harvey favored the classical epic of Vergil over the romantic epic of Ariosto.

The next reference to *The Faerie Queene* appears in Lodowick Bryskett's *A Discourse of Civil Life,* written before 1589, where the author describes a conversation in which Spenser, when asked to distinguish among the moral virtues, replies: "I have already undertaken a work tending to the same effect, which is in heroical verse, under the title of a *Faerie Queene,* to represent all the moral virtues, assigning to every virtue a knight to be the patron and defender of the same; in whose actions and feats of arms and chivalry the operations of that virtue whereof he is the protector are to be expressed, and the vices and unruly appetites that oppose themselves against the same to be beaten down and overcome."

In his dedicatory epistle to Raleigh in the first edition of 1590, Spenser explains that the purpose of the poem is "to fashion a gentleman or noble person in virtuous and gentle discipline." The twelve contemplated books, each divided into twelve cantos, were to portray the adventures of twelve knights, one of whom appears on each of the twelve days of feasting held by Gloriana, queen of Fairyland, whom Spenser identifies as Queen Elizabeth. Each knight was to represent allegorically one of the twelve virtues suppos edly described by Aristotle. All twelve virtues were to be combined in one character, Arthur, symbolizing "Magnificence" (a virtue kindred to magnanimity, or ideal nobility of character). Most scholars agree that Spenser did not follow this plan consistently. Only six of the projected books were completed and perhaps part of a seventh, the two so-called MUTABILITY CANTOS, an allegorical fragment appended to the 1609 edition. The nonextant remainder of the epic may have been destroyed in the burning of Spenser's Kilcolman Castle.

The epic is written throughout in nine-line stanzas rhyming *ab ab bc bc c,* the last line being an alexandrine. Spenser derived his stanza pattern from Chaucer's "Monk's Tale," which Chaucer took from an old French eight-line ballad stanza rhyming *ab ab bc bc.* In spelling, diction, and syntax the language is deliberately archaic and Chaucerian to convey the dignity of the subject matter. In addition to Chaucer, Spenser was chiefly influenced in style and subject matter by Vergil's *Aeneid* and eclogues, Homer's *Iliad* and *Odyssey,* Malory's *Morte d'Arthur,* and two Italian romantic epics of chivalry, Ariosto's *Orlando Furioso* and Tasso's *Gerusalemme liberata.* Among these influences Ariosto's was paramount.

Spenser's complex allegory has been approached on three levels: moral, religious, and political. The first of these is relatively clear, for the characters obviously represent conflicting virtues and vices. The second level, the religious, portrays the conflicts of the Church of England with the Reformed persuasion, Roman Catholicism, skepticism, atheism, and paganism. The political allegory, however, is obscure and probably inconsistent. Gloriana, the fairy queen, is certainly Queen Elizabeth; Arthur is at least initially the earl of Leicester, although Leicester's declining influence with the queen after 1580 and his death in 1588 affected Spenser's plans for him in the epic. Other characters in the political allegory, including Mary Queen of Scots as Duessa, have been identified with less certainty.

Consistent with Aristotle's prescription of epic structure, Spenser begins his story in *medias res* with a knight, a lady, and her dwarf already on a chivalric quest. (The account of the epic given below makes no attempt to emphasize Spenser's political allegory.)

Book I. The Legend of the Redcrosse Knight, or of Holiness. Redcrosse (Holiness), an inexperienced knight wearing the Christian armor of St. Paul, is riding forth with Una (Truth) and her dwarf (Humility) to rescue Una's parents, who have been imprisoned by a dragon. They first encounter the monster Error (representing false religious teaching), which Redcrosse defeats with the aid of Una. In the Wood of Error they meet the aged, apparently pious hermit Archimago (Hypocrisy), who takes them to his hut to spend the night. There Redcrosse, because of Archimago's magic, dreams that Una comes to seduce him, and with the dwarf he flees the hut in disgust. Later he meets the Saracen knight Sansfoy (Faithless) and his lady Fidessa (really Duessa, or Falsehood). Redcrosse slays Sansfoy and falls in with Fidessa. As he plucks a branch from a tree to make her a garland, the tree bleeds and identifies itself as the transformed Fradubio (Doubter), who accuses Fidessa of bewitching him. Redcrosse and Fidessa depart for the House of Pride, ruled by Queen Lucifera.

Meanwhile Una, pursued by Archimago disguised as Redcrosse, meets a friendly lion. Una and the lion spend the night at the hut of Abessa (Superstition), daughter of Corceca (Blind Devotion), and Abessa's violent servant Kirkrapine (Church-robber) is killed by the lion. Overtaken by Archimago disguised as Redcrosse, Una takes him to be her champion and is reconciled to him. Soon after, they encounter a Saracen, Sansloy (Lawless), who defeats Archimago and carries Una away into the forest, where the lion attempts to rescue her but is slain by Sansloy.

At the House of Pride, meanwhile, Redcrosse and the dwarf have been staying with Duessa, whom Redcrosse believes to be Una since she, like Archimago, can take any form she chooses. He enters the lists against Sansjoy (Joyless) and vanquishes him, but Sansjoy is rescued by Duessa's black magic. She takes Sansjoy to Hades to be healed of his wounds. Upon her return from the infernal regions, Duessa lures Redcrosse into drinking from an enchanted pool that takes away his strength; hence he is severely wounded and imprisoned by the giant Orgoglio (Pride). The dwarf flees, and Orgoglio makes Duessa his mistress.

Una is rescued from Sansjoy by the timely arrival of a band of fauns and satyrs, who bring her to their chief, the benign Sylvanus. Una remains with these "savage" folk until the arrival of the dwarf, who informs Una of Redcrosse's misfortunes and of the deceits played upon Redcrosse and Una by Archimago and Duessa. Una also meets Prince Arthur, a gallant knight devoted to Gloriana, and Arthur's squire Timias; in company with them, Una and the dwarf set out to rescue Redcrosse. Arthur slays Orgoglio, exposes Duessa as a witch, and frees the wounded Redcrosse.

After an exchange of gifts, Arthur and his squire depart to continue their quest of the beautiful fairy queen Arthur has seen in a dream, Redcrosse, Una, and the dwarf resume their journey. Encountering the specter Despair, Redcrosse is tempted to commit suicide but is restrained by Una. Disconsolate, he is taken by Una to the House of Holiness (virtuous counterpart to the House of Pride), where his wounds are healed and his Christian faith restored. He and Una journey to Eden, the kingdom of her parents, where Redcrosse slays the dragon. After another attempt to separate Una and Redcrosse, Archimago is captured and imprisoned, and Truth and Holiness are at last united in marriage. Redcrosse, however, soon must depart for further service on behalf of Gloriana.

Book II: The Legend of Sir Guyon, or of Temperance. Deceived by Archimago and Duessa's false report that Redcrosse has violated a virgin (portrayed by Duessa in disguise), Sir Guyon (Temperance) and Redcrosse narrowly avert a duel when each recognizes the Christian emblem on the other's shield. Later Sir Guyon and a palmer (Prudence) meet a dying mother, Amavia, who recounts how her deceased husband, Sir Mortdant, succumbed to the enchantress Acrasia (Intemperance), ruler of the Bower of Bliss. After Amavia dies, Sir Guyon takes her baby into his care and swears vengeance against Acrasia. He leaves the child with a lady called Medina. Soon after, Sir Guyon meets an unpleasant pair, Furor and his beastly mother Occasion [of sin], both of whom he subdues with great difficulty, Sir Guyon releases their captive, the squire Phedon, who explains how the wicked mother and son had caused him to slay his mistress Claribell and best friend Philemon.

At this point appears Atin (Strife, or Wrath), who warns Sir Guyon of the approach of Pyrochles (Firebrand), son of old Acrates (Self-indulgence) and Despight (Malice). Atin has been in pursuit of Occasion, and the palmer reproaches him for attempting to join "occasion to wrath." Atin departs after hurling a badly aimed poisoned dart at Sir Guyon. When Pyrochles arrives, Sir Guyon easily defeats him, but spares his life on promise of allegiance. At Pyrochles' insistence, Sir Guyon then releases Furor and Occasion from their chains, and the two monsters attack their own benefactor Pyrochles, who must be rescued by Sir Guyon. The palmer observes that Sir Guyon erred in bestowing pity on wickedness.

Meanwhile Pyrochles' brother Cymochles (Debauchery) leaves his mistress, the enchantress Acrasia, in the Bower of Bliss and, although in quest of revenge against Guyon for his defeat of Pyrochles, loses himself completely in the arms of Phaedria (Sensuality). The enchantress conducts Sir Guyon to Cymochles; the latter awakens from his torpor to attack the knight, but Phaedria prevents the combat by convincing them that "amours" are better than duels.

Mammon then escorts Sir Guyon to the House of Riches, but the knight refuses to be tempted. Finding Sir Guyon in a trance, the faithless Pyrochles and his wicked brother Cymochles are about to strip him of his armor when Arthur arrives. Arthur slays Pyrochles and Cymochles, and he and Sir Guyon journey to the Castle of Alma (Soul), which is under seige by Maleger (Evil unto Himself) and his twelve cohorts (the five senses plus the seven deadly sins). After a terrific struggle—whenever Maleger touches earth he is instantly revived—Arthur overcomes Maleger by squeezing him in midair and throwing his body into a lake. Sir Guyon and the palmer destroy the Bower of Bliss, capture Acrasia, and restore to normal shape all the lovers she has transformed into beasts.

Book III: The Legend of Britomart, or of Chastity. In this book Spenser abandons the style of the classical epic, with its sustained concentration on a single hero and continuous narrative development, and adopts the Italian or romantic style of Tasso's and Ariosto's epics, with their variety of main characters and loosely connected, episodic narration.

Arthur and Sir Guyon meet a knight and a squire on an open plain. The knight is really the lady Britomart (Chastity) in search of her lover Artegall, and the squire is Glauce, Britomart's aged nurse. Britomart unhorses Sir Guyon with her magic spear, but as Sir Guyon draws his sword, a palmer arrives and persuades the parties to reconcile, and all ride off together. In a deep forest they see a lady, later identified as Florimell, pursued by a lecherous forester. Sir Guyon and Arthur follow the lady, and Arthur's squire Timias pursues the forester.

Meanwhile Britomart and Glauce, who are not involved in these pursuits, come to the Castle Joyous, where they find six knights attacking a single opponent. Britomart routs all six, a victory that gives her title to the love of Malecasta (Unchastity), the lady of the castle for whose hand the knights were contending. That night Malecasta, thinking Britomart is a man, enters her bedroom intent on seduction; Britomart awakens with sword in hand. Malecasta's shrieks summon the six knights and Redcrosse (the last appearing here for the first time in Book III, as a guest at the castle). Redcrosse and Britomart put all to flight and depart the castle.

As they continue on their way, Britomart slyly inquires of her beloved Artegall, whom she pretends to be searching for to avenge an old grievance. Actually, she has never seen him in person; Merlin once showed her his image in a magic mirror and predicted that Britomart's marriage with Artegall would yield mighty descendants who would unite the Britons, Danes, and Normans under one nation. Eventually, Merlin prophesied, Britomart and Artegall, who are derived ultimately from the Trojans, would produce a lineage culminating in "a royal Virgin" (Queen Elizabeth) destined to "stretch her white rod over the Belgicke shore" and destroy "the great Castle" (Spain) forever. It was this prophecy that caused Britomart to don a man's armor and come to Fairyland in search of Artegall.

Thus Britomart is secretly pleased to learn from Redcrosse that her promised Artegall is a warrior of great reputation, although Redcrosse informs her that Artegall will prove difficult to find because he is always on far-flung missions of chivalry. Separating from Redcrosse and arriving at the sea coast, Britomart fends off an attack by Marinell, seriously wounds him, and departs, leaving him for dead. (Marinell's mother, Cymoent, was warned by the sea god Proteus that he would one day be harmed by a virgin. Hence Cymoent had raised Marinell to spurn all women.) Cymoent invokes the aid of Tryphon, physician of the sea gods, to restore her son to health and swears vengeance against Britomart.

Meanwhile Arthur and Sir Guyon follow the terrified Florimell, and Timias pursues the wicked forester. Separating from Sir Guyon, Arthur comes upon Florimell's dwarf, who informs him that his lady has long cherished unrequited love for the woman-hating Marinell.

In another part of the forest, Timias is ambushed by the forester and his two brothers; Timias kills all three, but falls gravely wounded. The virgin huntress Belphoebe (Chaste Love) nurses him to health, and he falls in love with her. But Spenser's account of her birth and parentage indicate that she is not a woman prepared for ordinary passions. Her mother begot her and her twin sister Amoret (Married Love) without cohabitation with a man, and these sisters were adopted by goddesses—Belphoebe being brought up by the huntress Diana to revere virginity, Amoret by Venus, in devotion to nuptial love. Amoret, Spenser relates, was transported after her birth to the Garden of Adonis (described in detail in Canto VI), where the seeds of all life are conceived, nurture, and die. Here Chaos supplies the raw materials of nature's eternal fecundity, and Form provides this raw generation and growth with ever-changing individuation and variation. In this mythic garden Venus realizes at last her love for Adonis, symbol of rebirth and of the paradoxical union of the eternal and the mutable in a single form. Other inhabitants of the garden include Cupid and Psyche with their daughter Pleasure. It is in this household that Amoret was raised. Symbolic of chaste nuptial passion, she is destined to love a gallant knight named Sir Scudamore (Shield of Love). As for Belphoebe, having been raised by the chaste Diana, she can love no man, and although she treats Timias' physical ills, he departs from her with deep wounds of the heart.

Poor Florimell experiences more perils. She stays at the hut of a witch, whose churlish son lusts after her. When she flees, the son goes mad, and the witch creates a hyena-like monster to pursue her. Florimell reaches a boat just in time to escape the beast, but the boatman proves to be as lecherous as the witch's son. She is rescued from him by Proteus, who takes her to the bottom of the sea. When she also resists his advances, he angrily confines her to a dungeon.

Back on the beach, a knight called Sir Satyrane struggles vainly to kill the monster who pursued Florimell. Finally, he binds the beast with Florimell's girdle left in the sand and leads the monster away. He next meets with an invincible giantess, who releases the monster and flees upon the approach of the Squire of Dames. The squire relates at length his many misfortunes in courtly love, telling how he was spurned by a courtesan because he lacked gold, by a nun because he lacked discretion, and by a woman of low birth because he lacked integrity. He has found no woman who has embraced chastity for its own sake.

Sir Satyrane and the Squire of Dames set out to find and destroy the witch's monster. They meet Sir Paridell (suggesting both "paramour" and Paris of Troy) and arrive at the castle of miserly old Malbecco (Jealousy) and his beautiful young wife Hellenore (suggesting both Helen of Troy and "whore"). The inhospitable Malbecco at first refuses to allow the company to enter, then finally relents and consigns his guests to a shed. Here a stranger arrives and is challenged by Sir Paridell, whom the newcomer easily defeats in combat. The strange knight turns out to be none other than Britomart.

At dinner that night Paridell slyly flirts with Hellenore and persuades her to steal her husband's gold and run away with him. When Paridell deserts her, she begins a dissolute life with a band of satyrs. Her miserly husband eventually finds her, but cannot convince her to return home. Having lost both money and wife, the jealous old cuckold grows asses' ears and crawls away to live in a cave.

Britomart and Sir Satyrane depart Malbecco's house to find Sir Scudamore, who laments that his Amoret is held prisoner by the enchanter Busirane. At Busirane's castle only the chaste Britomart can pass through the flames at the door. Britomart subdues Busirane and frees Amoret.

Book IV: The Legend of Cambel and Triamond, or of Friendship. Two knights, Blandamour and Paridell, in the company of Duessa and Ate (Discord), fight against Scudamore, who defeats Paridell. Sir Ferraugh arrives with a damsel he believes is Florimell, whom he has won by personal combat. In another trial at arms Blandamour in his turn wins the lady, but Paridell, goaded on by Ate, demands that Blandamour share her with him; the two knights, formerly friends, fight over what is really only a disguised witch. Later, they meet two other knights, Cambel and Triamond, and their ladies Cambina and Canace. All journey to a tournament held by Sir Satyrane, where the real Florimell's lost girdle is awarded to the lady judged to be the loveliest. The false Florimell wins the prize, but the girdle, which will not adhere to any except the virtuous, falls from her body.

Elsewhere Scudamore and Artegall are both unhorsed by Britomart, who recognizes Artegall as the man it has been prophesied she will marry (Book III). The two ideal lovers joyously declare their betrothal. The real Florimell, meanwhile, remains true to her hopeless love for Marinell and continues to reject the advances of Proteus, who has taken her to his sea chamber (Book III). At a banquet given by Proteus, Marinell, hitherto an enemy of love, overhears Florimell complain of her unrequited love for him, and he arranges her release from Proteus' prison.

Book V: The Legend of Artegall, or of Justice. The fairy queen sends Artegall (Justice) to rescue Irena (Ireland) from the tyrant Grantorto (Spain). To accompany him she furnishes a ruthless and violent groom, Talus (Punishment), who carries an iron flail that not only destroys wickedness but thrashes out truth from falsehood. Their first adventure is with a squire they find standing beside the beheaded corpse of a lady. The squire relates that his mistress was abducted by Sir Sanglier (Bloody), who left the decapitated woman in her place. Talus thereupon sets forth to intercept the abductor, and soon returns with Sanglier in custody. Sanglier, however, denies the squire's charges, whereupon Artegall decrees a strange judgment: the squire and Sanglier must each cut off and carry with them some part of the bodies of the dead and the living woman; whoever refuses must carry the deceased woman's head with him for a year. When the squire rejects this decision, Artegall realizes that his compassion proves him to be the true lover of the living woman.The squire's mistress is returned to him, and Sanglier is condemned to bear the dead woman's head.

Each of Artegall's adventures illustrates a different aspect of political, religious, or social justice. While enroute to attend the wedding of Marinell and Florimell, Artegall finds his way blocked by the Saracen Pollente (Corruption), who demands exorbitant tolls for crossing his bridge. Artegall kills the Saracen and instructs Talus to seize Pollente's daughter Munera (Bribery), who has profited from her father's extortion. Talus lops off her hands and feet and hangs them up as a warning to others.

In another adventure Artegall happens upon a giant who has gained the obedience of the people by what Artegall adjudges a perversion of justice: the giant divides the people's wealth equally and weighs everything—values as well as material objects—on a set of huge scales as if all were the same. Artegall proves the giant's philosophy false by placing one grain of truth on the scale that outweighs all the falsehood the giant can muster, whereupon Talus slaughters the giant and his multitude of followers.

After attending the marriage of Marinell and Florimell, Artegall and Talus meet a tribe of fierce Amazons led by Queen Ratigund, who makes her male captives wear women's clothes and perform domestic chores. Sir Turpine is about to be hanged for refusing to comply when he is rescued by Artegall. In battle with Ratigund, however, Artegall falls under the spell of her beauty and yields himself as her prisoner, although his loyalty to Britomart prevents him from becoming her lover. Because of this misplaced sympathy for Ratigund, poor Turpine is recaptured and hanged. (Hence he is not to be confused with the Sir Turpine of Book VI.)

Talus reports to Britomart on Artegall's submission, and she sets out with the groom to rescue him. On the way they come across the Temple of Isis, where Britomart dreams of a powerful crocodile tamed by the rod of Isis. The priests of the temple interpret her dream: Artegall is the crocodile, symbolic of the power of the law; Britomart is Isis, representative of mercy; and from their union will come a lion (the Tudors) that will devour the enemies of justice and truth.

In the land of the Amazons, Britomart slays Ratigund and frees Artegall, who resumes his mission. He meets Prince Arthur and Samient, a lady in the service of Mercila (Mercy, and also Queen Elizabeth), whose kingdom is threatened by the Souldan (Spain). Arthur challenges the tyrant, who is cut to pieces by iron hooks on his own chariot wheels. Samient conducts the victorious Arthur and Artegall to the court of Mercila, where they observe the trial of Duessa (here Mary Queen of Scots). Although the court finds her guilty of adultery, murder, and treason, Mercila compassionately refuses to execute her.

Arthur journeys alone to Belgae (the Netherlands), which has appealed for help against the tyrant Geryoneo (Spain). Arthur frees the people, puts an end to their idolatry (Roman Catholicism), and slays the tyrant.

On his own mission Artegall discovers that Irena (Ireland) is about to be executed by Grantorto (Spain), and that her only defender, Sir Burbon (Henry of Navarre), has been forced by a mob to throw down his shield (Protestantism) in disgraceful submission (i.e., to secure the French crown, he has converted to Roman Catholicism). Nevertheless, Artegall aids the knight against the rabble as the lesser of two evils. The repentant Sir Burbon regains the love of his lady, Flourdelis (France), although Artegall criticizes her for pardoning the knight so easily.

Opposed by Grantorto's horde of warriors, Artegall decides to avoid a general slaughter by engaging the tyrant in single combat. After a fierce struggle he beheads Grantorto, and returns to the court of the fairy queen. Upon his return to Irena, he discovers that two rapacious women, Envy and Detraction, have released the Blatant Beast (Slander) to create new havoc in the land. Thus Artegall learns that justice is difficult to achieve when opposed by lies and subversion.

Book VI: The Legend of Calidore, or of Courtesy. As in Book III, the titular hero appears in only about half of the action. Toward the end of the third canto, Calidore, the champion of courtesy, departs from the story and is replaced in this role by Arthur and Timias until the ninth canto, when Calidore again becomes a principal in the story.

Sir Calidore assumes the task of destroying the Blatant Beast released by Envy and Detraction at the end of Book V. On his quest he meets Briana (Female Discourtesy), whose knight Crudor (Male Discourtesy) requires that she shave the beards of knights and the locks of ladies in exchange for his love. Calidore slays Mallefort (Misdirected Courage), who had done Briana's shaving, and subdues Crudor, who gives up his strange requirements of love and is betrothed to Briana. The lovers promise to observe true courtesy in the future.

Calidore's next adventure involves a young woodsman, Tristram, who rescues a lady from mistreatment by her unchivalrous knight. Tristram turns out to be son of the king of Cornwall, a discovery that illustrates Spenser's dictum "Gentle blood will gentle manners breed." Calidore then meets Sir Calepine and his wife Serena, whom he rescues from the Blatant Beast after Serena has been wounded severely. The rude Sir Turpine (Turpitude) refuses to help the couple in their distress even at the urging of his lady, Blandina (Compassion). Sir Turpine not only refuses them the shelter of his castle, but wounds Sir Calepine and would perhaps do more harm but for the timely intervention of a "salvage man," a speechless primitive who is nevertheless benevolent. The savage heals the wounds of Sir Calepine with herbs, but finds that no medicine can cure the poisonous stings Serena received from the Blatant Beast.

One day while Sir Calepine is away, Serena and the savage meet Prince Arthur and Timias. Together they journey to a hermitage where a holy man administers to the wounds of Serena and Timias (also poisoned by the Blatant Beast) with spiritual teachings, for no physical therapy can heal wounds of the spirit. Aided by the savage, Arthur captures Sir Turpine, whom he unwisely spares when Blandina pleads for his life, for the false knight immediately conspires to slay Arthur. Finally Arthur hangs the villain from a tree by his heels.

Meanwhile Serena and Timias are restored to health and meet with Mirabella, a beautiful lady condemned by the court of Venus to roam through the world until she saves as many lovers as she has contemptuously rejected. She is guided by Disdain and whipped ahead by Scorn. When Timias attempts to rescue her, he is himself taken prisoner and the lady flees, whereupon Arthur and the savage appear. Mirabella returns to persuade Arthur and the savage to spare her oppressors because, she asserts, they are necessary if she is to achieve true atonement for her earlier pride in love. Serena and her husband are reunited when Sir Calepine saves her from death at the hands of cannibals.

In his pursuit of the Blatant Beast, Sir Calidore pauses to stay with a band of simple shepherds. Calidore (in this episode, Sir Philip Sidney) falls in love with Pastorella (the pastoral life. and also Frances Walsingham, who became Sidney's wife), the beautiful daughter of wise old Meliboe (Sir Francis Walsingham, Queen Elizabeth's secretary of state and Sidney's father-in-law). Calidore's ineffectual rival for Pastorella's love is Coridon, a clumsy shepherd Calidore treats with great courtesy and fairness. One day, in a beautiful and remote part of the forest, Calidore happens upon the three Graces, Euphrosyne (Mirth), Aglaia (Brilliance), and Thalia (Bloom), dancing to the pipe of Colin Clout (Spenser himself as poet). The Graces vanish as soon as Calidore makes his presence known, and Colin explains to Calidore that they symbolize all the virtues of courtesy:

These three on men all gracious gifts bestow,
Which decke the body or adorne the mynde,
To make them lovely or well favoured show,
As comely carriage, entertainement kynde,
Sweete semblaunt, friendly offices that bynde,
And all the complements of curtesie:
They teach us, how to each degree and kynde
We should our selves demeane, to low, to hie;
To friends, to foes, which skill men call Civility.
[VI, 23]

When brigands invade this pastoral land, Meliboe is killed, Coridon escapes, and Pastorella, after much difficulty, is rescued by Calidore, who takes her to the castle of Belgard, where the queen of the castle, Claribell, recognizes her to be a long-lost daughter.

Meanwhile Calidore comes upon the Blatant Beast ravaging a monastery, and engages the monster in a savage struggle; he is unable, however, to do more than muzzle and bind it. At the end of Canto 12 the Blatant Beast breaks its chains and escapes, proving again that slander and malice can never be destroyed nor permanently repressed.

Like Book III, Book VI owes much in structure and theme to Ariosto's *Orlando Furioso.* Also as in Book III, wherein characters are conceived as representatives of various gradations and aspects of love, Book VI relates every main episode to some important principle of courtesy. The theme of courtesy is sustained by other characters even when its primary embodiment, the hero, departs from the story. Spenser's view of courtesy has no counterpart in Aristotle's *Ethics,* but is found in such Renaissance conduct books as Castiglione's *Il Cortegiano* and Elyot's *The Governor.* Hence Calidore stands for all those virtues praised in the aristocratic books of COURTESY LITERATURE. The epitome of courtly graces, he is modest and humble, yet fearless and adroit in arms; deferential and flexible, yet firm of convictions and supremely confident. Many scholars see in Calidore a portrait of Sir Philip Sidney.

On the whole, *The Faerie Queene* is an artful blending of uniformity and variety, originality and imitation. Its most conspicuous quality is its style, characterized by archaisms and the "Spenserian stanza," described on page 144.

The effect of Spenser's closely woven rhymes concluding with the drawn-out alexandrine has been variously described as "difficult and unpleasing, tiresome to the ear by its uniformity and to the attention by its length" (Samuel Johnson) and "beautifully light . . . excellently adapted for describing a breathless chase on horseback or telling an amusing anecdote with a dash of impropriety in it" (C. S. Lewis). The tedium lamented by Johnson becomes most apparent in Spenser's rendering of direct dialogue, which often becomes prolix and repetitious. The same effect is not conveyed when Spenser gives a character's speech indirectly:

Then choosing out few words most horrible
(Let none them read) thereof did verses frame;
With which, and other spelles like terrible,
He bad awake blacke Plutoes griesly Dame,
And cursed heaven; and spake reproachfull shame
Of highest God, the Lord of life and light.
A bold bad man, that dar'd to call by name
Great Gorgon, Prince of darknesse and dead night,
At which Coctytus quakes, and Styx is put to flight. [I, 37]

Spenser's stanza triumphs most often in descriptive passages that express with Chaucerian vividness both swift action and details suggestive of character and ideas:

A gentle Knight was pricking on the plaine,
Y cladd in mightie armes and silver shielde,
Wherein old dints of deepe woundes did remaine,
The cruell markes of many a bloudy fielde,
Yet armes till that time did he never wield:
His angry steede did chide his foming bitt,
As much disdayning to the curbe to yield:
Full jolly knight he seemd, and faire did sitt,
As one for knightly giusts and fierce encounters fitt. [I, 1]

The language of *The Faerie Queene* is, as Milton observed, full of "sage and solemn tunes"—rich, sensuous, stately, and decorative. Unlike Ariosto, Spenser almost never alleviates his high seriousness with humor; the uniform tone of the epic is brooding, reflective, and melancholy. Spenser is also much less passionate in tone than Ariosto; Ariosto's Bradamante burns with passion and jealousy for her lover, but Spenser's Britomart is moved by concepts rather than emotions; her motives make connections with Spenser's moral and political allegory rather than with any feelings ordinary humans experience in actual life.

Although it is no longer fashionable to apply the adjective "dreamy" to Spenser's epic, the word nevertheless has some validity, for his memorable passages are those descriptive of paradisiacal and demonic dreams and visions —the House of Fame, the Masque of Cupid, the Garden of Adonis, or the dance of the three Graces. In such passages Spenser's languid descriptive power combines with his moral energy to express what is perhaps the most compelling quality of *The Faerie Queene,* an almost childish sense of wonder combined with a sure and complex order of values.

Much essential critical and scholarly material, as well as the definitive text, is in the Spenser Variorum Edition by E. A. Greenlaw, F. M. Padelford, C. G. Osgood, *et al.*, 10 vols. (1932-49). Although critical studies on *The Faerie Queene* are too numerous to cite in detail, a few important works include Josephine W. Bennett, *The Evolution of the Faerie Queene* (1942); M. Pauline Parker, *The Allegory of the Faerie Queene* (1960); Kathleen Williams, *Spenser's World of Glass: A Reading of the Faerie Queene* (1966); Paul J. Alpers, *The Poetry of the Faerie Queene* (1967); and Rosemary Freeman, *The Faerie Queene: A Companion for Readers* (1970).

Fair Maid of the West, The; or **A Girl Worth Gold.** A romantic comedy in two parts by Thomas HEYWOOD. It was first published in 1631 but performed much earlier, perhaps in 1610. Several years may stand between the writing of Part I and Part II. No source for the play is known. Based on imaginary episodes pertaining to an expedition to the Azores by the earl of Essex and Raleigh in 1599, the play is set in Plymouth and Fowey in England, Fayal in the Azores, and the Spanish Indies. The action is accompanied by dumb shows and a chorus.

Part I: In Plymouth, which bustles with preparations for the voyage to the Azores, young Spencer kills a man in defense of the beautiful and chaste Bess Bridges, barmaid of the Castle Tavern. Forced to flee the country, he bestows on his loving Bess the Windmill Tavern in Fowey and promises to return.

While her lover is gone, Bess prospers greatly in spite of the interference of a cowardly bully named Roughman, whom she manages to subdue. Meanwhile Spencer sends his friend Goodluck back to England to report on Bess's situation, and before Goodluck departs he hears a mistaken report of Spencer's death. The grief-stricken Bess purchases a ship, makes Goodluck its captain, and sets sail in the company of her drawer Clem, one Fawcett, and Roughman (now reformed); the purpose of the voyage, she announces later, is to bring Spencer's body home from Fayal. In the Azores, however, Bess learns that when Fayal was retaken by the Spaniards, Spencer's body was taken from holy ground and burned. In revenge Bess turns privateer against the Spanish; in an engagement she captures the ship in which Spencer happens to be prisoner, and although she recognizes him, she thinks he is a ghost sent to avenge Spencer's death. After many adventures described by the chorus, Bess's ship harbors in Morocco, and there, at the court of King Mullisheg, Bess and her lover are united in marriage.

Part II: After their marriage the lovers are set upon by the king of Fez, who is infatuated with Bess, and by his queen, Tota, who falls in love with Spencer. After several narrow squeaks, the lovers leave Fez only to become separated by piracy and shipwreck. Captured by bandits, Bess is rescued by the duke of Florence, who falls in love with her and endows her with money. At the end Spencer appears in Florence to claim Bess, and after several more scrapes, the lovers are made safe, wealthy, and happy.

Part II is less effective than Part I; unlike Part I, it is slow-moving, often farcical and pointlessly episodic. The great differences between the two parts may be the result of Heywood's attempt in Part II to reflect the sophisticated manner of Fletcher, whose style influenced Heywood in his later years.

Robert K. Turner has edited both parts for the Regents Renaissance Drama series (1970) with an informative critical discussion. For other commentary, see Ross Jewell, "Thomas Heywood's *The Fair Maid of the West,*" in *Studies in English Drama,* First Series, ed. Allison Gaw (1917).

Faithful Shepherdess, The. A pastoral tragicomedy by John FLETCHER, written about 1608-09 and first printed in an undated quarto about 1610. No definite source is known, although the play resembles the best known of such pastoral dramas, Guarini's *Il pastor fido.* Fletcher's play represents an effort to introduce the pastoral on the popular stage, an effort that Fletcher's preface to the first edition clearly states was a failure because the popular audience expected rural scenes of English "Whitsun ales, cream, wassail, and morris dances." The play enjoyed considerable popularity, however, at the court of Charles I (see PASTORAL).

The play dramatizes the "cross-eyed" loves of shepherds and shepherdesses during a night and a day in the traditional pastoral environs of Thessaly. The "faithful shepherdess" of the title is Clorin, who dwells apart in a shady grove, grows healing herbs, and devotes her life to mourning the death of her lover. In the same vicinity are various other shepherds and shepherdesses, come to attend a festival in honor of the god Pan: Perigot and Amoret, two chaste lovers, are representative of ideal love; Amarilles is more passionate than Amoret, and is hopelessly in love with Perigot. The Sullen Shepherd is incapable of any attachment except that of lust; and his female counterpart Cloe complicates the action by seeking sensual gratification from Thenot, an idealist devoted to Clorin, from Daphnis, a bashful shepherd, and from Alexis, a strong and equally passionate swain.

Most of the action concerns the transformations, misunderstandings, and reconciliations of these lovers who, in their different ways, symbolize for Fletcher the gradations and varieties of love, from the Platonic Clorin to the bestial Cloe. The play is distinguished by several delightful songs and passages of lyrical dialogue. For the most part, however, the work is tedious because of the absence of any compelling conflict and because, as W. W. Greg has pointed out, Fletcher seems to have experienced ambivalence and confusion with regard to the spiritual and Platonic ideals of love extolled in the play.

The Faithful Shepherdess was edited by F. W. Moorman for the Temple Dramatists series (1896) and is in *The Works of Beaumont and Fletcher,* ed. Arnold Glover and A. R. Waller, 10 vols. (1905-12), and in *Typical Elizabethan Plays,* ed. Felix Schelling and Matthew Black (1926). There is a lengthy analysis by W. W. Greg, *Pastoral Poetry and Pastoral Drama* (1905). For other commentary, see Frank H. Ristine, *English Tragicomedy* (1910), and W. W. Appleton, *Beaumont and Fletcher: A Critical Study* (1956).

Fall of Princes, The (wr. 1431-38). Translation from a French version of Boccaccio's *De casibus virorum illustrium* by John Lydgate (c. 1370-1449?), monk of Bury St. Edmunds whose poetry and translations dominated early fifteenth-century English literature. For the influence of *The Fall of Princes* on Renaissance writing, see BIOGRAPHY; CAMBISES; CHRONICLE PLAY.

Fatal Dowry, The. A tragedy by Philip MASSINGER, possibly in collaboration with Nathan FIELD. It was first performed in 1631 and printed in 1632 in a very corrupt text. No source is known. It was revised by Nicholas Rowe as *The Fair Penitent* (1703).

In Dijon, Burgundy, a valiant general has died in debtors' prison and his greedy creditors refuse to allow him burial until his debts are paid. Charalois, the general's virtuous son, and his lawyer Charmi take the case to trial but are defeated by a court dominated by Novall Senior, a corrupt old enemy of Charalois' father. As security for his father's debts, Charalois and an honest soldier named Romont voluntarily go to prison. They are released when Rochfort, ex-president of parliament and the general's old friend, becomes so impressed during the trial by Charalois' loyalty and Romont's blunt honesty that he pays the debts and even gives his daughter Beaumelle in marriage to Charalois. Beaumelle proves unfaithful, and Romont discovers her in the arms of Novall Senior's foppish son. At first Charalois refuses to believe Beaumelle's treachery, but Romont's report is confirmed when he discovers her and Novall Junior together. Charalois's revenge is swift: he goads the cowardly Novall Junior into a duel, kills him, and then sends for Rochfort to come and judge his daughter. When Rochfort condemns her, Charalois stabs her to death. Charalois is tried for her murder and Novall Junior's; acquitted, he is later killed by a friend of the Novall family. Romont, in turn, kills Charalois' murderer.

The standard edition was edited by T. A. Dunn in the Fountainwell Drama series (1969). There is another scholarly edition, with much commentary, by G. L. Lockert, Jr. (1918). Attribution, dating, and source are discussed by H. Cruickshank, *Philip Massinger* (1920) and G. E. Bentley, *The Jacobean and Caroline Stage,* 7 vols. (1941-67), IV.

Fenton, Sir Geoffrey (1539?-1608). Translator whose collection of prose tales taken from French versions of Italian novellas by Matteo Bandello was published as *Certain Tragical Discourses* (1567). Fenton also rendered (from French) writings of the Spanish Antonio de Guevara along with other authors, Latin, French, and Italian, which he issued as *Golden Epistles* (1575, 1577, 1582). See TRANSLATIONS.

fiction. Sixteenth-century English fiction reached its apogee in three works representative of three different narrative types—the idealistic romance, represented by Sir Philip Sidney's ARCADIA; the novel of manners, by John Lyly's EUPHUES; and the picaresque or rogue tale, by Thomas Nashe's THE UNFORTUNATE TRAVELLER.

Sidney's *Arcadia,* first published in 1590 (but circulated in manuscript for several years before) is itself a many-faceted composite of fictive types—the Italian novella, with its domestic intrigues and preoccupation with manners and social classes; the late Greek romance, with its variety of action and episodic conflicts of love and war; the Spanish chivalric romance, with its exaggerated adventures and refined sentiments; the pastoral romance, with its fantasies, love debates, and mingling of prose and verse; and even the picaresque tale, with its farcical low comedy and cynical attitudes. It is now acknowledged that Sidney did not dash off *The Arcadia* for the amusement of his sister, the countess of Pembroke, but painstakingly brought together these diverse types into a unified work which he intended to develop into a prose epic.

John Lyly's *Euphues, the Anatomy of Wit* (1578) and its sequel, *Euphues and His England* (1580), are a concoction of George Pettie's *A Petite Palace of Pettie His Pleasure* (1576) and Sir Geoffrey Fenton's *Certain Tragical Discourses* (1567), with some affiliations in content and purpose to COURTESY LITERATURE like Castiglione's *Il Cortegiano* or Roger Ascham's *The Schoolmaster.* Compared with Sidney's *Arcadia* or Nashe's *Unfortunate*

Traveller, Lyly's work is not so much fictive as rhetorical and social. His primary interest is in sentiment and manners, not character and motivation; his slender narrative is only an occasion for didactic monologues, lengthy epistles, and refined love debates. For his contemporaries the chief interest of Lyly's work was in its so-called EUPHUISM, a language made up from Pettie's excessive Ciceronian rhetoric, homely proverbs, and "unnatural natural history" from Pliny's *Historia naturalis,* as well as Isidore of Seville's medieval entomology and Bartholomew Anglicus' encyclopedia of animal lore.

Lyly's *Euphues* went through no fewer than sixteen editions during his lifetime and was followed by a wave of imitations. The resourceful Robert Greene capitalized on its popularity in *Mamillia* (wr. 1580, pr. 1583), and although Greene's subsequent fiction, such as PANDOSTO (1588) and *Menaphon* (1589), shows the paramount influence of the late Greek romances and of Sidney's *Arcadia,* his style continued to be affected by Lyly's euphuism. Indeed, the criteria most indicative of Lyly's influence during the sixteenth century are absence of action, uniformity of characterizations, and concern for style rather than substance. After *Mamillia,* Greene's tales reflect an increased interest in the legacy of *The Arcadia*—episodic adventures, lively characterizations, and genuine conflicts rather than rhetorical encounters. The subtitle of Greene's *Mamillia* (*A Mirror or Looking-Glass for the Ladies of England*) announces its debt to the feminist Lyly, and Greene's plot, such as it is, adheres to Lyly's as if *Euphues* were a recipe. Mamillia (a woman) arrives in Padua (instead of Naples) from Venice (instead of Greece) and is courted by Pharicles, who is in love with Mamillia's cousin Publia. Like Euphues, Pharicles is fickle, "conceited," and brashly "liberated," and Greene's tale, like Lyly's, is peppered with didactic harangues, sentimental epistles, and tortuously refined love debates. Like Lyly also, Greene brought out a sequel, *The Triumph of Pallas* (1593), in which the faithful Publia dies in a convent and Mamillia's father leaves his fortune to Mamillia on condition she does not marry Pharicles, who is in prison at Saragossa awaiting execution. After many adventures Mamillia rescues Pharicles, who gratefully gives her his love, and a benevolent Padua senate sets aside her father's will so the lovers can wed in prosperity.

The most popular imitation of *Euphues* was Thomas Lodge's ROSALYNDE, OR EUPHUES' GOLDEN LEGACY (1590), which Shakespeare used as a source for *As You Like It.* Like Sidney's *Arcadia,* Lodge's pastoral romance contains a number of eclogues, songs, and sonnets, and, following *The Arcadia,* gives more emphasis to villainous usurpation and war than does Shakespeare's play. A xenophobic condemnation of foreign travel, sermonized by Lyly (who found the theme in Ascham's *Schoolmaster*), is adopted also in Barnabe Rich's two part euphuistic romance *Don Simonides* (1581, 1584), whose hero travels to Italy and then to England, where he meets Euphues' comrade-in-love Philautus. Like Lyly, Rich writes his romance "for the amusement of our noble gentlemen as well as of our honourable ladies." A year earlier appeared Anthony Munday's *Zelanto,* in which euphuism is almost submerged in globe-trotting from Naples to Spain and England, and finally to Turkey. Hence most of these sixteenth-century imitations of *Euphues* tended to fuse the matter of the late Greek romances and of *The Arcadia*—shipwrecks, pirates, wars and invasions, peregrinations in search of kidnapped mistresses or enslaved lovers—with euphuistic debates, epistles, and monologues.

The wondrous and tangled adventures of the late Greek romances and Sidney's *Arcadia* are abundantly portrayed in one of the last heroic romances written by an Englishman, John Barclay's Latin work ARGENIS, printed in Paris in 1621 and in London in 1622. Although rendered into English in 1625 and again in 1628, Barclay's long tale of two idealistic lovers, interwoven with an abstruse political allegory on sixteenth-century rulers, was not as widely read in England as it was abroad, where it went through forty editions in the Latin text and was translated into ten European languages during the seventeenth century.

Among middle-class readers in England the refined courtly romance represented by *The Arcadia* and Barclay's *Argenis* was superseded by a new type of fiction. That new type emerges with Thomas Nashe's THE UNFORTUNATE TRAVELLER (1594), in which something of the realism of ROGUE LITERATURE supersedes the heroic idealism of *The Arcadia.* The *picaro,* or rogue hero, replaces both Sidney's noble courtiers and Lyly's fastidious gentlemen, and the rogue's farcical tricks and jests supplant Sidney's variegated adventures and Lyly's sentimental eloquence. Like much other Elizabethan fiction, Nashe's work is a medley of genres, and Nashe acknowledged its unorthodoxy in his dedicatory epistle to the first edition, where he describes the work as in "a clean different vein from my other former courses of writing." *The Unfortunate Traveller* has been variously classified as a picaresque novel in imitation of Diego Hurtado de Mendoza's *Lazarillo de Tormes,* as the first historical novel in English, as a melodramatic chronicle, as an extended JESTBOOK, and as a satire on other literary types such as jestbooks, chronicles, anti-Puritan tracts, and rogue pamphlets. In any case, the type represented by Nashe's novel, with its affinities to rogue literature and picaresque fiction, became linked with comic romances like Cervantes' *Don Quixote* to produce the later novels of Defoe and Fielding.

The French heroic romances, which were principally derived from the same late Greek romances that Sidney consulted in writing *The Arcadia,* began to be popular during the reign of Charles I, whose queen, Henrietta Maria, had been thoroughly indoctrinated at the French court in such *précieuse* fiction as Honoré d'Urfé's prodigious novel *L'Astrée,* Part I of which was rendered into English in 1620. Another heroic romance available in English was the *Polexandre* (1632) of Marin Le Roy, sieur de Gomberville, translated in 1647. Before this latter date, however, the court of Charles I, under the influence of Henrietta Maria and her coterie, was avidly reading and transforming into plays the continental romances of d'Urfé, Montemayor. La Calprenède, and the extremely fashionable Madeleine de Scudéry, whose prose romance *Ibrahim* ranges over Italy, Constantinople, and other less definite but exotic locales in following the peregrinations of a young Genoese enamored of the princess of Monaco. At the conclusion of *Ibrahim* the hero is saved from execution by the daughter of the Turkish emperor Solyman, who makes him grand vizier, but the hero remains true to his pledge of love and returns to Italy to seek the princess of Monaco's hand in marriage. As in most French heroic romances, *Ibrahim* features wars, shipwrecks, mistaken births and disguises, prolix digressions, lofty but recondite sentiments, and agonizing conflicts between love and honor.

Perhaps the most comprehensive imitation of the type in English was *Parthenissa* (1654-55) by Roger Boyle, earl of Orrery, who was conversant with not only the French heroic romances but the late Greek variety as well. In the Restoration period these romances, combined with their offspring in the CAROLINE DRAMA of the 1630s, produced the heroic plays of Boyle and Dryden. Except for their mastery of the heroic couplet, Dryden's *The Indian Emperor* (1665), *Conquest of Granada* (1670), and *Aureng-Zebe* (1676) are fairly indistinguishable from the Cavalier heroic dramas of the 1630s and the French romances of La Calprenède and Mlle. de Scudéry. Thus the main tributary of English romance, originating with Sidney's *Arcadia,* is fed briefly by the French heroic romances and the Cavalier drama, and trickles out forever after the brief spate of heroic plays in the Restoration.

Several types of realistic fiction prevailed well into the seventeenth century. The Italian novellas continued to be translated, and the enduring popularity of rogue fiction is apparent from the success of Richard Head and Francis Kirkman's *The English Rogue* (1665-72). The unadorned tale of actual human experience, begun with George Gascoigne's ADVENTURES OF MASTER F. J. (1573), continued unabated through the proletarian fiction of Thomas DELONEY and emerged in that brilliant mixture of realism and fantasy, John Bunyan's PILGRIM'S PROGRESS (1678).

The many aspects of Elizabethan fiction are treated in three important studies: J. J. Jusserand, *The English Novel in the Time of Shakespeare* (1908); Ernest A. Baker, *History of the English Novel,* 10 vols., II (1929); and Robert M. Lovett and H. S. Hughes, *History of the Novel in England* (1932).

Field, Nathan (1587-1620?) Actor and dramatist. Nathan Field was the son of John Field, a zealous Puritan minister and crusader against stage plays, and the brother of Theophilus Field, bishop of Llandaff, and of Nathaniel Field, a printer with whom the actor-dramatist is often confused. Field began his career in the theater at an early age, being taken from St. Paul's School around 1600 and forced into service as a boy actor in the company of the Children of the Chapel (later known as Children of the Queen's Revels).

Field was a protégé of Jonson and of several other dramatists. He affixed verses to editions of Jonson's *Volpone* and *Catiline,* and William

Drummond reported Jonson telling him that "Ned Field was his scholar, and he had read to him satires of Horace and some epigrams of Martial." In the 1614 edition of Jonson's *Bartholomew Fair* a character inquires," . . . which is your Burbage now?. . . Your best actor, your Field?" (VI, 119-20).

After the Children of the Queen's Revels joined the Lady Elizabeth's Company in 1613, Field became the leader of the troupe, commissioning new plays and negotiating for the players with Philip Henslowe and other theater managers. Around 1616 he joined the King's Men and remained with that company until his death, sharing leading roles with the great Richard Burbage and, in all probability, succeeding to Shakespeare's share in the company after the latter's death in 1616.

Field wrote at least two plays, *A Woman Is a Weathercock* (perf. c. 1609), composed in Jonson's satiric style for the Children of the Queen's Revels, and *Amends for Ladies* (perf. 1611) for the Lady Elizabeth's Company. He is believed to have collaborated with Fletcher in *Four Plays in One, The Honest Man's Fortune,* and several other plays. He may also have collaborated with Massinger in THE FATAL DOWRY (perf. 1631, pr. 1632).

The standard edition of Field's plays was edited by William Peery (1950). There is a critical biography by Roberta F. Brinkley, "Nathan Field, the Actor-Playwright," *YSE,* LXXVII (1928). See also W. W. Greg, "Nathan Field and the Beaumont and Fletcher Folio of 1679." *RES,* III (1927).

Fig for Momus, A (Thomas Lodge.) See SATIRE.

Fletcher, Giles, the Elder (1549?-1611). Poet and diplomat. The father of Giles and Phineas Fletcher was born at Watford, Hertfordshire, the son of the local vicar. He attended Eton and matriculated at King's College, Cambridge (B.A. 1569; M.A. 1573), where he was made a fellow in 1568.

In 1580 Fletcher was appointed to the diocese of Ely and a year later granted the degree of Doctor of Letters from Cambridge. He represented Winchelsea in Parliament after 1585 and in 1588-89 was employed by Sir Francis Walsingham in diplomatic missions to Scotland, Germany, and Russia. His experiences in Russia were recorded in *Of the Russe Commonwealth* (1591), which expressed such antipathy for the corruption, tyranny, and backwardness of the Russian court and aristocracy that Elizabeth's ministers ordered it suppressed. Fletcher's other noteworthy publication was *Licia, or Poems of Love* (1593), a sonnet sequence that includes a translation of Lucian's *Doris and Galatea* (see SONNET SEQUENCES). Fletcher's historical work in Latin, *De literis antiquae Britanniae,* was not published until 1633.

Fletcher's friend and patron Walsingham empowered him to examine Catholic priests and recusants in Bridewell prison in 1591. Later Fletcher was treasurer of St. Paul's (1597) and dean of the rectory at Ringword, Hampshire, his last office before his death in London in 1611.

Of the Russe Commonwealth appeared in abridged form in Richard Hakluyt's *Voyages* (1582) and Samuel Purchas' *Purchas His Pilgrims* (1625). It was first printed in its complete version by E. A. Bond in the Hakluyt Society (1856), with a recent edition by Albert J. Schmidt (1966). *Licia* is in *Elizabethan Sonnets,* ed. Sir Sidney Lee, 2 vols., (1904) II. *The English Works* has been edited by Lloyd E. Berry (1964).

Fletcher, Giles, the Younger (1588?-1623). Poet. Giles Fletcher was born in London the son of Giles Fletcher the Elder, LL. D., and younger brother of the poet Phineas Fletcher. He was educated at Westminster School and matriculated at Trinity College, Cambridge, around 1603, receiving his B.A. in 1606, when he was also elected a fellow of the College and made reader in Greek language and grammar.

Giles Fletcher completed most of his literary work early in life. In 1603 he contributed an elegy to a volume of poems commemorating Queen Elizabeth's death that year, and while still at Trinity College completed his best-known poem. *Christ's Victory and Triumph in Heaven and Earth, over, and after Death* (1610). *Christ's Victory* is in four parts: *Christ's Victory in Heaven, Christ's Victory on Earth, Christ's Triumph over Death,* and *His Triumph after Death.* All relate events from Christ's life with many descriptive digressions and allegories of vices and virtues. The eight-line stanzas rhyme *ab ab bc cc,* the last being an alexandrine. In the preface Fletcher acknowledges his debt to Spenser and to Du Bartas' epic *La Semaine* (1578). Fletcher's poem became a chief influence on Milton's minor epic *Paradise Regained.* In *Christ's Victory* the influences of Du Bartas and Spenser are fused with sensuous pagan mythology and Italianate richness and passion reminiscent of Giovanni Battista Marino and anticipatory of the exotic hyperboles and excesses of Richard Crashaw. Hence Fletcher's *Christ's Victory* is the principal example of baroque poetry between Robert Southwell's devotional poems and Milton's *On the Morning of Christ's Nativity.* Fletcher's four cantos in *Christ's Victory* on the birth, temptation, crucifixion, and resurrection of Jesus vied for popularity with Du Bartas' and Milton's epics well into the eighteenth century. Fletcher's other notable work, *The Reward of the Faithful* (1623), is a prose tract containing translations of Greek epigrams and selections by Boethius.

The definitive edition by F. S. Boas, 2 vols. (1908-09) also includes the poems of Phineas Fletcher. Joan Grundy has written a comprehensive critical essay, "Giles and Phineas Fletcher," in *The Spenserian Poets* (1969).

Fletcher, John (1579-1625). Dramatist. John Fletcher was born at Rye, Sussex, the son of Richard Fletcher, a distinguished clergyman who was, at various times, bishop of Bristol, Worcester, and London, as well as president of Corpus Christi College, Cambridge, and chaplain to Queen Elizabeth. Fletcher appears to have attended Corpus Christi, although almost nothing is known for certain of his early years. Fletcher's father fell out of favor with the queen while John was still attending college; he died in 1596, leaving only a very small inheritance to be divided among nine children. Under these impoverished circumstances, Fletcher may have been supported for a time by his uncle Giles Fletcher the elder, the diplomat and poet. The other Fletchers of literary renown, Phineas and the younger Giles, were John Fletcher's first cousins.

Like Francis Beaumont, Fletcher seems to have begun his literary career as a disciple of Ben Jonson, who affixed dedicatory verses to the undated (c. 1610) quarto of Fletcher's *The Faithful Shepherdess*. Fletcher probably wrote his earliest plays for the boys' companies at the private theaters in 1607-08, after which he began his brief but highly successful collaboration with Francis BEAUMONT. The two playwrights became intimate friends, sharing the same lodgings as well as "a wonderful consimility of fancy," according to John Aubrey, the seventeenth-century antiquarian. Their collaboration ended in 1612-13, when Beaumont married a wealthy Kentish heiress and retired from the stage. Because Fletcher after 1613 wrote all his plays for the King's Men, it is generally believed that he succeeded William Shakespeare as that company's leading dramatist after Shakespeare retired to Stratford. After 1625 Fletcher was succeeded in this role by Philip Massinger, a close friend of Fletcher's who collaborated with him on a number of plays. According to John Aubrey's account in *Brief Lives*, Fletcher died of the plague in 1625 and was buried at St. Savior's, Southwark, where his friend Massinger was buried nearly fifteen years later.

Because Fletcher was an extremely prolific dramatist who often collaborated with others, scholars have been confronted with some extremely difficult problems of attribution. In general, however, the Fletcher canon can be divided into five not entirely distinct categories:

(1) Plays written by Fletcher alone, including THE WOMAN'S PRIZE, OR THE TAMER TAMED (wr. c. 1604); THE FAITHFUL SHEPHERDESS (wr. c. 1608-09); *Bonduca* (wr. c. 1609-14); *Valentinian* (wr. c. 1610-14); *Monsieur Thomas* (wr. c. 1610-16); *Wit Without Money* (wr. c. 1614); *The Mad Lover* (wr. c. 1616); *The Chances* (wr. c. 1617); *The Loyal Subject* (wr. 1618; rev. 1633?); *The Humorous Lieutenant* (wr. c. 1619); THE ISLAND PRINCESS (wr. 1619-21); *The Pilgrim* (wr. c. 1621); THE WILD GOOSE CHASE (c. 1621); RULE A WIFE AND HAVE A WIFE (wr. 1624); and *A Wife for a Month* (wr. 1624).

(2) Plays written by Beaumont in which Fletcher is believed to have had only a small share, if any, such as THE WOMAN HATER (wr. c. 1606) and THE KNIGHT OF THE BURNING PESTLE (wr. 1607).

(3) Plays in which Beaumont and Fletcher collaborated more equally, although Beaumont is believed to have composed somewhat the larger share, such as *Four Plays in One* (wr. c. 1608); THE COXCOMB (1608-10); PHILASTER (wr. c. 1610); THE MAID'S TRAGEDY (wr. c. 1611); A KING AND NO KING (wr. 1611); *Cupid's Revenge* (wr. c. 1612); and THE SCORNFUL LADY (wr. 1613-16).

(4) Plays in which Fletcher collaborated with Philip Massinger, namely BARNAVELT (wr. c.

1619); *Thierry and Theodoret* (wr. c. 1617); *The Custom of the Country* (wr. c. 1619-20; rev. 1638?); *The Double Marriage* (wr. c. 1621); BEGGARS BUSH (wr. c. 1622); *The Spanish Curate* (wr. 1622); and *The Elder Brother* (wr. c. 1625).

(5) Plays in which Fletcher's hand is found together with authorship by two or more other playwrights, such as Francis Beaumont, Philip Massinger, Nathan Field, William Rowley, Ben Jonson, John Webster, and John Ford. These last include *The Queen of Corinth* (wr. 1616-17); *Rollo, Duke of Normandy, or The Bloody Brother* (wr. c. 1617; rev. 1627 30?); *The Noble Gentleman* (wr. c. 1625-26); and *The Fair Maid of the Inn* (wr. 1625-26).

Difficulties of attribution in all of these plays are further compounded by evidence that Philip Massinger and others may have revised some of Fletcher's plays for performances after his death. Thus, although the 1647 edition of Beaumont and Fletcher's works included thirty-four plays and the second edition of 1679 fifty-two plays, only relatively few were actually by both Beaumont and Fletcher, and of these Fletcher is now believed to have contributed a much larger number of plays than Beaumont.

Still another dramatist with whom Fletcher is presumed to have collaborated was William Shakespeare. They are said to have produced three plays together: TWO NOBLE KINSMEN, HENRY VIII, and *Cardenio* (a lost play). *Two Noble Kinsmen* was first printed in 1634 with the names of Fletcher and Shakespeare on the title page, and it was included in the 1679 edition of Beaumont and Fletcher's plays. It did not, however, appear in the Shakespeare First Folio (1623), nor in any subsequent edition of Shakespeare in the seventeenth century. The morris dance in *Two Noble Kinsmen* (III, *v*) was taken directly from Beaumont's *Masque of the Inner Temple and Gray's Inn,* performed at court on February 20, 1613; this episode from Beaumont's masque not only helps to establish a date for the play but to strengthen its connections with Beaumont's collaborator Fletcher. Fletcher's contribution to *Two Noble Kinsmen* is seen in the loosely connected double plot and the large number of lines with feminine endings. Most scholars agree that Shakespeare wrote the early scenes of Act I, the first scene of Act III, and most of Act V. The part of the jailer's mad daughter has been assigned entirely to Fletcher.

Henry VIII, also dated 1613, was included in the First Folio and not associated in any way with Fletcher until James Spedding presented his case in 1850 for Fletcher's collaboration. According to Spedding's now widely accepted view, Shakespeare wrote only the first two scenes of Act I, the third and fourth scenes of Act II, the first two hundred lines or so of Act IV, and the first scene of Act V.

The case for Fletcher's collaboration with Shakespeare on the lost play *Cardenio* stands on rather shaky ground. A play by that name was performed by the King's Men in 1613 and entered in the Stationers' Register in 1653 as having been written by Fletcher and Shakespeare. In 1727 Lewis Theobald, one of Shakespeare's early editors, produced a play on the stage called *Double Falsehood, or The Distressed Lovers,* which he claimed was based on a manuscript of Shakespeare's play handed down by the famous Restoration actor Thomas Betterton. Although *Double Falsehood* contains a number of lines reminiscent of Fletcher and Shakespeare, Theobald never produced his "manuscript," nor did he include the play in his edition of Shakespeare's complete works in 1733.

Since all three of the plays on which Fletcher and Shakespeare are believed to have collaborated are dated 1613, it is tempting to infer that at this time Shakespeare was grooming the younger playwright to take over as chief dramatist of the King's Men, or perhaps using Fletcher's fresh talents to strengthen his own waning powers. Nevertheless, the fact must be insisted upon that there exists no really solid evidence linking Fletcher and Shakespeare; Fletcher's authorship in *Two Noble Kinsmen* and *Henry VIII* is invariably argued on the probable but not entirely certain basis of what is deemed to be most saliently characteristic of Fletcher's style—spectacle and sentimentality, weak motivations of character, loose plot construction, and slackly accented end-stopped lines with feminine endings.

Beaumont and Fletcher's enormous popularity, which for a time in the 1630s and after 1660 was equal to if not greater than Shakespeare's, can be attributed to their mastery of a courtly mode of drama that came into fashion in the Stuart period with the drift away from the public playhouses and toward the private theaters such as Blackfriars. Derived from upper-class backgrounds themselves and thoroughly versed in the French and Spanish heroic romances, Beaumont and Fletcher formulated a type of TRAGICOMEDY perfectly suited to refined taste; the plots are ingenious and episodic, and set in such remote locales as Armenia, Messina, or Rhodes; the fragile characters find themselves painfully torn by hair-splitting distinctions regarding love and honor as whole kingdoms sway in the balance of their exquisite sentiments and soaring rhetoric. The hero is usually "lily livered" and totally ineffectual in spite of his flyting speeches and rodomontades, the heroine an equally garrulous *précieuse* who waxes pedantic over subtleties of deportment. In these plays, of which *Philaster* is the prototype, the emphasis is not, as in the earlier drama, on man confronting nature or struggling against divisive forces within himself, but on courtiers and ladies probing their conduct in the light of certain genteel conventions. Plays like *Philaster* suggest that Beaumont and Fletcher deliberately curtailed their emotional and intellectual range in response to the demands of an aristocratic audience that preferred esoteric manners to morality, fantasy to reality, and constant stimulation to any insights into life. All of these ingredients flowed from Beaumont and Fletcher into the extravagant Cavalier drama of the 1630s and 1640s (see CAROLINE DRAMA), and from there into the ranting heroic plays of love and honor like Dryden's *Aureng-Zebe* and *The Conquest of Granada* in the Restoration period.

Fletcher's comedies of manners proved to be equally influential. An early disciple of Ben Jonson, he cleverly converted comedies like Jonson's *Every Man in His Humour* into his own unique brand of sophisticated, amoral, and devastatingly witty comedies of manners in which a gay young rake genially fights the battle of the sexes, virile youths outsmart their stodgy elders, and gulls, doxies, coney-catchers, fops, and fantastics squabble over the spoils or just struggle to stay alive. The conflicts are above the surface of any real moral issues, and the characters are exaggerated social types rather than complex individuals. In such artful comedies of manners as *The Wild-Goose Chase* and *The Woman's Prize,* Fletcher set the stage for such similar comedies as William Wycherley's *The Plain Dealer* and George Etherege's *Man of Mode* in the Restoration.

Fletcher's forte is most apparent in tragicomedies like *The Loyal Subject, The Island Princess, The Humorous Lieutenant,* and *Monsieur Thomas,* plays that skillfully fuse comicality and high-blown sentiments, farce and romantic love, witty satire and didacticism. His main goal is simply diversion, variety, and constant entertainment, whether in graceful songs, wild farce, or amorous confrontations. In these qualities few Stuart dramatists matched his artifice and cunning. For over a decade after Shakespeare's retirement, Fletcher continued to supply the King's Men with at least three or four plays a year that represent the last surge of genuine vitality before the closing of the theaters. Significantly, perhaps, both Beaumont and Fletcher were among the last Stuart playwrights capable of continuing the glorious Elizabethan tradition of music and songs on the stage; in retrospect, their light and graceful lyrics represent a certain innocent vigor the English theater was never to experience again.

The Beaumont and Fletcher plays are most fully reproduced in *The Works of Francis Beaumont and John Fletcher,* ed. Arnold Glover and A. R. Waller, 10 vols. (1905-12). The incomplete Variorum Edition, under the general editorship of A. H. Bullen, 4 vols. (1904-13), contains twenty plays. Seven plays are in *The Dramatic Works in the Beaumont and Fletcher Canon,* ed. Fredson Bowers, 2 vols. (1966, 1970). An exhaustive effort to identify Fletcher's hand in collaboration with Beaumont, Massinger, and others was done by Cyrus Hoy in *SB,* VIII (1956); IX (1957); XI (1958); XII (1959); XIII (1960); XIV (1961); XV (1962). Important critical studies include E. H. C. Oliphant, *The Plays of Beaumont and Fletcher* (1927); Lawrence B. Wallis, *Fletcher, Beaumont, and Company* (1947); Eugene M. Waith, *The Pattern of Tragicomedy in Beaumont and Fletcher* (1952); W. W. Appleton, *Beaumont and Fletcher: A Critical Study* (1956); and Clifford Leech, *The John Fletcher Plays* (1962). The music from the plays was collected and edited by E. H. Fellowes, *Songs and Lyrics from the Plays of Beaumont and Fletcher* (1928); Fletcher's songs are discussed by E. S. Lindsay, "The Music of the Songs in Fletcher's Plays," *SP,* XXI (1924). Fletcher's collaboration with Shakespeare is studied by Paul Bertram, *Shakespeare and The Two Noble Kinsmen* (1965), and John Freehafer, "*Cardenio,* by Shakespeare and Fletcher," *PMLA,* LXXXIV (1969). There is a Concise Bibliography of Beaumont and Fletcher by S. A. Tannenbaum (1938), supplemented by D. R. Tannenbaum (1946) and updated in "Beaumont and Fletcher (1937-65)," ed. C. A. Pennel and W. P. Williams, in *Elizabethan Bibliographies Supplements,* VIII (1968).

Fletcher, Phineas (1582-1650). Poet. Phineas Fletcher was born in Cranbrook, Kent, the son of the author and diplomat Giles FLETCHER (d. 1611) and elder brother of the poet GILES FLETCHER THE YOUNGER. Phineas went to Eton and King's College, Cambridge (B.A. 1604, M.A. 1608), and was ordained in 1611. In 1615 he became chaplain to Sir Henry Willoughby at Risley, Derbyshire. His patron presented him with a living at Hilgay, Norfolk, in 1621, and there Fletcher spent the rest of his life.

Like his brother Giles, Phineas wrote most of his works early, chiefly during the period 1607-12. While at Cambridge he wrote a pastoral play about fishing, *Sicelides, a Piscatory,* performed at King's College in 1615 and printed in 1631. Fletcher's *Locustae vel pietas Jesuitica,* which appeared in English in 1627 with the title *The Locusts, or Appollyonists,* is an anti-Catholic satire on the Gunpowder Plot that may have given Milton some hints for the characterization of Satan in *Paradise Lost.*

Phineas Fletcher's chief poem, *The Purple Island, or The Isle of Man* (1633), which he described as "raw essays of my very unripe years," is even more baroque than Giles Fletcher's *Christ's Victory. The Purple Island* is an elaborate network of twelve seven-line stanzas that include seven autobiographical and piscatory eclogues (praised by that inveterate angler Izaak Walton), epithalamia, elegies, and a concluding poem by Fletcher's neighbor at Hilgay, Francis Quarles, who addresses him as the "Spenser of this age." (Fletcher himself pays extended tribute to his master Spenser in *The Purple Island.*)

The main part of *The Purple Island,* however, derives from the medieval theme of the "castle of the body" and develops the conceit of the island as the human body, in which the bones are the rocky foundations, the veins are brooks, and so forth, in meticulous detail based on the anatomy of Galen and Vesalius. The analogy is made by both Spenser (*Faerie Queene,* II. 9) and Du Bartas, but neither gives the subject Fletcher's peculiar mixture of scientific precision and didacticism. This portion of the poem ends with an epic catalogue and an allegorical battle between the vices and virtues to which the body is subject. The sensuous qualities of his brother Giles are only occasional in Phineas, whose allegory tends toward satiric realism and grotesque decoration, rather than pictorial presentation or envisioned narrative. Although Spenser was his master, Phineas is more immediately inspired by the emblems of Francis Quarles and the metaphors of medieval science (see EMBLEM BOOKS). Hence his language is less vivid and passionate than that of Giles, his imagination more concrete and literal.

Two of Fletcher's best works received little attention during his lifetime. *A Father's Testament,* a meditation in both prose and verse, did not appear until 1670. His manuscript of *Venus and Anchises* (falsely attributed to Spenser with the title *Britain's Ida* in 1628) was published in 1926 in an edition by Ethel Seaton and F. S. Boas.

The definitive edition of Phineas Fletcher's works, which includes the poems of his brother Giles, is by F. S. Boas, 2 vols. (1908-09). There is a comprehensive life and critical study by A. B. Langdale, *Phineas Fletcher, Man of Letters, Science, and Divinity* (1937), which contains a bibliography. There are critical essays by R. G. Baldwin, "Phineas Fletcher: His Modern Readers and His Renaissance Ideas," *PQ.* XL (1961), and Joan Grundy, "Giles and Phineas Fletcher," in *The Spenserian Poets* (1969).

Florio, Giovanni (or John) (1553?-1625). Linguist and translator. His Italian phrasebooks, *Florio His First Fruits* (1578) and *Florio's Second Fruits* (1591), were extremely popular, as was his Italian-English dictionary, *A World of Words* (1598), enlarged in 1611 with the title *Queen Anna's New World of Words.* He is best known for his translation in 1603 of Montaigne's *Essays.* See TRANSLATIONS.

Ford, John (1586-c. 1640). Dramatist. A

descendant of a prosperous Devonshire family, Ford may have attended Exeter College, Oxford, in 1601; he then studied at the Middle Temple, from which he was expelled for debt. Almost nothing is known of his personal life, perhaps because he lived much of the time in his native Ilsington, Devonshire. His first extant publication was an elegy, *Fame's Memorial* (1606), on the death of Charles Blount, earl of Devonshire, the second husband of Penelope Devereux (the celebrated "Stella" of Sir Philip Sidney's sonnet sequence). At his death Blount was in disgrace at court, and Ford's elegy can be interpreted as an early manifestation of his predilection for dealing with controversial or unpopular topics. Equally anticipatory of his later works is an early prose pamphlet, *Honor Triumphant, or The Peers' Challenge* (1606), in which four young nobles argue in euphuistic style the highly romantic notions that female beauty is the chief motivation for courage, that knights in the service of their ladies have no free will, that beautiful women are invariably moral, and, finally, that true wisdom is to be found only in ideal love. Such perverse treatment of ethical concerns was to become a main feature of Ford's plays.

Ford began his dramatic career in collaboration with Thomas Dekker and William Rowley on THE WITCH OF EDMONTON (wr. c. 1621), a domestic tragedy based on the recent execution for witchcraft of one Elizabeth Sawyer, whom the dramatists portray as having been virtually driven to witchcraft by her cruel and ignorant neighbors. The story of Dame Sawyer, with its mixture of buffoonery and stark realism, appears to be the work of Dekker and Rowley; the other plot, in which a young man wanders pathetically into committing murder and then attributes his sins to the omnipotence of fate, is probably Ford's contribution.

The chronology of Ford's plays is difficult to establish (according to legend, the cook of John Warburton, the eighteenth-century antiquary, inadvertently burned several plays). It is generally believed that his first independent production was a romantic tragicomedy, *The Lover's Melancholy,* performed in 1628 and first published in 1629. The melancholy lover in this slow-moving, brooding drama is a prince who grieves over the supposed death of his mistress, whose loss has also driven her father mad and prevented the marriage of her sister. The wholly artificial entanglements of the lovers enable Ford to devote lingering psychological analysis to his distraught characters, an analysis influenced directly by Ford's close study of Robert Burton's medical treatise *The Anatomy of Melancholy.*

Ford's psychological concern is also seen in what was probably his next play, *Love's Sacrifice* (perf. c. 1632). Here the duchess Bianca repulses the passionate advances of her husband's favorite Fernando, but later appears in his bedchamber and offers herself to him, although she swears to commit suicide after her submission. Fernando masters his passion for the duchess, but he is nevertheless doomed when the duke's sister, spurned by Fernando, enlists the aid of D'Avolos, a villainous courtier, in stirring up the duke's jealousy. Only after killing his wife does the duke become convinced of her innocence, whereupon he stabs himself and Fernando takes poison. In this play, the influence of Burton's *Anatomy of Melancholy* is again paramount, as is Shakespeare's *Othello,* especially in D'Avolos' devilish incitement of the duke's jealousy and his wife's Desdamona-like innocence.

Yet there is little of Shakespeare's earthiness in Ford's strangely alienated, lunar characters, whose arbitrary motives and inexplicable principles derive from Ford's own unconventional conceptions of heroism combined with Burton's psychological theories, Sidney's idealized views of aristocratic conduct in his *Arcadia,* and Beaumont and Fletcher's quixotic and arcane portrayals of "love and honor" in such plays as *Philaster.* These influences are consistently manifest in Ford's two major tragedies, 'TIS PITY SHE'S A WHORE and THE BROKEN HEART. In the first of these Ford deals with the theme of incest—previously treated with evasion and frivolity in Beaumont and Fletcher's *A King and No King*—with unequivocal compassion and honesty. As in *Love's Sacrifice,* the characters in *'Tis Pity* suffer mutely, live by isolated and esoteric principles, and make death a ritual of protest. The noblest character in the play is, ironically, the incestuous Giovanni, who is portrayed as a star-crossed, afflicted idealist whose helpless passion is contrasted to the ordinary, self-serving vices of his society—hypocrisy, cowardice, injustice, and cruelty. In spite of its bewildering maze of subplots, *'Tis Pity* remains a masterpiece of complex ironies and subtle, delicate characterizations.

In *'Tis Pity* the character Giovanni is isolated from his society by a strange and perverse idealism intelligible only to himself. In *The Broken Heart* this tragic isolation extends to include all the principal characters. Forced into a loveless marriage with a jealous old man by her brother Ithocles, the Ophelia-like Penthea rejects her former lover Orgilus and slowly starves herself to death. As they mourn beside her body, Orgilus traps her brother in a mechanical contrivance and murders him. In the final act the princess Calantha continues her dance at a wedding party as she receives successively news of the deaths of her father, of Penthea, and of her lover Ithocles; then, in a drawn-out ritual before an altar, she places a wedding ring on Ithocles' finger, announces the successor to her throne, and drops dead of a broken heart. For these haunted characters, obsessed with their own bizarre values and baffling purposes, the morality of society or the lure of conventional gratifications has little relevance; they are impelled by fate, by secret passions, and by ineffable concepts of idealized love and honor.

In Ford's other major work, PERKIN WARBECK, he adapts the chronicle play, long out of fashion, to his own unique style and complex perspectives. Basing the play on events described in Francis Bacon's *History of the Reign of Henry VII* (1622) and Thomas Gainsford's *True and Wonderful History of Perkin Warbeck* (1618), and on the dramaturgy of Shakespeare's later history plays, Ford portrays his titular hero as an idealist firmly convinced of his claim to the throne and the justice of his cause, and he leaves ambiguous and unsolved the question of whether or not Warbeck was in fact one of the little princes allegedly murdered by Richard III. The depiction of Henry VII as a shrewd but essentially benevolent man driven by political necessity is an extremely effective characterization. Thus, if *Perkin Warbeck* is not perhaps the "best specimen of the historical drama to be found out of Shakespeare," as Hartley Coleridge insisted, it is nevertheless equal to any non-Shakespearean history play except Marlowe's *Edward II.*

At the close of his career Ford turned to romantic comedy in *The Fancies, Chaste and Noble* (wr. 1631? or 1635-36) and *The Lady's Trial* (wr. 1638), both of which contain effective isolated scenes and situations but tediously prolix, improbable plots and subplots, and a variety of inconsistent or poorly conceived characterizations.

Ford's reputation rests securely on four plays: *Love's Sacrifice, 'Tis Pity She's a Whore, The Broken Heart,* and *Perkin Warbeck.* With Philip Massinger and James Shirley, he was the last of the great dramatists before the closing of the theaters, and in spite of his obvious links with Elizabethans such as Shakespeare, Jonson, and Beaumont and Fletcher, he was a highly individualistic and perhaps unique dramatist who probed hitherto unexplored regions of consciousness and morality. Readers who imagine Shakespeare to be a "psychological" dramatist must study Ford's plays to appreciate the differences between a writer who is fascinated with human variety and knows how to create illusions of life, and one like Ford, whose characters often illustrate specific theories of psychopathology.

Ford is sometimes charged with sharing in the "decadence" that overcame the stage in the 1630s, but the epithet cannot be applied without careful qualification. If Ford is decadent in the aesthetic sense, it is in his occasionally slack versification, languid dramatic pace, and carelessness of design; if decadent in a moral context, it is in his preoccupation with illicit passions, lawless idealism, and forbidden themes—i.e., with "abnormal psychology"—and yet he invariably treats these subjects with sensitivity, restraint, and compassion. Thus in many ways he was not so much "decadent" as modern, not so much a weak echo of an age in declension as a strong voice of an era yet to come.

William Gifford's edition of Ford's plays, revised by Alexander Dyce, 3 vols. (1869), is still essential, although it is not as scholarly as that by W. Bang and Henry de Vocht, 2 vols. (1908, 1927). Excellent paperback editions of *Love's Sacrifice, Perkin Warbeck, The Broken Heart,* and *'Tis Pity She's a Whore* are available in the Regents Renaissance Drama series (1971). The best critical studies are by M. Joan Sargeaunt, *John Ford* (1935); S. Blaine Ewing, *Burtonian Melancholy in the Plays of John Ford* (1940); and G. F. Sensabaugh, *The Tragic Muse of John Ford* (1944). There is a Concise Bibliography by S. A. Tannenbaum (1939), updated in "John Ford (1940-65)," ed. C. A. Pennel and W. P. Williams, in *Elizabethan Bibliographies Supplements,* VIII (1968).

Four PP, The. An interlude by John HEYWOOD, written about 1521 and printed in an undated edition between 1543 and 1547.

A palmer, pardoner, apothecary, and peddler meet by chance on an English country road and engage in a debate about the merits of their respective callings. After much wrangling, in which all reveal their mendacity and quackery, they agree to let the peddler judge a contest of tall tales to determine who is the greatest liar. The winner will have the right to bind the others as his servants. The apothecary tells as his tale how he once plugged up a female patient with a tampion which, when released explosively, destroyed castles ten miles away. The pardoner describes how he descended into Purgatory and Hell to obtain the release of a terrible shrew, one Margery Coorson. The palmer begins his tale by expressing doubt about the veracity of the pardoner's story, for he claims he has never in all his travels met a shrewish woman. According to him, all women are meek and compliant. At this turn all the participants agree that the palmer has won the contest as the greatest liar. After the palmer absolves the others of the penalty, they all depart in good humor, with the author concluding his satire against women by stating there has been no serious point or "offense" in the play.

As in all of Heywood's interludes, the plot of *The Four PP* is less important than the satiric characterizations and dialogue; Heywood's main influences are the medieval *débat* and *fabliau. The Four PP* is based on a medieval French farce, *D'un pardonneur, d'un triacleur, et d'une taverière.*

The play is in *The Dramatic Writings,* ed. J. S. Farmer (1905). For commentary, see Ian Maxwell, *French Farce and John Heywood* (1946), and T. W. Craik, "Experiment and Variety in John Heywood's Plays," *Renaissance Drama,* VII (1964).

fourteeners. See POULTER'S MEASURE.

Fowre Hymnes. Philosophical poems by Edmund SPENSER, published in 1596 with a dedicatory epistle to Margaret, countess of Cumberland, and to Mary, countess of Warwick. In the letter Spenser explains that the first two poems, on earthly love and beauty, were written "in the greener times of my youth," and that he would have suppressed them at the request of the countess of Warwick except that many copies were circulating in manuscript. All four poems are in rhyme royal. The first two, "Hymn of Love" and "Hymn of Beauty," develop the idea of love as an elemental creative force (as in Plato's *Symposium*) and show how man's moral being is influenced by his love of beauty on various levels. In the next two, "Hymn of Heavenly Love" and "Hymn of Heavenly Beauty," Christ replaces Cupid as symbol of creative love, and the Platonic ladder of ascent from earthly love to heavenly contemplation is based on the notion of a Christian God as ultimate reality. Heavenly beauty can be reflected in the physical world, Spenser suggests, but its essence exists in a separate sphere. The poems clearly express the influence on Spenser of Plato's Renaissance commentators Giordano Bruno, Baldassare Castiglione, Marsilio Ficino, and Pico della Mirandola. Although not distinguished as poetry, the four hymns are important expressions of Spenser's Platonism.

The standard edition is in *The Works,* ed. Edwin A. Greenlaw, F. M. Padelford, et al., 10 vols. (1932-49), I. There is a full analysis by Robert Ellrodt, *Neoplatonism in the Poetry of Spenser* (1960). See also J. B. Fletcher. "A Study in Renaissance Mysticism: Spenser's *Fowre Hymnes,*" *PMLA,* XXVI (1911); F. M. Padelford, "Spenser's *Fowre Hymnes,*" *JEGP,* XIII (1914); E. M. Albright, "Spenser's Cosmic Philosophy and His Religion," *PMLA, XLIV* (1929); J. W. Bennett, "The Theme of Spenser's *Fowre Hymnes,*" *SP,* XXVIII (1931); William Nelson, *The Poetry of Edmund Spenser* (1963); and Enid Welsford, *Spenser: Fowre Hymnes, Epithalamion. A Study of Edmund Spenser's Doctrine of Love* (1967).

Foxe, John (1516-1587). Reformation clergyman famous for his account of the persecution of Protestants during the reign of Mary Tudor (see ACTS AND MONUMENTS). Foxe was born at Boston, Lincolnshire, and attended Magdalen College, Oxford, but as a militant Puritan, he resigned his fellowship in 1545 in protest against the religious statutes of the college. In 1554 he took up residence on the Continent and began preparing the first draft of his religious history *Commentarii rerum in ecclesia gestarum,* which was published later that year at Strasbourg. The work is entitled *Acts and Monuments of the Christian Church* in the English version, and later became known as *The Book of Martyrs. Acts and Monuments* was condemned by Catholics as vicious bigotry, but this judgment on Foxe can be disputed: his *Christus triumphans* (1556) stands as a strong plea for religious tolerance. Upon his return to England after the accession of Elizabeth, Foxe held no important offices, although his friend Archbishop Edmund Grindal ordained him a priest in 1560 and made him canon of Salisbury in 1563. Four editions of his massive *Acts and Monuments* appeared during his lifetime.

The best biographical and critical account is J. F. Mozley, *John Foxe and His Book* (1940). There is an essay on Foxe's life and influence in Gordon Rupp, *Six Makers of English Religion, 1500-1700* (1957).

Friar Bacon and Friar Bungay. A romantic comedy by Robert GREENE, written about 1589 and first printed in 1594. It is based on a sixteenth-century chapbook, *The Famous History of Friar Bacon,* the earliest extant edition of which is 1627.

In thirteenth-century England, Edward, son of King Henry III, falls in love with Margaret, the beautiful daughter of the gamekeeper of rural Fressingfield. He assigns to his friend Lacy, earl of Lincoln, the task of representing him in courting Margaret while he journeys in disguise to Oxford to consult with the great magician Friar Bacon as to the most effective means of winning the chaste maiden. Bacon has worked for seven years to build a brass head that will utter profound wisdom.

At Oxford, Friar Bacon instantly penetrates Prince Edward's disguise and shows him in a "glass perspective," or magic mirror, the betrothal of Margaret to Lacy. Watching the lovers kiss, Edward furiously swears vengeance against his friend. Friar Bacon magically prevents his rival Friar Bungay from marrying the pair and conveys Bungay to Oxford on a devil's back.

At Hampton Court, King Henry entertains the German emperor, the king of Castile, and Castile's lovely daughter Elinor whom King Henry has betrothed to Edward. The royal party journeys to Oxford to see a test of skill between Friar Bacon and Jaques Vandermast, the emperor's magician. Bacon easily defeats the German magician. At Fressingfield, Edward angrily confronts Lacy and Margaret, but when they both express their willingness to die rather than separate, the prince magnanimously forgives his friend and relinquishes his claim to Margaret. Lacy and the prince depart for Oxford to see Edward's newly betrothed Elinor of Castile.

Friar Bacon, his seven years of labor on the brass head now completed, waits for his creation to speak. After watching and waiting for sixty days, he and Bungay are exhausted, and they leave Bacon's stupid servant Miles to watch the head. Bacon is hardly asleep before the head utters the words "Time is!" Miles finds the statement less than profound, so fails to awake his master. Next the head cries. "Time was!"—and again the clownish servant decides to wait for more profound utterances before awakening Bacon. Finally, the head says "Time is past!" and, to a clap of thunder, disintegrates. Bacon's magic leads to even greater misfortunes. In his glass perspective two Oxford scholars view their fathers killed in a duel over Margaret, and the two boys fatally stab each other. Realizing that his magic has been the cause of such grief, Bacon smashes his glass, abjures necromancy, and resolves to devote his future to God.

In his absence Lacy has written Margaret that their love was a mistake, and the grief-stricken girl vows to enter a nunnery. Hearing of her beauty, however, King Henry orders her to court, and Lacy hastens to Fressingfield, where he explains that his letter was only a ruse to test her constancy—an explanation Margaret promptly accepts. At court the lovers join with Edward and Elinor of Castile in a double wedding.

Greene's play may have been written in response to the popularity of Marlowe's *Doctor Faustus*; but not to contrast Faustus' black magic with Friar Bacon's white, for Bacon's use of the occult is as forbidden as that of Faustus, and at the conclusion of the play Bacon rejects magic and dedicates the rest of his life to God. Bacon's besting of the rival magician Vandermast does suggest, however, that Greene wanted his audience to appreciate the superiority of his true blue Englishman over Marlowe's German.

In his preface to Greene's *Menaphon*, Nashe praised Greene's plots, but that praise is difficult to justify in *Friar Bacon and Friar Bungay.* Lacy's cruel testing of Margaret in the fifth act is a new and unexpected conflict that does little for the story except associate Margaret with the Patient Grissel theme. On the other hand, Greene rather skillfully employs Bacon and Margaret as link characters unifying the multiple plots of magic and romantic love.

Greene's play has been edited by Daniel Seltzer in the Regents Renaissance Drama series (1963) and by J. A. Lavin in the New Mermaid series (1969). For criticism, see Waldo F. McNeir, "Traditional Elements in the Character of Greene's Friar Bacon," *SP,* XLV (1948); Frank Towne, "'White Magic' in *Friar Bacon and Friar Bungay?*" *MLN*, LXVII (1952); and Kenneth Muir, "Robert Greene as Dramatist," *Essays on Shakespeare and Elizabethan Drama in Honor of Hardin Craig,* ed. Richard Hosley (1962).

Fuller, Thomas (1608-1661). Anglican minister, essayist, and biographer, The son of the rector of St. Peter's in Aldwinkle, Northamptonshire, and of the daughter of the bishop of Salisbury, Fuller devoted most of his life in service to the Anglican Church. After ordination in 1631 and a degree in divinity from Cambridge in 1635, he began his preaching career at Netherbury, Salisbury, and Cambridge. With the outbreak of the Civil War he moved to London and preached with great success at the Savoy, a manor where he lived with various Royalist friends. For a time he served at Exeter as chaplain to the infant Princess Henrietta. Never a volatile or outspoken partisan, Fuller was frequently criticized for his lack of zeal by both Puritans and Royalists.

With the Restoration, Fuller resumed his clerical activities, but never managed to profit from the ministry. Instead, he determined to make the principal share of his living by soliciting subscriptions to a monumental biographical collection, *The History of the Worthies of England* (1662), which gives an account of distinguished Englishmen listed by the counties in which they were born.

Fuller was a prolix, indefatigable writer of sermons, histories, poems, epigrams, and translations. The work for which he was best known among his contemporaries, however, was *The Holy State and the Profane State*, published in (1642) (see CHARACTERS; ESSAYS). The work is divided into five parts: *The Holy State,* consisting of four books, and *The Profane State,* made up of one. Both deal chiefly with characters. In Book I Fuller describes nine domestic types—the ideal wife, husband, widow, son, master, servant, and so forth—and to each of these entertaining descriptions he appends pithy and easily digested moral observations. Five Christian biographies are included to illustrate these characters and to give further support to their didactic function. The ideal husband is represented by Abraham, the good wife by St. Monica, and so on.

Book II presents characters according to vocations—the ideal lawyer, physician, minister, patron, landlord, etc.—and thus Fuller extends his range from the home in Book I to society as a whole in Book II. In Book III he switches from typical characters to the more abstract subject of typical virtues, traits, and customs—moderation, hospitality, charity, piety, etc. Of these, moderation dominates the work as a whole; for it is Fuller's ideal of moderation, based on Aristotle's golden mean that prevents the many sins resulting from excess.

Book IV returns to the subject of Book I by emphasizing commonplace matters in a style peppered with maxims, witty turns of expression, and anecdotes. Here Fuller stresses practical problems of social conduct; one hears in his easy prose the voice of the congenial minister speaking from the pulpit to a congregation that accepts and enjoys his moral truisms. He is seldom waspish, polemical, or strident, and usually excoriates religious errors condemned by Puritans and Anglicans alike.

Fuller's contribution to literary history in *The Holy State and the Profane State* is in his perfecting of the character and the eulogized biography. His many characters—the ideal schoolmaster, the loyal servant, the dutiful son—helped to open a fresh dimension of psychological and social characterization that contributed to the development of the novel in the eighteenth century. His eulogized biographies of Lord Burghley and other public figures also played a part in the development of Stuart BIOGRAPHY

Fuller's many sermons, religious meditations, and other works (only a few of which are cited above) have been collected by M. G Walter, 2 vols. (1938). The standard biography is by J. E. Bailey (1874). D. B. Lyman, *The Great Tom Fuller* (1935), is shorter and more literary in emphasis. The most comprehensive study is by W. E. Houghton, *The Formation of Thomas Fuller's Holy and Profane States* (1938).

G

Game at Chess, A. An allegorical comedy satirical of the Catholic Church and of English and Spanish foreign relations, written by Thomas MIDDLETON in 1624 and produced the same year at the Globe Theatre by the King's Men. The English had been aroused to feverish anti-Spanish resentment as a result of the abortive efforts of Buckingham and Prince Charles to secure a marriage the year before to the Spanish Infanta, and by the Machiavellian maneuvers of the Spanish ambassador Gondomar. Thus the play is partly an allegory attacking the "Spanish match," partly a vehement satire against the Catholic Church and the Jesuits. After nine performances, the play was stopped because of protests by the Spanish ambassador. The theater was closed briefly and the King's Men prohibited by the Privy Council from further performances.

The prologue is spoken by Ignatius Loyola, founder of the Jesuits, who baldly confesses to his acquaintance Error his many vices and evil intentions toward England. In the game the White King represents James I; the White Knight, Prince Charles; the White Duke, Buckingham; the White Bishop, Archbishop George Abbot; the White Queen, the Church of England; the White Queen's pawn, the earl of Middlesex. In opposition to this White House (England) is the Black House (Spain). The Black King is Philip IV of Spain; the Black Duke, Philip's minister Olivares; the Black Bishop, the father general of the Jesuits; the Black Queen, the Roman Catholic Church; the Black Knight, the Spanish ambassador Gondomar, and the Fat Bishop, the archbishop of Spalato. The subplot involves the pawns of the White Queen, Black Queen, and Black Bishop.

In a letter of August 10, 1624, a Spanish aide in London. Don Carlos Coloma, angrily described the action of the play to the duke of Olivares:

> The subject of the play is a game of chess, with white houses and black houses, their kings and other pieces, acted by the players, and the king of the blacks has easily been taken for our lord the king, because of his youth, dress, and other details. The first act, or rather game, was played by their ministers, impersonated by the white pieces, and the Jesuits, by the black ones. Here there were remarkable acts of sacrilege and, among other abominations, a minister summoned St. Ignatius from Hell, and when he found himself again in

> the world, the first thing he did was to rape one of his female penitents... The second act was directed against the Archbishop of Spalato, at that time a white piece, but afterwards won over to the black side by the Count of Gondomar, who, brought on to the stage in his litter almost to the life, and seated on his chair with a hole in it... confessed all the treacherous actions with which he had deceived and soothed the king of the whites... The last act ended with a long, obstinate struggle between all the whites and the blacks, and in it he who acted the Prince of Wales heartily beat and kicked the "Count of Gondomar" into Hell, which consisted of a great hole and hideous figures; and the white king [drove] the black king and even his queen (into Hell) almost as offensively...

Among his sources were a number of anti-Catholic stories that Middleton found in such pamphlets as Thomas Scott's *Vox Populi* (1620) and *The Second Part of Vox Populi* (1624); Thomas Robinson's *The Anatomy of the English Nunnery at Lisbon* (1622); and *News from Rome: Spalato's Doom* (1624).

Although not a great play, *A Game at Chess* was extremely effective propaganda. No other seventeenth-century play provoked so many contemporary allusions and comments. As late as 1673 Sir William Davenant could expect his audience to understand his reference in *The Playhouse to Let* when he has a character remark, "There's such a crowd at the door, as if we had / A new play of *Gondomar.*"

The mass of contemporary allusions and references, as well as a close study of sources, can be found in the introduction and notes to the definitive edition of the play by R. C. Bald (1929). See also the New Mermaid edition by J. W. Harper (1967). Middleton's play is interpreted by E. C. Morris, "The Allegory in Middleton's *A Game at Chess,*" *Englische Studien,* XXXVIII (1907); and by J. R. Moore, "The Contemporary Significance of Middleton's *Game at Chess,*" *PMLA,* I (1935). See also Roussel Sargent, "Theme and Structure in Middleton's *A Game at Chess,*" *MLR,* LXVI (1971).

Gammer Gurton's Needle. A comedy attributed to William Stevenson (fl. 1550-60). The play is believed to have been written around 1550-53 and performed during that period at Christ's College, Cambridge; it was printed in 1575, but there may have been earlier editions. No single source is known. With *Ralph Roister Doister, Gammer Gurton's Needle* is important for being one of the earliest comedies in English to be based on classical models.

The play is divided into acts and scenes, and features the cunning slave of Latin comedy and the practical-joking Vice of the morality plays. It is racy and idiomatic in dialogue and realistic in its portrayal of English rural life. The song "Back and side, go bare, go bare" which opens the second act, was widely quoted by later dramatists.

The action begins when Diccon, an itinerant Bedlam beggar, steals some bacon from old Gammer Gurton's house and sells it at a tavern across the road for two pots of ale. Meanwhile Gammer Gurton's stupid man Hodge, whose breeches are torn, learns that she has lost her prize possession, her "goodly tossing spinner's needle."

At the tavern Hodge confides to the mischievous Diccon the reason the needle is so important: Hodge must have presentable breeches when he meets a young lady who is due to arrive on the morrow. Diccon promises to conjure up the Devil to find the needle, but the simple Hodge is terrified by Diccon's necromancy and flees, whereupon Diccon resorts to other mischief by telling Dame Chat, a contentious alewife and neighbor of Gammer, that Gammer's maid Tyb has accused her of stealing a cock. When Hodge returns, Diccon informs him that the Devil has revealed that the secret of the lost needle is "cat," "rat," or "chat"—i.e., Gib the cat ate it, Dr. Rat the curate found it, or Dame Chat stole it. When Hodge leaves to have his breeches sewn by a tailor. Diccon visits Gammer to inform her that Dame Chat stole the needle.

What follows is a furious battle between Gammer and Dame Chat. Consulted by Gammer, Hodge, and Diccon, the village curate Dr. Rat, a tippler, only compounds the growing confusion, and finally sends for Master Bailey, a constable, to settle the feud over the needle. Diccon confesses his intrigues and is ordered by Bailey to kneel down and swear an oath on Hodge's leather breeches. When the irrepressible Diccon whacks Hodge on the bottom, Gammer's needle is discovered where she left it in Hodge's half-mended breeches. The whole company rejoices and retires to the tavern to celebrate.

Although much of *Gammer Gurton's Needle* is written in the limpest doggerel, it is admirably constructed and fast-moving. The element of local realism is much more pronounced than in *Ralph Roister Doister,* the earliest extant classical comedy in the vernacular. One of the earliest university comedies on record, *Gammer* was performed for the amusement of the students at Christ's College, Cambridge, and its good-natured farce and exaggerated characterizations are expressive of a youthful ebullience and vitality. In avoiding the sophisticated wickedness of Plautus and Terence, the vulgarities of the interludes, and the didacticism of the morality plays, *Gammer* anticipates the congenial satire and festive exuberance characteristic of later Elizabethan comedy.

Gammer Gurton's Needle was edited by H. F. Brett-Smith for the Percy Reprints (1920), and is in *Elizabethan Plays,* ed. A. H. Nethercot, C. R. Baskervill, and V. B. Heltzel (rev. ed., 1971). C. W. Roberts questions Stevenson's authorship of the play in *PQ,* XIX (1940). For critical discussion, see A. H. Thorndike, *English Comedy* (1929), and David M. Bevington, *From Mankind to Marlowe: Growth of Structure in the Popular Drama of Tudor England* (1962).

Gargantua and Pantagruel (Rabelais). See UTOPIAN FICTION.

Gascoigne, George (1539?-1577). Poet and playwright. Educated at Trinity College, Cambridge, and at Gray's Inn, Gascoigne was a soldier, member of Parliament, and court entertainer. With Francis Kinwelmarsh (fl. 1566-80), he wrote the play *Jocasta* (1566), based on Lodovico Dolce's Italian version of Euripides *Phoenissae. Jocasta* was the first English translation of a Greek drama and one of the earliest tragedies in blank verse (see TRANSLATIONS). Gascoigne's SUPPOSES (also 1566), based on Ariosto's *I Suppositi,* was the first English comedy in prose (and became a source for the subplot of Shakespeare's *Taming of the Shrew*). It was first performed at Gray's Inn in 1566. Another pioneer work is Gascoigne's *The Steel Glass* (1576), one of the earliest formal satires in English. The poet's "steel glass" reveals the author's own faults, the abuses of the times, and the vices of kings, lords, and common men; another glass ironically reveals with "seemly show" the way things ought to be. At the conclusion of the poem a common plowman emerges as the ideal of moral conduct (see SATIRE).

In 1572-75 Gascoigne fought in the Low Counties and was captured by the Spanish. During his absence appeared an unauthorized edition of *Jocasta, Supposes,* and miscellaneous verses entitled *A Hundred Sundry Flowers* (1573), which the author repudiated and revised two years later with a new title, *The Posies of George Gascoigne* (see SONNET SEQUENCES). It contained the brief treatise *Certain Notes of Instruction,* the earliest extant essay in English on the subject of prosody (see CRITICISM, LITERARY).

The Glass of Government (1575), an innovative play on the theme of the prodigal son described as a "tragical comedy," is perhaps the earliest extant TRAGICOMEDY. Gascoigne worked with comparable ingenuity in prose; most notable is the narrative which some scholars consider the first English novel, THE ADVENTURES OF MASTER F.J. (1573). Other works include *The Complaint of Philomene* (1576), a narrative poem, and *The Grief of Joy* (1577), a collection of verse in honor of Queen Elizabeth.

Gascoigne was an imaginative but often crude writer with an impressive range; his *Tale of Hemetes the Hermit,* recited for the queen at Woodstock in 1575, is a prose tale combining elements of medieval and Renaissance romance; his *The Drum of Doom's Day* (1576) is a moralizing rendition of the medieval theme of *contemptus mundi;* and his straight prose tract *Delicate Diet for Dainty-Mouthed Drunkards* is a vehement and coarse temperance sermon. Hence Gascoigne is a writer constantly experimenting and changing, "a transitional poet—one in whom we see the golden quality coming to birth" (C. S. Lewis, *English Literature of the 16th Century* [1954]).

The definitive edition of *The Works* is by J. W. Cunliffe, 2 vols. (1907-10). There is a biographical and critical study by C. T. Prouty, *George Gascoigne: Elizabethan Courtier, Soldier, and Poet* (1942). S. A. Tannenbaum has a Concise Bibliography (1942), added to in

"George Gascoigne (1941-66)," ed. R. C. Johnson, in *Elizabethan Bibliographies Supplements,* IX (1968).

Gentle Craft, The. A prose narrative in two parts by Thomas DELONEY. As with most of Deloney's middle-class romances, *The Gentle Craft* is based on adaptations of euphuistic romances, chronicles, and JESTBOOKS. *The Gentle Craft* was written around 1596 and both parts were published in 1598. Deloney's tale of Simon Eyre, the shoemaker's apprentice who became lord mayor of London and founder of Leadenhall (London's center for the leather trade), became the principal source of Thomas Dekker's popular play THE SHOEMAKER'S HOLIDAY. According to M. E. Lawlis, Deloney originally planned *The Gentle Craft* as a trilogy, with Part I showing the origins of the shoemaker's trade, Part II how it flourished in London, and Part III its development throughout England. Deloney, who died in 1600, did not complete the third part.

Part I begins with an embellished version of the legend of Hugh and Winifred, patron saints of shoemakers. Hugh, son of a Welsh king, courts the young virgin Winifred, who rejects his passionate suit because, as a secret Christian convert, all her love is addressed to God. Forsaking women forever, the broken-hearted prince travels to Paris, Venice, and Sicily. After being shipwrecked and subduing several monsters, he sails to England, where at Harwich he learns the shoemaker's trade. Meanwhile the pagan tyrant Diocletian, legendary conquerer of England, imprisons Winifred for being a Christian. When Hugh visits her in prison, he confesses his admiration for her faith and courage and is himself imprisoned. Winifred is executed by bleeding to death and Hugh made to drink her blood. After their deaths Winifred is buried beside a sacred spring and Hugh's body thrown to vultures. Hugh had willed his bones to the "Gentlemen of the Gentle Craft," his friends the shoemakers, and both Hugh and Winfred become saints of that trade. Later a group of cobbler journeymen steal St. Hugh's bones to make tools, and to this day the shoemaker's tools are called "St. Hugh's bones."

In another tale, beginning in Chapter V, the wicked Roman emperor Maximinus seeks to kill all of England's noble youth. To protect her two sons Crispianus and Crispine, the queen of Logria sends them away to learn some humble trade. The boys meet a band of jolly shoemakers and become bound as apprentices for seven years. They grow so skilled that Maximinus employs them at court, where his daughter Ursula falls in love with Crispine. Ursula reveals her passion for Crispine after she sends for him on the pretext she is displeased with a pair of shoes. During their meeting Crispine expresses his own love, reveals his true identity, and swears Ursula to secrecy. They are later married by a blind friar, after which Ursula returns to court and Crispine to the cobbler's bench.

Crispianus, meanwhile, is pressed into the army to fight for the Britons in Gaul, where he so distinguishes himself that he wins the favor of Maximinus, who offers him Ursula's hand in marriage. Ursula's pregnancy outrages her father, but matters are righted when he learns that Crispine is a prince and the rightful father of Ursula's child. The shoemakers declare a holiday in honor of Crispine and Crispianus, whose careers have borne out the words of the Persian general Iphicrates to the king of Gaul: "A shoemaker's son is a prince born."

Chapter X begins the tale of Simon Eyre, the shoemaker who became lord mayor of London. In London every Sunday morning the apprentices meet for breakfast, and one Sunday Simon Eyre, unable to pay for breakfast, vows that when he is mayor he will treat all the apprentices in London. He marries a hard-working girl and opens his own shop. One of his journeymen is the Frenchman John Denevale, the first to introduce low-cut shoes to England. Denevale meets a Greek merchant whose ship carrying a cargo of linen has sprung a leak and has been taken to port. Denevale, Eyre, and his wife join in a scheme to buy the linen and resell it at one hundred percent profit. Soon afterward Simon and his wife, both richly attired, dine at the house of the lord mayor, who addresses Simon as "gentleman."

Denevale falls in love with Florence, Simon's maid, who is also loved by Haunce, a Dutch journeyman. Haunce manages to alienate the two lovers by lying to Florence and winning her promise to marry him. Denevale and Nicholas, a young journeyman, conspire to ruin the wedding by watering the wine, getting Haunce drunk, and substituting Nicholas for the bridegroom. Denevale tricks Nicholas into being arrested and goes himself to propose to Florence, but at this point Denevale's wife arrives from France to spoil his plans. Disgusted with all foreigners, Florence rejects both Denevale and Haunce, but Simon intervenes to save the day by releasing Nicholas from prison, arranging a marriage between him and Florence, and setting up the couple in a new shop.

As for Simon, his career flourishes. He becomes richer every day, is made sheriff of London, and finally lord mayor. In fulfillment of his promise made years before, Simon has a church bell (later known as the "Pancake Bell") rung every year on Shrove Tuesday to summon all the apprentices in London to a free breakfast. Toward the end of his illustrious career, Simon builds Leadenhall and decrees that every Monday leather will be sold at the hall for the convenience of shoemakers.

Part II begins with the shoemaker Richard Casteler's tangled romances. Two comely wenches, Meg and Gillian, compete unsuccessfully for his favor while Robin, a fat, jolly journeyman, baits the two girls with jokes and tricks. For his part, Richard Casteler is in love with a Dutch girl in London who is slow to reciprocate. When Richard finally wins her hand, Meg and Gillian come drunk to the wedding and accuse Richard of lightness in love. Meg departs to follow the English army to Boulogne, and eventually dies a repentant old woman in Islington. Gillian marries a worthy man and lives a full, happy life.

Richard Casteler's story is concluded in Chapter IV, which tells how he entertained the king at Whitehall with a chorus of shoemakers singing "The Song of the Winning of Boulogne." Unable to have children himself, when he dies Richard leaves his fortune to provide for fatherless children at Christ's Hospital, London.

Chapters V-VII describe the career of Peachy, a master cobbler who retains an entourage of finely dressed gallants. Two sea captains who are jealous of Peachy's finery are severely bested by Peachy and his men in a duel. Two lusty young apprentices who join Peachy's shop are Tom Drum and Harry Nevell. With Sir John Rainsford, a hot-headed but honorable knight, and thirty shoemakers, Peachy equips a force to aid the king in fighting the French on the Isle of Wight. After a successful campaign, the king pardons Sir John for a previous offense and makes Peachy his personal shoemaker.

In Chapter VIII Harry Nevell and Tom Drum woo a wealthy widow. She receives Harry but not the brash Tom, who is thrown out of the house after demanding "better entertainment" of the widow. (Hence "Tom Drum's entertainment" became an Elizabethan phrase synonymous with a violent reception.) Disgraced by his failure with the widow, Tom departs for Scotland to become a drummer in the army.

In Chapter IX Harry Nevell continues to pursue the widow, now in competition with a Dr. Burket. The widow, however, chooses as her husband the honest, humble William, an apprentice. Although beneath her socially, William is faithful, kind, and handsome. William and the widow are married happily for many years. In distress at losing the widow, Harry Nevell leaves Peachy's shop and tries one trade after another. After inheriting a fortune from his father, Harry gives a huge banquet for all his former masters and mistresses. To each one who complains of a wrong done while in service, Harry gives money, and ever afterward he retains in his house a member of each of the crafts he worked at while poor.

Chapters X-XI conclude Part II with the story of a little shoemaker of St. Martin's known as the "Green King" because he once dressed in green satin when he met the king. The Green King's one fault is extravagance, and after squandering much of his inheritance he leaves his wife and servant to seek his fortune in Holland. During the Green King's absence, his thrifty wife manages his affairs so well that he returns to find his business prospering.

The concluding tale relates how the Green King plays a trick on his wife and fellow shoemakers. When she complains that he never takes her walking, he promises to escort her to the fair on St. James's Day, July 25, and makes a wager with several shoemakers that they cannot walk with him to the fair. The group is led to believe that the fair is at Westminster; actually, the Green King continues the walk all the way to the fair at Bristol, and along the way the shoemakers fall by the wayside. The Green King's exhausted wife swears she will never again nag him about walking. When he dies at a ripe old age, the Green King is widely respected for his honesty and generosity to the poor.

Deloney's tales in *The Gentle Craft* combine the adventurous spirit of the aristocratic courtly romances with the sober morality and practical concerns of middle-class life. Hence Deloney's work is characterized by a mixture of exotic romanticism and mundane realism. He expresses little psychological interest in his characters, but as in the tales of Casteler and Peachy, he also refrains from making his protagonists paragons of virtue. Indeed, Casteler and Peachy show some of the wily resourcefulness of the heroes in ROGUE LITERATURE and picaresque fiction.

The definitive edition of *The Gentle Craft* was edited by Merritt E. Lawlis, *The Novels of Thomas Deloney* (1961). For a critical study, see Lawlis, *An Apology for the Middle Class: The Dramatic Novels of Thomas Deloney* (1961), and Llewelyn Powys, "Thomas Deloney," *VQR*, IX (1933).

Gentleman Usher, The. A comedy by George CHAPMAN, written and performed in about 1602 and first printed in 1606. In the main plot Chapman employs the familiar situation of a father and son in love with the same girl. The comic character for whom the play is named, Bassiolo, may have been inspired by Shakespeare's Malvolio in *Twelfth Night*.

The first two acts are dominated by a formal masque and burlesque dance. Prince Vincentio's courtship of Margaret, a lady of the Italian court, is frustrated by the fact that Duke Alphonso, the boy's father, is also in love with the girl. At the house of Count Lasso, Margaret's father, the duke is festively received and enlists the aid of a favorite, Medice, in winning Margaret. Suspecting that Margaret may have a secret lover, Medice plies Margaret's aunt Cortezza with liquor in order to learn the truth, but the old hag gives him nothing but flirtation. In his turn, Vincentio seeks the services of Count Lasso's clownish usher, Bassiolo, hinting broadly of great rewards that will be his when Vincentio becomes duke. The conceited, brash Bassiolo pretends to be a great authority on love, not realizing that both Vincentio and Margaret are laughing at him. The situation increases in gravity when Vincentio and Margaret engage in a secret marriage ceremony whereby they make their own vows and knit a scarf around each other's arm to signify their union.

When the duke discovers his son's love for Margaret, he threatens revenge, and he, Count Lasso, Medice, Cortezza, and Margaret's sister all hide in a room to surprise the lovers. Vincentio escapes pursued by Medice, and Margaret is left to face an enforced marriage to the duke. To avoid the marriage she covers her face with a caustic ointment that horribly disfigures her with blisters. Confronted by Margaret, who blames him for her condition, and by the news that Medice has treacherously wounded his son, the duke humbly retracts his threats and vows to atone for his behavior. All is made right when an ingenious doctor appears to cure Margaret of her blisters and Vincentio of his wounds. The base Medice is exiled, and the two fathers bless the marriage of Vincentio and Margaret.

In spite of its slow beginning and loose plot, *The Gentleman Usher* is, with *Monsieur D'Olive,* one of Chapman's liveliest comedies. After the first two acts it develops into a harrowing tragicomedy that averts disaster by the *deus ex machina* appearance of the doctor who cures Margaret of her disfigurement and by the sudden conversion to virtue on the part of the duke. Because of these fortuitous reversals, Chapman's comedy is considered a forerunner of the romantic tragicomedies of Beaumont and Fletcher.

The Gentleman Usher was edited by John Hazel Smith in the Regents Renaissance Drama series (1970), which contains full notes and criticism. Also valuable is the edition by T. M. Parrott, *The Plays and Poems,* 2 vols., II: *The Comedies* (1914). For criticism, see Paul V. Kreider, *Elizabethan Comic Character Conventions as Revealed in the Comedies of George Chapman* (1935), and Henry M. Weidner, "The Dramatic Uses of Homeric Idealism: The Significance of Theme and Design in George Chapman's *The Gentleman Usher,*" *ELH,* XXVIII (1961).

Glapthorne, Henry (1610-1643?). Dramatist. His play *Argalus and Parthenia* (wr. c. 1633) is discussed under PASTORAL.

Glaucus and Scylla. See SCYLLA'S METAMORPHOSIS.

Godwin, Francis (1562-1633). For comment on his *The Man in the Moon,* see UTOPIAN FICTION.

Golding, Arthur (1536?-1605). Translator of the most famous English rendering of Ovid's *Metamorphoses* (1565-67). See TRANSLATIONS.

Googe, Barnabe (1540-1594). Poet and translator. Little is known of Googe's early years except that he attended both Oxford and Cambridge. In the service of his kinsman Sir William Cecil, Lord Burghley, he traveled extensively in France and Spain before receiving a long-term post in Ireland (1574-85). Googe's first publication was an English version of the Latin poem *Zodiacus vitae* (Venice, c. 1531) by the Italian astrologer Marcellus Palingenius, born Pietro Angelo Manzolli (1501?-1543?). Entitled *The Zodiac of Life,* the first three books of Googe's version were published in 1560, the first six in 1561, and all twelve in 1565. Palingenius' compendium of astronomical lore and sermonizing in hexameters Googe renders into very slow-moving heptameters, or "fourteeners," in couplets. The work may have had some slight influence, as is claimed, on a line or two by Shakespeare, and Spenser may have been exposed to it when he and Googe were in Ireland.

In the dedicatory epistle to his only collection of original poems, *Eglogues, Epitaphs, and Sonnets* (1563), Googe states that he had intended his poems to be consigned to "continual darkness" until a friend caused "these trifles of mine to come to light" at the printer's while Googe was abroad. Googe's work contains epitaphs on John Bale, Richard Edwards, Nicholas Grimald, and Thomas Phaer; a few travel poems; complimentary "sonets" (short poems) in decasyllabic quatrains; and eight eclogues. Googe's eclogues, all in stumbling "fourteeners," are of historical interest, for the fifth and sixth are taken from Jorge de Montemayor's *Diana enamorada* and represent the first appearance of that influential Spanish romance in English literature. Moreover, Googe's eclogues mark the second publication of neoclassic pastorals in English after Alexander Barclay's imitations in 1515-21 of the eclogues of Mantuan (or Mantuanus), an Italian Carmelite monk whose voluminous eclogues satiric of the Roman Catholic clergy were widely used in English schools as exercises in Latin. Googe's versions of Mantuan's eclogues were followed by George Turberville's in 1567. The Mantuan eclogues of Barclay, Googe, and Turberville represent the extent of eclogues in English before the publication of Spenser's *Shepherd's Calendar* (1579), a work that heralded the golden era of Elizabethan poetry. Little if any of Spenser's admiration for Mantuan can be understood from Googe's didactic and somber eclogues, which hobble on "fourteeners":

> A piteous thing to be bewailed,
> a desperate act of love,
> O Destinies, such cruel broils
> have you power to move?

Googe's other works include an anti-Catholic miscellany, *The Popish Kingdom, or Reign of Anti-Christ* (1570), from the Latin of Thomas Kirchmayer (1511-1563), a German Lutheran known as "Naogeorg"; *A New Year's Gift* (1579), another anti-Catholic collection; a prose treatise on husbandry (1577), revised and enlarged in 1631 by Gervase Markham; and an English version of some Spanish proverbs by Inigo López de Mendoza (1398-1458).

For biographical data, see *The Dictionary of National Biography*. Rosemond Tuve has done a facsimile edition of *The Zodiac of Life* (1947). Googe's *Eglogues, Epitaphs, and Sonnets* was edited by Edward Arber in the English Reprints series (1871); *The Popish Kingdom* was edited by R. C. Hope (1880). For commentary, see T. P. Harrison, "Googe's *Eglogs* and Montemayor's *Diana,*" *University of Texas Studies in English,* V (1925); H. H. Hudson, "Sonnets by Barnabe Googe," *PMLA,* XLVIII (1933); Rosemond Tuve, "Spenser and *The Zodiake of Life,*" *JEGP,* XXXIV (1935); V. de Sola Pinto, *The English Renaissance, 1510-1688* (1938); and Paul E. Parnell. "Barnabe Googe: A Puritan in Arcadia," *JEGP,* LX (1961).

Gorboduc, or The Tragedy of Ferrex and Porrex. A tragedy by Thomas Sackville and Thomas Norton, written in 1561 and first printed in an undated edition around 1571. It was performed first at the Inner Temple during the Christmas season of 1561 and again before Queen Elizabeth at Whitehall, January 18, 1562. It is noteworthy for being the first

English tragedy in blank verse. The chief source of the play is an account in Richard Grafton's *Chronicles* (1556), which was taken from Geoffrey of Monmouth's *Historia regum Britanniae.*

In the dumb show with which the tragedy begins, six wild men clothed in leaves attempt unsuccessfully to break a bundle of sticks but easily snap them singly—an act symbolizing the strength of unity and the weakness of division. In the play proper, Gorboduc, king of Britain and descendant of Brut, decides to split his kingdom equally between his sons Ferrex and Porrex and retire from power. To his elder son Ferrex he awards the realm south of the Humber, to Porrex all land north of this boundary, and to each he assigns an aged and wise counselor. Almost at once the brothers begin to quarrel. Offended that his father has deprived him of the full inheritance due him by primogeniture, Ferrex rejects the advice of his counselor, the wise Dordan, and takes into his confidence the evil young Hermon, who urges Ferrex to kill his brother. Similarly, Porrex ignores the aged peacemaker Philander and heeds the advice of wicked young Tyndar, who urges violence against Ferrex.

Both Dordan and Philander flee to inform Gorboduc of impending disaster, and while they are in council news comes that Porrex has invaded Ferrex's land, murdered him, and usurped the realm. When Porrex appears before his father in an effort to justify these misdeeds, Gorboduc decrees that Porrex be banished, after which Queen Videna, to avenge the death of her favorite son Ferrex, stabs Porrex to death in his sleep. Incensed by these crimes, the people rebel and slay both Gorboduc and his queen. Fergus of Albany, an ambitious opportunist, raises an army against Gorboduc's chief ministers, Arostus and Eubulus, and the tragedy concludes with the chaos of civil war.

Gorboduc has little aesthetic value, but it is an interesting example of English tragedy at a stage of development when it was influenced by the medieval MORALITY PLAYS, the CHRONICLE PLAYS, and SENECAN TRAGEDY. Vestiges of the morality plays are evident in *Gorboduc* in the struggle between the good and evil counselors and in the destruction of the brothers when they heed false advisers. As in morality plays the names of the good advisers suggest their office: Eubulus means "good counselor" and Philander "friend of man."

Affinities to the chronicle plays are evident not only in the source and subject matter but in the heavy political moralizing in the manner of A MIRROR FOR MAGISTRATES, to which Sackville contributed his popular "Induction" to the tale of Buckingham. As in the *Mirror,* rulers can view in *Gorboduc* the terrible consequences of foolishly dividing a kingdom and of heeding flatterers and parasites, whereas commoners can see the evil fruits of rebellion and treason.

Gorboduc is often described as the first "regular" English tragedy, and much of its form derives from the Senecan five-act structure. In the style of Seneca, each act begins with a DUMB SHOW and concludes with a chorus (speaking in six-line stanzas rhyming *ab ab cc*). Also from Seneca is the use of the *nuntius* or messenger, who reports violence occurring offstage; the theme of revenge; the lengthy and didactic speeches couched in formally structured clauses; the cascades of interrogations, and the interlocked stichomythia. Unlike Seneca, however, the authors of *Gorboduc* do not observe the classical unities of time, place, and action, especially in the discontinuous and diffuse fifth act.

In characterization and theme *Gorboduc* takes a step away from medieval tragedy, for Gorboduc and his family are not destroyed by fortune's wheel but by evil forces within themselves. Like Shakespeare's King Lear, Gorboduc sets the tragedy in motion with his division of the kingdom, and the sons are brought to ruin through their own moral failures. At the conclusion of the tragedy Eubulus affirms that God will repair Gorboduc's shattered kingdom, "for right will always live, and rise at length," but the action of the play makes clear that history is formed by men:

Thus, then ensues, when noble men do fail
In loyal truth, and subjects will be kings.

Irby B. Cauthen has edited *Gorboduc* in the Regents Renaissance Drama series (1970). For commentary, see F. L. Lucas, *Seneca and Elizabethan Tragedy* (1922); Willard Farnham, *The Medieval Heritage of Elizabethan Tragedy* (1950); and Irving Ribner, *The English History Play in the Age of Shakespeare* (1957; rev. ed., 1965).

Gosson, Stephen (1554-1624). Preacher and

pamphleteer. Born in Kent, Gosson graduated from Corpus Christi College, Oxford, in 1576 and went to London to write plays for the popular theaters. According to Francis Meres, his dramas were "among the best for pastoral," but none of these is extant. In 1579 he underwent a religious conversion and vehemently attacked poetry and plays in a pamphlet entitled *The School of Abuse,* which he dedicated to Sir Philip Sidney and was, according to Edmund Spenser, "for his labor scorned." Soon after Gosson's attack Sidney wrote his famous defense of poetry and drama, *An Apology for Poetry* (also entitled *The Defense of Poesy*). It is not known whether Sidney wrote the essay in answer to Gosson specifically. Thomas LODGE responded directly, however, in *A Reply to Stephen Gosson Touching Plays* (1579), and Gosson continued the argument in an appendix to his *The Ephemerides of Phialo* (1579) and in a pamphlet aimed at Lodge personally, *Plays Confuted in Five Actions* (1582). (For these and other Puritan attacks on plays, see CRITICISM, LITERARY).

By 1584 Gosson was ordained and became rector of Great Wigborough (1591) and of St. Botolph's, Bishopsgate (1600). His *School of Abuse* is of interest chiefly for its euphuistic prose style, its clues to conditions on the stage in the 1570s, and its relationship (if any) to Sidney's great literary essay. In its content it offers little that is original in the long siege of invective against the stage that ran continuously from John Rainolds' lectures at Oxford in Henry VIII's reign to the interminable diatribes by William Prynne in the 1630s: plays were invented by the Devil, perfected by wanton Italians, and used to corrupt morals and damn souls.

The School of Abuse was edited by Edward Arber (1865, 1895). Gosson's *Plays Confuted* is in W. C. Hazlitt, *The English Drama and Stage* (1869). Gosson's biography is by William Ringler, *Stephen Gosson, A Biographical and Critical Study* (1941). For background, see E.N.S.Thompson, *The Controversy Between the Puritans and the Stage* (1903).

Governor, A Book Named the. A treatise on education by Sir Thomas ELYOT. It was the first English book on the subject of education and polite conduct (see COURTESY LITERATURE). First printed in 1531, it went through nine editions before 1600.

Elyot discusses the qualities of the ideal ruler, the origins and essence of true nobility, the desirable education of a gentleman, his appropriate forms of recreation, and the virtues he must cultivate. Unlike Machiavelli's *The Prince,* Elyot's book is not a manual on politics or statecraft. Elyot draws much of his philosophy from the Bible, classical literature (notably Plato, Aristotle, and Plutarch), Patrizi's *De regno et regis institutione,* and Erasmus' *Institutio principis Christiani.*

Elyot begins his treatise with a definition of the commonwealth: "A public weal is a body living, compact or made of sundry estates and degrees of men, which is disposed by the order of equity and governed by the rule and moderation of reason." He argues that the political order is coextended throughout natural creation, and like Plato, holds social justice to be the proper involvement of each member of society in the work for which he is best suited. Rejecting democracy as chaos, he insists that a strong and benevolent monarchy is the best form of government, for both nature and history testify that men are happiest under one ruler.

Elyot's chief concern is the proper education of such a ruler, who must be as wisely cultivated as a sensitive plant. Nursing attendants should be chosen with care, and in the earliest years only female nurses who speak Latin and the vernacular with great precision should be allowed near the infant prince. At the age of seven the child can be given over to a wise, gentle, and scholarly tutor, who will instruct him in Greek, Latin, and modern languages, all taught as natural conversation rather than mindless drill in grammar.

The classical authors Elyot recommends first are Homer and Vergil. At fourteen the prince may begin classical prose, oratory, history, cosmography—all accompanied by a regimen of regular exercises, especially tennis and the English longbow, but never football (which Elyot detested). Thus, consistent with the humanist tradition, Elyot values physical as well as intellectual development—an alert, learned mind in a vigorous body. At seventeen the prince may begin philosophy with Aristotle's *Ethics* and Cicero's *De officiis,* and thereafter Plato, the Proverbs of Solomon, the Old and

New Testaments. To accompany these studies Elyot recommends such constructive pastimes as dancing (to which he devotes several chapters), music, painting, and chess. Gambling and card playing he utterly condemns. Especially valuable in the moral cultivation of the prince is drama and poetry, which Elyot views as an extension of moral philosophy. Tragedies will caution the prince against tyranny, and comedy will make vice contemptuous.

Only the first of Elyot's three books of *The Governor* relates to education. The second deals with the cultivation of certain attitudes and experiences valuable for the prince as he assumes his office. The qualities Elyot emphasizes are piety, good will, mercy, generosity, love, and especially a capacity for developing true friends rather than mere flatterers, a distinction Elyot illustrates from Plutarch and Boccaccio. In the third and last book, Elyot systematically contrasts Aristotelian virtues and vices—courage versus cowardice, temperance versus prodigality, and so forth—always defining the ideal as a golden mean devoid of excess. The last three chapters provide some practical advice on the administration of government.

Unlike many courtesy books, such as Castiglione's *Il Cortegiano,* Elyot's has little to say about domestic life or the nuances of social relationships (see THE COURTIER). Instead, Elyot emphasizes the broadly humanistic values of liberal education, classical scholarship, morality, and political and social justice. In spite of some eccentricities, such as Elyot's xenophobic dislike of foreign travel and foreign manners, the book is rational, balanced, humane, and morally conventional. As a solid humanist treatise with little regard for either abstruse aesthetics or social niceties, *The Governor* found a wide and appreciative audience throughout the sixteenth century.

Elyot's *The Governor* is available in the Everyman's Library series, ed. Foster Watson (1907). A major study, complete with extensive bibliography, is Stanford E. Lehmberg, *Sir Thomas Elyot: Tudor Humanist* (1960). D. T. Starnes compares Elyot's and Henry Peacham's courtesy books in "Elyot's *Governour* and Peacham's *Compleat Gentleman,*" *MLR,* XXII (1927).

Great Duke of Florence, The. A tragicomedy by Philip MASSINGER, written and performed in 1627. The date of composition is highly conjectural. The play was first printed in 1636. For his source Massinger may have consulted an anonymous play, *A Knack to Know a Knave* (1594).

Giovanni, nephew of the widowed duke of Florence, has studied for three years at the home of the scholar Charomonte, whose daughter Lidia he secretly loves. When a messenger from the duke arrives at Charomonte's house to summon Giovanni back to court, he is so struck by Lidia's beauty that he gives the duke a glowing description. Impressed, the duke sends his courtier Sanazano to investigate the messenger's account. When Sanazano sees Lidia, he becomes himself helplessly in love and arranges with Giovanni to give a disparaging report of Lidia's appearance. Puzzled by these contradictory descriptions, the duke goes to Charomonte's house to see Lidia for himself. Giovanni, meanwhile, warns Lidia of the duke's approach, and the resourceful girl arranges for her maid to feign her identity. Unfortunately Charomonte, who has not been informed of the deception, inadvertently reveals the imposture. At first the duke is enraged, for he had planned to make Lidia his second wife; but then he recalls his earlier vow never to remarry, and his gracious blessings enable Giovanni and Lidia to join in marriage.

Many critics consider this romantic tragicomedy to be Massinger's greatest play. It is masterfully unified and cleverly plotted, and the characters—especially the courtly, modest Giovanni and his articulate and charming Lidia—are consistently well realized. On the title page of the first edition the play is described as "a comical history," a phrase pointing to its ultimate source in an old legend in which the Saxon king Edgar sends his subject Ethelwald to investigate the beauty of a prospective bride, whom the treacherous Ethelwald marries himself. King Edgar swears revenge, and the legend concludes tragically. The Elizabethan play *A Knack to Know a Knave* is the earliest known attempt to make a comedy of this originally unhappy legend, and Massinger may have simply reworked the characters and plot he found in the old play.

The sources, date of composition, stage history, and other details are fully discussed in the scholarly edition by J. M. Stochholm (1933). As in several of Massinger's other plays, S. R. Gardiner finds many significant political allusions; see his "The Political Element in Massinger," *Contemporary Review,* XXXVIII (1876). See also T. A. Dunn, *Philip Massinger: The Man and the Playwright* (1957).

Greene, Robert (1558-1592). Dramatist, novelist, pamphleteer, poet. Born in Norwich, Greene went to St. John's College, Cambridge in 1575 and graduated B.A. in 1580, M.A. in 1583. He married either in 1585 or 1586, and received an M.A. from Oxford in 1588. If several statements in his pamphlets are to be believed, before his marriage he traveled widely in Italy and Spain, where he gave himself over to debauchery and riotous living. Shortly after 1588 he deserted his wife and child to live a Bohemian existence in London. He was commissioned by the bishops to write pamphlets against the authors of the Martin MARPRELATE tracts, an assignment that seems to have outraged the Anglican minister Richard Harvey, Gabriel's brother, who condemned Greene's character in a religious tract. Greene responded with some contemptuous allusions to the Harvey family in *A Quip for an Upstart Courtier* (1592), and the exchange provoked the series of satiric pamphlets known as the Green-Harvey-Nashe controversey. (See HARVEY, GABRIEL). Greene later attacked Shakespeare as an "upstart crow" in the posthumous pamphlet A GROATSWORTH OF WIT (1592), which is famous for being the first reference to Shakespeare as an actor and dramatist. Greene died in London on September 3, 1592, in abject poverty, and, if his enemy Gabriel Harvey's account is true, expired of a surfeit of "pickled herring and rhenish wine."

Greene began his literary career with *Mamillia, a Mirror or Looking-glass for the Ladies of England* (1580), a prose work in imitation of John Lyly's *Euphues.* In Greene's tale Mamillia, daughter of the duke of Padua, is wooed by the dashing and faithless Pharicles, who pursues her for her wealth and station but is really in love with her friend Publia. When Mamillia discovers his deceit, Pharicles departs Padua for Sicily. The two women he deserts swear to remain loyal to his memory. As in *Euphues* there are many exchanges of letters, much *dubii* (lengthy discussions of the proprieties of love), and excrutiatingly prolix speeches of advice couched in Lyly's euphuism. Lyly's love triangle and theme of infidelity is also closely observed, except that Greene reverses the roles of his characters: in *Euphues* the two men are faithful, the woman unfaithful; in *Mamillia* the two heroines are faithful, the one man unfaithful. In the sequel, *Mamillia, the Second Part of the Triumph of Pallas* (1583), Greene discards the euphuistic style, gives less emphasis to genteel niceties of conduct, and tells an adventurous romance. At the court of Sicily Pharicles wins great distinction as a courtier and warrior, but is falsely accused of treason by a courtesan whose advances he spurns. Cast into prison and condemned to death, he is finally rescued by his faithful Mamillia, whom he marries at the end. Publia, who enters a convent at the beginning of the story, has almost no role in the sequel.

The first part of *Mamillia* is as much of a conduct book, or treatise on polite deportment, as it is a novel or romance. Following this imitation of Lyly's *Euphues,* Greene wrote a group of frame tales (stories within a story) supposedly—but not consistently—reflecting various vices and virtues. The earliest of the frame tales is *Arbasto, the Anatomy of Fortune* (1584), in which an old hermit in his cell tells a stranger a tragic story. Years before, the hermit was a powerful king and fell in love with the elder of two daughters of a neighboring monarch. When she did not return his love, he married the younger daughter out of spite and brought her back to his kingdom. Upon learning that he did not love her, she died of grief, whereupon the nobles of the kingdom, outraged at his mistreatment of his wife, sent him into exile. Although the tale clearly illustrates his own failings of character, the hermit concludes with a lengthy lamentation on the vicissitudes of fortune.

Greene's other frame tales include *Morando, the Tritameron of Love* (1586), which, as the title suggests, is patterned after Boccaccio's *Decameron* and Marguerite of Navarre's *Heptameron. The Mirror of Modesty,* published the same year, is, like *Penelope's Web* (1587), a collection of tales representing "a chrystal mirror of feminine perfection," each story illustrating one of the virtues Greene claims to have admired most in women—obedience, chastity, and silence. Of a somewhat different order is *Planetomachia* (1585), which contains an elaborate preface on astrological lore followed by two stories related by Saturn and two by Venus, each tragic tale designed to prove the god telling it had the greater influence on man's miseries. This type of prose narrative in the setting of a debate is also the plan of *Euphues his Censure to Philautus* (1587), in which several of Homer's Greeks and Trojans of both sexes meet and debate, by telling illustrative stories, which "wholesome precepts" are most essential to the forming of a perfect soldier. The apparent purpose of the four tales is, as in Baldassare Castiglione's *Il Cortegiano,* to set forth the qualities of the ideal courtier and soldier, but Greene's real concern is in telling "delightful tragedies." Greene's later frame tales include *Perimedes the Blacksmith* (1588), stories illustrating the virtues of lowly life, and *Green's Orpharion* (1599), narratives illustrating various cures for love melancholy.

In these frame tales Greene's usual method is to present a narrator or group of narrators who recount woeful stories of weak men and women ensnared by vice and betrayed by fickle fortune. The contradictions between human volition and fate are rarely acknowledged; the characterizations are weak, the tone consistently didactic. The theme most often repeated in Greene's frame tales is that of the prodigal son; hence the frame tales are not always distinguishable from the so-called "repentance pamphlets" such as *Greene's Mourning Garment* (1590); *Greene's Never Too late* (1590); *Francesco's Parting; or, The Second Part of Greene's Never Too Late* (1590); *Greene's Farewell to Folly* (1591); and the two posthumous pamphlets in 1592, *The Repentance of Robert Greene, Master of Arts,* and *A Groatsworth of Wit.* It is never entirely clear in any of these works whether Greene is referring to himself as a prodigal son or to some fictional character, although at times the narrative is interrupted by what appear to be autobiographical addresses to the reader. In *The Repentance,* for example, the narrator despairs at length over his misspent youth, and then, in the second part, Greene breaks in to describe his own early years in Norwich, his virtuous parents, and his incorrigible conduct as an adolescent. He confesses that he has abandoned wife and child. Now death yawns with its threats of retribution: "Hell (quoth I) what talk you of hell of me? I know if I once come there, I shall have the company of better men than myself." Rather unflatteringly, he dedicated this lugubrious sermon to "those gentlemen his quondom acquaintance, that spend their wits in making plays"—no doubt referring to Christopher Marlowe, Thomas Nashe, and George Peele. How much of this is genuine repentance and how much mere theatrical sop for Greene's sermon-loving readers is impossible to say with certainty.

At the same time that Greene was writing his moralizing frame tales and repentance pamphlets, he composed a number of romances of pure adventure and entertainment. Among these are *Gwydonius, the Card of Fancy* (1584); *Ciceronis amor, or Tullies Love* (1589); *Menaphon* (1589), a pastoral romance; and *Philomela, the Lady Fitzwater's Nightingale* (1592), which tells a rambling tale of a jealous husband who unjustly accuses his wife of infidelity (a favorite motif of Greene's that enabled him to link the prodigal son myth with that of Patient Grissel). Related to this romance in theme is PANDOSTO, THE TRIUMPH OF TIME (1588), which supplied Shakespeare with the main plot of *The Winter's Tale.*

The best of Greene's romances is *Menaphon* (1589), famous for its critical preface by Thomas Nashe referring to a Senecan *Hamlet* that may have been a source of Shakespeare's tragedy. Greene's pastoral romance begins with the shepherd Menaphon walking by the sea and meeting three shipwrecked people from Cyprus—a woman calling herself Samela (but really Sephestia, who has lost her husband in an earlier shipwreck); her son Pleusidippus; and an aged male servant. Sephestia joins Menaphon's company of shepherds and soon gains a reputation for her great beauty and virtue. One of the many shepherds who falls in love with her is Melicertus (who is, unknown to either of them, her long-lost husband); another wooer is Democles, king of Arcadia (actually her father). To complicate these relationships further, her son is stolen by pirates, grows up in Thessaly, and returns years later to join her company of suitors. Thus, unknown to any of them, she is courted by her father, husband, and son. Their true identities are not made known until an old woman appears and interprets correctly the words of an oracle.

One source of Greene's *Menaphon* was William Warner's *Albion's England* (1586),

Book IV, Chapter 20, but the main ingredients were taken from the late Greek romances—the improbabilities of the plot, the *dubii,* the frame tale digressions, the confused identities, coincidental encounters, pirates, and oracles. Like Sidney in *The Arcadia,* Greene interlards his pastoral romance with songs, such as the justly famous "The Shepherd's Wife's Song":

Ah, what is love? It is a pretty thing,
As sweet unto a shepherd as a king,
  And sweeter, too:
For kings have cares that wait upon a crown,
And cares can make the sweetest love to
  frown:
  Ah, then, ah then,
If country loves such sweet desires do gain,
What lady would not love a shepherd swain?

Toward the end of Greene's life he composed a series of so-called "coney-catching" pamphlets, dialogues and tales exposing the sharp practices of card cheats and confidence men (a "coney-catcher" being a cardshark, his victim a coney, literally a rabbit). The first of these, *A Notable Discovery of Cosenage* (1591) was based on an anonymous tract *A Manifest Detection of Dice Play* (1552), and, like Greene's subsequent coney-catching pamphlets, carries the motto *Nascimur pro patria* ("We are born for the benefit of our country"). That such lofty sentiment was coupled with practical commercial motives is suggested by the wide net Greene throws out in his dedication to "young gentlemen, merchants, apprentices, farmers, and plain countrymen," who are cautioned against the wicked practices of "coney-catchers" and "cross-biters" (extortionists posing as husbands of prostitutes). After telling two stories illustrating their nefarious techniques, Greene concludes his pamphlet with two quite unrelated stories about dishonest coal dealers.

The Second Part of Coney-Catching and *The Third and Last Part of Coney-Catching* (1591, 1592) expose such underworld activities as "prigging" (cattle rustling), "nipping" (cutting purses), "foisting" (picking pockets), and "courbing" (stealing out of windows with a hook). *The Second Part* contains nine tales, *The Third Part* ten. Later in 1592 Greene wrote three more pamphlets in this same vein of ROGUE LITERATURE: *A Disputation between a He Coney-Catcher and a She Coney-Catcher, The Black Book's Messenger,* and *A Quip for an Upstart Courtier. The Black Book's Messenger* is the fictitious biography of Ned Browne, "one of the most notable cutpurses, cross-biters, and coney-catchers that ever lived in England." Ned tells his story while standing at an open window with a halter around his neck (being in a French town that lacks a gallows); he relates how as a child he defied his virtuous parents, blasphemed, stole, and whore-mongered, and insists that he will never repent of his wickedness. In five tales he recounts how he cheated a malt seller, a priest, a gentlewoman, a man at St. Paul's, and, inadvertently, his own wife, who was cozened by the "coney" Ned had arranged to "cross-bite." Contrary to his promise, Ned does in fact repent at the end, just before he is pushed from the window and hanged. A postscript describes how wolves opened his grave and devoured his body.

A Quip for an Upstart Courtier presents a debate between a prodigal courtier named Velvet Breeches (representing pride) and an honest tradesman, Cloth Breeches (humility) to decide which is more representative of the national character. The disputants review in detail the disorders and vices of no fewer than sixty professions and trades, after which a jury of twenty-four citizens, under the leadership of a knight, is finally selected to judge the arguments on both sides. The jury decides in favor of Cloth Breeches, because he stands for honesty and simplicity as opposed to Velvet Breeches' cynicism and duplicity. *A Quip is* couched in fast-paced colloquial prose, representing some of Greene's best writing, but the satire is often pointless and dull. Over half of the pamphlet is taken up with the tedious business of selecting a jury, and the exposés of the various English trades and professions are neither very informative nor interesting.

All of Greene's plays were written from 1588 to 1590. The earliest is *The Comical History of Alphonsus, King of Aragon* (1599), a clumsy, ranting melodrama in imitation of Christopher Marlowe's *Tamburlaine.* Greene's next play, *The History of Orlando Furioso* (1594), another turgid melodrama, is based on the episode in Ariosto's epic in which Orlando goes mad with jealousy over Angelica. The bombast and rant were inspired by *Tamburlaine,* and the scenes of madness owe something to Thomas Kyd's *The Spanish Tragedy*. Equally undistinguished is a comedy, *A Looking-Glass for London and England* (1594), written in collaboration with Thomas Lodge shortly before Lodge sailed to the Canary Islands in 1588. Greene's last two plays, FRIAR BACON AND FRIAR BUNGAY (1594) and JAMES IV (1598), are unquestionably his best. As a dramatist he was weak and uneven in characterization and plot design; even his well-made *Friar Bacon and Friar Bungay* has glaring irrelevancies and character lapses, but all of his plays have the golden qualities of lyricism, fantasy, and entertaining romance. Some of his heroines, particularly Margaret of Fressingfield in *Friar Bacon and Friar Bungay* and Dorothea in *James IV,* are charming idealizations—intelligent, vivacious, steadfastly loyal to their men—and represent in Greene's mythology the antitheses of the omnipresent "courtesans" who lure his somewhat dull-witted heroes from paths of virtue. Such heroines may have influenced Shakespeare in his creation of Viola in *Twelfth Night* and Rosalind in *As You Like It.*

In view of Greene's short life and enormous productivity, he must have composed rapidly and rarely blotted a line. He produced an incredible variety of fictive and dramatic genres in his euphuistic and pastoral romances, conduct books, frame tales, pseudobiographies, rogue pamphlets, heroic dramas, Senecan tragedies, and festive comedies. Taken together, these suggest a writer who was both eclectic and original, innovative and repetitious, diligent and undisciplined. He perfected no literary type, developed no distinctive style, and evolved no coherent philosophy. He was not moved by ideas, but obsessed with certain mythic characters such as the prodigal son, the patient and long-suffering wife, and the heartless and whorish vamp. The vision that evoked his lyric and descriptive powers was an English pastoral of innocent milkmaids, sunlit glades and green fields, the paradisal opposite of the hellish world of his rogue tales and coney-catching pamphlets.

The Life and Complete Works was edited by A. B. Grosart, 15 vols. (1881-86). The most thorough biographical and critical study, John Clark Jordan's *Robert Greene* (1915), is concerned almost exclusively with the prose fiction; for Greene's plays, see Kenneth Muir, "Robert Greene as Dramatist," in *Essays on Shakespeare and the Elizabethan Drama in Honor of Hardin Craig,* ed. Richard Hosley (1962). There is a Concise Bibliography by S. A. Tannenbaum (1939), updated by "Robert Greene (1945-65)," ed. Robert C. Johnson, *Elizabethan Bibliographies Supplements,* V (1968). See also F. K. Darden, *A Bibliography and Study of the Coney-Catching Pamphlets of Robert Greene* (1952); Tetsumaro Hayashi, *Robert Greene Criticism: A Comprehensive Bibliography* (1971); and *The Predecessors of Shakespeare: A Survey and Bibliography of Recent Studies in English Renaissance Drama,* ed. Terence P. Logan and Denzell S. Smith (1973).

Greene-Harvey-Nashe Controversy. See HARVEY, GABRIEL.

Greville, Fulke, first Baron Brooke (1554-1628). Courtier, poet, and biographer. The son of a wealthy and distinguished Warwickshire family, Greville attended Shrewsbury School and Jesus College, Cambridge. It was at Shrewsbury that he became acquainted with Sir Philip Sidney, the subject of Greville's famous biography, *The Life of Sidney* (1652). Greville and Sidney came to Queen Elizabeth's court together. With Sidney, also, Greville is reputed to have joined the circle of intellectuals calling themselves the AREOPAGUS. Much favored by the queen, Greville held a number of important offices, including secretary for the principality of Wales (1583-1628). James I made him chancellor of the Exchequer (1614-21) and in 1621 elevated him to the peerage and granted him Warwick Castle and Knowle Park. In 1628 he was murdered by an offended servant.

With the exception of a closet drama, *Mustapha* (1609), and a few verses in the anthologies *The Phoenix* and *England's Helicon,* all of Greville's works were published posthumously. His great *Life of Sidney* was written in 1610-12, ALAHAM as early as 1601: but like all of Greville's posthumous works, *Alaham* is difficult to date with certainty. Like *Mustapha,* it is, as Charles Lamb observed, "more of a political treatise than a play." Although cast in remote places and involving exotic characters, both plays press hard on contemporary themes of power and authority, justice and tyranny in the state.

Greville's *Caelica* (1633) is a collection of sonnets, songs, and religious and philosophical poems in a wide variety of meters and on several different themes—Platonism, Calvinism, astrology, love, and courtly life. As a dramatist Greville is chiefly a curiosity; as a poet he is interesting for his occasional brilliance in a variety of styles from purest song to flat and prosaic meditations and biting satires. He is chiefly recalled as the biographer who drew vivid portraits of Sidney, William of Orange, and the queen he served so faithfully.

The standard edition is by G. Bullough, *The Poems and Dramas,* 2 vols. (1939). The best edition of Greville's *Life of Sidney* is that edited by Nowell Smith for the Tudor and Stuart Library (1907). There is an excellent critical study by M. W. Croll, *The Works of Fulke Greville* (1903), and two exhaustive biographical works: Ronald A. Rebholtz, *The Life of Fulke Greville, First Lord Brooke* (1971) and Joan Rees, *Fulke Greville, Lord Brooke, 1554-1628: A Critical Biography* (1971).

Groatsworth of Wit Bought with a Million of Repentance, A. A moral tale by Robert GREENE, first published in 1592. A pamphlet of ROGUE LITERATURE mingling prose with occasional verse, it has little intrinsic literary merit but offers some valuable commentary on English drama and provides the earliest notice of Shakespeare's presence in the London theater. The hero of the tale alludes to Shakespeare as "an upstart crow, beautified with our feathers, that with his tiger's heart wrapped in a player's hide, supposes he is as well able to bombast out a blank verse as the best of you; and being an absolute *Johannes factotum*, is in his own conceit the only Shake-scene in a country." The "you" of Greene's address may well have been such university graduates turned playwrights as Peele, Marlowe, and Nashe; Greene was warning such intellectuals that they could expect to be rivaled by common actors like Shakespeare.

Greene composed his tale during the last year of his life (allegedly on his deathbed), and related something of his own experience in the story of Roberto, a scholar who turns playwright and rogue. The plot begins with Roberto's father Gorinius, a miserly usurer, on his deathbed counseling Lucanio, his heir, to disregard all conscience and accumulate wealth by any means possible. To his other son Roberto, who had objected to the old man's greed, Gorinius bequeaths nothing but a single groat whereby he is advised to purchase "a groatsworth of wit." Roberto forswears all virtue and plots to cheat the ingenuous Lucanio out of his fortune by arranging a marriage between Lucanio and Lamilia, a common whore. Lamilia easily seduces the gullible Lucanio but cynically betrays Roberto, with whom she had originally agreed to share the spoils. Lucanio is bilked of his wealth and turned out into the street in poverty; he becomes a pimp and finally commits suicide. Roberto joins a troupe of actors as a playwright, but he fares scarcely better than Lucanio, turning to petty crime and the company of rogues and prostitutes. At last, despised and full of self-loathing, he is left with nothing but the single groat given to him by his father.

His tale concluded, Greene drops his narrator-hero and begins to speak candidly in his own voice on the vanity of human wishes. This is followed by ten rules for a happy life. Toward the end of the pamphlet (part of which is quoted above) Greene addresses his playwright friends, piously counseling them against atheism, slander (in the form of bitter satire), and actors (a treacherous lot). Aesop's fable of the grasshopper and the ant, Greene moralizes, is the story of his own misdirected life. Like the foolish grasshopper, he played all summer and came to misfortune in the winter. The pamphlet ends with the pious and penitential "A Letter Written to His Wife, Found with This Book after His Death."

A Groatsworth of Wit has been edited, with *The Repentance of Robert Greene*, by G. B. Harrison (1923). Felix E. Shelling's essay on Greene's pamphlet is in *The Queen's Progress and Other Elizabethan Sketches* (1904). See also J. Dover Wilson, "Malone and the Upstart Crow," *ShS,* IV (1951). Employing data gathered by computer, Austin Warren and others have recently concluded that *A Groatsworth* was actually written by Henry CHETTLE, whose apology for the attack on Shakespeare in *Kind Heart's Dream* (1593) represents Chettle's attempt to conceal his authorship. Since Chettle is known to have edited *A Groatsworth*, the hypothesis is not unlikely. At this point, however, evidence of Chettle's authorship remains inconclusive. See Warren, "Technique of the Chettle-Greene Forgery: Supplementary Material on the

Authorship of the *Groatsworth of Wit*," and Louis Marder, "Chettle's Forgery of the *Groatsworth of Wit* and the 'Shake-scene Passage,'" both in *ShN,* XX (1970).

Guarini, Giovanni Battista (1537-1612). Italian poet whose tragicomic pastoral drama *Il pastor fido* (Venice, 1580-89), translated as *The Faithful Shepherd* (by Edward Dymock, 1602; Jonathan Sidnam, 1630; Sir Richard Fanshawe, 1648), influenced the development of Stuart PASTORAL literature. See also TRAGICOMEDY.

Guevara, Antonio de (1474-1546). Spanish author famous in England for his *The Golden Book of Marcus Aurelius*, translated from the French version of René Bertaut in 1531, and rendered into English in 1534 by John Bourchier, Lord Berners. Guevara's *Golden Epistles,* a popular collection of letters, was translated by Sir Geoffrey Fenton in 1575. See LETTER-WRITERS.

Gull's Hornbook, The. A satirical pamphlet by Thomas DEKKER, first published in 1609. In Elizabethan slang a "gull" is a dupe or natural fool, a "hornbook" a child's alphabet mounted on a small board with a handle (and thus suitable, also, for beating on the child's bottom). Thus Dekker's title indicates that it purports to be an ironic primer or elementary teaching device to instruct gulls in the kind of conduct that will make them even more foolish and credulous. Dekker's chief source was a crude Latin poem, *Grobianus*, by Frederick Dedekind (c. 1525-1598); it first appeared in Latin in 1549, again in 1552 in an enlarged edition. It was translated from Latin into English in 1605 by one "R.F." as *The School of Slovenry; Or, Cato Turned Wrong Side Outward.* In Dekker's preface "To the Reader" in *The Gull's Hornbook* he acknowledges that his book contains a "relish of *Grobianisme*, and tastes very strongly of it in the beginning..."

Everything except the general idea of the satire, however, is uniquely Dekker's and based on his own sharp observation of the customs, fashions, and follies of his day. The book consists of a prologue and eight chapters. In the prologue he promises to sing like a cuckoo in June, but only to silly gulls. Chapter One continues the same line of mock solicitude for fools begun in the prologue; he promises to purge the age of its twin foibles of vanity (clothes) and luxury (gluttony and drunkenness), but such a cleansing, he notes, will prove more laborious than Hercules' labour in the Augean stables.

Chapter Two establishes the form of the mock precept or "rule" by which the gull must live if he is to perfect his folly, and the first of these is on arising in the morning: he must always sleep until noon because lolling in bed saves wear on clothes and the expense of breakfast. Chapter Three advises the gull on how to behave after arising, especially on a chilly day. Chapter Four offers advice on how to walk in public at St. Paul's, the natural habitat of all aspiring fools. Chapter Five recommends rules on how to behave at an inn during and after supper. Chapter Six, one of the liveliest and most vivid, explains conduct appropriate in a public playhouse. The gull is advised to sit on the stage, pass comments on the play during its progress, feel the clothes of the actors, and stalk out before the play is ended so that the audience will receive the full benefit of his elegant clothes and noisy judgment. Moreover, advises Dekker: "It shall crown you with rich commendation, to laugh aloud in the midst of the most serious and saddest scenes of the terriblest tragedy, and to let that clapper (your tongue) be tossed so high that all the house may ring of it..." In Chapter Seven the gull is instructed on deportment proper to fools in a tavern, and Chapter Eight takes the gull past the night watch and home to his "punk," or mistress. Thus Dekker's day in the life of a London gull, burlesque as it is, provides a rich source of information about Elizabethan manners and morals.

The standard edition of *The Gull's Hornbook* is by R. B. McKerrow (1904).

Gypsies Metamorphosed, The. A masque by Ben JONSON, first performed August 3, 1621, at an entertainment for James I at the marquess of Buckingham's estate, Burley-on-the-Hill, Rutlandshire. At the request of the king it was repeated two days later at Belvoir Castle in Leicestershire, and again at Windsor in September. Jonson made extensive revisions for the performance at Windsor, interpolating several allusions to the place and changing parts to suit male performers who had replaced the ladies at Burley. The masque was published in two editions in 1640, one in duodecimo, the other in Jonson's folio. His principal source was Dekker's *Lantern and Candlelight,* which he consulted for its gypsy cant.

The masque consists of five formal dances separated by songs and interludes. The second dance contains six "strains" or movements, between which the gypsies tell the fortunes of the nobles present. The fortune of the king, however, is read by the captain, a role taken by the marquess of Buckingham:

For this of all the world you shall
Be styled James the Just, and all
Their states dispose, their sons and daughters;
And for your fortune you alone,
Among them all, shall work your own
By peace and not by human slaughters.

A unique feature of Jonson's masque is the assignment of difficult speaking parts to nobles. Only the two hardest roles (of Jackman and Patrico) were taken by professional singers. *The Gypsies* is Jonson's most elaborate masque, a skillful blending of robust humor and delicate wit. For comment on other of Jonson's entertainments, see MASQUE.

The standard edition is in *Ben Jonson,* ed. C. H. Herford and Percy and Evelyn Simpson, 11 vols. (1925-53), VII. There is a manuscript version in the Huntington Library that has been reproduced by G. W. Cole for the Modern Language Association (1931). Stephen Orgel has edited *The Complete Masques* (1969) in the Yale Ben Jonson series. For commentary, see *Jonson's Masque of Gypsies: An Attempt at Reconstruction,* ed. W. W. Greg (1952), and Irena Janicka, "The Popular Background of Ben Jonson's Masques," *SJW,* CV (1969). See also John C. Meagher, *Method and Meaning in Jonson's Masques* (1966).

H

Hake, Edward (fl. 1574-79). See SATIRE.

Hakluyt, Richard (1552?-1616). Geographer. The younger of two cousins who bore the same name and who shared in collecting materials relevant to the maritime expansion of Elizabethan England, Richard Hakluyt compiled and published the encyclopedic *The Principal Voyages, Navigations, Traffics, and Discoveries of the English Nation . . .* (first ed. 1589; enlarged 3-vol. ed. 1598-1600). His older cousin was a lawyer of the Middle Temple. The renowned geographer was a clergyman who had been educated at Westminster School, London, and Christ Church College, Oxford. See HAKLUYT'S VOYAGES.

Hakluyt's Voyages. An anthology of explorations collected by Richard HAKLUYT. In 1582 he published his first collection, *Divers Voyages Touching the Discovery of America*, and in 1589 *The Principal Navigations, Voyages, and Discoveries of the English Nation Made by Sea or over Land;* these were enlarged to three volumes printed successively from 1598 to 1600 as *The Principal Navigations, Voyages, Traffics, and Discoveries of the English Nation.* It is this expanded version that is known as *Hakluyt's Voyages*. Their continuation was provided for when Hakluyt bequeathed his manuscripts to Samuel Purchas, who published *Hakluytus Posthumus, or Purchas His Pilgrims* in 1625.

Hakluyt's avowed purpose in collecting these accounts of English explorations from their legendary beginnings to the seventeenth century was to exhibit the daring and enterprise of his countrymen and thus "stop the mouth of our reproachers"—namely, the French. A more practical reason was to provide information about English overseas companies in order to attract investors; Hakluyt himself owned stock in the East Indies and Virginia companies.

Hakluyt's first volumes, *Divers Voyages,* describe thirty-eight explorations of the English from the mythical voyage of King Arthur to Iceland down to the defeat of the Spanish Armada and the earl of Essex's victory over the Spanish at Cádiz. The last account was dropped from the second edition after Essex's disgrace and execution.

Hakluyt's second collection, *Principal Navigations,* consists of sixty-three voyages, eleven of which took place before the Norman Conquest. The earliest is that of Helena, wife of a Roman emperor and daughter of Coelus, king of Britain, who went to Jerusalem in 337 A.D. to collect holy relics and construct churches. Several of these early voyages also tell of Englishmen who joined with other Europeans to help restore Jerusalem to Christianity during the Crusades.

Divers Voyages and *Principal Navigations* were incorporated into the expanded version, the last part of which is concerned entirely with discoveries in the Americas. The first account relates a voyage supposedly made to the West Indies in 1170 by Madoc, son of a Welsh prince; later voyages include those by John Cabot, John Davis, and Martin Frobisher in their search for a northwest passage to the fabulous riches of the Orient. There are also descriptions of voyages to Newfoundland, of explorations of the St. Lawrence River beginning with Sir Humphrey Gilbert's, of English and Spanish expeditions along the California coast, and of Sir Francis Drake's circumnavigation of the world. In a later and separate publication, *Virginia Richly Valued* (1609), Hakluyt made an effort to stimulate interest in Sir Walter Raleigh's Virginia colony. See RALEIGH, SIR WALTER.

The beautifully printed edition of the *Voyages* by the Hakluyt Society consists of no fewer than twelve large volumes containing over one hundred lengthy narratives by almost as many writers. Some of these accounts, scribbled into logbooks by ordinary sailors, are almost poignantly crude; others, like Raleigh's vivid and imaginary descriptions of strange places, customs, and peoples, and hair-breadth escapes from the hostile Spanish and the natural elements, are so well written as to make up a body of literature on the highest level of prose. Taken together, these volumes comprise a saga of the English people as strange and fascinating as any fiction, an epic of man's incredible determination and courage, his iron will and persistent dignity in the face of hunger, loneliness, and death.

In compiling his *Voyages* Hakluyt worked closely with his older cousin (also named Richard); the older Richard gathered much of the material that had been arranged, edited, and translated by the famous younger cousin.

Hakluyt's augmented edition of three volumes (1598-1600) has been reprinted by the Hakluyt Society, 12 vols. (1903-05). Selections from the *Voyages* have been edited by Laurence Irving (1926); Janet Hamden (1958), with an extensive bibliography; and Irwin R. Blacker in a Viking Portable Library edition (1965). The Hakluyt Society has published a collection of essays on Hakluyt, Purchas, and later anthologists in *Richard Hakluyt and His Successors,* ed. Edward Lynam (1946). See also G. B. Parks, *Richard Hakluyt and the English Voyages* (1928), and Samuel Eliot Morison, *The European Discovery Of America: The Northern Voyages, 500-1600* (1971); *The Southern Voyages, 1492-1616* (1974). For Hakluyt's life and times, see Foster Watson, *Richard Hakluyt* (1924), and *The Original Writings and Correspondence of the Two Richard Hakluyts,* ed. Eva G. R. Taylor, 2 vols. (1935).

Hall, Joseph (1574-1656). Poet, theologian, miscellanist. Hall was born at Bristow Park, Ashby-de-la-Zouch, the son of a deputy of the earl of Huntingdon. Hall's mother was a strict Puritan, a fact that may account to some degree for his tolerance of that sect in his later theological controversies. After attending grammar school at Ashby, Hall proceeded to Emmanuel College, Cambridge, in 1589, graduating B.A. in 1592, M.A. in 1596. A brilliant scholar, he was made a fellow in 1595 and later received two additional degrees (B.D., 1603; D.D. 1612).

Although Hall wrote a number of Latin verses, after Juvenal, *Virgidemiarum* (Books I-III, elegies, and pastorals at Cambridge, his first commendable work was a long satire modeled 1597; Books III-VI, 1598). Hall's roughhewn and scurrilous verses (the title means "a harvest of switches") were answered bitterly by John Marston, who was outraged by Hall's attack on contemporary writers, and the two authors exchanged satires so acerbic that John Whitgift, the Archbishop of Canterbury, ordered these diatribes burned in June 1599. In his preface to *Virgidemiarum,* Hall proudly deemed himself the "first English satirist," apparently unaware of previous satires by Skelton, Wyatt, Gascoigne, and others. Nevertheless, Hall's *Virgidemiarum,* if not unique, was partly responsible for launching the vogue for satire in the 1590s (see SATIRE).

Sometime around 1600 Hall took holy orders and was assigned to Halsted parish, where he wrote his first version of *Meditations and Vows Divine and Moral* (pr.1605). By 1603 he had published his last volume of secular verse, *The King's Prophecy, or Weeping Joy,* a collection celebrating the accession of James I. Shortly thereafter he resided for a time at Spa in the Low Countries, where, he later claimed, he disguised himself as a layman and disputed theological points with the Jesuits. His experiences in Spa are recounted in the second version of his prose *Meditations and Vows* (1606).

Hall's *Mundus alter et idem,* an important if not particularly distinguished contribution to utopian literature, was published in Latin at Frankfurt in 1605, later translated by John Healey into English in 1609 as *Discovery of a New World.* Described by Healey as a "political romance," Hall's utopia illustrates its author's penchant for experimenting in a wide variety of genres. Like Nicholas Breton, Hall produced a range of literature that represents almost every Elizabethan genre except the sonnet sequence—UTOPIAN FICTION, PASTORAL, SATIRE, LETTER-WRITERS, CHARACTERS, ESSAYS, meditations, and religious polemics.

Hall's career as a churchman prospered after his appointment in 1608 as chaplain to Prince Henry. He was made curate at Waltham, then bishop of Exeter (1627), and bishop of Norwich (1641). In 1616 he attended Lord Doncaster in a diplomatic mission to France, and upon his return the following year accompanied James I to Scotland for the purpose of introducing the Anglican liturgy in the Scottish kirks. Although Hall roused the king's anger for being excessively sympathetic to the Puritans, he was restored to favor by his diplomatic conduct at the Synod of Dort, where he advocated moderation, charity, and tolerance.

Hall continued to write prose works on a wide variety of subjects. His *Epistles* (1608) is an entertaining letter-writer intended as a practical guide for ministers; his *Characters of Vices and Virtues* (1608) is a collection of characters and essays that is important for introducing into English a type of character based on Theophrastus. Increasingly, Hall found himself engaged in religious controversy. He attacked the sectarian radicals called Brownists in *A Common Apology Against the Brownists* (1610), and under Charles I became a chief defender of episcopacy against the Puritans. Although Charles I favored him with the bishopric at Exeter, Archbishop Laud, suspecting Hall of latent Puritan sympathies, harassed him with spies and trumped-up allegations of disloyalty.

Hall became the target of John MILTON'S indignant pen when Hall published *A Humble Remonstrance to the High Court of Parliament* and *Episcopacy by Divine Right* (both in 1640), in which he defended the Anglican liturgy and church government against the Calvinists. Hall's tract was answered by five Puritans calling themselves "Smectymnuus." Hall responded with his *Defense of that Remonstrance,* which "Smectymnuus" answered with *A Vindication.* During these and subsequent exchanges, Milton contributed five tracts vigorously defending "Smectymnuus" and attacking Hall and the Anglican bishops.

In 1641, on the eve of the Civil War, Hall was among thirteen bishops recommended for impeachment by the Puritan-dominated Parliament. Ironically, he had been bishop of Norwich less than a year. After a brief incarceration in the Tower in December, Hall retired to Norwich, where he continued his pastoral duties until forced from the cathedral by the Puritans in April 1643. These difficult times are recounted in Hall's prose work *A Hard Measure* (1647). The last ten years of his life were spent at Higham, a small village near Norwich, where he finished his days in poverty and diligent study.

Not the least of Hall's literary achievements was a direct, plain, and energetic prose style that earned him the epithet "the English Seneca." In his essays and characters that terse and vigorous style marks him as a leading exponent of a Senecan prose in opposition to the ornate Ciceronian rhetoric popular during the sixteenth century. Only a few of Hall's voluminous theological works have been cited here. A single treatise, *Contemplations upon the Principal Passages of the Holy Story* (1612-26), comes to no fewer than eight lengthy volumes.

The definitive biography is by A. Davenport and T. E. Kinloch, *The Life and Works of Joseph Hall* (1951). The *Collected Poems* —all of Hall's English verse—was edited by A. Davenport (1949). Hall's *Virgidemiarum* is also in *The Works of the English Poets,* ed. Alexander Chalmers. 21 vols. (1810), V. Hall's prose style is analyzed in Philip A. Smith, "Bishop Hall, 'Our English Seneca,' " *PMLA,* LXIII (1948). The poems are discussed by Arnold Stein. "Joseph Hall's Imitation of Juvenal," *MLR,* XLIII (1948); H. H. Hudson *The Epigram in the English Renaissance*

(1947); and Bernard Harris, *Elizabethan Poetry* (1961).

Hamlet. A tragedy by William SHAKESPEARE, probably written in 1600-01 and first published in the pirated "bad quarto" of 1603. Two authoritative editions followed in 1604 and 1623 (First Folio). No source for the play has been found. It may have been derived from an "Ur-Hamlet," a nonextant earlier play known to have been performed in London in 1589. The author of the Ur-Hamlet may have been Thomas Kyd. Its characteristics have been inferred from a seventeenth-century German play, *Der Bestrafte Bruder-Mord* ("Fratricide Punished"), which is believed to have been based on the same source Shakespeare consulted in writing *Hamlet.* The story of Hamlet was orally established in Old Norse and Icelandic tales, and was first given literary form in a story in *Historiae Danicae* (c. 1200) by the Danish historian Saxo Grammaticus (1150?-1206). Saxo's version, with some changes, appears in the fifth volume of François de Belleforest's *Histoires tragiques* (1559), and Shakespeare, or the author of the Ur-Hamlet, may have read the story in Belleforest.

Prince Hamlet's mother, Queen Gertrude, is married with unseemly haste to her deceased husband's brother Claudius, who, as king of Denmark, must deal with two issues: Hamlet's deep resentment of the marriage, and the military ambitions of young Fortinbras, prince of Norway and son of the dead King Hamlet's old enemy, whose threats of invasion have turned Denmark into an armed camp.

King Hamlet's ghost appears to Hamlet, reveals that Claudius murdered him and usurped the throne, and demands that Hamlet take revenge against the new king (although of Queen Gertrude, whose complicity is left ambiguous, the ghost says, "leave her to heaven"). Several times during the play Hamlet reflects on his inability to act on the ghost's command. While he ponders how to exact revenge, he feigns madness, and in this guise frightens his beloved, Ophelia. Her father Polonius, aged counselor to Claudius, attributes Hamlet's odd behavior to melancholy induced by frustrated passion for Ophelia; Polonius had ordered his daughter to stop seeing the prince.

To goad Claudius into revealing his guilt, and test the validity of the ghost (and perhaps the extent of Gertrude's guilt), Hamlet arranges with a group of visiting actors to perform at court "The Murder of Gonzago," a drama that reenacts a murder much like that of King Hamlet. Claudius betrays his guilt when during the play he leaps up and flees to his chamber. Hamlet, unseen by Claudius, follows him there and observes him attempting to pray. After debating with himself, the prince spares Claudius, reasoning that a more condign revenge would catch the king in some mortal sin and thus send him to damnation. In Gertrude's bedchamber, Hamlet subjects his mother to a wild tirade about her hasty marriage and begs her not to bed again with Claudius. During this altercation the ghost reappears to Hamlet and reminds him of his "blunted purpose." Meanwhile, Polonius has been hiding behind an arras in the bedchamber; mistaking him for Claudius, Hamlet stabs him through the curtain.

Ostensibly to avoid scandal resulting from Polonius' death, Claudius sends Hamlet to England with the prince's former schoolmates Rosencrantz and Guildenstern. Two days at sea, Hamlet leaps aboard an attacking pirate ship, and the pirates take him back to Denmark. He tells his friend Horatio that, suspicious of a sealed document carried by Rosencrantz and Guildenstern, he had stolen it and found it was an order for his execution by the English king, signed by Claudius; whereupon he had forged a new commission ordering instead the deaths of his false friends.

During Hamlet's absence Ophelia, deranged with grief, has drowned herself. Her brother Laertes, who has sworn to take revenge against the killer of his father, fights furiously with Hamlet when the prince appears at Ophelia's burial. Later, Claudius easily enlists Laertes in a plot to destroy Hamlet. A fencing match is arranged, and both Laertes' sword and a goblet from which Hamlet is to drink between bouts are poisoned. In the final scene, however, Claudius' conspiracy miscarries: Gertrude drinks from the goblet; Laertes wounds the prince with the poisoned blade; then the weapons become switched and Laertes is flicked with his own sword. As he dies, Laertes confesses his guilt and names Claudius the culprit. Hamlet kills Claudius and as he himself dies in the arms of his friend Horatio, makes known his wish that Fortinbras succeed to the Danish throne.

Hamlet is made up of all the stock ingredients that went into that ragout of Senecan tragedy, Thomas Kyd's *Spanish Tragedy*—revenge, a ghost, real and feigned insanity, a play-within-the-play, suicide, court intrigue, and melancholy soliloquies—yet Shakespeare's powerful philosophical drama sublimely transcends this stale Elizabethan recipe. He complicates his hero's motives with ambiguous, enigmatic actions and speeches, and he employs the traditional soliloquy not to impart vital information to the audience but to obfuscate and even contradict the hero's thoughts and situation. Unlike Shakespeare's other tragedies, *Hamlet* is pure dissonance without any hint of resolution.

The main source of tension, Hamlet's delay, has caused enough critical speculation since the eighteenth century to fill a score of bookshelves. According to Goethe, Hamlet delays in fulfilling his obligation of revenge because he is a "sensitive plant" too delicate for such savage business. In an equally famous interpretation, Coleridge argued that Hamlet procrastinates because he is too intellectual for the kind of spontaneous action required for vengeance. A. C. Bradley proposed that Hamlet's delay is caused by a profound melancholy brought on by his father's death, and that Shakespeare's audience would have recognized Hamlet's behavior as clearly symptomatic of this mental disorder. Bradley's psychological perspective opened the way for Ernest Jones, Freud's disciple, who described Hamlet's derangement as the result of an unconscious incestuous attachment to Gertrude that caused him to identify with his mother's lover.

In spite of this recurring question of Hamlet's delay—and there are even critics who maintain there is none, contrary to Hamlet's own protestations—the play poses many equally baffling problems: Is Hamlet mad, or only feigning insanity? Is the ghost real or a hallucination? What is the extent of Gertrude's complicity in the murder of King Hamlet? What accounts for Hamlet's strange preoccupation with his own guilt? Why does he abuse Ophelia? Are his reasons for not killing Claudius at prayer what he claims (III, *iii*) or only rationalizations? These and many other enigmatic questions have made *Hamlet,* in C. F. Tucker Brooke's words, "a perfect tabernacle of the modern questioning brain," or, in James Joyce's facetious observation, "the happy hunting-ground for all those who have lost their minds."

The hero is so ambiguous that every actor who has distinguished himself in the role has portrayed a different character. John Barrymore's Hamlet was extroverted and wildly antic, whereas John Gielgud's was crisp, delicate, and introverted. In contrast, Maurice Evans presented a Hamlet who was virile, clean-cut, and a little shallow in the style of the American and English adolescents of the 1940s. Laurence Olivier's Hamlet (based largely on Ernest Jones' analysis) proved to be deeply neurotic and looked to be at least ten years older than Gertrude. To date, it would seem that actors and critics have not plumbed the heart of Hamlet's mystery.

The standard text is the New Cambridge edition, ed. J. Dover Wilson (1934). Goethe's analysis of Hamlet—actually a digression in a novel—is in his *Wilhelm Meister's Apprenticeship* (1795-96); Samuel Taylor Coleridge's observations can be found in his *Shakespearean Criticism,* ed. T. M. Raysnor (1960), and Bradley's work on *Hamlet* in *Shakespearean Tragedy* (1904). The book by Ernest Jones is *Hamlet and Oedipus* (1949). There is an exhaustive survey of *Hamlet* criticism from the seventeenth century to 1971 by Edward Quinn in *The Major Shakespearean Tragedies* (1973).

Harington, Sir John (1561-1612). Poet and translator, Harington was born at Kelston near Bath, the son of John Harington and Isabella Markham. His godmother was Queen Elizabeth. He attended Eton and King's College, Cambridge, proving himself a desultory and indifferent student, and enrolled at Lincoln's Inn. Upon his father's death he returned to Kelston in 1582 and occupied himself with various hydraulic experiments with new types of fountains.

There is a story that while at court Harington translated the naughty tale of Giacomo in Book 28 of Ariosto's *Orlando Furioso* and that as a penalty Queen Elizabeth ordered him to translate the whole epic before being allowed to return to court. In any event, Harington's version of *Orlando Furioso,* one of the major achievements of translation, was published in 1591 with a witty preface on the subject of heroic verse (see TRANSLATION).

Harington's Rabelaisian *Metamorphosis of Ajax* (1596) appeared under the pseudonym "Misacmos." Complete with diagrams, it is a comprehensive and often humorous plan for the installation of indoor plumbing, providing instructions on "how unsavory places may be made sweet." Harington's three sections on the water closet pun consistently on "jakes" (meaning "privy" and pronounced "jake-us") and may have inspired the name of Shakespeare's Jaques in *As You Like It.* Elizabeth, imagining some subtle allusions to Leicester in Harington's treatise, ordered him from court "till he be sober grown." Nevertheless, she had his water closet installed at Richmond Palace —making Harington's the first such plumbing facility in England.

By 1599 Harington was sufficiently restored to royal favor to accompany Essex to Ireland, probably as a spy reporting directly to the queen. During Elizabeth's declining years he secretly favored James VI as her successor and was knighted for his services when the king assumed the throne in 1603. Harington continued in favor at court until his death. In 1607 he published *A Brief View of the State of the Church* for the personal instruction of Prince Henry. His numerous letters were published in 1769 as *Nugae antiquae.*

Harington's *Epigrams* (pr. 1613, with many subsequent editions), his translations, and his works on hygiene show him to have been a keen student of classical and continental literature. A major influence on Harington's work was Rabelais, with whom he shared a bawdy wit, a penchant for mild irreverence, and a dedication to reason and science.

The standard edition of Harington's *Letters and Epigrams,* with a biographical account, is by N. E. McClure (1930). T. Rich has done a critical study of Harington as a translator in *Harington and Ariosto* (1940), and the influence of Rabelais is treated by Huntington Brown, *Rabelais in English Literature* (1933). Ian Grumble, *The Harington Family* (1957), contains a critical biography. See also T.G.A. Nelson, "Sir John Harington as a Critic of Sir Philip Sidney," *SP,* LXVII (1970).

Harrington, James (1611-1677). See UTOPIAN FICTION.

Hartlib, Samuel (d. 1670). For comment on his *Macaria,* see UTOPIAN FICTION.

Harvey, Gabriel (1545?-1630?). Scholar and critic. Born at Saffron Walden, Harvey was educated at Christ's College, Cambridge, and made lecturer of Greek at Pembroke Hall and later university professor of rhetoric. At Cambridge he began his famous friendship with Edmund Spenser, who portrayed Harvey as "Hobbinol" in *The Shepherd's Calendar* (1579). The two friends exchanged letters, two by Spenser and three by Harvey, in *Three Proper and Witty Familiar Letters* and *Two Other Very Commendable Letters* (both in 1580), which are of interest for their discussion of the adaptation of classical verse forms to English poetry (advocated by Harvey), Harvey's "rules for English versifying" (ignored by Spenser), and Spenser's literary opinions and influences (see CRITICISM, LITERARY, AREOPAGUS). In one of these letters Harvey was thought to have slighted the earl of Oxford, patron of John Lyly, and Lyly responded by twitting Harvey in his anti-Marprelate tract, *Pappe with a Hatchet* (1589). (see MARPRELATE, MARTIN.) To Lyly's side came Robert Greene and later Greene's friend Thomas Nashe; the ensuing exchange of satires is now known as the Greene-Harvey-Nashe controversy.

In the late 1580s the Anglican bishops commissioned Robert Greene to answer the Martin Marprelate tracts, a series of anti-prelatical satires. The extent to which Greene actually contributed his talents to the defense of the bishops is not known; but Gabriel Harvey's younger brother Richard, who was an Anglican minister, charged Greene with being too dissolute for this role in *Plain Perceval the Peace-Maker of England* (1590), and, in *Theological Discourse of the Lamb of God and His Enemies,* which he wrote about the same time, he castigated Thomas Nashe for his arrogant preface to Greene's *Menaphon.* Greene replied to Richard Harvey in *A Quip for an Upstart Courtier* (1592), a malicious ridicule of all the Harveys including their old father, a prosperous rope-maker of Saffron Walden, as well as the three brothers Gabriel, Richard, and John. Unknown to Greene, John Harvey, a physician, died while *A Quip* was at the printer's. When the outraged Gabriel came to London to take legal action against Greene, he learned that his adversary had just died ("of a surfeit of pickled herring and Rhenish wine," according to Harvey's account). To defend his family's honor against Greene's *A Quip,* Harvey began to write his *Four Letters* (1592), but in the middle of the work Nashe came out with *Pierce Penniless* (1592), which contained slurs at Richard Harvey's *Lamb of God.* Consequently, in the third epistle of *Four Letters* Harvey divided his attack between Greene and Nashe, although Harvey expressed his "earnest desire to begin and end such frivolous altercations at once." But the exuberant Nashe had discovered in Gabriel Harvey an ideal target for his venomous pen and dashed off *Strange News of the Intercepting of Certain Letters* (1592). Nashe's defense of Greene in that work expresses admiration for Greene's brilliance as a journalist:

> In a night and a day would he have yark'd up a pamphlet as well as in seven year, and glad was that printer that might be so blessed to pay him dear for the very dregs of his wit.

Nashe's address to Harvey illustrates the slangy, scatalogical style of the pamphlets on both sides throughout the controversy:

> Why, thou arrant butter-whore, thou cotquean and scrattop of scolds, wilt thou never leave afflicting a dead carcass, continually read the rhetoric-lecture of Ram Alley? A wisp, a wisp, a wisp, rip, rip, you kitchen-stuff wrangler...

Harvey's reply, *Pierce's Supererogation* (1593), is a prolix diatribe against not only Greene and Nashe, but John Lyly as well (belatedly, because of Lyly's anti-Martinist tract *Pappe with a Hatchet* in 1589). In the preface to *Christ's Tears Over Jerusalem* (1593), Nashe ventured some conciliatory words, but Harvey may not have read Nashe's preface before the publication of his next attack, *A New Letter of Notable Contents* (1593). In his preface to the second edition of *Christ's Tears* (c. 1594), Nashe angrily retracted his kind words about Harvey and renewed his assault with the most devastating satire of the controversy, *Have With You to Saffron Walden* (1596), a systematic razing of all Gabriel Harvey's literary works. Nashe mockingly dedicated the pamphlet to one Richard Lichfield, a barber at Cambridge. Hence Harvey put the barber's name on the title page as author of his rejoinder, *The Trimming of T. Nashe* (1597). This was the last shot fired, for on June 1, 1599, the bishop of London ordered all Nashe-Harvey pamphlets to be confiscated and prohibited their further publication.

In terms of intrinsic literary value, the Greene-Nashe-Harvey controversy was not very fruitful. Harvey's tracts are uniformly tedious in spite of their occasional outbursts of almost pathological rage; he writes at the top of his lungs, with very limited emotional range, and his satiric muse curses and fumes but rarely bites. Nashe is a verbal athlete with an easy and joyous mastery of all the tricks of satire—false panegyric, diminution, hyperbole, grotesque word coinage, mock solemnity, and the rest—but his flabby and ungainly opponent Harvey provides Nashe with little more than an occasion for burlesque and word games, not a viable moral challenge. After reading the pamphlets, one cannot resist thinking of the cliché "tempest in a teapot." The combatants never convince the reader that they feel their wounds very deeply.

The latent issues in the controversy—issues of which the disputants may not have been fully aware—were of considerable significance, for they underscored the changing role of the writer in Elizabethan society. As a self-conscious intellectual and academician, Gabriel Harvey identified himself with a tradition of erudition in literature extending from Chaucer to Sidney and Spenser. Hence Harvey's frequent invocation of the names of Sidney and Spenser in his pamphlets was more than what Nashe accused Harvey of, mere name dropping (although it was that also). Toward the end of Harvey's third epistle in *Four Letters* he lists the learned courtiers and classical scholars of that aristocratic tradition —George Buchanan, Sir Philip Sidney, Edmund Spenser, Richard Stanyhurst, Abraham Fraunce, Thomas Watson, Samuel Daniel, "and the rest whom I affectionately thank for their studious endeavors"—and makes clear that his attack on Greene and Nashe represents a defense of that tradition against all that Greene symbolized—"a lewd fellow and impudent railer," a "common scribbler" of euphuistic romances, popular plays, and journalistic pamphlets. "A mad world where such shameful stuff is bought and sold," lamented Harvey, "and where such roisterly varlets may be suffered to play upon whom they lust and how they lust. Is this Greene, with the running head and the scribbling hand, that never lins [ceases] putting forth new, newer, and newest books of the maker?" Underlying the personal and often trivial invective of the Greene-Nashe-Harvey controversy was Gabriel Harvey's defense of an intellectually elite literary tradition that he firmly believed was threatened by the new popular journalism of Greene and Nashe.

Harvey is best known as the hapless recipient of Nashe's excoriating *Have With You to Saffron Walden* and other satires—as the absurd "Gorboduc Huddleduddle" of Nashe's venomous pen—and as the critic who attempted to discourage Spenser from writing *The Faerie Queene* (he later retracted his objections to the "elvish queen") and unsuccessfully tried to persuade Spenser to adopt classical meters. He is also remembered for his allusion to Shakespeare in a marginal note of his copy of Chaucer's *Canterbury Tales:*

> The younger sort take much delight in Shakespeare's Venus and Adonis; but his Lucrece, and his tragedy of Hamlet, Prince of Denmark, have it in them to please the wiser sort . . .

There is a biography of Harvey by Hans Berli (1913). Harvey's Latin works have been edited by H. S. Wilson and C. A. Forbes (1945). The complete works were edited by A. B. Grosart, 3 vols. (1884-85). For a critical appreciation, see G. M. Young, "A Word for Gabriel Harvey," reprinted in *English Critical Essays: Twentieth Century,* ed. Phyllis M. Jones (1933); and H. S. Wilson, "The Humanism of Gabriel Harvey," *J. Q. Adams Memorial Studies* (1948). See also Virginia Woolf's essay "The Strange Elizabethans" in *The Second Common Reader* (1932). The Greene-Harvey-Nashe controversy is described in *The Works of Thomas Nashe,* ed. Ronald B. McKerrow, 5 vols., I (1904; new edition with corrections, ed. F. P. Wilson, 5 vols., I, 1958).

Have With You to Saffron Walden. See NASHE, THOMAS.

Henry IV, Parts I and II. A history play by William SHAKESPEARE. Part I, probably written in 1597, shortly after *Richard II,* was first printed in 1598 with the title "The History of Henry the Fourth, With the Battle at Shrewsbury, between the King and Lord Henry Percy, Surnamed Henry Hotspur of the North." Part II, written in 1598, was first printed in 1600. For his sources Shakespeare consulted the second edition of Holinshed's *Chronicles* (1587), Samuel Daniel's *The Civil Wars* (1595), and an anonymous play, *The Famous Victories of Henry V* (1594). In this last source Shakespeare found the name of Sir John Oldcastle, a Protestant martyr, which he changed to Sir John Falstaff when Oldcastle's relatives protested. Shakespeare's characterization of Owen Glendower is based on Thomas Phaer's contribution to *A Mirror for Magistrates* (1559). The reference to Hal's having been imprisoned briefly by the chief justice for misconduct (Part II) may have been taken from details in Sir Thomas Elyot's *The Governor* (1531). Shakespeare's *Henry IV,* Parts I and II, together with *Richard II* and *Henry V,* comprise a group of history plays referred to as the Henriad cycle or the second tetralogy (as opposed to the first tetralogy, consisting of the three *Henry VI* plays and *Richard III;* for the significance of these, (see CHRONICLE PLAY).

Part I recounts the rebellion of the Percys and the earl of Douglas, aided by the Welsh leader Owen Glendower and Edmund Mortimer, the latter the brother-in-law of young Henry Percy, nicknamed "Hotspur." While the rebels conspire to seize the crown from Henry IV, the heir to the throne, Prince Hal, sports away his time at the Boar's Head Tavern in the company of jolly Sir John Falstaff and his boon companions, Poins, Bardolph, and Peto. Hal and Poins lure Sir John into robbing some travelers at Gadshill, after which they return disguised to rob Falstaff himself. Afterward Hal is summoned before his father to whom he vows that he will redeem his tarnished honor. Meanwhile the rebels consolidate their powers against the king; Mortimer marries Glendower's daughter, and after some debate the map of England is divided among Hotspur, Glendower, and Mortimer. When the rebels confront the king's forces at Shrewsbury, however, neither Glendower nor Hotspur's father, the earl of Northumberland, appears in the field to support the valiant and rash Hotspur, who is killed by Hal in personal combat. The play concludes with the victory of the king's army at Shrewsbury and the reconciliation of Hal and his father.

Part II concerns the rebellion of Archbishop Scroop, Mowbray, and Hastings, and the conflict between Falstaff and the chief justice about Falstaff's lawlessness. Sent to recruit soldiers against the rebels, Falstaff meets his old schoolmate Justice Shallow and Shallow's colleague Silence, who are so impressed with the fat knight's bravado and alleged intimacy with Hal that Shallow imprudently lends the old rogue a thousand pounds. In Gaultree Forest the rebels meet John of Lancaster, Hal's younger brother, who persuades them that they will receive amnesty if they lay down their arms. When they comply, John of Lancaster executes the rebel leaders on grounds that his integrity does not require keeping his word to traitors. At court, meanwhile, Henry IV steadily declines in health. At his father's bedside, Hal, believing the king to be dead, places the crown on his own head. When Henry awakens to find the crown gone, he upbraids Hal for ingratitude, but after a scene of recriminations and repentance, father and son are reconciled. With the death of the king, Hal is crowned Henry V. When hailed joyously in the street by his old crony Falstaff, Hal angrily rebukes the fat knight, banishes him forever from his royal presence, and allows the chief justice to send him and his riotous companions to prison. Hence Part II concludes with Hal's reconciliation with the chief justice and his rejection of Falstaff.

As in all Shakespeare's historical plays, *Henry IV* alters the facts to improve the drama. Hotspur was really about the same age as Hal's father, but Shakespeare reduces his age to make him Hal's rival and foil. Although the two did not actually meet at Shrewsbury, Shakespeare makes their personal encounter in battle the effective climax of Part I. In his previous history plays, such as the *Henry VI* group, *Richard III,* and *Richard II,* Shakespeare had used comedy sparingly; in *Henry IV* about half the scenes depict the comic antics of Falstaff and his minions. This emphasis on comedy enabled Shakespeare to deal with his serious political story with greater concentration and selectivity; it also freed his genius to write some of the greatest comic scenes in dramatic literature. The scenes at court he cast in blank verse, the comic scenes in prose.

Most critics agree that *Henry IV,* Part I, marks the first totally successful product of Shakespeare's mature talent. The verse is lively and expressive, depending less on formal rhetoric than a sure sense of individual characters. The prose is consistently fluent and colloquial, as if Shakespeare had emerged from writing *Romeo and Juliet* with an inspired awareness of the great possibilities of the medium. Moreover, for the first time in any of his history plays, every character in the *Henry IV* plays is completely individuated by diction and speech rhythms. Hotspur's dialogue in Part I, for example, teems with its own peculiar energy from his first explosive speech in I, *ii,* where he explains his testy treatment of the king's messenger, to his haunting last words at Shrewsbury:

> But thought's the slave of life, and life
>   Time's fool,
> And Time, that takes survey of all the world,
> Must have a stop. Oh, I could prophesy,
> But that the earthy and cold hand of death
> Lies on my tongue . . .
>
> [V, *iv,* 81-85]

Shakespeare's theme in the *Henry IV* plays is the education of a prince, and in that education time must be mastered before men can be ruled effectively. Like Richard II, Hotspur is "Time's fool," a heroic and romantic figure who recklessly squanders advantages for the sake of gestures and impetuously plunges into disaster out of a prodigal disregard for timing. He seems to be the antithesis of Falstaff, for he lives only for honor whereas Falstaff refuses to acknowledge its validity; yet they are ironically similar, for both live a code unto themselves, and both, like children, exist without regard for the tragic element of time. "What a devil hast thou to do with the time of day?" Hal asks Falstaff. "Unless hours were cups of sack, and minutes capons, and clocks the tongues of bawds, and dials the signs of leaping houses, and the blessed sun himself a fair hot wench in flame-colored taffeta, I see no reason why thou shouldst be so superfluous to demand the time of day" (Part I: I, *ii,* 1ff).

Unlike Hotspur or Falstaff, Hal employs time cautiously. Like his father, he is calculating and wily, and even his feigned prodigality is only a stratagem for making time show him to best advantage:

My reformation, glittering o'er my fault,
Shall show more goodly and attract more eyes
Than that which hath no foil to set it off.
I'll so offend, to make offense a skill,
Redeeming time when men think least I will.
[I, *ii,* 236-40]

Falstaff is a kind of pot-bellied Peter Pan, a symbol of eternal childhood; but he is also patterned after a variety of types in drama, folklore, and myth, being derived from the sportive Vice of the morality plays, the mock King of Fools of medieval folk festivities, and the MILES GLORIOSUS of Roman comedy. His wit is indomitable, his sophistry as elusive as smoke. Much of the fun in Part I consists of Hal, Poins, and Bardolph attempting to drive the wily old fox into a hole. The efforts are futile because the quarry is so protean, so capable of turning himself at will into euphuistic courtier, moralizing Puritan, reckless highwayman, or true-blue Englishman. He is a confidence man *par excellence,* as well as whoremaster, thief, and glutton; miraculously, he is also innocuous and essentially innocent in his amorality, and Shakespeare is careful to preserve his comic integrity by never allowing his vices to tempt or taint the young prince. Thus the much-discussed debate over whether Falstaff was a "coward" may force the old rogue into a false role. To Falstaff "the better part of valor is discretion" (V, *iv,* 120) and honor "a mere scutcheon" (V, *i,* 142). In this context, ideas like honor and courage are not only inapplicable but destructive to Shakespeare's ironic contrast between Falstaff's amorality and Hotspur's illusory "honor."

In Part II Falstaff's vices become more coarse and threatening than in Part I, and this comic *hubris* prepares the way for Hal's brutal rejection of him at the end of the play. In Part I Falstaff's ironic counterpart was Hotspur, or immaturity personified; in Part II he is placed in direct opposition to the values represented by the lord chief justice and hence becomes Lawlessness. He also relinquishes some of the audience's sympathy when he fails to adjust to Hal's new role as king and thus betrays a signal absence of that flexible sense of humor which had been his one saving grace and source of power.

A standard edition of Part I is the new Arden, ed. A. R. Humphreys (1960); Part II has been edited for the New Variorum series by Matthias Shaaber (1940). Some important studies include J. Dover Wilson, *The Fortunes of Falstaff* (1943); E. M. W. Tillyard, *Shakespeare's History Plays* (1946); Lily B. Campbell, *Shakespeare's Histories* (1947); D. A. Traversi, *Shakespeare from Richard II to Henry V* (1957); Philip Williams, "The Birth and Death of Falstaff Reconsidered," *SQ,* VII (1957); C. L. Barber, *Shakespeare's Festive Comedy* (1959); Alvin Kernan, "The Henriad: Shakespeare's Major History Plays," *YR,* LIX (1969); and Elsa Sjoberg, "From Madcap Prince to King: The Evolution of Prince Hal," *SQ,* XX (1969). Criticism and sources are collected in *Shakespeare: Henry IV, Parts I and II: A Casebook,* ed. G. K. Hunter (1970).

Henry V. A history play by William SHAKESPEARE, written around 1599 and first printed in a very corrupt edition in 1600. As sources Shakespeare used the second edition of Holinshed's *Chronicles* (1587), Edward Hall's *Union of the Two Noble and Illustrious Families of Lancaster and York* (1548), and, to a lesser extent, Robert Fabyan's *New Chronicles of England and France* (1516). Shakespeare may also have relied upon a nonextant play referred to by the theater manager Philip Henslowe and performed by the Queen's Men during the period 1595-96. Another anonymous play, *The Famous Victories of Henry V,* entered in the Stationers' Register on May 14, 1594, is now known to be a later play than the lost one referred to by Henslowe and was probably not a source for Shakespeare's *Henry V.*

King Henry lays claim to the French crown by virtue of his descent from Isabella of France, mother of his great-grandfather, Edward III, and this claim is symbolically rebuked when the dauphin sends him a taunting gift of tennis balls—a contemptuous reminder of the king's less solemn and responsible youth. During the king's preparations for invading France, the earl of Cambridge, Lord Scroop, and Sir Thomas Grey are executed as traitors in league with the French. As in the *Henry IV* plays, Sir John Falstaff's friends play their comic roles, though the fat knight is absent. Mistress Quickly, hostess of the Boar's Head Tavern, tearfully reports the death of Falstaff to his cronies, Ancient Pistol, Nym, and Bardolph.

Unimpressed by the French king's offer of his daughter Katherine in marriage and a few small French dukedoms, Henry invades France and conquers the city of Harfleur. Advancing to Picardy in spite of famine and fatigue, Henry is met by the French herald Mountjoy, who brazenly cautions Henry of the great ransom he will have to pay if captured. The night before the battle at Agincourt, Henry walks incognito among his soldiers and reflects on the cares of kings. On the day of battle he proudly disclaims any privileges of ransom and inspires his outnumbered troops with an eloquent speech. In the battle that follows the English are victorious, and Henry completes his triumphs in France by gallantly winning the hand of the French king's daughter Katherine.

Henry V is the last play of the Henriad cycle, a tetralogy that includes RICHARD II and HENRY IV, Parts I and II (the last play being produced about a year before *Henry V*). (The earlier tetralogy included the HENRY VI plays and RICHARD III.) At the conclusion of *Henry IV,* Part II, the Epilogue had promised Falstaff's return to the stage:

> If you be not too much cloyed with fat meat, our humble author will continue the story, with Sir John in it, and make you merry with fair Katherine of France. Where, for anything I know, Falstaff shall die of a sweat, unless already a' be killed with your hard opinions, for Oldcastle died a martyr, and this is not the man.

One of the unsolved mysteries of *Henry V* is why Shakespeare chose not to keep this promise. The apologetic reference to Sir John Oldcastle, the Protestant martyr, in the Epilogue to *Henry IV,* Part II may indicate that his relatives were still complaining about Shakespeare's initial use of that name for Falstaff, and that Shakespeare decided to avoid further trouble by dropping the character. Or perhaps he simply wearied of the fat knight: Falstaff's weak characterization in THE MERRY WIVES OF WINDSOR certainly suggests an attrition of inspiration. On the other hand, Shakespeare may have feared that the sensational presence of Falstaff would overshadow that of his hero Henry V, the one English monarch he glorifies without any reservations.

Henry V is best described as a heroic play, for Shakespeare presents his titular hero as the ideal ruler—superb diplomat, courageous soldier, and charming lover. As in the *Henry VI* plays, the French are portrayed as cowardly and effete, scarcely a match for Henry's gallant band of Englishmen. Henry is also Shakespeare's greatest orator; he fires the spirits of his soldiers before Harfleur (III, *i),* calms their fears with quiet persuasion the night before Agincourt (IV, *i,* 247–301), and on the morning of combat delivers the most ringing battle exhortation in Elizabethan drama (IV, *iii,* 19-67). *Henry V* is a colorful pageant and patriotic ritual with little concern for either nuances of character or subtle philosophical discriminations. In the Prologue, Shakespeare invokes a "muse of fire" to inspire a stage large enough to encompass his epic scope:

> Can this cockpit hold
> The vasty fields of France? Or may we cram
> Within this wooden O the very casques
> That did affright the air at Agincourt?

In its own way *Henry V* is as ritualistic, formalized, and stately as *Richard II,* an appropriate paean to victory and political order with which to conclude Shakespeare's second tetralogy of English history plays. For Shakespeare's contribution to the genre, see CHRONICLE PLAY.

The standard text is the new Arden edition, ed. J. H. Walter (1954). For commentary, see W. B. Yeats, "At Stratford on Avon," in *Ideas of Good and Evil* (1903), which contrasts Richard II and Henry V; J. W. Cunliffe, "The Character of Henry V as Prince and King," *ShakS,* ed. Brander Mathews (1916); E. E. Stoll, *Poets and Playwrights* (1930); E. M. W. Tillyard, *Shakespeare's History Plays* (1946); Lily B. Campbell, *Shakespeare's Histories* (1947); Irving Ribner, *The English History Play in the Age of Shakespeare* (1957); D. A. Traversi, *Shakespeare from Richard II to Henry V* (1957); M. M. Reese, *The Cease of Majesty* (1961); and Alvin Kernan, "The

Henriad: Shakespeare's Major History Plays," *YR,* LIX (1969).

Henry VI, Parts, I, II, and III. A trilogy of history plays by William SHAKESPEARE. Part I was written around 1589-90 and first printed in the 1623 Folio; Part II was written in 1590 and printed in 1594; and Part III was written in 1590 and printed in 1595. Shakespeare's sources were Raphael Holinshed's *Chronicles* (1587 ed.) and Edward Hall's *The Union of The Two Noble and Illustrious Families of Lancaster and York* (1548). Joan of Arc's contention with fiends in Part I, V, iii may owe something to Reginald Scot's *Discovery of Witchcraft* (1584).

Part I deals with the wars in France during the early reign of young Henry VI; the rise and fall of Joan of Arc, portrayed as a charlatan and strumpet; and the defeat of the English under Talbot, a heroic leader betrayed or neglected by his countrymen at home. The few scenes taking place in England dramatize the beginning of the Wars of the Roses in 1455. As the play begins word reaches England that Talbot has been captured, Charles the Dauphin crowned at Rheims, and the French possessions won by Henry V are lost or in jeopardy. In London, meanwhile, the two chief counsellors of the youthful king, Humphrey of Gloucester, the lord protector, and Henry Beaufort, bishop of Winchester, compete for power. Even more dangerous to the realm is the quarrel between Richard Plantagenet, self-proclaimed heir of Richard II and head of the house of York, and his rival for the throne John Beaufort, earl of Somerset and head of the Lancastrian family. The Yorkist nobles pluck a white rose to symbolize their allegiance, the Lancastrians take a red, thus beginning the Wars of the Roses prophesied by the bishop of Carlisle at the deposition of Richard II. Richard Neville, earl of Warwick, makes an uneasy and temporary truce between the factions by persuading the king to restore Richard Plantagenet's estates, confiscated by Henry V, and creating him duke of York. The court sets out for Paris to attend Henry's coronation.

Joan of Arc seizes Orleans from the English, who recapture the city (Talbot having been released by ransom). Joan next captures Rouen, but soon loses this also to the heroic Talbot. Torn apart by intrigue between Yorkists and Lancastrians, the English court fails to send reinforcements to Talbot during the French seige of Bordeaux, and the English general dies of a broken heart with his dead son in his arms. The wily Henry Beaufort, newly made cardinal, negotiates a peace that is to be sealed by the marriage of King Henry to the daughter of the earl of Armagnac, but his scheme is dashed when the earl of Suffolk, a leader of the Lancastrians, so fires the king with descriptions of Margaret of Anjou's beauty that Henry breaks his agreement with Armagnac and announces his engagement to Margaret. Part I concludes with Suffolk's cynical prediction that Margaret will reign as queen but he will rule the realm.

In Part II the duke of Gloucester is disgusted to learn that Suffolk has negotiated a marriage with Margaret of Anjou that brings with it no dowry and stipulations the English will relinquish their claims in Anjou and Maine. The Lancastrians defend the marriage against his objections in an effort to remove him from office; Margaret has little affection for her new husband, who is weak-willed, dreamy, and pious, but she conspires with the Lancastrians out of jealousy of the duchess of Gloucester. Soon the duchess is arrested for sorcery and banished to the Isle of Man. Indeed, fiends have delivered to her a strange prophecy: a duke will depose the king, Suffolk will perish by water, and Somerset will suffer misfortune near a castle.

When Gloucester resigns as protector because of his wife's disgrace, the duke of York moves decisively toward the throne. He persuades the earls of Warwick and Salisbury of his rights to the crown, and is only momentarily delayed in his bid for power when Suffolk and Cardinal Beaufort manage to send him on a military expedition to Ireland. Before he departs, York incites the peasant leader Jack Cade to rebel so that he can return to England with an army and seize the throne on the pretext of restoring order. Cade's rebellion receives further impetus when the popular Gloucester is murdered at the behest of Suffolk and Cardinal Beaufort (who dies soon afterward of illness) and the commons demand Suffolk's banishment. The weak king agrees, and as Suffolk departs Queen Margaret confesses her passion for him and they become lovers. Later Suffolk is killed by pirates off the coast of Kent, thus fulfilling the second part of the duchess of Gloucester's prophecy.

Jack Cade invades London, is proclaimed king, but is soon assassinated by his volatile followers. Alarmed and rendered helpless by these developments, King Henry sends word to York that Somerset, York's chief enemy, will be put in the Tower if York agrees to peace. When the king fails in his promise, York joins with the earls of Warwick and Salisbury in battle against the king's forces at St. Albans. York's army is victorious, and in the battle his deformed son Richard (later Richard III) kills Somerset near Castle Inn, thus fulfilling the last part of the duchess of Gloucester's prophecy. As the Lancastrians flee in confusion, York hastens to London to proclaim himself king, an act completing the duchess' prediction.

In Part III York is already on the throne when the timid Henry comes to London to propose a settlement whereby he will remain king and York will be declared Henry's heir. York is inclined to accept, but is dissuaded by his ambitious sons Edward and Richard, who burn to occupy the throne at once. At this point Queen Margaret's army lands in England reinforced by French troops and defeats the Yorkist forces near Wakefield. York's youngest son Edward is tortured to death and York is stabbed by Queen Margaret and her general Lord Clifford after a mock ceremony in which York is crowned with a paper diadem. After the defeat at St. Albans, Warwick joins with York's sons Edward and Richard and defeats Queen Margaret's army. Edward is proclaimed Edward IV, his brother George made duke of Clarence, and Richard named duke of Gloucester. King Henry is clapped in the Tower, Lord Clifford beheaded, and Queen Margaret and her son Edward exiled to France. Warwick begins negotiations to marry the new king to Bona, sister-in-law to Louis XI, but as Warwick is in Paris completing the arrangements, news arrives that Edward has announced his engagement to Lady Elizabeth Grey, widow of Sir Richard Grey, slain at St. Albans. The enraged Warwick denounces the king and allies himself with Queen Margaret and her son, to whom Warwick gives his eldest daughter in marriage as a pledge of his faith.

Soon after Edward's coronation, the Yorkists split into factions, Richard supporting his brother prince Edward against Clarence, who firms up his own cause by marrying Warwick's second daughter. Queen Margaret's army lands in England with the support of Clarence, defeats the Yorkists, and restores Henry to the throne. The fearful Henry shortly abdicates in favor of Warwick and Clarence, pleading that he wishes to live a pious life in retirement. The former Edward IV escapes from prison to Burgundy, returns with an army and marches victoriously on London. Henry is again thrown in the Tower and Edward restored to the throne.

When King Edward meets Warwick and Clarence in battle, Clarence refuses to fight against his own brothers; the Lancastrians are defeated and Warwick killed. Edward later overcomes Queen Margaret in a decisive battle at Tewkesbury; she is captured and her son Edward murdered before her eyes. Edward takes Elizabeth Grey as his bride, Queen Margaret is ransomed by her father, and Richard of Gloucester, the "ragged fatal rock" and "deformed lump" of the house of York, secretly plots to wrest the crown from his elder brothers. His first step in that direction is hastening to London to murder Henry VI in the Tower.

The *Henry VI* trilogy, together with *Richard III,* comprise the first tetralogy of Shakespeare's history plays; the second tetralogy is the Henriad cycle consisting of *Richard II, Henry IV* Parts I and II, and *Henry V.* Shakespeare's treatment of history in the *Henry VI* plays is characteristically unauthentic. Part I, for example, covers events from the funeral of Henry V to the negotiations of marriage between Henry VI and Margaret of Anjou—a dramatic scope that prepares for the internecine wars of Part II—but Shakespeare far exceeds these time limits; the death of Sir John Talbot, powerfully dramatized in Act IV, did not really occur until nine years after these events, and the death of Joan of Arc, reported in Act V, did not happen until twenty-two years later.

The real problems in the *Henry VI* plays do not, however, pertain to historical authenticity—a matter of as little concern to Shakespeare's audience as to a modern one—but to the great difficulty he experienced in harnessing the chaotic events of his sources in the English chronicles. In the Wars of the Roses he found what he hoped was a single, controlling saga, and to this subject he brought a single theme that was both palatable to his audience and consistent with his own personal view of English institutions and history: that divisive factions motivated by ambition and vanity are the principal threat to a commonwealth, and that these factions must be curbed by a powerful central monarch sanctioned by hereditary right, justice, and wisdom. But neither subject nor theme proved sufficient to give dramatic unity to the bewildering variety of characters and episodes in the chronicles. This failure is especially evident in Part I, where the "noble-minded Talbot" emerges as the hero out of a vague mass of unrelated episodes.

Part II is much more emphatic in characterization, and conflict between opposing personalities is more boldly drawn. Young Queen Margaret is especially colorful as a power-hungry, sensual woman who despises her weak and submissive husband and beds with Suffolk out of both lust and political advantage; opposed to this Lancastrian virago is a worthy opponent in the ambitious Richard of York and his monstrous youngest son Gloucester, the emerging "bottled spider" of the Yorkist clan.

Part III is the most fast-moving of the three plays, for its main idea is brutal retribution in the destruction of the cynical Warwick, "the King-Maker," the downfall of proud Queen Margaret, and the cure for one-half of England's sickness in the bloody end of the Lancastrians. The triumph of the Yorkist faction at the conclusion of the play sets the stage for *Richard III,* which depicts the demise of the House of York and the restitution of moral order and political harmony in the almost Christlike deliverance by Henry Tudor, the future Henry VII and Queen Elizabeth's grandfather. For the relationship of the *Henry VI* plays to others of its type, see CHRONICLE PLAY.

Henry VI, Part I, is in the New Cambridge edition, ed. J. Dover Wilson (1952), as is Part II. Parts II and III are somewhat more fully annotated in the new Arden editions, ed. A. S. Cairncross (1957, 1964). Important studies of the plays are by Peter Alexander, *Shakespeare's Henry VI and Richard III* (1929); E. M. W. Tillyard, *Shakespeare's History Plays* (1946); Lily B. Campbell, *Shakespeare's Histories* (1947); F. P. Wilson, *Marlowe and the Early Shakespeare* (1953); C. T. Prouty, *The Contention and Shakespeare's 2 Henry VI* (1954); Irving Ribner, *The English History Play in the Age of Shakespeare* (1957); J. P. Brockbank, "The Frame of Disorder—*Henry VI,*" in *Early Shakespeare,* Stratford-Upon-Avon Studies 3 (1961); and M. M. Reese, *The Cease of Majesty* (1961).

Henry VIII. A history play by William SHAKESPEARE, written in collaboration with John FLETCHER in 1613 and first printed in the 1623 Folio. According to a theory first advanced by James Spedding in 1850 Shakespeare composed the first two scenes of Act I, the third and fourth scenes of Act II, the first two hundred lines of Act IV, and the first scene of Act V, and Fletcher wrote the remainder of the play. Most scholars assign a date of composition shortly before June 29, 1613, at which time the Globe theater burned down when the cannon salute to King Henry VIII in Act I, scene 4, set the playhouse afire. For his sources Shakespeare used Raphael Holinshed's *Chronicles* (1587 ed.) and Edward Hall's *Union of the Twō Noble and Illustrious Families of Lancaster and York* (1548), with some additional details from John Foxe's *Book of Martyrs* (1563) and, to a lesser extent, Samuel Rowley's *When You See Me You Know Me* (1603-05), a play about Henry VIII's reign.

When the duke of Buckingham and his son-in-law, Lord Abergavenny, stand opposed to an economic alliance with the French arranged by Cardinal Wolsey, the cardinal has Buckingham executed. Wolsey also questions the validity of King Henry's marriage to Katharine of Aragon, widow of Henry's brother Arthur, and advises the king to divorce Katharine and marry the duchess of Alençon, sister to the king of France. At a banquet Henry falls in love with Anne Boleyn, although he continues to profess admiration and respect for Queen Katharine. Nonetheless Henry expresses reservations about a marriage that has yielded no male heirs and called into question the legitimacy of his daughter Mary. At an assembly arranged by Wolsey, Katharine effectively defends her title and honor.

As Henry prepares to divorce Katharine and marry Anne Boleyn, Wolsey's scheming on behalf of the duchess of Alençon and his secret negotiations with Rome, together with his sumptuous living, increasingly alienate the king. Finally Henry discharges Wolsey, confiscates his property, and names Thomas Cranmer archbishop of Canterbury. As Henry and Anne Boleyn are married at Westminster Abbey, Katharine has a dream in which six white-robed figures appear to bid her a solemn farewell. The bishop of Winchester and Sir Thomas Lovell plot to discredit Cranmer, but the king expresses his confidence in his archbishop by naming him godfather of his new daughter Elizabeth. Holding the future Queen Elizabeth in his arms, Cranmer prophesies that she will bring "a thousand thousand blessings" and a golden age to England.

Henry VIII is more of a static and scenic pageant than a drama of strong conflicts and characters. The events portrayed were within the living memory of many of Shakespeare's audience, and the historical issues were still regarded as sensitive; Fletcher and Shakespeare do not, understandably, deal with these events and characters with much boldness. Henry is portrayed as the bluff, hearty, plain-spoken "King Hal" of the chronicles, and all the political misfortunes of the time are attributed to the discredited Cardinal Wolsey, who is shown as an ambitious schemer and manipulator with aspirations of becoming pope. In contrast, Thomas Cranmer is meek and self-effacing, but this subservience is not presented as being especially virtuous. The scene in which Henry falls in love with Anne Boleyn during a masque at Wolsey's palace is not in the chronicles and was wholly invented by the authors, who present the episode without any noticeable bias. The controversial Anne Boleyn is drawn with equal objectivity, albeit in one scene (II, *iii*) she reveals a somewhat scheming and cynical attitude. The one entirely sympathetic character is Katharine of Aragon, who delivers a moving speech at her trial (II, *iv,* 13-57); it is apparent that the authors thought of her as the innocent victim of Wolsey's Machiavellian intrigues.

A standard edition is the New Cambridge edition, ed. J. C. Maxwell (1962). The question of Fletcher's collaboration is studied by Marco Mincoff, "*Henry VIII* and Fletcher," *SQ,* XII (1961). For criticism, see Frank Kermode, "What Is Shakespeare's *Henry VIII* About?" *DUJ,* IX, New Series (1948); A. C. Partridge, *The Problem of Henry VIII Reopened* (1949); E. M. W. Tillyard, "Why Did Shakespeare Write *Henry VIII?*" *CritQ,* III (1961); H. Felperin, "Shakespeare's *Henry VIII:* History as Myth," *SEL,* VI (1966); G. Wilson Knight, *The Crown of Life* (1966); H. M. Richmond, "Shakespeare's *Henry VIII;* Romance Redeemed by History," *ShakS,* IV (1969); and Peter Milward, "The Shadow of Henry VIII in Shakespeare's Plays," *ELLS,* VII (1970).

Henslowe, Philip (d. 1616). Theater owner and manager, and author of the so-called Henslowe's Diary, a valuable memorandum and account book of plays and playwrights kept by Henslowe during the period 1592-1603 and preserved at Dulwich College, London.

The son of a gamekeeper in Sussex, Henslowe had little formal education. In the 1570s he married the wealthy widow of the master to whom he was apprenticed. Soon after, he began investing in theatrical properties. Perhaps inspired by the success of Burbage's Theatre, he built in 1587 the famous Rose Theatre on the Bankside. He was also active in other business ventures, such as the dye trade and a pawn brokerage. In 1592 he was made groom of the Queen's Chamber, and in 1603 gentleman sewer of the King's Chamber; both offices were chiefly sinecures. When the Lord Chamberlain's Men moved into the Globe on the Bankside, Henslowe built the Fortune across the Thames, and in 1613 constructed still another playhouse, the Hope, on the site of the old Bear Garden on the Bankside.

In 1592 Henslowe's daughter Joan married the great actor Edward Alleyn, who became closely associated with Henslowe in financing plays. As a theater manager, Henslowe's principal activities included the renting of theaters to the acting companies, the purchase of plays, and the buying of costumes and stage properties. He also advanced the acting companies money for the purchase of plays, and at times even paid dramatists to write exclusively for the Lord Admiral's Men. The company with which Henslowe and Alleyn were most closely affiliated was the Admiral's Men, and their dramatists included Thomas Kyd, Christopher Marlowe, Anthony Munday, Henry Chettle, Michael Drayton, Thomas Dekker, John Day, Thomas Heywood, and Samuel Rowley. Henslowe's contract required that he receive fifty percent of the receipts for places in the galleries, the best-paying section of the playhouse. Toward the end of his life Henslowe's power over the actors had grown so great that members of the company drew up a petition of grievances charging him with legal oppression, manipulation of their accounts, excessive charges for costumes, and even bribery.

Henslowe's authority was no less binding on the playwrights. The Diary provides the names of over twenty dramatists who wrote for the Admiral's Men and drew their money directly from Henslowe. On February 5, 1598, Henslowe paid two pounds to release Dekker from debtors' prison, then gave him what was apparently the balance of four pounds for his play *Phaeton.* Henry Chettle and Anthony Munday were also impoverished writers who became bound as "Henslowe's hacks" in order to avoid debtors' prison.

The inestimable value of Henslowe's famous Diary can be inferred from the statistics cited by Bernard Beckerman in *Shakespeare at the Globe* (1962): he counts sixty-seven plays that would not be known to exist if Henslowe had not mentioned them in this miscellaneous memorandum book in which he recorded (in a semi-literate shorthand) business transactions, medical prescriptions, stage expenses, profits, purchases of plays, dates of performances, loans to actors and playwrights, and payments to the master of the revels for licensing of plays. Of many dramatists, such as Thomas Heywood, almost nothing would be known except for Henslowe's Diary.

The Henslowe papers have been edited with much commentary by W. W. Greg (1904-08), and a supplement (1907); and by R. A. Foakes and R. T. Rickert (1961). For a discussion of Henslowe's activities, see E. K. Chambers, *The Elizabethan Stage,* 4 vols. (1923): T. W. Baldwin, "Posting Henslowe's Accounts," JEGP, XXVI (1927); and Thomas Marc Parrott and R. H. Ball, *A Short View of Elizabethan Drama* (1943).

Herbert, Edward, first Baron Herbert of Cherbury (1583-1648). Poet and philosopher. Herbert was born at Eyton-on-Severn near Wroxeter, the eldest son of Sir Richard Herbert of Montgomery Castle and of Magdalen Herbert, the friend and patroness of John Donne. Edward Herbert's brother was George HERBERT, the religious poet. A child prodigy, Herbert went to Oxford in 1596 at fourteen, already a master of Greek, Latin, and logic; and his early brilliance may in part account for his later egotism and eccentricity. At sixteen Herbert was betrothed to his cousin Mary. After his marriage he returned to Oxford in the company of his wife, mother, and younger brother George. There he distinguished himself as a scholar, especially in classical languages, and became a favorite of Queen Elizabeth. With the accession of James I Herbert was made Knight of the Bath and sheriff of Montgomeryshire in 1605. In 1608 he traveled with Aurelian Townshend to Paris, where, by his own account, he fought the first of his many duels. The Paris journey was the first of several adventurous missions abroad. He participated in the siege of Juliers in the Low Countries with the Prince of Orange and later traveled to Cologne and Italy, where he led an army of Protestants from Languedoc into Piedmont to assist the Savoyards against the Spanish. Later arrested in Lyon by the French, he was soon released and rejoined the Prince of Orange in the war against Spain.

In 1616 ill health required his return to London, where he renewed his acquaintance with such literati as Ben Jonson, John Donne, John Selden, and Thomas Carew. In 1619 Herbert was again on the Continent, this time as ambassador to France until his removal in 1621. It is believed that Herbert was the first to suggest to his friend and patron Buckingham the marriage between Prince Charles and the French princess Henrietta Maria. During Herbert's second residence in Paris, 1622-24, he wrote his philosophical treatise *De veritate.*

After petitioning Charles I to be relieved of his debts, Herbert was made lord of Cherbury (in Shropshire) in 1629. In 1632 he wrote his encomiastic *History of Henry VIII* (1649) and became active in several scientific schemes, including the improvement of warships, the modeling of new types of guns, and even the construction of a floating bathhouse on the Thames.

An ardent Royalist before the Civil War, Herbert accompanied Charles I to the Scottish wars in 1639 and spoke out so vigorously in the House of Lords on behalf of royal prerogative that he was imprisoned in 1642 by the Commons. He apologized for his intemperate behavior and was released from the Tower, and afterward grew increasingly neutral, showing little interest in the political and religious issues of the 1640s. His retirement to Montgomery Castle was interrupted by its seizure in 1643 and his eviction because of his previous service to the king. He died in London following a year's residence in Paris in 1647.

Herbert's fame derives from his *Autobiography,* first printed by Horace Walpole in 1764; his philosophical treatise in Latin, *De veritate* (Paris, 1624); and his single collection of poems in English and Latin (1665). Little of either the philosopher or the poet can be inferred from the swashbuckling *Autobiography*. Written when Herbert was past sixty, it ends in 1624 with his recall from Paris as ambassador, and may be tinged by an aged man's nostalgic recollections of duels and street brawls, intrigues at court, and amatory hits and near-misses. Herbert's themes are his own sensitive honor, quickness of wit, and monumental courage and virility—the self-portrait of a *miles glorious* (see AUTOBIOGRAPHY).

Herbert's *De veritate,* an immensely influential treatise, represents the first epistemological and metaphysical work by an Englishman. In the epistemological section Herbert identifies instinct as paramount among four human faculties of perception, implanted by God and functioning as the primary source of *a priori* knowledge. The three ancillary faculties include the "internal sense," or conscience; the "external sense," or sense impressions; and the "discursus," or reason (a discriminating faculty). These rationalist concepts were extended into religious speculations at the conclusion of *De veritate* and subsequently in *De religione laici* (published with *De causis errorum* in 1645) and the posthumous *De religione gentilium* (1663). All of these were in Latin and not translated into English until long afterward. The thrust of Herbert's theology is toward the substitution of reason for faith and the assertion of five fundamental propositions that could be accepted by all denominations. Hence *De veritate* represents a philosophical effort to establish a working position somewhere between sectarian dogmatism and skepticism. Herbert's five universal tenets of religious belief are: (1) God exists; (2) He ought to be worshiped; (3) virtue and piety are essential aspects of worship; (4) sins should be repented; and (5) rewards and punishments are dispensed in a future life.

Himself an orthodox Anglican, Herbert attempted in these articles to strip religion of its excrescences of priests, rituals, sacraments, and ambiguous revelations—those elements most controversial and divisive in his own times—and to establish a latitudinarian doctrine based on reason. His anti-Calvinist position is inherent in his de-emphasis of Scripture and insistence on free will and reason as opposed to predestination and total depravity. These implicit denigrations of Calvinism were recognized and attacked later by Richard Baxter in *More Reason for the Christian Religion* (1672). Herbert's *De veritate* gave impetus to the spread of deism in the eighteenth century and to latitudinarianism in the nineteenth. Both John Locke and Descartes were attracted by Herbert's theory of innate ideas.

Although Herbert's poetry was not published until 1665, he wrote most if not all of his poems before 1631. Hence Herbert was the first of the secular METAPHYSICAL POETS and, with his brother George, one of Donne's earliest disciples. Donne's rigorous logic and tight structure are evident everywhere in Herbert's verses, although he expresses none of Donne's turbulence and passion. Instead, Herbert conveys careful analysis, firm control, and closely woven dialectics. His stanzas are irregular but clearly calculated and classically architectonic. A convenient point of comparison between Herbert and his master is Donne's "Extasie" and Herbert's "An Ode upon a Question Moved, Whether Love Should Continue Forever." Unlike Donne, Herbert argues the question of love's transcendence over death at a tranquil distance from hands, lips, and eyes; yet Herbert's metaphysical source is clearly Donne's passionate excursion into the difficult relationship of body and soul:

> So when one wing can make no way,
> Two joined can themselves dilate,
> So can two persons propagate,
> When singly either would decay.

Herbert's "Parted Souls," dated May, 1608, closely echoes Donne's "A Valediction: Forbidding Mourning." Unlike Donne's poem, however, Herbert's is sonorous rather than colloquial, deliberate and reflective rather than spontaneous:

> I must depart, but like to his last breath
> That leaves the seat of life, for liberty
> I go, but dying, and in this our death,
> Where soul and soul is parted, it is I
> The deader part that fly away,
> While she, alas, in whom before
> I lived, dies her own death and more,
> I feeling mine too much, and her own stay.

Like Donne, Herbert is tough-minded, anti-Petrarchan, and intellectually precise. His recurring themes are those of Donne's secular poems—love's nooks and crannies, death's omnipresence, and the tensions of body and soul.

Herbert's poems were edited by G. C. Moore Smith (1923). The standard edition of Herbert's *Autobiography* is by Sir Sidney Lee (1886; rev. ed., 1906), which was reprinted in 1928 with an introduction by C. H. Herford. *De Veritate* was translated into English by M. H. Carré (1937). There is a full bibliography in H. R. Hutcheson's translation of *De religione laici* (1944). Herbert's philosophy is treated by Basil Willey, *Seventeenth Century Background* (1934), and his poems by G. Williamson, *The Donne Tradition* (1930); John Hoey, "A Study of Lord Herbert of Cherbury's Poetry," *RMS,* XIV (1970); and Catherine A. Herbert, "The Platonic Love Poetry of Lord Herbert of Cherbury," *BSUF,* XI (1971).

Herbert George (1593-1633). Poet and divine. Herbert was born at Montgomery on the Welsh border of a distinguished martial family on both sides, his father Sir Richard belonging to ancient English-Welsh aristocracy, his mother Magdalen the daughter of a rich landowner in Shropshire. George Herbert was the fifth child among seven sons and three daughters. One brother was EDWARD, LORD HERBERT OF CHERBURY, the poet, historian, and philosopher; another was Sir Henry Herbert, master of the revels to Charles I. George Herbert's father died when he was four, and he was raised by his strong-willed, pious, and intellectual mother, who was one of John Donne's closest friends and for whom Donne wrote "The Autumnal." Magdalen Herbert saw to it that her sons were "brought up in learning," according to Herbert's biographer Isaak WALTON, and she strongly urged that Herbert serve the Anglican Church. Accordingly, she assigned him to a special tutor at the great Westminster School, after which he proceeded to Trinity College, Cambridge, receiving the B. A. in 1612, the M. A. in 1616.

At Westminster and Cambridge Herbert proved to be a precocious, diligent scholar, especially in music, rhetoric, science, and classical languages. Consistent with his mother's ardent wish, he was also devout. After his first year at Cambridge, when he was only seventeen, he sent his mother as a New Year's gift two sonnets accompanied by a declaration of his intention to write for God's glory rather than for that of Venus: "For my own part, my meaning (dear Mother) is, in these sonnets, to declare my resolution to be, that my poor abilities in poetry shall be all, and ever, consecrated to God's glory." The first sonnet bears some of the colloquial forthrightness and intensity of Donne's *Holy Sonnets:*

My God, where is that ancient heat towards thee,
Wherewith whole shoals of martyrs once
  did burn,
Besides their other flames? Doth poetry
Wear Venus' livery? Only serve her turn?
Why are not sonnets made of thee? And
  lays
Upon thy altar burnt? Cannot thy love
Heighten a spirit to sound out thy praise
As well as any she? Cannot thy Dove
Outstrip their Cupid easily in flight?
Or, since thy ways are deep, and still the same,
Will not a verse run smooth that bears thy
  name?
Why doth that fire, which by thy power and
  might
Each breast does feel, no braver fuel choose
Than that which one day worms may chance
  refuse ?

True to this manifesto, Herbert wrote no secular poems during his lifetime; but at Cambridge a powerful ambition to succeed in the academic and political worlds, natural to the gifted scion of a proud family, soon came into direct conflict with an equally strong dedication to a religious life. On one side he was impelled by his early religious ideals and the wishes of his pious mother, and no doubt the counsels of his mother's close friend Dr. John Donne, all urging him toward the kind of ascetic monastic life exemplified in the Anglican community of Little Gidding established by Herbert's friend Nicholas Ferrar. On the other side were the secular gratifications of academic and political success represented by his circle of learned, rich, and powerful friends, including Francis Bacon. This conflict of vocation, never totally resolved, was to become the prevailing theme of his greatest poetry. Specifically, Herbert aspired to become university orator at Cambridge, a position that customarily led to important positions at court. Herbert's sympathetic biographer Walton states candidly that Herbert campaigned strenuously to persuade James I to grant him the appointment.

Herbert won the office in 1619, and his secular career flourished accordingly. He helped Bacon translate *The Advancement of Learning* into clear, forceful Latin, and in 1625 Bacon dedicated his *Translations of Certain Psalms into English Verse* to Herbert. In that same year, however, occurred the deaths of several of Herbert's patrons, including James I, and Herbert retired in distress to Kent, where he "lived very privately," according to Walton, debating "whether he should return to the painted pleasures of a court life, or betake himself to a study of divinity, and enter into sacred orders (to which his dear mother had often persuaded him)." Herbert's decision emerged gradually, after his mother's death in 1627 and his marriage to Jane Danvers (a friend of the Donne family). Finally, in 1630, he became ordained and, through the intercession of his kinsman the earl of Pembroke, Charles I granted him the rectorship of Fuggleston St. Peter in Bemerton, Wiltshire, where he devoted the remaining three years of his life to study, parish duties, and pious meditation.

From his deathbed Herbert sent to Nicholas Ferrar his only volume of poems, *The Temple,* together with its prose companion *A Priest to the Temple,* a manual of conduct for country parsons. He instructed Ferrar that his poems were to be either printed or burned, and that in *The Temple* Ferrar would read "a picture of the many spiritual conflicts that have passed betwixt God and my soul before I could subject mine to the will of Jesus my Master; in whose service I have now found perfect freedom." *The Temple,* published by Ferrar in 1633, became instantly popular and established Herbert as one of England's foremost religious poets. (*A Priest to the Temple* was not printed until 1652.) Even the stringent Puritan Richard Baxter, that crucible of religious integrity, wrote approvingly in 1681 of Herbert's poetry: "Herbert speaks to God like one that really believeth a God, and whose business in the world is most with God."

Baxter's observation goes to the heart of one difference between Herbert's poetry and that of his master Donne's, for Herbert's solid faith is never shaken by doubt. Herbert addresses himself as a humble son to the Father, and if the son is sometimes prodigal, it is because of the agonizing allurements of "painted pleasures" and wordly "snares"—temptations of the flesh that Baxter and other orthodox believers can accept as inevitable consequences of a Christian commitment. Unlike Donne, too, Herbert is always conscious of his verses serving a pastoral function. When his poems are not addressed directly to God, they often resemble homilies. Just as the student at Cambridge repudiated Venus for the Dove, the parson of Bemerton moved from Helicon to Jordan in *The Temple,* a long poem which opens with a stanza reasserting his manifesto in the New Year's sonnets at Cambridge:

Thou, whose sweet youth and early hopes
  enhance
Thy rate and price, and mark thee for a
  treasure,
Hearken unto a Verser, who may chance
Rhyme thee to good, and make a bait of
  pleasure.
A verse may find him who a sermon flies,
And turn delight into a sacrifice.

Although Herbert was as learned as Donne, and even more deeply schooled in Baconian science, the new learning, and classical literature, he deliberately avoided erudite or esoteric language in favor of what Coleridge describes as a "pure, manly, and unaffected diction," and drew his metaphors from common objects, nature, the Bible, and the liturgy. Yet these "plainly dressed" poems, so apparently spontaneous, informal, and colloquial, actually represent what can be described paradoxically as a simplicity of elaborate obliqueness—a homely, almost prosaic roughening of an underlying polish and sophistication. Herbert states his poetic strategies in "Jordan (I)":

Who says that fictions only and false hair
  Become a verse? Is there in truth no beauty?
Is all good structure in a winding stair?
May no lines pass, except they do their duty
  Not to a true, but painted chair?

• • • •

Shepherds are honest people; let them sing:
Riddle who list, for me, and pull for Prime:
I envy no man's nightingale or spring;
Nor let them punish me with loss of rime,
  Who plainly say, *My God, My King.*

In "Jordan (II)," similarly, Herbert attributes his inspiration to love rather than artifice and calculation:

As flames do work and wind, when they ascend,
So did I weave myself into the sense.
But while I bustled, I might hear a friend
Whisper, "How wide is all this long pretense!"

Like Sir Philip Sidney supposedly scorning the ecletic artificialities of Petrarchism and vowing merely to "look into his heart and write" in *Astrophel and Stella,* Herbert in these lines rejects the erotic "fictions" of the Cavalier love poets, the melodious pastorals of the Spenserians, and, presumably, the "winding stair" of intellectual complexities of the METAPHYSICAL POETS as well. His "plainly dressed," unpretentious poetry, he suggests, will seek its beauty not in Plato's famous chair (an imitation several times removed from reality) but from the living truth of plain Christian faith plainly stated.

In view of the astonishing complexities of Herbert's verse under its easy surface, Herbert's creed in "Jordan (I)" has puzzled his critics. In one sense, "Jordan (I)" can be read as the appropriately austere pose of the "plainly dressed" Bemerton parson, with a touch of Sidney's bravura in *Astrophel and Stella.* In another, quite compatible context, his words are accurate, for *The Temple* does in fact stand opposed to the main currents of Elizabethan poetry. And even Herbert's metaphysical qualities are not "winding" in the same way sophical or academic metaphors, rarely employs Renaissance literary conventions ironically, and pays no heed to those "wits" who are Donne's primary readers. Consistent with its plan, *The Temple* is a systematic yet intimate dialogue between its author and God, and Herbert expresses none of Donne's exhibitionism and theatricality. In Aldous Huxley's inimitable phrase, Herbert is the poet of "inner weather" rather than the spectacular performer as Donne's. Herbert abjures hard philo- on the dais, and the readers who best comprehend his self-effacing prayers and meditations are not courtly wits or academicians but devout Christians very much like Richard Baxter, "whose business in the world is most with God," and who have committed the Bible and liturgy to heart.

If, then, Herbert's readers are not the same as Donne's, it is nevertheless true that Herbert's poems are squarely in the metaphysical tradition for their incongruous and extended metaphors, violent transitions and shock effects, rigorous concentration and linear construction. In spite of their apparent simplicity, they are the result of assiduous revising, polishing, and metrical experimentation. Of the 169 poems in *The Temple,* 116 are in meters Herbert employs but once. An accomplished musician with an infallible ear, he often succeeds in conveying the subtlest nuances of emotion by artful manipulation of sound and rhythm. In "Church Monuments," for example, Herbert loosens the syntax to suggest the dissolution of both vain monuments and mortal flesh until, as Joseph Summers observes, "the sentences sift down through the rhyme-scheme skeleton of the stanzas like the sand through the glass; and the glass itself has already begun to crumble."

Such ingenuity occasionally leads Herbert into experiments Addison later condemned in the *Spectator Papers* (nos. 58, 62) as exemplary of "false wit": the use of "anagrams, chronograms, lipograms, and acrostics . . . whole sentences or poems cast into the figures of eggs, axes, or altars." In "Paradise" Herbert "prunes" his rhymes to form a rather broad visual conceit:

> I bless thee, Lord because I GRÓW
> Among thy trees, which in a RÓW
> To thee both fruit and order ÓW.

Influenced by *The Greek Anthology,* he employs "pattern" verses, as in "The Altar" and "Easter Wings," arranged on the page to form symbolic figures. As Professor Summers has shown, some of these patterns or emblem poems are expressive of significant Biblical and liturgical ideas. In "A Bunch of Grapes" and "Joseph's Coat" only the titles are emblematic. In the former the religious symbolism of the grapes and their relevance to the New Covenant does not become clear until the very end, and in the latter, Joseph's coat (not mentioned in the body of the poem) becomes a clue derived from Joseph's "coat of many colors" in Genesis 37:3.

If Herbert's poems are difficult, it is because they are often closely structured on Christian parables, Biblical allusions, liturgy, or intimate personal references. "The Pearl" is an emblematic allusion to Matthew 13:45: "Again the kingdom of Heaven is like unto a merchant, seeking goodly pearls, who, when he had found one pearl of great price, went and sold all that he had, and bought it." The poem refers to Herbert's own crisis of vocation and the price of his religious commitment, a price that increases the value of the "pearl," his life with God. Each stanza is devoted to a particular secular temptation—learning, honor (public office), and sensual pleasures:

> The propositions of hot blood and brains;
> What mirth and music mean; what love and
> wit

Have done these twenty hundred years, and more:
I know the projects of unbridled store:
My stuff is flesh, not brass, my senses live . . .

In each stanza the weight of details, the reasonings and justifications, are on the side of worldly involvement, yet these are turned back by the force of the plain and simple refrain "Yet I love thee." In the last stanza the metaphysical "silk twist" let down from heaven

Did both conduct and teach me, how by it
To climb to thee.

In "The Collar" the "silk twist" is a "rope of sands" which makes "good cable, to enforce and draw" the rebellious flesh to God's discipline. "The Collar" is as dramatic and forthright as any of Donne's argumentative poems:

I struck the board, and cried, No more!
I will abroad.
What? Shall I ever sigh and pine?
My lines and life are free; free as the road,
Loose as the wind, as large as store . . .

Once again the tension in the poem is Herbert's own crisis of vocation, the voice of the prodigal son or rebellious servant chafing under the harsh conditions of the master. As in many of Herbert's poems, the conclusion abruptly reverses direction:

But as I rav'd and grew more fierce and wild
At every word,
Me thought I heard one calling, Child!
And I replied, My Lord.

Out of Herbert's dark night of the soul his bright faith always appears like a warm dawn. The concluding poem in *The Temple* is entitled "Love (III)," and ends with two almost prosaic lines that summarize the spirit of Herbert's life and work:

You must sit down, says Love, and taste my meat:
So I did sit and eat.

The standard edition is *The Works,* ed. F. E. Hutchinson (2d ed., 1945). *The Latin Poetry* was edited by Mark McCloskey and Paul R. Murphy (1965). The most thorough critical biography is by M. Bottrall, *George Herbert* (1954), the most comprehensive critical study by Joseph H. Summers, *George Herbert, His Religion and Art* (1954). See also Rosamond Tuve, *A Reading of George Herbert* (1952); Joan Bennett, *Five Metaphysical Poets* (rev. ed., 1964); Louis L. Martz, *The Poetry of Meditation* (1954); T. S. Eliot, *George Herbert* (1962); and Mary E. Rickey, *Utmost Art: Complexity in the Verse of George Herbert* (1966). There is a Concise Bibliography by S. A. and Dorothy Tannenbaum (1946). See also Theodore Spencer and Mark Van Doren, *Studies in the Metaphysical Poets, 1912–38* (1939), and Humphrey Tonkin, "A Bibliography of George Herbert, 1960-67: Addenda," *SCN,* XXVII (1969).

Hermetic Philosophy. See VAUGHAN, HENRY.

Hero and Leander. A narrative poem by Christopher MARLOWE. It was probably written in 1593, the year of Marlowe's death, and was first published in its fragmentary form of two sestiads (some 800 lines) in 1598. Later in the same year the poem was published again, this time with four additional sestiads by George Chapman. The division into sestiads was made by Chapman, who named each section a "sestiad" after the principal location of the action, Sestos. (Similarly, Chapman's translation of Homer is divided into "iliads" because the action occurs near Ilium.) Although Marlowe was no doubt familiar with the story of Hero and Leander in Ovid's *Heroides,* translated by George Turberville in 1567, he used as his chief source the popular Greek version by Musaeus, an Alexandrine poet who lived around the sixth century A.D. The bare details of the story were taken from Musaeus, the sophisticated point of view and tone suggested by Ovid. All the beautiful flowering of descriptive language and characterization originates in Marlowe's romantic imagination.

The events of the tale are few and simple. Hero, a beautiful and virginal votress of Venus (paradoxically described as "Venus' nun"), resides at Sestos on the European side of the Hellespont and is wooed by Leander, a handsome youth who lives on the opposite shore at Abydos. Marlowe's first sestiad is given over to Leander's frantic pursuit of the virgin and to a lengthy digression on how Mercury's offense against the gods caused poverty among scholars. In the second sestiad Leander swims the Hellespont, spurns the flirtations of Neptune, and seduces Hero. At this point the manuscript concludes with the words *Desunt nonnulla* ("Something is lacking"). In the next four sestiads, by Chapman, Leander is guided in his swim across the Hellespont by Hero, who holds a lighted torch, but one stormy night Leander drowns and the distraught Hero throws herself into the sea.

The potential sentimentality of this tale of star-crossed lovers is counteracted by Marlowe's brittle couplets and by the tone of the narrator, who interlards his story with terse, worldly axioms like "Women are won when they begin to jar"; "All women are ambitious naturally"; "Love is not full of pity, as men say, / But deaf and cruel where he means to prey." In contrast to the cynical narrator, the lovers themselves are sensual innocents, by turns joyous and fearful in their erotic rapture, except in lines 199-294 of the first sestiad, when the previously naïve Leander suddenly turns "bold sharp sophister" and woos Hero in the language of a jaded roué. This patent inconsistency of characterization and the digression on Mercury and scholarship in the first sestiad (lines 385-484) are often cited as two blemishes in an otherwise flawless masterpiece.

Marlowe's poem is one of the greatest of the so-called Ovidian epyllia, erotic narratives in the tradition of Ovid, and belongs to a brief period that produced a number of similar poems: Thomas Lodge's SCYLLA'S METAMORPHOSIS (1589). Shakespeare's VENUS AND ADONIS (1593), and John Marston's METAMORPHOSIS OF PGYMALION'S IMAGE (1598). None of these was as popular as Marlowe's *Hero and Leander,* which was not only widely quoted but frequently published with three editions in 1598 and others in 1600, 1606, 1609, 1613, 1616, 1617, 1622, 1629, and 1637. By 1599 Marlowe's poem had become sufficiently well known to enable Thomas Nashe to write a lengthy parody of it in *Nashe's Lenten Stuff, or the Praise of the Red Herring.*

There are several equally good and well annotated editions of *Hero and Leander;* C. F. Tucker Brooke's in *The Works* (1910), L. C. Martin's in *The Poems* (1931), and Millar Maclure's in the Revels Plays edition of *The Poems* (1968). Excellent critical studies are in Douglas Bush, *Mythology and the Renaissance Tradition in English Poetry* (rev. ed., 1963); J. B. Steane, *Marlowe, A Critical Study* (1964); and Richard Neuse, "Atheism and Some Functions of Myth in Marlowe's *Hero and Leander,*" *MLQ,* XXXI (1970).

Heropaideia, or The Institution of a Young Nobleman. See COURTESY LITERATURE.

Herrick, Robert (1591-1674) Poet. Born in London the son of a goldsmith, Herrick was apprenticed after his father's death to his uncle Sir William Herrick, court jeweler to James I. Herrick grew up in Hampton, Middlesex, and attended Westminster School. Not succeeding as a goldsmith, Herrick was sent by his uncle to St. John's College, Cambridge, in 1613 and graduated B.A. in 1617, M.A. in 1620. Little is known of his activities during the years following graduation. By 1627 he had taken holy orders, for in that year he was an army chaplain on a military expedition to the Isle of Rhé. Upon his return Charles I assigned him the pastorate of Dean Prior in Devonshire.

The West Country of Devonshire is the scene of his collection of poems *Hesperides* (1648), which reveals Herrick's initial ambivalence toward his parish and its inhabitants. Apparently he missed the excitement of London, where he had been a disciple in the "tribe" of Ben Jonson. In Devonshire he was a bachelor of scholarly disposition isolated among rustic farmers and menials; eventually, however, he grew interested in their customs and the beauties of their country. With the victory of the Puritans he was ousted from his parish and returned to London, where he lived off the charity of friends and relatives until he was restored to Dean Prior at the Restoration. There he returned to his old life of books, dogs, cats, and an aged servant named Prudence Baldwin. He never married, and the passionate mistresses in *Hesperides* were doubtless only creations of his imagination.

The 1500 or more poems in *Hesperides* and *Noble Numbers* (1648), and the almost fifty additional poems discovered during the last two centuries, make up Herrick's *Works Both Human and Divine.* Most of the lyrics in *Hesperides* were composed in Devon when Herrick was vicar there in 1629-46. Of the earliest period of poetic apprenticeship before 1617 only one lyric remains, "A Country Life," a poem celebrating the rural environs of Middlesex. The sources of *Hesperides* are thoroughly classical, with roots in Anacreon, Catullus, Horace, and Theocritus. Herrick's Anacreonic theme of *carpe diem* and joy in the life of the senses is proclaimed in "The Argument of His Book":

I sing of brooks, of blossoms, birds, and bowers;
Of April, May, of June, and July flowers.
I sing of Maypoles, hock-carts, wassails, wakes,
Of bridegrooms, brides, and of their bridal cakes.
I write of youth, of love, and have access
By these, to sing of cleanly wantonness.
I sing of dews, of rains, and piece by piece,
Of balm, of oil, of spice, and ambergris.
I sing of Time's trans-shifting, and I write
How roses first came red, and lilies white.
I write of groves, of twilights, and I sing
The court of Mab, and of the fairy king.
I write of hell; I sing (and ever shall)
Of heaven, and hope to have it after all.

The lyric that best captures the spirit of Herrick's studious abandon is the famous "To the Virgins, to Make Much of Time," which begins "Gather ye rosebuds while ye may."

Among the CAVALIER POETS, Herrick has no peer. His lines are crisp, spare, and epigrammatic in the best classical manner, and when this economy combines with native ballad form, the result is a lyric of such pure delight as "Cherry-ripe":

> Cherry-ripe, ripe, ripe, I cry,
> Full and fair ones, come and buy.
> If so be, you ask me where
> They do grow, I answer, there
> Where my Julia's lips do smile.
> There's the land, or cherry-isle . . .

Whether his imaginary mistress is addressed as Julia, Corinna, Electra, or Anthea, Herrick's tone is always festive, spontaneous, and redolent of the "cleanly wantonness" of the purely literary lover. He abjures Donne's tough-minded realism and strives to emulate the exuberant grace of Jonson's "Still to be neat, still to be dressed." Yet *Hesperides* presents a variety of styles, "The Mad Maid's Song" recalls Shakespeare's airs, and "To Phillis" takes into account both Marlowe's pastoral invitation and Raleigh's mocking rejoinder:

Thou shalt have ribbands, roses, rings,
Gloves, garters, stockings, shoes, and strings
Of winning colors, that shall move
Others to lust, but me to love.
These (nay) and more, thine own shall be,
If thou wilt love, and live with me.

On other occasions, as in "The Cruel Maid," Herrick adopts a controlled stoic irony comparable to some of Andrew Marvell's best effects. Others of his poems are descriptive of nature ("To Daffodils"), a nature pastoral and literary rather than naturalistic, and the mythology that he creates from his world in Devonshire—pretty maids, May festivals, revels out of doors—is constructed on the golden verses of the Latin poets. Although Herrick was a devout man of the cloth, his *Hesperides* is a literary holiday in which he appears, as F. W. Moorman notes, "more of a Roman flamen than a Christian priest."

Herrick's *Complete Works,* with critical introduction and annotations, has been edited by J. Max Patrick for Anchor Books (1963). There is an excellent edition of *Hesperides* by L. C. Martin (1956; rev. ed. 1965). The best biographical and critical study is Frederick W. Moorman's *Robert Herrick* (1962). See also S. Musgrove, *The Universe of Robert Herrick* (1950); R. B. Rollin, *Robert Herrick* (1966); and A. Leigh DeNeef, "Herrick's 'Corinna' and the Ceremonial Mode," *SAQ,* LXX (1971). There is a Concordance by Malcolm MacLeod (1936) and a Concise Bibliography by S. A. Tannenbaum (1949), updated in "Robert Herrick (1949-65)," ed. G. R. Guffey, in *Elizabethan Bibliographies Supplements,* III (1968).

Hesperides. See HERRICK, ROBERT.

Heywood, John (c. 1497-c. 1578). Poet and dramatist. Little is known of Heywood's early years. He seems to have been born in London of middle-class parentage, and may have begun his career at the court of Henry VIII as a choirboy. In 1519 there is a record of Heywood's employment at court as a singer and entertainer of sorts. In the early 1520s he married Eliza Rastell, daughter of John Rastell, Sir Thomas More's brother-in-law. More's son-in-law William Roper refers to Heywood in *The Life of More* as being a close friend of More's. In *Scriptorum illustrium* (1557-58) John Bale describes Heywood as having been an accomplished musician and popular producer of INTERLUDES, masques, and other court entertainments.

The printer William Rastell, Eliza's brother, published four of Heywood's interludes in 1533: THE PARDONER AND THE FRIAR; *A Play of Love;* THE PLAY OF THE WEATHER; and JOHAN JOHAN THE HUSBAND, TYB HIS WIFE, AND SIR JOHN THE PRIEST.

Between 1543 and 1547 was published Heywood's THE FOUR PP (repr. 1569). Together with *Witty* and *Witless,* an interlude in manuscript, these comprise Heywood's extant plays. *Witty and Witless, A Play of Love,* and *Weather* are debates, *The Pardoner and the Friar* and *Johan Johan* are farces, and *The Four PP* is a combination of the two types. It is impossible to date these plays with any accuracy, although most scholars consider *Witty and Witless*, the dullest and least dramatic of the plays, as Heywood's earliest effort.

Heywood may have written many more plays than are extant. There are records of interludes and other entertainments at court from 1538 to 1559, and a play called "Of the Parts of Man" is paraphrased in part in the recently published *Autobiography of Thomas Whythorne*, edited in 1961 by James M. Osborn. Whythorne, author of one of the earliest autobiographies in English, served as Heywood's secretary from 1545 to 1548, and considered his master to be the literary equal of Chaucer.

Heywood's debates are rather prolix and tedious. In *A Play of Love* the characters represent various experiences in love—Lover-Loved, Lover-Not-Beloved, Neither-Lover-Nor-Loved, and Beloved-Not-Loving (a woman)—and exchange complaints and self-justifications. In the last hundred lines the disputants agree that there is little to choose among the pleasures and pains they represent and that love of God remains the one reliable and authentic passion. Heywood's *Weather* is more vivid of characterization and more firmly constructed. The characters who petition Jupiter for changes in the weather are drawn from a variety of trades, professions, and ages, and the simple plot enables Heywood to stress his favorite theme of man's ironic partiality of vision: man's ignorance, subjectivity, and pride render him incapable of apprehending the purposive design of things, whether that design is to be found in nature, as in *Weather,* or in love, as in *A Play of Love,* or in religion and society, as in *The Four PP.*

Heywood's fame as a dramatist rests on his two farces, *The Four PP* and *Johan Johan,* which represent the best comedies of the early Tudor period before *Gammer Gurton's Needle* and *Ralph Roister Doister* in the 1550s. None of Heywood's plays belongs in either the native or classical tradition that influenced the development of the later drama. The debates transfer the medieval poetic form to the stage, with some invigoration from Chaucer's "Pardoner's Tale" and Erasmus' *Moriae encomium,* whereas the farces derive directly from such French models as the anonymous *Dyalogue du fol et du sage,* which Heywood consulted in writing *Johan Johan.* In that play Heywood translates whole passages from the French farce, which he modifies by adding colloquial dialogue, exaggerated English types, and topical satire. In dramaturgy Heywood created little that was new or lasting; nevertheless, he deserves an important place in the early Tudor drama because of the high quality of at least two of his interludes and because his farcical interludes contributed to the growing secularization of the English drama.

Heywood's principal nondramatic works include *The Dialogue of Proverbs, The Epigrams,* and THE SPIDER AND THE FLY (1556). The first of these, published in 1546 with the title *A Dialogue Containing the Number in Effect of All the Proverbs in the English Tongue,* is a collection of proverbs poured into a long tale of halting tetrameter couplets. The lengthy narrative, or more precisely, the several stories of marriage within a frame tale, is divided into two parts, with thirteen chapters in the first part and eleven in the second. In the first part the narrator is visited by a young man seeking advice about whether to marry a poor young girl or a rich old widow—a debate that provides a frame for two of the narrator's stories illustrative of the young man's dilemma. After hearing the narrator's tale of the miseries of a young man who marries a rich old widow, the youth decides to choose neither the young girl nor the old widow. The youth's words illustrate how Heywood interlards his stories with proverbs: "Who that leaveth surety and leaneth unto chance, / When fools pipe, by auctoritee he may dance."

No doubt Heywood was strongly influenced by Sir Thomas More's circle at Chelsea, and More's *Epigrammata* (1518) may have inspired Heywood's *The Epigrams.* Heywood's rough-hewn and folksy epigrams, numbering six hundred in the last edition, are taken from native proverbs and owe little if anything to classical epigrammatists like Martial. Almost half of Heywood's epigrams are English proverbs of two lines given an original twist: "New broom sweepeth clean, which is thus understand: / New broom sweepth clean, in the clean sweeper's hand." Other epigrams are puns or short satiric jibes: "Love me, love my dog: by love to agree / I love thy dog as well as I love thee." Still others are much longer; "A Keeper of the Commandments," of almost a hundred lines, satirizes hypocritical violations of each of the commandments. In one epigram Heywood portrays his own personality:

Art thou Heywood with mad merry wit?
Yea, forsooth, master, that same is even hit.
Art thou Heywood that applieth
mirth more than thrift?
Yea, sir, I take merry mirth a golden gift.
Art thou Heywood that hath made
many mad plays?
Yea, many plays, few good works in all my days.
Art thou Heywood that hath made
men merry long?
Yea, and will, if I be made merry among . . .

Heywood published the first hundred of his epigrams in 1550, and enlarged upon these in editions in 1555 and 1560. In 1562 the total six hundred epigrams and *The Dialogue of Proverbs* were published as *John Heywood's Works.* Heywood's miscellaneous verses, some of which were included years later in Tottel's Miscellany, include an encomium to Princess Mary Tudor, verses in celebration of her marriage when queen to Philip II of Spain, and a satiric ballad condemning the seizure of Scarborough Castle by Thomas Stafford and other rebels in 1557. On less certain evidence, Heywood is also credited with writing an early and somewhat lame version of Desdemona's song "Sing all a green willow" in Shakespeare's *Othello.*

Late in Henry VIII's reign Heywood was in serious trouble over religion. In 1543 he was imprisoned after he and several other Catholic sympathizers accused Archbishop Thomas Cranmer of heresy. The king appointed Cranmer himself to conduct an investigation of these charges, and the affair concluded with several Catholics being executed and Heywood publicly recanting his alleged belief in papal authority. Sir John Harington, writing of the incident long afterward in his *Metamorphosis of Ajax,* indicated that Heywood narrowly escaped death through the kindly intervention of some unknown "gentleman" close to the king.

In spite of this contretemps, Heywood continued to enjoy the favor of the king, arranging entertainments at court and receiving emoluments as steward of the king's chamber. With the accession of Mary Tudor, his star rose sharply at court. He was made steward of the queen's chamber and received lands in Kent. Just before her death in 1558, Mary gave him a manor in Yorkshire, whereupon he resigned his court office, possibly in anticipation of retiring to his estates in the event of a Protestant succession. With the restoration of Protestantism under Queen Elizabeth, Heywood found his position increasingly difficult and departed England in July 1564, never to return. He died in Louvain in 1578.

John Heywood's daughter Elizabeth was the mother of John Donne, the poet. His son Jasper translated Seneca's *Thyestes, Hercules Furens,* and *Troas.* Both Jasper and Heywood's other son, Ellis, were prominent English Jesuits.

An excellent critical biography of Heywood is by Robert W. Bolwell, *The Life and Works of John Heywood* (1921), which contains an exhaustive bibliography. All Heywood's interludes except *A Play of Love* are edited by Rupert Da La Bare, *John Heywood, Entertainer* (1937), which also provides a critical biography and extensive bibliography. The standard edition of poems is *John Heywood's Works and Miscellaneous Short Poems,* ed. Burton A. Milligan (1956). The only complete edition of all Heywood's works is *The Works of John Heywood,* ed. John S. Farmer, 3 vols. (1905-08), which merely reprints early editions without introductions or notes. A good critical study of Heywood's plays and poems is by Robert C. Johnson, *John Heywood* (1970), which is followed by a lengthy annotated bibliography. For Heywood's interludes, see Ian Maxwell, *French Farce and John Heywood* (1946), and Pearl Hogrefe, *The Sir Thomas More Circle: A Program of Ideas and Their Impact on the Secular Drama* (1959). There is a Concise Bibliography by S. A. and D. R. Tannenbaum (1946), which is continued in "John Heywood (1944-60)," ed. Robert C. Johnson, in *Elizabethan Bibliographies Supplements,* IX (1968). For additional data on Heywood, see F. P. Wilson, *The English Drama: 1485-1585,* edited with a bibliography by G. K. Hunter (1969).

Heywood, Thomas (1573?-1641). Dramatist, poet, actor, and miscellanist. Born of a prosperous Lincolnshire family, Heywood attended Cambridge and was in London by October

1596, when Philip Henslowe recorded a payment for "Hawods booke." Except for dramatic records, allusions in prologues, and other literary data, little is known of Heywood's life. Hence the chronology and development of his work must be tentatively inferred from the uncertain evidence of publication dates.

By 1598 Heywood was well established as an actor and dramatist for the Lord Admiral's Men. In that year Henslowe contracted with Heywood to produce plays exclusively for the Admiral's Men for two years. Thus began Heywood's prolific and variegated career as actor, poet, and dramatist. For the next thirty-five years he acted on the popular stage for a number of dramatic companies, wrote pageants for the city of London, and, by his own statement in *The English Traveller* (1633), had "an entire hand in or at least a main finger" in 220 plays, of which about two dozen survive. These represent a variety of genres—the chronicle play, romantic comedy, comedy of manners, mythological drama, and domestic tragedy.

An early play, *Four Prentices of London,* was described by Heywood as having been done "in my infancy of judgment." An old-fashioned play employing chorus, dumb shows, and an episodic plot that ranges freely over several years and countries, *Four Prentices* portrays the adventures of four apprentices who accompany their father, the earl of Boulogne, on the First Crusade. Accompanying them are a sister and sweetheart, both disguised as boys, and in the end all the apprentices are made kings and the disguised sister marries the prince of Italy. This absurd dramatization of the romance of chivalry was later satirized in Beaumont and Fletcher's KNIGHT OF THE BURNING PESTLE.

Around 1599 Heywood had at least a share in writing the history play *Edward IV,* Parts I and II, a rambling saga that links very loosely five stories from the Wars of the Roses—the siege of London by the bastard Falconbridge, the farcical hijinks of Hobs the tanner, Edward's expedition in France, the murder of the young princes in the Tower, and Edward's tragic romance with Jane Shore. Although individual scenes contain some dramatic power and occasionally genuine pathos, the play as a whole reveals no effort at integration or thematic concentration. The next English history play attributed to Heywood, *If You Know Not Me, You Know Nobody,* written around 1604, displays this same structural weakness. Part I dramatizes, with considerable sentimentality, Elizabeth's heroic struggle for survival during the Catholic reign of Mary Tudor; Part II mingles William Parry's plot against Elizabeth's life in 1583, the career of Thomas Gresham, merchant prince and founder of the Royal Exchange, and the Spanish Armada. Heywood's Roman play, *The Rape of Lucrece* (1608), is less far-ranging topically but equally discursive in its recounting of history from the usurpation of Tarquin to his death in battle.

Heywood's most ambitious undertaking was an epical dramatization of Greek myth extending from the birth of Jove to the fall of Troy in five plays: *The Golden Age* (1611), *The Silver Age* (1613), *The Brazen Age* (1613), and *The Iron Age,* Parts I and II (1632). The most artistically successful and popular of these was the last, which features the love of Paris and Helen, the tragic tale of Troilus and Cressida, and the destruction of Troy and Priam's family.

During this same period Heywood worked assiduously with tragicomedy in *The Royal King and the Loyal Subject* (wr. c. 1602, pr. 1637), which is derived from the same tales in Matteo Bandello used later by John Fletcher in *The Loyal Subject* (1618). A comparison of the two plays reveals that Heywood had little talent for Fletcher's aristocratic style of romance. Like Fletcher, he dutifully endorses the Tudor theory of divine right of kings, but his patriotism is middle-class, pietistic, and humble; he totally lacks Fletcher's emotional concentration and lyrical prowess. More compatible with Heywood's middle-class romanticism are *Fortune by Land and Sea* (wr. c. 1607?, pr. 1655), written in collaboration with William Rowley, and THE FAIR MAID OF THE WEST, Parts I and II (1631). Part I of *Fair Maid of the West* begins at Plymouth during the preparation for the island voyage of Essex and Raleigh in 1599 and concludes with its hero and heroine at the court of King Mullisheg in Morocco. The main character is Bess Bridges, a resourceful, virtuous virago like the titular heroine of Dekker and Middleton's *Roaring Girl*—a saber-wielding hoyden with a true-blue English heart of gold. Part I was so successful that Heywood hurriedly wrote a sequel, but Part II, which bogs down in complicated love intrigues at the court of Morocco, lacks the dash, vigor and novelty of Part I.

Heywood's masterpiece A WOMAN KILLED WITH KINDNESS (wr. c. 1603, pr. 1607), was derived from two bloody Italian novellas of revenge that Heywood transformed into a domestic tragedy permeated with middle-class religious, economic, and social values. The novel idea of the cuckolded husband "forgiving" his errant wife was Heywood's own addition to the story, as was his portrayal of the villain Wendoll as weak, ambivalent, and guilt-stricken. No extant play by Heywood contains so many realistic scenes—the wedding festival of Frankford and his wife, the sudden, violent episode of the hunting party, the game of cards between Frankford and his wife and her lover, the discovery of Mistress Frankford's infidelity, and the final, almost serenely pathetic deathbed scene. And in no other play does Heywood so effectively link his multiple plots or instill each episode with such grim, continuous irony.

The remainder of Heywood's plays show little if any development beyond the two fine achievements of this early period, *Fair Maid of the West,* Part I, and *A Woman Killed with Kindness.* Yet his outpouring of plays, pamphlets, translations, and poems never slackened. *The Wise Woman of Hogsden,* (wr. c. 1604, pr. 1638) is a comedy of intrigue marked by realism suggestive of Jonson and Middleton, yet softened by the pathos and kindly sentiments reminiscent of Dekker. Heywood's young Chartley anticipates in some ways the careless rake of the Restoration comedy of manners, except that Heywood's middle-class sobriety and Protestant piety will not permit Chartley to outwit established values, and the rake is exposed, repents, and assumes responsibility for the maid he has deserted.

Unlike Chapman or Marston, Heywood never associated himself with the intellectual elite, the UNIVERSITY WITS, or the aristocratically minded dramatists who denigrated the popular stage and aspired to entertain courtly audiences exclusively. Like Dekker, he was something of an egalitarian sentimentalist with a fond vision of a socially congenial Merry England. Although as learned as Chapman or Marston, he felt a social kinship with the middle-class city fathers, for whom he prepared the lord mayor's annual pageants during the period 1631-39. With comparable good will, he wrote occasional pieces like *Love's Mistress, or the Queen's Masque* (1636), a mythological pageant in which Apuleius, representing poetry and learning, relates the story of Cupid and Psyche to an ignorant, ill-tempered Midas, symbolic of the general public. This conviviality, tolerance, and flexibility of Heywood's account to some extent for his scholarly *Apology for Actors* (1612), a prose tract written in defense of actors and playwrights against vituperative attacks by Puritan critics (see CRITICISM, LITERARY) In a restrained, dignified style, Heywood justifies professional acting on the historical bases of "antiquity," "ancient dignity," and "true use," and concludes with a rational, dispassionate defense of the moral values of the drama. Although the tract is too tepid and lusterless to inspire much literary interest, it reveals the author's intellectual integrity, modesty, generosity toward contemporaries, and instinctive kindness. The only anger expressed in Heywood's *Apology* is for those satiric dramatists who require the children's acting companies to mouth their venomous and scurrilous invectives.

Heywood was anything but a graceful or eloquent poet, and his voluminous verses are condignly neglected. Of uncertain date is the lengthy narrative poem *Troia Britanica, or Great Britain's Troy* (1609), a celebration of English monarchs down to James I. Equally ambitious and encyclopedic is his *Nine Books of Women,* which extols as "worthies" three Jews, three Gentiles, and three Christians. The strangest of Heywood's poems is the didactic, esoteric *Hierarchy of the Blessed Angels,* in nine books corresponding to the nine celestial orders, in which he discourses *ad infinitum* in verse and prose on demonic possession, astrology, necromancy, and other such matters "theological, philosophical, poetical, historical, apothegmatical, hieroglyphical, and emblematical."

A proper epitaph for Heywood as a dramatist might be lifted from one of his own prologues:

Of fairy elves, nymphs of sea and land,
The lawns and groves, no number
can be scann'd
Which we've not given feet to.

In his long career his indefatigable pen produced, with remarkable facility and ease, a steady stream of plays, but, allowing for only two or three exceptions, they reflect little genuine inspiration or concentration of powers. His characters are unrealized and inconsistent, his plots haphazardly conceived, and his dialogue frequently listless, uniform, and impotent. He rarely shows any sense of design or coherence, any conception of a play as an integration of plot, character, and language. His dramatic forte is in the creation of isolated scenes of poignant interaction and response, and even the best of these narrowly avert sentimentality. No doubt he thought of himself as a dramatic technician rather than an artist, and of his plays as ephemeral entertainments rather than literary works. Nevertheless, in at least one play, *A Woman Killed with Kindness,* he somehow transcended all these limitations with one thunderclap of purest genius.

The complete *Dramatic Works* was edited by R. H. Shepherd, 6 vols. (1874). The most comprehensive biographical and critical study is F. S. Boas, *Thomas Heywood* (1950). Two excellent critical studies from different perspectives are Otelia Cromwell, *Thomas Heywood: A Study in the Elizabethan Drama of Everyday Life* (1928), and F. M. Velte, *The Bourgeois Elements in the Dramas of Thomas Heywood* (1922; rev. ed., 1966). See also A. M. Clark, *Thomas Heywood, Playwright and Miscellanist* (1931). There is a Concise Bibliography by S. A. Tannenbaum (1939), continued in "Thomas Heywood (1938-65)," ed. Dennis Donovan, in *Elizabethan Bibliographies Supplements,* II (1967).

History of the Reign of King Henry VII, The. A history by Francis BACON. It was written in 1621-22, for the most part after Bacon's impeachment, and first published late in 1622. Bacon's principal sources were the sixteenth-century chroniclers, mainly Polydore Vergil. Bacon's history covers events from Bosworth Field in 1485, when Henry dethroned Richard III, to the last years of Henry VII's reign. The history follows a chronological development interrupted by speeches, dramatic dialogues, and extended authorial analysis of causes and effects. It concludes with a detailed interpretation of Henry VII's character, actions, and administration. What recommends Bacon's history is not only its lively, swift-moving, and lucid prose style, but its comprehensive grasp of legal complexities, for Bacon wrote with all the sure authority of one of England's greatest legal minds. Moreover, Bacon's analysis is also profoundly psychological, and he attempts to penetrate the opaque motives and strategies of a king who was independent, enigmatic, and notoriously devious. The Henry VII of Bacon appears as a man strangely similar to the author himself—practical, shrewd, cautious, and ruthlessly efficient. Bacon does not always admire these traits, but he acknowledges their necessity in a world of dangerous politics. The authority with which Bacon delineates that political world and its institutions gives his history a unique value. See BIOGRAPHY.

The standard edition is in *The Works,* ed. J. Spedding, R. L. Ellis, and D. D. Heath, 7 vols. (1857-59), VI. For commentary, see W. Busch, *England under the Tudors,* 2 vols. (1895) I; T. V. Wheeler, "Sir Francis Bacon's Historical Imagination," *TSL,* XIV (1969); and Edward Berry, "History and Rhetoric in Bacon's *Henry VII," Seventeenth-Century Prose: Modern Essays in Criticism,* ed. Stanley E. Fish (1971).

History of the World, The. See RALEIGH, SIR WALTER.

Histrio-Mastix. See PRYNNE, WILLIAM; CRITICISM, LITERARY.

Hobbes, Thomas (1588-1679). Philosopher Born at Westport, near Malmesbury, Wiltshire, the son of a country vicar of the Anglican Church, Hobbes later observed with characteristic wit that his mother was so alarmed by the Spanish Armada that she gave birth simultaneously to him and fear. The joke was not lost on Hobbes' contemporaries, who in later years mocked his pusillanimity in religion and politics. Hobbes attended Magdalen College, Oxford (1603-08); and, like Bacon and Milton, found college arid and stultifying for what in later years he contemptuously referred to as its "Aristotelity," or blind conformity to the scholastic disciples of Aristotle. After graduation he found employment as a tutor to William Cavendish (later second earl of Devonshire), an appointment that began a lifelong intimate friendship with the Cavendish family. In 1610 Hobbes conducted young Cavendish on a tour of France, Germany, and Italy, the first of his several sojourns on the Continent (others being in 1629-30; 1634-37; and 1640-51, chiefly in

Paris). Sometime during the period 1621-26 he was secretary to Francis Bacon, but it was not until he happened upon the mathematics of Euclid, in 1628 when Hobbes was forty, that he became wholly dedicated to the study of philosophy. His first publication was a translation of Thucydides in 1628.

Hobbes' initial philosophical treatise, *The Elements of Law, Natural and Politic,* was completed by 1640 but not printed until ten years later, when it appeared under two separate titles, *Human Nature* and *De Corpore Politico.* These developed the metaphysical materialism and mechanistic psychology that laid the groundwork for his best-known work on politics, LEVIATHAN (1651).

Alarmed by the angry deliberations of the Long Parliament, Hobbes became fearful that his life was somehow in danger and fled to Paris in 1640, where he remained for eleven years, part of that time acting as tutor to Prince Charles (later Charles II) and the sons of other English nobles in exile during the Civil War and the Cromwell regime. Hobbes enjoyed the company of French intellectuals, especially that of Pierre Gassendi (1592-1655), the astronomer and mathematician, friend of Pascal and Galileo (whom Hobbes had met in Italy in 1636), and caustic opponent of Aristotle and Descartes. In Paris Hobbes concluded another step toward his great *Leviathan* with the political treatise in Latin *De cive* (1642), which appeared in English with the title *Philosophical Rudiments Concerning Government and Society* (1651).

Although Royalists at the English court in exile approved Hobbes' spirited defense of absolute monarchy in these works, they began to suspect him of anticlericalism, materialism, and even atheism (despite Hobbes' protestations of piety), and in 1651, ever fearful of violent controversies, he returned to London and made his peace with Cromwell's government. In England he completed the last of his significant philosophical studies, *De corpore* (1655), rendered into English as *Elements of Philosophy, the First Section, Concerning Body* (1656), and *De homine* (1658).

With the return of monarchy to England, Hobbes was forgiven his defection and granted a pension, and resided quietly with the Cavendish family at their residences in London and Chatsworth, Derbyshire. Since his youth Hobbes had collected literary friends—Ben Jonson, Francis Bacon, Lord Herbert of Cherbury, Abraham Cowley, Sir Kenelm Digby, Edmund Waller, John Selden, and Sir William Davenant were all close acquaintances—and his conviviality, erudition, and wit were widely appreciated among intellectuals in the Restoration period. In his *Brief Lives* John Aubrey provides a lively firsthand account of Hobbes that includes such congenial quips as the philosopher's boast that he was not drunk over a hundred times in his life. Of amazing intellectual and physical stamina, Hobbes played a vigorous game of tennis while still in his seventies, and at eighty he completed a rhymed translation of Homer's *Iliad* and *Odyssey* (1673-75). His *Behemoth,* a candid interpretation of the causes of the Civil War, was written before 1668 and printed posthumously with his *Tracts* (1682).

Although primarily a philosopher, Hobbes made connections with literature at important points. His literary criticism, mainly in *Answer to Sir William D'Avenant's Preface before Gondibert,* printed with Davenant's *Preface of Gondibert* (1650), and in *Leviathan* (Part I, Chap. 8), represents the first treatment of literature in English based on systematic metaphysical and epistemological concepts (see CRITICISM, LITERARY). Hobbes' lucid definition of such terms as "fancy," "judgement," and "wit," which he linked to the functions of the mind and the operations of physical principles in nature, made a profound impression on literary criticism in the Restoration and eighteenth century, and the critical vocabularies of John Dryden, John Dennis, and Alexander Pope can be traced directly to Hobbes' ideas regarding the functions of reason, imagination, and judgment. Still another aspect of Hobbes' literary importance is his crisp, pungent, and utilitarian prose style that links Bacon's example of plain rhetoric with the practical style advocated by the Royal Society (of which Hobbes was never a member) and practiced by the prose masters of the eighteenth century.

A starting point for an explanation of Hobbes' philosophy is his terse definition of reality in *Leviathan,* Chapter 46, where he states that "every part of the universe is body, and that which is not body is no part of the universe: and because the universe is all, that which is no part of it is nothing, and consequently nowhere." Under its glaze of calculated abstractions, the passage conveys succinctly what Hobbes' contemporaries suspected he was suggesting but could scarcely believe he meant literally: that everything in the universe is material, and that which is not material simply does not exist except in the "decaying imagination." Unlike Donne, Sir Thomas Browne, or Descartes, therefore, Hobbes is not an "amphibian" divided between heaven and earth, soul and body, ideas and sensations; rather than sustain any such dualism, he jettisons the whole accumulation of Renaissance idealism—"Aristotelity," Platonism, and stoicism. Free will, the God-given moral faculty that Milton equated with reason, Hobbes describes as "last appetite," merely a mechanistic point of balance between delight and aversion, pleasure and pain. Since everything in the universe is material, man's experience is the result of external physical forces impinging upon internal physical faculties; in essence, man is a complex switchboard or computer sorting out and classifying data, and any Miltonic illusions of transcendence must be traced to the "decaying imagination," that most whimsical of faculties.

"Imagination therefore," notes Hobbes in *Leviathan,* "is nothing but decaying sense; and is found in men, and many other living creatures, as well sleeping as waking." In Hobbes' view, whatever is removed from the sensate world, wherein all "reality" resides, becomes suspect—imagination, passions, inspiration, and, of course, language itself. The implications for literature in these metaphysical assumptions and hypotheses are clear: imagination must be curtailed by judgment, spontaneity ordered by reflection, metaphors and symbols carefully grounded in sense data.

Clearly, Hobbes' mechanico-materialism heralded the final dissolution of the Renaissance spirit and the inception of a new Age of Reason in which restriction, not transcendence, became the cautious ideal; robust individualism and unfettered imagination became superseded by balanced, sane conformity and cool judgment carefully checked against established authority represented by the best classical authors and the acknowledged wits of the times. For Milton, an anachronism from an age that gave birth to Spenser and Shakespeare, the universe was penetrable by inspiration and metaphor; for Hobbes it can be understood only by systematic mastery of logical and mathematical principles.

Hobbes is a reminder that, in a sense, the sixteenth century had no need of philosophers because there were poets; in the sixteenth century, consciousness (a fact invariably embarrassing to Hobbes' psychology) was expanded to infinity by "correspondences" that are the essence of metaphor. Hobbes endeavors to constrict consciousness to a focal point in logical analysis—as in Pascal and Descartes, his recurring metaphor, significantly, is that of a watch or clock, appropriate counterparts of his metaphysical and psychological mechanico-materialism. In all matters pertaining to sense, he would reduce language to its tangible referent in physical "reality." Echoing Bacon's attack on imaginative language as one of man's "peccant humours," Hobbes maintains that "... the light of human minds is perspicuous words, but by exact definitions first snuffed, and purged from ambiguity. Reason is the pace, increase of science the way, and the benefit of mankind the end. And on the contrary, metaphors and senseless and ambiguous words are like *ignes fatui;* and reasoning upon them is wandering amongst innumerable absurdities . . ."

"Very nearly every statement of Hobbes," observes Basil Willey, "can be reduced either to hatred and contempt of schoolmen and clerics, or to fear of civil war and love of ordered living in a stable commonwealth." Hobbes could not forgive the scholastic philosophers for their abstruse "essences," "quiddities," and dissections of "soul," nor the clerics (chiefly the despised Puritans) for their divisive religious "enthusiasm," which, like Jonathan Swift, he identifies with the "decaying sense" of imagination and mindless passion. Moreover, these philosophical adversaries posited a conception of man that to Hobbes was conducive to an anarchic individualism.

A favorite irony of Hobbes is the contrast between the Renaissance illusion of man, a tissue of "nonsense" inflated by pompous metaphors, and his own concept of human nature, securely grounded in his own dialectical psychology and bleak materialism. Since there is nothing "real" of man except external stimuli, acted upon by his inner mechanism of wheels, springs, and wires, he responds between polarities of delight and aversion, attraction and revulsion, constantly in competition for a larger share of pleasure at the expense of another man's pain. By human nature, Hobbes always means Lear's "unaccommodated man" stripped of sublimation, golden metaphors, and the restraints of society. In such a state man is not deterred by "natural laws" or any of the other "innumerable absurdities" invented by "decaying sense"; his life, in Hobbes' famous phrase in *Leviathan,* is "solitary, poor, nasty, brutish, and short." In a way, Hobbes administers the *coup de grâce* to the expiring Renaissance ideal represented in the pastoral tradition, and it is small wonder that Milton's widow testified that the one author her husband "could not abide" was "Mr. Hobbes."

From Hobbes' grim view of human nature stems his idea of an artificial society in which men join to form a social contract for mutual self-preservation—to defend themselves, in effect, from their own bestial natures. In exchange for this security, they relinquish their freedom to the sovereign, who is the soul of this commonwealth, or "leviathan," and the first moral obligation of each member of the state becomes obedience. As Hobbes states in *Leviathan:* "This is more than consent or concord; it is a real unity of them all, in one and the same person, made by covenant of every man with every other man . . . This done, the multitude so united in one person is called a commonwealth, in Latin *civitas.* This is the generation of that great Leviathan, or rather (to speak more reverently) of that mortal god to which we owe under the immortal God our peace and defense."

This moral imperative of obedience in the social contract forms the basis of Hobbes' religion and ethics. It accounts for his extreme Erastianism, in which the church is totally subordinate to the monarch (another idea that inflamed some of Hobbes' contemporaries). It also explains how Hobbes' unequivocal materialism can be reconciled with the numerous Scriptural quotations and references to "God," "soul," and "faith" scattered throughout his writing. For Hobbes religion was dealt with on grounds of expediency even more simple than those of Pascal's famous "religious wager." Since religion (and even morality in any context except that of the original social contract) is a "fantasy" outside any corporeal reality, the whole problem returns to the simple question of which is more conducive to the peace and harmony of society—religious individualism and nonconformity, or obedience to a body of religious practices ordained by the monarch—and the tumultuous events of the 1640s and 1650s in England left no doubt in Hobbes' mind as to the proper answer. Hobbes was deeply distressed that his contemporaries construed his religious ideas as atheistic or cynical; indeed, his scrupulous effort to avoid such polemics was part of his own curious moral view that any idea or act must be judged by whether its consequences contributed to peace and order, the ultimate good, or to rebellion and anarchy, the worst of evils.

Thus it is ironic that Hobbes should find himself the center of emotionally violent controversy on all sides—from the church, the Royalists, the Puritans, the Cartesians, and almost every other organ and sinew of the leviathan. The most formidable of his opponents during the last twenty-five years of his life were the Cambridge Platonists, a group of university intellectuals that included Nathanael Culverwel (d. c. 1651); Ralph Cudworth (1617-1688), professor of Hebrew; Henry More (1614-1687), fellow of Christ's College; and John Smith (1618-1652). Except Culverwel, who died young and left only the posthumous work *The Light of Nature* (1652), the Cambridge Platonists were voluminous critics of Hobbes. Their basic ideas can be found in Cudworth's *The True Intellectual System of the Universe* (1678) and More's *Enchiridion ethicium* (1667) and *Divine Dialogues* (1668). They wrote in reaction against both Puritan dogmatism and Cartesian and Hobbesian materialism, insisting upon the spiritual nature of the universe, the soul and dignity of man, and the compatibility of Scripture and reason. In opposition to Descartes and Hobbes, they asserted the reality of a teleological universe of Platonic "forms," the validity of innate ideas, and the primacy of God-given reason over Hobbes' mechanistic psychic organs of fancy and judgment, and they argued that ethics were not determined by custom or expediency but by obedience to absolute laws corroborated by intuition, reason, Scripture, and even science.

In effect, the Cambridge Platonists revived the ancient controversy between the absolutist Socratics and relativistic, skeptical Sophists, and they lost because they shattered their lances against an iron-clad, systematic philosophy. It was the world described by Hobbes, not by the Cambridge Platonists, that conformed most nearly to the psychological and spiritual needs of Englishmen at the end of the Renaissance. The firm "reality" of Hobbes was devoid of ghosts, witches, and spiritual zeal, and if less mysterious and more constricted than Shakespeare's, it was also less chaotic and dangerous, or so it appeared to an age exhausted by religious controversy and desperately in search of lucidity, balance, and restraint.

The standard edition is still *The English Works of Thomas Hobbes,* ed. Sir William Molesworth, 11 vols. (1839-45). There is an excellent one-volume edition of *Leviathan* by Michael Oakeshott (1960). Two outstanding critiques are by T. E. Jessop, *Thomas Hobbes* (1960), and Leslie Stephen, *Hobbes* (1961). Hobbes' philosophy is treated by Basil Willey, *Seventeenth-Century Background* (1934); F. C. Hood, *The Divine Politics of Thomas Hobbes: An Interpretation of Leviathan* (1964); and J. W. N. Watkins, *Hobbes' System of Ideas* (1965). Samuel I. Mintz studies the development of Hobbes' philosophy in the seventeenth century in *The Hunting of Leviathan: Seventeenth-Century Reactions to the Materialism and Moral Philosophy of Thomas Hobbes* (1962). There is an extensive bibliography of Hobbes by Hugh Macdonald (1952).

Hoby, Sir Thomas (1530-1566). Diplomat and translator. Little is known of Hoby's early years. He attended St. John's College, Cambridge, for two years, studying Latin, Greek, and rhetoric under Roger Ascham and Sir John Cheke, and then traveled extensively in Europe after 1547 in preparation for a career in diplomacy. He took up residence in Strasbourg with Martin Bucer, the Protestant reformer and scholar whose views on divorce later influenced Milton. After translating several of Bucer's works, Hoby studied classical and Italian literature at the University of Padua. His diary of these and later years abroad until 1564 was published as *The Travels and Life of Sir Thomas Hoby* and gives an interesting picture of Hoby as an earnest student of French and Italian geography, customs, art, and literature.

Hoby's diplomatic career flourished under Edward VI, but with the accession of Catholic Mary Tudor he fled England to join his former master Sir John Cheke at Padua. According to Hoby's diary, it was here during the years 1554-56 that he completed the work for which he is famous, his translation of Baldassare Castiglione's *Il Cortegiano.* Castiglione's lively portrayal of several notable Catholic dignitaries translated by a militant Protestant like Hoby caused it to be kept from the press until Queen Elizabeth's reign. First published in 1561 as THE COURTIER, it was an immediate success, rivaling in popularity and influence such other great TRANSLATIONS as Arthur Golding's of Ovid's *Metamorphoses* (1565-67), Sir Thomas North's of Plutarch's *Lives* (1579), and John Florio's of Montaigne's *Essays* (1603). Additional editions of *The Courtier* appeared in 1577, 1587, and 1603; the 1587 edition was an elaborate version with translations in English and French in parallel columns. Five years after the first edition of *The Courtier* Hoby died in retirement as a gentleman landowner at Bisham, Berkshire.

Although Castiglione's Italian is rich and stately, Hoby renders it into crisp, plain, and concrete English. His motives in making the translation were set forth in his dedication to Lord Henry Hastings in the 1561 edition, wherein he proclaims his work to be appropriate for "princes and great men" as "a rule to rule themselves that rule others" and for "men grown in years" as a "pathway to the beholding and musing of the mind" as well as for young gentlemen as "an encouraging to garnish their mind with moral virtues and their body with comely exercises." He also intended the book to be read by gentlewomen as "a mirror to deck and trim themselves with virtuous conditions, comely behaviors, and honest entertainment toward all men." Hence *The Courtier* was an important contribution to COURTESY LITERATURE, but much of its popularity can be attributed to the fact it bears a relationship to several other genres much in vogue during the period—educational tracts, philosophical treatises and essays, and utopias.

The standard edition of *The Courtier* is by Walter Raleigh in the Tudor Translations (1900). *The Travels and Life of Sir Thomas Hoby, 1547-64* has been edited by Edgar Powell for the Camden Society, Series 3, IV (1902). For Castiglione, see Julia Cartwright, *Baldassare Castiglione,* 2 vols. (1902); for Hoby's methods as a translator, F. O. Matthiessen, *Translation: An Elizabethan Art* (1931)

Holinshed, Raphael (d. 1580?). Chronicler. Born at an uncertain date in Cheshire. Holinshed came to London as a minister, according to Anthony à Wood, and began his literary career as a translator for Reginald Wolfe, printer to the queen. Wolfe assigned Holinshed the monumental task of compiling and editing "a universal cosmography of the whole world" (in Holinshed's words) from the Flood to the reign of Elizabeth. After Wolfe's death twenty-five years later, his heirs settled for the less ambitious labor of publishing only the histories of England, Scotland, and Ireland. Although Holinshed had already done the bulk of these histories, William Harrison was contracted to write a topographical and social description of England, and Richard Stanyhurst of Ireland. The completed work was first published in 1577 as *The First Volume of the Chronicles of England, Scotland, and Ireland . . . Containing the Description and Chronicles of England from the First Inhabiting unto the Conquest.* Subsequently the history became known as simply "Holinshed's Chronicles." An elaborate publication, it contained illustrations of coronations, executions, and battles. The history of England was dedicated to Lord Burghley, that of Scotland to the earl of Leicester, and that of Ireland to Sir Henry Sidney. A second, enlarged edition was published in 1587, and it was this edition Shakespeare primarily consulted as the principal source of his history plays.

In the first edition several passages offensive to the government were deleted, and in the second some additional sections were expunged. Missing portions were restored in editions of 1722-23 and 1728; but the first complete and unexpurgated version of the chronicles, together with those by Edward Hall (1542) and Richard Grafton (1568), was edited by Sir Henry Ellis, 6 vols. (1807-08).

The portions of Holinshed used by Shakespeare were edited by Josephine and Allardyce Nicoll, *Holinshed's Chronicle Used in Shakespeare's Plays* (1927) and by Richard Housley, *Shakespeare's Holinshed: An Edition of Holinshed's Chronicles, 1587* (1968). F. J. Furnivall edited parts of Harrison's *Description of England,* 3 vols. (1877-81). For commentary on Holinshed, see W. G. Boswell-Stone, *Shakespeare's Holinshed: The Chronicle and the Historical Plays Compared* (1896); Jeanette Fellheimer, "Geoffrey Fenton's *History of Guicciardin* and Holinshed's *Chronicles* of 1587," *MLQ,* VI (1945); and Geoffrey Bullough, *Narrative and Dramatic Sources of Shakespeare,* 7 vols. (1972).

Holy State and the Profane State, The. See FULLER, THOMAS. CHARACTERS; ESSAYS.

Honest Whore, The. A comedy in two parts by Thomas DEKKER. Part I, written and first printed in 1604, is believed to be in small measure the work also of Thomas MIDDLETON. Part II, written 1605 but not printed until 1630, is entirely by Dekker.

Part I involves two main stories. In the first, Infelice's father, Gasparo, duke of Milan, who opposes his daughter's love affair with Count Hippolito, has arranged for Doctor Benedict to administer a sleeping potion to her. Gasparo convinces Hippolito that his daughter has died, and when Infelice awakens, he deceives her in turn into believing that Hippolito is dead. In the second story Candido, a linen draper, is so irritatingly patient that his wife Viola longs to see him angry. A visit from Viola's brother Fustigo enables her to put her husband's maddening patience to the test, but not even Fustigo's outrageous behavior can ruffle Candido's serenity.

After also failing to incite the patient Candido, a group of young courtiers pay a visit to a beautiful and vivacious prostitute, Bellafront, to whom Hippolito's friend Matheo also brings the reluctant count, still grieving over the supposed death of Infelice. Instead of seducing Hippolito, Bellafront is converted by his eloquent lecture on vice; she resolves to be chaste henceforth and to give her new "honest" love entirely to Hippolito, who scorns her advances. Doctor Benedict, after being rebuffed by Duke Gasparo, informs Hippolito that Infelice is still alive and offers to meet him in Bethlem Monastery, where the doctor promises to arrange Hippolito's wedding to Infelice.

As a last effort to break down Candido's patience, meanwhile, his wife has had him removed to a madhouse.

At Bethlem Monastery the lovers disguise themselves as friars; Gasparo and his courtiers appear in search of the lovers, and Bellafront, in the company of her former clients, reveals Hippolito and Infelice to Gasparo. When finally it is shown that the lovers have married, Gasparo accepts his new son-in-law, Bellafront contents herself with marrying Matheo, and the patient Candido is released from the madhouse.

In Part II, the "honest whore" Bellafront is a loyal and devoted wife to Matheo, who turns out to be a profligate scoundrel, whereas Hippolito, once impervious to Bellafront's blandishments, is now a weak and wavering husband sorely tempted by Bellafront's beauty. As for Candido, the patient and simple draper, his shrewish first wife has died, and Part II depicts his vicissitudes with his second, whom the bawds and gallants of the town vainly try to seduce in order to vex him out of his maddening equanimity.

Matheo is released from prison, where he was charged with murder, and returns home to drink, gamble, and torment his faithful wife Bellafront, who continues to reject Hippolito's passionate advances. Bellafront's father joins her household disguised as Pacheco, a serving man. After several episodes showing Matheo's disgraceful mistreatment of Bellafront, events bring the main characters to Bridewell prison, where all confticts are resolved. Hippolito defends Bellafront's loyalty to Matheo in the face of the husband's accusations, Pacheco reveals himself as Bellafront's long-lost father, Hippolito rejoins his wife, and Candido, wrongly imprisoned because of a trick played on him by town gallants, is released. In the end Matheo is warned to reform, Hippolito repents of his illicit infatuation, and only Bots, a common pander, receives punishment.

No source for *The Honest Whore* has been found. No doubt Dekker simply made improvisations on several very familiar characters and situations. As the names of the characters suggest, his comedy reflects the influence of Jonson's comedy of humours (see JONSON, BEN). Bellafront means "beautiful face," Infelice "unhappy," and Candido "honest" or "sincere." The reformation of the prostitute was a favorite topic with dramatists, and Dekker gives it a fresh look in Part I by having Bellafront rejected by a prudish Hippolito, who becomes the agent of her conversion. The linen draper Candido is a masculine rendition of the familiar Patient Grissel, a favorite character of Dekker, although some critics see him as a Christ figure, others as symbolic of Puritanism.

The differences between Part I and II of the play are sometimes explained by Middleton's absence from Part II, but it is more probable that in Part II Dekker simply found that he had exhausted his ideas in the first part and had to begin another story with changed characters. His most notable innovation was reversing the roles of Bellafront and Hippolito. In the second part Bellafront replaces Candido in the role of Patient Grissel, and in Part II Candido is anything but the forbearing man he was in Part I.

The standard edition is in Dekker's *Dramatic Works,* ed. Fredson Bowers, 4 vols. (1953-61). Important criticism is by Mary L. Hunt, *Thomas Dekker* (1911); Mary G. M. Adkins, "Puritanism in the Plays and Pamphlets of Thomas Dekker," *University of Toronto Studies in English* (1939); and James H. Conover, *Thomas Dekker: An Analysis of Dramatic Structure* (1969).

Hooker, Richard (1554-1600). Anglican theologian. Hooker was born at Heavitree, Exeter, and attended Corpus Christi College, Oxford, under the patronage of John Jewel, bishop of Salisbury. For several years Hooker was tutor to Edwin Sandys, son of the bishop of London, later archbishop of York, and to Thomas Cranmer's young nephew. In 1577 Hooker became a fellow of Corpus Christi and two years later a lecturer in Hebrew. He took holy orders in 1581, and in 1585 was given the mastership of the Temple church, where he became embroiled in a sustained theological controversy with Walter Travers, a brilliant Puritan lecturer. As the moderate and tolerant Hooker was to note later in the preface to his great work, OF THE LAWS OF ECCLESIASTICAL POLITY. the dissension between him and Travers was conducted with "such bowls of love, and such a commixture of that love with reason, as was never exceeded but in Holy Writ." Yet the lengthy controversy so troubled and wearied Hooker that he petitioned John Whitgift, archbishop of Canterbury, to be relieved of his duties at the Temple so that he might have leisure to prepare "a treatise in which I intend a justification of the laws of our ecclesiastical polity"—that is, a systematic defense of Anglican episcopacy against the arguments of its Calvinist critics.

In 1591 Hooker was permitted to resign his post at the Temple and given a rectorship at Boscombe, Wiltshire. In 1595 he accepted his last assignment, a country parsonage at Bishopsbourne, near Canterbury. After 1591 Hooker's treatise became his absorbing concern, and although the church he defended in the work forgot the project as soon as it was proposed, his labors were subsidized by his friend and patron Edwin Sandys and by his father-in-law. The first four books of Hooker's *Laws of Ecclesiastical Polity* appeared in 1594; the fifth book was printed in 1597. The sixth and eighth books were not published until 1648 and 1651, the seventh in 1662.

Hooker's work represents not only a solid compendium of philosophical ideas in support of ecclesiastical and secular hierarchy, but a reasoned proposal for an open and tolerant society based on mutual love and respect. The work is recognized as a monument of English prose style; appearing at the end of a century of stylistic evolution, it represents the high-water mark of a prose that is at once lucid and elegant, formally balanced and yet forceful and flowing.

The best life is still the lively and laudatory one written by Izaak Walton for the 1666 edition of the *Laws* and many times reprinted. Walton's errors have been corrected by C. J. Sisson, *The Judicious Marriage of Mr. Hooker and the Birth of "The Laws of Ecclesiastical Polity"* (1940). The standard edition of Hooker's works is still that by John Keble, 6th ed., 3 vols. (1874). Hooker's philosophy in the light of Anglican-Calvinist controversies is treated by F. J. Shirley, *Richard Hooker and Contemporary Political Ideas* (1949), and Peter Muntz, *The Place of Hooker in the History of Thought* (1952). See also *Richard Hooker: A Selected Bibliography,* ed. Egil Grislis and W. Speed Hill (1971).

Howard, Henry, earl of Surrey (1517-1547). Poet and courtier. Surrey was the eldest son of Thomas Howard, third duke of Norfolk, and descended from English kings on both sides of his family. At one time he was considered a candidate for marriage to Henry VIII's eldest daughter, later the queen Mary Tudor, and his sister married Henry's illegitimate son, the duke of Richmond. His cousin was Catherine Howard, Henry VIII's wife during the years 1540-42. Hence Surrey's life consisted chiefly of politics, court intrigue, and soldiering, with poetry his avocation and passionate amusement. He served at the French court as a companion to the duke of Richmond in 1532 and in 1536 joined the force under his father's command which put down the insurrection in Cornwall called the Pilgrimage of Grace. When accused of sympathizing with the rebels, he struck a courtier in the royal presence and was jailed for a time in 1537, an experience he describes in one of his most famous poems, "Imprisoned at Windsor."

Surrey's career depended largely on the fortunes of his cousin Catherine Howard and her supporters, and when she was the king's favorite and later queen, he was successively Knight of the Garter, seneschal of Norfolk, and steward of Cambridge University. After her execution in 1542, he fell prey to the growing power of the Seymour faction at court. In 1543 he was again imprisoned, for disturbing the peace and breaking Lent, an event he celebrates in a brilliant satire ("London, hast thou accused me") in which he mockingly protests that he was only trying to awaken the conscience of a wicked London by breaking its windows during Lent. He served heroically in the wars against France in 1544-46, being wounded before Montreuil and commanding the English forces at Boulogne. After losing a battle at St. Etienne, he was tried on trumped-up charges initiated by the Seymours and executed on Tower Hill in January, 1547. He was not quite thirty years old.

Like Sir Thomas WYATT, Surrey studied Italian poetry, especially the sonnets of Petrarch and he shares with Wyatt credit for introducing the sonnet form into English. Unlike Wyatt, however, Surrey favored the so-called English, or Shakespearean, sonnet of three quatrains and a couplet, which requires fewer rhymes than the Italian formula. The result is a smoother, more finely shaped sonnet than Wyatt achieved. One of Surrey's finest sonnets, "From Tuscan came my lady's worthy race," was written to Elizabeth, daughter of the ninth earl of Kildare, the "Geraldine" that seems to have inspired the entirely fictitious portrait of Surrey in Thomas Nashe's *The Unfortunate Traveller.* From the Italians Surrey also learned blank verse, which he introduced into English for the first time in his translation of Books II and IV of Vergil's *Aeneid* (1557). (See TRANSLATIONS.)

Surrey wrote a number of religious poems—some psalms and a paraphrase of Ecclesiastes I-V, chiefly in awkward POULTER'S MEASURE—but he is best remembered for the forty lyrics that appeared for the first time with Wyatt's in Tottel's Miscellany (1557). After their joint appearance in this popular anthology the phrase "Wyatt and Surrey" became synonymous with the "new poetry" of Henry VIII's reign. Yet there is little else to connect the two men except their mutual enthusiasm for Petrarch and other Italian poets. Surrey was in his twenties when Wyatt died, and though he expressed debt to the older poet and wrote a gracious elegy on his death, he was only casually acquainted with him.

Distinctions between Surrey and Wyatt must be underscored because they are too often lumped together as a result of their common berth in Tottel's Miscellany. Whereas Wyatt's forte is song and dramatic poems, Surrey has little facility in either. Surrey's best poems are plain, epigrammatic lyrics of the kind later perfected by Jonson, nostalgic verse epistles like "Imprisoned at Windsor," or adaptations of classical and continental poetic forms. This latter mastery enables Surrey to depart more radically than Wyatt from native rhythms and idioms and makes him much more confident and graceful in adapting Petrarch to English. Hence Surrey manages subtle modulations and elegance of diction rarely achieved in Wyatt's wooden translations from the Italian. It was Surrey's superior mastery of continental literary forms that accounts for the fact that Elizabethans generally preferred him to Wyatt, whose best verses were grown on native grounds. From a modern perspective, Surrey is hardly a major poet in the sense of being a Sidney or a Spenser; nonetheless, his importance in literary history remains considerable.

The standard edition of *The Poems* is by F. M. Padelford (rev. ed., 1928). Surrey's translation of Book IV of Vergil is edited by H. Hartman (1933). The best biographical and critical account is Edwin Casady, *Henry Howard, Earl of Surrey* (1938). See also J. M. Berdan. *Early Tudor Poetry* (1920), and Burton Fishman, "Recent Studies in Wyatt and Surrey," *ELR,* I (1971).

Howell, James (1594?-1666). For comment on his *Epistolae Ho-Elianae,* see ESSAYS; LETTER-WRITERS.

humours, comedy of. See JONSON, BEN.

Hyde, Edward, earl of Clarendon (1609-1674). Historian and statesman. Born in Wiltshire, Clarendon graduated B.A. at Magdalen College, Oxford, in 1626 and completed his legal training at the Middle Temple in 1633. During these years he was a close friend of Ben Jonson and other literati, including Thomas Carew, Sir William Davenant, John Earle, John Selden, Edmund Waller, Lucius Carey, and Viscount Falkland. As a member of Parliament in 1640-41 he proved mildly liberal on the issue of representative government, but the zeal of the Puritans drove him closer to monarchy. After the outbreak of the Civil War he lived for three years at Charles I's camp at Oxford, where he was knighted and appointed chancellor of the Exchequer and privy councilor. In 1646 he fled with Prince Charles to the Scilly Isles, where he began work on his *History of the Rebellion,* and in 1648 followed the prince and Queen Henrietta Maria into exile in France, where he was made lord chancellor of the exile government in 1658.

After the monarchy was restored in 1660, Clarendon held a number of important positions under Charles II, including chancellor of Oxford and speaker of the House of Lords. In spite of his loyalty, however, the king disliked him because of his rigid legality and constitutionality. In 1667 Charles II allowed Clarendon's enemies to make him the scapegoat of the Dutch wars, and he was deprived of his citizenship and exiled to France, where he died at Rouen in 1674. His body was returned to England and buried in Westminster Abbey.

Clarendon did not complete his monumental *History of the Rebellion* until 1671-72, after he had been exiled to France. He intended the work to be a primary source of reference rather than a history, and to this end he published it in several parts. It first appeared, under the editorial supervision of his son, in three volumes printed at Oxford in 1702-04. A companion volume covering most of the events recounted in the *History* is his autobiography, written in the third person and intended to be read by members of his immediate family; the autobiography appeared as *The Life of Edward Hyde, Earl of Clarendon, Being a Continuation of the History of the Rebellion* (1759). Although the events of Clarendon's history cover the period 1625 to about 1668, the primary focus is on the turbulent years 1642-60 (see AUTOBIOGRAPHY).

Clarendon was a first-hand witness to many

of the great events and personalities of these times, and he often had immediate access to government records. His view of the Civil War and the principal actors in that long struggle—Charles I, Queen Henrietta Maria, Cromwell, John Pym, General George Monk, and many others—is that of an unstinting Royalist, a devout Anglican, and a strict constitutionalist. Yet in spite of his apparent bias, he writes a meticulously substantiated and detailed account that reflects a deep awareness of the economic, political, and religious complexity of the issues. Clarendon's *History* created a model for later historical writing. In a plain style that is not as stately although as sweeping in philosophic range as Raleigh's *History of the World,* he writes a clear prose marked by persistent concreteness concerning people, places, and events. His characterizations of the vacillating Charles I and his impetuous queen are done with a compassionate sense of their inevitable tragedy. His view of historical events is seen through the ironic eyes of a temporizing constitutionalist who watched ambition and pride on both sides lead to abuse of power and national disaster.

The standard life is by Sir H. Craik, *The Life of Edward, Earl of Clarendon,* 2 vols. (1911). The best complete edition of Clarendon's *History of the Rebellion* is still that of W. D. Macray, 6 vols. (1888). Sir Charles H. Firth discusses the composition of the work in "Clarendon's *History of the Rebellion,*" *EHR,* XIX (1904); see also L. C. Knights, "Reflection in Clarendon's *History of the Rebellion,*" *Scrutiny,* XV (1948). *The Calendar of the Clarendon State Papers* in the Bodleian Library, an essential source for research in the Stuart period, was edited by O. Ogle, W. H. Bliss, W. D. Macray, and F. J. Routledge (1872-1932).

Hyde Park, A comedy of manners by James SHIRLEY, written about 1632 and first published in 1637. No source for the plot is known. The play was first performed in 1632 at the Phoenix Theatre by Queen Henrietta's Men, perhaps to celebrate the annual spring opening of Hyde Park to the public. The scene is London in the early seventeenth century.

The plot, which is very thin, concerns the courting of three pairs of lovers. The supposed widow Bonavent's merchant husband, lost for seven years abroad, returns in time to keep his wife from marrying again. Julietta, whose virtue is under siege by one Lord Bonvile, chooses instead the more honorable Trier, and Julietta's brother Fairfield, in love with Mistress Carol, wins his beloved only when he swears to her that he does not love her.

Shirley's *Hyde Park* illustrates that the comedy of manners was already well-developed in England before the Restoration period. The action of the play is hardly considerable, but the characters represent the comedy of manners at a sophisticated stage. The stereotyped characters of the genre are thoroughly represented—the gallant but good-hearted rake, the decayed nobleman, the garrulous city wife, and the stolid and only moderately bright merchant husband. The scenes in Hyde Park and the horse races shown on the stage are indicative of Shirley's efforts to achieve new dimensions of realism.

Hyde Park was edited for the Mermaid series by Sir Edmund Gosse (1888). Critical studies include R. S. Forsythe, *The Relations of Shirley's Plays to the Elizabethan Drama* (1914), and Theodore Miles, "Place-Realism in a Group of Caroline Plays," *RES,* XVIII (1942).

I

Ignatius His Conclave. A religious satire in prose by John DONNE. Of uncertain date of composition, it was first printed anonymously both in Latin and English editions in 1611. The chief object of Donne's venomous satire are the Jesuits, personified by Donne's monstrously proud and hypocritical Ignatius Loyola, founder of the Society of Jesus.

As Donne's body lies in a trance, or "extasie," his "sportful soul" sets forth on a journey through the universe until it arrives at the most distant room of hell, where Pope Boniface III and Mahomet are debating to determine who will occupy the highest room in hell, reserved by Satan for the greatest innovators. As Donne's soul listens, several others appear at Satan's gate and compete for admission. The first innovator to make his appeal is Copernicus, the astronomer, whom Satan is reluctant to admit because, although he is undeniably an innovator and a notorious heretic (from the Roman Catholic view), he is also dangerously individualistic and rebellious, for he has already turned the universe upside down, altered time, and even confused heaven and earth about saints' birthdays.

The next claimant to Satan's privileged domain is one "Philippus Aureolus Theophrastus Paracelsus Bombast of Hohênheim," the pompous name for Paracelsus, the German alchemist (1493-1541), who claims favorable treatment because his quack medicines killed most of the patients he promised to cure. At the right hand of Satan during this unholy conclave is Ignatius, jealous of the Jesuits' prerogatives, who denounces Paracelsus as a mere pretender since the Jesuits have practiced medicine far more perniciously than he. Paracelsus humbly submits to Ignatius' claim to superiority in medical trickery and skulduggery.

Next rises Machiavelli, who cunningly attempts to give Satan the impression that Ignatius would usurp the throne of hell. Slyly modest, Machiavelli insists that he can make no claims to innovation comparable to those by the ingenious Jesuits, even though he was their tutor, their political mentor, and hence an assiduous helper in populating hell. In response, Ignatius charges that Machiavelli worshiped his own wit instead of Satan, and that he conspired against Satan's chief helper, the pope. In praise of the pope's many contributions to hell, Ignatius provides a long list of papal sins, including imperialism, indulgences, flagrant countenance of vice, and usury. Obviously defeated, Machiavelli vanishes and Ignatius withdraws for a private and privileged consultation with Satan. Meanwhile hordes of other souls clamber for entrance to the highest room reserved for innovators. Among these are Christopher Columbus and St. Philip Neri (1515-1595), founder in 1575 of the Congregation of the Oratory, a society of secular priests. Finally, the uneasy Satan devises a plan whereby Ignatius can rule without threatening hell's sovereignty. He will ask the pope to employ Galileo to bring the moon closer to earth so that all Jesuits can go there and live under a "Lunatic Church" ruled by Ignatius. At the conclusion of Donne's vision, his soul returns to its body on earth.

The best editions are by C. M. Coffin (1941), and T. S. Healy (1970). Evelyn Simpson's *Study of the Prose Works of John Donne* (rev. ed., 1948) contains an important analysis. See also Marjorie Nicolson, "Kepler, the *Somnium,* and John Donne," *JHI,* I (1940), and Chris R. Hassel, Jr., "Donne's *Ignatius His Conclave* and the New Astronomy," *MP,* LXVIII (1971).

inkhorn terms. Words of native origin or common usage combined grotesquely with foreign words. During the sixteenth century, when English became influenced by Greek, Latin, Italian, and French, scholars like Sir John Cheke, Roger Ascham, and Thomas Wilson objected to the use of "ink-pot words" and sought to establish a plain English style "unmixed and unmangled with borrowings of other types." In *The Art of Rhetoric* (1553), Wilson cites this example of "strange words": "Now, therefore, being accersited to such splendent renown and dignity splendidious, I doubt not but you will adjuvate such poor adnichilate orphans as whilom ware condisciples with you and of antique familiarity in Lincolnshire. Emong whom I, being a scholastical panion, obtestate your sublimity to extol mine infirmity."

In his *Art of English Poesy* (1589) George Puttenham objects to such terms only when they are employed in place of English words already in common use. He accepts as legitimate such new "usurped Latin and French" words as *method, placation, function, assubtiling,* and *figurative,* but rejects as "ill-affected" *audacious, fecundity* (for "eloquence") and *compatible.* Some of these words, of course, came into common usage and ceased being "inkhorn terms." Others, like Costard's "honorificabilitudinitatibus" in *Love's Labour's Lost,* proved to be "easier swallowed than a flapdragon."

For a discussion of inkhorn terms and other aspects of foreign influence on English during the Renaissance, see A. C. Baugh, *History of the English Language* (1935)

Inns of Court. The four English law schools, consisting of the Inner Temple, the Middle Temple, Lincoln's Inn, and Gray's Inn. The Inner Temple appointed a master of revels as early as 1505, and throughout the sixteenth century all four Inns participated in staging plays and masques and in translating classical and contemporary foreign literature. Since the Inns of Court did not require a formal program of legal study until about 1700, many students before that spent their time writing or translating, biding time until a court or church appointment, or merely enjoying themselves at lighter pursuits. The famous literary figures who resided at the Inns include, at Lincoln's Inn, Sir Thomas More, Thomas Lodge, John Donne, and Francis Quarles; at Gray's Inn, George Gascoigne, Thomas Campion, Francis Bacon, and Sir John Suckling; at the Middle Temple, Richard Hakluyt, Sir Thomas Overbury, Sir John Davies, John Marston, John Ford, and Thomas Carew; and at the Inner Temple, Thomas Sackville and William Browne.

Toward the end of the sixteenth century masques became a favorite entertainment at the Inns of Court, especially at Christmas, Epiphany, Shrove Tuesday, Candlemas, and May Day. Sackville and Norton's *Gorboduc,* the first tragedy in blank verse, was initially performed at the Inner Temple; Gascoigne and Kinwelmarsh's *Jocasta,* the first English play based on a Greek drama, and his *Supposes,* the earliest English comedy in prose, both appeared for the first time at Gray's Inn. Chapman wrote at least one masque for the Middle Temple and Lincoln's Inn, a celebration of the marriage of Princess Elizabeth and the Count Palatine, and the same year Francis Beaumont and Francis Bacon honored the same event with *The Masque of the Inner Temple and Gray's Inn.* Several of Shakespeare's plays were performed at the Inns, including a performance of *The Comedy of Errors* at Gray's Inn on December 28, 1594, and one of *Twelfth*

Night at the Middle Temple in February 1601. More sophisticated than the audiences at the popular theaters, the residents at the Inns of Court consistently favored Beaumont and Fletcher's tragicomedies in the Jacobean and Caroline periods.

The most comprehensive study of the literary influence of the Inns is by A. Wigfall Green, *The Inns of Court and Early English Drama* (1931); see also Philip J. Finkelpearl, *John Marston of the Middle Temple* (1969).

Instauratio magna. See BACON, FRANCIS.

Institution of a Gentleman, The. See COURTESY LITERATURE.

Instructions to His Son. See RALEIGH, SIR WALTER.

interlude. A drama or dialogue, usually brief and farcical, that is not entirely distinguishable from the medieval MORALITY PLAY from which the interlude developed at the beginning of the sixteenth century. The term "interlude," which came into use around 1500, originally signified a play sufficiently brief to be performed between courses at a feast or between two parts of a longer play. Unlike the morality play, the interlude was performed for aristocratic audiences, frequently by professional actors. Although it often employs the allegorical figures and didacticism characteristic of the morality play, the interlude stresses wit, satire, and realism, and thus was instrumental in secularizing the native English drama.

The first known writer of interludes was Henry Medwall, chaplain to Cardinal Morton, whose first play of record, *Fulgens and Lucrece,* was acted at Lambeth Palace at Christmas 1497 to provide entertainment at a feast held for the Flemish and Spanish ambassadors. It is divided into two parts, the first given at the end of dinner in the afternoon, the second at the end of supper that evening. Based on a dialogue printed by William Caxton in 1481, it relates how the Roman heiress Lucrece chooses a worthy suitor of low degree in preference to a prodigal of noble birth, and it is the first English play to focus exclusively on a love story. Lucrece's servants and those of her suitors provide the kind of farcical subplot characteristic of the later drama.

The chief practitioner of interludes at the court of Henry VIII was John HEYWOOD, the king's court musician who composed seven lively and witty interludes: *Witty and Witless; Gentleness and Nobility;* JOHAN JOHAN THE HUSBAND, TIB HIS WIFE, AND SIR JOHN THE PRIEST; A PLAY OF LOVE; THE PARDONER AND THE FRIAR; THE FOUR PP; and THE PLAY OF THE WEATHER. Like most other writer's of interludes. Heywood incorporated, to varying degrees, three dominant influences: the morality play, the French farce, and the Latin school drama. From the last Heywood derived many of his character types—the pedantic schoolmaster, the wily servant, the jealous husband, and the braggart soldier. From the French farces he borrowed much of his low comedy and obscenity.

Another adaptation, and one that well illustrates ways in which the interludes were often grafted onto the old form of the morality plays, is John Redford's *Wit and Science* (c. 1530), written for performance by the boys at St. Paul's. The play portrays the efforts of young Wit to marry Lady Science, daughter of Reason and Experience. To prove himself worthy of the lady, Wit must ascend Mount Parnassus and slay the giant Tediousness, who guards its slopes. After some help from Diligence, Instruction, and Study, Wit overcomes the giant and wins the lady (represented by his college diploma). Hence in Redford's interlude the old theme of the struggle of the soul to achieve salvation, the principal conflict of the moralities, is humanistically altered to inspire achievement in secular education.

Also illustrative of the morality play in a state of transition is John Skelton's *Magnificence* (c. 1516), which is a morality play in its form and an interlude in its political content. Skelton's play tells how a well-meaning, prosperous prince is brought under the power of Adversity; Despair has almost seduced him into suicide when, true to the morality tradition. Good Hope and other virtues rescue him.

Other writers of interludes employed the interlude for the expression of religious propaganda, John Bale preaching anti-Catholicism in such interludes as *Comedy Concerning Three Laws* (c. 1538) and Nicholas Udall (if he was, in fact, the author) attacking Protestantism in *Respublica* (1553). Both plays reflect the influence of the Latin school drama in their use of the five-act structure.

The popularity of interludes waned after

the reign of Henry VIII and the rise of drama as pure entertainment rather than moral instruction. The aristocratic audiences that originally sponsored interludes grew weary of their simplistic extremes of solemn didacticism and obscene farce, and their brief vogue during the early Tudor period gave way to more sophisticated plays. Nevertheless, as with the morality plays, the interludes continued to influence the later drama, and as late as the 1590s Elizabethans were still referring to plays in general as "interludes."

Several of the best interludes are collected in J. Q. Adams, *Chief Pre-Shakespearean Dramas* (1924). For a critical discussion of the genre, see C. F. Tucker Brooke, *The Tudor Drama* (1911); F. S. Boas, *An Introduction to Tudor Drama* (1933); and J. E. Bernard, *The Prosody of the Tudor Interlude* (1939).

Island Princess, The. A tragicomedy by John FLETCHER, written around 1619-21 and printed in 1647. It is based in part on a Spanish history of the conquest of the Molucca Islands in the East Indies, Bartolomé Leonardo de Argensola's *La conquista de las islas Malucas* (1609), which Fletcher followed closely for the first three acts.

On the Island of Tidore, three men compete for the hand of Princess Quisara, whose father, the kindly king of Tidore, has been imprisoned by his neighbor, the tyrannical and villainous governor of Ternata. Her suitors are Ruy Dias, a Portuguese commander; Armusia, a daring Portuguese soldier; and her father's cruel enemy, the governor of Ternata. Under no circumstances, she announces, will she marry the last, but she will give her hand to the man who frees her father. Although she hopes that the victor in this contest will be the one she loves, Ruy Dias, it is Armusia who frees her father and demands the prize, whereupon she and Ruy Dias conspire to murder the noble Armusia rather than honor the pledge. Their would-be victim behaves so honorably and heroically, however, that Quisara transfers her love from Ruy Dias to Armusia. The governor of Ternata, disguised as a holy Moorish priest, causes the king of Tidore to suspect the integrity of all Portuguese, and after the king and his priest overhear Armusia declaim against Quisara's pagan religion, they have him thrown in prison, whence he is rescued by Ruy Dias as atonement for his previous treachery. Finally, the wicked governor of Ternata is deposed and imprisoned, the king of Tidore reconciled with his daughter, and Armusia betrothed to Quisara.

The Island Princess shows Fletcher at the zenith of his romantic imagination and lyric power, and it gives his unique dramatic qualities their purest expression—exquisitely refined sentiments, improbable reversals of action and motives, a fanciful charm combined with a certain coarseness. His poetry is more captivating than the characters who utter it. In *Paradise Lost* (II, 636 ff.), Milton may have recalled Fletcher's haunting description of the Molucca Islands:

Where every wind that rises blows perfumes,
And every breath of air is like an incense.
The treasure of the sun dwells here; each tree,
As if it envied the old Paradise,
Strives to bring forth immortal fruit . . .
[I. *iii,* 17–21]

In a play as romantic as *The Island Princess* the characters reach for an apex of eloquent idealism rather than any credibility of action. Hence Ruy Dias and Armusia seem to compete for the noblest concept of "honor" rather than to pursue Quisara like creatures of flesh and blood, whereas the airy princess outdoes them both in her ethical hair-splitting. After helping to bring Armusia to the brink of a Christian martyr's death, for example, she suddenly converts from paganism to Christianity and proclaims her love for Armusia in these terms:

Your faith and your religion must be like ye,
They that can show you these must be pure mirrors:
When the streams flow clear and fair, what are the fountains?
I do embrace your faith, sir . . .
[V. *ii,* 117 ff.]

Her statement is, of course, only a Fletcherian sleight of hand, in which considerations of motive are brushed off by verbalization. Fletcher's larger purpose is not verisimilitude but purest romance; not the creation of a reality but a rhapsodic celebration of heroic sentiments.

The Island Princess is in *English Drama 1580-1642,* ed. C. F. Tucker Brooke and N. B. Paradise (1933). For commentary see A. C. Sprague, *Beaumont and Fletcher on the Restoration Stage* (1926) and Clifford Leech, *The John Fletcher Plays (1962).*

J

Jack of Newbury, by Thomas Deloney. See JOHN WINCHCOMB, THE PLEASANT HISTORY OF.

James IV, The Scottish History of. A romantic comedy by Robert GREENE, written around 1591 and printed in 1598. For his story of the long-suffering, faithful queen, Greene consulted Giraldi Cinthio's *Hecatomithi;* his character Oberon, king of fairies, is from *Huon of Bordeaux,* a romance of the Charlemagne cycle. (Shakespeare borrowed from Greene's Oberon for *A Midsummer Night's Dream.)* The story of Bohan and his sons is apparently Greene's own invention.

The story of James IV is enclosed in a "frame-story" employing chorus, dances, and dumb shows. In the induction Oberon, diminutive king of fairies, meets Bohan, a Scot so misanthropic that he lives in his own tomb. Bohan has two sons, Slipper and Nano. Upon Nano, a dwarf, Oberon bestows a quick wit and a handsome countenance; to Slipper he gives a drifter's life and the promise that whenever Slipper needs help Oberon will come to his aid. As his sons depart (or, rather, leave the scene to participate in their father's play), Bohan promises to show Oberon the cause of his cynicism. The story he relates is the play itself—the story of James IV, "a king overruled with parasites"—and the actors are Bohan's own sons and countrymen.

The action begins with the marriage of James IV to the English princess Dorothea. Although she is of peerless beauty and grace, the king is enamored of a Scottish girl named Ida, daughter of the countess of Arran. Ateukin, a court parasite, promises the king that he will arrange Ida's submission in spite of her chastity and modesty; Ateukin hires Slipper and Nano, Bohan's sons come to court to seek their fortune, and an impoverished gentleman, Andrew Snoord, to help carry out his stratagems. To win the new queen's favor, Ateukin awards her the dwarf Nano. Meanwhile Eustace, a handsome young Englishman, arrives in Scotland to visit his aged friend Sir Bartram. Eustace has fallen in love in absentia with Ida, whose picture he received from Elinor, countess of Carlisle.

During the chorus interlude, Oberon amuses Bohan with a dance of fairies and, in return, Bohan has several Scottish gentlemen perform three dumb shows depicting the defeat of Semiramis, the Assyrian queen; the death of Cyrus the Great, Persian emperor;

and the murder of Sesostris, mighty conqueror of Asia, by his slaves.

Ateukin and Slipper arrive in Arran to woo Ida with gifts from the king, but the girl is already in love with Eustace. Rejected, Ateukin returns to court and advises the king to hire a Frenchman named Jaques to murder Queen Dorothea. Warned by Eustace's friend Sir Bartram, the queen disguises herself as a squire and flees the court in the company of Nano. Outraged by the king's perfidy and indulgence of "flatterers and parasites," the Scottish peers rise in rebellion.

The queen, still disguised as a squire, is attacked by Jaques and left for dead. Her faithful Nano takes the wounded "squire" to the house of Sir Cuthbert Anderson and his wife. The queen sends Nano to court to tell Sir Bartram that she is alive; her chief concern is to protect her foolish husband from harm. Meanwhile Eustace and Ida are married, and Ateukin now realizes his suit on behalf of the king is totally lost. Set upon by an invading English army led by Dorothea's indignant father, and disillusioned by Ida's marriage, the king now turns against the sycophants Andrew, Ateukin, and Slipper. The last escapes the king's wrath by the intercession of Oberon, who, true to his promise, carries him from harm. As James IV and the English king prepare to engage in single combat, Dorothea arrives to forgive her husband ("Youth hath misled; tut, but a little fault!") and beg her father to desist. Harmony is restored between the loving Dorothea and her repentant husband, and the English and Scots are reunited in friendship. Nano remains at court to serve his queen.

James IV skillfully combines elements of the medieval drama and the plays of Kyd, Marlowe, and Shakespeare. The situation of the foolish but well-meaning king overruled by false advisers and afflicted with lust is a familiar one in the morality plays, while the long-suffering Dorothea recalls medieval legends of Patient Grissel. Greene's play also foreshadows the later tragicomedy in its narrow escapes and last-minute reconciliations, and the crafty Ateukin, "a fair-spoken gentleman who can get more land by a lie than an honest man by his ready money," is a forerunner to the Machiavellian stage villain of the later drama.

James IV has been edited by Norman Sanders in the Revels Plays series (1970). For criticism, see Ruth Hudson, "Greene's *James IV* and Contemporary Allusions," *PMLA,* XLVII (1932); Waldo F. McNeir, "The Original of Ateukin in Greene's *James IV,*" *MLN* LXII (1947); and Kenneth Muir, "Robert Greene as Dramatist," *Essays in Shakespeare and Elizabethan Drama in Honor of Hardin Craig,* ed. Richard Hosley (1962).

jestbooks. Collections of comic prose tales, anecdotes, or witty remarks. To various degrees, these popular miscellanies were derived from the Latin *facetia,* the medieval *fabliau* and *exemplum,* the proverb and the epigram. In all probability jestbooks contain much of the material disseminated by traveling minstrels before the invention of the printing press.

Two medieval forerunners of the English Renaissance jestbook should be cited. The first is that by Petrus Alphonsus, whose *Disciplina clericalis,* written around the middle of the twelfth century, is a collection of *exempla* and apothegms derived from Arabic and Jewish tales and Aesop's *Fables.* Alphonsus' work was widely imitated and revised, and it gradually became absorbed as *fabliaux.* One of the earliest printed jestbooks was based on Alphonsus and his sources, with borrowings from classical literature. This was the enormously popular and influential *Liber facetiarum* of the Florentine papal secretary Poggio Bracciolini. Poggio's *facetia,* which he wrote to amuse himself and to help develop his Latin style, was printed posthumously in 1477. William Caxton published translated parts of Alphonsus and Poggio's *facetiae* as *The Fables of Alfonce and Poge* in 1484.

The first English jestbook, *A Hundred Merry Tales,* was printed in 1526 by John Rastell, Sir Thomas More's brother-in-law. Like most specimens of its type, it is coarse, colloquial, and realistic, although many jokes in the collection seem to have been chosen as a means of conveying parenthetical instruction on such religious topics as the Creed, the Pater Noster, and the Ave Maria. Without much evidence, William Hazlitt has attributed the work to John Heywood. The jestbook is ribald and irreverent, with several of its short tales involving ordinary people like village priests, millers, apprentices, and Oxford scholars. Tale 25 makes sport of an especially talented friar:

> A man there was that came to confess himself to a gray friar, and confessed that he had lain with a young gentlewoman. The friar then asked him in what place, and he said it was in a goodly chamber all night long in a soft warm bed. The friar, hearing that, shrugged in his clothes and said, "Now, by sweet Saint Francis, then wast thou very well at ease."

Soon after the popular *Hundred Merry Tales* appeared *Tales and Quick Answers* (wr. c. 1535), most of which is derived from Poggio's *facetiae,* a jestbook by the German Sebastian Brant, and some classical apothegms translated by Erasmus. Each jest is capped with a summary of its moral:

> There was a man upon a time which proferred his daughter to a young man in marriage, the which young man refused her, saying that she was too young to be married.
>
> "I wis," quod the foolish father, "she is more able than ye ween. For she hath borne three children by our parish clerk."
>
> Lo, by this tale ye see that fools cannot tell what and when to speak; therefore it were best for them to keep always silence.

Jokes at the expense of the clergy were popular, as were ethnic jests. Tales illustrating the ignorance and social ineptitude of Welshmen were especially plentiful in English jestbooks. In the sixteenth century so-called jest-biographies, jestbooks containing jokes attributed to a real or legendary person, became very numerous. One of the earliest of these was *Merry Tales Made by Master Skelton* (1567), which, although it appeared thirty-eight years after John Skelton's death and is entirely legendary, was responsible for Skelton's reputation as an unsavory rogue throughout the seventeenth and eighteenth centuries. Similar "jest-biographies" appeared in the sixteenth century purporting to be by or about George à Greene, Oliver Smug, John Tarlton, George Peele, and "Skoggan." Archie Armstrong, a court jester under James I and Charles I, published his own collection of favorite jokes in *A Banquet of Jests and Merry Tales* (1630). Like some modern joke books, Armstrong's jokes are given classifications such as "court jests," "college jests," and so forth.

Several Elizabethan authors wrote jestbooks. Thomas Dekker and George Wilkins were probably the authors of the popular *Jests to Make You Merry* (1607), which distinguishes between jokes that depend on language and those that rely on actions. John Taylor (the "Water Poet") wrote no fewer than three jestbooks: *Wit and Mirth* (1629), *Bull, Bear, and Horse* (1638), and *Taylor's Feast* (1638). According to his preface to *Wit and Mirth,* Taylor collected his jokes "out of taverns, ordinaries, inns, bowling greens, and alleys, ale-houses, tobacco shops, highways, and water-passages."

Francis Bacon's *Apothegms New and Old* (1625) is more pithy and less coarse than most jestbooks:

> Mr. Popham, when he was Speaker, and the Lower House had sat long and done in effect nothing; coming one day to Queen Elizabeth, she said to him, "Now, Mr. Speaker, what hath passed in the Lower House?" He answered, "If it please your Majesty, seven weeks."

Like the jokes one hears today, Elizabethan jestbooks contain nothing really original and little of aesthetic value. Jokes *per se* may be a form that defies originality, and an extemporaneous crudeness has always been their stock in trade, a kind of homely timelessness their salient characteristic. Thus our modern anthologies of jokes, done up with sprightly titles like *Fifty-one Funny Bones* and *Medical Jokes for Middle-Agers,* are scarcely distinguishable from their Elizabethan counterparts *The Mirror for Mirth* and *Pleasant Conceits of Old Hobson.*

The standard collection of Elizabethan and Jacobean jestbooks was edited by William Hazlitt, with the somewhat misleading title *Shakespeare Jest-Books,* 3 vols. (1864). There is a more recent collection of six jestbooks in *A Hundred Merry Tales and Other English Jestbooks,* ed. P. M. Zall (1963). The definitive scholarly study is by Ernest Schultz, *Die englischen Schwankbücher bis* 1607 (1912), summarized and brought up to date by F. P. Wilson in "English Jestbooks of the Sixteenth and Early Seventeenth Centuries," *HLQ,* II (1939). Wilson supplements Schultz's bibliography of English jestbooks printed before 1640.

Jew of Malta, The. A melodrama by Christopher MARLOWE, probably written around 1589 but not printed until 1632. Marlowe devised the plot from tales he had heard of a Jewish merchant in Constantinople, one David Passi, and combined these with ill-founded rumors of a Turkish attack on Malta in the 1580s. The story is totally dominated by Barabas, the Jew of Malta, who, although shown to be harassed unjustly by hypocritical Christians in the first part of the play, declines after Act III into a ludicrously villainous figure.

In a brilliant and lyrical opening, Machiavelli himself appears to introduce his disciple Barabas in his countinghouse, where he exults over his wealth but laments the ease of his financial conquests. His ruminations are interrupted by news that the Turks have demanded huge tribute from Malta and that the Christian governor has levied an exorbitant tax on Malta's Jews to meet the Turkish demands. After he refuses to submit to this extortion, Barabas' wealth is confiscated and his house seized and converted into a nunnery. Under the floor of the house, however, Barabas had concealed a store of riches, and he persuades his daughter Abigail to feign conversion to Christianity in order to gain admission to the new nunnery.

Abigail succeeds in finding the gold and giving it to her father. Meanwhile a Spanish fleet arrives with a cargo of Turkish slaves, and the governor of Malta, in defiance of the Turks, allows the Spanish to land and sell their shipment. At the slave market Barabas purchases a malicious, Christian-hating Arabian slave, Ithamore, whom he enlists in his unremitting feud against the Christians At the market, also, he meets two of his daughter's admirers, Don Lodowick, the governor's son, and Don Mathias, another gentleman. Taking them home, Barabas tricks them into a rivalry and duel fatal to both. Indignant over the death of Don Mathias, whom she genuinely loved, Abigail flees her father and becomes a convert. In retaliation Barabas donates a huge pot of poisoned rice to the convent in honor of the Eve of St. Jacques. The entire abbey is poisoned, but before she dies Abigail reveals her father's responsibility for the death of her two suitors to Friar Jacomo.

Barabas' stratagem is to play on the greed of the Christians. Feigning an inclination to conversion, he promises to give all his wealth to the friar who brings him into the church. At Barabas' house Ithamore strangles Friar Bernadine and props up the corpse; when Friar Jacomo, goaded into fury by Bernardine's competition for the Jew's wealth, strikes the corpse, he is persuaded that he has committed murder. Soon afterward Ithamore, with the help of a whore called Bellamira and her paramour Pilia-Borza, attempt to blackmail Barabas, but he appears before them disguised as a French lute player and poisons all three conspirators with a bouquet of tainted flowers.

Before they die, however, they accuse Barabas before the governor, who is in the midst of preparing the city against a siege by the Turks. Condemned to torture, Barabas feigns suicide by swallowing a special preparation of poppy and mandrake juice. The Christians hurl his body over the city walls, but he revives and joins the Turks. After he betrays the city, the Turks make him governor, but Barabas' habitual treachery now proves fatal. For a price he plots with the captive Christian governor to betray the Turks. Gunpowder is placed under the quarters of the Turkish troops and their officers invited to a splendid banquet in a hall with a collapsible floor under which Barabas has placed a boiling cauldron. At the given signal the Turkish troops are blown up, but the wily governor releases the mechanism that sends Barabas himself into the deadly cauldron.

The *Jew of Malta* is not as lyrical as Marlowe's *Tamburlaine,* as philosophical as his *Doctor Faustus,* nor as well plotted as his *Edward II.* In the first half of the play Barabas is motivated by fierce hatred of the hypocritical Christians who torment him, but about the point of Ithamore's appearance in Act III he deteriorates into a motiveless and macabre Vice skipping gleefully from one atrocity to another. At the end he has no real reason for betraying the Turks who have made him governor and put his Christian enemies at his feet, but the simple irony of the treacherous Machiavellian hoist by his own petard was apparently one that Marlowe could not resist.

The Jew of Malta is a melodrama of considerable intensity. The imagery concentrates on gold, jewels, and sumptuous wealth, yet the characters are as arid and cramped as the tiny island they inhabit, and the only virtuous person, Barabas' daughter Abigail, echoes the theme of the story with her plaintive inquiry, "Is there no virtue *anywhere?" The Jew of Malta* is often compared to Shakespeare's *The Merchant of Venice,* but the resemblances are superficial. In Marlowe's play the villainous misanthrope Barabas dominates the atmosphere completely, and his crass and bitter world is unalleviated by any hint of love or human goodness.

The *Jew of Malta* is in Marlowe's *Works,* ed. C. F. Tucker Brooke (1910). Other editions are by Irving Ribner in *The Complete Plays* (1963) and Richard W. Van Fossen in the Regents Renaissance Drama series (1970). For commentary, see Harry Levin, *The Overreacher, A Study of Christopher Marlowe* (1952); Howard J. Babb, "Policy in Marlowe's *Jew of Malta,*" *ELH,* XXIV (1957); Alfred Harbage, "Innocent Barabas," *TDR,* VIII (1964); J. B. Steane, *Marlowe: A Critical Study* (1964); and *The Jew Of Malta: Text and Major Criticism,* ed. Irving Ribner (1970).

jig. A brief dramatic farce accompanied by dancing and singing, and usually performed before or after a play. The name "jig" also designates certain ballads containing dialogue, such as "A New Northern Jig," "The Soldier's Farewell to His Love," and "Kit and Pegge," this last being a farcical dialogue between lovers. Many dialogue ballads printed in the sixteenth and seventeenth centuries, although not now recognizable as jigs, were designed as such when performed on the stage. The jig no doubt had affiliations with the popular song, which was appropriated for stage use by clowns. The best-known Elizabethan performer of jigs was the clown Richard Tarlton. The jig was also performed for satiric purposes, as when the Queen's Men joined in the Martin Marprelate controversy and attacked the Puritan writers from the stage. The dramatic jig, which had been employed at the end of the sixteenth century in pageants, festivities, and feasts, began to fade out in the early part of the seventeenth century.

The definitive study is by C. R. Baskervill, *The Elizabethan Jig and Related Song Drama* (1929), which contains a collection of Elizabethan jigs.

Johan Johan the Husband, Tyb His Wife, and Sir John the Priest. An interlude by John HEYWOOD, written sometime in the 1530's and printed in 1533.

The jealous husband Johan Johan suspects that his shrewish wife Tyb has cuckolded him with Sir John, the wily village priest. When his wife returns home late, however, the stupid husband is easily duped into believing Tyb's story of how she, two neighbor ladies, and the priest have baked the beautiful pie she has brought home. She even convinces her silly husband that he must invite Sir John to share the pie. After Johan Johan has meekly returned home with the priest, Tyb and Sir John begin eating while Johan Johan is assigned to several domestic chores. As he works feverishly, Tyb and Sir John leisurely finish the pie, after which Sir John narrates for Tyb's amusement didactic tales of three great miracles, all ironically related to a single theme. Sir John tells, first, how a sailor's wife miraculously bore seven children during her husband's absence, how a barren woman bore a child only a month after her return from a pilgrimage, and how another gave birth to a child only five months after her wedding. Discovering that his wife and the priest have devoured the pie, Johan Johan attacks his wife with a shovel of hot coals. When she flees with the priest, he follows in fear that she will cuckold him to avenge his domestic rebellion.

Heywood's interlude is based on a medieval French *fabliau, De Pernet qui va au vin,* which he extensively altered in scene, characterization, and dialogue. It is one of Heywood's liveliest and most popular satiric farces.

There is a facsimile edition by J. S. Farmer (1906). For commentary, see Ian Maxwell, *French Farce and John Heywood* (1946); Stanley Sultan, "The Audience Participation Episode in *Johan-Johan,*" *JEGP,* LII (1953); and Stanley Sultan, "*Johan-Johan* and Its Debt to French Farce," *JEGP,* LIII (1954).

John Winchcomb, The Pleasant History of. In His Younger Years Called Jack of Newbury. A prose romance by Thomas DELONEY (wr. c. 1596; pr. 1619), based on the supposed life of and legends concerning John Winchcomb, alias Smalwoode (d. 1520), a clothier of Newbury who became the subject of several pamphlets and chapbooks. He was reputed to have equipped several hundred men at his own expense and led them into battle at Flodden Field. For his sources Deloney made liberal use of Pedro Mexia's *The Forest, or Collection of Histories* (1571), translated from the French version into English by Thomas Fortescue, as well as several euphuistic romances and histories, including Stephen Batman's *The Doom* (1581) and Thomas Johnson's *Cornucopiae* (1595). As in all of Deloney's works, *Jack of Newbury* portrays ordinary Englishmen cast into the heroic mold of the traditionally aristocratic romance. Hence Deloney's fiction represents a movement away from the romantic narratives of Sidney, Lyly, Greene, and Lodge, with their pastoral background and eloquent noble lovers, toward a realistic setting using ordinary dialogue. Some chapters of *Jack of Newbury* are almost entirely in dialogue.

Chapter I gives an account of Jack's marriage in the days of Henry VIII. After three years of managing the weaving business of his deceased master, Jack is duped into a quick marriage at St. Bartholomew's by his master's attractive but much older widow. What follows is a lively struggle of wills as to which of the two will dominate in the marriage. Finally Jack's wit triumphs, and the two live harmoniously until the widow dies and leaves Jack to inherit her wealth.

Chapter II recounts Jack's second marriage to his faithful servant girl Nan, and his military achievements. When James IV of Scotland invades England in 1513, Jack equips 150 horsemen and foot soldiers, all lavishly attired in white coats, red caps, and yellow feathers. When called before Henry VIII's queen, Katherine of Aragon, Jack smears his face and white coat with blood, explaining to the queen that he was attacked by a dog-headed, poison-toothed ogre because of his avowed loyalty to the English monarch. Impressed by his fidelity and courage, the queen promises to favor Jack at court. On the way to encounter James IV at Flodden Field, Jack's army learns that the earl of Surrey, who is in command of the English during Henry VIII's absence in France, has already defeated the Scots. The grateful queen rewards her faithful followers, and especially Jack, to whom she gives a gold chain.

In Chapter III Jack meets Henry VIII, whom he amuses by telling how he became Prince of Ants. The king and queen visit Jack's house, where they are lavishly entertained by Jack's wife and his band of weavers. The grateful Henry declares that the weavers may have four deer each year from his park. When the king offers to knight him, Jack refuses because he prefers to remain a clothier, a king of his own laboring "ants and bees." Chapter IV tells of Jack's sport with Henry VIII's court fool, Will Sommers, whose pratfalls and idiotic actions amuse Henry and the queen. In Chapter V are described fifteen pictures in Jack's house that he shows to friends and servants because each represents a king, pope, or military hero who began his ascent from humble origins. Jack's sermons on these portraits stress that virtue is more important than birth or wealth. In Chapter VI the king's wars in France and the Low Counties have caused widespread unemployment among weavers, whose cause Jack pleads before the king. In spite of Cardinal Wolsey's obstructions and delays, Jack secures Henry's permission to resume free trade.

Chapter VII presents a variation on the familiar Elizabethan "bed switch" motif. When a young Italian merchant named Benedick is scorned by the Newbury maid Joan, he determines to get revenge by cuckolding Joan's kinsman John, a good-hearted weaver who learns of Benedick's scheme from his wife. John invites Benedick to supper with Joan, who pretends to promise affection and even an evening in bed. When Benedick slips into the bed anticipating Joan he finds, instead, the drugged sow that John has put there. Warned by John and his neighbors that Berkshire girls will never act the tart for any Italian, Benedick slinks out of town in disgrace.

In Chapter VIII Jack's wife listens to a gossip who objects to her generous treatment of her servants, and Jack angrily insists that his wife continue her good treatment and banish the gossip from the house. Chapter IX also deals with sound business management. Randoll Pert, a draper in debt to Jack for fifty-five pounds, is imprisoned for debt and ruined. Working as a lowly porter after his release, he happens to meet Jack, now a member of Parliament, when he is engaged to carry Jack's trunk. Jack recognizes his former acquaintance, feels distress that a tradesman has fallen so low, and offers to lend Pert five hundred pounds, payable when Pert becomes sheriff of London. Others laugh at the apparently absurd condition of this loan, but Jack shrewdly realizes that Pert has learned his lesson. He provides Pert with a shop and some cloth, and soon Pert's business prospers. Eventually Pert does become sheriff and repays the debt.

The meddling gossip of Chapter VIII is

baited mercilessly by Jack's servants, who cause her to get drunk and make a fool of herself. Jack's servant Tweedle has her carted through town in a basket and deposited at her own doorstep.

In the final Chapter XI, Jack is visited by Sir George Rigley, an impoverished knight returned from the wars. When Sir George gets Jack's servant girl Joan with child, he refuses to acknowledge the child and goes to London where Jack pursues him with a clever ruse. He tells Sir George of a wealthy and available widow, then dresses Joan in rich clothes to impersonate the great lady. After Sir George marries her, he is furious to learn her real identity, but he is finally mollified when Jack gives Joan a hundred pounds for her dowry and invites the knight and his new wife to stay with him at Newbury for two years. When Henry VIII learns of Jack's solution, he is so pleased that he provides Sir George, who is really a valorous soldier, with a comfortable living.

Deloney's episodic romance, in which one tale follows the other without integration, has little merit as fiction. The settings and dialogue are, for the most part, admirably realistic, but Deloney shows only occasional concern for motivation and virtually none for plot construction. Instead, he contrives situations in the style of the JESTBOOKS to reiterate the larger fantasies attractive to his middle-class readers: the saving grace of honest toil, the absence of class conflicts or antagonisms, the ability of common folk to achieve success and even glory by diligence and wit, and the essential benevolence of Merry England and its institutions of authority. To such calculated fantasies Deloney added a hero who is often entertainingly resourceful; but despite some superficial similarities, Jack of Newbury is not the *picaro* of ROGUE LITERATURE or the picaresque novel, for he succeeds in life without defying social standards. Indeed, those standards are shown to be the benevolent means by which Jack—and by implication, other hard-working and resourceful English tradesmen—can achieve a heroic stature previously reserved to the aristocracy. Such good news made Deloney's fiction popular. By 1619 *Jack of Newbury* had gone through eight editions, and by 1637, no fewer than thirteen.

Jack of Newbury was edited by George Saintsbury for the Everyman Library (1929), and by Merritt E. Lawlis, *The Novels of Thomas Deloney* (1961). For critical commentary, see Lawlis, *An Apology for the Middle Class: The Dramatic Novels of Thomas Deloney* (1961); and Max Dorsinville, "Design in Deloney's *Jack of Newbury*." *PMLA*, LXXXVIII (1973).

Jones, Inigo (1573–1652). Architect and designer. Jones began his career as a carpenter. Sometime before 1603 he traveled in France, Germany, and Italy to study art and architecture, and in Italy came under the influence of Andrea Palladio (1508-1580), whose architectural style, Palladianism, is characterized by monumental dignity, symmetry, and imaginative use of classical columns and colonnades. Like many of his contemporaries, Jones was also influenced by the Roman architect Marcus Vitruvius Pollio (first century B.C.). In 1604 Jones went to Denmark to plan several buildings for Christian IV, and upon his return to England in 1605 began to design scenery and costumes for masques at the court of James I, a task that had previously been left to the master of the revels. During the period 1605-31 Jones and Ben JONSON collaborated on a score of highly successful dramatizations beginning with Jonson's *Masque of Blackness.* To the English stage Jones introduced the first movable platform, revolving screens, and stage designs employing perspectives. From Italy he brought to England the concept of the picture stage with its curtain and proscenium arch. In 1631 the temperamental Jones and irascible Jonson ended their collaboration with a bitter personal quarrel, memorialized by Jonson's savage satire of Jones as Vitruvius Hoop in *A Tale of a Tub* (1633).

After the death of Prince Henry, for whom he was employed as a surveyor, Jones embarked on an extended tour of Italy with the earl of Arundel and spent several months at Vicenza to study its Palladian architecture. Upon his return in 1615 he was appointed surveyor to James I, an office he held into the reign of Charles I. Some of his most noteworthy achievements in architecture were Anne of Denmark's palace at Greenwich (completed in 1635), the banqueting house at Whitehall (constructed 1619-21), and the restoration of St. Paul's Cathedral (1634). The influence of the classical Palladio on these works by Jones made them models for architects in the eighteenth century.

A curious episode in Jones's career was his being commissioned by James I to discover the origins of the ruins at Stonehenge. Three years after Jones's death, John Webb published from Jones's notes *The Most Notable Antiquity of Great Britain, called Stone-Heng, Restored* (1655), in which Jones concludes that the Stonehenge ruins were the remains of a Roman temple. During the Civil War, Jones was heavily fined for his Royalist sympathies and died in the most abject poverty. His architectural and stage designs have been preserved in the library of the duke of Devonshire at Chatsworth. His *Architecture of Palladio,* in four volumes, was not published until 1715.

Jones's life, with an extensive bibliography of his works, is in J. A. Gotch, *Inigo Jones* (1928). The influence of both Jones and Palladio is described in John Summerson, *Architecture in England, 1530-1830* (1953). See also *Designs by Inigo Jones for Masques and Plays at Court,* ed. Percy Simpson and C. F. Bell (1924); James Lees-Milne, *The Age of Inigo Jones* (1954); and Stephen Orgel and Roy Strong, *Inigo Jones,* 2 vols. (1973).

Jonson, Ben (1572-1637). Poet and playwright. Descended from Scottish gentry, Jonson was born in Westminster a month after the death of his father, a minister. Jonson's mother soon afterward married a bricklayer, who put young Jonson to work in that trade after the boy attended Westminster School under the tutelage of the great William Camden. It was at Westminster School that Jonson became absorbed in classical studies, and years later he paid solemn homage to Camden's scholarly influence:

> Camden, most reverent head,
> to whom I owe
> All that I am in arts, all that I know . . .

It was Camden, Jonson stated, who taught him to write his verses first in prose and then rework them into meters.

Instead of attending a university Jonson joined the English army in the Low Countries, where he killed an enemy in a single combat staged between the English and Spanish lines. By 1592 he was back in London and married (to a "shrew," he testified later, but nevertheless "honest"). Little is known of his activities during the next five years, but it is probable he was engaged in some acting (at one time in the role of Hieronimo in Kyd's *Spanish Tragedy,* according to tradition) and collaborating on plays. By 1597 he was employed by the theater manager Philip Henslowe as an actor and dramatist, possibly completing a play begun by Thomas Nashe, *The Isle of Dogs,* which was presented at the Swan theater with Jonson as one of the actors. This play, now lost, so incensed the authorities for its seditious satire that the theaters were ordered closed and Jonson and two other actors were imprisoned. It was the first of several prison experiences for Jonson; a year later he went to jail for killing in a duel one of Henslowe's best actors, Gabriel Spencer, and barely escaped the death penalty by pleading benefit of clergy, a technicality enabling those who could read Latin (and thus presumably clergy) to avoid punishment in the secular courts. While in prison he converted to Roman Catholicism, and by his own statement to William Drummond, "remained a papist for twelve years."

Jonson's initial dramatic triumph was EVERY MAN IN HIS HUMOUR, performed in 1598 at the Curtain by the Lord Chamberlain's Men (including in the cast Richard Burbage, Will Kemp, and Shakespeare). There is a tradition, first recorded by Nicholas Rowe in the eighteenth century, that Shakespeare arranged to have the play performed by the Chamberlain's Men. On the surface *Every Man in His Humour* appears to be another of many Italian plays set in Venice, with the stereotyped Juvenalian conflict of wits between father and son and the high-handed intrigues of the familiar scheming servant. Actually it is a caustic satire on the foibles of Elizabethan manners and morals, as Jonson made plain when he revised the play for the 1616 folio and gave it a London setting and English characters and allusions. The idea of the "humours" was part of Jonson's satiric strategy, demonstrating that every man is afflicted by some excess in his nature, some dominant and overriding obsession that only the lash of hyperbolic satire can expunge.

Jonson's "comedy of humours" originates in the medieval medical theory that human disposition and temperament are determined by some imbalance of the essential bodily fluids of blood, choler, melancholy, and phlegm. Any excess of these is caused by the influence of the star under which a person is born. Melancholy people, for example, are influenced by Saturn and are thus described as being "saturnine." Such influence, however, was thought to be subject to modification by environmental factors such as climate, diet, nationality, or social position. In contrast to the "humorous" character is one in whom the vital fluids are harmoniously blended—that is, in modern usage, the "well-balanced" or "well-adjusted" person. One of the few such characters in Jonson's satiric comedies is Crites in *Cynthia's Revels* (1601), whom the author rather immodestly identified with himself. Crites is described as "a creature of a most perfect and divine temper . . . in whom all the humours and elements are peaceably met" (II. *iii*). In his induction to EVERY MAN OUT OF HIS HUMOUR (perf. 1599), Jonson is careful to distinguish between a genuinely "humorous" character and one who simply adopts a silly fashion in clothes:

So in every human body
The choler, melancholy, phlegm, and blood
By reason that they flow continually
In some one part, and are not continent,
Receive the name of Humours. Now thus far
It may, by *Metaphor,* apply itself
Unto the general disposition:
As when some one peculiar quality
Doth so possess a man, that it doth draw
All his affects, his spirits, and his powers,
In their conflutions, all to run one way,
This may be truly said to be a Humour.
But that a rook, in wearing a pied feather,
The cable hat-band, or the three-piled ruff,
A yard of shoe tie, or the Switzer's knot
On his French garters, should affect a Humour!
Oh, 'tis more than most ridiculous.

Jonson was not the first to use the humours in delineating characters on the stage. A year before Jonson composed *Every Man in His Humour* in 1598, Philip Henslowe recorded a performance at the Rose theater of George Chapman's *An Humorous Day's Mirth,* a loosely organized comedy in which several characters are ludicrously exaggerated to suggest some overabundance of a humour. Nor did Jonson employ his theory of the humours in comedy with any consistency, not even in *Every Man in His Humour.* It is important to recall in this regard that Jonson's comic characters, like their prototypes in Roman comedy, are types rather than individuals of psychological depth. In order to achieve consistency of character compatible with his adherence to the classical principle of decorum, Jonson focuses on a single dominant trait—love of intrigue, jealousy, or avarice—and the result is a character that owes as much to the stereotypical wily servant, jealous husband, or greedy parasite as to the rather limiting medical theory of the four humours.

Jonson's *Every Man Out of His Humour* was performed in 1599 by the Chamberlain's Men, at the newly constructed Globe theater. That Jonson prized the play highly can be inferred from its quick publication the next year with a dedication to that most prestigious body of literary critics, the gentlemen at the Inns of Court. Unlike *Every Man in His Humour,* however, *Every Man Out* was anything but a success. The plot is formless and discursive, and the characters, who have Italian names but inhabit the "Fortunate Island" (obviously England), are a dozen grotesques whose mad "humours" are systematically purged in the final act.

When the failure of *Every Man Out* cooled the desire of the Chamberlain's Men for more of Jonson's plays, he turned to the newly formed Children of the Queen's Chapel for the production of *Cynthia's Revels* at the Blackfriars. *Cynthia's Revels* is as acerbic a satire as Jonson's earlier plays. It also employs a greater variety of dramatic modes in its use of allegory, songs (including the famous lyric "Queen and huntress, chaste and fair"), and concluding masque—this last being a genre Jonson subsequently brought to perfection. In *Cynthia's Revels* Jonson also gave his critics an easy target by presenting himself as the character Crites, the self-appointed patriarchal judge of society and art confirmed in that office by Queen Elizabeth as Cynthia.

Cynthia's Revels was but one skirmish in the so-called War of the Theaters (or Poetomachia) begun when John Marston portrayed Jonson as the boorish Chrysoganus in *Histriomastix* (1599). Jonson retaliated by parodying Marston in *Every Man Out of His Humour* and *Cynthia's Revels.* Learning that Marston and Thomas Dekker were preparing still another satire at his expense, Jonson worked at top speed to anticipate their attack with *The Poetaster,* performed at the Blackfriars in 1601. In one scene of *The Poetaster* Jonson, in the role of Horace, feeds Marston, as Crispinus, an emetic that causes Marston to vomit whole passages of his pompous rhetoric. That Crispinus was in fact Marston is attested by William Drummond, who reported that Jonson claimed to have "had many quarrels with Marston, beat him, and took his pistol from him, wrote his *Poetaster* upon him." Soon after *The Poetaster,* Marston and Dekker produced SATIROMASTIX, OR THE UNTRUSSING OF THE HUMOROUS POET (wr. 1601) at both a private theater by the Children of Paul's and at the Globe by the Chamberlain's Men. It was the last shot fired in the "War of the Theaters." The exact nature of this dispute has long been debated by scholars. It may have been little more than a publicity stunt (Jonson was amiably collaborating with Marston on *Eastward Ho!* by 1605). On the other hand, it may have represented a struggle of competition between the popular public theaters and the exclusive private playhouses, or perhaps a commercial rivalry between the Admiral's Men and the Chamberlain's Men, or, as Alfred Harbage suggests in *Shakespeare and the Rival Traditions* (1952), a conflict between two opposing theories of drama, the popular tradition represented by Shakespeare, Dekker, and Heywood, and the intellectually elite style represented by Jonson and Marston.

After *The Poetaster* Jonson turned to tragedy. He wrote additions to Thomas Kyd's *Spanish Tragedy* for Henslowe in 1602, composed a play called *Richard Crookback* the same year, and in 1603 completed his first major tragedy, SEJANUS HIS FALL, produced by the Chamberlain's Men, as was Jonson's later Roman tragedy, *Catiline His Conspiracy* (1611). Neither tragedy was well received in the popular playhouses, a fact Jonson attributed in his prefaces to the "ignorance" of the "rabble." Both plays are historically accurate, realistic, observant of the unities, static, and overblown in the Senecan manner (see SENECAN TRAGEDY.) As Jonson must have been painfully aware, they lacked the profound characterization, rapid pace and powerful human interest of Shakespeare's extremely popular *Julius Caesar.*

After the failure of *Sejanus,* Jonson returned to writing masques and comedies (see MASQUE). In 1605 he began his collaboration with Inigo JONES, the masterful designer of stage scenes and machines, with *The Masque of Blackness,* produced at court on Twelfth Night with Queen Anne herself as a participant. Until Jonson and Jones quarreled and parted after their production of *Chloridia* in 1631, they produced a series of brilliant court spectacles, among which were *The Masque of Queens* (perf. 1609); *Love Restored* (perf. 1612); *Mercury Vindicated* (perf. 1615); *Pleasure Reconciled to Virtue* (perf. 1618), which influenced Milton's *Comus;* and *News from the New World* (perf. 1621). In spite of his growing favor at court as a result of his splendid masques—GYPSIES METAMORPHOSED (perf. 1621), which he did without Inigo Jones, was especially popular with James I—Jonson was always vulnerable to rough handling by the authorities; he served a term in jail for his part in collaborating with George Chapman and John Marston on EASTWARD HO! (1605), which made some dangerous jibes at the king's newly created Scottish knights.

The decade after *Sejanus* was also Jonson's most brilliant period of comedies, beginning in 1606 with VOLPONE, OR THE FOX, a savage mockery of human greed that established Jonson as England's greatest satiric dramatist. Immensely popular, *Volpone* was first performed by the King's Men at the public playhouses and later at both universities. Jonson was now able to apply himself to his comedies with the deliberation he had always wanted. (His slowness of composition, satirized by Dekker in *Satiromastix,* may have been the motive for the actors' taunting comparison of Jonson to Shakespeare, who, they reminded Jonson, "never blotted a line.") Jonson's next triumph was EPICOENE, OR THE SILENT WOMAN (wr. c. 1609), praised by John Dryden as being Jonson's masterpiece. It was performed by the Children of the Queen's Chapel for an exclusive audience at Whitefriars. Still another great comedy. THE ALCHEMIST, appeared in 1610. The three comedies are of various satiric tones: *Volpone* is bitter and poignant, often verging on tragedy; *Epicoene* a farcical exploitation of a single madcap situation; and *The Alchemist* a combination of serious satire and farce. *The Alchemist* takes place in the fashionable Blackfriars district where Jonson lived, and the action occurs during the plague of 1610. The neoclassic unities of time, place, and action are strictly observed; as in *Volpone,* the characters are all motivated by a single "humour"—to get something for nothing. With the exception of BARTHOLOMEW FAIR, first performed by the Lady Elizabeth's Company in 1614, Jonson was not again capable of equaling the comic artistry of *Volpone, Epicoene,* and *The Alchemist.*

In the spring of 1613 Jonson toured France as a tutor to the son of Sir Walter Raleigh, then a prisoner in the Tower. (According to his own account, Raleigh's son got him drunk and paraded him about the streets of Paris in a cart.) Upon his return he wrote *The Devil Is an Ass,* an inferior comedy produced in 1616 by the King's Men at Blackfriars. In 1616 Jonson assembled his poems, masques, and plays for the folio publication of his *Works.* Jonson's title *Works* was a literal translation of the Latin *opera,* a word used to describe collections by the greatest classical authors, and Jonson was much reviled for including stage plays, which were not widely regarded as being serious literature, in a volume bearing such a stately title. The 1616 folio, which Jonson carefully supervised through the press, represents one of the most elaborate and regal editions of the seventeenth century. It contained all of Jonson's poems written before 1613, which included *Epigrams* and *The Forest*; also included were *Every Man in His Humour; Every Man Out of His Humour; Cynthia's Revels; The Poetaster; Sejanus His Fall; Volpone; Epicoene; The Alchemist; Catiline His Conspiracy:* and eleven masques and a variety of other court entertainments. The bulk of Jonson's canon, including the poems written after 1613, appeared in the posthumous 1640 folio prepared for the press by Sir Kenelm Digby, Jonson's faithful friend and neighbor in Westminster. The 1640 folio was published in two volumes. The first volume contains, with some few minor additions, the works in the 1616 folio; the second volume consists of the collection of poems called *Underwoods;* Jonson's revised version of Horace's *Art of Poetry;* his *English Grammar, Mortimer; Timber; Bartholomew Fair; The Devil Is an Ass; The Staple of News; The Magnetic Lady; A Tale of a Tub; The Sad Shepherd* (a dramatic fragment); and the later masques and entertainments.

In 1616 Jonson received from James I a pension for life, the equivalent of being made poet laureate, and in 1618 embarked on a walking tour to Scotland, where he was entertained by William Drummond of Hawthornden. Drummond kept manuscript notes of Jonson's conversation that were published with Drummond's *Works* in 1711 as *Conversations of Ben Jonson with Drummond,* a priceless source of information about Jonson and his contemporaries. From *Conversations* one learns such things as "Shakespeare wanted art," Donne "for not being understood, would perish," and "only Fletcher and Chapman could make a masque." Much of what Jonson says is rambling *obiter dicta,* or the exaggerations of a self-important man of affairs trying to impress his ingenuous listener (which Drummond was not, for he concludes his notes with some caustic observations). For the most part, *Conversations* fills out the portrait of Jonson suggested by his prefaces, his notebooks, and the extant public records. He was, as Drummond noted, "passionately kind and angry," a robust man of prodigious appetites, powerful loyalties, and strong opinions. *Conversations* and other sources corroborate the fact that he was a man of keen intelligence and deep learning coupled with an almost child-like fancy. "He hath consumed a whole night," Drummond states, "in lying looking to his great toe, about which he hath seen Tartars and Turks, Romans and Carthaginians, fight in his imagination . . ."

Jonson's last important comedy was THE STAPLE OF NEWS (perf. 1625), a satire directed at the first English newspaper, *The Courant or Weekly News* (1622), for which the publisher Nathaniel Butter secured a "staple," or monopoly from the government. Characteristically, Jonson combined these details of contemporary London with a plot structure derived from Aristophanes' comedy *Plutus.* The main action concerns the absurd triangle of Pennyboy Junior, a young prodigal, Lady Pecunia, and Cymbal, who peddles fantastic rumors to a credulous public. Always sensitive to criticism, Jonson anticipates it by including four garrulous women who sit on the stage and, in the manner of the grocer and his wife in Beaumont and Fletcher's *Knight of the Burning Pestle,* twit the author's "decayed wit" and "scurvy" play.

Jonson's last years were marred by illness, personal misfortune, and declining creative power. His personal library, lovingly collected over the years from annual gifts from the earl of Pembroke, was destroyed by fire (an event treated in Jonson's seriocomic poem "An Execration on Vulcan"). His main efforts during these concluding years, *The Magnetic Lady* (perf. 1632) and *A Tale of a Tub* (perf. 1633), failed to win applause. One play, *The New Inn* (perf. 1634), combines romantic comedy and the comedy of humours to satirize the courtly vogue of Platonic love, and Jonson states in the preface that the audience, led by a band of angry courtiers, hooted the play off the stage. *The Sad Shepherd, or A Tale of Robin Hood,* probably his last composition (wr. c. 1636-37), is a charming but fragmentary pastoral consisting of two acts and part of a third. At his death he was buried in Westminster Abbey and celebrated in a collection of elegies by friends and disciples entitled *Jonsonus Virbius* (1638).

The bulk of Jonson's nondramatic poems includes his *Epigrams, The Forest,* and UNDERWOODS. His principal prose work is TIMBER (1640), a commonplace book recording his critical views, reactions to his reading, and comments on his contemporaries (see CRITICISM. LITERARY). Its most famous passage is the one regarding Jonson's friend William Shakespeare:

> I remember the players have often mentioned it as an honor to Shakespeare, that in his writing (whatsoever he penned) he never blotted out line. My answer hath been, "Would he had blotted a thousand," which they thought a malevolent speech. I had not told posterity this but for their ignorance who choose that circumstance to commend their friend by wherein he most faulted; and to justify mine own candor, for I loved the man, and do honor his memory on this side idolatry as much as any.

In his famous dedicatory poem to the 1623 Folio of Shakespeare's works, Jonson again paid tribute to his friend:

For if I thought my judgment were of years
    I should commit thee surely with thy peers,
And tell how far thou didst our Lyly outshine,
    Or sporting Kyd, or Marlowe's mighty line.
And though thou hadst small Latin and less Greek,
    From thence to honor thee I would not seek
For names, but call forth thund'ring Aeschylus,
    Euripides, and Sophocles to us,
Pacuvius, Accius, him of Cordova dead,
    To life again, to hear thy buskin tread
And shake a stage; or, when thy socks were on,
    Leave thee alone for the comparison
Of all that insolent Greece or haughty Rome
Sent forth, or since did from their ashes come.
Triumph, my Britain, thou hast one to show
    To whom all scenes of Europe homage owe.
He was not for an age, but for all time!
    And all the Muses still were in their prime,
When like Apollo he came forth to warm
    Our ears, or like a Mercury to charm!

As this tribute and *Timber* suggest, Jonson was the greatest English literary critic after Sidney and before Dryden. With Horace and Sidney, Jonson insisted that poetry instruct and delight, and he believed that both the grand style of Spenser and the metaphysical style of Donne sacrificed content for form. Hence in poetry as in drama. Jonson was a confirmed classicist standing squarely against what he saw to be the "excesses" of his romantic age. In verse he favored forms that required clarity, directness, and economy; epigrams, epitaphs; complimentary verses, and epistles. He called his *Epigrams* "the ripest of my studies." For all his extolling of classical virtues and art as "imitation," however, Jonson valued imagination as much as did any of his contemporaries, and although as a classicist he insisted that imagination required discipline and restraint, he was never a mindless minion of the ancients. As he states in *Timber* (XXI): "For to all the observations of the ancients we have our own experience, which if we will use and apply, we have better means to pronounce. It is true they opened the gates and made the way that went before us, but as guides, not commanders."

Jonson liked to think of himself as a literary and moral reformer, the "English Horace" and the first English poet to be thoroughly classical in theory and practice. Hence he looked disapprovingly upon nonclassical forms like sonnets, chivalric tales, allegory, and metaphysical conceits. He maintained that Spenser "writ no language" and that Donne, for not keeping the accent, "deserved hanging." His own spare, laconic style, inspired by Latin writers and grown to idiomatic grace on English soil, contains all the neoclassic virtues continued by Dryden and Pope.

Among his contemporaries Jonson was more influential than Spenser, Donne, or Shakespeare. His friends and admirers included the Sidney circle at Penshurst; the countess of Bedford's coterie (including Donne); the scholars at the Inns of Court (Francis Bacon, Sir Edward Hyde, John Selden); the wits at court (Sir Kenelm Digby, John Hoskyns, the earl of Pembroke): and many actors and dramatists of the popular stage. Beaumont and Fletcher were among Jonson's most ardent disciples.

After Jonson suffered a crippling stroke in 1628, he was bedridden for long periods, and although he continued to work at his plays and poems, his fame steadily declined. He was not forgotten, however, by a group of young wits who called themselves the "tribe of Ben" or the "sons of Ben." Unlike the French *Pleiade,* the "tribe of Ben" was mainly social, an informal gathering of young men drawn together out of esteem for Jonson, and they imposed no vow of loyalty nor required fidelity to any critical principles. After 1620 the Mermaid Tavern, where men of letters congregated earlier, was supplanted by the Apollo Room of the Devil and St. Dunstan Tavern, where Jonson's *leges convivales,* or "social rules," were emblazoned in gold letters over the fireplace. Among the "tribe of Ben" were Richard Brome, Thomas Carew, William Cartwright, Sir Kenelm Digby, Lord Falkland, Robert Herrick, James Howell, Shackerly Marmion, Jasper Mayne, Thomas Nabbes, Thomas Randolph, Joseph Rutter, and Sir John Suckling. In poetry, Herrick was the most accomplished and faithful follower of Jonson's classical precepts; in drama, Brome proved the most successful imitator of Jonson's satiric comedies. As a group, the "tribe of Ben" formed the nucleus of the CAVALIER POETS, who carried Jonson's classical style into the Restoration and eighteenth century. The motto of these "sons of Ben" conveys the flavor of their master's philosophy: "Live merrily and write good verses"—a motto as splendid as the laconic and ambiguous epitaph on Jonson's tomb in Westminster Abbey: "O rare Ben Jonson."

The standard edition of the plays and poems, which contains a wealth of essential information and commentary, is *Ben Jonson,* ed. C. H. Herford and Percy and Evelyn Simpson, 11 vols. (1925-53). Excellent editions of Jonson's plays have been published in several recent series: the New Mermaid, the Revels plays, the Regents Renaissance Drama series, and the Yale Ben Jonson series. (These are cited by separate editions in the entries to Jonson's individual works.) Jonson's complete poems have been edited by B. H. Newdigate (1936), G. B. Johnston (1955), and William B. Hunter (1963). Hunter's edition, *The Complete Poetry of Ben Jonson,* is a definitive work containing detailed notes and lists of variants. *The Complete Masques* was edited by Stephen Orgel (1969). A helpful companion to Orgel's edition is John C. Meagher, *Method and Meaning in Jonson's Masques* (1966), which contains Inigo Jones's sketches of costumes and stage designs.

The definitive biography is still Volume I of the Herford and Simpson edition of Jonson's works. There is a brief biography by G. Gregory Smith in the English Men of Letters series (1926). Two especially vivid accounts of Jonson's life and times are Byron Steel, *O Rare Ben Jonson* (1927), and Marchette Chute, *Ben Jonson of Westminster* (1953).

Outstanding critical studies of Jonson's poems are G. B. Johnston, *Ben Jonson: Poet* (1945); Wesley Trimpi, *Ben Jonson's Poems : A Study of the Plain Style* (1962); J. G. Nichols, *The Poetry of Ben Jonson* (1970); and J. B. Bamborough, *Ben Jonson* (1970), which contains an extensive bibliography. For important critical studies of the plays, see C. R. Baskervill, *English Elements in Jonson's Early Comedy* (1911); Helena W. Baum, *The Satiric and the Didactic in Ben Jonson's Comedy* (1947); Freda L. Townsend, *Apologie for Bartholomew Fayre: The Art of Jonson's Comedies* (1947); Edward B. Partridge, *The Broken Compass: A Study of the Major Comedies of Ben Jonson* (1958); and Jonas A. Barish, *Ben Jonson and the Language of Prose Comedy* (1960).

Various aspects of Jonson's art are studied by Willa M. Evans, *Ben Jonson and Elizabethan Music* (1919); T. K. Whipple, *Martial and the English Epigram from Sir Thomas Wyatt to Ben Jonson* (1925); C. F. Wheeler, *Classical Mythology in the Plays, Masques, and Poems of Ben Jonson* (1938); and G. E. Bentley, *Shakespeare and Jonson: Their Reputations in the Seventeenth Century Compared,* 2 vols. (1945).

S. A. Tannenbaum has a Concise Bibliography (1938), supplemented by S. A. and

D. R. Tannenbaum (1947) updated in "Ben Jonson (1947-65)," ed. G. R. Guffey, in *Elizabethan Bibliographies Supplements,* III (1968).

Jovial Crew, A; or The Merry Beggars. A comedy by Richard BROME, written and performed in 1641 and first printed in 1652. As sources Brome consulted Ben Jonson's *Gypsies Metamorphosed* and William Rowley's *The Spanish Gypsy.*

In spite of the efforts of his old friend Hearty to cheer him up, Squire Oldrents is profoundly melancholy. For one thing, a fortuneteller has predicted that his two daughters, Rachel and Meriel, will become beggars; for another, his much-loved and otherwise totally dependable steward Springlove is overpowered every May by a wanderlust. Springlove takes to the road for the summer with a band of jolly beggars who spend the winters in Oldrent's barn. When Rachel and Meriel tire of their father's melancholy. they persuade their two sweethearts Vincent and Hilliard to accompany them with Springlove's troop of beggars through the countryside. Thus, as Springlove reminds the girls, their father's melancholy will be relieved by this easy fulfillment of the fortuneteller's prophecy. Hearty convinces the kindly old squire to join in the merriment, and Oldrents, his melancholy temporarily alleviated, allows his tenants to stay on his property a year without rent, doubles his servant Springlove's wages, and joins his daughters in attending a gay celebration by the beggars.

The comedy increases when the girls and their sweethearts find the beggar's life not only raw and uncomfortable, but impossible to master in spite of Springlove's patient instructions. Joining the beggar band are two more lovers, Amie, niece of Justice Clack, and the boorish Martin, his clerk, who is also Hearty's nephew. Amie is not totally enamored of Martin, and Springlove, though expressing a willingness to help the couple find a preacher, is clearly desirous of having the girl for himself. When officers come to seek Amie, the beggar troop retires to Justice Clack's house. There the beggars perform plays that parallel the story Brome's audience has already seen: "The Two Lost Daughters," "The Vagrant Stewart," "The Old Squire and the Fortune Teller," etc. Before the plays conclude, Justice Clack genially forgives his niece and Martin, and Oldrents learns from the beggars that his loved steward is really his son—news that cures his melancholy utterly. Springlove takes Amie to wife, with her guardian's blessings, and Hearty promises to find another wife for his nephew Martin.

Brome's comedy is a mixure of realism, farce, and sentiment in the manner of Dekker's *Shoemaker's Holiday,* whereas several of the characters, notably Squire Oldrents and Justice Clack, owe a great deal to Jonson's comedy of humours (see JONSON, BEN). *A Jovial Crew* is Brome's most festive comedy, and probably the last good play on the English stage before the closing of the theaters in 1642.

Ann Hakker has edited *A Jovial Crew* in the Regents Renaissance Drama series (1966). For criticism, see R.J. Kaufmann, *Richard Brome, Caroline Playwright* (1961), and John W. Crowther, "The Literary History of Brome's *A Jovial Crew,* "in *Studies in English Renaissance Literature,* ed. Waldo F. McNeir (1962).

Julius Caesar, The Tragedy of. A tragedy by William SHAKESPEARE, written in 1599-1600 and first printed in the 1623 Folio. Shakespeare's chief source was Plutarch's *Lives of the Noble Grecians and Romans,* translated by Sir Thomas North (1579) from the French of Jacques Amyot (1559).

Julius Caesar has returned to Rome from his successful campaign in Spain (44 B. C.), which he celebrates under the guise of the Feast of Lupercal. Suspecting that Caesar aspires to a dictatorship, the republicans Cassius and Casca persuade Brutus to lead their conspiracy to assassinate him, and Brutus, long a friend of Caesar, reluctantly joins them in order to save Rome from tyranny. After Caesar is slain, his friend Antony incites a rebellion against the conspirators with a fiery speech at Caesar's funeral. Caesar's nephew Octavius, Antony, and Lepidus launch a purge against the conspirators in Rome, and then later bring an army to Philippi, where they defeat Brutus and Cassius (42 B. C.). Before the battle Brutus and Cassius quarrel bitterly and are then reconciled. Brutus learns of his wife's death, and the ghost of Caesar appears to warn him "Thou shalt see me again at Philippi." After their defeat both Brutus and Cassius commit suicide, and Antony proclaims over Brutus' body that "this was the noblest Roman of them all."

Julius Caesar represents an ingenious adaptation of historical material and mastery of dramatic structure. Shakespeare realized that his audience would come to the theater interested primarily in the great Caesar, and that his assassination in Act III would leave the remaining two acts devoid of momentum. Hence he effected a climatic plateau by following the assassination with Antony's stirring funeral oration in the Forum and the revolt of the populace against the conspirators; thereafter the presence of Caesar is consistently stressed as his spirit remains to pursue Brutus and Cassius to their destruction at Philippi. This subtle division of the play between the physical Caesar of Acts I—III and the spiritual force of IV—V provides a grimly ironic commentary on Brutus' expressed determination before the assassination to "come by Caesar's spirit./And not dismember Caesar" and his fear that Caesar's ambition will "change his nature" into that of a serpent's egg that must be killed "in the shell."

Shakespeare's Caesar is hardly the virile superman of popular imagination. He is hard-of-hearing, sterile, pompous, superstitious, and vain, and Shakespeare's reduction of his stature enables him to concentrate on the tragic hero Brutus, his most complex characterization before Hamlet. Incapable of any mean or selfish or even consciously personal political motives, Brutus is also helpless to effect any actual good, and his confused idealism finds its perfect foil in the burning personal envy of Cassius. Craven as he is at the beginning, however, Cassius grows more admirable in adversity after Act III, and his judgment is always superior to that of Brutus. Characteristically, the naive Brutus rejects Cassius' plea to destroy Antony because Brutus confuses virtue, his own cherished possession, with simple power, just as Richard II and Lear confuse symbols of authority with its substance. Moreover, Brutus is so insulated by his own self-righteousness that he cannot imagine how Antony, a frivolous night-reveler so different from himself, can possibly be effective. The great funeral speeches in the Forum (III, *ii*) dramatize this contrast between the idealistic Brutus and the realistic Antony. The latter is a playboy and carouser, but he knows better than Brutus the dark and vile recesses of human nature and is sufficiently ruthless never to be distracted by moral considerations. In the violent jungle of Roman politics, Brutus finds as Hamlet did that the "time is out of joint." In fact, Brutus' inner divisions, intellectual speculations, and agonizing hesitation anticipate the later dilemma of Hamlet.

A standard edition is the new Arden, ed. T. S. Dorsch (1955). For criticism, see M. W. MacCallum, *Shakespeare's Roman Plays and Their Background* (1910); G. Wilson Knight, *The Imperial Theme* (1931); John Palmer, *Political Characters of Shakespeare* (1945); R. A. Foakes, "An Approach to *Julius Caesar,*" *SQ,* V (1954); Earnest Schanzer, "The Problem of *Julius Caesar,*" *SQ,* VI (1955); Brents Stirling, *Unity in Shakespearean Tragedy* (1956); and Maurice Charney, *Shakespeare's Roman Plays: The Function of Imagery in the Drama* (1961).

K

King, Henry (1592-1669), Anglican bishop and poet. Born the son of the distinguished bishop John King, who ordained John Donne into the Anglican priesthood, Henry King was first and foremost a minister of the church and only occasionally a poet. He attended Westminster School and Christ Church, Oxford (B.A., 1611; M.A., 1614), and after holding several ecclesiastical offices, including that of prebend of St. Paul's, was appointed bishop of Chichester in 1642 and was expelled by the Puritans a year later. During the civil wars he lived on the charity of friends, but was reinstated in his bishopric after 1660. He was an intimate acquaintance of Jonson and, according to Izaak Walton, Donne's dearest friend and literary executor. The scholar H. J. C. Grierson states that King was responsible for the publication of the first edition of Donne's poems in 1633.

Except for a metrical version of the Psalms in 1651, all of King's verses are included in *Poems, Elegies, Paradoxes, and Sonnets* (1657), of which almost half are elegies and obituary poems reflecting the influence of Donne and Jonson. A few, however, are courtly love lyrics avoiding Donne's erotic heat but engaging freely in his metaphysical conceits, as in "The Double Rock":

Since thou hast view'd some Gorgon, and art grown
  A solid stone:
To bring again to softness thy hard heart
  Is past my art.
Ice may relent to water in a thaw;
But stone made flesh Love's chemistry ne'er saw.

King's most famous love poem is his "Sonnet" of eighteen lines beginning "Tell me no more how fair she is," which combines the more tender moments of Donne's *Songs and Sonnets* with Jonson's spare and economical love lyrics. Jonson's expressive restraint and colloquial concentration join with Donne's wit in "The Exequy," which laments with quiet grace the death in 1624 of King's young wife Anne. "Age, or grief, or sickness," he assures her, will "marry" his bodv to the "hollow vale" of death:

> But hark! My pulse, like a soft drum,
> Beats my approach, tells thee I come;
> And slow howe'er my marches be,
> I shall at last sit down by thee.

King wrote competent elegies on both Jonson and Donne, but his best notes are struck when, like his master Donne, he quietly reflects on his own death, as in "A Contemplation upon Flowers":

Oh, teach me to see death, and not to fear
But rather to take truce;
How often have I seen you at a bier,
And there look fresh and spruce.
You fragrant flowers, then teach me that my breath
Like yours, may sweeten, and perfume my death.

King's poems are available in the edition by John Sparrow (1925) and in *Minor Poets of the Caroline Period,* ed. George Saintsbury, (1921), III. Sparrow's introduction contains a full critical discussion, as does George Williamson, *The Donne Tradition* (1930). The fullest biographical account is by Laurence Mason, "The Life and Works of Henry King," *Transactions of the Connecticut Academy of Arts and Sciences (1913).*

King and No King, A. A tragicomedy by Francis BEAUMONT and John FLETCHER. It was written and performed in 1611 and first published in 1619. No source is known. Most scholars see Beaumont's hand in the arrangement of the plot. The scene is Armenia at some indefinite time.

The theme of the play is incest, which the clever resolution neatly evades. Arbaces, valiant young king of Iberia, falls passionately in love with his virtuous sister Panthea, whom he has not seen since childhood and for whom he has already arranged a marriage to Tigranes, the brave king of Armenia whom Arbaces has defeated in war. After kissing Panthea, Arbaces, in a violent fit of guilt, has her imprisoned. Later he repents of his impetuosity and sends Bessus, a cowardly braggart and buffoon, to represent him in his illicit courtship of Panthea. (Much of the comedy is conveyed by Bessus' clownish pretensions of "honor" and cowardly evasions of challenges and duels.) Matters are made increasingly difficult for the confused and vacillating Arbaces when his prisoner Tigranes confesses he is not in love with Panthea but with another lady, Spaconia. Visiting Panthea in prison, Arbaces writhes with guilt and desire as he begs her at one moment to submit to him, at another to reject him, and Panthea concedes that she too has felt more for him than a sisterly regard.

Half mad with desire, Arbaces now resolves to rape Panthea and then kill himself, but events are suddenly changed utterly by a strange revelation. Gobrias, the Iberian lord protector, and Arane, supposedly Arbaces' mother, announce that Arbaces is really Gobrias' son, conceived by another woman and given in infancy to the then barren Arane. Later Arane conceived by her husband, Iberia's king, and bore Panthea. Hence Arbaces is not a king, Panthea is not his sister, and nothing stands between the lovers. Arbaces retains his throne by marriage to Panthea, Tigranes and Spaconia are betrothed, and all ends happily.

With *Philaster, A King and No King* represents one of the fullest realizations of Beaumont and Fletcher's pattern of tragicomedy. The play was enthusiastically received when the King's Men performed it at court, Blackfriars, and the Globe in 1611, and it was often revived in the 1630s and Restoration period. John Dryden praised it highly in his *Essay of Dramatic Poesy,* and it exerted a pervasive influence on both the Cavalier drama in the reign of Charles I and the heroic plays of Dryden in the Restoration.

Although *A King and No King* is sprinkled with clever clues as to the true identities of Arbaces and Panthea—including the title of the play—suspense is sustained by the protean and volatile nature of Arbaces, who is by turns cruel and compassionate, craven and noble, foolish and wise; thus the audience is made aware that virtually anything can happen, and the *deus ex machina* at the conclusion comes as a gratifying release in a story taut with omnipresent possibilities of disaster. Although Panthea is a long-suffering, victimized heroine of the type Beaumont and Fletcher portrayed in *Philaster* and *The Maid's Tragedy,* she too is unpredictable, as when Arbaces blurts out his lust and she replies, "Methinks brothers and sisters lawfully may kiss."

The play is available in *The Works of Francis Beaumont and John Fletcher,* ed. Arnold Glover and A. R. Waller, 10 vols. (1905-12), IX. The play is edited by G. W. Williams in *The Dramatic Works in the Beaumont and Fletcher Canon,* ed. Fredson Bowers, 2 vols. (1966, 1970), II. The critical edition by Robert K. Turner, Jr., in the Regents Renaissance Drama series (1963) contains a fine introduction. For other commentary, see Arthur Mizener, "The High Design of *A King and No King,*" *MP* XXXVIII (1940); and Eugene

M. Waith, *The Pattern of Tragicomedy in Beaumont and Fletcher* (1952).

King John. A history play by William SHAKESPEARE of very uncertain date but usually assigned to the period 1596-97. It was first printed in the 1623 Folio. There is considerable dispute as to the source of the play. Those who argue for the date 1596-97 contend that the source is an anonymous two-part play, *The Troublesome Reign of John, King of England* (1591); those who insist on an earlier date claim that the anonymous play is merely a poor adaptation of Shakespeare's. The first of these views is the more widely accepted. Shakespeare's play, covering the whole period of King John's reign (1199-1216), deals chiefly with young Arthur, duke of Bretagne and son of King John's deceased elder brother Geoffrey.

The crown rests uneasily on King John's head. In France, King Philip demands that John relinquish the throne to young Arthur, and at the English court Philip the Bastard, thought to be the son of the late Sir Robert Faulconbridge, is revealed to be in reality the illegitimate son of Richard Coeur de Lion, King John's older brother. The Bastard denies any claim to the crown, and in France Arthur and Arthur's mother Constance meet with John to press Arthur's rights. In Angiers, where the confrontation occurs, the citizens attempt to restore harmony by arranging a marriage between Lewis, dauphin of France, and Blanch of Spain, John's niece.

The wedding festivities are interrupted by Cardinal Pandulph, papal legate, who excommunicates King John for denying Stephen Langton the office of archbishop of Canterbury, and fighting breaks out between the English and French. In the battle the Bastard kills the duke of Austria, and Arthur is captured by King John, who puts him in the custody of Hubert de Burgh. When Hubert is ordered by John to blind Arthur, Hubert takes pity on the boy and falsely reports his death. Unknown to either Hubert or King John, however, Arthur has been killed in a fall while attempting an escape. When Arthur's body is discovered by the English nobles Pembroke, Salisbury, and Bigot, they mistakenly assume that King John was the murderer.

When a French army lands in England, King John makes his peace with the church and attempts to placate the invaders. Lewis, the dauphin, however, persists in his claims to the throne. In battle against the French, King John falls ill with fever and is taken to Swinstead Abbey, where he is poisoned by a treacherous monk. At the conclusion of the play John names his son Prince Henry heir to the throne, and Cardinal Pandulph arranges an honorable peace with the French. The significance of these events is commented upon by the Bastard:

This England never did, nor never shall,
Lie at the proud foot of a conqueror,
But when it first did help to wound itself.
[V, *vii,* 112-14]

If Shakespeare did use the anonymous *Troublesome Reign of John* as his source, he followed the episodic plot very closely but altered many of the characterizations, changed the dialogue thoroughly, and deleted the virulent anti-Catholic sentiments. The result is a history play of very loose structure and unemphatic, sometimes inconsistent characterizations. In Act I, King John appears as a vividly drawn, energetic character dominated by his mother, the dowager Queen Elinor—a relationship that promises to become as interesting as that developed so effectively in *Coriolanus*—but Act II relinquishes all the advantages of this brilliant beginning by becoming bogged down in armies on the march, sieges, and turgid speeches. In Act III, moreover, John alters abruptly from an aggressive villain to a simpering weakling, and the Bastard from a witty cynic to a scrupulous spokesman of some of the most solemn passages of the play. *King John* achieves some dramatic success in isolated scenes and in its early portrayals of John and the Bastard, but these occasional flashes are not enough to give the work the coherence and direction of Shakespeare's other chronicle dramas. For other plays of the same type, see CHRONICLE PLAY.

A standard edition is the new Arden, ed. E. A. J. Honigmann (1954). *The Troublesome Reign* is discussed and reprinted in Geoffrey Bullough, *Narrative and Dramatic Sources of Shakespeare,* 7 vols. (1962), IV. For background and commentary, see Ruth Wallerstein, *King John in Fact and Fiction* (1917); E. M. W. Tillyard, *Shakespeare's History Plays* (1946); Lily B. Campbell, *Shakespeare's Histories* (1947); Adrien Bonjour, "The Road to Swinstead Abbey," *ELH,* XVIII (1951); Irving Ribner, *The English History Play in the Age of Shakespeare* (1957); M. M. Reese, *The Cease of Majesty* (1961); John R. Elliott, "Shakespeare and the Double Image of King John," *ShakS,* I (1965); J. L. Simmons, "Shakespeare's *King John* and Its Source: Coherence, Pattern, and Vision," *TSE,* XVII (1969); and Jonathan R. Price, "*King John* and Problematic Art," *SQ,* XXI (1970).

King Lear. A tragedy by William SHAKESPEARE, written in 1605–06 and first printed in 1608. The principal source is an old anonymous play, *The True Chronicle History of King Leir and His Three Daughters,* first published in 1605 but written and performed much earlier. Two additional sources include John Florio's translation of Montaigne's essays (1603) and Samuel Harsnett's *A Declaration of Egregious Popish Impostures* (1603). The story of Lear and his daughters was first told in Geoffrey of Monmouth's *Historia regum Britanniae* (1137), from which Raphael Holinshed derived his account in his *Chronicles* (1587 ed.). Shakespeare also read Spenser's version of the tale in the second book of *The Faerie Queene.*

In ancient Britain King Lear, a proud and foolish old man, decrees that he will divide his kingdom among his three daughters, Goneril, Regan, and Cordelia, according to how persuasively each is able to express her love for him. In the absurd love test that follows, Goneril and Regan declare their devotion with hypocritical eloquence, but Lear's favorite, Cordelia, states laconically that she loves her father "according to my bond" and cannot "heave my heart into my mouth." Enraged, Lear gives Goneril and Regan his entire kingdom and peremptorily disinherits Cordelia in spite of the protestations of the loyal earl of Kent, who is banished for his honest objections. Although Lear's daughters agree to maintain their aged father and his hundred knights, they soon reduce his retainers to nothing and drive the old man out into a storm in the company of his "wise fool."

Meanwhile, in another story, the earl of Gloucester disinherits his son Edgar on false suspicions engendered by Gloucester's unscrupulous illegitimate son Edmund, who aspires to appropriate Gloucester's lands. When Gloucester shows sympathy for Lear's cause, Regan and her cruel husband, the duke of Cornwall, put out Gloucester's eyes and send him to "smell his way to Dover" in search of Lear, at which point Cornwall's servant turns against the villain and gives him a mortal wound. Enroute to Dover, Gloucester is accompanied by his son Edgar, who conceals his identity from his father by an assumed voice and the disguise of a lunatic beggar.

Still accompanied by his court fool, and by the loyal Kent, who watches over the king in disguise, Lear raves insanely against his ungrateful daughters and the injustices of the world, proclaiming that he is "more sinned against than sinning," yet acknowledging his own harsh treatment of the faithful Cordelia. At Dover, Lear and his retinue are joined by Cordelia and an army raised by Cordelia's husband, the king of France. Meanwhile Lear's other daughters turn against each other out of jealousy over Edmund; Goneril poisons Regan, then commits suicide, and Edmund marches on Dover to defeat Cordelia's forces. Edmund orders Cordelia hanged, Lear dies of grief, and Edmund himself is killed in personal combat with Edgar. At the end the kingdom passes to the duke of Albany, Goneril's virtuous husband.

In all versions of the story except Shakespeare's, Lear escapes to France, where Cordelia restores him to his throne, crushes his enemies, and enables him to enjoy the last years of his life. The grinding agony of the outcome is Shakespeare's own conception, as are some of the most powerful elements of the play—Lear's madness, Kent's enduring devotion, the storm in Act III, and Cordelia's violent death. Perhaps Shakespeare's most radical innovation in the play is the invention of the fool, who performs the complex functions of ironic chorus and Lear's alter ego. He never appears except in Lear's company, and he departs from the play in Act IV as if an illuminated and reborn Lear no longer required his wisdom. He speaks in a bewildering variety of modes—moralizing songs, riddles, obscene jests, wise saws, and witty innuendoes; in the chaos of Lear's world, where the king has become a fool, the fool reigns as monarch of wit and philosophical insights. "Now thou art an O without a figure," he tells Lear after the old man has exiled Cordelia and given over his power to his wicked daughters:

I am better than thou art now. I am a Fool, thou art nothing. [*To Goneril*] Yes, forsooth, I will hold my tongue, so your face bids me, though you say nothing.
Mum, mum.
He that keeps nor crust nor crumb,
Weary of all, shall want some.

[*Pointing to Lear*] That's a sheal'd peascod.
[I, *iv,* 212-19]

Like *Hamlet, King Lear* is a massive, polyphonic dramatization of two families whose experiences reflect and comment on each other. The treachery of Lear's two daughters and the fidelity of the third is paralleled in the betrayal by Gloucester's illegitimate son Edmund and the loyalty of Edgar. In contrast to the ferocious Lear, however, Gloucester is temporizing and weak. His bitter revelation of life's futility is often cited as expressive of Shakespeare's own pessimism during the period of the great tragedies:

As flies to wanton boys are we to the gods.
They kill us for their sport.
[IV, *i,* 38-39]

Lear's revelation is more far-reaching. Beginning the play as little more than a spoiled child, he learns through suffering the fundamental values of love, responsibility, and human brotherhood. As in all Shakespeare's tragedies, the price of knowledge is exorbitant—madness, war, and death—yet Lear's reconciliation with Cordelia, however brief, and his total self-knowledge and human compassion signal a victory of spirit over both natural and moral evil.

King Lear concludes with no facile mitigation of its inevitable despair; there is neither poetic justice nor justification of evil in its outcome, and the death of Cordelia, as Samuel Johnson observed, is a gratuitous cruelty. Nevertheless, the loyalty of Cordelia, Kent, Edgar, and the poignant fool, as well as Lear's magnificent spirit, all combine to give the lie to any cynical or even totally despairing view of man's inhumanity to man.

A standard edition is the New Cambridge edition, ed. G. I. Duthie and J. Dover Wilson (1960). The new Arden edition, ed. Kenneth Muir (rev. ed., 1963), is also excellent. Criticism of *King Lear* is so voluminous that only a small portion of the important scholarship can be cited: A. C. Bradley, *Shakespearean Tragedy* (1904); Lily B. Campbell, *Shakespeare's Tragic Heroes: Slaves of Passion* (1930); G. Wilson Knight, *The Wheel of Fire* (1930) and *The Shakespearean Tempest* (1953); E. E. Stoll, *Art and Artifice in Shakespeare* (1933); Theodore Spencer, *Shakespeare and the Nature of Man* (1942); George Orwell, "Lear, Tolstoy, and the Fool," in *Shooting an Elephant and Other Essays* (1945); Harley Granville-Barker, *Prefaces to Shakespeare* (1946); Robert Heilman, *This Great Stage: Image and Structure in King Lear* (1948); John F. Danby, *A Dream of Learning* (1951); William Empson, "The Fool in Lear," *SR,* LVII (1949), repr. in Empson's *The Structure of Complex Words* (1951); Wolfgang H. Clemen, *The Development of Shakespeare's Imagery* (1951); and John Holloway, *The Story of the Night* (1961). *ShakS, 13* (1960), is devoted almost entirely to *King Lear; The King Lear Perplex* (1960), ed. Helmut Bonheim, contains sources, annotated bibliography, and excerpts of criticism from Nahum Tate's essay (1687) to William Elton's *King Lear and the Gods* (1960). The most exhaustive survey of criticism is in Edward Quinn, James Ruoff, and Joseph Grennen, *The Major Shakespearean Tragedies* (1973).

Kinwelmarsh, Francis (fl. 1566-80). Translator. With George GASCOIGNE, he translated Euripides' *Phoenissae* under the title *Jocasta* (1566), the first rendering into English of a Greek play. See TRANSLATIONS

Knight of the Burning Pestle, The. A satiric comedy by Francis BEAUMONT, written in 1607 and first performed by the Children of the Queen's Revels at the Blackfriars about 1608. The first edition appeared in an anonymous quarto in 1613. One obvious source of Beaumont's play is *Don Quixote.* Although the first part of Cervantes' novel was printed in Spain in 1607, an English version published in 1612 is known to have been translated five or six years before. Hence Beaumont may have read the English version in manuscript, or possibly have heard the story of Don Quixote from someone familiar with the original Spanish.

In the induction the actors at Blackfriars are about to perform a comedy of manners called "The London Merchant" when a boisterous grocer interrupts the prologue and demands to see, instead, a play "notably in honor of the commoners of the city" and not one that "girds at merchants," as he fears this comedy will, for the Blackfriars theater is notorious for its satires. The grocer is soon joined on the stage by his garrulous wife and his stage-struck apprentice Rafe. During the performance of "The London Merchant," the grocer and his wife will improvise their rival play, a heroic romance called "The Knight of the Burning Pestle," with the apprentice in the title role. Throughout the performance the grocer and his wife remain seated on the stage and make comments on the action in both plays.

In "The London Merchant," old Venturewell decides to marry his daughter Luce to the well-born but rather thick-witted Master Humphrey and to discharge his clever and industrious young apprentice Jasper Merrythought because Jasper has won his daughter's heart. Before Jasper leaves Venturewell's house, however, he arranges with Luce to meet in Waltham Forest. The lovers agree to elope, but Luce meanwhile mounts her own intrigue. Unknown to Jasper, she informs Humphrey that she will never marry except by elopement, and Humphrey agrees to take her away to Waltham Forest.

In "The Knight of the Burning Pestle," Rafe and two other grocers' apprentices, Tim and Little George, are inspired by reading the chivalric romance *Palmerin of England*; they determine to don armor and emulate Palmerin's heroism in order to bestow glory on the grocer's guild. Rafe dubs himself the Knight of the Burning Pestle; Tim becomes his squire, and Little George assumes the role of the squire's dwarf. The trio is further inspired by cheers of approval from the grocer and his wife.

Jasper goes home in the hope that his father Charles Merrythought will help finance his elopement, but finds that the jolly old soul is too taken with dancing and singing to earn a farthing; indeed, old Merrythought is so indifferent to work and so devoted to merrymaking that his parsimonious wife scrapes together what gold she has hoarded over the years and departs with her favorite son Michael. In Waltham Forest Merrythought's wife and Michael encounter Rafe as the Knight of the Burning Pestle, who frightens them out of their wits with his bombast and rodomontades.

When the unromantic Humphrey informs Venturewell of Luce's scheme to elope, the old man gives the plan his approval. As Luce has planned, in Waltham Forest she and Humphrey meet Jasper, who beats Humphrey and departs from the scene with Luce. The grocer and his wife are outraged by Jasper's conduct and demand that their champion Rafe teach the upstart a lesson. Jasper proves more than a match for the Knight of the Burning Pestle, who is left on the field of battle with a black eye and a cracked pate. With Michael and Dame Merrythought in tow, Rafe elects to recuperate from his wounds at the mysterious Castle of the Old Bell (otherwise known as the Bell Inn at Waltham).

When Humphrey informs Venturewell that Jasper has absconded with Luce, the old man angrily seeks out Charles Merrythought, who merely responds to Venturewell's complaints with lively dances and madcap songs. In Waltham Forest, meanwhile, Jasper reveals himself to be as quixotic as Rafe. In the bizarre manner of the heroes of the romances, he tests Luce's love and constancy by feigning jealousy of Humphrey and threatening her with a sword. The astonished girl proves steadfast enough, but unfortunately Venturewell and Humphrey arrive in the midst of Jasper's theatricals and carry her off before Jasper can explain his strange conduct.

At the suggestion of the grocer and his wife, the Knight of the Burning Pestle ventures forth from the Bell Inn to conquer a fearful giant called Barbaroso (alias Nick the barber), who terrorizes villagers with such ghastly tortures as drawing teeth, cutting hair, and giving purges. After Barbaroso is put to flight, the grocer is hard put to think of new adventures for his knight. The grocer is at first inclined to "let the Sophy of Persia come and christen him a child," but then recalls that the same event was dramatized only a week before at the Red Bull theater. Finally the grocer urges Rafe to woo the fair princess of Moldavia, but the doughty knight refuses to court any lady who "trusts in Anti-Christ and false tradition"; instead, Rafe chooses as his lady fair a true-blue English maid who works in a cobbler's shop in his own neighborhood.

In a letter Jasper informs Venturewell that he is dying and begs as his last request that the old man allow Luce to view him in his coffin. Once inside Venturewell's house, Jasper rises from his coffin and frightens Venturewell into promising to reject Humphrey as Luce's suitor.

Returning home in this role of a ghost, Jasper discovers that not even spirits can cool his father's enthusiasm for merrymaking; old Merrythought not only welcomes his son as a ghost, but even takes back his wife and Michael, providing they agree to join him in his endless dancing and singing. To Charles Merrythought's house also come Venturewell and Luce, whom Jasper now confronts without ghostly shrieks and sheets. Relieved, old Venturewell repents of his hard treatment of the lovers and gives their wedding plans his blessings. The grocer and his wife, wishing to add some pathos to this frothy comedy, require their champion to finish his role with an appropriately heroic death. Hence Rafe appears with an arrow stuck in his head, delivers a long eulogy in praise of his own past glories, and nobly expires to the loud sobs of the grocer's wife. Old Merrythought closes "The London Merchant" with a sprightly song, and the grocer's wife begs the audience to applaud her gallant Knight of the Burning Pestle.

The extraordinary artistry of Beaumont's comedy becomes most striking when it is compared with George Peele's THE OLD WIVES' TALE. Like Peele, Beaumont satirizes romances and heroic plays, but instead of employing his common folk as observers of the drama, as in Peele's frame tale, he converts them into a farcical chorus that remains on the stage to comment on the action in both stories—an idea Beaumont may have derived not only from Peele's play but from Thomas Kyd's *The Spanish Tragedy* (which Beaumont parodies in Rafe's finale). The target of Beaumont's mock-heroic comedy is brilliantly far-ranging and includes not only the old heroic romances like *Palmerin of England* but Elizabethan plays that glorified the achievements of ordinary citizens, such as George Peele's *Edward I,* Thomas Heywood's *Four Prentices,* or John Day's *Travels of Three English Brothers.* The aristocratic Beaumont pokes congenial fun at bourgeois sensibilities, which he accurately defines as humorless practicality mingled with sentimentality and childish credulity.

Beaumont wisely cast his comedy in a rough-hewn colloquial prose occasionally alleviated by old Merrythought's charming songs. *The Knight of the Burning Pestle* was the first full-length mock-heroic comedy on the English stage, a forerunner to such eighteenth-century classics as Buckingham's *The Rehearsal* and Sheridan's *The Critic.* Yet the anonymous dedicatory epistle to the first edition states that Beaumont's play was composed in only eight days and "utterly rejected" by its audience at Blackfriars. No doubt the London citizens, like Beaumont's vociferous grocer, could not abide a comedy that "girds at merchants." As might be expected, the play was a great success when revived for more sophisticated viewers at the Cockpit in Drury Lane in 1635.

The Knight of the Burning Pestle is available in several excellent modern editions: in the Regents Renaissance Drama series, ed. John Doebler (1967); the Fountainwell Drama series, ed. Andrew Gurr (1968); and the New Mermaid series, ed. Michael Hattaway (1970). It is also edited by Cyrus Hoy in *The Dramatic Works in the Beaumont and Fletcher Canon,* ed. Fredson Bowers, 2 vols. (1966, 1970), I. For criticism, see C. M. Gayley, *Beaumont, the Dramatist* (1914); Edwin S. Lindsay, "The Original Music for Beaumont's Play *The Knight of the Burning Pestle,*" *SP,* XXVI (1929); and Ian Fletcher, *Beaumont and Fletcher* (1967).

Kyd, Thomas (1558–1594). Dramatist. Born in London, the son of Francis Kyd, a prosperous scrivener or notary, Kyd attended the Merchant Taylors' School, where the humanist scholar Richard Mulcaster was headmaster and Edmund Spenser a fellow student. Kyd probably left school around 1583 and worked for a time as an apprentice scrivener. It is almost certain that he did not attend the university. In the 1580s his name appears as a playwright associated with the Queen's Men. In Thomas Dekker's pamphlet *A Knight's Conjuring* (1607), Kyd is referred to as "industrious," but the only publication to bear his name is *Pompey the Great, His Fair Cornelia's Tragedy* (1593), a translation from the French of Robert Garnier's *Cornélie* and inspired perhaps by the countess of Pembroke's translation in 1592 of another of Garnier's Senecan tragedies, *Marc Antoine.* Kyd dedicated the work to the young countess of Sussex, wife of Robert Radcliffe, Lord Fitzwalters, whose father Henry, fourth earl of Sussex, appears to have been Kyd's patron from 1587 to 1593. Kyd may have served the Sussex family during these years as a secretary and tutor.

There has been much speculation as to whether Kyd wrote an early version of *Hamlet,* now lost (called the "Ur-Hamlet" by German scholars), on which Shakespeare based his famous tragedy. Thomas Nashe seems to have been referring to Kyd as author of such a play in his preface to Robert Greene's *Menaphon* (1589), where he attacks "shifting companions" who "leave the trade of *Noverint* [i.e., scrivener] whereto they were born, and busy themselves with the endeavors of art," and who, lacking any true classical scholarship, find that "English *Seneca* read by candlelight yields many good sentences, as *Blood is a beggar,* and so forth; and if you entreat him fair in a frosty morning, he will afford you whole *Hamlets,* I should say handfuls of tragical speeches . . . which makes his famished followers to imitate the Kidde in *Æsop,* who enamored with the Foxes newfangles, forsook all hopes of life to leap into a new occupation . . ."

Another work attributed to Kyd is a prose pamphlet signed "T. K.," *The Householder's Philosophy* (1588), based on a story by Torquato Tasso. His authorship is made somewhat more probable because the publisher of the work was Thomas Hacket, a neighbor of Kyd's family in Lombard Street. In addition, Kyd has been named the author of three anonymous plays: *The Rare Triumphs of Love and Fortune* (1589), ARDEN OF FEVERSHAM (1592), and *The Tragedy of Soliman and Perseda* (1592). The last is a full-length version of the condensed play-within-the-play with which Kyd's best-known work, THE SPANISH TRAGEDY (wr. c. 1585), concludes. That Kyd was the author of *Soliman and Perseda* is likely but by no means certain, for someone else may have written the play to exploit the popularity of *The Spanish Tragedy.* Kyd's authorship of the domestic tragedy *Arden of Feversham* is equally questionable. Those who attribute it to Kyd usually find his hand also in an anonymous pamphlet, *The Murder of John Brewen,* which describes events very similar to those dramatized in *Arden of Feversham*—the murder of a husband by his wife and her lover, who were burned at Smithfield for the crime in June 1592. Others see little relationship among the pamphlet, *Arden of Feversham,* and works known to have been by Kyd.

The last few years of Kyd's life find him linked to another great dramatist of the period, Christopher Marlowe, with whom Kyd shared rooms in 1591. In May 1593, Kyd was arrested and imprisoned for allegedly writing ballads and pamphlets inciting English workers to riot against their foreign competitors in London. In the course of the investigation by the Privy Council certain presumably "atheistical" papers were discovered in Kyd's lodgings; actually, they were merely a partial transcription of a unitarian tract by John Proctor, *The Fall of the Late Arrian* (1549), but Kyd—already in serious difficulty over the incitement-to-riot charges and no doubt subjected to torture—blamed the composition of the controversial work on Marlowe, who was arrested, briefly examined about the matter, and released. A few days later Marlowe was killed at Deptford in a tavern brawl, and Kyd, still imprisoned and probably on the rack, went to great lengths to dissociate himself completely from his former friend, testifying to the Privy Council of Marlowe: "That I should love or be familiar friend, with one so irreligious, were very rare . . . He was intemperate and of a cruel heart, the very contraries to which, my greatest enemies will say by me."

It was during this time of anguish that Kyd published his *Pompey the Great* with a dedication to the countess of Sussex begging for some succor, and reminding the Sussex family of his past services. He also wrote Sir John Puckering, ex-officio head of the Privy Council, asking him to intercede with his erstwhile patron (presumably Sussex) to help him in his "pains and undeserved tortures," but there is no indication that the Sussex family made any effort to assist their former servant. After his release from prison Kyd lived another year, broken by poverty and ill health. He died at thirty-six on August 15, 1594, and was buried at St. Mary Colchurch, London.

Kyd was not generally known to be the author of *The Spanish Tragedy* until 1773, when Thomas Hawkins in *The Origin of the English Drama* cited a brief reference to Kyd as having written the play in Thomas Heywood's *Apology for Actors* (1612). *The Spanish Tragedy,* one of the most popular dramas of the English Renaissance, underwent numerous editions and revivals (including extensive additions done for Philip Henslowe by Ben Jonson in 1601-02). If Kyd had written no other play except this one, he would deserve recognition as a dramatist of primary importance, for it is a seminal work that decisively influenced the whole course of the English drama at a crucial stage of development. Later dramatists frequently alluded to it or echoed it mockingly in their comic scenes; by the reign of James I Kyd's tragedy was considered puerile, old-fashioned, and crude—the type of bombastic drama condemned by Hamlet in his address to the actors. In retrospect, however, *The Spanish Tragedy* is anything but inchoate or "primitive," and its highly sophisticated dramaturgy makes it difficult to believe that Kyd had not written several lost plays in preparation for his one extant triumph. No source has been found for Kyd's tragedy, and its many innovations are now seen to have been the result of his impressive originality.

The Spanish Tragedy was the first English tragedy of any real and enduring artistic merit—*Gorboduc* (1562) seems childishly inept by comparison—and the first English tragedy to incorporate all the principal Senecan elements: a plot structure firmly based on act divisions; the theme of revenge; a brooding, stoical hero; a ghost; and declamatory rhetoric and *sententiae* (the "handfuls of tragical speeches" referred to by Nashe). Kyd cleverly improvised on these ancient Senecan ingredients by eliminating the *nuntius,* or messenger, who reports violence occurring offstage, and dramatized murders, suicides, and mutilations with stunning visual effects; moreover, he abolished the archaic mythology and cast his story with a contemporary scene (see SENECAN TRAGEDY). He introduced character types of immense interest to his Elizabethan audience—the Machiavellian villain in Lorenzo and the scandalously daring and "liberated" female in Bel-imperia, for example. To these innovations Kyd brought some of the most effective conventions of the native English stage, such as the ingrained association of tragedy and statecraft, the play-within-the-play (an improvisation on the DUMB SHOW, a device well established since *Gorboduc*), the solemn ethical concerns of the morality plays, and the fast-paced action of the old Tudor interludes. Neither John Lyly nor Marlowe contributed more to the furtherance of a viable drama, and *The Spanish Tragedy* can be seen as a microcosm containing all the essential aspects of form and content characterizing English tragedy down to the closing of the theaters in 1642.

The standard edition of Kyd's works, which includes a comprehensive biographical and critical account, is by F. S. Boas, *The Works of Thomas Kyd* (1901). New biographical data is provided by Arthur Freeman, *Thomas Kyd, Facts and Problems* (1967). A full critical study, with bibliography, is by Peter Murray, *Thomas Kyd* (1970). There is a Concise Bibliography by S. A. Tannenbaum (1941), supplemented by "Thomas Kyd (1940-66)," ed. R. C. Johnson, in *Elizabethan Bibliographies Supplements,* IX (1968). See also *The Predecessors of Shakespeare: A Survey and Bibliography of Recent Studies in English Renaissance Drama,* ed. Terence P. Logan and Denzell S. Smith (1973).

L

Lady of May, The. See SIDNEY, SIR PHILIP.

Lady of Pleasure, The. A comedy by James SHIRLEY, written and performed in 1635 and first printed in 1637. Witty, satiric, and sophisticated, Shirley's play is a forerunner to the comedy of manners that became popular during the Restoration period. No source is known.

Sir Thomas Bornwell, an honorable country gentleman, has allowed his wife Aretina to persuade him to sell his rural estate and come to London, where the socially ambitious woman throws herself into party-going and gambling. She surrounds herself with a circle of fashionable wastrels, including Kickshaw, an admirer of French fashions; John Littlewit, an affected connoiseur of the arts; and Madame Decoy, a common bawd with pretentions of gentility. When Aretina's favorite nephew Frederick, a student at the university, arrives for a visit, she finds his dark clothes too melancholy, his erudition in Greek, Latin, and logic totally unfashionable, and she turns the lad over to her coterie for proper tutoring in fine clothes, tippling, gambling, and wenching. Sir Thomas, growing increasingly restive with these activities, determines to feign a wild extravagance to frighten his wife into frugality and common sense.

The natural rival to Aretina's social ambitions is a neighbor on the Strand, Celestina, Lady Bellamour, a coquettish young widow who shines in conversation, dancing, and amorous intrigues. She too has a coterie, chiefly Master Haircut, a perfumed gallant, and her two kinswomen, Isabella and Mariana Novice, whom, like Aretina with Frederick, she strives to make fashionable and sophisticated.

Aretina and her disciples fail miserably in their effort to humble the resourceful Celestina, who departs from a fiercely competitive encounter with Aretina's coterie with Aretina's husband on her arm. Equally disastrous for Aretina is an abortive liaison arranged by Madame Decoy. As her nephew Frederick enthusiastically slips into debauchery and her husband openly flirts with Celestina and threatens to sacrifice all their wealth for one month of pleasure, Aretina finally comes to her senses and resolves to devote herself to frugality and virtue. Sir Thomas confesses his threat was only a ruse and his courtship of Celestina feigned on both sides; the couple are reconciled, and agree to return to the country. A chastened Frederick goes back to his studies at school, and Madame Decoy and her entourage are dismissed by the Bornwells and advised to reform.

The Lady of Pleasure represents an important

link between Jonson's satiric comedy of humours and Jacobean comedy of manners like Fletcher's *The Wild-Goose Chase.* All of Shirley's characters are basically good, although Aretina is so volatile and foolish she must be redeemed from debauchery and libertinism by a resourceful husband and virtuous woman. The motive of the comedy is "to sport their follies, not their crimes," and the satire is sportive and witty rather than didactic. The widow Celestina, who is spirited and gracefully learned, is one of Shirley's brightest creations. Some scholars find the originals of Sir Peter and Lady Teazle of Sheridan's *School for Scandal* in Shirley's Sir Thomas Bornwell and Aretina.

The standard edition is still that by William Gifford and Alexander Dyce in Shirley's *Dramatic Works and Poems,* 6 vols. (1833). There is a more recent edition in *Jacobean Drama: An Anthology,* ed. Richard C. Harrier, 2 vols., (1963), II. For criticism, see R. S. Forsythe, *The Relations of Shirley's Plays to the Elizabethan Drama* (1914); Arthur Nason, *James Shirley, Dramatist* (1915); and G. F. Sensabaugh, "Platonic Love in Shirley's *The Lady of Pleasure,*" in *A Tribute to George Coffin Taylor* (1952).

Langland, William (1332?-1400?). For comment on the influence of *Piers Plowman* in English Renaissance literature, see SATIRE.

Lantern and Candlelight. A rogue pamphlet in prose by Thomas DEKKER, published in 1608 as a sequel to Dekker's THE BELLMAN OF LONDON, which appeared the same year. The lantern of the title refers to that carried by the bellman, or London nightwatchman, and to the lantern of Diogenes, the bitter cynic and satirist; the candle to the light that householders were required by law to display from windows on winter nights. The pamphlet, an encyclopedic expose of London's "villainies and abuses," is compiled from a variety of sources. Much of the first chapter is based on Thomas Harman's *A Caveat or Warning for Common Cursitors* (1566), a collection of anecdotes pertaining to twenty-three orders of criminals, and Robert Copland's doggerel verses in *The Highway to the Spital-House* (1536?), early examples of English ROGUE LITERATURE. Other sources include Thomas Nashe's *Pierce Penniless His Supplication to the Devil* (1592) and Gervase Markham's *Cavelarice, or The English Horseman* (1607), a rogue pamphlet dealing with the chicaneries of horse dealers.

In contrast to Robert Greene's "coney-catching" pamphlets, which are concerned chiefly with professional criminals (a coney being the prey of confidence men), Dekker's work searches out a wide variety of villainies and sharp practices at the ordinaries, at hunting and hawking, and in brothels, inns, prisons, and marketplaces. Following Harman's comprehensive guide, Dekker discourses on "canting" (the esoteric vocabulary of coney-catchers) and defines such underworld terms as "cursitors" (vagabonds), "Robert's men" (confidence men), "draw-latches" (thieves), "doxies" (whores), and "rufflers" (strong-arm robbers). A short and vivid second chapter shows a criminal sitting in hell thinking how best to retaliate against Dekker for his exposure of villainies in *The Bellman of London.* Instead of taking revenge upon "so mean a person as a bell-ringer," however, a devil sends a messenger to England "to work and win them by all possible means to fight under the dismal and black colors" of Lucifer. Hence Chapter 2, with its instructions of villainies to be patronized by the devil's messenger, represents a kind of prologue to the vices Dekker treats in the chapters that follow:

> Haunt taverns; there shalt thou find prodigals. Pay thy twopence to a player; in his gallery may'st thou sit by a harlot. At ordinaries may'st thou dine with silken fools. When the day steals out of the world thou shalt meet rich drunkards . . . Visit persons and teach gaolers how to make nets of iron there.

The most original chapters in *Lantern and Candlelight* pertain to the corruption and cruelty of English prisons, a subject Dekker was unfortunate enough to have learned from personal experience. He attacks the venality of prison warders and officials and expresses profound compassion for prisoners, especially those incarcerated for debt in these "block-houses of the law": "What scandal to Christianity! What derision to policy! But remember thou, whatsoever thou art, thou art a creditor and hast enclosed thy heart between walls of flint and marble—remember that a prisoner is God's image, yet man's slave and a scrivener's bondman. He is Christ's pawn, redeemed from one Hell and cast into another."

There is an excellent edition of *Lantern and Candlelight,* with critical commentary, annotations, and glossary, by E. D. Pendry in a Stratford-Upon-Avon Library edition (1967). Dekker's pamphlet is also reprinted by A. V. Judges, *The Elizabethan Underworld* (1930), and its influence on later pamphlet writers is traced by P. Shaw, "The Position of Thomas Dekker in Jacobean Prison Literature," *PMLA,* LXII (1947). For a comprehensive study of this and other rogue pamphlets by Dekker, see F. Aydelotte, *Elizabethan Rogues and Vagabonds* (1913).

Laws of Ecclesiastical Polity, Of the. A philosophical and theological treatise by Richard HOOKER defending the principles and practices of episcopacy against Calvinist critics who would abolish the authority of the Anglican bishops and replace it with presbyterian rule. Although Hooker's work was written during the period 1591-1600, only five of the eight books were printed before his death in November, 1600. The first four books were printed in 1594 by John Windet; the fifth and longest book appeared in 1597 as a separate volume. In 1604 the first four books were reprinted, and in 1611 a third edition of I-IV and a second of V. The sixth and eighth books were printed in 1648 and 1651, and in 1662 John Gander's edition introduced the seventh book. Izaak Walton's "Life of Hooker" was published with the 1666 edition. Books VI-VIII were probably brought together for publication from Hooker's notes and unfinished manuscripts after his death.

In the long history of theological debates from More to Milton, Hooker's defense of the Anglican Church contributes little if anything that is striking or original in its theology. Most of his ideas were commonplace justifications of ecclesiastical and secular hierarchy found in hundreds of sixteenth-century works. Yet Hooker's work is of immense value. First, it is a compendium of widely held cosmological, scriptural, and rational conceptions of divine and human order, or "degree," that affords a brilliant exposition of philosophical ideas on nature and society held by sixteenth-century writers like Sidney, Spenser. Shakespeare, and Milton. Second, it presents these ideas in an eloquent and lucid style that has come to be recognized as a monument of English prose. Finally, Hooker's treatise is almost unique in the history of Reformation polemics for its sustained tone of tolerance, good will, and benevolence.

Hooker strikes these attitudes in his lengthy preface, where he addresses his Calvinist adversaries who vehemently challenge the ecclesiastical and secular authority of the Anglican bishops and would reorganize the whole structure of church policy to conform to the presbyterian theocracies established in Geneva and Scotland. Hooker praises Calvin as a great theologian and sincere Christian, but in tracing the rise of Calvinism in England and the intransigence of Calvin's disciples, he points out that the presbyterian agitators would uproot the "social contract" on which English institutions are based and make their own consciences the standard to which others would be forced to conform. He charges the Calvinists with intolerance and repression, and pleads with them to "lay aside the gall of that bitterness wherein your minds have hitherto overabounded, and with meekness to search the truth."

Book I, the most magisterial and eloquent in style, is more philosophical than religious, for it deals with the general principles underlying divine, natural, and human laws. Some laws are temporal, others eternal, but their total operation, grounded in divine reason, constitutes a grand and universal harmony. To disturb one thread of this tapestry is to destroy the orderly design of the whole:

> Now if nature should intermit her course and leave altogether, though it were but for a while, the observation of her own laws; if those principal and mother elements of the world, whereof all things in this lower world are made, should lose the qualities which they now have; if the frame of that heavenly arch erected over our heads should loosen and dissolve itself; if celestial spheres should forget their wonted motions, and by irregular volubility turn themselves any way as it might happen; if the prince of the lights of heaven, which now as a giant doth run his unwearied course, should, as it were through a languishing faintness, begin to stand and to rest himself; if the moon should wander from her beaten way, the times and seasons of the year blend themselves by disordered and confused mixture, the winds breathe out their last gasp, the

> clouds yield no rain, the earth be defeated of heavenly influence, the fruits of the earth pine away as children at the withered breasts of their mother no longer able to yield them relief;—what would become of man himself, whom these things now do all serve? See we not plainly that obedience of creatures unto the law of nature is the stay of the whole world?

This view of a universal order in which divine, natural, and human laws and hierarchies are seen as an infinitely complex and integrated system of "correspondences" is essentially the same as that expressed in Ulysses' famous speech on "degree" in Shakespeare's *Troilus and Cressida* (I, *iii,* 85-126):

The heavens themselves, the planets,
  and this center,
Observe degree, priority, and place,
Insisture, course, proportion, season, form,
Office, and custom, in all line of order.
And therefore is the glorious planet Sol
In noble eminence enthroned and sphered
Amidst the other, whose med'cinable eye
Corrects the ill aspects of planets evil,
And posts like the commandment of a king,
Sans check, to good and bad. But
  when the planets
In evil mixture to disorder wander,
What plagues and what portents,
  what mutiny,
What raging of the sea, shaking of earth,
Commotion in the winds, frights, changes,
  horrors,
Divert and crack, rend and deracinate
The unity and married calm of states...

As order is in the heavens and in nature's divinely created plan, so it is with man and his institutions of government, church, education, and family. According to Hooker: "Thus we see how even one and the selfsame thing is under divers considerations conveyed through many laws, and that to measure by any one kind of law all the actions of men were to confound the admirable order wherein God hath disposed all laws, each as in nature, so in degree, distinct from other." To this cosmic and social order, or "degree," men give "uniform consent admiring her as the mother of their peace and joy," whereas the Calvinists, Hooker charges, would set against this complex, multiform harmony a single standard and single law of their own subjective improvisation: "Thus, by following the law of private reason where the law of public should take place, they breed disturbance..."

This medieval concept of corresponding hierarchies in which the sun "rules" the heavens, king rules the country, father governs the family, reason dominates over the passions, and even animals and matter find natural regulation by "degree," provided a coherent construction securing the individual's relationships to deity, nature, government, society, family, and dualistic self. Even as Hooker was writing, however, divisive forces were destroying this architectonic system of metaphors, and these forces were not, as Hooker feared, exclusively religious, although the Reformation with its inevitable proliferation of sects and its increasingly effective challenges to ecclesiastical and secular authority continued to play a major role in England far into the seventeenth century. The old cosmology and its elaborate façade of analogies also came steadily apart from the winds of the new learning of Coppernicus, Galileo, Bacon, Kepler, and others, just as it shook and sagged in the face of economic, political, and social changes. Viewing the disintegration of the old conception of order, John Donne wrote in "The First Anniversary":

And new philosophy calls all in doubt,
The element of fire is quite put out;
The sun is lost, and th'earth, and no man's wit
Can well direct him where to look for it.
And freely men confess that this world's spent,
When in the planets, and the firmament
They seek so many new; then see that this
Is crumbled out again to his atomies.
'Tis all in pieces, all coherence gone;
All just supply, and all relation:
Prince, subject, father, son, are things forgot,
For every man alone thinks he hath got
To be a phoenix, and that then can be
None of that kind, of which he is, but he.
This is the world's condition now . . .

Book II of Hooker's *Laws* is the briefest. It deals with the authority of scripture (the sole basis of Calvinist "discipline") and concludes that although indisputable Scriptural readings are infallible guides, they are not the only guides, for men also have recourse to natural law, reason, and even common sense. In Book III Hooker challenges the Calvinist contention that church discipline and practices are specifically prescribed or prohibited by Scripture. He argues that Scripture provides men with doctrines and beliefs but not with the externalities of worship or of government, matters which change with place and time. In fact, the Christian congregation is larger than any individual sect like Calvinist or Anabaptist and includes all mankind, even atheists and infidels. Hence Hooker's conception of what constitutes the church is much larger than Calvin's.

In Book IV Hooker defends the Anglican Church against the familiar libel that it is disguised Roman Catholicism, and he praises the Elizabethan compromise and settlement of 1559-61 as a truly "reformed religion" in its rites and ceremonies. Book V is a long and detailed analysis of the Book of Common Prayer; Books VI, VII, and VIII (the least interesting to modern laymen) explain and justify the many functionaries of the Anglican Church—deacons, elders, bishops, and kings.

The standard edition of Hooker's works is edited by John Keble, 6th ed., 3 vols. (1874). Books I-V are available in the Everyman's Library edition, ed. Christopher Morris, 2 vols. (1954). Hooker's style is discussed by D. C. Boughner, "Notes on Hooker's Prose," *RES,* (1939). The growth of the work and the practical problems of its writing and publication are discussed by C. J. Sisson, *The Judicious Marriage of Mr. Hooker and the Birth of "The Laws of Ecclesiastical Polity"* (1940). For philosophical background, see L. S. Thornton, *Richard Hooker: A Study of His Theology* (1924).

Lazarillo de Tormes (Diego Hurtado de Mendoza). See FICTION: ROGUE LITERATURE.

letter-writers. Formularies, or collections of model letters, ostensibly designed to provide instruction in epistolary skills. Actually, letter-writers came to have considerable literary significance and some intrinsic merit as forerunners of the essay, the novel, and the philosophical treatise. The earliest letter-writers were the medieval formularies based on the epistles of Cicero, Pliny, and Seneca; such formularies were often used as part of the *ars dictaminis* of the universities and were established in the curriculum as early as Charlemagne.

The best known of the early Renaissance letter-writers was Erasmus' *De conscribendi epistolas* (1522), which provided both principles of composition and *exempla* from classical epistles. Erasmus' model letters are divided into such categories as encomiastic, exhortatory persuasive, and "familiar" (informal letters on miscellaneous domestic topics). Except for the familiar letters, which Erasmus construed as a free form, his models follow the traditional pattern of classical orations, with their division into *exordium, narratio, propositio, confirmatio, conjuratio,* and *peroratio.* In discussing style he praises the virtues of brevity, clarity, and simplicity.

The line of descent is rather direct from Erasmus' formulary to the first letter-writer in English, William Fulwood's *Enemy of Idleness* (1568), which went through seven editions by 1600. Fulwood shrewdly dedicated his letter-writer to partially educated middle-class readers, whose ranks had grown rapidly during the reign of Elizabeth and who sought practical instruction in the niceties of deportment and communication. Fulwood's *Enemy of Idleness* consists of four books. Book I pertains to the rules of correct correspondence; Book II contains twenty-three model letters derived from Italian formularies; Book III, original letters dealing with problems of domestic life; and Book IV, letters about love. INKHORN TERMS, proper education, pedantry, and social levels of English usage.

The next popular letter-writer was Angel Day's *The English Secretary* (1586), printed at least four times before its revision in 1599 and three times after. Unlike Fulwood's, Day's manual was aimed at professional secretaries, men skilled in writing who were attached in service to some person of importance. In deference to them, Day expanded the later edition with a section on "Tropes and Figures" containing definitions and examples of ninety-three rhetorical devices such as antonomasia, catechresis, hyperbole, metalepsis, etc. Yet Day's book, a combined letter-writer and elocutionary rhetoric, is not devoid of human interest. Like Erasmus, he gives entertaining models and stresses the art of the familiar epistle. His informal letters concern such matters as a father urging his son to study, a friend writing condolences to a bereaved loved one, and a gentleman of means recommending a youth for employment. Hence Day's manual, like many letter-writers of the time, has affinities to COURTESY LITERATURE.

One of the sprightliest letter-writers of

the English Renaissance is Nicholas Breton's *A Post with a Packet of Mad Letters* (1602), a fascinating and often eccentric collection of letters aimed deliberately at conventional middle-class situations: a jealous husband roundly rebukes his wife, who answers his admonitions shrewishly; a son writes his father thanking him for a gift, and the father responds with Polonius-like advice. Breton's fulsome praise of the "honest" merchant trades of England leaves little doubt as to his intended audience, whom Breton also courts by emphasizing money matters, rustic piety, and "practical" subjects like mathematics rather than logic and the arts. Some of this emphasis can be attributed to Breton's own middle-class values; the rest he found in the didacticism of Guevara's famous letter-writer, *The Golden Epistles,* translated in 1575 by Geoffrey Fenton. To alleviate Guevara's heavy moralizing, Breton spices his formulary with slangy EUPHUISMS, intimate asides, and frequent jokes and witticisms. His liberal use of the informal letter, which was given a secondary role by Erasmus, Fulwood, and Day, makes Breton's letter-writer a small but nevertheless significant force in the evolution of the familiar essay.

An equally seminal work with affinities to several related genres is Joseph Hall's *Epistles,* in three volumes (I-II, 1608; III, 1611). Hall's master was Seneca, whom Hall employed as a point of departure for what he proclaimed to be "a new fashion of discourse, by Epistles; new to our language, usual to others, and (as novelty is never without some plea of use) more free, more familiar." By "free" Hall meant that his letters were less restricted in tone and subject than the treatise, less confined to rhetorical examples than the usual formulary. In fact, his *Epistles* mark the first effort in English to employ the letter-writer in an entirely literary way. Addressing himself to a much wider audience than Day or even Breton, Hall writes lengthy epistles on any subject that takes his fancy—death, dueling, courtship, celibacy, Scripture, or travel—and in style he is often as relaxed, clear, and simple as Bacon.

Another letter-writer that gave impetus to the development of the familiar essay was James Howell's *Epistolae Ho-Elianae* (1645; enlarged editions in 1647 and 1650), a collection of letters unique for its originality and sheer energy, its vivid descriptions of people, places, and events, and its author's conviction that the familiar letter was an important literary genre employed primarily to "express one's mind." Not all Howell's letters fit this description, for he wrote them in a variety of moods and apparently with several purposes in mind. Some letters obviously represent actual correspondence with friends, such as Jonson and Sir Kenelm Digby; others seem to be purely imaginary compositions Howell may have written while a prisoner in the Fleet. There are letters describing Raleigh's return from abroad and his execution; Henrietta Maria's arrival in London to marry Charles I; Bacon's arraignment and disgrace; and Howell's own experiences in Spain with Charles I and Buckingham during the abortive negotations for the hand of the Infanta. If one measure of epistolary skill is the writer's capacity for revealing himself to his readers, Howell certainly compares favorably with such masters of the form as Byron and Keats, for he projects his own inquisitive, extroverted, and gossipy self whether the topic is current affairs, astrology, Browne's *Religio medici,* or Howell's own curious "magical powders."

The letter-writer as a rhetoric or manual of instruction with model letters continued to fulfill its practical purposes throughout the seventeenth century (as it does in our own time), but its popularity was far exceeded by the free-ranging familiar epistles created by Hall and Howell. The familiar epistle was further developed by Margaret CAVENDISH, the indefatigable duchess of Newcastle, in *CCXI Sociable Letters* (1664). (Fifty-one of these letters appear also in her encomiastic *Life of William Cavendish, Duke of Newcastle.*) The *Sociable Letters,* though descending from the earlier letter-writers, are best described under the paradoxical rubric of epistolary autobiographical fiction, for the duchess's one and only subject, whether she writes of winter sports in Belgium or riots in Antwerp, is always her own vain, fanciful, and irresistible temperament. She is, in effect, the redoubtable and entirely fictitious Pamela of her own unconsciously composed novel.

Hence the letter-writer flows almost imperceptibly into that mainstream of seventeenth-century prose genres—picaresque tales, rogue literature, and characters—that culminate in the eighteenth-century novel. As the letter-writer became less utilitarian and more entertaining, and as model letters ceased to become illustrative of tropes and figures and more concerned with characterization and situation, with human problems and human conflicts quite analogous to those of today's journalistic letters of advice to the lovelorn or confessions to the wise and sympathetic columnist, it evolved into the complex epistolary novel begun by Samuel Richardson's *Pamela.*

The influence of letter-writers on the development of kindred genres is traced exhaustively in two studies: Katherine Gee Hornbeak, "The Complete Letter-Writer in English, 1568-1800," *Smith College Studies in Modern Languages,* XV (1934); and Jean Robertson, *The Art of Letter Writing: An Essay on the Handbooks Published During the Sixteenth and Seventeenth Centuries* (1942). A short account is by E. N. S. Thompson, "Familiar Letters," in *Literary Bypaths of the Renaissance* (1924).

Leviathan, or, The Matter, Form, and Power of a Commonwealth Ecclesiastical and Civil. A philosophical treatise on politics by Thomas HOBBES, first published in 1651.

The "Leviathan" of the title is the state, an artificial creation of man. Part I of Hobbes' book analyzes the nature of man, who creates society; Part II considers the essential nature of a commonwealth; Part III posits the relations between a Christian commonwealth and others: and Part IV, called "Of the Kingdom of Darkness," concludes the treatise with an attack on the Church of Rome.

According to Hobbes' mechanistic view, man is an organism conditioned to respond to stimuli from a wholly material world. All of man's ideas originate with sense impressions imposed externally; he cannot conceive what has not been pressed upon the senses by external objects. Conceptions such as "infinite" or "God" are not realities but merely words expressive of man's fears, hopes, or passions. Since Hobbes saw phenomena chiefly in terms of motion, he tends also to explain man's choices in the same terms: desire is a motion or reaction toward the "interior" self; revulsion is a motion away from the self—a motion inside the body reacting negatively to external motions. From this perspective, all men are indeed inherently "equal," but this equality does not imply equality of rights or freedom, for man's innate desires inevitably place him in competition with other men for the gratification of impulses. Out of the necessity for self-preservation, men enter into a contract by which they agree to transfer their individual strengths to some common power that will keep their passions in check. In view of man's nature the only alternative to such a transfer of power is a continual state of war and anarchy. The primary need of man, then, is self-preservation; and the chief end of the state, it follows, is the satisfaction of that transcendent need.

In Part II Hobbes moves from the nature of man to the kind of commonwealth that best serves his nature. The transfer of rights to a sovereign in order to achieve self-preservation for individuals in society is a contract made among those individuals, not between the individuals and the sovereign. Hence any attempt to overthrow the sovereign is a violation of this contract that individuals make with society as a whole and is never morally or expediently justified. Since civil war and anarchy are tantamount to the death of society—virtually a reversion to a "state of nature"—any ruler, however despotic, is preferable to rebellion as long as the ruler does not infringe upon the basic principle that motivates the subject's obedience—self-preservation. Thus the sovereign can expect obedience in every case except one: he cannot require the subject to destroy himself.

In this section Hobbes considers three types of commonwealth—monarchy, democracy, and aristocracy—and although he concedes certain advantages to others, he clearly favors an absolute monarchy as the most just and efficient form of government. As Hobbes sees matters, the imminent danger to a commonwealth results from too many limitations being placed on the monarch, not too few; Hobbes always expresses a greater fear of anarchy and civil war than of simple tyranny.

In Part III Hobbes argues for a total subordination of the church to the state. Even if the sovereign is an atheist or infidel, the Christian subject cannot rebel because the sovereign rules by natural laws, and to fulfill these the sovereign cannot share his power with popes or bishops. Hobbes compounds hundreds of Biblical citations to prove that there can be no dichotomy between man's obedience to God and his obedience to the sovereign.

Part IV is a condemnation of Roman Catholicism for its incursion into the realm of temporal power. According to Hobbes, the Catholic church has based its claim to secular authority on a perverse interpretation of Scriptures.

Hobbes' *Leviathan* aroused a storm of controversy from almost every quarter. Religious groups were incensed by its materialism and exclusively pragmatic justification of religious belief. The secular powers were equally aroused by its conception of authority as a necessary evil. Yet *Leviathan,* Hobbes' masterpiece, is perhaps the greatest defense ever written on behalf of political authoritarianism and the repression of freedom. Ironically, its content ran counter to the spirit of freedom engendered by the Renaissance, but its form—a vivid, lucid, eloquent prose—represents one of the glorious fulfillments of that same spirit.

An excellent one-volume edition of *Leviathan* has been edited by Michael Oakeshott (1960). There are excellent critical studies by F. C. Hood, *The Divine Politics of Thomas Hobbes: An Interpretation of Leviathan* (1964), and F. McNeilly, *The Anatomy of Leviathan* (1968). An erudite study from another perspective is by Samuel I. Mintz, *The Hunting of Leviathan: Seventeenth-Century Reactions to the Materialism and Moral Philosophy of Thomas Hobbes* (1962).

Life and Death of Mr. Badman, The. An allegorical dialogue by John BUNYAN, written and first published in 1680 as a companion piece to Bunyan's earlier prose work, PILGRIM'S PROGRESS (1678). Whereas *Pilgrim's Progress* describes the rise of a good man from despair to eternal salvation, *Mr. Badman* traces the steady decline of a wicked man from evil inclinations to total damnation. The dialogue is between Mr. Wiseman, who tells the story of Mr. Badman to Mr. Attentive, who occasionally asks questions and encourages the author's narrator to expand on certain details.

The character Mr. Wiseman describes has no redeeming qualities. He was, in fact, thoroughly evil virtually from birth:

> I will tell you that from a child he was very bad; his very beginning was ominous; and presaged no good end was in likelihood to follow . . . There were several sins that he was given to when he was a little one, that manifested him to be notoriously infected with original corruption; for I dare say he learned none of them of his father and mother nor was he admitted much to go abroad among other children that were vile, to learn sin of them . . .

In short, Mr. Badman's character is not attributed to environment, family, friends, or to any influence but his own innate nature totally corrupted at the outset by original sin and sustained by a depraved will that leads the villain headlong into a life of theft, atheism, drunkenness, philandering, lying, and cheating. Each account of a particular vice prompts a brief sermon from Mr. Wiseman or Mr. Attentive, who point out with numerous examples how horribly widespread sin is among men generally. As Bunyan plainly states in his prefatory address "To the Courteous Reader," evil is so widespread through the world that Mr. Badman can stand as a kind of world's body or culmination of mankind's instinctual bestiality. The point of Bunyan's unsavory example in Mr. Badman is to show vice for the ugly thing it is, and to warn sinners of the inevitable consequences of their folly.

The Life and Death of Mr. Badman, with Bunyan's *The Holy War,* has been edited by John Brown (1905). There is a psychological study of Bunyan's work in Mary E. Harding, *Journey into Self* (1956), and a thorough treatment of sources in J. B. Wharey, *A Study of the Sources of Bunyan's Allegories* (1904; repr. 1968).

Life and Death of Thomas Wolsey (George Cavendish). See BIOGRAPHY.

Life of Fisher (Richard Hall). See BIOGRAPHY.

Life of More (William Roper). See BIOGRAPHY.

Locrine. An anonymous tragedy first published in 1595. Mistakenly attributed to Shakespeare, it was printed in the Third (1664) and Fourth (1685) Folios. The title page of the first edition reads "newly set forth, overseen, and corrected by W. S." Some scholars believe the inscription indicates that Shakespeare edited the play for publication; others assign the editorship to William Smith, a poet. George Peele has also been suggested as the author. The source of the play is the legend of Locrine, or Logrin, told in Geoffrey of Monmouth's *Historia regum Britanniae* and Spenser's *Faerie Queene,* II, 10.

The beautiful German princess Estrildis is brought to England by King Humber, but she falls in love with Locrine, king of England, and bears his child, Sabrina. Locrine's jealous wife Gwendolen drowns both mother and child in the River Severn. Swinburne wrote a play on the legend in 1887.

A standard text is in *Shakespeare Apocrypha,* ed. C. F. Tucker Brooke (1908). For dating and authorship of *Locrine,* see E. K. Chambers, *The Elizabethan Stage,* 4 vols. (1923), IV.

Lodge, Thomas (1558-?1625). Poet and playwright. The son of Sir Thomas Lodge, mayor of London, he attended the Merchant Taylors' School, Spenser's alma mater, and Trinity College, Oxford, after which he entered Lincoln's Inn. Soon after 1578 he abandoned the study of law and set to work as a dramatist and pamphleteer. About 1579 he wrote his *Reply to Stephen Gosson Touching Plays* in answer to Gosson's notorious attack on plays and players in *The School of Abuse* (see CRITICISM, LITERARY). Since the title page of the first edition of Lodge's pamphlet is lost, the original title and date of publication are conjectural. Another pamphlet, *An Alarum Against Usurers* (1584), excoriates moneylenders in the pious and self-conscious manner of Robert Greene or Thomas Nashe.

Lodge's first considerable literary efforts were in pastoral romance and Ovidian epyllia. His first romance is *The Delectable History of Forbonius and Priscilla* (1584); his second is the Ovidian SCYLLA'S METAMORPHOSIS (1589), reissued in 1610 with the title *Glaucus and Scilla. Scylla's Metamorphosis* may have influenced Shakespeare's Ovidian poem *Venus and Adonis.* Lodge has other, less direct connections with Shakespeare. The crude but highly popular comedy MUCEDORUS (perf. c. 1589, pr. 1598), long attributed to Shakespeare, is thought by some scholars to be by Lodge, and the chronicle play *Leir,* which Shakespeare consulted in writing his tragedy, has also been attributed to Lodge. Neither of these attributions is very widely accepted, however. Lodge's euphuistic pastoral romance ROSALYNDE (1590), which he wrote while on a voyage to the Canary Islands in 1588, is known to have been a chief source of Shakespeare's *As You Like It.* Lodge has also been identified, with very little justification, as the Rival Poet in Shakespeare's Sonnets.

Lodge seems to have been goaded by necessity into a bizarre assortment of writings: pamphlets on usury, dialogues on magic and astrology, Nashe-inspired sermons on the seven deadly sins, and euphuistic romances. Quite possibly he wrote several plays, although only two can be assigned with certainty—*The Wounds of Civil War* (1594), and *A Looking-Glass for London and England* (1594), on which he collaborated with Robert Greene. Perhaps the most distinguished of his romances is *A Margarite of America* (1596), a prose tale in the heroic manner of Heliodorus' *Aethiopica* and Sidney's *Arcadia;* Lodge claimed to have read the tale in Spanish in a Jesuit library in South America. Lodge's chief work in lyric poetry is a sonnet collection called *Phillis* (1593), a sequence closely imitative of Ronsard and Desportes (see SONNET SEQUENCES).

Around 1600 Lodge abandoned the literary life, converted to Roman Catholicism, studied medicine in France and returned to receive an M.D. from Oxford in 1602. His later works became increasingly scientific and philosophical: *The Famous and Memorable Works of Josephus* (1603); *A Treatise of the Plague* (1603); *The Works, Both Moral and Natural, of Lucius Annaeus Seneca* (1614); and a commentary translated from the French upon a poem of Du Bartas (1625).

Lodge's *Complete Works* was edited by Sir Edmund Gosse, 4 vols. (1883). Important critical studies are by N.B. Paradise, *Thomas Lodge* (1931); C. J. Sisson, *Thomas Lodge and Other Elizabethans* (1933); and Wesley D. Rae, *Thomas Lodge* (1967). There is a Concise Bibliography by S. A. Tannenbaum (1940), with its supplement, "Thomas Lodge (1939-65)," ed. R. C. Johnson, in *Elizabethan Bibliographies Supplements,* V (1968). See also *The Predecessors of Shakespeare: A Survey and Bibliography of Recent Studies in English Renaissance Drama,* ed. Terence P. Logan and Denzell S. Smith (1973).

Love and Honor. A tragicomedy by Sir William DAVENANT, written and performed in 1634 and first printed in 1649. No source is known. The play is important historically as a link between the romantic tragicomedies of Beaumont and Fletcher and the heroic drama of the Restoration period. It was personally sponsored by Charles II in 1661 at Dorset Gardens and enjoyed considerable vogue for several seasons.

At the conclusion of the war between Milan and Savoy, the Savoyard general Count Prospero, a blunt and unrefined warrior, captures the Princess Evandra of Milan, her chief guard Leonell, and several ladies of her court. The cruel duke of Savoy has sworn to execute Evandra in retaliation for the supposed murder of his brother several years before. Opposing the duke's vow is his son Alvaro, a gallant, courteous young man in love with Evandra and far too delicate for such barbarities. Hence Alvaro orders Prospero to conceal the women and Leonell in a cave while he does what he can to appease the anger of his vindictive father.

When it is proclaimed that all women taken in the war are to be returned to Milan after a year, several Savoyard officers hurriedly court the ladies of their choice before the expiration date. Love entanglements confound these efforts, with a humorous subplot involving a coarse old colonel's courtship of a rich old Milanese widow. After many rivalries, mistaken motives, and hair-breadth escapes, Evandra is saved from execution by the noble Leonell's announcement that he must be substituted for her because he is really the son of the man who took the duke's brother prisoner. Leonell, in turn, is saved by the timely arrival of an ambassador from Milan who reveals himself to be the duke's supposedly executed brother. At the conclusion Prince Leonell marries Evandra, the other nobles and officers take suitable mates, and the rough warrior Prospero leaves to fight more wars.

The "love" of the title refers to the noble passions of Alvaro, Leonell, and Prospero for the beautiful Evandra, but these sentiments must wait upon demonstrations of "honor," which is construed largely as magnanimous self-sacrifice. Alvaro sacrifices duty to his father out of love for the heroine, Prospero is torn between love and military obligation, and Evandra herself offers her life to satisfy the duke of Savoy's revenge. Only Leonell is able to untangle these self-imposed moral knots, which he achieves when he reveals himself to be the duke of Parma's son and the real heir to Savoy's wrath. Such hair-splitting motives and lofty sentiments recall Beaumont and Fletcher's PHILASTER, a heroic tragedy of equally refined sentiments (see CAROLINE DRAMA).

The standard edition is by J. W. Tupper (1909). For criticism, see Alfred Harbage, *Sir William Davenant, Poet Venturer 1606-68* (1935), and Arthur H. Nethercot, *Sir William D'Avenant, Poet Laureate and Playwright-Manager* (1938).

Lovelace, Richard, (1618-1657?). Poet. Born the son of a knight and wealthy landowner in Kent, Lovelace grew up under the influence of an inflexible aristocratic code of loyalty and honor, and his life was ruined by the ill fortunes of his royal master Charles I. A brilliant and handsome youth, he attended the Charterhouse School at the same time as Richard Crashaw and proceeded to Gloucester Hall, Oxford, where, during the king's visit in 1636, Charles I was so taken by Lovelace's charm, humility and manliness that he ordered the M. A. degree to be given to him at once. In 1639 Lovelace led a company in the king's wars in Scotland, and in 1642 so outraged the House of Commons by his support of a pro-Royalist petition from Kent that he was imprisoned, during which time he wrote his famous lyric "To Althea, from Prison":

Stone walls do not a prison make,
 Nor iron bars a cage:
Minds innocent and quiet take
 That for an hermitage.
If I have freedom in my love,
 And in my soul am free,
Angels alone that soar above
 Enjoy such liberty.

During the period 1643-45 Lovelace was in Holland and France on the king's business, and in 1645 rejoined Charles I in England. The 1640s were years of adventure for Lovelace, and he completed most of his poems at this time, certainly before 1649. It is known that he wrote at least two plays, but none has survived. There is a legend that while fighting for the French in 1646 he was reported killed, and that his mistress Lucy Sacheverell, the "Lucasta" of his love poems, married another man. Actually, it is not known for certain whether Lucasta was a real person or a figment of Lovelace's romantic imagination.

In 1648 the unrepentant Royalist was again imprisoned by Parliament, this time for ten months, after which he published his only collection of poems, *Lucasta* (1649), prefaced with commendatory verses by Andrew Marvell. After the execution of the king and the collapse of the Royalist cause, Lovelace is believed to have slipped into poverty. He probably died in 1657, although little is known of his final years.

Lovelace was a soldier, scholar, and gentleman in the tradition of Sir Philip Sidney, an aristocrat of ideals comparable to those set forth in Castiglione's *Il Cortegiano,* and the themes of his poetry are the courtly ones of love and honor. As a poet, he was a gifted amateur variously influenced by Catullus, whom he translated, Giovanni Battista Marino, Ben Jonson, and John Donne. As a result he is associated with two schools of verse. See CAVALIER POETS and METAPHYSICAL POETS. On the whole he is classical in form—concise, economical, judiciously spare and lucid—and somewhat metaphysical in his paradoxical, often eccentric wit, although his instinctive restraint does not allow for free-ranging religious speculation. Instead, he strives to achieve intellectual resonance from apparently ingenuous subjects, as in his bestiary poems, "The Ant," "The Spider and the Bee," "The Snail," "The Falcon," and "The Grasshopper," inspired by his reading of Dutch EMBLEM BOOKS. Superficially his verse is suavely epicurean and archly witty, but the interior reverberates with ideas. In his libertine "Love Made in the First Age" the pastoral concept is strikingly anarchic and hedonistic:

Thrice happy was that golden age,
When compliment was constru'd rage,
  And fine words in the center hid;
When cursed No stain'd no maid's bliss,
And all discourse was summ'd in Yes,
  And Nought forbad, but to forbid.

Love then unstinted, love did sip,
And cherries pluck'd fresh from the lip,
  On cheeks and roses free he fed;
Lasses like autumn plums did drop,
And lads indifferently did crop
  A flower, and a maidenhead.

The standard edition of Lovelace's poems is by C. H. Wilkinson (rev. ed., 1953). The best biographical and critical study is O. H. Hartmann, *The Cavalier Spirit and Its Influence on the Life and Work of Richard Lovelace* (1925). See also Manfred Weidhorn, *Richard Lovelace* (1970); Randolph L. Wadsworth, "On 'The Snail' by Richard Lovelace," *MLR,* LXV (1970): and Raymond A. Anselment, "A Reading of Richard Lovelace's 'The Falcon,' " *JEGP,* LXX (1971).

Love's Labour's Lost. A comedy by William SHAKESPEARE, written around 1593-94 and first printed in 1598. No specific source is known, but the plot may have been derived from some account of a visit of Catherine de Medicis (1519-1589) and her daughter Marguerite de Valois, wife of Henry of Navarre, to Nérac in 1578, a visit arranged for the purpose of reconciling the long-estranged Henry and Marguerite. The influence of the Italian *commedia dell'arte* is especially apparent in Shakespeare's characterizations of Armado, Moth, and Holofernes.

Ferdinand, king of Navarre, persuades three of his lords, Dumain, Longaville, and Berowne, to dedicate themselves to rigorous study and avoid all company of women for a period of three years. On the periphery of this "little academe" of intellectuals is Don Adriano de Armado, a fantastic Spaniard given to boasting and grandiloquence; Costard, a slow-witted rustic; and Armado's page, Moth. Armado catches Costard wooing a country wench, Jaquenetta, in spite of the king's prohibition against women, and the culprit is made to fast for a week on bran and water. A graver threat to the king's self-imposed discipline occurs when the princess of France arrives on a diplomatic mission for her father. Although she and her three companions, Rosaline, Maria, and Katherine, are housed outside the royal park, the king and his lords visit them frequently and, of course, begin a number of love intrigues. Berowne, who formerly sneered at romance, finds himself in love with Rosaline, and the king, despite his vow, falls in love with the princess. For their turn, Dumain and Longaville are in love with Katherine and Maria, respectively.

The play concludes with much confusion resulting from the lords' wooing the wrong ladies while in disguise and a hilarious dramatic presentation of the Nine Worthies in which Costard plays Pompey, the curate, Sir Nathaniel is Alexander the Great, the pedantic schoolmaster Holofernes is Judas Maccabaeus, Moth is Hercules, and Armado the braggart is, appropriately, Hector. These festivities are interrupted by the news that the princess's father has died and she must return to France with her ladies. The princess ordains that the king and his lords must spend twelve months in total seclusion in order to win the ladies' hands. Berowne, the wittiest love cynic of the group, is given the task of visiting hospitals to cheer the sick. The play ends with a dialogue by Holofernes and Sir Nathaniel in praise of the owl and the cuckoo.

Love's Labour's Lost is Shakespeare's most esoteric and sophisticated comedy. Arthur Quiller-Couch and J. Dover Wilson, editors of the New Cambridge edition, surmise that it was written for performance "at some great private house, possibly the Earl of Southampton's." and although there is no real evidence to support their theory, the comedy certainly contains enough arcane references and cryptic contemporary allusions to suggest that Shakespeare intended the work for a coterie audience. Moreover, the Southampton circle would have been especially appropriate. The young earl had angered his guardian, Lord Burghley, by refusing to take a wife, and what could be more festive a subject to such a group than a play about four virile youths who spurn Cupid?

Shakespeare's comedy points to a number of other contemporary associations that would be meaningful to a courtly audience. The connection with Henry of Navarre has already been mentioned, but it should also be noted that unlike Shakespeare's scholarly ascetic, the historical Navarre was, in fact, a notorious Lothario. Then, too, the names of the main characters bear affinities to Navarre's French contemporaries. The name Berowne suggests the maréchal de Biron, Longaville the duc de Longueville, both generals who fought under Navarre in the French civil wars of 1589-92, and Dumain recalls the duc de Mayenne, who opposed Navarre in war and won great acclaim among the English for lending support to the earl of Essex's military expedition in 1592.

Still another well-known allusion to current affairs occurs in the play when the king criticizes Berowne's Rosaline as being "black as ebony." and adds:

O paradox! Black is the badge of hell,
The hue of dungeons and the school of night.
[IV, *iii,* 254-55]

Scholars detect here an allusion to the so-called school of night of Sir Walter Raleigh, attacked as a "school of atheism" by the Jesuit priest Robert Parsons in a pamphlet in 1592 (see Sir Walter RALEIGH). If the New Cambridge editors are correct in their surmise regarding Shakespeare's intended audience, the above allusion would have been especially amusing to the earl of Southampton's coterie, for Raleigh was one of Southampton's principal rivals at court during these years. Some scholars also maintain that Raleigh (or perhaps Gabriel Harvey) is represented satirically in the bombastic and vain Armado. Others see the clown Moth as Thomas Nashe and the pedant Holofernes as John Florio. There is no real evidence, however, for associating these characters with any actual persons.

A more likely source of these "fantastical" characterizations is the COMMEDIA DELL'ARTE; Berowne enumerates the familiar types when he refers to the "pedant, braggart, hedge-priest, the fool and the boy." The wildly pedantic Holofernes, babbling in INKHORN TERMS and pretentious metaphors crammed with "foolish, extravagant spirit, full of forms, figures, shapes, objects, ideas, apprehensions, motions, revolutions" (IV, *ii,* 67-69), conforms totally to the stock character of Italian comedy, whereas the huff-puff braggart Armado owes a great deal to the MILES GLORIOSUS without agreeing in every detail with that type; he does not boast of battles and sieges or of his conquest of women, for his vain swaggering pertains to his intellectual and linguistic pretensions—a kind of foppery that appeals to the "hedge-priest" or curate, Sir Nathaniel, who strives comically to impress him and Holofernes with his "sweetly varied" epithets.

What is most clearly emphasized as an object of satire in the comedy is romantic love, especially the delightful illusion of falling in love with love, a form of insanity accompanied by what Walter Pater described as "the foppery of delicate language," or what Berowne himself complains of as

Taffeta phrases, silken terms precise,
Thrice-pil'd hyperboles, spruce affection,
Figures pedantical; these summer-flies
Have blown me full of maggot ostentation.
[V, *ii,* 406-09]

In Berowne some scholars think they see a self-mocking portrait of Shakespeare, and in Rosaline, his beloved adversary in *débats de coeur,* a representation of the Dark Lady of the Sonnets. But in a comedy as delightfully artificial as *Love's Labour's Lost,* wherein the gossamer delicacy of the courtly circle dissolves at the first touch of reality with the news of the princess's father's death, it is perhaps foolish to seek anything more deeply meaningful than an astonishing exhibition of Shakespeare's masterful wit and absolute command of language.

Two editions are essential for texts and commentary: the New Cambridge edition, ed.

Arthur Quiller-Couch and J. Dover Wilson (1923), and the new Arden edition, ed. Richard David (1951). For criticism, see Frances A. Yates, *A Study of Love's Labour's Lost* (1936); H. B. Charlton, *Shakespearean Comedy* (1938); O. J. Campbell, *Shakespeare's Satire* (1943); C. L. Barber, *Shakespeare's Festive Comedy* (1959); D. A. Traversi, *Shakespeare's Early Comedy* (1960); J. Dover Wilson. *Shakespeare's Happy Comedies* (1962); Alfred Harbage, *"Love's Labour's Lost* and the Early Shakespeare," *PQ,* XLI (1962); Peter G. Phialas, *Shakespeare's Romantic Comedies* (1966); A. C. Hamilton, *The Early Shakespeare* (1967); and Gates K. Agnew, "Berowne and the Progress of *Love's Labour's Lost,*" *ShakS.,* IV (1969).

Lycidas. A pastoral elegy by John MILTON. It was first published in 1638 with other elegies written by Cambridge graduates in memory of the death of their classmate Edward King, who drowned in August 1637 in a shipwreck in the Irish Sea between the mouth of the River Dee ("Deva" in Milton's poem) and the Isle of Anglesea ("Mona") in Wales. As models for his elegy (one of the greatest in English) Milton consulted a host of classical sources, including Vergil's *Eclogues,* Moschus' *Lament for Bion,* and Theocritus' *Idyll* I.

In his own edition of the poem in 1645, Milton called it a "monody" in which he "bewails a learned friend, unfortunately drowned . . . And by occasion foretells the ruin of our corrupted clergy then in their height," a reference to Milton's attack on the Anglican bishops and their minions in lines 108-31, which conclude with the two obscure and much-disputed lines: "But that two-handed engine at the door / Stands ready to smite once, and smite no more." Whether the "two-handed engine" refers to the two houses of Parliament, St. Peter's keys to heaven and to hell, the two-handed sword of God in the Book of Revelation, or the two kingdoms of England and Scotland has provided occasion for virtually hundreds of erudite interpretations.

Milton's criticism of the corrupt practices of the Anglican clergy is, however, only an apparent digression that is carefully integrated with the sustained theme of natural evil—the problem, as in the Book of Job, of reconciling the suffering of the innocent with the ideal of divine justice. Hence the "two-handed engine" promises a kind of justice and retribution for evil, just as the combination of water and flower images and the many allusions culminating in that to Jesus ("So Lycidas, sunk low, but mounted high, / Through the dear might of him that walk'd the waves . . .") suggest a solution for the natural evil of death in the indestructibility of the human personality, in a nature guided by God's hand, and in man's covenant with Christ who rewards virtue with love and everlasting life.

There are well-annotated editions of *Lycidas* in *John Milton: Complete Poems and Major Prose,* ed. Merritt Y. Hughes (1957); *The Complete English Poetry of John Milton,* ed. John T. Shawcross (1963); and *The Complete Poetical Works,* ed. Douglas Bush (1965). There is a collection of critical interpretations in *Milton's Lycidas: The Tradition and the Poem,* ed. C. A. Patrides (1961). See also Patrick Murray, *Milton: The Modern Phase; A Study of Twentieth Century Criticism* (1967) and John Reesing, *Milton's Poetic Art* (1968).

Lyly, John (c. 1554-1606). Dramatist and novelist. Lyly was born in London, the son of Peter Lyly, an ecclesiastical notary in the employ (after 1562) of the archbishop of Canterbury. John Lyly's grandfather was William Lyly, the famous grammarian, master of St. Paul's School, and friend of Erasmus and Sir Thomas More. Lyly attended school at Canterbury, then proceeded to Magdalen College, Oxford, around 1569, graduating B.A. in 1573 and M.A. in 1575. In spite of his erudite parentage, Lyly was a dabbler rather than a scholar, "a dapper and deft companion," according to an early biographer, with an aversion to "crabbed studies." His character Euphues in *Euphues and His England* may be taken as a spokesman for the author's own experience at Oxford: "Yet may I of all the rest most condemn Oxford of unkindness . . . who seemed to wean me before she brought me forth, and to give me bones to gnaw before I could get the teat to suck." This dislike for academia did not prevent Lyly from petitioning his patron William Cecil, Lord Burghley, for an appointment to a fellowship at Oxford, an appeal Burghley rejected.

Lyly wrote most of his popular prose romance EUPHUES, *the Anatomy of Wit* (1578) while still at Oxford, and hurriedly followed up on this success with a rather inferior sequel, *Euphues and His England* (1580), which removes his arrogant young hero from Athens and Naples to London and Queen Elizabeth's court. In these romances Lyly popularized a fantastic style of writing called EUPHUISM, and a wave of "euphuistic" romances by Robert Greene and others filled the bookstalls throughout the 1580s. The 1632 edition of *Euphues* accurately recalls its great vogue at court: "All our ladies were then his scholars, and that Beauty in court which could not parley Euphuism was as little regarded as she which now there speaks not French." When he was "a little ape at Cambridge," Thomas Nashe later recalled, Lyly's romance caused the undergraduates to chatter "like idiots." For a decade or more, from the pulpit, in the academies, and at court Elizabethans found themselves, in the words of Michael Drayton's "Epistle to Henry Reynolds," "Talking of stones, stars, plants, of fishes, flies,

Playing with words and idle similes." Like most fads, Lyly's extravagant prose style was a very ancient vehicle done up in fresh veneer—Ciceronian rhetoric parodying its own mélange of triadic constructions, antitheses, and periodicities, plus some heavy doses of fantastic animal lore from Pliny's *Historia naturalis* and the medieval bestiaries. Shakespeare smiles to hear his genteel ladies and gentlemen in *Love's Labour's Lost* cutting their speeches to Lyly's absurd pattern.

With *Euphues* Lyly became the first of the so-called UNIVERSITY WITS to make a name for himself among the London literati. Others in this loose confederation of "wits" would follow: George Peele, Robert Greene, Christopher Marlowe, Thomas Lodge, and Thomas Nashe — academically trained writers who tried to find a large and discriminating audience somewhere between the masses who filled the popular theaters and the pedantic Gabriel Harveys at the universities and the Inns of Court. None of these writers, including Marlowe, rivaled the dizzying speed with which Lyly won the esteem of that large minority (present in every generation) who strain to be in the conspicuous vanguard of chic deportment. And yet *Euphues* represents a digression from Lyly's abiding interests and not inconsiderable literary talents, for his greatest achievements were in the drama.

Around 1583-84 Lyly took over Richard Farrant's lease of the fashionable Blackfriars theater and began to organize the boys of the Chapel Royal and St. Paul's chorus into an acting company bearing the name of Lyly's patron, Edward, earl of Oxford, Lord Burghleys' son-in-law. Ostensibly, Lyly's office required that he teach the boys Latin; actually, he trained them to perform in his own plays at the Blackfriars in preparation for presentations at court. The arrangement was characteristically brilliant, but did not prove as remunerative as he had hoped (he was in debtors' prison for a time in 1584). Within a decade Lyly produced eight sophisticated and witty comedies: *Alexander and Campaspe* (wr. and pr. 1548; see CAMPASPE); *Sapho and Phao* (wr. and pr. 1584); *Galathea* (wr. 1584-88; pr. 1591); ENDYMION (wr. 1588; pr. 1591); *Midas* (wr. 1589-90; pr. 1592); *Mother Bombie* (wr. 1587-90; pr. 1594); *Love's Metamorphosis* (wr. 1589-90?; pr. 1601); and *The Woman in the Moon* (wr. 1590-95?; pr. 1597).

Except for *The Woman in the Moon,* which is in blank verse, Lyly's comedies are in prose. *Mother Bombie* is a Plautine comedy of intrigue with a contemporary English setting; the others are allegories employing Ovidian characters and myths. The plots are very inconsequential and loosely assembled; dramatic effects depend upon sheer lyric variety—delicate verbal flourish, conceited love debates, scenic dances, and sprightly songs, which, though appropriate to the action, were not composed by Lyly. In essence, Lyly's comedies are colorfully ornamented tapestries woven on the loom of the old Tudor INTERLUDES. They represent the first comedies in English drama to achieve elegance, artifice, and verbal polish.

Lyly's prologue to *Sapho and Phao* suggests that he worked consciously to perfect a unique type of comedy: "Our intent was at this time to move inward delight, not outward lightness: and to breed (if it might be) soft smiling, not loud laughing; knowing it to the wise to be as great pleasure to hear counsel mixed with wit, as to the foolish to have sport mingled with rudeness." His comic theory required scrupulous avoidance of many elements in the native English tradition that he found inimical to "inward delight" and "soft smiling"—the boisterous farce of the interludes, the moral rigor of the morality plays, the verbal crudities of school dramas. His natural heir is not the festive and robust Thomas Dekker of *The Shoemaker's Holiday* but the charmingly artificial Shakespeare of *Love's Labour's Lost* and *A Midsummer Night's Dream* (both of which reflect Lyly's influence).

Lyly's comedies are philosophical without being cerebral; his recurring subject is the courtly one of love versus honor, with just enough Platonic vocabulary to command intellectual respect. He likes gracefully contrived situations rather than tense conflicts, and he rarely disturbs the perfect harmony of his art with dissonant moral anxieties from the real world. Like Oscar Wilde, to whom Lyly is often compared, he is a master at working surfaces to the highest possible glitter. With the exception of George Peele in *The Arraignment of Paris,* no Elizabethan after Lyly was able or perhaps inclined to imitate his limited but unique style of comedy.

Although some scholars have read Lyly's plays as *drames à clef* allegorizing important political events and personages, it is doubtful that they represent anything other than playful philosophical exercises and perfervid adulation of Queen Elizabeth. Lyly had shamelessly enlisted with other sycophants at court in the cult of the virgin queen, Diana chaste and fair, and heavenly Eros in *Euphues and His England,* and he persisted in these idealizations of the queen with his portrait of the virgin Sapho in *Sapho and Phao,* Cynthia in *Endymion,* and the queen of Lesbos in *Midas* (with Philip of Spain pictured as the gold-greedy Midas). Sadly enough, these frenetic tributes yielded Lyly none of the patronage he sought from the queen. He helped censor dramatic manuscripts for the bishop of London, probably authored at least one undistinguished pamphlet, *Pappe with a Hatchet* (1589), on the side of the bishops in the MARTIN MARPRELATE controversy, and served several terms in Parliament; but these were modest, unprofitable efforts of his own—no royal plum was dropped in his lap. His last hopes were dashed in 1597 when the office of master of the revels, which Lyly had wanted for years, was given to George Buck, a much less talented man.

The last of several petitionary letters by Lyly to the queen complaining of poverty and royal neglect is bitterly ironic: "My last will is shorter than mine inventory—but three legacies: patience to my creditors, melancholy without measure to my friends, and beggary not without shame to my family..." He died on November 30, 1606.

The standard edition is *The Complete Works,* ed. R. W. Bond, 3 vols. (1902). The best critical biographies are by J. Dover Wilson, *John Lyly* (1905), and G. K. Hunter, *John Lyly: The Humanist as Courtier* (1962). There is a Concise Bibliography by S. A. Tannenbaum (1940), augmented by "John Lyly (1939-65)," ed. R. C. Johnson, in *Elizabethan Bibliographies Supplements,* V (1968). See also *The Predecessors of Shakespeare: A Survey and Bibliography of Recent Studies in English Renaissance Drama,* ed. Terence P. Logan and Denzell S. Smith (1973).

M

Macbeth, The Tragedy of. A tragedy by William SHAKESPEARE, written in 1605--06 and first printed in the 1623 Folio. The principal source is the account of Macbeth in Raphael Holinshed's *Chronicles* (1587 ed.).

While returning from crushing a rebellion against Duncan, king of Scotland, the generals Macbeth and Banquo encounter three witches who prophesy that Macbeth shall be thane of Cawdor, thereafter king, and that Banquo shall beget kings but not be one himself. Even as the two generals ponder the meaning of the prophecies, a messenger from Duncan tells Macbeth that he has indeed been made thane of Cawdor. Lady Macbeth, when she learns of the auguries, urges her husband to make the second of them come true by murdering the king while he is their guest. Macbeth puts aside the promptings of conscience and slays Duncan; when he flees in horror from the chamber with bloodied daggers, Lady Macbeth berates him and takes the weapons to a room where the king's two grooms lie in drunken sleep. Fearing for their lives, Duncan's sons Malcolm and Donalbain go into hiding. They are suspected of the crime, and Macbeth is crowned king.

To prevent the fulfillment of the last of the witches' prophecies, Macbeth orders Banquo and his only son Fleance murdered as they come to his castle for a feast. In the banquet hall, a messenger tells Macbeth that Banquo is dead but his son has escaped. When the ghost of Banquo takes the king's chair at the table, Macbeth is terrified and makes arrangements to consult the witches again. They warn him to beware of Macduff, but assure him he cannot be harmed by any man born of a woman or be defeated until Birnam Wood shall come to Dunsinane.

When Malcolm raises an army against him and enlists Macduff's support, Macbeth has Lady Macduff and all her children slain. Meanwhile, Lady Macbeth, stricken with guilt, dies insane. Macbeth slowly apprehends the witches' trickery when the army of Malcolm and Macduff advances on Dunsinane Castle under camouflage of branches cut from Birnam Wood, and when Macduff in combat with Macbeth announces he was "from his mother's womb untimely ripped"—born, that is, by Caesarian section. Macduff kills Macbeth, fastens his head on a pike, and Malcolm is proclaimed king of Scotland.

It is often noted that *Macbeth* was written for the entertainment of James I, who would have been fascinated by the witchcraft scenes because he had written a tract on the subject several years before, and flattered by the Scottish history because he was himself a direct descendant of Banquo, for whose offspring the witches predict a glorious future. Yet however valid the historical background of the play, it does not begin to account for the awesome power of this great tragedy of conscience, with its atmospheric scenes of horror, its concentration of symbolic language, and its introspective, savage, and titanic hero. In only one previous play taken from history, *Richard III,* did Shakespeare make his hero a villain, and the differences between the two plays illustrate the enormous growth of Shakespeare's creative powers during the intervening twelve years. Unlike Richard III, Macbeth has no antagonist except the witches, Lady Macbeth, and himself; his real opposition is an evil completely self-absorbed and internal. That evil hangs over Scotland like an infectious vapor. Whereas Richard's malevolence is almost comic, his machinations self-conscious and artistically detached, Macbeth begins the play as thoroughly admirable—courageous, sensitive, and thoughtful of virtue—and only after his crime does he deteriorate into a fierce animal fighting for nothing except self-preservation.

The central theme of *Macbeth* is that of *virtù,* or self-assertion, which is presented as titanic pride yearning to achieve power over futurity. Appropriately, therefore, the element of fate is more stressed than in any of the other major tragedies, and its role in the play is profoundly ironic. The witches, or Fatal Sisters, somehow possess foreknowledge of a destiny preordained by the mysterious and ineluctible forces of will within the hero. For all their insight and gifts of prophecy, however, they do no more than nurture what Macbeth has already conceived in the seeds of time. At the inception of the play the traitor Macdonwald, whose "multiplying villainies of nature / Do swarm upon him," is brought down so that "noble" Macbeth may rise; but the chorus-like witches, unlike blind Duncan, "can look into the seeds of time / And say which grain will grow and which will not." It is pure accident that Macbeth encounters the witches "in the day of success" and learns he is thane of Cawdor; yet, unlike his companion Banquo, he is "rapt" by their prophecy, his whole sense of reality deeply shaken by "horrible imaginings." The prophecy originates with the witches, but its fatal effects are deeply rooted in Macbeth's own potentially evil nature:

This supernatural soliciting
Cannot be ill, cannot be good. If ill,
Why hath it given me earnest of success,
Commencing in a truth? I'm Thane of Cawdor.
If good, why do I yield to that suggestion
Whose horrid image doth unfix my hair
And make my seated heart knock at my ribs,
Against the use of nature? Present fears
Are less than horrible imaginings.
My thought, whose murder yet is but fantastical,
Shakes so my single state of man that function
Is smother'd in surmise, and nothing is
But what is not. [I, *iii,* 130-42]

Although Lady Macbeth fears his nature is "too full o' the milk of human kindness / To catch the nearest way," Macbeth's moral being is already so poisoned by wicked speculation and its consequent sense of unreality that he proves as easily seduced by her persuasions as he was by the witches' power of suggestion. The argument she gives that cracks his resolve is, finally, the ultimate one that challenges both his manhood and the very basis of their love: "From this time / Such I account thy love." If he will not murder Duncan, she tells him, then he is not the "man" she can henceforth love. To bring her courage to the sticking point, she must repress her instinctive goodness and change her "milk of human kindness" into bitter gall:

Come, you spirits
That tend on mortal thoughts, unsex me here,
And fill me, from the crown to the toe, topfull
Of direst cruelty! Make thick my blood,
Stop up th'access and passage to remorse,
That no compunctious visitings of nature
Shake my fell purpose, nor keep peace between
Th'effect and it! Come to my woman's breasts,
And take my milk for gall, you murd'ring ministers. . . [I, *v,* 41-49]

These are forced means to achieve her end, and when that end is realized, her nature reasserts itself and she collapses under afflictions of conscience and madness.

In contrast, Macbeth's cruelty grows, after his initial transgression, as if the unreality of Duncan's murder can only be endured by making evil the sole reality. What he experiences, also, is *habitude,* a spiritual process by which sin becomes easy through repetition. "My strange and self-abuse," he observes, "Is the initiate fear that wants hard use. / We are yet but young in deed." In this context, "self-abuse" signifies self-deception and "initiate fear" the hesitations of a novice. Having murdered Duncan and Banquo, he can alleviate his agony only by drowning all remnants of goodness in himself and becoming insulated in a subjective reality that perceives the only virtue to be self-preservation:

For mine own good
All causes shall give way. I am in blood
Stepp'd in so far that should I wade no more,
Returning were as tedious as go o'er.
Strange things I have in head that will to hand,
Which must be acted ere they may be scann'd.
[III, *iv,* 135-40]

In this tragedy Shakespeare's conception of sin is Protestant rather than Catholic, a spiritual condition rather than any act; in that depraved condition, man wanders lost in the nether world symbolized by the witches, and everything appears as both unearthly and starkly real, like a terrible nightmare. "Were such things here as we do speak about," asks Banquo,

Or have we eaten of the insane root
That takes the reason prisoner? [I, *iv,* 83-85]

A standard edition is the new Arden *Macbeth,* ed. Kenneth Muir (1951). Significant criticism of the play includes Thomas De Quincey, "On the Knocking at the Gate in *Macbeth,*" *London Magazine* (October 1823), repr. in *Macbeth: A Casebook,* ed. John Wain (1968); A. C. Bradley, *Shakespearean Tragedy* (1904); Levin Schücking, *Character Problems in Shakespeare's Plays* (1922); Lily B. Campbell, *Shakespeare's Tragic Heroes: Slaves of Passion* (1930); G. Wilson Knight, *The Wheel of Fire* (1930); Walter C. Curry, *Shakespeare's Philosophical Patterns* (1937); D. A. Traversi, *An Approach to Shakespeare* (1938; rev. ed., 1956); Cleanth Brooks, "The Naked Babe and the Cloak of Manliness," in *The Well Wrought Urn* (1947); H. B. Charlton, *Shakespearean Tragedy* (1948); Roy Walker, *The Time Is Free: A Study of Macbeth* (1949); Francis Fergusson, "*Macbeth* as the Imitation of an Action," *EIE* (1951), repr. in Fergusson's *The Human Image in Dramatic Literature* (1957); G. R. Elliott, *Dramatic Providence in Macbeth* (1958); John Holloway, *The Story of the Night* (1961); and Paul Jorgensen, *Our Naked Frailties: Sensational Art and Meaning in Macbeth* (1971). Essays on *Macbeth* are collected in *Approaches to Macbeth,* ed. Jay L. Halio (1966), and *Macbeth: A Casebook,* ed. John Wain (1968). There is a survey of criticism since the seventeenth century in Edward Quinn, James Ruoff, and Joseph Grennen, *The Major Shakespearean Tragedies* (1973).

Maid of Honor, The. A tragicomedy by Philip MASSINGER, written in 1621 and printed in 1632. The plot is derived, very broadly and with many changes, from William Painter's *The Palace of Pleasure* (1566-67). Some scholars find, with some justification, that Massinger's play is an allegory on the misfortunes of Charles I's brother-in-law Frederick, overthrown by the Spanish during the Thirty Year's War (1618-48); if this is true, the specific allusions in the play remain extremely obscure. The play is noteworthy for its sympathetic portrayal of Roman Catholicism, dramatized in the heroine's decision to enter a nunnery rather than to marry the man she loves.

When the duke of Urbino is defeated in war against the duchess of Siena, who has refused his hand in marriage, he appeals for help to the king of Sicily. When the king rightfully refuses on grounds that the war is unjust, the king's vainglorious and impetuous natural brother Bertoldo condemns the king as a coward and gathers a force of Sicilian hotheads to fight for Urbino. The king does not intervene, but he declares that no Sicilian captured in the war will be ransomed.

In Palermo Bertoldo woos the beautiful and chaste Camiola, who, though enamored of him, rejects his suit on grounds that as a Knight of Malta, he is pledged to celibacy. With Bertoldo gone to the wars, Camiola is set upon by a host of suitors. One is the base minion of the king, Fulgentio. When contemptuously rejected, he tries to destroy Camiola's reputation by slander, but her honor is defended in combat by the noble Adorni. In Siena, meanwhile, Bertoldo and his followers are defeated by the Sienese general Gonzago who—indignant that a Knight of Malta should wage such an ignoble war—strips Bertoldo of his Maltese cross and imprisons him at a very high ransom. True to his word, the king refuses ransom. Camiola, however, forgets all of her noble sentiments regarding Bertoldo's vow as a Knight of Malta and sends the trusted Adorni to Siena with the ransom money and a contract Bertoldo must sign pledging marriage to her in exchange for his freedom. Bertoldo quickly signs the agreement and is ransomed; once free, however, he forgets his agreement and falls in love with the duchess of Siena, who is infatuated with his handsome countenance and suave manner.

Returned to Sicily, Bertoldo is forgiven by the king, who gives his blessing to Bertoldo's planned nuptials with the duchess until Camiola appears and reveals the contract of marriage. Bertoldo laments his treachery and even the duchess agrees that he should return to Camiola. Although offered the man she loves, Camiola nevertheless renounces him when she enters with a company of friars to proclaim that she has determined to reject her lover and become a bride of the church—i.e.. a nun, or "maid of honor." As she departs for the convent, she awards the faithful Adorni a third of her wealth, and, after Gonzago restores Bertoldo as a Knight of Malta, bids her repentant lover to redeem his lost honor by fighting against the infidels.

In making his heroine a paragon of virtue given to theatrical gestures and lengthy speeches, Massinger skirts very close to a cloying sentimentality which he skilfully averts by creating a complicated moral relationship between Camiola and Bertoldo. She knows her duty, but cannot resist his charm; he is a vain and flighty courtier who gropes blindly toward some semblance of virtue at the end. Hence the conflict is between love and honor, and it is honor that receives the playwright's endorsement; love is looked upon as a trap, an inducement to the sliding irresolution represented by the lovers' repudiation of their solemn vows.

The standard edition is by E. A. W. Bryne (1927). For criticism, see S. R. Gardiner, "The Political Element in Massinger," *Contemporary Review,* XXXVIII (1876), who interprets the allegory; T. A. Dunn, *Philip Massinger: The Man and the Playwright* (1957); and Peter F. Mullany, "Religion in Massinger's *The Maid of Honor,*" *Ren D,* New Series, II (1969).

Maid's Tragedy, The. A tragedy by Francis BEAUMONT and John FLETCHER. It was written and performed around 1611 and first printed in 1619. No source is known, although the play makes liberal use of characters and episodes common to the late Greek romances as well as the French and Spanish heroic romances of the late sixteenth century. This play, together with Beaumont and Fletcher's *Philaster,* is considered to be a forerunner of the heroic drama of the Restoration because of its high-blown sentiments, episodic and improbable action, and turgid attitudinizing about love and honor by the chief characters. The scene of action is Rhodes at some unspecified time.

The great warrior Melantius returns from the wars to find his best friend Amintor engaged to his sister Evadne, a marriage ordered by the king. In obedience to the royal command, Amintor has broken his engagement to Aspatia, daughter of Calianax, the king's old adviser. At the masque celebrating Amintor's marriage to Evadne, a quarrel breaks out between Melantius and Calianax, but the king orders their reconciliation. Meanwhile the forsaken Aspatia sinks into profound melancholy.

On his wedding night Amintor learns the reason the king ordered his marriage to Evadne. For years the king has bedded with her, and the marriage has been arranged in order to conceal their illicit relationship. Because Amintor believes in the divinity of kings, he cannot do violence against the sacred body of his monarch; instead, he must endure his humiliation with patience, even in the face of the king's open mockery the morning after the wedding night.

As Amintor droops with shame, his friend Melantius succeeds in wringing Evadne's heart with remorse; she expresses contrition to the wronged Amintor and—not sharing Amintor's scruples about the divine right of kings—agrees to kill the king at the first opportunity.

Melantius' conspiracy succeeds. His sister stabs the king, and Melantius seizes the royal fort from Calianax. So strong is Melantius' cause that even the king's brother Lysippus pardons the rebels. At this point, however, events again go awry: Aspatia appears disguised as a soldier and, hoping to end her misery on Amintor's sword, engages him in a duel. As Aspatia falls wounded, Evadne arrives to announce the king's murder. When Amintor denounces her as a vile regicide, she takes her own life. Revealing herself to Amintor, Aspatia dies in his arms, and the grief-crazed Amintor kills himself. Lysippus views the tragic scene as an *exemplum* for both tyrants and rebellious subjects.

The Maid's Tragedy is a well-plotted, entertaining drama with many surprising turns. The complete court masque at the close of Act I is an effective *tour de theatre,* and the characters exude great emotional force. They often act in arbitrary, baffling ways, as when Amintor refuses to take revenge against the evil king, a decision that sets up a conflict between love and honor that is never made wholly convincing, or when Amintor suddenly attacks Evadne for killing the king even though her act has been, at least in part, in defense of his honor. Hence the characters are as extravagant in their actions and sentiments as any of the histrionic lovers of the heroic romances that inspired the play. Most of the work is by Beaumont, whose firm versifying is clearly evident in many scenes; Fletcher's clever dramaturgy and loose-flowing rhetoric are especially apparent in IV, *i* and V, *i-iii.*

The Maid's Tragedy is edited by R. K. Turner in *The Dramatic Works in the Beaumont and Fletcher Canon,* ed. Fredson Bowers, 2 vols. (1966, 1970), II. A. H. Thorndike edited the play in the Belles Lettres series (1906); Andrew Gurr in the Fountainwell Drama series (1968); and Howard B. Norland in the Regents Renaissance Drama series (1970). For criticism, see Eugene M. Waith, *The Pattern of Tragicomedy in Beaumont and Fletcher* (1952), and W. W. Appleton, *Beaumont and Fletcher: A Critical Study* (1956).

Malcontent, The. A tragicomedy by John MARSTON, written and performed in 1603, and printed in three editions in 1604. A third edition contains a famous induction by John Webster in which Richard Burbage, Henry Condell, John Lowin, and William Sly, members of the King's Men, converse with the audience about Marston's play, about a rival company of boy actors at the Blackfriars theater, and about the Globe playhouse itself. where *The Malcontent* is about to be performed with Burbage in the title role. Much of this conversation appears to refer to the so-called War of the Theaters (see JONSON, BEN). No source for Marston's play is known.

The corrupt court of Genoa, which is merely a puppet state of the duke of Florence, is ruled by the effete usurper duke Pietro Jacomo and his promiscuous duchess, Aurelia. Also at court is Genoa's former duke, disguised as Malevole, an all-licensed malcontent who vexes licentious courtiers and ladies with his acid tongue. Only the virtuous Count Celso knows that Malevole is really Duke Giovanni Altofronto, Genoa's wrongfully deposed ruler, whose faithful duchess, Maria, remains imprisoned in the citadel. The real power in Genoa is Mendoza, a treacherous courtier who cuckolds the present duke, but who also has a rival in Ferneze, a young courtier with whom Aurelia is currently enamored. In revenge, Mendoza informs Pietro of Aurelia's infidelity, and in a raid on her bedchamber Ferneze is stabbed by Mendoza. During these events Mendoza promises to help Aurelia avenge herself on her husband by murdering him. In reality, however, Mendoza plans to dispatch Aurelia, force the rightful duchess Maria to marry him, and seize power for himself.

Meanwhile the wounded Ferneze, who is thought to be dead, is carried to safety by Malevole, and the irate Pietro notifies the duke of Florence of his daughter Aurelia's disgraceful conduct. Shortly after, Mendoza foolishly tries to enlist Malevole's help in murdering Pietro, but Malevole reveals Mendoza's scheme to Pietro. After instructing Malevole to announce that he has committed suicide, Pietro takes on the disguise of a hermit and retreats to a cave. Mendoza banishes Aurelia, who meets her husband in the cave and they experience a conversion to virtue. Aurelia repents of her former lewdness, and the equally penitent Pietro relinquishes all claims to the throne he usurped from Altofronto. After much intrigue, events come to a crisis when all the chief characters are assembled at court to participate in a masque performed before Mendoza by Malevole, Pietro, Ferneze, and Celso. During the masque Malevole reveals himself to his duchess, and the masquers surround Mendoza with swords and pistols. Mendoza is contemptuously stripped of power. and Malevole, now once again in his old role of Altofronto, resumes power in Genoa.

In his preface to the first edition Marston describes his play as both a comedy and a satire, and in the Stationers' Register it is entered as a tragicomedy. Although employing many of the conventions of SENECAN REVENGE TRAGEDY, including declamation, lust, and violence, it avoids death at the end; moreover, the Machiavellian plotting of Mendoza is so closely superintended by the disguised Altofronto as to diminish any actual threat to the *status quo* of the characters.

That Marston's is a "humours" play is evident from the names of the *dramatis personae:* the name Mendoza suggests the Italian *mendoso,* or "correctable faults" (although his flaws are reformed by others rather than by himself); Malevole signifies "malevolent"; Altofronto denotes "lofty of countenance," and his loyal friend Celso has a name suggesting "noble" or "bright."

The Malcontent is very much in the mainstream of Elizabethan and Jacobean drama. It established the prototype for later malcontents like Jaques in *As You Like It* and Thersites in *Troilus and Cressida;* it portrays a Machiavellian villain in Mendoza who is more fully developed than any to be found at that time in the plays of Kyd, Marlowe, or Shakespeare; it continued the stage conventions of Senecan tragedy set by Kyd, including the play-within-the-play; and in Altofronto it presents a character who controls much of the action from within the play, and whose omnipotent counterparts are found in later dramas such as Cyril Tourneur's *Revenger's Tragedy* and Shakespeare's *Measure for Measure* and *The Tempest.*

The Malcontent has been edited by M. L. Wine in the Regents Renaissance Drama series (1964) and by Bernard Harris in a New Mermaid edition (1967). For commentary, see Anthony Caputi, *John Marston, Satirist* (1961), and Ejner J. Jensen, "Theme and Imagery in *The Malcontent,"* *SEL,* X (1970).

Mamillia. See GREENE, ROBERT; FICTION.

Mantuan (Giovanni Battista Spagunoli, 1448-1516). Italian poet and Carmelite monk whose vast output of Latin verse (over 50,000 lines) and, in particular, his eclogues reminiscent of Vergil (published as *Bucolica,* Paris, 1513), shaped Elizabethan poetry through the writings of Alexander Barclay. George TURBERVILLE. Barnabe GOOGE, and especially Edmund Spenser. See also PASTORAL.

Marino, Giovanni Battista (1569-1625). Italian poet. See CAREW, THOMAS; CRASHAW, RICHARD.

Markham, Gervase (or Jarvis, Jervis), of Cottam (1568?-1637?). Poet and author of courtesy books and manuals on horsemanship, farming, soldiering, and sports. Markham's place in literature is hopelessly confused by the fact that there were three Gervase Markhams: one, the third son of Robert Markham of Cottam, Nottinghamshire; another of Sedgebrook and Dunham, Nottinghamshire; and still another who was the plaintiff in a legal action in 1618 involving default of a wager by several Londoners, six of whom were actors at the Red Bull theater at the time. At present there is an uncertain consensus among scholars that Markham of Cottam was the poet and prolific prose writer, and that the plaintiff in the lawsuit was the playwright who collaborated with Lewis Machin on the comedy *The Dumb Knight* (wr. c. 1607-08) and with William Sampson on the tragedy *Herod and Antipater* (wr. 1621-22). The Markham referred to by Ben Jonson in *Conversations of Ben Jonson with Drummond* as "a base fellow" and no real poet could have been either of these Markhams. Gervase Markham of Dunham is not known to have been a writer.

Gervase Markham of Cottam served under Essex in the Low Countries and in Ireland, was a self-taught master of several languages, an accomplished veterinarian and breeder of horses—it has been said that he brought the first Arabian horse to England—and, judging from his eulogy *Devereux* (1597) on the death of Essex's brother Walter at the siege of Rouen in 1591, he was on familiar terms not only with Essex but with Penelope Rich (Sir Philip Sidney's "Stella") and with her sister the countess of Northumberland. The first of Markham's numerous treaties on the equestrian art was *A Discourse of Horsemanship* (1593). *The Most Honorable Tragedy of Sir Richard Grenville, Knight* (1595) is a poetic description of Sir Richard's heroic sea battle against the Spanish. (Tennyson consulted both Markham's poem and Sir Walter Raleigh's vivid prose account for details in writing his vigorous ballad "The Revenge." Tennyson could not have derived much inspiration from Markham's verses.) Markham's two long religious poems in six-line stanzas, *The Tears of the Beloved, or The Lamentations of Saint John* (1600) and *Mary Magdalene's Lamentations* (1601), suggest a direct influence of Robert Southwell, the Catholic martyr. Markham worked at a variety of other things, including an English version in 1608 of parts of Ariosto's *Orlando furioso,* but his abiding enthusiasms were horesemanship and soldiering, subjects he treated in an easy, familiar prose style. His many treatises on these topics are more than practical manuals and properly belong in the category of COURTESY LITERATURE.

There is no edition of Markham's complete works. Separate editions are listed in *CBEL,* ed. F. W. Bateson, 4 vols., I (1940); and in G. E. Noyes, *A Bibliography of Courtesy and Conduct Books* (1937). A work almost always assigned to John Marston was attributed to Markham by John H. H. Lyon in *A Study of "The New Metamorphosis" written by J. M., Gent* (1919). Largely because Markham dedicated his *Tragedy of... Grenville* to the earl of Southampton (among others), Robert Gittings identifies Markham as the "Rival Poet" of Shakespeare's Sonnets in *Shakespeare's Rival* (1960). F. N. L. Poynter attempts to untangle these and other problems in "Gervase Markham," *E&S,* XV (1962).

Marlowe, Christopher (1564-1593). Dramatist and poet. Born the son of a shoemaker in Canterbury, Marlowe attended King's School there and proceeded to a six-year scholarship at Corpus Christi College, Cambridge. The scholarship presumed the taking of orders, but for some reason Marlowe was not ordained. In 1587 he was absent from the university for several months, and his M.A. degree was granted in June of that year on the intervention of the Privy Council, which informed the college that during his absence "he had done her Majesty good service." What the "service" consisted of is not known, but some biographers speculate that he may have been at the English Catholic university in Rheims as a spy for the government.

During the next six years he was in London writing plays and possibly acting as a secret agent in some unknown capacity for Sir Francis Walsingham. While still at Cambridge he may have written his first play, *The Tragedy of Dido, Queen of Carthage,* and probably at least part of his first triumph, TAMBURLAINE THE GREAT, Part I, performed in 1587 by the Lord Admiral's Men with the great Edward Alleyn in the title role. The next year saw Part *II* of *Tamburlaine,* an equally popular sequel. Marlowe's other plays are of very uncertain date and order: *The Massacre at Paris,* THE JEW OF MALTA, DOCTOR FAUSTUS, and EDWARD II. He also translated Ovid's *Amores* (1597) and the first book of Lucan's *Pharsalia* (1600). His great narrative love poem HERO AND LEANDER was left unfinished at his death and completed (Cantos 3-5) by George Chapman. Marlowe's lyric "Come live with me and be my love," perhaps the most popular of the period, first appeared in the miscellany *The Passionate Pilgrim* (1599), later in *England's Helicon* (1600). It may have been this pastoral lyric Shakespeare remembered when he paid tribute to Marlowe as the "dead shepherd" in *As You Like It* (III, *v,* 81) and echoed the line from *Hero and Leander:* "Who ever loved that loved not at first sight?"

The records of the time indicate Marlowe was often in trouble with the authorities because of what seems to have been a rash, indiscreet temperament. His first known arrest occurred in 1589 when he and Thomas Watson, the poet, fought with William Bradley, an actor, in Hog Lane near the theater district. Bradley was killed, presumably by Watson, and both men went to jail, though they were later exonerated on grounds of self-defense. In May 1592 two constables swore a petition against Marlowe for habitual breach of the peace, and rumors began to circulate regarding his alleged atheism and homosexuality. These culminated in formal charges against him by a notorious informer, Richard Baines, who testified in June 1593 that Marlowe proclaimed, among other things, that "Christ was a bastard and his mother dishonest," that Christ and St. John the Evangelist were both homosexuals, that "they who love not tobacco and boys were fools," and that he, Marlowe, had as much right to coin money as the queen.

In May 1593, while Marlowe was in Kent visiting Thomas Walsingham, the authorities seized Thomas Kyd, with whom Marlowe had once shared rooms, and interrogated him on the rack. Under torture Kyd attributed certain atheistical papers found in his room to Marlowe (they were actually notes from a unitarian treatise) and linked Marlowe to the notorious skeptics in association with Sir Walter Raleigh (who was himself arraigned for atheism the following year). Marlowe was brought before the Privy Council and released on probation. What followed was not made public until the revelations by Leslie Hotson in his book *The Death of Christopher Marlowe* (1925). On May 30 Marlowe spent the day at a tavern in Deptford in the company of three men, all of whom had at one time or another served as government agents. Toward evening there was a dispute over the reckoning and one of them, Ingram Frizer, stabbed Marlowe in the eye. Marlowe was only twenty-nine at his death.

Many of Marlowe's contemporaries recognized his genius. He was praised by Chapman, Nashe, and Shakespeare. In his dedication to Shakespeare in the First Folio, Jonson wrote of "Marlowe's mighty line," and Michael Drayton, in a brief survey of the poets of his time, extolled Marlowe for "those brave translunary things/That the first poets had." Indeed, by 1593, the year of Marlowe's death, Shakespeare himself had not demonstrably exceeded that translunary genius, for Marlowe's *Edward II* compares favorably with Shakespeare's *Richard II,* and Marlowe's *Hero and Leander* is generally regarded as superior to Shakespeare's *Venus and Adonis*.

Standard is *The Works and Life,* ed. E. H. Case, 6 vols. (1930-33). There are single-volume editions of the complete plays by Irving Ribner (1963) and Roma Gill (1971). The standard biography is John Bakeless, *The Tragical History of Christopher Marlowe,* 2 vols. (1942), but there are excellent biographies by Leslie Hotson (1925), Una Ellis-Fermor (1927), Mark Eccles (1934), and F. S. Boas (1940; rev., 1953). Essential critical studies include Paul H. Kocher, *Christopher Marlowe, A Study of His Thought, Learning, and Character* (1946); Harry Levin, *The Overreacher, A Study of Christopher Marlowe* (1952); F. P. Wilson, *Marlowe and the Early Shakespeare* (1953); and J. B. Steane, *Marlowe, A Critical Study* (1964). There is a Concise Bibliography by S. A. Tannenbaum (1937), supplemented by "Christopher Marlowe (1946-65)," ed. R. C. Johnson, in *Elizabethan Bibliographies Supplements,* VI (1967). See also *Critics on Marlowe,* ed. Judith O'Neill (1970), and *The Predecessors of Shakespeare: A Survey and Bibliography of Recent Studies in English Renaissance Drama,* ed. Terence P. Logan and Denzell S. Smith (1973).

Marprelate, Martin. The pseudonym of the author or authors of seven prose satires printed on a secret press in 1588-89. "Martin Marprelate" attacked the authority of the Anglican bishops and argued for a presbyterian form of church discipline and government. These lively and imaginative pamphlets were occasioned by Archbishop John Whitgift's efforts to silence Puritan opposition to the bishops. In 1586, backed by Queen Elizabeth, he persuaded a reluctant Parliament to make himself and the bishop of London exclusively authorized to censor books and license printing presses.

Although all the alleged authors denied having any part in their publication, the Marprelate pamphlets seem to have been the work of Robert Waldegrave, a Puritan printer excluded from work by Whitgift's licensing law; a preacher named John Field, who, although dead by 1588, supplied notes later used in the pamphlets; John Penry, a Welshman; John Udall, a dissident parish priest at Kingston-on-Thames; and one Job Throckmorton. After the appearance of the seventh Marprelate tract, Penry, Udall, and Throckmorton were arrested. Udall died in prison, Penry was later executed, and Throckmorton, who is now believed to have collaborated on at least some of the pamphlets, was exonerated.

The seven extant Marprelate pamphlets are not significant for their theological profundity but for their literary value; they are among the liveliest prose satires to appear in the sixteenth century. The following passage from *The Epistle, or, Oh, Read Over, Dr. John Bridges, for It Is a Worthy Work* illustrates Martin's racy colloquialism and broad parody. Here Martin potrays Bishop Bridges "showing all his learning at once" while giving a sermon on his own first name:

> John, John, the grace of God, the grace of God, the grace of God! Gracious John, not graceless John, but gracious John. John, holy John, not John full of holes, but holy John! If he showed himself not learned in this sermon, then had he been a dunce all his life. In the same sermon, two several Johns, the father and the son, that had been both recusants, being brought publicly to confess their faults, this worthy doctor, by reason that the young man having been poisoned beyond the seas with popery, was more obstinate than his father, and by all likelihood, he was the cause of his father's perverseness: with a vehement exclamation able to pierce a cobweb, called on the father aloud in this pathetical and persuading sort: "Old John, old John, be not led away by the siren sounds and inticements of young John! If young John will go to the

> devil, the devil go with him." The puritans, it may be, will here object that this worthy man was endued with these famous gifts before he was B.[ishop]; whereas since that time, say they, he is not able to say boo to a goose.

One occasion for the first Marprelate satire was the confiscation of Waldegrave's press by the Star Chamber in April 1588 because Waldegrave had published a satirical dialogue against the bishops by John Udall. Waldegrave fled to Udall's parish at Kingston-on-Thames, assembled a new press, and printed not only another anti-episcopal work by Udall but also John Penry's *An Exhortation unto the Governors and People of Wales.* It was here that he published the first of the pamphlets actually signed "Martin Marprelate," *The Epistle,* a refutation of *A Defense of the Government established in the Church of England for Ecclesiastical Matters* (1587) by John Bridges. After printing the first pamphlet, Waldegrave moved his press to Fawsley House, Northamptonshire, always one step ahead of the aroused authorities, and there published another attack on Bishop Bridges. His next stop was Coventry, where he produced two more tracts. Fearing for his life, he fled to France, then to Edinburgh, where he settled down and prospered as a commercial printer duly licensed by King James. After a substitute printer was found, the anonymous Marprelate authors published three more pamphlets before the arrest of Penry, Throckmorton and Udall on August 14, 1589.

The seven extant Marprelate pamphlets (listed by their short titles) are *The Epistle, The Epitome, The Mineral Conclusions, Hay Any Work for Cooper?, Martin Junior, Martin Senior,* and *The Protestation. The Epistle* consists of anecdotes ridiculing not only Bridges' works, but also the private lives of three Anglican bishops, John Whitgift, archbishop of Canterbury, John Aylmer, bishop of London, and Thomas Cooper, bishop of Winchester. The style is terse, witty, and thoroughly irreverent, especially in its slangy innuendoes. Soon afterward appeared an attack on the bishop of London personally, *The Epitome,* to which Bishop Cooper addressed a pedantic, humorless rejoinder, *Admonition to the People of England* (1589). By this time it had become apparent that the bishops were no match for the sharp-witted, boisterous Martin, who responded to Cooper's *Admonition* with the amusing *Mineral Conclusions,* which purports to be thirty-seven "mineral and metaphysical schoolpoints to be defended by the several bishops"—i.e., thirty-seven ludicrous theological opinions, many of them twisted out of context from the *Admonition,* which Martin mockingly attributes to the prelates. The longest pamphlet was the next, *Hay Any Work for Cooper?* (the title taken from a popular street cry), which was also the least humorous, consisting of a point-by-point refutation of Cooper's argument for the civil authority of the bishops. The fifth pamphlet, *Martin Junior,* was the first to attempt a literary form. It is prefaced by Martin's address to the reader, followed by a text enumerating 110 points against episcopacy and a prologue in which Martin Junior describes how he found the tract in his father's handwriting.

The fictitous background of *Martin Junior* was continued a week later in *Martin Senior,* in which the supposed author, the eldest son of "Martin the Great," berates his younger brother Martin Junior for rushing into print with their father's treatise. The work concludes with eleven arguments against episcopacy and some doggerel verse attacking the anti-Martinists. The last of the Marprelate tracts, *The Protestation,* is the most bitter and vituperative; it rails against the tyranny of the bishops and challenges them to public debate on the issues of church government. If he should fail to refute his opponents in this open forum, Martin proclaims, he will gladly forfeit his life.

Forced to admit the patent ineffectiveness of Bishop Cooper's solemn *Admonition,* the bishops hired literary mercenaries to attack Martin Marprelate. A burlesque in verse, *A Whip for an Ape,* and a dialogue, *Mar-Martine,* both published in 1589, may have been by John LYLY and Thomas NASHE, respectively. In *A Countercuff Given to Martin Junior* (1589), a trifle of four pages, the prelates and their hirelings tried unsuccessfully to create an imaginary author as sportive and vivacious as Martin in a character signing himself "Pasquill." One tract by Pasquill, *Pappe with a Hatchet,* was almost certainly by Lyly. Of less definite authorship is *The Return of Pasquill,* a dialogue in which Pasquill, recently returned from abroad, argues over episcopacy with a feeble-witted Puritan.

Lyly's *Pappe with a Hatchet* precipitated still another controversy, for in that tract Lyly challenged Gabriel Harvey to join in the Marprelate debates and Harvey responded with *Advertisement to Papp-Hatchet* (1593), a pedantic and patronizing rejoinder that distributed blame for the controversy almost equally between prelates and Puritans. This viewpoint seems to have been shared by Gabriel Harvey's brother Richard, who in *Theological Discourse of the Lamb of God and His Enemies* castigates Martin Marprelate as a heretic and attacks the pro-episcopal dramatists Lyly, Nashe, and Robert GREENE. Greene answered with *A Quip for an Upstart Courtier,* which ridicules the Harvey family as social-climbing parvenus. After Greene's death in 1593 Nashe took up the torch to continue the war against the Harvey clan. The exchange of satires that followed during the next several years has become known as the Greene-Nashe-Harvey controversy (see HARVEY, GABRIEL).

The Martin Marprelate controversy ended with the confiscation of the illegal press. Martin's name was revived briefly during the anti-episcopal debates of the Long Parliament and the theological quarrels that followed. "Young Martin Marpriest" was the pseudonym of the author of *Hay Any Work* (1641). *A Dialogue* (1643), and four unimaginative and inconsequential attacks on the bishops in 1645.

For the texts of the 1588-89 pamphlets, see *The Marprelate Tracts,* ed. W. Pierce (1911). Pierce gives a detailed account of the debates in *An Historical Introduction to the Marprelate Tracts* (1908). Authorship is discussed by D. J. McGinn, "The Real Martin Marprelate," *PMLA,* LVIII (1943); the style of the tracts by Raymond A. Anselment, "Rhetoric and the Dramatic Satire of Martin Marprelate," *SEL,* X (1970).

Marston, John (1576?-1634). Dramatist. Marston's father was a distinguished lawyer, his mother the member of a prosperous Italian family of surgeons that had settled in London. Marston graduated B.A. from Brasenose College, Oxford, in 1594, and began the study of his father's profession but soon abandoned it for literature. His first publications appeared in 1598, THE METAMORPHOSIS OF PYGMALION'S IMAGE...AND CERTAIN SATIRES and *The Scourge of Villainy,* under the pseudonym "W. Kinsayder." Both were verse satires in the manner of Joseph Hall's *Virgidemiarum,* and both contained contemptuous references to Hall. *The Metamorphosis of Pygmalion's Image* was especially licentious; in 1599 the archbishop of Canterbury ordered it to be burned by the common hangman (see SATIRE).

Meanwhile Marston had temporarily joined Philip Henslowe and the Lord Admiral's Men as a playwright, later changing over to the Children of Paul's when that company was formed in 1599. He probably had at least a hand in rewriting for a performance in 1599 the anonymous play *Histriomastix,* which satirizes Jonson as the inane, pompous Chrysoganus and which may have precipitated the so-called War of the Theaters (see JONSON, BEN). Further attacks on Jonson came with Marston's *Antonio and Mellida* (1600), the anonymous *Jack Drum's Entertainment* (perf. 1600), in which Marston had a hand, and SATIROMASTIX (1602), which he probably wrote in collaboration with Dekker. William Drummond later recorded that Jonson had told him of the affair: "He had many quarrels with Marston, beat him and took his pistol from him, wrote his *Poetaster* on him; the beginning of them were, that Marston represented him on the stage."

Marston's quarrel with Jonson was apparently over by 1604, when Marston dedicated *The Malcontent* to Jonson and collaborated with Jonson and Chapman on *Eastward Ho!* (1605), a play that landed Jonson and Chapman (but not Marston) in jail for its satiric references to James I's Scottish knights. In his next play *Sophonisba* (1606), Marston returned to his caustic ridicule of Jonson. Marston was in prison in 1608, on some unknown charge perhaps unrelated to the stage. After beginning *The Insatiate Countess* (completed by the actor William Barksted and first published in 1613) Marston quit the stage, took holy orders, and married. In 1616 he became minister of Christ Church, Hampshire, remaining in this post until his retirement in 1631.

Marston's best-known and most accomplished plays are THE DUTCH COURTESAN, THE MALCONTENT, and *The Wonder of Women* (the last thought by T. S. Eliot and Marston himself to be the author's best). Like Marston's satires, these are bitter, exaggerated, often coarse, and occasionally brilliant, but with little sustained force or sense of form. His sensibilities are often compared with those of his best-known creation, Malevole, the exiled duke in *The Malcontent* who returns to his own court in disguise and rails vehemently against the corruption of the world. Like Cyril Tourneur, Marston was especially acerbic in his portrayal of women, who are usually monstrous hypocrites or immaculate saints; like John Webster, he seems to have been influenced, at least superficially, by Shakespeare, for his plays are full of echoes and reminiscences from *Richard II, Richard III, Julius Caesar, Hamlet,* and *Macbeth.* Like the early Elizabethan tragedians, Marston was an accomplished peruser of Seneca, especially of Seneca's *Thyestes* (see SENECAN TRAGEDY). His plays provide all of the emotional and physical violence of Kyd's *Spanish Tragedy* or Marlowe's *Tamburlaine* with little of their exuberance or heroism.

To the early Elizabethan formula of Senecan tragedy and seriocomic drama, Marston adds ingredients that are uniquely his own—a bitter acknowledgment of the futility of virtue or innocence, a cynical and passionate testimony to the universality of human wickedness.

Marston's *Collected Works* was edited by A. H. Bullen, 3 vols. (1887). The best critical biography is by Anthony Caputi, *John Marston, Satirist* (1961). A recent critical study is by Philip J. Finklepearl, *John Marston of the Middle Temple* (1969). There is a Concise Bibliography by S. A. Tannenbaum (1940), updated in "John Marston (1939-65)," ed. C. A. Pennel and W. P. Williams, in *Elizabethan Bibliographies Supplements,* IV (1968).

Marvell, Andrew (1621-1678). Poet. Marvell was the son of an Anglican minister of Calvinist leanings who served as master and preacher of an almshouse in Hull, where Marvell resided most of his life. Marvell entered Cambridge in 1633 and left with a degree in 1639. During his student days he was briefly converted to Roman Catholicism by a Jesuit, but his father persuaded him to return to the Anglican Church. After his father drowned in the Humber in 1641, Marvell went abroad for four years as a tutor (1642-46), traveling extensively in Italy, France, and Spain. In Rome he met Richard Flecknoe, the target of Dryden's later satire, whom Marvell lampooned mercilessly in one of his earliest poems, "Flecknoe, an English Priest at Rome."

Returning to England at the height of the Civil War, Marvell was a moderate Royalist, seeing in the king a constitutional force necessary to restrain factionalism and maintain political and social order, but he gradually transferred his loyalty to Cromwell. He took no part in the Civil War, and was able to maintain friendly relations with disputants on both sides. In 1651 he became a tutor to Mary, young daughter of Lord Fairfax, who retired that year to his family estate at Nun Appleton House in Yorkshire after a small dispute with Cromwell. In the rural setting of Nun Appleton, with its lush greenery and formal gardens, Marvell probably wrote his "Mower" poems and other famous pieces: "Upon Appleton House," "The Picture of Little T. C. in a Prospect of Flowers," "The Nymph Complaining of the Death of Her Faun," "The Coronet," and "The Garden." Since none of these or any of his major works were published during his lifetime, his poems are difficult to date exactly. He probably began his apprenticeship in poetry at Cambridge with minor Greek and Latin verse (pr. 1637).

Marvell's powers were fully developed by 1650, when he wrote his "Horatian Ode upon Cromwell's Return from Ireland," a remarkable poem not only for its mastery of Horace's style but its profound evaluation of two mighty political opposites, Cromwell and Charles I, whom Marvell treats with scrupulously balanced admonition and encomium. In a manner reminiscent of Shakespeare in *Richard II,* he presents the two antagonists as representatives of antithetical cosmic forces. Charles embodies justice, "ancient rights," and personal dignity; he is a "royal actor" on the stage of history, and at his execution performs his role on a "tragic scaffold,"

> While round the armed bands
> Did clap their bloody hands.
> He nothing common did or mean
> Upon that memorable scene.

From Marvell's providential view of history, Charles left a vacuum abhorred by nature, and the fates, or divine winds of destiny, make Cromwell the ineluctible force by which a new order must be born. The Cromwell at the beginning of the war, among his pears and roses in his "private gardens," Marvell contrasts to the "restless Cromwell" of divine election, urged on by his "active star" to obliterate all opposition "like the three-forked lightning":

> 'Tis madness to resist or blame
> The force of angry Heaven's flame;
> And, if we would speak true,
> Much to the Man is due.

Marvell's ode illustrates those qualities peculiar to his best poems—a complex sensibility of multiple perspectives, an apprehension of experiences with intellectual and emotional simultaneity, a tendency to nurture paradoxes and sustain opposites rather than to seek emphatic resolutions. These qualities put him squarely in the metaphysical tradition of John Donne (see METAPHYSICAL POETS). Characteristically, however, Marvell defies any such facile classification, for he expresses an integration of mid-seventeenth-century influences, poetic "schools," and philosophical impulses. Although his poetry owes much to Donne's "strong lines" and metaphysical images, it also has origins in Horace, Lucan, Theocritus, and the whole panoply of Greek and Latin poets. He also owes much to the classical school of Ben Jonson. Hence a poem like "Upon Appleton House," resembling Jonson's "To Penshurst" in many of its particulars, bursts out in lines reminiscent of Donne:

> Let others vainly strive t'immure
> The *Circle* in the *Quadrature!*
> These holy mathematics can
> In every figure equal Man.

To the lucidity, economy, and musical cadences of Jonson and the CAVALIER POETS Marvell joins the tensions, incongruities, and "strong lines" of Donne and the metaphysical poets. This difficult synthesis is only one aspect of other reconciliations—ascetic Puritan and passionate epicurean, Royalist and parliamentarian, contemplative recluse and man of public affairs, romantic lover of nature and urbane satirist, mystic and pragmatist. Unlike Milton (whose *Paradise Lost* he was, in 1674, among the first to praise), he is not a poet of easy resolution but of sharp dissonances, of meticulously refined ironies and paradoxes. In his "Dialogue Between the Soul and Body" the material lends itself to didactic debate, but Marvell shifts the conventional moral focus to an examination of a conflict within the order of nature itself. The soul complains of pains and restraints imposed by a tyrannical body; the body charges the soul with inflicting fear and grief, love and hate. The Platonist in Marvell could have tipped the argument in favor of the soul; instead, the poem merely concludes with the body's ironic observation:

> What but a Soul could have the wit
> To build me up for sin so fit?
> So architects do square and hew
> Green trees that in the forest grew.

In 1653 Marvell went to Eton to tutor Cromwell's ward, and it was there, after hearing of his host John Oxenbridge's adventures in Bermuda, that he wrote the exquisite "Bermudas." His "Ode to Cromwell" had shown the cruel but necessary destructive forces of nature; "Bermudas" portrays its quiet benevolence in a single, lyrically distilled scene of a boatload of Puritans, in flight from religious persecution at home, rowing toward the tranquil shore "safe from the storms, and prelate's rage." As in "The Garden", nature is shown to be rich and bountiful:

> He makes the figs our mouths to meet,
> And throws the melons at our feet.

At the conclusion, their song of praise to God (which is, in effect, the poem itself) joins with the rhythm of the pilgrims' rowing in a beautiful expression of man's rare harmony with nature:

> And all the way, to guide their chime,
> With falling oars they kept the time.

Marvell's recurring irony springs from his conception of man as in a middle state between heaven and hell, spirit and body, as in his "A Dialogue Between the Soul and Body":

> A Soul hung up, as 'twere, in chains
> Of nerves, and arteries, and veins.

Man is a transcendent, fluid creature of infinite consciousness and choices beset by his own inner oppositions and the cruelty of society and nature—a tragic condition Marvell responds to with analytical compassion or Augustan coolness coupled with passionate nostalgia. His capacity for apprehending the beauties of nature and humanity is immense, but it is always accompanied by a stoical awareness of the inevitability of suffering and loss. The myth of the Fall is omnipresent in most of his poems. In "The Picture of Little T. C. in a Prospect of Flowers" the child lives "golden days" as a "darling of the gods," naming the flowers and reforming "the errors of the spring." Someday, the poet suggests, she will break Cupid's bow and reign over adoring masculine hearts as she reigns over flowers. In the final stanza, however, these Cavalier compliments are tinged with a note of foreboding. This beautiful child "whom nature courts with fruits and flowers" must "spare the buds,"

Lest Flora angry at thy crime,
To kill her infants in their prime,
Do quickly make th' example yours:
And, ere we see,
Nip in the blossom all our hopes and thee.

The parallel between the child and the buds is clearly implicit, as is the contrast between nature's benevolence and cruelty, and the poem concludes with fine ambiguity and dissonance. In one sense it is a playful "picture" of witty gallantries; in another, a poignant reflection on human mutability.

In "The Nymph Complaining of the Death of Her Faun," Marvell renders a kindred theme in the subtlest allegory. Whether he intended to symbolize in the faun the Anglican Church may never be established for certain; it is clear from the Biblical echoes and sacramental imagery, and from the sustained use of colors Marvell habitually associated with sexual passion and innocence, that the poem allegorizes Platonic and Christian ideas on several levels. Less abstruse is "The Mower Against Gardens," which turns on the single conceit of the Fall as man's seduction of the world. In his cultivation of gardens man is shown to be a kind of rapist forcing innocent nature to "procreate without a sex" by grafting and hybridization,

While the sweet fields do lie forgot;
Where willing nature does to all dispense
A wild and fragrant innocence.

Of all Marvell's poems, "The Garden" is the most philosophically comprehensive, occupying a place in relation to his other mature poems that "The Extasie" bears to Donne's erotic verses in *Songs and Sonnets.* As with "A Drop of Dew," Marvell wrote two versions of the poem, one in Latin, the other in English. The Latin is more faithful to the Horatian conception of the *hortus conclusus* as a garden retreat from the tribulations of the world. In the English version the conventional tensions between the active and the contemplative life are represented by two established traditions of the garden myth itself—the sensual and libertine celebrated by the Italian and French pastoralists, and Marvell's own Platonic garden of meditation and spiritual transcendence. Hence the "uncessant labors" of the "busy companies of men," with their frenetic pursuit of glory, are mocked by the garden's verdant "flowers of repose." as in the classical *hortus;* but Marvell's pastoral is not a paradise of innocent sexuality, as it is in Tasso's *Aminta,* Spenser's *Faerie Queene* (IV, 10), or Randolph's "Pastoral Courtship." Marvell not only banishes women from his paradise but rejects their erotic "white and red" in favor of nature's more sensual "green":

No white not red was ever seen
So am'rous as this lovely green.

Women are metamorphosed into trees, as in the Greek myths, and the androgynous new Adam revels in the solitude of a Paradise wherein contemplation becomes joyously sensual and moral solitude renders the Fall itself innocuous:

What wond'rous life in this I lead!
Ripe apples drop about my head;
The luscious clusters of the vine
Upon my mouth do crush their wine;
The nectarine and curious peach
Into my hands themselves do reach;
Stumbling on melons, as I pass,
Ensnared with flowers, I fall on grass.

The climax of the poem occurs in a mystical moment of transcendence when the mind creates

Far other worlds, and other seas,
Annihilating all that's made
To a green thought in a green shade.

It is perhaps futile to discuss "The Garden" as either classical or metaphysical. With Donne's "The Extasie," Keats's "Ode on a Grecian Urn," and Yeats's "Sailing to Byzantium," it is a lyric of pure vision and miraculous imagination.

In Marvell's "To His Coy Mistress," the surface formality, lucidity, and regular meter invoke Jonson and the Latin poets, and the opening of the poem recalls, ironically, the artificialities of the conventional Cavalier invitation to love:

> Had we but world enough and Time,
> This coyness, Lady, were no crime.
> We would sit down, and think which way
> To walk, and pass our long love's day.

The first twenty lines of hyperboles, jogging iambic tetrameters, and banal rhymes dance gaily above the surface of temporal and spatial allusions to a past as remote as a "ten years before the Flood" and a future as distant and imponderable as "the conversion of the Jews," while the poet's love-making extends in space from the exotic Ganges to Marvell's own Humber River in Hull. In a metaphysical telescoping of images, the spatial and the temporal fuse in the lines:

> My vegetable love should grow
> Vaster than empires, and more slow.

The self-possessed tone changes suddenly with the twenty-first line and the beginning of the second movement, as if the awesome implications of his own metaphors suddenly begin to overtake the courtly wooer:

> But at my back I always hear
> Time's winged chariot hurrying near:
> And yonder all before us lie
> Deserts of vast eternity.

On one level, Marvell's poem is a seriocomic satire on such Cavalier lyrics as "To the virgins to make the most of time"; on another, an equally mocking dramatic demonstration of the seducer ironically seduced as the gallant wooer of the first twenty lines becomes in the second movement (lines 21-32) the victim of his own rhetoric, contemplating terrifying infinity (so comforting in the first movement) and space now reduced to claustrophobic tombs, ashes, and worms. Still another level of meaning is reached in the third transition, beginning in line 33 with the word "Now," for at this point the lover responds with wild passion to the metaphysical dilemma of mutability. The leisurely compliments of the first twenty lines are thrown into contrast to the frantic outbursts of the conclusion:

> Now let us sport us while we may,
> And now, like am'rous birds of prey,
> Rather at once our Time devour
> Than languish in his slow-chapped pow'r.

Thus a poem that begins as a courtly and complimentary invitation to love in the Cavalier mode concludes as a metaphysical speculation relating only tangentially to love, for the ultimate context of the poem pertains to the philosophical question of how man can preserve his temporal values against the inevitable destruction of time. To this grim question that haunted Shakespeare and Keats, Marvell's lover finds no answer except in the illusions of a heroic human subjectivity:

> Let us roll all our strength, and all
> Our sweetness, up into one ball;
> And tear our pleasure with rough strife
> Thorough the iron gates of life.
> Thus, though we cannot make our sun
> Stand still, yet we will make him run.

Characteristically, Marvell leaves off in dissonance, content to explore the multiple conflicts and tensions of the human condition rather than provide resolutions based on any single perspective. In this way he remains, in spite of his classical qualities, one of the most metaphysical, and in some ways, the most modern of the seventeenth-century poets.

Little is known of Marvell as a man except what can be inferred from his poetry. Milton apparently respected him greatly. As Secretary of Foreign Tongues, Milton strongly urged Parliament in 1653 to make Marvell his assistant, a post granted to Marvell in 1657. Marvell also served, actively and with great probity, as a member of Parliament for Hull in 1659-78, and, according to Milton's nephew Edward Philips, used his influence to free Milton from imprisonment after the Restoration. After Marvell's death his poems first appeared in 1681 in a volume published by a woman falsely claiming to be his widow.

Marvell's prose consists chiefly of his many newsletters written to his constituents on public men and events while he was a member of Parliament, and several letters and essays on ecclesiastical questions written between 1672 and 1677. After 1667 the body of his poetry consists of political poems in couplets that hark back to his Flecknoe satires. Thus the poet who began in the tradition of Jonson, and became as thoroughly metaphysical as Donne, concluded his career a satirist in the style of John Dryden.

The standard edition of Marvell's poems and correspondence is by H. M. Margoliouth, 2d ed., 2 vols. (1952; rev. 1971). A. B. Grosart's edition (1872-75) contains the prose, chiefly letters and political writings after the Restoration. See also *Selected Poems,* ed. Frank Kermode (1967) and *The Poems,* ed. J. Reeves and M. Seymour-Smith (1969). The standard biography is by P. Legouis, *André Marvell, poète, puritain, patriote* (1928; abridged and trans., 1965), which contains an essential bibliography. T. S. Eliot's essay on Marvell is in *Homage to John Dryden* (1924) and *Selected Essays* (1932); William Empson's discussion of "The Garden" is in *Some Versions of Pastoral* (1935). Some important critical studies are by J. B. Leishman, *The Art of Marvell's Poetry* (1966); J. M. Wallace, *Destiny His Choice: The Loyalism of Marvell* (1968); Ann E. Berthoff, *The Resolved Soul: A Study of Marvell's Major Poems* (1970); Patrick Culler, *Spenser, Marvell, and Renaissance Pastoral Poetry* (1970); and Donald M. Friedman, *Marvell's Pastoral Art* (1970). Bibliographies are by Theodore Spencer and Mark Van Doren, *Studies in Metaphysical Poetry, 1912-38* (1939) and "Andrew Marvell (1927-67)," ed. Dennis G. Donovan, *Elizabethan Bibliographies Supplements,* XII (1969).

masque. An entertainment consisting of combined dance, song, allegory, mimicry, music, costumes, and pageantry. In medieval England a procession of "masquers" would dance through the streets during holidays and stop at house after house to drink, dance, or play dice with the occupants. No doubt in primitive times these "mummings" and revelries were fertility rites comparable to the medieval St. George "Sword Dance" folk plays. During the reign of Henry VIII these festive disguisings were adopted by the court and became increasingly formalized and regulated. Frequently birthdays or holidays were celebrated by an unexpected visit to a house by a band of friends wearing masks, bearing gifts, and accompanied by singers and musicians. The first formal court masque in England may have been the so-called Epiphany Spectacle (1512), an elaborate celebration of dancing, singing, disguisings, and grotesque mimicry prepared for the court by Henry VIII himself. To these native elements of the masque were added certain influences from Italy, where the masque developed into a graceful operatic ballet, sometimes incorporated into pastoral comedies. At court the masque frequently became an adjunct to some other form of entertainment—as an allegorical dance or spectacle preliminary to a court ball or accompanying a wedding celebration or feast. Hence masques were ephemeral and occasional forms of entertainment either celebrating social events or incorporated into a play as a spectacle.

The masque had a considerable influence on poetry and drama. Spenser's *The Faerie Queene* includes two masques, the procession of the seven deadly sins (I, 4) and the Masque of Cupid (III, 12). What John Fletcher called "minute masques" were often incorporated into regular plays to achieve scenic, choral, or symbolic effects, as in Shakespeare's *Timon of Athens,* wherein the stage directions call for "Cupid, with a mask of Ladies as Amazons, with lutes in their hands, dancing and playing" (I, *ii*). In *The Tempest* a hymeneal masque is performed to celebrate the betrothal of Ferdinand and Miranda, and in *Henry VIII* to express Queen Katharine's dream.

The court masque did not reach its fullest development until the reign of James I, whose wife Anne of Denmark loved lavish spectacles. The first such fully developed and elaborate masque was Samuel Daniel's *Vision of the Twelve Goddesses* (perf. 1604), which celebrates allegorically the coronation of James I. Under James I and Charles I, exorbitant sums were lavished on costumes, scenery, complicated mechanical devices such as moving ships or castles on wheels, and huge thrones adorned with the Muses and carried by crowds of courtiers often assisted by professional actors. The modern reader of seventeenth-century masques can scarcely imagine from the songs and stage directions on the page their essential appeal to eye and ear. The staging, costumes, songs, and dances—often freely mingling amateur performers, professional actors, and audience—were vital aspects of these semi-dramatic courtly entertainments.

Many dramatists who wrote for the popular stage also created court masques—including George Chapman, Francis Beaumont, Thomas Campion, John Fletcher, Thomas Middleton, and James Shirley, to cite only a few—but the most successful master of the form was Ben JONSON. In collaboration with Inigo JONES, an artist trained in Italy who designed the stage scenery and machines, Jonson gave the court masque the full benefits of his lyric power, his sure sense of timing, and his erudition in classical mythology, folklore, history, travelers' tales, English manners and morals. He insisted that a masque be more than a spectacle in revelry; he required that it have poetic form, allegorical continuity, and moral edification. He often expressed in his masques not only grace and gaiety, which are found in abundance, but also social criticism and ethical concepts.

Jonson also introduced the anti-masque, a coarse and grotesque dramatization employed as a sharp contrast or "foil" to the dignified, more solemn spectacle. In *The Masque of Queens* (perf. 1609), for example, twelve hags sing and cavort grotesquely prior to the introduction of the twelve beautiful and stately queens in the House of Fame. Like all masques, Jonson's are thin in characterization, but he did strengthen the dramatic aspects of the genre by introducing classical character types and plot situations, chiefly derived from the comedies of Aristophanes. In addition to *The Masque of Queens,* Jonson's principal masques include *The Masque of Blackness* (perf. 1605); *The Hue and Cry after Cupid* (perf. 1608); *The Golden Age Restored* (perf. 1616); *Vision of Delight* (perf. 1617); THE GYPSIES METAMORPHOSED (perf. 1621); and *Love's Triumph Through Callipolis* (perf. 1631).

The masque is a semi-dramatic genre that blends into such other festivities as pageants, inauguration shows, progresses, and pastoral dramas. Milton's COMUS, for example, although originally described as a masque, is now generally considered to be a pastoral drama, as are Jonson's *The Sad Shepherd* (1641), Fletcher's *The Faithful Shepherdess* (c. 1610), and Thomas Randolph's *Amyntas* (1638). The masque ended as a form of court entertainment with the Civil War in 1642 and was not revived during the Restoration.

The origins of the masque in ritual and folklore and its continental development are described by Enid Welsford, *The Court Masque* (1927). A standard bibliography is by W. W. Greg, *A List of Masques, Pageants, etc.* (1902). See also Percy Simpson and C. F. Bell, *Designs by Inigo Jones for Masques and Plays at Court* (1924), and Allardyce Nicoll, *Stuart Masques and the Renaissance Stage* (1938). A standard reference work is E. K. Chambers, *The Elizabethan Stage,* 4 vols., (1923), I.

Masque of the Inner Temple and Gray's Inn, The. See BEAUMONT, FRANCIS.

Massinger, Philip (1583-1640). Dramatist. Massinger's father was a graduate of Oxford, a member of Parliament, and a trusted servant of Henry Herbert, second earl of Pembroke and brother-in-law of Sir Philip Sidney (after whom Massinger may have been named). Further connections with the Pembroke family are suggested by Massinger's birthplace, Salisbury, which is only a few miles from Pembroke's family residence, Wilton House, and by the numerous poems and dedications to plays Massinger later addressed to the Pembrokes. Massinger was educated at Oxford, which he left when his father died in 1606, and came to London as a debt-harassed collaborator in Philip Henslowe's stable of playwrights.

The first play to appear with Massinger's name on the title page was a tragedy, *The Virgin Martyr* (1622), in collaboration with Thomas Dekker, but Massinger had been writing plays for several years before this time, most of them in partnership with John Fletcher and Nathan Field. Some scholars have argued that it was Massinger, not Fletcher, who collaborated with Shakespeare in writing *Two Noble Kinsmen* and *Henry VIII.* In all probability, however, Massinger was only a disciple of Shakespeare rather than a collaborator; Shakespearean echoes occur frequently in Massinger's plays, especially in the first extant play known to be written by him alone, *The Duke of Milan* (wr. c. 1621, pr. 1623), which parallels *Othello* in situation and language. By this time Massinger was writing plays for both the King's Men and Lady Elizabeth's. The latter company performed his first notable production, THE BONDMAN (1624), published with a tribute to Philip Herbert, earl of Montgomery (one of the two men to whom Shakespeare's 1623 Folio was dedicated). Like several of Massinger's plays, *The Bondman* contains controversial political references, in this case satire aimed at an implacable enemy of the Pembrokes and favorite of James I, George Villiers, duke of Buckingham, for his neglect of the English fleet and his disastrous military adventures.

Only Thomas Middleton, whose allegorical A GAME AT CHESS caused an international incident, rivals Massinger in the audacity with which he represented controversial political and religious opinions on the stage. At a time when anti-Catholicism was an approved, almost omnipresent bias, Massinger's *Virgin Martyr* is sympathetic to Catholicism, and his *Renegado* (1630) depicts a Jesuit as the most virtuous character in the play. According to the office book of Sir Henry Herbert, master of the revels, Charles I read Massinger's *The King and the Subject,* a lost play, and deleted at least one passage with the note "This is too insolent, and to be changed." When still another of Massinger's plays, *Believe As You List* (wr. c. 1630, pr. 1849), was denied a license because the government feared offending Spain, Massinger changed the scene from modern Portugal and Spain to ancient Asia and Rome; but his thinly veiled allegory was understood by his audience if not by the unsuspecting censor. Under the guise of the mythical Asiatic king Antiochus, who is cruelly persecuted by the Romans, Massinger portrays Charles I's unfortunate brother-in-law Frederick V, elector palatine and titular king of Bohemia, who is helped in his hour of need by Queen Henrietta Maria, deserted by Charles I, and viciously conspired against by the Spanish ambassador and his English allies at court. (Massinger's allegory was first unraveled by S. R. Gardiner in "The Political Element in Massinger," *Transactions of the New Shakespeare Society* [1875-76]), Massinger returned to this dangerous game of attacking the government's policies toward Frederick in a later play, THE MAID OF HONOUR (1632), which in addition to its political implications, also suggests Massinger's unorthodox religious sympathies in his romanticization of the heroine Camiola's decision to enter a Catholic nunnery.

Although Massinger considered his bleak tragedy THE ROMAN ACTOR (1629) "the most perfect birth of my Minerva," none of his three extant tragedies equals his comedies in vivid characterization, energetic dialogue, and incisive wit. These qualities are most evident in A NEW WAY TO PAY OLD DEBTS (wr. c. 1622, pr. 1633) and *The City Madam* (wr. c. 1632, pr. 1658). The first is a brilliant comedy of manners that modernizes Middleton's A TRICK TO CATCH THE OLD ONE, written twenty years before. Characteristically, Massinger found his story in the intrigues and scandals of his times. His extortionist villain Sir Giles Overreach is patterned after the actual figure of Sir Giles Mompesson (1584-1651), an infamous usurer and protégé of Massinger's archenemy Buckingham, with perhaps some additional hints from Shakespeare's *Merchant of Venice.* Yet Massinger's monstrous Sir Giles bears as little resemblance in his tactics and life style to Shylock as Chaucer's Pardoner to Dickens' cunning old Tulkinghorn, for Massinger's clever charlatan plies his tyranny behind a phalanx of deeds, writs, subpoenas, lawyers, and corrupt judges. Equally updated is Massinger's hero Wellborn, a high-spirited rake and genial wastrel who served as the prototype for virile young Restoration sophisticates like Charles Surface in Sheridan's *School for Scandal.*

Massinger's other great comedy, *The City Madam,* is also based on an Elizabethan comedy, Chapman, Jonson, and Marston's EASTWARD HO! Massinger tones down some of the early comedy and adds to the *dramatis personae* the hypocritical Luke Frugal, a villain as monstrous in his own right as was Sir Giles Overreach in *A New Way.* Like Overreach, Luke is paradoxically crafty and obtuse, a schemer hoist by his own petard when he betrays the wife and daughters entrusted to his care by his equally deceptive but benevolent brother. In both *A New Way* and *The City Madam* Massinger develops villains of outrageous boldness and candor, then exults in the vindictive ritual of "stripping the Machiavel." *The City Madam* was revived by the great actor Edmund Kean under the title *Riches* in 1817.

In addition to these satiric social comedies, Massinger's best efforts were in romantic tragicomedies patterned after the examples of Fletcher. In collaboration with Fletcher he wrote BEGGAR'S BUSH (perf. 1622) and BARNAVELT (perf. 1619). His own THE GREAT DUKE OF FLORENCE (perf. 1627) illustrates Massinger's effectiveness in presenting a plot of amorous intrigues, quick turns of action, and sudden, unexpected revelations. Massinger was a master of plot design, and he could manage consistently coherent if not memorably lyrical dialogue. In stagecraft he was, with John Ford and James Shirley, one of the last genuinely gifted dramatists to appear before the closing of the theaters. His plays enjoyed a brief vogue at the court of Charles I, although in several of his prefaces he complains bitterly of the ignorance and indifference of his audience. His reputation improved in 1703 with the popularity of Nicholas Rowe's tragedy *The Fair Penitent,* which was based on Massinger's THE FATAL DOWRY (possibly in collaboration with Nathan Field). At the beginning of the nineteenth century the romantic poets made Massinger's name famous with their praise of *A New Way to Pay Old Debts.*

The Poems was edited by Donald S. Lawless (1968). An edition of the complete plays was edited in 1805 by William Gifford and reprinted by F. Cunningham, 4 vols. (1871). Although there is no modern collected edition, most of the individual plays have been thoroughly edited, and these are listed in S.A. Tannenbaum's Concise Bibliography (1938) and its supplement, "Philip Massinger (1937-65)," ed. C. A. Pennel and W. P. Williams in *Elizabethan Bibliographies Supplements,* VIII (1968). There is an excellent critical and biographical study by T. A. Dunn, *Philip Massinger: The Man and the Playwright* (1957). See also Henri J. Makkink, *Philip Massinger and John Fletcher: A Comparison* (1966) and Donald S. Lawless, *Philip Massinger and His Associates* (1967).

Matilda. See DRAYTON, MICHAEL.

Measure for Measure. A comedy by William SHAKESPEARE, written in 1604-05 and first printed in the 1623 Folio. The chief source is George Whetstone's two-part play PROMOS AND CASSANDRA (1578), which was based on Giraldi Cinthio's collection of tales, *Hecatomithi* (1565).

In order to avoid enforcing long-neglected laws against unchastity, Vincentio, the duke of Vienna, delegates all authority to his minter Angelo and apparently departs on the pretext of urgent business in Poland. In fact, however, he disguises himself as a friar and remains in Vienna to observe how Angelo will perform the office. Angelo, a rigorous moralist and ruthlessly literal judge, forthwith closes all brothels and condemns young Claudio to death for making Juliet pregnant. Although the lovers had entered into a "hand-clasp" marriage, it was not as yet solemnized in church because of a delayed dowry. As Claudio is led to prison to await execution, he sends his friend Lucio to ask Isabella, Claudio's sister and a novice in a nunnery, to intercede with Angelo.

Isabella's pleas for mercy do not move Angelo, but her beauty and virtue so inflame his lust that on her second visit he proposes that he will spare her brother in exchange for her virginity. When Isabella indignantly informs her brother of Angelo's offer, Claudio at first endorses her reaction, but then, faced with imminent death, begs that she accept the terms, whereupon Isabella attacks him as a coward and angrily departs. Meanwhile the duke learns of Angelo's duplicity, and in his disguise as a friar works to save Claudio. He persuades Mariana, formerly betrothed to Angelo and then jilted, to trick Angelo by going to bed with him as a substitute for Isabella. When Angelo, thus deceived into believing he has seduced Isabella, treacherously orders Claudio's execution nevertheless, the prison provost disobeys and sends Angelo another prisoner's head. The duke reappears in his own person, hears the appeals for justice from Isabella and Mariana, and when Angelo denies guilt, confronts him with the truth. Angelo confesses and repents; both Mariana and Isabella forgive him and plead movingly on his behalf. The play concludes with the duke taking Isabella in marriage and pardoning Angelo on condition he wed Mariana.

Criticism of the play has centered on three aspects: the legality of the "hand-clasp" marriage of Claudio and Juliet, the "bed trick" by which Mariana is substituted for Isabella, and the strange character of Duke Vincentio. Whether the hand-clasp betrothal was entirely acceptable to an Elizabethan audience is open to some dispute, but certainly such arrangements, although on the decline after the Middle Ages, were generally considered legal and binding. As for the bed trick, it is often considered coarse and unseemly; because of it, Coleridge condemned the play as "degrading to the character of woman." Thus much of the controversy stemming from *Measure for Measure* pertains to conventions—social conventions in the hand-clasp marriage, and dramatic conventions in the bed trick. To the latter can be added the arbitrary matings at the conclusion of the play when the duke unexpectedly takes Isabella to wife, forces Angelo to wed Mariana, and commands the clownish Lucio to wed his bawd. Unmotivated and unjustified as these pairings may strike a modern audience, they were totally consistent with the conventions of Elizabethan comedy. Perhaps one of the chief difficulties of the play is that Shakespeare combined these and so many other romantic conventions—disguises, quick turns of plot, distressed virgins, repentant would-be seducers—with starkly realistic scenes and complex characterizations.

A difficult moral problem is raised by the duke, who delegates authority to Angelo to deflect any criticism of harsh law enforcement away from himself. He has been described as the "duke of dark corners" who works elaborate stratagems behind the scenes: arranging that the onus of prosecutor will fall on Angelo; disguising himself as a holy friar; conceiving of the bed trick with Mariana, and trapping Angelo into a confession of guilt. Like Prospero in *The Tempest,* he virtually directs the action from inside the play; moreover, it can be brought to a resolution any time he chooses to reveal his identity. Hence many of the most powerful scenes, such as the emotional confrontation between Claudio and Isabella in Act III, Scene 1, and Claudio's long speech on the horrors of death in the same scene, are melodramatic and theatrical rather than genuinely poignant. Yet the dramatic omnipotence of the duke renders the action of the play ritualistic and points up its allegorical significance. It may be cruel for the duke to continue to deceive Isabella into believing her brother is dead, but without his deceptive manipulation and her suffering she could not have matured sufficiently to forgive Angelo.

As in *The Tempest,* the characters alter their moral perspectives through ordeal, and society is transformed by the consequent changes, not the least of which occurs in the duke himself, who qualifies justice with mercy. As the title of the play suggests, the old law of *lex talionis* is rejected in favor of a new order set forth in the Gospel of Matthew: "Judge not, that ye be not judged. For with what measure ye mete, it shall be measured to you again."

Most critics group *Measure for Measure* with *All's Well That Ends Well* and *Troilus and Cressida* as a "problem play," one that deals with sexual problems rather than the usual romantic love entanglements, mixes comedy with satiric and tragic elements, and conveys a realistic and somewhat abrasive tone. From one perspective, *Measure for Measure* is a tragicomedy, a play with all the imminent perils and moral concerns of tragedy but that ends happily; from another, it is a satire, with many of the serious moral concerns of Jonson's comedies.

The standard edition is the new Arden Shakespeare, ed. J. W. Lever (1965). The source of the play, Whetstone's *Promos and Cassandra,* is reprinted and discussed in Geoffrey Bullough, *Narrative and Dramatic Sources of Shakespeare,* 7 vols. (1972), II. For critical discussion, see W. W. Lawrence, *Shakespeare's Problem Comedies* (1931); E. M. W. Tillyard, *Shakespeare's Problem Plays* (1949); Ernest Schanzer, *The Problem Plays of Shakespeare* (1963); William B. Bache, *Measure for Measure as Dialectical Art* (1969); Jonathan R. Price, "*Measure for Measure* and the Critics: Towards a New Approach," *SQ,* XX (1969); and Herbert Weil, Jr., "Form and Contexts in *Measure for Measure,*" *Crit Q.* XII (1970). See also *Twentieth Century Interpretations of Measure for Measure: A Collection of Critical Essays,* ed. George L. Geckle (1970).

Medwall, Henry (fl. 1486). For comment on his *Fulgens and Lucrece,* see INTERLUDE.

Menaphon. See GREENE, ROBERT; NASHE, THOMAS.

Merchant of Venice, The. A comedy by William SHAKESPEARE. Written around 1596-97, it was first printed in 1600. For the story of the choice of caskets, Shakespeare made considerable innovations on a *novelle* in *Il pecorone* ("The Simpleton"), a collection of tales written around 1378 by a minor Italian writer, Ser Giovanni Fiorentino. The story is also told in John Gower's *Confessio Amantis* (1390), Boccaccio's *Decameron* (1348-58), and the anonymous *Gesta Romanorum* (1472), another compilation of tales. As for the story of Shylock's pound of flesh, Shakespeare may have read it in any number of versions, in an anonymous ballad, "The Cruelty of Geruntus," written before 1590; or in *The Orator* (1596), a collection of orations which includes "Of a Jew, who would for his debt have a pound of the flesh of a Christian," a work translated into English, perhaps by Anthony Munday, from *Les histoires tragiques* (1596), a French work of doubtful authorship. There is also a nonextant play, "The Venesyon Comodye," so spelled by Philip Henslowe in his diary, which may have been one source for Shakespeare's play. An occasion, if not a source, may have been the execution for treason of Roderigo Lopez, a Jewish-Portuguese doctor accused of conspiracy to assassinate both Queen Elizabeth and Antonio Pérez, pretender to the throne of Portugal. The wave of anti-Semitism following Lopez' execution may have inspired not only a revival of

Marlowe's *Jew of Malta,* played many times by the Lord Admiral's Men in 1594, but the popularity (if not the writing) of Shakespeare's play as well.

In Venice the impoverished Bassanio borrows three thousand ducats from his merchant friend Antonio in order to court Portia, a rich heiress in Belmont. With several of his ships about to return, but no cash in hand, Antonio borrows the sum from the usurer Shylock, who requires a "merry bond" by which Antonio must put up a pound of flesh if the money is not repaid on the day it falls due. In Belmont, Bassanio discovers that Portia's father left a will stipulating that she can marry only the suitor who selects her portrait concealed in one of three caskets. Among these caskets of gold, silver, and lead, Bassanio makes the right choice of lead and wins the lady for his wife, after which his friend Gratiano is betrothed to Portia's maid Nerissa.

The joy of the lovers is interrupted by news from Venice that Antonio's ships are lost and that the bitter Shylock, long abused by Antonio, now demands his pound of flesh. Unknown to their husbands, Portia appears at Antonio's trial disguised as a distinguished advocate and Nerissa as her legal clerk. When Portia's appeal to Shylock for mercy fails to soften his heart, she acknowledges the necessity of the payment but shrewdly requires, upon penalty of death, that Shylock exact no more nor less than one pound of flesh. Moreover, he must not spill a single drop of blood, for the bond provides for payment only of flesh. Baffled, Shylock relinquishes his claim against Antonio, and although the duke of Venice grants Shylock his life, he orders him to forfeit half his wealth to Antonio and half to the state, whereupon Antonio surrenders his claim to Shylock's wealth on condition the Jew turn Christian and give his property over to his daughter, Jessica, who was disinherited for eloping with a Christian. Still disguised, Portia and Nerissa require as payment for their legal services Bassanio's and Gratiano's wedding rings, which they had promised their wives to keep forever. When the husbands return to Belmont, Portia and Nerissa mildly rebuke them for surrendering the rings and reveal their true roles in Antonio's trial. As the play ends, Antonio learns of the safe arrival of his ships.

The Merchant of Venice is in some ways one of the most thoughtful and philosophical of Shakespeare's comedies. Its theme is essentially the same as that of MEASURE FOR MEASURE and THE TEMPEST, the opposition of mercy and justice, an idea Shakespeare articulates with quiet irony by almost systematically paralleling the various bonds motivating the characters: Antonio's bond to Shylock, Portia's to her father in the choice of caskets, and that symbolized by the wedding rings in Act V. The ultimate bond is the implicit one invoked by Portia in her appeal to mercy at Antonio's trial and blindly denied by Shylock in his lust for revenge—the bond of man's brotherhood with all men. This theme of love is not pressed on the audience in any didactic manner, and no doubt one of the ironies of the play is that it escapes the Christian characters as much as it does Shylock. At the end the Christians are transformed by love, but in their mindless joy they acknowledge no awareness of its deep cause.

The character of Shylock remains a paramount enigma. If Shakespeare intended him to be a conventional stage Jew and monstrous villain on the order of Barabas in Marlowe's anti-Semitic JEW OF MALTA, he quite obscured any such purpose by making him a sensitive, even poignant figure, as when Shylock exclaims:

> I am a Jew. Hath not a Jew eyes? Hath not a Jew hands, organs, dimensions, senses, affections, passions? Fed with the same food, hurt with the same weapons, subject to the same diseases, healed by the same means, warmed and cooled by the same winter and summer as a Christian is? If you prick us, do we not bleed? If you tickle us, do we not laugh? If you poison us, do we not die? And if you wrong us, shall we not revenge? If we are like you in the rest, we will resemble you in that...
>
> [III, *i,* 60ff.]

Yet this speech concludes ironically with a justification for his hatred and revenge, and not with any acknowledgment that the universality of blood and experience must lead to his own share in humanity, a truth he meanly denies again at Antonio's trial when he frantically intones "My bond! My bond! I will have my bond!" Nevertheless, it cannot be denied that he is sorely tormented by Christians, especially by the haughty Antonio, who spits on his gabardine and receives Shylock's ducats with sneering contempt.

Shakespeare stressed the valid causes of Shylock's hatred and made his motives more substantial than those of any of his other villains; but that he also deplored hatred itself is made evident everywhere in the play. The basic question is whether Shakespeare intended Shylock to be a villain at all, or whether the comedy is an ironically subtle satire at the expense of Christians. On the stage Shylock has appeared in blatantly anti-Semitic performances as a leering, hook-nosed, and fawning travesty of the stage Jew and in tearfully sentimental productions as a tragic hero of King Lear's stature, "more sinned against than sinning," cruelly persecuted by hypocrites and foully betrayed by his daughter.

The best of modern critics have avoided both extremes and studied the play as a whole, as a pattern of ideas in which Shylock is seen in a larger context with other characters such as Antonio, Bassanio, Portia, and even the clown Launcelot Gobbo, and in which Shakespeare's use of language and myth share an emphasis with Shylock's dissonant characterization. From this larger view, the play can be read as expressive of certain values relating to justice and mercy, hate and love, revenge and forgiveness, and all of these in the still larger context of the author's concept of an ailing but always redeemable humanity.

A standard text is the new Arden edition, ed. John Russell Brown (1955). Important criticism includes J. L. Cardoza, *The Contemporary Jew in Elizabethan Drama* (1925); E. E. Stoll, "Shylock, the Complete Villain," *ShakS* (1927); H. B. Walley, "Shakespeare's Portrayal of Shylock," in *Essays in Dramatic Literature* (1935); T. M. Parrott, *Shakespearean Comedy* (1949); J. R. Brown, *Shakespeare and His Comedies* (1957); Hermann Sinsheimer, *Shylock: The History of a Character* (1960); Barbara Lewalski, "Biblical Allusion and Allegory in *The Merchant of Venice*," *SQ*, XIII (1962); J. Dover Wilson, *Shakespeare's Happy Comedies* (1962); Peter G. Phialas, *Shakespeare's Romantic Comedies* (1966); Sigurd Burckhardt, *Shakespearean Meanings* (1968); Marvin Felheim, "*The Merchant of Venice*," *ShakS*, IV (1968); and Sylvan Barnet, "Prodigality and Time in *The Merchant of Venice*," *PMLA*, LXXXVII (1972).

Merry Devil of Edmonton, The. An anonymous comedy which has been attributed, without justification, to Michael Drayton or Shakespeare. It was written around 1603 and printed in 1608. It is often compared with *The Merry Wives of Windsor,* and its popularity is commented on by Jonson in the prologue to *The Devil Is an Ass.* No source is known.

In the induction to the play a Cambridge scholar named Peter Fabel, "the merry devil" of the title, is confronted by the real devil Coreb, with whom Fabel had signed a pact, now expired. Begging for more time, Fabel traps the devil in a necromantic chair in order to gain seven additional years, during which time the magician participates briefly in the action of the play that follows.

In the main story a different kind of pact is involved. Sir Arthur Clare and his wife, who betrothed their daughter Millicent to Raymond Mounchensey two years before in a handclasp marriage, now regret the union and plan to break it off by sending their daughter to a nunnery. After a time Sir Arthur and his wife will then give their daughter in a wealthier match to Frank Jerningham. The old magician Peter Fabel learns of this stratagem and informs Raymond, Frank, and Sir Arthur's son Harry, all of whom join to outfox Sir Arthur and his wife.

Meanwhile at Enfield Chase four merry rogues—a miller of Waltham, a drunken smith of Edmonton, an innkeeper of Waltham, and a carefree vicar of Enfield—gather to plan a poaching raid on the king's deer park. Amid the confused comings and goings of this band, Fabel works a number of tricks, e.g., disguising Raymond as a novice in order to steal Millicent from the nunnery and changing the sign of the Waltham innkeeper's tavern to confuse the parents in pursuit of their eloping children. In the end the run-away lovers are married by the deer-poaching vicar and both families join in celebration.

Whoever wrote *The Merry Devil* was gifted with a talent for inventing hilarious situations and a sure instinct for the taste of his Elizabethan audience. The main romantic plot is patiently developed with subtle implications of social satire, and the tale of Peter Fabel's magic resembles Robert Greene's *Friar Bacon and Friar Bungay.* The love entanglement, with its farcical nocturnal confusions on Enfield Chase, may have influenced certain scenes in *The Merry Wives of Windsor.*

The Merry Devil is in *Shakespeare Apocrypha,* ed. C. F. Tucker Brooke (1908; repr.

1967). Brooke's edition contains informative commentary, as do those by J. M. Manley in Charles M. Gayley's *Representative English Comedies,* 4 vols. (1903-36), II, and W. Amos Abrams (1942).

Merry Wives of Windsor, The. A comedy by William SHAKESPEARE, possibly written in 1600-01 (although 1597 is an equally probable date) and first printed in a corrupt version in 1602. No source is known. According to a doubtful statement by Nicholas Rowe in his "Life of Shakespeare" prefixed to the *Works* (1709), "Queen Elizabeth was so well pleased with that admirable character of Falstaff in the two parts of *Henry IV* that she commanded him [Shakespeare] to continue it for one more play and show him in love." The story passed on by Rowe was first recorded in an epistle to John Dennis' *The Comical Gallant* (1702), a rewriting of *The Merry Wives.*

An impoverished Sir John Falstaff decides to woo the wives of Ford and Page, two gentlemen of Windsor, because the ladies reputedly control their husbands' pursestrings, but Falstaff's disgruntled cronies, Nym and Pistol, notify the husbands of Falstaff's plan. Hence Falstaff's pursuit of the ladies results in farcical humiliations. The ladies hide him in a basket of soiled linen and dump it in a muddy ditch; on another occasion they disguise him as a woman and he is beaten by one of the husbands; finally he is set upon by Pistol, Mistress Quickly, and Mistress Page's daughter Anne disguised as fairies, after which the Fords and Pages reveal to the humiliated knight how completely he has been duped.

The secondary plot concerns the courtship of Anne Page by Doctor Caius, a choleric French physician; Slender, the clownish cousin of Justice Shallow; and a young gentleman named Fenton. Mistress Page favors Doctor Caius, and Master Page the idiotic Slender; but Anne herself prefers Fenton. At the conclusion Anne and Fenton trick their elders and elope.

The Merry Wives has suffered in reputation because Falstaff and his comic crew appear in very weakened condition when compared with their roles in the *Henry IV* plays. Falstaff appears as a witless dupe, and Justice Shallow, Pistol, and Bardolph are merely names without much comic vitality. Still, *The Merry Wives* is an entertaining farce, with several genuinely clever scenes and witty dialogue. Of some interest is the character of Nym, whose bombastic huff-puff may represent a satire on Edward Alleyn, chief actor of the Lord Admiral's Men, rivals of Shakespeare's company; Alleyn was famous for his ranting, turgid style of acting. Nym's preoccupation with the "humours" may be a genial satire on Jonson's currently popular comedies (see JONSON, BEN).

The standard text is the New Cambridge edition, ed. Arthur Quiller Couch and J. Dover Wilson (1921). Important criticism includes Bertrand Evans, *Shakespeare's Comedies* (1960); William Green, *Shakespeare's Merry Wives of Windsor* (1962); J. Dover Wilson, *Shakespeare's Happy Comedies* (1962); John M. Steadman, "Falstaff as Actaeon: A Dramatic Emblem," *SQ,* XIV (1963); and Jeanne Addison Roberts, "The Merry Wives: Suitably Shallow, But Neither Simple Nor Slender," *ShakS,* VI (1970).

Metamorphosis of Ajax, The. See HARINGTON, SIR JOHN.

Metamorphosis of Pygmalion's Image, The...and Certain Satires. A mythological poem and five verse satires written and published in 1598 by John MARSTON. The chief source of *Pygmalion's Image* is Ovid's *Metamorphoses,* with its traditional rendering of the familar myth, and the principal influences such Ovidian epyllia as Marlowe's *Hero and Leander* and Shakespeare's *Venus and Adonis.*

In the mythological poem, Marston follows the main outline of Ovid's tale of Pygmalion, the sculptor king of Cyprus who became so enamored of his statue of a beautiful woman that Venus brought it to life, but as narrator he often resembles what Marlowe's lascivious storyteller in *Hero and Leander* might have been like as an acrid malcontent. Marston dedicated the work to "the World's Mighty Monarch, Good Opinion," and signed it "W.K.," initials he later expanded in other works to "W. Kinsayder," derived from the word "kinsing," meaning a castrated dog.

In the satires almost everyone becomes the target of his acrimonious digressions—city dames, Roman Catholics, idealistic young lovers, Marston's readers, and even Marston himself:

> Censure myself, fore others me deride
> And scoff at me as if I had denied
> Or thought my poem good, when that I see

My lines are froth, my stanzas sapless be.

Unlike Marlowe, Marston cannot seriously entertain a romantic vision to any length; unlike Shakespeare, he cannot seriously believe in the imaginative integrity of his readers. Hence his poem is frequently interrupted by sly, lascivious winks at "gaping" and "wanton" readers who, through Marston's own patient preparation in descriptive hints and erotic episodes, are supposedly panting in expectation of some apocalyptic sexuality which Marston sadistically withholds. Of all the Elizabethan poets who adopted it to serve their respective purposes, Marston's use of Ovidian myth is the most curious: he employs the myth of Pygmalion as a bare frame on which to hang his misanthropy, sour views of women, vendettas against personal enemies like Joseph Hall, and his own bitter self-loathing.

The definitive edition of Marston's poem is in *The Poems,* ed. Arnold Davenport (1961). Gustav Cross analyzes the poem as a consistent satire in "Marston's *Metamorphosis of Pygmalion's Image:* A Mock-Epyllion," *EA,* XIII (1960).

metaphysical poets. A group of seventeenth-century English poets, beginning with John DONNE, who rejected Petrarchan love conventions, formal Elizabethan standards of rhetoric and decorum, and Spenserian narrative and mythological poetry. The poets most often designated as being metaphysical include, besides Donne: George HERBERT, Henry KING, Andrew MARVELL, Richard CRASHAW, John CLEVELAND, Thomas TRAHERNE, Henry VAUGHAN, and Abraham COWLEY. Although Thomas CAREW, Cleveland, and Richard LOVELACE are usually classified as Cavalier poets in the classical tradition of Jonson, some critics claim them for the metaphysicals. Actually, there was no formal "school of Donne," but merely a group of individual poets of different styles whose work reflects Donne's influence in various degrees. Since modern critics disagree in their definitions of "metaphysical" and since there was no formal literary criticism on the subject during the seventeenth century, any definition of the term, or classification of poets under that label, must remain somewhat tentative.

The term was first employed by John Dryden in *Discourse Concerning Satire* (1693) as a derogatory epithet describing Donne's poetry:

> He affects the metaphysics, not only in his satires, but in his amorous verses, where nature only should reign; and perplexes the minds of the fair sex with nice speculations of philosophy, when he should engage their hearts, and entertain them with the softnesses of love. In this (if I may be pardoned for so bold a truth) Mr. Cowley has copied him to a fault . . .

Dryden did not employ the word "metaphysics" to suggest what was philosophical or profound, but rather the academic and pedantic, or, in Elizabethan terms, what "smells too much of the lamp." In a poem on metaphysics, presumably, such arcane "speculations of philosophy" might be appropriate, but not in amorous verse, which Dryden assumed had a diction of its own. Thus Dryden associated metaphysical poetry with a vocabulary that was incongruous, academic or esoteric, and lacking in decorum and appropriateness to the occasion.

Before Dryden, poets too bold in their metaphors were described as using "strong lines"—that is, writing epigrammatic and ingeniously hyperbolic lines that have to be interpreted like riddles. Cleveland and Cowley were the poets most often charged with this pejorative phrase. In Cleveland's elegy on the death of Edward King, which appeared in the same volume with Milton's *Lycidas,* Cleveland writes "strong lines":

> When we have fil'd the rundlets of our eyes,
> We'll issue't forth, and vent such Elegies,
> As that our tears shall seem the Irish seas,
> We floating islands, living Hebrides.

William Drummond of Hawthornden, Jonson's friend, dismissed such "strong lines" as "scholastical quiddities," as did Francis Quarles; and Michael Drayton referred contemptuously to "strong-lined" writers as "chamber poets." Thus Dryden's attack on Donne and Cowley for affecting "the metaphysics" continues this seventeenth-century condemnation of incongruous, self-consciously intellectual and obscure "strong lines."

The metaphysical poets were first christened and analyzed in detail by Samuel Johnson in "The Life of Cowley" in his *Lives of the Poets* (1779). Taking up the discussion where Dryden left off, Jonson observed, "The metaphysical poets were men of learning, and to show their learning was their whole endeavour . . ." Like Dryden, Johnson believed that poetry should be decorous, smooth, and sublime (for Johnson, sublime in the manner of Gray's "Elegy") and that Donne's affecting of "the metaphysics" by writing of love in terms of astrology, astronomy, alchemy, mathematics, Aristotelian logic, and theological subtleties proved his originality but also made him deficient in the "sublime" and the "pathetic." To Johnson, Donne, Cleveland, and Cowley (the only poets he names as being "metaphysical") were wits rather than true poets, for they sacrificed emotional power for the sake of intellectual intensity. "Their courtship was void of fondness," he complains, "and their lamentation of sorrow." Instead of poetic sentiment and sublimity, they demonstrate a wit that was, in Johnson's now famous phrase, "a kind of *discordia concors;* a combination of dissimilar images, or discovery of occult resemblances in things apparently unlike."

It was this same strenuous exercise of wit that Coleridge noted when he wrote:

With Donne, whose Muse on dromedary trots,
Wreathe iron pokers into true-love knots;
Rhyme's sturdy cripple, fancy's maze and clue,
Wit's forge and fire-blast, meaning's press and screw.

For the rest of the romantics, the metaphysical poets had little to offer in an age newly enamored of Spenser's music, colorful narrative, rich mythology, and sensuous apprehension of nature—all qualities absent from the "forge and fire-blast" of the metaphysical poets.

At the beginning of the twentieth century the generally accepted conception of metaphysical poetry had not changed substantially since Johnson's essay. The term still suggested "strong lines," incongruous and far-fetched metaphors, archly difficult and obscure allusions and figures of speech, and strenuous displays of wit at the expense of sentiment and sublimity. Donne was admired or attacked for his eccentric wit, but most of his disciples, especially the once prestigious Cowley, were universally denigrated for what was felt to be their metaphysical excesses. It was generally recognized, also, that metaphysical verse was necessarily sub-lyrical because it was devoid of those qualities held to be most poetical in such Renaissance writers as Sidney, Spenser, Marlowe, Shakespeare, and Milton: appreciation of nature, vivid description, mellifluous and sonorous lines, conventional Petrarchan diction, pastoral idealism, and emotional response to myth and legend. In contrast to these virtues, the metaphysical poets seemed "harsh" and "rough," perversely obscure, intellectual without passion, ignorant of decorum and good taste—somewhat like precocious but incorrigible schoolboys not to be trusted in mature company.

The reputation of the metaphysical poets, and the whole conception of metaphysical poetry in general, changed profoundly after World War I. The seeds of change were planted by Sir Herbert Grierson's great edition of Donne's poems (1912) and his *Metaphysical Lyrics and Poems of the Seventeenth Century* (1921). The postwar generation of poets and critics, inspired by Grierson's eloquent introductions and accurate texts, praised as virtues in Donne what Dryden and Johnson had deplored as vices. Skeptical, suspicious of facile sentiment, in full revolt against Matthew Arnold's dialectics of "high seriousness," and in search of new perspectives and fresh modes of expression, the postwar generation seized upon Donne's poetry as an effective antidote to the whole panoply of Victorian disorders—Wordsworth's philosophical pretensions, Shelley's loose eloquence, Tennyson's complacency, and Browning's moral optimism. In his introduction to *Metaphysical Lyrics and Poems,* Grierson expanded upon the ancient canard of "scholastical quiddities" and defined metaphysical poetry as "a philosophical conception of the universe and the role assigned to the human spirit in the great drama of existence," wrenching Dryden's pejorative term "metaphysics" into an accolade meaning "pervasively philosophical" in the way of Dante and Goethe:

> It lays stress on the right things—the survival, one might say the reaccentuation, of the metaphysical strain . . . the more intellectual, less verbal, character of their wit compared with the conceits of the Elizabethans; the finer psychology of which their conceits are often the expression; their learned imagery; the argumentative, subtle evolution of their lyrics; above all the peculiar blend of passion and thought, feeling and ratiocina-

tion which is their greatest achievement. Passionate thinking is always apt to become metaphysical, probing and investigating the experience from which it takes its rise.

T. S. Eliot elaborated on these speculative distinctions by defining metaphysical poetry in terms of transhistorical sensibilities. Johnson's objection that in Donne, Cleveland, and Cowley "the most heterogeneous ideas are yoked by violence together" is cited by Eliot as a manifestation of their "unified sensibilities," a "fusion of thought and feeling" resulting from a "mechanism of sensibility which could devour any kind of experience." Far from being pedantic "chamber poets" affecting "scholastical quiddities," they were, in Eliot's words, "men who incorporated their erudition into their sensibility; their mode of feeling was directly and freshly altered by their reading and thought." Moreover, not content with limiting the metaphysical poets to Donne, Cleveland, and Cowley, as had Johnson, Eliot thought he heard the same reverberations of "unified sensibilities" in George Chapman, Thomas Middleton, John Webster, Cyril Tourneur, and, of course, Shakespeare. In his essays "The Metaphysical Poets," "Andrew Marvell," and "John Dryden," all written in the 1920s (and reprinted in his *Selected Essays,* 1917-32), Eliot made it clear that by "metaphysical" he meant (perhaps inadvertently) simply good poetry, and Eliot's critical disciples hastened to formulate two criteria to distinguish "good" metaphysical poetry from "bad" romantic verse—a "unified sensibility" that could, in Eliot's words, "devour any kind of experience" and blend "the most heterogeneous ideas," and, in metaphors, achieve "the elaboration... of a figure of speech to the farthest stage to which ingenuity can carry it."

The New Critics of the 1930s and their diligent engineers in the academies, equipped with highly sophisticated tools of literary analysis, began to unearth "metaphysical" sensibilities and metaphors and "telescoping of images" in poets from Chaucer to Robert Frost. Milton, however, was exempt, for Grierson and Eliot had agreed that, in Grierson's words, "Milton was no philosopher. The subtleties of theological definition and inference eluded his rationalistic, practical, though idealistic, mind." Elaborating on this parenthetical condemnation of Milton, Eliot later decreed that Milton was guilty of a "dissociation of sensibilities" because he "thought and felt by fits, unbalanced . . ." In a passage no doubt later repented of in view of what his followers made of it, Eliot converted this judgment into a historical dialectic in which after Donne, Marvell, and Henry King, "the language became more refined, the feeling became more crude," and although Shelley occasionally showed "traces of a struggle toward unification of sensibility," Tennyson and Browning only "ruminated."

Subsequent criticism of the metaphysical poets by scholars such as F.R. Leavis, Marjorie Nicholson, Mario Praz, Rosamond Tuve, and Helen C. White has freed this conception of metaphysical poetry from its singular preoccupation with "sensibilities" and its polarization of Donne and Milton, with the result that the English metaphysical poets are now seen against the background of similar movements and schools in Italy and Spain during the seventeenth century. Donne's radical metaphors and exaggerated conceits are also found in the followers of Giovanni Battista Marino (1569-1625) in Italy and Don Luis de Gongora y Argote (1561-1627), known as Gongora, in Spain, and can be viewed as part of the same baroque movement in the arts. One difficulty with this approach, however, is that the term "baroque" with reference to any of the arts except architecture and sculpture is as ambiguous as "metaphysical."

The thrust of recent inquiry has been toward establishing the unique characteristics of metaphysical poetry. According to one group of critics, metaphysical poetry represents a radicalization or deterioration of the Petrarchan *concetto* ("conceit"), the elaboration of metaphors as far as wit can extend them in order to establish the underlying correspondences of apparently disparate objects and experience—hence an effort to yoke "heterogeneous ideas by violence together." Another theory, expounded by Rosamond Tuve in *Elizabethan and Metaphysical Imagery,* holds that metaphysical poetry stems from the influence of Ramist logic, a view considerably weakened by the fact that many poets were disciples of Peter Ramus (1515-1572), including Milton, but did not write metaphysical poetry. Still another theory, originally put forth by Mario Praz, sees close connections between metaphysical poetry and EMBLEM BOOKS, finding affinities between metaphysical conceits and epigrammatic "strong lines" and the verbal and pictorial riddles of religious hieroglyphs like those in Francis Quarles's *Emblems* (1635). Although this theory has thrown considerable light on some seventeenth-century techniques of verse, it has not proved its claims except with reference to a few metaphysical poets, notably Richard Carshaw.

In conclusion, the definitions of metaphysical poetry set forth by Dryden and Johnson, however biased, now appear to have been substantially accurate. It is a poetry deliberately "deficient in the sublime and the pathetic," as Johnson noted, because it was written in reaction against the outworn language and sentiments of the Petrarchan sonneteers, the unrealities of the classical pastoralists, and the mellifluous simplicity of the Elizabethan song writers. Against these conventional modes the metaphysical poets posed their "strong lines," "unnatural thoughts," "violent fictions," obscure conceits, and their extended and often incongruous metaphors. The best writers of the school, like Donne, Herbert, and Marvell, added to these qualities a capacity for astonishing philosophical speculation, psychological realism, and fusion of thought and feeling. Their unique contribution to English poetry was accurately noted by Thomas Carew in his elegy on Donne as ruler of "the universal monarchy of wit":

The Muses' garden, with pedantic weeds
O'erspread, was purg'd by thee. The lazy seeds
Of servile imitation thrown away
And fresh invention planted...

Most of the criticism referred to in the discussion above is listed in the extensive bibliography by Theodore Spencer and Mark Van Doren, *Studies in Metaphysical Poetry* (1939). Of the vast commentary on the metaphysical poets, only a few important works can be cited here: George Williamson, *The Donne Tradition* (1930); F. R. Leavis, *Revaluation* (1936); Helen C. White, *The Metaphysical Poets* (1936); Rosamond Tuve, *Elizabethan and Metaphysical Imagery* (1947); Ruth Wallerstein, *Studies in Seventeenth Century Poetic* (1950); Louis Martz, *The Poetry of Meditation* (1954); Mario Praz, *The Flaming Heart* (1958); Joseph E. Duncan, *The Revival of Metaphysical Poetry: The History of a Style* (1959); Marjorie Nicolson, *The Breaking of the Circle* (rev. ed. 1960); A. Alvarez, *The School of Donne* (1961); Joan Bennett, *Five Metaphysical Poets* (rev. ed. 1964); and Louis Martz, *The Wit of Love: Donne, Carew, Crashaw, Marvell* (1969).

Michaelmas Term. A comedy by Thomas MIDDLETON, written around 1606 and first printed in 1607. No source is known. The scene is London during Michaelmas term, the autumn session of the law courts when quarterly rents are paid and magistrates elected. Michaelmas Term, his boy, and the "Other Three Terms" all appear as characters in the induction, who salute the follies and "familiar accidents" of the "six weeks whereof Michaelmas Term is lord."

Ephestian Quomodo, a wily and covetous London woolen draper, plots to improve his station in life by cheating young Richard Easy out of his wealth and property. Aiding Quomodo in this conspiracy are Falselight and Shortyard. The latter, disguised as Blastfield, makes the acquaintance of Easy, whom he hopes to debauch. Meanwhile Quomodo attempts to palm off his daughter Susan in marriage to Andrew Lethe, a worthless adventurer whom Quomodo mistakes as a gentleman. Quomodo's beautiful and virtuous wife Thomasine favors, instead, the suit of Master Rearage, a friend of Easy's.

After a series of shifty deals, Quomodo succeeds in possessing Easy's estates in Essex, but the foxy usurer goes too far when he pretends to be dead in order to see how his family will react to their new wealth. Disguised as a beadle at his own funeral, Quomodo hears himself maligned by his own son and sees his wife elope with Richard Easy. Now the trickster finds himself beguiled: if he admits to his pretense of being dead, he will have to explain how he has cheated the honest Easy out of his fortune. He decides to take his case before a magistrate. At the trial that follows, all the chicanery of the characters comes to light. Shortyard and Falselight are condemned to exile and Andrew Lethe is paired to the country girl he jilted. With some reluctance on the lady's part, Quomodo is returned to his wife and required to pay a fine. The daughter Susan is married to Rearage.

Michaelmas Term dramatizes a situation similar to that in Middleton's *A Trick to Catch the Old One*; the strategy of the plot is to catch "wily beguiled," or the avaricious extortioner hoist by his own petard. In the tradition of Jonson's moral satires, it portrays a society of dupes, gulls, sharp lawyers, and usurers, with little concern for polite or genteel people. Appropriately, Middleton has been called "the Hogarth of the seventeenth century" for his vivid portraits of daily life at St. Paul's, Fleet Street, Cheapside, and other London haunts. For its realism and biting satire, *Michaelmas Term* resembles Jonson's *Bartholomew Fair.*

Michaelmas Term was edited by Richard Levin in the Regents Renaissance Drama series (1966). For commentary, see W. D. Dunkel, *The Dramatic Technique of Middleton in His Comedies of London Life* (1925); Baldwin Maxwell, "Middleton's *Michaelmas Term,*" *PQ,* XXII (1943); and Charles S. Hallet, "Middleton's Overreachers and the Ironic Ending," *TSL,* XVI (1971).

Microcosmography (John Earle). See CHARACTERS.

Middleton, Thomas (1580–1627). Dramatist. Little is known of Middleton's personal life, and even the few details previously recorded regarding his birth and education have been corrected by Mark Eccles. Once presumed to have been born in 1570, Middleton is now known to be the "Thomas sonn of will: Middleton" born in London on April 18, 1580. The son of a prosperous bricklayer, Middleton did not attend Gray's Inn, as was generally believed, but entered Queen's College, Oxford, in 1598, at the age of eighteen.

Thus Middleton's early poems, previously viewed as the inept products of an adult, are now read as his somewhat precocious juvenilia. *The Wisdom of Solomon Paraphrased,* a long didactic poem in six-line stanzas, appeared in 1597, when Middleton was only seventeen. This initial work was followed by a rather feeble but interesting poem called *Micro-Cynicon, Six Snarling Satires* (1599) in imitation of Joseph Hall, and is assigned to Middleton solely on the basis of the signature "T.M. Gent." A narrative poem, *The Ghost of Lucrece,* appeared in print in 1600 but may have been written as early as 1596, when Middleton was only sixteen.

Middleton's prolific career as a dramatist began in 1602 when he became attached to the theater manager Philip Henslowe and collaborated with Thomas Dekker, Michael Drayton, and Anthony Munday on a number of plays now lost. He may have shared with Dekker in writing Part I of the highly successful THE HONEST WHORE (1604). Middleton scored his first success with a half-dozen sophisticated London comedies of manners for the children's companies from 1602 to 1608: *The Phoenix; The Family of Love; A Mad World, My Masters;* MICHAELMAS TERM; *Your Five Gallants;* and A TRICK TO CATCH THE OLD ONE. After the decline of the boy companies Middleton wrote, for Prince Charles' Company, THE ROARING GIRL in collaboration with Dekker, and *A Fair Quarrel* (wr. c. 1615-17) with William Rowley. The team of Middleton and Rowley became one of the most successful of the Jacobean period. This first period of comedy, which ends with *A Fair Quarrel* and Middleton's first extensive collaboration with Rowley, is characterized by realistic London scenes coupled with far-fetched and surprising turns of events, and by wily characters who outmaneuver cozeners and sharpsters. Although the dialogue, vacillating between verse and prose, is pungent and concrete, suggesting an intimacy with the cant and esoterica of lawyers, gulls, coney-catchers, astrologers, and merchants, it conveys a flat, one-dimensional effect, perhaps because the characters in this first group of comedies are social rather than moral beings, and their conflicts are seen not as a clash of values but as a series of swift-moving skirmishes between wit and knavery.

With the collaboration of Rowley in such plays as *A Fair Quarrel, The World Tossed at Tennis* (a masque wr. 1619-20), THE SPANISH GYPSY (wr. 1623), and THE CHANGELING (wr. 1622), a new element of romantic passion enters Middleton's dramas, as if imagination and genuine feeling had superseded detached observation and calculation. The greatest result of this collaboration was *The Changeling,* a tragedy inspired by the authors' reading of John Reynolds' *The Triumph of God's Revenge Against the Crying and Execrable Sin of... Murder,* published the year before. Most scholars assign the subplot and comic scenes to Rowley, the tragic main story of De Flores and Beatrice-Joanna to Middleton. In the source De Flores is a handsome young gallant, but Middleton ingeniously transforms him into a hideously deformed malcontent totally possessed by a maniacal passion for the beautiful Beatrice, who at first uses the ogre to destroy her lover's rival and later finds herself being used by the monster she employed. With relentless irony Middleton traces the steady erosion of Beatrice's flimsy virtue, until at last she is wholly destroyed by De Flores' corrosive evil.

Some of Middleton's new-found dramatic energy was suggested sometime before *The Changeling* in a loosely woven and discursive but often interesting tragicomedy, *The Witch* (wr. c. 1610-16), written by Middleton alone. Except for his masques, it is Middleton's first attempt at a purely romantic play, a coupling of two stories of intrigue and savage revenge aided by Hecate and her troupe of hags. Two songs of Middleton's witches were inserted into the text of Shakespeare's *Macbeth* in the 1623 Folio, but, as Charles Lamb pointed out in his famous comparison of Shakespeare's and Middleton's witches, few readers would find them similar:

> Hecate in Middleton has a son, a low buffoon: the hags of Shakespeare have neither child of their own, nor seem to be descended from any parent. They are foul anomalies, of whom we know not whence they sprung, nor whether they have beginning or ending. As they are without human passions, so they seem to be without human relations.... The Weird Sisters are serious things. Their presence cannot co-exist with mirth. But, in a lesser degree, the witches of Middleton are fine creations. Their power too is, in some measure, over the mind. They raise jars, jealousies, strifes, "like a thick scurf" over life. [*Specimens of Dramatic Poets* (1808)]

Middleton may have written *The Revenger's Tragedy,* a powerful work generally assigned exclusively to Cyril Tourneur. (See REVENGER'S TRAGEDY.) WOMEN BEWARE WOMEN, a tragedy indisputably Middleton's, was written in 1625-27 and not published until 1657, thirty years after Middleton's death. More concentrated and unified than most of Middleton's plays, this tragedy counterpoints two illicit passions that end in death: the incestuous love of Hippolito for his niece Isabella, and the adulterous relationship of a duke with a clerk's vain and proud wife. To an extent even greater than in *The Changeling, Women Beware Women* is reminiscent of the tense, alienated, and estranged worlds of Webster and Ford, with something of their preoccupation with inexplicable obsessions and all-pervasive moral sickness. Unlike these greater tragedians, Middleton unwisely sacrifices dramatic intensity with several obtrusive scenes of farcical clownery. As always with Middleton, his genius is felt in isolated scenes full of dramatic restraint and sustained irony rather than in the play as a whole. Most critics, like William Hazlitt, praise the beginning of the play and the climactic scenes while condemning the comic subplot and the extravagantly improbable conclusion: "In his *Women Beware Women* there is a rich marrowy vein of internal sentiment, with fine occasional insight into human nature and cool cutting irony of expression. He is lamentably deficient in the plot and dénouement of the story" (Hazlitt, *Lectures on the Dramatic Literature of the Age of Elizabeth* [1820]).

One of Middleton's last plays, A GAME AT CHESS, is a bold allegorical satire attacking the Catholic Church in general, the Spanish-English negotiations for peace, and the abortive expedition of Buckingham and Prince Charles to Spain to arrange a marriage with the Infanta. The King's Men played Middleton's political comedy for nine days to huge audiences at the Globe in August 1624 before the Privy Council imprisoned the author, shut down the theater, and prohibited any further performances. *A Game at Chess* is scandal-mongering anti-Catholicism of the most vicious kind, but it is also an imaginatively conceived, artful mixture of a comedy of ideas and outrageous farce. With *Women Beware Women,* it suggests that Middleton's closing years were characterized by continuous experimentation and growth.

In summary, Hazlitt's criticism of *Women Beware Women* could well serve as an accurate evaluation of Middleton's plays as a whole. He is a master of scenes in which a few sharp, pointed words cut through a character's identity to reveal a "vein of internal sentiment," and although he is spare of metaphors and often even blandly prosaic as a poet, he reveals in almost every play a fine insight into the complexities of character and the many laminations of irony implicit in the situations he ingeniously contrives. Yet none of his plays reveals any sustained control or clear vision, for he frequently surrenders realism to incongruous burlesque or wild improbabilities. At his worst, he resembles Dekker or Heywood, but devoid of their aptitude for song and romance; at his best, he compares favorably with Webster and Ford, but without their artistic coherence and philosophical range.

The standard edition of Middleton's *Works* is still that by A. H. Bullen, 8 vols. (1885-86). There is a biographical and critical study by R. H. Barker (1958). Mark Eccles has established several facts about Middleton's life in "Middleton's Birth and Education", *RES,* VII (1931). The best analysis of the tragedies is by Samuel Schoenbaum, *Middleton's Tragedies: A Critical Study* (1955). S. A. Tannenbaum's Concise Bibliography (1940) is continued in "Thomas Middleton (1939-65)," ed. Dennis Donovan, in *Elizabethan Bibliographies Supplements,* I (1967).

Midsummer Night's Dream, A. A romantic comedy by William SHAKESPEARE, written around 1595-96 and first printed in 1600. The plot is Shakespeare's own, although he borrowed selectively from a number of sources: Chaucer's "The Knight's Tale" in *The Canterbury Tales,* Sir Thomas North's translation of Plutarch's *Lives of the Noble Grecians and Romans* (1579), and Ovid's *Metamorphoses.*

At the court of Theseus in Athens, Egeus complains to the ruler that his daughter Hermia refuses to marry Demetrius and has chosen Lysander instead. Theseus orders Hermia either to obey her father in his choice of Demetrius or enter a nunnery for life. Hermia and Lysander agree to meet in a wood outside Athens in order to escape together. Hermia tells this plan to her friend Helena, who, in love with Demetrius, informs him of the elopement. The first night finds all four lovers spending the night in the fairy-haunted wood.

Also in the wood are Oberon and Titania, king and queen of fairies, who have come to Athens to attend the nuptials of Theseus and his Amazon queen Hippolyta. Oberon and Titania are quarreling over the ownership of a changeling boy whom Titania refuses to give up. To teach her a lesson, Oberon sends his minion Puck to press the juice of a magic flower into Titania's eyes while she sleeps; the potion will cause her to fall in love with the first person she sees when she awakens. Oberon also orders Puck to drop the potion in Demetrius' eyes, but Puck confuses the two lovers and gives the potion to Lysander, who awakens to see Helena and instantly falls in love with her. When the same potion is administered to Demetrius, he too awakens to see Helena, and with identical results. Hence both lovers are violently enamored of the same girl, and both now contemptuously spurn the bewildered Hermia.

Also in the forest are a company of menials who have gone there to rehearse a play, "Pyramus and Thisbe," to be performed in honor of Theseus' wedding. When Titania awakens, it is the most clownish of these tradesmen, Bottom the weaver, with whom she falls in love, in spite of the fact that Bottom wears an ass's head given to him by the mischievous Puck. When Titania agrees to surrender her changeling boy, Oberon ends the confusion. He releases Titania from her enchantment, removes the ass's head from Bottom, and applies a remedy to Lysander so that he will resume his normal affections upon awakening. The play concludes with the betrothal of the lovers (including Demetrius, forever enchanted with Helena), the reconciliation of Oberon and Titania, and a hilarious performance before Theseus and his court of "Pyramus and Thisbe" by Bottom and his fellow tradesmen.

Like *The Tempest, A Midsummer Night's Dream* employs a "river" plot involving three groups of characters who are kept apart until the assembly scene at the end: the "cross-eyed" lovers lost in the woods; Bottom and his Athenian "mechanicals" who rehearse and perform an idiotic play, "Pyramus and Thisbe"; and the fairies Oberon and Titania, who quarrel over possession of a foundling boy. All of these are related in some way with the sentimental romantic love the play genially satirizes, and all are involved in different ways with the wedding festivities of Theseus and Hippolyta.

Only Theseus and Hippolyta are immune to the moon-mad love afflicting both humans and fairies. Hippolyta is an Amazon taken prisoner by Theseus in war, and presumably her marriage is an act of state rather then the result of any heart-stricken passion. Theseus, with a long career of love and war behind him, is a practical rationalist who makes no distinction among lovers, lunatics and poets:

Lovers and madmen have such seething brains,
Such shaping fantasies, that apprehend
More than cool reason ever comprehends.
The lunatic, the lover, and the poet
Are of imagination all compact.

One sees more devils than vast hell can hold,
That is the madman. The lover, all as frantic,
Sees Helen's beauty in a brow of Egypt.
The poet's eye, in a fine frenzy rolling,
Doth glance from heaven to earth, from earth
  to heaven,
And as imagination bodies forth
The forms of things unknown, the poet's pen
Turns them to shapes, and gives to airy nothing
A local habitation and a name. [V, *i,* 4-17]

When taken as a whole, however, *A Midsummer Night's Dream* suggests that neither Theseus' unimaginative practicality nor Bottom's equally unimaginative literalism in the performance of his play adequately discriminates among lovers, lunatics, and poets. Certainly the young lovers in the woods are so lunatic that Oberon's potion makes no essential difference in their behavior. But the keenly discriminating imagination that went into the creation of *A Midsummer Night's Dream* gives the lie to Theseus' gross simplification and points up the vital differences between his own uninspired rationality, the madness of the lovers, and the zany performance by Bottom and his amateur "mechanicals."

The standard text is the New Cambridge edition, ed. Arthur Quiller-Couch and J. Dover Wilson (1924). Important criticism includes John Russell Brown, *Shakespeare and His Comedies* (1957); Ralph A. Olson, "*A Midsummer Night's Dream* and the Meaning of Court Marriage," *ELH,* XXIV (1957); C. L. Barber, *Shakespeare's Festive Comedy* (1959); Bertrand Evans, *Shakespeare's Comedies* (1960); David Young, *Something of Great Constancy* (1966); and Rose A. Zimbardo, "Regeneration and Reconciliation in *A Midsummer Night's Dream,*" *ShakS,* VI (1970).

miles gloriosus. The braggart soldier, a stereotyped character in Greek and Roman comedy and in the Italian COMMEDIA DELL'ARTE. The boastful, ineffectual soldier appears in Terence's *Thraso* and Plautus' *Miles gloriosus* (hence the term). In English drama the type first appeared in the interlude THERSITES (wr. c. 1537) and later in Nicholas Udall's RALPH ROISTER DOISTER, then became a familiar figure. Invariably the *miles gloriosus* is boastful but cowardly, boisterous, swaggering, and parasitical—an easy butt of ridicule and practical jokes. Some famous examples of the type include Captain Bobadil in Jonson's *Everyman in His Humour,* and in Shakespeare's Don Armado de Adriano in *Love's Labour's Lost,* Parolles in *All's Well That Ends Well,* and Ancient Pistol in *Henry V.*

For the origins and development of the *miles gloriosus,* see Daniel C. Boughner, *The Braggart in Renaissance Comedy* (1954).

Milton, John (1608-1674). Poet. The son of John Milton, a wealthy scrivener, musician, and composer, Milton was born in London and educated at St. Paul's School and Christ's College, Cambridge, receiving a B.A. in 1629 and M.A. in 1632. Milton's literary career is usually divided into three periods: the early poems and apprenticeship (1608-42); the prose works and political activity (1642-60); and major works and epics (1660-74).

While still at St. Paul's School, Milton aspired to become England's greatest poet, and the strict scholarly discipline and long hours of reading during these early years may have caused his later blindness. During the Cambridge period he wrote "On the Death of a Fair Infant Dying of a Cough," an elegy on the death of his sister's child that reflects some influence of the METAPHYSICAL POETS. He also completed "At a Vacation Exercise" and some Latin elegies and epigrams, but his first notable poem, written when he was twenty-one, was ON THE MORNING OF CHRIST'S NATIVITY, a polished and stately Christmas ode. Two short poems followed, on the death of one Hobson, a Cambridge University "carrier," or mailman. The predominant influences during these early years were the classical and Italian poets, and Edmund Spenser, whom Milton described in later years as "our sage and serious poet Spenser, whom I dare be known to think a better teacher than Scotus or Aquinas . . ."

After leaving Cambridge Milton resided for five years (1632-37) at his father's house at Horton, where he continued to prepare himself for the office of poet. At Horton he wrote two remarkably smooth and mature poems, L'ALLEGRO and IL PENSEROSO, and, with the composer Henry Lawes, two distinguished masques, ARCADES and COMUS. The latter was performed at Ludlow Castle near Horton in 1634 to celebrate the appointment of the earl of Bridgewater as president of Wales. Toward the end of this first period of apprenticeship, in 1637, Milton wrote LYCIDAS, one of the greatest elegies in the English language. It appeared originally as the last of several poems in memory of a Cambridge classmate of Milton's, Edward King, who drowned in the Irish Sea.

From 1637 to 1639 Milton traveled abroad, chiefly in Italy, where he was kindly received by John Baptista Manso, learned patron of Torquato Tasso, author of the Italian epic *Gerusalemme liberata.* Before departing from Naples, he acknowledged Manso's hospitality with a Latin poem, "Mansus." During his stay in Italy Milton also visited Hugo Grotius and Galileo. According to Milton's later statement, his Italian journey was interrupted by news of political and religious unrest at home, and in 1639 he began the journey northward, stopping at Geneva to stay with the father of Charles Diodati, Milton's best friend while at Cambridge and the recipient of several of his Latin and Italian verses, most notably the great pastoral elegy in Latin, EPITAPHIUM DAMONIS. Sometime in 1639 Milton was back in London as a tutor to his two nephews, Edward and John Philips, and a few other pupils.

In May 1641, Milton published his first prose tract, OF REFORMATION TOUCHING CHURCH DISCIPLINE IN ENGLAND, a vehement attack on episcopacy. An ardent Calvinist, Milton argued against the Anglican bishops on grounds that their authority was established neither by Scripture nor reason. *Of Reformation* was the first of several anti-episcopacy pamphlets, most of them in controversy with Bishop Joseph HALL. When five Presbyterian divines using the pseudonym "Smectymnuus" (i.e., Stephen Marshal, Edmund Calamy, Thomas Young, Matthew Newcomen, and William Spurstow) published a pamphlet attacking the bishops, Milton defended them against Bishop Hall in *Animadversions upon the Remonstrant's Defense Against Smectymnuus* (1641) and *Apology Against a Pamphlet . . . Against Smectymnuus* (1642), the latter of some literary importance for its digressions by Milton on the subject of his own early education and ambitions.

In June 1642, Milton entered a new phase of life with his ill-starred marriage to Mary Powell, a young and vivacious daughter of a Royalist family. The marriage may have been arranged by Milton's father, to whom the Powell family was in debt, and, in view of Milton's presbyterian convictions, intellectual severity, and considerable seniority, the marriage proved anything but compatible. Six weeks after the wedding Milton's wife begged to return to her family until Michaelmas; he agreed, and during the interim the Civil War broke out, separating the two for almost three years. For Milton, who had made chastity and married love cardinal sacraments, the failure of his first marriage was an ironic and cruel blow. Since the church refused to grant divorce except on grounds of adultery, Milton set out to change the divorce laws by writing a series of pamphlets attempting to establish, chiefly on the basis of the Old Testament, the Scriptural justification of divorce on grounds of incompatibility. The divorce tracts, ponderous with Scriptural documentation and scholarly arguments, include THE DOCTRINE AND DISCIPLINE OF DIVORCE (1643), *The Judgment of Martin Bucer Concerning Divorce* (1644), and *Tetrachordon* and *Colasterion* (1645). During this same period he wrote an informal, eight-page pamphlet reflecting his experience as a teacher, OF EDUCATION (1644), which he dedicated to Samuel Hartlib, a prolific writer and translator of one of John Amos Comenius' tracts on educational reform (published by Hartlib as *A Reformation of Schools* in 1642).

The divorce tracts created so much notoriety that they were mentioned in Parliament as a justification for reviving the rigid censorship laws that had been allowed to lapse after the reign of Charles I, and Milton's greatest pamphlet, AREOPAGITICA (1644), is a long and eloquent plea for the liberty of the press, or, more precisely, for the elimination of laws that would censor books prior to their publication.

Mary Powell returned with her impoverished family to live with Milton in 1645, and with the death of his father the next year, he was able to discontinue teaching and live comfortably on his inheritance.

The execution of Charles I in January 1649 created a shock of horror across Europe, and Milton defended the regicides in a pamphlet called THE TENURE OF KINGS AND MAGISTRATES (1649), a work that inspired the authorities to appoint him secretary of Foreign Tongues to the Council of State. Until his total blindness in 1652, Milton worked assiduously in this office, writing pamphlets in defense of Cromwell's government against its foreign and domestic critics. In answer to an emotional work called *Eikon Basilike,* purportedly written by Charles I "in his solitudes and sufferings" on the eve of execution, but actually done by a Royalist sympathizer, John Gauden, Milton wrote EIKONOKLASTES (1649), and in reply to Claude de Saumaise ("Salmasius"), whose *Defensio regia* in 1649 defended Charles I and condemned the regicides, Milton wrote *Pro populo Anglicano defensio* (*Defense of the English People,* 1650) and, later, *Defensio secunda* (*Second Defense,* 1654), the latter of great importance for its autobiographical digressions on Milton's education and literary aspirations.

Mary Powell died in 1652, leaving three daughters, and in 1656 Milton married Katherine Woodcock, possibly mourned in Sonnet XXIII ("Methought I saw my late espoused saint"). She died in 1658. He did not remarry until 1662, to Elizabeth Minshull, who survived him.

The death of Oliver Cromwell created an emergency in government, to which Milton responded with two complementary pamphlets, *A Treatise of Civil Power in Ecclesiastical Causes* (1659), a plea for religious liberty, and *Considerations Touching the Likeliest Means to Remove Hirelings out of the Church* (1659), an argument against official tithing under the new government of Richard Cromwell. On the eve of the restoration of Charles II in 1660, Milton published THE READY AND EASY WAY TO ESTABLISH A FREE COMMONWEALTH, which extols the virtues of parliamentary government and warns against the evils of monarchy. At the Restoration Milton was arrested, briefly imprisoned, and fined, whereupon he retired to a small house in Bunhill Row to devote the rest of his life to the completion of his major works, PARADISE LOST (begun as early as 1642), PARADISE REGAINED, and SAMSON AGONISTES.

Paradise Lost first appeared in ten books in 1667 and was published in twelve books in 1674. *Paradise Regained* and *Samson Agonistes* were printed together in 1671. Milton's last years also yielded his Latin grammar (1669) and *A History of Britain* (1670), a survey of events from legendary times to the Norman Conquest. He also completed a compendium of Peter Ramus' logic (1672), the treatise *Of True Religion, Heresy, Schism, and Toleration* (1673), *Familiar Letters* (1674), and *College Exercises* (1674), this last consisting mainly of Milton's PROLUSIONS, or "oratorical performances" in Latin that throw considerable light on his early poems. His *Brief History of Moscovia* (published posthumously in 1682) is based on accounts of Russia that Milton read in Richard Hakluyt and Samuel Purchas. Milton's most important posthumous work, the Latin treatise DE DOCTRINA CHRISTIANA, was not published until 1825, when it was translated by Bishop Charles R. Sumner. Several critical works such as Arthur Sewell's *A Study in Milton's Christian Doctrine* (1939) and Maurice Kelley's *This Great Argument* (1941) clearly show that *De doctrina Christiana* is not only an explanation of Milton's unique religious beliefs but also an essential clue to *Paradise Lost* and other poems.

Milton died in November 1674, "in a fit of the gout," according to an anonymous early biography (1686), and was buried beside his father in St. Giles', Cripplegate, London.

During his lifetime Milton was more widely known as a publicist than a poet. The divorce tracts had gained some notoriety, and after the Restoration he was both admired and reviled for his anti-prelatical and anti-monarchial prose. His best prose, most notably *Areopagitica,* attracted virtually no public notice. There were, however, some early signs that Milton was to have the "fit audience, though few" he had predicted for himself. Within twenty-five years of his death five biographies were in print—an unprecedented number even for a great statesman, which he was not. These include an anonymous biography of uncertain date, but probably composed around 1686-87 by Milton's early pupil and lifelong friend Cyriack Skinner; John Aubrey's account in Anthony à Wood's *Athenae Oxonienses* (1691); the very full but unreliable *Life of John Milton* (1694) by Edward Philips, Milton's early pupil and son of his sister Anne; a lengthy biographical sketch by John Toland prefixed to his edition of Milton's prose works (1698); and a discussion of Milton's last years and the writing of *Paradise Lost* and *Paradise Regained* in the autobiography of Milton's young Quaker friend Thomas Ellwood (1714). The first edition of *Paradise Lost* sold thirteen hundred copies in a year and a half—a moderately successful record by publishing standards in Milton's time, especially in view of Restoration taste for light humor and satire rather than solemn religious poetry—and the brisk printing of subsequent editions in 1674, 1678, 1688, 1692, and 1695 reflects a steady increase in Milton's readers.

During the Restoration period Milton's reputation can best be described as ambivalent and mixed. Among Royalists he was a despicable ally of the hated regicides, as William Winstanley vehemently declared in his *The Lives of the Most Famous English Poets* (1687): "John Milton was one, whose natural parts might deservedly give him a place amongst the principal of our English poets, having written two Heroic Poems and a Tragedy . . . But his fame is gone out like a Candle in a Snuff, and his Memory will always stink . . . a notorious Traitor, and most impiously and villainously bely'd that blessed Martyr King Charles the First." More cerebral critics like Sir John Dennis, Charles Gildon, and John Dryden were quick to appreciate Milton's genius as a poet. Given a copy of *Paradise Lost,* Dryden was so stunned with its beauty he read all through the night, later exclaiming, "This man cuts us all out, and the ancients too!"

According to John Aubrey, Dryden went to Milton to request permission to adapt the epic to the stage in an opera subsequently entitled *The State of Innocence and the Fall of Man,* which Dryden rendered in heroic couplets: "John Dryden, Esq., Poet Laureate, who very much admires him, went to him to have leave to put his *Paradise Lost* into a drama in rhyme. Mr. Milton received him civilly and told him he would give him leave to tag his verses." In view of Milton's strictures against rime prefaced to *Paradise Lost* (1667 ed.), his permission was magnanimous, and Dryden responded in kind in his preface to the 1677 edition of the opera, where he conceded the superiority of Milton's epic, praising it as "one of the greatest, most noble and most sublime poems, which this age or nation has produced." In his "Essay on Satire" (1693) Dryden continued this line of praise but qualified his adulation with reservations about Milton's avoidance of rhyme and "irregularities" of diction and versification.

The first detailed and extensive evaluation of *Paradise Lost* came in 1712 with eighteen essays by Joseph Addison in *The Spectator,* issued on consecutive Saturdays from January 5 (No. 267) to February 9 (No. 297). In the first six essays Addison dealt with the work as a whole, in the next twelve with one book of the epic in each essay. His primary motive was to measure *Paradise Lost* "by the rules of epic poetry, and see whether it falls short of the *Iliad* or *Aeneid*, in the beauties which are essential to that kind of poetry." After careful analysis of plot ("fable"), characters, sentiments, and language, Addison concluded that, although somewhat flawed in all these, Milton's epic contained "all the greatness of plan, regularity of design, and masterly beauties which we discover in Homer and Vergil."

After Dryden's encomia and *The Spectator* essays Milton's eighteenth-century reputation rose to the airy and insecure heights of "divine," "sublime," "grand," and "noble," with little grounding in tangible critical facts; indeed, when critics descended to diction and imagery, Milton was often found to be "rough," "harsh," or "foreign." Thus Milton's poetry was somewhat vulnerable, although highly regarded, when Samuel Johnson wrote on Milton in the *Rambler* essays in 1751 and his famous essay "The Life of Milton" in *The Lives of the Poets* in 1779. A devout Anglican and monarchist, Dr. Johnson was not inclined to write favorably of a free-thinking unitarian and republican like Milton, and although he conceded some virtues to *L'Allegro* and *Il Penseroso,* and much grandeur to *Paradise Lost,* he found the sonnets barely mediocre, *Comus* "elegant, but tedious," and *Lycidas* a grotesque fraud. Of *Lycidas* he wrote: "Of this poem there is no nature, for there is no truth; there is no art, for there is nothing new. Its form is that of a pastoral, easy, vulgar, and therefore disgusting: whatever images it can supply, are long ago exhausted..." In general, Johnson viewed Milton as a poet of obscure and uncertain conceptions and eccentric language larded with awkward Latinisms—in effect, a bore: "*Paradise Lost* is one of the books which the reader admires and lays down, and forgets to take up again. None ever wished it longer than it is. Its perusal is a duty rather than a pleasure. We read Milton for instruction, retire harassed and overburdened, and look elsewhere for recreation . . ." Johnson's harsh judgment, a mixture of refreshing candor, lucid objectivity, and mean bigotry, became the customary point of departure for "Miltonoclasts" for the next hundred and fifty years.

Among pre-romantics like James Thomson and William Cowper, Milton was a standard around which to rally in their attacks on the Age of Reason, with its circumscriptions on free imagination and inspiration, its confining heroic couplets, its fixation with "rules," its suspicions of religious "enthusiasm," supernaturalism, and transcendence of mechanistic reason and bleak materialism. Blake named one of his prophetic books *Milton* and made engravings of scenes from Milton's poems that represent brilliant new dimensions in literary criticism. Both Blake and Shelley penetrated deep into Milton's theology to discover the most mystical and radical deviations from orthodoxy. "The reason Milton wrote in fetters when he wrote of Angels and God," observed Blake in *The Marriage of Heaven and Hell* (1793), "and at liberty when of Devils and Hell, is because he was a true poet and of the Devil's party without knowing it." In *A Defense of Poetry* (1821), Shelley described Milton's Satan as a moral being "far superior to his God," repeating the "Satanist" interpretations of Dryden and Blake that Satan was the real hero of *Paradise Lost.*

Among other romantics, Coleridge, Wordsworth, Lamb, Hazlitt, and Keats were, to various degrees, all disciples of Milton. In Coleridge's lectures on Milton in 1818 (preserved in *Literary Remains* [1836]), he specifically defended Milton's "exquisitely artificial" language, and in Hazlitt's lectures the same year he compared Milton favorably to Shakespeare and defended Milton's style against Dr. Johnson's criticism. Keats, on the other hand, admired the many "wonders" of *Paradise Lost* but condemned Milton's "foreign idiom" as "a corruption of our language—it [*Paradise Lost*] should be kept as it is unique—a curiosity—a beautiful and grand curiosity" (Letters, September 21, 1819).

In the American colonies Milton's *Paradise Lost* had long vied for popularity with the Bible, William Shakespeare, Alexander Pope, and John Bunyan (in that order of esteem), no doubt because the poem was read as representing the most ardent Christian orthodoxy. The New England Transcendentalists William Ellery Channing and Ralph Waldo Emerson gave Milton criticism in America a secular aspect; both largely ignored Milton's theology and concentrated on characterization, imagery, and prosody. In spite of the publication of Milton's *De doctrina Christiana* in 1825, a similar emphasis on formal aesthetics rather than theology persisted in England as Walter Savage Landor, John Ruskin, and Alfred Tennyson dealt with "Miltonic style"—Latinate diction, convoluted syntax, and massive "organ music"—and generally dismissed Milton's thought as being "Puritan." Thomas Babington Macaulay's strangely vacuous and uniformative essay on Milton, occasioned by the publication of *De doctrina Christiana,* ignores Milton's theology altogether and makes stylistic comparisons with Dante.

The late Victorian period saw a new trend in Milton criticism as attention turned from matters of style to the poet's life. The transition toward biography, no doubt inevitable in view of the Victorians' passionate enthusiasm for that genre, began with the publication of David Masson's massive *The Life of John Milton: Narrated in Connection with the Political, Ecclesiastical and Literary History of His Times* (1859–94), which portrays a fascinating but somewhat repellent Milton, austerely Puritan, profoundly obsessed and demon-driven—an egalitarian in principle but a rigid authoritarian in practice, especially in the home. Masson's work began the search for the "human" Milton, however grotesque—a kind of anodyne for the "divine" and aloof abstraction of an earlier age. Biographies such as Robert Garnett's *The Life of Milton* (1890), Sir Walter Raleigh's *Milton* (1900), S. B. Liljegren's *Studies in Milton* (1919), culminating in Denis Saurat's eminently readable *Milton: Man and Thinker* (1925), produced a composite portrait of a very "human" poet and thinker of innumerable eccentricities and foibles, perhaps blinded by syphilis, perhaps even, as one biographer suggested, an albino, but always, in the words of Rose Macaulay in her *Milton* (1934), a towering, stricken genius who was both "exotic" and "monstrous."

The pinnacle of Milton's reputation, or perhaps the nadir, depending upon the perspective, was reached in 1888 with Matthew Arnold's pontifical declaration: "That Milton, of all our English race, is by his diction and rhythms the one artist of the highest rank in the great style whom we have; this I take as requiring no discussion, this I take as certain." Obviously, such "high seriousness" required hushed reverence or crashing boredom, but little of the wonted "recreation" Dr. Johnson had thought readers missed in Milton.

This concern for biography of the "debunking" variety, combined with the Victorian institutionalizing of Milton as a literary monument mounted on platitudes left Milton dangerously vulnerable to the hard-headed, sophisticated attacks that followed World War I. The assaults began in the 1920s from Ezra Pound, whose legendary conversations on Milton's deficiencies can only be imagined long afterward from Pound's *Make It New* (1934), where he refers to Milton's "asinine bigotry, his beastly hebraism, the coarseness of his mentality." These opinions were more demurely conveyed by T. S. Eliot, Pound's avowed disciple, in *The Sacred Wood* (1920). According to Eliot, after Shakespeare Milton erected a "Chinese wall" behind which English blank verse steadily deteriorated, and in a later essay, "A Note on the Verse of John Milton" (1936), he condemned Milton's use of language—his abstractions, inversions, and auditory imagination totally devoid of visual apprehension—as a "bad influence." The beginning of Eliot's essay is characterized by a certain slyness he often employed when on the subject of Milton's poetry: "While it must be admitted that Milton is a very great poet indeed, it is something of a puzzle to decide in what his greatness consists."

As Eliot himself later noted, most twentieth-century criticism hostile to Milton was abetted by Dr. Johnson's authoritative denunciation of Milton's language, a charge Eliot effectively amplified by attributing to Milton a "dissociation of sensibilities" in contrast to the "fine" integration of thought and feeling represented by John Donne and the metaphysical poets. According to Eliot, in *Paradise Lost* Milton *argues* his sectarian philosophy rather than simultaneously *experiencing* it through mind and nerves and flesh, as did Dante and Donne. His criticism of Milton, coming at a time when Eliot's reputation as a poet was ascending, and carrying with it a stock of dialectical theories and catch phrases, stunned the Miltonists in the academies. Moreover, Eliot was soon joined by an alliance of skillful polemists from Cambridge University and from the "New Critics" in America: Bonamy Dobrée, F. R. Leavis, F. L. Lucas, and Herbert Read, among others. Perhaps the most acerbic detraction of Milton after Pound's came from F. R. Leavis in *Revaluation: The Tradition and Development of English Poetry* (1936), which, echoing Eliot's theory of Milton's "dissociation of sensibilities," contends that Milton "displays a feeling *for* words, rather than a capacity for feeling *through* them," and that Milton's versification is "almost as mechanical as bricklaying." "Milton's dislodgment in the past decade, after his two centuries of predominance," Leavis announced rather complacently, "was effected with remarkably little fuss."

After World War II it became increasingly evident that "Milton's dislodgment" had not really taken place and was not likely to occur. For one thing, the Miltonists proved fully capable of producing critical studies and research of the highest order, and after the war historical Milton scholars such as Douglas Bush, C. S. Lewis, Marjorie Nicolson, Sir Herbert J. C. Grierson, Irene Samuel, E. M. W. Tillyard, and Charles Williams were joined by equally gifted scholars using a variety of critical approaches—Cleanth Brooks, Don Cameron Allen, Northrop Frye, Maurice Kelley, Helen Gardner, B. Rajan, Arnold Stein, and John Steadman. In most instances they wrote enthusiastically of both Donne and Milton and therefore weakened the false antithesis between those two poets created by Eliot, Pound, and Leavis. By 1947, in his lecture on Milton before the British Academy, Eliot considerably softened his criticism of Milton, and his retrenchment in that lecture clearly reflects the influence on his judgment of Lewis, Tillyard, and Williams.

Looking back on this readjustment of Milton criticism after World War II, Douglas Bush recalls the importance of the "historical and interpretative process" in "recovering the whole Milton and the nature and background of his thought" (*John Milton: A Sketch of His Life and Writings* [1964]), a process which involved the broadening of the exclusively "Puritan" or "Spenserian" Milton into the more authentic role of the Christian humanist of the Renaissance who was, by turns, radical and conservative, eclectic and innovative, inspired and methodically rational—indeed, a poet of emotional and intellectual complexity equal to John Donne's. From this contemporary perspective, Milton's reputation, shorn of its denigration and divinity, seems now to rest on grounds more secure than ever.

The standard edition of Milton's works is *The Works of John Milton,* ed. Frank A. Patterson, 18 vols. (1931-38), complete with a helpful index in two volumes (1940). This is the so-called Columbia Milton edition, the work of many editors and translators. It contains the most reliable texts of the poems and prose. Another basic source for a study of Milton's prose is *The Complete Prose Works of John Milton,* ed. D. M. Wolfe, 5 vols. (1953-71), by the Yale University Press, and also the work of numerous hands. There are many excellent shorter editions of the prose and/or poems cited in separate entries of Milton's works.

The fullest biography is David Masson, *The Life of John Milton,* 7 vols. (1859-94), but most readers will prefer the concise and more factual study by William Riley Parker, *Milton, A Biography,* 2 vols. (1968). Volume I contains the life, Volume II the commentary, notes, and index. There are several well-written shorter biographies: Denis Saurat, *Milton: Man and Thinker* (1925; rev. ed., 1944); James Holly Hanford, *John Milton, Englishman* (1944); Kenneth Muir, *John Milton* (1955); Edward C. Wagenknecht, *The Personality of Milton* (1970); and William Hayley, *The Life of Milton* (1796), ed. J. A. Wittreich, Jr. (1970).

James Holly Hanford's *A Milton Handbook* (1926; rev. ed., 1933; 5th ed., 1970) is still an indispensible reference work and general introduction to Milton. There is a concordance to the poems by John Bradshaw (1894).

Critical studies of individual poems and prose works are listed in the separate entries, but some essential commentaries on Milton's work as a whole are cited here: E. M. W. Tillyard, *Milton* (1930), *The Miltonic Setting* (1938), and *Studies in Milton* (1951), all three quite different in slant and emphases; David Daiches, *Milton* (1957); Marjorie Nicolson, *John Milton: A Reader's Guide to His Poetry* (1963); and Douglas Bush, *John Milton: A Sketch of His Life and Writings* (1964). Merritt Y. Hughes is the general editor of a projected comprehensive study of all Milton's poems, *A Variorum Commentary on the Poems of John Milton.* Two volumes have been published: *The Latin and Greek Poems,* ed. Douglas Bush, I (1970), and *The Italian Poems,* ed. J. E. Shaw and A. Bartlett Giamatti, II (1970).

James Holly Hanford has compiled a convenient bibliography of Milton in the Goldentree Bibliographies series (1966). Two bibliographies are standard references: David H. Stevens, *A Reference Guide to Milton from 1800 to the Present Day* (1930), continued by Calvin Huckabay, *John Milton: An Annotated Bibliography, 1929-68* (1969).

Mirror for Magistrates, A. A collection of tragic monologues in verse spoken by characters from English history and legend. It was inspired by John Lydgate's *The Fall of Princes* (1494), which, in turn, was based on Boccaccio's gloomy recital of tragic lives, *De casibus virorum illustrium.* The printer Richard Tottel published an edition of Lydgate's work in 1554, John Wayland another one a year later, and it was the latter who conceived the idea of continuing Lydgate's tales with "the fall of all such as since that time were notable in England, diligently collected out of the chronicles." Wayland's projected edition was prohibited by Mary Tudor's ministers, who apparently feared any such portrayal of recent English history.

At the beginning of Queen Elizabeth's reign, William BALDWIN was granted a license to publish *A Mirror for Magistrates* (1559), written by Baldwin, George Ferrers, and five other authors, and consisting of nineteen monologues by historical personages from the reign of Richard II to that of Edward IV (roughly spanning 1377-1483): Tresilian, Mortimer, Gloucester, Mowbray, Richard II, Owen Glendower, Northumberland, Cambridge, Salisbury, James I of Scotland, Suffolk, Jack Cade, York, Clifford, Worcester, Warwick, Henry VI, Clarence, and Edward IV. After a brief introduction in prose by one of the authors, each of these characters steps forth to lament his misfortunes and follies. The stated purpose of the moralizing, lugubrious monlogues is to warn rulers against tyranny and their subjects against rebellion. In his address to "princes" in this first edition, Baldwin explained the significance of his title: "Here, as in a looking glass, you shall see if any vice be in you, how the like hath been punished in others heretofore; whereby admonished, I trust it will be a good occasion to move to the amendment."

This didactic purpose notwithstanding, the more practical motive of Baldwin's *Mirror* was to render vivid and personal the English chronicles of Edward Hall and Robert Fabyan, Baldwin's chief sources, and to provide a series of tragedies more dramatic, variegated, and relevant to Elizabethans than Lydgate's tedious recitation in 36,000 lines of rhyme royal. Baldwin's experiment was only partially successful. Most of his characters speak in rhyme royal (thought to be appropriate to people of lofty position), although the monologue of Henry VI is in POULTER'S MEASURE, that of Edward IV (probably written long before 1559 by John Skelton) in twelve-line stanzas, and that of Richard II in doggerel ten-line stanzas. Moreover, in spite of the often interesting prose links, wherein the authors discuss characters and events in the chronicles, the plaintive monologues become as monotonous as the lamentations of "fate" and "fortune's wheel" in Chaucer's *The Monk's Tale.*

In Baldwin's second edition (1563) eight new monologues were added, those of Woodville, Hastings, Buckingham, Collingbourne, Richard III, Shore's Wife, Somerset, and the "Blacksmith." Of the many editions of the *Mirror* the 1563 is the most distinguished because of two selections, Thomas CHURCHYARD'S "Shore's Wife" and Thomas SACKVILLE'S "Induction" to "The Complaint of Henry, Duke of Buckingham." Of Jane Shore, the simple merchant's wife who became the mistress of Edward IV and suffered persecution under Richard III, Churchyard makes a pathetic heroine in a poignant domestic tragedy. In his biography of Richard III Sir Thomas More had apologized to his readers for describing such a woman of mean estate, but Churchyard seizes upon Jane Shore's humble station to exploit its sentimental value and makes her a pathetic lamb among ravenous wolves. In a famous couplet Churchyard summarizes her star-crossed career:

They broke the boughs and shak'd the tree by sleight,
And bent the wand that might have grown full straight.

Marlowe's alert eye picked up Churchyard's lines, which he appropriated in *Doctor Faustus* to describe his own tragic character: "Cut is the branch that might have grown full straight."

A more assured and polished contribution to the 1563 edition is Sackville's "Induction," with its description of a winter evening, the poet's encounter with the ghostly abstraction Sorrow, and a descent into Hades. Sackville's verbal ease and concentration of imagery give rhyme royal a renewed vitality:

And sorrowing I to see the summer flowers,
The lively green, the lusty leas forlorn,
The sturdy trees so shattered with the showers,
The fields so fade that flourished so beforn,
It taught me well all earthly things be born
To die the death, for nought long time may last;
The summer's beauty yields to winter's blast.

Sackville's dreary portrayal of winter, nature's blight, prepares the way for equally lugubrious descriptions of medieval specters such as Revenge, Misery, Old Age, Famine, Malady, and Death, and a climactic apostrophe to the greatest of mutability's devastations—fabled Troy:

Not worthy Hector, worthiest of them all,
Her hope, her joy, his force is now for nought;
O Troy, Troy, Troy, there is no boot but bale.
The hugy horse within thy walls is brought:
Thy turrets fall, thy knights, that whilom fought
In arms amid the field, are slain in bed,
Thy gods defiled and all thy honor dead.

Other editions followed in 1571, 1574, 1575, 1578, 1587, and 1610. Those of 1574, 1578, and 1610 contain significant additions. *The First Part of the Mirror for Magistrates* (1574) was so named because it presented lives up to the birth of Christ and hence before Baldwin's time span. John Higgins, who wrote all the material, included such pre-Christian Britons from history and legend as Albanact, Humber, Locrinus, Elstride, Sabrine, Mardan, Malin, Mempricius, Bladud, Cordilia, Forrex, and Porrex. *The Second Part of the Mirror for Magistrates* (1578) by Thomas Blenerhasset continues Higgins' work by covering the period A.D. 44 to 1066 and includes such English notables as Guiderius, Carassus, Helena, Vortiger, Uther Pendragon, Cadwallader, Sigebert, Lady Ebbe, Edric, and Harold.

The edition by Richard Niccols (1610) is the final version adhering to the original purpose of the series. The largest of the *Mirrors,* it includes ninety-one tragedies, over fifty by Higgins and Blenerhasset and the rest by Niccols himself, and covers the period from Albanact to the end of Queen Elizabeth's reign. The concluding selection, "England's Eliza," is a tribute by Niccols to the glories of that last era. Niccols' edition of 1610 appeared after popular enthusiasm for historical monologue and verse "complaint" had subsided. The printer lost money on the publication, and subsequent reissues under different titles in 1619, 1620, and 1621 can be taken as futile efforts to recoup financial losses rather than as a sign of popular interest. None of the editions after Baldwin showed any poetic ability, and only the 1563 edition succeeded in attracting really talented writers.

The best that can be said for the *Mirror* series is that it helped to freeze Elizabethan poetry in late-medieval narrative styles and verse forms, and thus made the thaw of Spenser much more necessary and appreciated than it might have been. Yet the influence of *A Mirror* far outweighs its minuscule aesthetic value. It became an important source of reference for over thirty history plays written before 1600, and its medieval preachments of *contemptus mundi, hubris,* and fate worked a pervasive influence on Elizabethan and Jacobean conceptions of tragedy. Moreover, its popularization of the "complaint," especially in Churchyard's lament of Jane Shore in the 1563 edition, is responsible for such imitations of that genre as Samuel Daniel's *Rosamond,* Shakespeare's *Rape of Lucrece,* and Michael Drayton's historical monologues (Drayton's "Cromwell" was included in Niccols' edition of the *Mirror*). A less direct but no less effective contribution of the *Mirror* was that it inspired popular interest in national history and thus helped pave the way for such superior works as Daniel's *Civil Wars,* Drayton's *Barons' Wars* and *England's Heroical Epistles,* William Warner's *Albion's England,* and perhaps even Shakespeare's history plays.

A Mirror for Magistrates, including the editions of 1559-78 with valuable commentary, has been edited by Lily B. Campbell (1938, repr. 1960). Campbell has also edited *Parts Added to the Mirror for Magistrates by John Higgins and Thomas Blenerhasset* (1946). As commentary, an early work by W. F. Trench, *A Mirror for Magistrates: Its Origin and Influence* (1898), still has some value. For the influence of the *Mirror* on the formulation of Elizabethan tragedy and attitudes toward history, see Campbell, *Tudor Conceptions of History and Tragedy in a Mirror for Magistrates* (1936), and Willard Farnham, *The Medieval Heritage of Elizabethan Tragedy* (1936).

miscellanies, poetical. Collections or anthologies of poems and songs. The most popular single collection of assorted verses by various hands in the sixteenth century was the famous *A Book of Songs and Sonnets* (or Tottel's Miscellany), published by Richard Tottel in 1557. It established a vogue, and by 1600 the proliferation of similar miscellanies numbered nearly twenty. Tottel's Miscellany featured the poems of Thomas Wyatt, Henry Howard, earl of Surrey, and other COURTLY MAKERS. Subsequent miscellanies, varying greatly in quality and quantity, included a wide variety of lyrical types. Variety itself and a fondness for alliterative poems seem to have guided the choice of selections in *A Gorgeous Gallery of Gallant Inventions* (1578), whereas Richard Edwards' *A Paradise of Dainty Devices* (1576) favored religious and didactic verses. *A Handful of Pleasant Delights* (1584) consists mainly of ballads, and *England's Parnassus* (1600), made up chiefly of quotations and lyric fragments, has the appearance of a commonplace book.

Selections in poetical miscellanies were often printed with no more than their authors' initials, and many of these were falsely ascribed and the poems inaccurately reproduced. Occasionally a whole miscellany was attributed to a single major author when, in fact, it was composed by several minor poets. Hence *The Passionate Pilgrim* (1599) was attributed to Shakespeare (no doubt because the publisher realized the sales value of his name), though only a few poems in that miscellany were by him. Similarly, it is impossible to date a poem by its appearance in a miscellany, for several of Tottel's lyrics continued to be published into the seventeenth century side by side with new poems.

Justice Shallow in Shakespeare's *Henry IV,* Part II, proclaimed that he would never be without his "Songs and Sonnets," and his affection for the poetical miscellany was widely shared by his contemporaries. Hence Tottel's Miscellany and its offsprings in the sixteenth century were the lyrical ancestors of the *Oxford Book of Modern Verse* and Louis Untermeyer's numerous anthologies. For consistent quality, three poetical miscellanies stand out among the rest: Tottel's Miscellany, *The Phoenix Nest* (1593), and *England's Helicon* (1600).

Sixteenth- and seventeenth-century miscellanies are listed in *CBEL,* I, and in A. E. Case, *A Bibliography of English Miscellanies, 1521-1750* (1935). Hyder E. Rollins has edited *The Phoenix Nest* (1931; reissued 1959); *England's Helicon,* 2 vols. (1935); and *Tottel's Miscellany, 1557-1587,* 2 vols. (rev. ed. 1965). There is a thorough study by Elizabeth W. Pomeroy, *The Elizabethan Miscellanies: Their Development and Conventions* (1973).

Miseries of Enforced Marriage, The. A comedy by George WILKINS, written and printed in 1607. Like the anonymous A YORKSHIRE TRAGEDY, Wilkins' play is based on an account in John Stowe's *Annals* of one Walter Calverly, executed for murder in 1605. Wilkins' play deals with Calverly's life before the murder and ends happily; *A Yorkshire Tragedy* continues Calverly's ill-fated career after 1604 (see DOMESTIC TRAGEDY).

A rich and ingenuous young orphan of Yorkshire, William Scarborow, proposes marriage to Clare, daughter of Sir John Harcop, but soon afterward William is forced into marriage to Katherine, the niece of his stern guardian Lord Falconbridge. When Clare commits suicide, Scarborow slips into a life of dissipation, falls prey to faithless friends and usurers, neglects wife and children, and feuds with his two brothers, Thomas and John.

These miseries precipitated by Scarborow's enforced marriage are alleviated, after much intrigue, by the Scarborow family's faithful old butler. The brothers are reconciled, and William repents of his dissolute life and accepts responsibility for his wife and children.

The liveliest characters in Wilkins' play are William's parasitical companion, the prodigal Sir Francis Ilford, and Ilford's debauched cohorts, Bartley and Wentloe; William himself is as insipid and docile to "fate" as is his wife Katherine. Except for the aged butler of the Scarborow family, whose resourcefulness brings about a happy ending, the good characters are uniformly flat and ineffectual. In 1677 Aphra Behn made *The Miseries* into a comedy of intrigue entitled *The Town Fop, or Sir Timothy Tawdry.*

The Miseries was edited by J. S. Farmer in the Tudor Facsimile series (1913). For commentary, see Glenn H. Blayney, "Enforcement of Marriage in English Drama (1600-1650)," *PQ,* XXXVIII (1960).

Monsieur D'Olive. A comedy by George CHAPMAN, written about 1604 and first published in 1606. The chief interest is in the subplot and the hilarious fop of the title. Chapman aims his satire at the conduct of foreign embassies and James I's wholesale creation of knighthoods. The scene is an independent principality bordering on France.

Vandome returns from his travels to learn that his good friend Marcellina, wife of Count Vaumont, has been living in exile and total seclusion because Vaumont had falsely accused her of having an affair with Vandome. He also learns that Count St. Anne so grieves for his dead wife, Vandome's sister, that he has refused to bury her. Instead, he has had her body embalmed and spends his days worshiping at her feet and lamenting her loss. When Vandome pleads with Marcellina to abandon her seclusion and return to her husband, she refuses. Marcellina's sister Eurione accompanies Marcellina in retirement from the world, but wearies of the life because, she confides to Vandome, she is secretly in love with St. Anne.

Meanwhile Duke Philip decides to send Monsieur D'Olive, an officious buffoon and self-styled sophisticate, to petition the king of France to have St. Anne's wife buried at once. This conflict is settled when St. Anne, carefully guided into the situation by Vandome, falls in love with Eurione. St. Anne thereupon buries his wife, and D'Olive's mission to France is cancelled. Monsieur D'Olive had so exaggerated his preparations and so passionately engaged himself in the forthcoming mission that some substitute is required for his boundless energies. Hence D'Olive's friends Roderique and Muger forge a letter to D'Olive from Hieronime, a lady of the court, asking him to come disguised to her chamber, and the eager D'Olive quickly assents. Meanwhile Vandome tries to coax Marcellina from her seclusion by telling her that her husband has become a philanderer and is pursuing Hieronime. If Vaumont is caught with the courtesan, states Vandome, he could be penalized with castration or death. To save her husband, Marcellina foresakes her retreat to go to Hieronime's chamber. There D'Olive is hoodwinked by his friends, Marcellina rejoins her husband, and Duke Philip soothes the humbled D'Olive with assurances of further service.

The definitive edition is in *The Plays,* ed.

T. M. Parrott, 2 vols., II: *The Comedies* (1914). For criticism, see Paul V. Kreider, *Elizabethan Comic Character Conventions... of Chapman* (1935), and A. P. Hogan, "Thematic Unity in Chapman's *Monsieur D'Olive*," *SEL*, XI (1971).

Montagu, Walter (1603?-1677). Stuart courtier whose pastoral drama *The Shepherd's Paradise* was written for and performed by Queen Henrietta Maria in 1632. See CAROLINE DRAMA; PASTORAL.

Montaigne, Michel Eyquem de (1533-1592). French philosopher and essayist. John Florio translated his *Essays* into English (1603). See ESSAYS; TRANSLATIONS.

Montemayor, Jorge de (1521?-1561). Portuguese poet whose pastoral romance *Diana enamorada* (pr. Valencia, c. 1550), translated into English from Spanish by Bartholomew Yong as *Diana* (completed 1582, pr. 1598), influenced Barnabe Googe, Spenser, Sidney, Shakespeare, and others. See PASTORAL; TRANSLATIONS.

morality play. A medieval and early Renaissance drama characterized by personified moral abstractions such as Vice and Virtue, cast in an allegorical plot designed to teach a moral lesson. Hence the chief ingredients of the morality play are abstract characterizations (Everyman, Charity, Humility, Pride, etc.), allegory, and didacticism. About thirty morality plays survive, most of them from the fifteenth century. Whereas the medieval miracle and mystery plays dramatize episodes from the Bible or from the lives of saints and martyrs, the moralities are acted sermons portraying the struggle between vices and virtues for the possession of the soul. Some of the best-known moralities include *The Castle of Perseverance* (c. 1415), *Pride of Life* (c. 1420). *Mankind* (c. 1470), and especially *Everyman* (c. 1529).

Morality plays continued to be performed for popular audiences, often by amateur actors from the trade guilds, well into the sixteenth century. John Skelton's *Magnificence* (wr. c. 1520) portrays a well-meaning prince rescued from Vice by Charity, Good Hope, Perseverance, and other virtues, and its theme is as much political as religious. Another political innovation on the morality play is John Bale's *King John* (wr. before 1540), in which King John struggles to save Widow England and her blind son Commonalty, who are not rescued from Sedition and Roman Catholicism until the timely intervention of such virtues as Imperial Majesty and Verity. At about this time Sir David Lindsay produced *The Satire of the Three Estates* at the Scottish court of James V. Lindsay's morality portrays Rex Humanitas, a young king, persistently neglecting Good Counsel and Verity (represented as carrying a New Testament translated into English by Protestants) until he is lectured into virtue by Divine Correction. In two parts, *The Satire of the Three Estates* excoriates in the name of the character John the Commonweal the corrupt three estates of clergy, nobility, and merchant class. These later morality plays illustrate a development away from the older, more generalized themes of the medieval moralities toward political and theological propaganda. As this development proceeds into the sixteenth century, the morality play becomes increasingly difficult to distinguish from the INTERLUDE, a brief allegorical play that came into vogue during the reign of Henry VIII.

Morality plays continued to exert influences on the more sophisticated Elizabethan drama long after they had ceased to be regularly performed. They contributed to the pervasive didacticism of later drama, and their character stereotypes, especially those of Vice and Virtue, reappear in the plays of Marlowe, Kyd, Dekker, Jonson, Shakespeare, and others. The morality character Vice, invariably a sportive, clownish wag, reappears for instance in Robert Greene's *Friar Bacon and Friar Bungay* as the servant Miles, who rides the Devil's back, and as Wagner in Marlowe's *Doctor Faustus.* Elsewhere in DOCTOR FAUSTUS old morality influence is felt very directly in the debates between the Good Angel and the Bad Angel and in the Devil's presentation of the seven deadly sins. Some scholars find Shakespeare's delineation of Richard III, Falstaff, and Iago equally influenced by the character Vice in the morality plays. The extent to which an Elizabethan audience was aware of the moralities is implicit in Richard III's description of his own duplicity: "Thus, like the formal vice Iniquity, / I moralize two meanings in one word."

Morality plays are treated extensively by E. N. S. Thompson, "The English Morality Play," *Transactions of the Connecticut Academy of Arts and Sciences,* XIV (1910); A. P. Rossiter,

English Drama from the Early Times to the Tudors (1950); and David M. Bevington, *From Mankind to Marlowe* (1962). For the influence of moralities on Shakespeare's *Othello,* see Bernard Spivack, *Shakespeare and the Allegory of Evil* (1958).

More, Sir Thomas (1478-1535). Scholar, statesman, and Roman Catholic martyr and saint. More was raised in the household of John Cardinal Morton, archbishop of Canterbury, and went to Oxford to become the pupil of the early humanists John Colet, William Grocyn, and Thomas Linacre. In obedience to the wishes of his father, a justice of the court of King's Bench, More studied law at the New Inn, London (1494), and at Lincoln's Inn (1496). From 1499 to 1503 he was indecisive about a career, possibly aspiring to the priesthood and the rigorous ascetic habits of a Carthusian monk. Finally choosing an active life, he became a member of Parliament in 1504 and a year later married Jane Colt, who bore him three daughters and a son.

More's estate at Chelsea became a gathering place for a group of humanist scholars, including the great Erasmus. It was at More's suggestion that Erasmus wrote his satire *Encomium moriae* ("Praise of Folly," with a pun on More's name). In 1509 More became a bencher of Lincoln's Inn, in 1510 under-sheriff of London. An anonymous manuscript fragment, THE BOOK OF SIR THOMAS MORE, passages of which have been attributed to Shakespeare, dramatizes this portion of More's career and describes him in his office of under-sheriff as "the best friend the poor ever had" (see CHRONICLE PLAY).

Shortly after the death of Jane Colt in 1511, More married Alice Middleton, a widow with one daughter. At this time More was greatly in favor with Henry VIII, who admired More's scholarly attainments and personal integrity. It was while on a diplomatic mission for the king in 1515 that More began his literary masterpiece UTOPIA. As More's friendship with Henry increased so did his several offices: privy councilor (1518), knighthood (1521), subtreasurer (1521), speaker of the House of Commons (1523), and chancellor of the duchy of Lancaster (1525). On behalf of the king, More wrote an attack on heretics that caused the pope to bestow on Henry the accolade "Defender of the Faith," a title still retained by English monarchs. During these years More was a prolific writer of Latin treatises attacking Anabaptists, Lutherans, and other reformed sects; many of these are coarse, scurrilous, and personally abusive—a style customary among religious polemicists of the time.

When Cardinal Wolsey failed to secure Henry's divorce from Katharine of Aragon so that he might marry Anne Boleyn, the king appointed More lord chancellor to succeed Wolsey. More at first refused the office but was at last persuaded to accept. As Katharine's case became increasingly pressing, More's situation as chancellor grew more difficult. He accepted the king's temporal authority but refused to acknowledge his spiritual supremacy over the claims of Rome. With the Act of Supremacy (1534), which acclaimed the king supreme head of the English church, More refused to sign the oath and was committed to the Tower (April 17, 1534). In prison he wrote his poignant apologia, *A Dialogue of Comfort Against Tribulation.* Despite strong pressure to accept the oath, More remained steadfast and was at last condemned to die. On July 7, 1535, still affirming his political loyalty to the king but insisting on the spiritual hegemony of the Roman church, he went to his death with great courage and dignity. In recognition of his loyalty to the church, Pope Pius XI canonized More in 1935.

In addition to his voluminous writings in Latin, most of which pertain to religious controversy, More's chief works include a translation of Pico della Mirandello's brief *Life of John Picus, Earl of Mirandola* (1510); *Utopia* (1518), written in Latin and translated into English in 1551 by Ralph Robinson (see UTOPIAN FICTION); and THE HISTORY OF RICHARD THE THIRD (written in about 1513–14), a vivid, dramatic portrait probably based on a Latin work by Cardinal Morton (see CHRONICLE PLAY). It is recognized as the first modern historical narrative in English and influenced Shakespeare's *Richard III.* Other works in English include *Supplication of Souls* (1530), a defense of the clergy against Simon Fish's attacks in *A Supplication for the Beggars,* and *An Apology of Sir Thomas More* (1533), a defense of his own religious beliefs and attitudes. *The Jests of Thomas More,* a collection of jokes reprinted throughout the sixteenth century, is not by More but reflects his reputation as a wit and humorist (see JEST-

BOOKS). Two important biographies of More were written by his contemporaries: the first a brilliant work written about 1558 by his son-in-law William Roper (1496-1578), *The Life of More* (wr. c. 1558; pr. 1626); and a lesser book by Nicholas Harpsfield, of uncertain date of composition and not printed in its entirety until 1932.

The standard edition of More's writings is the Yale edition of *The Complete Works,* ed. Edward Surtz, J. H. Hexter, et. al., 5 vols. (1963-69). See also *The Correspondence of Sir Thomas More,* ed. Elizabeth F. Rogers (1947), and *Thomas More's Prayer Book,* ed. Louis L. Martz and Richard S. Sylvester (1969). Although partisan, R. W. Chambers' *Thomas More* (1935) is still the best biography. Important critical studies include Enid Routh, *Sir Thomas More and His Friends* (1934); W. E. Campbell, *Erasmus, Tyndale, and More* (1949); and Edward Surtz, S. J., *The Praise of Wisdom* (1957).

Mother Hubberd's Tale, or Prosopopoia. A satiric verse allegory by Edmund SPENSER, first published in *Complaints* in 1591. Its verse form is rhymed iambic pentameters, its chief source the popular French stories of Reynard the Fox translated and published by William Caxton in the late fifteenth century. The object of Spenser's satire was the corruption of the clergy and the venality of false courtiers.

In the first part of the poem, the Fox and the Ape disguise themselves as beggars and set out to seek their fortune. Their first victim is a simple farmer who listens sympathetically to the Ape's woeful description of how he came by his soldier's wounds. The gullible farmer hires them to guard his sheep, and the wily pair ruin their benefactor and then escape.

Tired of begging, the Fox and the Ape next disguise themselves as learned clergymen. On the advice of a corrupt priest, the Fox poses as a minister and the Ape as his learned clerk. Finally exposed by their ruthlessly exploited parishioners, the two next seek their fortunes at court. The Ape dresses in the latest style and masters some necessary skills, such as fortunetelling, juggling, dancing, and parlor magic. Indeed, the Ape's doggerel verses, aimed only at the seduction of women, and his mastery of silly entertainments instead of the affairs of state make him a seriocomic travesty of the ideal courtier described in Castiglione's *Il Cortegiano* (see THE COURTIER) and later of the virtuous men in Spenser's own *Faerie Queene.* As the Ape plies his false trade, the Fox plays the role of his confidential servant and practices all the kinds of trickery Spenser condemns in Elizabeth's own court—accepting fees in exchange for empty promises of preferment, taking bribes, and bilking honorable men of their wealth.

In the second part, the Ape and the Fox are again discredited, and here Spenser's tale is confined entirely to the bestiary. They discover a Lion asleep in a wood with crown and scepter, which they steal to usurp his throne. The Fox in the tale acts as the Ape's power-behind-the-throne and chief mentor, and many scholars see in this a satirical portrait of Elizabeth's lord treasurer, William Cecil, Lord Burghley. The Fox so ravishes the land with his injustices (including his persecution of poets and scholars) that the Olympian gods interfere to save the kingdom. Jupiter sends Mercury to arouse the sleeping Lion, who puts to flight all flatterers, soundly thrashes the Fox, and cuts off the Ape's ears and tail. The poem concludes purporting to be a mythic explanation of why the ape has no tail to this day.

The standard edition is in *The Works,* ed. Edwin A. Greenlaw, F. M. Padelford, et al., 10 vols. (1932-49), VII. For criticism, see Harold Stein, *Studies in Spenser's Complaints* (1934); Brice Harris, "The Ape in *Mother Hubberd's Tale,*" *HLQ,* IV (1940-41); and William Nelson, *The Poetry of Edmund Spenser* (1963).

Mucedorus. A comedy performed around 1589 and printed anonymously in 1598. It has been falsely attributed to Shakespeare and, with much uncertainty, to Thomas Lodge. Additions made to the play, probably for a court performance, appear in the 1610 edition. The plot and names of characters may owe something to Sir Philip Sidney's *Arcadia.* The burlesque of pastoral romance and the absurd chivalry in *Mucedorus* are a mixture difficult to trace to any one source. Extremely popular but of only moderate dramatic value, the play was performed frequently at the Globe and elsewhere by the King's Men and went through no fewer than fifteen editions between 1598 and the Restoration period.

In the induction, Comedy and Envy engage in debate as to which shall dominate the play. Envy threatens to turn mirth into blood and tears, Comedy maintains it will overcome any such "tragic stuff."

Mucedorus, prince of Valencia, travels to Aragon in the disguise of a shepherd to seek Princess Amadine, whose beauty has become legend. He rescues Amadine from a bear as she and her betrothed, the cowardly Lord Segasto, are walking in the forest. Segasto tries several ways to avenge the humiliation of Mucedorus' rescue of Amadine: he sets a murderer loose on the prince, falsely accuses him of homicide, and finally seeks his banishment. Mucedorus and Amadine agree to meet in the forest and escape Aragon together, but at the rendezvous the princess is carried off by Bremo, an atavistic woodsman, who boorishly forces his affections on her. Mucedorus, in the garb of a shepherd, sets out in search of Amadine.

The king of Valencia, Mucedorus' father, arrives in Aragon in quest of his son, whose best friend, Anselmo, has revealed the prince's whereabouts. Changing his disguise from that of a shepherd to a hermit, Mucedorus is captured by the wild man Bremo, who keeps him prisoner with Amadine. One day Mucedorus kills Bremo with a crab-tree staff and reveals his true identity to Amadine. Lord Segasto appears and pays suit to Amadine, who chooses Mucedorus, and Segasto gallantly relinquishes his claim. The lovers return to court and are pardoned by the king of Aragon. The king of Valencia arrives and identifies his lost son, and the court rejoices in the nuptials of Mucedorus and Amadine.

In the epilogue, Envy threatens to divert these happy events to tragedy, and even to cause trouble for the actors. At the conclusion of the 1610 edition, both Comedy and Envy kneel before James I and ask his indulgence for any inadvertent errors they may have committed in the performance.

Mucedorus served up for popular consumption all the old ingredients of medieval metrical romances like *Guy of Warwick* and *Huon of Bordeaux,* but whoever wrote the play was well versed in Elizabethan taste and stage conditions; he may have been a disciple of the UNIVERSITY WITS assigned to revise an old play for performance at court by the King's Men. In any event, he was a competent versifier and storyteller; the romantic plot of Mucedorus and Amadine is skillfully contrasted to the low-humor farce by Mouse, Segasto's roguish servant, and Bremo, the wild man of the wood who somewhat resembles Caliban in *The Tempest.* In spite of its simple facade, *Mucedorus* is a clever, albeit contrived and artificial, concoction of romantic characters and situations very dear to ordinary Elizabethans.

Mucedorus is in *Shakespeare Apocrypha,* ed. C. F. Tucker Brooke (1908). For commentary, see R. H. Goldsmith, "The Wild Man on the Elizabethan Stage," *RES* (1958), and George F. Reynolds, "*Mucedorus,* Most Popular Elizabethan Play," in *Studies in English Renaissance Drama in Honor of Karl Holzknecht,* ed. J. W. Bennett, Oscar Cargill, *et al.* (1959).

Much Ado About Nothing. A comedy by William SHAKESPEARE, written in 1598–99 and first printed in 1600. As his sources Shakespeare used a variety of dramatic and nondramatic works, including Matteo Bandello's *Novelle* (1554) in Belleforest's French translation *Histoires tragiques* (1559) and Spenser's *Faerie Queene,* II, 4.

To Messina comes Don Pedro, the prince of Aragon, with two gallants in his company, Claudio and Benedick, to visit Duke Leonato, father of the beautiful Hero and uncle of Beatrice. Claudio woos and wins Hero, but Beatrice and Benedick, two witty enemies of love, have a more tempestuous relationship, and their friends arrange that Benedick shall overhear Don Pedro and Claudio describe Beatrice's love for him and, at the same time, that Beatrice shall eavesdrop on how much Benedick loves her. The stratagem is successful, and the two become lovers.

Meanwhile, Don Pedro's bastard brother Don John conspires to ruin the love between Claudio and Hero by having his friend Borachio converse lovingly at night with Hero's maid Margaret, who is dressed like Hero. When Don Pedro and Claudio witness this assignation, they think that Margaret is Hero and become immediately convinced of Hero's infidelity. At their wedding ceremony, Claudio brutally denounces Hero, who swoons from shock, whereupon the wise Leonato, on the advice of a friar, takes her away and falsely announces her death. Encouraged by Beatrice, Benedick demands revenge for Claudio's slandering of Hero, but at this point Borachio is forced to confess to the plot he and Don John had concocted: night watchmen hired by the constable Dogberry had overheard Borachio boast drunkenly of the trickery.

Claudio accepts the blame for Hero's death, and tells Leonato he will perform any penance the governor may prescribe. Leonato commands Claudio to marry Hero's "cousin," who at the ceremony turns out to be Hero herself. The play concludes with the double marriage of Benedick and Beatrice, Claudio and Hero.

Much Ado About Nothing is one of Shakespeare's most successful comedies. It effectively coordinates three stories: that of Hero and Claudio, a plot utilizing the same situation of a woman falsely accused as *The Winter's Tale* and *Cymbeline*; of Beatrice and Benedick, who are comically trapped into love; and of the villain Don John, whose plot to subvert Hero's love and reputation is foiled by the bumbling Dogberry and his night watchmen. The comedy is not as philosophically deep or suggestive as some others by Shakespeare, but it has proved to be highly successful on the stage because it combines skillful timing with some superbly staged scenes. Dramatic irony and suspense are exploited to the fullest. When Beatrice and Benedick learn of each other's love, for example, Shakespeare keeps them apart for several scenes in order to wring the greatest comic effects possible from their first confusing encounter as lovers.

Equally effective is Shakespeare's handling of Dogberry's slowness in imparting the vital news of Don John's plot. Dogberry's evidence of Hero's innocence, maddeningly interrupted and delayed, is finally given to the guests at the wedding only after they believe Hero is dead. Indeed, this play well illustrates an essential aspect of Shakespeare's comic method. Rather than deceive his audience until a series of surprising revelations at the end, as was the technique of John Fletcher, Shakespeare chose to confuse his characters while keeping his audience fully informed. *Much Ado About Nothing* exemplifies the wisdom of that comic theory.

The standard text is the New Cambridge edition, ed. Arthur Quiller-Couch and J. Dover Wilson (1923). For sources, see C. T. Prouty, *The Sources of Much Ado About Nothing* (1950). For critical commentary, see David L. Stevenson, *The Love-Game Comedy* (1946); Barbara Everett, "*Much Ado About Nothing,*" *CritQ,* III (1961); J. Dover Wilson, *Shakespeare's Happy Comedies* (1962); and Peter G. Phialas, *Shakespeare's Romantic Comedies* (1966). Walter R. Davis has edited *Twentieth Century Interpretations of Much Ado About Nothing: A Collection of Critical Essays* (1969).

Munday, Anthony (1560-1633). Poet and dramatist. The son of a London draper, Munday was apprenticed to the printer John Allde and introduced to the stage as a boy actor. While apprenticed to Allde, he began to write verses and obtain introductions at court. Around 1578 Munday went to Boulogne and later to the English College at Rome as a government spy against Roman Catholics. Upon his return he published an expose of what he described as Catholic treasons in *The English Roman Life* (1582). He was instrumental in the capture and execution of several Catholics, including the Jesuit priest and poet Edmund Campion, and wrote a virulent anti-Catholic diatribe, *A Watchword to England* (1584), attacking " popish traitors."

Munday's first literary publication was a long verse and prose romance, *Zelauto, or The Fountain of Fame* (1580), an imitation of John Lyly's *Euphues*. What was probably his first extant play, *Fedele and Fortunio* (1585), is a free adaptation of Luigi Pasqualigo's Italian prose comedy *Il fedele* (1575), though George Chapman and Stephen Gosson have also been suggested as translators. It is believed that Shakespeare may have borrowed a hint or two from Munday's play in writing *Much Ado About Nothing.*

Until the end of Elizabeth's reign Munday worked steadily as one of Philip Henslowe's stable of dramatists. Francis Meres in *Palladis Tamia* referred to him as among "our best plotters," a phrase suggesting that he wrote outlines of plays completed by others. According to Henslowe's diary, Munday was one of four dramatists paid to write *Sir John Oldcastle* (1600), a play performed to restore the damage inadvertently done to that Protestant martyr's reputation by Shakespeare's "old John of the castle," Falstaff in the Henriad plays. Munday wrote an old-fashioned chronicle history by himself, *The Downfall of Robert Earl of Huntingdon* (1600), and its sequel, *The Death of Robert Earl of Huntingdon* (1601) in collaboration with Henry Chettle. Munday may have been author of part of the manuscript version of the play THE BOOK OF SIR THOMAS MORE, which also contains three pages some experts say are in Shakespeare's handwriting. (See I. A. Shapiro,

"Shakespeare and Munday," *Shakespeare Survey,* XIV [1961] and the McMillin article cited below.)

Munday worked without particular distinction in a variety of literary forms—translations of French and Italian chivalric romances (*Palmerin D'Oliva* [1588], Book I of *Amadis of Gaul* [1590], and *Palmerin of England* [1596, 1602]), lyric poems, and ballads. After Munday retired from the stage around 1603 and opened a drapery shop in London, he wrote several pageants for the lord mayor and contributed additions to John Stowe's *Survey of London* in the editions of 1618 and 1633.

Munday's slender literary talents were chiefly dramatic; he demonstrated some ingenuity in writing plots, but for the most part he was a plodding workman rather than a gifted poet.

For Malone Society reprints of Munday's plays, see *CBEL,* I, 535 ff. There is a full biographical and critical account by Celeste Turner, *Anthony Munday: Elizabethan Man of Letters* (1928), and a Concise Bibliography by S. A. Tannenbaum (1942), updated in "Anthony Munday (1941-66)," ed. R. C. Johnson, in *Elizabethan Bibliographies Supplements,* IX (1968). See also Scott McMillin, *"The Book of Sir Thomas More:* A Theatrical View," *MP,* LXVIII (1970).

Mutability Cantos, The. Two cantos by Edmund SPENSER affixed to the six completed books of *The Faerie Queene* in the 1609 folio with the title "Two Cantos of Mutabilitie: Which, both for Forme and Matter, appear to be parcell of some following Books of the Faerie Queene, Under the Legend of Constancie." Although traditionally listed as Book VII, Cantos 6 and 7, their precise affinities to *The Faerie Queene* is a matter of dispute. Philosophical allegories employing ideas from Aristotle, Lucretius, Ovid, and Justus Lipsius, the two cantos describe how the Titaness Mutability overthrows the laws of Nature, Justice, and Policy. Deprived of the moon goddess Cynthia's light, the world appeals to Jove, but Mutability denies Jove's authority and proclaims her omnipotence. On Arlo's Hill (Spenser's residence in Ireland) Dame Nature presides over the conflict between Jove and Mutability, and finally decides against the omnipotence of Mutability because, although everything is subject to alteration and fluctuation, the essence of life and matter does not change. Hence Spenser's theodicy is based on his concept of the relationships of nature and change to deity. All things in nature change, but mutability is not an attribute of God.

The standard edition is in *The Works,* ed. Edwin A. Greenlaw, F. M. Padelford, et. al., 10 vols. (1932-49), I. For commentary see Evelyn M. Albright, "Spenser's Cosmic Philosophy and His Religion," *PMLA,* XLIV (1929); Edwin Greenlaw, "Spenser's *Mutabilitie,*" *PMLA,* XLV (1930); William Nelson, *The Poetry of Edmund Spenser* (1963); and Alice F. Blitch, "The Mutability Cantos 'In Meet Order Ranged,'" *ELN,* VII (1970).

N

Nashe, Thomas (1567–1601). Poet and pamphleteer. Born the son of a minister at Lowestoft, Suffolk, Nashe received a B.A. at St. John's College, Cambridge, and left one term short of earning his M.A. degree. He began his literary career in London in 1588.

Nashe's first known publication was a preface to his mentor Robert Greene's prose romance *Menaphon* (1589), in which Nashe wrote breezily about the faults of his literary contemporaries and excoriated ignorant actors and uneducated dramatists. Addressed to the "gentlemen students of both universities," Nashe's preface attacks inkhorn terms, the "swelling bombast of a bragging blank verse" of Senecan tragedy, and unoriginal writers who "in disguised array vaunt Ovid's and Plutarch's plumes as their own." He praises the early humanist scholars, especially Sir Thomas More, Sir Thomas Elyot, Sir John Cheke, and Roger Ascham, and, coming closer to his own age, celebrates the works of George Gascoigne, George Turberville, Arthur Golding, and Thomas Phaer. Spenser he calls "the only swallow of our summer," although he also has kind words for poets like Matthew Roydon, Thomas Atchelow (contributor of some lyrics to *England's Parnassus* [1600]), and George Peele (for his *Arraignment of Paris*). Of Richard Stanyhurst's version of the first four books of Vergil's *Aeneid* in hexameters, praised by Gabriel Harvey, Nashe has nothing but contempt for such "thrasonical huff-snuff."

Nashe continued his derisive attack on contemporary literature in his first pamphlet, *The Anatomy of Absurdity* (1589), which also denounces women, Puritans, astrologers, and ballad-makers. Characteristically Nashe courses freely over any number of other topics that momentarily seize his interest. The euphuistic style indicates that in this early work Nashe was influenced by Greene's romances.

With John Lyly, Nashe was asked by the Anglican authorities to reply to Martin MARPRELATE, the pseudonymous Puritan author of some brilliant anti-prelatical tracts, and Nashe may have written a series of anti-Puritan satires under the pen name "Pasquill," although his authorship of these tracts has not been ascertained. Certain parenthetical jibes at the Harvey family in these anti-Martinist pamphlets, together with Gabriel Harvey's belittling of Nashe's friend Robert Greene, provoked an energetic, scurrilous exchange of satires known as the Greene-Nashe-Harvey controversy (see HARVEY, GABRIEL) Nashe's original contribution to the controversy, *Pierce Penniless His Supplication to the*

Devil (1592), is not only a lampoon of the Harveys and a defense of plays (reversing some of his earlier judgments in Greene's *Menaphon*) but a lyrical mock homily on the seven deadly sins. In one passage rich with Rabelaisian wordplay and earthy wit, Nashe inveighs against the recent vogue of heavy drinking among the English, a passage that may have inspired Hamlet's digression on excessive drinking by the Danes in Act I, scene 4. (Nashe's *Pierce Penniless* is often cited because of its reference to "brave Talbot . . . new embalmed with the tears of ten thousand spectators," which provides a terminal date for Shakespeare's *Henry VI,* Part I.)

Nashe continued his feud with Harvey in *Strange News of the Intercepting of Certain Letters* (1592), in which he defends Robert Greene's life and works against Gabriel Harvey's denunciations. Nashe's last pamphlet was his best on the subject, *Have With You to Saffron Walden, or Gabriel Harvey's Hunt Is Up* (1596). Here Nashe accuses Harvey (who was fiercely proud of his family and origins) of being ashamed of his provincial town and of his father (a rope-maker of Saffron Walden): Wouldn't it be more justified, inquires Nashe waggishly, for Dr. Harvey to repent of his snobbery? his boasting of friendship with Sidney? his ignorance and superstitions? The humorless Harvey was no match for Nashe, who used the controversy as a release for his virile wit and astonishing verbal powers. Like Rabelais, Nashe exulted in false panegyric, hyperbole, anecdotes, word coinage (Harvey is addressed as Gorboduc Huddleduddle, Timothy Tiptoes, Braggadochio Glorioso, Gilgilis Hobberdehoy), outrageous mimicking and insolent displays of erudition. As C. S. Lewis has observed, Nashe's irreverant, colloquial prose anticipates the style of Shakespeare's Sir John Falstaff. Minuscule as the Greene-Nashe-Harvey controversy was in intellectual content, it yielded some brilliant satires by Nashe.

Nashe's hyperbolic, violent, and essentially journalistic style had its origins not only in Juvenal and Rabelais but in Nashe's avowed Italian master, Pietro Aretino (1492-1556), whose scabrous and sensational manner of writing Nashe admired and (omitting Aretino's pornography) consciously imitated. The paramount features of that style are declamation, exhortation, hyperbole, and unrelieved emotional intensity, whether the emotion be love, scorn, or piety.

Nashe's *Christ's Tears Over Jerusalem* (1593) adopts a more solemn tone than his previous pamphlets. A long, anguished sermon by Jesus is followed by a lurid description of the siege and destruction of Jerusalem. It concludes with a pious exhortation to London to forsake its evil ways lest it suffer the fate of the Biblical city. In a personal digression Nashe asks pardon of his enemies, and "even of Master Dr. Harvey" (a magnanimous gesture Nashe deleted from the second edition of 1594). It has been suggested that *Christ's Tears* reflects some profound religious conversion in Nashe, but that change was probably less spiritual than stylistic. Like Greene, Nashe often assumed a pietistic, penitential tone; the minister's son found the role of the Prodigal Son instinctively congenial.

The Terrors of the Night (1594) is a discursive meditation on demonology, oneiromancy, satanism, and witchcraft. The same year Nashe published, with a dedication to Shakespeare's patron the earl of Southampton, his remarkable adventure THE UNFORTUNATE TRAVELLER, OR THE LIFE OF JACK WILTON, which has been variously described as the earliest picaresque novel, a prose romance, and a satiric narrative (see FICTION).

In 1597 Nashe collaborated with Ben Jonson on the satiric *The Isle of Dogs,* an Aristophanic comedy (now lost) that so incensed the authorities because of its scurrility that Philip Henslowe's license was revoked, Jonson was clapped in the Fleet Prison and Nashe thought it prudent to absent himself from London and live inconspicuously in Yarmouth, a town he celebrated in *Nashe's Lenten Stuff* (1599), a panegyric in prose on red herring, the principal commerce of Yarmouth. The pamphlet is notable because it sustains a single theme (unusual for Nashe), contains a plethora of comic literary devices, and shows Nashe at the height of his powers as a prose stylist. He recites a host of legends about herring, tells a hilarious story of a pope's dinner, and gives a seriocomic rendition of Marlowe's *Hero and Leander.* Nashe's last work to be published was a strange, masque-like entertainment and his only drama, *Summer's Last Will and Testament* (perf. 1592; pr. 1600). It was named after Will Summer, Henry VIII's court jester, and contains the famous and haunting litany written in the plague year: "Brightness falls from the air. / Queens die young and fair."

The standard edition of Nashe's works is by R. B. McKerrow, 5 vols. (1904-10); Volume V contains the definitive biography and a full account of Nashe's role in the Martin Marprelate and Harvey controversies. An excellent recent edition, with a convenient glossary and index, is by Stanley Wells, *Thomas Nashe: Selected Writings* (1965). There is a full-length critical study by G. R. Hibbard, *Thomas Nashe: A Critical Introduction* (1962), and a Concise Bibliography by S. A. Tannenbaum (1941), updated in "Thomas Nashe (1941-65)," ed. R. C. Johnson, in *Elizabethan Bibliographies Supplements,* V (1968). See also *The Predecessors of Shakespeare: A Survey and Bibliography of Recent Studies in English Renaissance Drama,* ed. Terence P. Logan and Denzell S. Smith (1973).

Nashe's Lenten Stuff. See NASHE, THOMAS.

New Atlantis, The. Utopian tale in prose by Francis BACON. First printed in 1627, it was inspired by Plato's *Republic,* Sir Thomas More's UTOPIA, and Bacon's own philosophy of the new science (see UTOPIAN FICTION).

On a voyage from Peru to the Orient, the narrator and the ship's crew find themselves lost in the South Seas. Arriving at the port of a large city, they are at first forbidden to land by the inhabitants, then permitted to do so if they will swear as Christians that they are not pirates and have killed no one during the past three months. Taken ashore, they are billeted in the House of Strangers. Here they learn from the governor that the city is called Renfusa, that they may remain for six weeks, and that, centuries before, the island's inhabitants were converted to Christianity when St. Bartholomew sent an ark to them containing the Old and New Testaments. Moreover, the narrator and his friends discover, the island traded centuries before with Phoenicia, China, and Atlantis (later named America), but when Atlantis was destroyed by a flood, the islanders (inhabitants of New Atlantis) were persuaded by their wise monarch Solomon to cut off outside communications, become self-sufficient, and strictly regulate immigration and visitations of foreigners.

This monarch also founded the wondrous Solomon's House, a society of scientists dedicated to studying "all the works and creatures of God." Every twelve years six scientists of Solomon's House are sent throughout the world to gather new inventions, books, and ideas from foreign countries. Meanwhile the scientists of Solomon's House continue experiments in such areas as refrigeration, soil cultivation, animal breeding, transportation, and production of synthetic materials. Labor is divided so that each group of scientists can work systematically at one aspect of their field—communication, research, statistics, theory, experimentation, production, or distribution. Their work has not only rendered New Atlantis prosperous and self-sufficient but given the country a technology far superior to any in the world. The scientists have developed weather stations (towers high in the air), machines for flying and for traveling under water, and pipes through which sound can be sent over great distances. After describing these achievements to the narrator, the director of Solomon's House gives permission for the narrator to write them down for the edification of the rest of the world.

The New Atlantis, with critical commentary, is included in *Famous Utopias of the Renaissance,* ed. Frederic R. White (1949). See also two articles by Judah Bierman, "Science and Society in the *New Atlantis* and Other Renaissance Utopias," *PMLA,* LXXVIII (1963) and "*New Atlantis* Revisited," *S Lit I,* IV (1971).

New Way to Pay Old Debts, A. A comedy of manners by Philip MASSINGER. It was written around 1622 and first printed in 1633. The main plot is based on Massinger's reworking of Thomas Middleton's A TRICK TO CATCH THE OLD ONE (1608). Massinger also exploits public hostility toward two recently convicted extortioners, Sir Giles Mompesson and Sir Francis Michell, whom he portrays in his play as Sir Giles Overreach and Justice Greedy (the latter having only a minor role as Sir Gile's hireling). Massinger's villains are not historically accurate but are made to express attitudes and conduct business in ways that suggest the notorious Mompesson and Michell of real life.

Young Frank Wellborn, whose prodigality and careless dependence on his greedy uncle Sir Giles has brought him utterly to ruin, meets Allworth, who introduces him to his rich and attractive stepmother, Lady Allworth. The widow receives Wellborn graciously and promises to help restore his tarnished reputation. Also paying respects to Lady Allworth is Lord Lovell, who promises, for his part, to help young Allworth in a clandestine courtship of Sir Giles' daughter Margaret. Sir Giles is also scheming in matters of the heart: he plots to get the rich, distinguished Lovell to marry Margaret, and to win Lady Allworth for himself. When Lovell visits Sir Giles, he pretends to court Margaret, much to Sir Giles' glee, but actually represents Allworth's suit. Sir Giles is tricked in another way. His courtship of Lady Allworth is not for love but her money; if, as he hopes, his prodigal nephew marries the widow instead, Sir Giles can still get her money by ruining Wellborn and making the widow responsible for Wellborn's debts. Meanwhile Lady Allworth joins in Wellborn's conspiracy to dupe Sir Giles into thinking Wellborn is her choice as a suitor. In the glow of Lady Allworth's favor, Wellborn sees his creditors vanish when Sir Giles, anticipating the imminent marriage of his nephew and the widow, pays all Wellborn's debts for him so the youth can afford the cost of the courtship.

The outfoxing of the greedy Sir Giles and his factotum Justice Greedy continues apace. Thinking that Lovell is to marry Margaret, Sir Giles eagerly sends a letter to his chaplain instructing him to wed Margaret to the gentleman accompanying her to the church; Allworth instead of Lovell goes to the ceremony, and thus Sir Giles is tricked into blessing the wrong marriage. Then, too, Sir Giles' servant Marrall steals and destroys the deeds to Wellborn's estates, which Sir Giles had managed to confiscate. Wellborn is now free of Sir Giles and of the debts the greedy uncle had unwisely paid. When Sir Giles learns that Margaret and Allworth are married, he goes beserk and tries to stab his daughter. The gallant Lovell intervenes, announces his own betrothal to Lady Allworth, and promises to help Margaret and Allworth gain their due portion of Sir Giles' wealth.

A New Way represents one of Massinger's most skillful and sophisticated comedies. The plot is confidently executed, each scene moving inevitably toward the farcical denouement that sees Sir Giles snared by his own treacheries. That conclusion is made inevitable as early as the end of Act I, where Lady Allworth whispers to Wellborn that he is to be the recipient of unlimited credit. From that point the comedy depends for its effects on dramatic irony rather than suspense. The character of Wellborn is noteworthy as a forerunner of the cynical and charming spendthrifts of Restoration comedy.

The standard edition is by T. W. Craik (1964). *A New Way* has also been edited by A. H. Cruickshank (1926) and Muriel St. Claire Bryne (1949). The relation of the play to Middleton's comedy and to historical characters and events is described by R. H. Ball, *The Amazing Career of Sir Giles Overreach* (1939). For critical commentary, see T. A. Dunn, *Philip Massinger: The Man and the Playwright* (1957) and F. M. Burelbach, Jr., *"A New Way to Pay Old Debts:* Jacobean Morality," *CLAJ*, XII (1969).

North, Sir Thomas (c. 1535-c. 1601). Translator. After attending Peterhouse, Cambridge, North studied at Lincoln's Inn, where he translated his first work, Antonio de Guevara's *El relox de principes,* from a French version of the original Spanish. This was North's *Dial of Princes* (1557). After giving up a career in law, he returned to Cambridge, was knighted in 1591, and pensioned by the queen in 1601. Little is known of his life.

North's next translation was *The Moral Philosophy of Doni, or The Fables of Bidpai* (1570), a collection of Indian beast tales in Arabic that North took from the Italian. His next and greatest work was his translation of Plutarch's *Lives of the Noble Grecians and Romans* (1579), which he derived from a French version by Jacques Amyot (1559). Amyot's translation was a great work in its own right—the first book to be honored by the French Academy as a modern classic—and North's became a landmark of English prose and the chief source for Shakespeare's Roman plays. Shakespeare's high opinion of North's concrete, lively, and colloquial style is implicit in the fact that he borrowed more extensively and more literally from North than from any of his other sources (see TRANSLATIONS).

North's Plutarch has been edited by George Wyndham in the Tudor Translations series (1895). For North's style and methods, see F. O. Matthiessen, *Translation: An Elizabethan Art* (1931), and C. H. Conley, *The First English Translators of the Classics* (1927).

Northern Lass, The. A comedy of manners by Richard BROME, written in 1629 and printed in 1632. It was the first of Brome's plays to be published. No source is known.

Sir Philip Luckless is engaged to marry Mistress Fitchow, but as his kinsman Tridewell reminds him in vehemently opposing the match, there are some grave obstacles: she is too old and domineering, and her pampered brother Widgine is a complete fool. Sir Philip's marital plans become still more complicated when Mistress Traynewell informs him that he had promised to marry Constance, a northern lass placed in her care by her uncle, Sir Paul Squelch, a bachelor judge with whom Mistress Traynewell is secretly in love. When Mistress Traynewell produces a note from the northern lass signed "Constance," Sir Philip assumes that it comes from Constance Holdup, a prostitute with whom Sir Philip had been acquainted, and he throws Mistress Traynewell out in the belief she is the bawd's madam. Meanwhile Tridewell visits Mistress Fitchow to dissuade her from the marriage by citing all of Sir Philip's faults, but the lady shrewdly outmaneuvers him by feigning such admirable loyalty to her fiancé that Tridewell finds himself falling in love with her.

Fearing that Constance Holdup is plotting to forestall his marriage by blackmail, Sir Philip hastens to Mistress Fitchow, and demands they elope at once. She eagerly accepts, but must first placate her disconsolate and pampered brother Widgine by telling him that he too will soon enjoy the fruits of marriage—to the beautiful northern lass Constance, whose childless uncle has, she claims, promised a rich dowry. Actually, Judge Squelch has little to offer as dowry and plans for Constance to marry Master Nonsense, a wealthy Cornish gentleman.

In conversation with the northern lass, Mistress Traynewell learns that the naïve girl misinterpreted Sir Philip's courtly compliments in a letter as an outright proposal of marriage, and Mistress Traynewell conducts Constance to Sir Philip's house to clear matters. There Sir Philip, just returned from his elopement, discovers that the northern lass is not Constance Holdup. Smitten with her beauty, and regretful he did not follow up on his earlier tentative wooing by correspondence, Sir Philip begins to realize that he has married the wrong woman. This suspicion is confirmed when his bride, angered by Sir Philip's gallant treatment of Constance, flies off in a huff and sends word he is barred from her bedroom. Through Tridewell as intermediary, Mistress Fitchow later consents to an annulment—a relatively easy matter to effect since the marriage was not consummated—but only on condition the northern lass take a husband—who, of course, she hopes will be her brother Widgine.

Squelch, however, is still determined that the northern lass will marry Master Nonsense, although the girl clearly detests the fop. When Mistress Traynewell tries to dissuade him, Squelch angrily denounces both women and decides to get revenge by living like a libertine. Hence he allows Tridewell and Sir Philip to arrange an assignation in his apartment with a comely "country lass," who is really Constance Holdup, a bane Sir Philip is eager to dispose of in any way he can. To avoid scandal, Sir Philip and Tridewell let it be known that the girl in the apartment is the northern lass, and acting on this misinformation, Widgine comes to the apartment, makes love to Constance Holdup, and proposes marriage. Ambitious of sharing Widgine's imaginary wealth and social position, the prostitute readily agrees, and the two depart in search of a minister to perform the ceremony. Unware of their elopement, Squelch comes to the apartment disguised as a Spanish courtier to keep his appointment with the "country lass"; instead, he finds Mistress Traynewell, who, also in disguise, has substituted herself for the prostitute to baffle Squelch's impetuous career as a rake. This confusion is compounded still further when a constable arrests them as disorderly persons and takes them to Squelch's house to be arraigned. There Squelch and Mistress Traynewell reveal their true identities, and Squelch, humbled by his misadventure, frees the northern lass from an enforced marriage and proposes marriage to a delighted Mistress Traynewell. Soon afterward Widgine arrives at the judge's house, having discovered his marital blunder, and is required to pay Constance Holdup a handsome sum for his freedom. When Sir Philip and Mistress Fitchow learn that their marriage is void because the priest was an imposter, Sir Philip is free to marry the northern lass and Tridewell to wed Mistress Fitchow.

The Northern Lass, praised in prefatory verses affixed to the 1632 edition by Thomas Dekker, John Ford, and Ben Jonson, proved to be a favorite on the stage well into the Restoration period. Brome's comedy is a clever satire on English marriage conventions, an entertaining series of confrontations involving mistaken identities and misplaced aspirations in which the northern lass of the title performs rather passively as the prize of deceived fortune hunters. The characterizations are hardly noteworthy, but the plot is skillfully executed and the satire congenial—a successful blending of native festive comedy with Jonson's satiric comedy of manners.

The Northern Lass was edited by R. W. Shepherd in *The Dramatic Works of Richard Brome,* 3 vols., (1873), III. For criticism, see Harvey Fried, "The Early Quartos of Brome's *The Northern Lasse,*" *Papers of the Bibliographical Society of America,* LIV (1960); and R. J. Kaufmann, *Richard Brome, Caroline Playwright* (1961).

Norton, Thomas (1532-1584). See GORBODUC.

Nosce Teipsum. See DAVIES, SIR JOHN.

Notable Discovery of Cosenage, A. See GREENE, ROBERT.

Nymphidia, The Court of Fairy. A mock-heroic narrative poem by Michael DRAYTON, first printed in 1627. It is based chiefly on Chaucer's tale of "Sir Thopas" in the *Canterbury Tales* and Shakespeare's A MIDSUMMER NIGHT'S DREAM. In 705 lines of eight-line stanzas rhyming *aa ab cc cb,* Drayton recounts the vicissitudes of the fairy king Oberon's court as described to him by Nymphidia, an attendant on Oberon's Queen Mab. The cause of Oberon's tribulations is Pigwiggin, Queen Mab's courtly lover who arranges to meet the errant lady in a cowslip. The jealous husband, aided by his servant Puck, sets off in pursuit of the lovers and finally encounters Pigwiggin, who challenges Oberon to personal combat. The two rivals are mounted on earwigs with little cockleshells for shields. Their deadly combat is interrupted by Proserpine, goddess of fairyland, who spreads Lethe water on the two rivals so that Pigwiggin forgets his passion for Mab and Oberon loses all jealousy. At the conclusion all participants retire to a feast with "mickle joy and merriment." The poem is noteworthy for its sustained hyperbole, genial satire on courtly love and heroic poetry, and graceful, delicate imagery.

The standard edition is in *The Works of Michael Drayton,* ed. J. William Hebel, Kathleen Tillotson, and Bernard H. Newdigate, 5 vols. (1931-41), I. For critical discussion, see Oliver Elton, *Michael Drayton: A Critical Study* (1905).

O

Observations in the Art of English Poesy (Thomas Campion). See CRITICISM, LITERARY.

Of Reformation Touching Church Discipline in England. A pamphlet written in opposition to Anglican episcopacy by John MILTON, first printed in 1641. It was the first of Milton's prose works, and the first of five anti-prelatical tracts. The Root and Branch Bill, before Parliament in June 1641, proposed to abolish archbishops and bishops completely and to reorganize the authority of the Anglican Church on the lines of Presbyterianism. This controversy in Parliament was the occasion for Bishop Joseph HALL'S defense of prelatical authority in his tracts *Episcopacy by Divine Right* (1640) and *A Humble Remonstrance to the High Court of Parliament* (1640, 1641). A group of Calvinist ministers calling themselves "Smectymnuus" replied to Hall, among them Thomas Young, Milton's former tutor, and Hall replied to their tract with still another. In May 1641 James Ussher, archbishop of Armagh, also answered Smectymnuus. Milton's *Of Reformation,* appearing about a month after Ussher's retort, is a systematic rebuttal of both Hall and Ussher, and a defense of the Smectymnuus authors. Milton attacks the bishops for their pomp, pride, tyranny, superstition, and lack of Scriptural authority. Still a monarchist in 1641, Milton argues that neither civil welfare nor monarchy need depend on the authority of bishops.

Of Reformation is notable for its expression of Milton's early religious views, praise of Wycliff, account of the English Reformation under Henry VIII and Elizabeth, and condemnation of episcopacy as an institution destructive of monarchy, "whose towering and steadfast height rests upon the immovable foundations of justice, and heroic virtue...[not] the painted battlements and gaudy rottenness of prelatry..."

The standard edition is in *The Works,* ed. Frank A. Patterson, 18 vols. (1931-38), III. There are well-annotated editions in *The Student's Milton,* ed. Frank A. Patterson (1930); *The Complete Prose Works,* ed. D. M. Wolfe, 5 vols. (1953-71), I; and *The Prose of John Milton,* ed. J. Max Patrick (1967). For commentary, see Arthur Barker, *Milton and the Puritan Dilemma, 1641-1660* (1942); A. Chew, *Joseph Hall and Milton* (1950): William Riley Parker, *Milton, A Biography,* 2 vols. (1968), I; and D. M. Wolfe, *Milton and His England* (1971).

Old Fortunatus. A comedy by Thomas DEKKER written in 1599 and presented that year by the Lord Admiral's Men at court during the Christmas season. It was first printed in 1600. The story is largely derived from an old German folk tale.

The goddess Fortune bestows on old Fortunatus, a beggar, the choice of wisdom, strength, health, beauty, long life, or riches, and the old man foolishly chooses the last. Fortune gives him a magic purse from which he can draw ten gold pieces whenever he wishes, after which she departs for Cyprus to attend a tree-planting by her assistants Vice and Virtue. The tree of Vice is rich and flourishing, that of Virtue barren; Fortune, however, is indifferent as to which tree flourishes.

At the court of Soldan of Babylon, Fortunatus puts on a magic hat that transports him to Cyprus, where he joins his two sons, Ampedo and Andelocia. He lives in luxury until Fortune and the Destinies cut off his life; he dies repentant of his wrong choice and attempts without success to return the purse. His two sons agree to share by turns their inheritance of the magic purse and hat.

With the purse Andelocia travels to England to the court of Athelstane, whose wicked daughter Agripyne steals the purse, whereupon Andelocia returns to Cyprus and filches the magic hat from his brother. Transported back to England by the hat, Andelocia takes Agripyne to a desert, where he is tricked into eating from the tree of Vice, which transforms him into a horned monster. Virtue appears to offer him her fruit as an anodyne; reformed by Virtue's remedy, he is given by Fortune another chance to make good use of the purse and hat.

Returning disguised to the English court, Andelocia feeds Vice's fruit to Agripyne, and to Montrose and Longaville, two courtiers, who are all duly changed into monsters. Again disguised, this time as a French physician, Andelocia cures his victims with Virtue's fruit, after which both brothers are captured, thrown in the stocks, and die. At this point Virtue and Vice debate over which has won, and Virtue appeals her case to Queen Elizabeth herself, who is present at the performance. With a hymn in praise of the queen, true Virtue's deity, the play concludes.

Old Fortunatus displays Dekker's unique talents at their primitive best. To a classicist like Jonson. Dekker was a "very simple honest fellow" and merely "a dresser of plays" yet *Old Fortunatus* is a brilliant appeal to Elizabethan popular taste for airy romance, folk tales, and sentimentality. There is little in the play that is very original or experimental: its affinities to the MORALITY PLAYS are apparent from the allegorical characters and the theme of the vanity of human wishes.

The standard edition is in *The Dramatic Works,* ed. Fredson Bowers. 4 vols. (1953-61). For the view that the play is a satire critical of the earl of Essex. see Fredson Bowers. "Essex's Rebellion and *Old Fortunatus.*" *RES,* III (1952). Other criticism is by Mary L. Hunt. *Thomas Dekker* (1911): J. W. Ashton. "Dekker's Use of Folklore in *Old Fortunatus. If This Be Not a Good Play.* and *The Witch of Edmonton.*" *PQ.* XLI (1962): and J. H. Conover. *Thomas Dekker: An Analysis of Dramatic Structure* (1969).

Old Wives' Tale, The. A comedy by George PEELE, written between 1591 and 1594 and first printed in 1595. One source was Robert Greene's *Perimedes the Blacksmith* (1588), which gave Peele the idea of telling his story within a story. The play is a loose medley of episodes from folk tales, legends, and medieval chivalric romances.

At the opening of the play, Antic, Frolic, and Fantastic, lost in a wood at night, arrive at the cottage of Clunch the blacksmith, whose wife Madge welcomes them with food and drink and "an old wives' winter's tale" that forms the body of the play—a narrative full of knight-errantry, magic, accidental encounters, and strange prophecies.

Three pairs of knights set out to rescue Delia, daughter of the king of Thessaly, who has been kidnapped and enchanted into forgetfulness by the wicked sorcerer Sacrapant. Each of the knights encounters at a crossroad the supposed Senex, who is in fact the youth Erestus, magically transformed by Sacrapant into a white bear by night and a crooked old man by day who speaks only in riddles. In return for alms, each knight hears an enigmatic prophecy. Erestus utters this riddle to Delia's gallant brothers, Calypha and Thelea:

> Be not afraid of every stranger;
> Start not aside at every danger;
> Things that seem are not the same;
> Blow a blast at every flame;

For when one flame of fire goes out,
Then comes your wishes well about.

The braggart Huanebango and his clownish squire Corebus, who refuse to give Erestus alms, hear a quite different prophecy:

He shall be deaf when thou shalt not see.
Farewell, my son. Things may so hit,
Thou mayst have wealth to mend thy wit.

Another knight, Eumenides (who acquires his helper enroute), is Delia's loyal suitor, and to him Erestus predicts good fortune if he can keep his wits about him:

Son, I do see in thy face
Thy blessed fortune work a pace,
I do perceive that thou hast wit;
Beg of thy fate to govern it.
Bestow thy alms, give more than all,
Till dead men's bones come at thy call.

Near this same crossroads dwells Lampriscus, a beggar who has two daughters—the beautiful but spoiled and shrewish Zantippa and the good-natured but very ugly Celanta. In gratitude to Lampriscus for giving him honey to sustain him when in the form of a bear, Erestus promises that the beggar's unpleasing daughters will marry and receive dowries: "Send them to the well for the Water of Life; there shall they find their fortunes unlooked for."

Erestus' prophecies to the knights are fulfilled. Delia's brothers brave Sacrapant's thunder and lightning, but his furies carry them off to slavery. They learn, however, that Sacrapant's power resides in a flame enclosed in glass, and that he can perform magic only as long as the flame burns. None can break the glass "but she that's neither wife, widow, nor maid," and the sorcerer cannot die except by a dead man's hand.

Huanebango and Corebus are easily defeated by Sacrapant, who knocks the braggart off his horse, deafens him and blinds Corebus. These two soon fall in with the beggar's daughters. Zantippa comes to the Well of Life, whence a head appears to her and begs to be stroked; instead, she angrily strikes it with her cup and awakens Huanebango, who lies enchanted near the well. Thus Zantippa receives for her pains a fool for a husband. The ugly sister fares better when she marries Corebus, who in his blindness believes she is beautiful. When she obligingly strokes the head at the well, she receives a huge sum of gold in return.

The rescuer of Delia is Eumenides, who donates money to help bury a stranger named Jack, whose grateful ghost appears and offers to help free Delia from the magician. It is Jack who defeats Sacrapant and reveals the whereabouts of the magic flame. He also summons Venelia, Erestus' betrothed, who, since she is neither maid, wife, nor widow, easily extinguishes Sacrapant's flame and destroys his power. Erestus is restored to his youth and is reunited with Venelia, the brothers are released from slavery, and Eumenides is betrothed to the liberated Delia. In the closing episode Jack demands a share of Eumenides' gains in return for his services; Eumenides reluctantly offers to give him Delia, but the exacting ghost demands that Eumenides cut her into two equal parts, since both of them deserve exactly half of the girl. At the last minute, however, Jack announces that his demand was merely a test of Eumenides' faith and disappears into the ground. The lovers depart for Thessaly, and the old wife who has told the tale rises to prepare breakfast.

Peele's comedy is a sprightly satire on the chivalric romances cleverly designed to appeal to both popular and aristocratic taste (see PASTORAL). Some scholars have described the play as the first literary SATIRE on the English stage. The bombastic Huanebango is a burlesque of Huon de Bordeaux, hero of the *chanson de geste,* and perhaps also a satire at the expense of Gabriel Harvey, who advocated the use of hexameters and Latin quantitative meters like those of Richard Stanyhurst in his 1583 translation of the *Aeneid.* Peele's Huanebango quotes liberally from Stanyhurst's hexameters.

The standard edition is in *The Works,* ed. C. T. Prouty, 3 vols., III: *The Old Wives' Tale,* ed. Frank S. Hook (1970). For commentary, see Harold Jenkins, "Peele's *Old Wives' Tale,*" *MLR,* XXXIV (1939); M. C. Bradbrook, "Peele's *Old Wives' Tale:* A Play of Enchantment." *ES,* XLIII (1962); and Laurilyn J. Rockey, "*The Old Wives' Tale* as Dramatic Satire," *ETJ,* XXII (1970).

On the Morning of Christ's Nativity. An ode by John MILTON, written in 1629 and first published in his *Poems* (1645). The first four stanzas, the Induction, are in rhyme royal (*ab ab bc c,* the last line an Alexandrine), the same stanza pattern as Milton's "On the Death of a Fair Infant Dying of a Cough"; the twenty-seven stanzas of the "The Nativity Hymn" are in irregular accents rhyming *aa bc cb dd;* they begin with Christ's appearance to the shepherds before dawn and conclude with the Virgin laying the babe to sleep as night falls. The chief "conceit" is the idea that the poem will be a gift for the Christ-child arriving in advance of those given by the Magi; an important theme is the conventional one that Christ's birth routed pagan deities and silenced their oracles. Stanzas XI-XXV anticipate Milton's review of the pagan deities in *Paradise Lost,* (I, 392-540).

The Nativity ode represents Milton's first major effort. During the Christmas vacation of 1629 he referred to the composition of the poem in some Latin verses addressed to his friend Charles Diodati:

> . . . I am singing the heaven-descended King, the bringer of peace, and the blessed times promised in the sacred books—the infant cries of our God and his stabling under a mean roof who, with his Father, governs the realms above . . . These are my gifts for the birthday of Christ—gifts which the first light of its dawn brought to me. [*Elegy VI,* trans. Merritt Y. Hughes, in Hughes, ed., *John Milton: Complete Poems and Major Prose* (1957)]

The standard edition is in *The Works of John Milton,* ed. Frank A. Patterson, 18 vols. (1931-38), I. Other excellent editions are in *The Complete English Poetry of John Milton,* ed. John T. Shawcross (1963), and *The Complete Poetical Works,* ed. Douglas Bush (1965). Cleanth Brooks and J. E. Hardy have done a close analysis of the Nativity ode in their edition of the *Poems* (1951), as has Malcolm M. Ross in *Poetry and Dogma* (1954). See also Alan Rudrum, *A Critical Commentary on Milton's Comus and Shorter Poems* (1967).

Orchestra, or A Poem...of Dancing. See DAVIES, SIR JOHN.

Osburn, Francis, Advice to a Son. See COURTESY LITERATURE.

Othello. A tragedy by William SHAKESPEARE, written in 1604-05 and first printed in 1622. The principal source is Giraldi Cinthio's *Hecatomithi* (1565), a collection of Italian prose tales. No English version of the story is known to have been available to Shakespeare, though he may have read it in a French version by Gabriel Chappuys (1584).

When Othello, a valiant Moorish general in the employ of the Venetian state, elopes with Desdemona, her father Brabantio accuses him before the senate of having seduced his daughter by witchcraft and "spells bought of mountebanks." Othello ably defends himself against these charges, and Desdemona testifies to confirm his innocence. Equally important in Othello's exoneration is the fact that his services are needed against the Turks, who are reported to be advancing upon Cyprus. As Othello departs with Desdemona for Cyprus, Brabantio angrily warns him that Desdemona "betrayed her father, and will thee." Others leaving for Cyprus include Cassio, whom Othello has promoted to lieutenant; Iago, who is secretly plotting to destroy the Moor; and Roderigo, a rich Venetian fop whom Iago has duped out of his money with the promise that he will arrange matters so that Roderigo will have an affair with Desdemona.

On Cyprus it is learned that the Turks have gone elsewhere, and the treacherous Iago initiates his plot against the Moor. He begins by getting Cassio drunk and so discrediting him that Othello discharges him from office. He then slyly insinuates to Othello that Cassio is Desdemona's lover, an accusation he attempts to make plausible by having Desdemona appeal to Othello to restore Cassio's rank and by arranging that a handkerchief given to Desdemona by Othello be found in Cassio's possession. Crazed by jealousy, the Moor strangles Desdemona while Iago sends Roderigo to assassinate Cassio. When Roderigo fails, he is silenced by Iago's sword, but the wounded Cassio survives. Meanwhile Othello learns from Iago's wife Emilia that Desdemona is innocent, and her testimony is confirmed by Cassio and some letters found on Roderigo. Realizing how he has been deceived into murder by Iago, the grief-stricken Othello takes his own life. Iago is led away to torture, and Cassio assumes the governorship of Cyprus.

Of Shakespeare's four major tragedies, *Othello* is the most concentrated in action. After the expository first act, which lays the groundwork for Iago's plot against the lovers and reaches an eloquent climax in Othello's trial before the Venetian senate, the intensity eases until Act III, Scene 3—the long confrontation between Iago and Othello that concludes with the distraught Moor giving himself over utterly to Iago ("Now art thou mine lieutenant") —after which the action moves relentlessly toward its chilling peak in the murder of Desdemona.

Criticism of the play has centered mainly on Othello's character and the motives of Iago. A. C. Bradley saw Othello as noble and heroic, one whose idealism made him tragically vulnerable to Iago's artful deception, and, like Coleridge, Bradley insisted upon accepting Othello's own testimony that he was not by nature "jealous." This view of Othello was challenged by F. R. Leavis, who described the Moor as a pompous dullard who is rapidly seduced in Act III, Scene 3, simply because Iago appeals to everything that is indigenous to Othello's real nature. Leavis even suggests that Othello is so emotionally unstable that Iago's elaborate stratagems were unnecessary in causing the tragedy. Few critics have been as willing as Leavis to reduce Othello's stature, or as inclined as Bradley to praise the Moor's perfections. Most have come to view Othello, as does Robert Heilman, as a hero of great stature deeply flawed by pride and naïveté, and painfully ignorant of the values of love represented by Desdemona.

It was Coleridge who began the pursuit of Iago's elusive motives with his famous reference to "the motive hunting of a motiveless malignity," and, to be sure, Iago expresses a number of different reasons for his hatred. The first is his resentment of Othello's choice of Cassio rather than himself as lieutenant, a rebuke especially cutting to him because Cassio is a "theoretician" without experience in the field. Later he states that he hates the Moor for having cuckolded him (I, *iii,* 392-93); II, *i,* 305-06), and even hints that he himself has a lust for Desdemona (II, *i,* 300). Finally, he complains bitterly that Cassio's virtues cast a shadow over his own depraved life: "He hath a daily beauty in his life / That makes me ugly" (V, *i,* 19-20). One explanation for this "motive hunting" is that Iago's schemes represent the rationalizations of a man sickened with hatred and paranoia, a misanthropic villain who would reduce others to his own cynical nihilism and despair. Another explanation, suggested by Bernard Spivack, is that Iago requires no rational motives because his Elizabethan audience recognized him as the dramatic descendant of the Vice of the morality plays, who is by definition opposed to all goodness. Hence Iago's antic disposition, for Vice sports in deceiving others and in sneering at virtue. His only ally is the Devil, a fact Othello instinctively realizes at the end of the play when he stares at Iago's feet expecting to find them cloven.

A standard text is the New Cambridge edition, ed. Alice Walker and J. Dover Wilson (1957). Equally rich in data and criticism is the new Arden *Othello,* ed. M. R. Ridley (1958). Essential criticism includes A. C. Bradley, *Shakespearean Tragedy* (1904); F. R. Leavis, "Diabolic Intellect and the Noble Hero," in *The Common Pursuit* (1952); Robert Heilman, *Magic in the Web* (1952); and Bernard Spivack, *Shakespeare and the Allegory of Evil* (1958). There is a history of *Othello* criticism from the seventeenth century to the present in Edward Quinn, James Ruoff, and Joseph Grennen, *Shakespeare's Major Tragedies* (1973).

Overbury, Sir Thomas (1581-1613). Courtier, essayist, and poet. Born of a distinguished Warwickshire family, Overbury was educated at Queen's College, Oxford, and at the Middle Temple. He became a close friend of James I's favorite, Robert Carr, later earl of Somerset, and was knighted in 1608. Soon afterward he traveled in France and the Low Countries, where he wrote *Observations in His Travels upon the State of the Seventeen Provinces as They Stood 1609* (1626). Overbury's *The Remedy of Love,* a translation from Ovid in two parts, is of uncertain date of composition and was not printed until 1620.

Upon his return from abroad, Overbury's career continued to flourish; he courted Lady Rutland, Sir Philip Sidney's daughter, to whom according to Overbury's friend Ben Jonson, he wrote the poem "A Wife." His fortunes declined abruptly, however, when he vehemently opposed the marriage of the earl of Somerset to Frances Howard, divorced wife of the earl of Essex. The match was much favored by the powerful Howard family and by James I himself, and Overbury was arrested on trumped-up charges of treason and clapped in the Tower, where he was slowly poisoned to death by four men allegedly in the service of the countess of Essex. In the trial that followed (1615-16), Francis Bacon acted as prosecutor; the countess and Somerset were convicted of murder but were soon pardoned by the king. The four agents were hanged. Many of the details of the scandal remain obscure to this day.

Overbury is best known for his collections of CHARACTERS, beginning with *A Wife Now the Widow of Sir Thomas Overbury,* published posthumously in 1614. It contains the second edition of Overbury's poem "A Wife" and twenty-two characters by Overbury and "other learned gentlemen his friends." In the many subsequent editions down to 1622, the collection grew to include eighty-three characters, many of them by professional authors. The dramatist John Webster contributed twenty-two characters to the 1615 edition; Thomas Dekker wrote six poignant characters on debtors' prisons in the 1616 edition; and John Donne composed the character of a dunce and "Essay on Valor" for the 1622 edition.

Although the Overbury scandal accounted for much of the popularity of the collection, it has many intrinsic literary virtues (see ESSAYS) that set it off from its predecessor, Joseph Hall's *Characters of Virtues and Vices* (1608). The Overburian characters are less didactic, more detailed and vivid than Hall's, and in their concentration on social types resemble the characters of humours developed by Ben Jonson in his satiric London comedies. A few of the Overburian characters are idealized rather than satiric portraits, notably Webster's dignified encomium "An Excellent Actor," which he may have composed in answer to the character "A Common Player," an attack on actors in John Stephens' *Satirical Essays. Characters, and Others* (1615). Some believe Webster's character was modeled on the late Elizabethan actor Richard Burbage. The most popular idealized portrait in the Overbury collection is the prose lyric "A Fair and Happy Milkmaid," which Sir Isaak Walton recalled joyously in *The Compleat Angler.* Most Overburian characters are, however, pungent satires on such familiar social types as "A Puritan," "A Roaring Boy," "A Courtier," "An Affectate Traveler," "A Braggadochio Welshman, and "A Pedant." The prevailing style of the collection is described in the first edition by Overbury himself in his definition of the character as "a quick and soft touch of many strings, all shutting up in one musical close; it is wit's descant on any plain song."

There are brief biographical accounts of Overbury in C. E. Gough, *The Life and Characters of Sir Thomas Overbury* (1909), and Charles Whibley, *Essays in Biography* (1913). The definitive edition of the characters is *The Overburian Characters,* ed. W. J. Paylor (1936). Overbury's "A Wife" and his *Observations* are in *The Miscellaneous Works in Verse and Prose,* ed. E. F. Rimbault (1856). The Overbury murder and trial is the subject of Sir E. A. Parry's *The Overbury Mystery* (1925) and William McElwee's *The Murder of Sir Thomas Overbury* (1952).

P

Painter, William (1540?-1594). Author and translator of prose tales collected in *The Palace of Pleasure* (1566-67). See TRANSLATIONS.

Palladis Tamia (Francis Meres). See CRITICISM, LITERARY.

Pandosto, the Triumph of Time. A prose romance by Robert GREENE. It was first published in 1588, and in subsequent editions given the title *Dorastus and Fawnia.* For the plot Greene consulted such late Greek romances as Longus' *Daphnis and Chloe* and Heliodorus' *Aethiopica.* Shakespeare based the plot of *The Winter's Tale* on Greene's romance.

While visiting king Pandosto of Bohemia, king Egistus of Sicily is falsely accused of adultery with Pandosto's wife Bellaria. To escape the jealous rage of the Bohemian king, Egistus returns to Sicily and Pandosto puts Bellaria in prison and casts away his infant daughter Fawnia, whom he wrongly believes to have been conceived by Egistus. At Bellaria's trial an oracle proclaims her innocent and predicts Pandosto will not have an heir unless Fawnia is recovered. Meanwhile Fawnia is cast ashore on the coast of Sicily where she is found by a shepherd, who keeps the jewels she wears but nonetheless takes pity on the babe and raises her as his daughter. During Fawnia's life as a shepherdess she is courted by many swains but does not relinquish her heart until she meets Dorastus, son of Egistus who has come to view her fabled beauty. Fleeing the wrath of Egistus, who opposes the marriage of his son to a commoner, the lovers leave Sicily and are shipwrecked in Bohemia, where Pandosto falls in love with Fawnia, not realizing she is his daughter. Finally, she is recognized when her foster father arrives and shows Fawnia's jewels to Pandosto, who then laments his unjust treatment of his deceased wife and abandoned daughter, and the lovers are betrothed.

In THE WINTER'S TALE Shakespeare made some critical changes in Greene's story. He changed the countries and the monarchs, giving the part of Pandosto of Bohemia to Leontes of Sicily, and that of Egistus of Sicily to Polixenes of Bohemia. He renamed several other characters and increased the importance of three he invented himself—Antigonus, Autolycus, and Paulina. He omitted completely the episode of Pandosto's falling in love with his daughter, and he kept Pandosto's wife, as Hermione, alive: she becomes the central figure in one of his most moving scenes. Moreover, he attenuated Greene's strong emphasis on coincidence or fate, an element Greene derived from the Greek romances. Most important, perhaps, Shakespeare vitalized the listless, puppet-like characterizations he found in Greene's tale and eliminated all traces of Greene's euphuism and inflated rhetoric.

Pandosto was edited by P. G. Thomas (1907) and Kenneth Muir, *Shakespeare's Sources,* 2 vols. (1957) I. Greene's debts to the Greek romances and Shakespeare's use of Greene's story in *The Winter's Tale* are discussed by Samuel L. Wolff, *The Greek Romances in Elizabethan Prose Fiction* (1912), pp 445-58. See also John Lawlor, *"Pandosto* and the Nature of Dramatic Romance," *PQ,* XLI (1962).

Paradise Lost. An epic poem by John MILTON, originally published in 1667 in ten books, then rearranged by Milton into twelve books in the second edition of 1674. Although Milton did not work on the epic continuously until about 1658, he probably started it as early as 1642, after his return from his journey to Italy. In the manuscript at Trinity College, Cambridge, which is dated 1640-42, are four drafts for a drama on the fall of man, part of which is preserved in the finished epic in Satan's address to the sun in Book IV, lines 32-41. As Milton notes in his invocation to Book IX, his subject of the Fall was "long choosing, and beginning late," the culmination of a lifetime of prodigious learning, social and political aspirations and disillusionments, personal successes and defeats, and changing religious beliefs.

Hence Milton's epic is not only a compilation of his own unorthodox religious concepts as set forth in the posthumous Latin treatise DE DOCTRINA CHRISTIANA, but a medley of intellectual and aesthetic sources such as the classical epics of Homer and Vergil, the Italian epics of Ariosto and Tasso, Spenser's *Faerie Queene* and other writings, Hesiod's *Theogeny,* Ovid's *Metamorphoses,* Lucretius' *De rerum natura,* Du Bartas's popular epic *La Semaine,* translated by Joshua Sylvester as *Divine Weeks* (read by Milton as a child), and even rabbinical writings and medieval mystery plays. Many other sources could be added to these, and the list will doubtless increase as scholars continue to learn more about Milton's vast intellectual experience and complex sensibilities.

Book I: Milton announces his theme as being "of Man's first disobedience," original sin, which brought death to the world "till one greater Man / Restore us, and regain the blissful seat," and promises in the epic to "assert Eternal Providence, / And justify the ways of God to Man." As in classical epics, Milton begins *in medias res,* in the middle of the story, presenting Satan and his host of fallen angels on a burning lake in Hell (called Pandemonium) after their ignominious defeat and fall from Heaven:

Nine times the Space that measures Day and Night
To mortal men, he with his horrid crew
Lay vanquisht, rolling in the fiery gulf
Confounded though immortal: But his doom
Reserv'd him to more wrath; for now the thought
Both of lost happiness and lasting pain
Torments him; round he throws his baleful eyes
That witness'd huge affliction and dismay
Mixt with obdurate pride and steadfast hate:
At once as far as Angels' ken he views
The dismal situation waste and wild,
A dungeon horrible, on all sides round
As one great Furnace flam'd, yet from those flames
No light, but rather darkness visible
Serv'd only to discover sights of woe,
Regions of sorrow, doleful shades, where peace
And rest can never dwell, hope never comes
That comes to all; but torture without end
Still urges, and a fiery Deluge, fed
With ever-burning Sulphur unconsum'd . . .
[I, 50-69]

Satan awakens his stunned legions, announces that a world has been created for a new creature called Man, and summons a council to deliberate their next action.

Book II: Satan's council debates whether to attempt a new assault on Heaven. The first to speak is the pagan god Moloch, who advises "open war." The next speaker, Belial, counsels appeasement with Heaven's hosts, "ignoble ease, and peaceful sloth." Next speaks Mammon, who recommends a policy of total isolationism wherein the fallen angels might seek their own good, however hard and painful. Finally, Satan's minion Beelzebub proposes that they seek revenge by seducing to their party God's newly created creature Man. Satan volunteers to journey up to earth for this purpose. He departs from Pandemonium, meets his concubine Sin and her loathesome offspring Death at the Gates of Hell, and rises through the realms of Chaos and Ancient Night.

Book III: From the Empyrean, God views Satan's approach to earth and announces that Satan will succeed in corrupting Man, whereupon the Son magnanimously offers himself as ransom. God accepts his offer, and all the hosts of Heaven's angels praise the Son's glory and the ultimate victory of Man. Meanwhile Satan lands on the world's outermost orb, the Limbo of Vanity, then passes the Gate of Heaven and proceeds to the sun, where he meets the angel Uriel. Disguised as a minor angel, Satan learns from Uriel the direction of earth. He lands on mount Niphates, part of the Taurus range in Armenia.

Book IV: In the Garden of Eden Satan first sees Adam and Eve in all their bliss, and his heart burns with mingled guilt, malice, and spite ("Which way I fly is Hell; myself am Hell"). He overhears the pair speak of the forbidden Tree of Knowledge and determines to make this prohibition the occasion of their corruption:

Yet let me not forget what I have gain'd
From their own mouths; all is not theirs it seems:
One fatal Tree there stands of Knowledge call'd,
Forbidden them to taste: Knowledge forbidd'n?
Suspicious, reasonless. Why should their Lord
Envy them that? can it be sin to know,
Can it be death? and do they only stand
By Ignorance, is that their happy state,
The proof of their obedience and their faith?
O fair foundation laid whereon to build
Their ruin! Hence I will excite their minds
With more desire to know and to reject
Envious commands, invented with design
To keep them low whom Knowledge might exalt
Equal with Gods; aspiring to be such,
They taste and die. . . [IV, 512-27]

Adam and Eve discuss their creation and first meeting, their love for each other, and their joyous work in Paradise. As Eve sleeps, Satan tempts her with a dream; he is discovered by the angels Gabriel and Uriel, who, supported by an "angelic squadron," evict him from the Garden.

Book V: When Eve relates her dream to Adam, he comforts her with the idea that "Evil into the mind of God or Man / May come and go, so unapprov'd and leave / No spot or blame behind." Raphael is sent from Heaven by God to warn Adam of the coming temptation. At Adam's request, Raphael relates the story of Satan's rebellion and defeat.

Book VI: Raphael describes how the archangels Michael and Gabriel led God's legions against Satan and his rebels. The battle remained indecisive until the Son overwhelmed Satan's followers and drove them into Pandemonium.

Book VII: Raphael relates how and why the world was created, and how the Son and his angels were sent by God to complete the Creation in six days, after which the Son was glorified and reascended into Heaven.

Book VIII: Adam inquires of Raphael concerning the motions and laws of the heavenly bodies in the universe, and is "doubtfully answered" that although the heavens be a "book of God before thee set," it would be preferable for Adam to know "that which before us lies in daily life" and to "speak of things at hand." Adam recalls his own creation, and confides his abiding passion for Eve. Disturbed by this confession of uxoriousness, Raphael warns Adam, who fears nature has made Eve too lovely to resist, "Accuse not Nature, she hath done her part," and leaves the Garden.

Book IX: Changing into a serpent, Satan laments his fallen state ("For only in destroying do I find ease") and reasserts his determination to corrupt Man in spite of the consequences to himself ("spite then with spite is best repaid"). Although Adam protests, Eve convinces him that they can work more effectively if they divide their labors, and thus Satan comes upon Eve alone in the Garden. Satan persuades her with flattery and promises of divinity to eat from the forbidden Tree of Knowledge, and Eve, fearing death or exile as a result of her sin, decides to seduce Adam into eating the fruit ("Adam shall share with me in bliss or woe"). Horrified with Eve's transgression, Adam nevertheless joins her in sin:

She gave him of that fair enticing Fruit
With liberal hand: he scrupl'd not to eat
Against his better knowledge, not deceiv'd
But fondly overcome with Female charm.
Earth trembl'd from her entrails, as again
In pangs, and Nature gave a second groan,
Sky low'r'd, and muttering Thunder, some sad drops

Wept at completing of the mortal Sin
Original; while Adam took no thought,
Eating his fill, nor Eve to iterate
Her former trespass fear'd, the more to soothe
Him with her lov'd society, that now
As with new Wine intoxicated both
They swim in mirth, and fancy that they feel
Divinity within them breeding wings
Wherewith to scorn the Earth: but that false Fruit
Far other operation first display'd . . .
[IX, 996-1012]

After this euphoria, they fall to dalliance and violent lust, then awaken to engage in bitter recriminations.

Book X: In Heaven Man's fall is announced, and God asserts Man's total responsibility ("No decree of mine / Concurring to necessitate his Fall"). The Son is sent to earth to pass judgement. Eve is cursed with pain in childbirth and submission to her husband, and Adam condemned to earn his bread by the sweat of his brow. Both they and their descendants will taste sickness and death. Meanwhile Satan returns to Hell to announce his victory, but is met with hisses as he and his followers are changed into serpents. In the Garden Adam and Eve humbly acknowledge their mutual responsibility and are reconciled.

Book XI: Seeing their repentance, the Son intercedes on behalf of Adam and Eve. God agrees to temper justice with mercy, but sends the archangel Michael to evict them from Paradise. Michael takes Adam to a high hill, from which he unfolds a vision of Man's future misery until the time of the Flood.

Book XII: Michael continues his narration of Man's destiny with emphasis on events after the Flood—the coming of the Messiah to redeem Man for original sin, the Crucifixion, and the Resurrection. Elated, Adam praises the grace of God ("O goodness infinite, goodness immense") and sees that all Satan's evil and his own will turn to good, and he even expresses some doubt whether he should repent or rejoice over a sin destined to give "God more glory, more good will to Men . . ." Counseled by Michael to seek "a paradise within thee, happier far," Adam and Eve depart from Eden hand in hand: "The World was all before them, where to choose / Their place of rest, and Providence their guide."

For generations *Paradise Lost* was read as an orthodox account, but since the publication of Milton's *De doctrina Christiana* in 1825 the epic has been read in the light of his individualistic theology, and several important deviations from conventional Christian theology now appear evident. For one, Milton believed that the Son was created after the Father and, though immortal, subject to Him. He portrays the Holy Spirit as a symbolic manifestation rather than an actual part of a Trinity. And he depicts God as creating the world from His substance rather than from nothing, and argues at some length (V, 468 ff.) that matter, formed from the substance of divinity, is in no way inferior or even separable from spirit.

Although *Paradise Lost* has been described as a "Puritan epic," it is totally alien to Calvinism in its philosophy. Whereas Calvinism stresses predestination and man's utter helplessness in effecting his own salvation, Milton makes free will and human responsibility the ideological core of his poem. God proclaims on several occasions that Adam's fall, though known to Him in advance, is an act of unqualified volition. Moreover, Calvinism saw man as totally depraved and irrational, whereas Milton emphasizes man's dignity and makes reason the cornerstone of his attempt to "justify the ways of God to man," for Milton insists that reason and free will are aspects of the same God-given human faculty. And finally, whereas Calvinism found inspiration in the omnipotent and judicial God of the Old Testament, Milton portrays the loving and merciful God of the New. The God of *Paradise Lost* is not, therefore, in the tradition of Calvinism but of Christian humanism, the doctrine that fuses Judeo-Christian theism with classical reason and humanitarianism.

Milton's implicit theology emerges from a systematic juxtaposition of ironic oppositions—reason versus passion, order versus anarchy, love versus hate, humility versus pride—with Satan the chief exponent of the deadliest vices of pride, spite, and irrationality, and the Son the exemplar of the saving virtues of humility, love, and reason. Between these two titanic figures stands Man, the microcosm containing within himself a potentiality, not actualized until the Fall, for all the extremes of sin and virtue represented by Satan and the Son. Adam's fall in Book IX is brought about through Eve, who enervates his reason as she inflames his passion, and who becomes the agent through which Man is conducted to Satan. It is Man, not Satan, who is the central character of the epic, for it is Adam who holds the key to the outcome of the drama.

Satan was not conceived to be the hero of the poem until Blake and Shelley elevated Satan's pride and malice to a heroic defiance of God's "tyranny." This tendency to ennoble Satan stems perhaps from the romantics' view of evil as being more interesting than good (the Son being rather bland in contrast to Satan), perhaps from the natural inclination to sympathize with the underdog (Satan being hopelessly impotent throughout the poem), or perhaps from the overwhelming vividness of Satan's titanism when he is introduced in Books I-II. This last impression is a point of departure for Milton's irony, however, for Satan degenerates from leviathan in Books I-II to vulture in Book III, wolf, thief, and cormorant in Book IV, and reptile in Book IX. Though colorful and energetic, at least until the conclusion of Book IX, Satan is ironically powerless to effect anything without God's despised authority and is miserably enslaved by his own tormenting passions. As the epitome of evil, he represents the prototype of all the real and imaginary people Milton found despicable. He is Machiavellian stage villain, morality play Vice, pompous Anglican prelate, and, in the temptation scene with Eve in Book IX, cavalier lover of Petrarchan eloquence and sophistry. Paradoxically, he is both dynamic and impotent; he is all style without substance, energy without productivity, intelligence without wisdom.

As Milton was aware, *Paradise Lost* is a unique poem. It adopts many of the conventions of the Homeric and Vergilian epics—invocations, catalogues of heroes (Books I-II), prophecies, descents into Hades, extended allusions and similes—yet unlike either the classical epics or the Italian romantic epics of Boiardo, Tasso, and Ariosto, or the *Faerie Queene* of Spenser, *Paradise Lost* is cast in the form of a "great argument," a systematic philosophical defense of Milton's own theodicy that consciously employs its central myth to confront the complex problems of the living present: How did evil come into the world? Why is human history a chronicle of misery, cruelty, injustice, and failure? How can man, once fallen, gain redemption? For Milton the answers began with his synoptic conception of man as a creature endowed by God with reason, the moral faculty enabling him to make choices unfettered by determinism or predestination. As the angel Raphael tells Adam before the Fall:

God made thee perfect, not immutable;
And good he made thee, but to persevere
He left it in thy power, ordained thy will
By nature free, not over-ruled by fate
Inextricable, or strict necessity.
Our voluntary service he requires,
Not our necessitated. . . [V, 524-30]

Eve capitulates to Satan out of irrational impulses of vanity, ambition, and even levity (according to Adam, she is "too much of ornament, in outward show / Elaborate, of inward less exact"), and Adam, "overcome by female charm," allows passion to usurp reason when, like a uxorious husband, he surrenders to Eve's blandishments. Their punishment for disobedience is eviction from Paradise, loss of everlasting life, sweating labor, pain, and death; but their tragedy is alleviated by the Son's offer of himself in atonement. At the conclusion of the epic the archangel Michael takes Adam to a hill and shows him a vision of man's future in which Satan is crushed, and man redeemed and resurrected, and Adam rejoices in the paradox of the *felix culpa,* the "fortunate fall," a concept that enables Milton to conclude his poem with optimism and joy. "O goodness infinite, goodness immense!" exclaims Adam:

That all this good of evil shall produce,
And evil turn to good; more wonderful
Than that which by creation first brought
 forth
Light out of darkness! Full of doubt I stand,
Whether I should repent me now of sin
By me done and occasioned, or rejoice
Much more, that much more good thereof
 shall spring,
To God more glory, more good will to Men
From God, and over wrath grace shall abound.
[XII, 468-77]

The standard edition of *Paradise Lost* is in *The Works of John Milton,* ed. Frank A. Patterson, 18 vols. (1931-38), II, which has an index in two volumes. Editions especially helpful for notes and commentary are *The Student's Milton,* ed. Frank A. Patterson (1930; rev. ed., 1933); *The Poetical Works of John Milton,* ed. Helen Darbishire, 2 vols. (1952-55), II; *John Milton: Complete Poems and Major Prose,* ed. Merritt Y. Hughes

(1957); and *The Complete Poetical Works of John Milton,* ed. Douglas Bush (1965). Newcomers to Milton's paradise will find these introductions helpful: Marjorie Nicolson, *John Milton: A Reader's Guide to His Poetry* (1963), and Harry Blamires, *Milton's Creation: A Guide Through Paradise Lost* (1971).

Milton's style is studied closely in Christopher Ricks, *Milton's Grand Style* (1963), and Burton J. Weber, *The Construction of Paradise Lost* (1971). The relationship of Milton's epic to other works of the same or similar type is studied in Gilbert Murray, *The Classical Tradition in Poetry* (1927); C. M. Bowra, *From Virgil to Milton* (1945); E. M. W. Tillyard, *The English Epic and Its Background* (1954); and Dennis Burden, *The Logical Epic* (1967).

Milton's religious views are discussed from various perspectives in Maurice Kelley, *This Great Argument* (1941); William Empson, *Milton's God* (1961); John M. Evans, *Milton and the Genesis Tradition* (1968); and Joseph E. Duncan, *Milton's Earthly Paradise: A Historical Study of Eden* (1972). Milton and science are treated in Marjorie Nicolson, *Science and Imagination* (1956) and *Breaking of the Circle* (rev. ed., 1960); and K. Svendsen, *Milton and Science* (1956). Themes are emphasized especially in C. S. Lewis, *A Preface to Paradise Lost* (1942); Douglas Bush, *Paradise Lost in Our Time* (1945); John S. Diekhoff, *Milton's Paradise Lost: A Commentary* (1946); B. Rajan, *Paradise Lost and the Seventeenth Century Reader* (1947); and Lawrence Babb, *The Moral Cosmos of Paradise Lost* (1970).

Twentieth-century criticism of *Paradise Lost* is studied by A. J. A. Waldock, *Paradise Lost and Its Critics* (1947); Robert Adams, *Ikon: Milton and the Modern Critics* (1955); and Patrick Murray, *Milton: The Modern Phase* (1967). Detailed analyses are by Arnold Stein, *Answerable Style* (1953); John Peter, *A Critique of Paradise Lost* (1960); and Bernard Wright, *Milton's Paradise Lost: A Reassessment of the Poem* (1962).

Paradise Regained. A narrative poem in four books by John MILTON. It was first published in 1671 with *Samson Agonistes.* Designed to be a "short epic" in the manner of the Book of Job, *Paradise Regained* is an expanded account of Christ's temptation in the wilderness as described in the Gospel of Luke. According to Thomas Ellwood (1639-1713), a Quaker friend of Milton's, *Paradise Regained* originated in Milton's mind from a chance remark by Ellwood after reading *Paradise Lost:* "Thou hast said much here of Paradise Lost, but what hast thou to say of Paradise Found?" (from Ellwood's autobiography, *the History of the Life of Thomas Ellwood* [1714]).

As a sequel to *Paradise Lost, Paradise Regained* shows Christ the man triumphing over a cunning Satan who offers three temptations: to make bread out of stone, to rule over the world's kingdoms, and to test God by leaping from the pinnacle of a temple in Jerusalem. All these temptations represent Satan's efforts to make Christ express vainglory and lust for power.

Upon learning of Christ's baptism by John and the heavenly proclamation that he is the Son of God, Satan summons his council to plot Christ's downfall. After Christ has been in the wilderness for forty days, Satan appears to him disguised as an old man and asks him to perform a miracle by changing the desert stones into bread. Christ immediately penetrates the disguise and sternly upbraids Satan.

Satan returns to confer with his peers while Andrew and Simon seek after Christ, and the Virgin Mary expresses her anxiety over his long absence. Satan tempts Christ with the vision of a richly laden banqueting table, but is scornfully rebuked. Satan next offers earthly power and wealth, but these too are rejected. Finally, Satan appeals to Christ as a liberator of his people by reminding him that the house of David is under the tyranny of Rome. He takes Christ to a high peak and shows him a vision of the eastern world divided between Romans and Parthians, and suggests how Christ might cover himself with glory by freeing the Jews.

Satan continues the lure of political commitment to seduce Christ. That failing, he offers Christ another kind of power—the great achievements of the Greek poets, philosophers, and scholars—but in a famous passage (II, 309-52), Christ rejects humanistic learning ("Alas! what can they teach, and not mislead; / Ignorant of themselves, of God much more ..."). At last Satan takes Christ to the top of a temple and bids him jump to "show thy progeny," whereupon Christ replies, "Tempt not the Lord thy God." Smitten with amazement at Christ's strength, Satan himself falls in "ruin, and desperation, and dismay, / Who durst so proudly tempt the Son of God." Jubilant angels bear the victorious Christ home to his mother.

The standard edition of the poem is in *The Works,* ed. Frank A. Patterson, 18 vols. (1931-38), II; other editions are by John Gawsworth, *The Complete English Poems* (1953); John T. Shawcross, *The Complete English Poetry* (1963); and Douglas Bush, *The Complete Poetical Works* (1965). Some important critical interpretations are by Merritt Y. Hughes, "The Christ of *Paradise Regained* and the Renaissance Heroic Tradition," *SP,* XXXV (1938); Elizabeth M. Pope, *Paradise Regained: The Tradition and the Poem* (1947); Arnold Stein, *Heroic Knowledge* (1957); Barbara K. Lewalski, *Milton's Brief Epic* (1966); John M. Steadman, *Milton's Epic Characters* (1968); and *Calm of the Mind: Tercentenary Essays on Paradise Regained and Samson Agonistes in Honor of John S. Diekhoff,* ed. Joseph A. Wittreich (1971).

Pardoner and the Friar, The. An interlude attributed to John HEYWOOD, written sometime before 1521, and first printed in 1533.

A mendicant friar and an avaricious pardoner from Rome arrive at an English village to raise alms. While the friar preaches against covetousness and avarice, the pardoner attempts to peddle his collection of relics—a holy glove with the power to increase grain production, an arm of St. Sunday to protect travelers, a great toe of the Holy Trinity to cure toothache and cancer, the French hood of the Virgin to help pregnant women, and so forth. When the friar accuses the pardoner of avarice and fraud, the pardoner maliciously brands him as a heretic. When their debate turns to fisticuffs, the curate, assisted by Neighbor Pratt, attempts to evict the combatants from the church but is beaten for his efforts. As the friar and the pardoner depart, the curate and Neighbor Pratt lament that they ever agreed to let the church to such rascals.

Heywood's interlude is a simple but effective attack on corrupt pardoners and beggarly friars, two popular objects of satire in the Middle Ages. It is written from a staunchly Catholic perspective, however, and the honest curate serves as a foil to the wicked characters who would tarnish the image of the church.

J. S. Farmer has done a facsimile edition (1906). For commentary, see R. W. Bolwell, *The Life and Works of John Heywood* (1921); Ian Maxwell, *French Farce and John Heywood* (1946); and James Bryant, "*The Pardoner and the Friar* as Reformation Polemic," *Ren P* (1971).

Parnassus Plays, The. An anonymous trilogy of satiric plays written in 1598-1602 and performed at St. John's College, Cambridge, before 1603. The first part was printed in 1606, the other two parts not until 1773. They are bitterly critical of the neglect of learning, the pitfalls of patronage, and the uncertain plight of scholars after graduation. The plays contain allusions to many contemporary writers, such as Dekker, Greene, Jonson, Lyly, Marlowe, Nashe, Peele, and Shakespeare.

The first play, *The Pilgrimage to Parnassus,* is an allegory describing the "pilgrimage" of two idealistic scholars, Philomosus and Studioso, to Mount Parnassus to drink from the holy spring of learning. They journey through the trivium of logic, rhetoric, and philosophy. In logic they encounter a bewildering maze created by the conflicting schools of Aristotle and Peter Ramus; in rhetoric, or poetry, they meet with equal disillusioment; in philosophy, the steepest ascent of all, they encounter Ingenioso, who curses learning because it has impoverished him. At the end of four years they reach Parnassus, i.e., the B.A. degree.

The second play, *The Return from Parnassus,* Part I, finds the two pilgrims in search of a living after graduation. In London they again meet Ingenioso (perhaps Robert Greene), who scratches for work from ignorant printers and miserly patrons, and Luxurioso, a profligate would-be poet. At the end of the play all four are reduced to mean labor, abject poverty, and total despair.

The third play, *The Return from Parnassus,* Part II (subtitled *The Scourge of Simony*), shows the scholars in even more desperate straits. Philomosus and Studioso, failing miserably as quack doctors, turn to "the basest trade"—the theater. Richard Burbage and Will Kemp, chief actors in the Lord Chamberlin's Men, try to teach them acting, suggesting they might do well in Kyd's *Spanish Tragedy* or Shakespeare's *Richard III.* In the end both scholars abandon all hope of profit and retire to Kent to become sheepherders.

The Parnassus Plays represent not only the best of English academic drama but a vivid account of the woes of college-trained intellectuals of the Elizabethan period. Few scholars were fortunate enough to find patronage or even gainful employment after graduation. Most drifted into the church, or languished at the doors of nobles, or worked at shoddy journalism. The plays are also a tour through the popular literature of the times. In Part I of *The Return* Ingenioso falls in with Gullio, a literary dandy who compares himself to Sidney and quotes breezily from Shakespeare's *Venus and Adonis* and *Romeo and Juliet.* In Part II, the richest for its literary allusions, a corrector for the press leafs through the latest poetic miscellany passing epigrammatic judgment on Daniel, Drayton, Marlowe ("happy in his buskined muse"), Shakespeare, Spenser, and many others, and the actors at the Globe furnish the interesting observation that "Few of the university men pen plays well; they smell too much of that writer Ovid... Why, here's our fellow Shakespeare puts them all down."

All three parts of the Parnassus group were edited by W. D. Macray (1886) and J. B. Leishman (1949). For commentary, see F. S. Boas, *University Drama in the Tudor Age* (1914); G. C. Moore Smith, *College Plays Performed in the University of Cambridge* (1923); and Marjorie L. Reyburn, "New Facts and Theories about the Parnassus Plays," *PMLA,* LXXIV (1959).

pastoral. A literary work depicting shepherds, shepherdesses, or other rustic folk in a rural setting. (This literal definition, however, does not take into account the many variations and symbolic representations of the form.)

The originator of pastoral poetry was the Greek poet Theocritus (c. 316-c. 260 B.C.), a native of Syracuse. Because many of the colonizing Greeks of Sicily came from Arcadia in southern Greece, a primitive rural area, and spoke the Doric dialect, the words "Arcadia" and "Doric" have long been associated with the pastoral. Theocritus' poems are in the form of "idylls" (selections, or brief "pictures") portraying the simple lives of herdsmen and fishermen. Vergil later adopted these idylls as "eclogues" (often spelled "eglogues" by Elizabethans in the belief the word came from the Greek *aix,* meaning "goat"; hence "goat songs"). Theocritus' bucolics (from the Greek *bukolos,* meaning "herdsman") are relatively realistic descriptions of Sicilian peasantry at work and play, and he introduced most of the pastoral episodes that adhered to the form for centuries: improvised singing contests, complaints of unrequited love, *dêbats,* lamentations over the death or absence of a lover, and interweaving of mythology and contemporary regional lore.

Theocritus was an objective poet who expounded no philosophy, yet his idylls are not without implicit comment. They describe a world that had already passed away when he wrote; his happy, independent, and unfettered peasants had become the serfs of rich landowners, and his idylls are thus tinged with a yearning for a passed golden age—a sentiment his readers at the sophisticated court of Alexandria found especially appealing. Hence what were to become abiding qualities of the pastoral were already established in the idylls of Theocritus: nostalgia for a lost golden age, and a strong sense of contrast between the innocence and simplicity of rural life and the sophistication and complexity of court and city.

Theocritus' successors in the pastoral were Bion and Moschus, poets of the second century B.C. Bion's most famous pastorals are lamentations for the dying god Adonis and were probably written to be sung at religious ceremonies. The best-known poem attributed to Moschus is a pastoral elegy in which, as Daphnis, a simple shepherd swain, he laments the untimely death of Bion. It became a model for three of the greatest elegies in English—Milton's *Lycidas,* Shelley's *Adonais,* and Matthew Arnold's *Thyrsis.*

The great Latin poet Vergil (70-19 B.C.) based what is thought to be his earliest work, *The Eclogues,* on the pastorals of Theocritus. Vergil totally idealized the pastoral life in contrast to his own Augustan world of economic competition and civil wars; his shepherds and nymphs neither sow nor reap, but passively accept the gifts a mysteriously benevolent nature showers upon them. Vergil was the first pastoralist to express political and religious themes, which he develops in allegory. His sixth eclogue has the satyr Silenius explain the creation of the world in terms of the Epicurean philosophy in Lucretius' *De rerum natura;* his fourth eclogue, the so-called Messianic, prophesies the coming of a golden age (described by Plato and Hesiod) with the mysterious birth of a child. Vergil was actually celebrating the birth of an heir to a Roman consul, but throughout the Middle Ages and Renaissance his eclogue was read as an inspired prophecy of the birth of Christ.

The prose pastoral began in the late Greek period with the romance *Daphnis and Chloe* by a Greek writer known only as Longus (c. 350

B.C.?). To the poetic pastorals it adds harrowing adventures, sensual love relations, and numerous digressions narrating tales within tales. Angel Day rendered *Daphnis and Chloe* into English in 1587 from the French of Jacques Amyot, and Sir Philip Sidney probably used Longus as one source for THE ARCADIA.

The classical pastoral, with its apotheosis of earthly joys, did not appeal to ascetic medieval sensibilities, but the pastoral idea was kept alive in other forms: in the English legends of Robin Hood and his merry band in Sherwood Forest, the Mayday and Whitsuntide festivals, and minor literary types like the *pastourelle,* a dialogue between a knight bent on seduction and an unwilling shepherdess. Other pastoral elements are in the Towneley mystery plays of the fifteenth century, most notably in the comic episodes of the shepherd Mak. The Nativity, of course, is a pastoral scene, and this too was celebrated in music and liturgy. Moreover, Biblical stories are pervaded by pastoral associations: the hero of the Old Testament, David, was a shepherd as well as a poet (especially praised for his Twenty-third Psalm beginning, "The Lord is my shepherd: I shall not want"); Abel, one of the few examples of divinely favored virtue in Genesis, was a shepherd (in contrast to his wicked brother Cain, a farmer—a difference of vocations often noted by Renaissance moralists); and Christ was portrayed as the Good Shepherd in songs and sermons. The Elizabethan poet Michael Drayton pointed out these Christian associations when he wrote in one of his prefaces: "In the angels' song to the shepherds at our Saviour's Nativity, pastoral poesy seems consecrated."

Both Petrarch and Boccaccio wrote Latin eclogues in imitation of Vergil, but the most influential pastoralist of the Renaissance proved to be a Carmelite monk of Mantua known as Mantuan or Mantuanus (1448-1516). His eclogues were widely read in English schools as exercises in Latin; his verses were appropriately easy for pedagogical purposes, his descriptions of nature pleasant, his didacticism edifying, and his satire on the ignorance and corruption of his fellow Catholic clergymen entirely congenial to Protestants. (In Shakespeare's *Love's Labour's Lost* Mantuan is a favorite of the pedantic schoolmaster Holofernes.) Mantuan was more successful than any previous pastoralists in turning bucolic conventions like the *débat* among shepherds into thinly veiled religious satire.

Alexander BARCLAY was the first to render into English some of Mantuan's Latin eclogues, in a very clumsy and faltering version printed around 1515. Barnabe GOOGE did little better in his eclogues from Mantuan and Montemayor in *Eglogues, Epitaphs, and Sonnets* (1563), set in POULTER'S MEASURE and "fourteeners." George TURBERVILLE followed with all nine of Mantuan's eclogues in *The Eglogs of the Poet Mantuan Turned into English Verse* (1567). These Elizabethans stressed in their versions what their contemporaries found delightful in Mantuan's pastorals—sentimental complaints of forsaken lovers, the innocuous pleasantries of country life over the frustrations and vices of court and city, and anti-Catholic propaganda (Mantuan's anti-clericalism being given this sectarian twist by his zealous Protestant translators). None of these inept adaptations of Mantuan gives any indication of the great vitality the pastoral was to achieve later in the sixteenth century.

On the Continent, however, several far more gifted pastoralists than these early Elizabethans were destined to have far-reaching influence on English poets. The French poet Clément Marot (1496-1544) wrote a series of brilliant Vergilian eclogues using French names and setting; in Italy, Torquato Tasso (1544-1595) and Giovanni Battista Guarini (1537-1612) adapted the pastoral to the drama in two seminal tragicomedies, *Aminta* (Venice, 1573) and *Il pastor fido* (Venice, 1580-89), respectively. During the same period the Italian poet Giacomo Sannazaro (1458-1530) wrote *Arcadia,* and the Portuguese Jorge de Montemayor (c. 1521?-1561) composed *Diana enamorada,* both pastoral romances in prose. (Montemayor's *Diana enamorada,* it will be recalled, was the *chef d'ouevre* of that connoisseur of romances, Don Quixote.) What attracted later Elizabethans to these continental pastoralists was their dazzling virtuosity, graceful artifice, and easy mastery of conventions.

The first English poet to rival their achievements was Edmund SPENSER in THE SHEPHERD'S CALENDAR (1579), a publication that marks a new era not only of the pastoral but of English poetry in general. Employing twelve eclogues in a calendar design under the rubrics "plaintive," "moral," and "recreative," Spenser courses skillfully through the whole panoply of pastoral modes—love *débats, blazons* (songs in praise of female charms), satire (attacking the Roman clergy as "false shepherds"), allegorical autobiography, and literary criticism—and all of this in an amazing and totally unprecedented variety of difficult meters and stanza patterns. A brief passage from Spenser's praise of Queen Elizabeth in the April eclogue demonstrates his matchless eloquence:

> See, where she sits upon the grassy green,
> (O seemly sight)
> Yclad in scarlet, like a maiden queen,
> And ermines white:
> Upon her head a cremosin coronet,
> With damask roses and daffadilies set:
> Bay leaves between,
> And primroses green,
> Embellish the sweet violet.

In his autobiographical pastoral COLIN CLOUT'S COME HOME AGAIN Spenser is well within the tradition of Vergil when he contrasts the innocent joys of rural life with the cynicism and vanities of court—a motif played upon by Shakespeare, with considerable irony, in *A Midsummer Night's Dream, As You Like It,* and *The Winter's Tale.* In two pastoral elegies, *Daphnaida* and *Astrophel* (the latter on the death of Sir Philip Sidney), Spenser continues the custom established by Vergil (who, as Daphnis, eulogized Julius Caesar) and widely imitated by Clément Marot and other continental pastoralists.

In Book VI of *The Faerie Queene* Spenser uses the pastoral with more thematic ambiguity when his knight of courtesy, Sir Calidore, interrupts his chivalric mission to dwell for a time in Arcadia with a band of shepherds and shepherdesses. Although Sir Calidore wins the love of Pastorella (her name signifying the delights and beauties of her world), he forsakes his bucolic life and resumes his knightly quest at the end of the story. The episode raises the vital question of what the pastoral symbolized for Spenser and his contemporaries. If it meant an escape from cares and obligations, then Sir Calidore's resumption of his mission indicates Spenser's acknowledgment that pastoral retirement and chivalric commitment are incompatible ideals, that the simple gratifications of Colin Clout are irreconcilable with the stern duties of Sir Calidore. On the other hand, Spenser may have intended the pastoral episode to suggest not merely escapism but the classical concept of *otium,* a state of inner contentment and self-realization removed from society's frenetic scramble after position, power, and wealth. From this latter perspective, the pastoral is not incompatible with chivalry but represents another side of a manifold ideal of life, like the twofold Christian virtues of monasticism and evangelism—Christ in the desert, alone with God, and Christ preaching in teeming cities, converting sinners. From one perspective the pastoral life symbolizes a temptation Sir Calidore must resist; from another, it can be construed as a vital phase of his growth toward achieving true virtue as a knight.

As the above illustration makes clear, the meaning of "pastoral" is not to be contained within the borders of Arcadia, with its nymphs and swineherds, singing matches, forlorn complaints of lovers, and dainty images of "Fair-lined slippers for the cold, / With buckles of the purest gold." Since its origins in Theocritus and Vergil, the pastoral has manifested what might be called, in contrast to its strictly poetic conventions, certain "inner" psychological formulations: acknowledgment of tensions between the real and the ideal, and nostalgia for a golden age. Such visions find a perfect parallel, of course, in the Christian myth of Eden, which can be imagined either as existing or having existed in historical time, in a geographical location, or in the mind—or, as in Milton's *Paradise Lost,* in a fusion of all three. Once entered, that strange Garden may take different symbolic forms. It might become the *hortus conclusus* of Epicurean, Stoic, and Platonic conceptions, a place of retreat from the physicality of the world into an intellectual quietism and illumination such as Andrew Marvell's "green thought in a green shade" in his poem "The Garden." In a sense, of course, the pastoral has always been motivated by a desire for escape—escape from economic stress, domestic cares, urban frustrations, all the ravages of normative living—but the heuristic question is not whether the poet has chosen to escape by means of the pastoral, but which of many avenues of escape he has chosen.

For a Renaissance poet there were many routes besides the ones leading into the Christian Eden or the *hortus conclusus* of repose. Tasso's pastoral drama *Aminta,* for example, inverts the Christian ideal by extolling a golden age before "cold honor" brutally imposed repressions on "natural" instincts. Tasso's chorus proclaims that the pursuit of instinctual gratification is the purest virtue, and his Eden is shown to be a banquet of sensual delights. Montaigne's essays extolling the virility of "nature" over the decadence of pretentious "custom" (as in "Of the Cannibals") represents another variation on the libertine Eden, as does Gonzalo's magniloquent description of his imagined pastoral utopia in Shakespeare's *The Tempest:*

I' th' commonwealth I would by contraries
Execute all things; for no kind of traffic
Would I admit; no name of magistrate;
Letters should not be known; riches, poverty,
And use of service, none; contract, succession,
Bourn, bound of land, tilth, vineyard, none;
No use of metal, corn, or wine, or oil;
No occupation; all men idle, all;
And women too, but innocent and pure;
No sovereignty. [II, *i,* 147-56]

Gonzalo's pastoral paradise would, he exclaims, "excel the golden age," but the villainous Sebastian cynically inquires, "No marrying 'mong his subjects?" and Antonio retorts, "None, man, all idle—whores and knaves." The New World explorations provided impetus for speculations such as Montaigne's and Gonzalo's. John Donne refers to the newly discovered tropics as

That unripe side of earth, that heavy clime
That gives us man up now, like Adam's time
Before he ate...

It was easy to go a step further than the libertine view and begin to see uncivilized man as a "noble savage"—an idea already suggested by the innocent rustics of the pastorals. With the New World discoveries art began to imitate life; the already existing tensions between nature and art underwent even more complex permutations.

There were many objections raised to the association of the pastoral with liberation from moral restraints. Guarini devoted much of his pastoral drama *Il pastor fido* to refuting the idea by presenting three sets of bucolic lovers in a hierarchy of love relationships extending from crude sexual appetite to purely spiritual fulfillment. Andrew Marvell also answers the amoral conception of Eden in his "The Garden," with its paradoxically sensuous intellectual raptures, and in *Lycidas* Milton takes note of the fact that in the pastoral world there still exist moral alternatives to austere self-denial:

Alas! What boots it with uncessant care
To tend the homely slighted Shepherd's trade,
And strictly meditate the thankless Muse?
Were it not better done as others use,
To sport with Amaryllis in the shade,
Or with the tangles of Neaera's hair?

In Book IV of *Paradise Lost,* the most idyllic portion of his epic, Milton turns the tables on the pastoral "naturalists" by portraying Adam and Eve's unrestrained physical love as both totally gratifying and divinely blessed; after the Fall, ironically, genuine ardor becomes mere titillation and postlapsarian "sexual maladjustment."

It is impossible to describe briefly the many and complex affinities of the pastoral with the ideal of a golden age, or to trace the vast "garden" literature, of which Milton's *Paradise Lost* is only a small part, or to discuss adequately the influence of the pastoral on Renaissance man's changing concepts of the relationship of nature and art. These intricate aspects of the pastoral, so easily distorted in any short survey such as this, are patiently analyzed in the works cited at the end of this discussion.

To make matters even more complicated, the pastoral in England never existed as an isolated genre but blended with mythological love poems based on Ovid, such as Marlowe's *Hero and Leander* and Shakespeare's *Venus and Adonis,* just as it readily absorbed the poetic diction and love conventions of the Petrarchan sonnet and filtered into the whole literature of Elizabethan songs and madrigals. In effect, the Renaissance pastoral was not so much a genre or literary type as an omnipresent metaphor permeating all the activities of Renaissance culture—poems, dramas, romances, masques, iconography, sculpture, gardening, royal progresses, and entertainments of every variety.

The most prolific Elizabethan and Jacobean pastoralists were the followers of Spenser. The Spenserians share certain poetic qualities that set them off from both the neoclassic disciples of Ben Jonson and the metaphysical poets: close imitation of Vergilian bucolic conventions; harmony and decorum; clear diction and smooth cadences; sensuous description and mythopoeic elaboration; philosophical idealism and firm thematic resolution rather than dissonances of ambiguity, paradox, and contradiction.

One of the most productive Spenserians was Michael DRAYTON, whose *Idea, the Shepherd's Garland Fashioned in Nine Eclogues* (1593, with enlarged editions to 1619) envisions an Edenic age when man lived in harmony with God and nature. *The Muse's Elysium* (1630), his last collection of eclogues, is straightforward pastoral idealism in the manner of Spenser, and stands out as something of an anachronism among the cynical pastoral lyrics of the CAVALIER POETS and the eccentric perspectives of Andrew Marvell's nature poems. Perhaps the high-water mark of the Spenserian-type pastoral described above was the publication in 1600 of the voluminous pastoral miscellany *England's Helicon* (see MISCELLANIES, POETICAL). It contains a great deal of verse written before *The Shepherd's Calendar,* but the selections nevertheless serve as an extended illustration of the harmonious meters, spontaneous songs, mythic richness, and gold-bright imagery of that romantic school of pastoralists best represented by Spenser.

William BROWNE, another Spenserian, is more noted for his industry than genius. His *Shepherd's Pipe* (1914), written in collaboration with George Wither, was followed by his pastoral magnus opus in decasyllabic couplets, *Britannia's Pastorals* in three books (I, 1613; II, 1616; III, 1852 in a Percy Society edition). Like most Spenserians, Browne demonstrates a genuine feeling for nature, especially for the beauties of his native Devonshire, and he was ingenious enough as a myth-maker to influence Milton, Coleridge, and Keats.

Phineas FLETCHER'S eclogues, *Britain's Ida* (1628), came out in the first edition with his master Spenser's name on the title page. Fletcher's "piscatory eclogues," published with his *The Purple Island* (1633), are written in cunning imitation of Theocritus' *Idyll,* XXI, which dramatizes the labors and entertainments of fishermen rather than shepherds, although Fletcher's direct source was Sannazaro's piscatory eclogues (Venice, 1526). Fletcher's eclogues are of interest for their attack on the Anglican prelates, whom he depicts as shabby parodies of St. Peter, Christ's "fisher of men":

Some stretching in their boats supinely sleep,
Seasons in vain recall'd, and winds neglecting;
Others their hooks and baits in poison steep,
Neptune himself with deathful drugs infecting.

Some such passage in Fletcher's anti-prelatical satire influenced Milton's vehement digression on the venality of the Anglican clergy in LYCIDAS.

Milton's *Lycidas* remains one of the greatest elegies in English. Milton's ultimate source was the ancient lamentation of Bion on the death of Adonis, but he also echoes passages from a whole chorus of pastoralists from Theocritus to William Browne. Pastoral elements in Milton are for the most part from the early works—i.e., "On the Morning of Christ's Nativity," *Arcades, L'Allegro* and *Il Penseroso, Comus,* and *Epitaphium Damonis.* Because Vergil's first poems were pastorals, it became traditional in the Renaissance for young poets to test their wings in that form, and the tradition was still being observed by such later writers as Alexander Pope and Lord Byron.

In the nature poems of Andrew MARVELL the pastoral conventions of *The Shepherd's Calendar* are dismantled and rearranged to accommodate angular metaphysical wit, enigmatic paradoxes, and incongruous speculations. In Marvell's two epithalamia on the marriage of Lord Fauconberg and Lady Mary Cromwell he demonstrates that he can, when so inclined, make his Hobbinol, Phillis, and Tomalin sing orthodox Spenserian harmonies as well as Michael Drayton; for the most part, however, he chooses to energize the old conventions with new motives—psychological analyses, sexual realism, and multiple perspectives. He portrays a nature that is sentient and vitalistic, a "mystic book" of "scatter'd Sybils' leaves" that serves as a mysterious emblem of infinite symbolic interpretations: a shepherd's garland is suddenly seen as Christ's thorns; a chance stumble on grass recapitulates the primordial Fall; a garden's verdancy is annihilated by consciousness into "a green thought in a green shade." Frank Kermode rightly observes that English pastoral poetry in the tradition of Spenser terminates with Marvell; one senses that Marvell's pastorals are less akin to *The Shepherd's Calendar* than to Wordsworth's philosophical "Ode on Intimations of Immortality."

In conclusion, a word must be said of the pastoral drama, the least appealing of the forms discussed. Two seminal pastoral dramas have already been noted, Tasso's *Aminta* and Guarini's *Il pastor fido,* both of which are essentially Vergilian eclogues joined together into related scenes to form tragicomedies. They appealed to courtly audiences because of their delicate lyricism, exquisite sentiments, and timely *débats* on various aspects of love and passion. Although extremely influential, neither play comes even close to equaling Shakespeare's romantic comedies in human interest. The first considerable adaptation of these Italian pastoral tragicomedies to the English stage was John Fletcher's THE FAITHFUL SHEPHERDESS, performed in 1608 and published in an undated edition around 1610. A failure on the popular stage, it was revived with great applause at court in 1632. This finest of English pastoral tragicomedies illustrates the intrinsic limitations of the genre: as a play *The Faithful Shepherdess* is a melange of vacuous emotive confrontations, but as a poem it has effective rhetorical variety and lyric grace.

Many of Charles I's courtiers flooded the royal stages of Whitehall and Hampton court with garrulous imitations of Tasso, Guarini, and Fletcher until the outbreak of the Civil War in 1642, but it would be cruel to attempt their resurrection here. After the Restoration pastoralism continued to be popular in poetry, but with renewed polish and coloration appropriate to the standards of the Age of Reason.

Some important studies of the pastoral are by W. W. Greg, *English Pastoral Poetry and Pastoral Drama* (1906); William Empson, *English Pastoral Poetry* (1938; pr. in England as *Some Versions of Pastoral*); Frank Kermode, *English Pastoral Poetry* (1952); Thomas G. Rosenmeyer, *The Green Cabinet; Theocritus and the European Pastoral Lyric* (1969); and Harold E. Toliver, *Pastoral Forms and Attitudes* (1971).

Peacham, Henry (1576?-1643?). See COMPLETE GENTLEMAN, THE; ESSAYS.

Peele, George (1556-1596). Dramatist. Peele was born in London, the son of James Peele, chief administrator of Christ's Hospital and a man of some minor literary achievements. James Peele wrote the first known book on double-ledger accounting, composed works in verse on mathematics, and arranged civic pageants. After attending school at Christ's Hospital, where he received a thorough classical education in languages, George Peele matriculated at Broadgates Hall (later Pembroke College), Oxford, in 1571, then transferred to the college most famous at the time for its writing and performing of plays, Christ Church, receiving his B.A. in 1577 and his M.A. in 1579. At Christ Church Peele rendered one of Euripides' *Iphigenia* plays into English; Peele's version is lost, but it is known through two commendatory poems by William Gager, distinguished for his Latin plays. Gager describes Peele as one inclined to mix jests and solemnities, who was "strangely short of leg, dark of complexion, and red-haired," and urges Peele to continue doing classical translations. In 1580 Peele married Anne Cooke, the sixteen-year-old daughter of a merchant near Oxford, and in the following year came to London to seek his fortune as a writer. His prefatory verses appeared with those of John Lyly and other Oxonians in Thomas Watson's sonnet sequence *Hecatompathia, or A Passionate Century of Love* (1582).

Peele's earliest extant play, THE ARRAIGNMENT OF PARIS, published anonymously in 1584, was performed around 1582-83 before the queen by the Children of the Chapel. At the conclusion of Peele's lyrical pastoral he achieved a memorable *tour de théâtre* by having the legendary golden apple bestowed not upon Venus but upon Queen Elizabeth in the audience. In spite of this auspicious beginning at court, Peele turned to the popular stage with a number of plays written for the Lord Admiral's Men, led by the great actor Edward Alleyn and financed by Philip Henslowe. After *The Arraignment of Paris,* Peele wrote *The Battle of Alcazar* (wr. c. 1589; pr. 1594); *Edward I* (wr. c. 1593; pr. 1593); *David and Bethsabe* (wr. 1594-99; pr. 1599); and THE OLD WIVES' TALE (wr. 1591-94; pr. 1595). In addition to the translation of Euripides, Peele wrote several lost plays: *The Hunting of Cupid,* of which only a fragment survives (wr. after 1591); *The Turkish Mahomet and Hiren the Fair Greek* (after 1594); and *The Knight of Rhodes,* a play of very uncertain date and known only by a reference to it in a jestbook falsely attributed to Peele, *The Merry Conceited Jests of George Peele* (1607). Like William Rowley in a later period, Peele is very often assigned authorship of any anonymous play that coincides with the time of his literary activity, but few of these attributions are supported by any evidence.

Peele is ranked with John Lyly, Robert Greene, Christopher Marlowe, Thomas Lodge, and Thomas Nashe as one of the UNIVERSITY WITS—talented young men from Oxford and

Cambridge who came to London seeking their fortunes by appealing to audiences more sophisticated than the crowds at the popular theaters but not so dry-as-dust as the academicians they left behind them. In Greene's "Address to the Gentleman Scholars of Both Universities" in *A Groatsworth of Wit* (1592) he singled out Marlowe, Nashe, and Peele among the university wits in warning them against being exploited by common actors (Shakespeare among them). Greene refers specifically to Peele as one who, like himself, was "driven to extreme shifts" of poverty by being forced to rely upon actors for a meager livelihood:

> And thou no less deserving than the other two, in some things rarer, in nothing inferior; driven as myself to extreme shifts, a little have I to say to thee; and were it not an idolatrous oath, I would swear by sweet *St. George* thou art unworthy better hap, sith thou dependest on so mean a stay. Base-minded men all three of you, if by my misery ye be not warned.

By 1596 Peele was in such "extreme shifts" that he sent his daughter to Lord Burghley with a copy of his mythological poem *The Tale of Troy,* a very early piece written before *The Arraignment of Paris,* and a pathetic letter appealing for alleviation of his illness and poverty. He died the same year, of syphilis if one believes Francis Meres, who noted curtly in *Palladis Tamia* (1598): "As Anacreon died by the pot: so George Peele, by the pox." Soon after his death, and certainly by the time of the publication of the bawdy jestbook *The Merry Conceited Jests of George Peele,* Peele had a reputation for debauchery and prodigality. Whether that reputation is justified remains uncertain, but recent biographers such as David Horne (cited below) find it to have been highly exaggerated.

Peele's unique contribution to Elizabethan drama was remarked upon by Thomas Nashe in his preface to Greene's *Menaphon* (1589); "I dare commend him to all that know him, as the chief supporter of pleasance now living, the *Atlas* of poetry, & *primus verborum artifex:* whose first increase, *The Arraignment of Paris,* might plead to your opinions, his pregnant dexterity of wit, and manifold variety of invention, wherein (*me iudice*) he goeth a step beyond all that write." With John Lyly, Peele brought to the drama an unprecedented elegance and grace, especially in *The Arraignment of Paris;* Peele's *primus verborum artifex* praised by Nashe represents a contemporary's acknowledgment that he wrote the finest blank verse of the period, and Nashe's phrase "variety of invention" points to the almost bewildering heterogeneity of Peele's dramatic production—Ovidian mythology, Senecan blood-and-thunder melodrama, chronicle history, Biblical story, and folk tale.

Like Lyly, Peele conceived of a play as a medley of semi-autonomous scenes rather than an integrated logical and thematic development. *The Battle of Alcazar* and *Edward I* consist of loosely related episodes held together by concentration on lyrical pathos and bombastic rhetoric, and in both plays Peele attempts to "out-Herod Herod," or more precisely, to emulate the emotional violence and verbal hyperbole of Marlowe's *Tamburlaine.* (*The Battle of Alcazar* and the lost *The Turkish Mahomet and Hiren the Fair Greek,* it will be recalled, were much admired by Shakespeare's swaggering *miles gloriosus,* Ancient Pistol, in *2 Henry IV,* II, *iv.*) The Senecan flourishes in *The Battle of Alcazar,* with its half-crazed villains, lugubrious ghosts, and mutilations, make Peele's play read like a parody of Thomas Kyd's *The Spanish Tragedy,* as when the brooding Muly Mahomet, apparently drunk on Senecan alliteration, curses his unsalubrious destiny:

> Ye elements of whom consists this clay,
> This mass of flesh, this cursed crazed corpse,
> Destroy, dissolve, disturb and dissipate
> What water, earth and air congealed.

David and Bethsabe is more equal to Peele's great lyric skill, with its exotic imagery in imitation of the Song of Songs; but it is as episodic and meandering in plot as his other plays, recounting not only David's passion for Bethsabe but the rape of Thamar, the revolt of Absalom, and even the succession of Solomon, with little effort to integrate these episodes. *The Old Wives' Tale* is equally diffuse, but here the sudden transitions, variety of events, and episodic narration are in keeping with the fairytale and folklore atmosphere, and convey the impression of being tales within the old wife Madge's larger narrative frame. It is an astonishing confirmation of Peele's "variety of invention" to compare the exquisitely artificial and lyrical *The Arraignment of Paris* with *The Old Wives' Tale,* with its colloquial prose, boisterous rural characters, and robust humor. A comparison of Peele's variegated plays tends to justify the praise of both Greene and Nashe, that he was, in some ways, unequaled by his contemporaries—and especially in his sure sense of language and virile imagination; yet these talents, lacking discipline and a concept of organic form, yielded, with the exception of *The Arraignment of Paris,* dramas of only occasional flashes of inchoate genius.

The standard edition is *The Works of George Peele,* prepared under the general editorship of C. T. Prouty (1952-). Three volumes have been published: *The Life and Minor Works,* ed. David Horne (which includes the definitive biography), I (1952); *The Dramatic Works* (*Edward I,* ed. Frank S. Hook, and *The Battle of Alcazar* ed. John Yoklavich), II (1961); and *The Dramatic Works* (*The Araygnement of Paris,* ed. R. Mark Benbow; *David and Bethsabe,* ed. Elmer M. Blistein, and *The Old Wives' Tale,* ed. Frank S. Hook), III (1970). There is a critical biography by L. R. N. Ashley, *George Peele* (1970), and a Concise Bibliography by S. A. Tannenbaum (1940), augmented by "George Peele (1939-65)," ed. R. C. Johnson, in *Elizabethan Bibliographies Supplements,* V (1968). See also *The Predecessors of Shakespeare; A Survey and Bibliography of Recent Studies in English Renaissance Drama,* ed. Terence P. Logan and Denzell S. Smith (1973).

Penseroso, Il. See ALLEGRO, L'.

Pepys, Samuel (1633-1703). Diarist. The son of a tailor, Pepys was born in London, attended Huntingdon Grammar School and St. Paul's, entered Trinity College, Cambridge, and, as a sizar, graduated from Magdalen College with a B.A. in 1653, and M.A. in 1660. After his marriage in 1655 to Elizabeth St. Michael, daughter of a French Huguenot, Pepys' father's first cousin, Sir Edward Montagu, later earl of Sandwich, secured Pepys a minor clerical post in government. Through Montagu's influence again, Pepys was appointed to a post in the navy and became on good terms with the duke of York (later James II). After 1665 Pepys was surveyor general of supplies for the Admiralty, and rose to become secretary and one of the most distinguished naval administrators in British history. In 1679 and again in 1685 he represented Harwich in Parliament, and in 1684 and 1685 was president of the Royal Society. His career was ruined by the revolution of 1688 and his long friendship with James II. Enemies falsely accused him of sending naval information to the French, and he was periodically arrested and imprisoned during the period 1688-90. At his death his manuscripts went to the Bodleian Library at Oxford.

Although Pepys published a few official works, his one famous writing is the diary he kept during the years 1659-69. Written in a code mingling Latin, Greek, Spanish, French, German, and his own improvised cipher, it was intended solely for his own amusement and was not decoded and published until the partial, selective edition of 1825. It consists of a day-by-day account of Pepys' many activities—public affairs, marriage problems, civic events, theater- and party-going, philandering—and reveals with total candor a strange, witty, gregarious, and utterly captivating personality. Like the diary of John EVELYN, it records momentous events such as the great plague and the London fire, but unlike Evelyn, Pepys was an outgoing, gossipy man who wrote with unmitigated honesty because he wrote exclusively for himself. The diary is not only an invaluable historical document (and a primary source for students of the Restoration stage), but a vivid portrait of a man who loved every moment of his life and times.

The definitive edition, and the first complete one to appear, is edited by Robert Latham and William Matthews, 3 vols. (1972); it contains copious notes and commentary. The bibliography by E. Chappell, *Bibliographia Pepysiana* (1933), has been added to by "Samuel Pepys (1933-68)," ed. Dennis Donovan, *Elizabethan Bibliographies Supplements,* XVIII (1970).

Pericles, Prince of Tyre. A play by William SHAKESPEARE, written around 1608-09 and first printed in a corrupt quarto in 1609. Pericles was not included in the First Folio of 1623 nor in the second of 1632. Some scholars doubt that Acts I and II are by Shakespeare; others have assigned portions of the play, and even the whole work, to John Day, Thomas Heywood, William Rowley, or George Wilkins. The primary source is the old Latin tale retold by John Gower as "Apollonius of Tyre" in *Confessio Amantis* (1390). Another source is Laurence Twine's prose tale *The Pattern of Painful Adventures,* which appeared in two early editions, one undated and the other in 1607. In 1608 George Wilkins published *The Painful Adventures of Pericles, Prince of Tyre,* a prose version combining both Twine's tale and Shakespeare's play.

Pericles is presented to the audience by the poet Gower, who, as the Chorus, comments on the story at the beginning of each act and delivers the Epilogue. The play opens with Gower's description of an evil situation. Wicked King Antiochus of Antioch, guilty of incest with his daughter, prevents her from marrying by subjecting her suitors to a riddle they must solve under penalty of death. When young Pericles passes the test and discovers the king's secret crime, Antiochus orders Thaliard, a lord, to kill the prince. Pericles flees to Tyre, but soon realizes he must leave or be assassinated by Thaliard. Pericles places his trusted old councilor Helicanus in charge of Tyre and sails to the city of Tarsus, which he relieves of a terrible famine when he arrives with a large shipload of grain. Cleon, governor of Tarsus, and his wife Dionyza are grateful and urge him to remain, but Pericles, learning that Thaliard is still in pursuit, sails from Tarsus and is shipwrecked at Pentapolis. There he weds Thaisa, daughter of King Simonides.

At Pentapolis, Pericles learns that Antiochus and his daughter are dead and that the people of Tyre intend to make Helicanus their king unless Pericles returns. While en route to Tyre, Pericles' ship encounters a storm during which Thaisa dies giving birth to Marina. Buried at sea in a wooden coffin, Thaisa is washed ashore at Ephesus, where Lord Cerimon, skilled in medicine, brings her back to life. Believing that Pericles and Marina have perished in the storm, the grieving Thaisa retires into seclusion as a votaress in the temple of Diana. Meanwhile, Pericles leaves Marina in the care of Cleon and Dionyza at Tarsus.

Gower describes how as the years pass Marina becomes so universally admired for her beauty and virtue that Dionyza, resentful because she outshines her own daughter, plots to have Marina murdered. Dionyza's servant Leonine is about to kill Marina when she is abducted by pirates, who sell her to brothel keepers in Mytilene. In the brothel Marina proves so virtuous, however, that she converts her would-be clients to a better life and wins the admiration of Lysimachus, governor of Mytilene. Her employers, convinced she will never be anything but chaste, consent to her request to leave the brothel to do humble but honest domestic labor.

Years later Pericles returns to Tarsus and is informed by Cleon and Dionyza that Marina has died. On his return to Tyre, Pericles is driven to Mytilene by a storm, and there Lysimachus, hoping to raise Pericles, fallen spirits, has Marina entertain him with singing. Pericles recognizes her as his lost daughter. Later, in a dream, he is informed that he must tell his tale to a votaress at the temple of Diana at Ephesus. The votaress, of course, turns out to be Thaisa. Pericles, Marina, and Thaisa are reunited; Lysimachus and Marina are betrothed; and the treacherous Cleon and his wife are executed for their mistreatment of Marina. Upon hearing of Simonides' death, Pericles proclaims that he and Thaisa will rule in Pentapolis and their daughter and Lysimachus will reign in Tyre. In the Epilogue Gower explains that each of the principal characters illustrates a particular vice or virtue.

If *Pericles* is, in fact, by Shakespeare, it represents a radical change in style and sensibilities after the period of his great tragedies—perhaps his response to the new fashion for dramatic romances and tragicomedies set by John Fletcher. The rambling plot, which, like *The Winter's Tale,* narrates the tangled tribulations of two generations of characters, the high-flown sentiments, and the improbable turns of plot all point to the influence of Fletcher. Although extremely popular in Jacobean and Caroline times, *Pericles* was rarely performed after the seventeenth century and is generally considered inferior to Shakespeare's other romances, *The Winter's Tale, Cymbeline,* and *The Tempest.*

A standard text is the New Cambridge edition, ed. J. C. Maxwell (1956). For commentary, see Edward Phillips, "An Approach to the Problem of *Pericles,*" *ShS,* V (1952); Kenneth Muir, *Shakespeare as Collaborator* (1960); and Frank Kermode, *Shakespeare: The Final Plays,* Writers and Their Work Series No. 155 (1963).

Perkin Warbeck, The Chronicle History of. A history by John FORD, probably written sometime between 1622 and 1632 and first printed in 1634. As sources Ford consulted Thomas Gainsford's *True and Wonderful History of Perkin Warbeck* (1618) and Francis Bacon's *History of the Reign of King Henry VII*

(1622). The historical Warbeck (c. 1474-1499) was a commoner set up by Henry VII's enemies to destroy the Tudor claim to the throne by pretending to be one of two young princes supposedly slain by Richard III. Unlike Ford's character, he confessed his imposture before he died. Ford's play covers happenings in England and Scotland during the period 1495-99. To these events Ford added a number of ironic actions and much subtlety of character, especially in his ambiguous portrayal of the titular hero, who, unlike the outright imposter of the historical sources, is sympathetically portrayed by Ford as being sincerely convinced of his own authenticity. In the prologue Ford apologizes for his use of the chronicle play, now "so out of fashion, so unfollowed." Nevertheless, many readers have found it to be Ford's psychological masterpiece.

From the long and bloody wars of the Lancaster and York factions has emerged the Tudor monarch Henry VII, but his crown does not rest easy because Margaret of Burgundy, Richard III's sister, supports two pretenders to the throne, Lambert Simnel, who is rumored to be Edward, son of George, duke of Clarence, and—a much more powerful menace to Henry VII—Perkin Warbeck, who claims to be Richard, younger son of Edward IV. Simnel's threat is so dissipated that he has accepted a menial office in King Henry's household, but the young and handsome Warbeck is cordially received by James IV in Scotland, where Warbeck proclaims himself Richard IV. Indeed, Warbeck so impresses the Scottish court with his grace and elegance that James IV gives his kinswoman Katherine Gordon in marriage to Warbeck in spite of her father's vehement objections to the match. Even Lord Daliell, Katherine's gallant young suitor, lends his support to Warbeck's cause. James IV, however, only tentatively joins forces with Warbeck to press the young man's hereditary claims.

In London Henry VII has not been idle. He puts Warbeck's sympathizers to the block, crushes a Cornish uprising, and negotiates peaceful relations with Spain by a marriage between the Spanish king's daughter and Arthur, prince of Wales. Henry also secures closer ties with France and Germany, for the shrewd king will soon use these alliances to force James IV from his support of Warbeck. Under these pressures, intensified by Henry's promise of his daughter Margaret's hand in marriage to the bachelor James IV, the Scottish king agrees to banish Warbeck and his followers. Cut off from James IV, Warbeck's fortunes rapidly decline. Twice defeated in the field, he is finally captured and imprisoned. The kindly Henry VII treats him with tolerance at first, but eventually Warbeck goes to the block, still insisting that he is Richard IV and the last of the Plantagenet monarchs. To the very end Warbeck's loving wife remains loyal to him.

The triumph of Ford's *Perkin Warbeck* is that he employs in the chronicle play the same psychological intensity of a tragedy like *The Broken Heart.* Although the chronicles agreed that Warbeck was a fraud—an allegation Ford cleverly leaves unresolved—Ford creates a Warbeck whose nobility stems from his sincere conviction that he is in fact "the fair white rose of England" and "sole heir to the great throne of old Plantagenets." The claim is insupportable, yet Warbeck the imposter is more kingly than the real thing. Like Marlowe's *Edward II,* however, Warbeck is surrounded by sychophants, such as the dangerous Stephen Frion, "a subtle villain," and by common rabble like Heron, a bankrupt mercer, and Skelton, a mere tailor. These sordid characters, together with the politic James IV and Henry VII, provide effective foils to Warbeck's futile but glowing idealism. Adding to the poignancy of Warbeck's life is his star-crossed love with Katherine, who is steadfast in her faith as he goes to the block amid jeers and execrations.

Perkin Warbeck was edited by Donald K. Anderson in the Regents Renaissance Drama series (1966), and by Peter Ure in the Revels Plays series (1968). For commentary, see Clifford Leech, *John Ford and the Drama of His Time* (1957); Alfred Harbage, "The Mystery of *Perkin Warbeck,*" *Studies in the English Renaissance Drama in Memory of Karl Julius Holzknecht,* ed. J. W. Bennett, Oscar Cargill, and Vernon Hall, Jr. (1959); Winston Weathers, "*Perkin Warbeck:* A Seventeenth-Century Psychological Play," *SEL,* IV (1964); and Jonas A. Barish, "*Perkin Warbeck* as Anti-History," *EIC,* XX (1970).

Petrarch (or Petrarca), Francesco (1304-1374). Italian poet, diplomat, classicist, and critic. His chief Italian writings, *Canzoniere* and the *Trionfi,* as well as his Latin prose and poetry, influenced every facet of Renaissance literature. His love sonnets, translated into English by Sir Thomas WYATT and Henry HOWARD, earl of Surrey, introduced to English poetry the principal conceits as well as the mode of lyric expression subsequently naturalized in the Elizabethan SONNET SEQUENCES. See also PASTORAL; TRANSLATIONS.

Philaster, or Love Lies A-Bleeding. A tragicomedy by Francis BEAUMONT and John FLETCHER, written around 1610 and first printed in 1620. No source is known. In characterization, plot, and theme, it is a forerunner of the heroic plays of the Restoration period. In 1695 Elkanah Settle rewrote the play as an opera. The scene is Sicily at some indefinite time.

Prince Philaster, the noble and rightful heir to the kingdoms of Sicily and Calabria, languishes under the tyranny of the present king, who has betrothed his daughter Arethusa to an empty-headed, vacuous fop, Pharamond, prince of Spain. At court Philaster boldly insults Pharamond, and Arethusa, who is in love with Philaster, openly scorns the Spanish "popinjay." Philaster assigns his young page Bellario to enter Arethusa's service; Pharamond takes as his mistress a lascivious courtesan named Megra. When the king discovers Pharamond's disgraceful conduct, Megra threatens to proclaim to the world that Arethusa is bedding with her page Bellario. Disturbed by these accusations, Philaster dismisses Bellario and indignantly accuses the loyal and virtuous Arethusa of infidelity. During a hunting party Philaster, Arethusa, and Bellario happen to meet in the forest, and Philaster, after offering his sword to Arethusa and Bellario so they can end his misery, wounds his mistress and her page, whereupon a simple country bumpkin arrives on the scene to wound Philaster, who creeps away into the woods. As Bellario is being accused of assaulting Arethusa, Philaster reappears, confesses to the assault, and is carried off to prison.

The common people rise in revolt to free the popular Philaster and imprison Pharamond in retaliation, whereupon the king pleads with Philaster to stop the uprising. In obedience. Philaster frees Pharamond and persuades the mob to disperse. After Megra again accuses Arethusa of wrongful relations with Bellario, the king demands proof of his daughter's innocence. In a melodramatic, tearful scene Bellario reveals himself to be really Euphrasia, daughter of a nobleman; she has adopted her disguise as a boy in order to serve Philaster, with whom she has long experienced a deep Platonic love. Vowing never to marry, the idealistic Euphrasia pledges her life to Arethusa's service. Pharamond departs in disgrace for home, and the lovers Arethusa and Philaster are joyously betrothed with the blessings of the king.

Philaster contains the ingredients of the heroic romances dear to Beaumont and Fletcher's aristocratic audience—delicate sentiments, artfully staged emotional scenes, disguised ladies, plenty of surprises and sudden turns of plot. Philaster became the prototype of the "lily-livered" and ineffectual protagonist of the Cavalier romances of the 1630s and the heroic dramas of Dryden in the Restoration period. Although constantly extolled by others as being "noble" and even "divine," Philaster never draws his sword in any formidable combat; instead, in one scene he stabs his mistress and is cudgeled by a commoner. His flyting speeches are squandered on Pharamond, an effeminate coward:

Let me alone,
That I may cut off falsehood whilst it springs!
Set hills on hills betwixt me and the man
That utters this, and I will scale them all,
And from the utmost top fall on his neck,
Like thunder from a cloud, [III, *i,* 73-8]

He prates endlessly of his own great "honor," proclaiming proudly: "When any fall from virtue,/I am distracted; I have an interest in it." Yet he is curiously indifferent to honor when he accuses Arethusa of infidelity and cowardly attacks her and her page. Such perverse conduct can only be attributed to his sensitivity and melancholy, maladies that presumably set Philaster off from less refined mortals.

The similarities between *Philaster* and Shakespeare's *Cymbeline* are often noted. Both portray falsely accused heroines and girls disguised as boys, and draw situations and characters from the stock ingredients of romance. Even at his most romantic, however, Shakespeare does not create characters as humorlessly ethereal as Euphrasia. At the conclusion of the play she reveals that she has pursued Philaster out of a Platonic love engendered by her father's praise of Philaster's "noble virtues," and that she intends to dedicate her life to his happiness:

Never, Sir, will I
Marry; it is a thing within my vow:
But, if I may have leave to serve the princess,
To see the virtues of her lord and her,
I shall have hope to live. [V, *v,* 187-92]

Such sentiments were as incomprehensible to an Elizabethan popular audience as to the modern reader, but they endeared *Philaster* to Beaumont and Fletcher's refined patrons precisely because they were unworldly, incredible, and strangely "heroic."

The play is in *The Works of Francis Beaumont and John Fletcher,* ed. Arnold Glover and A. R. Waller, 10 vols. (1905-12), I; and edited by R. K. Turner in *The Dramatic Works in the Beaumont and Fletcher Canon,* ed. Fredson Bowers, 2 vols. (1966, 1970), I. Andrew Gurr has edited *Philaster* in the Revels Plays series (1969). For criticism, see James Tupper, "The Relation of the Heroic Play to the Romances of Beaumont and Fletcher," *PMLA,* XX (1905); John Danby, *Poets on Fortune's Hill* (1952); Eugene M. Waith, *The Pattern of Tragicomedy in Beaumont and Fletcher* (1952); and Harold S. Wilson, "*Philaster* and *Cymbeline,*" in *English Institute Essays 1951* (1952).

Phoenix and the Turtle, The. An untitled allegorical elegy of sixty-seven lines attributed to William SHAKESPEARE. It first appeared as one of several dedicatory verses appended to a long poem by Robert Chester, *Love's Martyr; Or, Rosalind's Complaint* (1601), and was later published again in John Benson's *Poems: Written by Wil. Shake-speare. Gent.* (1640). An obscure allegory cast in trochaic tetrameter, it laments the deaths of the phoenix and the turtle (turtledove) but celebrates the transcendent powers of their "mutual flame," a mystical union created by love. The last fifteen lines, the "threnos," makes clear that the phoenix symbolizes beauty and the turtle, fidelity.

The poem has been interpreted in a number of ways: as a celebration of the relationship of Essex and Elizabeth; a tribute to the spiritual integration of male and female in sexual love; and even a religious poem on the Trinity. For a discussion of these and other theories, see the standard editions: the New Variorium Edition of *The Poems,* ed. Hyder E. Rollins (1938); and *Poems,* the new Arden Shakespeare, ed. F. T. Prince (1960). See also J. V. Cunningham, "Essence and the Phoenix," *ELH,* XIX (1952) and G. Wilson Knight, *The Mutual Flame* (1955).

Piers Gaveston. See DRAYTON, MICHAEL.

Piers Plowman (William Langland). See SATIRE.

Pilgrim's Progress, The. A religious allegory by John BUNYAN, first published in 1678 (Part I) and added to and revised by the author in the three editions of 1678-1679. Part II was published in 1684. Written in a plain, direct style influenced by the Authorized Version of the Bible and by Puritan devotional literature such as *The Plain Man's Pathway to Happiness,* Bunyan's *Pilgrim's Progress* has been aptly described as a Puritan epic. By 1800 it had gone through over ninety editions and been translated into 108 different languages.

In Part I the author has a dream in which he sees his hero Christian reading a book that warns him to flee from the City of Destruction. Unable to convince his family to leave, Christian sets out alone to find a haven in the distant Celestial City. On his journey through such places as Slough of Despond, Interpreter's House, Palace Beautiful, Valley of Humiliation, and Vanity Fair, Christian meets at various times the allegorical characters Worldly Wiseman, Faithful, Hopeful, and Giant Despair.

In Part II Christian's wife experiences a vision that convinces her of the truth of the prophecy read by her husband, and she too departs the City of Destruction to seek the Celestial City. Accompanied by her children and her neighbor Mercy, as well as by Great Heart, who protects them all from Giant Despair and other monsters, she finally arrives at her destination and is reunited with Christian.

Pilgrim's Progress is one of the few literary classics to be acclaimed initially by the lower economic classes and only long afterward recognized by the literati. Though Bunyan was self-taught and widely read, he deliberately aimed at a style that would combine the simple folk tale and the emotive pulpit oratory of the Low

Church denominations. The result is a manner of writing that combines the offices of evangelist and poet:

> Now I saw in my dream that these two men went in at the gate, and lo! As they entered, they were transfigured, and they had raiment put on that shone like gold. There was also [those] that met them with harps and crowns and gave them to them; the harp to praise withall, and the crowns in token of honor. Then I heard in my dream that all the bells of the city rang for joy; and it was said unto them, "Enter ye into the joy of your Lord." I also heard the men themselves, that they sang with a loud voice, saying, "Blessing, Honor, Glory, and Power be to him that sitteth upon the throne, and to the Lamb forever and ever!"
>
> Now, just as the gates were opened to let in the men, I looked in after them, and behold! The city shone like the sun, the streets also were paved with gold, and in them walked many men with crowns on their heads, palms in their hands, and golden harps to sing praises withall...

Hence the style is densely parabolic, intimate, simple and direct, and rarely departs from its images and metaphors taken from the Authorized Version.

Two excellent editions are by J. B. Wharey (1928) and James Thorpe (1969). Bunyan's allegorical methods and affinities to Spenser and Milton are treated by Wharey in *A Study of the Sources of Bunyan's Allegories* (1904; repr. 1948). See also Richard L. Greaves, *John Bunyan* (1970); Stanley E. Fish, "Progress in *The Pilgrim's Progress,*" *ELR,* I (1971); and Brigitte Scheer-Schäzler, "Heracles and Bunyan's Pilgrim," *CL,* XXIII (1971).

Play of Love, A. See HEYWOOD, JOHN.

Play of the Weather, The. An interlude written by John HEYWOOD and printed in 1533.

The god Jupiter sends his court crier Merry Report, the Vice, to announce that anyone who objects to the weather should come to court and suggest a remedy. Eight petitioners appear, each with a different request. The gentleman pleads for warm, dry, and windless weather, ideal for hunting; the merchant wants clear weather with only moderate winds to aid his ships; the ranger, representing gamekeepers, petitions for strong winds because he makes extra money from clearing fallen trees after storms. Next appear two millers, one dependent upon water, the other upon wind to grind their grain. After a lengthy debate between these two, a gentlewoman arrives to plead for what amounts to an elimination of all weather because heat, cold, wind, and rain are all equally harmful to her complexion, whereupon a laundress complains that she needs both sun and wind to dry clothes. Finally, a boy comes forth to argue for frost and snow, ideal weather for catching birds and making snowballs.

Although the wily Merry Report despairs of a solution in view of these contradictory demands, Jupiter proposes one. Since no one kind of weather is suitable for all, each shall have, by turns, the weather he requests. The disputants then depart praising Jupiter's wisdom and justice.

Heywood's interlude is a clever farce adapted from some unknown French *débat.* The plot is slight, being little more than a protracted joke, but the characters are lively and the dialogue racy and vivid. Some scholars have found deep allegorical meanings in the play, but like most of Heywood's interludes, this one would appear to be pure entertainment.

There is a modern edition by J. S. Farmer (1908). For criticism, see K. W. Cameron, *John Heywood's Play of the Weather: A Study in Early Tudor Drama* (1941), and David M. Bevington, "Is John Heywood's *Play of the Weather* Really About the Weather?" *RenD,* VII (1964).

Pléiade, La. A group of French poets formed around 1547 at the College de Coqueret in Paris under the teacher Jean Dorat, who attempted to revitalize French literature by repudiating medieval courtly poets in favor of ancient Greek and Renaissance Italian writers. The chief members of la Pléiade include Pierre de Ronsard, the most distinguished of the group, his disciple Joachim du Bellay, Jean-Antoine de Baïf, Rémy Belleau, and Jacques Peletier. Their manifesto, signed by Du Bellay, was *Défense et illustration de la langue francaise* (1549), which attacked medieval court poets (especially the prestigious Clément Marot) and medieval Latin scholars, argued for the use of the vernacular instead of Latin, and called for a new poetic system based on Greek and Renaissance Italian themes and forms. It also repudiated the old image of the poet as a court entertainer and exalted him to the dignified role of sage and seer. The Renaissance English poets most influenced by la Plêiade were Edmund SPENSER and Sir Philip SIDNEY.

For a discussion of la Plêiade, see R. J. Clements, *The Critical Theory and Practice of the Plêiade* (1942) and G. Castor, *Pléiade Poetics* (1964). Specimens of their poetry are in *A Survey of French Literature,* ed. Morris Bishop, 2 vols., I (rev. ed., 1965); for their criticism, see *Critical Prefaces of the French Renaissance,* ed. B. Weinberg (1950).

Poetomachia, or **War of the Theaters.** See JONSON, BEN; MARSTON, JOHN; SATIROMASTIX.

Poly-Olbion. A topographical verse description of England by Michael DRAYTON. Although Drayton worked on the poem from 1603 to 1622, it remains unfinished. It consists of thirty parts (called "Songs"), each comprising 300 to 500 lines of hexameter couplets. Drayton planned the poem to be a national epic. The title means "land of many blessings," and Drayton intended it to inspire appreciation for the achievements and beauties of England. His itinerary covers the extreme southwest to Chester, through the Midlands to London, through the eastern counties to Lincoln, and finally, from Lancaster and Yorkshire to Northumberland and Westmoreland. He describes the topographical features of each county, with particular emphasis on rivers and streams, and gives an account of the region's history, legends, birds, animals, and plants. The thirty songs of the poem are divided as follows; (1) the founding of England by Brut, son of Aeneas; (2) Dorsetshire, with an account of the adventures of Sir Bevis of Southampton; (3) Somerset; (4) the rivers of England and Wales; (5) Sabrina, genius of the Severn, judges which rivers belong to England and which to Wales; Merlin is discussed; (6) the salmon and beaver of Twy; the story of Sabrina, the druids and poets of Wales; (7) celebration of Hereford; (8) conquest of Britain by the Romans and Saxons; (9) celebration of Wales; (10) Merlin's prophecies, Winifred's well, a defense of the Brut legend; (11) Cheshire, the religious Saxon kings; (12) Shropshire and Staffordshire, Saxon kings, and Guy of Warwick; (13) Guy of Warwick concluded; (14) Gloucestershire; (15) marriage of Isis and Thane; (16) Roman roads and Saxon kingdoms; (17) Surrey and Sussex sovereigns of England from William the Conquerer to Queen Elizabeth; (18) Kent, England's generals and sea captains; (19) Essex and Suffolk, English navigators; (20) Norfolk; (21) Cambridge and Ely; (22) Buckinghamshire, England's civil wars; (23) Northamptonshire; (24) Rutlandshire, the British saints; (25) Lincolnshire; (26) Nottinghamshire, Leicestershire, Derbyshire, with the tale of Robin Hood; (27) Lancashire and the Isle of Man; (28) Yorkshire; (29) Northumberland; and (30) Cumberland.

The standard edition is in *The Works of Michael Drayton,* ed. J. William Hebel, Kathleen Tillotson, and B. H. Newdigate, 5 vols. (1931-41), IV-V. For commentary, see Oliver Elton, *Michael Drayton: A Critical Study* (1905); Edmund Blunden, *Votive Tablets* (1931); and William H. Moore, "Sources of Drayton's Conception of *Poly-Olbion,*" *SP,* LXV (1968).

Porter, Henry (fl. 1596-99). See TWO ANGRY WOMEN OF ABINGDON.

poulter's measure. Alternating twelve- and fourteen-syllable lines in iambic couplets. The term was introduced by George Gascoigne in *Certain Notes of Instruction* (1575) and derives from the custom of London poulterers giving a customer fourteen eggs in the second dozen. Although Sir Thomas WYATT employed this singsong measure in a few poems, Henry HOWARD, earl of Surrey, established its vogue by using it in his popular verse translations of Ecclesiastes and the Psalms. Thereafter poulter's measure and its derivative, the "fourteener" couplet, dominated devotional poetry for several generations. Thomas Sternhold and John Hopkins used both poulter's measure and fourteeners in their enormously popular metrical version of the Psalms (1547). According to C. F. Tucker Brooke, "One might say that the progress of poesy in the Elizabethan age was largely a matter of disentangling it from poulter's measure and developing blank verse" (*A Literary History of England,* ed. A. C. Baugh [1948]).

Preface to Menaphon. See GREENE, ROBERT; HARVEY, GABRIEL; NASHE, THOMAS.

Preston, Thomas (1537-1598). See CAMBISES, KING OF PERSIA.

prolusions. The title generally given to John MILTON'S "oratorical performances," seven academic exercises he published in Latin in 1674 with the title *Johannis Miltoni prolusiones quaedam oratoriae.* These preliminary essays, or disputations, written while Milton was a student at Christ's College, Cambridge (1625-32), include (in translation): (1) "Whether Day or Night Is the More Excellent"; (2) "On the Music of the Spheres"; (3) "Against Scholastic Philosophy"; (4) "In the Destruction of Any Substance There Can Be No Resolution into First Matter"; (5) "Partial Forms Are Not Found in an Animal Beside Its Whole Form"; (6) "That Sportive Exercises Are Occasionally Helpful to Philosophic Studies"; and (7) "Learning Makes Men Happier Than Does Ignorance." For the most part, the prolusions are characterized by Platonism, Baconian optimism, hostility to false learning, and adherence to classical humanism rather than medieval scholasticism. They have been studied as clues to Milton's early thought. E. M. W. Tillyard (*The Miltonic Setting* [1938]) has found prolusions 1 and 2 to be keys to L'ALLEGRO and IL PENSEROSO.

The standard Latin text is in *The Works of John Milton,* ed. Frank A. Patterson, 18 vols. (1931-38), XII. The best English translation is by Phyllis B. Tillyard in *John Milton's Private Correspondence and Academic Exercises,* introduction by E. M. W. Tillyard (1932). Merritt Y. Hughes has translated the prolusions in *John Milton: Complete Poems and Major Prose* (1957). An essential critical analysis, with texts and notes, is by Katherine McEuen in *The Complete Prose Works of John Milton,* ed. D. M. Wolfe, 5 vols. (1953-71), I. For other commentary, see David Masson, *The Life of John Milton,* 7 vols. (1859-94), I; and D. L. Clark, *Milton at St. Paul's School* (1948).

Promos and Cassandra. A play in two parts by George WHETSTONE, first published in 1578. Four years later Whetstone published a prose version in a collection called *An Heptameron of Civil Discourses.* Although not strictly a tragedy, it was one of the earliest plays to deal seriously with domestic problems, and Shakespeare used it as a source for MEASURE FOR MEASURE. Whetstone's own source was the fifth novel of the eighth decade in Giraldi Cinthio's *Hecatomithi* (1565). According to the title page of the first edition. Whetstone's play is a "history" in two "comical discourses." Nevertheless, the tone is didactic and solemn throughout.

Lord Promos, viceroy to Corvinus, king of Hungary and Bohemia, revives a long-neglected law requiring a man guilty of adultery to be beheaded and the woman offender to wear a disguise for the rest of her life as a badge of her disgrace. When Promos convicts Andrugio and his mistress under this harsh statute, Andrugio's beautiful sister Cassandra petitions Promos for a pardon, which he at first grants and then retracts, demanding Cassandra's virginity in exchange for Andrugio's freedom. When Andrugio begs her to comply, she reluctantly agrees, on condition that Promos marry her afterward.

Having satisfied his lust, Promos refuses to keep his promise. Instead, he orders Andrugio to be executed and his head sent to Cassandra. Andrugio's jailer, however, releases Andrugio and presents Cassandra with the mangled head of an executed felon whom she takes to be her brother. Distraught to the point of suicide, Cassandra reveals Promos' treachery to the king, who orders Promos to marry her and then to be executed. Once married to Promos, however, Cassandra earnestly pleads for his life, a suit the king refuses to grant until Andrugio throws off his disguise and adds his plea for clemency to that of his sister's. The king pardons Andrugio on condition that he marry the girl he has wronged and spares Promos after he promises to love Cassandra and forgive Andrugio.

In Whetstone's play King Corvinus does not enter the story until Part II, and even here his participation is limited to pretending ignorance of Promos' crime and of the corruption of Promos' assistant Phallax, and of dispensing justice at the end. In *Measure for Measure,* Shakespeare makes Duke Vincentio, wily counterpart of King Corvinus, the chief strategist in the snaring of Angelo (Promos). Moreover, he has Isabella (Cassandra) refuse to submit to Angelo, substituting instead the famous "bed trick" involving Mariana, Angelo's former betrothed. By the invention of Mariana as a character, Shakespeare is able to preserve Isabella as a pure and perhaps even somewhat self-righteous woman destined, unlike Whetstone's Cassandra, for marriage to the duke himself. Equally important, Shakespeare adds humor to Whetstone's coarse characters of prison and brothel. eliminates Whetstone's didactic treatment, and instills in the play his own theme of mercy and justice.

Promos and Cassandra is in the Shakespeare Classics series, ed. Sir I. Gollancz (1909). Geoffrey Bullough's *Narrative and Dramatic Sources of Shakespeare,* 7 vols. (1972), II, contains a translation and discussion of Cinthio's tale and the complete text of Whetstone's play.

Prosopopoia (Spenser). See MOTHER HUBBERD'S TALE.

Prothalamion. A wedding song by Edmund SPENSER, first printed in 1596. The poem celebrates the double marriage of Lady Elizabeth and Lady Katherine Somerset, daughters of Edward Somerset, earl of Worcester, to Henry Gilford and William Peter in August 1596. Two main influences on Spenser's poem were John Leland's *Cygnea cantio* (1545) and William Vallans' *A Tale of Two Swans* (entered in the Stationers' Register in 1590 but not printed until Thomas Hearne's edition of Leland's *Itinerary of John Leland the Antiquary* [1710-12]). Like both poems, *Prothalamion* employs the motifs of the two swans on a journey, a marriage of two rivers, and topographic descriptions of historic places on the banks of the Thames and the Medway.

Prothalamion is less formal in structure and only about half the length of Spenser's other great wedding song. EPITHALAMION, *Prothalamion* consists of ten eighteen-line stanzas, each concluding with the refrain "Sweet Thames, run softly till I end my song." The poem begins with a description of a beautiful summer day; water nymphs scatter flowers before two lovely swans, and one nymph sings a tribute to the marriage of the swans. Spenser praises his own home of "merry London, most kindly nurse" and the great houses of Leicester and Essex. The earl of Essex, the queen's favorite, Spenser describes as

> Great England's glory and the world's wide wonder,
> Whose dreadful name late through all Spain did thunder,
> And Hercules' two pillars standing neere
> Did make to quake and feare:
> Faire branch of Honor, flower of Chivalrie . . .

The standard edition is in *The Works,* ed. Edwin A. Greenlaw, F. M. Padelford, et. al., 10 vols. (1932-49), V. Sources and background are discussed by T. M. Greene, "Spenser and the Epithalamic Convention," *CL,* IX (1957). See also Harry Berger, "Spenser's *Prothalamion:* An Interpretation," *EIC,* XV (1965).

Prynne, William (1600-1669). Puritan pamphleteer and historian. Prynne attended the Bath grammar school and Oriel College, Oxford, then became a barrister at Lincoln's Inn. A zealous and outspoken presbyterian and prolific author of political, historical, and religious tracts, he wrote over two hundred books and pamphlets. His best-known work relates to the controversy between the Puritans and the stage, *Histrio-Mastix. The Players' Scourge or Actor's Tragedy,* published late in 1632 (with the date 1633 on the title page). It is a huge tome of over a thousand pages bristling with Scriptural quotations and commentary, and much historical documentation; yet it is totally barren of any information regarding the Caroline drama. Prynne attempted to chart all the evils of the theater from Roman times to his own, and his diatribe was too general to give offense except in a single short passage wherein he charged that any woman who performed in a play was a whore (see CRITICISM, LITERARY). Unknown to Prynne, Queen Henrietta Maria and her ladies at court performed in a masque while the book was being printed, and for this inadvertent slander Prynne was singled out for exemplary punishment. In 1634 the Star Chamber stripped him of his law degree, fined him heavily, and condemned him to be mutilated, pilloried, and imprisoned.

Prynne's punishment in the pillory became a *cause célèbre* attended by thousands of sympathizers protesting the tyranny of the bishops, the Roman Catholic influence at court, and Henrietta Maria's extravagant patronage of "lewd and lascivious" dramatists. Thus Prynne's *Histrio-Mastix* and his trial and punishment for seditious libel created vague but highly emotive associations among Puritans and Royalists. After *Histrio-Mastix,* support of the court drama was often interpreted as an expression of loyalty to the monarch and bishops; opposition could be construed as symbolic of religious independence and defiance of the government.

Prynne continued to attack the bishops even from the Tower, and in 1637 was again mutilated, this time branded on the cheeks with the letters S. L. ("seditious libeler"). In 1640 a sympathetic Parliament declared his conviction illegal and he was released, but the indefatigable controversialist soon began attacking Cromwell's

Independents for their religious toleration, which Prynne equated with anarchy. In 1660 Prynne penned a strong defense of monarchy, for which Charles II rewarded him by making him keeper of records in the Tower, an office he served in with great diligence and erudition. During the Restoration he served as member of Parliament for Bath.

The fullest accounts of Prynne's life and works are by Ethyn W. Kirby, *William Prynne* (1931), which contains a bibliography, and William M. Lamont, *Marginal Prynne, 1600-69* (1963). Prynne's attack on the drama is discussed by E.N.S. Thompson, *The Controversy between the Puritans and the Stage* (1903); Alfred Harbage, *Cavalier Drama* (1936); G. F. Sensabaugh, "Love Ethics in Platonic Court Drama, 1625-1642," *HLQ*, I (1938); and Edmund S. Morgan, "Puritan Hostility to the Theatre," *PAPS*, CX (1966). See also Lamont, "Prynne, Burton, and the Puritan Triumph," *HLQ*, XXVII (1964).

Puritanism. A religious movement that flourished in England from the beginning of Elizabeth's reign to the Restoration, and in America from the settlement of the Puritans in Massachusetts in 1620 to the establishment of the new charter in 1691. The word "Puritan" was originally an opprobrious term used to describe anyone who believed in reforming or eliminating the rule by bishops of the Anglican Church and replacing episcopacy with some form of church government resembling that established in Geneva by Calvin and later in Scotland by Knox. According to Thomas Fuller in his *Church History of Britain* (1655), the "odious name of Puritan" came into use in 1564 when the Anglican bishops attempted to impose strict conformity of ritual and vestments in the Anglican Church. By John Bunyan's time the word had became more generalized, for in *The Life and Death of Mr. Badman* (1680) Bunyan refers to "a goodly old Puritan, for so the godly were called in time past." By the end of the seventeenth century the word had assumed its present connotation of describing a person of very strict moral or religious principles. In *Reliquiae Baxteranae* (1696), Richard Baxter recalls that his father was reviled as being a "Puritan" and "Precisian" because he preferred to read Scripture on Sunday rather than join the village dances.

Puritanism developed directly out of the so-called Elizabethan compromise, an effort to establish a moderately ritualistic and authoritarian church that would be generally acceptable in dogma and discipline to the widely divergent sects that proliferated during the Protestant Reformation. Thomas Cranmer's Book of Common Prayer, an episcopal hierarchy independent of Rome, and a ritualistic church service in English had all been established during the brief reign of Edward VI (1547-53), only to be abrogated during the stringent persecutions of Protestants under the Catholic Mary Tudor (1553-58). When Elizabeth came to the throne she revived her father's Act of Supremacy and secured the Anglican Church firmly to the secular control of the crown. Unlike her sister Mary Tudor, Elizabeth viewed religion largely in terms of political strategy; although thoroughly Protestant, she feared and despised Calvinists, whose defiance of episcopacy she recognized as a threat to her own political absolutism.

With the third Act of Uniformity in 1559, the Book of Common Prayer of 1552 became the sole guide for liturgy and church discipline, and through her bishops Elizabeth proposed to force it on a reluctant and Calvinist-inclined Parliament. The 1552 Prayer Book was anathema to Puritans because it omitted much anti-Catholic matter from previous versions and because of its "popish remnants" with regard to priestly vestments, ecclesiastical terminology, ceremonial observances, and holidays. The Puritans emerged as a visibly unified faction when Archbishop Matthew Parker issued his Advertisements (1566) directing the churches to observe strict uniformity in priestly vestments. In 1570 Thomas Cartwright aroused widespread Puritan sympathy when he was ousted from his chair at Cambridge for opposing episcopacy as "popish" and unauthorized by Scripture. Two Puritan "admonitions" to Parliament appeared in 1572 attacking "Romish" practices in the Prayer Book, communion without prior sanctification, and episcopacy. Especially repugnant to Puritans were restrictions on preaching and such practices as the sign of the cross, kneeling instead of sitting during communion, and the use of the wedding ring. Their primary objection, according to the admonitions of 1572, was to episcopacy itself, "as the names of Archbishop, Archdeacons, Lord Bishop, Chancellor, etc.... drawn out of the Pope's shop together with their offices. So the government which they use... is anti-Christian and devilish, and contrary to Scriptures."

Although the seeds of Puritan rebellion were

planted in the second decade of Elizabeth's reign, they grew unobtrusively underground until the reign of James I. Elizabeth's excommunication by Rome, her crises with Catholic Spain, and her relentless persecution of Jesuits were demonstrable evidence of her anti-papal sentiments; moreover, she was immensely popular with the Puritan-dominated upper middle class, whose economic interests she consistently protected. As she grew older, the more restive Puritans chafed under episcopacy and optimistically anticipated a new order of things under the future James I, who as James VI of Scotland had consented to the establishment of the presbyterian church government. Meanwhile Elizabeth's efforts to enforce uniformity erupted into the Martin MARPRELATE tracts between Puritans and bishops, and the long and bitter pamphlet controversy between the Puritan Thomas Cartwright and Archbishop John Whitgift culminated in Richard Hooker's temporizing defense of episcopal authority in OF THE LAWS OF ECCLESIASTICAL POLITY.

Those Puritans who had looked to the accession of James I with optimism were soon disillusioned. The Millenary Petition presented by the Puritans to the new king in 1603 was restrained and moderate in its condemnation of episcopal "abuses," but James responded with anger and contempt, later summarizing the issue succinctly in his famous dictum "No bishop, no king." Nevertheless, he arranged the Hampton Court conference in 1604 to enable the dissidents to air their grievances against the bishops. The conference concluded with a rejection of the Puritans' charges, a few minuscule reforms, and the establishment of a nonsectarian committee to translate a new version of Scripture that would be universally acceptable for use in the churches. This last proposal resulted in the publication of the great Authorized Version (or King James Bible) of 1611 (see BIBLE TRANSLATIONS).

By the time of the Hampton Court conference two main groups of Puritans were clearly identifiable—the Congregationalists, who wished to effect reforms within the Anglican Church, and the Separatists, who wished to break away completely. Both groups advocated the full Calvinist panoply of election, predestination, limited atonement, total depravity, irresistible grace, and final perseverance, but remained irreconcilable on the issue of whether to reform the existing ecclesiastical structure or destroy it completely. (The Congregationalists settled the Massachusetts Bay Colony, the Separatists the colony at Plymouth, and the two settlements remained distinct until the new charter of 1691.)

For the most part, the lot of the Puritans was the same under James I as it had been under Elizabeth. Some (but certainly not all) recoiled with disgust at seeing the godless attending plays or violating the Sabbath with dancing and games. They were occasionally fined for flagrant defiance of restrictions on preaching or censored for vitriolic attacks on the bishops. Nevertheless, James I's archbishop of Canterbury, George Abbot, was far less tyrannical than Elizabeth's Whitgift and later, Bancroft, and Puritans of any tact or flexibility could not have found life under James I wholly intolerable.

All this changed abruptly with the accession of Charles I in 1625 and the systematic persecution of Puritans by Archbishop William Laud, whose motto "Thorough, thorough" was driven home by an Ecclesiastical High Commission that painstakingly examined and harshly punished consciences and made efforts to impose "Laud's liturgy" on the presbyterian kirks of Scotland. It was the tyranny of Charles I and the zeal of Archbishop Laud that caused the first mass migrations of Puritans to Holland and the New World.

It was Laud's hated "Romish" liturgy that provoked the Scots to revolt in 1639, after which Charles was forced to convene the Long Parliament of 1640, without whose cooperation he could not have financed the Scottish wars. Economic motives had also prompted Charles's defiance of Parliament after 1629, when he imposed arbitrary taxes on English shipping. Hence religious and economic issues were inextricably fused, for the wealthy middle classes most vulnerable to arbitrary taxation also made up the body of England's best-educated and most militant Puritans. The fuse was lighted when Charles demanded that financially successful Puritans submit to confiscatory taxation that would undermine their own ideals on behalf of the despised institution of episcopacy; the explosion came when the Puritans realized that any parliamentary opposition to these harsh policies would bring death or imprisonment.

When war came in 1642 the Puritans and other religious dissenters, driven together to defend themselves against the common peril, represented anything but uniformity. Nor was

Parliament itself wholly Puritan, some members opposing the monarch on legal and political rather than religious grounds. Among the Puritans, few at the outbreak of hostilities were either Separatist or anti-monarchist. The political and religious development of John Milton during the 1640s provides an illustration of the broad spectrum of alternatives among Puritans. A monarchist in 1642, Milton gradually changed in the direction of republicanism; from Congregationalist, he moved with the events of the time toward Separatism, Independence, and finally, concluding that "new presbyter is old priest writ large," denounced the theocratic rule of the Calvinists and concluded his life as a total non-conformist. Nevertheless, Milton can still be described from first to last as a "Puritan," for he rejected episcopacy, decried the whole medieval accumulation of rituals, traditions, and forms as pagan superstitions, and believed Scripture to be the sole authority and revelation of truth.

Among the many varieties of Puritanism, the Calvinist presbyterian Separatists of the Geneva declension proved to be the most militant, austere, and uncompromising. These were the Puritans who settled Plymouth Colony, exiled Roger Williams, and provoked Milton's angry defiance. Other Puritans, in spite of stereotyped portraits of them as pleasure-fearing fanatics in literary works such as Jonson's BARTHOLOMEW FAIR and Samuel Bulter's *Hudibras,* were socially diversified. Some, like Milton, loved music, dance, and drank wine; others did not. Some, like John Bunyan, lived in fear of the flesh and the devil; others, like Andrew Marvell, were self-possessed rationalists or stoics.

With the return of monarchy in 1660, Charles II restored episcopacy and initiated the new Act of Uniformity in 1662 to prohibit the religious and political divisiveness of such unlicensed Baptist preachers as John BUNYAN. That act makes clear that the crown interpreted Puritanism for what it had always been—a revolt against the authority of bishops, a demand for "purification" of all the "popish" residue (real or imagined) in the Elizabethan compromise, and insistence on the Word of God in Scripture as the one and only authority in all spiritual matters.

Four scholarly studies of Puritanism are noteworthy: G. M. Trevelyan, *England Under the Stuarts* (16th ed., 1933); William Haller, *The Rise of Puritanism* (1938); M. M. Knappen, *Tudor Puritanism* (1939); and Alan Simpson, *Puritanism in Old and New England* (1955).

Purple Island, The. See FLETCHER, PHINEAS.

Puttenham, George (d. 1590). For comment on his *Art of English Poesy* (1589), see CRITICISM, LITERARY; INKHORN TERMS.

Q

Quarles, Francis (1592-1644). Poet and essayist. Born in Romford, Essex, the son of a surveyor-general, or conveyor of supplies, for the Navy, Quarles graduated from Christ's College, Cambridge, in 1608 and went on to study law, with very little interest in the subject, at Lincoln's Inn. In 1613 he was with the diplomatic mission accompanying Princess Elizabeth to the Palatinate, and from 1620 to about 1630 was in Ireland as secretary to James Ussher, archbishop of Armagh, the Biblical scholar now remembered for his attempt to give precise historical dates to events in the Old Testament.

Quarles' first book, *A Feast of Worms Set Forth in a Poem of the History of Jonah* (1620), is a grim Biblical paraphrase in pentameter couplets setting the tone of his subsequent Scriptural narratives in verse, among which are *Hadassa, or the History of Queen Ester* (1621); *Job Militant: with Meditations* (1624); *Sion's Sonnets* (1625), a rendition of the Song of Solomon in couplets with interspersed prose meditations; and *The History of Samson* (1631). His *Divine Poems* (1630) include all of his previously published works except the poem *Argalus and Parthenia* (1629), a secular romance in imitation of Sir Philip Sidney's *The Arcadia. Divine Fancies* (1632) consists of moral epigrams, spiritual meditations, and satirical observations in verse on contemporary manners and mores. All of these were extremely popular, but none so much as *Emblems* (1635) and *Hieroglyphics of the Life of Man* (1638), both printed with the title *Emblems* after 1639.

Quarles' *Emblems* is now generally considered to have been the most popular book of the seventeenth century. Each of its five books contains fifteen "emblems," woodcut engravings accompanied by a quotation from Scripture and a brief poem interpreting the illustration. (For other works of this type, see EMBLEM BOOKS.) Quarles borrowed his illustrations from two Jesuit emblem books; his verses were inspired by the allegorical poems of Phineas Fletcher and the French epic of the Creation, *La Semaine* (1578) by Guillaume Salluste Du Bartas (1544-1590) in the English version (1592-99; complete edition, 1605) by Joshua Sylvester. A typical poem in Quarles' *Hieroglyphics of the Life of Man,* beginning "Behold how short a span," is headed by an emblem and a quotation from Job 14:2: "He cometh forth like a flower, and is cut down." Like George Herbert's "The Altar" or "Wings," Quarles' poem is "patterned": the first line of each stanza, italicized by Quarles, makes a couplet stating the theme of the poem as a whole: *"Behold / Alas, / Our days / We spend / How vain, / They be / How soon / They end."*

The final stanza, pyramided on the page to suggest both an altar and man's ironic growth into nothingness, illustrates Quarles' plain, simple diction and penchant for the medieval theme of *contemptus mundi*:

They end
When scarce begun;
And ere we apprehend
That we begin to live, our life is done;
Man, count thy days, and if they flee too fast
For thy dull thoughts to count, count every day thy last.

Such quaint verses may have been scorned by intellectuals in the seventeenth century, but as Horace Walpole said: "Milton was forced to wait till the world had done admiring Quarles." In a way, Quarles was ideally equipped for the office of poet laureate of the Protestant masses: his sensibilities were baroque, his style vaguely metaphysical; he conveys George Herbert's piety and simplicity without taxing readers with Herbert's angular wit and emotional depth; he riddles in hieroglyphics like Richard Crashaw, another baroque poet, but he avoids Crashaw's "papist" ritualism and humid sensuality. Like George Wither and John Bunyan, Quarles was greatly admired by Puritans, whom, as a devout Anglican and Royalist, Quarles heatedly attacked in two prose pamphlets, *The New Distemper* (1645) and *Judgment and Mercy for Afflicted Souls* (1646).

On the brink of the Civil War Quarles succeeded Thomas Middleton to the office of chronologer of London, and published a series of prose pamphlets which, although anti-Puritan, were moderate and temperate for the times. His prose is more brisk and good-humored than his poetry, but just as plain. His *Enchiridion* (1640; enlarged edition, 1641) is a collection of moral counsels in verse and epigrammatic prose reflecting the twin influences of Machiavelli and Francis Bacon. Quarles' only known play, *The Virgin Widow,* a comedy written around 1641-42 and published five years after his death, is a somewhat inept but always interesting allegory in verse and prose of Lady Albion (England) beset by conflicts of church and state.

In 1618 Quarles married Ursula Woodgate, of St. Andrews, Holborn, the "dear Ursula" to whom he always referred with devotion, and after his death she wrote his memoir, "A Short Relation of the Life and Death of Mr. Francis Quarles," in *Solomon's Recantation, Entitled Ecclesiastes, Paraphrased* (1645), in which she complains bitterly of her husband's persecution by the government (possibly because of his authorship of the anonymous pamphlet *The Loyal Convert* [1644], which ironically—in view of Quarles' lifelong anti-Catholicism—was branded as "papist" in sentiment). When Quarles died, Ursula and her nine surviving children (she bore eighteen in all) were left completely destitute.

The standard edition is still the unsatisfactory *The Complete Works in Prose and Verse of Francis Quarles,* ed. A. B. Grosart, 3 vols. (1880-81), which contains a biography, bibliography, and engravings with the poems. There is a good selection of Quarles' *Emblems* in *Seventeenth-Century Prose and Poetry,* ed. A. M. Witherspoon and F. J. Warnke (2d ed. 1957).

Quip for an Upstart Courtier, A. See GREENE, ROBERT.

R

Raleigh (or Ralegh), Sir Walter (1552?–1618). Courtier, explorer, historian, and poet. Born of a poor but distinguished family in Devonshire, Raleigh went to Oriel College, Oxford, at age fifteen and left in 1572 without taking a degree. During his early years he campaigned in France with a Huguenot army, accompanied his half-brother Sir Humphrey Gilbert on several expeditions to the West Indies and the St. Lawrence River, and went on raids against Spanish ships and ports.

After a brief residence at the Middle Temple around 1575, Raleigh commanded a company of infantry in Ireland, where he earned a reputation for daring against the enemy and insolence to his superiors. By 1581 he was at court as a protégé of Robert Dudley, earl of Leicester, and for the next decade Raleigh was the cynosure among the queen's favorites, rivaled only by Essex after 1587. Raleigh was dashingly handsome, dressed flamboyantly, and moved about with easy confidence in a circle of notables that included Lord Burghley, Leicester, and the queen's personal astrologer and mathematical wizard, John Dee. Raleigh also cultivated the friendship of Edmund Spenser, who praised Raleigh's poetry in *Colin Clout's Come Home Again;* after visiting Spenser at Kilcolman, Raleigh accompanied him to England to publish the first three books of *The Faerie Queene* and promote the poem at court. Raleigh has also been associated with a group of intellectuals that included Thomas Hariot, the great mathematician, Henry Percy, ninth earl of Northumberland, and the poets George Chapman, Christopher Marlowe, and Matthew Roydon.

According to some modern scholars, Raleigh's coterie became known as the "school of night" because of its atheistic views and study of occultism, Shakespeare employs the phrase in *Love's Labour's Lost:* "Black is the badge of hell, / The hue of dungeons and the school of night" (IV, *iii,* 254-55); the character of Armado in that play has been identified, on very slender evidence, with Raleigh. Although the existence of the "school of night" has never been ascertained, it is a fact that Raleigh was regarded by many of his contemporaries as a skeptic and perhaps even a "lewd atheist," a reputation no doubt encouraged by his bitter rivals for the queen's favor in the Essex faction, which included, among others, the young earl of Southampton, Shakespeare's patron.

Most of the thirty or forty extant poems attributed to Raleigh were probably written during the ten years he basked in the queen's favor. As appropriate to a gentleman of power and influence, he demurred from publishing his poems, which circulated in manuscript until printed, often anonymously or with pseudonyms, in miscellanies such as *The Phoenix Nest* (1593), *England's Helicon* (1600), and Davison's *Poetical Rhapsody* (1602), or in the songbooks of William Byrd. As a result, Raleigh's poetry presents extremely difficult problems of attribution and dating. In style, the poems stem from no single literary school or tradition; many are colloquial and rough-hewn in the manner of Wyatt, others taut and brittle of wit in a way suggestive of Donne, but with little of Donne's humor or philosophical and metrical complexity. Raleigh's recurring themes are mutability and the vanity of human wishes, his prevailing tone an acrid disillusionment coupled with stoical resignation to the injustices and miseries of the world:

> What is our life? a play of passion;
> Our mirth, the music of division;
> Our mothers' wombs the tiring-houses be
> Where we are dressed for this short comedy.

In "The Nymph's Reply to the Shepherd" Raleigh ruthlessly strips away the pastoral idealism of Marlowe's popular lyric "Come live with me and be my love":

> Thy gowns, thy shoes, thy beds of roses,
> Thy cap, thy kirtle, and thy posies
> Soon break, soon wither, soon forgotten—
> In folly ripe, in reason rotten.

In "The Lie" Raleigh angrily orders his soul to cast the lie of virtue into the teeth of a hypocritical world:

> Go, soul, the body's guest
> Upon a thankless errand;
> Fear not to touch the best;
> The truth shall be thy warrant.
> Go, since I needs must die,
> And give the world the lie.

If such lines seem to foreshadow Donne's unadorned directness, it is not because Raleigh is "metaphysical," but simply individualistic, relatively independent of the golden lyricists of his time, and totally anti-Petrarchan.

A major poem on a somewhat different order is Raleigh's *A Book of the Ocean to Cynthia,* a fragment that survives as the eleventh and part of the twelfth book of what Raleigh may have intended to be an epic in praise of Queen Elizabeth. Not printed until 1870, it consists of 520 lines in decasyllabic quatrains in which Raleigh rather tediously laments his unrequited love for the queen. This only extant version of the poem may represent a hastily composed redaction done while Raleigh was in the Tower in 1592 and out of favor with Elizabeth. It is not, in all probability, the same version that Raleigh read to Spenser at Kilcolman and that Spenser praised in *Colin Clout's Come Home Again* and in his dedicatory epistle to Raleigh in the first edition of *The Faerie Queene.* The tone of the fragment is uniformly lugubrious. Love and beauty are shown to be "All slaves to age, and vassals unto time, / Of which repentance writes the tragedy," although Raleigh generates occasional excitement in recalling his past glories in the service of the queen:

> To seek new worlds for gold, for praise, for glory,
> To try desire, to try love severed far;
> When I was gone she sent her memory,
> More strong than were ten thousand ships of war...

Few courtiers, and none of such relatively humble origins, prospered so well and so rapidly at the hands of the tight-fisted Queen Elizabeth. She granted Raleigh lease to the regal Durham House on the Strand, formerly occupied by the bishops of Durham, and gave him an estate at Sherborne and 40,000 acres in Munster. Moreover, she granted him monopolies such as the export of certain cloths and imports of wines, and made him lord warden of the stannaries, a lucrative position enabling him to share in the profits of the West Country tin mines. In addition, he was knighted (1584), made lieutenant of Cornwall (1585), and captain of the Queen's Guard (1587). His honors, emoluments, and involvements must have seemed endless, and his brain seethed with a thousand schemes—agricultural and alchemical projects, shipbuilding, colonization in Ireland and North America, plans for looting riches from the hated Spaniards. Yet Raleigh's career, even at the acme of his powers, remained ominously circumscribed. Although he served in Parliament and took an avid interest in affairs of state, the queen refused to admit him into any of the inner chambers of actual decision making and responsibility. As if in tacit acknowledgment of some instability in his nature, the queen kept him from the Privy Council, the Star Chamber, and the really important governorships and military commands.

Raleigh's paradoxical status at court, together with his early training at sea and his visionary disposition, impelled him to seek his fortunes abroad. When Sir Humphrey Gilbert drowned off the Azores in September 1583, Raleigh received his kinsman's patent for establishing an English colony in North America. The first of Raleigh's three expeditions to Virginia sailed in two small ships under the command of two of Raleigh's friends, Arthur Barlowe and Philip Amadas (the latter only twenty years old); they followed the tradewind route of Columbus and Verrazano to the West Indies, went up the North Carolina coast, and landed at what is now Roanoke Island. They returned to England the same year with two young Indians to display at Queen Elizabeth's court. At Raleigh's request, Richard Hakluyt printed Barlowe's account of the expedition in *A Discourse Concerning Western Planting,* a work calculated to persuade the queen and other would-be investors that Virginia could be cultivated into a vast plantation of bananas, sugarcane, pineapples, and sassafras (the last greatly in demand for treating syphilis), and contained enough gold in its mountains to equal the treasures of Mexico.

The second expedition, launched in 1585, only seven months after the return of the first, represents Raleigh's greatest administrative achievement. The queen did not permit him to accompany any of the Virginia expeditions; his task was to raise funds, select the key members of the crew, outfit the ships, and plan the objectives of the mission. While his ships were abroad on these expeditions, Raleigh kept the interest of his countrymen alive by feeding Richard Hakluyt's presses with descriptions of vast natural resources waiting to be exploited in the New World. As Sir Philip Sidney wryly observed, Hakluyt sometimes served in the capacity of "Raleigh's trumpet" heralding the dawn of an English empire that would dwarf the awesome powers of Spain.

The chief obstacle to Raleigh's ambition was money; he exhausted all his own wealth on the Virginia enterprise (over £40,000), begged and cajoled others to invest, and ordered his commanders to plunder Spanish ships and Caribbean settlements to help finance the expeditions. For Raleigh's second expedition to Virginia the queen donated gunpowder and *The Tiger,* a ship of the line (mentioned in Shakespeare's *Macbeth,* I, *iii*). Sir Francis Walsingham, Lord Burghley, and other wealthy statesmen eagerly invested in the second voyage, for England and Spain had severed relations and the queen gave permission to loot Spanish ships wherever they were found.

Raleigh gave command of the second expedition to his cousin, Sir Richard Grenville, later celebrated for his heroism in Raleigh's stirring *Report of the Fight About the Isles of the Azores* (1591). As governor of the colony Raleigh appointed Ralph Lane, who had served with him in Ireland. The other key members of the company attest to Raleigh's admirable foresight, for he also sent Thomas Hariot, his tutor in mathematics and navigation, who was assigned the tasks of studying the Indians, describing natural resources, and mapping the terrain. In preparation for this work Hariot learned some Algonquian from the two natives brought to England by Barlowe. Raleigh also included in the company an artist and surveyor, John White, who was to make illustrations of Virginia and the Indians. Hariot's detailed description of the second Virginia voyage was later published, together with White's drawings, as *A Brief and True Report of the New Found Land of Virginia* (1588). Translated into Latin, French, and German by Theodor de Bry, Hariot's account served for more than a century as a definitive source of information about the New World.

The second expedition sailed for the "City of Raleigh" on April 9, 1585, in seven ships with about five hundred men, including 108 colonists. Other ships not yet outfitted were held in reserve as a relief force scheduled for departure in June. Sir Richard Grenville, who was more concerned with booty than colonization, captured several rich prizes in the West Indies and Puerto Rico, landed Ralph Lane and the colonists on Roanoke Island, and returned to England. After many hardships the colonists were relieved by an unexpected visit from Sir Francis Drake's squadron; they abandoned Roanoke in June 1586 and returned to England with Drake. Two days later Raleigh's reserve force arrived, found the settlement deserted, and also headed for home.

Even before their return, Raleigh was preparing a third expedition to Virginia. This one, however, he intended to be a self-perpetuating community rather than a trading post or—as the Spanish believed—a naval base for operations against the Spanish in the Caribbean. To colonize Virginia, Raleigh recruited fourteen families (which he planned would become the future aristocracy of the New World), numbering eighty-nine men, seventeen women, and eleven children. They sailed from Plymouth on May 8,

1587, touched in at Puerto Rico, and landed on Roanoke Island on July 22. Soon the colony was beset by troubles with the Indians, and the new governor, John White, returned to England to ask Raleigh for reinforcements. After long delays resulting from England's preparations against the Spanish Armada, the relief force finally sailed in March 1590, and in August Raleigh's men arrived at Roanoke to find the colony razed and totally deserted. To this day it remains uncertain what happened to Raleigh's lost colony of Roanoke.

Any further expeditions to Virginia were forestalled by a sharp decline of Raleigh's fortunes at court. In 1592 the queen was outraged to learn of Raleigh's secret marriage to Elizabeth Throckmorton, one of her maids of honor, and Raleigh was sent to the Tower for several months. In 1594 he was charged with atheism, the substance of the allegation being that he had made certain controversial observations on the nature of the soul while dining with a clergyman.

Thus a primary motive of Raleigh's expedition to the Orinoco River in 1595 was not only to discover the fabled riches of El Dorado but to recover the favor of the queen. At the mouth of the Orinoco, Raleigh was forced back by heavy floods on the very threshold of what he believed to be the mythical El Dorado. He returned to England with some gold, only to discover widespread rumors to the effect that he had never been to Guiana at all but had remained in Cornwall and sent ships to Barbary to purchase gold. Partly to squash such absurd slander, Raleigh wrote a vivid description of the voyage, *The Discovery of the Large, Rich, and Beautiful Empire of Guiana, with a Relation of the Great and Golden City of Manoa Which the Spaniards Call El Dorado* (1596), which Hakluyt later added to his *Voyages* (1598 ed.).

When James I came to the throne, Raleigh found himself the vassal of a monarch who thoroughly despised him. Although men like Lord Henry Howard rushed forth to poison the new king's opinion even before meeting Raleigh, "England's Solomon" would doubtless have scorned Raleigh even without the assistance of Raleigh's army of enemies at court. James I glowed with dogmatic piety, whereas Raleigh was widely reputed to be an atheist; the king had blamed most of man's vices and physical infirmities on "drinking tobacco" in his much-touted treatise *A Counterblast to Tobacco,* whereas Raleigh celebrated the "divine weed" as a salubrious gift of the gods. Most important, however, James was determined to keep peace with Spain, even at the price of appeasement, and Raleigh was England's most notorious warmonger where Spain was concerned.

Shortly after James came to power Raleigh was arrested on the incredible charge of conspiring with Lord Cobham and several others to overthrow the king on behalf of the Spanish. The crown's shameful case against Raleigh was prosecuted zealously by Sir Edward Coke, the attorney general; and one of Raleigh's most hated enemies, Lord Henry Howard, was among the judges. On the way to his trial the angry populace tried to mob the man they had loathed for years because of his arrogance and wealth, but Raleigh behaved with such dignity and probity during the hearings that popular opinion soon changed and he was viewed as the victim of a sordid conspiracy. Nevertheless, he was found guilty and sentenced to death, although the sentence was suspended at the last moment. For the next thirteen years Raleigh lived in the Tower with his wife and two sons.

It was in the Tower that he wrote the bulk of his prose works, many of them dedicated to young Prince Henry, who frequently visited Raleigh to hear the versatile courtier discourse on agriculture, law, politics, trade and commerce, and navigation and naval affairs. Most of the prose works Raleigh wrote during this period were published posthumously, including a treatise on government and politics, *The Prerogative of Parliaments in England* (1628); a courtesy book, *Instructions to His Son* (1632); a collection of didactic rules on statecraft for the edification of Prince Henry, *The Prince, or Maxims of State* (1642): a medley on various topics, including a long treatise on improving the design of ships, *Judicious and Select Essays and Observations* (1650); a book of philosophical meditations, *Sir Walter Raleigh's Skeptic, or Speculations* (1651; entitled in the 1657 edition and afterward *The Remains*); and still another treatise on statecraft, *The Cabinet-Council* (1658), which John Milton published from manuscript.

The best-known product of Raleigh's restless energy during these years in the Tower was his ambitious *History of the World* (1614), a huge fragment of a work in which he planned to trace the hand of Providence from the creation of the world to his own times. The book includes a lengthy preface, four chapters on the Creation, the history of the Jews, early Egyptian history, Greek mythology, and early Roman history to the Roman conquest of Macedon in 130 B.C. Raleigh's theme is summarized in his observation that "the judgments of God are forever unchangeable," a fact the reasonable man must accept with stoical resignation and unflinching Christian faith. The simple piety and religious vitalism of Raleigh's essentially medieval view of history confirms that his "atheism" was an allegation chiefly promulgated by his enemies. His skepticism, however, is pervasively felt throughout his preface, but it is directed at secular rulers rather than God. Indeed, he finds nothing complimentary to say of any English monarch except James I. He is especially critical of Henry VIII, father of Queen Elizabeth (now safely deceased): "If all the pictures and patterns of a merciless prince were lost in the world, they might all again be painted to the life out of the story of this king." While accepting the literal truth of Scripture, Raleigh belittles a variety of secular authorities such as Aristotle, scholastic philosophers, and most kings and magistrates from the Maccabees to the Tudors. In his preface he sardonically apologizes for sparing more recent rulers from his indictment because "whosoever, in writing a modern history, shall follow truth too near the heels, it may happily strike out his teeth.'

For Raleigh, history was a mirthless tragicomedy in which man's lust for power and glory is mocked by mutability, death, and God's unfathomable purposes. Significantly, perhaps, Raleigh's most frequent allusions and paraphrases are from Ecclesiastes, but not even that eloquent text in the Authorized Version exceeds the sharp poignancy of Raleigh's magnificent apostrophe to death toward the conclusion of his *History of the World:*

> O eloquent, just, and mighty death! whom none could advise, thou hast persuaded; what none hath dared, thou hast done; and whom all the world hath flattered, thou only hast cast out of the world and despised; thou hast drawn together all the far-stretched greatness, all the pride, cruelty, and ambition of man, and covered it all over with these two narrow words: *Hic jacet!*

Another work from this period is Raleigh's *Instructions to His Son* (1623), the brief popularity of which (it went through six editions by 1636) owes more to the reputation of its author than to any artistic merits of the work, for it reflects all the maudlin formality and stiffness of the usual "advice to a son" type of writing then in vogue among conduct books (see COURTESY LITERATURE). Although presumably addressed to Raleigh's younger son Carew, born in the Tower in 1605, it is remarkably devoid of parental warmth or even of concern for the psychological and spiritual problems of life. Instead, Raleigh assumes the posture of Polonius or Francis Bacon, sermonizing on more practical matters like career and acquaintances, clothes and deportment. Pelucid reason (by which Raleigh means a faculty enabling one to make unimpassioned choices) must be the guide in all matters pertaining to career, friendship, and marriage. Something of the ruthless Elizabethan courtier cuts through Raleigh's rhetoric when he cautions his son: "Make election rather of thy betters than thy inferiors, shunning always such as are poor and needy."

In one sense, Raleigh's *Instructions* is strangely revealing of the author, who, in effect, earnestly counsels his son to be everything Raleigh was not. Thus the passionate and headstrong father advises the son to be rational and prudent in all matters, especially marriage; disparages ostentatious and expensive clothes; and cautions against indiscretions in private conversations, which Raleigh ruefully describes as "whirlpools and quicksands." Although Raleigh's *Instructions* is not very autobiographical—albeit at one point he vehemently attacks his old enemy Essex—it sustains the same tone of grim realism and manly stoicism characteristic of his poems and *History of the World.* He mingles a sometimes ruthless practicality with rustic piety and resignation to the folly and brutality of men. "All is vanity and weariness," he observes of the world, "yet such a weariness and vanity that we shall ever complain of it and love it for all that."

In 1616, when Raleigh was almost sixty-five, he was released from the Tower to lead another expedition to the Orinoco in search of gold. The king stipulated that Raleigh do nothing to antagonize Spain, but this condition was made impossible to obey when Raleigh's enemies leaked news of the expedition to the Spanish. While Raleigh lay ill of fever in Trinidad, a party led by his son Walter was ambushed by the Spanish near St. Tomas, and in the ensuing battle the settlement was burned and Raleigh's son killed. Returning to England in a rotting ship carrying nothing more valuable to the king than starving seamen, Raleigh was arrested on the old charges of 1603; largely to appease the Spanish, he was executed at Westminster on October 29, 1618.

There are several excellent biographies of Raleigh, including Stephen J. Greenblatt's *Sir Walter Raleigh (1973).* See also Willard M. Wallace, *Sir Walter Raleigh* (1959); and Margaret Irwin, *That Great Lucifer: A Portrait of Sir Walter Raleigh* (1960). Raleigh's philosophical activities and ideas are studied in Muriel C. Bradbrook, *The School of Night: A Study in the Literary Relationships of Sir Walter Raleigh* (1936); C. F. Tucker Brooke, "Sir Walter Raleigh as Poet and Philosopher," *ELH,* V (1938): Eleanor Grace Clark, *Ralegh and Marlowe* (1941); and Ernest Strathmann, *Sir Walter Ralegh: A Study in Elizabethan Skepticism* (1951). *The Poems of Sir Walter Ralegh,* ed. Agnes M. C. Latham (1929; rev. ed., 1950), is the standard edition and contains a full discussion of sources and texts. The standard edition of Raleigh's prose works, including his letters and *History of the World,* is still *The Works of Sir Walter Raleigh,* ed. William Oldys and Thomas Birch, 8 vols. (1829). There are more recent editions of the prose (including Raleigh's letters) by G. E. Hadow (1917) and W. R. Macklin (1926). The best edition of *The Discovery... of Guiana* is by V. T. Harlow (1928); of *Instructions to His Son* by C. Whibley (1927). Raleigh's *History of the World* is treated at length by Sir C. Firth, *Essays Historical and Literary* (1938).

Ralph Roister Doister. A comedy attributed to Nicholas UDALL, written around 1553 and first printed in an undated edition in 1566 or 1567. It is based on the comedies of Plautus and Terence. *Ralph Roister Doister* combines the Roman five-act structure and classical unities with boisterous native humor and a rural English setting. The prologue refers to Plautus and Terence and describes the play as a "comedy or interlude."

The titular hero is an arrogant braggart who seeks the hand of Dame Christian Custance, a rich and virtuous widow betrothed to Gawyn Goodluck, a merchant absent from the village on business abroad. Ralph is accompanied by a sidekick, Matthew Merrygreek, a carefree, wily parasite and practical joker, and two servants, Harpax and Dobinet Doughty. On behalf of Ralph, the servants insinuate themselves into the confidence of Dame Christian's maids Tibet Talkapace, Annot Alyface, and old Madge Mumblecrust, who receive a scolding from their mistress when they present Roister Doister's ring and love tokens.

When Ralph learns from Matthew Merrygreek that Dame Christian finds him totally unacceptable, he is overwhelmed by melancholy. Merrygreek contrives to arouse him by bringing him face to face with Dame Christian, but when she roundly spurns him again Ralph falls into a swoon. He revives in time to hear Merrygreek read his love letter to Dame Christian in such a way that Merrygreek's punctuation turns all of Ralph's flattery into insults. Ralph now threatens revenge against the Scrivener who composed the letter. The Scrivener, however, faces the braggart down and proves he wrote the letter correctly. Merrygreek then admits he misread the letter and promises to set matters straight with Dame Christian.

Meanwhile Gawyn Goodluck's servant Sym Suresby returns home, sees Ralph and Merrygreek at Dame Christian's house, and receives the false impression that she has betrayed her troth to his master. Thereupon the outraged lady emphatically spurns the unwelcome suitor and Ralph retaliates by threatening to burn her house down. A wild melee ensues between Dame Christian's household and Ralph's entourage, with the ever-wily Merrygreek switching allegiance and conspiring with the lady against his master. Ralph is humiliatingly routed by the "Amazons"; Gawyn Goodluck returns, is reconciled with his lady, and presents a banquet to which he invites the repentant Merrygreek and even Roister Doister. The play concludes with a song in praise of Queen Mary Tudor.

Ralph Roister Doister is the earliest extant example of an English comedy in the vernacular written to conform to classical models. It also marks an early popularization of those staples of Roman comedy, the MILES GLORIOSUS, or "braggart soldier," here portrayed in Ralph, and the "parasite," seen in Merrygreek. Merrygreek's role also suggests the Vice character of the morality plays and the parasite of the Italian COMMEDIA DELL'ARTE. Although strictly conforming to the classical unity of place, *Ralph Roister Doister* exceeds the unity of time by portraying actions that occur over a period of almost three days. It is less concentrated in action than GAMMER GURTON'S NEEDLE, the other early example of adaptation to classical five-act structure, and considerably more sophisticated in characterizations and theme. In *Roister Doister* there may even be the suggestion of class consciousness in its presentation of a competition for the role of ideal lover among the soldier (Ralph), the scholar (Scrivener), and the merchant (Goodluck), with the accolade bestowed on the newly arrived merchant class. In spite of its doggerel verse and farcical trials by combat, *Roister Doister* is more thoughtfully constructed than it may appear on the surface, much of its broad comedy being satire aimed at the love encounters of the chivalric romances.

An excellent modern text is in *Elizabethan Plays,* ed. A. H. Nethercot, C. R. Baskerville, and V. B. Heltzel (rev. ed. by Nethercot, 1971). Classical and native characterizations are studied by E. P. Vandiver, "The Elizabethan Dramatic Parasite," *SP,* XXXII (1935); and the satiric elements by G. W. Plumstead, "Satirical Parody in *Roister Doister:* A Reinterpretation," *SP,* LX (1964).

Randolph, Thomas (1605-1635). Poet and dramatist. At an unknown date, Randolph entered Westminster School, where he distinguished himself as a precocious poet and scholar, and in 1624 entered Trinity College, Cambridge, on a scholarship. His brief play *The Drinking Academy,* preserved in a Huntington Library manuscript, may have been written as early as 1623 for a production at Westminster, and many of his best plays have been assigned to the Cambridge period, including *Aristippus, or the Jovial Philosopher* (1630), *The Conceited Peddler* (1630), *Hey for Honesty* (1651), and perhaps an early version of *The Muses' Looking Glass* (1638) as well as Randolph's celebrated pastoral drama *Amyntas, or the Impossible Dowry* (wr. 1630). In 1632 one of his best plays, *The Jealous Lovers,* was performed by members of his college before the king and queen, and triumphed over *The Rival Friends,* written for the same occasion by Randolph's rival in drama at Cambridge,Peter Hausted.

Sometime late in 1629 or early 1630, when Cambridge was closed for several months because of the plague, Randolph probably engaged himself to the King's Revels as a regular contributor of plays performed at the Salisbury Court Theater, preceding Richard Brome, another "son of the tribe of Ben," in that capacity of dramatist of the King's Revels. In 1629-30 Randolph was probably in London, where he became an ardent disciple of Ben Jonson, to whom he pays deference in several poems. By 1631 he was back at Cambridge to receive his M. A. degree, and it was here, at the request of the master of Trinity, that he wrote *The Jealous Lovers.* Randolph left Cambridge soon after 1631 and became tutor to the son of one Captain William Stafford of Blatherwick, where Randolph died and was buried March 17, 1655.

With Richard Brome, Randolph was one of the most gifted and precocious of Jonson's followers, a capable poet and a dramatist of minor but considerable talents, and, although his reputation declined after the Restoration, his contemporaries praised him as a rival to both Shakespeare and Jonson. G. E. Bentley in *The Jacobean and Caroline Stage* mentions nearly a hundred allusions to Randolph in the seventeenth century. In his dedicatory poems, elegies, epithalamia, classical translations, and pastoral verses Randolph is more witty and facile than genuinely inspired. In his best-known poem, "A Gratulatory to Mr. Ben Jonson," he acknowledges himself to be a gifted amateur rather than a fully dedicated writer: "I was not born to Helicon, nor dare / Presume to think myself a Muse's heir."

Randolph's poems and plays were collected by W. Carew Hazlitt, 2 vols. (1875). Two convenient editions are those by J.J. Parry, *The Poems and Amyntas of Thomas Randolph* (1917), and G. Thorn-Drury, *The Poems of Thomas Randolph* (1929). There is a Concise Bibliography by S. A. Tannenbaum (1946), supplemented by "Thomas Randolph (1949-65)," ed. G. R. Guffey, in *Elizabethan Bibliographies Supplements,* III (1968).

Rape of Lucrece, The. A narrative poem by William SHAKESPEARE. It was written in 1593-94 and published in the latter year with a dedication by Shakespeare to Henry Wriotheseley, earl of Southampton. *Lucrece* consists of 1,855 lines in rhyme royal (seven-line stanzas rhyming *ab ab bc c*). The story of Lucrece was first told in Ovid's *Fasti,* a poem not translated into English until 1594, although the tale was paraphrased in a number of sources, including William Painter's *Palace of Pleasure* (1566-67), Chaucer's *Legend of Good Women* (c. 1386; lines 1680-1883), and John Gower's *Confessio Amantis* (1390). The style of Shakespeare's poem closely resembles Samuel Daniel's "The Complaint of Rosamond" (1592), in which Rosamond Clifford, Henry II's mistress, mourns her tragic fate in a manner similar to that of characters in *A Mirror for Magistrates.*

Lucrece, beautiful and virtuous wife of Collatinus, is raped by Sextus Tarquinius, son of King Tarquin of Rome, after she graciously entertains him on behalf of her absent husband. Afterward Lucrece sends for her father and husband, to whom she appears attired in mourning habit. She names her assailant, demands revenge, and stabs herself. Her body is taken to Rome to illustrate the tyranny of the Tarquins, and the people are so moved that they exile the Tarquin family and change the government from a monarchy to a republic.

In his dedication to the earl of Southampton of *Venus and Adonis* the year before the publication of *The Rape of Lucrece,* Shakespeare had promised "some graver labor," and *Lucrece* may represent his conscious effort to atone for scandalized reactions to the earlier poem. In any event, *Lucrece* is a solemn and even lugubrious work, heavy with didacticism and emotive rhetoric. The throbbing, often tedious meter is derived from rhyme royal, the same stanza pattern as Daniel's The diction is stilted, the characters wooden, and the action confined largely to long passages of moralizing and declamation. Lucrece devotes over eighty lines to dissuading Tarquin from rape in such tortuously sermonizing lines as these:

And wilt thou be the school where Lust shall learn?
Must he in thee read lectures of such shame?
Wilt thou be glass wherein it shall discern
Authority for sin, warrant for blame?
To privilege dishonor in thy name,
  Thou back'st reproach against long-living laud,
  And mak'st fair reputation but a bawd.

The standard version is in the New Variorum Edition of *The Poems,* ed. Hyder E. Rollins (1938). Two important studies of background and form include Douglas Bush, *Mythology & the Renaissance Tradition in English Literature* (1932, rev. ed., 1963), and Don Cameron Allen, "Some Observations on *The Rape of Lucrece,*" *ShakS,* XV (1962).

Ready and Easy Way to Establish a Free Commonwealth, The. A political pamphlet by John MILTON, written and published in 1660 on the eve of the restoration of Charles II. Milton's tract warns the nation of the dangers inherent in abolishing parliamentary government and returning to monarchy. If king and bishops return, warns Milton, "we may be forced perhaps to fight over again all that we have fought, and spend over again all that we have spent..." It was probably for this defiant tract that Milton was arrested and imprisoned briefly upon the return of the monarchy. It is generally believed that Milton was spared more severe punishment by the intercession of his friend Andrew Marvell. As an alternative to monarchy, Milton proposes a Grand Council chosen by a small electorate serving life terms in office, a scheme partly based on the Netherlands government and partly on Plato's *Republic,* with its guardian class. *The Ready and Easy Way* denounces both democracy and one-man rule.

The standard edition is in *The Works,* ed. Frank A. Patterson, 18 vols. (1931-38), X. Other editions, containing notes and commentary, are in *Of Education, Areopagitica, The Commonwealth,* ed. Laura E. Lockwood (1911); *Areopagitica and Other Prose Writings of John Milton,* ed. William Haller (1927); *The Complete Prose Works,* ed. D. M. Wolfe, 5 vols. (1953-71), V; *John Milton: Complete Poems and Major Prose,* ed. Merritt Y. Hughes (1957); and *The Prose of John Milton,* ed. J. Max Patrick (1967). For additional commentary, see Arthur Barker, *Milton and the Puritan Dilemma,* 1641-1660 (1942), and William Haller, *Liberty and Reformation in the Puritan Revolution* (1955).

Redford, John (d. 1547). For comment on his *Wit and Science,* see INTERLUDE.

Revenge of Bussy D'Ambois, The. A tragedy by George CHAPMAN, written around 1610 and first printed in 1613. Although ostensibly a sequel to Chapman's BUSSY D'AMBOIS, it differs widely in characterization and philosophy from the earlier tragedy. *The Revenge* is based on William Grimestone's *General Inventory of the History of France* (1607). The hero and most of the main characters are entirely Chapman's invention.

Bussy D'Ambois's ghost has appeared to his brother Clermont and demanded revenge against the two men most responsible for his death, the count of Montsurry and the duke of Guise. In addition to Clermont, two others swear vengeance against the murderers—

Montsurry's wife Tamyra and Bussy's fiery and courageous sister Charlotte. For Clermont, however, revenge is problematical: Montsurry refuses to accept an honorable duel and lives barricaded in a house surrounded by guards, and the duke of Guise leads the Catholic faction to which Clermont himself belongs. Meanwhile Charlotte's search for revenge is frustrated by her Machiavellian husband Baligny, who only feigns an alliance with Charlotte while conspiring with Henry III to destroy Guise, Clermont, and the Catholic party at court. At Charlotte's house Clermont is arrested by Henry's soldiers, but is later released by the vacillating king at the urging of Guise. Goaded on by a second appearance of Bussy's impatient ghost and by Charlotte's open scorn, Clermont enlists the aid of Bussy's ghost to get into Montsurry's house and forces the murderer into a fatal duel. As Montsurry dies, the two enemies forgive each other.

In a separate episode Baligny and the king arrange the assassination of Guise. Clermont first learns of Guise's death when he sees the duke's ghost dancing about the body of Montsurry. Revenge against a king is unthinkable for Clermont, but his political loyalty to Guise is like the "cement of two minds." Torn between an impossible revenge and loyalty to the Catholic faction of the duke, Clermont recoils with disgust at "the horrors of the vicious time" and commits suicide. Charlotte and Tamyra retire to a nunnery to live out their lives in penance.

Although Clermont D'Ambois finally succeeded in killing his brother's enemy Montsurry in Act V, he clearly felt revulsion for his own deed. As a protagonist he lacks the impetuous nature of Bussy; he is at once too intellectual and too noble for the barbaric code of revenge. "Rome's Brutus is revived in him," a character notes, and it might be added that Clermont also contains much of Hamlet as well.

The standard edition is in *The Plays and Poems,* ed. T. M. Parrott, 2 vols., I: *The Tragedies* (1910). Robert J. Lordi has edited *The Revenge* in the Regents Renaissance Drama series (1971). For criticism, see Richard H. Perkinson, "Nature and the Tragic Hero in Chapman's Bussy Plays," *MLQ,* III (1942); John W. Wieler, *George Chapman: The Effect of Stoicism Upon His Tragedies* (1949); and Geoffrey Aggeler, "The Unity of Chapman's *Revenge of Bussy D'Ambois," Pacific Coast Philology,* IV (1969).

Revenger's Tragedy, The; or The Loyal Brother. A Senecan tragedy usually attributed to Cyril TOURNEUR, although some scholars have assigned the play to Thomas Middleton. It was first printed anonymously in 1607 as having been performed by the King's Men. No source is known. The scene is Italy during the Renaissance.

Vindice swears revenge against the aged duke who has poisoned Vindice's mistress Gloriana because she would not consent to be his concubine. At the suggestion of his brother Hippolito, Vindice enters the service of the duke's wicked son Lussurioso disguised as a bitter malcontent called Piato. The duke's court is totally corrupt: Lussurioso assigns the malcontent to arrange the seduction of Vindice's own sister Castiza; the duchess is incestuously bedding with the duke's illegitimate son Spurio; and the duke's youngest son (not named in the play) has been arraigned for raping a nobleman's virtuous wife.

Still disguised as Piato, Vindice offers his mother gold in exchange for Castiza's virginity, and although the mother weakens, Castiza stoutly refuses. To put Lussurioso off the track of his sister, Vindice informs him of the duchess's incestuous affair, and the hot-head bursts into her chamber only to find the duke, who angrily throws him in prison on suspicion of attempted murder. Lussurioso's two envious stepbrothers, Supervacuo and Ambitioso, pretend to defend him while actually seeking his execution; in a mixup resulting from their intrigues, however, their youngest brother is executed instead of Lussurioso.

Soon Vindice finds an opportunity for revenge on the duke. As Piato the malcontent, he has been hired by the duke to conduct a lady to a rendezvous; instead, Vindice poisons the skull of Gloriana, which the duke kisses in the dark. As he dies, the duke is forced to watch his son Spurio make love to the duchess.

When the duke's body is discovered, only Piato is accused. Lussurioso ascends to his father's throne, and his first act as duke is to banish the duchess and decree his stepbrother's execution. Two groups plot Lussurioso's assassination. The first, led by Vindice and Hippolito, succeeds; the second group, led by Ambitioso, Supervacuo, and Spurio destroys itself when they fall upon each other in a melee of mutual homicides. A nobleman, Antonio, restores order. Corrupted by their hatred, Vindice and Hippolito are sent away to be executed, and Antonio succeeds to the dukedom.

The Revenger's Tragedy is among the most gruesome and macabre of the Jacobean stage. It turns many of the devices of Senecan revenge tragedy into startling new effects, intensifying both incongruity and realism (see SENECAN TRAGEDY). Only John Marston matches Tourneur's moral revulsion, only John Webster his unmitigated gloom and foreboding. The miserable Vindice, whose lost idealism is symbolized by the decayed head of his mistress, gradually begins to live the role he at first only assumed as the malcontent Piato, "whose brain time has seasoned." The word for Piato is "sick" —an idea worked thoroughly into the language of the play—but the only term for the other characters is "foul," a word that hangs in the dialogue like a cloud of pollution. Although *The Revenger's Tragedy* employs the actions and conventions of Senecan tragedy, its pervasive moral tone and characterizations owe a great deal to John Marston's biting satires and to Thomas Middleton's comedies of intrigue.

The standard edition is in *The Works,* ed. Allardyce Nicoll (1930; repr. 1963). Lawrence J. Ross has edited *The Revenger's Tragedy* for the Regents Renaissance Drama series (1966); R. A. Foakes for the Revels Plays (1966); and Brian Gibbons for the New Mermaid series (1966). For commentary, see Robert Ornstein, "*The Revenger's Tragedy* and Renaissance Naturalism," *SP,* LI (1954); Samuel Schoenbaum, *Middleton's Tragedies* (1955); Fredson Bowers, *Elizabethan Revenge Tragedy 1587-1642* (rev. ed., 1959); Alvin Kernan, *The Cankered Muse* (1959); Peter Lisca, "*The Revenger's Tragedy:* A Study in Irony," *PQ,* XXXVIII (1959); and Peter B. Murray, *A Study of Cyril Tourneur* (1964), which has an exhaustive bibliography.

Rich, Barnabe (1540?-1617). Prose writer and translator. Rich is best known for two prose works: *Rich His Farewell to Military Profession* (1581), a collection of eight tales, and *The Strange and Wonderful Adventures of Don Simonides* (1581, 1584), a two-part romance inspired by John Lyly's *Euphues.* (See FICTION). See also BANDELLO, MATTEO; ROGUE LITERATURE; TRANSLATIONS.

Richard II. A history play by William SHAKESPEARE, written around 1595-96 and first printed in 1597. For his historical material Shakespeare consulted Raphael Holinshed's *Chronicles* (1587 ed.), the first four books of Samuel Daniel's poem *The Civil Wars* (1595), and an anonymous play of uncertain date, *Thomas of Woodstock.*

The first conflict in the play is between Henry Bolingbroke, son of John of Gaunt and cousin of King Richard, and Thomas Mowbray, duke of Norfolk, whom Bolingbroke accuses of embezzlement and complicity in the recent murder of Thomas of Woodstock, duke of Gloucester and Richard's uncle. A trial of combat between Bolingbroke and Mowbray is interrupted by Richard, who banishes them both—Mowbray for life, Bolingbroke for ten years, a sentence Richard later reduces to six at the plea of John of Gaunt. When the aged Gaunt dies, Richard confiscates his lands and wealth to finance a campaign against the Irish, whereupon Bolingbroke returns to England with an army to redeem his patrimony. Bolingbroke's cause is aided by Henry Percy, duke of Northumberland, Lord Ross, Lord Willoughby, and later even by Richard's own weak-willed brother, the duke of York. At Flint Castle Richard meets with Bolingbroke and, after some vacillation, gives over his crown. In spite of the objections of the bishop of Carlisle, who argues that no sovereign anointed by God can be legitimately deposed, Bolingbroke announces that he intends to ascend the throne. Richard's queen is sent to France and Richard to prison at Pomfret Castle, where he is murdered by Sir Pierce of Exton, who does the deed after overhearing Bolingbroke lament the hazards of leaving Richard alive.

After Bolingbroke's coronation as Henry IV, the duke of York discovers that his son Aumerle is implicated in a plot to kill the new monarch, and York, in spite of his wife's pleas, exposes the plot to the king. Magnanimously, the new Henry IV pardons Aumerle, but does not extend his clemency to the other rebels. Although he admits that he wanted Richard dead, Bolingbroke repudiates any complicity in the murder and resolves at the end of the play that he will atone for Richard's death by a crusade to the Holy Land.

Richard II, the first of the second tetralogy of history plays—the so-called Henriad Cycle—which also includes HENRY IV, Parts I and II, and HENRY V, marks a significant advance over Shakespeare's earlier histories and a step in the direction of the later tragedies. Richard is the first of Shakespeare's introspective, melancholy heroes, a character far more complex than the antic villain Richard III. *Richard II* is also the first play of Shakespeare's to portray a fatal conflict between two "mighty opposites" (Richard and Bolingbroke), antagonists representing contrasting personalities and antithetical values. Richard is dreamy, impetuous, and incompetent—a man of words rather than actions; Bolingbroke is practical, shrewd, and cooly efficient—a doer rather than a talker. Richard, the last of the colorful Plantagenet kings, symbolizes all the romantic pageantry and ritualism of the fading medieval past; Bolingbroke heralds the new order with its political utilitarianism and purposive energy.

The contrast between Richard and Bolingbroke also personifies conflicting claims to authority. Richard is arrogant, corrupt, and tyrannical, but he is God's anointed king ruling by divine right; Bolingbroke is competent, and his cause against Richard is just, but he bears no legal claim to the throne. Rather than resolving this tension between the claims of divine right and superior ability. Shakespeare distributes arguments on both sides. He makes Richard headstrong and vain, but not villainous. His complicity in the assassination of his uncle Thomas of Woodstock, which is clearly stated in the chronicles, is only hinted at in the play, and Shakespeare cultivates great sympathy for Richard as his power declines. Bolingbroke, on the other hand, is no ordinary usurper. He returns from exile only to regain the lands that are rightfully his; he moves toward power almost imperceptibly, and he receives the crown from Richard's own hands.

Shakespeare's *Richard II* is often compared with Marlowe's EDWARD II, for both plays find the dramatists at similar stages of development, and their dramas represent significant innovations on the genre of the CHRONICLE PLAY. Both plays revive the latent affinities of Elizabethan tragedy to history, an association evident since *Gorboduc,* and in both plays the chronicles provide occasion for profound and ironic character study. Neither play quite reaches the limits of tragedy, however, for both Richard and Edward are weak and vacillating men whose vision remain pathetically circumscribed by petty vanities. Yet both rise in stature as their powers wane, and the ironic contrast that emerges is that of men odious in public office but admirable in personal life. Marlowe limits the political implications of his drama by making Edward's antagonist Mortimer a scheming Machiavellian motivated solely by personal ambition. What sweeps Shakespeare's Bolingbroke to the throne is the tide of ineluctible history, and the impotent Richard, for whom the time is out of joint, melts like a snowman under Bolingbroke's rising sun.

For text, commentary, and notes, two editions are essential: the New Cambridge Edition, ed. J. Dover Wilson (1939), and the New Variorum Edition, ed. Matthew Black (1955). Important criticism includes E. M. W. Tillyard, *Shakespeare's History Plays* (1944); Irving Ribner, *The English History Play in the Age of Shakespeare* (1957); M. M. Reese, *The Cease of Majesty* (1961); and Robert R. Reed, Jr., *Richard II: From Mask to Prophet* (1968). See also *Twentieth-Century Interpretations of Richard II: A Collection of Critical Essays,* ed. Paul M. Cubeta (1971).

Richard III. A history play by William SHAKESPEARE, probably written in 1592-93, and first printed in 1597. For his historical sources Shakespeare consulted the second edition of Raphael Holinshed's *Chronicles* (1587), which, in turn, took its material about Richard III's reign from Edward Hall's *The Union of the Two Noble and Illustrious Families of Lancaster and York* (1548). Hall derived much of his account from Sir Thomas More's *History of Richard III* (wr.c. 1513-14) and Polydore Vergil's *Anglica Historia* (1534). Shakespeare's play dramatizes historical events from the death of Edward IV (1483) to the defeat and death of Richard at Bosworth Field (1485).

As Edward IV, head of the Yorkist faction, lies sick and dying, his brother, the diabolical Richard, plots a devious course to the throne. First, he connives to have his brother George, duke of Clarence, imprisoned in the Tower on trumped-up charges, then later murdered. Next, he successfully wins the hand of Lady Anne, widow of the Lancastrian Edward, prince of Wales, at the very bier of her dead father-in-law, Henry VI, although Richard openly admits to her that he was responsible for the murders of both king and prince. Next he engineers the execution of Lords Hastings, Rivers, and Grey, whereupon, through the aid of the Machiavellian duke of Buckingham, Richard assumes the throne. Other atrocities soon follow—the murder of the little princes in the Tower, the execution of Buckingham for treason, and Richard's cynical efforts to rid himself of Lady Anne and marry his niece Elizabeth of York, whom he plots to kill soon after the ceremony. Richard's star declines with the rise of Henry Tudor, earl of Richmond, who gathers a force against the "bloody boar." Richard is defeated at Bosworth Field by Henry Tudor, who becomes Henry VII, first of the great Tudor monarchs. Henry ends the long feud between the houses of Lancaster and York by announcing his betrothal to Edward IV's daughter, Elizabeth of York.

Richard III is the last play of the so-called first tetralogy, which includes HENRY VI, Parts I-III. *Henry VI,* Part III, ends with Richard's murder of Henry VI in the Tower, and *Richard III* extends his villainy to making him a symbol of the curse laid on the House of Lancaster because of Henry's usurpation of the throne. The play owes as much to the SENECAN TRAGEDY of Kyd and Marlowe as to the chronicles. Following Marlowe's *Tamburlaine* and *The Jew of Malta,* Shakespeare unifies his play around one titanic figure, a method he had not used in the episodic *Henry VI* plays, and he imitates Marlowe also by introducing his character with a long and bold soliloquy:

And therefore, since I cannot prove a lover,
To entertain these fair well-spoken days,
I am determined to prove a villain
And hate the idle pleasures of these days.
[I, *i*, 28-31]

There is nothing subtle in Shakespeare's delineation of Richard. Unlike Macbeth, he is utterly lacking in any virtues, and he exults in his Machiavellian malevolence. Even Richard's audacity is equated with bestiality, for he is described as England's "bottled spider," "mad dog," and "ravaging boar." The grotesque cripple performing the role of a virile courtly lover as he gilds Lady Anne's vanity with eloquence establishes the image of how far and wide the protean Richard can range in lurid perversity. He is a bustling arranger of horrors, an assiduous artist full of playful cruelty and murderous intensity. His lurid character stems from all the theatrical conventions that went into his making—sportive Vice of the morality plays and scheming Machiavel of Kyd and Marlowe's Senecan dramas. His nightmare world is the milieu of Seneca's turgid closet dramas—violence, revenge, ghosts, bombastic speeches, dire prophecies, and curses. His diabolism anticipates such later creations as Edmund in *King Lear* and Iago in *Othello.*

A standard text is the New Cambridge edition, ed. J. Dover Wilson (1954). For criticism, see E. M. W. Tillyard, *Shakespeare's History Plays* (1944); Irving Ribner, *The English History Play in the Age of Shakespeare* (1957); M. M. Reese, *The Cease of Majesty* (1961); Ruth L. Anderson, "The Pattern of Behavior Culminating in *Macbeth,*" *SEL,* III (1963); A. L. French, "The World of *Richard III,*" *ShakeS,* IV (1969); and Waldo F. McNeir, "The Masks of Richard the Third," *SEL,* XI (1971).

Richard the Third, The History of. A biography in both Latin and English by Sir Thomas More. Written in about 1513-14, and considered one of the earliest biographies in English, More's work is probably derived from a lost Latin biography by John Morton, archbishop of Canterbury; it became a chief source for Shakespeare's *Richard III* (see BIOGRAPHY). Left incomplete in the middle of a speech by Buckingham a week after Richard's coronation, the English version was completed by Richard Grafton and published in the chronicles of Hardyng and Hall (1543). More's nephew William Rastell published a separate edition in English in 1557. More originally planned the work to describe events through the reign of Henry VII, but put the project aside sometime in 1518.

More's *Richard the Third* is noteworthy as the most brilliant historical study before Bacon's HENRY VII. It is not only a masterpiece of English prose, but a classic for its ironic characterizations and dramatic episodes. As history, More's account is not entirely reliable, being derived largely from hearsay by such enemies of Richard as More's friend Cardinal Morton, but it excels as pure literature as More ingeniously manipulates characters and events to strengthen his pervasive theme of the evils of usurpation and tyranny. Hence Richard is portrayed as a monster—lustful, insatiable, deformed both physically and mentally; and the unfortunate characters surrounding More's titanic Richard—Jane Shore, Buckingham, the two Elizabeths—are drawn with ambiguity, irony, and compassion. More's instinct for drama is apparent in his emphasis on Richard's cat-and-mouse game with Edward IV's widow, Richard's ghastly dreams, Lord Stanley's prophetic nightmare of Richard as a ravenous boar, the famous episode of the Bishop of

Ely's strawberries, and the equally familiar episode in which Buckingham and the mayor of London try to persuade an unresponsive crowd of citizens to proclaim Richard the true king. All these scenes, and many other ironic events and nuances of character, Shakespeare incorporated into his history play.

The standard edition is by Richard S. Sylvester in the Yale edition of *The Complete Works,* ed. Edward Surtz, S. J., J. H. Hexter, et al., 5 vols., II (1963-69), which contains much scholarly data. Other important commentary is in *The English Works of Sir Thomas More,* ed. W. E. Campbell, R. W. Chambers, et al., 2 vols., I (1931). See also Leonard F. Dean, "Literary Problems in More's *Richard the Third,*" *PMLA,* LVIII (1943).

Roaring Girl, The; or Moll Cutpurse. A comedy by Thomas MIDDLETON and Thomas DEKKER, written around 1610 and printed in 1611. It was based on the activities of one Mary Frith (c. 1584-c. 1660), a notorious thief, fortuneteller, and street-brawling virago.

When his father opposes his marriage to Mary Fitzallard, Sebastian Wengrave pretends to court the "roaring girl," two-fisted, tobacco-smoking Moll Cutpurse, who, though knowledgeable in the ways of the London underworld, is basically virtuous and kindly. Old Wengrave sends his parasite Trapdoor to destroy Moll, but she succeeds in eluding the old man's stratagems and bringing about the marriage of Sebastian and Mary.

In other intrigues, the lecherous Laxton attempts to seduce Mistress Gallipot, an apothecary's wife; Jack Dapper pursues the elusive Mistress Tiltyard, a feather merchant's spouse; and young Goshawk tries to convince Mistress Openwork that her husband is unfaithful so she will cuckold him in revenge. In the end all these housewives retain their virtue, the gallants are exposed in their schemes, and all parties join in a convivial dinner.

The play is a happy union of talents—Middleton's genius for situation of intrigue, and Dekker's gift for genial satire and festive comedy. Both writers were thoroughly learned in the ways of London daily life. Sir Alexander Wengrave, Sebastian's covetous father who is outwitted at his own game by Moll, is characteristically Middleton, while the good-hearted, "mad, merry Moll" is limned with the same sentimentality that went into the creation of Dekker's Bellafront in *The Honest Whore.*

Havelock Ellis edited the play in the Mermaid series, 2 vols., II (1890). For commentary, see M. Dowling, "A Note on Moll Cutpurse—The Roaring Girl," *RES,* X (1934); and R. H. Barker, *Thomas Middleton* (1958). For a historical account of the heroine, see Denis Meadows, "Mary Firth, the Roaring Girl" in *Elizabethan Quintet* (1956).

rogue literature. English tales of rogues and ruffians in the sixteenth and seventeenth centuries. These narratives had many medieval tributaries and a variety of different Elizabethan forms—pseudo-biographies, confessional pamphlets, CHARACTERS, essays on crime and criminals, JESTBOOKS, and picaresque novels. Medieval drama and poetry foreshadowed much of this rogue literature. Many of Chaucer's pilgrims in the *Canterbury Tales*—the Pardoner, Monk, Friar, Summoner, Shipman, and Doctor of Physic—are confidence men, extortionists, or common brigands, and the General Prologue is especially rich in revelations of their sly methods of cheating and stealing. Rogues also abound in the miracle and morality plays, the sportively wicked character of Vice being especially familiar, and early Tudor INTERLUDES continued this tradition in such farces as John Heywood's portrayal of priestly roguery in THE PARDONER AND THE FRIAR. Rogue literature is also evident in the medieval legends of Robin Hood, celebrated in May Day pageants and countless ballads, and in tales of such playful scoundrels as Robin Goodfellow, Robert the Devil, and Friar Rush.

From this background in folklore emerged the Elizabethan jestbook, narrated presumably by someone with a reputation for practical jokes or waggish humor, such as Thomas More, John Skelton, or George Peele. *A Nest of Ninnies* (1608), ascribed to Robert Armin, and *Tarlton's Jests* (1638), attributed to Richard Tarlton, were jestbooks of this type. Armin was an actor who played the witty fool with the Lord Chamberlain's Men; Tarlton, a famous clown with the Queens Men, was Queen Elizabeth's favorite fool. It is doubtful if either actor was the author of the jestbook associated with his name, but the attribution sold copies.

By the end of the sixteenth century rogues became prominent in plays such as the anonymous *A Knack to Know a Knave* (perf. 1592), with its coney-catcher Cutbert Cutpurse, and in the popular tales of Thomas DELONEY, especially his portrayal of the roguish if not picaresque hero in JOHN WINCHCOMB. Rogues in drama and fiction were followed by several studies of criminal types in character collections, notably Nicholas Breton's *The Good and the Bad* (1616) and Geoffrey Minshull's *Essays and Characters of a Prison and Prisoners* (1618).

The most highly developed and enduring genre of rogue literature was the picaresque novel, which reached its perfection in the Spanish classic *Lazarillo de Tormes,* first published in Spanish in 1554-55 and in English in 1586, and probably written by Diego Hurtado de Mendoza. Certainly *Lazarillo de Tormes* conforms totally to the definition of the picaresque novel set forth by Frank W. Chandler: "It possesses . . . two poles of interest—one, the rogue and his tricks; the other, the manners he pillories" (*The Literature of Roguery,* I, 5). To these criteria might be added both the ingenuity and ingenuousness of the hero, who in spite of his amoral efforts at survival is shown to be more clever and certainly less depraved than the social types he encounters. The principal motive of the *picaro,* or rogue hero of picaresque fiction, is survival and perhaps a little well-earned profit or pleasure in the face of society's greed and cruelty. Hence Lazarillo recounts his adventures as the son of a poor miller who begins his career as a guide to a wicked old blind man, whose money and food he steals to stay alive. Thereafter he encounters a miserly priest, a haughty nobleman, a venal seller of indulgences, and other craven and unscrupulous types, until at last he becomes town-crier of Toledo. The travelogue enables the author to provide a satiric panorama of social types and institutions.

The first English fiction of this type was Thomas Nashe's THE UNFORTUNATE TRAVELLER (1594), which is only partially picaresque. Like *Lazarillo de Tormes,* to which its relationship remains highly conjectural, *The Unfortunate Traveller* is an episodic travelogue, its hero witty and ingenuous; but it does not consistently satirize contemporary manners and morals—indeed, at times the hero is portrayed as being something of a conforming prude—and Nashe's tale, especially in the first part, may have been intended initially as a jestbook to which the author added episodes as they occurred to him. Nevertheless, in spite of its discursive form and inconsistencies in characterization and point of view, Nashe's novel is the most remarkable piece of rogue fiction before Defoe.

Still another important contribution to Elizabethan rogue literature were "coney-catching" pamphlets describing contemporary criminal types and exposing their techniques—a coney being a small rabbit, and hence the dupe or prey of the confidence man. Among the earliest of these were the so-called beggar books describing various kinds of rogues. The anonymous *Fraternity of Vagabonds* (1561) is a "beggar book" pamphlet describing twenty-five types of beggars and thieves, such as the "Abraham Man," who feigns madness, the "Ruffler," who begs or steals in the disguise of a discharged soldier, the "Whipjack," who poses as a shipwrecked sailor, and the "Prigman," a common thief.

The great master of coney-catching pamphlets, Robert GREENE, learned his art not only from earlier beggar books but out of his own experiences in the Elizabethan underworld. His thinly disguised confessional tracts such as *Greene's Mourning Garment* and *Greene's Never Too Late* (both 1590) mix pastoral and picaresque with the confessions of a prodigal son. Greene's first two coney-catching pamphlets were straight exposés of criminal practices in Elizabethan London, *A Notable Discovery of Cosenage* (1591) and *The Second Part of Coney-Catching* (1592). In the second of these Greene informs his readers that a gang of rogues had threatened to mutilate him in retaliation for his revelations, and he boasts, "I live still, and I live to display their villainies," a promise he fulfilled a year later with *The Third and Last Part of Coney-Catching,* ten tales recounted by rogues. Another pamphlet of the same year is a dialogue, *A Disputation Between a He Coney-Catcher and a She Coney-Catcher,* in which the rogues Laurence Foist and Nan a Traffique exchange tales. Greene's last work of this kind, *The Black Book's Messenger* (1592) is a pseudo-biography of one notorious Ned Browne, who tells of his adventures as he awaits execution in France. Ned's breezy account combines the jestbook, the coney-catching exposé, the picaresque tale, and the didactic exordium. "I lived wantonly," Ned confesses, "and therefore let me end merrily, and tell you two or three of my mad pranks and so bid you farewell." Nevertheless, after recounting a life devoted to purse picking, horse stealing, church robbing, extortion, and adultery, Ned concludes his tale on the homiletic note characteristic of Greene's pamphlets. "If any be profited," states Ned piously, "I have the desired end of my labor."

Contemporaneous with Greene's pamphlets appeared several erroneously bearing his name, or, like the anonymous *Cuthbert Coney-Catcher's Defense of Coney-Catching* (1592), answering Greene's revelations by telling tales illustrating how roguery is not confined exclusively to professional criminals but is also practiced by usurers, sharp lawyers, millers, and common tradesmen. This tendency to develop from exposé to satire is continued in Samuel Rowlands' pamphlet *Greene's Ghost Haunting Coney-Catchers* (1602), fifteen stories depicting chicanery by colliers, innkeepers, and others.

Harking back to the beggar book is Thomas Dekker's BELLMAN OF LONDON (1608), which, according to the title page, gives "a discourse of all the idle vagabonds of England, their conditions, their laws among themselves, their decrees and orders, their meetings, and their manners of living." Dekker followed this in the same year with a sequel, LANTERN AND CANDLELIGHT, which devotes twenty-four chapters to "abuses and villainies" as practiced in ordinaries, inns, marketplaces, and prisons. The first chapter deals with "canting," or rogue terms, and almost a third of the book reveals the venality and cruelty of English prison life—a subject Dekker unfortunately became familiar with from personal experience.

To an extent far greater than Greene, Dekker was influenced in his rogue pamphlets by a very early and comprehensive beggar book by Thomas Harman entitled *A Caveat or Warning for Common Cursitors Vulgarly Called Vagabonds* (1566), a collection of anecdotes pertaining to twenty-three criminal orders. It was Harman's work, crudely written but encyclopedic, that continued to be widely consulted by writers of picaresque fiction and coney-catching pamphlets well into the seventeenth century. It was Harman, not Greene or Dekker, who, together with several Spanish romancers of roguery, inspired the artless but vastly influential picaresque work by Richard Head and Francis Kirkman, *The English Rogue Described in the Life of Meriton Latroon,* first printed in 1665 and subsequently enlarged to five parts by 1672. As wide-ranging and episodic as any Greek romance, *The English Rogue* takes the picaresque hero Meriton Latroon through prisons and dives in London to adventures in the East Indies, all accompanied by bloody fights with pirates and erotic engagements with a succession of mistresses and wives. The natural descendants of Meriton Latroon were Defoe's Moll Flanders and Fielding's Jonathan Wild.

There are collections of rogue literature in *The Elizabethan Underworld: A Collection of Tudor and Early Stuart Tracts and Ballads,* ed. A. V. Judges (1930), and *The Counterfeit Lady Unveiled, and other Criminal Fiction of Seventeenth-Century England* (1961). The full and many-sided story of rogue literature, only touched upon here, is told by Frank W. Chandler, *The Literature of Roguery,* 2 vols. (1907). Volume I, complete with extensive bibliographies, pertains to rogue literature in the Renaissance. There is an almost equally comprehensive study by Frank Aydelotte, *Elizabethan Rogues and Vagabonds* (1913). Two standard bibliographies are Arundell Esdaile, *A List of English Tales and Prose Romances Printed before 1700* (1912); and Charles C. Mish, *English Prose Fiction, 1600-1700* (1952).

Roman Actor, The. A tragedy by Philip MASSINGER, written about 1626 and first published in 1629. Massinger's principal sources were *The Lives of the Twelve Caesars* by Suetonius and the *Roman History* of Dio Cassius, with some borrowings from Tacitus and Eutropius.

During the tyranny of the Roman emperor Domitian in the first century A.D., the actor Paris and his troupe are arrested as slanderers and spies by Domitian's factotum Aretinus. When the emperor returns from the wars, the actors are released to perform a play, "The Cure of Avarice," to help break the miserly habits of the father of Parthenius, an impoverished gallant. In another play performed at court, the emperor's new wife Domitia interferes with the play when Paris, playing a rejected lover, threatens suicide. The jealous court ladies and Aretinus quickly notify Domitian of his wife's suspicious conduct, and Domitian agrees to spy on a meeting between the two. Paris at first rejects Domitia's passionate advances out of loyalty to the emperor, who bursts in while the pair are embracing. Domitian confines Domitia to her room, peevishly orders Aretinus' execution, and throws the court ladies in jail.

Domitian's punishment of Paris takes place

when the two men act out a play called "The False Servant," with Domitian in the role of a cuckold. In the scene where the husband of the play discovers his wife's infidelity, Domitian kills the Roman actor. Far from repenting of her infidelity, Domitia taunts Domitian, but he is too struck with her beauty to have her executed. Instead, he places her name in his book of condemned people.

Meanwhile an astrologer predicts that the tyrant will soon die and the astrologer himself be eaten by dogs shortly before Domitian's death. To prevent these predicted events, the terrified Domitian orders the astrologer burned and surrounds himself with soldiers and tribunes. Part of the prophecy comes true when rain puts out the fire kindled for the astrologer's execution and dogs attack the astrologer's body. Domitia, Parthenia, and several court ladies discover their names in Domitian's book of the condemned, and in order to forestall their executions they dupe Domitian into thinking the hour predicted for his death has passed. When the relieved Domitian dismisses his bodyguards, the conspirators fall upon him and stab him to death.

The Roman Actor is not only a condemnation of tyranny but a spirited vindication of the despised profession of acting. In his eloquent speeches in defense of actors, Massinger may have been replying to an anonymous pamphlet, *A Short Treatise Against Stage-plays,* addressed to Parliament and published in May 1625. In the dedication to the 1629 edition, Massinger called *The Roman Actor* his best play, "the most perfect birth of my Minerva."

A standard edition is by William L. Sandidge (1929), whose introduction gives original information on sources and stage history. For a critical discussion, see W. D. Briggs, "The Influence of Jonson's Tragedy in the Seventeenth Century," *Anglia,* XXXV (1912), T. A. Dunn, *Philip Massinger: The Man and the Playwright* (1957); and A. P. Hogan, "Images of Acting in *The Roman Actor,*" *MLR,* LXVI (1971).

Romeo and Juliet. A tragedy by William SHAKESPEARE, written around 1595-96 and first printed in 1597. For his primary source Shakespeare used a poem by Arthur Brooke, *The Tragical History of Romeus and Juliet* (1562), which was based on a tale in Belleforest's *Histoires tragiques* (1559).

In this tragedy of what the prologue describes as two "star-crossed lovers," the Veronese families of Montague and Capulet carry on an ancient feud. Romeo, a Montague, appears disguised with his friend Mercutio and others at a ball given by old Lord Capulet, and there Romeo falls in love at first sight with Capulet's young daughter Juliet. With the aid of Friar Laurence, the couple are secretly married the following day. Shortly after, Romeo's friend Mercutio brawls with Juliet's cousin Tybalt, and although Romeo tries to prevent violence, Mercutio is slain. In revenge, Romeo kills Tybalt and is banished for the crime. Meanwhile, old Capulet promises Juliet's hand in marriage to Count Paris. Desperate, she consults with Friar Laurence, who devises a plan whereby she will drink a sleeping potion and feign death, then be brought from the tomb to join Romeo in Mantua. The friar's plot miscarries, however, when his message fails to reach Romeo, who hears from another source that Juliet is dead. At Juliet's vault Romeo kills the grieving Paris, and with Juliet asleep next to him, he drinks poison and dies. When Juliet awakens to find Romeo dead, she stabs herself to death. Confronted by these tragic consequences of their hatred, the two families of Capulet and Montague end their long feud.

The prologue provides a synopsis of the story in the form of a sonnet:

Two households, both alike in dignity,
In fair Verona where we lay our scene,
From ancient grudge break to new mutiny,
Where civil blood makes civil hands unclean.
From forth the fatal loins of these two foes
A pair of star-cross'd lovers take their life,
Whose misadventur'd piteous overthrows
Doth with their death bury their parents' strife.
The fearful passage of their death-mark'd love,
And the continuance of their parents' rage,
Which, but their children's end, nought could remove,
Is now the two hours' traffic of our stage;
The which if you with patient ears attend,
What here shall miss, our toil will strive to mend.

Romeo and Juliet does not follow the form of Shakespeare's later tragedies. In spite of the "piteous overthrows," the play holds out the possibility of ending happily down to the very point of Romeo's death in the fifth act. The lovers are innocent pawns rather than flawed progenitors of their own destiny. It is mere chance that brings Romeo to the Capulet ball where he meets and falls in love at first sight with Juliet, and chance that places Mercutio and Tybalt on a collision course in the street. Unfortunate timing also puts Paris into the story with his proposal of marriage, prevents Friar Laurence's letter from reaching Romeo, and brings the friar to Juliet's tomb too late to avert disaster. In none of the later tragedies is fate such a decisive factor.

Moreover, the hero and heroine are not nearly as interesting and well drawn as the minor characters. The garrulous nurse, a character created from the *balia* of the COMMEDIA DELL'ARTE, is a creature of unprecedented vitality on the Elizabethan stage, and writing her lines no doubt helped convince Shakespeare of the limitless capabilities of colloquial prose, a medium he used with equally great results in *Henry IV,* Parts I and II. The nurse is also one of Shakespeare's earliest characters to speak at considerable length without having any necessary role in the plot; her crowning justification for being in the story is that she is intrinsically entertaining.

Mercutio is equally vivid as the love cynic whose obscene quips provide a choral commentary that furnishes an effective antidote to the otherwise saccharine sentiments of the idealistic lovers. The fussy and meddlesome Friar Laurence and the benevolent but choleric old Capulet are also memorable.

Romeo and Juliet is a tragedy of distinct polarities of light and dark images, night scenes of love and day scenes of violence, exalted sentiments in the young lovers and flippant cynicism in Mercutio and the nurse. The one indivisible unity is the love of the hero and heroine, blasted by the hatred of their parents.

The play has all the signs of Shakespeare's early works. He suspends action with Mercutio's lengthy digression on Queen Mab (I, *iv,* 54-103), writes euphuistic speeches of extended conceits, as in Lady Capulet's analogy of Paris to a "book" for Juliet to read (I, *iii,* 81-94), dramatizes the first meeting of the lovers as a *ballet de coeur* of interlocking dialogue (II, *ii*), and fills the play with conceits, puns, and obscure witticisms. Miraculously, such artificiality does not vitiate the ingenuity of the plot or the energy of the characters, and *Romeo and Juliet* remains among the greatest of Shakespeare's plays.

The New Cambridge edition, ed. G. I. Duthie and J. Dover Wilson (1955), is standard for text and commentary. Arthur Brooke's poem is reprinted and discussed by Kenneth Muir, *Shakespeare's Sources,* 2 vols. (1957), I. For criticism, see Harley Granville-Barker, *Prefaces to Shakespeare,* II (1930); H. B. Charlton, *Shakespearean Tragedy,* (1948); and Clifford Leech, *Shakespeare's Tragedies* (1950); Hans Zeisel, "In Defense of Shakespeare's *Romeo and Juliet,*" *ShStud,* VI (1967-68); Ruth Nevo, "Tragic Form in *Romeo and Juliet,*" *SEL,* IX (1969); and *Twentieth-Century Interpretations of Romeo and Juliet: A Collection of Critical Essays,* ed. Douglas Cole (1970).

Rosalynde, or Euphues' Golden Legacy. A pastoral romance by Thomas LODGE, written "to beguile the time with labor" while Lodge was on a sea voyage to the Canary Islands in 1588. It was first published in 1590 and was so popular it went through nine editions by 1614. It supplied Shakespeare with the main source of AS YOU LIKE IT. Lodge's principal source was *The Tale of Gamelyn,* a fourteenth-century metrical romance that he consulted for his tale of the wronged brother. Other influences were the late Greek romances, Sir Philip Sidney's *Arcadia,* Robert Greene's *Menaphon* and *Pandosto,* and, as Lodge's secondary title indicates, John Lyly's *Euphues.*

Upon the death of Sir John of Bordeaux, his eldest son Saladyne plots to disinherit his two brothers, Fernandyne, a scholar away at Paris, and Rosader, the youngest. In another story, Torismond has seized the throne of France from Gerismond, who lives in exile in the forest of Arden. At Torismond's court reside his virtuous daughter Alinda and her best friend Rosalynde, Gerismond's beautiful daughter.

To make the French peers forget their banished king, Torismond stages a tournament featuring a giant Norman wrestler who frequently kills his opponents. Saladyne encourages Rosader to challenge the Norman, but secretly promises the Norman gold if he will break Rosader's neck. At the tournament Rosader defeats the Norman, and Rosader and Rosalynde fall in love at first sight. Observing the admiration of the French peers for Rosalynde, Torismond fears that one of them will marry her and claim the usurped throne; hence, in spite of Rosalynde's protest that she is innocent of plotting treason, and Alinda's pleas on behalf of her friend, Torismond orders Rosalynde to "either wander to her father or else seek other fortunes." Alinda disguises herself as a humble shepherdess named Aliena, and Rosalynde as a boy called Ganymede, and the two set out for the forest of Arden.

Meanwhile Saladyne puts Rosader in chains with orders that no one in the house is to comfort or feed him, but Adam Spencer, Sir John of Bordeaux's loyal old servant, frees Rosader and provides him with weapons. After Rosader and Adam beat Saladyne and his retainers out of the house, Saladyne returns with the sheriff and Rosader and Adam flee to the forest of Arden to join Gerismond, who warmly welcomes them. Torismond, in a plot to seize Saladyne's land, pretends to be outraged by his cruel treatment of Rosader and banishes Saladyne for life. Now repenting of his evil ways, Saladyne goes off in search of Rosader.

In the forest of Arden, Aliena purchases a large plot of grazing land, and Ganymede acts the role of adviser in love for Rosader, who pines for Rosalynde. Ganymede also counsels the young shepherd Montanus, whose passion is spurned by the haughty Phoebe, especially after Phoebe falls in love with Ganymede. Although secretly in love with Rosader, Ganymede (Rosalynde) feigns contempt for all these lovers who sigh their hearts out and hang amorous verses on trees:

> "I can smile," quoth Ganymede, "at the sonettos, canzons, madrigals, rounds, and roundelays that these pensive patients pour out when their eyes are more full of wantonness than their hearts of passions. Then, as the fishers put the sweetest bait to the fairest fish, so these Ovidians, holding *amo* in their tongues when their thoughts come at haphazard, write that they be wrapped in an endless labyrinth of sorrow, when walking in the large leas of liberty they only have their humours in their inkpot."

Lost in the forest of Arden, Saladyne is rescued from a lion by Rosader, and the two brothers are reconciled. When Saladyne later saves Rosader, Aliena, and Ganymede from a band of brigands, Saladyne and Aliena fall in love and soon become betrothed. Their wedding is to be on "a Sunday," and Ganymede promises Rosader that on that date will appear "by necromancy and magic" his beloved Rosalynde; on the same day, Ganymede announces, Phoebe will have "an answer of her loves, and Montanus either to hear the doom of his misery or the censure of his happiness." On the day of the ceremony Rosalynde appears in a women's attire and is at once recognized by her father, who joyously gives her in marriage to Rosader. Phoebe disavows her passion for Ganymede and takes Montanus as her husband.

During the wedding feast of the three couples, Fernandyne, the "middle brother," arrives from Paris to announce that the peers of France have risen against Torismond. In the ensuing battle Torismond is killed, and the peers restore Gerismond to the throne. Rosader is made heir to the kingdom; Saladyne's lands are returned; Montanus is created "lord over the forest of Arden"; and Adam Spencer becomes captain of the king's guard.

In Lodge's *Rosalynde,* the influence of Lyly's *Euphues* is most apparent in the highly stylized, occasionally euphuistic and didactic soliloquies, and that of Sidney's *Arcadia* in the interspersed songs and sonnets as well as the chivalric idealism of the characters, although Lodge makes no attempt to imitate Sidney's stately language. An elaborate masterpiece of Arcadian fiction, *Rosalynde* is one of the last great pastoral romances before the advent of the more prosaic and realistic fiction of Greene, Nashe, and Deloney.

An excellent edition of Lodge's *Rosalynde* is by W. W. Greg in the Shakespeare Classics Series No. 1 (1907; reissued 1931). E. A. Tenney discusses Lodge's romance in *Thomas Lodge* (1935). See also Marco Mincoff, "What Shakespeare Did to *Rosalynde,*" *SJ,* XCVI (1960), and Robert B. Pierce, "The Moral Languages of *Rosalynde* and *As You Like It,*" *SP,* LXVIII (1971).

Rowley, William (c. 1585-1626). Actor and dramatist. Almost nothing is known of Rowley's life except what can be learned from title pages, actors' lists, and dedicatory poems attached to works by other playwrights. His name first appears as the author of a dedicatory epistle to the family of James Shirley, the dramatist, prefixed to the 1607 edition of the play *The Travels of Three English Brothers,* which Rowley wrote in collaboration with John Day and George Wilkins. Rowley probably began his career as an actor with the Queen Anne's players; for a time he was with the Duke of York's Men and, after 1609, with Prince Charles' company, for which he acted comic roles and wrote several plays for performance at court. His several dedications of plays to Prince Charles' company attest to his friendship with members of that group. Around 1622-23 he was with the Lady Elizabeth's Men, and after 1623 joined the King's Men. He was buried at St. James', Clerkenwell, in February 1626.

By his contemporaries Rowley was praised as an actor rather than a dramatist. He took little interest in the publication of plays, received little notice for his writing, and preferred to collaborate with others rather than work alone. He is believed to have been something of a "play doctor," touching up plays by John Fletcher, John Ford, Ben Jonson, Philip Massinger, Thomas Middleton, and William Shakespeare. To Rowley alone have been assigned, with varying degrees of uncertainty, several comedies: *A Shoemaker a Gentleman* (wr. c. 1608); *A New Wonder, a Woman Never Vexed* (1632); *A Match at Midnight* (1633); and *The Birth of Merlin* (1662). Several other plays attributed to Rowley, including *The Fool Without a Book* and *A Knave in Print* (both entered in the Stationers' Register in 1653), are lost.

As a collaborator Rowley usually contributed low comedy scenes in fluent, colloquial prose; he is believed to have had little talent for characterization or versification. Plays for which there is some external evidence of his collaboration include *All's Lost by Lust* (wr. c. 1619-20). with Thomas Middleton; THE CHANGELING (wr. 1622), with Middleton; *A Cure for a Cuckold* (wr. c. 1624-25), with John Webster; *A Fair Quarrel* (wr. c. 1615-17), with Middleton; *Fortune by Land and Sea* (wr. c. 1607?), with Thomas Heywood; *The Maid in the Mill* (wr. 1623), with John Fletcher; *A Match at Midnight,* of very uncertain date, and possibly with Middleton; *The Old Law* (wr. c. 1618?), with Middleton and Philip Massinger; THE SPANISH GYPSY (wr. 1623), with Middleton; *The Travels of Three English Brothers* (wr. 1607), with John Day and George Wilkins; THE WITCH OF EDMONTON (wr. c. 1621), with John Ford and Thomas Dekker; and *The World Tossed at Tennis* (wr. c. 1619-20), with Middleton.

For biographical data and canon, see E. K. Chambers, *The Elizabethan Stage,* 4 vols. (1923); III, G. E. Bentley, *The Jacobean and Caroline Stage,* 7 vols. (1941-67), V.; and D. M. Robb, "The Canon of Rowley's Plays. *MLR,* XLV (1950). *All's Lost by Lust* and *The Spanish Gypsy* were edited in the Belles-Lettres series by Edgar C. Morris (1908); *All's Lost by Lust* and *A Shoemaker a Gentleman* were edited by C. W. Stork (1910). For Rowley's collaboration with Middleton, see P. G. Wiggin, *An Inquiry into the Authorships of the Middleton-Rowley Plays* (1897).

Rule a Wife and Have a Wife. A comedy by John FLETCHER, written in 1624 and first printed in 1640, It is based in part on Miguel de Cervantes' story "El casamiento engañoso" in *Novelas ejemplares* (1613), which was not translated into English until 1624. The scene is Valladolid, Spain.

Two women, one noble and the other common, aspire to marriage but for quite different reasons and by different techniques of courtship. Donna Margarita, a wealthy and proud lady, needs a husband as a respectable façade behind which she may pursue her enthusiasm for loose affairs, masques, and revels. One of her many advisers in this matter, Altea, convinces her that Don Leon, Altea's own brother, is a perfect choice because he appears to be stupid, totally subservient, and credulous—indeed, a born cuckold. Meanwhile Donna Margarita's witty and vivacious servant, Estifania, seeks no advice; on her own initiative she dupes Michael Perez, a genial but conceited man who boasts that he knows all about women, into marrying her in the mistaken belief that she is the mistress of Margarita's splendid house. Soon Perez learns that his new wife is an impostor; they quarrel bitterly and separate.

The marriage of Margarita and Don Leon proves equally stormy. Soon after the wedding, at a party to which Margarita invites her would-be lover, the duke of Medina, her formerly stupid and servile husband turns out to be shockingly intelligent and masterful. The duke tries to deceive Don Leon into leaving his bride by pretending to offer him an army commission; Don Leon not only sees through the ruse but succeeds in winning his wife's respect for his manliness. Now loyal to her husband, she tricks the duke into making a fool of himself and repenting of his attempts on her chastity. In the end the duke gives a real commission to Don Leon, and the wily Estifania earns her husband's affection by bestowing upon him a thousand ducats that she managed to swindle from a rascally usurer.

Rule a Wife, one of Fletcher's last and best plays, is a comedy of manners based on the familiar shrew-taming theme he had employed in one of his earliest comedies, THE WOMAN'S PRIZE, OR THE TAMER TAMED. The characters in *Rule a Wife* are ironically contrasted and very carefully developed with attention to their variety and vitality. The haughty Donna Margarita has a foil in the roguish Estifania, while the strong and silent Don Leon is sharply contrasted to the blustering Perez.

The standard edition is that edited by R. W. Bond in the Variorum Edition by A. H. Bullen, 4 vols. (1904-13), III. For commentary, see O. L. Hatcher, *John Fletcher, A Study in Dramatic Method* (1905); Baldwin Maxwell, *Studies in Beaumont, Fletcher, and Massinger* (1939); and Clifford Leech, *The John Fletcher Plays* (1962).

S

Sackville, Thomas, earl of Dorset (1536-1608). See GORBODUC; MIRROR FOR MAGISTRATES, A.

St. Peter's Complaint. See SOUTHWELL, ROBERT.

Samson Agonistes ("Samson the Athlete"). A tragedy by John MILTON, first published with *Paradise Regained* in 1671. Its form is based on Greek tragedy, its plot on the last episode of Samson's life as suggested by the account in the Book of Judges (XVI). In the preface to the first edition, "Of That Sort of Dramatic Poem Which Is Called Tragedy," Milton describes tragedy as "the gravest, moralest, and most profitable of all other poems," criticizes contemporary drama for "intermixing comic stuff with tragic sadness...or introducing trivial and vulgar persons," and interprets Aristole's *catharsis* as a homeopathic principle whereby tragedy is seen as a powerful "salt to remove salt humours." Consistent with the neoclassical "unities," Milton concludes: "The circumscription of time wherein the whole drama begins and ends, is, according to ancient rule and best example, within the space of twenty-four hours."

Like *Paradise Regained, Samson Agonistes* is systematically structured on episodes of temptation. The scene opens with Samson, blinded and enslaved by the Philistines, recalling God's promise that he would liberate his people and being futilely comforted by the chorus, which, as in Sophocles' *Oedipus Rex,* consists of a group of tribal elders. Samson's first temptation occurs with the arrival of his father Manoa, an aged, defeated man who urges Samson to seek self-preservation by paying a ransom and retiring to his home to convalesce ("Repent the sin, but if the punishment / Thou canst avoid, self-preservation bids..."). Next comes Dalila, who blames her "common female faults" for her treachery and offers Samson the "delights" of "domestic ease" with her, a temptation he angrily rejects, though he reluctantly manages to forgive her ("At distance I forgive thee, go with that"). Next comes Harapha, the boastful strong man of the Philistines, who tries to goad Samson into a facile satisfaction by challenging him to personal combat, a challenge Samson contemptuously refuses. Finally Samson is summoned by a messenger to appear before the Philistine lords to show his strength for their amusement, and at first he refuses.

When the messenger comes a second time, however, Samson experiences some "rousing motions" that urge him to consent. As the Philistines celebrate their feast to the pagan god Dagon, Samson pulls down Dagon's temple upon their heads, a feat reported by a messenger, or *nuntius*, and the chorus concludes: "All is best, though we oft doubt, / What th' unsearchable despise/Of highest wisdom brings about. . . " (lines 1745-47).

The standard edition of *Samson Agonistes* is in *The Works of John Milton,* ed. Frank A. Patterson, 18 vols. (1931-38), I. Two scholarly editions are *John Milton: Complete Poems and Major Prose,* ed. Merritt Y. Hughes (1957), and *Milton's Dramatic Poems,* ed. Geoffery and Margaret Bullough (1958). Important critical studies are by C. E. Kreipe, *Milton's Samson Agonistes* (1926); F. M. Krouse, *Milton's "Samson" and the Christian Tradition* (1949); C. M. Bowra, *Inspiration and Poetry* (1955); William Empson, *Milton's God* (1961); and Watson Kirkconnell, *That Invincible Samson: The Theme of Samson Agonistes in World Literature with Translations of the Major Analogues* (1964). See also *Samson Agonistes: The Poem and Materials for Analogues,* ed. Ralph E. Hone (1966); *Twentieth Century Interpretations of Samson Agonistes: A Collection of Critical Essays,* ed. G. M. Crump (1968); and *Calm of the Mind: Tercentenary Essays on Paradise Regained and Samson Agonistes in Honor of John S. Diekhoff,* ed. Joseph A. Wittreich (1971).

satire. A variety of explanations have been offered to account for the increase of formal satire at the end of the sixteenth century. According to some scholars, cynicism and despair became widespread among intellectuals after the disgrace and execution of Essex; others suggest that there was a deepening of pessimism after the defeat of the Spanish Armada and the anticlimactic years that followed; still others attribute the satiric mood of the 1590s to a general malaise or sense of *fin de siècle,* or to increased class tensions and economic instability. A more philosophic reason may be inherent in Renaissance man's growing consciousness of his own paradoxical identity. In a work like Pico della Mirandola's *De hominis dignitate (On the Dignity of Man),* he saw himself as an exalted being created in God's image and gifted with divine reason; in the essays of Montaigne, on the other hand, he is shown to be distinguishable from beasts only by his pride and vanity.

Still other scholars see the roots of sixteenth-century English satire not in classical literature but in the native tradition represented by the plain style and social awareness of late medieval satires like William Langland's *A Vision of William Concerning Piers Plowman* (wr. late 14th c.) According to Hallett Smith: "The importance of the Piers Plowman tradition in English satire is that it emphasized the unity of religious and social concerns, strengthened and kept alive the medieval manner of considering society as a group of the various 'estates' and trades which made it up, and gave prestige to a style that was uncouth, rough, or plain, devoid of rhetoric, and trying for single truth and rugged honesty rather than for polished wit" (*Elizabethan Poetry* [1952], p. 210). Hence early English Renaissance satire was not so much inspired by the sophisticated wit of Horace or Juvenal as by the homely, plain-spoken Langland, who excoriated social abuses and religious hypocrisy.

These aspects of the native tradition in satire are evident in the poems of John SKELTON, whose BOWGE OF COURT (i.e., "court rations"), a dream-allegory in rhyme royal, employs a stock medieval form to express a sense of moral outrage that anticipates the spirit of the Reformation. *Ware the Hawk* satirizes Skelton's fellow priests who are more given to hunting than to pastoral duties. *Philip Sparrow,* a dramatic monologue of a Norfolk schoolgirl named Jane Scroop lamenting the killing of her bird by a cat, is a congenial, sportive *tour de force* in the manner of Chaucer's "Nun's Priest's Tale"; whereas his *Tunning of Eleanor Rumming,* with its rough alliterative rhythms, may reflect the direct influence of William Langland. More caustic and scurrilous are the three satires Skelton wrote in 1521-22 against Cardinal Wolsey—*Speak, Parrot!, Colin Clout,* and *Why Come Ye Not to Court?* Although Wolsey is Skelton's principal target, he widens his attack to include the corruption of the ruling classes and the evils of the new anti-scholastic humanism of the schools.

Other early English satirists after Langland include Alexander Barclay, who translated Sebastian Brant's *Narrenschiff* as *Ship of Fools* in 1509 with pointed references to English follies and vices, and John Heywood, whose many interludes during the reign of Henry VIII made congenial sport of busybody housewives, self-serving and sybaritic priests, and other social types (see INTERLUDE). Heywood's major effort in satire was a lengthy poem of thousands of lines in rhyme royal, THE SPIDER AND THE FLY (1556), inspired by the pseudo-Homeric battle of the frogs and mice. In style the work is medieval for its allegorical debate and linking of the bestiary with satire, but Heywood's point of attack is England's political and religious situation rather than any of the seven deadly sins. The villainous spider of the piece is obviously the Protestant leader Thomas Cranmer, and Mary Tudor the maid who sweeps out the spider with her broom. The flies are England's common people, who are mainly Catholic, and the spiders England's middle class, dominated by Protestants.

The spirit of William Langland is also manifest in the satires of the Puritan Robert Crowley, who printed *Piers Plowman* in 1550, then brought out in the same year his own satires in *One and Thirty Epigrams,* in which he attacks a variety of social abuses—usury, blasphemy, drunkenness, gambling, and exploitation of the poor. In *The Voice of the Last Trumpet* (1549) Crowley systematically divides sinners into twelve classes, or "lessons." This cataloging of evils in the commonweal is also seen in George GASCOIGNE'S *The Steel Glass* (1576), a blank-verse satire in which thirty-six crafts and trades are classified according to their vices, although Gascoigne also finds time to castigate greedy landlords and vain women. An equally broad, Langland-like condemnation of social abuses is Edward Hake's *News Out of Paul's Churchyard,* first published in a nonextant edition in 1567 and revised and published again with a dedication to the earl of Leicester. A crude poem in heptameters, or "fourteeners," Hake's satire rails against the venality of doctors, lawyers, landlords, and merchants as well as the cruelties of cock fighting and bull baiting and the evils of prostitution. From these satires in the 1550s to the 1580s by Crowley, Gascoigne, and Hake, the profit motive condemned in the reign of Henry VIII in More's *Utopia* again emerges as the chief vice of a society becoming increasingly acquisitive, mobile, and ostentatious with the disintegration of the old feudal amenities, obligations, and observances. It would appear that the same abuses that outraged William Langland in the fourteenth century and More in the early sixteenth—exploitation of labor, enclosures, usury, extortion, and legal chicanery —were recurring toward the end of the sixteenth century as a result of accelerated economic and social changes brought on by a complex of causes that neither the government of Queen Elizabeth nor the moralizing satirists fully understood. Hostility toward the profit value and idealization of fading medieval institutions are stressed in Spenser's satire MOTHER HUBBERD'S TALE (wr. c. 1580; pr. 1591). Spenser's allegorial bestiary in couplets was inspired by Chaucer, but exhibits little of Chaucer's willingness to suffer greedy fools and charlatans with genial tolerance. Spenser's Ape and Fox, symbolic of man's bestiality, are rapacious confidence men and spoilers who invade every estate of the commonweal—husbandry, church, law, even the highest councils of government—until their blatant attempt at usurpation incites the Lion (symbolic of a powerful and enlightened Tudor monarchy) to put a halt to their insatiable greed.

In the second half of the sixteenth century formal and sophisticated modes of satire began to develop to rival the popularity of Langland's passionate, simple, and didactic style. The chief conveyors of these new techniques were the classical satirists Horace, Juvenal, and Persius. Thomas Drant's metrical version of Horace's satires, *A Medicinable Moral* (1566), suggests an unprecedented awareness of satire as a distinctive literary genre in its prefatory analysis of the etymology of the term. According to Drant, the word "satire" derives from the Latin word for "cutting" and is hence biting and sharp; from the word "Saturn," which calls attention to the melancholic nature of the malcontent; and from the Latin word *satur,* meaning "full," that is, enriched by artifice. Drant also reconciles the classical forms with the native tradition by relating the term to "satyr," a word he believes connects satire with what is rough, coarse, and "shaggy."

Two early satires based on Horace and Juvenal are Thomas Lodge's *An Alarum Against Usurers* (1584), a prose pamphlet, and *A Fig for Momus* (1595), a collection of eclogues, epistles, and satires. Following Spenser, Lodge adopts the iambic pentameter couplet but casts his satires in epistolary form.

Lodge's *A Fig* is a tentative effort, a "by-pleasure" rather than a polished work, as he suggests in his preface "To the Gentlemen Readers Whatsoever," and he is careful to avoid slander by designating his lechers, wastrels, and hypocrites by such names as "Anphidius," "Rollus," and so forth. In *Wit's Misery and the World's Madness* (1596), another prose pamphlet, Lodge linked satire with the CHARACTER, a genre that proved entirely compatible.

The great triumvirate of satirists at the end of the sixteenth century were John DONNE, Joseph HALL, and John MARSTON. Many of Donne's *Songs and Sonnets* are broadly satiric of the Petrarchan vogue, and he wrote five formal satires during the period 1593-97, all in couplets and in the style of Horace. *Satire I* ridicules certain social types, such as a perfumed courtier, a pedant, a discharged captain, and thus combines verse satire, the character, and the medieval theme of vanity. *Satire II* attacks hypocritical, doggerel love poetry and venal lawyers; *Satire III* concerns religion; *Satire IV* the court; and *Satire V* the law courts. *Satire III,* the best of these, is less a satire on religion than an exhortation to seek religious truth. Something of a skeptic himself at this time, Donne felt more compassion than scorn for those sincerely in quest of God, however erroneous their beliefs:

Kind pity chokes my spleen; brave scorn forbids
Those tears to issue which swell my eyelids;
I must not laugh, nor weep sins, and be wise;
Can railing then cure these worn maladies?

Donne describes the "peccant humours" of each persuasion—Catholic, Calvinist, Anglican, latitudinarian—in erotic terms of courtship. For Donne a glaring irony of his times was that men risked their lives to explore the New World, fought wars, and battled over mistresses, yet feared to combat the devil and enrich their own souls. Religious truth, however difficult to discover, is nevertheless accessible, but it cannot be dictated by any secular ruler or power, only by God himself:

So perish souls, which more choose men's unjust
Power from God claimed, than God himself to trust.

The forerunner of the great English satirists of the eighteenth century was not Donne, but Joseph Hall, whose *Virgidemiarum,* Books I-III (1597) and IV-VI (1598), won enthusiastic praise from both Joseph Warton and Alexander Pope. Apparently ignorant of satires by Gascoigne, Lodge, and other earlier Elizabethans, Hall described himself in the prologue to Book I as the first English satirist. The first three books Hall labeled "toothless" satires, the next three "biting." As his later antagonist John Milton was to point out, the distinction is obscure if not tautological. Hall apparently meant by "toothless" an attack on general vices rather than on individuals, and by "biting" an attack more specific and violent. He states the difference by comparing "lightning to a thunderclap." Nevertheless, it is not difficult to recognize his targets in Books I-III as the "halfpenny muses" of popular poets and dramatists such as Peele, Marlowe, Greene, Marston, and Nashe. Only twenty-three when he wrote *Virgidemiarum,* Hall was surprisingly conservative for one so young. He heaps scorn on every literary fashion of the times—historical monologues like *A Mirror for Magistrates,* Ovidian mythological poetry, sonnet sequences, all plays that ignored the classical unities, and even blank-verse iambic pentameters:

Too popular is tragic poesy,
Straining his tiptoes for a farthing fee,
And doth beside on rhymeless numbers tread;
Unbid iambics flow from careless head.
Some braver brain in high heroic rhymes
Compileth worm-eat stories of old times...

From Hall's unqualified praise of Spenser ("whom no earthly wight / Dares once to emulate, much less dares despite") and Gabriel Harvey and his condemnation of virtually all other contemporaries, it becomes clear that Hall's youthful idealism rested on a quixotic, elitist attitude that literature was too sacred for the profane multitudes. In the "biting" satires of Books IV-VI Hall moves his attention from "Parnassus turned to the stews" toward the corrupt practices of the propertied classes—colonialism, enclosures, profiteering, and usury. Although he disavows any direct influence of satirists other than Juvenal, Hall was probably familiar with Spenser's *Mother Hubberd's Tale,* Ariosto's satires, and perhaps even Rabelais's.

In marked contrast to Hall's self-described "quiet style" is Marston's scurrilous and vehement *Scourge of Villainy* (1598). Except for brief sallies against Hall for his literary judgments and pretensions, Marston's satire aims its darts at vice, which Marston sees almost exclusively in terms of lust. Marston (who, ironically, had the same year written the pornographic *Metamorphosis of Pygmalion's Image*) inveighs against smutty literature as vehemently as does Hall. His pen fairly bristles with indignation when he writes of Petrarchan love poetry:

If Laura's painted lip do deign a kiss
To her enamored slave, "Oh heaven's bliss!"
Straight he exclaims, "not to be matched with this!"
Blaspheming dolt! Go, threescore sonnets write
Upon a picture's kiss, Oh raving sprite!

In *Scourge of Villainy* Marston assumes the guise of the carping malcontents in his own plays; like Thersites in Shakespeare's *Troilus and Cressida,* Marston has but one theme—"wars and lechery, all wars and lechery." In his own metaphor, Circe has turned all men into swine. Unlike the imperious and stoical Joseph Hall, Marston feels revulsion even for himself. "He that thinks worse of my rimes than myself," he notifies his readers, "I scorn him, for he cannot; he that thinks better is a fool." Since Marston sees himself and others as being too depraved for redemption, he must look to his ideal in the philosophical principle of "synderesis," a process by which pure energy gives life to souls:

Return, return, sacred Synderesis!
Inspire our trunks! Let not such mud as this
Pollute us still. Awake our lethargy;
Raise us from out our brainsick foolery!

Like Marston's *Scourge of Villainy,* Edward Guilpin's *Skialetheia* (1598) imitates Hall's Juvenalian obscurity and harshness. Published anonymously, Guilpin's book contains seventy satiric epigrams, most in couplets or alternating rhymes, directed at familiar London types and personalities under such pseudonyms as "Titus" or "Clodius." Guilpin's satirical portrait of Essex as "great Felix" parodies a famous passage in Shakespeare's *Richard II:*

For when great Felix, passing through the street,
Vaileth his cap to each one he doth meet,
And when no broom-man that will pray for him
Shall have less truage [i.e., homage] than his bonnet's brim,
Who would not think him perfect courtesy,
Or the honeysuckle of humility?
The Devil he is as soon—he is the Devil
Brightly accoust'red to bemist his evil.

The satires of Hall and Marston, and the flyting exchange of prose between Gabriel Harvey and Thomas Nashe known as the Greene-Harvey-Nashe controversy (see HARVEY, Gabriel) aroused considerable public attention. On June 1, 1599, the archbishop of Canterbury and the bishop of London, scandalized by the increasing vehemence of these satires, ordered all of them—those by Harvey, Nashe, Hall, and Marston—to be burned.

It was not this action that caused a decline in the publication of satires, but rather a growing disaffection with the genre. John Weever's *Faunus and Melliflora* (1600) is an Ovidian mythological poem followed by three formal satires, yet Weever attacks both Hall and Marston for writing in what he confesses is an inferior mode. *The Whipping of the Satyr* (1601) by one "W.I." criticizes Breton, Marston, and Jonson for writing satire, a form the author believes causes civil disharmony and unquiet in the state. Breton apparently answered this criticism in his pamphlet *No Whipping nor Tripping but a Kind Friendly Snipping* (1601), in which he agrees with "W.I." and recommends that writers devote themselves to religious themes rather than social satire.

Although the vogue for verse satire declined after 1600 and was not revived except sporadically until the Restoration, satire on the stage continued unabated, largely through the influence of Jonson's satiric comedies. Jonson's comedy of humours is based on the classical concept that one function of satire is to "purge" the excessive "humours" that make men deviate from rational moderation. In a larger context, however, Jonson saw himself as Horace defending the civilized values of Augustan Rome against the excesses of his own barbarous age. In his *Poetaster,* in fact, he portrays himself as Horace administering an emetic to Marston, who vomits up his pornographic poems and ill-tempered satires. As an absolutist in the moral vein that runs from Juvenal and Plautus to William Langland to Swift, Jonson in his satiric comedies portrays how men fall short of an ideal—indeed, the moral outrage of this tradition is predicated on a clear recognition of such an ideal—whereas the less populated path from Chaucer to Shakespeare, which is more congenial and relativistic, shows how the ideal somehow always falls short of men's expectations. In Jonson's *Volpone* hypocrisy is righteously whipped and sent to the galleys;

in *A Midsummer Night's Dream* and *As You Like It* the lovers are gradually relieved of their illusions. After the Restoration it was Jonson's concept of satire that prevailed, reaching its apogee in the polished and urbane satires of Dryden, Swift, and Pope.

The standard work on Renaissance English satire is R. M. Alden, *The Rise of Formal Satire in England* (1899). Connections between verse satire and satiric comedy are studied by L. C. Knights, *Drama and Society in the Age of Jonson* (1937), and O. J. Campbell, *Comical Satire in Shakespeare's Troilus and Cressida* (1938). See also Ruth Mohl, *The Three Estates in Medieval and Renaissance Literature* (1933); John Peter, *Complaint and Satire in Early English Literature* (1956); and Alvin Kernan, *The Cankered Muse: Satire of the English Renaissance* (1959).

Satire of the Three Estates, The (Sir David Lindsay). See MORALITY PLAY.

Satires I-V (Donne). See SATIRE.

Satiromastix, or The Untrussing of the Humorous Poet. A play by Thomas DEKKER, written in 1601 and published in 1602. Although Dekker's name is the only one on the title page of the first edition, he was probably assisted by John MARSTON. The "humorous poet" satirized in the role of Horace is Jonson, who shortly before had caricatured Dekker and Marston in *The Poetaster.* In *Satiromastix* Dekker introduces no fewer than three plots, the satiric, the tragicomic, and the comic. The three are not effectively integrated. The central, tragicomic plot concerns the triangle involving Sir Walter Terrill, his bride Caelestine, and King William Rufus; the comic subplot deals with the totally unrelated courtship of Mistress Miniver by three knights; and the satiric subplot with characters and situations taken from Jonson's *Poetaster.* The action takes place around 1100 A.D. in England.

King William Rufus attends the wedding festivities of Sir Walter Terrill and Caelestine. Enamored of the bride, the king dares Terrill to allow Caelestine to appear at court, and the foolish bridegroom impetuously accepts the invitation. Also at the wedding are three knights, Sir Quintilian, Sir Adam Prickshaft, and Sir Vaughan ap Rees, all of whom are eager for the hand of a widow, Mistress Miniver. Hired to supply wedding verses for the occasion is the bumbling poet Horace, who is unable to complete his doggerel verses although he has labored on them for three days. Captain Tucca, a bombastic swaggerer, upbraids Horace for his incompetence and curses him for some previous slanders. Also angry about Horace's acerbic satires are two bright young poets, Crispinus and Demetrius, who are preparing a play in which Horace is to appear as a bricklayer.

Horace is hired by Sir Vaughan to write torrid love letters to Mistress Miniver. The wealthy widow prefers Sir Adam, though he is completely bald, whereupon Sir Vaughan puts on a banquet at which he reads Horace's satire on baldness. Sir Adam's champion, Captain Tucca, appoints Crispinus and Demetrius to write verses in praise of baldness.

Meanwhile King William Rufus eagerly awaits the arrival at court of Caelestine, whom he plans to seduce. To save her honor, however, she takes poison and Terrill takes her body to court to present to the king. Overcome with shame, the king laments his tryannical conduct, at which point Caelestine recovers from the poison, which was only a potion administered by her father, Sir Quintilian. Terrill and his wife are joyously reunited.

Such solemnity requires Crispinus to present an interlude at court in which Horace and his protégé Bubo appear wearing horns. Horace is crowned with nettles instead of laurels and, under Captain Tucca's threats, agrees to give up writing waspish satires. Captain Tucca announces his betrothal to the rich widow, the three knights cheerfully accept their misfortunes in love, and the play concludes with a dance. In the epilogue, Captain Tucca promises more satiric plays about Horace, Crispinus, and Demetrius.

In *Satiromastix,* Crispinus is Marston, Demetrius is Dekker, and Horace is Jonson. An episodic and disorderly work, the play is nevertheless important and often interesting as still another salvo fired in the so-called War of the Theaters involving these three dramatists (see JONSON, Ben). The one outstanding feature of the play is Dekker's brilliant caricature of Jonson as Horace, a fumbling malcontent who, like Jonson, has a mountainous belly, a pock-marked face, and an amorous disposition, and is given to self-righteous satires, slowness of composition, and flattery of social superiors.

The best edition of Dekker's play is in *The*

Dramatic Works, ed. Fredson Bowers, 4 vols. (1953-61). For a discussion of *Satiromastix* and the "War of the Theaters," see Josiah H. Penniman, *The War of the Theatres* (1897), and R. B. Sharpe, *The Real War of the Theatres* (1935). See also James H. Conover, *Thomas Dekker: An Analysis of Dramatic Structure* (1969).

Schoolmaster, The. See ASCHAM, ROGER; COURTESY LITERATURE.

Scornful Lady, The. A comedy of manners by Francis BEAUMONT and John FLETCHER. It was written around 1613-16 and first published in 1616. No source is known.

The "scornful lady" of the title is the beloved of Elder Loveless, who has offended her by stealing a kiss from her in public, and she angrily requires that he spend a year abroad as atonement. Elder Loveless leaves his house and fortune in the hands of his wild, spendthrift brother Young Loveless, who gathers around him a captain, a traveler, a poet, and a tobacconist to help squander Elder Loveless's estate by drinking, eating, and wenching. Elder Loveless does not, however, go abroad. Instead, he gives out false news of his own death and assumes a disguise to observe the conduct of both his lady and Young Loveless.

Meanwhile the lady receives at her house another suitor, Welford, a handsome young man she respects but does not love. When Elder Loveless appears in a disguise to report his death, the lady penetrates the disguise and pretends to be totally unaffected by the news. When Elder Loveless angrily reveals himself. she berates him for breaking his promise to go abroad. Welford takes this quarrel as an opportunity to press his suit with the lady, and when she rejects him outright, her sister Martha steps forth to offer herself as a second choice.

Meanwhile, Young Loveless borrows huge sums from a usurer, Morecraft, by putting up Elder Loveless's estate as collateral. When Morecraft and the rich widow he is wooing come to take possession of Elder Loveless's house, Young Loveless refuses to return Morecraft's money or relinquish the house. When Elder Loveless appears, the whole transaction is made void, and Morecraft loses both his money and the widow, who rejects Morecraft and takes up with the shrewd and gay Young Loveless.

Elder Loveless determines on one last effort to win his scornful lady. He disguises Welford as his future bride and presents her to the lady. Fearful of losing him to another, the lady offers to marry Elder Loveless at once. Out of pity for what she thinks is an abandoned woman, Martha takes Welford to her bed. The next morning Elder Loveless reveals the plot, Welford and Martha hurry to church to marry, and Young Loveless arrives in the company of his new bride, the rich and beautiful widow. Morecraft swears to give up usury and become a wastrel in the former style of the now virtuous Young Loveless.

The Scornful Lady is important as an early forerunner of the Restoration comedy of manners. Beaumont and Fletcher's brilliant comedy has all the ingredients of the later genre—a young rogue who escapes the consequences of his prodigality by marrying a rich widow, the gulling of a usurer or extortioner, a contrast of social types, an emphasis on the battle of the sexes, and an artifical, light-hearted treatment of sexuality. Not surprisingly, the play was often revived throughout the later seventeenth century.

A scholarly edition of the play is edited by Cyrus Hoy in *The Dramatic Works in the Beaumont and Fletcher Canon,* ed. Fredson Bowers, 2 vols. (1966, 1970), II, which contains a thorough treatment of sources, stage history, influences, etc. For additional commentary see Baldwin Maxwell, *Studies in Beaumont, Fletcher, and Massinger* (1939), and W. W. Appleton. *Beaumont and Fletcher: A Critical Study* (1956).

Scourge of Villainy, The. See MARSTON, JOHN; SATIRE.

Scylla's Metamorphosis (entitled *Glaucus and Scylla* in the 1610 edition). A narrative poem by Thomas LODGE. It was first printed in 1589 but probably written several years earlier, possibly during Lodge's years at Oxford University in the mid-1570s. Hence it is the earliest of the erotic narrative poems based on Ovid that appeared in the 1590s: Shakespeare's *Venus and Adonis* (1593), Drayton's *Endymion and Phoebe* (1595). Marlowe's *Hero and Leander* (1598), and Marston's *Metamorphosis of Pygmalion's Image* (1598). Lodge's stanzaic pattern rhyming *ab ab cc* is the same as that of Shakespeare's *Venus and Adonis.*

Scylla, a nymph beloved by Glaucus, son of Thetis and a sea deity, arouses the jealousy of Circe, who drops magic herbs into Scylla's fountain that turn the nymph into a monster who terrifies mariners as they pass by the whirlpool of Charybdis. This is Ovid's version. The tale told by Lodge concerns the efforts of Thetis to overcome Glaucus' great passion for Scylla prior to the nymph's metamorphosis. Glaucus was indifferent to love and contemptuous of female beauty before he was smitten by Scylla, who scorns his wooing. Thetis advises her son to seek reason rather than passion:

Come, wend with me, and midst thy father's bower
Let us disport and frolic for a while
In spite of Love, although he point and low'r.
Good exercise will idle lusts beguile;
  Let wanton Scylla coy her where she will,
  Live thou, my son, by reason's level still.

When Glaucus will not heed her advice, Thetis prays for the aid of Venus, who commands her son Cupid to shoot another arrow that will relieve Glaucus of his passion, after which Thetis has Cupid shoot an arrow of desire into the proud and aloof Scylla, who is smitten with desire and changed into a hag by Ate's grisly crew of Fury, Rage, Despair, Wanhope, and Woe. In the envoy Lodge addresses his moral to the ladies:

Lest through contempt, almighty Love compel you
  With Scylla in the rocks to make your biding—
  A cursed plague for women's proud backsliding.

The title page of the 1589 edition underscores the moral implications of the story by proclaiming it "very fit for young courtiers to peruse, and coy dames to remember." Actually, Lodge was combining the genre of the love complaint, made popular by *A Mirror for Magistrates,* with the theme of the female's coldness for her lover in the Petrarchan sonnet sequences. Much of the first portion of the poem consists of Glaucus' complaints of unrequited love, the last part of Scylla's lamentations for her past disdain and present afflictions of the heart. Although omitting any cumbersome allegory, Lodge cannot resist the appeal of that form's attendant spirit of didacticism. Another aspect of the myth that Lodge obviously savored was the idea of a disdainful man being passionately pursued by a female, a motif Shakespeare continued in *Venus and Adonis.*

Lodge's poem is in his *Complete Works,* ed. Edmund Gosse, 4 vols. (1883, repr. 1963). The poem is discussed at length in the introduction to the Arden edition of Shakespeare's *Venus and Adonis,* ed. C. Knox Pooler (rev. ed., 1927), and by Douglas Bush in *Mythology and the Renaissance Tradition in English Poetry* (rev. ed., 1963).

Sejanus His Fall. A tragedy by Ben JONSON, written in 1603, performed the same year by the King's Men, and printed in 1605. For the story of Aelius Sejanus (fl. 30 A.D.), favorite of the emperor Tiberius, Jonson consulted Dio Cassius, Tacitus, and a host of other Roman historians, most of whom Jonson notes in the margins of the 1605 edition.

From the most humble origins, Sejanus has risen by guile and flattery to great heights of power in the Rome of Tiberius Caesar. Now Sejanus plots to increase his power even more by destroying his chief enemies, Agrippina, widow of the great Germanicus, and her sons. Further, he conspires with Livia, the wife of Tiberius' son Drusus Senior, and with her physician Eudemus to poison Drusus and marry Livia. In spite of Sejanus' demonstrated perfidy, the indolent and lascivious Tiberius does nothing until after Drusus dies and Sejanus asks his permission to marry Livia. Now fully aware of his minion's insatiable ambition, Tiberius departs from Rome for a spell of voluptuous living in the country, but leaves behind the wily and unscrupulous Macro to report secretly on Sejanus' activities. At the height of Sejanus' triumph, as it appears he is about to be acclaimed tribune, Tiberius sends the senate a letter condemning his former favorite. Sejanus is arrested for treason, and the Roman mob, incited by Macro, tear him to pieces.

Sejanus illustrates Jonson's requirement that tragedy convey "truth of argument," by which he meant not only dramatic probability but verisimilitude and even historical authenticity, and his *Sejanus* attempts to provide a Roman tragedy less romantic and more factual than Shakespeare's popular *Julius Caesar.* The result is a very learned, solemn, and often sententious tragedy that is Senecan in style and medieval in theme (see SENECAN TRAGEDY). The prolixity, *sententia,* and gravity of the speeches recall Seneca; the theme harks back to Lydgates

Fall of Princes and *A Mirror for Magistrates* in its portrayal of the vanity of human aspirations and the uncertainty of fickle fortune. Jonson's deeper meaning is the Stoic idea that only virtue and wisdom can withstand fortune's calamities. As Lepidus observes as he witnesses Sejanus' fall:

Fortune, thou hadst no deity, if men
Had wisdom; we have placed thee so high
By fond belief in thy felicity. (V, *vi*)

When *Sejanus* was performed at the Globe theater in 1603 by the King's Men, it was hooted off the stage. In the first edition Jonson states that "a second hand has had good share" in revising the stage version for publication. Most scholars agree that Jonson's collaborator was George Chapman.

The standard edition is in *Ben Jonson,* ed. C. H. Herford and Percy and Evelyn Simpson, 11 vols. (1925-53), IV. Jonas A. Barish has edited *Sejanus* in the Yale Ben Jonson series (1965) and W. F. Bolton in the New Mermaid series (1966). For commentary, see L. C. Knights, "Tradition and Ben Jonson," *Scrutiny,* IV (1935); Robert Ornstein, *The Moral Vision of Jacobean Tragedy* (1960); D. C. Boughner, "*Sejanus* and Machiavelli," *SEL,* I (1961); K. W. Evans, "*Sejanus* and the Ideal Prince Tradition," *SEL,* XI (1971); and Gary D. Hamilton "Irony and Fortune in *Sejanus,*" *SEL,* XI (1971).

Senecan tragedy. Tragedies influenced by those of Lucius Annaeus Seneca (c. 4 B.C.-A.D. 65), known as Seneca the Younger. Seneca's tragedies were widely imitated during the Renaissance. His extant plays include *Agamemnon, Hercules Furens, Hercules Oetaeus, Medea, Oedipus, Phaedra, Phoenissae, Thyestes,* and *Troas.* All were based on or influenced by the late Greek tragedies of Euripides; like those of Euripides, they are all in five acts. Without exception they are "closet dramas" or "speakings," that is, not intended for performance in a theater (though Renaissance writers and critics were ignorant of this fact).

Seneca's tragedies are characterized by : (1) the theme of revenge; (2) a chorus that moralizes about the action but does not directly participate; (3) a *nuntius,* or messenger, who reports violent events not visually presented; (4) a dramatic focus on the emotional climax of the story rather than an episodic progression toward the climax; (5) a five-act division; (6) a ghost, often returned from the dead to seek revenge; (7) the use of stock characterizations—the cruel tyrant, the faithful friend or servant, the female confidante; (8) an introspective, moralizing stoic hero; (9) an emphasis on violent and sensational situations drawn from Greek tragedy and mythology—insanity, incest, mutilation, suicide, adultery, infanticide—with these transgressions providing the motive for revenge; and (10) a style characterized by bombast and rant, turgid descriptions, introspective soliloquies, and stichomythia.

The popularity of Senecan tragedy can be attributed, first, to the fact that Seneca, the only surviving Roman tragedian, was diligently studied in Elizabethan grammar schools, where Latin was the language of instruction. The great Greek tragedians Aeschylus, Sophocles, and Euripides were relatively unknown to Elizabethans and not translated until the seventeenth century. Then, too, Senecan rhetoric, didacticism, and sensationalism were wholly compatible with the Elizabethan temperament. Medieval writers like Dante and John Lydgate had extolled Seneca's tragedies for their rhetoric and stoic moralizing.

Seneca's tragedies were first performed before sophisticated audiences at the Inns of Court and the universities. One of the earliest adaptations from Senecan tragedy was Sackville and Norton's GORBODUC, written in blank verse and presented before Queen Elizabeth in 1562. Sackville and Norton embellished their Senecan source by using DUMB SHOWS derived from Italian drama, showing violence on the stage rather than having it described to the audience by a *nuntius,* relating a story from British history rather than from Greek mythology, and intensifying gloomy dialogue with violas, cornets, flutes, hautboys, and drums. *Gorboduc* was followed four years later by George Gascoigne and Francis Kinwelmarsh's *Jocasta,* produced at Gray's Inn and borrowed from an Italian version of *Phoenissae* rather than directly from Seneca. *Gismorde of Salerne in Love,* written by five different authors and produced at the Inner Temple in 1567, combines a tale from Boccaccio with close imitation of Senecan dialogue and dramatic form.

These productions of Senecan tragedy were addressed to elite audiences, and Mary Herbert, countess of Pembroke, and the sister of Sir Philip Sidney, used her influence as the most notable patroness of poets to promote "pure" imitations of Seneca's tragedies. It remained for Thomas Kyd, and after him Christopher Marlowe, to popularize the genre to such an extent that subsequent Elizabethan tragedy became synonymous, to a large degree, with improvised Senecan tragedy. Kyd's triumphant innovation was THE SPANISH TRAGEDY. produced in the popular. playhouses around 1585-87 and possibly before. It set off a wave of imitations reaching its zenith in Shakespeare's HAMLET fifteen years later. Kyd's innovations were even more radical than those by the authors of *Gorboduc* a generation before. He not only eliminated Seneca's tedious *nuntius* and showed horrors on the stage; he made his main plot a modern tale of love and war occurring in Spain and Portugal—lands of great popular interest just before the Armada—and embellished this story of court intrigue with a rich mixture of subplots calculated to satisfy the Elizabethan appetite for polyphonic narrative. Unlike Marlowe, he was not so much a poet as an ingenious designer of plots, and he imitated Seneca's rhetoric and disregarded his slow-moving narrative methods. He substituted for Seneca's flat characters a whole troop of types fascinating to his Elizabethan audience—a fully developed Machiavellian villain, a convention-defying, aggressive heroine, a swaggering cutthroat of the Renaissance court, and a volatile hero who raves and weeps, curses and philosophizes, prays like a Christian and murders like a pagan.

Senecan violence and declamation are apparent in Marlowe's first play. TAMBURLAINE, and in some ways this play is more thoroughly Senecan than Kyd's, for Marlowe shows less concern for plot and, like Seneca, concentrates on a relentless articulation of a few related emotions—love, glory, ambition—rather than on any artful arrangement of events. In Marlowe's wake came Shakespeare's early plays, many of which clearly reflect Senecan elements. Shakespeare's earliest tragedy, TITUS ANDRONICUS, probably derived its cannibalistic banquet from the most frequently translated of Seneca's tragedies, *Thyestes.* Many of Shakespeare's chronicle plays from *Henry VI* to *Richard II* can be read as variations on the Senecan theme of the hereditary curse.

Several characteristics of Elizabethan tragedy in general have their origins in Seneca—the five-act division, the revenge motive, the ghost, the preoccupation with insanity, the declamation and bombast, and the brooding, stoical hero. These features occur regularly in the tragedies of Ben Jonson, George Chapman, Cyril Tourneur, and John Webster.

Some significant studies of Senecan tragedy include J. W. Cunliffe, *The Influence of Seneca on Elizabethan Tragedy* (1893, repr. 1907); F. L. Lucas, *Seneca and Elizabethan Tragedy* (1922); and H. B. Charlton, *The Senecan Tradition in Renaissance Tragedy* (1946).

Shadow of Night, The. A book of poems by George CHAPMAN. First published in 1594, it is Chapman's first work to appear in print. The book includes two long, allegorical, and tortuously obscure philosophical poems, "Hymnus in Noctem" and "Hymnus in Cynthiam." The first hymn consists of 403 lines addressed to night, the "great goddess" who appears as chaos, ignorance, and time. Consistent with Chapman's view that poetry must be opaque, it is night that governs the muses and promotes "silence, study, ease, and sleep," whereas day governs the routine, mundane affairs of ordinary living. Chapman invokes the spirit of night to aid him in his pursuit of Platonic absolutes, hidden realities, and revelations of the soul, as opposed to the mere intellect or common reason: "No pen can anything eternal write / That is not steeped in humor of the Night."

The poet laments that in the formation of the world chaos (night) was removed to the remotest regions in order to permit the advent of light, for this creation of form necessitated a fatal separation of chaos from order and harmony. Hence disorder since the creation has not been an intergral part and function of being but a separate, always threatening element. In the world of day, men struggle with banalities and pursue wickedness, for chaos and disorder are no longer intermingled with other elements but located in their hearts and souls. "In Noctem" concludes with a sermon on the corruption and ignorance of the world, and on the role of the poet as philosopher, truth seeker, and moral redeemer.

"Hymnus in Cynthiam" is somewhat longer and even more abstruse. It is addressed to Cynthia, the moon goddess, who is, in one ambiguous symbol, both universal power and Queen Elizabeth. As in the first hymn, night is symbolic of eternity, truth, and inspiration, all paradoxically associated with the ever-changing moon. In a lengthy, complex invocation Chapman asks Cynthia to fill his soul with ecstasy so that he may glorify her and penetrate the obscure shadows of night. The poem concludes with the wish that Cynthia might release her powers on the ignorant world in disasters and upheavals that would reveal her omnipotence.

The Shadow of Night is an esoteric philosophical poem of deliberate and almost perverse obscurity. Although the frame of philosophical reference is Platonic, the symbols are personal and cryptic, hence unconventional and often non-Platonic in associations. Chapman's two subjects, the divine origins and destiny of the creative soul and the condemnation of worldly folly and injustice, lend themselves to sermonizing and dogmatism, tones not native to the style of METAPHYSICAL POETRY, though *Shadow of the Night* has sometimes been classified as such. Some scholars have read the work as the poetic manifesto of a coterie of skeptics and atheists headed by Sir Walter Raleigh and including Chapman, Christopher Marlowe, the mathematician Matthew Roydon, and the astronomer Thomas Harriott. Shakespeare is believed to have satirized this coterie of intellectuals as "the school of night" in *Love's Labour's Lost,* but there is little to substantiate this interpretation. It is more probable that *The Shadow of Night* is a product, not of any atheistic coterie, but of Chapman's own elitist conceptions of poetry and his own blurred, personalized Platonism.

A scholarly edition is in *The Poems,* ed. Phyllis B. Bartlett (1941, repr. 1962). For detailed explication, see M. C. Bradbrook, *The School of Night* (1936), and Roy W. Battenhouse, "Chapman's *The Shadow of Night:* An Interpretation," *SP,* XXXVIII (1941).

Shakespeare, William (1564-1616). Dramatist and poet. Christened on April 26, 1564, in Holy Trinity Church, Stratford-on-Avon, Shakespeare was, it is assumed, born on April 23. He was the eldest of four boys and two girls born to John Shakespeare, a prosperous glover on Henley Street, and Mary Arden, daughter of a small landowner in nearby Wilmcote. John Shakespeare held several important municipal offices in Stratford, including that of bailiff (the equivalent of mayor). Although the school records at Stratford have not survived, Shakespeare no doubt attended the grammar school established by the city fathers to prepare their sons for entering the universities. The curriculum was of a very high quality but extremely narrow and rigid by modern standards, the subject of concentration being exclusively Latin.

There is no evidence that Shakespeare attended either of the universities. At eighteen he married Ann Hathaway, twenty-six, on November 27, 1582; on May 26, 1583, she gave birth to their first child, Susanna. On February 2, 1585, two more children followed, the twins Hamnet and Judith. The son was named for a Stratford family, and the name "Hamnet" is not known to have any but a coincidental relationship to the title of Shakespeare's most famous tragedy.

Nothing whatever is known of Shakespeare's whereabouts or activities from the time of his marriage until Robert Greene's reference to him as an actor and playwright in *A Groatsworth of Wit* (1592). According to one legend, he left school to work in his father's business, another has him a schoolteacher in the country, and still another makes him a butcher's apprentice. Perhaps the best guess is that sometime during this so-called lost decade he was in London serving his apprenticeship as an actor. It is chiefly in that capacity Greene described him in 1592:

> Yes, trust them [i.e., actors] not; for there is an upstart crow, beautified with our feathers, that with his tiger's heart, wrapped in a player's hide, supposes he is as well able to bombast out a blank verse as the best of you; and being an absolute *Johannes factotum,* is in his own conceit the only *Shake-scene* in a country.

When Shakespeare's friends protested this attack, Henry Chettle, who had published Greene's pamphlet, absolved himself of any responsibility. In the preface to his *Kind Heart's Dream,* Chettle wrote of Shakespeare in these commendable terms:

> ...divers of worship have reported his uprightness of dealing, which argues his honesty and his facetious grace in writing that approves his art.

Shakespeare was probably an original member of the Lord Chamberlain's Men, the distinguished acting company that included the popular comedian Will Kempe and the great tragedian Richard Burbage. After the accession of James I in 1603, the company changed its name to the King's Men and became official members of the royal household, an honor that entitled them to wear the king's livery on his coronation day. Unlike many dramatists, Shakespeare was fortunate in not having to depend upon his writing to make a living; he was not only a principal actor with London's most prosperous company but also part owner, or "sharer," in the Globe theater, constructed by the Lord Chamberlain's Men on the Bankside in 1599. By 1597 he was sufficiently affluent to purchase New Place, one of the most imposing houses in Stratford and he continued to invest in real estate and other business ventures in Stratford throughout his life.

Shakespeare probably resided in London without his family until his retirement from the theater around 1611-12. There is record of his living for a time with a Huguenot family in London. No doubt he returned to Stratford for brief visits to attend to business and family matters. In 1596, while the Lord Chamberlain's Men were on tour, his son Hamnet died. His father's death came in 1601, his mother's in 1608. His eldest child Susanna married a Calvinist physician, John Hall, in 1607; Judith did not marry until 1616.

It is impossible to date precisely many of Shakespeare's plays and poems. Important evidence of terminal dates for some of the works is a passage in Francis Meres' *Palladis Tamia* (1598):

> As the soul of *Euphorbus* was thought to live in *Pythagoras:* so the sweet witty soul of *Ovid* lives in mellifluous & honey-tongued *Shakespeare.* Witness his *Venus* and *Adonis,* his *Lucrece,* his sugared sonnets among his private friends, etc.
>
> As *Plautus* and *Seneca* are accounted the best for Comedy and Tragedy among the Latins: so *Shakespeare* among the English is the most excellent in both kinds for the stage; for Comedy, witness his *Gentlemen of Verona,* his *Errors,* his *Love labours lost,* his *Love labours wonne,* his *Midsummer night dream,* and his *Merchant of Venice;* for Tragedy his *Richard the* 2, *Richard the* 3, *Henry the* 4, *King John, Titus Andronicus,* and his *Romeo and Juliet.*

Of those plays mentioned by Meres, among the earliest were probably A COMEDY OF ERRORS (c. 1592-93) and TITUS ANDRONICUS (c. 1593-94), which find Shakespeare beginning his apprenticeship by working in two well-established Elizabethan genres, the first a comedy drawn from Plautus, a favorite Latin dramatist at the universities and Inns of Court, the second a SENECAN TRAGEDY derived from Thomas Newton's popular English translation, *Seneca, His Ten Tragedies* (1581). About the same time as *A Comedy of Errors* and *Titus Andronicus,* Shakespeare began the first of his two tetralogies on the Wars of the Roses, HENRY VI, Parts I-III, and RICHARD III. For most critics the *Henry VI* plays are the least satisfactory of Shakespeare's chronicle dramas. The verse is stiffly formal, the action as episodic and loosely connected as in Shakespeare's two principal sources, Raphael Holinshed's *Chronicles* (1587 ed.) and Edward Hall's *The Union of the Two Noble and Illustrious Families of Lancaster and York* (1548). Shakespeare's view in these first history plays is nationalistic and xenophobic; the French are shown to be foolish and corrupt, Joan of Arc is portrayed as a fraudulent strumpet, and the principal hero is Talbot, the English general who is defeated in France only because of treachery at home. The political lesson that emerges from the Henry VI plays is clear and unequivocal: civil war is hectic in the body politic, and the only healthy state is one ruled by a strong and just central monarchy.

In these early history plays Shakespeare's future greatness can be felt in a few powerfully drawn characters such as Henry IV, Queen Margaret, and Jane Shore, and, most tellingly, in several brief, vivid scenes imaginatively developed out of details seized upon in Holinshed and Hall. This confident handling of the chronicles is most consistently realized in the last play of the tetralogy, *Richard III,* a powerful, highly concentrated melodrama reflecting the influence of Marlowe's *The Jew of Malta* and *Edward II.* It was from Marlowe that Shakespeare learned not only the "mighty line" of unrhymed iambic pentameter but also the technique of focusing on a single, dominant character in order to distill the raw and chaotic details of the chronicles, and in *Richard III* he unifies a multitude of characters and events around one awesome villain who combines the evil frivolity of the character Vice from the morality plays with the ruthless calculation of the Machiavellian villain. In *Henry VI,* Part III, Richard had vowed to "set the murderous Machiavel to school," and in this melodramatic climax to the tetralogy of the Wars of the Roses, Richard emerges a full-blown Marlovian titan with just enough human weakness and lyrical introspection to prevent him from being an absurd caricature:

But I, that am not shaped for sportive tricks,
Nor made to court an amorous looking-glass;
I, that am rudely stamped, and want love's.
  majesty
To strut before a wanton ambling nymph;
I, that am curtailed of this fair proportion,
Cheated of feature by dissembling nature,
Deformed, unfinished, sent before my time
Into this breathing world, scarce half made up,
And that so lamely and unfashionable
That dogs bark at me as I halt by them...
[I, *i,* 14-23]

With *Richard III* Shakespeare's earliest, experimental period came to an end. In his next series of plays he turned from Plautine comedy, Senecan revenge tragedy, and English history plays to the COMMEDIA DELL'ARTE and Italian romantic comedy in THE TAMING OF THE SHREW, TWO GENTLEMEN OF VERONA, and LOVE'S LABOUR'S LOST (all wr. c. 1593-95). The last represents his most archly sophisticated, lyrical, and witty achievement before A MIDSUMMER NIGHT'S DREAM in 1595-96. Like *The Taming of the Shrew, Love's Labour's Lost* is audacious and sophisticated farce, from the hilarious characterization of the pedant Holofernes to the love debates between nimble-witted Rosaline, a "light wench" and "lightly wanton with a velvet brow," and her adversary Berowne (a character some have identified as representing Shakespeare himself).

For about eighteen months during the period 1593-94 the public theaters were closed because of the plague, and Shakespeare turned to writing nondramatic verse. From this time dates VENUS AND ADONIS (1593), an erotic Ovidian narrative poem dedicated to the earl of Southampton. No doubt the work caused some scandal, for the following year, as if in atonement, Shakespeare wrote a narrative poem describing a woman who dies rather than accept the humiliation of sexual violation. Like the first poem, THE RAPE OF LUCRECE (1594) was dedicated to the earl of Southampton, a generous patron of the arts from whom Shakespeare was no doubt seeking financial compensation. "The younger sort take much delight in Shakespeare's *Venus and Adonis,"* observed Gabriel Harvey in one of his letters, "but his *Lucrece,* and his tragedy of *Hamlet*...have it in them to please the wiser sort."

It was about this time, also, that Shakespeare began the 154 "sugared sonnets" referred to by Meres (see SHAKESPEARE'S SONNETS). They may have circulated among his friends for a decade or more in manuscript, being added to a little at a time until their first publication, apparently without Shakespeare's authorization or supervision, by Thomas Thorpe in 1609. In any event, Shakespeare's enthusiasm for sonnets was at its height around 1593 to 1596, for *Love's Labour's Lost* and ROMEO AND JULIET, both written during this period, are redolent with their influence. Thorpe's edition is dedicated to one "Mr. W. H.," variously identified as Henry Wriothesley, third earl of Southampton (1573-1624), and William Herbert, third earl of Pembroke (1580-1630). As for the identification of the principal figures praised or villified in the Sonnets—the Young Patron, the Rival Poet, and the Dark Lady—scholarly speculation has been endless (see *Shakespeare's Sonnets,* New Variorium Edition, ed. Hyder E. Rollins [1944]).

The period during or shortly after Shakespeare wrote his nondramatic poetry was marked by a spectacular outpouring of variegated plays, including RICHARD II (wr. 1595-96), *Romeo and Juliet* (1595-96). *A Midsummer Night's Dream,* THE MERCHANT OF VENICE (1596-97), and KING JOHN (wr. 1596-97). The first two contain the basic elements of Shakespeare's later tragedies. Although *Romeo and Juliet* depicts two "star-crossed lovers" destroyed by fate, medieval and Senecan qualities are mixed with two astonishing innovations of characterization from the *commedia dell'arte*—the nurse, inspired by the Italian *balia,* and Mercutio, a combination of the comic "enemy of love" and the MILES GLORIOSUS. *Romeo and Juliet* contributed little toward Shakespeare's mature conception of tragedy, but these two characters, especially the nurse, illustrate that at this point in his career he had mastered two related principles—the dramatic impact of rapid-fire, colloquial prose, and the emotional value of a character who, although not essential to the story as a whole, remains on stage simply "to talk himself alive" by virtue of intrinsically fascinating vitality of expression. These two principles contributed greatly to the creation of such memorable characters as the later Falstaff, the gravediggers in *Hamlet,* the porter in *Macbeth,* and many others.

Written about the same time as *Romeo and Juliet* was *Richard II,* the first of the second tetralogy of history plays that includes HENRY IV, Parts I and II, and HENRY V. Although a history play, *Richard II* marks a significant step toward Shakespeare's major tragedies, for the protagonist Richard is not, like Romeo, "star-crossed" but deeply flawed. Moreover, Richard displays many of the qualities of Shakespeare's later tragic heroes—complex consciousness, introspection, isolation, indecision coupled with impulsiveness, and profound inner conflicts. In this play the tragic formula may have been derived in part from Marlowe's *Edward II.* Both plays present the theme of deposition with almost calculated ambiguity; both heroes are weak, vacillating, and prone to flattery—faults which, in fact, Essex complained of in Queen Elizabeth. Indeed, the night before Essex's abortive uprising the rebels commissioned the Lord Chamberlain's Men to perform *Richard II,* "Know you not I am Richard II?" Elizabeth angrily asked one of her privy councilors, and after the rebellion the actors were required to exonerate themselves before the council. Their defense served to excuse both the dramatist and the players, for they explained that *Richard II* was "an old play" (hence not relevant to any recent crisis) which they performed without awareness of its immediate political implications.

Shakespeare's remarkable versatility was well established by 1600. All the elements of his greatest tragedies are fully realized in JULIUS CAESAR, in which the hero Brutus continues the genealogy of indecisive, introspective, self-deceived and ironically idealistic heroes that extends from *Richard II* to *Hamlet.* In Shakespeare's comedy his range, variety, and sheer quality are as impressive as in tragedy. *A Midsummer Night's Dream* is a fantasy of purest imagination, a brilliant synthesis of fairy lore and romance, myth and satire, whereas *The Merchant of Venice,* written and performed about a year later (and perhaps influenced by Marlowe's *Jew of Malta),* ranges far beyond Marlowe's melodrama, not only in its sensitive and complex characterization of Shylock but in its richly suggestive use of myth and ironic, vivid social contrasts. Taking a hint perhaps from Robert Greene's heroines, Shakespeare also enlivened his comedy with Portia, a vivacious, witty, and resourceful girl who served as the prototype for the later Viola in TWELFTH NIGHT and Rosalind in AS YOU LIKE IT.

This period also saw Shakespeare's perfection of the CHRONICLE PLAY in Parts I and II of *Henry IV,* written around 1597-98—two history plays vastly superior to his rather faltering *King John* that came immediately before. Here Shakespeare again demonstrates superbly his ability to integrate the polyphonic Elizabethan plot and the variegated details of the chronicles. A comparison of the *Henry IV* plays with even such a masterpiece of a similar kind as Thomas Dekker's SHOEMAKER'S HOLIDAY underscores Shakespeare's unquestionable superiority. Dekker's Lacey and Shakespeare's Hal are both prodigal sons, but Dekker's is only the occasion for innocuous intrigue, Shakespeare's a complex individual whose antithesis in Hotspur is made to represent not only opposing temperaments but conflicting value systems. Dekker's Simon Eyre is a character whose dramatic effectiveness largely depends on sentimentality and verbal repetition; Shakespeare's Falstaff is a monarch of wit, a protean magician, a mime of a thousand masks, and a brilliant dramatic descendant of the wise clown, the festive king of fools, and the Vice of the morality plays. Falstaff's rejection by Hal has caused centuries of angry comment, but the most brutal rejection of the fat knight was by Shakespeare himself. According to legend, he was asked by Queen Elizabeth to "show Falstaff in love" and, around 1600-01, wrote the farcical MERRY WIVES OF WINDSOR, wherein the previously indomitable old rogue is outwitted by Mistress Anne Page and her provincial cronies.

By 1599-1600 romantic comedy had become for Shakespeare an easy formula, and his effortless mastery is perhaps suggested by the titles of the so-called golden comedies—*As You Like It; Twelfth Night, or, What You Will;* and MUCH ADO ABOUT NOTHING. All the efforts of Shakespeare's predecessors and contemporaries such as John Lyly, Robert Greene, George Peele, Thomas Heywood, and Thomas Dekker seem laborious when compared with the easy grace of these ebullient plays.

After 1600 Shakespeare never returned to the gaiety and optimism of the golden comedies. What followed in the next period were the great tragedies and what F. S. Boas was the first to describe as "problem plays" (ALL'S WELL THAT ENDS WELL, TROILUS AND CRESSIDA,

MEASURE FOR MEASURE). What precipitated this "dark" period of Shakespeare's career? Some attribute it to disillusionment following the execution of the earl of Essex, others to some unknown illness or personal grief. It has been suggested, also, that Shakespeare was merely reflecting the general *Weltschmerz* of his contemporaries, or that perhaps he fell under the influence of Jonson's caustic and realistic comedies. In any event, these problem plays, unlike the earlier comedies, feature savagely cynical malcontents such as Lavache in *All's Well* or Thersites in *Troilus and Cressida.* The love relationships are misalliances or unsavery sexual affairs, the plots multiple, complex, and thematically ambiguous.

During this same period Shakespeare completed his four major tragedies, HAMLET (wr. c. 1600-01), OTHELLO (wr. c. 1604-05). KING LEAR (wr. c. 1605-06), and MACBETH (wr. c. 1605-06). Each of these has its own unique complexity, yet all are tragedies of character rather than fate, and all explore with great concentration of language and action man's starkest confrontations with himself, with other men, and with the gods. One need only put any one of Shakespeare's tragic heroes in the other's situation to see how different each hero is in temperament: How successful would Iago have been against Hamlet? Would Claudius have survived a day if Macbeth had been prince of Denmark? Yet all Shakespeare's tragic heroes are by turns and in various degrees violent and compassionate, savage and sensitive, profoundly introspective, articulate, proudly defiant, isolated and wholly obsessed and deeply divided within themselves over some secret ideal—revenge, honor, love, or ambition. Like the heroes of ancient Greek tragedy, they grope in darkness toward their own destruction, writhing in self-deception until released by a revelation that comes too late. For Hamlet illumination and death follow so hard upon each other he cannot utter what he has learned from suffering:

Had I but time—as this fell sergeant death.
Is strict in his arrest—oh, I could tell you—
But let be Horatio, I am dead,
Thou livest... [V, *ii,* 347-50]

Othello states that "he threw a pearl away richer than all his tribe." Macbeth sees at last the duplicity of the witches and tastes the bitter irony of his vaulting ambition:

I have lived long enough. My way of life
Is fall'n unto the sear, the yellow leaf;
And that which should accompany old age,
As honor, love, obedience, troops of friends,
I must not look to have... [V, *iii,* 22-26]

And Lear, who began his ordeal with the frivolous question "How much do you love me?" ends it with Cordelia dead in his arms and asking, like Job, the very meaning of life itself:

Why should a dog, a horse, a rat, have life,
And thou no breath at all? Thou'lt come no more,
Never, never, never, never, never!
[V, *iii,* 306-08]

King Lear was Shakespeare's last philosophical tragedy. His turn toward romance may have begun with ANTONY AND CLEOPATRA (wr. c. 1606-07), the most poetic and episodic of his tragedies. The star-crossed, passionate Antony, who gives "all for love and the world well lost," can be imagined as Romeo in middle age, whereas his dark "gypsy" queen may bear some arcane relationship to the Dark Lady of the Sonnets. Yet any such indications that Shakespeare was turning back to earlier associations are belied by two other plays he wrote at about this time, TIMON OF ATHENS and CORIOLANUS (both wr. c. 1607-08). Timon is in the bitter style of John Marston, less of a tragedy than a satire directed at human nature, and *Coriolanus,* Shakespeare's last tragedy, is also his most political. Of all Shakespeare's tragic heroes, Coriolanus is the least conscious and articulate, for he is merely a petulant boy deprived of maturity by early war experiences and a domineering mother. The principal character of the play is Rome itself, the victim over which the various political factions fight like dogs over a bone.

Sometime after *Coriolanus,* Shakespeare wrote his last four plays. PERICLES, CYMBELINE, THE WINTER'S TALE, and THE TEMPEST. In contrast to his earlier work, all these are exotic in setting and full of sudden and improbable turns of plot. Perhaps they represent an appeal to the more aristocratic audience at the newly built Blackfriars theater, or the influence of John FLETCHER, with whom Shakespeare is believed to have collaborated in TWO NOBLE KINSMEN and in his last play, HENRY VIII. In any event, he was not only turning away from the popular playhouses but perhaps anticipating his retirement to Stratford. Prospero's speech in *The Tempest,* written in 1611, is often interpreted as Shakespeare's own farewell to the stage:

Our revels now are ended. These our actors,
As I foretold you, were all spirits, and
Are melted into air, into thin air;
And, like the baseless fabric of this vision,
The cloud-capp'd towers, the gorgeous palaces,
The solemn temples, the great globe itself—
Yea, all which it inherit—shall dissolve
And, like this insubstantial pageant faded,
Leave not a rack behind. We are such stuff
As dreams are made on, and our little life
Is rounded with a sleep. [IV, *i,* 148-58]

Records show that Shakespeare spent the last four years of his life in Stratford. On March 25, 1616, he made his will, leaving his possessions to his family and some money to buy memorial rings for John Heminges, Richard Burbage, and Henry Condell, his fellow actors in the King's Men company. His monument in the Stratford church states that he died on April 23, 1616. In 1623 Heminges and Condell arranged for the publication of the First Folio, which includes all of Shakespeare's plays except *Pericles* and *Two Noble Kinsmen.*

No systematic investigation of Shakespeare's life was made until Nicholas Rowe's first biography in 1709, although anecdotes, legends, and general notices were recorded in late seventeenth- and early eighteenth-century collective biographies by John Aubrey, Charles Gildon, Gerard Langbaine, Edward Phillips, and William Winstanley. Two reliable biographies that reproduce most of the documents related to Shakespeare as well as critical analyses of previous works on the subject are J. Q. Adams, *Life of William Shakespeare* (1923), and E. K. Chambers, *William Shakespeare: A Study of Facts and Problems,* 2 vols. (1930). Much of this data is conveniently summarized by G. E. Bentley, *Shakespeare: A Biographical Handbook* (1961). Some new information about Shakespeare's life and neighbors in Stratford is set forth by Mark Eccles, *Shakespeare in Warwickshire* (1961), a further contribution to the work done by Edgar I. Fripp in *Shakespeare's Stratford* (1928) and *Shakespeare Studies: Biographical and Literary* (1930). For a survey of Shakespeare's biographers, see Samuel Schoenbaum, *Shakespeare's Lives* (1970).

Any extensive study of Shakespeare's works requires use of the New Variorum editions begun in 1871 by H. H. Furness and now under the continuing sponsorship of the Modern Language Association, whose editor since 1966 has been James G. McManaway (succeeding J. Q. Adams and Hyder E. Rollins). Of the New Variorum series only *Titus Andronicus* and *The Comedy of Errors* remain to be edited. Another standard scholarly edition is the new Arden Shakespeare, originally edited 1899-1924 in 37 volumes and later extensively corrected, revised, and supplemented (1951-). The vast criticism and scholarly research on Shakespeare are listed in three convenient bibliographies: Walthan Ebisch and L. L. Schücking, *Shakespeare Bibliography* (1931), and its Supplement (1937), which are continued by Gordon Ross Smith, *Classified Shakespeare Bibliography, 1936-1958* (1963). More recent listings are in Ronald Berman, *A Reader's Guide to Shakespeare's Plays* (1965), and the annual Shakespeare bibliography in *SQ,* (1950-). Convenient one-volume reference works are *The Reader's Encyclopedia of Shakespeare,* ed. Oscar James Campbell and Edward G. Quinn (1966), and *A New Companion to Shakespeare Studies,* ed. Kenneth Muir and Samuel Schoenbaum (1971).

Shakespeare's Sonnets. A sequence of 154 sonnets by William SHAKESPEARE, first printed in 1609 by Thomas Thorpe, probably without the author's permission or supervision. The many problems regarding the dating of the Sonnets, their sources and influences, and the identities of the personages referred to are copiously set forth in the New Variorium Edition by Hyder E. Rollins (1944). Although most scholars assign the Sonnets to the period 1592-95, they cannot be dated with certainty. The first reference to the Sonnets occurs in Frances Meres's *Palladis Tamia* (1598), which alludes to Shakespeare's "sugared sonnets among his private friends," but it cannot be ascertained that these sonnets circulating privately in manuscript were those printed by Thorpe in 1609. Scholars are equally doubtful as to whether they are autobiographical or merely literary exercises. The latter view is persuasively argued by Sir Sidney Lee in his chapter "Vogue of the Elizabethan Sonnets" in *Life of William Shakespeare* (1915), where he cites numerous analogies from Italian, French, and English poets.

Those who read the Sonnets as autobiographical find a fascinating story involving four chief characters—the Poet, his young Patron, a Dark Lady, and a Rival Poet. The first 126 sonnets are generally regarded as having been written to the young Patron (most often identified, with little if any evidence, as the earl of Southampton or the earl of Pembroke), whom the Poet begs (in the first seventeen poems) to marry and have children, to guard his reputation against slander, and to live wisely and without dissipation. There are several poems lamenting the Poet's absence from the Patron, and at one point the Patron's affections seem to have been taken by the Rival Poet (George Chapman? Michael Drayton? Thomas Lodge? Christopher Marlowe?), whose verses the Poet cannot equal. Not until after the first 126 sonnets does the Dark Lady become a main character. Judging from the poems, she is a brunette utterly lacking in conventional beauty, yet has a powerful sexual hold on the Poet. At one point she seduces the young Patron, causing a crisis of friendship between the Poet and the Patron. Like the Poet, she is married, and is unfaithful not only to her husband but to the Poet as well. He addresses her angrily as "the bay on which all men ride" and as a common bawd who dispenses her favors too liberally. Attempts to identify the Dark Lady have not been successful. At present the chief candidate for the role is Mary Fitton, a maid of honor at Queen Elizabeth's court with connections to the earl of Pembroke. (See Thomas Tyler, *The Herbert-Fitton Theory of Shakespeare's Sonnets* [1898].) One obstacle to reading a coherent "story" in the Sonnets is that the arrangement of the sequence by Thorpe may not at all represent the one intended by Shakespeare.

The last two poems of Shakespeare's sequence, 153 and 154, are paraphrases of the same epigram in the Greek Anthology, a collection of 4,500 Greek poems assembled in the tenth century by a Byzantine scholar, Constantinus Cephalas. In all probability Sonnets 153 and 154 were paraphrased from some unknown intermediate source rather than translated directly from the Greek.

With the exception of *Hamlet,* no literary work has aroused so much speculation and diverse interpretation as Shakespeare's Sonnets. The identity of the "W. H." to whom they are dedicated remains as baffling as that of the "fair youth" and "dear boy" addressed from time to time in Sonnets 1-127, and almost every detail of the sequence, from the identity of the mysterious "W. H." to that of the Dark Lady and the Rival Poet, has created endless speculation, little of it having much basis in solid fact. Even the meaning of the sequence as a whole remains ambiguous, for if Sir Sidney Lee reads the Sonnets as literary exercises, others like Coleridge find them to be candid and heartfelt confessions. For some readers Shakespeare's celebration of the "fair youth" represents an expression of the highest ideals of friendship in the Renaissance tradition, a purely Platonic relationship of soul to soul; to other readers these tributes are conclusive evidence of the author's homosexuality. Some read the Sonnets as they would a modern novel, finding a clearly delineated plot and thoroughly developed characterizations; others prefer to see them as an orchestration of medleys on loosely related themes, a concatenation of moods and ideas without much narrative coherence or continuity.

Several philosophical themes receive repetitive emphasis in the Sonnets. One is the Petrarchan and Platonic conflict of reason and passion, at first represented by the Poet's stress on his own moral choices and those of the young Patron, and later by the terrible struggle within the Poet between his ideals and his deep sexual desires. As in VENUS AND ADONIS, also composed about this time, sexuality is experienced as a "fever, longing still / For that which longer nurseth the disease," and the Poet's sense of his spirit's humiliating capitulation to sensuality gives rise to some of the most passionate Sonnets in the sequence, especially the so-called angry Sonnet (129):

The expense of spirit in a waste of shame
Is lust in action, and till action, lust
Is perjured, murderous, bloody, full of blame,
Savage, extreme, rude, cruel, not to trust...

Although in Sonnet 147 the Poet sees "desire as death," he is "past cure," and his agony finds expression in the only unequivocally religious poem in all of Shakespeare's works, Sonnet 146:

Poor soul, the center of my sinful earth,
My sinful earth, these rebel powers that thee
  array,
Why dost thou pine within and suffer dearth,
Painting thou outward walls so costly gay?

Like Sir Philip Sidney's "Leave Me, O Love," Sonnet 146 is both prayer and palinode, concluding with the resolution that henceforth he will "buy terms divine in selling hours of dross," and "within be fed, without be rich no more."

Another theme of the Sonnets is that of mutability, personified by the protean character of Time as the cankerworm destroying the rose, as the subtle thief, as the power-proud tyrant, as the merciless old man with sickle. Time is the villain who relentlessly destroys all creation and beauty, as in Sonnet 65:

How with this rage shall beauty hold a plea,
Whose action is no stronger than a flower?

Against the enemy Time and his allies death and "all-oblivious enmity," the Poet places his faith in man's few but precious means of transcendence—procreation, love, and art. The beginning of Sonnet 55 gives magnificent expression to this affirmative idea in the Sonnets as a whole:

Not marble, nor the gilded monuments
Of princes, shall outlive this powerful rhyme.
But you shall shine more bright in these contents
Than unswept stone besmeared with sluttish
time.

The definitive text and best summary of the vast textual, biographical, and critical problems of the Sonnets can be found in the New Variorum Edition, ed. Hyder E. Rollins, 2 vols. (1944). For specialized topics, consult the *CBEL*, I, and supplement; and Walter Ebisch and Levin L. Schücking, *A Shakespeare Bibliography* (1931), together with its supplement to 1935. Ebisch and Schücking are continued to 1958 by Gordon Ross Smith, *Classified Shakespeare Bibliography* (1963). The fullest bibliography to 1939 is by S. A. Tannenbaum (1940). A few interpretations of the Sonnets can be cited for their influence or particular aesthetic value: John Crowe Ransom, "Shakespeare at Sonnets," *The World's Body* (1938); Edward Hubler, *The Sense of Shakespeare's Sonnets* (1952); J. B. Leishman, *Themes and Variations in Shakespeare's Sonnets* (1961); and J. Dover Wilson, *An Introduction to Shakespeare's Sonnets* (1964).

Shepherd's Calendar, The. A pastoral poem by Edmund SPENSER in twelve eclogues (selections), published in 1579 with the anonym "Immerito" (worthless one"). The first edition contained a dedication to Sir Philip Sidney, a prefatory letter to Gabriel Harvey, and a detailed gloss by "E. K.," who is generally believed to have been Edward Kirke (1553-1613), a friend of Spenser's at Pembroke College, Cambridge.

Other less likely candidates for "E. K." are Fulke Greville, Thomas Watson, and Spenser himself. The last of these is least probable because "E. K." in his gloss occasionally misinterprets the poem, cites incorrect sources, and defines words inaccurately.

Spenser made use of a wide range of pastoral poets for his sources. Although Theocritus and Vergil are frequently referred to in the gloss, Spenser more often consulted Mantuan, Giocomo Sannazaro, Clément Marot, Jorge de Montemayor, and the early Tudor poets who imitated and translated Mantuan, Alexander Barclay and Barnabe Googe. Spenser's use of the calendar was taken from *Le Compost et Kalendrier des bergiers,* a fifteenth-century French almanac or cyclopedia mingling pious meditations with expositions of the pater noster or creed with astrological lore and practical wisdom. Each month was headed by a woodcut with appropriate zodiacal signs; Spenser employs a similar device but uses emblems illustrating the theme of each eclogue.

According to "E. K.," Spenser's eclogues are subsumed under three rubrics: "plaintive" (1, 6, 11, 12); "moral" (2, 5, 7, 9, 10); and "recreative" (3, 4, 8). The "plaintive" he describes as combining love poems with compliments to certain personages; the "moral" as being satiric of religious abuses. The "recreative" he does not define, but suggests they were intended to be purely entertaining. These distinctions are only accurate in a very general way and do not account for Spenser's concatenation of themes on love, religion, poetry, and statecraft. The most obvious thread running through the eclogues is the hopeless love of Colin Clout (a name taken from John Skelton's poems), representing Spenser, for the cold and haughty shepherdess Rosalind, whose identity remains a mystery. Scholars have learned little more about her than E. K.'s brief explanation that the girl's name is "a feigned name, which being wel ordered, wil bewray the very name of hys [the poet's] love and mistresse, whom by that name he coloureth." Other characters can be identified: Hobbinol is certainly Gabriel Harvey; Eliz is Queen Elizabeth; Roffy (or Roffyn) is bishop John Young, master of Pembroke College during Spenser's years at Cambridge; Tityrus is variously Vergil or Chaucer; and Lobbin, though less certain of identification, is probably Robert Dudley, earl of Leicester. These fictive names are not conventional in the classical or Renaissance pastoral; Spenser seems to have chosen them for their English sound or associations. In the "May" eclogue the name and much of the characterization of the shepherd-priest Piers recall William Langland's satire *Piers Plowman.*

"E.K." defended Spenser's archaic diction on grounds that it "maketh the style seeme grave, as it were reverend"—effects not shared by all of Spenser's contemporaries. Ben Jonson observed that Spenser "writ no language," and Sir Philip Sidney, though praising the poem on the whole, expressed objections in *An Apology for Poetry* to his friend's "old rustic language": "That same framing of his style to an old rustic language I dare not allow, sith neither Theocritus in Greek, Vergil in Latin, nor Sannazaro in Italian did affect it." Spenser conveys this rusticity by improvisations of orthography, dialectical words, Chaucerian imitations, and occasional use of the perfective prefix *y.* In a sense, therefore, Jonson's statement that Spenser "writ no language" is true if the assumption can be made that language cannot be invented. Spenser's artifice certainly renders *The Shepherd's Calendar* uneven of effects and quality. In some eclogues the language succeeds in being "reverend," as in "October," which has as its argument the "celestiall inspiration" of the true poet; on rare occasions, however, the reader is tempted to agree with Samuel Johnson's opinion of Spenser's contrived language as "studied barbarity."

Few readers have failed to admire the subtle rhythms of *The Shepherd's Calendar,* and Spenser fairly overwhelmed his contemporaries with his amazing variety of verse forms, including elegiac quatrains, ottava rima, heroic couplets, ballad measure—thirteen different types in all, and even one instance of a sestina. The result is what James Russell Lowell described in 1875 as "a variety, elasticity, and harmony of verse most grateful to the ears of man." To the eye Spenser's poem may seem at times grotesque; to the ear it never falters. For Spenser's generation it was the mellifluous sound of the "new poetry," as revolutionary and as decisively breaking with the past as Wordsworth's *Lyrical Ballads* in the nineteenth century. In his dedication "To His Book," Spenser echoes, in all humility, his master Chaucer's words in *Troilus and Criseyde* (V, 1786): "Goe little booke: thy selfe present, / As child whose parent is unkent [unknown]." At the conclusion of *The Shepherd's Calendar,* however, his prediction is more worthy of his work:

> Loe I have made a Calender for every yeare,
> That steele in strength, and time in durance
> shall outweare:
> And if I marked well the starres revolution,
> It shall continewe till the worlds dissolution.

The standard edition is in *The Works,* ed. Edwin A. Greenlaw, F. M. Padelford, et al., 10 vols. (1932–49), I, which contains a wealth of scholarly data. For criticism, see A. C. Hamilton, "The Argument of Spenser's *Shepheardes Calender,*" *ELH,* XXIII (1956); R. A. Durr, "Spenser's Calendar of Christian Time," *ELH,* XXIV (1957); Paul E. McLane, *Spenser's Shepheardes Calender: A Study in Elizabethan Allegory* (1961); S. K. Heninger, "The Implications of Form in *The Shepheardes Calender,*" *S Ren,* IX (1962); and William Nelson, *The Poetry of Edmund Spenser* (1963).

Shirley, James (1596–1666). Dramatist and poet. Shirley was born in London in September 1596 and entered the famous Merchant Taylors' School in October 1608, after which he proceeded to St. John's, College, Oxford, in 1612, then transferred to Cambridge in 1615 and graduated in 1617. Most of the few details about Shirley's personal life derive from Anthony à Wood's *Athenae Oxonienses,* which states that Shirley took orders at Cambridge and settled near St. Albans, Hertfordshire, as a clergyman. In 1621 he was appointed master of the grammar school at St. Albans, probably through the influence of his young wife Elizabeth Gilmet, whose family was prominent in the town. His career as clergyman and teacher ended in 1624 when he converted to Roman Catholicism and returned to London, where he entered Gray's Inn and began writing plays. His first play was probably *Love Tricks, or The School of Compliment* (perf. 1625, pr. 1631). By 1633 he was firmly in favor with the Catholic Queen Henrietta Maria, and his witty, fast-moving comedies were enthusiastically received at court. In 1633 *The Young Admiral* was performed to celebrate the king's birthday, and according to the master of the revels, Sir Henry Herbert, Charles I himself suggested the plot for Shirley's highly successful comedy *The Gamester* in 1634. These honors were capped the same year by Shirley's commission to write *The Triumph of Peace,* a graceful masque, which the four Inns of Court presented to the king and queen.

With the outbreak of the plague and closing of the London theaters in May 1636, Shirley's career took a new turn when he accepted an invitation from John Ogilby to visit Dublin, where Ogilby had opened the city's first theater in 1635. Here Shirley remained, except for brief trips to London, for the next five years, during which time he wrote and produced *The Royal Master, The Doubtful Heir, The Constant Maid,* and *St. Patrick for Ireland.*

Upon his return to London in 1640, Shirley became the leading dramatist for the King's Men, filling the position left vacant by Philip Massinger's recent death and remaining until the closing of the theaters in 1642. With the outbreak of the Civil War, Shirley left his wife and children in London to enter the Royalist service with his patron, William Cavendish, earl of Newcastle. After Cavendish fled England following the king's defeat at Marston Moor in 1644, Shirley returned to London and enlisted the patronage of a wealthy scholar and Royalist sympathizer, Thomas Stanley; for the next few years Shirley devoted himself to tutoring, compiling Latin grammars, and doing translations for Ogilby's editions of Homer and Vergil. In 1646 Shirley published a collection of his poems, consisting chiefly of epithalamia, elegies, prologues, and songs from plays, all reflecting the acknowledged influence of Jonson. A short quasi-dramatic piece based on Ovid's *Metamorphoses* appeared in 1659 as *The Contention of Ajax and Ulysses for the Armor of Achilles,* which contains the closing dirge that became one of the famous lyrics of the seventeenth century:

> The glories of our blood and state
> Are shadows, not substantial things...

After the Restoration, Shirley's plays were enthusiastically received, especially such comedies of manners as HYDE PARK (perf. 1632) and *The Gamester* (perf. 1634), but he wrote no new plays. Two months after suffering injuries in the Great Fire of London in 1666, Shirley and his second wife Frances died on the same day.

Most of Shirley's forty or more plays have survived, and among these the best are of two types, revenge tragedies and comedies of manners. The best of the tragedies, THE TRAITOR (wr. c. 1631, pr. 1635) and THE CARDINAL (wr. c. 1641, pr. 1652), hark back to the violent and bloody Elizabethan tradition of Kyd, Shakespeare, and Webster. The comedies of manners, represented superbly by THE LADY OF PLEASURE (wr. 1635, pr. 1637), look back to sophisticated comedies like Fletcher's *The Wild-Goose Chase* and Jonson's satiric comedies of humours. Of less quality but greater in number are Shirley's romantic comedies (about fourteen in all), which are best described as tragicomedies. The scene is usually Italy, the *dramatis personae* made up of nobles and courtiers, and the main plot treated with more solemnity than in his comedies of manners. The plots, many of them drawn from Spanish sources, are complicated and episodic, the characters sentimental or overdrawn, the action full of sudden shifts and suspense. Shirley's tragicomedies represent the very best of a courtly type of play that emerged with the demise of the popular theaters in the early 1630s. (see CAROLINE DRAMA). Tragicomedies like *Love's Cruelty* (perf. 1631), *The Young Admiral* (perf. 1633), and *The Royal Master* (perf. 1637) may often seem sensational, overblown, and loosely constructed when compared with the best of that genre by Beaumont and Fletcher, but they represent the finest tragicomedy on the stage just before the closing of the theaters. Few Cavalier dramatists matched Shirley's wit and poetic facility; although his tragicomedies are often bland and tiresome, they are superior in every way to pedestrian efforts of courtiers like William Cartwright, Lodowick Carlell, Thomas Killigrew, or Walter Montagu. In these declining years of the theater, when the Cavalier writers were rushing in to hasten the demise of a formerly robust tradition, Shirley's plays were among the few to give even a hint of a more glorious past.

The definitive edition of Shirley's *Dramatic Works and Poems* is still that by William Gifford and Alexander Dyce, 6 vols. (1833). Shirley's *The Traitor* was edited by J. S. Carter for the Regents Renaissance Drama series (1971). A comprehensive biography is by Arthur Nason, *James Shirley, Dramatist* (1915). Robert S. Forsythe, *The Relations of*

Shirley's Plays to the Elizabethan Drama (1914), is an important critical study. There is a Concise Bibliography by S. A. Tannenbaum (1946), updated in "James Shirley (1945-65)," ed. C. A. Pennel and W. P. Williams, in *Elizabethan Bibliographies Supplements,* VIII (1968).

Shoemaker's Holiday, The; or, The Gentle Craft. A romantic comedy by Thomas DEKKER written in 1599 and first performed by the Lord Admiral's Men at court during the Christmas season of that year. It was first printed in 1600. Dekker based his play on Thomas Deloney's THE GENTLE CRAFT (wr. c. 1596), a prose tale of a cobbler who rose to become lord mayor of London in the fifteenth century. The love story of Rose and Lacy may owe something to Robert Greene's *Friar Bacon and Friar Bungay,* and the play also borrows elements from Shakespeare's *Henry V* and *Romeo and Juliet.*

Sir Hugh Lacy, earl of Lincoln, and Sir Roger Oteley, lord mayor of London, are both eager to see the earl's nephew Rowland Lacy off to the king's wars in France because neither approves of his wooing of Oteley's beautiful daughter Rose. Young Lacy, however, has other plans; he tells his cousin Askew that he will join his regiment at Dover or in Normandy, and takes on the disguise of a Dutch shoemaker.

Also mustered to the wars is Rafe Damport, journeyman shoemaker for Simon Eyre, "the mad shoemaker of Tower Street", and "one of the merriest madcaps" in London. Before departing for France, Rafe gives his loving wife Jane a pair of shoes to remember him by.

Disguised as Hans and speaking a barely comprehensible English, Lacy secures a journeyman's place in Simon Eyre's shop at the urging of Eyre's two workers Hodge and Firk, and over the protest of his garrulous wife Dame Margery. As "Hans," Lacy not only proves a skillfull worker but helps Eyre's career by lending him money to purchase at great profit a cargo of spices newly arrived in port from Candia. Prosperous and richly arrayed, Eyre is made alderman.

Meanwhile Oteley's daughter pines away for her lover Lacy, and her father encourages her betrothal to a prosperous neighbor, Master Hammond. Spurned by Rose, Hammond begins courting Rafe's wife Jane, who, although remaining steadfastly loyal to the memory of her husband, believes that he has been killed in the wars. The plot deepens further when the earl of Lincoln's shifty servant Dodger returns from France to inform his master of Lacy's absence from the war, and the earl sends Dodger to London to snoop out Lacy's whereabouts.

Rafe returns badly wounded, only to find his wife gone and his inquiries about her at Eyre's shop drowned out by the jubilation caused by Eyre's election to the office of sheriff. Dame Margery humorously swaggers under the weight of her new status, and the ebullient Eyre gives his shop to Hodge, elevates Firk to foreman, and promises rich returns to "Hans" for his loan. At the lord mayor's dinner Eyre's "merry Mesopotamians" join in the revels, and Rose recognizes her lover among the shoemakers. Matters do not fare well for poor Rafe. Hammond's man comes to the shop with Jane's shoe, to be used as a pattern in making a new pair for Hammond and Jane's wedding. Confronted at the very church door by Rafe and his shoemaker friends, Hammond returns Jane to her husband. Simon Eyre, meanwhile, has been proclaimed lord mayor, and he gives his blessings to the marriage of Lacy and Rose. Sir Hugh and Sir Roger, still disapproving of the match, decide to protest to the king, who has just arrived in London and has arranged a meeting with the now famous "madcap" Simon Eyre.

The king appears at a jolly feast of the shoemakers. Delighted with Eyre and his merry crew, he decrees that a new hall be erected for the shoemakers in Cornhill, pardons Lacy for his absence from the wars, knights the young man on the spot, and gives his blessings to the wedding. The play ends with the king joining in the feast.

In some respects *The Shoemaker's Holiday* is a pastoral-like idealization of Merry England basking in universal conviviality and free of all social stratification. All classes from cobblers to rich merchants rejoice in their robust independence; only the earl of Lincoln and the snobbish Oteley express any social exclusiveness, and their attitude is denounced by the king himself at the end of the play. Yet, beneath this surface optimism, Dekker gently satirizes the garrulous and often insensitive Margery Eyre as a social climber, and gives a poignant account of poor Rafe, railroaded to the wars and glibly patronized upon his return. The mixture of sentimental romance and festive comedy of ordinary life, all occasionally modified by touches of grim realism, characterize Dekker's distinctive genius.

The definitive edition is in Dekker's *Dramatic Works,* ed. Fredson Bowers, 4 vols. (1953-61), a valuable work for its copious notes and learned commentary. Paul C. Davies has edited the play in the Fountainwell Drama Series (1968). Other criticism is by Arthur Brown, "Citizen Comedy and Domestic Drama," *The Jacobean Theatre, Stratford-upon-Avon Studies* (1960); James H. Conover, *Thomas Dekker: An Analysis of Dramatic Structure* (1969); and Michael Marken, "The Construction of *The Shoemaker's Holiday,*" *SEL,* X (1970).

Sidney, Sir Philip (1554-1586). Poet. Sidney was born at his family's ancestral manor at Penshurst, Kent, the son of Sir Henry Sidney, lord president of Wales (after 1560) and later lord deputy of Ireland. Sir Philip's mother was Mary Dudley, daughter of John Dudley, the earl of Northumberland, who was executed for leading the attempt to place Lady Jane Grey on the throne in 1553. Lady Mary's brothers were the powerful Ambrose Dudley, earl of Warwick, and the queen's favorite Robert Dudley, earl of Leicester. Sir Philip's godfather was Philip II of Spain, a personal friend of his father's during the reign of Mary Tudor.

Sidney attended school at Shrewsbury in Shropshire, where the curriculum was said to consist of "Vergil and Calvin," a combination of classical studies and Presbyterian theology. In 1567 or 1568, he matriculated at Christ Church, Oxford, noted as a center of activity in drama, especially for its performances of Latin plays written by William Gager. There is no indication, however, that Sidney took much interest in plays while at Oxford; he seems to have favored philosophy, in particular Aristotle, whose *Rhetoric* he partially translated in later years.

Sidney left Oxford in 1572 without taking a degree and went abroad to study foreign languages and to prepare himself for a career in diplomacy and politics. He went first to Paris, where he spent three months with Sir Francis Walsingham, the English ambassador and later his father-in-law. In Paris Sidney became friends with Admiral Gaspard de Coligny, leader of the Huguenots; Peter Ramus, the great logician; and Hubert Languet, a Huguenot diplomat and scholar who took a fatherly interest in young Sidney's education. While in Paris Sidney witnessed the St. Bartholomew's Day massacre, in which thousands of Huguenots were put to the sword, and the atrocity sharpened Sidney's fear of Catholic power and his detestation of religious intolerance.

By August 1574, after travels that had taken him to Heidelberg, Strasbourg, Venice, Rome and Padua, Sidney was at Vienna with his mentor Languet and Edward Wotton, half-brother of the statesman Sir Henry Wotton. It is this period at the court of Emperor Maximilian II to which Sidney refers in the pleasant opening of his *An Apology for Poetry,* where he describes how he and "the right virtuous Edward Wotton" studied horsemanship under the emperor's Italian equerry John Pietro Pugliano, whose eloquence on the subject of horses was so great, Sidney humorously recalled, "that, if I had not been a piece of a logician before I came to him, I think he would have persuaded me to have wished myself a horse."

Sidney returned to England by late spring of 1575, preceded by a flow of encomia and honorary titles from the many foreign princes favorably impressed by his erudition, charm, and courtly deportment, and the queen, in deference to Sidney's growing popularity at home and abroad, bestowed on him the honorary title of cupbearer. It is evident she would have preferred that Sidney—articulate, handsome, and versatile—remain a mere ornament, but the young courtier was filled with ambition, political ideas, and considerable independence. While on the Continent he had met with several leaders, including William of Orange, to discuss the forming of a Protestant league that would unite England with the Netherlands and the principalities of the Holy Roman Empire against Catholic France and Spain, and upon his return to England he allied himself at court with the bellicose anti-Spanish faction. Since Elizabeth's policy was to maintain a delicate balance of power between France and Spain while avoiding direct confrontation with either, Sidney's energetic efforts on behalf of the league very probably hampered his prospects at court. Moreover, the queen complained petulantly about the cost of Sir Henry Sidney's policies in Ireland, and Sidney, with characteristic integrity, visited his father there and returned to write a stout defense of those policies in *A Discourse on Ireland* (1577), in which he praised Sir Henry's administration, recommended increased military forces to suppress the rebels, relief for the poor, and new taxes on rich landowners. This last suggestion was especially objectionable to the queen, who found her staunchest supporters among the wealthy Irish gentry.

In Ireland the queen favored quick and economical solutions, not long and expensive programs of reform, and that unyielding island continued to be a swamp of despond for ambitious Tudor statesmen. In 1576 a recent casualty was Walter Devereux, first earl of Essex, who, having failed utterly to quell the Irish rebels, aspired to shore up his flagging career by marrying his daughter Penelope to a member of the illustrious Dudley family. Penelope Devereux (the "Stella" of Sidney's later sonnet sequence *Astrophel and Stella*) was only eleven at the time Essex began negotiating with Sir Henry Sidney, and it is doubtful if the marriage plans ever reached the stage of a formal engagement. Toward the end of 1576 Essex died, marriage negotiations terminated, and Penelope became secretly affianced to Charles Blount (later Lord Mountjoy). After this engagement was broken, she married Lord Robert Rich in 1581, divorced him years later, and wedded her first betrothed Lord Mountjoy.

In December 1576, Sidney was given his first important diplomatic assignment when he was sent by the queen to convey her condolences to Rudolph, the new Holy Roman emperor, on the death of his father Maximilian, and to congratulate him on his succession. Sidney was also ordered to take the same message to the Palatinate, where the elector had recently died and been succeeded by his son Louis. Sidney's real mission was more than a gesture of courtesy; for he was instructed to appraise the degree of support these rulers might give England in the event of a confrontation with Spain. Sidney was well received in Vienna and Germany, and while he was on his way home Sir Edward Dyer brought the queen's permission for Sidney to represent the earl of Leicester as godfather at the baptism of William of Orange's daughter. William of Orange was so favorably impressed with Sidney that he offered his sister's hand in marriage, a proposal of such political implications that the queen hastily forbade Sidney from continuing any further negotiations in the matter. The queen's mission afforded Sidney an ideal opportunity to further his own plans for a Protestant league, and at one point his old friend Languet wrote letters cautioning Sidney against exceeding authority by meeting independently with William of Orange to discuss military operations against the Spanish.

After Sidney's return to England in June 1577 the queen treated him warmly, acknowledged the success of his mission and the many plaudits he had received from abroad, but she continued to confine him to largely ceremonial assignments. On two occasions in 1579 she angrily banned him from court, once when he and the earl of Oxford exchanged challenges to a duel (which the Privy Council interceded to prohibit), and again when Sidney wrote a letter (probably instigated by Leicester and Walsingham) opposing Elizabeth's negotiations of marriage with D'Alençon, duke of Anjou, a match strongly supported by Sidney's enemy the earl of Oxford.

These years of relatively light political involvement afforded Sidney ample time for literary activity. His only dramatic work, the pastoral entertainment *The Lady of May,* was performed before the queen when she visited Leicester at Wanstead near Greenwich, probably in May 1578. The entertainment, first printed in 1598, may be described as a "quasi-masque" or satiric farce. It shows the influence of the *commedia rusticali,* comic interludes very popular at the time in northern Italy, in which rustic folk debate about some aspect of love before a sophisticated audience. Sidney may have seen dramatizations of the type during his travels. In his pastoral, the May Lady asks Queen Elizabeth to judge a dispute between two suitors, Espilus, a shepherd, and Therion, a forester, the shepherd representing contemplative withdrawal from life and the forester active involvement. There is some evidence that Sidney's uncle Leicester identified himself with Therion and that the queen, contrary to Leicester's hopes, chose Espilus as the superior suitor. In preparation for just such a "wrong" choice, Sidney wrote an epilogue denouncing the forester and his friends and thus divorcing Leicester from their faction in the dispute over the May Lady's hand.

It has been conjectured that about 1578-79 Sidney began meeting for literary discussions at Leicester House with a loosely organized group that included Edmund Spenser, Thomas Drant, Sir Edward Dyer, Abraham Fraunce, Fulke

Greville, and Gabriel Harvey. In correspondence of October 1579 Spenser and Harvey refer, rather playfully, to the group as the AREOPAGUS, the name of an ancient Athenian tribunal. One topic discussed was the use of classical quantitative meter in English poetry, with Harvey arguing in favor of employing quantitative scansion and classical hexameters. Although a few of Sidney's songs in THE ARCADIA are in classical meters, the bulk of his other poetry, as well as Spenser's *The Shepherd's Calendar* (1579), show clearly that neither Sidney nor Spenser held very firmly to the idea of adopting classical prosody to English verse.

It was probably in the summer of 1580, when Sidney was *persona non grata* at court because of his authorship of the letter about the queen's proposed marriage, that he began the first version of his prose romance *The Arcadia.* It was composed at Wilton, the country estate of his sister Mary, countess of Pembroke, to whom Sidney dedicated "this idle work," as he calls it in his preface, "being done in loose sheets of paper, most of it in your presence, the rest by sheets sent unto you, as fast as they were done"—a statement suggesting that he did the major portion of the romance at Wilton and perhaps sent his sister the remainder after he departed. Consisting of five books resembling acts in a tragicomedy, with each act divided by prose and verse "eclogues" or interludes, *The Arcadia* seems to have been, at first, merely an amusing summer diversion. Later, however, while working on *An Apology for Poetry* around 1581-83, he was compelled to return to some important aesthetic ideas that had preoccupied him during his Aristotelian studies at Oxford and, doubtless, in his conversations with the "Areopagus" group at Leicester House. Consequently, in about 1584 he began a thorough revision of *The Arcadia* with a view toward making the romance conform to certain critical precepts he had developed regarding epic and heroic poetry.

Whereas the "Old" *Arcadia,* Sidney's first version, is essentially a love story of adventure and intrigue, the "New" *Arcadia* is on the scale of a heroic prose poem in which the argument concerns not only love but education, courtesy, politics, and war. In the "New" *Arcadia* the first part of the story is revised completely to begin *in medias res,* as Aristotle required of epic narrative, and a host of new characters and events are introduced. In addition, Sidney elevated the language, deepened the philosophical ideas, elaborated on descriptive passages, and gave increased attention to subtleties of motive and action. No doubt he intended to expand his romance to twelve books to give the whole an epic structure, but the revision was never completed and the story breaks off in the middle of what appears to have been Book III.

Since *An Apology for Poetry,* written sometime in 1581-83, was not published until 1595, some years after Sidney's death, the occasion for its writing and its exact date of composition are difficult to ascertain. Sidney's literary essay, known also as *The Defense of Poesy,* may have been intended as a rejoinder to an attack on literature dedicated to Sidney, Stephen Gosson's *The School of Abuse* (1579), a treatise purporting to be "a pleasant invective against Poets, Players, Jesters, and such like caterpillars of a commonwealth" (see CRITICISM, LITERARY). Gosson, a former dramatist recently converted to austere religious views, may have dedicated his work to Sidney with the mistaken idea that Sidney's known championship of Protestantism was attended by a concomitant hostility to the arts. If so, a letter of Spenser to Harvey on October 15, 1579, shows how completely Gosson was misled. "New books I hear of none," wrote Spenser, "but only of one that writing a certain book called the *School of Abuse,* and dedicating it to Master Sidney, was for his labour scorned, if at least it be in the goodness of that nature to scorn."

Sidney makes no mention of Gosson in *An Apology for Poetry.* Instead, he defends poetry against its detractors on grounds of its antiquity, universality, and unique moral utility. From Aristotle and his Renaissance commentators Sidney derives a concept of poetry as imitation, or *mimesis,* "that is to say, a representing, counterfeiting or figuring forth...a speaking picture: with this end, to teach and delight." It is this moral function, asserts Sidney, more than any necessary form, that is the essence of poetry. Thus mere versification is "but an ornament and no cause to poetry, sith there have been many most excellent poets that never versified, and now swarm many versifiers that need never answer to the name of poets." By such criterion Plato and Xenophon, writing in prose, are considered poets as well as Homer and Vergil, for "...it is that feigning notable images of virtues, vices, or what else, with that delightful teaching, which must be the right describing note to know a poet by." It was with this conception of poetry that Sidney returned to revise *The Arcadia* into an "absolute heroical poem," a phrase Sidney used to describe Xenophon's prose biography of Cyrus the Great.

In his *Apology* Sidney complained that the love poetry of his time was without any genuine passion—or, as he stated in using the term from Aristotle—without *energia*—a fault he brilliantly rectified in his sonnet sequence ASTROPHEL AND STELLA, written sometime between Penelope Devereux's marriage to Lord Rich in 1581 and his own betrothal to Frances Walsingham in 1583. No doubt Penelope was little more than the occasion for Sidney's literary outpourings; after all, a sonnet sequence in the Petrarchan mode requires a mistress, even if one does not exist in real life. The theme of Sidney's 108 sonnets and eleven songs was succinctly summarized by Thomas Nashe in his preface to the 1591 edition: "The argument cruel chastity, the prologue hope, the epilogue despair." The course of Astrophel's turbulent courtship is charted by "calendar" sonnets commemorating public events and holidays; by passionately charged confrontations with Stella as well as emotion recollected in tranquility; and by witty exchanges between Astrophel and his friends at court. Sidney cleverly denies the slightest influence of Petrarch while following most of the Petrarchan conventions—witty conceits and antitheses, anguished conflicts of physical desire and Platonic idealism, fits of exuberance and melancholy, and prolonged writhing of futile reason in the clutches of tyrannical passions—all of which give his sequence an admirable *energia.*

In his *Apology* Sidney had praised the Psalms as the highest order of poetry; not surprisingly, therefore, he rendered forty-three into English from the Vulgate. A portion of Sidney's version of the famous Twenty-third Psalm illustrates his metrical ingenuity:

> The Lord, the Lord, my shepherd is,
> And so can never I
> Taste misery,
> He rests me in green pasture his:
> By waters still and sweet
> He guides my feet.

Another religious work by Sidney was his English rendition of *De la vérité de la religion Chrétienne* (Paris, 1581) by his Huguenot friend Philippe de Mornay. Sidney wrote an English preface and six chapters; the remainder was completed by Arthur Golding, the translator of Ovid's *Metamorphoses,* who published it after Sidney's death with the title *A Work Concerning the Trueness of the Christian Religion* (1587).

Although Sidney was elected to Parliament in 1581, he was consistently denied any powerful or remunerative position at court. Even his knighthood in 1583 was granted to him only because Count Casimir of Germany requested Sidney to act as proxy at Casimir's installation as a Knight of the Garter, a ceremony requiring knighthood of its participants. Sidney's financial situation remained that of many Elizabethan courtiers, as he sank into debt while attempting to maintain appearances without any substantial source of income. On several occasions he invested in the sea voyages of Martin Frobisher and Sir Francis Drake in expectation of fabulous profits, but these dreams came to nothing. At one point, in August 1585, apparently discouraged by meager prospects at home, Sidney arranged to accompany Drake on a voyage to the Indies, but at the last moment the queen forbade him to leave.

Sidney's destiny was to lie in the Old World, not the New. Shortly after his attempt to sail with Drake he was made governor of Flushing, an English fortress in the Netherlands, where he helped organize an effective military force against the Spanish. As he led an attack against a Spanish column near Zutphen, he discarded his thigh guards in a gesture of contempt for his personal safety and was struck in the leg by a musket ball. For sixteen days he languished in great pain and extraordinary fortitude at Arnhem, where he died on October 17, a month before his thirty-second birthday.

Only a few of Sidney's minor poems were published during his lifetime. As a man of public affairs, he considered himself an amateur poet, "having slipped into the title" of his "unelected vocation," as he stated in his *Apology.* This casual attitude was, of course, part of his calculated pose of *sprezzatura,* that gentlemanly trait of performing difficult tasks without the slightest show of effort; but Sidney's relegation of poetry to an ancillary place in his life is also consistent with his disciplined endeavor to make himself the embodiment of a cultural ideal requiring a variety of accomplishments and virtues. In contrast to Milton, who aspired to become England's greatest poet, Sidney attempted to represent the perfect courtier, a living example of the noble prototype set forth in courtesy books such as Baldassare Castiglione's *Il Cortegiano.* In the light of this ideal (consistently manifest in Sidney's correspondence with his father, his brother Robert, and Languet), poetry was secondary to such cardinal commitments as obedience to God, service to the queen, defense of Protestant truth against Catholic falsehood, cultivation of reason through humanistic education, and unrelenting attention to personal integrity.

Nevertheless, his literary achievements were immense. *The Arcadia,* the first prose pastoral romance in English, caused a wave of "Arcadian" imitations. *An Apology for Poetry* is notable for being the first literary essay in English worthy of the name of criticism, for Sidney was the first to emphasize a coherent body of aesthetic principles and to treat literature from the standpoint of appreciation and judgment rather than as a branch of rhetoric requiring crabbed analysis of figures and tropes. And although Sidney's *Astrophel and Stella* is not the first sonnet sequence in English, it is certainly the first of any genuine emotional power and poetic sophistication, and it began a vogue that culminated in Shakespeare's great sequence, in comparison to which Sidney's is certainly not inferior. But perhaps Sidney's greatest achievement was that in his fiction, literary criticism, and poetry he introduced into English literature ideas and literary forms from Italian, French, and Spanish writers that opened the doors of Europe to the English Renaissance. In spite of his burning political aspirations as a man of affairs, this literary achievement remains his finest contribution to the country he served so well

The standard edition is *The Complete Works,* ed. Albert Feuillerat, 4 vols. (1912-26). Some additional letters and political tracts are in Feuillerat's edition of *The Prose Works,* 4 vols. (1962). *The Poems of Sir Philip Sidney,* ed. William A. Ringler, Jr. (1962), is indispensable for texts, introductions, and notes. The standard edition of Fulke Greville's *The Life of Sir Philip Sidney* (1652) is edited by Nowell Smith (1907). There is no definitive biography but several works are excellent: M. W. Wallace. *The Life of Sir Philip Sidney* (1915; repr. 1967); Mona Wilson, *Sir Philip Sidney* (1932); Roger Howell, *Sir Philip Sidney, the Shepherd Knight* (1968); and Robert Kimbrough, *Sir Philip Sidney* (1971). There is a Concise Bibliography by S. A. Tannenbaum (1941), continued in "Sir Philip Sidney (1941-65)," ed. G. R. Guffey, in *Elizabethan Bibliographies Supplements,* VII (1967). See also *Sir Philip Sidney: An Annotated Bibliography of Modern Criticism,* ed. Mary A. Washington (1972).

Silex Scintillans. See VAUGHAN, HENRY.

Sir John Van Olden Barnavelt. See BARNAVELT.

Sir Thomas More, The Book of. A fragment of a dramatic manuscript in the Harleian collection of the British Museum, believed by some scholars to have been written in part by Shakespeare. The manuscript contains twenty folio pages in seven different handwritings; the various hands are usually referred to as S (who wrote about half) and A-E. The so-called Hand D in the manuscript, which covers only three pages, is the one attributed to Shakespeare. Most scholars assign S to Anthony Munday; other portions of the work have been attributed to Henry Chettle (A), Thomas Heywood (B), an anonymous bookkeeper (C), and Thomas Dekker (E). The seventh hand is believed to be by Sir Edward Tilney, Queen Elizabeth's master of the revels, who seems to have marked some objectionable passages and rejected the manuscript as too controversial. The earliest known owner of the work was John Murray, an eighteenth-century book collector. It was first published in 1844 by Alexander Dyce in a modernized edition, and in 1908 C. F. Tucker Brooke included it in his *Shakespeare Apocrypha,* a collection of plays not in the First Folio. In 1910 J. S. Farmer produced the first photographic facsimile, and in 1911 W. W. Greg edited a typographical facsimile for the Malone Society.

Although Shakespeare's authorship was claimed by Richard Simpson as early as 1871, few scholars seriously considered his argument until Sir Edward Maunde Thompson, a distinguished paleographer, revived the controversy while preparing his chapter on handwriting in *Shakespeare's England* (1916). Thompson concluded that Hand D matched Shakespeare's six extant signatures, a claim challenged by S. A. Tannenbaum, an expert in handwriting equal to Thompson. To explore the question still further, A. W. Pollard prepared a symposium, *Shakespeare's Hand in the Play of Sir Thomas More* (1923), in which several scholars examined the work from perspectives other than that of paleography. J. Dover Wilson accepted the three pages in question as being by Shakespeare because he discovered that the abnormal spellings of Hand D corresponded closely to those in the quartos, and R. W. Chambers pointed out that More's speech on loyalty and order on those pages agreed in sentiment and style with several passages in plays known to be by Shakespeare. The scene covered by the three pages portrays More attempting to placate an angry mob of Londoners who are threatening to attack and expel the city's foreigners because they believe the aliens are responsible for economic inflation. Chambers considered the following speech by More as characteristic of Shakespeare's style and concept of civil order:

You shall perceive how horrible a shape
Your innovation bears. First, 'tis a sin
Which oft the apostle did forewarn us of,
Urging obedience to authority;
And 'twere no error if I told you all
You were in arms 'gainst your God himself,
All. Marry, God forbid that!
More. Nay, certainly you are:
For to the King God hath his office lent
Of dread, of justice, power, and command,
Hath bid him rule, and willed you to obey:
And, to add ampler majesty to this,
He hath not only lent the King his figure,
His throne and sword, but given him his own name,
Calls him a god on earth. What do you then,
Rising 'gainst him that God himself installs,
But rise 'gainst God? What do you to your souls
In doing this? O desperate as you are,
Wash your foul minds with tears, and those same hands,
That you like rebels lift against the peace,
Lift up for peace, and your unreverent knees,
Make them your feet to kneel to be forgiven!
[II, *iv,* 114-35]

Chambers' argument for Shakespeare's authorship was further substantiated by Caroline Spurgeon's close analysis of Hand D's imagery, and yet when all the evidence is considered, it appears very tenuous indeed. The only really objective evidence is that of the handwriting experts, who remain almost equally divided on the issue. The dating of the manuscript is also uncertain. The contributors to Pollard's book in 1923 generally agreed on 1593-95, but that date is now rejected in favor of a later period, perhaps 1599-1607, although this span is also based on very shaky internal evidence.

The arguments for and against Shakespeare's authorship are summarized by R. C. Bald in *ShakS,* II (1949). Spurgeon's study of imagery is in *RES,* VI (1930). For additional details on the manuscript, see Harold Jenkins, "A Supplement to Sir Walter Greg's Edition of *Sir Thomas More,*" *Malone Society Collections,* VI (1962).

Skelton, John (1460?-1529). Poet. Skelton was born at Diss, Norfolk, and attended Oxford and Cambridge, both of which named him poet laureate in his later years. Little is known of his life, and his poems, which survive in corrupt editions, cannot be dated precisely. For several years he was tutor to the future Henry VIII and was highly praised for his learning by Erasmus in an ode called "De laudibus Britanniae." Ordained at forty in 1498, Skelton was made rector of a church at Diss for most of his life, but it is not known whether he actually lived there for any length of time.

In his *Garland of Laurel* (wr. c. 1520), a lengthy dream-allegory in imitation of Chaucer's *House of Fame* and prologue to the *Legend of Good Women,* Skelton gives a list of his own writings in English and Latin, many of which are lost. He claims to have written three morality plays (of which only *Magnificence* survives; see INTERLUDE), an English grammar, a pedagogical treatise for his pupil Prince Henry, and a lost English version of the French poet Guillaume de Deguilleville's lengthy *Pèlerinage de la vie humaine* (1330-31), which Skelton claimed he translated as *Of Man's Life the Peregrination.* Elsewhere William Caxton praises Skelton's translations of Cicero and Diodorus Siculus. Widely read in at least four languages, Skelton found the main inspiration for his poems in Juvenal and the English poets Chaucer, Gower, and Lydgate.

Skelton's earliest masterpiece, THE BOWGE OF COURT ("bowge" meaning court rations), is a satirical dream allegory in seven-line stanzas imitative of Chaucer. Aboard the ship of state the poet finds himself with a sinister group symbolizing the venality of court life—Favel (flattery), Disdain, Riot, Deceit, and others,—and at the end leaps overboard to escape these macabre "friends." The poem is a trenchant, wry satire, a major achievement in English verse between Chaucer and Wyatt and Surrey (see SATIRE).

In *Colin Clout* (wr. c. 1519) Skelton began to pursue the dangerous course of satirizing the powerful Cardinal Wolsey, attributing to that proud clergyman most of England's religious and social ills. In *Colin Clout* the English bishops neglect their flocks to engage in frivolities and vices, and alcoholic priests and dissolute nuns follow the wretched example of their superiors. At the apex of this hierarchy of corruption is Wolsey himself, power-hungry and self-seeking, who is assailed even more directly in Skelton's *Speak, Parrot!* (wr. c. 1520) where the parrot of a noble lady chatters of Wolsey's ambition and pride. The most audacious of these anti-Wolsey satires is *Why Come Ye Not to Court?* (wr. c. 1552-23), in which the cardinal is charged with all the evils of church and state—mismanaged foreign affairs, widespread poverty, ecclesiastical neglect and wickedness. The satire concludes with the admonition "God send him sorrow for his sins!" Wolsey prevented publication of these satires for several years, and from 1519 until his death Skelton was forced to seek occasional sanctuary at Westminster.

The best known of Skelton's verses are *Philip Sparrow* (wr. c. 1508) and *The Tunning of Eleanor Rumming* (wr. c. 1509). The first of these is written in so-called Skeltonics—short and irregular dimeters and trimeters in loose patterns of consecutive rhymes. Suggested by a mock elegy by Catullus on the death of a sparrow, it laments the death of a pet bird belonging to one Jane Scroop, a pupil of the Black Nuns at Carrow near Diss. The poet cleverly works his colloquial Skeltonics into the words of the Office of the Dead in the Vulgate Version:

> And when I said "Phip! Phip!"
> Then he would leap and skip,
> And take me by the lip.
> Alas, it will me slo,
> That Philip is gone me fro!
> *Si in i qui ta tes,*
> Alas, I was evil at ease!
> *De pro fun dis cla ma vi,*
> When I saw my sparrow die!

Skelton describes the horrifying death of the sparrow in the jaws of a cat and assembles an epic flock of feathered mourners (including Chaunticleer, Pertelote, and Pliny's fabulous phoenix). Philip Sparrow's bereaved mistress Jane is amazingly articulate and learned—she alludes to Homer, Ovid, Chaucer, Gower, and Lydgate—but at the end she proclaims that "our language is so rusty, / so cankered and so full" that she must give her peroration in a limping epitaph in Latin rather than English.

It was probably the acerbic, coarse satire *Eleanor Rumming* that prompted Pope's famous epithet "beastly Skelton," and yet this vivid description of an alewife and her drunken cronies is one of the most brilliant satires of the Tudor period. In a racy, colloquial style, the poem enumerates the household items the blowsy housewives bring to Eleanor's tavern in exchange for ale:

> And some brought sour dough,
> With "Hey," and with "Ho!"
> Sit we down a row,
> And drink till we blow,
> And pipe "Tirly Tirlow!"

Because of his rough Skeltonics, or because he cast crude scorn on most of the humanistic and liberal movements of the early English Renaissance, Skelton's reputation steadily waned after the middle of the sixteenth century. In recent times, however, W. H. Auden and others have praised his ingenuity, originality, and realism. His one surviving play, *Magnificence,* is now recognized as an important link between the religious MORALITY PLAY and the secular allegorical drama. The titular hero of the play is brought to ruin by such frivolous companions as Counterfeit, Countenance, Liberty, and Folly, and is saved at the end by Goodhope, Redress, Sad Circumspection, and Perseverance. The conflict is not the conventional one of good versus evil, however, but of misdirected political liberality versus strict civil discipline. The stakes are not the usual ones of salvation versus damnation but of sound government versus civil chaos. In *Magnificence,* as in many of his poems, Skelton declares himself to be an orthodox Catholic and a political conservative hostile to any challenges to the medieval order.

Skelton's *Complete Poems* was edited by Philip Henderson (1931, rev. ed., 1948); *The Poems* by Robert Kinsman (1969). There are two essential biographical and critical studies:

William Nelson, *John Skelton, Laureate* (1939), and I. A. Gordon, *John Skelton, Poet Laureate* (1943). For criticism, see also S. E. Fish, *John Skelton's Poetry* (1965). W. H. Auden's appreciative essay is in *The Great Tudors,* ed. Katherine Garvin (1935). Bibliographies are in the works by Nelson and Gordon, and in Burton Fishman, "Recent Studies in Skelton," *ELR,* I (1971).

Skialetheia (Edward Guilpin). See SATIRE.

Smectymnuus. See Joseph HALL; John MILTON: OF REFORMATION TOUCHING CHURCH DISCIPLINE IN ENGLAND.

songbooks. Few periods in history have been as musical as the Elizabethan. Catches, glees, rounds, madrigals, and airs were sung, and flutes, lyres, and virginals played, in every shop and tavern as well as at court. The courtier was thought to be a dolt who could not take his part in a spontaneous "three-man's song" or sight-read a madrigal score, and the barber or shoemaker or servant who could sing or play an instrument was always preferred for employment. In *The Gentle Craft* Thomas Deloney observes that every journeyman shoemaker was expected to "sound the trumpet, or play upon the flute, and bear his part in a three-man's song, and readily reckon up his tools in rhyme." Songs were the invariable concomitant of pageants, feasts, festivals, and tavern gatherings, and were written to accompany every social activity—dancing, drinking, and love-making. At the court of Henry VIII simple and direct lyrics, such as those by Sir Thomas Wyatt, were set to music. Even the king himself could write a graceful lyric:

> Green groweth the holly, so doth the ivy.
> Though winter blasts blow never so high,
> Green groweth the holly...

Although the first secular songbook was published by Wynkyn de Worde as early as 1530, the next did not appear until 1571, the date of Thomas Whythorne's *Songs of Three, Four, and Five Voices.* The growing popularity of songbooks can be attributed to the introduction of the madrigal from Italy and the development of the air, long known in England but given renewed interest because of its great popularity in Spain in the sixteenth century. The madrigal is a short lyric consisting of six to thirteen lines with three rhymes, and sung by three to six voices. Unlike the part-song, the madrigal is polyphonic, all voices carrying the melody without subordination. Shakespeare's song "Take, O take those lips away" in *Measure for Measure* illustrates the type. Printed in small quarto volumes, each volume containing the part for a single voice, songbooks of madrigals were popular in homes, shops, schools, and taverns. The first songbook of Italian madrigals was Nicholas Yonge's *Musica transalpina* (1588); about the same time William BYRD published the first collection of English madrigals, *Psalms, Sonnets, and Songs.*

Equally popular were songbooks of airs, lyrics written for singing to the accompaniment of lute or lyre. The first of these was printed in 1597 by John Dowland, an accomplished lutist. Airs were printed so they might be sung with the highest solo accompanied by a lute, or occasionally by a viol de gamba, or were written as a part-song with the highest voice carrying the melody and the others in accompaniment. The most popular books of airs were those by Thomas CAMPION, one of which contains the famous air:

> There is a garden in her face,
> Where roses and white lilies grow;
> A heav'nly paradise is that place,
> Wherein all pleasant fruits do flow.
> There cherries grow which none may buy
> Till "Cherry-ripe" themselves do cry.

Unlike most composers, who fitted music to verses written by others, Campion wrote both music and lyrics for at least the first half of his *Book of Airs* (1601), a songbook issued in collaboration with Philip Rosseter, a musician. In his preface to this edition Campion described his airs as "ear-pleasing rhymes without art," and consciously worked to achieve brevity, clarity, and simplicity: "What epigrams are in poetry, the same are airs in music; then in their chief perfection when they are short and well-seasoned...The subject of them is, for the most part, amorous, and why not amorous songs as well as amorous attires? Or why not new airs as well as new fashions?" In his subsequent volumes, *Two Books of Airs* (1613) and *The Third and Fourth Books of Airs* (1617), Campion wrote both words and music.

Another popular composition for songbooks was the ballet, a less complex and polyphonic form than the madrigal and hence more suitable for dancing. Noting the great variety of types and sheer volume of production, Douglas Bush estimates that from the 1590s to 1630s there appeared "about ninety collections of madrigals, airs, canzonets, and ballets; of madrigals alone there were nearly a thousand" *(English Literature in the Earlier Seventeenth Century* [1945].) The most prolific writers of these, after Byrd and Campion, were Thomas Morley (1557-1606), Thomas Weelkes (c. 1575-1623), and John Wilbye (1574-1638). Especially interesting is Morley's collection *The Triumphs of Oriana, to Five or Six Voices* (1601), twenty-five songs in praise of Queen Elizabeth by almost as many composers, one of them John Milton's father.

Although a few distinguished composers flourished in the reign of Charles I, notably William and Henry Lawes (the latter collaborating with Milton on the production of *Comus*), songbooks declined in popularity with the rise of Puritanism, which hastened the demise of vocal music by abolishing church liturgy and choirs. During the Restoration instrumental music and more regular forms were introduced to replace the free, spontaneous lyrics of the Elizabethan songbooks.

There is an excellent brief survey of Elizabethan music and composers by W. Barclay Squire in *Shakespeare's England,* 2 vols. (1916) II. The definitive study of the madrigal is by E. H. Fellowes, *The English Madrigal* (1925). See also M. C. Boyd, *Elizabethan Music and Musical Criticism* (1940). The most exhaustive collections of lyrics from songbooks are by E. H. Fellowes, *The English Madrigal School,* 36 vols. (1913-24), and *The English School of Lutenist Song-Writers,* 15 vols. (1920).

sonnet sequences. To Elizabethans the sonnet, or "sonet," was associated with Petrarch and with any short lyric of metaphoric complexity on the subject of love. The quatorzain, or scheme of fourteen lines, was not invariably observed, but the Elizabethans enthusiastically borrowed the other distinguishing features of the Petrarchan sonnet: its *concetto,* or "conceit" (a witty or striking analogy, as in the poem by Sir Thomas WYATT: "The lover compareth his heart to an overcharged gun"); its stock of similes (the lover compared to a ship at sea, the mistress to a town under siege, the lover's bed to his "living tomb"); and its never-ending analyses of passions.

Italian poets a hundred years before Petrarch—Dante in *La vita nuova* among others—had employed the sonnet sequence, but it was Petrarch, the "final blossom and perfection of the troubadours," in Coleridge's apt phrase, with his incredible outpouring of about four hundred sonnets in his *Canzoniere* (songbook), also called *Rime,* who gave the sonnet sequence unprecedented energy and variety. For over forty years, from around 1330 until his death in 1374, Petrarch probed every facet of his obsession for Laura, a woman he first met in the Church of Santa Chiara in Avignon on April 6, 1327, and who became, although scarcely known to him and married to another, the great idol and spiritual symbol of his sonnets. There are sonnets devoted to Laura's name; "calendar" sonnets celebrating anniversaries of their infrequent encounters, or to her birth date, or to the inception of his love; sonnets cataloging her graces or physical attractions; elaborating paradoxes; expressing Platonic ideas; and lamenting the poet's alienation, loneliness, grief, and painful awareness of love's futility. As in this sonnet translated by Wyatt, the recurring theme is the conflict of reason and passion, and the rhetorical modes are paradox, antithesis, and contrariety. Characteristically, the lover is a prisoner tortured by love's cruelty and his own masochistic fixation:

I find no peace and all my war is done.
I fear and hope, I burn and freeze like ice,
I fly above the wind, yet can I not arise,
And naught I have and all the world I seson;
That looseth nor locketh holdeth me in prison,
And holdeth me not; yet can I 'scape nowise;
Nor letteth me live nor die at my devise,
And yet of death it giveth none occasion.
Without eyen I see; and without tongue I plain;
I desire to perish, and yet I ask health;
I love another, and thus I hate myself;
I feed me in sorrow, and laugh in all my pain.
Likewise displeaseth me both death and life,
And my delight is causer of this strife.

No English translation can begin to convey Petrarch's sophistication of language—his subtle rhymes, ingenious metaphors, shrewd puns and allusions. His favorite technique is to limit his rhymes to two in the octave (first eight lines), then open to another rhyme in the sestet (last six lines) with no concluding couplet but a sense of dissonance or "opening up" at the end. Unlike English, Italian is a language with an almost infinite stock of rhymes, and Petrarch could freely tap these resources where his English translators could not.

A Petrarchan sonnet frequently begins with a *concetto,* which the poem ingeniously elaborates. In the Wyatt version above, it consists of a catalog of contrarieties; in another sonnet it may be a comparison between the lady and a bloody tyrant; in still another, it is the metaphor of the lover as a prisoner welcoming the lashes of his captor. Often but not invariably there is a marked transition between octave and sestet, a contrast between the general and the particular, between metaphor and personal application, between some event in the external world and the lover's inner tumult.

Aside from his extraordinary technical facility, Petrarch was admired and imitated for the almost sensational qualities of his humanism—for boldly thrusting himself into the fiery emotional center of his lyrics, for making a febrile relationship with a woman a philosophical issue of cardinal importance, and for exploring the byways of his own sensitive, complex nature. Moreover, he was able to create a highly imitable, almost systematic poetic correlation to these impulses in a language derived from both neo-Platonism and the religion of love of the troubadours, and his erotic vocabulary gradually established itself as a refluent mode of expression among Renaissance love poets. Indeed, even today many figures of speech with reference to love are Petrarch's once fresh and ingenious metaphors worn into clichés by endless repetition.

The Petrarchan sonnet was first introduced into England by Sir Thomas WYATT and Henry HOWARD, earl of Surrey, in the first edition of *A Book of Songs and Sonnets* (1557)—also known as Tottel's Miscellany—which among its 271 poems included sixty sonnets, most of them adaptations or very literal translations from Petrarch. Of Wyatt's thirty-two sonnets seventeen are from Petrarch; in twenty-eight of the sonnets Wyatt employs an approximation of Petrarch's rhyme scheme in the octave (*ab ba ab ba*) and sestet (*cd dc ee*), and uses the concluding couplet in only one. Of Surrey's fifteen or sixteen sonnets in Tottel's Miscellany, ten are of the so-called English or Shakespearean pattern of three quatrains and a couplet; included among these is Surrey's most original and successful sonnet, "From Tuscan came my lady's worthy race."

Although Tottel's Miscellany went through no fewer than seven editions during the period 1557-84, it did little to increase the popularity of the sonnet form. In France, however, Petrarch's influence took secure hold with Clément Marot and later with the geniuses of LA PLÉIADE, especially Joachim du Bellay and Pierre de Ronsard. Perhaps as early as 1569 Edmund Spenser was writing imitations of Petrarchan sonnets learned from Marot and Du Bellay, although Spenser's work was not generally known until the publication of his *Complaints* in 1591.

Most of the English sonneteers between Wyatt and Surrey and Sir Philip Sidney were mere dabblers. Only two poems in Barnabe Googe's *Eclogues, Epitaphs, and Sonnets* (1563) were in sonnet form, and George Turberville's *Epitaphs, Epigrams, Songs, and Sonnets* (1565? 1567) contains no poem of fourteen lines. Obviously Googe and Turberville employed the word "sonnet" in their titles merely to exploit the popularity of Tottel's Miscellany and not out of any interest in the formal aspect of the genre. George Gascoigne's *A Hundred Sundry Flowers* (1573) included thirty sonnets, most of them translations from Petrarch's French disciples, although some may be original. Gascoigne offered a more concise definition of the sonnet than was generally understood by his contemporaries: "I can best allow to call those Sonnets which are fourteen lines, every line containing ten syllables." In his own sonnets Gascoigne employed the Italian scheme of a limited number of rhymes without a concluding couplet.

Another early disciple of Petrarch was Thomas Watson, Christopher Marlowe's friend, who in his youth had translated all of Petrarch's sonnets from Italian into Latin. Almost all of Watson's sonnets are eighteen lines. The best of these he rendered into English in *Hecatompathia* (1582), an inflexibly literal and scholarly work that received little notice among his contemporaries.

About the same time as Watson's *Hecatompathia* appeared, Sidney was writing ASTROPHEL AND STELLA, the sequence of 108 sonnets that sparked an enormous outburst of Petrarchan sonnet imitations and improvisations throughout the 1590s. Although Sidney's work had circulated in manuscript, it was not published until 1591, when three pirated editions appeared. (The first authorized edition was published by the countess of Pembroke in 1598.) In the first quarto of 1591 Thomas Nashe's dedicatory epistle signaled the advent of a new era of the sonnet form:

> Put out your rush candles, you poets and rimers, and bequeath your crazed quarter-

> zains to the chandlers; for lo, here he cometh that hath broken your legs. Apollo hath resigned his ivory harp unto Astrophel...

The occasion for the writing of *Astrophel and Stella* seems to have been Sidney's brief courtship of Penelope Devereux, daughter of Walter Devereux, first earl of Essex, and sister of Robert, Queen Elizabeth's great favorite. Their engagement, which was never formal, was terminated when Penelope was still only fourteen, and at nineteen she was betrothed to Lord Rich. (Sidney's Sonnet 37, which attacks Lord Rich by name, was not published until Lady Pembroke's authorized version of 1598.)

The courting of Stella described in the sequence, however, scarcely needed reference to any actual relationship with Penelope Devereux, for Sidney's sonnets are shot through with imaginative theatricality and literary fantasy of the most sophisticated order. To heighten the verisimilitude of his passion, Astrophel proclaims that he is "no pick-purse of another's wit" nor imitator of "Petrarch's long-deceased woes," yet Sidney's brilliant sequence is redolent of Petrarch and Petrarch's French and Italian disciples. From them Sidney borrows his conflict of passion versus reason, his erotic posturing and theatrical torments, his radical conceits, antitheses, and paradoxes. But he revitalizes the tradition by creating in Astrophel a persona of charming ingenuousness, arrogance, and wit, and by energizing the whole texture of the work with a sense of drama, immediate scene, and swift action. Not "emotion recollected in tranquillity," but spontaneous responses to the moment characterize many of the sonnets. "Fly, fly, my friends, I have my death's wound, fly; / See there that boy, that murdering boy, I say" assaults the reader with some of the colloquial spontaniety of John Donne's later *Songs and Sonnets.* In the first sonnet Sidney claims to write for Stella's eyes alone, "that she, dear she, might take some pleasure of my pain," and yet he addresses a variety of readers, expanding his audience to include court gossips, pedants, literati, lovers, and would-be lovers. In spite of its affiliations with Petrarch's contemplative, self-examining style, *Astrophel and Stella* is the most gregarious, joyously extroverted, and variegated of the Elizabethan sonnet sequences. This variety is also apparent in the rhyme schemes. Sidney favors one pattern in the octave (*ab ba ab ba*) but uses any number of combinations, including the couplet, in the sestet. (If he has a preference in the sestet, it is for the *cd cd ee* and *cc de ed* patterns.)

It was perhaps inevitable that Samuel DANIEL should be the first to follow in Sidney's steps. His patron was Sidney's sister, the countess of Pembroke, and twenty-eight of Daniel's sonnets had supplemented Thomas Newman's edition of *Astrophel and Stella* in 1591. Daniel's *Delia* (1592) employs the so-called "Shakespearean" form of three differently rhymed quatrains and a couplet (*abab/cdcd/efef/gg*), which he handles with smooth if prosaic competence and studious attention to his French master, Philippe Desportes, who in turn was often copying quite literally from Tasso. Like Daniel, Henry Constable in his *Diana* (1592), a collection of twenty-three sonnets, illustrates Sidney's caveat in *Astrophel and Stella* that "stolen goods will come to light," for most of Constable's poems have been shown to be bald copies of sonnets by Desportes and other continental Petrarchans. During the sonnet craze of the 1590s it became a widely adopted practice to pilfer from Desportes, Claude de Pontoux, Sannazaro, Du Bellay, and other Petrarchans.

In 1593 appeared four notable sonnet sequences: Thomas Watson's posthumous *Tears of Fancy,* which despite its title is dull and scholarly, and three livelier contributions, Barnabe Barnes's *Parthenophil and Parthenophe,* Giles Fletcher the Elder's *Licia,* and Thomas Lodge's *Phyllis.* The most listless and eclectic of these is Lodge's; the most widely divergent from the conventional quatorzains is Fletcher's sonnets, some of which contain as many as eighteen lines. Fletcher frequently employs an effective transition between octave and sestet, and he uses the Shakespearean form with a competence just short of concise, Surrey-like elegance:

Like Memnon's rock, touched with the rising sun,
Which yields a sound and echoes forth a voice;
But when it's drowned in western seas is done,
And drowsy-like leaves off to make a noise;
So I, my love, enlightened with your shine,
A poet's skill within my soul I shroud—
Not rude, like that which finer wits decline,
But such as Muses to the best allowed.

Barnabe Barnes's collection encouraged a sparse sequence of twenty sonnets from his friend William Percy, son of the earl of Northumberland, whose pedestrian *Coelia* appeared in 1594. That same year saw the publication of Michael Drayton's first version of *Idea,* consisting of fifty-two sonnets in a variety of rhyme patterns, which Drayton continued to revise and amplify until the final recension of 1619, the edition in which first appeared one of the greatest sonnets of this or any period, "Since there's no help, come let us kiss and part." Aside from that one gem, Drayton's verse lacks the comprehensive strategies and artful passion of Sidney's sequence. Yet a half-dozen or so of Drayton's sonnets convey strong lines couched in thoughtful irony, as in the sonnet "How many paltry, foolish, painted things," or the strangely ambivalent and unconventional mockery of his lady's present beauty:

There's nothing grieves me but that age
  should haste
That in my days I may not see thee old,
That where those two clear sparkling eyes
  are plac'd
Only two loopholes then I might behold.
But when your figure and your shape is gone,
I speechless am, like as I was before;
Or if I write, my verse is filled with moan,
And blurred with tears by falling in such store;
  Then muse not, Licia, if my muse be slack,
  For when I wrote I did thy beauty lack.

The height of the sonnet vogue came with the publication of Spenser's AMORETTI in 1595, about the time Shakespeare was writing his climactic sequence. Spenser's eighty-eight sonnets describe his courtship of Elizabeth Boyle, his second wife, and their marriage is celebrated in the long descriptive poem EPITHALAMION appended to the sequence. In contrast to Petrarch's prolonged agonies and Sidney's futile passion, Spenser's sequence represents a Platonic, Christian appropriation of the literary traditions associated with the sonnet form. One requisite of the Petrarchan tradition is that love be frustrated, irrational, isolated from society, and tragically abortive. Spenser's *Amoretti* tells a love story that ends in joyous and sacramental consummation, and the passion of the lover is presented as being communal, consistent with reason, and infinitely gratifying in spite of the vicissitudes attending the relationship. Unlike Drayton, Spenser is more than occasionally Platonic; his Platonism is intellectual and purposive rather than merely figurative or poetically dualistic. Hence *Amoretti* tends to be at once philosophical, formal, and personal—a reflective moral analysis of an emotional experience filtered through some of the usual Petrarchan literary frames of reference such as blazons of the lady's beauty, complaints of her coldness, momentary seizures of erotic frustration, meditations on mutability and the eternizing powers of poetry, and occasional digressions on literary topics, e.g., his delay in completing *The Faerie Queene:*

Great wrong I do, I can it not deny,
To that most sacred empress, my dear dread,
Not finishing her Queene of Faery,
That mote enlarge her living praises, dead.

Published in the same year as Spenser's *Amoretti* was George Chapman's "A Coronet for His Mistress Philosophy," ten arcane and moralizing sonnets which he appended to his *Ovid's Banquet of Sense.* "A Coronet" is actually a clumsy translation of Gilles Durant's poem *Le Zodiac amoureux* together with an adaptation of a contemporary English pastoral, "The Amorous Contention of Phyllis and Flora" by one "R.S.," probably Richard Stapleton. Another illustration of how far the English sonnet was growing away from its amorous Petrarchan origins can be seen in Richard Barnfield's curious *Cynthia* (1595), a panegyric on Queen Elizabeth followed by twenty sonnets purporting to be addressed not to a lady but to a boy named Ganymede for whom the poet expresses his romantic passion. Equally dim lights flickered in Bartholmew Griffin's *Fidessa,* sixty-two sonnets, and Robert Tofte's *Laura* (both 1597), forty sonnets in a variety of rhymes and meters. Fulke Greville's *Caelica,* written about this time but not published until 1633, consists of 109 short poems, only about a third of which are of fourteen lines. (Until well into the seventeenth century Elizabethans referred to any comparatively short poem as a "sonnet.")

As the quality of sonnets steadily declined after 1595, the vogue for satire increased, with the result that the patent artificiality and eclecticism of the Petrarchan literary conventions became vulnerable to the arrows of parody and scorn. Mercutio in *Romeo and Juliet* mocks the absurdities of the sonnet fashion: "Now is he for the numbers that Petrarch flowed in: Laura to his lady was but a kitchen-wench; marry, she had a better love to berhyme her" (II, *iv,* 40). Shakespeare's Sonnet 130 playfully ridicules the Petrarchan fad of idealizing the mistress:

My mistress' eyes are nothing like the sun;
Coral is far more red than her lips' red;
If snow be white, why then her breasts are dun;
If hairs be wires, black wires grow on her head.

About the same time John Davies was circulating in manuscript his nine "gulling sonnets" which parodied the emotional attitudinizing of Petrarchan sonneteers, and Donne was writing his *Songs and Sonnets,* a collection of lyrics that, in their sexual realism and brittle, unsentimental language, represent a reaction against the whole Petrarchan movement.

By 1600 the sonnet sequence was no longer necessarily associated with love. As early as 1593 Henry Lok had published a devotional sonnet sequence, *Sundry Christian Passions Contained in Two Hundred Sonnets,* augmented by 128 sonnets in the second printing of 1597, and in 1593 Barnabe Barnes ceased praising the beauties of Parthenophe and dedicated his hundred or more sonnets in *Divine Century of Spiritual Sonnets* to God, "the great Disposer of all great honors."

Sir William Alexander's *Aurora* (1614), Alexander Craig's *Amorous Songs, Sonnets, and Elegies* (1606), and Patrick Hannay's songs and sonnets in *The Nightingale* (1622), however undistinguished, are evidence that the Petrarchan sonnet was not entirely extinct after 1600. The fact remains, nevertheless, that the Petrarchan hegemony had all but expired and that the amorous sonnet sequence no longer served the new poets. That the sonnet form itself was still exceedingly virile is attested by Donne's magnificent and moving *Holy Sonnets,* first published with his *Songs and Sonnets* in 1633 and reprinted at least seven times in the seventeenth century, and by the sonnets of John Milton, the most accomplished master of the Italian form in the English language.

Most of the Elizabethan sonnet sequences are in the collection edited by Sidney Lee, *Elizabethan Sonnets,* 2 vols. (1904). See also Janet Scott, *Les Sonnets élisabéthains* (1929). Petrarchan literary and love conventions are treated by L. E. Pearson, *Elizabethan Love Conventions* (1933), and L. C. John, *The Elizabethan Sonnet Sequences* (1938).

Southwell, Robert (1561–1595). Poet and Catholic martyr. Southwell was born of an ancient East Anglian family in Horsham St. Faith near Norwich. Most of his early education was with the Jesuits. When very young he left England to study at the English college at Douai, then went to Paris at fifteen to attend a Jesuit seminary. He spent two years as a novitiate at Tournai, where he began to write devotional poems in both English and Latin. In 1580 Southwell went to Rome to teach at the English college there; ordained in 1584, he volunteered for the dangerous English mission, expressing in a letter to Claudio Aquavia, the Jesuit general, his desire for martyrdom. (Under an English law of 1584 any Englishman ordained in the Roman Catholic Church after 1557 and residing in England longer than forty days was subject to execution.)

Southwell landed in England in 1586 with another Jesuit, Henry Garnett, and their arrival was duly noted by Sir Francis Walsingham's government agents. In London and Sussex, Southwell lived with the family of Philip Howard, earl of Arundel, under the alias of Robert Cotton. To conceal his identity, he studied sports, especially falconry (hence a recurring metaphor in his poems). By 1591 Southwell had written at least four religious works that circulated in manuscript: "An Epistle of Comfort to the Reverend Priests," addressed to his patron Arundel, then in the Tower for treason; "Triumphs over Death," a consolation on the death of Arundel's half-sister Margaret; "Mary Magdalene's Funeral Tears;" and "A Humble Supplication to Queen Elizabeth," a plea for tolerance of Catholics.

Southwell's arrest came in June 1592. He was residing at Uxenden Hall, Harrow-on-the-Hill, with the family of Richard Bellamy, whose kinsman Jerome Bellamy had been executed for conspiracy in the Babington Plot. The notorious government agent Richard Topcliffe seized Bellamy's daughter Anne, who was forced to reveal Southwell's identity. Topcliffe subjected Southwell to the most sadistic tortures for a week without success in an effort to learn the plans of the Jesuit mission in England, reporting his activities daily to the queen in written reports. Southwell's incredible heroism under torture elicited detached curiosity and reluctant admiration from some of Elizabeth's ministers, who came to observe Topcliffe's professional activities. The impatient queen, awaiting promised revelations of diabolical Jesuit plots, cursed Topcliffe as a "fool." Southwell was removed to the Tower, where he languished for three years. During his trial at Newgate, Southwell defended himself with great dignity and candor against the Tudor legal invention of "equivocation," or Jesuitical evasion—actually, a law designed to prevent the defendant from avoiding self-accusation. He was drawn and quartered at Tyburn on February 21, 1595. He was beatified by Pope Pius XI in 1929.

Three volumes of Southwell's works appeared after his death. *St. Peter's Complaint with Other Poems* (1595) was published anonymously and reissued twice in the same year as well as in 1597, 1599, and 1602 (enlarged edition). By 1638, thirteen editions had appeared. Another collection of Southwell's poems, *Maeoniae, or Certain Excellent Poems and Spiritual Hymns,* was published the same year as *St. Peter's Complaint.* Still other poems were printed with his prose tract *Mary Magdalene's Funeral Tears* (Douai, 1616). *St. Peter's Complaint* is a poem of 792 lines, with stanzas rhyming *ab ab cc,* accompanied by Scriptural glosses. The subject is the story of Christ's passion and St. Peter's remorse for his wavering faith and betrayals, but the underlying theme is Peter's parallel with every Christian believer. An extended meditation, the poem is tranquil, carefully measured, and serene in spite of its elaborate rhetoric and conceits:

With mildness, Jesu, measure my offense;
Let true remorse thy due revenge abate.
Let tears appease when trespass doth incense;
Let pity temper thy deserved hate.
Let grace forgive, let love forget my fall;
With fear I crave, with hope I humbly call.

Southwell's prose tends to be artificial and euphuistic, but his best poems—all of them devotional—are charged with meaning and complex emotions. Jonson confessed to William Drummond that he would destroy some of his own poems if he could have written Southwell's "Burning Babe":

As I in hoary winter's night
  stood shivering in the snow,
Surprised I was with sudden heat
  which made my heart to glow;
And lifting up a fearful eye
  to view what fire was near,
A pretty babe all burning bright
  did in the air appear...

The vision concludes with some of the delicate piognancy of George Herbert's devotional poems:

With this He vanish'd out of sight
  and swiftly shrunk away,
And straight I called unto mind
  that it was Christmas day.

With Herbert, Southwell is one of the most original and inspiring religious poets of the English Renaissance. Although repetitious and even occasionally cloying when his pathos descends to bathos (a danger, also, with Herbert), he is always vigorous and original. His best poems have been described as metaphysical, his least effective as simply drab in the manner of early Tudor poets like Wyatt (see METAPHYSICAL POETS). In truth, Southwell's poetry springs from no distinct era or tradition, neither early Tudor nor metaphysical nor baroque, but from the incandescence of a faith in conflict with temptation and struggle. His themes arise from adventures of his soul on pilgrimage, and his voice is uniquely his own.

The definitive edition of the poems is by James H. McDonald and Nancy P. Brown (1967). There are two distinguished critical biographies; Pierre Janelle, *Robert Southwell the Writer* (1935), and Christopher Devlin, *The Life of Robert Southwell: Poet and Martyr* (1956). James H. McDonald has compiled an extensive bibliography (1937). See also Helen C. White, "Southwell: Metaphysical and Baroque," *MP,* LXI (1964), and Carolyn A. Schten, "Southwell's 'Christ's Bloody Sweat': A Meditation on the Mass," *EM,* XX (1969). *An Humble Supplication to her Majesty by Robert Southwell,* ed. R. C. Bald (1953) describes the persecution of Jesuits in Elizabethan England.

Spanish Gypsy, The. A tragicomedy by Thomas MIDDLETON and William ROWLEY, written in 1623 and printed in 1653. The sources are two stories by Cervantes, "La gitanilla" and "La fuerza de la sangre" in his *Novelas ejemplares* (1613). The first story is about an exiled Spanish nobleman who returns to Spain in disguise and becomes leader of a band of gypsies in Madrid, teaching them to forsake their old ways of cheating and stealing and adopt a utopian life as actors, dancers, and singers. The second story relates the passionate love affair of Roderigo and Clara. The scene is Madrid in the early seventeenth century.

One night, while in the company of his two friends Louis de Castro and Diego in the suburbs of Madrid, Roderigo, the impetuous young son of Fernando, corregidor of Madrid, drunkenly accosts a beautiful girl and her family. While his friends detain the family, Roderigo forces the girl to his chambers and rapes her. When she departs, she takes from his rooms a crucifix by which she hopes to identify her assailant. When Roderigo rejoins his friends, falsely swearing he has done the girl no harm, he is horrified to learn that his victim is Clara, daughter of a distinguished nobleman and beloved of his friend Louis.

Now secretly in love with Clara himself, Roderigo tells his father he is going to Salamanca to study; actually, he disguises himself as an Italian poet and joins a band of gypsies in Madrid so that he can observe Clara without being recognized. The leader of the gypsies is Alvarez de Castilla, returned to Spain in disguise after being exiled for killing the father of Louis de Castro, who is petitioning Fernando for Alvarez's return in order to avenge his father's death. Also in the gypsy band is the beautiful Constanza, Fernando's long-lost daughter, who bides her time in hope of somehow securing Alvarez's pardon, and John, disguised son of a Spanish nobleman, who has joined the group because Constanza, with whom he is in love but whose true identity is unknown to him, has required that he live with the gypsies for two years before she will consent to marry him.

When the gypsies perform a play at Fernando's palace, Fernando instantly recognizes his son among the actors but shrewdly keeps silent. Louis sends for Clara to join the audience at Fernando's, but en route she faints and, by sheer coincidence, is taken to rest at Roderigo's chambers, the scene of her violation. When Fernando arrives, she produces the missing crucifix to prove her charge against Roderigo, and the shocked Fernando swears to have his son executed. Clara pleads for Roderigo's life, and, temporarily mollified, Fernando rejoins the festivities at his palace in the company of Clara, who takes on a disguise to prevent being recognized by Roderigo. It is apparent that both Clara and Fernando are hoping for some turn of events that will enable Roderigo to learn his lesson without fatal consequences.

During the course of the entertainments at the palace, John's courtship of Constanza meets with new difficulties. A rich patroness of the gypsies, Cardochia, incensed by John's spurning of her advances, goads her suitor Diego into attacking John during the performance of a play, and when Diego is bested in the fight, Cardochia accuses John of theft. As judge in these matters, Fernando sends John to prison, then turns to his son, proclaims Roderigo's identity to the audience, and condemns him to death for Clara's rape. Roderigo shamefully acknowledges his guilt, but proposes an alternative to the sentence: he will agree to marry an ugly heiress or any girl in the audience who will accept him. Fernando consents, guessing that Roderigo's choice will be the disguised Clara, who, in fact, readily accepts the proposal of marriage. After the ceremony, Clara reveals her real identity to her husband, renews her plea to Fernando that Roderigo be forgiven, and father, son, and wife are happily reconciled.

The complications of Constanza and John, and Louis' desire for revenge against Alvarez, remain to be resolved. To persuade Louis to help effect John's release from prison, Alvarez magnanimously abandons his disguise and agrees to submit to Louis' vengeance. Confronted by this display of Alvarez's courage and honor, Louis realizes that revenge is no longer important. At the conclusion of the play Cardochia is shown to be a liar unworthy of Diego's affection, and John is released from prison, reveals himself as a nobleman, and is betrothed to Constanza, whose identity is also made known. To celebrate these happy events, the principal characters join with the gypsies in a sprightly dance.

As this summary indicates, *The Spanish Gypsy* has an extremely convoluted plot full of coincidences, incredible disguises, quick turns of action and motive, and spectacular scenes. The three complex stories of Roderigo and Clara, John and Constanza, and Alvarez and Louis, together with their many ancillary characters and events, are interwoven with an adroitness equaled only by Francis Beaumont and John Fletcher in their most ingenious tragicomedies. The characters in *The Spanish Gypsy* are lightly drawn and the various disguises very thinly motivated; individual scenes, however, are portrayed with exceptional skill and lyric grace, especially those depicting the pastoral-like gaiety of the gypsies. The melodramatic, dissonant opening episode, beginning with Roderigo's frivolous antics and concluding with his intensely passionate violation of Clara, is unique in its psychological realism and sexual candor.

There are editions of *The Spanish Gypsy* by Edgar C. Morris in the Belles-Lettres series (1908) and by C. M. Gayley in *Representative English Comedies,* III (1914). For critical commentary, see R. H. Barker, *Thomas Middleton* (1958). Dugdale H. Sykes argues for the authorship of John Ford in *Sidelights on Elizabethan Drama* (1924).

Spanish Tragedy, The. A Senecan revenge tragedy by Thomas KYD, written around 1585. The first edition is undated; the next two editions, one described as "newly corrected," appeared in 1602. No source is known.

The Spanish Tragedy is the first successful attempt to adapt Senecan dramatic devices and conventions (with the exception of the *nuntius)* to the popular stage: the revenge theme, the ghost, the play-within-the-play, the dumb show, the soliloquy, the declamation and bombast, the emphasis on macabre brutalities, insanity and suicide (see SENECAN TRAGEDY). To these Kyd added several innovations, e.g., a Machiavellian villain, a resourceful, aggressive heroine, and a contemporary scene of great political interest—the war between Spain and Portugal in 1580.

A common source (now lost) or an earlier version of *The Spanish Tragedy* may have provided the plot for *Hamlet,* although the affinities of Kyd's play to Shakespeare's remain obscure. *The Spanish Tragedy* held its popularity for at least twenty years, in spite of the ridicule of later dramatists; by 1633 it had gone through ten editions. In 1601-02 Ben Jonson was paid by Philip Henslowe to revise the play for a revival by the Lord Admiral's Men at the Rose Theatre.

In the induction the ghost of Don Andrea, a Spanish courtier, describes how he was slain in the war between Spain and Portugal by Don Balthazar, son of the Portuguese viceroy. In the company of Revenge, Andrea has returned from Hades to serve as Chorus to the ensuing tragedy and to see the woman he loved, Bel-imperia, take revenge against Balthazar for his death.

The king of Spain learns of the victory over Portugal, of Andrea's death, and of the capture of Balthazar by Horatio, Andrea's dearest friend and son of Hieronimo, marshal of Spain. When the Spanish army arrives, however, Lorenzo, haughty son of Don Cyprian, duke of Castile, and the nephew of the king, claims credit for the capture of Balthazar. To settle this dispute between Horatio and Lorenzo, the king awards Horatio whatever ransom is to be paid by the Portuguese for Balthazar and gives his brother's son Lorenzo the honor of taking custody of Balthazar until peace negotiations with the Portuguese are settled. Meanwhile Balthazar is to be treated as an honored guest of the Spanish court rather than as a prisoner.

In Portugal, the viceroy hears conflicting reports of his son's fate in battle. The viceroy's honest minister Alexandro testifies that Balthazar was taken prisoner; the treacherous Villuppo accuses Alexandro of having shot the prince in the back. Without giving Alexandro an opportunity to defend himself, the viceroy sends him to prison to await execution.

Horatio relates to Bel-imperia how her lover Andrea was slain, and after he departs she delivers a soliloquy lamenting Andrea's death, swearing vengeance against Balthazar, and resolving to make Horatio her lover in order to have a trusted ally against Balthazar. Encouraged by Bel-imperia's shrewd brother Lorenzo, who hopes to profit by the match, Balthazar has already made overtures of love to her. When Balthazar again addresses her in amorous terms, she angrily rejects him and departs. As she leaves she deliberately drops her glove just as Horatio appears, so that Horatio and not Balthazar retrieves it. Her warm gratitude to Horatio informs the humiliated Balthazar that Horatio has thus bested him in love as well as war.

At a banquet for the Portuguese ambassador, Hieronimo, who has a reputation for staging court theatricals, presents a dumb show which, he explains, symbolizes three past victories of little England over Spain; since Spain has known three such defeats, Hieronimo suggests,

Portugal should not be shamed by being vanquished. The king is pleased with this diplomatic presentation, but the ghost of Andrea impatiently inquires of Revenge if they have come from Hades only to witness spectacles of harmony, and Revenge grimly promises, "I'll turn their friendship into fell despite, / Their love to mortal hate, their day to night."

Lorenzo can be even more hopeful that his sister's marriage to Balthazar will somehow rebound to his own gain, for the king announces that in the event of such a union, the first son of Balthazar and Bel-imperia is to inherit the joint kingdoms of Portugal and Spain. Bel-imperia's father Don Cyprian assures his brother the king that Bel-imperia will "follow my advice, / Which is to love him, or forego my love."

To Balthazar, however, Bel-imperia's scorn makes the courtship seem hopeless, and Lorenzo vows to discover and remove the cause of her coldness. At dagger point he forces her servant Pedringano to disclose that she has taken Horatio as a lover. Accompanied by Pedringano and Balthazar's servant Serberine, Lorenzo and Balthazar surprise the lovers at night in Hieronimo's bower. They hang Horatio from a tree, stabbing him to death as he strangles, and carry Bel-imperia away to be held in Lorenzo's custody. Aroused from his bed by the melee, Hieronimo discovers his son's mutilated body and becomes wild with grief. Dipping his handkerchief in Horatio's blood, he swears not to part with it or to bury the body until he has learned the identity of the murderers and exacted his revenge.

Again Andrea bitterly complains, this time that he has been brought from Hades to see his best friend slaughtered and his mistress shamefully abused, and Revenge replies, "The sickle comes not till the corn be ripe. / Be still, and ere I lead thee from this place, / I'll show thee Balthazar in heavy case."

The conflict between the truthful Alexandro and deceitful Villuppo is quickly resolved at the beginning of Act III when news of Balthazar's capture arrives from Spain. Alexandro is freed and Villuppo sent to his execution.

Hieronimo, meanwhile, keeps Horatio's murder a secret in the hope the culprits will betray themselves. One day, as he is passing Don Cyprian's house, a letter written in blood and addressed to him is dropped at his feet; purporting to be from Bel-imperia, it accuses Balthazar and Lorenzo of Horatio's murder and implores Hieronimo to seek revenge. Suspecting the letter may be a trap, the cautious Hieronimo attempts to confirm its validity by making inquiries of Lorenzo about Bel-imperia's whereabouts. Lorenzo tells him she has been sent away from court by Don Cyprian as punishment for her rejection of Balthazar.

Hieronimo's questioning however, disquiets Lorenzo, who determines to eliminate the two witnesses to Horatio's murder, Serberine and Pedringano. Lorenzo dispatches Pedringano to murder Serberine, and at the same time alerts the watch so that Pedringano is arrested for the killing. With Machiavellian duplicity, Lorenzo convinces Pedringano that a reprieve is absolutely certain; thus Pedringano swaggers confidently through his trial—presided over by Hieronimo—and arrogantly mocks the hangman on the gallows. There is, of course, no reprieve, and Pedringano dies with frivolous jests still on his lips. Lorenzo's stratagem miscarries when the hangman discovers a letter by Pedringano to Lorenzo which clearly implicates Lorenzo and Balthazar in Horatio's murder, and which he gives to Hieronimo. With this confirmation of Bel-imperia's letter, Hieronimo resolves to take his plea for justice directly to the king.

Several developments prevent Hieronimo from accomplishing his mission. Bel-imperia (held prisoner by her brother) is mysteriously absent from court and cannot testify; and Hieronimo's wife Isabella loses her wits with grief over Horatio's death and commits suicide, an event that badly shakes Hieronimo's resolve. Moreover, before Hieronimo can present his case, Lorenzo and Balthazar go to the king with an elaborate explanation for the absence of Bel-imperia and Horatio. They contend that they were impelled to have the lovers removed from court because their illicit relationship threatened both Bel-imperia's honor and the royal marriage planned by the king. Hieronimo cannot effectively counteract these lies because his deranged conduct at court has convinced the king that he is hopelessly insane.

Plans for the marriage of Bel-imperia and Balthazar proceed on schedule. At Lorenzo's suggestion, Don Cyprian arranges an outward show of reconciliation between his son and Hieronimo. The ghost of Andrea again protests this mockery of vengeance, whereupon Revenge presents a dumb show in which the torches of Hymen are quenched by blood. Understanding the meaning of this grim pantomime, Andrea eagerly anticipates the horrors to come.

Finally Bel-imperia returns to court and

rebukes Hieronimo for his delay in avenging Horatio's murder. Hieronimo promises to strike at the first propitious moment, and Bel-imperia pledges her support. Hieronimo's opportunity comes when the king asks him to put on a play to entertain the visiting viceroy of Portugal and to celebrate the impending nuptials. Hieronimo's tragedy, entitled "Soliman and Perseda," tells of a beautiful Italian lady called Perseda (played by Bel-imperia), who is married to a knight of Rhodes named Erasto (acted by Lorenzo) and wooed by the Turkish emperor Soliman (taken by Balthazar). Soliman's pasha (played by Hieronimo) advises Soliman to have Erasto killed so that he can have the lady for himself. Unknown to the royal audience, at this point in the play Bel-imperia and Hieronimo become real rather than feigned murderers. As the pasha, Hieronimo actually stabs Lorenzo to death, and Bel-imperia as Perseda kills Balthazar and then herself.

The reality of what has happened does not occur to the audience until Hieronimo steps out of his role, exults in his revenge, and exhibits the slain. After a futile effort to hang himself, Hieronimo is seized and threatened with torture to make him reveal his "accomplices," whereupon he bites out his own tongue. Pretending to agree to write a full confession, he calls for a knife to mend his pen, and with this he stabs Don Cyprian and then himself. The tragedy concludes with Andrea expressing satisfaction with these "spectacles," and Revenge promising comfort to Andrea's slain friends and more torments for his enemies in Hades:

Then haste we down to meet thy friends and
    foes:
To place thy friends in ease, the rest in woes;
For here though death hath end their misery,
I'll there begin their endless tragedy.

The Spanish Tragedy is a fast paced *tour de théâtre* that makes all earlier Senecan adaptations seem tedious by comparison. To ordinary Elizabethans, Kyd's inflated language conveyed the romantic passion and wild frenzy of his characters:

O eyes! no eyes, but fountains fraught with
    tears;
O life! no life, but lively form of death;
O world! no world, but mass of public wrongs...

Kyd larded his dialogue with the stylized devices familiar to every educated Elizabethan—cascading interrogations, apostrophes, balanced clauses, alliteration, and stichomythia.

Mocked and parodied (as well as imitated) as it was by later playwrights, *The Spanish Tragedy* is anything but a crude or primitive play. Although more of a rhetorician than a poet, Kyd was nevertheless a masterful designer of plots and ingenious scenes. The staging of Horatio's murder, Pedringano's execution, and the play-within-the-play are all illustrative of Kyd's adroitness in presenting multiple perspectives and startling contrasts. Moreover, his characterizations are as innovative and sophisticated as his dramaturgy; his Bel-imperia ended forever the stereotyped image of the passive, listless female on the English stage, and his Lorenzo gave birth to Machiavellian villains like Marlowe's Barabas in *The Jew of Malta* and Mortimer in *Edward II,* and to the legion of crafty schemers on the stage after Marlowe. Kyd's influence was still apparent in such later dramatists as John Ford and James Shirley.

Although the standard edition is in Kyd's *Works,* ed. F. S. Boas (1901), there are several excellent editions of more recent vintage, including those by Philip Edwards in the Revels Plays (1959); A. J. Cairneross in the Regents Renaissance Drama series (1967); and T. W. Ross in the Fountainwell Drama series (1968). For criticism, see Fredson T. Bowers, *Elizabethan Revenge Tragedy, 1587-1642* (1940); William Empson, *"The Spanish Tragedy," Nimbus,* III (1956); S. F. Johnson, "*The Spanish Tragedy,* or Babylon Revisited," in *Essays on Shakespeare and Elizabethan Drama in Honor of Hardin Craig,* ed. R. Hosley (1962); Ejner Jensen, "*The Spanish Tragedy:* The Play Explains Itself," *JEGP,* LXIV (1965), and Philip Edwards, *Thomas Kyd and Early Elizabethan Tragedy* (1966).

Spenser, Edmund (1552-1599). Poet. Born in London, Spenser attended the Merchant Taylors' School, administered by the great humanist and stern teacher Richard Mulcaster. Spenser went on a scholarship in 1569 to Pembroke College, Cambridge, where he graduated B.A. in 1573, M.A. in 1576. At Cambridge he began his lifelong friendship with Gabriel HARVEY, the "Hobbinol" of Spenser's first great poem, THE SHEPHERD'S CALENDAR (1579), and of the autobiographical pastoral COLIN CLOUT'S COME HOME AGAIN (1595). Harvey and Spenser published their correspondence in *Three Proper and Witty Familiar Letters* and *Two Other Very Commendable Letters* (both in 1580). In a letter of April 1580, Spenser requested Harvey's criticism of an early draft of *The Faerie Queene,* and Harvey made clear in his reply that he regarded Spenser's work on the "elvish queen" as a foolish sacrifice of the "garland of Apollo" (representing true poetry) to the fantasies of "Hobgoblin" (representing fairyland). In these letters also, Spenser refers to a circle of friends meeting at Leicester House called the AREOPAGUS, which he describes as gathering to discuss "certain laws and rules of quantities of English syllables for English verse"—that is, the use of classical quantitative prosody in English poetry.

After his marriage to Machabyas Childe, who bore him two children, Spenser served briefly in the household of Robert Dudley, earl of Leicester (later represented as Arthur in *The Faerie Queene*). Although about this time Spenser made many influential literary and political friends, including, in addition to Leicester, Sir Philip Sidney, Sir Francis Walsingham, Sir Walter Raleigh, and others, his career is believed to have been hindered by the opposition of William Cecil, Lord Burghley, whom Spenser attacked in a satiric bestiary. MOTHER HUBBERD'S TALE, written around 1580 but not published until 1591.

In 1580 Spenser went to Ireland as secretary to Lord Grey of Wilton, the queen's lord deputy, and except for two brief periods in England, 1590-91 and 1595-96, he spent the last eighteen years of his life there, chiefly at Kilcolman Castle, situated between Limerick and Cork. There he took his second wife, Elizabeth Boyle; their courtship is the theme of Spenser's sonnet sequence AMORETTI (1595) and their marriage in 1594 the occasion for the great nuptial hymn EPITHALAMION (printed with *Amoretti*). Other minor poems by Spenser include COMPLAINTS (1591), a collection of early and late verse on the theme of mutability and the vanity of human wishes; *Daphnaïda* (1591), an elegy on the death of a lady; *Astrophel* (wr. 1586, pr. 1595), a pastoral commemorating Sidney's death; PROTHALAMION (1596), a wedding song in honor of the marriages of Elizabeth and Katherine Somerset, daughters of Edward Somerset, earl of Worcester; and FOWRE HYMNES (1596), a group of Platonic poems celebrating the subjects of love, beauty, heavenly love, and heavenly beauty.

Spenser's principal work, THE FAERIE QUEENE, to which was affixed the MUTABILITY CANTOS, was begun in 1580 and composed chiefly in Ireland during the period 1589-96. The first three books were printed in England in 1590, the next three in 1596. His last published work was a prose tract, *A View of the Present State of Ireland* (wr. c. 1596, pr. 1633), in which he urges repressive policies against the Irish rebels. In 1598 Spenser's estate in Ireland was burned during the Tyrone rebellion and Spenser fled to England. After his death on January 16, 1599, he was buried in Westminster Abbey.

Spenser was the most influential English poet between Wyatt and Surrey and the golden age of verse in the 1580s and 1590s, an era Spenser helped inaugurate with his *Shepherd's Calendar* (see PASTORAL). Although this pastoral allegory of shepherds and shepherdesses discoursing on love, poetics, politics, and religion may hold little interest for modern readers, its influence in its own time is incalculable, for it marks the first major poem after Chaucer to demonstrate a sustained mastery of native accents and rhythm at a time when English poets, perplexed by changes in pronunciation, were groping for some viable alternatives to POULTER'S MEASURE and classical hexameters. (In their above-mentioned correspondence, Spenser's friend Gabriel Harvey urged him to adopt classical quantitative meters, but Spenser wisely demurred in favor of a prosody best suited to the natural syllabic stresses of the language.)

Spenser's philosophy and theology have been the subject of considerable scholarly speculation. The extent of his commitment to Calvinism is an especially difficult question. Cambridge in Spenser's time was a center of Calvinism, and Calvinism dominated the Sidney circle at Leicester House, where Spenser was a frequent guest before he took up residence in Ireland. It is important to remember however, that Spenser, eclectic and susceptible to a bewildering variety of intellectual influences, rarely adopted ideas without transforming and modifying them to suit his own unique disposition and sensibilities. Thus, though *The Shepherd's Calendar* satirizes Roman Catholic churchmen, such criticism is not necessarily Calvinist. That Spenser believed in some form of predestination is apparent from his *Fowre Hymnes* and from a familiar passage in *The Faerie Queene* where

Una asks the Redcross Knight: "Why shouldst thou despair, that chosen art?" (I, 9, 53). Yet the doctrines of predestination and election were expounded not only by Calvin but also by St. Paul, St. Augustine, and Luther.

Spenser's philosophy cannot be attributed to any one sect or ideology but flows into his works from a variety of literary and religious tributaries. He was staunchly Protestant, strongly anti-Catholic, selectively Platonic, and thoroughly nationalistic, and to these persuasions he combines a passion for classical mythology, folklore, and medieval chivalry. His chief mythic source was the Bible, to which he brings his own adaptations of symbolic story from Ovid and Natalis Comes. Any close study of the classical mythology in *The Faerie Queene* will reveal that he often changes details of myth to suit his own narrative purposes. He was also well read in the neo-Platonists Marsilio Ficino and Pico della Mirandola, but again, he borrows from them only selectively to implement his own ideas and literary needs, so not even his *Fowre Hymnes,* although influenced by the Italian Platonists, can be said to be entirely derivative, or even wholly Platonic. Petrarch, Mantuan, Marot, Du Bartas, and the poets of the PLEIADE he knew intimately and often imitated in the technical aspects of his poetry, but their influence upon him emotionally seems to have been negligible Major influences on *The Faerie Queene,* of course, are Boiardo. Ariosto, and Tasso, from whom he borrowed liberally for characters, situations, and plot structure. His chief inspiration, however, was neither classical nor contemporary French or Italian sources but medieval, especially the allegorical romances of Malory and Chaucer, although he read these authors in corrupt and apocryphal texts. Equal to the literary influence of medieval romances was medieval iconography—paintings, tapestries, architecture and sculptures—the crumbling magnificence of pictorial symbolism and allegory that left its traces everywhere in his work.

The pattern that emerges is that of an omnivorous sensibility easily digesting heterogeneous sources and converting them into concrete images, scenes, and characters. What energized Spenser's imagination was myth, ritual, and story, not ideas *per se;* Platonism, Lucretian materialism, and even Protestantism, however sincerely advocated, gave only a peripheral coloration to characters in action, and none of his works compares in artistry to *The Faerie Queene,* the all-absorbing project that makes his other poems appear as digressions from the main flow of his instincts and genius. In this sense he was the most thoroughly literary of the Elizabethan poets before Shakespeare, and his philosophical ideas are fused with concrete characterizations, narration, and description. Dislocated from their necessary and highly emotive context of fable, his ideas were not radically different from the commonplace conceptions of good and evil held by Sidney, Drayton, Lodge, or Shakespeare. He loathed courtly love as hypocritical bestiality, and viewed courtship as a union of the physical and spiritual faculties leading to the sacramental relationship of marriage. He valued sincerity, loyalty, courage, and generosity; he despised hypocrisy, treachery, cowardice, and selfishness—the virtues and vices his characters symbolize are rarely more complex or esoteric than these.

Spenser's influence on English poetry continued well into the nineteenth century. Just as Donne's work gave rise to the metaphysical poets and Jonson's to the classical and Cavalier lyricists, Spenser's poetry created a romantic tradition of pastoralism, mythological symbolism, and narrative verse that profoundly influenced Drayton, Shakespeare, William Browne, Giles and Phineas Fletcher, and Spenser's last great disciple in the seventeenth century, Milton. During the eighteenth century Spenser's genius was acknowledged by Dryden, Rhymer, and Pope, although their enthusiasm was often qualified with strictures against Spenser's alleged obscurity and "fanciful and chimerical" language. Dr. Johnson praised Spenser's moral perspectives but condemned his language as "difficult and unpleasing"—indeed, Ben Jonson's complaint that Spenser "writ no language" has been consistently reiterated down to the present. Addison's famous essays on *The Faerie Queene* in 1752 helped to keep Spenser's reputation alive, as did Thomas Warton's appreciative essay *Observations on the Faerie Queene* in 1754.

In the second half of the eighteenth century pre-romantics such as Cowper and Blake rallied around Spenser's poetry in defense of their anticlassical aesthetics, and the Romantic poets in the age of Wordsworth elevated him to the level of Shakespeare. To Lamb, Spenser was a "poet's poet" (an epithet that has endured). and in his *Lectures on the English Poets* in 1818

Hazlitt praised him as "the poet of our waking dreams" who "invented not only language, but a music of his own for them." The decline of Spenser's status at the end of the nineteenth century might well have begun as early as 1830 with the immensely influential essay by Macaulay, who identified Spenser's cardinal weakness as "the fault of tediousness"—a complaint frequently echoed by twentieth-century readers.

After World War II occurred a resurgence of Spenserian scholarship, a systematic analysis of Spenser's sources, philosophical ideas, and literary techniques, with the result that his limitations and capabilities now seem to have been established with greater accuracy than in the past. He is now viewed, in general, as a syncretic poet of sophisticated narrative skills, uneven but occasionally awesome verbal power, and incredible imaginative range. That a poem as long as *The Faerie Queene* will cause readers to nod occasionally is no longer denied; that it remains a monumental literary achievement has been confirmed with each new critical study.

The standard edition of Spenser's works is the Variorum Edition, ed. E. A. Greenlaw, F. M. Padelford, *et al.,* 10 Vols. (1932-49). The standard biography by A. C. Judson is in Volume VIII of the Variorum Edition and also published separately (1945). Single-volume editions are by J. C. Smith and E. de Selincourt (1912), which has a fine introduction and full glossary, and by Hugh Maclean (1968), which is admirably annotated. The vast Spenserian scholarship is best traced in four bibliographies: F. N. Johnson, *A Critical Bibliography of the Works ... Printed Before 1700* (1933); Jewel Wurtsburgh, *Two Centuries of Spenserian Scholarship* (1936); D. F. Atkinson, *Edmund Spenser: A Bibliographical Supplement* (1937); and W. F. McNeir and F. Provost, *Annotated Bibliography of Edmund Spenser, 1937-60* (1962). See also *Essential Articles for the Study of Edmund Spenser,* ed. A. C. Hamilton (1972).

Spenserian stanza. For definition, see FAERIE QUEENE, THE.

Spider and the Fly, The. An allegorical mock-heroic bestiary in rhyme royal by John HEYWOOD. It was first printed in 1556 but, according to Heywood's epilogue, was begun nineteen years earlier. The time span between composition and publication may account in part for the generally acknowledged obscurities and inconsistencies of Heywood's political and religious allegory. Heywood's poem is nearly as long as Milton's *Paradise Lost.*

As in most of Heywood's works, a modicum of plot is enlarged upon by liberal use of the medieval *débat*. The Fly, caught in the Spider's web, is allowed to plead his case for clemency before the Spider, who promises to judge the plaintiff according to reason, law, custom, and conscience. This lengthy debate satirizing courts and legal procedures is made even more convoluted when the Fly appoints a butterfly and the Spider an ant to act as advocates. When all legal arguments fail, the Spider and the Fly summon their allies and prepare to settle the dispute by war. The flies capture the ant and prepare to execute him, but the eloquent ant manages to win a reprieve. After the attack of the flies against the cobweb castle is repulsed, both sides agree to a truce, but not until an extremely long debate over how the territory (a window) is to be divided. In the midst of this controversy the Spider reopens the original litigation and decrees that the Fly must be condemned to death. Before execution can take place, however, a maid appears and threatens to kill the Spider, who then must plead for his own life. His appeals fail; the maid crushes the Spider, lectures the flies and spiders on the necessity of peace and order, and both factions depart in amity. At the conclusion of the poem the narrator urges his readers to emulate the harmony reached by the spiders and flies:

> Let us here
> Play our parts in this part, all parts to appear
> To this maid as spiders and flies to that maid.
> Let our banners of obedience be display'd,
> Of love the badge, of rejoicing the right root,
> And of our own wealths the right and full boot.

There is little doubt that the maid of Heywood's poem is Mary Tudor, who attempted to crush Protestantism and restore Roman Catholicism to England, and that Heywood, a devout Catholic, had to wait almost twenty years for religious developments in England to provide him with a suitable conclusion to his poem. The other principals in the poem are less easy to identify, possibly because Heywood sometimes refers to issues and personages in Henry VIII's reign and on other occasions to events in Mary Tudor's. In the first part of the poem the flies seem to represent the commons, the spiders the nobility and rich landowners, and the issue appears to be land enclosures (although not consistently); in the second part the flies appear to be Roman Catholics, the spiders Protestants, and the issue religious conformity. Early in the poem the Fly caught in the web could represent Sir Thomas More and the Spider Cardinal Wolsey; later the crushed Spider suggests Archbishop Thomas Cranmer, executed by the Catholics in 1556. Obscure as Heywood's allegory is, it is nevertheless recognizable as being patently pro-Catholic, an allegation the author was at pains not to publicize until the restoration of Roman Catholicism under Mary Tudor.

The best edition of *The Spider and the Fly* is still that by A. W. Ward (1894), which has an excellent introduction. The most thorough study of the allegory is by Jacob Haber, *John Heywood's "The Spider and the Fly"* (1900). See also Robert C. Johnson, *John Heywood* (1970).

Stanyhurst, Richard (1547-1618). Poet and translator. Born in Dublin the son of a member of the Irish House of Commons, Stanyhurst graduated from Oxford in 1568 and studied at one of the Inns of Court. He contributed "A Description of Ireland" to the 1577 edition of Raphael Holinshed's *Chronicles.* His sole volume of verse is *The First Four Books of Virgil His Aeneas Translated into English Heroical Verse* (Leyden, 1582; London, 1583). (See TRANSLATIONS.) In his epistle to the reader, Stanyhurst defends his use of hexameters and argues, in agreement with Roger Ascham and Gabriel Harvey, that Latin quantitative verse can be effectively imitated in English—an idea then being discussed by Harvey, Spenser, and others in the Sir Philip Sidney circle. Although Harvey approved of Stanyhurst's experiment with classical hexameters, it was justifiably ridiculed by William Puttenham, Joseph Hall, Thomas Nashe, and many others of Stanyhurst's contemporaries. Stanyhurst's translation contains many absurdities of versification, diction, and orthography, such as: "But lo! to what purpose do I chat such janglery trim-trams?" Or: "The wavery commons in kim-kam sects are haled." Of Stanyhurst's translation, Hyder E. Rollins has observed that "no amount of scholarship and no theory of metrics and orthography, however labored, could teach Stanyhurst to tell a hawk from a handsaw in matters of poetry," and Rollins' opinion was generally shared by Elizabethans.

After the death of his wife in 1579 Stanyhurst went to the Low Countries and converted to Roman Catholicism. He remained abroad for the rest of his life, devoting most of his time to writing the saints' lives in Latin.

Stanyhurst's version of Vergil was edited by Edward Arber (1880) and D. Van der Haar (1933). Portions of the translation, together with Stanyhurst's dedication and preface, are in *The Renaissance in England,* ed. Hyder E. Rollins and Herschel Baker (1954). A. C. Southern, *English Recusant Prose* (1950), contains commentary and bibliography.

Staple of News, The. A comedy by Ben JONSON, written in 1625 and printed in 1631. As sources, Jonson consulted Aristophanes' *Plutus* (for its theme of money worship) and an anonymous play, *The London Prodigal* (1605), which portrays characters similar to Jonson's three Pennyboys and a father who feigns death in order to reform his prodigal son. Jonson's play satirizes the credulous reception of the public to the first English newspapers and other news pamphlets begun in the 1620s by Nathaniel Butter (satirized as Nathaniel, a "decayed stationer," in Jonson's play). The "staple of news" in Jonson's time was a news service roughly comparable to the modern Associated Press or Reuters. There is another satire on the new journalism in John Fletcher's *Fair Maid of the Inn* (1626).

The induction, or "Intermeans," is a satiric chorus similar to those used in Jonson's *Every Man Out of His Humour* and Beaumont and Fletcher's *The Knight of the Burning Pestle:* the mistresses Expectation, Censure, Mirth, and Tattle, four "women of fashion" who have come to the play "to see and be seen," sit on the stage, interrupt the prologue, and babble about the play at the end of each act.

Having inherited "above two thousand a year" from his father, whom he believes is dead, Pennyboy Junior sets out to purchase a clerkship at the newly established office of the Staple of News for his friend Tom the barber. Accompanying Pennyboy Junior in the disguise of a beggar is his father, Frank Pennyboy, "a right kind-hearted man" who is afraid that his prodigal son will squander his patrimony. At the Staple of News, Pennyboy Junior learns from his attorney Picklock that the proprietor of the news agency, Cymbal, is courting Lady Pecunia, the ward of Pennyboy's miserly uncle Richer Pennyboy. Indeed, Pecunia is a coquette with an army of suitors, but Pennyboy Junior resolves to win the lady's heart for himself.

At the Apollo Room of the Devil Tavern, Pecunia is flattered and wooed by Cymbal, Pennyboy Junior and the fops, hacks, and fantastics who have gathered around the Staple of News. Angry with his prodigal son, Frank Pennyboy doffs his disguise and, except for the gift of a tattered cloak, disinherits his son on the spot. Impoverished and deprived of Pecunia, Pennyboy Junior redeems himself by outwitting the unscrupulous lawyer Picklock, who tries to ruin his father. Pennyboy Junior is reconciled with his father, inherits his uncle's wealth, and marries Lady Pecunia.

Like Jonson's other comedies, *The Staple of News* satirizes abuse of wealth, money worship, and credulous enthusiasm for innovations and fads. Although less compact of plot than either *Volpone* or *The Alchemist,* its characterizations are equally vivid, and individual scenes, such as the riotous wooing of Lady Pecunia at the Devil Tavern in Act IV, are as wildly funny as any in Jonson. In spite of a bewildering variety of characters as numerous as in *Bartholomew Fair, The Staple of News* achieves unity and concentration by employing the new journalism as a dominant satiric metaphor.

The standard edition is in *Ben Jonson,* ed. C. H. Herford and Percy and Evelyn Simpson, 11 vols. (1925-53), VI. Devra R. Kifer has edited *The Staple of News* in the Regents Renaissance Drama series (1971). Much background information is in Folke Dahl, *The Beginnings of English Journalism* (1950). For commentary on the play, see Esther C. Dunn, *Ben Jonson's Art: Elizabethan Life and Literature Reflected Therein* (1925); Helena W. Baum, *The Satiric and the Didactic in Ben Jonson's Comedy* (1947); G. E. Bentley, *The Jacobean and Caroline Stage,* 7 vols. (1941-67), IV; and James E. Savage, "Ben Jonson and Shakespeare: 1623-1626," *UMSE,* X (1969).

Stationers' Register. A record of book titles entered for publication by the Worshipful Company of Stationers and Papermakers of London. Formerly a guild or company engaged in the production and distribution of paper parchment, pen quills, and other writing materials, it was granted an absolute monopoly by Queen Mary Tudor in 1557 of the "art or mystery of printing." The charter required all printers to serve an apprenticeship with the company and to record titles intended for publication in the company's Register. Only books printed for the first time were entered. The Register includes titles of books published or intended for publication from 1554 to 1709. (Records for the years 1571-76 are lost).

Once a title was entered, no other member of the company was permitted to publish the book. Thus the company protected the rights of its members, not those of authors; what is now called "copyright" has no real bearing on the activities of the company. Nor did an entry indicate approval by those responsible for censorship and licensing—representatives of the master of revels for dramatic works, of the archbishop of Canterbury or bishop of London for nondramatic literature. Ronald B. McKerrow stresses the commercial nature of the Stationers' Company: "The important thing is that the entry was essentially a trade matter concerning the right in the book entered by one member of the company as against others..." (*An Introduction to Bibliography for Literary Students* [1927]).

A title was normally entered shortly before publication. In some instances, however, a title was recorded but the book was never published; not infrequently, several months or even years elapsed between date of entry and publication. In still rarer cases, a book was published without being entered. The Register is of little use, therefore, in establishing dates of composition and first publication. Instead, it provides certain evidence that at the date of entry a work was in existence or at least contemplated for publication.

The standard editions are *A Transcript of the Register of the Company of Stationers of London, 1554–1640,* ed. Edward Arber, 5 vols. (1875–94); and *A Transcript of the Register of the Worshipful Company of Stationers from 1640 to 1709,* ed. G. E. B. Eyre, 3 vols. (1913-14). Arber's work contains in its introductions and appendices much scholarly information about the company. For the legal proceedings of the company, see *Records of the Court of the Stationers' Company, 1576 to 1602,* ed. W. W. Greg and E. Boswell (1903). For discussion of the company's activities, see A. W. Pollard, "The Reputation of the Book Trade in the Sixteenth Century," in *Shakespeare's Fight with the Pirates* (1917; repr. 1920); Ernest Kuhl, "The Stationers' Company and Censorship, 1599-1601," *Library,* IX (1929); W. M. Clyde, *The Struggle for the Freedom of the Press from Caxton to Cromwell* (1934); Graham

Pollard, "The Company of Stationers Before 1557," *Library,* XVIII (1937); and Cyprian Blagden, "The 'Company' of Printers," *SB,* XIII (1960).

Stevenson, William (fl. 1550-60). See GAMMER GURTON'S NEEDLE.

Stowe (or Stow), John (1525?-1605). Antiquarian and chronicler. Born in London, the son of a tallow chandler, Stowe was apprenticed early in life to a tailor, and was admitted to the Merchant Taylors' Company in 1547. A self-educated merchant, Stowe was able to continue his historical studies by grants of money from the Merchant Taylors' Company, Archbishop Matthew Parker, William Camden, and Robert Dudley, earl of Leicester.

Stowe's first publication was an edition of Geoffrey Chaucer (1561). This was followed by *A Summary of English Chronicles* (1565, with many subsequent editions both abridged and enlarged, and a continuation by Edward Howe after 1607). A more famous work was an English history from the legendary Brut to Elizabethan times, *The Chronicles of England* (1580), reprinted thereafter with the title *The Annals of England* (1592). Stowe's *A Survey of London* (1598; revised and enlarged in 1618 and in later editions by Anthony Munday and others) is a detailed description of the architecture, history, institutions, streets, customs, and recreations of Elizabethan London. Stowe died in London and was buried at the church of St. Andrew Undershaft, where his wife erected a statue that still stands.

The standard edition of *A Survey of London* was edited, with a biography of Stowe and a bibliography of his works, by C. L. Kingsford, 2 vols. (1908; rev. ed., 1927). John Gairdner edited *The Annals* for the Camden Society publications, XXVIII (1880). There is an edition of *A Survey of London* in the Everyman's Library series, ed. Ernest Rhys (1906; repr. 1940), and another edition by Henry Morley (1908). For commentary on Stowe, see T. S. Dorsch, "Two English Antiquaries: John Leland and John Stow," *E&S,* XII (1959).

Suckling, Sir John (1609–1642). Poet and dramatist. Suckling was born at Whitton, near Twickenham, Middlesex, of a distinguished and titled family. In 1623 he matriculated at Trinity College, Cambridge, but left without a degree. After a brief residence at Gray's Inn, the death of his father left him with the means of extensive travel abroad after 1628. He was knighted in 1630, and the following year accompanied the marquis of Hamilton with six thousand men to serve with Gustavus Adolphus. In these wars, according to Gerard Langbaine in *An Account of the English Dramatic Poets* (1691), Suckling was "present at three battles, five sieges, and as many skirmishes." He returned to England as a court messenger in 1631. Between his return from Germany and his departure to the Scottish wars in 1639, he wrote four plays, earned a reputation as a lady's man, gambled for high stakes at bowls and cards, and, according to John Aubrey's account in *Brief Lives,* invented the game of cribbage. His reputation as a rake and reveler originated in Puritan accounts, but they are confirmed by his own self-portrait in his satiric poem "Session of the Poets."

In 1634 Suckling fell into disgrace when he was publicly beaten by Sir John Digby, brother of Sir Kenelm, for his objectionable attentions toward a lady at court. Nor was Suckling's reputation enhanced by his farcical conduct during the Bishops' War against the Scots in 1639, when he outfitted a hundred cavalrymen in gorgeous red and white uniforms at a personal cost of £12,000. A Puritan critic acerbically noted that Suckling's perfumed troopers were better arrayed for "dalliance" than for war, and the complete rout of the king's army north of the Tweed made Suckling's gaudy warriors appear totally ludicrous.

After the abortive Scottish expedition, Suckling turned to politics, serving in the Long Parliament of 1640 and publishing a pamphlet of political advice for Charles I in 1641 (reprinted in a posthumous collection of his writings, *Fragmenta Aurea,* [1646]). He conspired with several other Royalists, including his close friends Sir William Davenant and Henry Jermyn, to force the earl of Strafford's release from the Tower, where the king's favorite languished under condemnation of death, and for this intrigue Suckling was charged with high treason by Parliament. He fled to the Continent, and after a period of extreme poverty, ended his life with poison in 1642.

Suckling's work consists of an anti-Socinian tract titled *An Account of Religion by Reason,* some letters, miscellaneous poems and ballads, and his plays. His best-known poems are his satire on his contemporaries, "Session of the Poets" (1637; See CRITICISM, LITERARY), and the lyric "Why so pale and wan, fond lover?" See CAVALIER POETS. These and other poems, together with three of his plays, are contained in *Fragmenta Aurea* and *Last Remains* (1659).

His four plays include *Aglaura* (wr. 1637); *Brennoralt, or The Discontented Colonel* (wr. c. 1639); *The Goblins* (wr. 1638); and an unfinished tragedy, *The Sad One* (wr. c. 1637?). His most successful play was his first, *Aglaura,* a tragedy performed at court during the Christmas season in 1637 by the King's Men, on whom Suckling characteristically lavished a fortune in costumes for the production. *Aglaura* apparently did not win unqualified applause. Suckling changed the fifth act to give it a happy ending, whereupon its second appearance at court, in 1638, was a great triumph, especially with the queen. Both versions of the fifth act were printed in the 1638 edition with a prologue referring to the tragedy of the Christmas performance that became the happy tragicomedy of the Easter production in 1638:

'Tis strange, perchance, you'll think, that she that died
At Christmas, should at Easter be a bride.

Aglaura, a typically turgid Cavalier romance, continued to be popular well into the Restoration, and as late as 1691 Langbaine describes it as "much prized." Nevertheless, Suckling's reputation derives not from his plays but his cynical, careless lyrics in the mood of John Donne's "Go and catch a falling star" and "I long to talk with some old lover's ghost." Unlike most Cavalier poets, Suckling was only indifferently attentive to Jonson's poems, which required too much discipline and restraint. As he wrote to Thomas Carew, his own muse was "easy and free," and his best poems are audacious derisions of Petrarchan love conventions like "Out upon it! I have loved" and "Why so pale and wan, fond lover"—sportive songs of bravura that imitate Donne's occasional cynicism but little of his rigorous wit.

The Works, ed. A Hamilton Thompson (1910; repr. 1964) has been superseded by *Sir John Suckling's Poems and Letters from Manuscript,* ed. Herbert Berry (1960) and *The Works,* ed. Thomas Clayton (1971). Important critical studies are by Kathleen M. Lynch, *The Social Mode of Restoration Comedy,* University of Michigan Publications in Language and Literature, III (1926); F. O. Henderson, "Traditions of *Precieux* and *Libertin* in Suckling's Poetry," *ELH,* IV (1937); L. A. Beaurline, "The Canon of Sir John Suckling's Poems," *SP,* LVII (1960); and Beaurline and Clayton, "Notes on Early Editions of *Fragmenta Aurea,*" *SB,* XXIII (1970).

Supposes. A comedy by George GASCOIGNE, written in 1566 and printed in 1573. A free translation of Ludovico Ariosto's *I Suppositi* ("The Substitutes" [1509]), this is the first English comedy written entirely in prose, and it established the fashion for Italian settings that prevailed for almost a hundred years. The episode of the master exchanging roles with the servant is from Plautus' *Captivi,* and the one in which the lover disguises himself as a girl in order to enter his mistress' house is from Terence's *Eunuchus.* Several other situations and character types are derived from Roman comedy. Shakespeare found in this play the Bianca-Lucentio subplot for his *Taming of the Shrew.*

Damon, a prosperous widower of Ferrara, has a beautiful daughter, Polynesta, who is wooed both by Cleander, a ridiculous old doctor of laws, and by the supposed Erostrato, a student. Secretly, however, Polynesta has given her love to a young man who she thinks is Damon's trusted young servant Dulippo but who, unknown to either Polynesta or her father, is in fact the real Erostrato in disguise. Meanwhile the real Dulippo has exchanged identities and "become" Erostrato, suitor of Polynesta. Through Pasiphilo, a knavish parasite, the feigned Erostrato learns that Damon favors Cleander for his daughter because of Cleander's huge fortune. He persuades Damon to postpone his decision for two weeks, until the arrival of Erostrato's father, Philogano, who will match Cleander's promised marriage settlement. He then dupes an old Sienese gentleman into posing as Philogano.

Damon discovers his daughter's romance with the supposed Dulippo, who is arrested and thrown in prison. Meanwhile the real Philogano, a doting father, arrives in the company of his shrewd and practical servant Litio. At Erostrato's house he is turned away violently by the feigned Philogano. All of this confusion begins to clear with Dulippo's repentance and the discovery of some "miraculous" births. Dulippo turns out to be Cleander's long-lost son, captured in childhood by the Turks. The real Philogano proves he is the father of Erostrato and the social equal of Damon, who now accepts Erostrato as son-in-law. At the conclusion of the play, all identities are made known and Cleander, cured of his marital aspirations, invites the mischievous Pasiphilo to dinner.

Gascoigne's comedy is a very competent rendition of two versions of Ariosto's *I Suppositi,* the first done by Ariosto in prose in 1509, the second in verse about twenty years later. Gascoigne's own prose is colloquial and fluent, his dramatic sense exceptionally well developed for an Englishman writing in the 1560s. His *Supposes* and *Jocasta* were both acted by students at Gray's Inn in 1566, perhaps in friendly rivalry to Sackville and Norton's GORBODUC, produced at the Inner Temple and at Whitehall the year before.

The standard edition is in *The Works,* ed. J. W. Cunliffe, 2 vols. (1907-10), I. There are other editions in *Early Plays from the Italian,* ed. R. W. Bond (1911), and *Elizabethan and Jacobean Comedy,* ed. Robert Ornstein and Hazelton Spencer (1964). The staging of Gascoigne's comedy is discussed by Lily B. Campbell, *Scenes and Machines on the English Stage during the Renaissance* (1923). For other commentary, see C. T. Prouty, *George Gascoigne: Elizabethan Courtier, Soldier, and Poet* (1942).

Surrey, earl of. See HOWARD, HENRY.

T

Tamburlaine the Great. A play in two parts by Christopher MARLOWE. Part I may have been written in an early draft before Marlowe left Cambridge in 1587, Part II a year later after the success of Part I, performed by the Lord Admiral's Men with the great actor Edward Alleyn in the title role. Both parts were printed in 1590. For the story of Tamburlaine, the famous Timur of Persia, Marlowe consulted Pedro Mexia's *Silva de varia leccion,* translated into English in 1571 by Thomas Fortescue as *The Forest,* and Petrus Perodinus' *Magni Tamerlanis Scytharum imperatories vita* (1553), and for background, a number of works by Herodotus, Plato, and Xenophon. The geography is taken from Abraham Ortelius' *Theatrum orbis terrarum* (Antwerp, 1570).

Part I is an episodic, lyrical recital of Tamburlaine's spectacular rise from Scythian shepherd to titanic world conqueror and "scourge and wrath of God." In Act I the effeminate weakling King Mycetes of Persia vainly attempts to put down Tamburlaine, "that sturdy Scythian thief" who robs his merchants and ravishes the countryside, but Mycetes is himself overturned by his wily brother Cosroe. Act I dramatizes two easy conquests of Tamburlaine. He wins the heart of his captive princess Zenocrate, daughter of the sultan of Egypt, and converts to his cause Theridamas, the Persian general sent by Mycetes with a huge army to conquer him. Presumably Tamburlaine is an ineluctible demigod of destruction who "turns fortune's wheel in his hands."

At first Cosroe enlists Tamburlaine as an ally, but the Scythian thirsts for a crown of his own and defeats Cosroe in battle. Next Tamburlaine conquers Bajazeth, emperor of the Turks. He places Bajazeth and his queen Zabina in a cage, mocks them, and teases them with food as if they were animals. Tamburlaine then marches on Damascus, where Zenocrates' father and the king of Arabia have joined forces to oppose him. At the siege of Damascus he slaughters a deputation of virgins sent to plead for mercy. His captives Bajazeth and Zabina go insane and dash out their brains against their cage. It is clear that Tamburlaine's cruelty and bloodlust are insatiable. With Damascus overthrown, the sultan bows to Tamburlaine's might and Zenocrate is crowned queen of Persia and betrothed to the Scythian conqueror.

Part II suggests a more critical view of Tamburlaine, "the monster that hath drunk a sea of blood, and yet gapes still for more to quench his thirst." The Turkish vassals of

Bajazeth—Orcanes, Gazellus, and Uribassa—join with their ancient enemies the Christians, led by Sigismund of Hungary, to oppose Tamburlaine. The Christians treacherously violate the truce on grounds that no oath made to an infidel need be honored, and the outraged Turks retrench their forces and defeat the perfidious Christians. Meanwhile at Tamburlaine's camp Zenocrate dies of illness, and the grief-crazed Tamburlaine burns the town and surrounding countryside.

Although in Act IV Tamburlaine defeats Orcanes and Gazellus and their Turkish allies, he suffers a personal setback when one of his three sons, Calyphas, remains behind the battle to play cards because, unlike his father and brothers, he has no taste for war. His furious father kills Calyphas and refuses to give him appropriate burial.

At the siege of Babylon Tamburlaine commits further atrocities. He has the governor of the city hung in chains, drowns all its citizens, and orders the Koran burned. As other enemies gather forces, Tamburlaine sickens and dies.

Tamburlaine, Part I, introduced to Elizabethans what Jonson later called "Marlowe's mighty line," a pounding, resonant torrent of iambic pentameter blank verse crammed with euphonious allusions, alliteration and assonance, and soaring hyperboles. That Marlowe was aware of his innovation is apparent from his manifesto-like Prologue to Part I:

From jigging veins of riming mother wits
And such conceits as clownage keeps in pay,
We'll lead you to the stately tent of war,
Where you shall hear the Scythian Tamburlaine
Threat'ning the world with high astounding
  terms,
And scourging kingdoms with his conquering
  sword.
View but his picture in this tragic glass,
And then applaud his fortunes as you please.

Part I appears to be anything but a "tragic glass," for it chronicles Tamburlaine's rise from common bandit to emperor of western Asia, and at the conclusion he stands triumphant over a dozen principalities. Part I recounts these victories episodically: Tamburlaine's conquest of Mycetes in Act I, Cosroe (II), Bajazeth (III-IV), and the sultan of Egypt at Damascus (V). Hence Part I is more of a heroic poem than a tragedy.

Part II describes Tamburlaine's victories over Callapine, Bajazeth's son, and his followers, but the Scythian's fortunes begin to wane after the death of Zenocrate in Act II. Tamburlaine can no more keep Zenocrate alive than his captain Theridamas is able to keep his beautiful captive Olympia from suicide in Act III; hence the Scourge of God and his minions have power only to destroy—an impression reinforced by the defection and execution of Tamburlaine's son Calyphas and Tamburlaine's own death in Act V.

Critics are divided as to the ultimate meaning of the play. Some read it in terms of its subtitle in the 1590 edition as being "two tragical discourses," a continuous two-part tragedy in which Tamburlaine rises to great heights until the second half of Part II, when his vaunted mastery of fate proves ironically hollow in the face of death. Others see the play as Marlowe's glorification of Renaissance individualism and self-assertion, citing speeches like the following to illustrate Tamburlaine's defiance of man's limitations and bold repudiation of the medieval concept of *contemptus mundi:*

Nature that fram'd us of four elements,
Warring within our breasts for regiment,
Doth teach us all to have aspiring minds.
Our souls, whose faculties can comprehend
The wonderous architecture of the world,
Still climbing after knowledge infinite,
And always moving as the restless spheres,
Will us to wear ourselves and never rest,
Until we reach the ripest fruit of all,
The perfect bliss and sole felicity,
The sweet fruition of an earthly crown.

Critics who interpret these lines as expressive of Marlowe's own values rather than those of a Tamburlaine stricken with *hubris* may be hard-pressed, however, to reconcile their concept of the play with Marlowe's view in *Doctor Faustus,* a tragedy which cautions against such aspirations in the style and tone of a morality play, or in *Edward II,* which grimly refutes in the destinies of Edward and Mortimer the proud claim that "everything is in a man's own hands."

A standard edition is in *The Works,* ed. C. F. Tucker Brooke (1910). Equally valuable for notes and commentary are editions by R. H. Case, *The Works and Life,* 6 vols. (1930-33), I, and Irving Ribner, *The Complete Plays* (1933). John D. Jump has edited Parts

I and II in the Regents Renaissance Drama series (1967), J. W. Harper in the New Mermaids series (1971). For important criticism from different perspectives, see Una Ellis-Fermor, *Christopher Marlowe* (1927); Paul H. Kocher, *Christopher Marlowe, A Study of His Thought, Learning, and Character* (1946); Harry Levin, *The Overreacher, A Study of Christopher Marlowe* (1952); Irving Ribner, "The Idea of History in Marlowe's *Tamburlaine*," *ELH,* XX (1953); and Roy W. Battenhouse, *Marlowe's Tamburlaine: A Study in Renaissance Moral Philosophy* (1941; rev. 1964).

Taming of the Shrew, The. An early comedy by William SHAKESPEARE, probably written in 1593-4 and first printed in the 1623 Folio. The relationship of this play to the anonymous *The Taming of a Shrew,* printed in 1594, 1596, and 1607, is much disputed by scholars; the latter has been described as an earlier version, a poor imitation of Shakespeare's play, or another version of the same source from which Shakespeare's comedy was derived. Certainly the anonymous play is markedly inferior to Shakespeare's. For his subplot Shakespeare used George Gascoigne's Italianate comedy SUPPOSES (1566), a translation of Ariosto's *I Suppositi* (1509).

In a lengthy Induction a drunken tinker, Christopher Sly, is picked up on the heath by a lord and his huntsmen, who, as a joke, tell him that he is really a nobleman who has slept for fifteen years, and that the play to be performed by a group of strolling players is for his sole amusement.

The main story performed for the tinker concerns Petruchio, a witty Veronese who elects to marry Katharina, the spoiled and volatile eldest daughter of Baptista, a wealthy gentleman of Padua. To tame his shrewish bride, Petruchio subjects her to the most outrageous treatment; he appears late for his wedding dressed in rags, refuses to feed her or allow her to sleep, and declares that neither food nor bed is adequate to her extraordinary requirements. Meanwhile, Katharina's sister Bianca is wooed and won by Lucentio, disguised as a schoolmaster, and Bianca's spurned suitor, Hortensio, wins a widow. At the marriage feast for these couples Petruchio triumphantly wins a good-natured dispute over which bridegroom has the "tamest" and most obedient wife when the two brides curtly reject summonses from their husbands but Katharina meekly comes at once.

The *Taming of the Shrew* is one of Shakespeare's most delightful early comedies if the reader does not, with George Bernard Shaw, view the play as an attempt to portray realistically the efforts of a cynical fortune hunter to break the spirit of an innocent woman by humiliation and starvation. Far from being realistic, *The Shrew* is an overt fantasy, a play-within-a-play couched between the mundane low comedy scenes of the drunken tinker. Moreover, Katharina is anything but a passive victim of Petruchio's will, for she is resourceful enough to suggest such strong-willed and articulate heroines as Rosalind in *As You Like It* and Viola in *Twelfth Night,* and she often makes clear that she really wants and enjoys her man. The play is one of Shakespeare's best-humored and most festive farces, a wild spoof on the eternal battle of the sexes.

A standard text is the New Cambridge edition, ed. Arthur Quiller-Couch and J. Dover Wilson (1928). There is a full text of *The Taming of a Shrew* in Geoffrey Bullough, *Narrative and Dramatic Sources of Shakespeare,* 7 vols. (1972), I. The two versions are compared by Hardin Craig, "*The Shrew* and *A Shrew,*" in *Elizabethan Studies in Honor of George F. Reynolds* (1945). See also Richard Hosley, "Sources and Analogues of *The Taming of the Shrew,*" *HLQ,* XXVII (1964). For criticism, see H. B. Charlton, *Shakespearean Comedy* (1938); Derek Traversi, *Shakespeare: The Early Comedies* (rev. ed., 1964); and Richard Henze, "Role Playing in *The Taming of the Shrew,*" *SHR,* IV (1970).

Tasso, Torquato (1544-1595). Italian poet whose pastoral play *Aminta* (Venice, 1573) and epic poem *Gerusalemme liberata* (written in 1575, printed in revised form as *Gerusalemme conquistata* in 1593) were widely admired by English Renaissance poets. Thomas WATSON rendered the play into Latin as *Amyntas* (1585), which was translated into English hexameters by Abraham Fraunce as *The Lamentations of Amyntas for the Death of Phillis* (1587), in which form it ran through four editions by 1596. See PASTORAL; TRANSLATIONS.

Taylor, John (c. 1580-1653). Miscellanist and poet, known as the "Water Poet." Taylor was born the son of a surgeon in Gloucester, attended school there, and became apprenticed to a London waterman, one who ferries passengers and supplies on the River Thames. At eighteen Taylor went on the Cadiz expedition with Essex, enlisted in the Royal Navy, and made sixteen or more sea voyages, several of these to the Azores. Discharged from service because of a leg injury, he settled in London as a waterman and began writing numerous pamphlets in verse, prose, and mixtures of both.

A boisterous exhibitionist, Taylor performed much-publicized feats such as rowing to Queenborough in Kent in a paper boat, and traveling from London to Edinburgh and back without spending a penny of his own. Very often Taylor solicited advance subscriptions to pamphlets he promised to write describing such sensational events. In *The Penniless Pilgrimage* (1618) Taylor recounts how he met Ben Jonson ("my long approved and assured good friend"), also on a tour, who gave him a gold piece and wished him well. Taylor assiduously cultivated the acquaintance of literati, and it did not disturb him in the least that Jonson, Thomas Dekker, Nicholas Breton, and others made sport of him as a hackneyed scribbler.

Taylor's bulky folio, *All the Works of John Taylor the Water Poet* (1630), which in spite of its title represents only a small fraction of the canon, contains no fewer than sixty-three works, including his "Urania," a didactic poem in eighty-six stanzas of faltering ottava rima; a long treatise on beggars; a diatribe against usurers; and doggerel sonnets, anti-Catholic epigrams, and assorted satires and eulogies in verse and prose. Part of that collection had appeared as *The Sculler* in 1612, a work Jonson acridly noted was praised by James I. Taylor scribbled pamphlets on every subject imaginable—food, navigation, penology, alcoholism, fashions in clothes, religion (always pro-Anglican and scornful of Puritan "Amsterdamners"), English taverns, manufacturing, husbandry, housewifery, agriculture; his pen fairly leaked, and he could spread ink with authority and aplomb on any topic. Especially popular were his "thumb Bibles," verse summaries of the Old and New Testaments, and his travel guides, seventeenth-century Baedekers describing the great houses, roads, taverns, and inns around London and its environs. Taylor was, in fact, the lineal ancestor of those modern travelers who write books on how to live away from home on five dollars a day.

Incredibly resourceful, Taylor was able to make a living by his pen; his eager public read his pamphlets virtually to pieces, and the lengthy list of his publications must represent only a portion of his output. During the plague of 1625 he left London and went to Oxford, where he may have studied for a time at Oriel College. He opened a tavern there at the outbreak of the Civil War, and when Oxford fell to the parliamentarians in 1645 he purchased another public house in London. The last year of his life, at seventy-five and partially lame, he went from London to Gravesend and back on his final tour. He died in London in 1653.

Taylor provides painful evidence, if any were needed, that all Elizabethans did not sing like birds. His execrable verses were written with a cast-iron ear, and his prose style waddles like a fat man on crutches. There is every evidence that at times Taylor quixotically aspired to write like Thomas Nashe, but he had little of Nashe's erudition and wit. That he shared with Nashe a fascination with language is evident from one of Taylor's most competent pamphlets in verse, *The Essence, Quintescence, Incence, Innocence, Lye-Sence, and Magnificence of Nonsence upon Sence* (1653), which is one of the earliest "jabberwocky" nonsense poems in English.

Taylor's writings, too numerous to cite here, are listed in *CBEL,* ed. F. W. Bateson, 4 vols., (1940), I. There are biographical accounts by Willard Thorp, "John Taylor, Water Poet," *Texas Review,* VIII (1922); and Wallace Notestein, *Four Worthies* (1957).

Tempest, The. A play by William SHAKESPEARE, written in 1611 and first printed in the 1623 Folio. No principal source is known. Minor or indirect sources include John Florio's translation of Montaigne's essay "On Cannibals" (1603), a marine pastoral type of play in the Italian *commedia dell'arte,* and pamphlets describing shipwrecks in the New World.

For twelve years Prospero, former duke of Milan, and his daughter Miranda have lived on a remote island far from Milan, where Prospero's brother Antonio rules illegally. Here Prospero has cultivated the art of magic, and retains in his service Caliban, a witch's son who is half fish and half man, and Ariel, a good-willed sprite. By causing a storm, Prospero manages to bring to the island a ship carrying the king of Naples, his son Ferdinand, the king's brother Sebastian, Prospero's brother Antonio, the benevolent counselor Gonzalo, and several others. The marooned party is divided into three groups on the island. Antonio, the king of Naples, Gonzalo, and Sebastian are terrorized by illusions created by Ariel, while on another part of the island two common fellows, the clownish Trinculo and the drunken Stephano, are worshiped as gods by the savage Caliban. Believed to have been drowned, Prince Ferdinand is washed ashore, meets Miranda, and the two fall in love. Their courtship is closely supervised by Prospero, who subjects the dutiful and humble Ferdinand to several unpleasant tasks to prove his devotion to Miranda.

At the end of the play all of the island's inhabitants have been subjected to various ordeals, and they assemble before Prospero to be judged. The king of Naples joyfully receives his son, Antonio repents his evil-doing and restores Prospero's dukedom, and Ferdinand and Miranda are betrothed. Prospero forgives his former enemies, gives up his magic, and prepares to depart from the island.

The Tempest, Shakespeare's last comedy, is both a unique play and a reworking of his own previous themes and situations. The motif of reconciliation is the same as that in *Cymbeline* and *The Winter's Tale;* the idea of the superiority of mercy over harsh justice and of forgiveness over revenge appears also in *The Merchant of Venice* and *Measure for Measure.* In *The Tempest,* however, these values are dramatized without any of the abrasive realism or dissonance of the earlier comedies. Fantasy and myth have an even greater role than in *A Midsummer Night's Dream,* and Shakespeare sets his play in a locale appropriate to his vision of ideal harmony—an enchanted island ruled by a benign magus who controls the action from within the play to an extent even greater than did Duke Vincentio in *Measure for Measure.* Like the duke, Prospero had been an irresponsible ruler, and his pardon of others' sins represents his own atonement. Thus he partakes of both individual humanity and symbolism; as a man he is as fussy, garrulous, and petulant as old Capulet or Polonius, but as a symbol he stands for humane justice and reason.

In Prospero's rejection of magic (V, *i,* 33ff.) readers imagine they hear Shakespeare's own voice, and it is perhaps inevitable that in another of Prospero's speeches they listen to Shakespeare bidding farewell to the stage as he prepares to return to Stratford:

Our revels now are ended. These our actors,
As I foretold you, were all spirits, and
Are melted into air, into thin air.
And, like the baseless fabric of this vision,
The cloud-capp'd towers, the gorgeous palaces,
The solemn temples, the great globe itself—
Yea, all which it inherit—shall dissolve
And, like this insubstantial pageant faded,
Leave not a rack behind. We are such stuff
As dreams are made on, and our little life
Is rounded with a sleep.

[IV, *i,* 148–58]

In *The Tempest* Shakespeare employs these images of sleep, dreams, illusions, and idle fancies to express some of his firmest convictions regarding the value of mercy and the meaning of true freedom.

The Tempest is the only one of Shakespeare's plays to observe the classical unities of time, place, and action, as if in this last play, as Alfred Harbage fancifully suggests, Shakespeare were saying to the classicist Jonson, "See, Ben, I could have done it every time!"

A standard text is the new Arden edition, ed. Frank Kermode (1954). Affinities to the masque are considered by Enid Welsford, *The Court Masque* (1927), and symbolism is interpreted by G. Wilson Knight, *The Shakespearean Tempest* (1932). For other important commentary, see E. M. W. Tillyard, *Shakespeare's Last Plays* (1938); Derek Traversi, *"The Tempest," Scrutiny,* XVI (1949); Frank Davidson, *"The Tempest:* An Interpretation," *JEGP,* LXII (1963); Rose Zimbardo, "Form and Disorder in *The Tempest," SQ,* XIV (1963); John Fraser, "*The Tempest* Revisited," *CR,* XI (1968); Stanley E. Hyman, "Portraits of the Artist: Iago and Prospero," *Shenandoah,* XXI (1970); and M.C. Bradbrook, "Romance, Farewell! *The Tempest,*" *ELR,* I (1971). Non-Shakespearean adaptations are collected in *After The Tempest,* ed. G. R. Guffey (1969). See also *The Tempest: Twentieth Century Views,* ed. Hallett Smith (1969).

Temple, The. See HERBERT, GEORGE.

Tenure of Kings and Magistrates, The. A political pamphlet by John MILTON, first published in 1649. The second edition (1650) contains some emendations and an appendix of extracts from Protestant reformers justifying tyrannicide. The arraignment of Charles I by a faction in Parliament aroused a storm of shock and indignation at home and abroad, and Milton's pamphlet argues "that it is lawful, and hath been held through all ages, for any, who have the power, to call to account a tyrant or wicked king, and after due conviction, to depose and put him to death if the ordinary magistrates have neglected or denied to do it." Milton's tract is based on the idea of a temporal social contract between governors and governed, and on the natural law that "all men were naturally born free." Characteristically, he supports his arguments by appeals to Scripture, ancient and modern history, reason, and prestigious testimony.

After Milton's tract fortuitously appeared in February, hard upon Charles I's execution, a grateful Parliament appointed him secretary for foreign tongues in the Council of State, a post he retained until his total blindness in 1652.

The Tenure of Kings and Magistrates is in the *Prose Works,* ed. M. W. Wallace for World's Classics (1925); *The Complete Prose Works,* ed. D. M. Wolfe, 5 vols. (1953–71), III; and *John Milton: Complete Poems and Major Prose,* ed. Merritt Y. Hughes (1957). Important commentaries include E. N. S. Thompson, *Essays on Milton* (1914); William Haller, "Before *Areopagitica,*" *PMLA,* XLII (1927); D. M. Wolfe, *Milton in the Puritan Revolution* (1941); and Merritt Y. Hughes, "Milton as a Revolutionary," *ELH,* X (1943).

Thélème, The Abbey of (Rabelais). See UTOPIAN FICTION.

Thersites. An INTERLUDE sometimes attributed to Nicholas UDALL. Of uncertain authorship and date, it was probably written around 1537 and was first printed in an undated edition that appeared between 1561 and 1563. *Thersites* has for its source a Latin dialogue by J. Ravisius Textor, professor of rhetoric at the College de Navarre and later (1520–24) rector of the University of Paris. Derivative of Plautus, *Thersites* marks the first appearance of the braggart soldier, or MILES GLORIOSUS, on the English stage. The episode of the combat with a snail, however, is a familiar medieval satire against the Lombards.

Purporting to show "how that the greatest boasters are not the greatest doers," the farce presents Thersites, a swaggerer; Mater, his mother; Mulciber, an armorer; a Snail; Miles, a knight; and Telemachus, son of Ulysses. Returned from the Trojan War with only a club, Thersites purchases combat weapons from Mulciber and then, over his mother's protests, challenges all the great heroes of history to single combat. Only the Snail accepts his boastful challenge; after a hot fight the cowardly Thersites succeeds only in getting the Snail to retract his horns. Next Thersites is beaten by Miles, an undistinguished common soldier from Calais. Thereafter young Telemachus arrives in search of a cure for worms. Mater restores him to health with a charm. Although Telemachus had previously beaten Thersites in combat, he no longer bears the braggart a grudge. Nevertheless, Thersites continues to rail until driven from the stage by Miles.

There is an edition by J. S. Farmer in *Six Anonymous Plays* (1905).

Thomas of Reading. A prose narrative by Thomas DELONEY, written around 1596 and published in 1612 (fourth edition). Like all Deloney's middle-class tales, *Thomas of Reading* is an episodic, disconnected narrative based on adaptations from euphuistic romances, historical chronicles, and JESTBOOKS. *Thomas of Reading* celebrates the clothier's craft.

On his way to Wales, King Henry I is astonished at the richly laden carts of Thomas Cole of Reading and of other clothiers shipping goods to London. The king is embroiled in a war with his brother Robert, duke of Normandy, and the earls of Moraigne and Shrewsbury, and has turned their families out of their homes. Margaret, daughter of the banished earl of Shrewsbury, hires herself out as a servant at the home of Master Gray of Gloucester.

The chief clothiers of England meet with Henry I to request three favors: that England adopt a single standard of measurement, that the people be made to accept cracked money as viable currency, and that clothes thieves be hanged. The king complies by making the length of his arm one yard, by ordering all coins to be split, and by permitting clothiers to hang without trial anyone caught stealing cloth.

Shortly before Thomas of Reading prepares a feast at Gerard's Hall for King Henry and his two sons, the clothier Cuthbert is caught in an assignation with the pretty young wife of Old Bosom, keeper of an inn that is a haunt of the clothiers. The old man hangs Cuthbert in a basket from the ceiling; he is not to be lowered until the king's sons themselves ask for his release. After the banquet the princes adjourn to the inn and, much to the amusement of the clothiers, arrange for the chagrined Cuthbert's freedom.

Robert, duke of Normandy, meets Margaret at Master Gray's house and falls in love with her. Thinking she is a common servant, he knows the king will never grant him permission to marry her. The lovers elope and are captured by the king's men. Margaret is spared but Robert is blinded, after which Margaret reveals her true identity, gives all she has to the poor, and enters a nunnery. Robert vows to be buried in Gloucester, where he first met her.

In still another episode, Thomas of Reading encounters the wicked Jarman family, keepers of the Crane Inn who murder wealthy merchants in their sleep. After two futile attempts to dispatch Thomas, the Jarmans finally succeed. Before he is murdered, however, Thomas experiences premonitions of death; he recalls that his daughter wept at his departure from Reading, and his nose bleeds (an ominous sign). He writes a letter in which he agrees to lend his clothier friend Tom Dove two hundred pounds, and makes out a will leaving his wife and children his great fortune and granting Dove the money as a gift in the event of his death. After Thomas' murder, the Jarmans are caught and hanged: Dove uses the money to pay his debtors and enjoys a prosperous business thereafter. Henry I is so grieved over Thomas' death that he refrains from all business for a week and orders the Crane Inn to be destroyed. Since that day the river into which Thomas Cole of Reading's body was thrown has been called Cole River, and the town where he died Colebrooke.

Thomas of Reading is edited by Merritt E. Lawlis, *The Novels of Thomas Deloney* (1961). For a critical analysis, see Lawlis' *An Apology for the Middle Class: The Dramatic Novels of Thomas Deloney* (1961).

Three Proper and Witty Familiar Letters. See HARVEY, GABRIEL; SPENSER, EDMUND.

Timber, or Discoveries Made upon Men and Matter as They Have Flowed out of His Daily Readings. A collection of commentary, notes, personal observations, and paraphrases and translations of authors by Ben JONSON. *Timber* was first published in the posthumous two-volume 1640 folio of Jonson's works, edited by Sir Kenelm Digby. It is especially interesting as a record of Jonson's prodigious reading of Horace, Vives, Erasmus, Machiavelli (whom Jonson frequently condemns), Justus Lipsius, and Francis Bacon (who was very influential with Jonson for both his scientific ideas and prose style). It also contains much criticism of Jonson's contemporaries, including Shakespeare, whom Jonson charged with "wanting art" but in general greatly admired. The last portion of *Timber,* although lacking any apparent arrangement, consists of brief essays that Jonson may have planned to develop into a treatise on literary principles, writing techniques, and classification of genres (See CRITICISM, LITERARY).

The impression of Jonson that emerges from *Timber* is that of a rigorous literary and moral disciplinarian, a staunch neoclassicist, and a very talented prose stylist. With characteristic good sense, he believed that classical authors were to be studied thoroughly, but not supinely imitated or blindly obeyed: "For to all the observations of the ancients we have our own experience, which if we will use and apply, we have better means to pronounce. It is true they opened the gates and made the way that went before us, but as guides, not commanders."

"Pure and neat language I love," Jonson observes, "yet plain and customary." *Timber* provides an informative introduction to Jonson's classical ideas and his own lean, spare poetic style. "For a man to write well, there are required three necessities," he states: "to read the best authors, observe the best speakers, and much exercise of his own style." Since about four-fifths of *Timber* consists of paraphrases and translations of classical and continental authors, it has little significance for its originality; its importance stems from the fact that it represents one of the earliest expressions of a body of criticism based on discipline, decorum, and attention to form—principles of criticism that gained increasing acceptance in the seventeenth century.

The standard edition of *Timber* is in *Ben Jonson,* ed. C. H. Herford and Percy and Evelyn Simpson, 11 vols. (1925-53), VIII. The editions of Felix E. Schelling (1892) and M. Castelain (1906) trace most of Jonson's sources. There is a more recent edition by G. B. Harrison (1923). For commentary, see the introductions and notes of the editions cited above, and Ralph S. Walker, "Ben Jonson's *Discoveries:* A New Analysis," *E&S,* New Series, V (1952); Frank B. Fieler, "The Impact of Bacon and the New Science upon Jonson's Critical Thought in *Timber,*" *RenP,* (1958-60); and Daniel G. Calder, "The Meaning of 'Imitation' in Jonson's *Discoveries,*" *Neuphilologische Mitteilungen,* LXX (1969).

Timon of Athens. A tragedy by William SHAKESPEARE written in 1607 or 1608 and first printed in the 1623 Folio. Part of the story Shakespeare derived from Sir Thomas North's translation of Plutarch's *Lives of the Noble Grecians and Romans* (1579), the rest from an anonymous play, *Timon,* written between 1581 and 1590 and first printed by Alexander Dyce for the Shakespeare Society in 1842. Shakespeare may also have consulted Lucian's dialogue *Timon Misanthropus* in a Latin or French translation.

Having squandered a fortune by his generosity and liberality, Timon turns to his rich Athenian friends for assistance and is contemptuously spurned. Enraged, he invites a large group of his former friends and hangers-on to a feast, at which he serves nothing but warm water and curses. Afterward he leaves the city and lives as a hermit in a cave. One day while digging for roots, he uncovers a vast treasure. Now rich again, Timon cynically gives gold to thieves, whom he praises for their sincerity, and to his devoted servant Flavius, whom he declares to be the only honest man in the world. He also bestows money on Alcibiades, a rebellious general returned from exile, and urges him to burn Athens and destroy its inhabitants. When some Athenian senators appeal to the ailing Timon for aid against Alcibiades, Timon advises them to hang themselves. At the gates of Athens, Alcibiades promises to spare all except those who have personally offended him. As this agreement is reached, word comes to Athens that Timon has died in his cave and been buried by the sea in a tomb inscribed: "Here lie I, Timon; who, alive, all living men did hate."

In *William Shakespeare: A Study of Facts and Problems,* R. W. Chambers contends that *Timon of Athens* represents an unfinished play added to the 1623 Folio from Shakespeare's "foul papers," and the early text certainly contains enough amorphous lines, mixed rhyme and blank verse, and general unevenness to suggest a rough draft. The eminent critic Sir Walter Raleigh suggested, rather unconvincingly, that *Timon* is an early draft of *King Lear,* and the style does in fact resemble that of the later tragedies in some of its dialogue. Timon's ravings echo on occasion Lear's mad speeches, and Timon's execrations against Athens and all humanity (IV, *i,* 1-40; IV, *iii,* 1-43) resemble Coriolanus' curses on Rome (III, *iii,* 120-35). Nevertheless, *Timon* is totally lacking in the complex characterizations, thoughtful philosophy, and artful design of Shakespeare's later tragedies such as *Antony and Cleopatra, King Lear,* and *Coriolanus.*

Coleridge described *Timon* as "A *Lear* of the satirical drama," and a main problem of the play is just this uncertain vacillation between satire and tragedy, for its titular hero can be seen as being either a great man of flawed virtue who, like Lear, is "more sinned against than sinning," or as himself an object of satire, a mean and twisted prodigal blaming others for his folly. Most critics incline to the second view, for Timon is a character of little stature or consciousness, and at the end of the play he expresses no more awareness of his true situation than at the beginning. Edward Dowden and other critics have attempted to explain the incoherent pessimism of *Timon* as being the heart-felt expression of some great calamity or disillusionment that occurred to Shakespeare during the period he wrote the play. Yet the character of the railing misanthrope was well established on the Elizabethan stage, and Shakespeare employs the type in such characters as Jaques in *As You Like It* and Thersites in *Troilus and Cressida.* Perhaps *Timon* represents Shakespeare's unsuccessful effort to elevate this familiar type to the stature of a tragic hero.

A standard text is the New Cambridge edition, ed. J. Dover Wilson and J. C. Maxwell

(1957). Important commentaries are by G. Wilson Knight, *Wheel of Fire* (1930), and O. J. Campbell, *Shakespeare's Satire* (1943). Francelia Butler gives a history of the criticism of the play in *The Strange Critical Fortunes of Shakespeare's Timon of Athens* (1966); sources are considered by E. A. J. Honigmann, "*Timon of Athens*," *SQ*, XII (1961). For other commentary, see Willard Farnham, *Shakespeare's Tragic Frontier* (1950); G. Wilson Knight, "*Timon of Athens* and Its Dramatic Descendants," *REL*, II (1961); L. C. Knights, "*Timon of Athens*," in *The Morality of Art: Essays Presented to G. Wilson Knight by His Colleagues and Friends*, ed. D. W. Jefferson (1969); and Anne Lancashire, "*Timon of Athens:* Shakespeare's Dr. Faustus," *SQ*. XXI (1970).

'Tis Pity She's a Whore. A tragedy by John FORD. It was probably written sometime between 1629 and 1633, and was first published in 1633. A major influence on Ford's play was an Italian drama of incest by Sperone Speroni, *Canace é Macareo* (1546), and perhaps the real-life trial in 1631 of Sir Giles Allington, convicted of marrying the daughter of his half-sister.

In Parma the young Giovanni secretly harbors a passion for his beautiful sister Annabella. In spite of the rigorous moralizing of his tutor, Friar Bonaventura, the proud and headstrong youth confesses his love to her. Although horrified by his disclosure, she reveals that she shares his illicit passion. After exchanging vows of love, the brother and sister consummate their relationship.

Meanwhile Annabella is beset by legitimate suitors. Especially competitive are Soranzo and Grimaldi, who fight and plot bitterly to gain advantage in the suit. There is also the half-wit suitor Bergetto, whose only qualification is that he is the nephew of Donado, a close friend of Annabella's father, Florio. Soranzo's suit is impeded by a former affair with a married woman, Hippolita, who, believing her husband Richardetto, to be dead, now seeks to marry Soranzo. When Soranzo spurns her in hopes of marrying Annabella, Hippolita plots with Vasques, Soranzo's servant, to get revenge. Unknown to any of the others, however, Richardetto is not really dead but is in Parma disguised as a physician. He waits for the propitious moment to punish Soranzo for making him a cuckold.

After both Florio and Donado have dismissed the imbecile Bergetto as an impossible choice, Soranzo is chosen as a suitable husband for Annabella. When Annabella begins to experience nausea as a result of being made pregnant by Giovanni, the disguised Richardetto prescribes marriage as a remedy for her "maidenly ills." Richardetto also gives Grimaldi poison to use against his rival Soranzo. Tipping his sword with the poison, Grimaldi strikes out in the dark and kills Bergetto, who had bungled into the ambush set for Soranzo. Seeking refuge at the cardinal's house, Grimaldi admits the murder to Donado, Florio, Richardetto, and the arresting officers, but is protected by the cardinal on grounds that Grimaldi is a Roman of noble blood. The arresting party departs in disgust at this patent contempt for justice.

At the wedding feast of Soranzo and Annabella, the surly Giovanni burns with jealousy, but his anger goes unnoticed as Hippolita arrives disguised with several masked ladies to perform an entertainment in honor of the bride and groom. When Hippolita calls for wine to make a toast, the treacherous Vasques slips her the poisoned cup intended for Soranzo. Hippolita dies cursing the marriage, and Friar Bonaventura expresses his fear that her death is a sinister omen of evil.

Soon after the wedding, Soranzo discovers Annabella's pregnant condition and furiously demands to know the father. The wily Vasques convinces Soranzo to treat Annabella with kindness until he, Vasques, can ferret out the culprit. Putana, Annabella's duenna, is tricked into revealing the father to Vasques, who has the simple woman carried off and blinded.

Meanwhile Annabella writhes with guilt for her transgression, seeks penance from Friar Bonaventura, and pleads with her brother to repent. Giovanni receives a letter from Annabella informing him that their incestuous love has been discovered, but he refuses to believe it. Soon afterward he accepts an invitation to Soranzo's birthday feast in spite of the friar's warning not to attend. Realizing the approach of disaster, the friar flees from Parma.

At Soranzo's feast Giovanni suddenly emerges from his sister's bedchamber with her heart on his dagger. To the horrified company he reveals his incestuous love and defies their indignation. His father dies of shock, Soranzo falls mortally wounded in the ensuing fight, and Giovanni is stabbed by Vasques and his band of cutthroats. The haughty Giovanni dies still unrepentant and defiant.

'Tis Pity treats its delicate subject of incest with rare sensitivity and understanding. The illicit lovers are neither vicious nor monstrous; indeed, their solemn and idealistic union expresses a beauty not to be found in the crass relationships of other lovers such as the vindictive Hippolita, the hypocritical Soranzo, or the clownish Bergetto. The "pity" of the title points to the tragic waste of beauty, exalted passion, and idealism represented by two sinful lovers viewed against the background of society's routine cruelty and banal corruption. Of the venal society, *'Tis Pity* takes an almost satirical perspective, an unambivalent moral view; the lawless lovers, in contrast, are portrayed compassionately. Without approving of their folly, Ford shows them to be tragically wasted and hence worthy of our tears.

The best recent editions are by Brian Morris in the New Mermaid series (1969) and N. W. Bawcutt for the Regents Renaissance Drama series (1970). One of the few Jacobean plays still frequently performed, its stage history to modern times is described by M. Joan Sargeaunt, *John Ford* (1935). The influence of Robert Burton's *Anatomy of Melancholy* on *'Tis Pity* and other plays by Ford is treated by S. Blaine Ewing, *Burtonian Melancholy in the Plays of John Ford* (1940). Distinguished critical studies include G. F. Sensabaugh, *The Tragic Muse of John Ford* (1944); Clifford Leech, *John Ford and the Drama of His Time* (1957); Donald K. Anderson, "The Heart and the Banquet: Imagery in Ford's *'Tis Pity* and *The Broken Heart,*" *SEL,* II (1962); and Kenneth A. Requa, "Music in the Ear: Giovanni as Tragic Hero in Ford's *'Tis Pity She's A Whore,*" *PLL,* VII (1971).

Titus Andronicus. A tragedy by William SHAKESPEARE, written in 1593-94 and first printed in the 1623 Folio. Several sources have been suggested: the Philomela legend in Ovid's *Metamorphoses,* Book VI, Seneca's *Thyestes,* and a nonextant chapbook entered in the Stationers' Register in 1594.

The Roman general Titus Andronicus and his four sons return to Rome after long warfare with their prisoners, Tamora, queen of the Goths, her Moorish lover Aaron, and her three sons, Alarbus, Demetrius, and Chiron. Despite Tamora's pleas for mercy. Titus executes Alarbus to appease the souls of the Andronici killed in the wars. Soon afterward the vacant imperial throne is offered to Titus, who refuses it in favor of Saturninus, son of the deceased emperor, to whom Titus betroths his daughter Lavinia. Another competitor for the crown, Saturninus' brother Bassianus, formerly affianced to Lavinia, abducts her with the aid of her brothers. When Mutius, one of Titus' sons, tries to prevent his father from pursuing the abductors, Titus kills him. Saturninus, falsely suspecting that Titus has arranged the abduction, conspires with Tamora in seeking revenge against the Andronici.

At Aaron's suggestion, Tamora's sons kill Bassianus and ravish Lavinia, cutting off her tongue and hands to prevent her from testifying against them. They also convince Saturninus that Titus' sons are guilty of murdering Bassianus; two of Titus' sons are condemned to death, a third banished. Aaron tells Titus that the emperor will spare the sons if they will cut off their hands as a token of submission, whereupon Titus has Aaron lop off his hand instead. When Titus' hand and the heads of his treacherously executed sons are returned to him, Titus swears revenge against his enemies.

Discovering from Lavinia the real culprits in her mutilation and in Bassianus' murder, Titus sues to the court for justice, but Saturninus is even more irritated by Titus' apparently demented ravings than he is concerned with justice; Saturninus is also distracted by news that Lucius, Titus' son and a claimant to the throne, is marching on Rome with an army of Goths. Disguised as Revenge, Tamora appears to Titus with her two sons, dressed as Murder and Rape, and Titus, throwing off his feigned insanity, cuts her sons' throats while Lavinia holds a basin in her stumps to catch the blood.

At a banquet for Lucius and the emperor, Titus serves up Tamora's sons to his guests, reveals what they have eaten, kills Lavinia to end her shame, and stabs Tamora. Saturninus, in turn, kills Titus and is himself slain by Lucius. The treacherous Aaron is condemned to death by starvation, Tamora's body thrown to the vultures, and Lucius proclaimed emperor of Rome.

Although Senecan to the core, *Titus Andronicus* owes less to the Roman dramatist than to Thomas Kyd and Christopher Marlowe, whose Senecan adaptations were drawing huge audiences to the popular theaters. The extravagant characterizations and carefully staged horrors are obviously derivative of Kyd's *The Spanish*

Tragedy, and Shakespeare's Machiavellian Aaron descends directly from Marlowe's monstrous Barabas in *The Jew of Malta.* This earliest extant tragedy of Shakespeare's is purest Senecan brew, a heady concoction of real and feigned insanity, ghastly mutilations, barbaric revenge, awesome villainies, and titanic bombast and rant. Many scenes are as farcical as *The Comedy of Errors,* as when Lavinia departs from the stage with her father's hand in her teeth because she is without hands, or when Tamora and her sons appear in the roles of Revenge, Murder, and Rape. Most modern critics view the play with such distaste that they would prefer to assign it to another dramatist, but as Jonson testily observed in his induction to *Bartholomew Fair,* Shakespeare's play vied with *The Spanish Tragedy* as a favorite of Elizabethan audiences "these five-and-twenty or thirty years." In retrospect, Senecan tragedy appears to have been as much a bloody ritual as a play in any ordinary sense. *Titus Andronicus,* for better or worse, represents that ritual in its purest form (see SENECAN TRAGEDY).

An excellent modern text is the new Arden edition, ed. J. C. Maxwell (1953). The play is discussed by H. B. Charlton, *Shakespearean Tragedy* (1948), H. T. Price, *Construction in Shakespeare* (1951); R. F. Hill, "The Composition of *Titus Andronicus,*" *ShakS,* X (1957); and Jack E. Reese, "The Formalization of Horror in *Titus Andronicus*" *SQ,* XXI (1970).

Tottel's Miscellany. Originally entitled *A Book of Songs and Sonnets,* this famous collection of verse was published by Richard Tottel in 1557. See MISCELLANIES, POETICAL.

Tourneur, Cyril (c. 1575-1626). Dramatist and poet. Except that he was the author of an obscure verse allegory, *The Transformed Metamorphosis* (1600), and THE ATHEIST'S TRAGEDY (1611), little is known for certain of Tourneur's life and literary activities. THE REVENGER'S TRAGEDY, published anonymously in 1607, is attributed to Tourneur on the strength of tradition rather than indisputable evidence, and some scholars assign the play to Thomas Middleton. In 1611 there was entered to Tourneur in the Stationers' Register a play called *The Nobleman,* apparently never published but acted by the King's Men in 1612. In 1613 Tourneur, Thomas Heywood, and John Webster (all composing plays for the King's Men at the time) wrote *Three Elegies on the Most Lamented Death of Prince Henry.* The same year Robert Daborne commissioned Tourneur to write one act of a play called *The Arraignment of London,* but this, too, was never printed.

Tourneur's "Funeral Poem upon the Death of ...Sir Francis Vere" connects the dramatist with service abroad. Vere was lieutenant governor of the fortress of Brill in Holland, a position previously held by one "Richard Turnor," possibly the author's father. Tourneur is known to have acted as a courier to Brussels in 1613 and to have received a pension for services to the Dutch. In 1625 he accompanied Sir Edward Cecil as personal secretary on an unsuccessful expedition against Cádiz. On the voyage Tourneur fell sick and was put ashore at Kinsale, Ireland, where he died several weeks later.

The two plays on which Tourneur's reputation rests are almost parodies of elements of Elizabethan revenge tragedy—Machiavellian villainy, mutilations and perversities, unspeakable cruelties and calculated horrors. Although Tourneur lacked Webster's poetic facility, he resembles Webster in his tendency to concentrate imagery patterns powerfully suggestive of sexual depravity, animal ferocity, or total moral corruption. In *The Revenger's Tragedy* Vindice carries with him the skull of his murdered mistress; like D'Amville, the atheist in *The Atheist's Tragedy,* Vindice is so macabre an exaggeration of earlier villains by Marlowe, Kyd, and Marston as to appear strikingly original.

The standard edition of Tourneur's plays is *The Works,* ed. Allardyce Nicoll (1930; repr. 1963). The most exhaustive critical study is by Peter B. Murray, *A Study of Cyril Tourneur* (1964), which contains an extensive bibliography. See also Fredson Bowers, *Elizabethan Revenge Tragedy 1587-1642* (rev. ed., 1959), and Alvin Kernan, *The Cankered Muse* (1959). There is a Concise Bibliography by S.A. Tannenbaum (1946), updated in "Cyril Tourneur (1945-65)," ed. Dennis Donovan, in *Elizabethan Bibliographies Supplements,* II (1967).

Toxophilus. See ASCHAM, ROGER.

tragicomedy. A play that presents in its plot and characters certain effects more suitable to tragedy and yet concludes happily. The tone suggests a serious theme (regicide, revenge, etc.), and the action leads toward a tragic denouement that is suddenly reversed by an unexpected turn of events—the throwing off of a disguise, the discovery of a lost son or daughter, the timely arrival of a crucial character, or, perhaps, the sudden conversion of a villain. Beaumont and Fletcher's many tragicomedies established a vogue that reached its peak in the 1630s, and John FLETCHER's epistle to his *Faithful Shepherdess* (c. 1610) accurately defines the genre: "A tragi-comedy is not so called in respect of mirth and killing, but in respect it wants deaths, which is enough to make it no tragedy; yet brings some near it, which is enough to make it no comedy; which must be a representation of familiar people with such kind of trouble as no life be questioned; so that a god is as lawful in this [tragicomedy] as in a tragedy, and mean people as in a comedy."

Fletcher's definition agrees essentially with that set forth by Giovanni Battista Guarini, the author of the famous pastoral *Il pastor fido,* in *Il compendio della poesia tragicomica* (*Compendium of Tragicomic Poetry* [1599]): "He who composes tragicomedy takes from tragedy its great persons but not its action, its verisimilar plot but not its true one, its movement of the feelings but not its disturbance of them, its pleasure but not its sadness, its danger but not its death..."

Tragicomedy not only juxtaposes comedy and tragedy, noble and base characters (often to contrast exalted and gross love), but combines the most exaggerated contrasts of heroism and villainy with sudden, unmotivated turns of action, episodic and sensational events, and situations of charged emotions that invite surprising and unpredictable consequences. Wars or rebellions provide the usual background for courtly intrigues, jealousies, usurpations, treachery, and self-sacrifice. The prototype of the genre is Beaumont and Fletcher's *Philaster; or Love Lies A-Bleeding,* produced with great success in 1611. Shakespeare's *Measure for Measure, Cymbeline,* and *The Winter's Tale* also conform largely to the type. Under the influence of Sir William DAVENANT and John Dryden, tragicomedy evolved into heroic drama during the Restoration period.

Two studies of the classical origins and later development of the genre are by F. H. Ristine, *English Tragicomedy* (1910), and Marvin Herrick, *Tragicomedy: Its Origin and Development in Italy, France, and England* (1955).

Traherne, Thomas (1637-39?-1674). Poet. Little is known of Traherne's life, and his poetry and prose were not discovered until the twentieth century. Owing to the research of Gladys Wade, it is now known that Traherne was born between 1637 and 1639, the son of a Hereford shoemaker who seems to have found the friends or resources to send his son to Brasenose College, Oxford, in 1652. Traherne graduated B.A. in 1656 and was given a country parish in 1657 at Credenhill, Herefordshire, through the influence of the dowager countess of Kent. The appointment could have been little more than a sinecure, for while holding the post Traherne was able to earn an M.A. (1661) and B.D. (1669) from Oxford. Sometime later he became chaplain to Sir Orlando Bridgeman, the lord keeper, and when Bridgeman was discharged from office in 1672 Traherne accompanied him into retirement in Teddington, where Traherne was buried in 1674.

A. B. Grosart discovered Traherne's manuscripts in a London bookstore in 1896 and assumed them to be works by Henry Vaughan. Before Grosart's death, he turned the manuscripts over to Bertram Dobell, who identified them as Traherne's and published the poems in 1903 and the prose work *Centuries of Meditations* in 1908. In 1910 H. I. Bell edited Traherne's *Poems of Felicity* from manuscripts in the British Museum, altering Dobell's text and printing thirty-eight new poems by Traherne and two by Traherne's brother Philip. The only work Traherne published during his lifetime was *Roman Forgeries* (1673). His *Christian Ethics* (1675) and *A Serious and Pathetical Contemplation of the Mercies of God* (1699) appeared posthumously, the latter not identified as being by Traherne until Dobell's research in the twentieth century. It contains Southwell's free-verse series of poems entitled "Thanksgivings."

Traherne's poems, inspired by the religious verse of George HERBERT, are concerned chiefly with the Christian theme of felicity—how joy in life and God is lost and then reclaimed. Even to a greater extent than Herbert's, Traherne's poetry is openly evangelical; he brings the good news of the Gospels to the hearts of his readers and tells how men can be reborn by love. In "Wonder" the child comes into the world like Wordsworth's "best philosopher" and joyous sage, but earthly concerns soon seal his senses, stifle his spontaneity, and close his mind to creation's wonders. "How like an angel down came I!" Traherne exclaims, "How bright are all things here!" The child soon learns, like Wordsworth's youth, to imitate the glitter of other men's values. In "Wonder" Traherne's dialectics are startlingly similar to those of Vaughan and Blake:

Proprieties themselves were mine,
And hedges ornaments;
Walls, boxes, coffers, and their rich contents
Did not divide my joys, but all combine.
Clothes, ribbons, jewels, laces, I esteem'd
My joys by others worn;
For me they all to wear them seem'd
When I was born.

The child comes into the world to find it Eden; the wisdom of the man is in reclaiming the ecstasy and wonder of the child. The miraculous powers of appreciation are celebrated in the "The Salutation":

From dust I rise,
And out of nothing now awake;
These brighter regions which salute mine eyes,
A gift from God I take:
The earth, the seas, the light, the lofty skies,
The sun and stars are mine; if those I prize.

Like Herbert, Traherne works in a variety of meters, not always successfully. His poems have vigor, sincerity, and frequent sparkle; yet they lack the ingenuity of Herbert's or the clear confidence of Vaughan's. Traherne's tone is so uniformly zealous as to become flat, and almost every stanza contains a stumbling accent or lapse of precision. Nevertheless, his poetry remains one of the great discoveries of the twentieth century, adding one more link in the chain of religious verse on childhood and innocence from Herbert and Vaughan to Blake and Wordsworth.

Traherne's prose is, in many ways, more "poetic" than his verse. His *Centuries of Meditations* consists of brief reflections on the same themes of wonder and joyous discovery as in the poems, but the prose is often more passionate, rich in suggestion, direct and forceful:

> The first Light which shined in my infancy in its primitive and innocent clarity was totally eclipsed; insomuch that I was fain to learn all again. If you ask me, "How was it eclipsed?" Truly, by the customs and manners of men, which like the contrary winds blew it out; by an innumerable company of other objects—rude, vulgar, and worthless things that like so many loads of earth and dung did overwhelm and bury it; by the impetuous torrent of wrong desires in all others whom I saw or knew that carried me away and alienated me from it; by a whole sea of other matters and concernments that covered and drowned it; finally, by the evil influence of a bad education that did not foster and cherish it...

Traherne's complete works in poetry and prose have been edited by Gladys Wade (rev. ed., 1932), who also wrote the definitive biography, *Thomas Traherne: A Critical Biography* (1944), which contains a bibliography of criticism compiled by R. A. Parker. Additional biographical material is in Angela Russell, "The Life of Thomas Traherne," *RES,* VI (1955). An edition equal to Wade's in importance—because there are great differences among editors regarding the text of Traherne's poems—is *Thomas Traherne's Centuries, Poems, and Thanksgivings,* ed. H. M. Margoliouth, 2 vols. (1958). Traherne's *Meditations on the Six Days of the Creation* has been edited by G. R. Guffey (1966), and *Christian Ethics* by Carol L. Marks (1968). Anne Ridler has edited *Poems, Centuries, and Three Thanksgivings* in the Oxford Standard Authors series (1966). For criticism, see Louis Martz, *The Paradise Within: Studies in Vaughan, Traherne, and Milton* (1964); K. W. Salter, *Thomas Traherne: Mystic and Poet* (1964); A. L. Clements, *The Mystical Poetry of Thomas Traherne* (1969); Alison J. Sherrington, *Mystical Symbolism in the Poetry of Thomas Traherne* (1970); and Stanley N. Stewart, *The Expanded Voice: The Art of Thomas Traherne* (1970). For bibliographies, see Theodore Spencer and Mark Van Doren, *Studies in Metaphysical Poetry* (1939); A. L. Clements, "Thomas Traherne: A Chronological Bibliography," *LC,* XXXV (1969); Edward E. Samaha, Jr., "Richard Crashaw and Thomas Traherne: A Bibliography, 1938-66," *SCN,* XXVII (1969); and "Traherne and the Seventeenth-century English Platonists (1900-1966)," ed. G. R. Guffey, *Elizabethan Bibliographies Supplements,* XI (1969).

Traitor, The. A tragedy by James SHIRLEY, written around 1631 and first published in 1635. Shirley's source may have been the twelfth novel of Marguerite of Navarre's

Heptameron, or perhaps some little-known Florentine history. *The Traitor* was falsely attributed to an obscure Jesuit who died in Newgate Prison, but the play is now known to be Shirley's.

The scene is Florence toward the end of the fifteenth century. The "traitor" of the title is Lorenzo, Machiavellian kinsman of the young Alexander, duke of Florence, whom Lorenzo had helped bring to power and now plots to unseat under the pretext of establishing a free republic. When the duke expresses desire for the beautiful Amidea, betrothed to Pisano, Lorenzo schemes to appease the duke's lust and also provoke the wrath of Amidea's rash and violent brother, Sciarrha. As Sciarrha and his brother Florio test their sister's ability to resist the duke's offers, Pisano arrives to announce that he no longer loves Amidea but is now enamored of Oriana, his friend Cosmo's fiancée. Actually, the villainous Lorenzo had planted his agent Petruchio in Pisano's house in order to persuade Pisano to break the engagement with Amidea so that she will be free to be enjoyed by the duke. For her part, Oriana remains loyal to Cosmo and rejects Pisano as a suitor.

To prevent the duke from violating their sister, Sciarrha and Florio invite him to a masque showing the evils of treachery, then lure him into Amidea's bedchamber, where they plan to murder him. When Amidea confronts the duke with her decision to seek death rather than dishonor, the duke repents of his passion and promises to reform, whereupon the brothers, who have been hiding nearby, congratulate the duke on his virtue and vow to discover the instigator of this confrontation between them and the duke.

When his plot against the duke's life miscarries, Lorenzo begins to fan anew the young man's lust for Amidea and to encourage Sciarrha's resentment of Pisano for jilting her. When Pisano refuses to answer Sciarrha's angry challenge, Sciarrha cuts him down in cold blood as Lorenzo watches. Faced with the prospect of execution for murder, Sciarrha finally agrees to bring his sister to the duke's bed. At Amidea's insistence, however, Sciarrha kills her and places her body in the bed. After kissing her cold lips, the duke realizes she is dead and cries out in anguish. At this point Lorenzo and Petruchio stab the duke to death and, hoping to lay the blame for the murder on Sciarrha, place his body in bed beside Amidea's. Sciarrha turns on Lorenzo, kills him, and receives a mortal wound himself. Cosmo marries Oriana and succeeds as ruler of Florence.

Shirley's *The Traitor* is an anachronistic tragedy of blood and bombast harking back to the Senecan plays of Kyd, Marlowe, and Shakespeare (see SENECAN TRAGEDY). Like Shirley's other great tragedy of revenge, THE CARDINAL, this one contains most of the Elizabethan ingredients of the genre—violent passions and illicit loves, murder, and Machiavellian villainy. Although some of the dramatic situations echo the Elizabethan masters, Shirley's considerable poetic skills are entirely his own. For almost a century after its first performances by Queen Henrietta's Men at the Phoenix in the early 1630s, *The Traitor* continued to be greeted as one of the world's greatest tragedies. John Genest records performances as late as 1704 (*Some Account of the English Stage from 1660 to 1830,* 10 vols, II [1832]).

The Traitor is in *The Dramatic Works and Poems,* ed. William Gifford and Alexander Dyce, 6 vols. (1833). A more recent edition in paperback is that by John Stewart Carter for the Regents Renaissance Drama series (1971). Critical commentaries include those by R. S. Forsythe, *The Relations of Shirley's Plays to the Elizabethan Drama* (1914); Arthur Nason, *James Shirley, Dramatist* (1915), and A. P. Riemer, "A Source for Shirley's *The Traitor,*" *RES,* XIV (1963).

translations. The flood of English translations from Greek, Latin, Italian, French, and Spanish sources that began toward the end of Henry VIII's reign and continued unabated into the seventeenth century was chiefly motivated by curiosity and love of adventure, patriotism, and practicality. Like the sea adventurers Drake and Frobisher, Elizabethan translators were discoverers of new worlds; to render into English the works of Castiglione or Montaigne was to explores strange seas, exploit exotic riches, and plant the English flag on alien soil. The emotional and intellectual effects of these translations, like those of the New World explorations, was to give Englishmen new ideas and perspectives. Like most world travelers, however, the English translators brought their own cultural values with them and did not hesitate to impose them on the foreigners they aspired to conquer. Sir

Thomas North's Greeks and Romans wear Elizabethan doublets and hose and speak in the idiom and cadences of Elizabethan gentlemen; Arthur Golding's Ovid is converted from joyous pagan to profoundly allegorical Calvinist, and Richard Stanyhurst's Dido is not so much a love-crazed Carthaginian queen as a jilted English girl expressing her indignation in colloquial Elizabethan: "Shall a stranger give me the slampam?"

As John Florio noted of his own translation of Montaigne, Elizabethan translators gave their readers "meat without sauce," or, more accurately, the original author's meat simmered in the translator's own spice and garnish. Most Elizabethan translators were vaguely aware of their obligation to render the spirit as well as the letter of the original; they frequently cited Horace's dictum on translation in *Ars poetica: Qui quae desperat nitescere posse, relinquit* ("He who despairs of excelling, leave off"). George Chapman's statement of the translator's role in his preface to the translation of Homer is equally cogent and objective: "The work of a skillful and worthy translator is to observe the sentences, figures, and forms of speech proposed in his author, his true sense and height, and to adorn them with figures and forms of oration fitted to the original in the same tongue to which they were translated."

Yet few Elizabethan translators, including Chapman, paid any heed to this statement or to Horace's caveat. Instead, they consistently changed their original authors into mirrors of themselves, bringing the art of translation to the very boundaries of ingenuous plagiarism, and yet a plagiarism comparable to that prized by Dryden in describing Jonson: "He invades authors like a monarch, and what would be theft in other poets, is only victory in him." This disregard of the Elizabethan translators for the style and spirit of the original can be attributed to the fact that few translators were scholars, or even familiar with the original languages of their authors. George Gascoigne and Francis Kinwelmarsh translated Euripides' *Phoenissae* from an Italian version; Sir Thomas North read Plutarch in the French translation of Jacques Amyot; and Petrarch's sonnets were frequently translated from versions by French poets.

In this great period of intellectual discovery many of the most fertile lands nevertheless remained *terra incognita* to the English Renaissance translators. Plato, whose influence was omnipresent *via* Latin, French, and Italian, was not translated into English until well into the seventeenth century. Only one text of Aristotle's came to light, the *Nichomachean Ethics,* poorly rendered into English from Italian by John Wilkinson in 1547. The Greek tragedians, Aeschylus, Sophocles, and Euripides, were—curiously enough in this great age of drama—totally neglected except for the single adaptation of Euripides' *Phoenissae* as the tragedy *Jocasta* (1566) by Gascoigne and Kinwelmarsh. Only one translation of Plautus appeared in the Elizabethan period, William Warner's version of *Menaechmi* (1595), which gave Shakespeare some details for his *A Comedy of Errors.*

The inferior Roman dramatist Seneca, on the other hand, was frequently translated, doubtless because his Latin made him much more accessible to Elizabethans than were the Greek tragedians (See SENECAN TRAGEDY). Moreover, Seneca's Stoicism became very popular in schools and universities. Robert Whittington rendered Seneca's colloquies as *A Dialogue Between Sensuality and Reason* and *The Remedies Against All Casual Chances* in 1547; Arthur Golding did a version of Seneca's *De Beneficiis* as *The Work . . . Concerning Benefiting* in 1578; and Thomas Lodge translated most of Seneca's prose works in 1614. Philemon Holland, an indefatigable translator of Roman historians, did a version of Plutarch's popular *Moralia* in 1603.

The most prestigious of the classical writers were Homer, Vergil, and Ovid. The Scottish writer Gawin Douglas translated the complete *Aeneid* as early as 1512, but his literal and drab version attracted little interest. More notable is the earl of Surrey's version, the first English translation in the Renaissance of a great classic and the first specimen of blank verse in the English language. Surrey's work first appeared in an edition of Book IV printed by William Owen (or Awen) in 1554; Books II and IV were published by Richard Tottel as *Certain Books of Virgil's Aeneid* (1557). Surrey's translation, in unrhymed decasyllables, was probably written as early as 1538-40. The next of Vergil's translators was Thomas Phaer, who did the first seven books in jogging heptameters, or "fourteeners" (1558), then did books eight and nine and most of ten (1562). In 1573 Thomas Twyne completed Phaer's

English version of the *Aeneid,* and included in a later edition the apocryphal but ever-popular "thirteenth book" of the Italian humanist Mapheus Vegius (1584). Phaer's sing-song ballad measure often slips from mediocrity to downright doggerel, yet his work enjoyed sole authority until Richard STANYHURST'S immensely influential translation of the first four books in hexameters (1582). Stanyhurst's Vergil received the praise of Gabriel Harvey as being a triumphant experiment in transplanting the quantitative prosody and hexameters of Vergil and Ovid to native English soil, but Thomas Nashe's criticism that "this clime of ours he cannot thrive in" represents a superior judgment. Stanyhurst's limping hexameters are unbearably tedious, and his coined words, slangy diction, and excessive alliteration are comically grotesque, as the following passage from Book II illustrates:

The wavering commons in kim-kam sects are hailed.
First, then, among others, with no small company guarded,
Laocoon, storming from princely castle, is hast'ning
And afar off bellowing, "What fond, fantastical, harebrain
Madness hath enchanted your wits, you townsmen unhappy?
Ween you, blind hoddypecks, the Greekish navy returned?
Or that their presents want craft? Is subtle Ulysses
So soon forgotten? My life for an halfpenny, Trojans . . .

The works of Homer enjoyed more skillful sponsorship than Vergil's. Before Chapman's much-praised translation of Homer, little was done in spite of Homer's towering prestige. Thomas Purfoote produced a pedestrian segment, *The Crown of Homer's Works, the Battle of the Frogs and Mice* (1579), and Arthur Hall translated in doggerel fourteeners ten books of the *Iliad* from the French (1581). These efforts were dwarfed by Chapman's version—"the work that I was born to do," he said. Working from the original Greek, which he collated with Italian and French versions, Chapman completed the whole of the *Iliad* in 1612, the *Odyssey* in 1614. In 1616 both epics appeared in an elaborate, handsome edition, *The Whole Works of Homer,* dedicated to Prince Henry, son of James I. Although Chapman's *Iliad* is cast in rhyming fourteeners, a stubborn and difficult measure, his sheer energy and considerable poetic skill justify Keats's famous praise. The *Odyssey,* in pentameter couplets, speaks out even more "loud and bold" than does the *Iliad,* as in the famous passage of the sirens:

Come here, thou worthy of a world of praise,
That dost so high the Grecian glory raise!
Ulysses, stay thy ship! and that song hear
That none passed ever but it bent his ear,
But left him ravished, and instructed more
By us than any ever heard before.

Chapman's titanic achievement, though not generally acknowledged until the romantic period, is now thoroughly appreciated. If Chapman has faults, they are those shared by most great Elizabethan translators—the imposition of his own style and even his own ideas on the original. He requires his Homeric heroes to talk like Stoic philosophers, interlards the text with his own conceits, and attributes to Homer his own conception of poetry as a form of arcane symbolism. "Poesy is the flower of the sun and disdains to open to the eye of a candle," he writes in his "Preface to the Reader." "So kings hide their treasures and counsels from the vulgar." If Chapman errs, it is in his firm conviction that Homer shared this elitist conception of poetry.

George Turberville rendered Ovid's *Heroides* as *Heroical Epistles* in 1567, and in 1569 Thomas Underdowne produced a fragment, *Invective Against Ibis.* While still at Cambridge Marlowe did Ovid's *Amores* as *All Ovid's Elegies,* and Chapman produced a very broad and characteristically obscure version of Ovid's erotica in *Ovid's Banquet of Sense* (1595). Ovid's most popular work, and one that became an encyclopedia of mythology for Renaissance writers from Spenser to Milton, was the *Metamorphoses,* the first four books of which were translated by Arthur Golding in 1565, the completed version of fifteen books in 1567 with a dedication to Robert Dudley, earl of Leicester. Golding's translation in rhyming heptameters presents Ovid's witty and urbane classic with often bizarre solemnity, yet Golding's almost prosaic clarity and sustained fluency made it a convenient reference work for Shakespeare and other dramatists. Few writers have been so totally incompatible of disposition and temperament as Ovid, the cynical sophisticate, and Golding, the Puritan translator of Calvin's treatises as well as author of commentaries on the Psalms and of sermons on Galatians, Job, Ephesians, and Deuteronomy. But the erotic pagan poet and his Puritan translator were reconciled on the level of allegory, for Golding firmly believed that the *Metamorphoses* was an edifying moral derived from the Pentateuch. In his verse dedication to the earl of Leicester, Golding proclaims:

What man is he but would suppose the author of this book
The first foundation of his work from Moses' writings took?
Not only in effect he doth with *Genesis* agree,
But also in the order of creation, save that he
Makes no distinction of the days . . .

Golding's Ovid reigned supreme until the publication of George Sandys' translation in 1626.

After Homer, Seneca, Vergil, and Ovid, the classical authors most frequently translated were the Greek and Roman historians. One "B.R." (possibly Barnabe Rich) translated the first two books of Herodotus in 1584; Thomas Nicolls did Thucydides (1550); Thomas Paynell, Sallust's *Felicius, the Conspiracy of Catiline* (1557); and Antony Cope, a fragment of Livy (1544). Alexander Barclay had translated Sallust's *Jugurthan War* as early as 1520, and Thomas Heywood both *Jurgurtha* and *Catiline* in 1608. Tacitus' *Histories* and *Agricola* were translated by Sir Henry Saville (1591), his *Annals and Description of Germany* by Richard Greenway (1598). The most prolific of these translators of classical historians was the scholarly Philemon Holland with his versions of Livy's *Roman History* (1600), Pliny's *Natural History* (1601), Suetonius' *Twelve Caesars* (1606), Ammianus Marcellinus' *Roman History* (1609), and Xenophon's *Cyropaedia* (1632).

The most popular and artistic of the history translations was Sir Thomas North's rendition of Plutarch's *Lives of the Noble Grecians and Romans,* translated into English in 1579 from the great French version by Jacques Amyot (1559). An invaluable biographical source for Elizabethan dramatists, North's translation was the principal reference for Shakespeare's *Julius Caesar, Antony and Cleopatra,* and *Coriolanus,* and a contributing source for *A Midsummer Night's Dream* and *Timon of Athens.* It is small wonder that Shakespeare often borrowed word for word from North's Plutarch, for it is one of the great monuments of Tudor prose style. That North was a master of concrete and vivid English is illustrated in his description of Antony's first meeting with Cleopatra. Shakespeare followed it very closely in Enobarbus' speech beginning "The barge she sat in, like a burnished throne" (II, *ii,* 191–245):

> Therefore, when she was sent unto by divers letters, both from Antonius himself and also from his friends, she made so light of it, and mocked Antonius so much, that she disdained to set forward otherwise, but to take her barge in the river of Cydnus; the poop whereof was of gold, the sails of purple, and the oars of silver, which kept stroke in rowing after the music of flutes, hautboys, citterns, viols, and such other instruments as they played upon in the barge. And more for the person of her self, she was laid under a pavilion of cloth of gold of tissue, apparelled and attired like the goddess Venus, commonly drawn in picture: and hard by her, on either hand of her, pretty fair boys apparelled as painters do set forth god Cupid, with little fans in their hands, with which they fanned wind upon her. Her ladies and gentlewomen also, the fairest of them, were apparelled like the nymphs Nereids (which are the mermaids of the waters) and like the Graces; some steering the helm, others tending the tackle and ropes of the barge, out of the which there came a wonderful surpassing sweet savour of perfumes, that perfumed the wharf's side, pestered with innumerable multitudes of people...

Like most Elizabethan translators, North viewed history as moral allegory, and his version of Plutarch—dedicated to Queen Elizabeth—was motivated by both patriotism and piety, by the belief that no writer "teacheth so much honor, love, obedience, reverence, zeal, and devotion to princes as these Lives of Plutarch do."

The stream of Elizabethan translations not only represented a revival of interest in classical literature, but also brought the European Renaissance to England in a flood of translations from Italian, French, and Spanish masterpieces. Dante was not translated from Italian and thus remained unknown except to scholars, but other Italian writers of epics became familiar through Edward Fairfax and Richard Carew's versions of Tasso's *Gerusalemme liberata* in ottava rima (both entitled *Godfrey of Bolloigne* and printed in 1594 and 1600, respectively) and Sir John Harington's translation in eight-line stanzas of Ariosto's *Orlando Furioso* (1591), done at the request of Queen Elizabeth. Occasionally pedantic and slangy, Harington's translation was nevertheless justly admired by his contemporaries for its vividness, energy, and rhetorical conciseness:

Of dames, of knights, of arms, of love's delight,
Of courtesies, of high attempts I speak:
Then when the Moors transported all their might
On Afric seas, the force of France to break,
Drawn by the youthful heat and raging spite
Of Argramant, their king, that vow'd to wreak
The death of King Trayano (lately slain)
Upon the Roman emperor Charlemain.

An even more influential translation was William Painter's collection of 101 tales (most of them from the Italian), *The Palace of Pleasure,* published in two volumes (1566, 1567). Painter's original purpose was to present a series of stories from Livy, but the Roman writer's style proved uncongenial and Painter turned to translating erotic novellas from Boccaccio, Bandello, and Queen Margaret of Navarre. Painter's lucid style and patient concern for nuances of characterization and situation made his *Palace of Pleasure* a storehouse of sources for Elizabethan and Stuart dramatists.

Another collection of novellas is Sir Geoffrey Fenton's *Certain Tragical Discourses* (1567), consisting of thirteen tales of the Italian Matteo BANDELLO translated from the French of Boaistuau and Belleforest. Inspired by the success of Painter's rich and multifarious collection, Fenton's is limited by his puritanical restriction to tales of "chaste ladies in distress," his tedious sermonizing (not found in his sources), and his highly affected, self-conscious prose style. Nevertheless, Fenton's collection proved almost as popular as Painter's, and both works were important in introducing Elizabethans to the sophisticated narrative methods and secular values of the Italian novellas.

Perhaps the most successful Elizabethan translation from Italian was Sir Thomas HOBY'S version of Baldassare Castiglione's *Il Cortegiano,* in four books, published in 1561 (see THE COURTIER). In his dedication to Lord Hastings, Hoby declared that he intended his work for the elderly as "a pathway to the beholding and musing of the mind," to young gentlemen "to garnish their mind with moral virtues and their body with comely exercises," to ladies as "a mirror to deck and trim themselves with virtuous conditions," and to all readers in general as "a storehouse of most necessary implements for the conversation, use, and training-up of man's life with courtly demeanors..." True to the translator's intention, Castiglione's idealized portrait of the elegant conversations of noble lords and ladies at Urbino became a conduct book to Elizabethans, a guide to Renaissance eloquence and courtly deportment (see COURTESY LITERATURE). The fourth book, dominated by the rapturous dialectics of Cardinal Bembo, had an especially pervasive influence on the philosophical vocabulary of Spenser and other Elizabethan poets.

Machiavelli's influence was less direct but equally powerful. Although *Il Principe* (wr. 1513; pr. Rome, 1531) was a practical conduct book for Thomas Cromwell, Gabriel Harvey, Francis Bacon, Lord Burghley, the earl of Leicester, and others, and although the Machiavellian villain was a well-established figure on the Elizabethan stage, *Il Principe* was not translated until 1640. Machiavelli's lesser works *The Art of War* and *A Florentine History* were translated by Peter Whitehorne in 1560-62 and Thomas Bedingfield in 1595, respectively. Elizabethans did not, in fact, derive their fear and awe of Machiavelli from *Il Principe* but from a vehement attack in a book by a French Huguenot, Innocent Gentillet's *Contre-Machiavel* (France, 1576). Gentillet's hostile and distorted work, translated into English by Simon Patrick in 1602 but well known in the French version long before, helped to spread among Englishmen the bizarre impression of Machiavelli's *Il Principe* as a monstrous, atheistic, and totally amoral handbook written for the devil's disciples.

French was the foreign language best known to Elizabethans, and their translations from this tongue were both the most numerous and most faithful to the originals. John BOURCHIER, second Lord Berners, the translator of Froissart's *Chronicles,* contributed to a revival of interest in the Charlemagne romances with his version of *Huon of Bordeaux,* written about 1534, which became a primary source for Spenser and many Elizabethan dramatists. Also important was Joshua Sylvester's translation into decasyllabic couplets of Du Bartas's epic *La Semaine* as *Divine Weeks and Works* (1590-92), which influenced both Spenser and Milton.

Another major Elizabethan translation was John Florio's version (1603) of Montaigne's *Essays* and *Apology for Raymond Sebond.* Florio, a literary enterpriser of extravagant wit and inflated eloquence, felt nothing of the translator's usual humility. For him translation was an opportunity to daub at the author's canvas with his own brush. In his dedication "To the Courteous Reader" in the 1603 edition of Montaigne, he expresses his method with disarming candor: "Why, then, belike I have done by Montaigne as Terence by Menander, made good French no good English. If I have done no worse, and it be no worse taken, it is well. As he, if no poet, yet am I no thief, since I say of whom I had it, rather to imitate his and his author's negligence than any backbiters' obscure diligence. His house I set before you, perhaps without his trappings, and his meat without sauce..." Florio, author of an Italian-English lexicon, *The World of Words* (1598), was a passionate enthusiast of language, a linguistic innovator of great vitality, and he did not hesitate to convert Montaigne's lean and crisp French into an ornate English that fascinated Shakespeare, who borrowed considerably from Florio in *The Tempest* and *King Lear* and may have satirized Florio's pedantic garrulity in the character of Holofernes in *Love's Labour's Lost.*

Characteristically, English translators ignored some of the greatest French writers. A strange hiatus is Rabelais, who, like Machiavelli, was widely quoted and influential, yet not available in English until Sir Thomas Urquhart's version of the first two books of *Gargantua and Pantagruel* in 1653, the third, fourth, and final book as late as 1693. A translation of a fragment of the work, entitled *Gargantua His Prophecy,* was entered in the Stationers' Register in 1592 but, if ever published, has not survived.

Most of the great Spanish writers were translated relatively early in the Elizabethan period. Sir Thomas North translated Antonio de Guevara's *Relox des principes (Dial of Princes,* 1557), which is often cited as an early source of EUPHUISM, and the anonymous *Lazarillo de Tormes* was made available in English in 1586 by David Rowland. Cervantes' *Don Quixote,* first published in Spanish in 1605, was rendered into English (Part I, 1612; Part II, 1620) by Thomas Shelton, but unlike the Spanish original, the English version did not attract popular notice for several generations. Jorge de Montemayor's prose pastoral *Diana enamorada,* however, achieved early recognition in England. It was translated into French by Nicolas Colin (1578) and into English from Spanish by Bartholomew Young (trans. 1582; pr. 1598). Sidney may have borrowed something from Montemayor in his *Arcadia,* and Shakespeare probably consulted Young's translation for the portions of *Diana* he used in *Two Gentlemen of Verona.*

Thus the story of translations in the English Renaissance, of which only a small part can be told here, is one that touches on every aspect of English literature during the period. In retrospect, it is evident that this intellectual movement proved effective in dispelling a lingering Tudor provincialism, in broadening the scope of English consciousness and sensibilities, and in exposing Elizabethans to new ideas, new techniques, new styles of thought and expression.

Many of the translations discussed above are available in the Tudor Translations, first series, 32 vols., (1892-1903); second series, 12 vols. (1924-27). Two introductions to the subject are by C. H. Conley, *The First English Translators of the Classics* (1927), and F. O. Matthiessen, *Translation: An Elizabethan Art* (1931).

Treatise of Moral Philosophy, Containing the Sayings of the Wise, A. See BALDWIN, WILLIAM.

Tribe of Ben. See JONSON, BEN.

Trick to Catch the Old One, A. A comedy of manners by Thomas MIDDLETON, written in 1604-06 and first printed in two editions in 1608. No source is known. It was rewritten around 1622 by Philip Massinger as A NEW WAY TO PAY OLD DEBTS.

Old Pecunius Lucre, young Witgood's usurious uncle, has profited from his nephew's riotous living by lending him money at exorbitant interest, and the now impoverished wastrel plots with his common whore to regain the squandered inheritance. Witgood will take the courtesan to London as the rich "Widow Medler" and, aided by a wily friend, the Mad Host, set her up in a great house and pass her off as his fiancée. Surely, Witgood surmises, Lucre and Witgood's army of other creditors will be tricked into renewed generosity if they believe he has prospects of marrying a wealthy widow.

Witgood's stratagem works brilliantly. Lucre opens his pursestrings to help finance the courtship, delighted to see his nephew plunge even further into bankruptcy and certain that the widow will make good on all debts, and old Walkadine Hoard, Lucre's rival in avarice, begins to maneuver madly to compete for the widow's hand in marriage. Meanwhile, unknown to Lucre or her uncle, Witgood pays court to Mistress Joyce, Hoard's beautiful and prosperous niece. Unaware, of course, that Widow Medler is a prostitute, Hoard secretly marries her; when Lucre discovers Hoard's marriage, he indignantly demands compensation on grounds of the widow's breach of promise. To this charge Widow Medler stoutly maintains what nobody can deny: though falsely claiming to be rich, Witgood was actually heavily mortgaged to Lucre. In the hope that the widow will reconsider his nephew's proposal, Lucre foolishly restores Witgood's wealth and makes him his heir. Witgood then cunningly presents the widow with a fake legal action for breach of promise, a suit that Hoard—still under the illusion his wife is fabulously rich—settles out of court by paying Witgood's debts.

At his wedding dinner Hoard learns from a gleeful Lucre what Witgood revealed reluctantly only to persuade Lucre to attend the feast—that is, that Hoard has married an impoverished prostitute. Undaunted, the bride answers that she had never actually claimed to be wealthy, that all the deception was really Hoard's, and that, in any event, she is not a bad catch for an old man. Hoard resigns himself to the marriage in good humor, Lucre admits that he has been outfoxed at last, and a prosperous and reformed Witgood announces his secret betrothal to Joyce, whereupon the whole company retires to supper in celebration of the double nuptials.

Middleton's play resembles Ben Jonson's satiric comedies of London life, but refrains from expressing any of Jonson's moral rigor; for Middleton instinctively favored moral underdogs to the self-righteous majority. Thus he looks benignly on Witgood's prodigality and deceits, and finds more to praise than blame in the courtesan's clever stratagems. As in Middleton's *Michaelmas Term* and *The Honest Whore,* he makes his comedy an entertaining game in which half-dead old skinflints are outwitted by a younger generation bent on simple gratifications that affirm life in opposition to the tired old vices of avarice, hoarding, and usury. Hence there is something picaresque in Middleton's comedy that is absent from Massinger's adaptation *A New Way to Pay Old Debts,* which changes Middleton's simple knave Pecunius Lucre into the monstrous Sir Giles Overreach, a predatory villain bent on destroying the lives of decent ladies and gentlemen. Unlike Massinger, Middleton loved the seamy side of London life; he viewed civilization largely in terms of a fascinating struggle for survival among bawds, crooked barristers, coxcombs, and charlatans, with victory going inevitably not to the most moral but to the swiftest in vitality and wit. Middleton's *A Trick to Catch the Old One* represents the triumph of that comic vision.

A Trick has been edited by Charles Barber in the Fountainwell Drama series (1968) and by Robert G. Lawrence in the Regents Renaissance Drama series (1971); both contain excellent critical introductions. For additional commentary, see W. D. Dunkel, *The Dramatic Techniques of Middleton in His Comedies of London Life* (1925); T. S. Eliot, "Thomas Middleton," in *For Lancelot Andrewes* (1928); R. H. Barker, *Thomas Middleton* (1958); and Richard Levin, "The Dampit Scenes in *A Trick to Catch the Old One,*" *MLQ,* XXV (1964).

Troilus and Cressida. A play by William SHAKESPEARE, written in 1601-02 and first printed in 1609. Although Shakespeare made some use of Chaucer's *Troilus and Criseyde* and George Chapman's translation of Homer's *Iliad,* his chief sources were William Caxton's *Recuyell of the Histories of Troy* (1475), John Lydgate's *The Troy Book* (c. 1412-20), and Robert Henryson's *Testament of Cressid,* the last printed in Thynne's edition of Chaucer (1532).

Troilus, youngest son of King Priam of Troy, falls in love with Cressida, daughter of the Trojan priest Calchas, who has defected to the Greeks. The lovers consummate their relationship under the guidance of Cressida's cynical uncle Pandarus, but their brief raptures end when

Cressida is exchanged for the Trojan general Antenor. Although the lovers pledge eternal fidelity, the moment Cressida arrives in the Greek camp she strikes up a liaison with Diomedes, to whom she gives the scarf that was Troilus' love token.

Alternating with this tale of treacherous love are the military actions of the Greeks and Trojans. Proud Achilles sulks in his tent with his favorite, Patroclus, and refuses to fight until goaded into action by his envy of the clownish Ajax and by Hector's slaying of Patroclus. As the bitter malcontent Thersites reminds the audience, the noble cause of the Greeks degenerates into "wars and lechery, wars and lechery," and the shrewd Ulysses tells Agamemnon and Nestor that the failure of their cause must be attributed to their total disregard for "degree," or observance of proper political and social hierarchy. At the end of the play Achilles and his Myrmidons treacherously murder Hector when they find him helpless and unarmed, and Troilus seeks out Diomedes to gain revenge, but their encounter concludes indecisively. Shakespeare's denigration of the Greek and Trojan heroes, who are shown to be little more than vain, petty, and ignorant fools, has caused the play to be described as both "comical satire" and "tragical satire."

A major critical problem has been to establish the unity of a play so evenly divided between the argument of Mars and the theme of Venus. The love story is portrayed as being anything but ideal; Troilus is completely absorbed by a sensuality that Cressida cynically exploits to heighten her own jaded pleasure, and once separated from Troilus she slips easily into another sexual relationship. As for the war story, it is almost as sordid as the judgment of the choral character Thersites: "All the argument is a cuckold and a whore." When Hector urges the return of Helen of Troy and an end to the war because she is "not worth what she doth cost" and "Tis mad idolatry / To make the service greater than the god," Troilus sophistically argues that all values, including courage and honor, are valid for the very reason they are subjective. For his part Paris wants the war continued in order to exonerate himself:

> But I would have the soil of her fair rape
> Wiped off in honorable keeping her.

To such fatuous arguments Hector weakly yields out of deference to "our joint and several dignities," but there is neither honor nor dignity on either side.

In a contrasting scene, the Greeks debate the causes of their failure against the Trojans. Ulysses attributes it to factionalism and neglect of "degree," or proper consideration for rank and position. His long speech (I, *iii,* 83-126 in its entirety) is often cited as illustrative of Shakespeare's own ideal of order in man, society, and nature:

> Degree being vizarded,
> Th' unworthiest shows as fairly in the mask.
> The heavens themselves, the planets, and this center
> Observe degree, priority, and place,
> Insisture, course, proportion, season, form,
> Office and custom, in all line of order.

In spite of this high-sounding speech, Ulysses concludes the scene with the crafty scheme of pitting Achilles and Ajax against each other. Ajax will win the right to battle Hector by a lottery rigged by Ulysses. If Ajax loses to Hector, the Greeks can then denigrate Ajax and put in combat Achilles as their "better man"; if Ajax wins, the Greeks can "dress him up in voices." Either way, suggests Ulysses, "Ajax employed plucks down Achilles' plumes" and "two curs shall tame each other." The canine image sets the moral tone of the Greek camp, where dog eats dog.

It is not always clear what philosophical ideas are being emphasized in *Troilus and Cressida,* but one key to Shakespeare's meaning may be Ulysses' long speech on the relationship of time to value (III, *iii,* 145-90), which has some affinities to his earlier discourse on "degree." Just as in Ulysses' speech on reputation, time makes a mockery of fame; it also destroys the love of Troilus and Cressida and tarnishes the once bright illusion of the heroic myth of the Trojan wars. Thus in this bitter and pessimistic drama, both love and heroism are "subjects all/To envious and calumniating time."

For text, notes, and commentary the New Cambridge edition, ed. Alice Walker and J. Dover Wilson (1957), is excellent. Equally valuable is the New Variorum Edition, ed. H. N. Hillebrand (1953). Essential works of criticism include W. W. Lawrence, *Shakespeare's Problem Comedies* (1931); O. J. Campbell, *Comicall Satyre and Shakespeare's Troilus and Cressida* (1938); Kenneth Muir, "Troilus and Cressida," *ShakS,* VIII (1955); Brian Morris,

"The Tragic Structure of *Troilus and Cressida,*" *SQ,* X (1959); Arnold Stein, "*Troilus and Cressida:* The Disjunctive Imagination," *ELH,* XXXVI (1969); and Jarold W. Ramsey, "The Provenance of *Troilus and Cressida,*" *SQ,* XXI (1970).

Turberville (or **Turbervile), George** (c. 1544-c.1597). Poet and translator. Turberville was born of an illustrious Dorsetshire family, the same as that described in Thomas Hardy's novel *Tess of the D'Urbervilles.* Little is known of Turberville's early years, and his biography is made difficult by the fact that there were at least five George Turbervilles living in Dorsetshire during the Elizabethan period. Turberville was at New College, Oxford, in 1561 but left without taking a degree and entered one of Inns of Court, where he made the acquaintance of George Gascoigne, Barnabe Googe, and Arthur Brooke—all assiduous translators of classical and continental authors. In several poems Turberville describes himself as a diligent scholar of Plato, Cicero, Ovid, Plutarch, and Seneca.

From June 1568 to September 1569, Turberville was in Russia with the English ambassador Thomas Randolph and forty other "gentlemen desirous to see the world" and to negotiate trading agreements on behalf of an English company. The expedition was later described in Richard Hakluyt's *Principal Navigations* with some verse epistles by Turberville. In his letter to Sir William Cecil, Lord Burghley, dated August 12, 1568, Turberville criticizes the Russian clergy as corrupt and hypocritical, the peasantry as barbarous, and the nobility as savage and tyrannical.

All of Turberville's works were written and published during the decade 1565-75. His biographer John E. Hankins speculates that Turberville discontinued literary activity after 1574, when he married a wealthy woman and settled in Devonshire to look after his estates. Turberville's works include *Heroical Epistles* (1567), an English version of Ovid's *Heroides;* a collection of largely original poems, *Epitaphs, Epigrams, Songs, and Sonnets* (pr. 1565? 1567); a translation of the Latin eclogues of the influential Italian pastoralist Mantuan (1448-1516), *The Eglogs of the Poet Mantuan Turned into English Verse* (1567); *A Plain Path to Perfect Virtue* (1568), a version of the Latin devotional poem *De quatuor virtutibus* (c. 1516) by the German scholar Dominicus Mancinus; a compilation of ten novellas called *Tragical Tales* (pr. 1574? 1576? 1587), seven from Boccaccio's *Decameron* and three from Mambrino da Fabriana's *La selva* (Lyons, 1556), an Italian version of the Spanish *Silva* of Pero Mexia; and two manuals on the art of hawking and hunting, *The Book of Falconry or Hawking* (1575) and *The Noble Art of Venery or Hunting* (pr. 1575? 1576).

Turberville's translations are in wooden "poulter's measure" (alternating twelve-and fourteen-syllable lines) and "fourteeners." Of his twenty-four epistles from Ovid, twelve are in poulter's measure, six in fourteeners, and six in iambic pentameter blank verse, which Turberville may have learned from the earl of Surrey's translation of Vergil's *Aeneid.* Turberville's version of nine eclogues from Mantuan has some literary importance in continuing the neoclassic pastoral, initiated around 1515-21 with Alexander Barclay's rendition of Mantuan's Latin eclogues and continued by Turberville's friend Barnabe Googe, who imitated six of Mantuan's eclogues in *Eglogues, Epitaphs, and Sonnets* (1563). No doubt Spenser read all these versions of Mantuan when he composed his *Shepherd's Calendar* in 1579. Like Googe's, Turberville's prosody is execrable; of Turberville's nine eclogues from Mantuan, five are in halting fourteeners, four in poulter's measure.

Turberville's *Epitaphs, Epigrams, Songs, and Sonnets* reflects the influence of Wyatt, Surrey, and Nicholas Grimald as represented in Tottel's Miscellany—that is, a certain diligence without flair or fire. None of Turberville's "sonnets" (which in the 1560s still meant any short lyric on the subject of love) is in fourteen lines. Like his translation of Mancinus, the original poems are dedicated to Anne Russell, countess of Warwick and wife of Ambrose Dudley, brother of Robert Dudley, earl of Leicester. Anne Russell is addressed in the poems as "Pandora" or "Pyndara," Turberville as "Tymetes," and his collection represents the first group of poems in English to celebrate a mistress. As Turberville notes in his address to the reader, his vicissitudes of love with Pandora are "fantasies" rather than expressions of genuine passion, and his love poems are, in fact, more respectful of the lady than amorous. One of the better-known poems to Pandora is "To his love, that sent him a ring wherein was graved 'Let reason rule.'" The source is, of course, Petrarch, but it is Petrarch sifted through his imitators in Tottel's Miscellany:

Shall reason rule where reason hath no right,
Nor never had? Shall Cupid lose his lands?
His claim? his crown? his kingdom? name of
  might?
And yield himself to be in reason's bands?
No, friend, thy ring doth will me thus in vain.
Reason and love have ever yet been twain...

Turberville's epigrams were influenced by those of Erasmus and John Heywood. Like Heywood's, they derive from the native tradition and owe little if anything to classical sources:

At night when ale is in,
  Like friends we part to bed;
In morrow grey, when ale is out,
  Then hatred is in head.

Turberville's verses bear evidence of most of the main forces at work in English poetry before the advent of the golden age of Sidney and Spenser—Chaucer in John Stowe's apocryphal edition, Erasmus, Mantuan, John Heywood, and Tottel's Miscellany. For the most part, Turberville's achievements were on the minor scale of Alexander Barclay or Barnabe Googe.

There is no complete edition of Turberville's works. His version of Ovid's epistles was edited by Frederick Boas, with illustrations by Hester Sainsbury (1928). *Epigraphs, Epigrams, Songs, and Sonnets* was reprinted by Alexander Chalmers in his *English Poets,* II (1810), and by J. P. Collier in the Elizabethan Poetical Miscellanies series (1870). Turberville's version of Mantuan's epilogues was edited with an introduction by Douglas Bush (1937). There is an anonymous edition of *The Noble Art of Venery or Hunting* in a Tudor and Stuart Library edition (1908). John E. Hankins has done a critical biography, *The Life and Works of George Turbervile* (1940). See also Hyder E. Rollins, "New Facts about George Turbervile," *MP,* XV (1918); and W. E. Sheidley, "George Turberville and the Problem of Passion," *JEGP,* LXIX (1970).

Tusser, Thomas (1524?-1580). Agricultural writer and poet. Born in Rivenhall, Essex, Tusser served as a choirboy at St. Paul's Cathedral, attended Eton School and King's College and Trinity College, Cambridge, which he left without a degree because of frequent illnesses. At Eton his master was Nicholas Udall, notorious for his pedagogical cruelties and famous for his comedy *Ralph Roister Doister.* After a stint at court as a musician, Tusser married and moved to Suffolk, where he settled as a farmer; when his wife died he remarried and went to live in Ipswich. He is known to have been a singer at the cathedral in Norwich and to have died in a London debtors' prison.

It was from his farm in Suffolk that Tusser sent to the publisher Richard Tottel the first version of the one work for which he is famous, *A Hundred Good Points of Husbandry* (1557). Reprinted several times, it was combined with a book on housewifery (1571) and augmented to take its final form as *Five Hundred Points of Good Husbandry* (1573), one of the most popular books in the sixteenth century. A forerunner the modern Farmer's Almanac, it is an encyclopedia in doggerel verse of such practical matters as planting, tillage, forestry, weather, and household economy combined with autobiographical digressions, homespun wisdom, genial humor, and piety. Like Benjamin Franklin's Poor Richard, Tusser knew his readers well. He emphasizes rustic good sense and practical advice and adjures any "rhetoric fine":

What look ye for more in my book?
  Point needful and meet to be known?
Then daily be sure to look,
  To save, to be sure, thine own.

The 1573 edition was reprinted by W. Payne and S. J. Herrtage for the English Dialect Society (1878) and in a facsimile edition by D. Hilman (1931). The 1557 edition was edited by D. Hartley (1931). For commentary, see G. E. Fussell, "'Farmers' Calendars from Tusser to Arthur Young," *Economic History,* II (1933); and C. S. Lewis, *English Literature of the Sixteenth Century* (1954), which has an annotated bibliography.

Twelfth Night; Or, What You Will. A comedy by William SHAKESPEARE, written in 1601-02 and first printed in the 1623 Folio. Shakespeare's principal source is Barnabe Rich's "Apolonius and Silla," the second story in his *Rich His Farewell to the Military Profession* (1581), a tale derived from the prose versions of an anonymous Italian play, *Gli' Ingannati* (1537), found in Bandello's *Novelle* (1554) and Belleforest's *Histoires tragiques* (1559).

Viola and Sebastian, twin sister and brother, are separated after a shipwreck off the coast of Illyria, where Viola disguises herself as Caesario, a boy, and becomes a page to Duke Orsino, with whom she secretly falls in love but who is vainly wooing Olivia, a lady too distracted by her brother's death to heed Orsino's persistent courting. Orsino sends Caesario to Olivia to plead his suit, and the lady soon becomes enamored of the disguised Viola. Meanwhile Sebastian, in the company of Antonio, captain of the ship that rescued him, arrives in Illyria in search of Viola and joins a merry crew of revelers at Olivia's house—Olivia's hard-drinking uncle Sir Toby Belch, her maid Maria, the clown Feste, and Sir Toby's thick-witted friend Sir Andrew Aguecheek, who dreams of winning Olivia's hand. Much of the comedy stems from the torments these merry-makers impose on Olivia's pompous and puritanical steward Malvolio.

When Antonio is arrested on an old charge, he asks Viola, still disguised as Caesario, and very much resembling her twin brother Sebastian, to return a purse he left in trust, and the baffled Viola refuses. Other mixups result when the cowardly Aguecheek attacks the fierce Sebastian, whom Aguecheek takes to be Caesario, and Olivia actually marries Sebastian, believing the astonished youth to be Caesario. Matters are cleared up when the main characters assemble at Olivia's house and Viola throws off her disguise. Orsino is betrothed to Viola, and Sebastian remains happily wedded to Olivia. Only the bad-humored Malvolio refuses to join in the concluding festivities.

Twelfth Night belongs with *As You Like It* and *Much Ado About Nothing* as one of Shakespeare's light-hearted and festive "golden comedies." The main romantic plot of *Twelfth Night* is derived from a situation in the COMMEDIA DELL'ARTE wherein the heroine attempts to redeem herself with her lover by taking the disguise of a boy and becoming his page. Shakespeare alters the pattern by having Viola shipwrecked and donning a male disguise to protect herself from men. This romantic story is interwoven with the farcical subplot in which the retainers and guests of Lady Olivia's household engage in baiting Olivia's steward Malvolio, who prudishly objects to the night revels of Sir Toby Belch and his cohorts.

The characters and action of the plot bear some resemblance to Jonson's realistic and satiric comedies of humour (see JONSON, BEN). Sir Toby is drawn from the Elizabethan social type of the impoverished and idle knight (like Falstaff), and his minion Maria represents the shrewd wench bent on improving her social position by marrying a gentleman of title, no matter how paunch-fallen and seedy he might be. Sir Andrew Aguecheek represents the familiar Elizabethan country gull or dupe aspiring to be chic and debonair. He also longs to be a courtly lover, and to that end attaches himself to Sir Toby, who genially bilks him of money while holding out vague promises of marriage to Olivia. Feste is the earliest of Shakespeare's "wise fools," and he may have been created expressly for Robert Armin, the comic actor who played fools more subtle than the raucous clowns portrayed by Will Kempe, who is known to have quit Shakespeare's company in 1599. Shakespeare realizes the wise fool only partially in Feste, whose wit is sometimes blunt and tedious compared with the razor-sharp humor of Touchstone in *As You Like It* or the fool in *King Lear.* Feste's songs, however, are exquisite, especially the one that concludes the play: "A great while ago the world begun, / With hey, ho, the wind and the rain..."

The most "humorous" character in the Jonsonian sense is, as his name suggests, the pride-obsessed Malvolio. Considering himself superior to Sir Toby's jocund company, he proves to be as absurd as Aguecheek once Maria traps him into thinking his mistress Olivia is smitten with him. To purge him of these mad humors, Sir Toby and the others bind and whip him, and when he is released at the end of the play his hot rage strikes the one dissonant note in an otherwise harmonious conclusion: "I'll have my revenge on the pack of you!" Olivia concedes that he has been "notoriously abused," and Orsino sends servants after him to "entreat him to a peace." As the lovers depart Feste steps forth with an appropriate song to conclude this most musical of Shakespeare's comedies.

A standard text is the New Cambridge edition, ed. Arthur Quiller-Couch and J. Dover Wilson (1926). A theory on the historical occasion for the first performance is proposed by Leslie Hotson, *The First Night of "Twelfth Night"* (1954). C. L. Barber studies the genre of the play in *Shakespeare's Festive Comedy* (1959). Additional important criticism includes Joseph Summers, "The Masks of *Twelfth*

Night," *UR*, XXII (1955); J. Dover Wilson, *Shakespeare's Happy Comedies* (1962); Clifford Leech, *Twelfth Night and Shakespearean Comedy* (1965); Peter G. Phialas, *Shakespeare's Romantic Comedies* (1966); and John R. Brown, *Shakespeare's Dramatic Style* (1971).

Two Angry Women of Abingdon, The Pleasant History of. A comedy by Henry Porter (d. 1599), written in 1598, acted by the Lord Admiral's Men that year, and printed in 1599. It is in both blank verse and prose. No source is known.

The two angry women of the title are Mistresses Barnes and Goursey, who quarrel bitterly at a dinner party. The next day Master Barnes attempts to mend the breech between the families by offering his daughter Mall in marriage to Goursey's son Francis. Mistress Goursey determines to cross the match. Much of the action concerns the efforts of the mild, reasonable husbands to placate their tempestuous wives, and of the young lovers to pursue their courtship in spite of the petulant antagonisms of their mothers. The ladies are not brought to their senses until Barnes and Goursey feign a duel to show them the consequences of their malice. The ladies repent of their anger, are reconciled, and all the characters retire to supper to celebrate the nuptials of Mall and Francis.

Porter's play illustrates the progress made by Elizabethan comedy during the fifty years following GAMMER GURTON'S NEEDLE. Both are comedies of English rural life, but in contrast to Porter's play, *Gammer Gurton's Needle* appears to be little more than a farcical interlude. Porter elevates his characters to the middle class, widens the plot with a romantic love story, employs a great deal of intrigue rather than depending entirely on farce, and relegates the coarsest comedy to two lower-class buffoons, Dick Coomes, a tipsy "roaring boy," and Nicholas Proverbs, a servant afflicted with a "humour" that causes him to dress like a fop and utter nothing but proverbs. Although a simple comedy with typed characters, *Two Angry Women* represents the kind of popular drama that links *Gammer Gurton's Needle* and *The Merry Wives of Windsor.*

W. W. Greg has edited Porter's play, with an introduction, in the Malone Society reprints (1912), and Havelock Ellis in the Mermaid series (1888). It is also in *Representative English Comedies,* ed. C. M. Gayley, I (1903). For commentary, see A. H. Thorndike, *English Comedy* (1929).

Two Gentlemen of Verona, The. A comedy by William SHAKESPEARE, written in 1594-95 and first printed in the 1623 Folio. The main plot is derived from the story of Felix and Felismena in Jorge de Montemayor's Spanish pastoral romance *Diana enamorada* (1542? 1559?), possibly in the French translation by Nicolas Collin (1578, 1587). There was also a lost play acted at court in 1585 called *The History of Felix and Philiomena.* The last scene of the play is based on the history of Titus and Gisippus in Book II, Chapter XII, of Sir Thomas Elyot's *The Governor* (1531).

Proteus remains in Verona to woo Julia while his life-long friend Valentine departs to seek adventure in Milan, where he falls in love with Silvia, the duke of Milan's daughter, who returns his regard. Arriving in Milan, Proteus also is smitten with the beautiful Silvia, and in violation of his vows to Julia, seeks to win Silvia for himself. He betrays his friendship to Valentine by informing the duke that Valentine and Silvia plan to elope. Banished by the duke, Valentine becomes a bandit leader. Meanwhile Julia, disguised as a boy, arrives in Milan and gains employment as Proteus' page. When her father attempts to force her marriage to one Thurio, Silvia sets out to join Valentine but is captured by robbers and rescued by Proteus, who attempts to force his affections on her. Valentine then arrives to rescue Silvia from Proteus. Upbraided by Valentine for disloyalty and unseemly lust, Proteus so sincerely expresses his contrition that the magnanimous Valentine actually offers to give up Silvia in his favor. Hearing this, Julia swoons, and her true identity is discovered by Proteus, who reaffirms his love for her. At the conclusion Thurio resigns his claim on Silvia, the duke accepts Valentine as son-in-law, and all ends happily for the lovers. Launce and Speed, the clownish servants of Proteus and Valentine respectivily, provide much of the farce and low comedy.

Many of the characters and situations in *Two Gentlemen* reflect the influence of the COMMEDIA DELL'ARTE, and the inflated sentiments, the conceited prose and word play can be attributed to the vogue of John Lyly's *Euphues.* In the *commedia dell'arte* the situation of the lady wooed by two rival friends and a boorish third party (Thurio, in this case) was conventional, as was that of a lady assuming the disguise of a boy in the service of her lover, as Julia does for Proteus, and carrying love messages to her lady rival (Shakespeare employed similar situations in *Twelfth Night* and *As You Like It*). Equally derivative of the *commedia dell'arte* are contrasted clowns such as the witty Speed and the thick-brained Launce.

Critics have devoted much attention to the episode in Act V, Scene 4, where Proteus is about to force his love on Silvia when Valentine arrives and reproaches him for his base conduct. Shamed by this reprimand, Proteus begs Valentine's forgiveness, and when Valentine magnanimously offers to let Proteus have Silvia as a token of their friendship, the poor lady swoons—as have many of Shakespeare's readers. Yet such perverse etiquette as Valentine's can be found in any number of episodes in the late Greek romances, and in Montemayor's *Diana* and Sidney's *Arcadia,* wherein noble characters fulfill some ideal sentiment rather than act upon real-life impulses or motives. Hence *Two Gentlemen* is one of Shakespeare's most refined plays, full of fluent verse and delicate songs like "Who Is Silvia?" but it has never been a favorite of popular audiences.

A standard text is the New Cambridge edition, ed. Arthur Quiller-Couch and J. Dover Wilson (1921). For criticism, see H. B. Charlton, *Shakespearean Comedy* (1938); John F. Danby, "Shakespearean Criticism and *Two Gentlemen of Verona,*" *CritQ,* II (1960); A. C. Hamilton, *The Early Shakespeare* (1967); and Robert Weimann, "Laughing with the Audience: *The Two Gentlemen of Verona* and the Popular Tradition of Comedy," *ShakS,* XXII (1969).

Two Lamentable Tragedies (Robert Yarington). See DOMESTIC TRAGEDY.

Two Noble Kinsmen, The. A romance by John FLETCHER and William SHAKESPEARE, written in 1612-13 and first printed in 1634. Most scholars agree that Shakespeare wrote Act I, Scenes 1-3; Act III, Scene 1; and all of Act V except Scene 2. The principal source is Chaucer's "Knight's Tale" in *The Canterbury Tales.*

The wedding festivities of Theseus, duke of Athens, and his bride Hippolyta are interrupted by three queens who have come to demand that Theseus avenge the murders of their husbands by Creon, king of Thebes. Theseus and his general Pirithous conquer the city and receive the gratitude of the three women. Palamon and Arcite, two noble Thebans who have reluctantly but heroically fought for their uncle Creon, are captured in battle and imprisoned. From their prison window they see Hippolyta's sister Emilia, and both immediately fall in love with her. Soon afterward Arcite is banished from Thebes, and Palamon contrives to have the jailer's daughter, who falls in love with him, arrange his escape from prison. Arcite and Palamon meet in a wood outside Thebes, and although the two friends eat and drink together with great conviviality, Palamon insists they must fight for the favor of Emilia.

Meanwhile, the jailer's daughter, deserted by Palamon and hearing that her father is to be hanged for Palamon's escape, wanders about in madness until she meets a group of country folk, who take her to a dance performed at the Theban court. There Palamon and Arcite prepare to fight over Emilia. Their combat is interrupted by the arrival of Theseus, who, on the advice of Emilia and Hippolyta, decrees that the youths will meet in combat a month hence and that the winner will marry Emilia, the loser be executed.

When the jailer is pardoned, he engages a physician to cure his daughter of madness, and the doctor prescribes a wooer to impersonate Palamon. When Arcite is victorious in the combat, Palamon is sent to the executioner's block; his death is prevented, however, by news that Arcite has been accidentally killed and that Theseus has given Emilia to Palamon. At the conclusion the jailer's daughter is cured and marries, and the court of Theseus observes the funeral of Arcite and the nuptials of Palamon and Emilia.

Although the wedding of Theseus and Hippolyta also provides the setting for *A Midsummer Night's Dream,* and several other details in *Two Noble Kinsmen* suggest either Shakespeare's hand or influence, the romance bears all of the marks of Fletcher's high-blown tragicomedies. The characters entangle themselves in rhetoric while remaining shallow and unmotivated, and they account for their actions by lofty sentiments rather than by any plausible impulses. The titular heroes are individuated, but in quite arbitrary ways: Palamon is practical and aggressive, Arcite idealistic and more gentle. The heroine herself cannot choose between them, and when they fight for her hand she only hopes that the one who survives will not be disfigured.

The jailer's daughter typifies Fletcher's delineation of lower-class characters. Her passion for Palamon is wholly sensual and coarse, her longing for a high-born gentleman totally ludicrous. In her madness she rails obscenely in a way that caricatures the pathos of Ophelia and Lady Macbeth. The conclusion of the play is also characteristic of Fletcher's romances: all the conflicts are resolved in a rush of fortuitous events, and the characters depart with ritualistic observations on the omnipotence of fate and true love.

G. L. Kittredge included the play in his *Complete Works of Shakespeare* (1936), which contains much criticism of sources and style, and G. R. Proudfoot has edited the play in the Regents Renaissance Drama series (1970). See also Theodore Spencer, "*Two Noble Kinsmen,*" *MP,* XXXVI (1938); Kenneth Muir, *Shakespeare as Collaborator* (1960); Clifford Leech, *The John Fletcher Plays* (1962); and Paul Bertram, *Shakespeare and The Two Noble Kinsmen* (1965), which contains an extensive bibliography.

Two Treatises...of the Immortality of Reasonable Souls. See DIGBY, SIR KENELM.

Tyndale, William. (1494?-1536). Biblical translator and Protestant martyr. Born of common farmer stock in Gloucestershire near Wales, Tyndale entered Oxford in 1506 and Cambridge about 1518. By 1522 he was engaged as a tutor to the children of Sir John Walsh near his home in Gloucestershire. After completing a translation of Isocrates (which has not survived), he did an English version of Erasmus' *Enchiridion militis Christiani* (1503) as *The Manual of the Christian Knight* (1533). Erasmus' manual of religious conduct and devotions had a lasting influence on Tyndale. Fired by Erasmus' work, Tyndale disputed so vehemently with visiting clergymen that he was haled before the local diocese and threatened with expulsion from the church. His response to this attempted repression was an avowed determination "to cause a boy that driveth the plough" to know more of the Scriptures than a priest, and to this end he began his life-long effort to translate the Bible into the vernacular and circulate it among ordinary people.

Tyndale sought the support of Cuthbert Turnstall, bishop of London, in translating the New Testament, but that failing, he went to Hamburg and later to Wittenberg, where he met Luther. The printing of Tyndale's English translation of the New Testament was begun in Cologne, where it was stopped by the Catholic church authorities, and finally completed in Worms in 1525. Tyndale's translation was opposed by Protestant and Catholic officials alike, not only because they looked askance upon any unauthorized version of Scripture, but because Tyndale's prologues and marginal glosses were unorthodox and hotly controversial. Copies that were smuggled into England were hunted out and burned by Henry VIII's bishops. Cardinal Wolsey attempted to have Tyndale arrested at Worms, but Tyndale found refuge at Marburg with a friendly Lutheran prince, Philip, the landgrave of Hesse. In 1531, in reply to demands by Henry's bishops that he return to England, Tyndale offered to "humbly submit myself at the feet of his royal majesty, offering my body to suffer what pain and torture, yea, what death his grace will," providing only that the king allow but one man to translate the Bible into English. Tyndale's offer was, of course, ignored by the king and his anti-Lutheran advisers.

That same year, Tyndale engaged in a bitter theological controversy with Sir Thomas More, whose *Dialogue Against Heresy* was countered by Tyndale's *Answer unto Sir Thomas More's Dialogue.* In this and other polemical pamphlets Tyndale's position remained consistently firm. He denied More's charges of heresy but avowed himself to be a militant anti-papist and a Zwingli-style reformer who stopped short of Calvin's political radicalism. He believed, with Luther and Zwingli, in a separation of church and state, but also gave the secular authority of the monarch—and monarchy for Tyndale was a necessary evil—unmitigated hegemony in the secular realm. The one overpowering idea he reiterated tirelessly was Luther's concept of the priesthood of all believers guided by the truth of God as expressed in Holy Scripture.

In 1535 Tyndale was arrested by Catholic authorities near Antwerp, taken to Vilvorde, and executed in spite of Thomas Cromwell's efforts to save him. Within a few years of his death the Great Bible, a somewhat revised version of Tyndale's translation, found a place in every parish church in England. Tyndale's vig orous, lucid prose in this work contributed an important foundation for the King James Version of 1611. See BIBLE TRANSLATION

Tyndale's New Testament, with comparative texts of all earlier English translations, has been edited by A. W. Pollard (1926). See also Pollard's *Records of the English Bible* (1911). An authoritative biography is J. F. Mosley's *William Tyndale* (1937).

U

Udall, Nicholas (1504?-1556). Dramatist and schoolteacher. Virtually nothing was known of Udall until recently, and even now the bits and pieces of biographical data accumulated by scholars leave large gaps in his life. The only extant play that can be assigned to him with any certainty is RALPH ROISTER DOISTER, written in the early 1550s, and even this work would not have been assigned to Udall were it not that in the third edition of Thomas Wilson's *Rule of Reason, Containing the Art of Logic* (1552) a letter by Udall's character Roister Doister is introduced as having been "taken out of an interlude by Nicholas Udall." Another early interlude, THERSITES, has also been attributed to Udall, but on less certain grounds.

It is known that Udall was born in Southampton between 1504 and 1506 and attended St. Mary's School in Winchester in 1517-20. He entered Corpus Christi, Oxford, in 1521 and graduated B.A. in 1526, M.A. in 1534. He left Oxford for a time in 1529 as a result of his involvement in religious disputes on the side of the Lutherans. There is a record of his appointment in 1533 to a London grammar school, where he wrote verses and songs in celebration of Anne Boleyn's coronation and where, in the following year, he published *Flowers for Later Speaking,* a textbook based on the works of Terence. In 1534 also, Udall took a position at Eton, where he is known to have produced and directed plays performed by the boys there. Some of these dramas were attended by Henry VIII's chancellor, Thomas Cromwell.

The records also indicate that Udall was imprisoned for several months in Marshalsea debtors' prison; that he was charged with stealing; and that on one occasion he confessed to sodomy with his students. In 1542 he translated Erasmus' *Apothegmata,* and was for a time befriended by Catherine Parr when she was queen. At her request Udall edited Erasmus' paraphrase of the Gospel of St. Luke and was responsible for its distribution in the churches. His last post seems to have been at Westminster School, where he died in 1556. John Bale refers to "several comedies" by Udall, and Udall is known to have written plays performed before both Mary Tudor and Elizabeth. Of these only *Ralph Roister Doister* has survived, although many anonymous comedies and interludes have been attributed to him.

G. Scheurweghs' definitive edition of *Ralph Roister Doister* in Bang-De Vocht, *Materials for the Study of the Old English Drama,* XVI (1939), is accompanied by many new facts about Udall's life. Other biographical and critical details have appeared in *N & Q* by W. L. Edgerton,

CXCV (1950); Herbert T. Webster, CXCVI (1951); and A. W. Plumstead, New Series, X (1963).

Underwoods (or Under-wood). A collection of poems by Ben JONSON, first published in the second volume of the folio of 1640. The first three poems are devotional; the next group are love poems, including ten related lyrics called "A Celebration of Charis." Other poems include "A Nymph's Passion," "Dream," some eulogies (most notably Jonson's great dedicatory poem to Shakespeare), a sonnet to Lady Mary Wroth (to whom Jonson dedicated *The Alchemist;* she was the daughter of Sir Philip Sidney's brother Robert), several epistles (including "An Epistle to a Friend, to persuade him to the wars"). A series of four elegies are in imitation of John Donne, and the second of these (viii) appeared in the 1633 edition of Donne's poems. Also included in *Underwoods* are "An Execration upon Vulcan," "Eupheme" (to Lady Venetia Digby, wife of Jonson's friend Sir Kenelm Digby), and the famous Pindaric ode on the death of Sir Henry Morison, nephew of the traveler Fynes Morison, which begins "It is not growing like a tree/In bulk, doth make men better be . . ." The epitaph on the countess of Pembroke, now included in *Underwoods,* was not printed in that collection until Peter Whalley's edition of 1756.

The epigraph to *Underwoods* is from Martial's *Epigrams*: *Cineri, gloria sera venit* ("Glory comes too late to the ashes of the dead"). The opening poem, "To the Reader," explains the title of the collection and its link to Jonson's *The Forest* (1616):

> With the same leave the ancients call'd
> That kind of body *Sylva,* or ὕλη, in
> Which there were works of divers nature,
> And matter congested; as the multitude
> Call timber-trees, promiscuously growing,
> A *Wood,* or *Forest*: so am I bold to entitle
> These lesser poems, of later growth, by
> This of *Underwood,* out of the analogy
> They hold to the *Forest,* in my former
> Book, and no otherwise.

The standard edition of *Underwoods* is in *Ben Jonson,* ed. C. H. Herford and Percy and Evelyn Simpson, 11 vols. (1925-53), VIII. Two excellent editions are in *The Poems of Ben Jonson,* ed. B. H. Newdigate (1936), and *The Complete Poetry of Ben Jonson,* ed. William B. Hunter, Jr. (1963). Critical analyses of separate poems are in G. B. Johnston, *Ben Jonson: Poet* (1945), and Wesley Trimpi, *Ben Jonson's Poems; A Study of the Plain Style* (1962).

Unfortunate Traveller, The; or The Life of Jack Wilton. A prose tale by Thomas NASHE. It was first printed in 1594 with a dedication to the earl of Southampton, Shakespeare's patron. It has been variously classified as a picaresque novel, the first historical novel in English, and a prose satire (see FICTION). In the dedication Nashe acknowledges the difficulty of classifying the work, for it is in a "clean different vein from other my former courses of writing." Nashe drew on a variety of different sources, including Diego Hurtado de Mendoza's *Lazarillo de Tormes,* translated into English by David Rowland (1586), historical chronicles, ROGUE LITERATURE, and JESTBOOKS. Most of the historical events and personages portrayed in the story are Nashe's inventions.

Jack Wilton, the resourceful young hero, begins his tale by telling of the jokes he played on his elders when he was a page at the court of Henry VIII during the English siege of Tournay. After recounting several pranks, Jack describes his adventures after being whipped out of Tournay for his roguery. He journeys to Münster in time to witness the defeat of the Anabaptists and the execution of their leader John of Leyden. Later Jack meets the earl of Surrey and becomes his page; they head for Italy, meeting along their circuitous way the great Erasmus and Sir Thomas More as well as the Italian poet Pietro Aretino. At Wittenberg they hear Luther disputing theology, a subject Jack finds incomprehensible. Later Jack takes up with an Italian courtesan and poses as the earl of Surrey. When Surrey discovers the imposture, he dismisses it in good humor. In Florence, Surrey defeats all comers in a tournament where he challenges his opponents in the name of his "fair Geraldine" (the subject of Surrey's most famous sonnet in Tottel's Miscellany, "From Tuscany came my lady's race"). Leaving Surrey, Jack accompanies his courtesan to Rome, which Nashe describes vividly. The courtesan is captured by two villains, and Jack, accused of murder but later exonerated through the intercession of a kindly Englishman, falls in with a concubine of the pope. After several hairbreadth escapes, Jack vows to mend his loose and wild ways.

He marries the courtesan and travels to France, where the story concludes with Jack at Henry VIII's camp on the Field of the Cloth of Gold.

There are many evidences in *The Unfortunate Traveller* of what Nashe himself described as "extemporial writing." In the early portions of the work Nashe seems to have intended to write a jestbook, turned to a parody of EUPHUISM, and then to a satire on foreign fashions and manners, chronicles, and travel tales. The point of view in the work is equally uncertain. In his account of the Anabaptist uprising at Münster, Nashe switches to a form that is, in his words, "more than duncified twixt divinity and poetry," and moralizes from his own rather than Jack Wilton's point of view. At this stage in the story Nashe may have been planning a didactic conclusion, but the idea of introducing the earl of Surrey as a character opened fresh possibilities for his narrative. After Jack separates from Surrey and arrives in Rome, Nashe again discards his youthful narrator and describes the beauties of Rome and Tivoli in the eloquent cadences of the poet. *The Unfortunate Traveller* has, in fact, not one but three narrators: Jack Wilton of the fictive past; Jack of the present (passing on the wisdom of his experience to the "gentlemen pages" to whom the tale is addressed); and Nashe himself, the virtuoso poet and preacher who usurps Jack's role whenever a subject impels him.

Claims for *The Unfortunate Traveller* as the first historical novel in English rest on tenuous grounds, for Nashe rarely exhibits any deep concern for the historical events his hero witnesses. Nor does *The Unfortunate Traveller* conform entirely to the essential requirements of the picaresque novel, wherein the *picaro,* or rogue hero, employs a defensive amorality to survive in an oppressively unjust and hypocritical society. Nashe expresses little if any criticism of society *per se,* and Jack—except in the very early portion of the narrative—is not so much a rogue as an innocent observer, and, on some occasions, even something of a prude. The importance of *The Unfortunate Traveller* does not, however, stem from any conformity to other modes of fiction but from its unprecedented vitality of language, raw realism, and energetic narrative pace.

The definitive edition of *The Unfortunate Traveller* is in Nashe's *Works,* ed. R. B. McKerrow, 5 vols. (1904-10). There is also an excellent edition, with a helpful glossary, by Stanley Wells, *Thomas Nashe: Selected Writings* (1965). For critical commentary, see the edition by H. F. B. Brett-Smith in the Percy Reprint series (1927); Fredson Bowers, "Thomas Nashe and the Picaresque Novel," *Studies in Honor of John Calvin Metcalf* (1941); Agnes C. Latham, "Satire on Literary Themes and Modes in Nashe's *The Unfortunate Traveller,*" *English Studies 1948* (1948); and Bruce E. Tests, *Sweet Smoke of Rhetoric* (1964).

university wits. A term used to signify the first wave of Oxford and Cambridge graduates to engage in literary activities in London during the period 1585-95. The forerunners of this group were John Lyly and George Peele, who were followed by Christopher Marlowe, Thomas Lodge, Samuel Daniel, Thomas Watson, Matthew Roydon, Robert Greene, and Thomas Nashe, among others. Their particular contributions during this period included the use of dramatic blank verse (popularized in Marlowe's "mighty line"), the perfection of Senecan revenge tragedy, romantic comedy, historical drama, and pastoral romance. There is little to justify considering the so-called university wits as a cohesive group or organized literary movement; instead, the term designates a cultural phenomenon—the exodus of gifted young dramatists and poets from the universities to the London theaters and court circles. Some of these writers, such as Greene and Marlowe, made an effort to earn a living by their pens. Greene expresses an awareness of this migration from the universities to London in his pamphlet A GROATSWORTH OF WIT, in which he cautions the "gentlemen scholars of both universities" against coming to London to seek fame and fortune in the public theaters.

See Felix E. Schelling, *English Literature During the Lifetime of Shakespeare* (1910, 1927); and Ernest W. Talbert, *Elizabethan Drama and Shakespeare's Early Plays* (1963).

Utopia. A description of an ideal commonwealth written by Sir Thomas MORE in Latin in 1515-16 and published in Louvain (1516) and Basle (1518). The second book was composed when More was in Flanders on a diplomatic mission for Henry VIII in 1515, the first in 1516 upon More's return to England. It was first translated into English by Ralph Robinson in 1551. In Book I More is introduced by his friend Peter Giles to an alleged companion of Amerigo Vespucci, Raphael Hythloday ("teller of tall tales"), who condemns the conditions he found in England under Henry VII: excessive punishment for theft, unjust taxation, unequal distribution of wealth and property, enclosures, the avarice of the rich and the desperation of the poor. In Book II these deplorable conditions are contrasted to those in the ideal land once visited by Hythloday, the state of Utopia ("nowhere"), where war, religious turmoil, crime, poverty, private wealth, and money do not exist. An interesting feature of Utopia is its total religious toleration, an idea which More himself did not embrace in his own controversial writings. To Hythloday's praise of Utopia, More concludes ambivalently that "many things be in the Utopian weal public which in our cities I may rather wish for than hope for."

More's *Utopia* was influenced by Plato's *Republic,* St. Augustine's *De civitate Dei,* Vespucci's accounts of New World voyages, and Erasmus' *Institutio principis Christiani.* For other Renaissance utopias, see UTOPIAN FICTION.

The standard edition is in the Yale edition of *The Complete Works,* ed. Edward Surtz, S. J., J. H. Hexter, et al., 5 vols., IV (1963-69), which includes the Latin text and an extensive bibliography. Important critical studies include H. W. Donner, *Introduction to Utopia* (1945); Russell Ames, *Citizen Thomas More and His Utopia* (1949); J. H. Hexter, *More's Utopia: The Biography of an Idea* (1952); and Edward Surtz, S. J., *The Praise of Pleasure* (1957). There is a collection of essays in *Twentieth Century Interpretations of Utopia,* ed. William Nelson (1968).

utopian fiction. Although the two most distinguished utopias of the English Renaissance, Sir Thomas More's UTOPIA (1516) and Francis Bacon's NEW ATLANTIS (1627), were both inspired ultimately by Plato's *Republic,* they also have indirect connections with two medieval works, St. Augustine's *De civitate Dei* (fourth century), which is mystical and philosophical, and the fantastic, purely entertaining travel accounts of the sixth-century English monk St. Brendan. The roots of utopian fiction are to be found in both Augustine's expression of transcendent truth and Brendan's tall tales. More's *Utopia* and Bacon's *The New Atlantis* illustrate admirably how these motives of truth-telling and entertainment can combine. More's *Utopia* means "nowhere,"; the name of his chief character, Hythloday, signifies "teller of tall tales," yet More's work is not only a charming fantasy but a serious attack on religious hypocrisy, political folly, and social injustice.

More concludes *Utopia* with an ambivalent reaction to Hythloday's praise of Utopia as being morally and intellectually superior to Christian Europe: ". . . I needs confess and grant that many things be in the Utopian weal public which in our cities I may rather wish for than hope for." No such ambiguity is expressed by the optimistic Bacon, who dedicated his *New Atlantis* to James I, the "English Solomon," in hope that the king would support some of his scientific schemes and "projects." In the first part of *New Atlantis* Bacon describes in fictive style the journey of the sailors, the storm that blows them off course, and their shipwreck near Atlantis; this much he concedes to St. Brendan's legacy of simple adventure. All the rest is Augustinian vision and prophecy except that Bacon's focus, unlike Augustine's, is on man in this world and on man's need to organize his intellectual resources to conquer nature. Like Bacon's *The Advancement of Learning, The New Atlantis* is little concerned with human nature or with political institutions. The social conditions on Bacon's imaginary Pacific island of Bensalem receive some attention, but his chief interest is in "Solomon's House," a model of a scientific college dedicated to "the producing of great and marvelous works for the benefit of man." The scientists in Solomon's House experiment with refrigeration, vivisection, telephone communications, submarines, and airplanes. (Bacon's imaginary college, "dedicated to the study of the works and creatures of God," later helped inspire the founding of the Royal Society.)

In the spirit of Bacon's *New Atlantis* are Francis Godwin's *The Man in the Moon* (1638) and Samuel Hartlib's *Description of Macaria* (1641). Bishop Godwin, a forerunner of Jules Verne and H. G. Wells, was inspired not only by Bacon but also by Galileo and Kepler. Godwin's Spanish hero is an amateur scientist or "projector" (as the type was to be called in the eighteenth century) who trains a flock of swans to carry him to the moon, where he finds an ideal climate, a pleasant society, and several corroborations of Baconian theories regarding heat and motion. Although Godwin was a crude dabbler in fiction, his whimsical tale influenced the seventeenth-century French poet Cyrano de Bergerac and went through twenty-five editions in four languages by the end of the eighteenth century.

Hartlib's *Macaria* is so Baconian and practical as to be almost drab. The only concession Hartlib makes to literary appeal is to cast the work as a dialogue between a scholar and a traveler. Addressed to Parliament, *Macaria* is really less a utopia than a practical treatise proposing a systematic reorganization of England's agricultural and economic institutions. Unlike More and many other utopian writers, Hartlib is not collectivistic or communistic. His *Macaria* is a utopia in which capitalism is regulated by a supreme council of bureaucracies subdivided into departments of husbandry, fishing, domestic trade, foreign trade, and so forth.

A mass of educational and scientific utopian literature sprang up in England during the revolutionary period of the 1640s and 1650s. The defeat of monarchy and the rapid development of new institutions sparked a visionary zeal and millenarian spirit among supporters of the new commonwealth. Paradoxically, in this climate of political and religious millenarianism utopias became increasingly less fictive and more expository, less concerned with wondrous narration than with argumentation. Representative of this new style of utopia is James Harrington's influential *Commonwealth of Oceana* (1656). In his dedication to Oliver Cromwell, who appears in the work as the benevolent Olphaeus Megalator, Harrington refers appropriately to *Oceana* as a "political romance." Essentially a treatise on government in the form of allegory, *Oceana* sets forth practical proposals for the complete renovation of the English constitution. In Harrington's utopia participation in government is limited to a propertied middle class who elect representative elders to rule for short periods; the amount of land that can be owned is strictly regulated to ensure distribution of wealth, and property owners are guardians of the working class, described therein as "servants." For Harrington both power and freedom are incumbent on "possession of the earth," and his ideal constitution is aimed at consolidating the Stuart hegemony of landowners and gentlemen farmers. The legislature of Oceana, however, is anything but traditionally aristocratic, for Harrington advocates the abolition of the House of Lords in favor of a bicameral parliament in which one group of representatives votes and the other debates. Although Cromwell's aides made sport of *Oceana* as an impractical fantasy, it proved to be of considerable influence in the American colonies. It was enthusiastically endorsed by John Adams and James Otis, and played an important part in the writing of the constitutions of the Carolinas, Massachusetts, New Jersey, and Pennsylvania.

Harrington's was the last influential utopia before the Restoration period. Of little interest is Samuel Gott's *Nova Solyma* (1648), a work in Latin once falsely attributed to John Milton. In Gott's pedestrian work two young men, Eugenius and Politan, visit an imaginary commonwealth that is, in effect, an inadvertent parody of Calvin's Geneva for its religious bigotry, social narrowness, and political tyranny. An equally lame effort is John Sadler's *Olbia, the New Island Lately Discovered* (1660), a long and tedious account of a pilgrim shipwrecked on an imaginary island in the New World. *Olbia* consists of little more than a long fragment in which a pilgrim meets a sermonizing hermit who digresses painfully on the subject of numerical mysticism and the vanity of human wishes.

Four important utopias were written abroad during this period and not published in English until some years later. These include Tommaso Campanella's *The City of the Sun* (written in 1602 in Italian, revised in 1611, rewritten in Latin in 1613 and again in 1630, and first translated into English by T. W. Halliday in 1886); Joseph Hall's *Mundus alter et idem* (printed in Frankfurt in 1605 and translated into English by John Healey in 1609 as *Discovery of a New World*); Francois Rabelais's "The Abbey of Thélème" in *Gargantua and Pantagruel* (translated into English by Thomas Urquhart in 1653); and Johann Valentin Andreae's *Christianopolis* (first published in Germany in 1623 but not translated into English until 1916).

Campanella's *City of the Sun* is a dialogue

in which a Genoese seaman describes an ideal civilization in the New World to a Knight Hospitaler whose responses are confined largely to exclamations of wonder and disbelief. Not surprisingly, in view of the fact it was written by a Calabrian monk who was tortured for years by the Inquisition, *City of the Sun* is a pastoral vision of a just and tolerant society which, like More's *Utopia,* reflects on the corruption and cruelty of Renaissance institutions. Joseph Hall's *Discovery of a New World,* which was published anonymously (and may have been written not by Hall but by an Italian jurist who lived in England, Alberico Gentili), is an abrasive attack on Roman Catholicism and European vices. The new world described in this utopia is an allegorical one divided into Crapulia, a kingdom inhabited by people with dreadful headaches induced by their own strict laws against fasting; Yvronia, a land of drunkards; Viraginia, ruled over by fierce viragoes who enslave all men; Moronia, inhabited entirely by fools; and Lavernia, domain of thieves, murderers, and common rogues.

Less satirical is Rabelais's famous description of life at the Abbey of Thélème and Andreae's utopia on education. Rabelais's refined ladies and gentlemen at Thélème live by the motto "Do as you will," and their cooperative spirit, dignity, and pursuit of intellectual excellence represent a humanist's faith in the essential goodness of men once freed from the stultifying influences of traditional discipline. Resembling Castiglione's description of the genteel coterie of Urbino in *Il Cortegiano,* Rabelais's account of Thélème is also a vision of an ideal society of humanistic and totally cultivated aristocrats—latter-day counterparts of Plato's philosopher-kings.

Andreae's *Christianopolis,* the work of a German humanist scholar and Lutheran, was inspired by the author's enthusiasm for Calvin's Geneva. In Andreae's ideal city of Caphar Salama there is no private property, no money, no profit motive, and the whole of society is dedicated to increasing the dignity of honest labor. The city is a decentralized complex of enclaves divided into various trades and ruled by medieval guilds. Andreae's chief concern in *Christianopolis* is educational reform, and his recommendations for a practical, humanistic educational system influenced other reformers like Comenius, Hartlib, and Milton.

Three excellent studies of utopian fiction are M. L. Berneri, *Journey Through Utopia* (1950); A. L. Morton, *The English Utopia* (1952); and S. B. Liljegren, *Studies in the Origin and Early Tradition of English Utopian Fiction* (1961).

V

Vaughan, Henry (1622-1695). Poet. Henry Vaughan and his twin brother Thomas were born at Newton on Usk in Brecknockshire of a Welsh family of impoverished gentility. After the conclusion of his formal education, Vaughan resided at Newton most of his life, signing his work "Silurist" after a local Welsh tribe called Silures by Tacitus. The natural beauties of the country where Vaughan spent his childhood played a large part in the love of nature expressed in his poetry.

Vaughan entered Jesus College, Oxford, in 1638, but unlike his brother Thomas, did not graduate. Instead, after two years at Oxford, Vaughan went to London to study law, but spent most of his time translating Latin poems and making the acquaintance of literati. Judging from the war poems in his later *Olor Iscanus,* Vaughan saw action in the Royalist army sometime before 1646, after which he settled in Newton with his wife and father. Sometime after the Civil War he received an M.D. and began a medical practice in Newton. In response to a letter of inquiry from John Aubrey, Vaughan wrote in 1673 that he had been a physician for several years "with good success." Vaughan's medical interest is reflected in his translation of Heinrich Nolle, *General System of Hermetic Medicine* (1655). After 1655 Vaughan seems to have written little poetry.

His earliest publication, *Poems, with the Tenth Satire of Juvenal Englished* (1646), is an undistinguished collection of translations and five poems reflecting Vaughan's years in London. By 1647 he had finished another volume of verses, *Olor Iscanus* (1651), which consists, like the first collection, of occasional poems, prose and verse translations, and a few original Latin poems.

There is little in these first two works to suggest the powerful and original *Silex Scintillans* (1650; enl. ed., 1655), the preface of which pays tribute to George Herbert, "whose holy life and verse gained many pious converts (of whom I am the least)..." Whereas Vaughan's first two volumes are entirely secular, *Silex Scintillans* is profoundly religious, often mystical and pietistic, suggesting that sometime between the writing of *Olor Iscanus* in 1647 and *Silex Scintillans,* Vaughan experienced a religious conversion, perhaps as a result of his war experiences or the death in 1648 of his younger brother William (who seems to be the person eulogized in several poems in *Silex Scintillans*). Whatever the occasion for Vaughan's conversion, it rendered him susceptible to the religious inspiration not only of Herbert, but of John Donne, the Jesuits, Owen Feltham, the writers of emblem books, and the Hermetic-Christian philosophers (the latter introduced to him by his brother Thomas).

Hermeticism was an occult philosophy attributed to the Greek god Hermes as he was identified with the Egyptian god Thoth, and who became popularly known in the Renaissance as the legendary philosopher Hermes Trismegistus ("Thrice-greatest Hermes"). The earliest Hermetic texts date from the second and third centuries B.C. and reflect an intermingling of Greek science and rationalism with Egyptian mysticism. The principal tenet of this vague cult is that truth derives from arcane revelations rather than from reason, and in the Renaissance the Hermeticists insisted that religious, historical, and scientific truths were somehow revealed by the transformations of matter in such occult sciences as alchemy and astrology. Hence the mystical Soul of the World became emanate through alchemical transmutations. In the constantly changing cosmos, all matter and life collect evil and corruption as metal exposed to oxygen and moisture accumulates rust, and the evils of time can be purged by alchemical refinements and astrological and magical divinations. These last Hermetical concepts are especially evident in Vaughan's poems "Resurrection and Immortality" and "Regeneration" in *Silex Scintillans* (the title, meaning "sparkling flint," suggesting both matter and revelation or illumination).

To these Hermetic ideas, which his brother Thomas expounded in several theosophical and quasi-scientific treatises during the period 1650-55, Vaughan brought a powerful response to nature, sensitive invocations of childhood, and searching analyses of soul. The recurring theme of *Silex Scintillans* is the paradoxical one of man's loss of God and his occasional revelations of God's glory. For Vaughan, life in the world is tantamount to exile and slavery:

> These bonds, this sad captivity,
> This leaden state, which men miscall
> Being and life, but is dead thrall.

This Platonic and Hermetic view of the world as the prison of the soul is contrasted to the transcendent visions that become occasions for Vaughan's mystical poems. In Vaughan's "The Retreat," which may have influenced Wordsworth's "Ode: On Intimations of Immortality," reminiscences of childhood spent in nature suggest, as in Wordsworth's poem, that the soul existed in sublimity before its fall into the darkness of the material world:

> Happy those early days! When I
> Shined in my angel-infancy,
> Before I understood this place
> Appointed for my second race,
> Or taught my soul to fancy aught
> But a white, celestial thought . . .

Like Blake and Wordsworth, Vaughan extols childhood as a spontaneous, joyous time in which God's creations in nature manifested a preëxistent glory, a prelapsarian unity with God that splintered into alienation when man fell into the corruption of flesh and world. Putting the Renaissance concept of the microcosm and macrocosm to mystical Christian application, Vaughan sees the "fulness of the Deity" in a single leaf or violet. In one of his greatest poems. "They Are All Gone into the World of Light," the Hermeticist needs no "perspective" or telescope to "dispense these mists" between man and the heavens if the alembic of pure memory can recall God's glory, or pious meditation reveal "brighter dreams" to his soul.

With Donne and Herbert, Vaughan is among the best of the METAPHYSICAL POETS. His radical contrasts and explosive transitions do not, however, result from insatiable wit or emotional tension, but from his sustained, mystical conception of consciousness as a vacillating state between the polarities of total darkness and blinding illumination. Between man and God nature stands like a gossamer veil. As a poet, Vaughan is rarely on the dark side of life, and hence his religious poems convey the serenity of glowing faith or the ecstasy of mystical revelation rather than the anxieties, perplexities, and tensions of other metaphysical poets.

Vaughan's mystical poems were little heeded during his lifetime and totally neglected throughout the eighteenth century. Blake read him with interest, however, as did Wordsworth and Coleridge. It was not until the latter part of the nineteenth century that Vaughan's poems began to be read widely, especially among orthodox Anglicans who found inspiration in his brilliant synthesis of orthodox theology, scripture, mysticism, and personal sentiment. The enthusiasm for the metaphysical poets after World War I secured Vaughan as one of the finest minor poets of the seventeenth century.

The standard edition, which includes the prose, is by L. C. Martin (2nd ed., 1957), also available in a shorter version, *The Poetry and Selected Prose* (1963). *The Complete Poetry* (1964) was edited by French Fogle. The standard biography is by F. E. Hutchinson (1947). Essential criticism is by Elizabeth Holmes, *Henry Vaughan and the Hermetic Philosophy* (1932); Helen C. White, *The Metaphysical Poets* (1936); Ross Gardner, *Henry Vaughan: Experience and the Tradition* (1959); E. C. Pettet, *Of Paradise and Light* (1960); and R. A. Durr, *On the Mystical Poetry of Henry Vaughan* (1962). There is a comprehensive bibliography by E. L. Marilla (1948).

Venus and Adonis. A narrative poem by William SHAKESPEARE, written in 1592 and first printed in 1593 with a dedication by Shakespeare to Henry Wriothesley, earl of Southampton. Shakespeare refers to his poem as "the first heir of my invention," meaning either that it was his first published poem or that it was his first effort at nondramatic verse. For his principal source he consulted the stories of Venus and Adonis and of Hermaphroditus and Salmacis in Ovid's *Metamorphoses,* probably in the English translation by Arthur Golding (1567). The six-line stanzas rhyming *ab ab cc* were derived from a similar erotic poem by Thomas Lodge, SCYLLA'S METAMORPHOSIS (1589), which describes the wooing of the bashful Scylla by the virile sea-god Glaucus. Shakespeare's poem is often compared with another great Ovidian epyllion published the same year, Marlowe's HERO AND LEANDER.

Venus and Adonis is characterized by vivid descriptions of nature, lengthy and often turgid dialogue, and realistic characterization, particularly of the feverishly erotic and aggressive Venus. The goddess of love passionately pursues the coy youth Adonis, who resists her advances as mere "lust" rather than true love. He refuses her invitation to meet with her on the morrow, preferring the hunt to her embraces. At dawn she hears the sounds of the hunt and finds him killed by a boar. The poem concludes with her lament.

Shakespeare's poem departs radically from Ovid in both content and style. Whereas Ovid writes in a lean, economical, and fast-moving style, depending largely on narrative summary to tell his story, Shakespeare plots his poem by simple encounters providing occasion for rich description and prolix speeches. Ovid's imagery is artificial, decorative, and traditional for his time; Shakespeare's is vivid and naturalistic, full of detailed descriptions of birds and animals, and he peppers his diction with archly witty conceits, puns, and word play. Ovid's attitude toward sex is sophisticated, playfully witty, and amoral, whereas Shakespeare's—if, indeed, he is entirely serious in the poem—is thoroughly didactic and even ambivalent.

In *Venus and Adonis* sex is neither Ovid's winsome game nor Marlowe's titillating eroticism, but a fever of the blood in which Venus preys on Adonis like a hawk tearing at a dove. Adonis is described as a victim rather than a lover, and Venus smothers him with lust and wrestles him to earth like an Amazon. In a way curiously similar to Sonnet 129 ("The expense of spirit in a waste of shame"), sex is depicted as predatory and violent:

Now quick desire hath caught the yielding prey,
And gluttonlike she feeds, yet never filleth,
Her lips are conquerers, his lips obey,
Paying what ransom the insulter willeth.

"Call it not love," the prudish Adonis berates Venus, "for love to heaven is fled / Since sweating lust on earth usurped his name."

For text and commentary the New Variorum Edition of *The Poems,* ed. Hyder E. Rollins (1938), is standard. Also essential for criticism and notes is the new Arden Shakespeare edition of *The Poems,* ed. F. T. Prince (1960). Several critics have compared Shakespeare's poem with Marlowe's *Hero and Leander:* W. B. C. Watkins, "Shakespeare's Banquet of Sense," *SoR,* VII (1942); Hallett Smith, *Elizabethan Poetry* (1952); and C. S. Lewis, *English Literature in the Sixteenth Century* (1954). G. Wilson Knight has a provocative interpretation in *The Burning Oracle* (1939).

Virgidemiarum. See HALL, JOSEPH; SATIRE.

Volpone, or The Fox. A comedy by Ben JONSON, written in 1606 and printed in 1607. For the most part the plot was invented by Jonson, although the theme of legacy hunting is found in sources as ancient and familiar as Lucian's *Dialogues.* Instead of the comedy of humours, Jonson employed in this play the bestiary, assigning to each principal character a parallel bird or animal. Volpone is the fox; his parasite Mosca is the fly; Peregrine, the falcon; Sir Pol, the parrot; Voltore, the vulture; Corbaccio, the crow; and Corvino, the raven. (For comment on comedy of humours, see JONSON, BEN.)

Volpone, an old and avaricious Venetian noble who is unmarried and childless, feigns a fatal illness in order to lure Voltore, Corbaccio, and Corvino into bestowing gifts on him in expectation of being named the old man's sole heir. To each of these Volpone's wily servant Mosca gives assurances that the old villain is near death. The greedy Corvino even goes so far as to offer his beautiful young wife Celia to Volpone as a token of his esteem. In a secondary plot Sir Politic Would-be (Sir Pol), a silly Englishman, and his wife Lady Politic Would-be, a garrulous social climber, are chastised severely by another Englishman in Venice, the rather sensible Peregrine, who is especially irritated by Sir Politic's absurd claims of being cognizant of state secrets in both Venice and England. Sir Politic is cured of his eccentricity when Peregrine pretends to have him arrested for treason.

After many complications, in which the would-be heirs outrival each other in avarice, Mosca tricks his master out of his wealth, but is in turn exposed by Volpone in a public trial. Mosca is whipped and confined to the galleys. Volpone's wealth is given to a hospital for incurables, and he himself sent to prison to become the sick man he pretended to be. Volpone's greedy dupes are also severely punished by the Venetian magistrates.

Volpone is the earliest of Jonson's comic masterpieces, and in many ways his most savage for its portrayal of the main characters as beasts and its harsh punishments meted out at the end. Volpone is like an orchestra leader tuning up and masterfully directing all the venalities of the other characters, and he himself is so protean a confidence man that he can turn himself into a dozen shapes and forms from mountebank to cavalier lover. The play is remarkable for its singular concentration on the theme of avarice, and for its dialogue replete with learned allusions to alchemy, astrology, medicine, law, and other sciences and pseudosciences, yet Jonson's amazing learning never becomes ponderous or pedantic. Except for Celia and Corbaccio's son Bonario, who are passive characters of bewildered innocence, the *dramatis personae* are all greedy birds and animals distinguishable only by their gradations of wit and levels of corruption. In spite of its harsh overtones, *Volpone* established Jonson as the leading satirist of his time (see SATIRE), and his own high opinion of the comedy can be inferred from the fact that he dedicated it to the "most noble and equal sisters," Oxford and Cambridge. In his prologue Jonson proclaims his observance of the neoclassic unities of time, place, and action.

The standard edition is in *Ben Jonson,* ed. C. H. Herford and Percy and Evelyn Simpson, 11 vols. (1925-53), V. More recent editions are by Alvin B. Kernan in the Yale Ben Jonson series (1962); Jay Halio in the Fountainwell Drama series (1968); and Philip Brockbank in the New Mermaid series (1968). Other excellent editions are by Janet Brunoski (1970) and Morris Venables (1970). The edition by Venables contains an extensive bibliography. Important criticism is by Harry Levin, "Jonson's Metempsychosis," *PQ,* XXII (1943); Helena W. Baum, *The Satiric and the Didactic in Ben Jonson's Comedy* (1947); Edward B. Partridge, *The Broken Compass: A Study of the Major Comedies of Ben Jonson* (1958); Robert E. Knoll, *Ben Jonson's Plays: An Introduction* (1964); William Empson, "*Volpone,*" *Hud R,* XXI (1968); Allan C. Dessen, *Jonson's Moral Comedy* (1971); Charles A. Hallett, "Jonson's Celia: A Reinterpretation of *Volpone,*" *SP,* LXVIII (1971); and Ian Donaldson, "*Volpone:* Quick and Dead," *EIC,* XXI (1971).

W

Waller, Edmund (1606-1687). Poet. Born of wealthy landed gentry in Coleshill, Buckinghamshire, Waller was educated at Eton and King's College, Cambridge. He left Cambridge without taking a degree and studied law at Lincoln's Inn. There is evidence that he was a member of Parliament at age sixteen. In 1631 he married a London heiress, whose death three years later added to his already impressive wealth. During the years 1636-39 he courted unsuccessfully Lady Dorothy Sidney, daughter of the second earl of Leicester, whom he celebrates as the beautiful but unresponsive "Sacharissa" in many of his love poems.

Waller's checkered political career reflects the vagaries of public issues and events in the 1640s. Renowned for his eloquence in Parliament, he championed religious toleration and opposed the bishops on the eve of revolution (as in his tract *Speech against Prelates' Innovations* [1641]), but switched to the king's cause at the outbreak of hostilities. In 1643 he was convicted of plotting to deliver London to the king's army. Fined and banished, he spent several years in Paris in the company of his friends John Evelyn and Thomas Hobbes, the latter serving for a time as tutor to Waller's son. In 1651 he secured permission to return to England, and rewarded Cromwell's magnanimity with "A Panegyric to My Lord Protector." With the Restoration Waller was restored to Parliament and the king's good favor. When Charles II observed that Waller's poetic tribute to him was artistically inferior to the panegyric on Cromwell, Waller is said to have replied, with characteristic wit: "Sire, we poets never succeed so well in writing truth as in fiction."

Waller wrote about half of his poetry after 1660. He continued to fight for religious toleration, and became one of the first members of the Royal Society. Three editions of his poems had appeared in 1645, all of which he repudiated in his first authorized edition of 1664. His *Divine Poems* was published in 1685, and a fuller edition came out in 1686. A posthumous second part of the secular lyrics was printed in 1690, with a preface by Francis Attebury praising Waller's perfection of the heroic couplet, his admirable clarity, and his avoidance of Donne's syncopated rhythms and monosyllabic diction.

Thus Waller's trim and elegant verses, couched in heroic couplets, link the neoclassicism of Ben Jonson and Robert Herrick to the Age of Reason. Overlooking the use of heroic couplets by Michael Drayton, Ben Jonson, Sir John Beaumont, and George Sandys, John Dryden and other Restoration critics praised Waller as being the chief innovator of that poetic form. Waller himself stated that he learned his "harmony of numbers" from Edward Fairfax (d. 1635), who rendered into English couplets Torquato Tasso's *Gerusalemme liberata* as *Geoffrey of Bulloigne, or The Recovery of Jerusalem* (1600). Alexander Pope commended Waller for his orderly verses in *Epistle to Augustus* and *Essay on Criticism,* and imitated Waller's style in his early *Pastorals* and *Windsor Forest.* Waller's reputation in the eighteenth century was further enhanced by Samuel Johnson, whose "Life of Waller" is among the best essays in his *Lives of the Poets* (1779-81).

The hallmark of Waller's poetry is wit, a quality that recalls Andrew Marvell's metaphysical archness combined with rhetorical balance and grace, as in Waller's popular "On a Girdle":

That which her slender waist confined
Shall now my joyful temples bind;
No monarch but would give his crown,
His arms might do what this has done.

It was my heaven's extremest sphere,
The pale which held that lovely deer;
My joy, my grief, my hope, my love,
Did all within this circle move . . .

Yet the similarities to Marvell's "Definition of Love" are superficial; what informs Waller's clever metaphors is not metaphysical tension but adroit rhetoric in the service of courtly compliments. His true masters are not Donne and Marvell. but Jonson and Herrick, whose imaginative strength and occasional fire he lacks. In one justifiably popular lyric, "Go, lovely rose," Waller achieves, at least in the first stanza, just the right balance of epigrammatic wit and emotional restraint:

Go, lovely rose,
Tell her that wastes her time and me
That now she knows,
When I resemble her to thee,
How sweet and fair she seems to be.

Characteristically, the three remaining stanzas fail to sustain this classic economy and inevitability of phrase. A highly precocious writer whose poems date back as early as 1623, Waller wrote steadily for sixty years without appreciable change or growth, and in a way suggestive of his career as a whole, even his best poems rarely fulfill the splendid promise of their first stanzas. What he lacked was the quality Sidney described as *energeia,* or passionate conviction, and his real forte was not, as occasional successes like "Go, lovely rose" might suggest, love poetry. The poems to Sacharissa, more calculated than amorous, recall to mind that his best verses were polished compliments to such diverse personages as Jonson (in *Jonsonus Virbius,* 1638), Sir William Davenant, Henry Lawes (who set Waller's lyrics to music in 1638), Charles I, Oliver Cromwell, John Evelyn, Charles II, Sir William Killigrew, and the prince of Orange. One of Waller's last poems, "Of the Last Verses in the Book," conveys the rhetorical mastery and cool restraint that earned him the admiration of the Augustan age:

The soul's dark cottage, battered and decayed,
Lets in new light through chinks that time has
made;
Stronger by weakness, wiser, men become
As they draw near to their eternal home;
Leaving the old, both worlds at once they view,
That stand upon the threshold of the new.

Still standard, with an excellent brief biography, is G. Thorn-Drury's edition of the *Poems* for the Muses' Library, 2 vols. (1905). Samuel Johnson's "Life of Waller" in *Lives of the Poets* is still of great value. For Waller's life and times, see Julia Cartwright, *Sacharissa* (1901), and Kurt Weber, *Lucius Cary, Second Viscount Falkland* (1940). Critical commentary on Waller's poetry is in R. L. Sharp, *From Donne to Dryden* (1940), and Warren L. Chernaik, *The Poetry of Limitation; A Study of Edmund Waller* (1968).

Walton, Izaak (1593-1683). Biographer and miscellanist. Born of yeoman stock in Stafford and apprenticed at an early age to a London ironmonger, Walton owned his own shop in Cornhill before he came of age, and by 1618 had moved to Fleet Street as a freeman of the Ironmongers' Company. By this time Walton was probably already a wealthy man, a devout Anglican who gave time and money to the church. Walton's priest at St. Dunstan's Church near Fleet Street was the poet John Donne, who introduced the likeable Walton to Michael Drayton, Ben Jonson, Sir Henry Wotton, and other literati. A quiet, self-taught, simple man of many cultural interests, Walton sought out the company of ministers, poets, and dramatists, writing only a few mediocre verses himself but enjoying the friendship and conversation of more eloquent men.

In 1626 Walton married Rachel Floyd, great-grandniece of Thomas Cranmer. When she died in 1640 after bearing seven children, none of whom survived infancy, Walton married Anne Ken, stepsister of the bishop of Bath and Wells, by whom he had three children. During the Civil War, Walton remained a Royalist, working quietly and unobtrusively at his business of ironmongering and his lifelong passion of lake and stream fishing. Walton's first publication was a memoir attached to a posthumous edition of poems by his friend Sir Henry Wotton in 1640; this memoir was published separately as *The Life of Sir Henry Wotton* (1651).

The work for which Walton is best known. THE COMPLEAT ANGLER, first appeared in 1653, and he continued to revise and amplify it until 1676. Some of the lore about fly-fishing (of which Walton knew little) was supplied in the first part of the book by Thomas Bowker, a retired cook. Walton's young friend Charles Cotton contributed the dialogue of Venator, the hunter. Besides Venator, the others who debate the superiority of their favorite sport are a fisherman. Piscator (Walton himself) and a falconer, Auceps. The ostensible point is to show the merits of fishing over other sports—a dispute Piscator unquestionably wins—but in substance Walton mingles his charming apostrophe to angling with digressions on manners and morals, general theology and commonplace philosophy, and loving descriptions of the beauties of outdoor living. The whimsical, ingenuous nature of the author shines through on every page, and millions of readers who have never baited a hook have fallen in love with Walton's treatise. Part II, added to the fifth edition (1676), was written by Charles Cotton.

The author's personality is equally diffused throughout his biographies of the four great Anglican divines who were his personal friends: John DONNE (1640), Richard HOOKER (1665), George HERBERT (1670), and Robert Sanderson (1678). These are humble, adulatory biographies in which the author pays tribute to the steady Christian faith, humility, charity, and learning of his subjects. Walton shows little interest in subtleties of character; he is bent chiefly on showing how fully his subject presents a portrait of the Anglican saint. Nevertheless, he is always richly informative, quoting from letters, sermons, or poems and interpolating his own opinions when these seem appropriate. He also reports conversations, frequently in the first person, and provides full details of his subject's family background, education, professional achievements and talents (see BIOGRAPHY). The most famous of Walton's *Lives* is that of Donne. Walton mainly emphasizes the later years of Donne's career and touches only lightly on the "rake" and "frequent visitor of ladies" who wrote the *Songs and Sonnets.* Characteristically, the reverential Walton focuses on the great divine, author of *The Holy Sonnets* and stirring preacher of St. Paul's Cathedral, who, reports Walton, "preached like an angel on a cloud." Walton also traces the painful development of Donne's religious views from Roman Catholic to Anglican, from religious and social renegade to the king's trusted servant, and he sympathetically treats of the great financial suffering and domestic happiness that stemmed from Donne's marriage.

The last years of Walton's life were spent at Winchester, where his son-in-law served as prebendary.

All of Walton's major works were edited by Geoffrey L. Keynes, *The Compleat Walton* (1929). The best edition of *The Lives* is by S. B. Carter (1951). The standard biography is by Margaret Bottrall (1955). For criticism, see H. J. Oliver, "Izaak Walton's Prose Style," *RES,* XXI (1945) and D. Novarr, *The Making of Walton's Lives* (1958). Bibliographies are by J. E. Butt, "A Bibliography of Izaak Walton's *Lives,*" *Proceedings of the Oxford Bibliographical Society,* II (1930) and Dennis G. Donovan, "Recent Studies in Burton and Walton," *ELR,* I (1971).

Warning for Fair Women, A (anon). See DOMESTIC TRAGEDY.

War of the Theaters or **Poetomachia.** See JONSON, BEN; MARSTON, JOHN; SATIROMASTIX.

Water Poet, The. See TAYLOR, JOHN.

Watson, Thomas (1557?-1592). Poet and translator. Now little read, Watson was highly esteemed by his contemporaries for his mastery of classical and continental literature. He attended Oxford before studying civil and canon law abroad. In 1581 he published his Latin version of *Antigone* translated from Greek (see TRANSLATIONS). His first English work, *Hecatompathia, or A Passionate Century of Love* (1582), sought to educate English readers to the delights of the Petrarchan mode by offering one hundred poems taken from Italian, French, and classical sources, rendered into eighteen-line "sonnets" and accompanied by a short explanatory gloss. Watson was also one of the first to introduce the Italian lyric, publishing in 1590 his *First Set of Italian Madrigals Englished* (see SONGBOOKS). His popular Latin version of Tasso's pastoral *Aminta* (1585) was translated into English by Abraham Fraunce, in which form it went though several printings (1587, 1588, 1589, 1596; see PASTORAL). His Latin pastoral *Amintae gaudia* was published posthumously in 1592; his *Tears of Fancy,* containing sixty English sonnets in imitation of Petrarch and Ronsard, appeared in 1593 (see SONNET SEQUENCES). He is said to have written plays, but none attributable to him has been identified.

Watson's *Poems* was edited by E. Arber (1895), his *Hecatompathia* by S. K. Heninger (1964). For biographical details see Mark Eccles, *Christopher Marlowe in London* (1934).

Webster, John (1580?-1634?). Dramatist. Very little is known for certain about Webster's life. In his preface to *Monuments of Honor* (1624) he describes himself as "born free of the Merchant Taylors' Company," a bit of information that has helped to identify him as the son of John Webster, a freeman of that guild and perhaps the "cloth-worker," who died in London in September 1625. Webster's name first appears in Philip Henslowe's Diary in 1602, when he recorded payment to Webster, Munday, Middleton, Drayton, "and the rest" for a lost play, *Caesar's Fall.* In 1604 Webster wrote the induction to John Marston's *The Malcontent* and is believed to have worked in a minor capacity with Thomas Dekker on *Westward Ho!* (perf. 1604) and *Northward Ho!* (perf. 1605). In the preface to his *The Devil's Law-Case* (1623), Webster refers to another play by him, *The Guise,* but this too is lost. Webster contributed twenty-two sketches, such as "A Fair and Happy Milkmaid" and "A Roaring Boy," to the 1615 edition of Sir Thomas Overbury's collection of characters (see CHARACTERS).

Although many plays or parts of plays have been attributed to Webster, the only extant plays known for certain to be his—in addition to the masque *Monuments of Honor* and the tragicomedy *The Devil's Law-Case*—are two of the greatest tragedies of the period, THE WHITE DEVIL (1612) and THE DUCHESS OF MALFI (perf. 1614, pr. 1623). Both are drawn from near-contemporary events of revenge and blood lust recounted in Italian novellas and dramatized with all the stark intensity of Shakespeare's *Othello* and *Macbeth* (albeit, as R. W. Dent has shown in *John Webster's Borrowing* [1960], Webster derives little in the way of language directly from Shakespeare).

Webster's characters, and especially his noble, passionate, and strangely obsessed heroines, are creatures of great complexity. His villains, such as Ferdinand and Bosola in *The Duchess of Malfi* or the ambition-crazed Flamineo in *The White Devil,* clearly derive from the early Elizabethan revenge tragedies but somehow transcend these affinities by their wholly credible confusions and afflictions. For Webster evil is not motivated by any perceptible goals but by some anguished compulsion darkly conveyed in ominous metaphors and images.

More than any Elizabethan dramatist except Shakespeare, Webster poetically weaves his themes in imagery patterns and repeated symbols, in muted ironies and profoundly affective motifs. His two masterpieces are obviously the works of a slow, patient craftsman who strove for total integration of plot, language, and character. In replying to those who had criticized his slowness of composition. Webster wrote: ". . . I confess I do not write with a goose-quill winged with two feathers, and if they will needs make it my fault, I must answer them with that of Euripides to Alcestides, a tragic writer: Alcestides objecting that Euripides had only in three days composed three verses, whereas himself had written three hundred: 'Thou tell'st true,' (quoth he) 'but here's the difference—thine shall only be read for three days, whereas mine shall continue three ages'" (Preface, *The White Devil,* 1612 edition).

The standard edition of Webster's *Works* is edited by F. L. Lucas, 4 vols. (1927; rev. ed., 1958), which includes Webster's characters in the Overbury collection. *The Devil's Law-Case* was edited by Frances A. Shirley in the Regents Renaissance Drama series (1972). Two excellent critical studies are Clifford Leech, *John Webster* (1951), and Travis Bogard, *The Tragic Satire of John Webster* (1955).

Essays on Webster have been collected in two anthologies: *John Webster,* ed. G. K. and S. K. Hunter (1969); and *John Webster,* ed. Brian Morris, in the Mermaid Critical Commentaries series (1970). There is a Concise Bibliography by S. A. Tannenbaum (1941), updated in "John Webster (1940-65)" ed. Dennis Donovan, in *Elizabethan Bibliographies Supplements,* I (1967).

Whetstone, George (1544?-1587). Poet and prose writer. Whetstone was one of five sons born to Robert Whetstone, a haberdasher of Westcheap, London. Very little is known of Whetstone's life. He may have been at one of the Inns of Court around 1576. In 1578 he accompanied Sir Humphrey Gilbert on an abortive expedition to discover a northwest passage to China, and in 1580 travelled to Italy, a visit he describes in *An Heptameron of Civil Discourses* (1582). Thomas C. Izard has shown that almost all previous accounts of Whetstone's military service are erroneous: Whetstone was not a soldier in the Low Countries until 1587, and it was Whetstone's brother Bernard who was with Sir Philip Sidney when the latter was killed at Zutphen, not the poet. Mark Eccles has produced evidence to show that Whetstone was killed in 1587 in a duel with an English captain ("Whetstone's Death," *TLS* [August 27, 1931]).

As a man of letters Whetstone put his hand to almost every genre in vogue—novellas, pastorals, prose romances, "complaints," conduct books, and didactic treatises. His first published work was *The Rock of Regard* (1576), a series of prose tales interspersed with verse "complaints" illustrating the sad plights of dissolute women like Cressida. Some of Whetstone's verses in *The Rock* have vigor, particularly his "Invective Against Dice," with its brilliant little scene of the gambler just before he is fleeced of his winnings by a greedy tart:

Then roists he in his ratling [corded] silks,
And sorts with Venus' dames,
Whose loving looks enforce his heart
To fry in Cupid's flames.

Whetstone is best remembered for his unacted tragicomedy in two parts, PROMOS AND CASSANDRA (1578), which supplied Shakespeare with the main plot of MEASURE FOR MEASURE. Having written the play in fourteeners and "poulter's measure," Whetstone went back to his source, the fifth novel of the eighth decade of Giraldi Cinthio's *Hecatomithi* (1565), and reworked the story into a prose tale in *An Heptameron of Civil Discourses,* a long prose work describing the genteel customs, or "exercises," of Italian nobility.

A Mirror for Magistrates of Cities and *A Touchstone for the Time,* two prose works originally published together in 1584 under the first title, were reprinted as *The Enemy to Unthriftness* (1586). This work marks Whetstone's development away from storytelling and toward relatively nonfictive didactic exposition and sermonizing. It does not, as many scholars have stated, represent Whetstone's conversion to Puritanism or his repudiation of stage plays. Whetstone's *The Honorable Reputation of a Soldier* (1585) is somewhat unique in being a conduct book setting forth "moral rules of those that follow Mars" and emphasizing philosophical topics like duty, courage, honor, and military justice instead of fortifications and tactics. Whetstone's plain statement that at the time of writing he was without any military training would appear to be supported by the fact that he takes most of his military lore from Roman historians rather than from his own experiences.

The English Mirror (1586), dedicated to Queen Elizabeth, is a prose encyclopedia of vices and virtues that reads like a supplement to Whetstone's *A Mirror for Magistrates of Cities,* except that the latter treatise more or less concentrates on the sin of envy and envy's opposite, peace (since strife, by Whetstone's reasoning, invariably springs from envy). Whetstone's next publication, *The Censure of a Loyal Subject* (1587), describes the executions of the fourteen men condemned for their roles in the Babington Plot, the conspiracy to assassinate Queen Elizabeth and replace her on the throne with Mary Stuart. Since Whetstone chose to narrate events in dialogue form, it is not very informative.

Whetstone's main shortcoming is one he shared with many of his Elizabethan contemporaries: he tends to obscure a subject in a fog of didacticism or encomia. This trait is especially manifest in his six elegies, or "metrical biographies," on his personal friend George Gascoigne (1578?), Sir Philip Sidney (1587?), and other notables.

There is no edition of Whetstone's complete works. The standard biography and critical study by Thomas C. Izard, *George Whetstone: Mid-Elizabethan Gentleman of Letters* (1952), corrects many erroneous conceptions of Whetstone's life and writings. His prose is discussed by George Krapp in *The Rise of English Literary Prose* (1915).

White Devil, The. A tragedy by John WEBSTER, written around 1609-12 and printed in 1612. It is based on actual events involving the murder of Vittoria Accoramboni, on December 22, 1585. Webster's play was adapted for the eighteenth-century stage by Nahum Tate as *Injured Love, or The Cruel Husband* (1707).

Paulo Giordano Orsini, duke of Brachiano, falls in love with Vittoria Corombona, who is married to Camillo, a foolish, impotent old man. Brachiano is married to the virtuous but phlegmatic Isabella, sister of the powerful Francisco, duke of Florence, and of Cardinal Lorenzo de Monticelso. Brachiano enlists the services of Vittoria's unscrupulous brother Flamineo in his love suit, and during their first interview Vittoria slyly recounts a dream that clearly suggests Brachiano should murder both Camillo and Isabella. Flamineo commissions a quack doctor to poison Brachiano's picture, and Isabella dies after dutifully kissing it before retiring for the night. Flamineo also arranges for Camillo to break his neck while exercising on a vaulting horse. Cardinal Monticelso and the duke of Florence agree that Brachiano is too powerful at the moment to accuse of these crimes, although his now open love affair with Vittoria makes him a suspect in the murders. Since Vittoria was in her husband's house at the time of his murder, and because she is less powerful than Brachiano, she is brought to trial by the cardinal and the duke of Florence as an accessory in Camillo's murder.

At her trial Vittoria boldly faces down her accusers, proclaiming her innocence of the murders and charging her judges with hypocrisy. Nevertheless, she is sent to be confined in a religious house. Brachiano invades the convent, carries her out of confinement, and marries her. Soon afterward Cardinal Monticelso is elected pope, and he promptly excommunicates the lovers.

The duke of Florence, disguised as Mulinassar, a Moor, and accompanied by Count Lodovico and Gasparo disguised as Knights of Malta, visit Brachiano's palace at Padua. Lodovico poisons Brachiano's helmet as he is about to enter the lists, and while he lingers in agony on his deathbed, Lodovico and Gasparo attend him in the disguise of Capuchin priests rendering the last rites. As Vittoria watches, they strangle Brachiano in his bed.

Brachiano's ghost later appears to Flamineo and warns him of a terrible death. When Flamineo's demand for blood money is spurned by his sister Vittoria, he threatens to kill both her and her maid Zanche. Lodovico and his followers arrive to stab all three to death. Shortly thereafter the young prince Giovanni arrives to arrest Lodovico and punish everyone responsible for the bloodshed.

The White Devil is a powerful portrayal of illicit passion, Machiavellian intrigue, revenge, and murder. The heroine is neither tempted nor misled by her brutal lover; unlike Lady Macbeth, she is not motivated by ambition for herself or for another, nor even by revenge, as was Bel-imperia in Kyd's *The Spanish Tragedy.* Instead, Vittoria is consumed by the rawest lust and depravity of will, and she remains contemptuous of any virtue except the iron courage she herself personifies. Like the duchess of Malfi, the heroine of Webster's other distinguished tragedy, she faces death with the same fortitude with which she defied moral conventions, but unlike the duchess, who is serenely composed and reflective at her end, asking only that her children be given their medicine and proclaiming proudly that she is "the Duchess of Malfi still," Vittoria faces down Flamineo and her murderers like a snarling vixen set upon by dogs. The difference between the two heroines suggests the essential contrast between the two tragedies. In *The White Devil* the instinct to love is either unbridled lust, as with Vittoria and Brachiano, or mindless obsession, as with Brachiano's doting wife; and sexual desire is not a life force but an urge to destroy. Like Shakespeare's *Othello, The White Devil* is a "nocturnal" tragedy, darkened by images of sleep and dreams, tombs, and passions nurtured in shadows. "This place is hell," Vittoria cries, and the villainous Lodovico concludes this darkest of Jacobean tragedies with the grim observation, "I limned this night-piece, and it was my best."

The definitive edition is in *The Works,* ed. F. L. Lucas, 4 vols. (1927; rev. ed., 1958). John Russell Brown has edited *The White Devil* for the Revels Plays (1960); Elizabeth M. Brennan in a New Mermaid text (1966); and J. R. Mulryne in the Regents Renaissance

Drama series (1969). Important criticism is in Lucas' edition; in *John Webster: A Critical Anthology,* ed. G. K. and S. K. Hunter (1969) which contains critical essays from the seventeenth to the twentieth century; and in *John Webster,* ed. Brian Morris, in the Mermaid Critical Commentaries series (1970). See also Cliford Leech, *John Webster: A Critical Study* (1951); Travis Bogard, *The Tragic Satire of John Webster* (1955); Gunnar Boklund, *The Sources of The White Devil* (1957); and J. R. Mulryne, *"The White Devil* and *The Duchess of Malfi,"* in Stratford-upon-Avon Studies, I (1960).

Whythorne, Thomas (1528-96). See AUTOBIOGRAPHY.

Wild-Goose Chase, The. A comedy by John FLETCHER, written around 1621 and printed in 1652. No source is known. A witty and sophisticated comedy of manners that anticipates those by William Congreve and George Etherege during the Restoration period, Fletcher's play was revised in 1702 by George Farquhar as *The Inconstant.* The theme of the playful rake caught in matrimony by a virtuous lady became a favorite one in the comedy of manners after 1660.

Returning home to Paris from Italy is old La Castre's wild young son Mirabel and his two equally madcap friends, Belleur and Pinac. La Castre would like to see Mirabel, the "wild goose," settle down in marriage to his betrothed, the beautiful and witty Oriana, but the rake wants no part of matrimony. Meanwhile Oriana conspires with her brother De Gard to capture this wild goose as her husband. Most of the action concerns Oriana's stratagems and those of Monsieur Nantolet's two beautiful daughters, the gay, vivacious Rosalura, and the austere and learned Lillia Bianca, to snare Belleur and Pinac. In the end the wild goose and his friends are tricked into declarations of love and proposals of marriage.

Few comedies of manners rival Fletcher's fast-paced and robust battle of the sexes. Unlike the Restoration comedies of this type, Fletcher's conveys a wholesome and innocent vitality rather than a leering cynicism. His Mirabel is more like a boy playing hooky than a polished roué, while his antagonist Oriana is almost evenly balanced between a modest lass and a fierce vixen. Although episodic and rambling, the play contains well-constructed individual scenes, and Fletcher's colloquial blank verse often expresses vividly a character's situation and attitude in a few lines, as in this comment on Mirabel by Monsieur De Gard:

He marry? he'll be hanged first!
                                        he knows no more
What the conditions and the ties of love are,
The honest purposes and grounds of marriage,
Nor will know, nor be ever brought to endeavor,
Than I do how to build a church! [I, *i*]

The Wild-Goose Chase is in *Elizabethan Plays,* ed. Hazelton Spencer (1933), and in *The Development of the English Drama,* ed. G. E. Bentley (1950). For criticism, see A. C. Sprague, *Beaumont and Fletcher on the Restoration Stage* (1926), and Clifford Leech, *The John Fletcher Plays* (1962).

Wilkins, George (fl. 1604-08). See MISERIES OF ENFORCED MARRIAGE, THE.

Wilson, Thomas (1525?-1581). For comment on his *Art of Rhetoric,* see CRITICISM, LITERARY; INKHORN TERMS.

Winter's Tale, The. A romance by William SHAKESPEARE, written in 1610-11 and first printed in the 1623 Folio. The source of the main plot is Robert Greene's popular prose romance PANDOSTO, OR THE TRIUMPH OF TIME (1588), which Shakespeare followed closely.

Leontes, king of Sicilia, wrongly believes that his virtuous wife Hermione has committed adultery with his life-long friend Polixenes, king of Bohemia, who is visiting the court of Sicilia. When Hermione becomes pregnant, Leontes is convinced that Polixenes is the real father, and even imagines that his son Mamillius is not really his own. Crazed with jealousy, he imprisons Hermione on trumped-up charges and persuades the virtuous Lord Camillo to poison Polixenes. Camillo balks at the deed, however, and flees to Bohemia with Polixenes.

When a daughter, Perdita, is born to Hermione, Leontes disowns the child and orders Antigonus, husband of Hermione's serving-lady Paulina, to leave the child in some deserted place. At her trial Hermione courageously defends herself, and her innocence is further indicated by the arrival of messengers who convey to Leontes the words of Apollo's oracle: Hermione is chaste and Leontes a tyrant destined to "live without an heir, if that which is lost be not found." When Hermione learns that Mamillius has died of grief over his father's brutal treatment of her, she collapses and her serving-lady Paulina returns to inform Leontes that Hermione has died. Leontes nevertheless persists in his jealousy and rejects the oracle as false.

Hermione's daughter Perdita ("that which is lost") was abandoned on the seacoast of Bohemia by Antigonus, who was soon afterward eaten by a bear. Hence Perdita's whereabouts could not be reported to Leontes. Perdita was rescued by an old shepherd and raised as if she were his own. In Bohemia she later meets Florizel, son of Polixenes, disguised as a shepherd, and the two fall in love. These events involving Perdita and Florizel take place sixteen years after Hermione's trial and presumed death. Polixenes is enraged to learn his son is enamored of a commoner, and the lovers flee to Sicilia, pursued by Polixenes and Camillo in disguise. There Perdita's true identity is discovered by her now repentant father, who makes amends with Polixenes. At Paulina's house Leontes views a statue that bears an amazing resemblance to Hermione, and when he kisses it, the statue descends from its pedestal and embraces him. It is, of course, the living Hermione, who has remained in seclusion all these years awaiting the fulfilment of the oracle. Leontes begs her forgiveness, and the reconciled husband and wife, together with Polixenes, joyously prepare to celebrate the nuptials of the widow Paulina to Camillo as well as those of Perdita and Florizel.

The changes Shakespeare made in his source were chiefly to give Greene's romance additional motivation and coherence. Unlike Greene's characters, Shakespeare's have some reasons for acting as they do and are not blown between Sicilia and Bohemia entirely by winds of chance. Nevertheless, *The Winter's Tale* is one of Shakespeare's most episodic and fortuitous tales and retains many of the traditional elements of the old wives' tale suggested by the title—oracles, damsels in distress, disguises, abandoned waifs, and miraculous encounters. Leontes' jealousy is as unaccountable and perversely arbitrary as Lear's division of his kingdom, and like Lear's Leontes' madness is only healed by time and suffering. Like *Cymbeline* and *The Tempest, The Winter's Tale* is a benign romance of reconciliation, its underlying theme the optimistic one that the sins of the father need not be visited upon the next generation—that ancient crimes can be atoned for and men reborn through the redeeming power of love.

A standard text is the new Arden edition, ed. J. H. P. Pafford (1963). Shakespeare's use of Greene's romance is analyzed by Kenneth Muir, *Shakespeare's Sources,* 2 vols. (1957), I. E. M. W. Tillyard discusses the play at length in *Shakespeare's Last Plays* (1938), as does S. L. Bethell in *The Winter's Tale* (1947), which interprets it as a Christian allegory. See also R. G. Hunter, *Shakespeare and the Comedy of Forgiveness* (1965); Fitzroy Pyle, *The Winter's Tale: A Commentary on the Structure* (1969); Joan Hartwig, "The Tragicomic Perspective of *The Winter's Tale,*" *ELH,* XXXVII (1970); William Blissett, "The Wide Gap of Time: *The Winter's Tale,*" *ELR,* I (1971); and Philip M. Weinstein, "An Interpretation of Pastoral in *The Winter's Tale,*" *SQ,* XX (1971).

Witch of Edmonton, The. A tragedy by Thomas DEKKER, John FORD, and William ROWLEY, written around 1621 and printed in 1658. Some scholars believe John Webster may also have collaborated on the play. For the witchcraft story the authors used a pamphlet by Henry Goodcole, *The Wonderful Discovery of Eliz. Sawyer, a Witch Late of Edmonton* (1621), describing the execution of Elizabeth Sawyer for witchcraft on April 19, 1621. No source is known for the other plot, which is on the popular theme of the miseries of forced marriage.

Frank Thorney, the young servant of Sir Arthur Clarington, secretly marries another servant in Sir Arthur's household, Winnifrede, whom Frank has made pregnant. Fearful that his father Old Thorney will disown him if he learns the circumstances of the marriage, Frank sends Winnifrede to live with her uncle while he plays for time in which to reveal the truth gradually to his father. Sir Arthur soon learns of Frank's transgression and, ignorant of the marriage, offers Frank a large dowry if he will marry the girl; Frank joyfully accepts the money and informs Sir Arthur of the secret wedding. Sir Arthur promises not to reveal this information until Frank can prepare his father for the news. Sir Arthur's concern for Winnifrede, however, is anything but altruistic: it was he, not Frank,who first seduced her, and he now offers her gold if she will remain in his household as Frank's wife and maintain an illicit relationship with him.

Winnifrede spurns the offer, proclaiming her love for Frank and her moral reform from "a loose whore to a repentant wife."

Old Thorney, meanwhile, arranges to have Frank marry Susan Carter, daughter of Old John Carter, a wealthy Hertfordshire yeoman. Before the marriage Susan was courted by Warbeck, a swaggering braggart, and her sister Katherine by Somerton, a virtuous young landowner. Old Carter yields to Susan's choice of Frank, whom she had fallen in love with some years before.

In another part of Edmonton, Mother Sawyer, an ignorant and wretchedly poor old crone, is slowly driven to witchcraft by the persecution of her neighbors. Her chief tormentor is Old Banks, who curses and beats her whenever she trespasses on his property hunting for a few sticks to warm herself. One day a black dog called Tom with miraculous powers of speech appears to Mother Sawyer, reveals its identity as a disguised devil, and promises her revenge against her neighbors in exchange for her soul. At first her vengeance is merely farcical, consisting of making Old Bank's clownish son Cuddy stumble into a muddy pool while pursuing a flirtatious spirit he believes to be Katherine Carter, with whom he is enamored; but soon Tom arouses the whole community to hysteria as livestock begin to sicken mysteri ously and women miscarry.

Once married, Susan finds her husband acting strangely—occasionally calling her Winnifrede and muttering enigmatic riddles about his past. Blinded by love, however, she attributes his conduct to anxiety over her former suitor Warbeck's having challenged him to a duel. Frank conceives a treacherous plot: pretending to go on an extended business trip, he will abscond with Old Carter's dowry and escape abroad with Winnifrede disguised as his groom. The plan miscarries when Susan, refusing to be separated, follows him into a lonely grove, where he blurts out the truth about his past. When the dog Tom rubs against his leg, Frank is seized by a violent passion and stabs Susan to death. At the devil's suggestion, he slashes his arms and ties himself to a tree to make the murder appear to be the work of brigands. He then concocts the story that he knows the assailants but is bound by oath not to reveal their names; however, he slyly describes them in such a way that Warbeck and Somerton are arrested for Susan's murder.

Called in by the justice of the peace to examine Mother Sawyer for witchcraft, Sir Arthur hears her contemptuously define "witch" as one who, among other things, offers a maiden gold in exchange for her virtue, and he is convinced that she harbors supernatural knowledge dangerous to his reputation. Her guilt is further established when her old enemy Ann Ratcliffe goes mad and commits suicide, and when Tom ferociously attacks Old Banks and his followers. Frank Thorney is convicted on much stronger evidence: a bloody dagger is found in his coat; the dog Tom frolics about his bed; and when Susan's body is brought into his room, it bleeds profusely in his presence. At Tyburn both Frank and Mother Sawyer confess their crimes, repent, and are hanged. Somerton weds Katherine, and Sir Arthur, having confessed to his abuse of Winnifrede, is made to pay the girl a thousand pounds.

The Witch of Edmonton is not a great tragedy, but it is an interesting play for its use of the drama as a vehicle for journalism. It is apparent that the playwrights believed firmly in witchcraft, yet they also viewed Mother Sawyer compassionately as a helpless victim of a bigoted and ruthless community. The domestic tragedy of Frank Thorney, in spite of its didacticism and improbabilities, is an effective counterplot to the witchcraft story. It is impossible to assign with much certainty the respective shares of the collaborators. The farcical scenes with Cuddy are usually attributed to Rowley, largely because he is known to have performed low comedy roles. The sympathetic treatment of Mother Sawyer and the scenes of rural life bear the stamp of Dekker, reknowned for his ability to combine realism and sentiment. The domestic tragedy may have been conceived by Ford, whose recurring theme is forbidden and tormented marriage, and the sensitively drawn characterization of Winnifrede recalls several of Ford's other long-suffering heroines.

The standard edition is in *The Dramatic Works,* ed. Fredson Bowers, 4 vols. (1953-61), III. There is a Mermaid edition by Ernest Rhys (1949). For criticism, see Mary L. Hunt, *Thomas Dekker: A Study* (1911), and Edward Sackville-West, "The Significance of *The Witch of Edmonton,*" *Criterion,* XVII (1937).

Wither, George (1588–1667). Poet and miscellanist. Born in Bentworth near Alton, Hampshire, Wither attended Oxford for three years, then returned to his father's farm. He enrolled in Lincoln's Inn in 1615 but did not proceed to the bar; instead, he went to court, where his poems on Prince Henry and Elizabeth of Bohemia, *Henry's Obsequies* and *Epithalamia* (both 1612), attracted favorable comment. His hopes for preferment were dashed when he was imprisoned for several months because of his satiric *Abuses Stripped and Whipped* (1613). As Charles Lamb observed, it is impossible to explain how Wither's castigations of such abstractions as Hate, Envy, and Avarice could have aroused personal resentment. Wither's next work, *Shepherd's Hunting* (1615), was a verse pastoral in imitation of those by his friend William Browne (see PASTORAL), with whom he collaborated in writing the collection of pastorals *The Shepherd's Pipe* (1614).

Wither served as captain in the Royalist cavalry in 1639, and with the Civil War joined the Parliamentary army and rose to the rank of major-general of forces in Surrey. According to a legend recorded by the seventeenth-century antiquary John Aubrey, the poet John Denham saved Wither's life: "It happened that George Wither was taken prisoner, and was in danger of his life, having written severely against the king, etc. Sir John Denham went to the king, and desired his majesty not to hang him, for that whilest George Wither lived *he* should not be the *worst* poet in England" (*Brief Lives,* ed. Andrew Clark, 2 vols. [1898], I, 221).

Wither seems to have been personally responsible for the ignominous defeat of his own soldiers in Surrey, an action for which he blamed another officer in a book called *Justiciarus justificatus* (1646). The accused, Sir Richard Onslow, sued Wither for libel; the book was burned and Wither stripped of his military offices. With the Restoration, he was imprisoned for three years (1663-67), possibly for his satires against Charles I, perhaps for his outspoken criticism of both parliamentarians and royalists. After his release he lived quietly in London until his death.

The best of Wither's verse was written before 1620, the year in which his *Works* appeared without his authorization. (His volume *Juvenilia* is the same collection, printed in 1622 with his supervision.) After 1620 Wither produced prodigious quantities of religious verse, satires, pastorals, prose meditations, emblem poems, prophecies, and even a history of a plague and a translation of Nemesius' *The Nature of Man* (1636). None of his hundred or more works matches the modest achievement of his early poems, which have an occasional cavalier grace and lyric ease. Edmund Gosse's judgment of Wither is generally accepted: ". . . a very curious and perhaps unique instance of a tiresome and verbose scribbler, to whom in his youth there came unconsidered flashes of most genuine and exquisite poetry" (*Jacobean Poets* [1894]).

Wither's poems were edited by Frank Sidgwick, 2 vols. (1902), with extensive bibliography, and his *History of the Pestilence* by J. Milton French (1932). Charles Lamb wrote an essay on Wither's poetry in 1818. See also Sir C. H. Firth, "George Wither," *RES,* II (1926) and Charles S. Hensley, *The Later Career of George Wither* (1969).

Woman Hater, The; or The Hungry Courtier. A comedy by Francis BEAUMONT, written in about 1606 and first published in 1607. Although John Fletcher may have contributed some scenes, the play is believed to be almost wholly Beaumont's. The chief influence on the play is Ben Jonson's comedy of humours. The scene is Milan in the early seventeenth century.

The duke of Milan receives an umbrana, a rare and tasty fish, which he sends to the "woman hater" Gondarino, a general. The duke has little interest in food because his one passion is Oriana, a beautiful fifteen-year-old girl who longs to appear at court in spite of the warnings of her anxious brother Valore, who fears court life will corrupt her. The glutton Lazarillo, on the other hand. has no interest in life except food. When he learns that Gondarino has received the umbrana, he frantically busies himself to get an invitation to dinner.

Oriana arrives at Gondarino's house to seek shelter in a hailstorm, and the woman-hating general violently reviles her. Also at Gondarino's house appear the duke, the courtiers Arrigo and Lucio, and the ravenous Lazarillo—still hotly in pursuit of the fish—accompanied by Valore, who finds Lazarillo's gluttony amusing.

Several characters are being playfully manipulated. Oriana amuses herself by tormenting Gondarino with feigned affection when she is actually in love with the duke. Valore's intelligencers are recording every imprudent syllable of Lazarillo in order to charge the fool with "high treason." Even Oriana is being toyed with, for Gondarino blackens her reputation with the duke by telling him monstrous tales of her unchastity.

Perhaps the most tormented character of all is Lazarillo, whose much-desired fish continues to elude him. Gondarino has given the fish to his mercer, to whom he is in debt and hopes to mollify; the mercer, in turn, gives it to a pander, who, pretending to be a scholar and master of magic, promises to enchant a rich heiress into marrying the mercer. The "heiress," of course, is one of the pander's prostitutes, to whom he gives the fish. Finally, Lazarillo tracks the precious umbrana to the brothel, but as he prepares to sit down to dinner with Julia, a prostitute, he is arrested for "high treason." As he is dragged away, he promises Julia he will marry her upon his release from prison if only she will save the umbrana until his return.

Meanwhile the duke arranges to have Oriana's virtue put to the test. He has the courtier Arrigo inform her that she is condemned to death and can only be saved if she beds with him. When she stoutly refuses, the duke emerges from his hiding place and claims her for his virtuous bride. The slanderous Gondarino is punished by being bound to a chair while ladies of the court smother the "woman hater" with kisses. The glutton Lazarillo is released from jail, marries Julia, and dines triumphantly on his long-awaited umbrana.

Beaumont's fast-moving comedy is a close imitation of Jonson's comedy of humours (See JONSON, BEN); all the main characters are motivated by some singular obsession or passion—Lazarillo by his gluttony, Gondarino by his violent abhorrence of all women, the duke by his jealousy, and Oriana by her practical joking. In contrast to Jonson's comedies of this kind, however, *The Woman Hater* seldom rises above farce, the situations being both trivial and overdrawn. Yet the witty, vivacious Oriana is intrinsically entertaining enough to enable the audience to forget that her tormenting of Gondarino is really no more motivated and credible than Lazarillo's obsession with the fish.

The Woman Hater is edited by G. W. Williams in *The Dramatic Works in the Beaumont and Fletcher Canon,* ed. Fredson Bowers, 2 vols. (1966, 1970), I. Fletcher's possible share in the play is considered by E. H. C. Oliphant, *The Plays of Beaumont and Fletcher* (1927). For commentary, see A. W. Upton, "Allusions to James I and His Court in Marston's *Fawn* and Beaumont's *Woman Hater,*" *PMLA,* XLIV (1929), and Baldwin Maxwell, *Studies in Beaumont, Fletcher, and Massinger* (1939).

Woman Killed with Kindness, A. A domestic tragedy written around 1603 by Thomas HEYWOOD, and printed in 1607. It was based on three tales from Bandello in William Painter's *The Palace of Pleasure* (1566-67). The scene is Yorkshire in the sixteenth century. Two quite distinct plots are sustained: the infidelity of Anne Frankford with Wendoll, her husband's friend, and the financial misfortunes of Sir Charles Mountford and his sister Susan.

The play begins with the joyous wedding of Anne and John Frankford, an apparently ideal couple whose felicity is shattered when Frankford takes into his house an impoverished gentleman named Wendoll. While Frankford is absent on business, the treacherous Wendoll seduces Anne, who submits easily although she expresses little affection for him. Meanwhile Sir Charles Mountford loses his temper while hawking with Sir Francis Acton, Anne Frankford's brother, and kills two of Acton's huntsmen. Almost ruined by the resulting litigation, Sir Charles and his sister Susan are driven to borrow money from one Master Shafton, whose feigned generosity is really a stratagem to bring about their bankruptcy.

At Frankford's house, meanwhile, the groom Nick discovers Anne's infidelity and reports what he has learned to his master, who catches the illicit lovers in bed. Wendoll flees the house. and Anne, in an agony of guilt and contrition, is given a strange punishment by her husband. Frankford orders her to remove all her belongings and depart, never to see him or their children again. He will not revenge her treachery with blood but let her soul languish in guilt and "kill her even with kindness."

Sir Charles and Susan suffer further humiliations. The ruthless usurer Shafton has Sir Charles imprisoned for debt, and to save his family estate Sir Charles must appeal to his enemy Sir Francis, who determines to get revenge by forcing Sir Charles to trade his sister in exchange for financial assistance. Susan agrees to the match only because of her devotion to her brother; secretly she carries with her a dagger to preserve her honor. Sir Francis, however, is not capable of such dishonor as he originally intended. Moved by Sir Charles' willingness to sacrifice his sister to pay a debt, and stricken with love and admiration by Susan's beauty and purity, Sir Francis takes the dowerless sister as his cherished bride and magnanimously releases the brother from all his debts.

The happily married couple and the now prosperous Sir Charles join Master Frankford and his children in a concluding scene that takes place at Anne's deathbed. Anne has virtually starved herself to death, and Frankford is touched by her repentance. As she dies, he at last forgives her, weds her again with a kiss, and orders that these words be inscribed on her tomb: "Here lies she whom her husband's kindness killed."

Heywood's play is among the best domestic tragedies of the seventeenth century (See DOMESTIC TRAGEDY). His theme is the superiority of Christian forgiveness to the barbaric aristocratic code of revenge, which he may have believed was glorified in Senecan tragedies. He shows no indication of the attitude felt by most modern readers of the play—that Anne Frankford's psychological suffering may be as cruel as any physical punishment. Indeed Master Frankford is portrayed as a peerless husband, a Christ-like man betrayed by the Judas he befriends. In the subplot Sir Francis' refusal to exact revenge and his magnanimous forgiveness of Sir Charles parallels Frankford's conduct in the main story, and Susan's heroic chastity is contrasted to Anne's easy submission to Wendoll. In both stories passion is the cause of tragedy. Sir Charles gives in to it when he kills Acton's huntsmen in a fit of rage, as does Anne when she joylessly surrenders to Wendoll. The rejection of revenge by both Frankford and Sir Francis represents, then, a triumph over that same passion that conquers Anne and Sir Charles. Irving Ribner reads a Biblical allegory in the three principal characters, identifying Frankford with Christ, Anne with Eve, and Wendoll with Satan (*Jacobean Tragedy: The Quest for Moral Order* [1962]), but this view is difficult to reconcile with the subplot.

R. W. Van Fossen has edited *A Woman Killed with Kindness* in the Revels Plays series (1962). The play is also in *Elizabethan Plays*, ed. A. H. Nethercot, C. R. Baskervill, and V. B. Heltzel (rev. ed., 1971). Hallett Smith reviews criticism of the work in "*A Woman Killed with Kindness*," *PMLA*, LIII (1938). For other criticism, see Freda L. Townsend, "The Artistry of Thomas Heywood's Double Plots," *PQ*, XXV (1946); David Cook, "*A Woman Killed with Kindness:* An Un-Shakespearean Tragedy," *ES*, XLV (1964); and John Canutsen, "The Theme of Forgiveness in the Plot and Subplot of *A Woman Killed with Kindness*," *RenD*, New Series. II (1969).

Woman's Prize, The; or The Tamer Tamed. A comedy by John FLETCHER, written around 1604 and first published in 1647. The play is believed to have been extensively revised about 1610. The source, and occasion for writing the play, was Shakespeare's *The Taming of the Shrew.* Although the characters have Italian names, the setting is London.

Petruchio, the "wife-tamer," had lived so miserably with his first wife that most of his friends agree his second marriage will prove difficult. Urged on by her cousin Bianca, however, the bride Maria does not submit meekly to Petruchio's bad disposition and tyrannical ways. Once submissive and gentle, she now becomes a fire-eating virago boldly resolved to "tame the wife-tamer." She refuses to bed with Petruchio, bolts herself and Bianca in a bedroom with a month's supply of food, and proclaims that she will remain barricaded until Petruchio signs the agreement she has drawn up. Petruchio prepares for a lengthy siege.

Meanwhile Maria's sister Livia is also experiencing man troubles. She is secretly engaged to Rowland but fears that her father will force her to marry Moroso, a rich old man. The practical Livia decides that she must plan a way in which she can have Rowland without sacrificing her dowry. She deliberately offends Rowland, who departs cursing all women, is equally rude to Moroso, and then joins Maria and Bianca in their sealed chamber. A whole troop of townswomen arrive to celebrate this "battle of the sexes" with drinking and dancing. Finally, the men are vanquished and the women end their siege. Petruchio consents to give Maria fine clothes and liberty; Moroso agrees not to force a marriage on Livia for at least a month; and the jubilant Bianca proclaims a total victory for the women.

These conditions, however, are grossly abused by the madcap Maria, who squanders huge sums on clothes, refurnishes the house, and then even threatens to move the house to another location. To humiliate Petruchio further, she announces to her friends that he is sick with the plague and claps him up in the house like a prisoner. Desperate, he threatens to leave on a long journey, an announcement Maria calmly accepts. He has himself brought to her in a coffin surrounded by mourners complaining that Maria's mistreatment caused his death, but this ruse only causes her to weep because Petruchio, she states, had led such a wasteful, foolish life. Completely defeated, Petruchio sits upright in his coffin and is embraced by Maria, who announces that now the "wife-tamer" himself has been tamed, she will prove an obedient and affectionate mate. A reformed and much wiser Petruchio gladly receives his new wife. In the subplot of Rowland and Livia, another ruse brings equally happy results. Feigning to be on her deathbed, Livia demands that both Moroso and Rowland sign documents renouncing all claims upon her. Both, of course, oblige, but Rowland is elated to discover on his way home that his document is a wedding license. Thus the wily Livia wins both her dowry and the man of her choice.

Fletcher's *The Woman's Prize* is an attempt to outdo Shakespeare's *The Taming of the Shrew,* and it almost succeeds. Instead of having the wife a shrew, as in Shakespeare's play, Fletcher makes the husband a tyrant and, like Shakespeare, writes a wild farce exploiting a rather static and limited situation. Unlike the heroine of Shakespeare's play, however, the recalcitrance of Fletcher's Maria extends far beyond credulity or even dramatic necessity, and Fletcher's Petruchio lacks the vivacity, wit, and energy of Shakespeare's wily "woman-tamer." Like Fletcher's *Wild-Goose Chase,* his *Woman's Prize* is a fast-paced, witty comedy one that might well have been more highly regarded if Shakespeare had not written *The Taming of the Shrew.*

The standard edition is by George B. Ferguson (1966). For criticism, see E. H. C. Oliphant, *The Plays of Beaumont and Fletcher* (1927); Baldwin Maxwell, *Studies in Beaumont, Fletcher, and Massinger* (1939); and Clifford Leech, *The John Fletcher Plays* (1962).

Women Beware Women. A tragedy by Thomas MIDDLETON, written around 1625–27 but not published until 1657. The main plot is based on popular accounts of a notorious adulteress, Bianca Capello. For the subplot Middleton consulted the anonymous French romance *Les Amours tragiques d'Hypolite et Isabelle* (Paris, 1610). The scene of Middleton's play is Florence in the early seventeenth century.

Leantio, a young Florentine of modest means, imprudently marries Bianca, a beautiful Venetian girl of a rich and distinguished family. During a religious procession the duke of Florence sees her on the balcony of Leantio's house and immediately vows to possess her. The duke persuades Livia, the corrupt sister of two Florentine gentlemen named Fabricio and Hippolito, to lure Bianca into his net. At the duke's palace Leantio learns that he is to become governor of a remote city and that Bianca, who has become enamored of the duke, is to remain at the palace as the duke's mistress. Hence Leantio becomes easy prey for the wealthy, sensual Livia, who takes him as her lover. When Livia's proud brother Hippolito learns of her affair with Leantio from the duke, Hippolito swears to kill Leantio. Hippolito, meanwhile, has entered into an incestuous relationship with his niece Isabella. When Livia discovers that Hippolito has murdered Leantio, she resolves to reveal her brother's incestuous relationship and for her part, Isabella vows to leave Hippolito and silence Livia. The climax to these multiple betrayals and perverse love affairs occurs during a masque in celebration of the duke's marriage to Bianca. Isabella and Livia are poisoned by incense, Hippolito stabs himself, Bianca poisons the duke to avenge Leantio's murder and then drinks from the poisoned cup.

Although Middleton's tragedy lacks unity and concentration, it is nevertheless impressive for its swift action, vivid characterization, and effective single scenes. Especially memorable are Middleton's portraits of his two principal women characters, the passionate Livia and the shifting, fickle, and uncertain Bianca. The concluding masque utilizes a dramatic device grown conventional since Kyd's *The Spanish Tragedy,* but Middleton's use of it conveys an entirely original and effective ironic balance between moral horror and outright farce.

Two excellent editions are by Roma Gill in the New Mermaid series (1967) and by Charles Barber for the Fountainwell Drama texts (1969). Significant critical discussions are by Samuel Schoenbaum, *Middleton's Tragedies* (1955); Christopher Ricks, "Word Play in *Women Beware Women*," *RES*, XII (1961); Edward Engleberg, "Tragic Blindness in *The Changeling* and *Women Beware Women*," *MLQ*, XXIII (1962); George Core, "The Canker and the Muse: Imagery in *Women Beware Women*," *Ren P 1968* (1969); and Inga-Stina Ewbank, "Realism and Morality in *Women Beware Women*," *E & S*, XXII (1969).

Wonderful Year, The. A pamphlet by Thomas DEKKER describing three momentous events of the year 1603: the death of Queen Elizabeth, the accession of James I, and the London plague. Printed in the same year it describes, Dekker's pamphlet is based on his own personal experiences, first-hand reports, gossip, and his reading of moralizing ballads and jestbooks.

Dekker begins with a lengthy and eloquent eulogy on Elizabeth's death:

> The report of her death, like a thunder-clap, was able to kill thousands. It took away hearts from millions. For having brought up even under her wing a nation that was almost begotten and born under her, that never shouted any other *ave* than for her name, never saw the face of any prince but herself, never understood what that strange outlandish word "change" signified—how was it possible but that her sickness should throw abroad an universal fear, and her death an astonishment?

After several short poems celebrating her funeral, Dekker pays tribute to the new order established by James I: "The loss of a Queen was paid with the double interest of a King and Queen. The cedar of her government, which stood alone and bare no fruit, is changed now to an olive upon whose spreading branches grow both kings and queens."

Meanwhile, the frightful scourge of the pestilence creeps relentlessly upon London:

> Imagine then that all this while Death, like a Spanish leaguer—or, rather, like a stalking Tamburlaine—hath pitched his tents, being but a heap of winding-sheets tacked together, in the sinfully polluted suburbs.

Like most of his predecessors writing about the plague, Dekker portrays it as punishment for sin, and his description of the catastrophe, though occasionally detailed and realistic, is more often interwoven with didacticism, sermonizing, anecdotes, and even grim jokes. In fighting the plague, none of man's customary greed, vanities, and pursuits is effective; the power of medicine is as pitifully futile as the courtier's vaunted sword:

> Galen could do no more good than Sir Giles Goosecap. Hippocrates, Avicenna, Paracelsus, Rhazes, Fernelius, with all their succeeding rabble of doctors and watercasters, were at their wits' end—or I think rather at the world's end, for not one of them durst peep abroad, or, if any one did take upon him to play the venturous knight, the plague put him to his *nonplus*.

Thus Dekker's pamphlet, written in a dazed "wonder" over the "wonders" of 1603, is a bitter comment on the vanity of men and of their failures of courage and resourcefulness. Unlike Defoe's later *Journal of the Plague Year*, Dekker's work often abjures journalistic detail in favor of grim irony and mockery. Amid the carnage of the plague, Dekker focuses on panic and horror but never loses the moralist's view of man's abiding folly.

The two best editions of the pamphlet, complete with critical commentary and annotations, are those of F. P. Wilson, *The Plague Pamphlets of Thomas Dekker* (1925), and E. D. Pendry, *Thomas Dekker: Selected Writings* (1967).

Wood, Anthony a (1632-1695). Antiquary and historian. Born in Oxford, Wood attended New College School, Thame School, and Merton College, where he resided throughout most of his life, dying in the house where he was born. His single great achievement was *Athenae Oxonienses* (1691-92), a two-volume biographical compilation of all the Oxford graduates from 1500 to 1690 who in any way distinguished themselves. The work is an invaluable biographical reference for literary historians of the English Renaissance. It caused a storm of controversy when it first appeared because of Wood's candor and alleged recording of gossip and scandal. In 1693 Henry Hyde, second earl of Clarendon, had Wood convicted of libel for stating that Clarendon's father sold public offices, an accusation Wood recorded from the notes of his assistant John AUBREY. Wood was notoriously irascible and tactless.

After he and Aubrey quarreled, Aubrey took from Wood much of the biographical data he had accumulated for twenty-five years. This material was published long afterward as Aubrey's *Brief Lives* (1813). Unlike Aubrey, a witty anecdotist with a lively prose style and eye for details of human interest, Wood was an indefatigable collector of facts with little concern for vividness or literary polish. Except for *Athenae Oxonienses* and *The History and Antiquities of the University of Oxford,* in Latin (1674, English translation in 1792-96), Wood's writings were published posthumously from his voluminous manuscripts at Oxford. These include *Modius salium* (1751), a collection of Oxford humor; and *The Life and Times of Anthony Wood,* autobiographical writings published by Thomas Hearne in 1730.

Athenae Oxonienses, ed. P. Bliss, 4 vols. (1848), is still standard. *The Life and Times of Anthony Wood,* ed. Andrew Clark, 5 vols. (1891-1900), contains Wood's diaries and other autobiographical papers. There is an abridged edition of Wood's *Life and Times* by L. Powys (1932).

Worthies of England, The History of the. See FULLER, THOMAS.

Wyatt, Sir Thomas (1503-1542). Courtier and poet. Born at Allington Castle in Kent and educated at St. John's College, Cambridge, Wyatt spend most of his life in service to Henry VIII on diplomatic missions abroad, first as ambassador to Spain (1537-39), later as Henry's representative in France and Italy. More than any writer after Chaucer and before Spenser, Wyatt was responsible for importing foreign verse forms into England. With his friend Henry HOWARD, earl of Surrey, he introduced the sonnet form of Dante and Petrarch. He wrote adaptations or translations of Petrarch, twenty-eight in the Petrarchan rhyme scheme, and three in the so-called English or Shakespearean formula of three quatrains and a concluding couplet. He experimented in Horatian verse epistles, terza rima, ottava rima, and epigrams adapted from French and Italian poetry (see SONNET SEQUENCES). Wyatt also wrote fifty or sixty lyrics relatively free of foreign influence—unadorned songs with simple refrains written for accompaniment to the lute, and these graceful songs are the most affective lyrics to come from the native tradition in the English Renaissance. "Take heed betime" and "Blame not my lute" are illustrative of the genre.

Wyatt encountered serious trouble during his political career. He was imprisoned in the Tower in 1536 by Henry VIII as the suspected lover of his first cousin Anne Boleyn during the government's investigations of her alleged infidelities. In 1541 he was again imprisoned, this time for his friendship with the disgraced chancellor Thomas Cromwell; but on both occasions Wyatt was exonerated and regained the king's confidence.

None of Wyatt's poems was published during his lifetime. His first printed works were translations and adaptations of the Psalms (1549) in a variety of meters, including POULTER'S MEASURE; but his best-known poems appeared in 1557 with Surrey's in Tottel's Miscellany, also known as *A Book of Songs and Sonnets* (see MISCELLANIES, POETICAL). "I had rather than forty shillings I had my book of Songs and Sonnets here," says Justice Shallow in *The Merry Wives of Windsor,* expressing the general opinion of the times; for Wyatt's songs, sonnets, and rondeaux continued to capture popular interest until the end of the century. Wyatt was sometimes awkward and ineloquent, especially in his translations, close paraphrases, and adaptations of French and Italian poems expressive of servility to love, female adulation, and other soft Petrarchan sentiments; but his lyrics achieved two vital breaks with the medieval past—his spontaneous songs demonstrated the virility of a poetry free of both narrative and allegory, and his importation of foreign verse forms reopened long-sealed English doors to the invigorating influence of the French and Italian Renaissance (see COURTLY MAKERS).

The standard edition of Wyatt's poems is by Kenneth Muir in the Muses Library (1940), revised as *The Collected Poems of Sir Thomas Wyatt,* ed. Kenneth Muir and Patricia Thomson (1969). Biographical and textual matters are treated by E. K. Chambers, *Sir Thomas Wyatt and Some Collected Studies* (1933). There are excellent critical discussions in E. M. W. Tillyard's edition, *The Poetry of Sir Thomas Wyatt* (1929) and Patricia Thomson, *Sir Thomas Wyatt and His Background* (1964). See also Michael C. O'Neel, "A Wyatt Bibliography," *Bulletin of Bibliography,* XXVII (1970) and Burton Fishman, "Recent Studies in Wyatt and Surrey," *ELR,* I (1971).

Y

Yorkshire Tragedy, A. An anonymous DOMESTIC TRAGEDY written around 1606 and printed in 1608. It was falsely assigned to Shakespeare on the title page of the first edition. The play is based on an account in John Stowe's *Annals* of Walter Calverly, who was executed at York for murder in 1605.

A man weds a virtuous woman, who does not realize that her new husband, although of good family, is a bigamist, a drunkard, and a profligate; indeed, he has mortgaged his property and made his younger brother, an honest university student, security for his enormous gambling debts. When the brother is jailed for debt, the master of his college travels to Yorkshire to seek aid. The husband reacts with such rage and guilt that in his passion he kills two of his sons and a servant who interferes. Brought to justice, he laments his wickedness and is taken off to prison to await trial.

A Yorkshire Tragedy is based on the same sensational crime that inspired George Wilkins' THE MISERIES OF ENFORCED MARRIAGE. Wilkins relates events from Walter Calverly's life before the murders and ends his play happily. *A Yorkshire Tragedy* continues Wilkins' story and assumes (judging from its beginning) a familiarity with the earlier play.

In *A Yorkshire Tragedy* the characters are referred to simply as "Husband," "Wife," "First Son," etc, and they are rigidly typed: the wife is a Patient Grissel, virtuous and incredibly enduring; the husband is a prodigal hopelessly addicted to a demonic lust for gambling. Nothing alleviates his mad obsession until he is brought under the shadow of the gallows, whereupon he collapses in remorse and self-loathing. The moral of the tragedy is sternly underscored: "And 'tis set down by Heaven's just decree / That Riot's child must needs be Beggary."

The standard edition is in *Shakespeare Apocrypha,* ed. C. F. Tucker Brooke (1908). Brooke has discovered one episode in the play that influenced *King Lear* (see "*King Lear* and *A Yorkshire Tragedy, MLN,* XXVII [1912]). For other criticism, see H. H. Adams, *English Domestic or Homiletic Tragedy 1595-1642* (1943), and Michel Grivelet, *Thomas Heywood et le drame domestique élizabéthain* (1957).